The BRISTOL BABEL

The First 100 Years of BRISTOL CITY F.C.

By David Woods

Published by

YORE PUBLICATIONS

12 The Furrows,
Harefield, Middx,
UB9 6AT

Printed by:
THE BATH PRESS

ISBN 1 874427 95 X

Published by:
Yore Publications
12 The Furrows, Harefield,
Middx. UB9 6AT.

© David Woods 1994

British Library Cataloguing-in-Publication Data.
A catalogue record for this book
is available from the British Library.

ISBN 1 874427 95 X

It has been necessary to copy or re-photograph much of the illustrative material contained herein.
Consequently such illustrations may not have always reproduced to as high a standard as preferred.
However, in view of the significance of such illustations they have been included.

DEDICATION

This book is dedicated to all past and present players, officials, and supporters of the Bristol City and Bedminster Football Clubs, including their predecessors.

In memory of the author's father, Edward David Woods, who followed the 'Babes' from the mid 1920's until his death on February 28th, 1969.

Also in memory of that great City player John Atyeo who died on June 8th, 1993. He gave much enjoyment to the author's early years of watching the Club.

And in conclusion a special dedication to the author's children, Andrew (11), Nicholas (9), and Helen (8), who are carrying on the Family tradition of supporting Bristol City that was started by both grandfathers of the author.

ACKNOWLEDGEMENTS

This book would not have been possible without the great help and assistance of Mervyn Baker in regard to research (who is hoping to produce a complete *Who's Who* on Bristol City in the near future), or without the immense contribution made by Andrew Crabtree to an earlier work, and post-war programme information from David Clarke. Many others have also helped, including numerous members of the Association of Football Statisticians, but special thanks are due to the following individuals:- Mark Adams, the late John Atyeo, George E. Baker, Mike Bondy, Kevin Brake, Mark Britton, Keith Brookman, John Clapp (Bristol City), Denis Clarebrough, Tony Cook, John Cox (Bristol City), Ron Cranfield, Mike Davage, W.A. Davies, Jantzen Derrick, David Farmer, Peter Farrell, David Foot, Beryl Fudge (Bristol City), Peter Godsiff, Bill Harvey, Leslie Heal, John Helliar (West Ham United), Brian Hobbs, Tom Hopegood, Bryan Horsnell, Mike Hunter, Mike Jay, Alan Jenkins, Alan Lacock, Mitchelle (Portsmouth), Jonathan Morgan, Cara Palmer (Hereford United), Adam Parsons, S.J. Paynter, Lorna Parnell (Football League), Gerry Pearce, Geoff Rose, Rev. Nigel Sands (Crystal Palace), Peter Sas (Bristol City), Roy Shoesmith, Mike Skinner, Steve Small, Kevin Smith, Monica Spencer, Matthew Stevens, Roly Stubbins, Mike Swain, James Thomas, Colin Timbrell (Gloucestershire F.A. Historian), Phil. Tottle (Bristol City), Don Tuckfield, John Watkins, Mrs. W.J. Wedlock, Brian Wilkinson, Alan Williams, Tony Williams, the late Ted Woodriffe, James Woodrow, and Clayton Worlock.

Gratitude is also expressed to the many soccer historians who have produced books, especially in the last ten years, and the late Thomas Bowden who had compiled a contemporary record of Bristol City - in marvellous copperplate handwriting - covering the period 1897 to 1915, together with the staff at the British Newspaper Library, and those of the Bristol Central Library who have been of great assistance.

Contents

FOREWORDS

For those who enjoyed reading the author's first book 'Bristol City A Complete Record 1894 - 1987', you will undoubtedly have gleaned that Bristol City's historical origins are complicated to say the least.

There are two 'family lines'. One originating from Southville, which was formed in 1887, and Bedminster which was formed two years later in 1889. The second 'family line' is from Bristol South End formed in 1894 and Bristol City, our historical namesake, formed in 1897.

The change to professionalism and the adoption of the club's name to Bristol City occurred in 1897. Accordingly it is fitting that 1997 will mark the occasion of the official centenary celebrations of the event.

This new book by David Woods, 'The Bristol Babe' is a most welcome commemoration of the hundred years from the formation of Bristol South End (1894), the current club's immediate predecessor, to the present day.

This book was already underway when an E.G.M. in November 1993 voted a new Board of Directors to the helm at Bristol City Football Club. The change heralded a new chapter in the history of the Club and for those of us who hold the Club close to our hearts there is now the exciting opportunity to successfully shape the future events of our Club and change the face and fortunes of football at Ashton Gate.

'The Bristol Babe' is a singular tribute to the author's dedication, painstaking research, meticulous attention to detail and remarkable statistical analysis. It is too a testimonial to those involved with the formation and survival of Bristol South End and all the players and others who during the intervening years have contributed to the administration, management and development of Bristol City Football Club.

John Clapp (Director)

We are delighted and honoured to write this foreword to the centenary history of Bristol City Football Club. As players at the same time as John Atyeo we appreciate the opportunity of taking this task from our erstwhile colleague, whose death last year was such a great shock.

Being active members of the Old Players Association we feel able to give appreciation on behalf of all the players in respect of this labour of love that David Woods has produced, especially as his regular supporting of the Robins started at about the same time as our careers at Ashton Gate.

It is fascinating to follow the history of the Babe of Bristol football from its birth as Bristol South End on April 12th 1894, as well as the career of Bedminster from their formation as Southville in 1887 right up to their amalgamation with Bristol City in 1900. This book, 'The Bristol Babe', is a welcome addition to the little that has previously been published on the Club, and it is to be appreciated that the deeds of the early pioneers, John Durant, Bill Hodgkinson, Fred Keenan, Harry Locke, Ted Locke, W.R.Nurse and Col.Plant, are able to be celebrated with a Centenary History, as without their foresight and enterprise there would not be any Bristol City Football Club today.

Of the six major clubs in Bristol during the Victorian era only three survive, and in following Bristol St.George, who celebrated their centenary in 1992 despite closing down for a season in 1899-1900 when they re-formed as an amateur organisation, and Bristol Rovers in 1983 (formed as the Black Arabs in 1883), it is to be hoped that Bristol City will soon recapture the vision that brought about their early rise to fame.

Jantzen Derrick

Alan Williams

Musings

Recent events in the history of Bristol City Association Football Club, culminating in an Extraordinary General Meeting at Whitchurch Sports Centre on the evening of Friday, November 12th 1993, caused the writer to reflect on the early pioneers of the Club, and the likely sense of deja-vu they would have experienced had it been possible for any of them to have been present.

The Club has been subjected to a number of F.A. Inquiries throughout its existence, and it was another such inquiry that acted as a catalyst for the actions of the self-styled, 'Reform' group who gained control as a result of this meeting. This served to set up a situation comparable to the early times, when the Club's rapid rise to eminence brought about the 'Babes' nickname.

The vote was won by a combination of factors, but the main influence was the commitment to play exciting, entertaining football in pursuit of the target of Premiership status within 2 to 5 years, and the winning of a major trophy to gain entry into European competition within 4 to 10 years.

As the Club is now embarking on its second century it is likely that this takeover appears to offer a chance to recapture the vision of the early founders, and gives opportunity to address the woeful lack of achievement following the Babes first relegation experience in 1911. The Reform group saw fit to focus on this lack of achievement, and remarked on the Club's potential to be one of the best, so it is now incumbent upon the current custodians of Bristol City Association Football Club to realise such potential for the long suffering local football public.

Beginnings

Internal dissention within the ranks of Bedminster Association Football Club (who had been founded as Southville in Queen Victoria's Jubilee Year of 1887), coupled with the decision of Bristol South A.F.C. to disband, led to erstwhile Bedminster members Fred W. Keenan and John Durant calling a meeting. Bristol South disbanded despite having just secured the inaugural Championship of the South Bristol & District League, when the top of the table looked thus:-

	P	W	D	L	F	A	Pts
BRISTOL SOUTH	14	9	3	2	41	22	21
Frenchay	14	10	0	4	51	20	20
Willsbridge	14	9	2	3	38	17	20

The meeting was held in the front parlour of the residence of the former, Bovey Tracy House, Milford Road, Southville, to discuss the future of the association game in South Bristol. This meeting was held on Thursday, April 12th 1894, when eighteen football enthusiasts were in attendance to agree on the formation of a new club.

The discussion was chaired by Harry Locke, and those present included W.B. Hodgkinson, one time Secretary of Eastville Rovers, Arthur Jones and Hammer Clements - notable local players - and J.A. Stevens, Secretary of the Bristol & District League, who was acting in an advisory capacity. After much discussion it was resolved to form a new club, calling such organisation - in accordance with the proposal of J.A. Stevens - who, being an admirer of Preston North End, voiced the thought, *"why not Bristol South End?"* The sum of £6.8s.6d was pledged before the meeting broke up, this money being used to set up an administration. Four days later in the back room of Rock Lodge, Southville Road, the home of affluent local businessman John Durant, officials were appointed. Bill Hodgkinson became Secretary with Fred Keenan as his assistant, Harry Locke and his brother Ted shared the role of Treasurer, W.R. Nurse was chosen as Chairman, while Col. Plant became President with John Durant as his deputy.

Rebuffed

From the outset the newly formed Club was ambitious and not just interested in taking over the niche left by Bristol South. Wishing to compete with the premier local clubs - Bedminster, Clifton, Eastville Rovers, St. George, and Warmley - it was resolved that application be made for admission to the Bristol & District League (this League changing its name to the Western League in 1895) at such organisation's meeting on April 25th.

However, their ambitions met with early rebuff, their application being flatly refused on the basis that; *"the League cannot entertain a club without any history".* Swindon Athletic also failed in their bid for election, but the applications of Hereford Thistle and Swindon Wanderers were favourably received. On the day preceding this rejection the establishing of the Bristol South End Club proceeded apace with a General Meeting being held in the General Elliot public house in East Street, Bedminster, when a Committee of fourteen was elected to assist the Club officers. Colours of red shirts and navy blue knickers were chosen, and it was agreed that the annual subscription would be five shillings for gentlemen, and two shillings and sixpence for the ladies.

Not dismayed by the rejection received from the Bristol & District League, the Club responded with the resourcefulness that was to show itself on many occasions in the early years. Friendlies were arranged against any team that would play them, including the likes of Preston North End, Swindon Town, and Tottenham Hotspur. They were also heartened by being granted affiliation to the Gloucestershire F.A. as this opened the way for their participation in the various cup competitions.

Another setback though occurred on May 23rd when the Reserves were denied admittance to the South Bristol & District League (at a meeting held in the Hope & Anchor, Redcliffe Hill), further salt being rubbed into the wound by the fact that Bedminster's 3rd XI (Extras) were successful.

Ground

A field was obtained at St. John's Lane, Bedminster, on lease from the trustees of the Ashton Court Estate at an annual rent of £20, and several sub-committees were formed to co-ordinate the work necessary to prepare the site as a suitable venue for the association game. Frenzied activity throughout the summer brought the ground ready for the Club's first match on Saturday, September 1st 1894, when the following advertisement appeared in that morning's Western Daily Press.

FOOTBALL
This Day (Saturday) September 1st,
1894
at
St. John's Lane, Bedminster
SWINDON TOWN (Champions of the
West of England)
V. BRISTOL SOUTH END
Kick-off 3.30
Admission 3d. Enclosure 3d extra

After the Match, both teams will visit the Theatre Royal, by special invitation of the Lessee.

First Match

In gloriously hot weather a crowd of 3,500 was entertained prior to the kick-off by the Bristol South Brass Band, under the conductorship of George A. Godfrey, such gentleman being destined to continue in this role for the first 53 years of the Club's existence, making his final appearance in this role at Ashton Gate on Saturday, August 23rd 1947. The kick-off saw the ball being started on its career by the South End Club Vice-President, John Durant - on behalf of the visitors - after the home captain, Arthur Jones, had won the toss and elected to play against the sun.

Trestrail, the homester's custodian, returned the initiative kick and the ball was carried up the left wing. After a little reversal a hot tussle resulted in South End rushing the first goal, Lewis having hit a post with a shot just before. This served to prompt Swindon into activity and it wasn't long before they responded, a centre by Mills giving Walman the opportunity to restore parity. Trestrail then had to make a couple of good saves to prevent the visitors from going ahead before South End came again to take the lead for a second time when Fry put away a left wing centre from Lewis. The homesters now had their tails up and Swindon were hard pressed to keep them out, being particularly indebted to the prowess of their goalkeeper Williams, but prior to half-time the visitors snatched an equaliser thanks to their captain R.L. Jones.

After an interval that was greatly appreciated by the players, owing to the immense heat, Swindon warmed to the task, the South End proved resilient, and it wasn't until the half was well advanced that the visitors took the lead. Trestrail misjudged a corner, allowing the ball to enter the net after hitting his person. This stirred the homesters, but after having a number of attempts to level matters they succumbed yet again, this right on the final whistle, when Selwood shot into the net after the ball had been dropped.

South End's first match thus ended in a 4-2 defeat, but the local press - the *Western Daily Press* and the *Bristol Times & Mirror* - was full of praise, describing the game as exciting and well contested throughout. Great credit was extended to the newly organised team for their gallant stand and their frequent unselfish play and clever tactics. For this match the two sides lined up as follow:-

South End
Trestrail, Welham, Taylor, Davis, A.Jones, G.Jones, Walters, Fry, Lewis, Clements, Mayger.

Swindon
Williams, Allen, Richardson, Webb, Dibsdall, Spackman, Ricks, Jones, Walman, Selwood, Mills.

Another Rebuff

After the game the players and officials were entertained to a burlesque performance of the Water Babies, as guests of the lessee of the Theatre Royal, and so concluded a week that also brought another rebuff of hopes of Bristol & District League membership. Swindon Wanderers had withdrawn in consequence of financial problems which saw them give up their County Ground home to Swindon Town, and South End applied to take over their fixtures. The League however, resolved to continue with one club less, though a later improvement in Wanderers' circumstances allowed them to take up membership from October 1894, thus leaving South End feeling they had a case to prove. The opportunity to make their point soon presented itself as Swindon Wanderers were the visitors to St. John's Lane on the second Saturday of the campaign when in winning by the overwhelming score of 11-0, South End gave clear indication to the League that they might well have been in error to refuse them.

All in all an auspicious start for a club that had gathered sufficient support to acquire a membership of 300, including 50 players, during the summer. Of the players a number had been attracted from the Bedminster Club, including Frank Mayger, one of the Minsters' star performers, who was appointed Vice-Captain, Hammer Clements, and the Jones brothers.

1895 - Bristol South End in action at St.Johns' Lane

Formation

April 12th 1894 is therefore the date of the formation of the Club that was to be re-named Bristol City in 1897, but the Club's genealogical tree is complicated by the amalgamation with Bedminster at the end of the 1899-1900 season.

The Bedminster organisation was formed, as Southville, in 1887, and they played their first match on October 15th of that year when, on their home pitch in Bedminster Park (now known as Greville Smyth Park) they defeated Criterion 1-0 thanks to a second-half goal from McCarthy. Southville's inaugural campaign coincided with the commencement of the Gloucestershire Senior Cup competition, and they, and their opponents Globe, had the honour of appearing in the very first match in this tournament. This historic game took place on November 12th when a 1-1 stalemate was played out on Durdham Down.

Early Bristol Football

Organised association football was a late starter in Victorian Bristol, the locality being a hot bed of interest in boxing, cricket, and the rugby code. This meant that it wasn't until 1882 that a local club was formed to play the dribbling game. It is the Warmley Club that had the distinction of pioneering the game in the area, and it is fitting that this organisation, up to the time of their unfortunate demise in 1898, was the most successful of the local teams. St. George were formed in the same year, on October 21st, and the intense local rivalry, which was to end in the closure of both them and Warmley, soon developed. The first recorded round ball game in the local press is the match played between St. George and Warmley which took place on the ground of the former on Saturday, December 2nd 1882 when St. George won 2-0. The return took place on January 6th 1883 when Warmley obtained revenge by the odd goal in three.

The following season saw the birth of the Black Arabs (this being the original name of Bristol Rovers), and also the Clifton Association Club, who produced Bristol's first international player in C.Wreford-Brown. He represented England against Ireland in 1889 when he was playing for Oxford University in term time, and his home Club, Clifton, during vacations. Further caps were gained in 1894 and 1895 versus Wales, and in 1898 against Scotland. For this latter match he was a member of the F.A. Selection Committee and was prevailed upon by his colleagues to captain the side that beat the Scots 3-1 in Glasgow on April 2nd. He also played for the Corinthians and the Old Carthusians, winning the F.A. Amateur Cup with the latter in 1894 and 1897, as well as representing Gloucestershire and London in County matches.

Professional Clubs

The formation of Bedminster, as Southville in 1887, and Bristol City, as Bristol South End, in 1894, completed the list of what can be termed the major local clubs, though the Clifton organisation - who disbanded in December 1897 - never embraced professionalism, which came to Bristol for the 1897-98 season when Bristol City, Bristol St. George, Eastville Rovers and Warmley took the plunge. The following campaign saw Bedminster follow suit to set up an unsustainable situation in a City the size of Bristol with local enthusiasts being required to support the activities of five professional clubs. By 1900 the survival of the fittest had reduced this number to the two we have today, with Bristol Rovers (as they had by then become known) being the sole survivor on the other side of the River Avon.

Gloucestershire Football Association

The early roots of the association game in Bristol were in the east of the City, but it wasn't long before clubs sprung up south of the river, much interest being kindled in consequence of the first County match played by Gloucestershire on Tuesday, April 7th 1885, when the following advertisement appeared in that morning's Bristol Times & Mirror:-

> *Association Football*
> *GLOUCESTERSHIRE*
> *V*
> *SOMERSETSHIRE*
>
> *This Day (Tuesday), April 7th*
> *Bedminster Cricket Ground*
> *Kick-off at 3.15*
> *Admission 6d.*

A crowd of 600 turned up to witness the event, and although Somersetshire were firm favourites to win, it was Gloucestershire who triumphed in a keenly fought encounter, thanks to Pocock who obtained the game's solitary goal with a rather fluky shot a few minutes prior to the interval. On this day the teams lined up as follows:-

Gloucestershire

G.Godfrey (Warmley), H.F. Semple (Clifton), F.Channing (Eastville Rovers), G.T.Pocock (Clifton), W.H.Vickery (Gloucester), J.W. Clarke (Warmley), T.Coleman (Warmley), J.R.Riddell (Warmley), E.C.Newnham (Clifton), J.H.Fletcher (Gloucester), C.Lacy-Sweet (Clifton).

Somersetshire

J.Adams (Street), A.Andrews (Wells), G.Broughton (Street), T.Pursey (Street), T.Denning (Bridgwater), T.Thorne (Shepton Mallet), T.Ball (Street), J.Ware (Street), J.C.Moreland (Glastonbury), W.Stacey (Street), W.Ball (Street)

Referee   Umpires

H.A.Williams   J.A. Tayler (Glos.) and H.Cooper (Somerset.)

The following season saw further fixtures being fulfilled by a Gloucestershire XI, these including an engagement with Aston Villa at Perry Barr when they succumbed to the tune of 10-1 against their illustrious hosts, but it wasn't until Tuesday, September 7th 1886 that the official formation of the Gloucestershire Football Association took place. This was followed by the instigation of the Gloucestershire Senior Cup competition the next year, and the Junior Cup tournament in 1889.

Western League

The first League competition locally was the Bristol & District League, which was formed following a meeting at the Earl Russell Hotel, Lawrence Hill, Bristol, on Wednesday, March 30th 1892, when representatives of the Bedminster, Clifton, Eastville Rovers, Mangotsfield, St. George and Warmley clubs were in attendance. This League, which was to become known as the Western League in 1895, kicked-off on Saturday, September 24th 1892 with the following results:-

St. George	2	Clevedon	0
Warmley	1	Trowbridge	4
Wells	2	Mangotsfield	0

The other teams in the League commenced their programme later, their inaugural games being:- October 1st; Mangotsfield 3 Eastville Rovers 1; October 8th; Clifton 1 Warmley 3; October 22nd; Wells 2 Bedminster 2.

Gloucestershire Senior Cup Finals

It was however, the Gloucestershire Senior Cup Final that was the highlight of the season in the early years, the first Final ending in a 1-1 draw between Clifton and Warmley on March 10th 1888, when approximately 2,000 turned up on the old St. George ground, near the Lord Rodney public house at Two Mile Hill. The replay was held at the same venue a week later, when Clifton took the trophy after disposing of their opponents by 4 goals to 1. In the first meeting, H.H.Francis scored for Clifton, and J.R. Riddell was on the mark for Warmley, but unfortunately all the endeavour of research have not so far yielded up information in regard to scorers and the attendance for the replay when the sides lined up as follows:-

Clifton F.J.Baines, W.F.Gorton, P.F.Newnham, G.Innes-Pocock (Capt.), C.Wreford-Brown, G.R. Lowndes, R.Innes-Pocock, C.Lacy-Sweet, C.H.Russell, A.B.Colthurst, H.H.Francis.

Warmley G.Godfrey, G.Gay, S.Peacock, J.Peacock, W.Noble, H.Williams, T.Nelmes, J.Mackay, J.R. Riddell, P.Fussell (Captain), W.Bowler.

Referee F.M. Ingram (Essex County)

Umpires Dr W.G.Grace (Wanderers), W.J.Somerton (Eastville Rovers).

The Warmley team line-up was the same as for the initial match, but Clifton brought in C.Wreford-Brown, C.H. Russell & A.B.Colthurst for C.H.Newnham, H.Falcon and A.W.Francis.

It wasn't until the 1907-08 campaign that the competition became a straight forward contest between Bristol City and Bristol Rovers, when the instigation of the Gloucestershire Intermediate Cup allowed the more junior clubs, such as Bristol Amateurs, Bristol East, St. Francis, Staple Hill etc., to take part in a more suitable tournament, but the demise of Clifton, Warmley, St. George and Bedminster meant that from 1900-01 the Finals became the province of the two remaining professional clubs. Up to this time the Cup had been won most often by Warmley, with four successes, followed by Bedminster, Bristol City, Clifton and St. George with two, then Eastville Rovers with one. Attendances had reached a high of 11,433 with receipts of £356-1-9 for the match on the new St. George ground at Bell Hill in 1899. However, the following campaign brought a drop to 1,975 with receipts of £61.9s.3d for the clash on the Bristol Rovers ground between Bedminster and Bristol City, such a poor turnout being ascribed to lack of interest in consequence of the forthcoming amalgamation of the two clubs involved.

The results of the Finals from 1889 to 1900 were:-

April 6th 1889;   Eastville Rovers 1 -   Warmley 0
(St. George)

March 22nd 1890; Clifton 5   -   St. George 0
(St. George) 3000

March 28th 1891; Bedminster 2   -   Warmley 0
(St. George)

March 12th 1892; Warmley 2   -   Bedminster 1
(Kingswood Athletic Ground) 6,000 (£100)

April 1st 1893; Warmley 4   -   Gloucester 1
(The Chequers) 3,500

March 31st 1894; St. George 3   -   Eastville Rovers 1
(The Chequers) 4,000

April 15th 1895; St. George 4   -   Gloucester 3
(The Chequers) 2,000 (£51)

April 6th 1896; Warmley 1   -   Eastville Rovers 0
(Bell Hill) 5,651 (£161.12.2)

April 19th 1897; Warmley 2   -   Bedminster 0
(Bell Hill) 6,705 (£191.15.5)

April 11th 1898; Bristol City 2   -   Warmley 1
(Eastville) 11,186 (£348.6.3)

April 3rd 1899; Bristol City 2   -   Bristol Rovers 1
(Bell Hill) 11,433 (£356-1-9)

April 30th 1900; Bedminster 3   -   Bristol City 1
(Eastville) 1,975 (£61.9.3)

Southville - Formation

The formation and first match of Southville - later Bedminster A.F.C. - is well recorded, but the actual date of their inception remains unknown, unlike that of their opponents in the inaugural Gloucestershire Cup match, the Globe Club. This organisation for old boys of Queen Elizabeth's Hospital School was born on August 29th 1887, at a meeting held in the Bristol Coffee Tavern. At a small gathering of Southville Cricket Club members, the decision was taken to form a football section. The first Captain elected was W.G. Griffiths, but this honour only lasted about three minutes as owing to some informality another poll was taken, and this time A.Brown just secured the coveted position. However, after only two months in office, Mr Brown resigned, and H.G. Harris a popular figure known as Happy Harry, was elected in his place. The post of Vice-Captain was taken by W.G. Griffiths, and the important positions of Honorary Secretary and Treasurer were filled by Fred W. Gyles and W.H. Burland respectively.

This initial campaign for Southville brought some fine wins, including the double over North Rovers - 4-0 at home and 2-0 away - but in the Gloucestershire Cup they eventually went out 1-0 in a second replay against Globe, following draws of 1-1 and 0-0. Those who turned out for the Villains in this first season were:- C.E.Gyles* (goalkeeper), A.Brown*, J.Bucknell, W.H.Burland, W.H.Fox*, C.A.Green, W.G.Griffiths*, F.W.Gyles*, H.G.Harris, S.J.Harris*, A.Latham, R.Lewis, J.F. McCarthy*, F.Merchant, B.Morris, H.Morris* and V. Parker (* The full line-up in regard to the Club's first ever match against Criterion on October 15th has not been traced, but from match reports it is known that these players took part).

Changes were made to the Committee for the following campaign, Charlie E. Gyles taking over as Secretary from his brother, and J.F. McCarthy assuming the role of Vice-Captain. The Gyles brothers were stalwart members of the Club, and Fred later founded the well known local sports shop that is still operating today. He died after a lengthy illness on December 2nd 1918. The season produced a 9-1 home win over North Rovers, but the Villains scope for advancement to rank with the top local clubs that their team sometimes suggested it was capable of, was limited by their playing in a public park.

Catalyst

The catalyst for change was provided by Dr W.G. Grace, the colossus of Victorian Cricket, who was so impressed by Southville's performance in a 2-1 defeat in a Gloucestershire Cup match he refereed at Warmley on February 9th 1889, that he wrote and advised of their staying together as they had the makings of being a fine combination. This encouragement from such a prominent personality, together with the active help of Dr Ernest H.Cook, brought about the association with Bedminster Cricket Club (formed in 1847 and still going strong today). Season 1889-90 therefore saw the adoption of the Bedminster name - and the team - in their maroon and old gold colours, ensconced at the cricket ground in Greenway Bush Lane, where facilities were such that gate money could be taken.

The stage was now set for a club from South Bristol to rival the principal local clubs on the other side of the river, these being Clifton, Eastville Rovers, St. George, and Warmley. However, before leave is taken of the doings of the old Southville Club, it is worthy to record the Villains playing summary. Information is as given in the Bristol Evening News of September 15th 1894, and as contained in Half Back's Stray Leaves column in the Bristol Evening Post of November 9th and 16th 1935; research having failed to establish complete lists of results for their two seasons of operation.

1887-88 record:- P18 W9 D6 L3 F22 A4
1888-89 record:- P19 W5 D3 L11 F27 A16.
The players used in 1888-89 were:- C.E.Gyles(Goalkeeper), G.Beard, S.Bendall, A.Brown, W.H.Fox, G.Gerrish, W.G.Griffiths, F.W.Gyles, R.Hanover, E.T.Harris, H.G.Harris, S.J.Harris, T.Hemmens, J.F.McCarthy, B.Morris and H.Morris.

Bedminster - Early Success

The newly named Club opened their campaign with a 6-0 defeat at Clevedon, and whilst they had a few more heavy reverses during the season, notable wins were obtained over St. Agnes 10-2, St. Simon's 8-0, and Warmley 7-0, to produce a final record of:- P20 W8 D1 L11 F54 A53, such record including a shock Gloucestershire Cup defeat at the hands of Craigmore College in the 1st Round, the influenza hit Minsters going down 2-0 on their own ground.

Season 1890-91 brought the first changes to the Committee since 1888. H.G. Harris resigned as Captain in consequence of a twisted knee, which was sustained in the last match of the previous campaign and took a long time to heal, with F.W. Gyles taking his place. The positions of Secretary and Treasurer were filled by W.M. Cleverdon and Arthur Smith respectively. This was a notable season as it saw the Minsters emerge on top of the pile when they disposed of Warmley 2-0 in the Final of the Gloucestershire Cup which was played on the old St. George ground on March 28th. Their path to secure this top prize in the local scene was highlighted by their revenge over Craigmore College, who they annihilated 12-0 in the Semi-Final. The record for the campaign shows only three defeats, fifteen matches being won, three drawn, and with seventy eight goals being scored against twenty two conceded.

F.A. Cup Debut

The third year at Greenway Bush Lane (sometimes called the Coronation Road Ground) saw Bedminster entering the F.A.Cup for the first time, treading in the pioneering footsteps of Clifton and Warmley who took part in the 1st Qualifying Round the previous season with the following results:-

Clifton 1 - Wednesbury Old Athletic 7
(County Ground)
Warmley 0 - Walsall Town Swifts 12
(Tennis Court Ground) 2,200

The Minsters received a bye in the 1st Qualifying Round, and a walkover in the 2nd, when their opponents the 93rd Highlanders scratched. Therefore it wasn't until November 14th that they made their debut in this competition when they were hosts to Luton Town. Unfortunately it wasn't an auspicious debut as the visitors, who were 3-0 up at half-time, won 4-1 with the help of two own goals, Bachelor notching Bedminster's reply. In the Gloucestershire Cup the Minsters attracted a new record crowd to Greenway Bush Lane on February 27th, when 1,300 spectators turned up to witness their favourites beat St. George 2-1 and thereby set up another confrontation with Warmley in the Final. This took place two weeks later on the Kingswood Athletic Ground, but this time, in front of a new record Final crowd of 6,000 paying receipts of £100, the White Shirts of Warmley extracted revenge by winning 2-1.

Visit of the F.A. Cup Winners

The season brought the first visit to Bristol of a Football League club when the famous West Bromwich Albion side played a Gloucestershire XI on the St. George ground on April 20th. The visitors delighted the 1,730 people present by bringing with them the F.A. Cup of which they were the holders having beaten Aston Villa 3-0 at the Oval on March 19th. The Baggies proved much too strong for the homesters, winning 7-0, after being 3-0 ahead at the break. Their scorers were Dyer (2), Geddes (2), McLeod(2) and Nicholls. On this day the sides lined up as follows:-

Gloucestershire XI
G.Speck (Gloucester), M.L.Owen (Clifton), J.H.Bloor (St. George), J.M.Cutteridge (Clifton), A.Farrant (St.George), F.Winstone (St. George) J.F.McCarthy (Bedminster), H.H.Francis (Clifton), E.D.Compton (Clifton), O.T.Powell (Gloucester), D.Baugh (St. George).
Albion
J.Reader, M.Nicholson, T.McCulloch, J.Reynolds, C.Perry, W.Groves, W.Bassett, R.McLeod, S.Nicholls, F.Dyer, A.Geddes.

Fancy Dress

The Minsters brought their campaign to a close by putting on a Fancy Dress match at Greenway Bush Lane on April 19th. A crowd of about 1,500 were in attendance when W.G. Griffiths (Ally Sloper) pitting his side against a team organised by H.G. Harris (Lady Muldoon). There was a variety of fancy dresses on display; Bluejacket, Chimney Sweep, Cricketer, Drayman, Fireman, Highlander, Irishman, Masher, Minnie Palmer, Mrs Slap Cabbage, Policeman, Postman, Red Indian, Jack Tarr, but the most popular guise was, what in this present day and age would be called, a native of Africa. Great entertainment was had by all, though no one was sure as to which side had won, and it was resolved to hold further such events in the future.

Bedminster had made one alteration to their Committee for 1891-92 with S.J. Harris taking over as Vice-Captain in place of J.F. McCarthy, but further changes were made for 1892-93 when at a meeting on September 19th the Rev. A.B. Macfarlane was elected as Captain, with C.E. Gyles as his deputy. For the 2nd XI A.T. Wright was chosen as Captain, taking over from A. Latham who had been elected in 1890-91, and his Vice-Captain was E.T. Harris. The Reserves had a successful campaign, winning fifteen matches, drawing one, and losing five, scoring sixty-eight goals and conceding thirty-two.

League Action

The season saw the commencement of what was to become known as the Western League, though at this time it was called the Bristol & District League, this competition being formed at the instigation of W.A. Deakin (Chairman of Bedminster) and G.T. Bryant (St. George). The Minsters, as one of the founder members, ended the campaign in a creditable fourth place when the table looked thus:-

	P	W	D	L	F	A	Pts
Warmley	16	11	3	2	72	19	25
Trowbridge Town	16	10	4	2	66	17	24
St. George	16	9	5	2	36	22	23
BEDMINSTER	16	6	5	5	30	34	17
Clevedon	16	6	4	6	25	36	16
Eastville Rovers	16	6	3	7	36	40	15
Clifton	16	4	2	10	27	61	10
Mangotsfield	16	3	2	11	19	45	8
Wells	16	1	4	11	14	51	6

Extras

Bedminster formed a 3rd XI for this 1892-93 season, calling this team the Extras, but the only result that has come to light for the campaign is a 8-1 defeat away to St. Pauls Reserves on October 21st. The 2nd XI which had been running since the 1888-89 season went out of the Gloucestershire Junior Cup in what appears to be strange circumstances. They had been leading their 2nd Round match 4-2 at home to St. John's on November 19th when the game had to be abandoned in the 78th minute due to fading light, this in consequence of the referee, S.Fry, turning up 30 minutes late. However, despite this fact, the Gloucestershire F.A. at their meeting in the Earl Russell Hotel, Lawrence Hill, Bristol, on November 29th, ordered the match to be replayed on the St. Pauls ground on December 3rd when the Minsters lost 3-2. All the other fixtures played by the Reserves this campaign were Friendlies, but the following season brought expansion of the Bristol & District League and the election of the team to the Second Division of such organisation.

Local Leagues

The commencement of League competition locally stimulated interest and brought about similar arrangements for the junior clubs. 1893-94 saw the birth of the South Bristol & District League, this was followed by the East Bristol & District League, and the North Bristol & District League for 1894-95. In 1897-98 the South Bristol & District League tried to change their name to the Western Counties Alliance, but as such title wasn't acceptable to the Gloucestershire F.A. it was eventually called the Bristol & District Alliance, this organisation folding at the end of the campaign. Obviously the trend set by the Bristol & District League in changing their name to the Western League for 1895-96 had set a vogue, and in 1899-90 the East Bristol & District League adopted the original title of the Western League, hence the Bristol & District League of today, and in 1906-07 the North Bristol & District League became the Bristol & Suburban League. From the earliest days all manner of sport had been played on the Downs, and it was used extensively by rugby and soccer clubs, but it wasn't until 1905-06 that the Downs League was formed. Wednesday football was popular in Bristol from the mid-1890's and this brought about the establishment of the Bristol Wednesday League in 1907-08, thus leaving the later development of Sunday football which resulted in the formation of the Bristol & District Amateur Sunday Football League in 1966.

Rugby

The increasing numbers of league competitions reflected the enormous growth in the association game, and indeed sport in general, in 19th Century Bristol. The rugby code was flourishing much earlier than the round ball game with Clifton R.F.C., after being formed in 1872, becoming a major club and entertaining the likes of Cardiff - who they beat on at least two occasions in 1881 and 1883. Numerous local teams were operating, these included the Arabs (source of inspiration for the first name of Bristol Rovers), Ashley House, Bedminster, Brighton House, Bristol Rangers, Bristol Swifts, Carlton, Cotham, Frenchay, Harlequins, Hornets, Oakfield, Redland Park, Rockleaze, Westbury Park and Vauxhall Rangers. The last named Club played on the site of the current Ashton Gate stadium. The Arabs rose to become one of the prominent local sides, being good enough to confront the might of Newport on the Downs in front of 2,000 spectators on March 7th 1885.

Early Floodlights

At Western-super-Mare in 1881, a rugby match took place between the local side and Clifton R.F.C., when a crowd of 4,000 turned up to witness the novelty of the game being played under electric lights. Bristol R.F.C. came rather late on the scene, being the result of an amalgamation between Carlton and Redland Park in 1888, and they played their home fixtures on the County Ground which, as the new headquarters of Gloucestershire County Cricket Club, was opened for the summer game on April 22nd 1889.

Cricket

Cricket had been long established in the City, with clubs such as Clifton founded as early as 1821, Bedminster (1847), Downend, Knowle and St. George. The County side was formed in 1870, and performing in the County Championship they won the competition in 1874, 1876 and 1877, as well as sharing the honour with Nottinghamshire in 1873.

News Coverage

This growth in sporting pursuits, especially in regard to the association game, coupled with education reform which produced a society where most members were able to read, brought response from the Bristol Evening News in that they published a Special Saturday Football Edition, the first issue of which appeared on October 14th 1893. Eventually this developed into a sports paper in all but name, so it wasn't until April 5th 1919 that the proprietors of the Western Daily Press, of which the Evening News was a part, saw fit to produce the Sports News to rival the Sports Times that had first appeared towards the end of 1909. The weekly Bristol

Observer also carried a regular football column during the winter months, this commencing on February 9th 1895 and continued until March 3rd 1917.

Bristol South A.F.C.

The first Champion's of a local junior League were Bristol South who took top place in the South Bristol & District League in 1893-94, whereupon they took the decision to disband, though according to remarks in the local press the suggestion is that they amalgamated with the newly formed Bristol South End Club. This suggestion however, would not appear to be borne out by events, as when Bristol South's withdrawal from the League was accepted at a meeting held in the Hope & Anchor, Redcliffe Hill, on May 23rd, South End's Reserves failed in their bid for election to an enlarged competition, such combination of events indicating the likelihood that the two clubs were not connected. Bristol South, who appear to have been formed in the close season of 1891, played their home fixtures on the Chessels Fields, Bedminster.

Amateur Cup

Returning to the exploits of Bedminster we find them, in 1893-94, as entrants in the initial F.A. Amateur Cup competition, but after receiving a bye in the 1st Qualifying Round, they lost 3-0 to Home Park (Plymouth) at Greenway Bush Lane on November 4th. Trouble in the camp this campaign saw the departure of two of their keenest supporters, John Durant and Fred W. Keenan, who had been enthusiastic behind the scenes workers. They became prominent instigators in the formation of Bristol South End, this situation perhaps going someway towards explaining the rivalry between these two clubs which always appeared to owe more to the principal people on both sides, rather than the average supporter. However, despite this rift, public interest in the Minsters continued to develop and the attendance record, set the previous campaign when 3,000 were present to witness a 2-0 League win over Warmley on January 21st, was raised to 4,000 on the occasion of the visit of St. George in the Semi-Final of the Gloucestershire Cup on February 24th which was drawn 2-2. The start of the season had seen the composition of the Committee being changed with the position of Secretary being shared between Dr J.T. Wallace and W.H.Burland, and the role of first XI Captain taken by J.W.Wallace, with W.G.Griffiths as Vice-Captain.

First Six-a-Side Tournament

The campaign was brought to a conclusion with Bedminster involved in the inaugural Six-a-Side Tournament organised by the Bristol & District League. This event took place on the Chequers Ground, Kingswood (where Messrs. G.B.Britton Limited had their new shoe factory built in 1960), on April 21st when Eastville Rovers destroyed the Minsters hopes 21-0 in the 2nd Round.

New Rivals

Season 1894-95 dawned with the new upstart Bristol South End operating almost in Bedminster's backyard, and whilst this babe of the local scene had been denied entry to the Bristol & District League, they had arranged such an attractive list of friendly fixtures, including games against Preston North End,

Tottenham Hotspur and Swindon Town, that there was extremely hot competition for the uncommitted spectator. The first meeting of the new rivals took place at Greenway Bush Lane on March 23rd when a crowd of 4,000 saw the visitors win 2-0, thanks to first-half goals from Clements and Luffman.

The oddest match the Minsters were ever involved in occurred during this campaign, on March 9th, when they travelled to do battle with Mangotsfield in a League match. Their opponents only had two players available in consequence of suspensions, but still decided to fulfil the fixture as they assumed that they would be able to stop Bedminster from scoring because of the offside rule, which at this time required three players in front of the ball. This apparently worked for ten minutes or so, but then the Minsters were awarded a corner from which they subsequently put the ball in the net, whereupon Mangotsfield left the pitch to give the game to the visitors!

Alteration to the Committee saw Dr. I.T. Wallace assuming sole responsibility for the position of Secretary, F.E. Skeates becoming 1st team Captain with W.G. Griffiths as his deputy, F.Harris as Captain of the Reserves, and C.M. Tallack being Captain of the Extras. On December 15th, the Club held - reported as - their 2nd Concert, which took place at the Hope & Anchor, Redcliffe Hill, with H.G. Taskerin in the Chair.

Famous Visitors

This 1894-95 season, which had commenced with Bedminster winning through to the Final of the Trowbridge Six-a-Side Tournament on September 1st when they went down 10-5 to Southbroom, brought the only visit of a Football League club to Greenway Bush Lane. This occurred on November 26th when Stoke arrived to oppose a Bristol & District Representative XI and a crowd approaching 2,000 turned up and saw the First Division side take the lead after only two minutes when Evans scored. At half-time this advantage had been increased to 2-0 thanks to a goal from J. Robertson, and with this player notching two more after the break, as well as a successful strike from Dickson, without eliciting any response from the homesters, the final whistle found the team from the Potteries easy 5-0 winners. On this day the sides composed the following:-

Bristol & District League XI
F.W.Gyles (Bedminster), W.Grundy (Staple Hill), F.Lovett (Eastville Rovers), J.P.Ormiston (Clifton), S.J.Milne (Bedminster), F.Winstone (St.George), H.E.Smith (Bedminster), H.H.Francis (Clifton), C. Leese (St. George), N.Britton (St.George), W.Phipps (Warmley).
Stoke
Clawley, Forster, Eccles, Turner, T.Robertson, Brodie, Evans, Dickson, J.Robertson, Wilkes, Meston.

Visits by famous clubs were a regular feature of Bristol football at this time and, apart from matches covered elsewhere, these were as follows:-
Dec 22 1888 Gloucestershire 0 - Corinthians 10 (County Ground) 1,500
Mar 23 1894 Bristol & Dist.Lge. 0 - Sunderland 9 (The Chequers) 9,000
Mar 28 1894 Gloucestershire 1 - Corinthians 5 (The Chequers) 500

Oct 15 1894 Bristol & Dist.Lge. 0 - Aston Villa 8 (Bell Hill*) 6,000
Apr 16 1895 Bristol & Dist.Lge. 3 - Wolverhampton Wanderers 6 (Bell Hill) 5,500
Apr 30 1895 Bristol & Dist.Lge. 4 - Blackburn Rovers 7 (Bell Hill) 2,000
Apr 7 1896 Western League 2 - Aston Villa 0 (Bell Hill) 5,380 (£143.1s.6d)
Apr 9 1896 Clifton 0 - Corinthians 6 (The Chequers) 100
Apr 3 1897 Eastville Rovers 0 - Aston Villa 5 (Eastville*) 5,000
Apr 20 1897 Western Lge.1 - Nottingham Forest 9 (Bell Hill) 2,000
Apr 22 1897 St. George 1 - Derby County 7 (Bell Hill) 300
* Ground openings.

For important games Bedminster used to erect temporary stands at Greenway Bush Lane, but by the time of the Gloucestershire Junior Cup Semi-Final that was played on the ground on December 22nd 1894, when Warmley Reserves defeated the home Reserves XI 1-0, a permanent grandstand had been built, and was in use for the first time.

Lady Footballers

Towards the end of the campaign, on April 16th, the Lady Footballers came to Bristol, putting on a match at Greenway Bush Lane in front of 2,000 curious spectators. Unfortunately three of the ladies were indisposed, so two young men went in goal, and the Blues side, who beat the Reds 5-2, played one short.

Re-election

The Minsters finished the season fourth from the bottom of the First Division of the Bristol & District League, this requiring them to seek re-election for the first time. The Club had to go through this re-election ordeal on May 7th when the Bristol & District League held their meeting at the Earl Russell Hotel. The Minsters, along with the other retiring clubs, Mangotsfield and Swindon Wanderers (Clevedon having resigned), went into the ballot with aspiring teams, Barton Hill, Cardiff and St. Pauls, for the four places in the First Division. This resulted in Bedminster maintaining their status by topping the poll as follows:- Bedminster 12 votes, Cardiff 11, Swindon Wanderers 9, St. Pauls 9 (all elected), Mangotsfield 6, Barton Hill 1. With this hurdle safely surmounted the Minsters were hopeful of improving the situation in 1895-96 when the League, in consequence of a decision taken at this meeting, changed its title to the Western League.

New Record Attendance

The second match of the new campaign saw Bedminster's home attendance record raised again, when 5,000 spectators assembled on September 14th to witness the Minsters 6-3 triumph in an attractive Friendly against Mr J.A. Stevens Bristol City XI. This gathering at Greenway Bush Lane was destined to remain the highest at this venue, as, by the commencement of the following season, Bedminster were to be in their new home at Ashton Gate.

Limited Company

It was at a meeting held in the offices of the Bedminster Club solicitor, W.H. Brown, on December 12th 1895 that it was reported that Bedminster Cricket & Football Club, recently formed as a Limited Company for the purpose of acquiring a new ground (due to the fact that Greenway Bush Lane was to be built on), had been successful in obtaining a lease, on advantageous terms, from Sir Greville Smyth, for 11 acres of land opposite Bedminster Park. Dr E.H. Cook stated that agreement had been made with the Cricket section, and that negotiations were pending with the football fraternity in regard to the use of the new venue. A Company prospectus was being prepared, and work was to go ahead in the laying out of the ground and proceeding with the erection of the necessary pavilion and stands. Talks were also taking place with Bristol Bicycle & Tricycle Club, and if terms could be agreed it was intended that a cycle track be laid down. It was also hoped that in due course Somerset County Cricket Club would play some of their matches there.

Tragic Fatality

This last season at Greenway Bush Lane was a disappointing one as again the team finished fourth from bottom of the League, though the reduction in numbers saw them in 8th place compared to the 9th of the previous campaign. In both the F.A. and the Amateur Cup they fell at the first stage, but in the Gloucestershire Cup the Minsters won through to the Semi-Final before losing to Eastville Rovers at Greenway Bush Lane on March 28th, when the death of the homesters forward Herbert Edward Smith overshadowed all other events of this season.

Herbert, sustained a head injury early in the match when challenging for the ball with Lovett of Eastville Rovers. He continued after receiving treatment, but twice went off for further attention before finally retiring from the match in the second-half. Unfortunately no one realised the seriousness of his condition, and he returned home where he collapsed later that evening and died at approximately 6 o'clock the following morning, without regaining consciousness. As a mark of respect for this 27 year old, Bedminster cancelled their Easter fixtures.

Crowd Disorder

On March 7th, crowd disorder reared its head three weeks prior to the tragic event chronicled above, when, in a Western League Division Two fixture, Barton Hill came to Greenway Bush Lane and defeated the Minsters 2nd XI by the only goal of the game. This so unsettled the locals that the referee, Sam Peacock, was in fear for his safety. He had to be protected and escorted back into Bristol in order to be kept out of the hands of a number of youths, this incident making Mr Peacock assert that he had no wish to referee again in the future. The Western League Committee though were hopeful that he would eventually change his mind, and at their fortnightly meeting, held at the Conservative Club, Old Market, Bristol, on March 11th, they considered what measures to take in regard to the incident. After much deliberation they ordered Bedminster to print and exhibit 1,000 handbills warning of ground closure should the disgraceful scenes be repeated.

On February 19th a change was made in regard to the position of Secretary, J.F. McCarthy taking over from C.M. Tallack who had only been installed in this office at the commencement of the campaign.

The season was brought to a conclusion with the Minsters engaged in another Six-a-Side Tournament organised by the Western League, and April 23rd found them facing Eastville Rovers in a Semi-Final at Staple Hill. Unfortunately Bedminster were unable to gain revenge for the defeat suffered in the inaugural event two years previously as they succumbed yet again, though this time by the score of 16-9.

Another Re-election Ordeal

Bedminster's disappointing League position meant that for the second time they had to face up to a re-election ordeal. This should have taken place at the Western League meeting held at the Conservative Club, Old Market, on May 6th, but the matter of electing clubs was adjourned until a meeting held at the same venue a month later on June 3rd. After this delay Bedminster were safely restored to League membership, being voted in with Bristol South End.

Opening of Ashton Gate

Season 1896-97 saw the Minsters at Ashton Gate, though then known as the Bedminster Athletic Ground, and the first game at this venue was a Friendly against Staple Hill on September 12th. This was won by Bedminster 4-2 despite the Hillians, through Bracey, having the honour of obtaining the first goal on the ground. On this momentous occasion the teams lined up as follows:-
Bedminster
F.W.Gyles, A.F.Salter, G.H.Hemmens, D.Baugh, S.J.Milne, O.McAuliffe, J.F.McCarthy, E.T.Harris, G.Cottle, G.A.Pearson, W.Burley.
Staple Hill
W.Hudson, Grundy, Britton, Nicholls, Max Brain, Davis, Drury, Brimble, Punter, Bracey, Millard.
Referee J.A. Stevens.

The official opening however, was staged for the Western League match against Warmley two weeks later when 3,000 witnessed a 1-1 draw. At this time the football pitch wasn't where it is today, this area being the cricket ground. The winter game was confined to a corner of the site where the Bowling Green is now to be found. The cricket pitch didn't come into use until the following year when Dr W.G. Grace's team of twelve from Gloucestershire scored 212, and V.T. Hill's Somerset XII made 68 for 8 in reply. This fixture, which was effected by wet weather, took place on Friday, April 30th and the following day.

In the Gloucestershire Cup Bedminster reached their third Final, but meeting up with Warmley yet again they succumbed 2-0 in front of almost 7,000 spectators, paying receipts of £191.15s.5d, on the new St. George ground at Bell Hill on April 19th. This season brought the first League meetings between Bedminster and the South End Club, the honours being shared with each club winning their respective away fixture. The F.A. Cup and the Amateur Cup also produced clashes with South End, and again honours were shared with the Minsters accounting for the Garibaldians - as South End were popularly known - in the F.A. Cup, and their rivals gaining revenge in the lesser competition.

Charity Cup

A new tournament commenced locally this campaign with teams competing on a knock-out basis for a handsome bowl donated by C.H. Flook Esq. This competition was entitled the Bristol Charity Cup, and Bedminster won through to the Semi-

Finals before going out to their old adversaries from Warmley. This Charity Cup continued on a knock-out basis until being allowed to lapse for 1900-01, whereupon it was revived the following season as a League competition, and continued in this form until being concluded during the period of World War Two.

Gloucestershire Junior Cup Success

The Minsters ended their Western League campaign in third place, a new high, behind South End and Champions Warmley. But it was their 2nd XI to whom the honours went as they secured the Gloucestershire Junior Cup, demolishing Eastville Wanderers 6-0 in the Final played on the Ridgeway Ground on Christmas Day. April 11th saw Bedminster putting two sides in the field to contest the 7th Annual Warminster Six-a-Side Tournament that was held on the Holly Lodge Ground. The senior team received a bye in the 1st Round, but the Reserves disposed of Westbury 10-0 to progress through to the next stage where they went down 12-0 to Chippenham 'A'. This 2nd Round also brought the Minsters 1st team into the fray, and they took care of Trowbridge Conigre 15-1 to set up a Semi-Final confrontation with the conquerors of their Reserves. Unfortunately though they were unable to extract revenge as they lost by the narrow margin of 1-0.

Second A.G.M.

On February 1st 1897, Bedminster Cricket & Football Company Limited held their 2nd Annual General Meeting, at the Ford Memorial Hall, Bedminster. Chairman Dr E.H.Cook, in giving details of their 1st Annual Statement, reported that in the period from September 26th to December 31st 1896, gate receipts totalled £260.10s.5d, and profits amounted to £6.15s.3d. Directors G.Bracher and D.Thomas successfully offered themselves for re-election, and auditor Clement Gardiner was re-engaged for another year. Dr Cook said that the Company had taken possession of the new ground on March 25th the previous year, and following the achievement of having it ready for the start of the football season, it was expected that all would be well for the cricket opening on April 30th when the pavilion should be completed.

Special Match

However, before the grand cricket opening the Minsters' directors arranged a special exhibition soccer match to take place on the Bedminster Athletic Ground, inducing Derby County and West Bromwich Albion to play each other for a money prize, on Wednesday April 21st 1897. A crowd approaching 5,000, who paid receipts of £123.13s.6d turned up and saw the Rams beat the Baggies 2-1 with goals from John Goodall and the great Steve Bloomer, in response to the strike by Roddy McLead five minutes after the break. Derby did well to win as they were without the services of their goalkeeper Robinson. After being injured during the first-half, John Goodall took over in the first period, but at half-time Leiper took his place. On this day the sides lined up as follows:-

County
Robinson, Methven, Leiper, Cox, A.Goodall, Stanley, J.Goodall, Bloomer, Miller, Stevenson, McQueen.

Albion
Reader, Horton, Williams, Jones, McManus, Banks, Dean, Flewitt, McLeod, Richards, Garfield.

Prior to the above match early arrivals were treated to a schoolboys game; Redcliffe Boys beat a Bristol West XI 1-0.

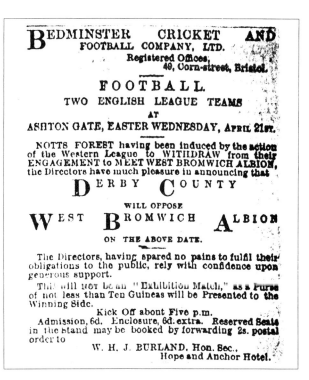

BEDMINSTER CRICKET AND FOOTBALL COMPANY, LTD.
Registered Offices,
49, Corn-street, Bristol.

FOOTBALL.
TWO ENGLISH LEAGUE TEAMS
AT
ASHTON GATE, EASTER WEDNESDAY, April 21st.

NOTTS FOREST having been induced by the action of the Western League to WITHDRAW from their ENGAGEMENT to MEET WEST BROMWICH ALBION, the Directors have much pleasure in announcing that
DERBY COUNTY
WILL OPPOSE
WEST BROMWICH ALBION
ON THE ABOVE DATE.

The Directors, having spared no pains to fulfil their obligations to the public, rely with confidence upon generous support.
This will not be an "Exhibition Match," as a Purse of not less than Ten Guineas will be Presented to the Winning Side.
Kick Off about Five p.m.
Admission, 6d. Enclosure, 6d. extra. Reserved Seats in the Stand may be booked by forwarding 2s. postal order to
W. H. J. BURLAND, Hon. Sec.,
Hope and Anchor Hotel.

The expenses incurred in putting on this venture amounted to £124.4s.9d, including £11 spent on seat improvements, so with gate receipts plus £3 in respect of programme sales it can be appreciated that little profit accrued from this enterprise.

The Big Divide

Professionalism came to Bristol for 1897-98, with Bristol City (after changing their name from Bristol South End), Eastville Rovers, St. George (now titled 'Bristol St. George'), and Warmley all taking the plunge. Eastville Rovers and Bristol St.George gained admittance to the Birmingham & District League, but the more ambitious Bristol City were elected to the First Division of the Southern League, much to the chagrin of Warmley who on joining the competition the previous year had had to start in the Second Division. Bedminster however, decided to remain amateur, but wishing to broaden their horizons, they, together with Bristol St. George, put themselves up for election to the Second Division of the Southern League at this organisation's Annual General Meeting on May 8th 1897. Unfortunately a proposition was carried to the effect that the Division be limited to twelve clubs, and following the re-election of Maidenhead, only one (St. Albans) of the ten hopeful applicants was successful. The Minsters were therefore obliged to play in the newly formed Amateur Section of the Western League, the competition having been split into a single Professional Division, and two Amateur Divisions. Bedminster were obviously in the top Division of the Amateur competition, and they romped away with the Championship, only losing one match, this the last game of the campaign.

Last Charity Cup Defeat

The Bristol Charity Cup was also divided between professionals and amateurs, with the latter taking part in a two section qualifying knock-out, the winners of each section meeting to decide the team to go forward and join battle with the professionals in the competition proper. The Minsters emerged as the side to carry the amateur colours after disposing of Barton Hill 5-1 in the Amateur Final, but they were brought down at the first time of asking by the professionals, losing 4-0 to old rivals Warmley. This was destined to be Bedminster's last defeat in the tournament, since during it's remaining life as a knock-out competition, the Minsters won the trophy on each occasion. Bedminster followed in the footsteps of Warmley who had won the trophy during the first two years, beating Bristol South End 2-1 in 1896-97 and accounting for Reading 3-0 in front of 2,000 spectators on the St George ground at Bell Hill on April 25th 1898.

Third A.G.M.

February 7th saw the 3rd Annual General Meeting of the Bedminster Cricket & Football Club, held at the Hope & Anchor, Redcliffe Hill, when Dr E.H.Cook declared a profit of £49.5s.0d, which went to the credit of the redemption fund, together with the previous profit of £6.15s.3d. New directors were appointed in A.W.Francis and E.J.Pilliers, in place of J.G.Russell-Harvey and W.Howell-Davies who did not offer themselves for re-election.

Professionalism

Feeling left behind by their old rivals, the Minsters decided to embrace professionalism and the 1898-99 campaign saw Bedminster in the First Division of the Southern League, along with Bristol City and Warmley, the latter club having gained promotion from the Second Division.

Warmley

Warmley were, without doubt, the elite club of early Bristol football. They won the Western League Championship and the Gloucestershire Cup on four occasions, but their record in the Second Division of the Southern League for 1897-98 was remarkable even for them. Promotion was achieved after finishing runners-up behind the Royal Artillery (Portsmouth) in both the League and a series of Test Matches. They completed an amazing record of not conceding a single goal in their home League programme. Unfortunately they rather blotted their copybook by letting in three in their two home Test Matches. This strong defence was greatly helped by the activity of their forwards who weighed in with 108 goals in the twenty-two League games, and another 14 in the last four Test Matches, to graphically illustrate the truth of the old maxim that 'attack is the best form of defence'. With the renowned White Shirts of Warmley also winning the Bristol Charity Cup and reaching the Final of the Gloucestershire Cup during the campaign, it can be realised what a momentous season it was for them, and makes the fact of their demise in January of the following year such a sad event.

Warmley's time in the First Division of the Southern League was a disaster. They suffered greatly with injuries to players, this serving to produce such poor form that it wasn't until December 10th that they were able to secure their first Southern League success, beating Sheppey United 4-0 on the Chequers Ground. This poor form, allied to inclement weather which coincided with their home games, brought about gates well under that required to meet their financial obligations, and matters came to a head following crowd trouble during and after a 5-1 home defeat by Millwall Athletic on January 7th. It was thought likely that this trouble would lead to an F.A. Inquiry, and in consequence a meeting was held four days later in the Kingswood Hotel, under the Presidency of F.Maggs, when the small number of people present were informed by the Secretary, T.B. Summers, that the Club was in debt by approximately £900.

During the summer, wages and expenses came to £320 of which only £90 was realised from calls on shareholders, and as gates receipts were only £547.4s.7d (£320.7s.9d in respect of matches at the Chequers), losses were of the order of £22 per week.

With the situation being considered untenable it was decided to adjourn and arrange a legally summoned meeting for the purpose of winding up the Club. A number of shareholders felt that if the situation was explained to the players they might be willing to complete the season's fixtures by only taking the balance of gate money following deduction of expenses. Accordingly T.B. Summers met with the players the following day, and they decided to continue the operation of the Club on the understanding that they would take all the gate money and accept responsibility for the payment of all expenses.

This agreement ensured the playing of two more matches, a 3-2 defeat at Brighton United on January 14th and a home loss 2-1 against the Royal Artillery the following week. The players, being by then fully acquainted with the inherent problems, realised they had little alternative than to let the famous old Club die, especially as the F.A. Inquiry into the incidents at the Millwall game - held at the Royal Hotel, College Green, Bristol on January 28th - ordered the closure of the Warmley ground for four weeks from January 30th.

Southern League Debut

Bedminster made their debut in the Southern League on September 10th 1898, when they obtained a commendable 1-1 draw with Tottenham Hotspur at Northumberland Park. Harry Smith had been engaged as the Minsters first manager, and under his capable direction the first success was gained, in their sixth match, on November 12th, when New Brompton were beaten 4-1 on the Bedminster Athletic Ground, this setting up a sequence of four successive wins. The first local derby brought a clash with Bristol City at St. John's Lane on December 17th, when in front of 10,250 spectators they went down 5-2 after holding their rivals 1-1 at half-time. The next weekend produced another derby clash, though this time with Warmley on the Chequers Ground, and again the Minsters were unable to find their form as they lost 3-2. The home fixture with Bristol City was brought off on March 4th, when revenge was extracted in front of a record 7,000 crowd, thanks to a goal in the second-half from Leonard.

Early Stars

The stars of the first professional Bedminster side included Robert Kelso, a Scottish International signed from Dundee, who Bedminster appointed Captain, James Whitehouse, a talented goalkeeper from Aston Villa, and Robert Crone, an Irish International who should have become the only player to be capped whilst at the Club. He was selected for the game against Wales on March 4th 1899, but had to decline the honour as Bedminster insisted that he turn out in the local derby played on this day.

The Minsters ended the campaign with a run of four successive wins to attain a final League placing of 8th, and they secured the Bristol Charity Cup by beating Reading 2-1 in front of 1,911 spectators at St. John's Lane on April 24th. The receipts, after the deduction of expenses, were given as £42.13s.6d.

(Right) An early Football Annual

(Below) Notice of a local derby match
(24th September 1898)

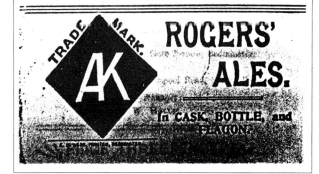

BRISTOL CITY FOOTBALL GROUND.

TO-DAY (SATURDAY), at 3.30,

ST. GEORGE v. BRISTOL CITY.

Admission as usual.

Alderman W. HOWELL DAVIES, J.P., has kindly
promised to kick off.

N

J. DAVERIDGE,
FAMILY WINE & SPIRIT MERCHANT,
"STAR" HOTEL,
North St., Bedminster.

Choice Old Wines & Spirits of various Brands in Stock.
Bass's Ale & Guinness's Stout.   First-Class Billiard Room.

HEAD-QUARTERS BRISTOL CITY FOOTBALL CLUB.

BRISTOL CITY
FOOTBALL ANNUAL
CONTAINING
Photos & Biographies of Players 1897-98.
PRICE 3D.

ROGERS'
ALES.

TRADE MARK. AK

In CASK, BOTTLE, and
FLAGON.

Bristol South End A.F.C

Minutes season 1897 8

A meeting of members of the above Club
was held on April 3 1897 at the
Albert Call Bedminster to hear
the Report of the Committee in the
running the Club as a Professional
one and to devise the best means of
carrying it on as such

There was a very large attendance
of members presided over by the
Chairman of the Club. Mr. Jarvis Jarvis
who explained the reason for a more
this were met and called in the
Secretary of the Investigation committee
Mr. W. Councilman to give their
report — which was adopted

Mr. Locke explained the character
scheme which the Committee of
Management recommended the
members to adopt and was supported
by Mr. Turns and other members of
the Committee

After much discussion it was
Resolved on the proposition of
Mr. A. Boone seconded by Mr. H. Fox
"That we adopt professionalism"
This was carried unanimously

(Above) Handwritten minutes of the Bristol South End meeting
held on the 3rd April 1897.

BRISTOL CITY ATHLETIC GROUND.

GREAT ENGLISH CUP TIE.

SATURDAY NEXT, JANUARY 28TH, at 2.45.

SUNDERLAND
v.
BRISTOL CITY.

Referee: Mr T. HELME (Bolton).
Linesmen: Messrs. P. A. Timms (London), and G. H. Skar-
rington (Ipswich), Members of the Football Association.

Tickets can be obtained up to 7 p.m. on Friday Next, the
27th, at the following places, viz:—Headquarters, Angel
Hotel, Redcliff Street; Star Hotel, North Street, Bedminster;
Prince Hotel Totterdown; P. O'Brien, East Street, Bed-
minster; T. Willis, Newsagent, East Street, Bedminster;
Maxwell's Restaurant, Nicholas Street, L. H. Rydell, Book-
seller, Union Street; and of the Secretaries, at the following
prices, viz.:—
To Ground 6d, No. 2 Enclosure 1s (including admission to
Ground), Stand Enclosure 2s (including admission to
Ground), Numbered Reserved Seats:—Whole of Covered
Stand 3s each, on field of play 6s each, may be booked at
Headquarters, Angel Hotel, Redcliff Street, or through the
Secretaries.
NOTE:—Prices on Day of Match will be—
                     To Ground. No. 2 Enc. Stand Enclosure
Adults   . . 1s . .   1s extra . . . . 1/6 extra
Boys   . . 3d . .   6d extra . . . . 1/- extra
        SEASON TICKETS NOT AVAILABLE.

(Above) From the Bristol Evening News -
details of the F.A.Cup clash on 28th January 1899

First International Match in Bristol

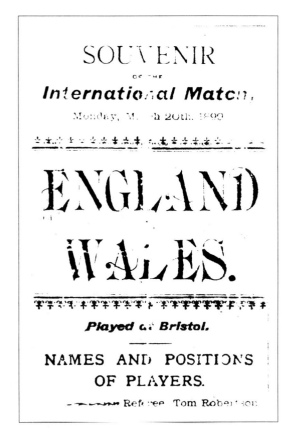

SOUVENIR
of the
International Match,
Monday, March 20th, 1899

ENGLAND
WALES.

Played at Bristol.

NAMES AND POSITIONS
OF PLAYERS.

Referee Tom Robertson

The highlight of the season was the first International match played in Bristol, though the selection of the Bedminster ground for the game against Wales caused much local jealously, as many thought that Bristol City's St. John's Lane ground should have been the chosen venue. It is difficult to understand the reasons for this disagreement, as there appears little doubt that the Bedminster Athletic Ground was the best choice, only the Rovers ground at Stapleton Road (Eastville) being a realistic alternative.

The jealously served to keep the attendance down to 6,000, with receipts of £320, on March 20th, when England won 4-0 thanks to goals from Steve Bloomer (2), Ernest Needham and Fred Forman. On this historic occasion the line-up was as follows:-
England
Robinson (Southampton), Thickett (Sheffield Utd), Williams (West Bromwich Albion), Frank Forman (Nottingham Forest), Crabtree (Aston Villa), Needham (Sheffield Utd), Athersmith (Aston Villa), Bloomer (Derby County), G.O. Smith (Corinthians), Settle (Bury), Fred Forman (Nottingham Forest).
Wales
S.Jones (Druids), Arridge (New Brighton Tower), Blew (Wrexham), Richards (Druids), Buckland (Bangor), Harrison (Wrexham), Vaughan (Druids) Meredith (Manchester City), Owen (Crewe Alexandra), Morris (Nottingham Forest), Atherton (Hibernians)
Referee
Tom Robertson (Queens Park)

The Strange Case of the Missing Cash

At this time the football section of the Bedminster Club was run by a Syndicate Committee, who paid one third of all home gate receipts as rent to the main company, and it was this Committee who had the task of making the necessary arrangements for the successful staging of this great honour for Bristol soccer. This duty was admirably discharged by the following:- F.N.Bacon, H.J.Ball, W.H.Burland, G.J.C.Labdon, F.V.Larway, J.H.Leakey, F.W.Mapson, E.J.Pillers and D.Thomas, but the end of the game produced problems and a mystery for W.H.Burland, the Financial Secretary, who was responsible for the gate money of £320. On taking the money for banking, Mr Burland found he was £5 short, a sum he was obliged to make up himself as a search failed to reveal the location of the deficit; however a fortnight later a bag with the missing money turned up in one of the dressing rooms.

Fourth A.G.M.

A profit of £61.17s.10d for the year-ending December 31st 1898 was announced by Chairman Dr E.H.Cook at the 4th Annual General Meeting, held at the Bedminster Hotel, East Street, Bedminster, on February 6th 1899, this profit again going towards the redemption fund which now totalled £117.18s.1d. J.Lawson was elected to the Board in place of E.J. Pillers, who did not seek re-election, and Dr E.H. Cook and A.J. Beavon in offering themselves for further service were successfully returned.

New Manager

However, despite this profit, finance was a problem. A meeting of supporters on April 19th saw £500 being raised to produce hope that the 1899-1900 campaign, with Sam Hollis taking over as manager after resigning from Bristol City, would see them challenging for honours. The appointment of Samuel Woodroffe Hollis in the dual role of Secretary/ Manager at a salary of £225 per annum plus a bonus for certain levels of success, was confirmed at a Committee meeting held on April 26th, and with Robert Crone being the only player re-signed for the new season Mr Hollis got to work in his usual fashion to gather together a team.

Newcomers

The players he recruited included goalkeeper George Toone from Notts County, forwards Francis Becton from Sheffield United, and Albert Flewitt from West Bromwich Albion - all three being English internationals. Hugh Wilson, a utility player and Scottish International, came from Sunderland and was appointed Captain, forward Tommy Boucher from Notts County, and half-back Peter Chambers ex-Blackburn Rovers, were also signed. During the course of the campaign, fullback George Barker joined from Bristol City. He was described as the best player in his position in the Southern League.

Best F.A. Cup Run

The Minsters commenced their Southern League season with three successive wins. The worst playing sequence was just two consecutive defeats (apart from the last month when amalgamation with Bristol City had been agreed upon), and Bedminster ended with a final placing of 6th. This served to make the Minsters the most successful of the local clubs. This fact was further emphasised when they retained the Bristol Charity Cup on March 24th, when they gained a well merited 4-1 victory over Bristol Rovers at St. John's Lane in front of 6,034 spectators who had paid receipts of £172.11s.7d. The F.A. Cup saw Bedminster having their best ever run as they managed to win through to the Final Qualifying Round before succumbing 2-1 at home to Portsmouth, a match watched by a 6,000 crowd on December 9th.

Fifth A.G.M.

Sam Hollis found problems in combining the role of Secretary/Manager with that of his business interests in the licensed trade, so Mr Mapson took over the duties of Football Club Secretary on February 28th 1900. A profit of £57.1s.2d was declared for the year-ending December 31st 1899, by Financial Secretary W.H. Burland at the 5th Annual General Meeting of the Bedminster club, which was held under the Presidency of Dr E.H. Cook at the Bedminster Hotel, on February 5th.

No doubt this continuing profitability, together with the success of the team, probably gave the Minsters' supporters every expectation of continued enjoyment in watching their favourites. Behind the scenes however, despite denials to the contrary, moves were afoot that were to change these expectations. Disappointment was expressed in regard to the fact that Somerset Cricket Club had still not played on the ground, they being of the opinion that the outfield was substandard, and had not seen fit to make financial contributions, apart from £1.15s.0d, towards the cost of the ground drainage and improvements. The retiring directors W.E. Gardner and F.V. Larway in offering themselves for re-election were successfully returned to office, and Clement Gardiner, the auditor, was re-engaged as normal for another year. The meeting concluded with a financial presentation to W.H. Burland in respect of his recent marriage.

Amalgamation

The Bedminster Board, particularly W.H. Burland and A.W. Francis, were mindful of the fate of the two oldest rivals in the east of the City - Bristol St. George and Warmley - who in not acting on amalgamation proposals put forward in the Spring of 1897, eventually disbanded; Warmley, as previously mentioned, in January 1899, and St. George at the end of the 1898-99 season. Therefore it was considered a wise move that consideration be given in regard to the establishment of one professional club in south Bristol. The first moves were made by Bedminster in the 1898-99 campaign, this remarked upon at the A.G.M. on February 7th 1899, in that an approach to Bristol City had been rebuffed. Not deterred however, they continued with the suggestion, and Bristol City responded during the first week of April 1900 by making clear that they were only prepared to consider amalgamation on the basis that everything Bristol City would be retained at the expense of Bedminster.

Not surprisingly most people, including the local press, thought this would be an end to the matter, despite the general feeling that amalgamation was necessary, but the wise members of Bedminster refused to be deterred. Mr Francis organised a further meeting, and eventually a compromise was sorted out which was put to the Bristol City shareholders at the Temperance Hall, Bedminster, on Tuesday, April 10th. The meeting accepted the compromise that the Board of the amalgamated club would comprise equal members of Bedminster and Bristol City directors, and acknowledged that Bristol City would continue as the going concern with their colours and inferior ground at St. John's Lane being retained.

Though it was thought expedient, in order to attract the erstwhile Bedminster supporter, that home matches during the initial campaign be shared between Ashton Gate and St.John's Lane.

Following this amalgamation agreement the Minsters suffered a loss of form bringing about three successive Southern League defeats, but they bounced back with a fine 4-1 home win over Queens Park Rangers on April 25th when the attendance was reported as only totalling one hundred. The Club then brought their Southern League career to an end with a goalless draw at Reading on April 28th, leaving one more game to play, a clash with Bristol City in the Final of the Gloucestershire Cup.

Final Rites

Bedminster were firm favourites for this match played on the Bristol Rovers ground at Eastville (at this time referred to as Stapleton Road), on April 30th, when the Minsters seized the opportunity to go out on a high and leave no one in any doubt as to their status as the 'best team in Bristol'. The fact of amalgamation was responsible for a lack of interest in the game, this restricting the attendance to less than 2,000, paying receipts of £61.9s.3d, who saw Bedminster do most of the early attacking after losing the toss. However, they didn't achieve an early breakthrough, despite City losing the services of Jones for a while to have his injured nose attended to, and it wasn't until their opponents were back to full strength that they went in front, Boucher seizing on a back pass from McDonald to put the ball between the sticks. This advantage was then doubled within a short while, Geddes easily beating Lewis in putting away a cross from the right. City then responded with a spell of attacking and obtained an indirect free-kick that Robson unfortunately put into the back of the net without anyone else touching it. The Minsters pressed at the start of the second-half, but it wasn't until five minutes before the call of time that the score was added to, a miskick by McDonald setting up another goal for Geddes. This served to produce a positive response from City in the very next minute. Russell tricked Barker, and crashed in a shot that hit the crossbar, which rebounded into the net off one of the Bedminster backs, to complete the scoring with the Minsters 3-1 ahead, and therefore winners of the Gloucestershire Cup for the second, and last, time.

Bedminster
Toone, Barker, R.H. Davies, Draycott, W.H. Davies, Chambers, Whelan, Flewitt, Boucher, Wilson, Geddes.
Bristol City
Lewis, McDonald, Robson, Downie, McLean, Hamilton, Potter, Blessington, Jones, O'Brien, Russell.
Referee
T. Armitt (Leek)

So passed into history the maroon and old gold shirts of the renowned Minsters, who in 1893 had one of the largest followings in local football with a membership of some 400. The future of the association game was now to principally rest with the City and Rovers' Clubs, though both Bristol St. George and Warmley later reformed as amateur organisations.

CHAPTER FOUR - BRISTOL SOUTH END

Early Days

Following the auspicious start to the career of this new club, they faced up to their first local derby on September 15th 1894, but the same line-up that had put eleven goals past Swindon Wanderers the previous Saturday was unable to register at St. George, where they went down 2-0. This however, proved to be a temporary hiccup as they then embarked on a seven match unbeaten run, winning six, before succumbing 4-2 at home to Hereford Thistle on November 10th when they made their debut in the F.A. Amateur Cup. A further run of three consecutive wins then followed before losing 4-2 on December 15th when Clifton were the visitors. This left South End with the record of having won ten of the fifteen matches played - one being drawn - scoring forty goals and only conceding nineteen. After this though the Garibaldians' (red shirts were worn by the followers of Italian revolutionary Garibaldi) form deserted them, and the remaining twenty two matches only produced five wins. During this disappointing spell they made their debut in the Gloucestershire Cup, but again failed to live up to their early reputation, going out at the first time of asking, 2-0 at Mangotsfield on January 19th.

This inaugural season saw the club also operating a 2nd XI, and a 3rd XI (Extras), but both of teams suffered the same fate as the senior side by being denied entry to any League. They also had to content themselves with the playing of Friendlies, the only exception being the Reserves' involvement in the Gloucestershire Junior Cup. In this competition they successfully negotiated two hurdles, beating Eastville Rovers Reserves 2-1 away, and Mangotsfield Reserves 3-1 at home, before going out at Frenchay 5-3.

The star performers of the South End Club were Hammer Clements and Frank Mayger, these two being so highly thought of that comparison was made with the great Billy Bassett of West Bromwich Albion and England fame. It was said that *'whilst Midland spectators might boast of Bassett, local enthusiasts thought that none could compare with Mayger and Clements when playing for South End'*.

Hamlet Horatio Clements

Variously referred to as Hammer and Hamer, Clements was a popular player for both the Bedminster and Bristol South End clubs. He was born in August 1874 and he learnt his football at the City School in Bristol, later turning out for the Redcliffe team that played at Windmill Hill. The Bedminster Club were impressed, and he made his debut for the Minsters in 1893-94, playing in the same forward line as Frank Mayger, a left-wing partnership that continued in the first two seasons of the South End Club. Hammer was equally at home in the forward or half-back line and, with Frank Mayger and Phil Britton (Warmley), he was regarded as one of the leading amateur players in the district. This was a status that he retained throughout his career, as even after the adoption of professionalism by Bristol City and Bedminster, he still made appearances for them. Clements, who also turned out for the Gloucestershire Representative XI, stood 5ft 9in tall, weighed

around 12st 4lbs, and was a resourceful player whose great asset was a fine turn of speed. He was a keen sprinter and a member of Bristol Athletic Club, becoming their assistant Honorary Secretary. He brought his football career to a close when playing in the same Arlington Rovers side as Billy Wedlock around the turn of the century. Unfortunately he suffered an early death, being found lying by the roadside at 10.05pm on Tuesday March 29th 1910. According to the Inquest he had died about an hour earlier, after getting off the train and making his way up the hill to his Nailsea home, having had a massive heart attack. In memory of this fine player, Bristol City held a minute's silence before the home game with Woolwich Arsenal on April 2nd.

HAMMER CLEMENTS.

Frank Ernest Mayger

Together with Hammer Clements, Mayger was the star of the Bristol South End team, and such was his ability that he was asked to turn professional by the Bristol City manager Sam Hollis. However, he resisted all such overtures as he had a good job with Messrs. Colthurst & Harding Limited, from where he eventually retired as their Chief Accountant. He attended Redcliffe School, and started his footballing career by turning out for the Redcliffe Club who played at Windmill Hill. Frank joined Bedminster in 1892 and he achieved folklore status when he notched all five of his side's goals in a Gloucestershire Cup Success over Craigmore College on January 28th 1893. He moved across to St. John's Lane to become part of the fledgling Bristol South End team in 1894, where he made 48 appearances and scored 12 goals in two seasons. Frank played for the Gloucestershire Representative side. He was very active in politics, being Secretary of the local Conservative & Unionist Association for twenty years until his resignation in 1928. He was born on October 16th 1873 and died on January 7th 1960, when he was living in Bloomfield Road, Brislington, having moved there in the early 1950's, from Rose Cottage, Dundry, where he had lived for many years. Frank married for the second time on July 10th 1937, to Miss M. Edwards, and this union was blessed with a daughter, Monica, in 1940.

The Tilley Sisters

On February 27th, a special match was put on at St. John's Lane, in aid of the Lord Mayor's Relief Fund for the Unemployed, when the South End players put two suitably dressed teams in the field for a match to be played between the Lady Impersonators and the Gentlemen. A crowd said to be in excess of 3,000 paying receipts of £31.13s.3d were in attendance to see the Lady Impersonators take the honours by winning 5-3 after being level at the break 2-2. The Tilley sisters - star variety performers of the time - were also present to lend support to the fund raising activities, and by going round the ground in Italian costume with a barrel organ and tambourines, they bolstered the fund by a further £3.6s.0d. Photographs were taken of the players with the Tilley sisters prior to Amy starting the game for the Gentlemen, her sister Nellie doing likewise for the Lady Impersonators after the break. For this worthy cause the sides lined up as follows:-

Lady Impersonators
A.Bellamy, S.Pitman, H.Elvin, F.Millard, A.Jones, S.Davis, H.Williams, F.Elmes, W.Lewis, H.Clements, F.Mayger.
Gentlemen
A.Jackson, G.Jones, Hale, R.Hunt, W.Cranfield, A.Gridland, F.Luffman, S.S.Martell, A.Cleak, W.Hollister, M.Cranfield.

The Old Invincibles

The 1st Annual Dinner was held, under the Presidency of W.R. Nurse, at the Ford Memorial Hall, Mill Lane, Bedminster, on May 29th 1895. Harry Locke (Treasurer) declared a profit of £62.4s.4d., in respect of the first season. Gate receipts were £400.9s.4d, which included £49.12s.7d taken for the fixture against Preston North End on April 6th. It was considered to be quite a coup that this newly formed amateur side was able to induce such a famous club as the Old Invincibles of Preston (founder members of the Football League and first Champions in 1888-89 when they didn't lose a match and also won the F.A. Cup) to come to Bristol and play at St. John's Lane.

Not surprisingly South End proved no match for their illustrious visitors. Clements scored a disputed goal for the homesters, in front of a 2,000 crowd who had assembled despite the torrential rain, but Proud Preston obtained six. The game was refereed by South End Committee man George Elmes who did little to conceal his excitement when awarding his team's goal, running back to the centre-circle exclaiming *"Goal! Goal"* !

Total income for the season came to £651.5s.6d., due to the addition of subscriptions totalling £109.10s.1d, and the proceeds of a bazaar which raised £139.17s.8d, plus £1.8s.5d from the sale of hat cards. Expenditure came to £589.1s.2d., which included ground improvement costs of £109.9s.2d, rent of £20 and away match expenses of £62.0s.6d.

First Honours

A meeting of South End Club members on April 13th issued this communique, after deciding by a large majority not to make application for membership of the Bristol & District League for 1895-96:- *"This meeting of Bristol South End Football Club desires to add its appreciation of the good work done by the Bristol & District League and that this resolution is in no way antagonistic to that body. This Club will always be glad to work and cordially co-operate with the League for the advancement of football in the district".* In consequence another season of Friendlies were arranged, but the 2nd XI (changing their name to South End Athletic) and the 3rd XI were, however, successful in securing election to Divisions One and Two respectively of the South Bristol & District League, at meeting held at the Angel Hotel, Redcliffe Street, on May 22nd. It was the Athletic who had the distinction of obtaining the Club's first honour by winning the Championship at their initial attempt.

South End Wednesday

The 1895-96 campaign also saw the formation of the team to play on Wednesdays, such team being known as Bristol South End Wednesday. They commenced their career on November 20th when, thanks to a solitary goal from Grindley, Redland Grove College were beaten at St. John's Lane. For the home match that was won 4-0 with goals from Grindley (3) and Macfarlane, against Mr J.A. Stevens Bristol City XI on Christmas Day in front of 2,000 spectators, a virtual 1st XI was fielded, the two sides lining up thus:-

South End Wednesday
A.Jackson, Binding, A.Jones, R.Grey, H.Clements, M.Cranfield, F.S.Davis, A.B.MacFarlane, W.H. Grindley, W.Lewis, C.Taylor.
Mr J.A. Stevens Bristol City XI
G.Speck (Gloucester), Grundy (Staple Hill), A.Britton (Staple Hill), S.J. Milne (Bedminster), Peacock (Staple Hill), Nicholls (Staple Hill), H.Williams (South End Athletic), A.Taylor (Clifton), W .Rooke (Staple Hill), Phipps (Staple Hill), Thomas (Clifton).

F.A.Cup Debut

The end of the season for this midweek side saw them with the record of having won five of their sixteen games, drawing five and losing six, with thirty five goals being scored and thirty-two conceded.

The campaign was notable in that it brought the Club's first foray in the F.A. Cup (then commonly known as the English Cup), and a successful start was made with Slough being disposed of 5-1 in a Preliminary Round match played at St. John's Lane on October 5th when Clements notched a hat-trick. Unfortunately they went out in the next round a week later, 1-0 at home to Great Marlow, after putting up a great fight with only nine men from the 20th minute. Arthur Jones and Taylor collided when the latter player headed away.

Officials

The officials of the Club, in this their second season, comprised the President John Durant, twelve Vice-Presidents Col. Sir E.S.Hill K.C.B., M.P. J.Barnes, E.Carpenter, M.Clancy, A.E.Denby, W.E.Gardner, P.Harding, J.Harris, W.A. Latham, Dr Rudge, Capt. Trestrail, and A.Whittington. A Main committee with eighteen members:- B.Barnes, J.Barnes, A.J.Bellamy, H.Clements, J.Crompton, A.E.Denby, G.Elmes, H.C.Ewens, A.Hone, T.Humpage, A.Jones, F.Millard, W.E.Poole, H.Prescott, F.W.Saunders, A.Whittington, A.Williams, and J.Worth. A Selection Committee comprising eleven members:- A.J.Bellamy, H.Clements, J.Crompton, G.Elmes, E.Ford, A.Jones, F.Millard, H.Prescott, A.Smith, W.F.Ward, and J.Worth. The post of Secretary remained in the hands of W.B.Hodgkinson, but he now had W.G.Tozer as his assistant. James Barnes was Chairman with George Elmes as his deputy, and the position of Treasurer remained the tandem operation of the Locke brothers. On the playing side, the 1st XI Captaincy was still in the capable hands of Arthur Jones, but his Vice-Captain was now Fred Millard, the latter retaining his interest in the Club right up to his death on January 26th 1952 at the age of 78, being then employed as gate supervisor at Ashton Gate. The Athletic Captain was A.J. Bellamy, with A.Cleak as his second, and J.Haig was Captain of the Extras.

Rules

At this time the Rules of the Club, as given in the handbook for 1895-96, were:-

1. That the Club be known as the Bristol South End A.F.C. and that the Club colours be Red Shirts and Dark Navy Blue knickers.
2. That the affairs of the Club be managed by a committee consisting of the Officers and 14 members, to be annually elected at the 1st General Meeting in each season.
3. That a General Meeting be held at least twice a year.
4. That at a General Meeting at the end of the season, the Secretary shall present a statement of the affairs of the Club and that should such statement show a deficit it shall be met in such a manner as the General Meeting shall suggest.
5. That candidates be proposed and seconded by Members of the Club; the proposer to deposit the subscription at the time of nomination. In the event of any candidate being rejected, the subscription shall be refunded to the proposer.
6. That the annual subscription be, for bona fide players 2/6d. per annum, non-players 5/- per annum, and ladies 2/6 per annum, payable on or before the 1st day of September.

The season was brought to a conclusion with the Club holding their 2nd Annual Dinner on May 12th at the Ford Memorial Hall, Mill Lane, Bedminster, when Mr Locke presented the balance sheet that showed the financial position to be healthy. Congratulations were offered to goalkeeper Jackson who appeared in all the 1st team games.

The expulsion of Cardiff from the Western League at the turn of the year following their failure to fulfil fixtures and pay fines, brought about a change of heart from South End, and they decided to offer to take over the fixtures of the Welsh club.

This offer was considered at a Western League meeting held at Earl Russell Hotel, Lawrence Hill, on January 15th 1896, when the committee voted 9 to 7 to reject South End yet again, issuing this statement:- *"The Western League thank the South End Club for their offer, but regret that they cannot see their way clear, owing to the question of points and other various difficulties of the case, to accept it, but the League trust that the South End Club will renew it's application next season, and the South End Club is further assured that this resolution has nothing to do with any personal matter between the League and the South End Club".*

The Garibaldians were not pleased by this further rejection, but good sense prevailed by the end of the season when they resolved to make another application for Western League membership. Accordingly they therefore stood for election at a meeting held at the Conservative Club, Old Market Street, on June 3rd when at last, they were successful.

It didn't take long for South End to justify their Western League membership as they were early leaders in the chase for the Championship, by winning their first four games. They were however, no match for the eventual Champions, Warmley, losing 4-0 on the Tennis Court Ground in front of 4,464 spectators on December 28th, and going down 3-0 on their own patch on April 24th watched by a crowd numbering some 2,500. The Garibaldians ended their inaugural League campaign as runners-up, the completed table looking thus:-

	P	W	D	L	F	A	Pts
Warmley	16	13	2	1	42	9	28
SOUTH END	16	11	0	5	28	22	22
Bedminster	16	8	2	6	32	16	18
St. George	16	8	1	7	27	23	17
Eastville R.	16	7	2	7	25	23	14*
Trowbridge T.	16	5	3	8	21	30	13
St. Pauls	16	3	5	8	29	31	11
Staple Hill	16	5	0	11	18	39	10
Clifton	16	4	1	11	19	48	9

* Two points deducted for playing an ineligible man.

The McClean Affair

On losing their home League game against Eastville Rovers, 3-1 on January 9th, South End lodged a complaint in regard to the playing of an ineligible man. This was upheld by the Western League Committee in that Rovers had played John McClean, an ex-professional with Burslem Port Vale, who had been paid 15 shillings per week to work on the ground of the Eastville Club. The Rovers were fined £1, had two points deducted and were ordered to replay all matches in which the player had appeared. There was, however, an exception to this latter instruction, with the game against South End that started the matter off, as it appears that the Garibaldians were less than straightforward in regard to their protest as they had endeavoured to induce the self-same John McClean to turn out for them by offering him £1.5s.0d. to work at St John's Lane!

Record Defeat

South End lost to Bedminster in the F.A.Cup, but in gaining their revenge in the Amateur Cup, they went on to reach the

1st Round proper before they received their come-uppance, against the eventual winners, the Old Carthusians. This fixture took place at St. John's Lane on January 30th, when South End had the misfortune to suffer their worst defeat, going down 10-0.

The visitors, who had been the very first winners of this tournament in 1893-94 (when they beat the Casuals 2-1 at Richmond), arrived at full strength and after surviving early home pressure took control. Half-time arrived when the Old Carthusians led 2-0, thanks to goals from Smith and Tringham, and by the final whistle they had increased this by a further eight with strikes from Smith (4), Tringham (2), Buzzard and a Clements own goal to thereby register double figures.

South End
G.Speck, E.Robson, A.P.Frith, H.Clements, J.S.Ross, G.E.Hockin, W.Thompson, J.Quinlan, H.Porter, A.Fielding, F.Fielding.

Old Carthusians
B.K.R.Wilkinson, E.H.Bray, W.W.Timmins, E.C.Bliss, C.Wreford-Brown, S.Darvell, E.M.Jameson, E.M.Tringham, G.O.Smith, E.F.Buzzard, C.D.Hewitt.

Referee
P.R.MacLaughlin (Freemantle)
Linesmen
T.B.Summers (Warmley) and C.Fuller (Hampshire Association).

Professionalism

This heavy defeat served to confirm the thoughts of the South End Committee in that they had progressed as far as they were able with local amateur players, and gave added thrust to the moves that were already in motion in regard to exploring the possibilities of adopting professionalism and gaining admittance to the First Division of the Southern League.

At this time the affairs of the Club were in the hands of Albert E.Denby (President), James Barnes (Chairman), H.C. Ewens and A.Howe (Joint Treasurers), Walter G.Tozer & Arthur Jones (Joint Secretaries), and on field matters were under the direction of Hammer Clements (Captain) and Robert Skelding (Vice-Captain); notable absentees being John Durant, W.B.

Hodgkinson and E.J. Locke. There was some discord in the camp on gaining Western League status and although John Durant was unanimously re-elected President, he declined the post, and Albert Denby took over. The absence of W.B.Hodgkinson and E.J.Locke was more of a mystery, but as the move to professionalism became known all was revealed.

The absentees felt their hands would be tied by being officially connected to the Club, so they relinquished office to work tirelessly for the secret Investigation Committee that had been founded to explore the possibility of South End's adoption of professionalism and gaining entry to the Southern League. This Committee comprised James Barnes, James Crompton, Albert Denby, H.C. Ewens, W.B. Hodgkinson, T.Humpage, E.J. Locke and Walter E. Tozer. Meetings were held regularly at Albert Denby's home, reporting on - amongst other things - their frequent contact with Nat Whittaker, the Southern League Secretary, and S.R. Carr, a Southern League Committee member.

At last all was ready for the results of their labours to be announced, and on April 3rd 1897, a meeting of all Club members was held at the Albert Hall, Bedminster, when professionalism was adopted, all members being asked to become guarantors at ten shillings each. Messrs Whittaker and Carr both spoke at the meeting, Whittaker guaranteeing that South End would be elected to the First Division of the Southern League and Carr stating that the Club's interests would be best served by having the smallest possible Management Committee. This meeting was adjourned until April 27th for a further report from the Investigation Committee, and then adjourned again until May 10th - two days after South End had secured election to the First Division of the Southern League.

This latter meeting saw the Albert Hall overflowing when James Barnes (Chairman) called on W.B.Hodgkinson to give his report, and then arrange for the election of the Management Committee. Albert E.Denby (Chairman), W.B.Hodgkinson (Secretary), E.J.Locke (Financial Secretary), James Crompton, H.C.Ewens, F.H.Hawksby and Walter G.Tozer were duly elected. Two dozen representatives of the Southern League were present at this meeting, they having been regally entertained at the Mitre Hotel before the start, and the help given by Messrs Whittaker and Carr was gratefully acknowledged by the presentation to them of silver cigarette boxes.

Unfortunately, the guarantee system wasn't a success, so another scheme was put forward, that of turning the Club into a limited liability company, and at the Albert Hall on June 4th, members gave their approval. Accordingly, a Board of Directors was elected, it's members being Albert E.Denby (Chairman), James Crompton, H.C.Ewens, F.H.Hawksby, and Walter G.Tozer. Later, the size of this Board was increased to eight with the appointments of James Barnes, William P.Kingston (on July 19th) and Joseph Daveridge (on August 4th). The capital of the company was £2,500 in £1 shares of which 1,400 were offered to the public.

New Name

Whilst all these meetings were taking place, the name of the Club had not been settled. The Investigation Committee had decided early in their deliberations that the Club needed a new identity, and in settling for Bristol City, this was considered by the Gloucestershire Football Association at their meeting held at the Full Moon Hotel, North Street, Stokes Croft, Bristol, on April 27th 1897. The initial response wasn't encouraging as the Gloucestershire F.A. ruled that *"it would be detrimental to the interests of the clubs in the city and neighbourhood if any one club was allowed to take the name of Bristol City"*, causing the Bristol Times and Mirror of the following day to comment that *"This ruling should put a stopper on any club calling itself by this name and even had they not taken this action, surely the Bristol Rugby Club would have the right to protest"*. However, this didn't stop the ambitions of the Garibaldians, for they continued to press for the right to adopt the name of *Bristol City* which, as intimated by the Bristol Times and Mirror, brought forth protest by Bristol R.F.C. who complained to the Rugby Union that they considered the name to be too similar to their own. Eventually, the South End club received approval for the change of name on August 7th after the Gloucestershire F.A. had checked as to whether the older established clubs, such as Eastville Rovers, had any objections. In addition a visit to London was made by Walter Tozer, in order to appeal directly to the Football Association.

This hold-up delayed the issue of the subscription list for £1 shares, but was eventually opened from the 1st to the 11th September 1897. 1,400 were offered to the general public by subscription (2/6d. on application, the same on allotment, 5/- after allotment, and the balance - if and when required, but not before 1st May 1898 - for a further two calls at one month's notice, of 5/- each). Only 531 were purchased however, and a precedent was set - that was to be repeated 85 years later - whereby the Directors had to make good the poor response of the local public, although on this occasion the shortfall was ascribed to the delay in issuing the Prospectus. According to the Prospectus, H.C.Ewens had taken over from Albert Denby as Chairman, and the following year both gentlemen decided to retire from the Board. They were no doubt exhausted by their efforts to establish the Club at the forefront of the professional game in Southern England.

During the summer, improvements to the St Johns Lane Ground were put in hand and this brought about banking at both ends and the erection of a canvas screen, to block out the free view that spectators watching from Mutton Hill at the Northern end of the ground had of the proceedings. This screen, hoisted when a match was in progress, comprised of canvas sheets attached to a number of 30ft poles, such resourcefulness serving to increase attendances and further improve income by the fact that such sheets became ideal advertisement hoardings.

The last season as an amateur club had seen South End return to Gloucester, from where they had obtained the prolific goalscorer Percy Stout in 1894-95, and secure the services of goalkeeper George Speck, together with the talented Fielding brothers.

This gave the Garibaldians a fairly strong side, as demonstrated by their runners-up position in the Western League, but it still didn't help them allay their Gloucestershire Cup jinx. This time they went out to Western League Division Two side Fishponds, the only consolation being that they obtained their first goal in the competition, this by courtesy of an opposition defender. They had more success though in the newly instigated Bristol Charity Cup, winning through to the Final, which was played on the Rovers ground at Eastville when they went down 2-1 to Warmley on April 30th.

The Bristol Charity Cup

The Reserves finished in fourth place in the South Bristol & District League Division One, and reached the Semi-Finals of the Gloucestershire Junior Cup when they succumbed 5-2 at St. John's Lane against Bedminster Reserves. The Extras improved slightly on their wooden-spoon position of 1895-96, as they ended the campaign in sixth place (out of eight clubs) in Division A of the South Bristol & District League. The Wednesday team again operated, winning four of their six games played, losing the other two. They scored nineteen goals and conceded twelve.

Percy Wyfold Stout

Stout played soccer for Corinthians, Gloucester, Bristol South End, Western League and Gloucestershire Representative XI's. He was better known as a rugger player for Gloucester, Richmond, Bristol, Gloucestershire, Barbarians and England, with five rugby caps in 1898 and 1899, making his debut against Scotland on March 12th 1898. Born November 20th 1875, he died on October 9th 1937. During World War One he was acting Captain with the Machine Gun Corps, and for action in Gaza he was awarded the D.S.O. in 1917; he was mentioned in despatches no less than five times, and was awarded the Order of the Nile 4th Class.

Coming of Sam Hollis

With the adoption of professionalism it became clear that if the Club was to make its mark in the soccer world then it would be wise to engage the services of a manager. Of those that applied the name of Samuel Woodroffe Hollis stood out like a beacon. He had been trainer of Woolwich Arsenal for the previous three years, and he was invited to Bristol by Mr. Denby on Easter Wednesday, April 21st 1897, when he took in the exhibition match between Derby County and West Bromwich Albion on the Bedminster Athletic Ground at Ashton Gate. Afterwards he walked back to Mr. Denby's house for tea, where he agreed to take on the task of being the Club's first manager even though they had little money and no professional players.

After staying the night, when he met prominent members of the Club, Sam Hollis returned to London where he got to work straight away by tapping up a number of his Woolwich Arsenal players and found that there were those willing to sample West Country life provided the money was satisfactory. Accordingly Messrs. Denby and Ewens went to Southampton a week later to meet up with Hollis at the Hampshire County Cricket Ground, where his Arsenal team beat Southampton St. Mary's in a Friendly by five goals to one. After the game Mr. McMinns, the Southampton Secretary, offered the Bristol representatives not only support for their Southern League membership application but also the offer of some of the Saints' surplus players as well. The first offer was gratefully accepted but the second brought forth a 'No thank-you' from Mr. Hollis, *"if they are not good enough for you, they're not good enough for us. We want players that you want"*. Big words indeed, especially as Mr. Hollis had still not seen the colour of the money that was available for bargaining.

Do Your Best

It was therefore time to talk money and Hollis insisted on knowing where he stood before he left Southampton to return to London. *"What time does your train go?"* asked Mr. Denby. *"6.05p.m."* responded Mr. Hollis. *"How much do you want?"* *"£20 or £30 - £30 I should say"*. *"All right I will be at the station with it'*. Mr. Hollis got to the station at five minutes to six, but there was no sign of Mr. Denby. The minutes indeed were flashing past, when at 6.03 Mr. Denby dashed up in a hansom and thrust a cheque for £30 into Hollis's hands and parted with the words *"Do your best for us"*.

There was no limit as to the fee a man could have for signing on, so £30 was hardly a princely sum with which to build a team, but Mr. Hollis proved equal to the task. On the return trip to London his smooth tongue worked overtime as he persuaded four of his Arsenal players - Alex 'Sandy' Caie, 'Paddy' O'Brien, 'Jock' Russell and Finlay Sinclair - of the honour to play for the Club, that they agreed to sign without asking for even a penny signing-on fee. This brilliant bit of business gave him the scope to set his sights a little higher for other newcomers, and with the addition of a further £10 from Mr. Denby he secured Jack Hamilton, Billy Jones and Hugh Monteith from Loughborough, Albert Carnelly and Harry Davy

from Leicester Fosse, Billy Higgins from Grimsby Town - to become the Captain - Tommy Wyllie from Bury, and George Mann from Manchester City.

Colours Changed

Sam Hollis had certainly done his best, in fact he had achieved a minor miracle as the team he assembled for £40 was to prove almost good enough to secure the Southern League Championship. However, prior to League action getting underway, the players were introduced to the supporters at a Club Concert held at the Bedminster Town Hall on August 11th. The musical portion of the evening brought contributions from Alex Caie and 'Hammer' Clements after the presentation of silver matchboxes to the members of the 'Investigation Committee'. These were in appreciation of the work they had done in bringing about the professional Bristol City Club, a club that saw fit to change their colours by introducing white knickers in place of navy blue. The day following this Concert saw City begin ball practice at St. John's Lane, when a crowd numbering between 700 and 800 were present to observe the proceedings. Similar well attended practice sessions were then held on every Tuesday and Thursday evening throughout the rest of the month.

Great Start

The campaign commenced with a 3-1 home win in a Friendly on September 1st over a 'Saints' team that had dropped the St. Mary's part of their title. This victory was followed by further home Friendly wins over Swindon Town 3-1 and Chorley 6-2, before the first Southern League engagement on September 11th.

This saw Wolverton at St. John's Lane in front of a 6,000 crowd who witnessed a rampaging first forty five minutes of action from the City which put them 6-1 ahead at the break, and seemingly on course for a double figure score. The visitors though had other ideas and they fought back to 6-4 before the homesters made the game safe to produce a final score line of 7-4. 'Jock' Russell had the honour of obtaining City's first Southern League goal, the other scorers being Alex Caie (3), Albert Carnelly (2) and Billy Higgins. Wolverton responded through Worsley (2), Radford and Poole. For this fixture which kicked-off at 4p.m. the sides lined up as follows:-

City: Monteith; Davy, Sinclair, Mann, Higgins, Hamilton, Wyllie, Carnelly, Caie, O'Brien, Russell.
Wolverton: Waller; Moss, Worker, Mack, Edwards, Dormer, Wesley, Radford, Worsley, Poole, Frost.
Referee: J.H. Beanland (Swindon)

The following Saturday brought the formidable challenge of an away fixture against Millwall Athletic, the previous campaign's Runners-up, and Champions in 1895-96, and City astounded the soccer world by coming away from 'East Ferry Road' with a tremendous 6-2 success. The Great Western Railway operated a special excursion from Bristol so there were many City supporters among the 6,000 crowd. Their favourites turned out first in their bright scarlet jerseys and white knickers that caused the local reporter to remark that they strongly reminded him of the Arsenal. Higgins won the toss for City and set Millwall to face the slight breeze which didn't hinder them as the 'Lions' attacked straight away to force Monteith to save at the expense of a corner. However it wasn't long before City made their presence felt as Caie after only five minutes put the ball in the net from a centre by Wyllie. This advantage was then doubled thanks to O'Brien before Davies pulled one back for Millwall before the break, and in the second-half Carnelly obtained number three before Almond notched another for the 'Lions'. The visitors then responded with a hat-trick from O'Brien, taking his total to four, to clinch victory. On this day the line-ups were as follows:-

Athletic: C. Traynor; Graham, Robson, King, Almond, Curley, Davies, Calvey, A. Traynor, Davis, Geddes.
City: Monteith; Davy, Sinclair, Mann, Higgins, Hamilton, Wyllie, Carnelly, Caie, O'Brien, Russell.
Referee: A. Cecil-Knight.

A Sad Lament

The local Millwall newspaper, 'The East End News', of Wednesday, September 22nd in reporting the game, concluded with this lament:-

Oh, Traynor, my tears sadly flow for thy keeping
The goal, when thy efforts were wanted the most
For thee in deep sorrow and grief I am weeping
To find thou wert letting the ball pass the post.

The last time I saw thee I thought 'twas the rain, or
Shall I say grief? that thy vision obscured
As the ball found thy net, my dear little Traynor,
And goals by the foemen were quickly secured.

Not surprisingly this was Charlie Traynor's only game for Millwall, and he soon returned to Abercorn for whom he was playing the previous season when he appeared for the Scottish League against the Irish.

Western League Champions

This great start by the City was maintained throughout the campaign as the newcomers, or the 'Bristol Babe' as they were soon known, did not sustain their first defeat in the Southern League until New Year's Day. They held pole position for over a third of the season, but in the end had to settle for the not inconsiderable achievement of finishing as Runners-up. In the Professional Section of the Western League though they were not to be denied after taking over top place at the turn of the year, being described by J.A. Stevens (League Secretary) as being, *"the best team ever seen in the competition"*. Indeed such was their renown that Eastleigh, after having previously suffered 14-1 and 10-3 defeats at the hands of the City during the season, scratched from their home match with the Babes on

March 2nd. The points were subsequently awarded to the City which served to produce the following final table to give the Club it's first major honour.

	P	W	D	L	F	A	Pts.
BRISTOL CITY	14	11	1	2	51	16	23
Swindon Town	14	9	1	4	32	15	19
Reading	14	7	2	5	29	25	16
Bristol St. George	14	6	3	5	25	27	15
Eastville Rovers	14	6	2	6	38	25	14
Warmley	14	5	3	6	36	27	13
Eastleigh	14	3	2	9	22	55	8
Trowbridge Town	14	2	0	12	15	58	4

Gloucestershire Cup Success At Last

In the F.A. Cup the 'Citizens', as City were also called, reached the 3rd Qualifying Round on October 30th, when in succumbing 2-0 to Southampton - who went on to reach the Semi-Finals - they experienced their first defeat as a professional club. The campaign brought an end to the Gloucestershire Cup jinx, and after achieving their first win in the competition when Eastville Rovers were dispatched 2-0 on February 26th, the Babes went on to reach the Final, after disposing of Bristol St. George following two attempts in the Semi-Final. The Final was played on the Rovers ground at 'Stapleton Road' on April 11th when a record crowd of 11,186 (paying receipts of £348.6s.3d.) were in attendance to see City become the sixth club to win the trophy, after beating the previous holders Warmley 2-1. It was quite a season for new attendance records, which was only to be expected with the adoption of professionalism, but a new high was reached for the Southern League match against Southampton at St. John's Lane on January 15th, as the 12,170 (£379.16s.2d.) spectators present was a record for any club in the competition up to that time. The same situation also occurring in the Western League a few months later when the visit of Warmley on April 8th brought forth a crowd in the region of 10,000 who paid receipts of £264.18s.0d.

City didn't operate any Reserve, Extras or Wednesday sides this term, indeed they were to manage without any juniors' sides - apart from a Reserve XI playing a series of Friendlies in 1899-1900 - until 1903-04. They did, however, enter the Bristol Charity Cup again, but after beating Eastleigh 10-3 in a 1st Round match at St. John's Lane, they were surprised on their own ground by Warmley who won 1-0 in the next round.

Sketch in Bristol Observer: Toone the Notts County goalkeeper saves from Carnelly, in a Friendly at St.John's Lane on 12 February 1898.

Bid For Football League Status

Quite a momentous inaugural season then for the professional Bristol City, and this served to make the ambitious members of the Club try for Football League status. Accordingly at the Football Annual General Meeting held in Manchester on May 20th, 1898, they entered the ballot with the three Second Division clubs that were up for re-election, Lincoln City (for the fourth time in six seasons), Darwen and Loughborough Town, together with non-League Burslem Port Vale, Nelson and New Brighton Tower. However, their application didn't impress the delegates and the Babes finished bottom of the poll when the voting went as follows:- Lincoln City 21 (re-elected), Burslem Port Vale 18 (elected), Loughborough Town 16 (re-elected), Darwen 15, New Brighton Tower 13, Nelson 3 and Bristol City 1.

Following this vote it was decided to increase the size of the two divisions of the Football League and this saw one place being immediately filled by Darwen and another meeting being arranged eight days later when New Brighton Tower, Glossop North End and Barnsley gained admission in an apparently uncontested election. Quite why Nelson and Bristol City were not involved, or why they were not granted League status at the same time as Darwen, which was within half-an-hour of the original poll, is not clear, but whatever the reason the City were obliged to try again for Southern League honours in 1898-99.

Second A.G.M.

The 2nd Annual General Meeting of Bristol City Football Club Limited was held at the Temperance Hall, East Street, Bedminster on the 5th July 1898, when the 1st Annual Report was accepted, which showed that the new Company had managed to make a small profit of £18.2s.4d. The total income of £3,448.2s.9d. included gate receipts of £3,263.16s.4d. and season ticket sales of £101.2s.6d. Expenditure came to £3,430.0s.5d., which included wages of players, team-manager and groundsman amounting to £1,670.9s.6d., players bonuses of £169.9s.6d., travelling expenses of £244.15s.6d., guarantees and share of gates £674.11s.11d. The value of Club property, including the small grandstand, fittings, furniture and tollhouse was valued at £347.7s.6d.

Changes to the Board saw William P. Kingston taking over as Chairman with James Crompton as his deputy, the other members being:- Joseph Daveridge, F.H. Hawksby, Harry King, G.J. Maggs, R.E. Melville, N.E. Poole, Walter G. Tozer and E.C. Tyack.

Tragedy

The achievements of the 1897-98 campaign were celebrated with City holding a Complimentary Dinner at the Prince Hotel, Totterdown on April 18th, 1898, but it is right to record the tragedy that had attended their very first professional match (against Southampton on September 1st) which had been played in appalling weather - gale force winds, torrential rain, and a half-flooded pitch. A little girl, taken to the match by her parents, was drowned in the swollen waters of the brook that ran alongside the ground.

New Players

For the City's second Southern League campaign the side was strengthened by the singing of William Langham, John Murphy and Arthur Potter from Notts County, Patrick Finnerhan from Liverpool, John McLean from Grimsby Town, and George Barker a full-back from Everton - who had taken part in an International trial six months earlier. There was also a change of Captain as William Higgins moved on to Newcastle United and he was replaced by William Stewart who had been Captain at Everton for three of the five previous years he had been at Goodison Park.

Another good Southern League season with City not suffering their first defeat until January 11th meant that the Citizens went into their last match against Southampton on April 29th at the head of affairs, but needing to win to be sure of capturing the Championship. Such though were the complexities of the 'Rules of the Competition', that a draw - despite the fact of the Saints' superior goal average - would still give an opportunity to capture the prize as Rule 8 made it clear that should there be a tie on points, then a deciding match on neutral territory would be necessary.

Bitter Defeat

Naturally great interest manifest itself for this vital match and a new record Southern League crowd for the St. John's Lane ground of 13,000 paying receipts of £440, were present when Southampton turned out first in white shirts and black shorts. City won the toss, which offered little advantage as the wind was blowing almost straight across the pitch, and defended the 'Lane End'. McLean kicked-off for the visitors, but this was no advantage, as the homesters getting the ball at once attacked with Hamilton causing the Saints' custodian Robinson to effect a clearance. City soon took the lead when Caie passed to Langham who registered with a great shot that caused Robinson to strain himself in making a vain effort to save. This injury caused Robinson to leave the field for a while, being replaced by Haynes, who was immediately tested in saving another shot by Langham. Upon the keeper's return the City were unlucky in that the referee, Captain Simpson, overlooked a handball by the visitors right-back Meehan, but it wasn't long before City turned their almost complete control of the game to good account, as a brief bout of passing involving Caie, O'Brien and Langham saw the latter player put them further ahead. The homesters kept up the pressure to half-time but were unable to increase their advantage further.

After the break the City took up where they had left off, but six minutes into the half the Saints got back into the game when Chadwick beat Monteith with a long shot. This roused the visitors and although Stewart and Davy kept them out for some time with excellent defensive work, Monteith misjudged a dropping shot by Wood and the ball rolled into the net for the equaliser. From the kick-off City responded and Caie put in a great header that brought out the best in Robinson who effected an accomplished save. From another City attack the visitors broke away, and although Stewart got to the ball his faulty clearance went to McLean who had all the time in the world to put his side ahead with a clinking shot in the sixty-eighth minute.

The Saints made the game safe eight minutes before the end when after much City pressure Wood turned a well placed corner to good account, though the homesters had the last word when Caie scored the final goal of this amazing game to make the score: Bristol City 3 Southampton 4, such a scoreline allowing the Saints to clinch their third successive Championship.

City: Monteith; Davy, Stewart, Jones, McLean, Hamilton, Langham, Finnerhan, Caie, O'Brien, Russell.

Southampton: Robinson; Meehan, Durber, Meston, Chadwick, Haynes, Yates, McLeod, McLean, Wood, Robertson.

Referee: Captain Simpson.

To lose the Championship in this way was a bitter blow to Sam Hollis, for what was his last match in charge. He had announced his intention to resign on March 18th due to increasing interference by the Directors, including some of the conditions attached to the new offer of a £200 per annum contract, and he had agreed to takeover as Secretary/Manager of local rivals Bedminster.

United League

As well as performing in the Southern League the City operated in the United League in preference to the Western League, but after winning their first four fixtures, their form fluctuated and in the final table they only managed to secure fifth place viz:-

	P	W	D	L	F	A	Pts.
Millwall Athletic	20	14	3	3	42	19	31
Southampton	20	12	1	7	53	33	25
Tottenham Hotspur	20	11	2	7	36	25	24
Woolwich Arsenal	20	10	4	6	40	31	24
BRISTOL CITY	20	11	0	9	43	31	22
Reading	20	8	5	7	36	25	21
Brighton United	20	10	1	9	51	42	21
Wellingborough	20	7	1	12	33	40	15
Kettering	20	8	1	11	21	33	15*
Rushden	20	6	1	13	26	45	13
Luton Town	20	2	3	15	24	71	7

* Two points deducted for ineligible player.

F.A. Cup Success

In the F.A. Cup the City became the first local club to reach the 1st Round proper, and in meeting Sunderland at St. John's Lane on January 28th the ground record was beaten out of sight when 16,945 people, paying receipts of £524.1s.6d., were present to witness the famous visitors progress to the next round by scoring four goals to two by the Citizens. The F.A. Cup run however was marred by tragedy, as during the match away to Bristol St. George on November 19th, a spectator fell from a tree and was killed. City sent £10 to the widow and a relief fund was launched for her and her dependants.

In the Gloucestershire Cup, the City in accounting for Bristol Rovers 2-1 on the Bristol St. George ground at Bell Hill on April 3rd, retained their hold on the trophy in front of a record crowd of 11,433 who had contributed receipts of £356.

Supporters Match

On April 15th 1899, the City supporters had the opportunity to show what that they could do as the St. John's Lane ground was given over for them to put on their own match. This resulted in a 4-3 win for those who frequented the Totterdown End over the Bedminster End, after drawing 2-2 at the break.

Season Tickets

For the 1898-99 Season the City players had been paid £3 per week basic, plus £2 for a win and £1 for a draw. Season tickets were priced at 15/-, 12/6 & 10/-. A Congratulatory Banquet was held for Players and Directors at the Club Headquarters, the Angel Hotel, Redcliffe Street, on 22nd April, and the Club Complementary Dinner took place at the Prince Hotel, Totterdown on May 13th.

Board

The Board for 1899-1900 comprised William P. Kingston (Chairman), James Crompton (Vice-Chairman), Joseph Daveridge, Albert E. Denby, F.H. Hawksby, Harry King, G.J. Maggs, Walter G. Tozer, E.C. Tyack and E.H. Webb. The position of Financial Secretary remained the domain of E.J. Locke, but the departure of Sam Hollis also brought to an end W.B. Hodgkinson's tenure in the role of General Secretary.

New Manager

Robert Campbell the General Secretary & Manager of Sunderland was engaged in a similar capacity, at a salary of £270 per annum, to take over from Sam Hollis at St. John's Lane, and he recruited what appeared to be a good set of players for 1899-1900. Pre-season trial matches were held, which produced total attendances of 7,000, and all seemed set clear for a strong challenge to secure the Southern League Championship.

Humiliation

Alex Crawford was signed from Clyde, together with Alex McDonald. Alex Downie came from Third Lanark, Adam Godsman from Inverness, Fred Molyneux from Stoke, and ex-City and Bedminster player A.E. (Talbot) Lewis returned from Everton. Yet despite this infusion of talent and the engagement of James Blessington from Derby County in October, a poor season ensued with City struggling to finish in ninth place, just above Bristol Rovers on goal average. The local honours were taken by Bedminster who occupied sixth place, and also beat City in the Gloucestershire Cup Final before amalgamating with them at the season's end. The City re-entered the Bristol Charity Cup this term, but this brought more humiliation, as after a creditable 1-1 away draw with Bedminster in the Semi-Final they fell apart in the replay, going down 6-0 at St. John's Lane on February 21st.

Annual Sports

On August 12th 1899, St. John's Lane saw the staging of Bristol City's 1st Annual Sports, such information being given in the Club Handbook for the 1899-1900 season, which also details the following song:-

Play up, Play up, "BRISTOL CITY"
(Air:- 'Tramp, Tramp, Tramp the Boys are Marching')

Once more on the Football ground,
Let our ringing cheers resound,
For the Boys well-known both far and near
They're the heroes of to-day,
And the game they love to play,
Is to Bristol City Sportsmen ever dear

Chorus

Play up, play up, Bristol City,
Add more glory to your name,
You're the Champions of the West,
And are equal to the best -
At the jolly old Association game.

They have gone from town to town,
Meeting teams of great renown,
And have gained their matches nearly every one;
They've made famous left and right,
Our old colours Red and White.
They will fight until the English Cup is won.

Play up, Play up etc.

Boys! let us stand to those,
Who strike terror to our foes.
And have made old Bristol famous for it's sport,
Who in the football field
To no players ever yield,
But will bring 'The Bristol City' safe to port.

Play up, Play up etc.

Obviously this song didn't inspire the team during the season as their performances in the Southern District Combination and the Professional Section of the Western League were as poor as their record in the Southern League. The final tables showing City in sixth spot in the Combination and in bottom place in the Western League viz:-

SOUTHERN DISTRICT COMBINATION

	P	W	D	L	F	A	Pts.
Millwall Athletic	16	12	2	2	30	10	26
Tottenham Hotspur	16	10	3	3	41	18	23
Portsmouth	16	8	2	6	28	18	18
Woolwich Arsenal	16	8	1	7	27	22	17
Southampton	16	6	2	8	24	29	14
BRISTOL CITY	16	5	3	8	25	32	13
Reading	16	4	4	8	16	28	12
Chatham	16	5	2	9	12	37	12
Queens Park Rangers	16	4	1	11	19	28	9

WESTERN LEAGUE

	P	W	D	L	F	A	Pts.
Bristol Rovers	6	3	1	2	8	6	7
Bedminster	6	3	1	2	10	12	7
Swindon Town	6	3	0	3	7	7	6
BRISTOL CITY	6	2	0	4	12	12	4

In consequence of their F.A. Cup exploits of the previous season City were granted exemption until the 1st Round Proper, when in defeating Stalybridge Rovers in front of approximately 5,000 spectators who paid receipts of £131 at St. John's Lane, they won through to the 2nd Round for the first time. This brought them the reward of a trip to the most famous club in Victorian England, the mighty Aston Villa, and special excursions were laid on to get local supporters to Villa Park for the game on February 10th. Unfortunately City were no match for their hosts going down 5-1, but they had the consolation of a share in the gate receipts of £533.

Boer War

The start of the Second Boer War in October 1899 saw the City lose the services of full-back Alex Milligan and goal-keeper Joseph Watts. Milligan was recalled to the colours of the Scots Guards at the outbreak of hostilities along with the old Bedminster player Andrew Hargett (Royal Engineers) who was to play for the Citizens between 1903 and 1905, but Watts didn't join the fray until January 1900. Hargett became quite a hero seeing action in twenty two engagements, including Spion Kop, Colenso, and the Relief of Ladysmith, receiving only a slight finger wound in the process.

The loss of Milligan to these momentous events in Southern Africa possibly goes someway towards explaining City's poor form, as it may be of some significance that the three matches he played in prior to his departure were all won. But be that as it may, the end of the campaign amalgamation with Bedminster - which appears to have been more like a takeover of the older club by the younger - brought about a clear out of Citizens players. Only four City players were retained - William Jones, John McLean, Patrick O'Brien and David Robson, compared with six erstwhile Bedminster members - George Toone, Robert Davies, Hugh Wilson, Peter Chambers, Michael Whelan and Alfred Geddes. Even Robert Crone later teamed up at St. John's Lane, joining as trainer 12 months later and making two appearances in Friendly games, against Bridgewater and Clapton in 1901-02.

Sponsorship

The home Southern League game against New Brompton on December 16th, 1899, illustrates the business acumen of the City Directors as this game was sponsored by the United Kingdom Commercial Travellers Association, perhaps the earliest match to be so sponsored?

A special game took place at St. John's Lane on October 9th when a side of locally based English players took on a team of locally based Scottish players in aid of Western League Funds. A crowd numbering 1,911 turned up to see the English side win 2-1 thanks to two first-half goals from Jack Jones, with Alex Crawford replying for the Scots after the break. On this occasion the two sides lined up as follows:-

English Players: Toone (Bedminster); Shutt (Swindon Town), R.H. Davies (Bedminster), Bramley (Bedminster), W. Jones (Bristol City), Chambers (Bedminster), Langham (Bristol City), J. Jones (Bristol Rovers), Boucher (Bedminster), Lewis (Bristol Rovers), Wilson (Swindon Town).

Scottish Players: Monteith (Bristol City); Ritchie (Bristol Rovers), McDonald (Bristol City), Lamont (Bristol Rovers), Henderson (Swindon Town), H. Wilson (Bedminster), Brown (Bristol Rovers), Crawford (Bristol City), Caie (Bristol City), Thompson (Bristol City), Paul (Bristol Rovers).
Referee: A. Farrant

The City held their Celebration Dinner, even though there was little to celebrate, thanks to the kind offices of A. Cattle Esq., who paid for the event held at the Exchange Hall, Bedminster on the 26th March 1900.

New Signings

In the close season Bob Campbell strengthened his squad, that comprised of the retained members of the previous season's Bedminster and City players, and he signed Phil Bach and William Fulton from Sunderland, David McDougall from Partick Thistle, William Michael from Heart of Midlothian, David Nicol from Millwall Athletic, and James Stevenson from Newcastle United. All therefore was set for the re-constituted club to once again put in a strong challenge for Southern League honours in 1900-01.

Another Near Miss

This time they did live up to their promise, although they failed to gain the Championship, despite challenging strongly throughout the campaign. In fact the City held top spot for over a third of the season, but had to settle as Runners-up again for the third time in four seasons at the finish, when the table looked as follows:-

	P	W	D	L	F	A	Pts.
Southampton	28	18	5	5	58	26	41
BRISTOL CITY	28	17	5	6	54	27	39
Portsmouth	28	17	4	7	56	32	38
Millwall Athletic	28	17	2	9	55	32	36
Tottenham Hotspur	28	16	4	8	55	33	36
West Ham United	28	14	5	9	40	28	33
Bristol Rovers	28	14	4	10	46	35	32
Queens Park Rangers	28	11	4	13	43	48	26
Reading	28	8	8	12	24	25	26
Luton Town	28	11	2	15	43	49	24
Kettering	28	7	9	12	33	46	23
New Brompton	28	7	5	16	34	51	19
Gravesend United	28	6	7	15	32	85	19
Watford	28	6	4	18	24	52	16
Swindon Town	28	3	8	17	19	47	14

Delay

In an enlarged Western League Division One the start was delayed because approval from the Football Association wasn't given until November 12th, this resulted in a number of the previously arranged fixtures being played as Friendlies. It fell to the City to kick-off the Professional Western League programme when they beat Southampton 4-1 in front of 5,000 at St. John's Lane two days later, but this excellent form wasn't maintained and at the end of the campaign they were to be found in fifth place viz:-

	P	W	D	L	F	A	Pts.
Portsmouth	16	11	2	3	26	22	24
Millwall Athletic	16	9	5	2	33	14	23
Tottenham Hotspur	16	8	5	3	37	19	21
Queens Park Rangers	16	7	4	5	39	25	18
BRISTOL CITY	16	6	4	6	25	26	16
Reading	16	5	5	6	24	29	15
Southampton	16	5	2	9	20	29	12
Bristol Rovers	16	4	1	11	18	42	9
Swindon Town	16	2	2	12	9	35	6

Matches on the Bedminster Ground

Following the amalgamation with Bedminster, fourteen games were played on the Bedminster Athletic Ground. For the Southern League match against Bristol Rovers played at this venue on October 20th, a new record crowd for this ground of 15,500 - paying receipts of £380 - were present to witness City's 1-0 success.

The F.A. Cup brought an exit at the hands of Reading in a 1st Round Proper 2nd Replay at the County Ground, Swindon, but City got back to winning ways in the Gloucestershire Cup, demolishing the Rovers 4-0 in the Final at St. John's Lane on April 29th when the receipts from a small crowd of 2,800 amounted to £84.5s.4d. On January 10th the City held a Smoking Concert and during the proceedings Sandy Caie was presented with two handsome easy chairs as a wedding present from his fellow players.

****

City (in white shirts) attack the Woolwich Arsenal goal in the League match at St.Johns' Lane on 26th October 1901
(Note the canvass screens in the background which prevented a free view from Mutton Hill)

Election to The Football League

Even though the Club had been successful on the field the finances for the 1900-01 campaign had revealed a loss of £974.5s.11d.,which allied to the deficit of £1,163.16s.11d. incurred during the previous season meant that total losses were in excess of £2,000. The message was clear in that City should cut back on their ambitions in order to trim expenses, but as ever the bold members of the Club resolved to take the opposite approach and in pushing their ambitions further made another application for membership of the Football League.

This time their boldness was rewarded with success when they stood for election along with the three clubs up for re-election - Walsall, Stockport County and Burton Swifts - together with non-League Crewe Alexandra, Darwen, Doncaster Rovers and Stalybridge Rovers. City finished joint top of the poll as follows:- Bristol City 23 (elected), Burton Swifts 23 (re-elected and changed name to Burton United on amalgamation with Burton Wanderers), Doncaster Rovers 16, Stockport County 16, Stalybridge Rovers 7, Walsall 7, Crewe Alexandra 5 and Darwen 0.

For the remaining vacant place a second ballot was held between the clubs tied in third place, and this resulted in Stockport County with 21 votes retaining their Football League status in preference to Doncaster Rovers who polled 13. However, Doncaster's disappointment was to be shortlived as just prior to the start of the season New Brighton Tower resigned and they took over the vacancy.

Return of Sam Hollis

Following this fine achievement in securing Football League status just seven years after the formation of the Club, the Babes lost the services of the main architect of their successful application. Robert Campbell resigning from his three year managerial contract following major disagreement. The Directors then turned again to Sam Hollis, who had been out of the game following Bedminster's amalgamation, and he agreed to return on the clear understanding that he would not brook any interference.

The Same Problem

Again Hollis was faced with building a side with little money so he introduced economies that included a reduction in his own salary and called upon Club benefactors to give financial assistance. His appeal raised £345 and enabled him to set off on a player-signing mission. He obtained Joseph Connor, Arthur Flynn and William Tuft from Walsall, Wally Moles from Tottenham Hotspur, Joseph Bradbury (Barnsley), Walter Cookson (Nelson), Thomas Boucher (Bristol Rovers), Steven Jones (Aberdare), Herbert Banks (Aston Villa), James Robertson (New Brompton), Harry Clay (Kimberley St. John's), James Jay (Bristol East) and Ernest Vickerstaffe (Eastville Athletic). These players together with those retained from the previous campaign, Robert Davies, William Jones, Peter Chambers, Patrick O'Brien and John McLean proving good enough for City to end the Season in sixth place in the Second Division, though among those released was one who might well have proved an asset had he not been playing for Aberdare during the next four years. This was the peerless William John Wedlock who was to become one of the best centre-halves ever to play for England. After joining City from local club Arlington Rovers he made two appearances but was allowed to leave as the Citizens were well served at centre-half by the outstanding John McLean who only missed performing in thirty-five of the two hundred and fifty sides that took the field (including Friendly and abandoned games) for the Club during the period from 1898 to 1902.

Winning Debut

Saturday, September 7th, 1901 saw the start of the career of the Bristol Babe in the Football League when two goals from Paddy O'Brien brought a 2-0 away success over Blackpool at Bloomfield Road, and after being brought back to earth by a 3-0 defeat at Burslem Port Vale on the following Monday the first home League game took place at St. John's Lane on September 14th when Stockport County were beaten 3-0 in front of 7,000 spectators. The experiment of sharing home games between City's ground and the old home of Bedminster was discontinued following election to the Football League, and all matches until the move to Ashton Gate for the start of the 1904-05 campaign would be played at St. John's Lane.

F.A. Cup Shock

In the F.A. Cup the Babes had a reprieve against local rivals Bristol Rovers when the fog descended at Stapleton Road on November 16th, forcing the abandonment of the game after eighty minutes with City trailing 2-0. Unfortunately this reprieve wasn't turned to good effect as after managing a 1-1 draw in the re-arranged game they succumbed 3-2 at St. John's Lane in the replay to give Rovers their first ever win over Football League opposition.

A Profit At Last

Ever conscious of the need to increase revenue the City held their 1st Annual Six-a-Side Tournament at St. John's Lane between Easter Tuesday, April 1st and Saturday the 5th of April, and on Saturday the 17th of May put on what was billed as an Old English Sports and Archery Tournament. These events helping towards the declaration of a profit for the season of £39.14s.9d. to stem the losses of the previous two campaigns. However, despite this small profit the figures from the Statement of Accounts do not indicate any great benefit was gained from Football League membership as gate receipts only increased from £3,526.8s.11d. to £3,835.7s.11d., and total income from £3,695.13s.9d. to £4,099.8s.2d. In fact season ticket sales even went down, from £132.16s.10d. in 1900-01 to £75.3s.9d.

Further ways of increasing revenue brought about the playing of Rugby Union at St. John's Lane at the start of the following season with Bristol beating Lydney 11-0 on September 13th., and Bristol Rovers use of the ground for their home Southern League 1-0 success over Tottenham Hotspur on October 17th, 1903, when a crowd in the region of 8,000 was reported to have been in attendance.

Season 1902-03 saw top place in the Second Division being reached for the first time on September 20th, when Manchester United were defeated, but this position could not be maintained. A final placing in fourth spot though was a creditable performance and this helped to increase the profit to £360.10s.10d. Gate receipts improved to £4,756.14s.5d. and total income to £5,304.18s.5d. Season Tickets sales reached £117.9s.4d. and £450 was paid out in transfer fees. The highlight of the campaign was in the F.A. Cup when City travelled to Bolton and achieved a giant killing act by beating the First Division side 5-0.

The final league placing of fourth was repeated on each of the following three seasons, the end of which saw Sam Hollis leaving the Club for the second time, and he was replaced by Harry Thickett who had played in fourteen League matches for the Babes in 1904-05, the first season at the new Ashton Gate. The last campaign at St. John's Lane had seen the attendance record for the ground raised to 17,909 (£754.11s.9d.) on the occasion of the F.A.Cup match against Sheffield United on February 6th, 1904, and this made the Board realise that they needed to develop the ground or move to a more suitable venue. Unfortunately they only held a short lease on St. John's Lane and being unable to come to agreement with the Ashton Court Estate Trustees in regard to extending it for a further ten years they took the decision to move to Ashton Gate.

Record Crowd At St. John's Lane

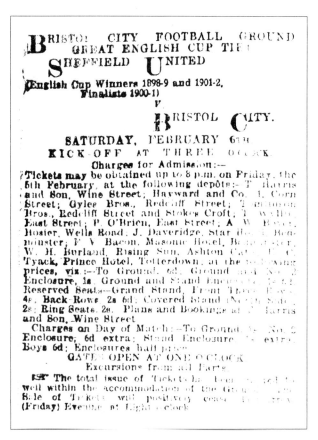

The pairing of City with Sheffield United in the draw for the 1st Round Proper of the F.A. Cup had all Bristol agog with excitement, as not only were the Blades a renowned Cup team (winners of the competition in 1899 & 1902, plus Finalists in 1901), but they were holding a position at the head of affairs in Division One. So great was the interest, the City Directors decided to increase the seating accommodation at St. John's Lane, and a temporary Covered Stand to hold 500 people was erected at the Lane End of the ground. In addition 1,000 Ring Seats were provided within the railings, a single row along each side and a double row behinf both goals. For those who obtained tickets by the Friday before the game admission prices were:- Ground 6d; Number 2 Enclosure 1/-; Stand Enclosure 1/6d. But on the match day, entrance to these areas of the ground cost a further 6d. Reserved seats were charged at 4/- and 2/6 in the Grandstand, 2/- in the New Covered Stand, and 2/- for the Ring Seats, tickets for these seats only being obtainable from Messrs. Harris & Son, Wine Street, Bristol.

With the rain falling at midday there were many who, being acquainted with the peculiarities of the St. John's Lane ground, were very dubious as to whether the match would be played, but Referee T. Kirkham of Burslem had no doubt when he inspected the pitch half-an-hour later. Therefore a start was made at 3 o'clock, with Morris kicking-off for the City who were attacking the Lane End. Little was seen of the United forwards for the opening five minutes but in their first real attack a minute later, Priest beat Clay with his header from a corner to put the visitors ahead.

This set City aback for a little while and the Blades nearly got another goal before the Babes again put the pressure on. Corbett and Wombwell missed chances to equalise in this spell before United broke away again to go two up, when Johnson lifted the ball splendidly into the net. Not disheartened though, the City continued to press and just before half-time they gained their reward when Hosie headed in Dean's corner from the right. Coming out after the break with their tails up City went straight on the attack. After a raid by Corbett was repulsed, Fisher put the ball into the goalmouth for Dean to put it between the posts, only for Foulke to scoop it out, although it was over the line. Despite protests by the City players the Referee refused to consult his linesman, and the homesters were robbed of an equaliser. Thus reprieved the Blades made the game safe shortly before the end when in a heavy storm, Bennett netted from what many thought was an offside position.

City: Clay; Gilson, Tuft, Jones, Hosie, Chambers, Dean, Corbett, Morris, Fisher, Wombwell.
United: Foulke; Boyle, Thickett, Needham, Wilkinson, Johnson, Lipsham, Priest, Brown, Common, Bennett.

The breakdown of the gate receipts for this game makes interesting reading:-

		£	s	d
Number of people who paid 6d. prior to the day of the match	15,255	381	7	6
Number of people who paid 1/- on the day	2,614	130	14	0
	17,869			
Add complimentaries	40			
	17,909			
Enclosures raised over and above the 6d. to ground		142	1	3
Stands and ring seats over and above the 6d. to ground		100	9	0
		754	11	9

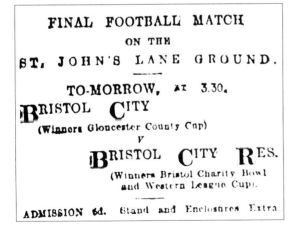

FINAL FOOTBALL MATCH
ON THE
ST. JOHN'S LANE GROUND.

TO-MORROW, AT 3.30.
BRISTOL CITY
(Winners Gloucester County Cup)
v
BRISTOL CITY RES.
(Winners Bristol Charity Bowl and Western League Cup.)

ADMISSION 6d. Stand and Enclosures Extra

This last match took place on 30th April 1904

Opening of Ashton Gate

The first view that spectators had of the new Ashton Gate was at the Public Trial match on the 27th August 1904, when 5,000 were in attendance to see a side billed as the '1st XI' beat a 2nd XI 9-0 after holding a 2-0 advantage at half-time. They found the venue much changed from City's last match here on April 20th, 1901, as the pitch had been moved from the South East corner of the site to the central position it holds today.

Bolton's Revenge

The ground was officially opened on September 3rd when visitors Bolton Wanderers rather spoilt the occasion by winning an exciting game 4-3, in front of 14,000 spectators who paid receipts of £300. Among those present were F.J. Wall (Secretary of the Football Association), J.A. Tayler and J.R. Riddell (President and Chairman respectively of the Gloucestershire Football Association) and G. Humphreys (Chairman of Bristol Rovers), who saw the Babes winning the toss and setting themselves to attack towards the Covered End. The opening goal was obtained after the match had been in progress for twelve minutes, this to the account of the visitors when Tuft in attempting to clear a shot by Marsh only succeeded in knocking the ball up onto his own crossbar from whence it went into the net.

City equalised through Dean after twenty-five minutes, and gained the lead six minutes later when Gilligan scored from a corner taken by Wombwell. City pressed strongly after this, but Bolton got back into the game when Marsh registered with rather a tame shot two minutes before the break. The second-half saw City keeping up the initiative and eventually Wombwell put the homesters ahead after a run from the half-way line which ended with a magnificent shot that sped into the top corner of the net. This lead was maintained until near the finish when with the time running out Marsh was able to equalise matters for the visitors with a nice effort, and then almost on the final whistle Yenson obtained the winner with City appealing for offside.

City: Clay; Gilson, Tuft, Jones, Hosie, Chambers, Dean, Corbett, Gilligan, Capes, Wombwell.
Wanderers: Davies, Ostick, Struthers, Clifford, Greenhaigh, Boyd, Stokes, Marsh, Yenson, White, Taylor.
Referee: A. Cooknell

International Trial

The 13th of February 1905 saw the club being honoured with the playing of an International Trial Match at Ashton Gate. A 7,500 crowd paying receipts of £230 turned up to see the North beat the South 3-1 after leading 1-0 at half-time.

Record Breaking Season

The momentous 1905-06 Season saw the Babes become the first club to win thirty Football League games in a campaign, create a new points record, and equal the winning run of fourteen consecutive League matches set by Manchester United the previous year. This run still remains a record (apart from being equalled by Preston North End in 1950-51), and remains beyond reach, though Reading in 1985-86 with thirteen wins, looked to have had the achievement within their grasp.

City's debut match in the First Division on 1st September 1906 - a 1-2 defeat to Manchester United. The original cover at this end was demolished in December 1917.

Closer examination of the record of the three clubs that share the record demonstrates that City's run was contained in an unbeaten sequence of twenty four League games, Preston's in twenty, and United's in eighteen, so perhaps City are able to lay claim to their's being the better overall accomplishment. Promotion to the First Division therefore was achieved during Harry Thickett's first season in charge, and helped to produce a profit of £425.19s.0d. Gate receipts totalled £5,275.12s.4d., total income £5,505.8s.1d., and season ticket sales £250.10s.4d. Only £290 was expended on transfers. For the vital home match with Manchester United on December 30th gate receipts were given as £726.4s.3d. Such a high figure for a recorded attendance of around 19,000 was due to those spectators who didn't purchase tickets in advance, and had to subsequently pay increased prices on the day of the match.

The start of the 1905-06 campaign didn't suggest that such a record breaking season was to be in prospect, as after the Public Trial Match on August 23rd, when 4,000 spectators turned up to see the Greens beat the Reds 2-1, the opening game took the Babes to the 'Clayton' ground in Manchester where United destroyed them to the tune of 5-1. This, however, didn't have any adverse effects as City immediately embarked on their twenty four match unbeaten run, not being defeated again in the League until the visit of Leicester Fosse on February 17th, who surprised the Babes in winning 2-1. These were the only League defeats suffered during the campaign, but in the F.A. Cup the City were the victims of another giant killing act, going down to a shock 2-1 defeat at Brentford on the same day as local team Staple Hill were putting up a great fight in this competition at Manchester United, though after scoring first they eventually lost 7-2.

To celebrate promotion a Banquet and Smoking Concert was held at the Royal Hotel, College Green, when the Lord Mayor Alderman A.J. Smith and the High Sheriff H.L. Riseley were in attendance. The menu was fit for a king, and there were twenty-one speeches interposed with the piano playing of Percy Smith plus performances by various artistes including the Apollo Glee Party, and J.M. Dingle singing the Club song *"Play up! Play up! Bristol City"*. At this time the Board comprised of William P. Kingston (Chairman) W.H. Burland (Vice-Chairman), Frank N. Bacon, J.H. Leakey, Joseph Daveridge, F.V. Larway and F.H. Thomas; The Hon. Secretary was E.J. Locke.

Hottest Day

Season 1906-07 therefore saw the Babes mixing with the elite for the first time and after the playing of a Trial Match when the 'Reds', through Jones (4), Stainforth and Critchley beat the 'Blues' 6-0 in front of about 2,500 spectators on August 20th, the great day of the opening engagement duly arrived. September 1st was the hottest day that had been recorded for League Football in this country, and the City were faced at Ashton Gate by their promotion partners Manchester United. Unfortunately it wasn't a winning debut as despite scoring first, thanks to a fifth-minute penalty by Bennett, United fought back to equalise through Roberts five minutes later, and complete the scoring before half-time when Picken did the necessary. On this day the crowd number was said to be in the region of 21,000, but with receipts of £485, the figure was more likely to have been around 18,000.

Runners-up

However, despite this disappointing start the team soon found it's feet in higher company and by the turn of the year were in the running for the Championship, a prize which only just eluded them at the finish due to suffering three successive defeats - two at home - over the Easter period.

Although finishing as Runners-up, three points behind Newcastle United, the City did have the consolation of gaining another Football League record as this was the highest position obtained by a Club on gaining promotion to the top Division; this record was equalled by Charlton Athletic in 1936-37 and eventually eclipsed by Ipswich Town in 1960-61 when they secured the Championship.

'India Rubber Man'

At Goodison Park on February 16th, 1907, Billy Wedlock became the second Bristol City player to be capped for England, the first having been Billy Jones who made his one and only appearance in a 3-0 win over Ireland at Southampton on March 9th 1901. Billy 'Fatty' Wedlock, playing at centre-half, helped England to a 1-0 success over Ireland and he went on to make a total of twenty-six appearances (twenty-five consecutive) for his country in the centre-half position between 1907 and 1914. He also played three times for the Football League, versus the Scottish League at Villa Park on February 29th, 1908, the Irish League in Belfast on October 10th, that year, and the return against the Irish League at Boundary Park on October 9th, 1909; these games were won 2-0, 5-0 and 8-1 respectively.

Wedlock was only 5ft 5inches tall, but such was his athletic ability he was an outstanding player, nicknamed amongst his contemporaries as the 'India Rubber Man', and reckoned to be one of the best players of his generation. At this time England had another outstanding player in this position, namely Charlie Roberts of Manchester United. Roberts though was a great believer in players rights and he was a prime mover in the formation of the Players Union, such action incurring the wrath of the Football Association which possibly explains why he only gained three England caps, though he did turn out eight times for the Football League. The arguments as to who was best still rumble on to this day, shades of the North and South divide, but whatever prejudices one might bring to bear on the matter, one fact is indisputable. Here were two great players, both being the product of that era, and this fact would result in one missing out on International appearances.

Record Profit

The Babes first season in the top flight produced a profit of £3,048.12s.6d. with gate receipts increasing to £8,829.5s.5d. Total income was £9,147.9s.6d., season ticket sales £464.16s.9d. and transfer fees paid £205, these figures being declared at the Annual General Meeting held at the Temperance Hall, Bedminster on Monday the 24th June, 1907. Highest home gate receipts for the season were achieved at the game against Woolwich Arsenal on October 13th when £621.14s.8d. was taken from a crowd totalling about 22,000.

City Programme

A Banquet was held to celebrate the achievements of the Season, though this time it was held at the Grand Hotel, Broad Street, on May 27th, 1907. The campaign is notable in that this is the earliest season that the modern type of programmes for the City are known to exist, though comment in the Bristol City Handbook for 1899-1900 in reference to 'Observer's' Notes in the Bristol City Football Club Match Programme suggests the possibility that a proper programme, as opposed to a team sheet, was also published at this time. Single sheet programmes were produced during the initial campaign of Bristol South End, and one for the game against Preston North End on April 6th, 1895 still exists. This consists of a pink sheet sized 7½ x 4¾ inches, containing match line-up on one side and forthcoming attractions on the other. The programmes produced during 1906-07 consisted of eight pages, 8 x 5 inches, containing a potted history of the visitors on page two, Editors Notes on page three, Men of Mark on page four, 'Kandid Konfessions of the Kute Kid' on pages five, and six, an advertisement on page seven, and team line-ups on the back page. These programmes were good value at 1d., exactly the same price as the team sheets had been. For 1907-08 the size of the programme was increased to twenty pages measuring 9½ x 7¼ inches, but remained priced at 1d. Regular features were 'Our Visitors', 'Notes by the Editor', 'The Kute Kid' column, 'The Passing Breeze', 'In the Smoke', the code for half-time scores, first & reserve team results, a two page spread for team line-ups, and five pages of advertisements - including those on the front page. Biographies and photographs of players were often included, and the programme of September 21st for the game against Newcastle United contained The Kute Kids Limerick Selection, and the issue for the match against Bolton Wanderers on April 18th included an appreciation in respect of The Passing of Walter Bennett.

Following the success of the first season amongst the elite City supporters were hopeful of their team going one better in 1907-08 and they turned up in some numbers to see the Public Trial match on August 21st when the 'Reds' beat the 'Blues' 2-0, with goals from Burton and Maxwell, this scoreline being repeated in the Private Trial a week later when Burton and Gilligan were the scorers. However, after a brilliant start that brought a 3-2 home win over Everton and a 4-0 away success against Woolwich Arsenal form fluctuated. A run of sixteen matches from Christmas Day until April 11th, brought only one win and saw City just one off the bottom with only four games left to play. They then proceeded to put an unbeaten run together, three games being won, and ended the campaign in tenth place.

Benefits

Harry Clay became the fourth Bristol City player to have a Benefit Match, he took the game against Nottingham Forest on November 30th when he received £129. The first recipient of a Benefit was Billy Jones who obtained £102.6s.6d. from a match versus Third Lanark on April 14th, 1903, followed by Peter Chambers who received £100 from the League match with Chesterfield on January 21st, 1905, and then Billy Tuft who pocketed £140.14s.0d. from a game with Southampton on February 25th two years later.

Death of Walter Bennett

All Bristol was saddened to hear of the death of ex-City player Walter Bennett on April 6th, 1908. Walter had been released by the Club at the end of the previous season and he returned to his native heath on deciding to retire from the professional game. He commenced employment in Denaby Main Colliery where he met his untimely death, being buried under tonnes of rock following a cave in.

The lack of success in 1907-08 was reflected in the balance sheet which showed a profit of only £757.18s.10d. Gate receipts dropped significantly to £6,998.7s.6d. Total income was £7,449.14s.4d. and season ticket sales £429.3s.11d. Transfer fees paid totalled £225. Highest receipts were for the game against Sunderland on April 20th when a 19,500 crowd generated £529.

First City Man To Play For The Football League XI

Frank Hilton became the first City player to be honoured by the Football League, playing and scoring for their Representative XI in a 6-3 win over the Irish League at Roker Park on October 12th, 1907.

Rugby International

Rugby Union came to Ashton Gate on the 18th January 1908, when in foggy conditions England succumbed to a 28-18 defeat by Wales in front of 21,000 spectators who paid receipts of £1,600.

F.A. Cup Final

The third campaign in the First Division in 1908-09 would, with an end of season position of eighth, suggest an untroubled and successful League campaign, but this wasn't the case. Closer inspection of the League indicates why, for it can be deduced that if Manchester City had not been beaten thanks to a late own goal in the last match, the Babes would have finished thirteenth, and if the visitors had managed to have won, the final placing would have been eighteenth. Despite the Club's second highest ever Football League placing, the campaign was not notable in respect of League 'doings', but it was still what many supporters of the time maintain as the Babes most memorable season, due to their exploits in reaching their one and only F.A. Cup Final to date.

Progress to the Final at the Crystal Palace Grounds at Sydenham, London, on April 24th, 1909, was certainly achieved the hard way, as in every round - except the Third - replays were needed, and in the first Semi-Final at Stamford Bridge on March 27th the Babes only survived against Second Division Derby County thanks to a penalty by Willis Rippon with the last kick of the game. In the replay at St. Andrews four days later the City, in giving a much better performance, were full value for their 2-1 success, though again they were indebted to another penalty by Rippon after forty three minutes. Davis equalised for Derby three minutes after the break, but the Babes notched the winner through Robert Hardy six minutes later.

The F.A.Cup 3rd round match at Ashton Gate. City beat Southern League Norwich City 2-0 on February 20th.
(From the Bristol Times and Mirror - the earliest known local newspaper action photograph of City)

(Left) Harry Clay about to clear for the City, in the F.A. Cup Semi-final at Stamford Bridge against Derby County. Billy Wedlock (in the dark shirt) is on the extreme right.

(Below) In the Cup Final at the Crystal Palace, Clay is in action again. The player with arm raised is City's Archie Annan.

The City's Cup Final opponents were Manchester United who, despite finishing lower in the League, were favourites for what was also their first Final, due mainly to the fact that they had won the Championship the previous season, and injuries had robbed the Babes of two key players in Rueben Marr and Rippon. Both teams had to wear alternative strips due to a colour clash. United took the field in white shirts with a thin red 'V' running from their shoulders to their stomach, with the red rose of Lancashire on their left breast. City turned out in royal blue shirts with a white shield bearing, in red silk, the Bristol Coat of Arms on their left breast. The only goal of the game was obtained by Sandy Turnbull for United after twenty-two minutes, and whilst the Babes had opportunities to equalise it would appear that the victors were deserving of their success.

The City players spent the night previous to the game at the Queens Hotel, Norwood, having departed from Temple Meads Station on the 2.30p.m. train, but the majority of their supporters travelled up on the Saturday in the dozens of special trains laid on by the Great Western Railway, helping to produce a crowd of 71,401, which is the largest any City team has performed in front of. On this great occasion the sides lined up thus:-

City: Clay; Annan, Cottle, Hanlin, Wedlock, Spear, Staniforth, Hardy, Gilligan, Burton, Hilton.
United: Moger; Stacey, Hayes, Duckworth, Roberts, Bell, Meredith, Halse, J. Turnbull, A. Turnbull, Wall.
Referee: J. Mason (Burslem)

So ended a season that had started with a crowd of only 1,000 attending the Trial game on August 26th, when the 'Blues' beat the 'Reds' 3-2, and at the Annual General Meeting held at the Temperance Hall, East Street, Bedminster on June 30th, 1909 a profit of £3,133.18s.11d. was declared. Gate receipts were £12,619.8s.6d., this including £3,051.15s.2d. which was City's share of the proceeds from the Final and Semi-Final. Total income was £13,253.6s.6d., season ticket sales totalled £430.0s.10d., and £425 was paid out in transfer fees. March 5th brought the death of the Club Vice-Chairman W.H. (Billie) Burland at the age of only 37. This ex-Bedminster player, Treasurer, Secretary and Director, who joined the City following the amalgamation in 1900, died at his residence at the Rising Sun, Ashton Gate. He was buried in Arnos Vale, Cemetery on March 9th.

Liberal Success

On February 10th a special match took place at Ashton Gate involving local politicians, when the Liberals decimated the Conservatives to the tune of 13 goals to 2, after being 5-0 ahead at half-time.

Bill Demery took the Middlesbrough match on October 24th as his Benefit and he received £134.13s.9d. Receipts of £660.11s.9d. were taken for the home game against Bradford City on Boxing Day, and £780.9s.3d. for the clash with Manchester United on Easter Monday.

Third International

Joe Cottle became the third Bristol City player to be capped by England when he played, with Billy Wedlock, in the team that beat Ireland 4-0 on the ground of Bradford Park Avenue on February 13th, 1909.

⚽ Match to Remember

Bristol City 4 Nottingham Forest 0 Football League Division One: Saturday, 30th April, 1910

The last match of the campaign brought Nottingham Forest to Ashton Gate and the visitors, after winning the toss, were the first to look dangerous, for in the first minute Whitchurch sent a pass into the middle which threatened trouble, but West in stumbling in his attempt to get at the ball let in Cottle to clear for the homesters. Annan next had to do battle against Armstrong, but he neatly tricked and punted off up the field where Burton securing possession sent out to Shearman who raced off and drove a great shot just behind the bar. Forest then took up the attack but Hooper's centre was well attended to, and immediately the ball was transferred to the other end where Cowell, receiving from Staniforth, was unable to beat the two players between him and the goal. Staniforth then drove a shot behind and Horrocks getting away put in a centre which Wedlock intercepted. But in the same moment things looked very queer in front of the City goal as in endeavouring to clear, the ball slipped off Annan's foot towards his own goal, putting West clear, but fortunately for the homesters he mis-kicked and the ball was then bundled out of danger.

City then took control of the game, Cowell coming close, then Burton shooting over the bar, before they took the lead after nineteen minutes had elapsed. *Cowell* secured possession from a Staniforth cross, and with the visitors custodian Hassell on his knees he had a comparatively easy task in driving the ball into the net.

From the re-start Forest got away on the left and when the ball came across, West got in a good header that went narrowly over the cross-bar. City came again however and were on top for the

Although the visitor's defence wasn't giving anything away, at this stage their forwards were letting them down. West, in the centre, was well plying his wings, but very little was made of the ensuing chances as Forest only managed to shoot in fits and starts. For the City, Hardy and Staniforth had Needham in a hopeless position practically every time they came down, and in one of these advances Hardy cannoned in a shot which Hasell saved but being tackled by Cowell the ball ran to Burton who drove across. Hardy put in a header which hit the visitors custodian to rebound to the City inside-right who hit his second chance behind. After this a mistake by Maltby enabled Hardy to get close in before shooting but his attempt, though very close, skimmed the upright and went wide. However not dismayed the homesters kept at it, and with the half twenty-five minutes old they scored their second goal when *Cowell* found the net with his drive after receiving from Burton who had taken the ball through the Forest defence. Almost from the kick-off the City gained possession again. Hardy was going through the visitors defence, and as the ball was centred he was fouled in the penalty area. The resultant penalty saw *Cowell*, with a fast rising drive, netting his own and his side's third goal. The Robins were now well on top and swarming round Nottingham's goal, but it wasn't until five minutes from the end that the fourth and final goal was obtained this again being to the credit of *Cowell*.

CITY: Clay, Annan, Cottle, Young, Wedlock, Hanlin, Staniforth, Hardy, Cowell, Burton, Shearman.
FOREST: Hassell; Gibson, Maltby, Hughes, Wolfe, Needham, Armstrong, West, Hooper, Whitchurch, Horrocks.
Referee: J.T. Hawcroft   Attendance: 11,000
(Source: Sports Times, 30th April, 1910)

Wednesday Team Again

The campaign saw City starting up a Wednesday team again after a lapse of eleven seasons, and playing in the Bristol Wednesday League they were to dominate the competition until the side disbanded just prior to the start of the 1912-13 Season in protest over a decision by the Gloucestershire Football Association to remove the Club from participation in the League Cup Competition. City Wednesday achieved the League and Cup double for the four seasons that they operated, and it wasn't to be until the 1920's that they would again run such an XI for a period - Champions in 1928-29 - and this was followed by another revival in 1949-50 when they won the Second Division Championship of that League.

Anti-Climax

Season 1909-10 was an anti-climax, for in the F.A. Cup - despite disposing of Liverpool in the 1st Round - the Babes went out, after a replay, to West Bromwich Albion at the next stage. The League matches saw a struggle to avoid the dreaded drop (but being successfully avoided this time didn't prevent such a calamity befalling them the following campaign). Gate receipts went down to £7,612.7s.6d., total income £8,237.0s.5d. and this served to produce a deficit of £78.0s.10d. Despite the interest generated by their F.A. Cup run in the previous season it is somewhat perplexing to note that season ticket sales also went down, in fact to the lowest figure in their First Division career, a total only amounting to £327.3s.6d. Sammy Gilligan had the match against Aston Villa on March 19th as his Benefit when he received £228.8s.3d.

Relegation For The First Time

As previously mentioned the 1910-11 campaign brought an end to the Babes tenure in the First Division, despite the boost of a great 1-0 win at Newcastle on the opening day, this success going somewhat towards restoring the Club's pride against the 'Magpies' as on April 25th, 1910, they had come to Ashton Gate and obtained a 3-0 win with what was virtually a Reserve side, such a team being fielded due to their involvement that week in three League games as well as the F.A. Cup Final Replay.

Return Of Hollis Again

Relegation at the end of 1910-11 was a calamitous blow to the ambitions of the Club, but the warning signs were clear from an early stage with only one win, one draw, and one goal in the opening seven matches. Manager Harry Thickett was dismissed on October 6th and Director Frank Bacon took over in a temporary capacity until requesting to be relieved after the Babes suffered one of the greatest pre-First World War F.A. Cup shocks when non-League Crewe Alexandra came to Ashton Gate on January 14th and won 3-0. The Directors then turned to Sam Hollis for the third time and he took over again on January 19th.

In the League there had been some improvement in form prior to the F.A. Cup defeat, with the Babes reaching fourteenth place after completing the double over Newcastle United on

New Year's Eve, but the barren period that was without a single win between February 11th and April 14th left the Club at the bottom of the table with only three matches left. However, two successive wins gave them a chance of escaping and if full points could have been secured against Everton who were the visitors to Ashton Gate in the final game, then survival would have been achieved. Unfortunately it wasn't to be as the Babes succumbed to the only goal of the game and so lost their First Division status.

Benefits

Three Benefits were awarded during the campaign, Billy Wedlock taking the Manchester United game on October 8th when he received £354.3s.2d., Andy Burton receiving £210.19s.6d. from the Aston Villa fixture on November 5th, and Archie Annan and Arthur Spear each receiving £200 from their Joint Benefit match against Everton on April 29th.

Flight of M. De Lessops

The flight of M. de Lessops in his aeroplane over Nottingham whilst City were engaged in the quest for points with Notts County on October 1st brought play to a halt and caused the referee, J.W. Marsh, to blow for time four minutes early due to his failure to allow for the interruption. When this was brought to his notice he decided to rectify his error and the players were obliged to return to the field of play to complete the game, though this produced no alteration to the score.

Massive Loss

The unsuccessful fight against relegation with expenditure on players of £1,657.2s.2d. in a vain effort to beat the drop, produced a massive loss of £3,842.5s.4d. and a fall in gate receipts to £5,828,19s.8d. These figures were given at the Annual General Meeting held at the Temperance Hall on June 30th, when the only encouraging information was that the season ticket sales had increased to £359.11s.8d. Total income of £6,450.16s.3d. included monies received in respect of Bedminster Cricket Club holding a Carnival at Ashton Gate on July 2nd, 1910.

Another Struggle

A crowd of 1,500 turned up for the Trial game on August 26th when the 'Reds' beat the 'Whites' 2-1. Brand and Forbes scored for the winning side, and Ball for the losers. A successful start was made to life back in the Second Division when the Babes beat Fulham 1-0 at Ashton Gate on September 2nd, but life was to prove much harder in this sphere than previously. The 1911-12 campaign proving to be a fight against having to apply for re-election, this eventually being avoided with a final placing of thirteenth.

The lower status was reflected in the gate receipts which decreased to £4,228.13s.2d. (including £302.17s.11d. in respect of the Reserves), and season ticket sales reducing to £199.15s.6d. A loss of £817 was revealed at the Annual General Meeting held at the Temperance Hall on June 26th, such loss mainly on account of transfer fees being paid which amounted to £709.19s.10d.

Rugby League

In order to increase revenue a Rugby League match was staged at Ashton Gate on December 20th when the touring Australians beat a Combined West of England and South Wales side by 23 points to 3.

Return Of Popular Jack Hamilton

The popular A.J. (Jack) Hamilton returned to the City on September 16th when he took over in charge of the Reserves, and he was to become caretaker manager of the Babes during the period of the Great War.

Big Win

Promotion was a confident forecast of supporters for 1912-13 and with no defeats, though only two wins, in the opening seven games suggested the possibility that this might be the case, form subsequently deteriorated, and the end of the campaign saw the Babes down in sixteenth spot. The Season has started with 6,000 supporters attending the Club Trial on August 24th and they saw the 'Reds' through Harris, Owers and Bowyer, beat the 'Blues' 3-0, and it wasn't until October 19th that the Babes suffered their first defeat when, despite Wedlock obtaining a rare goal, they went down 3-1 at Glossop. After winning their next game, at home to Clapton Orient the following Saturday, another win was not achieved until December 21st. This set up a sequence of three successive victories in the League, followed by two defeats before some real form was found for the home fixture against Stockport County which was won 7-2 on January 18th. Unfortunately only two more wins were obtained in the remainder of the League programme to leave the fans feeling rather disgruntled.

Marr's Benefit

Reuben Marr, who had been sent off in the match at Wolverhampton on September 7th due to dangerous studs, had his Benefit on the occasion of Burnley's visit on February 8th. He received £300 which also included approximately £156 in respect of a special benefit performance at the Princes Theatre.

Increased Receipts

The increased optimism of the public was reflected in the gate receipts which improved to £5,086.19s.11d. (this sum included £445.15s.4d. from Reserve matches) and season ticket sales of £318.1s.8d. However despite this rise, which helped produce a total income of £6,526.5s.6d., a loss of £987.2s.7d. was announced at the Annual General Meeting held at the Ford Memorial Hall, Mill Lane, Bedminster on June 26th, when the Directors in attendance were:- E.G. Murdock (Chairman), W. Pont, Joseph Daveridge, G.H. Bacon, F.H. Thomas and F. Vowles. Frank Bacon was absent due to illness, but Hon. Secretary E.J.Locke was present, as was new Manager George Hedley who had taken over from Sam Hollis on April 23rd.

Home International

On the 17th March 1913, the City had the honour of staging at Ashton Gate the Home International between England and Wales when a crowd numbering some 9,000, paying receipts of £393, turned up to witness England's 4-3 success. Billy Wedlock had been selected at centre-half for England but he had to withdraw due to injury. That day the teams lined up as follows:-

England: Scattergood (Derby County), Crompton (Blackburn Rovers), Pennington (West Bromwich Albion), Moffatt (Oldham Athletic), McCall (Preston North End), Bradshaw (Blackburn Rovers), Wallace (Aston Villa), Fleming (Swindon Town), Hampton (Aston Villa), Latheron (Blackburn Rovers), Hodgkinson (Blackburn Rovers).

Wales: Bailiff (Llanelly), Hewitt (Chelsea), Lloyd Davies (Northampton Town), Hughes (Manchester City), Peake (Liverpool), J.T.Jones (Stoke), Meredith (Manchester City), Wynn (Manchester City), Davis (Millwall), Lot Jones (Manchester City), Llew Davies (Wrexham).

Referee: A.A. Jackson (Scotland).

Death of E.J.Locke

After spending £678.7s.10d. in transfer fees in 1912-13, the Board speculated even more during the following campaign in an effort to reclaim First Division status. They expended £1,459.2s.0d. out of gate receipts that rose to £6,976.18s.1d. (including £426.18s.5d. for Reserve matches), but the only achievement was an improved final placing of eighth, as the loss of £968.17s.1d. was comparable to that of the previous season. A notable absentee at the Annual General Meeting at the Ford Memorial Hall, on June 29th was the erstwhile Hon. Secretary E.J. Locke who died during the course of the campaign. Frank Hill, who had been Locke's assistant, took over as Secretary. A testimonial fund was set up and this saw the selection of a Combined City & Rovers team for the first time when they faced F.A. Cup holders Aston Villa at Ashton Gate on April 29th, 1914. A crowd of about 4,000 spectators turned up to see the Villa win 3-0 thanks to an own goal by Bennett after 20 minutes, then two strikes by Boyne in the following fifteen minutes.

Bristol XI: Stansfield (Rovers); Kearns (City), Bennett (Rovers), Moss (City), Wedlock (City), Mainds (Rovers), Neesam (City), J.C. Shervey (Rovers), Morton (City), Crompton (Rovers), Harris (City).

Aston Villa: Hardy, Lyons, Weston, Barker, Morris, Leach, Wallace, Stephenson, Boyne, Bache, Edgley.

The Howarth Affair

The sensation of the season concerned the Babes newly acquired centre-forward Tommy Howarth who, whilst on leave from the Army and visiting a friend in Bristol over Christmas 1913, played in a Trial game for the Club. He performed well enough for the City to arrange - after the usual notice - for him to purchase his discharge, and then find him suitable employment. However on Howarth taking up this employment the Football Association stepped in and this brought about his suspension for twelve months - from April 1914 - together with his loss of amateur status. The Club were fined £50 for their involvement in a practice that the F.A. were determined to stamp out since at the same meeting they also dealt with Manchester United who had been playing an army man under an assumed name.

The Great War

The commencement of the Great War in August 1914, and the decision of the football authorities to continue with League and Cup football, gave the 1914-15 campaign an unreal feel to it, and the City - after starting well - fell away to be in thirteenth place when normal League football came to a close for four years. The Annual General Meeting held at the Ford Memorial Hall on June 30th 1915, revealed a loss of £1,417.6s.4d., this was mainly due to reduced gate receipts of £4,625.3s.11d. and season ticket sales of only £79.9s.0d., the latter compared to £280.3s.6d. the previous campaign. Transfer fees of £99.12s.4d. reflected the general uncertainty of the times.

Death of W.B. Hodgkinson

The season saw the death of the man who had done so much to establish Bristol City in the football world - W.B. Hodgkinson. He was at this time Secretary of the Gloucestershire Football Association and was buried in Arnos Vale Cemetery on March 14th, 1915 following his death in the Bristol General Hospital on March 10th.

Purchase of The Ground

In many areas of the Country during the war years, the Football League operated various competitions, but the Bristol clubs were isolated in the football sense. Apart from playing in the South West Combination in 1915-16, they were denied the opportunity of reasonable competition when this competition was discontinued the following campaign, due to Portsmouth and Southampton joining the London Combination. This situation eventually brought about the formation of the Bristol County Combination which operated in the 1917-18 and 1918-19 seasons, the City being Champions in the first year and Runners-up the next. It was a difficult struggle to keep going throughout this period, but not only was this achieved it was the great foresight of the Directors at this time, that was to provide the platform that ensured the Club's survival in 1933 and 1982. The move was the purchase of the ground following the expiry of the lease on the 17th March 1917, an act that must have taken much courage given that losses of £809.6s.7d. and £537.17s.9d. for the two previous seasons had been declared. Additionally in 1916 the Covered End was so badly damaged by gale force winds that it had to be demolished in December 1917. It wasn't until 1928 that this cover was replaced, becoming initially known as the 'Keating Stand' though nowadays for some unbeknown reason it is often referred to by the geographically incorrect title of the 'East End'. Another loss of £555.8s.2d. was announced for 1917-18, but the final season of wartime football produced a profit of £264.4s.10d.

During the first season of the war City continued to publish their match programme, but it is not known whether this continued throughout the rest of this period.

(How the Sports Times viewed the Howarth affair)

Killed in Action

A number of Babes players served at the front and Arthur Moss won military distinction in 1917. Tragically Tommy Ware and Edwin Burton were killed in action, Ware in June 1915 and Burton in August the following year. Also killed at the front was Sergeant A. Edwards, who made four appearances for City in 1912-13, he was hit in the head by a piece of shrapnel in 1918.

Secretary Frank Hill was called up in 1917, but he survived to take over from Arthur Glass, the temporary Secretary, at the end of hostilities in 1918. City Vice-Chairman Frank Bacon who was a popular figure at Ashton Gate died on January 25th, 1918. He had been goal keeper for Arlington Rovers at the same time as Billy Wedlock played for them.

Baseball

The Ashton Gate ground was used for other events around this time, with a Sacred Concert being held on a Sunday evening in June 1919, but perhaps the most unusual use was the staging of a baseball match. This took place on July 13th, 1918, when a team representing the United States of America beat Canada 6-5 in front of 2,000 spectators.

Joe Palmer

Prior to the re-starting of League Football in 1919-20, the City were perturbed by a report that suggested they may not be allowed to automatically retain their Second Division status. However, in the event this suggestion was not acted upon, and the return of peacetime football saw the Babes lining up with familiar old rivals. At this time City had a new man in charge, Joe Palmer, who took over from Jack Hamilton - the man in charge during the difficult war years. Palmer thus returned to Ashton Gate where he had been a trainer under George Hedley before the War.

Supporters Club

City fans got together to form a Supporters Club on April 25th, 1919, when they held a meeting at the Bedminster Hotel. At this meeting W.G. Sarle was elected Chairman, W. Reid Hon. Secretary, and Mr. Sweet Hon. Treasurer. This Club would appear to have been the second such organisation to have been formed by City supporters as there had been one in existence for a while during the St. John's Lane days. This pioneer Club did not survive very long since certain officials of the Football Club were not kindly disposed towards it. The first year of this new Supporters Club proved very successful as at their Annual General Meeting one year later, on April 30th, they declared a profit of £225.5s.3d., prior to giving the Football Club £41.2s.8d. for the painting of the Stand, £92.2s.3d. to the Bristol Royal Infirmary, and making other donations totalling £6.7s.0d. The Supporters Club officials for 1920-21 were:- C.H.C. Taylor (President), Captain F. Plunkett O.B.E. (Chairman), C.M. Ackerman (Secretary) and W. Sandford (Asst. Secretary). Membership cost 2s. per annum.

The City started the 1919-20 Season with two Trial Matches, these seeing Blues beating the Reds 1-0 on August 16th in front of 2,000 spectators, and the Reds gaining revenge a week later when they won 7-1. They opened their League Programme on the last day of the month when they beat Bury 1-0 at 'Ashton Gate' in front of 10,000 spectators. It was to be quite a season for crowds throughout the country, and City had more than their share as demonstrated by their record gate receipts for the campaign of £30,769.5s.2d., though this was greatly helped by reaching the Semi-Finals of the F.A. Cup.

F.A. Cup Semi-Final

In contrast to the Babes last successful run in the F.A. Cup, this time they were not involved in any replays. They accounted for two First Division sides, in Arsenal and Bradford City, on the way to the Semi-Final confrontation with Second Division Huddersfield Town at Stamford Bridge on March 27th, 1920. Their injury hit side had the fates conspire against them to make up for the luck they experienced in saving the Semi-Final at this venue eleven years previously. City suffered two injury setbacks in the early stages, John Wren being a virtual passenger after the eighth minute, followed seventeen minutes later by Dickie Reader had to go off for the remainder of the half after being rendered unconscious and sustaining damaged ribs. Reader's injury resulted from a collision with Mutch, the Huddersfield custodian.

POPULAR AT CHELSEA. THE PENSIONER (To Bristol City): " Very pleased to see you here again, sir, and by way of a secret, I shan't be half glad if you're up here again next month for the final."
(How the Sports News saw the Bristol Babe at Chelsea)

However this wasn't all the bad luck they experienced as City were denied the lead after twenty-three minutes due to the poor positioning of the officials. Centre-forward Tommy Howarth put in a header that was reported as being a good foot over the goal line when it was cleared by a Huddersfield defender. After this the score remained deadlocked until the sixty-fifth minute, when Taylor scored for the 'Terriers', and things looked all up for the City when he added a second only three minutes later. The Babes showed great spirit though, this being emphasised by the return of Reader at the start of the second-half, and Howarth got City back into the game with a great shot with nineteen minutes left. Unfortunately they were unable to turn to good account other opportunities that came their way in the time left. They were therefore obliged to become an early victim of Huddersfield's remarkable rise from being threatened with closure only four months previously, to becoming giants of the game in the 1920's when they became the first club to win three successive League Championships. On this day in front of 35,863 spectators paying receipts of £4,643.12s.9d., the line-ups were as follows:-

City: Vallis; Treasure, Banfield, Wren, Wedlock, Nicholson, Reader, Neesam, Howarth, Pocock, Harris.
Town: Mutch; Wood, Bullock, Slade, Wilson, Watson, Richardson, Mann, Taylor, Swann, Smith.
Referee: A. Warner (Nottingham)

Defensive Record

The 1920-21 season saw a strong bid being made for promotion, but the Babes eventually finished in third place, being headed by newly elected Cardiff City, and Birmingham. The credit for this high placing was mainly due to the defence which, despite being without Billy Wedlock after the opening five games, conceded a Club record low of 29 goals in 42 League matches. The following campaign however saw them let in exactly twice this number, this being a big factor in the Babes relegation to the Third Division (South), which had been formed in 1920-21. So poor was City's form that their situation looked hopeless by December 28th, when Alex Raisbeck was appointed as Secretary-Manager in succession to Joe Palmer who had been sacked on October 19th.

Yo-Yo City

Proving too strong for the lower division, City romped away with the Championship, heading the table from December 16th, but the euphoria of this success was dispelled when a disastrous return to the Second Division action ended in demotion again at the end of the 1923-24 campaign. That season saw the Babes in a relegation position from September 29th, when they suffered their worst home Football League defeat, going down 8-0 to Derby County. This defeat came seven days after winning 3-2 at the Baseball Ground.

Boardroom Unrest

This Yo-Yo existence had its repercussions in the Boardroom, grumblings of discontent first rearing it's head in 1921 and bringing about E. Gwynne Vevers' replacement of Ernest Murdock as Chairman on March 15th. This action was followed by the Club's share capital being increased from £12,500 to £15,000. This disharmony continued throughout the relegation campaign of 1921-22 even though a so called 'Healing Meeting' took place at the Grand Hotel on December 5th, 1921. In consequence a special meeting was held at the Ford Memorial Hall on June 2nd, 1922, when Chairman Vevers blamed the attitude of Murdock and his boardroom ally, W.J. Giles, for the poor position of the Club. It was therefore decided that all the Directors would resign en-bloc, and a fresh Board would be elected fourteen days later. Accordingly at this same venue on June 16th, nearly 200 shareholders were in attendance to vote on the fifteen nominations for the ten places. Among those putting themselves forward was Sam Hollis who was now Chairman of the Shareholders Association, but he together with Murdock and Giles were defeated. George Jenkins though just scraped in and he was to later play a major part in the history of the Babes, following an F.A. Inquiry into the dealings of the Club.

F.A. Inquiry

This Inquiry into the affairs of Bristol City cut short the promotion celebrations in 1923, as six Directors - Vevers, W. Pont, G.H. Bacon, H. Pruett, F.H. Thomas and W. Weeks - were suspended for life from any activity in regard to the running of a football club. Secretary/Manager Alex Raisbeck was fined £50 and the Club £250. Only three Directors remained when the Annual General Meeting was held at the Ford Memorial Hall on July 19th - Harry Drewett, the new Chairman, former Secretary Frank Hill, and George Jenkins. Seven more Directors, including Percy Daniell who became Vice-Chairman, were elected at this meeting which went on until 12.30 a.m. The inquiry had been held 'in camera' on June 9th and the suspensions announced three days later, this being confirmed following an appeal that was dismissed by the F.A. Appeals Committee sitting at the Queens Hotel, Birmingham on June 29th. However, after much campaigning by Alex Raisbeck the ban was eventually lifted, City being notified in a telegram from the F.A. on January 25th, 1926.

Dick Kerr's Preston Ladies

These early years following the end of the Great War saw Ashton Gate staging Ladies Football and Rugby Union games as well as a Schoolboys International Trial. Bristol R.F.C. played two matches here in 1921, beating Newport by 13 points to 6 in front of 12,500 spectators on February 5th, and losing to Leicester 10-7 on March 26th when 10,500 were present. The Ladies first played at Ashton Gate on the 20th April 1921, when Bath City Ladies beat Brantocco Ladies (Southampton) 2-1, watched by a 12,500 crowd in support of the Bristol City Memorial Fund. Five months later the famous Dick Kerr's Preston Ladies XI turned up to take on a South of England Ladies XI. The latter game was played on September 28th when 4,500 spectators saw Dick Kerr's side win 5-0. It was on April 4th, 1923, that the best of England's schoolboy footballers came to Ashton Gate when a team representing the South beat the North 4-2 in front of 4,000.

Neutral Venue

The ground was also used as a neutral venue for a number of F.A. Cup matches at this time. Ashton Gate had first been used for this purpose in 1911 when Merthyr Town beat Exeter City 2-1 in a 2nd Replay of the Second Qualifying Round when 2,000 spectators were present, but interest was much greater when Chelsea and Plymouth met on the 28th February 1921, to resolve their Third Round tie, 26,007 turning up to see the 'Pensioners' win 2-1. The following year, on January 16th, Swansea Town beat West Ham United 1-0 in the First Round watched by 8,976 spectators. Four more games of this nature took place prior to the Second World War:-

Dec. 8th 1924 Exeter City 1 Newport County 0
5,000 (5th Qual.Round)
Dec. 7th 1925 Reading 2 Torquay United 0
3,765 (1st Round)
Nov. 5th 1928 Yeovil & P.U. 3 Barry Town 1
650 (4th Qual.Round)
Dec. 5th 1932 Torquay United 3 Bournemouth & B.A. 2
2,000 (1st Round)

Ashton Gate was also used to stage Bath City's 1-1 draw in a Friendly with Blackburn Rovers on May 5th, 1932, when the attendance was 2,000. The fixture was switched due to the fact that the Twerton Park pitch was flooded.

Attendance Records

As previously mentioned crowds were high in the period following the ending of the Great War and this brought many changes to attendances and receipt records. City's pre-war record had been achieved on February 20th, 1909, when

Southern League Norwich City were beaten 2-0 in the Third Round of the F.A. Cup, the receipts of £868.0s.9d. being generated by a crowd of 24,009. This attendance was beaten for the first time on the 31st January 1920, when 25,900 people were present to witness City's 1-0 success over Arsenal in the F.A. Cup, but this did not remain the record for long. The League visit of Clapton Orient that same year, on October 30th, saw the figure being raised to 26,022, then up to 34,710 two months later (December 27th) when Laurie Banfield took the League match against Port Vale as his 1st Benefit, receiving £400 from gate receipts of £2,038.13s.5d.

Receipts Records

Receipts in excess of £1,000 were achieved for the first time on the occasion of Fulham's visit on Saturday, October 4th, 1919 when £1,150 was taken. This day was originally scheduled for Fulham's home fixture against the City, but the Football League authorities ordered the switch in consequence of the 'Cottagers' failure to turn up at Ashton Gate the previous week due to a national rail strike. This directive annoyed Fulham as it meant that their home fixture with City would have to be re-scheduled as a weekday match with a consequential loss of revenue. However, in coming to Ashton Gate and winning 3-0 to take City's unbeaten record, it would appear that this compensated them for such an annoyance. It didn't take long however for the £1,150 figure to be exceeded, and on February 21st, it rose to £3,551.7s.6d., this being the amount taken for the F.A. Cup match against Cardiff City that day.

Benefits

As well as Laurie Banfield's 1st Benefit match, a number of other City players had League matches for their Benefit games throughout the 1920's:-

Bob Young	April 10th, 1920	v. Hull City (£300)
Edwin Jones	March 12th, 1921	v. Birmingham (£400)
Joe Harris	April 17th, 1922	v. Coventry City (£600)
Bert Neesam	Oct. 14th, 1923	v. Swansea Town
Laurie Banfield	Jan. 19th, 1924	v. Bradford City
(2nd Benefit)		
Frank Vallis	Dec. 13th, 1924	v. Merthyr T. (£400)
Billy Pocock	March 4th, 1925	v. Luton Town (£400)
Bob Hughes	Jan. 30th, 1926	v. Aberdare Athletic
Bert Neesam	April 10th, 1926	v. Newport County
(2nd Benefit)		
Sandy Torrance	Jan. 15th, 1927	v. Gillingham
Johnny Paul	Feb. 18th, 1928	v. Clapton Orient
Ernie Glenn	Nov. 24th, 1929	v. Tottenham H.

'Jock' Nicholson though 'bucked the trend' as he arranged a Friendly for his Benefit, taking an unknown sum from a match with Cardiff City on September 22nd, 1920. This policy was also adopted by Edwin Jones for his 2nd Benefit three years later, against Swansea Town on May 2nd, and by Andy Smailes from a game with Cardiff City on the 10th April 1929.

Billy Wedlock retired at the end of the 1920-21 campaign, and he arranged as his 2nd Benefit for an International XI to take on a Combined Bristol XI at Ashton Gate at the conclusion of that season on May 4th. The International team included many retired players, and not surprisingly the Bristol side won 3-2, despite being 1-0 behind at half-time. A crowd of about 8,000 turned up to see Pocock (2) and Wilcox score for the Bristol team, with Wall and Woodward doing the necessary for the Internationalists. On this day the sides were made up as follows:-

Bristol XI: Vallis (City); Panes (Rovers), E. Jones (City), Neesam (City), Sims (Rovers), Nicholson (City), Walter (Rovers), Crompton (Rovers), Wilcox (City), Pocock (City), Harris (City).

International XI: S. Hardy (Aston Villa); F.M. Milne (late Corinthians), J. Blair (Cardiff City), R. Young (late Bristol City), W. Wedlock (Bristol City), F. Keenor (Cardiff City), J. Cottle (late Bristol City), S. Bloomer (late Derby County), V.J. Woodward (late Chelsea), W. Jones (late Bristol City), G. Wall (Oldham Athletic).

(Note: Three of the International side had to cry off, so old Bristol City favourites Young, Cottle and Jones turned out)

Meeting the Future King George VI

The City players being introduced to the future King George VI prior to kick-off at Clapton Orient on 22 April 1922.

The season following Wedlock's retirement brought, as previously related, relegation to the Third Divisions (South) for the first time. The only highlight that campaign was the win at Clapton Orient on April 22nd, when the players on both sides were introduced to a distinguished spectator - the Duke of York (the future King George VI).

The deaths of Edward Hanlon and Ernest Murdock

After the 'Yo-Yo' campaigns the Babes were back in the Third Division (South) in 1924-25, and this time their sojourn was to be of longer duration. It took them three seasons before they captured the Championship and were once again able to progress to greener pastures. Between times they finished third in 1924-25 and fourth in 1925-26, the events in the latter campaign being overshadowed by the death, at the age of forty, of the Babes trainer Edward Hanlon on September 10th. Hanlon had died following a fall down the stairs at 4 a.m., after a disturbed night's sleep which was brought about by his wartime experiences with the Royal Engineers. At this time he was living with his wife in club property - the flat above the shop at the entrance to Ashton Gate. Following his death an appeal fund was set up, and including the £160 taken from a Benefit match against Cardiff on September 30th, enough money was raised to buy a house in Southville for his widow.

(Above) Matthews of City challenges with Southampton's Ball at Ashton Gate - 13 October 1923
(Below) At the Nest, Norwich - in the F.A.Cup on 12 January 1924.
The homesters goalkeeper Williamson comes out to clear a corner from Pocock.

The 1925-26 season starts in cartoon style
(Sports Times)

Match to Remember

Bristol City 9 Gillingham 4
Football League Division Three (South)
Saturday, 15th January, 1927

City turning out at Ashton Gate in their new shirts of darker red than normal - crimson almost instead of scarlet - were holding 4th spot in the table. They were some fourteen points and sixteen places higher than the visitors Gillingham, who having transferred their smart Scot - Marshall - to Brentford a few days previously, brought in Arblaster.

*Wadsworth won the toss for the homesters and Coggins was put to guard the Entrance End goal. The first few minutes ruled all in favour of the Robins, with Keating and then Gilhespy coming near to scoring. Keeping up the pressure City eventually took the lead after the game had been in progress for six minutes, when **Martin** scooped the ball into the back of the net from a splendid centre by Rankin. Walsh had played a prominent part in the movement, and his hard following up and persistence nearly led to another score just after, when he squared the ball across the area with Pickering closing on him, but the visitors goal remained intact by the skin of it's teeth. However, the citadel wasn't long in succumbing for a second time as following plucky attempts by Arblaster and Meston to forge their way through for the visitors, Martin and Gilhespy got going for the City. Gilhespy lost the ball but in cannoning back to him off of Nichol, he centred to such effect that **Walsh** was able to burst past the backs, met the leather with his head, and beat Ferguson, in the twelfth minute. Continuing to press, the homesters were shocked when in a break-away after twenty-two minutes, **Amos** took a centre in his stride, dashed forward and kept his head to beat Coggins with a well judged shot. The goalkeeper could scarcely make any movement in a forlorn effort to save. The game now became more even with both sides creating and missing chances, with the Robins being denied a penalty when Gilhespy looked to be fouled in the area. Referee Captain Linnett, became unpopular with the crowd, when he waved play on. Just prior to half-time that man Amos struck again when he staggered the 11,000 crowd to notch an equaliser for the Gills after their forwards had passed and re-passed, being given too much rope by the City defence. **Amos** found himself close to goal with the ball, and though both home backs tried to stop him, he recovered possession with telling effect, thus making the interval score:-*

BRISTOL CITY 2 GILLINGHAM 2.

*Coming out after the break, and determined to set matters right, the Robins got back into the lead after five minutes had elapsed, **Gilhespy** doing the necessary after a good centre by Rankin had found him close to goal. This had followed a spell of intense City pressure that had brought them three corners. Four minutes later the lead was increased still further when **Walsh** netted from a scrimmage in front of the goal, this at first being disallowed by Captain Linnett. But on consulting with his linesman he reversed his decision much to the anger of the Gillingham players. Almost immediately afterwards the referee incurred the wrath of the visitors still further when penalising them for 'handball', **Walsh** netting easily from the spot for the homesters after fifty-five minutes.*

*With their tails now up the City were on the rampage and minutes later Tot **Walsh** struck again, beating Ferguson with a well placed shot to put the Robins 6-2 ahead, before the Gills hit back when **Arblaster** beat Coggins all ends up with a shot from just outside the penalty area. However, scarcely had the game restarted, than **Walsh** got his fifth goal of the match. Although Gillingham responded by coming on the attack, they soon found themselves 9-3 down as **Walsh**, and then **Keating** scored. But they had the last say in a thoroughly entertaining game when **Arblaster** scored the final goal of the match after eighty minutes to make the score:*

BRISTOL CITY 9 GILLINGHAM 4.

City: Coggins, Hughes, Glenn, Neesam, Wadsworth, Smailes, Gilhespy, Martin, Walsh, Keating, Rankin.

Gillingham: Ferguson, Robertson, Pickering, Rogers, Mason, Nichol, Meston, Arblaster, Amos, Hillier, Bradley.

Referee: Captain Linnett (London)

Attendance: 11,081

(Source: Sports News - The Pink 'Un, Bristol, Saturday, 15th January, 1927.

The end of the 1925-26 season saw the death of City's popular ex-Chairman Ernest Murdock, on the 18th of May, at the Bedminster Cricket Club. He appeared to be in good health, but after taking his turn at batting in the nets, he returned to the pavilion and suddenly collapsed and died. He was 60 years old, and was the headmaster of Christ Church Boys School in Clifton. During the Great War he had attained the rank of Major.

Champions Again

In winning the Third Division (South) Championship in 1926-27 the City set a new points record for the Division, plus new Club records in the Football League by beating Gillingham 9-4 on January 15th and notching 104 goals. This was certainly the season for goals with twenty-nine being obtained in six matches from Christmas Day, when the Babes won 7-3 at Aberdare, until February 5th when a 5-2 success was gained at Coventry. Attendances received a welcome boost and 31,417 paying receipts of £1,833 were present for the important match against Swindon on March 12th. A profit of £1,913.1s.9d. was declared at the Annual General Meeting held at the Ford Memorial Hall, on June 30th when gate receipts were given as £23,076.9s.6d. This was a big improvement over the previous campaign when a loss of £651.12s.10d. had been announced.

A Good Start

Back in the Second Division it looked as though City were intent on regaining First Division status as the first five games were won, but they then began to fall away and at the campaign end they were in twelfth position.

Christmas 1927: the cartoon illustrates City's need of points

The following four seasons for the Babes in this Division were a constant struggle, before they suffered relegation yet again. In 1929-30 it took the securing of twelve points from their last nine games to enable an escape to be made at the expense of Hull City who City had beaten 1-0 on the Anlaby Road ground in the penultimate game.

Fire at Ashton Gate

Alex Raisbeck resigned on June 29th, 1929 and he was succeeded by Joe Bradshaw on August 14th who remained in the Ashton Gate hot seat for three difficult campaigns before resigning on February 4th 1932. The opening day of the 1929-30 Season on August 31st, brought City a 3-1 defeat at Notts County, but the real drama occurred at Ashton Gate when a fire, discovered by a policeman on point duty at Ashton Bridge at 9.40 p.m., destroyed a considerable portion of the Number Two Grandstand. It took firemen 1½ hours to bring the blaze under control, when 120ft of the Park End was gutted, though the refreshment room underneath was saved.

21 September 1929 - Ashton Gate. Action from the match with Hull City, The fire damaged Number Two Stand can be seen in the background.

This fire obviously set a trend as a few years later, on April 18th, 1931, the same misfortune afflicted the main Number One Grandstand, when a fire was discovered in the Press accommodation forty-five minutes after the end of the game with Tottenham Hotspur. This time though plenty of people, including the players, were on hand to deal with the blaze.

Worst Ever Season

With positions of twentieth, twentieth and sixteenth in the three seasons leading up to 1931-32, it is unlikely that anyone thought the campaign was going to be anything other than difficult, but it is doubtful that such a disastrous time was envisaged. The Babes finished firmly at the bottom of the table with a Club record low of twenty-two points, such form bringing about a financial crisis. This saw the offloading of seven players, with Bertie Williams being transferred to Sheffield United, Alan Sliman (who was later killed in an air crash in 1945 while serving in the Royal Air Force), moving to Chesterfield, Tot Walsh to Millwall, Sid Elliott to Notts County, Joey Johnson to Stoke City, and Arthur Mercer plus Cuthbert Robson both going to Chester. This helped to keep the 'wolf from the door' for a while as a profit of £1,092.12s.0d. was declared by Chairman George Jenkins, who had taken over from Harry Drewett in 1924-25, at the 1932 Annual General Meeting at the Ford Memorial Hall on June 23rd. Unfortunately this decimation of the playing strength made it difficult for the Club to recover and regain the confidence of their public, bringing about financial problems in the following season that threatened their very survival.

Coming of Bob Hewison

Bob Hewison took over as Manager, his first match in charge being a 1-1 draw at Southampton on the 23rd April 1932, and he had to assemble an almost completely new look team for 1932-33, only Ernie Brinton, Sid Homer, Wally Jenkins and Jock Taylor remaining.

A bright start saw the 'Robins', as City were now sometimes called, in second place on October 1st, but a subsequent decline saw them having to fight against the possibility of falling into a re-election spot, a fate which they avoided by finishing fifteenth.

Financial Problems

Finance proved to be a real headache with the overdraft standing at £16,500, and this brought about a Public Meeting at the Provident Hall, Prewett Street, Redcliffe on May 5th, when George Jenkins made an appeal for the £10,000 share capital still available to be bought. Gifts of £227 were pledged, this adding to that raised by the Knowle Stadium Company who, on March 4th, came to City's aid by holding a special Benefit Greyhound Meeting with all the proceeds being donated to the Club.

Knowle Stadium

Knowle Stadium was built for greyhound racing and was opened for it's initial meeting on July 23rd, 1927, continuing such operation until it's last meeting on January 28th, 1961 following the sale of the site for housing development five days earlier. Many other events also took place at this venue, including a Womens Soccer International on June 1st, 1936 (when England beat France 4-1 in front of 3,000 spectators), but to generations of Bristol sports enthusiasts it was best known as the home of Bristol Bulldogs Speedway. 22,000 was the highest crowd at this venue, and was achieved by the Bulldogs when they were defeated 50-45 by Belle Vue on May 22nd 1949.

Four more seasons of struggle followed with positions of nineteenth, fifteenth, thirteenth and sixteenth respectively, but the gloom was lifted somewhat by the winning of the Welsh Cup in 1933-34 when Tranmere Rovers were beaten 3-0 in a replay at Chester after a 1-1 draw at Wrexham. Goals from Riley (2) and Scriven secured the trophy before a crowd of 5,000 (£252 receipts).
The babes line-up consisted :-
Scattergood, W.Roberts, Birks, C.Morgan, Parker, E.Brinton, Homer, Molloy, Riley, Loftus and Scriven.

Record Attendance

The following campaign a magnificent F.A. Cup run saw the 'Robins' progress to the 5th Round in the process of which the Ashton Gate attendance record was twice broken. The record hitherto was for the League match against Everton on April 3rd, 1931, when a crowd of 36,985 produced receipts of £2,080.8s.8d., but these figures were easily beaten for the visit of Portsmouth in a Fourth Round F.A.Cup replay on January

30th 1935. The official attendance was given as 42,885 (£2,570), though with the gates being rushed many people gained access without paying, and it was reported that at least 50,000 were in the ground. This figure of around 50,000 has never been surpassed, but the official attendance at the Pompey game was beaten a few weeks later at the next stage of the competition when the 43,335 (£3,208.15s.1d.) present for the match with Preston North End on February 16th set a record that remains to this day.

Film Star 'Robins'

This Cup run brought much extra business to the local cinemas as the Hippodrome and the Stoll Cinema (Bedminster) showed film of the Preston game, plus City's matches against Cardiff City and Bradford from 1920, during the week commencing February 18th . The star attraction though was the showing of the 1909 F.A. Cup Final at the Bedminster Town Hall for the week commencing February 4th, 1935. This film had first been shown locally at the Palace and the Empire Theatres the week following the Final, the Babes and the Manchester City players attending the second house at the Empire following their match at Ashton Gate on April 28th, 1909. What has happened to this film since 1935 is unknown, though it is possible that it was lost during the blitz, as no footage has come to light in the intervening years.

Death of William P. Kingston

Unfortunately the day of one of City's greatest Cup victories coincided with the funeral of 72 year old William Panes Kingston who had been Chairman when the Babes had reached the Final in 1909. He died at his Long Ashton home on January 27th, 1935, and his local church was packed with many mourners, including Harry Drewett representing the football club, for the midday funeral service three days later.

Pools Dispute

The 1935-36 season brought to a head the dispute the Football League were having with the Pools' Companies over the use of their fixtures. This resulted in the cancellation of the scheduled games for February 29th plus March 7th, and the substitution of secret matches in their place. However, this strategy wasn't continued, for following a meeting attended by 84 of the 88 League Clubs, in Manchester on Monday March 9th,the ploy was dropped. The fixtures originally scheduled for February 29th were played on March 14th. Bristol City, together with Bournemouth & B.A., Exeter City and Gateshead, were the four Clubs who did not attend the meeting.

Poor Reserves

City's poor League form was reflected by the Reserves in the London Combination, a competition to which they were elected to the Second Division for 1930-31. They gained admission to the First Division on March 10th, 1932, after finishing fifth and ninth respectively in the lower division. The Babes ended 1932-33 in twenty-first place (three off the bottom), and although this improved to seventh the following campaign, the remaining years up to the Second World War brought positions of twentieth, twenty-fourth (bottom), twenty-first, seventeenth, and twenty-first respectively.

The F.A.Cup run of 1934-35

Harston (marked 'x'), heads the equaliser against Bury at Ashton Gate

Bristol City 2 Portsmouth 0 F. A. Cup 4th Round Replay
Wednesday, 30th January, 1935

Cup fever was at it's height in Bristol for this F.A. Cup replay versus the previous season's finalists Portsmouth, and a new record for both attendance (42,885) and receipts (£2570) was set for the Ashton Gate ground. However, this attendance figure only represents those that paid for admittance as an hour before the afternoon kick-off the ground was full to capacity with thousands locked outside. This led to the main gates being forced open and the crowd was swelled to an estimated 50,000 as thousands poured in without paying. Shortly after the match started some railings collapsed and hundreds of spectators were forced onto the pitch by the pressure of the crowd behind, while many fans climbed onto the roof to the Covered End for a view of the field. After a short delay the referee persuaded the good-natured crowd who had spilled onto the playing area to retreat behind the touch-lines where they massed eight deep and the game then continued.

At the outset both teams settled down to play at a terrific speed, the ball being lashed about in midfield in breathless fashion. Pompey defended with good length kicks, but could not get the forwards moving. City's first real attack came just before the crowd had spilled onto the pitch, and saw Landells and Harston feed Hodge with the ball, but in running through he was overwhelmed by the visitors defence. The crowd incident brought the proceedings to a halt for five minutes. Following the re-start both sets of forwards made desperate efforts and Rutherford was prominent for the visitors before Hodge obtained a corner for the City from which Brinton put in a fast shot that went narrowly wide.

*There was no score in the first-half but the honours belonged to the home side, therefore the crowd were in great anticipation of a famous cup upset when the teams returned for the second-period. Dolman, in the City goal, collected from a corner soon after the re-start and he also saved several surprise shots by Salmond before the homesters got their act together, with Harston rushing through and forcing Gilfillan to make a precarious save. Give-and-take play then ensued and following a misunderstanding on the part of the City players, Worrall broke clean through, but when all seemed lost for the home team, Bridge saved the day by conceding a corner and suffering injury in the process. After seventy-five minutes came the first goal of the game when the Robin's right-wing broke clear and Hodge centred wide of the Pompey backs for **Harston** to head through a brilliant goal.*

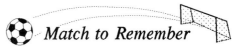

Match to Remember

*This success produced frantic scenes, and Portsmouth attacked with desperation, but within another seven minutes the visitors found themselves two down following a movement on City's left-wing. Landells lobbed the ball over to Banfield who headed to **Hodge,** and the latter player from close in drove the ball smartly inside the post, which produced more cheering and added to the din of rattles and bells.*

This further set-back didn't subdue Pompey completely, however, as just prior to the final whistle they forced Dolman to make a great save, but at the end of the day there was no doubt that the Robins were fully deserving of making progress into the 5th Round of the Competition where they were due to face further First Division opposition in Preston North End.

CITY: *Dolman; Roberts, Bridge, Riley, Pearce, E. Brinton, Hodge, Banfield, Harston, Landells, Cainey.*
POMPEY: *Gilfillan; Mackie, W. Smith, Nichol, Salmond, Thackeray, Worrall, J. Smith, Weddle, Easson, Rutherford.*
Referee: J.Millward (Derby)
Attendance: 42,885 (Receipts £2570)
(Source: Western Daily Press, Thursday 31st January, 1935)

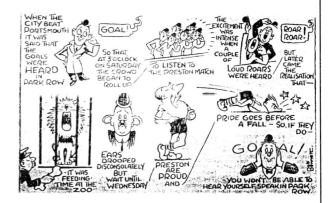

Ashton Gate was host to its official record attendance of 43,335 for the 5th round match with Preston North End, which ended as a scoreless draw.

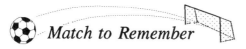

Match to Remember

Walsall 2 Bristol City 8
Football League Division Three (South)
Saturday, 26th February, 1938.

For this Football League Division Three (South) match, Walsall had Bristol City as visitors to Fellows Park, the home team being unchanged from the previous Saturday, whilst the City had Dryden in for Colquhoun at outside-left.

Winning the toss Walsall kicked towards the Entrance End and they were soon on the attack, which necessitated Brook clearing from Morgan, who had put the ball well towards the visitors goal. The City however responded, but their attack came to nought when with the ball going across the goal to Peters, he was pulled up for offside. Both ends were rapidly visited in the early stages and Walsall conceded a corner in their efforts to stop Dryden. For the homesters Payne put the ball up the centre to Evans who tried, without success, to get through, but, keeping up the pressure for the next few minutes Prew and Askew both went close for them. City them nearly obtained a goal when Rowles just missed with a header and Bourton tested Williams with a fast straight drive.

However, the first score wasn't long in coming, for after 22 minutes **Peters** obtained an excellent goal when he rounded Morgan on the right and netted with a fast cross shot which beat Williams. This goal for the City was the prelude to a sensational four minutes as within a minute **Rowles** had added a second for the visitors in rushing and netting a centre by Peters, then **Brain** made it 3-0 a minute later before Walsall responded through **Evans** in the 26th minute. Dryden then tested Williams with a long shot which the custodian did well to save and Woolhouse nearly got through for Walsall, but City when they got away always looked the more dangerous with Peters putting over several good centres. Walsall however never relaxed their efforts, Evans attempting to take advantage of a long forward pass from Woolhouse, but the ball went out, and then appealing for a penalty later when following a scuffle near goal Evans was knocked over. Two minutes before the interval a long pass upfield found the homesters in disarray and **Rowles**, gaining possession, lobbed the ball over the advancing custodian's head to make the half-time score:- Walsall 1 Bristol City 4.

Coming out after the break in a determined frame of mind, Walsall put the City defence under pressure but were unable to reduce the arrears though Evans did get through on one occasion, but was pulled up for off-side. However, goals were not long in coming as a foul by Bennett at the other end produced a free kick which **Brook**, not being deterred by the fact that it was a long way out, sent directly into the corner of the net. Then in the 55th minute Peters beat two Walsall defenders on the left-wing before passing to **Bourton**, who scored City's sixth goal with a fast cross shot. After this the homesters seldom looked like scoring, though Woolhouse tried a straight drive which went outside. Excellent play by Bourton, tricking two defenders before touching the ball to **Peters**, enabled the latter to rush in and score City's seventh after 73 minutes. Woolhouse then tried to pass back to his custodian Williams, but **Rowles** got there first and scored the visitors eighth goal ten minutes before time. It was then left to Walsall to have the last say when Evans after previously getting through on the left and shooting wide when tackled, got a surprise score when Prew breaking away sent the ball across the goal for **Evans** to edge the ball through to produce a final score of:

WALSALL 2 BRISTOL CITY 8.

Walsall: Williams, Shelton, Bennett, Askew, Morgan, Payne, Prew, Woolhouse, Evans, Robinson, Redwood.

City: Dawson; Brook, Turner, Morgan, Pearce, Armstrong, Peters, Bourton, Rowles, Brain, Dryden.

Referee: R.G. Rudd (London)

Attendance: 4,368

(Source: Sports Argus, Birmingham, 26th February, 1938)

(Above) Programme cover from the record away victory

Improved form brought forth some bumper attendances, the best being that for the home game with Cardiff City on March 5th when 38,953 were present (paying receipts of £2,330) to see their favourites concede two valuable points to their Welsh visitors.

Renaissance

However despite lacking suitable Reserve team strength, 1937-38 brought a renaissance to the Club's League fortunes, and after an exciting tussle throughout the campaign with Millwall, Queens Park Rangers, Watford and Brighton & Hove Albion, the 'Lions' of Millwall pipped the Babes by one point for the Championship. This season brought to light the goalscoring talents of Alf Rowles who set the football world alight with his exploits following the notching of a hat-trick on his League debut in the Babes 4-1 win over Exeter City at Ashton Gate on January 15th. He went on to create a Football League record for consecutive scoring by a debutant when hitting the target in the next five games, obtaining a further nine goals in the process. Unfortunately his promising career was cut short following an injury sustained in the home game with Notts County on September 7th, 1938. Despite attempts at a comeback he was eventually forced to retire, and so a player of great potential was lost to the Club, very much in the same way as they were to lose the services of Paul Cheesley almost forty years later. The following campaign saw a decline in form with the Babes finishing in eighth place, but this was due in no small part to

another investigation into the affairs of the Club. A joint Football Association and Football League Inquiry into illegal payments to amateurs resulted in the censuring of the Club Directors and Secretary, while Manager Bob Hewison was suspended from his position from October 3rd, 1938 to May 6th, 1939. Club Captain Clarrie Bourton took over as player-manager, and he did well, despite the turmoil at Ashton Gate, to steer the team into a respectable position in the top half of the table. The end of the campaign saw Hewison - after working as chief scout during the period of his suspension - taking over once again the reins of manager, and it was hoped that the forthcoming season would bring about another serious challenge for the Championship. Unfortunately due to the madness that was to engulf mankind this hope was never tested.

Declaration of War

Despite the War clouds gathering over Europe, the 1939-40 campaign started as normal, but after the playing of three League games the competition was abandoned following Britain's declaration of War with Germany on September 3rd. At this time the City occupied ninth place in the table, having gained three points from their record of parity:- P3 W1 D1 L1 F5 A5. This marked the end of normal League football for seven years, but after an interval of seven weeks, during which time Friendly matches were played, various League and Cup Competitions were organised under the auspices of the Football League.

The 'Blues' beat the 'Reds' in the trial match, 12 August 1939. The attendance was 3,440. (Note the No.1 Stand that was later bombed)

Duke, the Norwich City goalkeeper pushes the ball round the post for a corner, on 30 August 1939.
This became the penultimate Football League match at Ashton Gate before War caused the abandonment of the competition.

Only Two Players

The composition of the Babes team varied greatly from week to week depending on the availability of players who were based locally, this situation accounting for the fact that many players on the books of other clubs - such as Ronnie Dix, Jack Hargreaves, Bill Mitchell, Bob Paisley, Jack Preece, Ted Roberts, Bob Shankly, Alec Stock and George Tadman - turned out in City's colours.

Sometimes sides were fielded that included spectators to make the numbers up, this being highlighted by the South Regional League match at Southampton on Christmas Day 1941 when City lost 5-2. For this fixture the Babes players travelled in three cars, but the breakdown of one of the vehicles in Warminster brought about the arrival of only one car containing two players in time for the kick-off. The missing personnel didn't turn up until the game was well under way with City having their depleted resources supplemented by six Southampton players, including their trainer Gallagher - who scored one of City's goals - and three spectators, Aldersea, McNess and Waterman.

Marathon Match

Highlights of wartime football for City were their reaching the Third Round of the War League Cup in 1942-43 and the amazing Second Round, 2nd Leg match in the same competition against Cardiff City at Ninian Park on April 14th, 1945. This game which also counted in the League competition was won for that purpose by the Babes 2-1, but as Cardiff had won the 1st Leg at Ashton Gate by the same score a week previously the tie was still undecided. Consequently ten minutes extra-time was played, which in producing no alteration to the score brought a continuance of the fixture on a sudden death principle. It wasn't until a record 3 hours 22 minutes had been played that the tie was decided in favour of Cardiff, when Billy Rees managed to summon enough energy to put the ball into the net and bring the proceedings to a halt. This record length of a game was not however destined to stand for long, as on March 30th the following year a fixture between Stockport County and Doncaster Rovers lasted for a further three minutes before bad light stopped play.

End of the War

The War in Europe ended on May 7th, 1945, but with the possibility of the conflict in the Far East with Japan looking likely to drag on (though this did eventually finish on August 14th that year), and with numerous players in the Forces, the football authorities decided not to recommence normal peace time activity until 1946-47. However, the F.A. Cup did start up again, on a two-legged basis for the first and only time to date. Attendances boomed during this last campaign of wartime football, giving an indication of the great surge of interest that was to manifest itself in the immediate post-war years.

Air Raids

The War had brought about the loss of the main Grandstand at Ashton Gate, when it was bombed in January 1941. The actual date of the destruction has been impossible to accurately determine, though sequences of events (including the switching of the scheduled home fixture with Cardiff City to Ninian Park on January 11th) indicate that it occurred during the air raid on the night of January 3rd/4th and not on January 16th which was given in the 'Pink 'Un Sports Annual' for 1946-47.

Portrayed in his 1930's goalkeeper days

BILL DOLMAN

Due to building restrictions in post-war Britain it was to be over ten years before work began to build a replacement for what was known as the Number One Grandstand, and it was often thought as being unfortunate that the Luftwaffe did not instead rid the Club of Number Two Grandstand (which was also known as the 'Cow Shed'), on the opposite side of the ground. This structure lasted until being condemned as unsafe and was demolished in the close season of 1966 prior to the building of the Dolman Stand in 1970.

The Germans though made an attempt to hasten things up as they returned on the night of April 11th/12th, 1941 and two bombs fell on the pitch, which brought about the cancellation of the home match with Bath City in the West Regional League scheduled for the following day. This raid also brought about the death of former Bristol City player Sandy Torrance and his wife, amongst many others.

2nd XI

The City operated two teams throughout the War years, though their 2nd XI was named the 'Colts' for the first four campaigns, and then the 'Athletic' for two seasons, before reverting to being Reserves again when the official Western League commenced again for 1945-46. The first season of the War brought about temporary suspension of the Western League from September 8th to October 21st when it reformed with clubs who wished to continue. City Colts finished the campaign in sixth place as follows:-

	P	W	D	L	F	A	Pts
Trowbridge Town	20	18	0	2	87	31	36
Bristol Aero.Co	20	13	4	3	78	33	30
Radstock Town	20	12	1	7	68	54	25
Peasedown Miners Welfare	20	9	5	6	45	36	23
Glastonbury	20	9	5	6	49	43	23
BRISTOL CITY COLTS	20	9	2	9	54	43	20
Chippenham Town	20	7	2	11	51	78	16
Welton Rovers	20	6	1	13	44	65	13
Wells City	20	6	1	13	37	66	13
Bath City Res.	20	4	3	13	35	69	11
Paulton Rovers	20	3	4	13	34	64	10

The following two campaigns saw the continuance of the Western League competition, though it is possible that these were not officially organised by the Western League Committee as no mention was made in the centenary history of this body ('A View From The Terraces' by Sandie & Doug Webb). The City Colts finished in fourth place in 1940-41 when the League comprised:- Aero Engines, Bath City, Clevedon, Paulton Rovers, Peasedown Miners Welfare, and Soundwell, as well as Bristol City.

Clarrie Bourton, the Robins captain, breaks through the Swansea defence in the Ashton Gate match on 31 August 1940

Season 1941-42 brought an improvement to third place with this record:- P10 W6 D2 L2 F34 A16 Pts.14 when the Colts opponents were Aero Engine, Bath City, National Smelting Co., Paulton Rovers, and Soundwell. It is not clear as to whether this so called Western League operated in 1942-43. There are certainly fixtures detailed as matches in this competition given in the local newspaper, and a summary has been found which purports to be the Colts Western League record viz:- P10 W10 D0 L0 F42 A5 Pts. 20. The team though was also engaged in the Bristol & Suburban League this campaign, when their record as given in the local Press on February 20th was:- P10 W10 D0 L0 F49 A8 Pts.20, and as it has not been possible to find any Western League results it can be realised why doubt exists. In the Bristol & Suburban League that season the Colts were clear Champions only dropping one point in their sixteen matches, scoring seventy eight goals and only conceding seventeen. They also reached the Semi-Final of the Gloucestershire Senior Amateur Cup when they went down 2-0 to the Bristol Aeroplane Company on March 27th.

Gloucestershire Senior Amateur Cup Success

Continuing in the Bristol & Suburban League in 1943-44, though now being called Bristol City Athletic, they finished as runners-up, their record on April 27th being:- P22 W20 D0 L2 F85 A20 Pts.40. Consolation for missing out of the Championship was gained in the Gloucestershire Senior Amateur Cup as this trophy was secured for the first, and only time, when they beat Hollygrove 5-1 at the 'Aero Engines Ground' on April 14th. To win this competition they had beaten Eden Grove (a) 4-2 on December 11th in the 2nd Round after receiving a 1st Round bye, then accounted for the National Fire Service (a) 6-0 on January 15th to set up a Semi-Final confrontation with Aero Engines at the 'Douglas Ground' on February 12th. This hurdle proved more difficult and in only being able to obtain a 2-2 draw a replay took place at the same venue a week later, but this time the Athletic hit their true form and in achieving a 5-2

victory they gained access to the concluding stage of the competition. In the Final Hollygrove proved no match for City and goals from Collis, Tovey, Artus, Collins and Bishop brought about a comprehensive success.

High Scoring Athletic

Season 1944-45 again saw the Athletic reach the Final, but this time, after a 1-1 draw at Eastville Stadium on May 19th, their opponents - the Royal Electrical and Mechanical Engineers - proved too strong four days later when a return to Eastville brought a 4-1 defeat in front of 1,458 spectators. However the Championship of the Bristol & Suburban League was secured with this record:- P26 W23 D1 L2 F108 A33 Pts.47. The only defeats were against the National Fire Service (a) on December 23rd and Hollygrove (h) on February 17th. The best wins were obtained in the home games versus R.A.F. (Filton) on March 3rd and Papworth Athletic on December 16th these ending with scores of 11-1 and 8-1 respectively.

The marathon match with Cardiff City on 14th April 1945

Bristol Charity League

The war years saw the end of the long established Bristol Charity League competition. After commencing as a knock out tournament in 1896-97 it had become a League competition in 1901-02 and continued in this vein until 1941-42 when it appears likely that the City Colts took the honours. There were only two clubs taking part in this last season, but as only one result has come to light - Bristol City Colts 3 National Smelting Company 2, on March 28th - it has not been possible to ascertain who secured the Championship, or even establish as to whether the competition was satisfactorily concluded. With the exception of this last campaign the winners of the League competition from 1901-02 are as follows:-
1901-02 Bristol Rovers Res; 1902-03 Bristol Rovers Res; 1903-04 Bristol City Res; 1904-05 Bristol Rovers Res; 1905-06 & 1906-07: Shared between Bristol City Res and Bristol Rovers Res following inconclusive play-offs; 1907-08 Kingswood Rovers; 1908-09 Bristol City Res; 1909-10 Bristol

Rovers Res; 1910-11 Bristol Rovers Res; 1911-12 Welton Rovers; 1912-13 Bath City; 1913-14 Bath City; 1914-15 Unknown; 1915-16 to 1918-19 No competition; 1919-20 Bristol Rovers Res; 1920-21 Bath City; 1921-22 Yeovil & Petters United; 1922-23 Bristol Rovers Res; 1923-24 Bristol Rovers Res; 1924-25 Bristol Rovers Res; 1925-26 Trowbridge Town; 1926-27 Welton Rovers; 1927-28 Bristol City Res; 1928-29 Bristol City Res; 1929-30 Bath City; 1930-31 Bath City; 1931-32 Bristol City 'A'; 1932-33 Bristol Rovers Res; 1933-34 Bristol Rovers Res; 1934-35 Bath City Res; 1935-36 Bristol Rovers 'A'; 1936-37 Bristol City 'A'; 1937-38 Clevedon; 1938-39 Gloucester City; 1939-40 Unknown; 1940-41 Clevedon.

These results produce a summary that shows Bristol Rovers well ahead with twelve outright wins, City next with six, (both Clubs also sharing the Championship twice), Bath City six, Clevedon two, Welton Rovers two, and then Gloucester City, Kingswood Rovers, Trowbridge Town, and Yeovil & Petters United with one apiece.

City Programme

The restrictions on newsprint during the Second World War brought about changes to the City programme which had remained the large size style (9½ inches x 7¾ inches) that had been adopted during First Division days. The programme cover for 1907-08 had been pale blue with black printed advertisements, but by 1910-11 it had evolved into a red cover, displaying the Bristol Coat of Arms in a prominent position above the advertisements. This style of cover was to remain, though the colour changed to pink, right through until the 1936-37 season when a 'Robins' team group displaced the coat of arms, this then being continued until the end of the initial wartime campaign of 1939-40. The 1910-11 programme contained sixteen pages, but by 1919-20 this had been reduced to twelve, and remained the same until 1929-30 when sixteen pages were again adopted. This number however didn't last long as the next campaign brought a further increase to twenty, 1933-34 to twenty-four, and finally up to thirty-two in 1935-36. Unfortunately this increase in the number of pages was mainly in response to the need for additional advertising space, and the actual reading matter didn't vary much throughout the inter-war years. The content included Editor's Notes; fixtures, results and League tables for 1st, Reserve and 'A' teams; programme of music (usually played by the Bristol South Band), half-time scoreboard, and team line-ups (on centre-pages). The First World War brought an increase in the price from 1d. in 1910-11, to 2d. in 1919-20, and this was the last change (except for that occasioned by Second World War issues) until a rise up to 3d. was made during the 1949-50 campaign.

The 1940-41 season brought forth a single sheet (10¼ inches x 8 inches), printed on both sides and folded in half, costing 1d., but the following campaign the single sheet issue (8¼ inches x 5 inches) only contained printing on one side, though still at a cost of 1d. Variations on single sheet issues continued throughout the war, and after until the end of 1946-47. Very few programmes have come to light for this period, but for the F.A. XI game against the R.A.F. at Ashton Gate on January 22nd, 1944, a four page issue (8¾ inches x 5¾ inches) was on sale at a cost of 3d.

A programme was certainly published during the initial campaign of the First World War, as the 'Sports Times' of January 22nd, 1916, makes reference to the fact, though what sort of programme it was and whether it continued throughout the duration of the War has not proved possible to determine.

****

Free Scoring Attack

A free scoring attack on the return to Football League fare in 1946-47 saw Don Clark with 36 goals from thirty-seven League games head the Third Division (South) scorers, this enabling the 'Babes' to finish in third place behind Queens Park Rangers and Champions Cardiff City. The campaign had started with the Blues beating the Reds 4-1 in the Trial Match on August 20th, and the first League fixture on the last day of the month brought an unexpected 4-3 reverse at Aldershot. However, after this poor start the 'Babes' found a rich vein of form going thirteen matches without defeat. This run included the League match which was won 1-0 against Bournemouth & Boscombe Athletic on October 12th (the game was Cliff Morgan's 2nd Benefit and attracted an attendance of 21,802). Ten of the twenty-one home League games produced attendances in excess of 20,000 and the important fixture with Cardiff City on April 4th brought 32,535 (£2,209) into Ashton Gate to witness a 2-1 home success. This figure however was well beaten for the return three days later, a Third Division (South) record crowd of 51,621 being present for a 1-1 draw.

(Above) City's 1st leg 4th round victory over Brentford in the 1945/46 F.A.Cup
(Below) And how the Bristol Evening Post saw the shock defeat to non-League Gillingham in 1946/47

New Record Profit

Not surprisingly these high attendances helped produce a record profit, of £5,450.2s.5d., that was declared at the Annual General Meeting held at the Club Offices on February 10th, 1948. The meeting only lasted 45 minutes, sixteen shareholders being present together with Directors G. Jenkins (Chairman), A.R.P. Bray (Vice-Chairman), C.W. Crawford, H.J. Dolman, W.J. Kew and A.S. Sperring.

Record League Win

The return fixture with Aldershot on December 28th brought about City's record League success of 9-0, this after the previous five games had failed to yield a victory. The 'Babes' scored in their first attack with Hargreaves shooting into an empty net after Williams had collided with Gage the Aldershot custodian. In the fifth minute the advantage was doubled when Hargreaves netted again, his cross being misjudged by Gage. Another mistake by the goalkeeper in the tenth minute saw City further in front, a shot by Clark straight at Gage somehow passing under his body. By half-time the 'Babes' were leading by six goals, Clark heading in a free kick for the fourth, Hargreaves getting the fifth after thirty-six minutes when his shot through a crowd of players was reached by Gage but somehow escaped his grasp and went into the net, and the sixth just before the interval when Williams with an excellent header converted a Hargreaves corner. After the break the action slowed down somewhat, and it wasn't until the seventieth minute that another goal was obtained, Chilcott's centre being headed in by Clark following the best move of the afternoon. Jones secured the eighth goal with a tremendous left-foot drive from outside the penalty area five minutes from the end, and the scoring was brought to a halt two minutes later when Clark easily registered with a penalty after Williams had been brought down.

City: Eddolls; Morgan, Fox, Peacock, Roberts, Jones, Chilcott, Thomas, Clark, Williams, Hargreaves.
Aldershot: Gage; Rogers, Shepperd, Fitzgerald, Rowland, Brown, Hobbs, White, Brooks, Griffiths, Hassell.
Attendance: 17,690.

Expectation

Expectation was high for a strong promotion challenge in 1947-48 but following an excellent start with a 6-0 win over Southend United at Ashton Gate on the opening day of the campaign, and ten wins in the first thirteen fixtures (with scores of 7-2 at Reading, and 6-0 at home to Leyton Orient and Norwich City, together with Southend United) saw City in second place throughout October and putting in a strong challenge for the one promotion place. Unfortunately a 2-1 home defeat at the hands of Watford on October 25th 'burst the bubble' and the following seven League games up to the end of the year only produced one win and seven goals, though scoring form did return for the F.A. Cup first round replay against Dartford on December 6th, when City notched up a 9-2 victory. Things didn't improve much in the New Year, the one highlight being a 5-2 home success over Bristol Rovers on February 14th, and with only seven more wins to the end of the campaign they ended in a disappointing seventh place. The 'Babes' though did again supply the top scorer in the Third Division (South), Len Townsend leading the way with 31 goals if the local Press can be relied upon (other sources give 29). Attendances continued to be high with eleven home League games producing crowds in excess of 20,000. For the match against the glamour team of the Division, Notts. County (Tommy Lawson et al) on January 3rd, a gathering of 35,287 paying receipts of £2,227.16s.9d. turned up to see Towsend score the solitary goal of the contest and raise false hopes that City were coming back to form, such hope being demolished in the following fixture when they lost 6-1 at Swansea.

A Loss

This time however the high attendances didn't produce a profit despite the fact that season ticket sales had increased from £383.3s.6d. to £2,493.15s.6d., the reason being partly due to the transfer fee expenditure of £6,750 for players such as Hyam Dimmer (Aldershot), Idris Hopkins and Len Townsend (Brentford), and Harry Osman (Millwall). At the stormy Annual General Meeting (more on this later) at the Grand Hotel, Broad Street, Bristol, on March 15th 1949, a loss of £2,222.11s.4d. was declared even though gate receipts had risen from £30,742.19s.11d. to £34,492.1s.1d.

Resignation of Bob Hewison

The team's slide continued in 1948-49 with a final position of sixteenth, this bringing about the resignation of both the Chairman and the Manager. Following a row with the Board over team selection Bob Hewison resigned on March 8th, only three months after having his contract renewed. He had just completed forty years in professional football, and in 1946 had been given a long service medal by the Football League in recognition of his outstanding achievement of engagement in football management for twenty-five years. Born at Blackworth, Newcastle, on March 25th, 1889, he played for East Hollywell Villa and Whitley Athletic before joining Newcastle United as a wing-half in July 1908. He stayed at St. James Park until the First World War when he began playing for Leeds City, and in 1919-20 - while recovering from a broken leg - he acted as Secretary during the period that the Club was being wound up. He then returned to Newcastle and played a

few games before joining Northampton Town as Player-manager, from there he took over at Queens Park Rangers in the summer of 1925. He remained at Loftus Road until the summer of 1931 and joined Bristol City in April 1932. On leaving City he was appointed Manager to Gateshead in May 1949, but only stayed until October of the same year, and the next year, on June 1st, he commenced a three year term in charge of Guildford City. He then scouted for Bristol Rovers until May 1957 when he took over as Manager of Bath City, staying in this position until retiring from the game at the conclusion of the 1960-61 campaign. He died in Bristol in the Spring of 1964.

The Going of George Jenkins

On February 16th 1949, the Board saw the addition of new Directors in the Rev. F.C.Vyvyan Jones (Vicar of St. Michaels', City), George Jones (Managing Director of Wessex Coaches), Norman Bowers-Jones (Proprietor of Willsbridge Motor Company) and Arthur Joseph Amor. However, this new blood didn't prevent the storm clouds that were gathering. Matters came to a head at the Annual General Meeting that year, which was preceded by a special meeting to change the articles of association. Within a couple of minutes unanimous agreement was reached, but in the A.G.M. that followed, Chairman George Jenkins who was offering himself for re-election, together with Arthur Sperring, was voted off the Board by a show of hands when he was the only Director out of ten who refused to loan the Club £1,000. As the major shareholder he then demanded a poll which would have been likely to have guaranteed his re-election, but a vote of no confidence was called, and in the light of the hostile attitude of the 140 shareholders present he withdrew his nomination and left the Board, declining the offer of life membership. A sad end for a man who gave much to Bristol City, and who had guided the Club through many difficult years. He died at the age of 73 in Stapleton Hospital, Bristol, on September 3rd 1955.

Harry Dolman Takes Over

Henry James 'Harry' Dolman succeeded George Jenkins as Chairman at the next Board Meeting on the 23rd March 1949, and he was to continue in this capacity until deciding to step down on March 13th 1974, becoming the first President of the Club. Harry, who was born on August 6th, 1897, has often been described as a benevolent dictator who knew what he wanted, but for all that he never achieved his dream of getting City back into the First Division. Fortunately though he lived long enough to see it happen, for he died on the 9th November 1977, during the Club's second season back in the big-time. After living his childhood in his birthplace of Yatton Keynell, Wiltshire, and one of seven children, he became an engineering apprentice on leaving school at the age of 14. During the First World War he served with the Wiltshire Yeomanry on the Somme and at Ypres, following which he spent eighteen months at the Merchant Venturers Technical College, Bristol before joining the Bristol engineering firm of Brecknell, Munro & Rogers as a junior draughtsman in 1921. Here his talent for design came to the fore and in 1928 he was made a Director of the Company, eventually taking it over during a financial crisis when it became Brecknell, Dolman & Rogers. Harry played soccer in his youth, and was a qualified referee, but his early football affiliation was to Bristol Rovers. He was asked whether he wanted to join the Board of the 'Eastville' Club, but after attending two meetings he was perturbed that the main subject of discussion was, what he thought as a retrograde step, the sale of the stadium to the greyhound company who ran meetings there. He allowed himself to be persuaded by ex-Rovers Manager Captain A.J. Prince Cox that he would be better off with City. Prince Cox then introduced him to George Jenkins, and soon after, in 1939, Harry Dolman was elected to the Ashton Gate Board. On becoming Chairman in 1949 the original intention was that he would only hold such office for twelve months with Arthur Sperring taking over the following year, but the death of Sperring brought about Dolman's unanimous re-election in 1950.

The Bob Wright Interlude

The new Chairman's initial task was the selection of a Manager. The first choice was Peter Doherty the flame-haired Irish International who was playing for Huddersfield Town but as Doherty took up the position of Player-manager with Doncaster Rovers, the Chairman had to look elsewhere. He approached Bill Dodgin at Southampton and Arthur Rowe at Chelmsford, but then settled on a lesser-known candidate, Bob Wright, who was assistant to Jimmy Seed at Charlton Athletic. He was appointed as the new Bristol City Manager on April 13th, at a salary of £850 per annum, and was promised a free hand.

Charlton's assistant trainer Eddie Nash was brought in by the Manager as trainer, resulting in demotion for long-serving City stalwart 'Lemmo' Southway who became his deputy. In compensation 'Lemmo' was given a benefit match, and this brought about a Combined Bristol XI (containing one guest) taking on an All Star Team on April 25th, 1950. There was much interest in the fixture and a crowd totalling 21,419 paying receipts of £1,570.12s.2d. turned up at Ashton Gate to see Williams, after seventy minutes, obtain the only goal of the game to give the Combined XI victory. This Bristol team comprised the following players:- Stretton (Luton Town); Bamford (Rovers), Bailey (City), Pitt (Rovers), D. Roberts (City), Peacock (City), Boxshall (City), Eisentrager (City), Rodgers (City), Lowrie (City), Williams (City).

This benefit was followed by another eight days later when City took on Brentford, for Maurice Roberts who had gone blind shortly after being signed from the London Club. Unfortunately this worthy cause was not so well supported, only 4,500 (£262.13s.0d.) being present for City's 4-1 success.

Bob Wright's reign however was only destined to last one season, even though after a disappointing campaign that saw City occupying fifteenth place in the final table, he had been offered a three year contract. Returning from the Club's second foreign tour (the first was to Denmark in 1946), the Manager handed in his resignation, complaining that he had not been given the free hand he was promised, and he left on June 11th. Much had been spent on new players, including £10,000 for Welsh International George Lowrie from Newcastle United (this beating City's previous record of £5,000 for Len Townsend), and £4,450 to Huddersfield Town for Arnold Rodgers.

It was therefore no great surprise, even though attendances continued to be high, that a record loss of £24,328.13s.7d. was revealed for the year-ending June 30th, 1950, at the Annual General Meeting held at the Grand Hotel on August 10th the following year.

Supporters Club

The 1949-50 campaign saw the formation of the current Supporters Club, this being the fourth such body connected with Bristol City. The second Supporters Club which was mentioned earlier discontinued sometime during the 1920's or 1930's and this void was filled by the Bristol City Supporters Association which came into being following a meeting, convened by Mr. A.H. Wookey and presided over by J.G. Ure, at the Ford Memorial Hall, Bedminster on October 16th, 1936. This Association survived for some time, and at their Annual General Meeting, at the Grosvenor Hall, the Arcade, Bedminster on the 11th August 1939, a credit balance of £42.1s.3d. was declared from income of £110.17s.7d.

Again, however, it is not clear how long this body remained in existence, but the fact that no such group was operating in the early post-war years brought about the birth of the present Supporters Club at a meeting held at the Crown & Dove Hotel, Bridewell Street, Bristol on October 9th, 1949. The original Committee comprised R. Hurley (Chairman), L. Derrick (Secretary), Les Cutmore (Treasurer), W. Burn and A. Taylor. This organisation has done much good work for the Football Club in the intervening years, raising many thousands of pounds. Their help towards the building of the Grandstand in the period 1951 to 1953 was much appreciated by the Board and this led to them being granted space in the stand for their Clubroom, which was opened in August 1955, and subsequently enlarged to twice the size ten years later. Having these premises, coupled with the benefit of City's promotion, produced a boom in membership and by 1957 this was in excess of 5,000 supporters who had each paid a fee of 1s.9d. Arthur Fowler who was to be much involved with the Club until a coup on December 18th, 1984, became the first Steward of the Clubroom. Ex-City player Billy Pocock was Chairman in 1955-56.

The first donation made to the Football Club was £80 in 1950, having been collected by the raffle of an autographed football, and the following year the Supporters Club took over the catering rights at Ashton Gate. In 1958 they paid half of the £6,400 fee to obtain the services of Bert Tindill from Doncaster Rovers, and the following year took responsibility for paying the £12,000 cost of relaying the pitch. They started organising trips to away matches in 1951, and opened the first Club Shop in the old offices at the Park End in 1967, this being moved to the officials car park opposite the Grandstand in 1969 when it was named the Robbie Robin Shop. July 1967 saw the formation of the Young Robins Club, the original Committee consisting of Mike Draper, Norman Hook and Don Tuckfield.

There is currently a thriving London Branch of the Supporters Club, and even further afield, City's fame took root with the formation, by Goran Pedersen, of the 'Scandanavian Supporters Club of Bristol City' in July 1990.

Action from City's 3-1 victory over Borussia Monchengladbach in Germany on 28 May 1950.

Pat Beasley & Promotion At Last

Albert 'Pat' Beasley took over as Player-manager at Ashton Gate on July 24th, 1950, coming from Fulham for whom he had been playing since 1945. He turned out for Arsenal in their Championships seasons of 1933-34 and 1934-35 then moved to Huddersfield Town, appearing in their 1937 F.A. Cup Final team, and then obtained his solitary England Cap when he scored in a 2-1 win in Scotland in 1939. He was given a five year contract, the longest awarded by the Club up to then, and this appointment was to set the 'Robins' (this nickname which had been in use since the 1930's now having completely taken over from the famous 'Babe') on course for better things. The team improved to claim tenth place in 1950-51, sink to fifteenth in 1951-52, and then start to take off by being fifth the following year, third next year, before securing the promotion prize in 1954-55.

Outstanding Champions

An outstanding team took the Championship of the Third Division (South) for a record-breaking third time after an exciting battle with Leyton Orient. The Robins started with an unbeaten run of thirteen League games, and took over pole position in the table when they beat Colchester United at Ashton Gate on September 14th when a crowd of 18,710 (£2,012.18s.6d.) saw Arnold Rodgers (3) and John Atyeo do all the scoring. A shock 4-1 home defeat by Gillingham on December 18th brought a drop to second place, but a 2-1 home win over Reading in the next game restored them to the head of affairs. However after completing the double over Reading two days later the team hit rough water in the New Year when they suffered three successive defeats, including a 4-1 hammering at rivals Leyton Orient. The 1-0 home defeat by Norwich City on January 8th pushed them down to second place again, and although they gained revenge at Norwich on January 29th to set in motion an unbeaten run to the end of the campaign, they didn't regain top place until February 26th. On this day City made amends for the defeat at the hands of Southend in the F.A. Cup on November 20th. Jimmy Rogers (2) and Atyeo scored to give the Robins a 3-2 victory in front of a

20,837 crowd who had paid receipts of £2,313.19s.3d. It was the signing of England International Arthur Milton from Arsenal in February that kept the momentum going, and it was disappointing to City that he chose to retire at the end of the season to concentrate on his cricket for Gloucestershire, later playing in Test Matches for England to become the last double international. His performances for City were a big help in seeing the Robins equal the seventy points record for the Division which had been set by Nottingham Forest four years previously.

Scoring Honours

The goal scoring honours belonged to John Atyeo with 28, and Jimmy Rogers, who despite playing over half his games at outside-right, notched 25. Rogers was a brave, fast raiding winger whose goals tally would have made many centre-forwards proud. His departure to Coventry City in 1956 proved to be a major mistake by Pat Beasley, and it was no surprise when Peter Doherty signed him back in 1958.

John Atyeo

Of all the players who have performed for Bristol City it is Billy Wedlock and John Atyeo who are the most illustrious. It was due to the endeavours of Harry Dolman that the services of Atyeo were obtained on June 14th, 1951, agreeing a number of conditions to prevent the possible loss of this fine player to Portsmouth, or even Bristol Rovers. These conditions were:

(i) He should always be on top wages.

(ii) He should be allowed to live at home to continue his apprenticeship as a quantity surveyor, attending Ashton Gate for training on Tuesdays and Thursdays.

(iii) He should be allowed to drive a car to Bristol for training.

(iv) A donation of £100 should be given to his amateur club, Westbury United.

(v) A 1st team Friendly should be played at Westbury at the end of the following season.

(vi) He would not be put on City's transfer list without his father's consent.

The signing of Atyeo was quite a coup as he had already played two games as an amateur in the Portsmouth side that won the League Championship in 1950-51, as well as gaining five England Youth caps in 1949-50.

Atyeo went on to become the first City player since the days of Billy Wedlock to play for England, winning six caps and scoring five goals between 1955 and 1957. He made a scoring debut for England when Spain were beaten 4-1 at Wembley on November 30th, 1955, and he bowed out with a goal in the last seconds of the vital World Cup Qualifying match with the Republic of Ireland in Dublin on May 19th two years later, his header enabling England to go forward to the Final stages in Sweden in 1958. He became a legend in his time at Bristol City staying with the Club until the end of his career, despite being sought after by the likes of Chelsea, Liverpool and Tottenham Hotspur. By the time he retired at the end of the 1965-66 campaign he had amassed a Club record 645 appearances and 350 goals in the Football League, F.A. Cup and the Football League Cup. In the F.A. Cup he held the record for the total number of goals (30), but this was later overtaken by Denis Law.

In all games for the City, including Welsh Cup, Gloucestershire Cup, Friendlies etc., Atyeo made a total of 700 appearances and registered the staggering total of 395 goals. Of these goals the one he obtained after nine seconds in the game with Bury on March 16th, 1957, has it's place in the Club records as it is Bristol City's fastest.

He bade his playing farewell at Ashton Gate in his testimonial match against Leeds United on October 10th, 1966 when receipts of £3,930 were obtained from 17,425 spectators. Unfortunately it wasn't a scoring farewell, Jantzen Derrick and Gerry Sharpe netting for City in a 4-2 defeat. Atyeo was never cautioned by a referee throughout his career, and it was fitting that on April 28th, 1964, he became the sixth holder of the Harry Bamford Memorial Trophy.

Following on from the success of 1954-55 the Robins took the Second Division by storm in the first half of the next season, heading the table from November 19th to Christmas Eve. They were acknowledged as an outstanding team, and a poll of various soccer experts carried out by the 'Daily Herald' in December 1955 demonstrates this view as City finished top of the voting to find the promotion favourites:- City 48; Sheffield Wednesday 36; Liverpool 26; Leeds United 10; Swansea Town 9; Leicester City 7; Stoke City 7; Bristol Rovers 3; Port Vale 2 and in voting for the outstanding player of the season John Atyeo was in sixth place with 3 votes. Unfortunately the impetus wasn't maintained, and although they remained in the promotion race until the closing weeks of the campaign they eventually finished a disappointing eleventh, some ten points behind the Champions Sheffield Wednesday. However such was the interest in the Club it brought about their appearance on television, the highlights of a 1-1 draw with Leicester City at Ashton Gate on February 25th being shown on B.B.C.

Schoolboy Internationals

After the Robins had completed their programme when they suffered a Gloucestershire Senior Professional Cup defeat by the Rovers the ground was used to stage a Schoolboys International on May 12th. This brought forth a bumper crowd of 17,400 paying receipts of £2,400 to see England beat Wales 3-1 after drawing 1-1 at half-time.

This was only the second time that Ashton Gate had been used to host such a match, it being just over twenty-four years since England Schoolboys had disposed of Wales 1-0 thanks to a Phil Taylor goal right on the final whistle, this game being played in front of 9,800 spectators on April 9th, 1932. In the intervening period though Ashton Gate was used to stage a Schoolboy Trial, this on April 2nd, 1949 when a crowd of approximately 10,500 put in an appearance to witness England beat The Rest 2-0.

Jimmy Rogers beats Gill in the Brighton goal to put City ahead at Ashton Gate on 19th February 1955. Williams is in the centre, and Atyeo on the right

City Captain Jack White is presented with the Third Division (South) Championship Shield on 23 April 1955.
Other players: (left to right) Williams, Thresher, Boxley, Atyeo, Rogers, Peacock.

(Left) Jimmy Rogers in goalscoring mood, when Lincoln City were beaten 5-1 at Ashton Gate on 3rd December 1955. John Atyeo is on the right.

Tommy Burden races through to score against Blackburn Rovers in the 2-0 home win on 21st April 1956.

Misfortune Against The Cup Winners

Season 1956-57 saw the Robins repeat their familiar pattern of struggle against relegation following a good initial campaign in a higher sphere, but this was successfully avoided with a somewhat flattering final placing of thirteenth, their status being saved by a dramatic improvement in form from the turn of the year, nine wins and three draws being obtained from the last seventeen games. This improved form also brought about the first F.A. Cup run since 1953-54. Rotherham United were beaten 4-1 on January 5th and then the giant-killers of Rhyl (3-0) three weeks later to set up a clash at Aston Villa on February 16th. Over 15,000 fans travelled to Birmingham, helping to produce a crowd of 63,099, this being the largest to see the City play since the Cup Final of 1909. For this fifth round tie the pitch was an absolute mudbath, and the atmosphere was electric when John Atyeo, with a twenty-five yard blockbuster (the photograph of this goal appearing on the front of the City Programme from 1957 to 1959), equalised a strike by Peter McParland that had put the Villa ahead. Jackie Sewell restored Villa's lead following the interval and City looked to be down and out when Ernie Peacock went to hobble in the centre-forward position after sustaining a leg injury.

Not dismayed though the Robins kept battling away, and with only a few minutes left Atyeo whipped the ball into the middle where Peacock found himself in front of an open goal. Unfortunately due to his injury the chance was lost and so Villa escaped to win what their Captain John Dixon later said was their hardest match on the way to securing the trophy.

Five-A-Side Winners

The City brought their season to a close by taking part in a five-a-side tournament at St. James Park, Exeter on May 10th, winning the A.S. Line Cup by beating Exeter City 17-10 in the Final watched by 1,773 spectators, after disposing of Barnstaple Town and Bideford.

Floodlights

With more and more clubs installing floodlights throughout the 1950's they were eventually allowed to be used for competitive games, and City's first Football League match wholly played under 'lights was the home clash with Notts County on February 20th, 1957. Bristol City's initial experience of playing under artificial light had been at Swindon Town on April 2nd, 1951, when they lost 2-1, and this led to City Chairman Harry Dolman putting his inventive mind to work to design and manufacture a set of floodlights for the Club. These cost £3,500 and by present standards they were very primitive, being a series of metal poles with a cluster of three lights on top.

They were ready for their first match which was scheduled for January 20th, 1953, when the famous Wolverhampton Wanderers were to make a visit. Unfortunately fog intervened and it was a week later - on January 27th - when the fixture was played. A crowd of 24,008 turned up for this first floodlight game in Bristol, and despite seeing the visitors win 4-1, the lighting and the spectacle they seemingly produced was pronounced an outstanding success. At this time the lights were fitted on a total of fourteen pylons, seven on each side of the pitch, but this was later augmented by six more, with three at each end.

These pylons were approximately 40ft high and they were to remain a feature of Ashton Gate until the end of the 1964-65 campaign when they were sold to Southern League Burton Albion for £2,000. The receipts for the Wolves game came to £2,969, fully justifying Harry Dolman's gamble in making Bristol City one of the early pioneers of floodlit football.

With receipts from further such matches ranging from £1,345 against Stuttgart Kickers on November 8th, 1955, to a high of £3,821 versus Arsenal on March 30th the previous year, the beneficial effect it had on the Club's finances can well be realised. These finances were also helped by Bristol Rugby Football Club using the ground for a number of floodlit matches.

Alick Jeffrey Tragedy

By now the facilities at Ashton Gate were good enough for the Club to be chosen to host an Under-23 International, and on October 17th 1956, receipts of £4,610 were received from 25,817 spectators who were present to see a goalless draw with France. Unfortunately the event was marred by tragedy, as Alick Jeffrey - a talented goal-scorer with Doncaster Rovers - sustained a broken leg early in the match, an injury from which he never fully recovered. In subsequent years four more Under-23 Internationals have been staged at Ashton Gate and the ground has also been used for an Under-21 International and a Football League Representative fixture. The Football Association have also made further use of the facilities on offer, though when their Representative XI came to Ashton Gate on November 22nd, 1941, and on the 22nd January 1944 (losing 7-2 and 4-2 respectively to an R.A.F. XI) these facilities were very basic. Things had improved however by the time of their next visit on March 2nd, 1954, when they opposed a Western League XI in a Diamond Jubilee match. Unfortunately heavy snow fell, obliterating the pitch markings, bringing about abandonment after sixty-five minutes. This led to another game being arranged for March 22nd the following year, when the F.A. XI won 3-0 in front of a crowd of 4,278. Their fifth, and last, visit took place on October 8th, 1958 when 14,157 spectators saw an R.A.F. XI beat the F.A. XI side 4-1, John Atyeo scoring the losers' solitary goal.

The first floodlight game at Ashton Gate - Wolves beat City 4-2 on 27th January 1953.

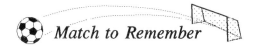

Match to Remember

Bristol City 4 Bristol Rovers 1
Gloucestershire Senior Professional Cup Final
Tuesday, 29th April, 1958.

The City's display in winning this derby clash was sheer perfection for two-thirds of the game which produced a succession of non-stop thrills for the County Trophy, at Ashton Gate. The match consisted of crowd-pulling soccer with the Robins being a vastly superior team to that of the Pirates.

*Right from the start, with City defending the Open End goal, the homesters appeared to set their minds on a win, and win they did at a canter, despite going a goal down in six minutes, when **Geoff Bradford** receiving the ball from Alfie Biggs, steered the ball past an advancing Bob Anderson from eight yards. This produced the Rovers best spell and play at this stage indicated that the Pirates were about to wrench the magnificent trophy from the City's grasp. However, this form didn't last and the homesters - after launching raid after raid on the retreating visitors rearguard - secured the inevitable equaliser. Dermot Curtis stabbed the ball out to Johnny Watkins on the wing, and the centre that followed was masterly glanced by **Bobby Etheridge** past the diving Howard Radford into the far corner of the goal, with the game thirteen minutes old.*

*Keeping up the pressure Etheridge missed a good opportunity, Curtis hit the crossbar from Wally Hinshelwood's corner kick, Etheridge and Watkins between them messed up a chance. Watkins hit the base of the post and Atyeo put the resulting rebound over the bar but after thirty-six minutes the goal that City so richly deserved eventually came. Hinshelwood pushed the ball across to Curtis who flicked it inside for **Atyeo** to hammer it accurately past Radford's right hand from the edge of the penalty box, to put the homesters 2-1 ahead. This scoreline remained until half-time, though the Robins could so easily have scored four goals and maybe even more.*

A marvellous save by Radford just after the restart prevented City going further ahead. Hinshelwood outpaced Josser Watling, he centred for Watkins to hook back to Etheridge who was standing ten yards from goal, and his first time shot zoomed towards the net. A certain goal, until the Rovers goalie managed to somehow block it.

*The Pirates now came back into the match to some degree, Peter Hooper having a good opportunity to level matters, but he shot straight at Anderson. Then Ray Mabbutt, in only tapping the ball towards the corner of the net, gave Anderson the chance to leap across and turn the ball wide. City responded, and Alan Williams now frequently wandering upfield, twice had shots at the visitors goal, before the best move of the night produced the Robin's third goal after seventy-four minutes. Mike Thresher burst past Dai Ward and Mabbutt, before sending a long crossfield ball to Hinshelwood who tore past Watling and centred from the by-line. **Curtis** easily controlled, and shot comfortably past Radford from six yards. Five minutes later victory was then put beyond doubt, when **Etheridge** beat Radford with a tremendous drive, after Atyeo had headed on Thresher's free kick.*

City: *Anderson; Peacock, Thresher, McCall, A. Williams, Burden, Hinshelwood, Atyeo, Curtis, Etheridge, Watkins.*
Rovers: *Radford; Bamford, Watling, Sykes, Hale, Sampson, Mabbutt, Biggs, Bradford, Ward, Hooper.*
Referee: *Reg Leafe (Nottingham)*
Attendance: *10,590*
(Source: Bristol Evening Post, Wednesday 30th April, 1958)

Sheffield Wednesday 2 Bristol City 3
Football League Division Two
Saturday, 15th November, 1958

*A crowd of 30,164 at mist shrouded Hillsborough bore witness to one of City's greatest fighting performances. They became, that season, the first side to take any points from the Wednesday at Hillsborough, the first visiting team to score at the ground for five matches, and the team who netted three goals against a defence which had conceded only three goals in eight previous home games that season. The visitors started well and the game had only been in progress for two minutes when John Watkins had a fiery shot saved by the Wednesday custodian Springett. Shortly afterwards the left-winger drove the ball onto the upright but after eleven minutes the homesters took the lead when **Finney**, after speeding past Gordon Hopkinson, and having his first shot blocked by Tony Cook, then cracked the rebound through a ruck of players into the net. Six minutes later **Finney** struck again when he headed McAnearney's free kick over Cook's hands from the edge of the penalty-area to put the homesters firmly in the driving seat with a 2-0 advantage. However, not dismayed, the Robins fought back and after twenty-seven minutes they gained their reward when Bert **Tindill** obtained the best goal of the game, following a move started by Bobby Etheridge, who flicked the ball onto Peter McCall, who then shattered the homesters defence with a 25 yard gem of a ground pass. This found the scorer running into an open space before thumping the ball into the net from 20 yards past Springett's right hand. Just on half-time McCall had a rasping 35 yard drive tipped onto and over the cross-bar by Springett. This was an amazing shot that deserved to equalise matters and would have been a fair refection of the first-half play.*

*After the re-start the Wednesday were well on top for the first fifteen minutes, and they went near to increasing their lead on several occasions. Suddenly the homesters appeared to have burnt themselves out and City took command for the remaining two-thirds of the half. But by the dying minutes they looked to be condemned as unlucky losers, for by that stage there had been no alteration to the score. Then it happened. Watkins blasted the ball across into the six-yard box, Tindill nodded it down and John Atyeo scooped it out of Springett's arms for Alan **Williams**, up with his forwards, who steer the ball into the net for the equaliser. The City now with their tails up kept on the attack, and from the re-start Hopkinson broke up a Sheffield raid and hit the ball up to Etheridge who passed back for McCall to find Atyeo on the half-way line. Etheridge then received the centre-forward's pass and passed it on to Tindill who gave it to Wally Hinshelwood. The right-winger supplied a pin-point ground level centre that was slammed home from ten yards by **Atyeo**, with a few seconds left for play. This finale produced an amazing win for the Robins by 3 goals to 2.*

Wednesday: *Springett; Martin, Curtis, T. McAnearney, Swan, Gibson, Wilkinson, Froggatt, Shiner, Fantham, Finney.*
City: *Cook; Hopkinson, Thresher, McCall, A. Williams, Burden, Hinshelwood, Tindill, Atyeo, Etheridge, Watkins.*
Referee: *L. Howarth (Beverley)*
Attendance: *30,164*
(Source: Bristol Evening Post, Monday, 17th November, 1958)

Historical Note: This turned out to be Sheffield Wednesday's only home league defeat in the 1958-59 Season, when they finished up winning the Second Division Championship.

64

The Coming of Peter Doherty

The 1957-58 campaign saw the Robins struggle again, and the situation looked distinctly ominous on December 21st when the Club found itself in a relegation position following their 4-3 defeat at Liverpool. This brought about the dismissal of Manager Pat Beasley on January 6th. Club Physiotherapist Les Bardsley and Chairman Harry Dolman then ran the team for a short while until Jimmy Seed became Caretaker-Manager for nine days, before leaving on January 22nd to take over as Manager of Millwall. However it wasn't to be long before City had a new man at the helm, Harry Dolman securing the services of the man he had wanted nine years earlier. The great Peter Doherty, after resigning from Doncaster Rovers, joined City on January 28th when he signed a three year contract. As luck would have it his first match in charge brought a quick return to Belle Vue three days later, where the City lost 2-1 to his old club Doncaster Rovers, to sink the Club into the relegation frame yet again. However, the inspired signing of Bert Tindill from Doncaster for £6,400 on February 3rd eventually brought about an improvement in form that produced seven wins and two draws in the final third of the campaign. This pushed the Robins up to seventeenth in the table, and had 'Ashton Alf' thinking fondly of the possibility of promotion in the following season.

Williams and Anderson combine to thwart Charlton's attempt to score, at the Valley. 14 September 1957.

Post-War Record

A brilliant start to 1958-59 saw City create a post-war Football League record with thirteen goals being obtained in their first two League matches, a 6-1 success over Rotherham United at Ashton Gate on August 23rd being followed by an amazing 7-4 win at Barnsley four days later. But despite being in the promotion race for two thirds of the campaign the Robins eventually finished a disappointing tenth. The F.A. Cup produced an epic match against Blackpool in the fourth round.

This was considered to have been the best cup-tie played by the Club since the War, and 42,594 spectators paying receipts of £5,569.15s.6d. saw Mike Thresher keep a firm grip on Stanley Matthews. The crowd witnessed one of Wally Hinshelwood's great days, which when they came made him one of the best right wingers in the Football League. This season was probably the finest that Hinshelwood ever had as he played well throughout and also produced another outstanding performance in the 4-0 demolition of Swansea Town on October 11th.

Alan Williams. Played in the Blackpool game

Watkins scores with a typical power shot in the Swansea match.

City's left winger Johnny Watkins also had a good campaign, his cannonball shot breaking the net against Ipswich Town on March 27th, and it was a major shock to supporters to find this popular player placed on the transfer list at the season's end.

He was sold to Cardiff City and in playing a major part in their promotion the following campaign saw service with them in the First Division in 1960-61 before joining Bristol Rovers in 1961-62.

Harry Bamford Memorial Fund Match

The end of the season saw another Combined Bristol XI match, on this occasion it was for the Harry Bamford Memorial Fund. All Bristol was saddened by the death of this fine Bristol Rovers full-back, who was renowned as a gentleman both on and off the field. He died on October 31st, 1958, following a road accident three days earlier when he was riding his scooter to Clifton College to take a coaching session. The match was played at Eastville Stadium on May 8th when a crowd of 28,347 helped swell the fund by £3,709.6s.6d. Arsenal provided the opposition, and the end of an exciting game saw the Bristol side triumph by a score of 5-4, Bradford (2), Atyeo (2) and Ward being the homesters scorers, with Groves (2), Clapton and Henderson replying for the Gunners.
Combined Bristol XI: Cook (City); Burden (City), Watling (Rovers), Sykes (Rovers), Alan Williams (City), Mabbutt (Rovers), Hinshelwood (City), Atyeo (City), Bradford (Rovers), Ward (Rovers), Hooper (Rovers).
Arsenal: Sims (Aston Villa); Wills, Evans, Everett, Docherty, Bowen, O'Neill (Clapton 45 mins), Groves, Charles, Bloomfield, Henderson.

In memory of Harry Bamford a trophy was put up for award each season to a local footballer who exhibited his great sportsmanship, and the recipients until the award was discontinued in 1972 were:- 1958-59 Geoff Bradford (Bristol Rovers); 1959-60 Colin Mitchell (Clifton St. Vincents); 1960-61 Bob Anderson (Bristol City); 1961-62 Burt Britton (Avonmouth); 1962-63 Albert Allen (Parson Street Old Boys); 1963-64 John Atyeo (Bristol City); 1964-65 Ray Mabbutt (Bristol Rovers); 1965-66 Ray Bean (Soundwell); 1966-67 Jack Connor (Bristol City); 1967-68 Bert Biggs (St. Philips Marsh Adult School); 1968-69 Harold Jarman (Bristol Rovers); 1969-70 Terry Bush (Bristol City); 1970-71 John Honeyfield (St. Adhelm's); 1971-72 Bobby Jones (Bristol Rovers).

Trouble In The Camp

The start of the 1959-60 campaign, with City having signed the left wing pairing of Malcolm Graham and John McCann from Barnsley for a Club record deal valued at £20,000 (this involving £14,500 cash and the transfer to Oakwell of Bert Tindill), filled Bristol with expectation that this was to be the season that brought the long awaited return to First Division football. These thoughts were shared by the national newspapers who made the Robins one of the favourites for the promotion prize. Unfortunately things didn't turn out as expected and instead of going onto higher things the Club found themselves suffering relegation after a dismal campaign saw them finish at the bottom of the Second Division table with only twenty seven points. Problems arose in the close season when John Atyeo, Tommy Burden and Mike Thresher refused to re-sign following a dispute over wages. The trio insisted on being paid the maximum of £20 per week in the season and £17 in summer as had been promised when the Club was promoted. After the Chairman's intervention they were restored to full wages, but this obviously undermined the

Manager's position and the Club polarised itself into two camps. This naturally had its effect on the field and the team struggled throughout the campaign with relegation being almost inevitable from the turn of the year. City's situation wasn't helped by the injury problems of new signing Malcolm Graham who didn't make his debut until October 31st when he scored twice in a 3-1 win at Stoke City. Unfortunately after scoring two more goals in the next three games the problems with regard to his injured left knee returned and he wasn't fit enough to return to the side until February 6th when he scored in a 2-2 home draw with Sheffield United. At the end of the campaign he had scored eight goals in fourteen appearances, so it can be appreciated what a loss he was to the team. However, despite his potential he was allowed to leave Ashton Gate and he joined Leyton Orient for £5,250, helping them to gain promotion to the First Division in 1961-62. Johnny McCann also had a difficult time at Ashton Gate. This Scottish 'B' International broke his leg during a 4-1 win at Plymouth on Boxing Day, and it was no surprise when this skilful player moved to Huddersfield Town in September 1960, in an exchange deal that brought the popular Jack Connor to the City.

Goal Problem

Goals were in short supply in the relegation campaign and in attempting to rectify the problem City Manager Peter Doherty gave centre-half Alan Williams a run out at centre-forward against second in the table Middlesbrough (Brian Clough, Peter Taylor et al) on September 26th. He scored in a 2-0 success, but after a 3-0 defeat in the next match against Derby County the experiment was discontinued. There were some good wins during the season to demonstrate what the side might have been capable of achieving if they had all been pulling together, the most exciting being a 1-0 victory over Liverpool at Ashton Gate on September 1st, but overall form was so poor that it was inevitable that the Manager's head would roll. Peter Doherty had relinquished his position as Manager of the Northern Ireland team to concentrate solely on City's plight, but this wasn't enough to save him when results didn't improve, and with reports of fights by players in training, he was dismissed on March 15th.

Committee

Team affairs were then taken over by a Committee comprising Les Bardsley, Harry Dolman, Vice-Chairman W.J. (Bill) Kew, Director the Rev. F.C. Vyvyan-Jones, and player Tommy Burden - who had been reinstated as captain, taking over from Tommy Cavanagh who had been signed the previous summer for £2,500 from Doncaster Rovers. Performances improved somewhat after this, one such performance ending in an unlucky 2-1 defeat at Villa Park on April 9th. Roger Collinson scored a fantastic first-half goal with a shot from a position by the right touchline, just inside the Villa half, which put the Robins in front, before Villa hit back with two dubious second-half penalties to clinch promotion. Another good display produced a more successful outcome, against Ipswich Town at Ashton Gate on Easter Monday, when the visitors were beaten 5-1, but by then relegation was almost a certainty, a situation which was made fact by a 3-1 defeat at Leyton Orient in the following match on April 23rd.

The Appointment of Fred Ford

There were sixty applicants for the vacant manager's job at Ashton Gate, but they didn't include the man that Harry Dolman wanted. He had sounded out Fred Ford, who was coach with Bristol Rovers, but had been initially turned down. However whilst on a coaches and trainers course at Lilleshall, where he met up with Les Bardsley and Bill Harvey (coach) of

John Atyeo shows his international style in the unlucky defeat at Villa Park - April 1960 (Other City player in the foreground is Tommy Burden)

Bristol City it was made clear to him that the job was his for the asking, and thinking that he would be mad to turn his back on the opportunity he made contact by telephone with Harry Dolman. Accordingly therefore Fred Ford was appointed Manager of Bristol City on July 14th, 1960, when he signed a three year contract worth £2,750 per annum.

Wonderful Gift - Pity About The Proviso

He inherited a Club that had all it's debts - which were in excess of £55,000 - wiped out by Harry Dolman who donated enough share holding stock in his Company (Brecknell, Dolman & Rogers) to clear this sum. There was however a proviso to this gift in that he demanded, and got, the resignation of Directors the Rev. Vyvyan-Jones and George Jones, though the reasons as to why he wished the removal of these two hard-working Board members has never been made public. Fred Ford later remarked that on his first morning's training he had to sort out a couple of the older professionals, for the Club was notorious at this time for its dressing room atmosphere that one could cut with a knife, in consequence of the bitter pro- and anti-Doherty factions. The fact that Ford succeeded in making it a remarkably happy club - and even won over the fans who initially did not take kindly to his coming from arch-rivals Bristol Rovers - speaks volumes for the man, and his period in charge was characterised by the entertaining football that was played.

High Scoring

The following five campaigns saw the Robins performing in the national Third Division, which had been formed in 1958-59 when the top halves of the North and South Sections joined together, the remainder making up the Fourth Division. In this period the City attack was in great form, and they never scored less than fifty League goals at home in each of the five seasons. However this notwithstanding the 1960-61 campaign almost brought further demotion - mainly due to poor away form - but improvement from the middle of January saw a rise

from eighteenth to fourteenth place at the season's end. The F.A. Cup brought footballing fireworks on Guy Fawkes Day when Chichester City came to Ashton Gate, this First Round match being switched from their ground. City ran up their top score in the competition, putting eleven goals past the luckless amateurs, a score that would have been even higher if the players hadn't spent the second-half trying to create opportunities for Jantzen Derrick to register a goal. Their efforts were in vain however, and an 8-0 half-time score-line was only increased by three after the break, and was someway behind the Club's record First team competitive match victory of 14-1 against Eastleigh in the Western League on January 26th, 1898.

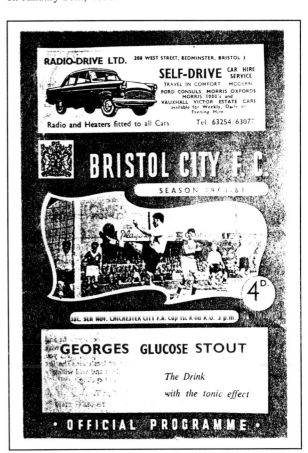

 **Match to Remember**

A 'Guy Fawkes Day' spectacle was served at Ashton Gate when the luckless amateur's from Sussex, who forfeited home advantage, were destroyed by a City side that after taking a 8-0 interval lead appeared to spend the second-half attempting to set up a goal for Jantzen Derrick, the only forward who failed to score for the homesters.

It was apparent from the first minute that the City were several yards faster than their opponents and later in the game their superior stamina showed through as well. The score could easily have been as high as 20 if the homesters had not become careless with their shooting and approach work. Bobby Williams had a most enjoyable game playing some masterful football and with his namesake, Adrian, was much too clever for their ponderous opponents, making and missing some six chances. Three times in the space of the first eight minutes of the second-half, he cut through the defence, walked round centre-half Bailey and calmly steered open goal opportunities wide of the posts.

Manager Fred Ford dismissed the game's missed chances by saying "People expected us to win 6-0, we got 11 so there can be no complaints. It takes some doing to get 11 goals in any type of football as it doesn't even happen in lighthearted practise games".

Complacency crept in during the second-half with players attempting tricks which would never come off in League matches and some defenders anxious to score goals often neglected their elementary defensive duties.

The match, naturally belonged to the City forwards, John Atyeo topping the list with five goals, scoring his first three in the space of eleven minutes towards the end of the first half, when his team were already three up. Atyeo's best goal was also the best of the game, this being his second, when he neatly lobbed Connor's pass first time into the top corner of the net - an effort that would have beaten most goalkeepers. Bobby Williams netted twice, the second being a deflection off Bailey's leg, Alex Tait got one and Adrian Williams - who scored the opening goal after five minutes - obtained three, but Derrick, who with Tait played wide on the flanks in accordance with instructions, didn't shine as brightly as he might have done. Atyeo's mobility, his chasing back and his excursions to both flanks to collect the ball impressed the onlookers and produced the hope that he would show a similar yearning for work in future - especially away from home.

For the visitors left-winger Peter Harris made occasional break-aways and also had the two best chances for them.

Bristol City: Cook; Collinson, Thresher, Connor, Alan Williams, Etheridge, Tait, Robert Williams, Atyeo, Adrian Williams, Derrick.
Chichester City: P. Thomas, A. Cunningham, F. Knotts, J. Rumsey, D. Bailey, D. Aburrow, D. Green, N. Hillier, G. Gilfillan, M. Blythman, P. Harris.
Referee: R. Reddaway (Kettering)
Attendance: 12,577 (£2,074.10.0)
Source: Bristol Evening Post, Monday, 7th November, 1960.

Fireworks on Guy Fawkes Day 1960 As portrayed in the Bristol Evening Post

League Cup

This success over Chichester set the Robins off on a cup run that saw them beat Kings Lynn, after a replay, and achieve a fine win over Second Division Plymouth Argyle, before going out to eventual Finalists Leicester City at Filbert Street 4-1 after the first meeting had been abandoned at half-time due to a waterlogged pitch. The season was notable for the commencement of the Football League Cup, the very first match - by virtue of the fact that it kicked off earlier than the other games played on that night - being Bristol Rovers 2-1 success over Fulham at Eastville Stadium on September 26th.

City received a bye in the First Round, but the next stage saw them drawn to play at Aldershot on October 10th, where despite being reduced to ten men due to Gordon Hopkinson being injured, they gained a creditable draw, thanks to a goal from Jack Boxley. In the replay on October 25th a comfortable 3-0 success was achieved, a game that saw Adrian Williams turn in an outstanding performance and fully deserve his goal. This was to be City's only win in the competition for almost eight years, and being drawn at Nottingham Forest in the Third Round it wasn't surprising that their losing streak started off against a Club who had often proved difficult opponents. At this time Forest didn't have floodlights and it was hoped to play on the Notts County ground at Meadow Lane, but the Football League ruled against this. The match therefore went ahead on the afternoon of Tuesday, November 15th when only 3,690 spectators were present to see Forest win 2-1.

Wessex Youth League

The 1960-61 campaign also brought to fruition the brainchild of Peter Doherty the recognition of the need for a local Youth League. At this time City had a successful and productive youth policy, their youngsters having reached the Semi-Finals of the F.A. Youth Cup in 1955-56 & 1959-60, and attracting an attendance as high as 18,181 for their meeting with Chelsea Youth at Ashton Gate on the 5th April 1960. Accordingly a Wessex Youth League commenced operation, and City's initial game took place on the County Ground, Bristol, on September 17th when they played out a goalless draw with Weymouth Town Youth. This competition continued for seven seasons, City winning the Championship in 1961-62, 1964-65, 1965-66 & 1966-67, as well as finishing Runners-Up in 1960-61, 1962-63 & 1967-68.

The Bristol Evening Post portrays the 6-0 victory over Notts County in the 1961/62 season.

Barnsley's Revenge

Promotion was a real possibility in 1961-62 but the Robins were twice put in their place by an outstanding Portsmouth side who ran the City off the park by winning 4-0 at Ashton Gate on March 6th, and 5-0 at Fratton Park eighteen days later. The campaign had started with a Public Trial Match on August 12th when 1,476 spectators were at Ashton Gate to see the Reds beat the Whites 3-2, this destined to be the last such match, as in future years the role of such games were to be taken over by pre-season friendlies. The Third Division action got underway on August 19th when City were the first visitors to Notts County in their Centenary Season. This game ended in an unlucky defeat, County scoring the only goal with a last minute penalty.

John Atyeo (no.8) scores from close range at Ashton Gate, in City's 2-1 success over Bournemouth - 2nd December 1961

More action in the 1961/62 season. versus Crystal Palace.

But this bad luck evened itself out in the next fixture, when John Atyeo who was standing yards offside was gifted the opportunity to steal the points when he was the recipient of a back pass by courtesy of the Northampton Town defence. After losing their first two away matches, things picked up on August 29th when the double was completed over Northampton, but it was the following match at top of the table Peterborough United that City started to show their potential. They won 4-3 in a thrilling game to inflict on the 'Posh' their first defeat in the Third Division, and this sort of form was to show itself again in away successes of 4-3 at Halifax Town, and 4-0 at Swindon Town. On November 11th City were involved in another high scoring game at Barnsley, but this time the Oakwell lads were able to extract revenge for the heavy reverse of three years previously by winning 7-3. City's best away performance though was on December 9th when they recovered from a 2-0 half-time deficit against Crystal Palace to win 3-2 thanks to scintillating performances by Jantzen Derrick and John Atyeo. High scoring was a feature of many of the home games, wins of 6-0 against Notts County, 6-1 versus Bradford Park Avenue, as well as successes of 5-0 and 5-3 against Reading and Swindon Town respectively. In the F.A. Cup this form again came to the fore with a 5-2 win in a replay at Hereford United when Alex Tait managed to score from an amazing angle, and an 8-2 demolition of Dartford. All in all a satisfactory season with a final placing of sixth to leave 'Ashton Alf' to enjoy his summer break with every expectation of promotion in 1962-63.

'St Mary Redcliffe Restoration Appeal'

Arsenal came to Bristol again to face another Combined XI on August 8th, though this time it was at Ashton Gate in a special match in aid of the 'St. Mary Redcliffe Restoration Appeal'. The 'Gunners' won 2-1 with both their goals being scored by Barnwell (one penalty), and the Bristol side replied through Keith Williams. A crowd of 19,962 who paid receipts of £3,400 turned up to see the following players:-

Combined XI: Million (Rovers); Bradford (Rovers), Thresher (City), Sykes (Rovers), Connor (City), Casey (City), Savino (City), Atyeo (City), K. Williams (Rovers), R. Williams (City), R. Jones (Rovers). Substitute: Derrick (City) replacing Savino. **Arsenal:** McKechnie; Magill, McCullough, Clamp, Neill, Sneddon (Brown), McLeod (Strong), Barnwell, Baker, Eastham, Skirton.

Another Record

The serious football started ten days later when newly promoted Millwall gained a 2-2 draw at Ashton Gate, and it wasn't until the fifth match of the campaign that City obtained their first success, winning 2-0 at home to Port Vale. Form fluctuated throughout the season, but still the goals kept flowing with notable away wins of 5-2 at Bradford Park Avenue, Carlisle United and Halifax Town. Unfortunately the Robins' poor defensive record, which saw ninety-two League goals being conceded, doomed them to a lowly fourteenth position, even though the attack notched up exactly a century, this record giving the Club an unusual record in achieving the lowest placing for a team scoring a 100 goals or more. The away match with Queens Park Rangers on March 2nd took place at the White City Stadium, when despite scoring first through Alex Tait, they lost 3-1. The best home win was achieved on April 16th, with Barrie Meyer marking his last appearance by scoring three times in a 6-3 victory over Southend United. This was a match that the writer and three other City supporters thought might be missed, as the previous evening had seen us stranded in Reading when returning from the away fixture at Roots Hall.

Trials and Tribulations

The Supporters Club hired two Wessex Coaches for this Easter Monday trip, and on the return journey stopped for the normal refreshments at a public house on the outskirts of Reading. We four lads were pleased to find that there was a games room on the premises, but after making use of such facilities we were disconcerted to find that our transport has disappeared, being afterwards informed that due to people switching over coaches, an error had been made in the counting of the passengers. After waiting around for a while in the hope that a coach would return, it was finally decided to start walking along the A4 and try to thumb a lift, having a modicum of success - after walking about five miles - by obtaining two lifts to eventually reach Hungerford. Being now past midnight we tried our best to sleep in a shop doorway, but after waking early we were fortunate in obtaining a lift right back to Bristol, actually arriving home in time for some of us to go to work. For our pains we were given a free trip to another away game.

Bristol Rovers' Goalkeeper - Hall - leaps high to tip a shot over the bar in the 1963/64 season opening match, won 3-0 by City.

The Big Freeze

The winter of 1962-63 was the worst since 1948, with heavy snowfall at the turn of the year and freezing conditions persisting right through until March. This brought about much delay in settling City's F.A. Cup match with Aston Villa. The match was originally scheduled to be played at Ashton Gate on January 5th and was twice postponed before a 1-1 draw was achieved on January 16th. This set up a sequence of nine more postponements before the tie was finally brought off at Villa Park on March 7th, where the Robins put up a fine performance before going down 3-2.

Great Goalkeeper

The defence was much stronger for 1963-64, the signing of Mike Gibson from Shrewsbury Town towards the end of the previous campaign proving to be a major factor in this regard. He was probably the best goalkeeper ever to have played for the Robins and he was to be a stalwart in the side for the next nine seasons. The League programme commenced with a 3-0 win over Bristol Rovers on August 24th, and this was followed by a great performance in winning 2-1 at newly promoted Brentford, but a 4-1 defeat at Port Vale on August 31st brought everyone back to earth. After a 2-0 home win over Notts County a week later, form slumped in a sequence of eight games without a win, although a 3-1 home win over Peterborough United on October 11th restored confidence.

The campaign's end saw the Robins in fifth place and being well equipped for a promotion push in 1964-65.

Alick Jeffrey Returns To Ashton Gate

The F.A. Cup saw City reaching the Fourth Round. On the way to this stage they were rather fortunate in beating non-League Corby Town 3-1 before taking care of Exeter City 2-0, to earn an away game against Doncaster Rovers. A keen tussle at 'Belle Vue' on January 4th saw City escape with a 2-2 draw after Brian Clark equalised in the last minute. The replay brought Alick Jeffrey to Ashton Gate for the first time since breaking his leg in the Under-23 match in 1956, such injury having kept him out of the English game for many years. He came through his ordeal without any mishap, but was unable to prevent Rovers from losing 2-0, to leave City contemplating an away trip to Sunderland in the next round.

Hot & Cold

This fixture created a lot of interest and a special train was put on to get the fans to Roker Park, bringing about a journey that many City supporters will never forget. The fare was £1.10s.0d. (£1.50) and when the trip started from Parson Street Station at 11.20 p.m. on Friday, January 24th the heating of the carriages was such that despite the extremely cold weather, the windows were opened so as to be able to cool down. This however proved to be a move that was soon to be regretted as it wasn't long before the heating system broke down, and it was a very cold train load of supporters who shivered outside Birmingham for three to four hours in the early hours of the morning, while a cow on the line was dealt with! This meant that arrival in Sunderland was about 11 a.m., instead of the scheduled 8.02 a.m., depriving many supporters of what was the interesting feature of such trips in the days before police over-involvement - the time to become acquainted with a new area. This certainly added to the writer's experience of many trips around this time, for without the motorway network we have today the coach (usually just one) would leave Ashton Gate around 11 p.m. for northern grounds, with arrival at the destination often reached by 8 a.m., and hence leaving time free to explore new territory. Such excursions allowed a visit to the docks in Kingston-upon-Hull, an early monring tour (conducted by the groundsman) of the Bradford Park Avenue ground, and enjoyment of the delights of the beach at Cleethorpes! An abiding memory of these trips is of the huge transport cafe at Newcastle-under-Lyme that we used to arrive at in the wee small hours.

A Brilliant Sunderland Team

We arrived at Sunderland optimistically thinking that a win would be suitable recompense for the ordeal of our long journey, but it wasn't to be. The City didn't play badly, but Sunderland were absolutely brilliant - putting on a display in winning 6-1 that the writer hasn't seen bettered in his thirty-six years of regular football attendance. As well as the individual skill of their players, they never stopped fighting for the ball, harrying and chasing City in all areas of the pitch as though they were the potential giantkillers. In the 'Rokerites' team was Johnny Crossan who City had signed from Colerane in October 1958, only to have his registration refused by the Football League due to allegations that he had been paid while still an amateur. He was later banned from playing football in England, but wishing to play in a higher grade of football he signed for Dutch Club Sparta Rotterdam, and later took part in the European Cup with Standard Liege of Belgium. The Football League eventually lifted the ban and he joined Sunderland in October 1962.

Unique Double

Peter Hooper scored with one of his typical blockbusters from thirty-five yards to bring City back into the game at 2-1, but by half-time they had conceded another goal to the smooth running Roker machine. The second period was nearly all one way traffic, and by the finish Sunderland were clear victors with goals from Herd (2), Crossan (2), Sharkey and Hurley to inflict on City their record defeat in the F.A. Cup. This was to form the first part of a unique double as Sunderland were to come to Ashton Gate almost twenty-seven years later and by winning 6-1 in the Football League (Rumbelows) Cup, inflict on City their heaviest defeat in this competition also. However, on the latter occasion, the Robins were most unlucky as the score does not give a true indication of the play. So City were out of the F.A. Cup in a most emphatic manner, and all we poor supporters could do was to wend our way to the station in time for the 6.50 p.m. train that eventually got us back to Bristol at about 3 a.m. on Sunday morning. The 46,201 spectators who were present at the game will no doubt well remember the Sunderland team as being:- Montgomery; Irwin, Ashurst, Harvey, Hurley, McNab, Usher, Herd, Sharkey, Crossan, Mulhall. It is little wonder that this fine combination gained promotion to the First Division at the season's end, and also reached the Sixth Round of the F.A. Cup when it took Manchester United three attempts to get past them.

Promotion Again

City opened their 1964-65 League campaign at newly relegated Scunthorpe United on August 22nd, receiving the shock of their lives when they were defeated 5-2, though it was remarked that they had suffered similarly in their first match

in 1905-06 but still had gone on to claim the promotion prize. The players seemingly took heart from this observation, and in the following six matches twenty-five goals were scored and only four conceded in the process of winning five and drawing one, to go top of the table on September 14th. A slump in form however brought a drop to ninth by the time the leaders, Bristol Rovers, came to Ashton Gate on February 13th, but in winning this game 2-1, after falling behind, the Robins embarked on an amazing run of success which saw only one more fixture being lost. This form was good enough to bring the side through to claim the second promotion spot on goal average from Mansfield Town, City's average being 1.6727 compared to 1.5574 of Mansfield. It is however interesting to note that under the present system Mansfield would have got the verdict as they scored ninety-five goals compared to City's ninety-two. Under the goal difference method that applied until recently, the decision would have held good as the Robins had +37 compared to the +34 of the 'Stags'.

The last Bob Bennett Bristol City cartoon, on 15th March 1965.

'The Robin'

City brought out a supporters magazine during the year, entitled 'The Robin', and the first issue made it's appearance on February 13th. It wasn't however a long lived venture and after the selling of issue number two on April 24th it would seem that it appeared no more.

New Floodlights

The close-season of 1965 saw City's first set of floodlights being sold, for £2,000 to Southern League Burton Albion, but it wasn't until December 28th, 1965, that the new lights were ready for the 'big switch-on'. Wolverhampton Wanderers were again the visitors, though this time in a Second Division fixture, and they inflicted on City their first home defeat in twenty matches. This new system cost £27,000 and consisted of forty-eight lamps on each angled head, set atop four 160ft high pylons which were situated at each corner of the ground. These floodlights were to be a feature of Ashton Gate for the next twenty-seven years, and many felt that the ground lost much of it's character when the pylons were removed on June 8th, 1992, to find a new home with Wigan Athletic at Springfield Park. City's third set of lights were erected on the roofs of the Grandstand (named the 'Des Williams Stand' on June 4th, 1992) and the 'Dolman Stand', and were fully in use for the first time on the 5th November 1991, when Plymouth Argyle succumbed 2-0 in a Second Division game.

A star returns. Cary Grant (born in Bristol) watched the 4-0 victory over Charlton on 6th September 1966

Successful Return

Another successful return to Second Division life saw the Club only just miss a further promotion due to unluckily dropping three points to Southampton over Easter. In the home match on Good Friday the 'Saints' were outplayed but still managed to gain a 1-0 win, and in the return three days later at the 'Dell', a last minute goal by Terry Paine prevented City gaining full revenge, though this time it was just reward for Southampton's persistence as they had what they thought was an equaliser disallowed by the referee a minute earlier. The difference between success and failure is very slim and in City's case it was in consequence of not being able to obtain three points from these two games, the 'Saints' gaining the promotion prize with the Robins finishing in fifth place.

'Daily Mail Fair Play League'

The City however did gain some reward for their football by winning the *Daily Mail Fair Play League* for the Second Division, finishing tenth in the combined table for all the Football League Clubs, with an average for the season of 76.50. This gave them a double as the previous campaign they took the award for the Third Division with an average of 74.64.

Farewell John

The game with Ipswich Town at Ashton Gate on May 10th, 1966, brought an era to an end as it was John Atyeo's final League match, and it was entirely appropriate, and in the nature of the man, that he marked his farewell by obtaining the two goals necessary for him to reach the grand total of 350 in League & Cup for the City. He only played once more at Ashton Gate, during the following campaign, when he turned out for the Robins on the occasion of his Benefit Match. This game was brought off on October 10th when a crowd numbering 17,425 (paying receipts of £3,930) turned up to see Leeds United win 4-2. On this evening John's goal touch eluded him, but what with the emotion of the event and the fact that Leeds brought along the 'World Cup' (Jules Rimet Trophy) which England had won in the Summer, this didn't spoil the enjoyment for one and all.

Bristol & District Amateur Sunday Football League

While England were winning the World Cup, the Summer of 1966 heralded the last phase of Bristol's soccer development, with the formation of the first local Sunday League. Upon hearing news of this competition, a group of Bristol City supporters (including the writer) formed a Club in the hope of joining it. At the Kings Head, Bedminster Down, on the 14th July, Bristol Casuals came into being, the name as well as conveniently representing the attitude of the players, also had the same initials as the 'parent' Club.

Record Fee

Continuing City's usual trend, the 1966-67 campaign brought a decline and four successive defeats at the outset set up a relegation struggle. However the signing of John Quigley - one of the best players ever to turn out for the Club - from Huddersfield Town in October, followed by the purchase of Chris Crowe from Nottingham Forest in January and Hugh McIlmoyle in March, electrified the team and supporters. The arrival of John Quigley brought City a cheque of £2,500 as Brian Clark went to 'Leeds Road', but Chris Crowe cost the Robins a £15,000 fee, this figure being beaten a few months later when a Club record £27,000 was found to obtain the services of Hugh McIlmoyle from Wolverhampton Wanderers. The season ended with the Club in the security of sixteenth place, and hopes were high that the following campaign would bring about an involvement in the promotion battle.

Greaves Shows How

It was the F.A. Cup that provided Robins supporters with some of their best memories of 1966-67, the City progressing through to the Fifth Round after disposing of Halifax Town and Southampton. This round for the last sixteen teams found the Club, along with a following of about 10,000, at White Hart Lane on March 11th taking on the might of Tottenham Hotspur, and those supporters were dismayed when Jimmy Greaves put the Spurs ahead within the first eleven minutes.

However the opportunity to equalise presented itself after fifty-five minutes when the Robins were awarded a penalty when Mike England handled a corner from Jantzen Derrick. This kick was entrusted to Tony Ford and he hit his shot low and true, but Pat Jennings fell on his right to save. However, the referee (Ken Burns) ruled that the keeper had moved before the kick was taken so City had another chance. This time Chris Crowe took on the responsibility, but all he could do was to put the ball two yards wide. It was left to Jimmy Greaves to demonstrate how such kicks should be taken, when he rubbed salt into City's wound, by easily slotting one in during the last minute, after Gordon Low had handled.

Drink Up Thee Cider

The Cup run brought about the adoption of a new song by City supporters, a popular melody by 'Adge Cutler and the Wurzels' entitled *'Drink Up Thee Cider'*, this being a feature of many a game from February onwards, and was especially noticeable during the 1-0 F.A. Cup win over First Division Southampton on February 18th.

Loss of an International Fixture

Ashton Gate was selected as the venue for an Under-23 International between England and Wales on October 12th, but the Football Association moved the fixture to Wolverhampton as they thought that the attendance would suffer with John Atyeo's benefit taking place during the same week.

The season at Ashton Gate was brought to a conclusion with the ground being given over to the Bristol & District Amateur Sunday Football League for the playing of their Cup Final (which according to their Chairman was only the second time that a Football League ground had been used for such a match).

False Hopes

Despite the euphoria brought about by the influx of new players the previous campaign, 1967-68 started badly with another run of four straight defeats. This form brought about the dismissal of Manager Fred Ford on September 19th, and the appointment of Alan Dicks - who had been Jimmy Hill's assistant at Coventry City during the period of the 'Sky Blues' renaissance when they were renowned as great innovators. Alan Dicks, or 'AD' as he wished to be known, was engaged as the new Manager following a meeting with Harry Dolman on October 5th, but he didn't take up full time duties until eleven days later. His first match in charge was at Fratton Park on October 21st when, in a travesty of a game, the Robins seemingly operating with an eleven man defence, reaped their just desserts by going down 2-0. However as the season progressed more adventurous policies were adopted and the signing of John Galley for £25,000 from Rotherham United - even though with his leg in plaster he was unable to play for a month - proved to be a master stroke. His first game for the Robins at Huddersfield Town on December 16th saw him notch all City's goals in a 3-0 success and he ended the campaign with sixteen League goals plus two in the F.A. Cup. Galley's prowess in the goalscoring stakes was a significant factor in the side's escape from relegation, and the occupancy of nineteenth position at the season's conclusion.

Support for Fred Ford

The sacking of Fred Ford brought forth a tremendous display of support for this popular man. A deputation of players visited Chairman Harry Dolman at his Chew Magna home to try to persuade him to give Fred another chance, and many letters in the pages of the *'Green 'Un'* - including ex-player Tony Cook - clearly indicated the high esteem in which Ford was held. He went on to become coach at Swindon Town before returning to Bristol Rovers in April 1968, when he took over as team Manager, staying for eighteen months before linking up with Swindon again where he was in charge for two years. He then had a spell as coach at Torquay United before being appointed youth coach at Oxford United in 1974. In January 1981 he was given a special award for his service to football, but on October 16th that year, he died within a few days of his great friend Bill Shankly.

John Galley scored this goal after only two minutes play. City beat Norwich 4-0, on 20th September 1969.

League Cup Success

The events of the next three campaigns didn't bring much improvement with positions of nineteenth, fourteenth and nineteenth respectively, but for some unaccountable reason this continuing run of failure had no effect on the position of Alan Dicks. However, it is likely that his tenure of the Ashton Gate hot seat was saved by the Club reaching the Semi-Finals of the Football League Cup in 1970-71. City had reached this stage of the competition for the first time after disposing of Rotherham United, Blackpool, Leicester City and Fulham, but the luck they experienced in beating Fulham in a Quarter-Final Replay at Ashton Gate on November 24th was to completely desert them in their two-legged clash with Tottenham Hotspur in the Semi-Final. The first leg was played at Ashton Gate on December 16th, a week later than scheduled in consequence of a power workers dispute. 30,022 fans paid receipts of £13,931 and saw Alan Skirton put City ahead only for Alan Gilzean to grab a vital equaliser for the Londoners. The second leg at White Hart Lane on December 23rd brought forth a magnificent battling defensive performance by City, and this coupled with the squandering of a good opportunity by Gerry Sharpe, took the tie into extra-time. Unfortunately though the defence cracked in this period and goals by Martin Chivers and Jimmy Pearce dashed City's hopes of their first major Cup Final appearance in sixty-two years.

Old Players Matches

This season brought Jack Connor's career at Ashton Gate to a close after his playing over 400 games for the Club in all competitions. He arranged for Wolverhampton Wanderers to turn out for his Benefit, and on March 15th they beat City 2-1 at Ashton Gate in front of 7,800 spectators. This netted around £2,000 which was added to the proceeds from various other events that had been organised throughout the year. Among these was an 'Old Players Match' involving favourites from yesteryear. This game between City and Rovers took place at 'Eastville' on May 2nd when goals from Hamilton and Biggs gave the homesters a 2-0 victory in revenge for defeat in a similar fixture on December 1st seven years earlier. On the earlier occasion the game was organised for the Benefit of the 'Friends of Frenchay Hospital' and a crowd totalling 3,289 were present at Eastville to see City Old Players win 6-3 with goals from Arnold Rodgers (3),

Jimmy Rogers (2) and Tommy Burden, the Rovers replying with strikes from Geoff Fox, Georgie Petherbridge and Geoff Bradford. A third match in this series was played on February 28th, 1978, prior to the start of Les Bardsley's Benefit, when City lost 2-1 to Bobby Charlton's XI. This Old Players match lasted only twenty minutes each way, Rovers winning 1-0 thanks to a goal from Geoff Bradford. The last of this type of game at Ashton Gate took place as a curtain raiser to Geoff Merrick's Benefit on May 12th, 1980, and ended in a 0-0 draw.

Top of the Table for a While

Comparative success was achieved in 1972 and 1973, with final placings of eighth and fifth. Top place in the table was actually attained on September 11th, 1971, but the following campaign the opposite situation applied, for almost a year later - on September 2nd - the Robins found themselves right at the bottom. A strange season as five games were won away before the first home win.

The ball, together with Ian Broomfield and Millwall goalkeeper Brian King. Six goals were shared in February 1971

John Emanuel scores in the Glos. Cup Final versus Rovers, in May 1972.
The match was settled for the first time with a penalty shoot-out (City lost 4-2).

(Right)   Eight months later this home match versus Sheffield Wenesday was abandoned - the reason is apparent from the photo' !

(Below)   February 1973.   Plenty of action in the F.A.Cup at Molineux, which was won by Wolves.

City players from the left: Merrick (6), Drysdale, Sweeney (2), Tainton, Gould (9) and Gow.

(Above) Gerry Gow scores against Portsmouth at Ashton Gate on 3rd March 1973.

(Right) Tom Ritchie and Bobby Gould express dismay as another chance is missed against Blackpool - the visitors won 1-0 in October 1973.

(Below) Sweeney's penalty is saved. However, the kick was re-taken, and the resulting goal gave the Robin's a 1-0 victory over Bolton in the first game of 1975/76 - which proved crucial at the season's end.

Hold the Front Page

Season 1973-74 found City holding pole position in mid-September but a decline in performance during the second-half of the campaign saw the Robins dropping to a lowly sixteenth place in the final table. However despite this disappointment it was a notable campaign due to City's exploits in the F.A. Cup, national fame being achieved after beating Leeds United 1-0 in a fifth round Replay at Elland Road on February 19th. Donnie Gillies scored after seventy-three minutes to produce one of the greatest shocks in the Competition, and this served for City to become the first football side to have their exploits covered on the front page of 'The Times'. This defeat of the Cup favourites was sensational as not only was it the first loss - apart from going down in the Football League Cup to Ipswich Town - that the 'Peacocks' had suffered home or away during the season, but they were the team that was to go on and take the Championship honours. City's run came to an end however at the next stage, when they unluckily lost 1-0 at Ashton Gate to a Liverpool side that was to eventually win the trophy, leaving the homesters to think on what might have been. This taste of success though was to be the springboard to better things over the following few years when the confidence gained in beating such a side as Leeds, and giving Liverpool a hard game, was to bear fruit.

The home cup-tie with Leeds on February 16th, when Keith Fear scored a great goal after sixty-five minutes to equalise a first-half strike by Billy Bremner, saw the use of closed circuit television for crowd control at Ashton Gate for the first time, sixteen cameras being brought in specially for the game.

Unlikely Goalscorer

Of the thirty-one League and Cup goals City scored at home this season there was one that will remain long in the memory of all the 10,711 fans who were present on September 18th to see it. Hull City were the visitors on a windswept Tuesday evening, and were much the better side in the opening half, taking the lead through Stuart Pearson after twenty-four minutes. After the break though the Robins came back and Tom Ritchie equalised within two minutes, to set the scene for an unlikely goalscoring hero to emerge. Goalkeeper Ray Cashley, who had a faultless game between the posts, volleyed his clearance from a yard inside his own penalty area at the 'Covered End'. The ball sped through the air, bounced just before the Hull penalty area and soared high into the net with Jeff Wealands groping about ten yards off his line. A fantastic goal to give the Robins the lead for the first time in the match. Cashley said afterwards that "*It was a wonderful moment for me, and it came at a great time for the team, but I obviously wasn't trying for goal. I couldn't really believe I scored even though I had been getting some good distances with kicks on my left side, but this was a really big one in the wind*". This goal put the Robins in charge and eight minutes before time Bobby Gould snapped up a chance to clinch the game 3-1 and put the homesters on top of the table. On this night the teams were as follows:-
City: Cashley; Sweeney, Drysdale, Emanuel, Rodgers, Merrick, Tainton, Ritchie, Gould, Gow, Fear.
Hull City: Wealands; Banks, DeVries, Kaye, Deere, Blampey, McGill, Lord, Pearson, Wagstaff, Greenwood.
Referee: B.H. Daniels (Rainham).

A Near Miss then Success At Last

A low scoring attack, hampered progress to some extent during the 1974-75 campaign, but a 1-0 success at Southampton on Good Friday, March 28th - City's first ever League win at the 'Dell' - gave the Robins a marvellous chance of promotion. Unfortunately the opportunity was tossed away in the following day's game at Ashton Gate when Norwich City took both points with a 1-0 win, this result accounting for the fact that at the season's end the 'Canaries' were promoted in the third promotion spot, the second year that the three-up and three-down had been in operation, instead of the Robins. The difference resulted in a final placing of fifth.

This time however success wasn't long delayed as the following campaign saw promotion to the First Division achieved at long last, when the City finished the season as Runners-up to Sunderland. They threw away the opportunity of winning the Championship in consequence of two 2-1 defeats in the closing weeks - away to Blackpool and at home to Notts County in the last match, after promotion had already been secured.

The crucial matches during the campaign proved to be the opening game when City secured the points, against Bolton Wanderers (thanks to the referee Mike Taylor ordering an unsuccessful penalty kick to be re-taken), and the fixture against West Bromwich Albion on March 17th. The later game was won 1-0 despite the almost incessant pressure exerted by the Baggies. It is pertinent to consider what might have been the final outcome if the Football League had not allowed a late postponement (on February 28th, the original date of the fixture), when a number of the Robins' players were suffering with influenza. From such situations are promotions won, and there is little doubt that the City supporters at the Hawthorns realised the importance of their team's success that night. They celebrated with almost as much gusto as that displayed when the great prize was ultimately achieved, when Portsmouth were beaten 1-0 at Ashton Gate, on the never-to-be-forgotten night of April 20th.

Gerry Gow - eleven years with Bristol City

Match to Remember

West Bromwich Albion 0 Bristol City 1
Football League Division Two
Wednesday, 17th March 1976.

The winning of this match, that was postponed from the 28th of February due to the City players suffering from influenza, convinced the supporters of the Robins that their team were destined to be one of the promoted clubs at the Season's end.

Ian Greaves, manager of close rivals Bolton Wanderers - who enjoyed the atmosphere, the excitement and the sheer professionalism of City's defensive performance - was also convinced that the Robins would make it. But Albion player-manager Johnny Giles complained about the chances his side missed in the second-half, and how the luck of the Irish deserted his side on St. Patrick's Day, when shots by Alistair Brown and John Wile cannoned off the woodwork in the last five minutes. However, Bolton boss Greaves taking a neutral, dispassionate view, said "The better side won, City played superbly in defence, they looked to be a side with a future".

City manager Alan Dicks praised the Robins endeavours stating "We worked tremendously hard and deserved this breaks in the last few minutes because of the wholehearted way we played. If Paul Cheesley had scored from an open-goal chance before Albion's late rush, that would have sealed it up".

The Baggies slow build-ups and insistence in pushing the ball around pedantically at the back and in the midfield, were countered by City's persistence, centres and deep passes being snapped up eagerly by the dominant Gary Collier and Geoff Merrick. Close attention by Gerry Gow, Gerry Sweeney and Trevor Tainton (who all never stopped working in midfield) on Giles, prevented the Irishman launching his normal penetrative passes, and up front Cheesley and Tom Ritchie chased endlessly. Clive Whitehead also impressed with his willingness to tackle back, and it was he that set up the only goal of the game right on the stroke of half-time. His long run down the right ended with a low cross that rebounded off of Giles, for **Sweeney** to lash a shot from eight yards into the net at the Birmingham Road End. The match facts show that the homesters had four shots on target and ten off-target, compared with City's tally of three and three respectively.

This win consolidated the City's place at the top of the Second Division, three points in front of Bolton and four ahead of Sunderland, though their rivals had two games in hand.

Albion. Osborne, Mulligan, Robson, T. Brown, Wile, Robertson, Martin, Cantello (A.Brown 83 minutes), Mayo, Giles, Johnston.

City: *Cashley; Sweeney, Drysdale, Gow, Collier, Merrick, Tainton, Ritchie, Gillies,   Cheesley, Whitehead, (Mann 82 minutes).*

Referee: Malcolm Sinclair (Guildford)

Attendance: 26,640

(Source: Bristol Evening Post, Thursday, 18th March, 1976)

Arsenal 0 Bristol City 1
Football League Division One
Saturday, 21st, August 1976

Bristol City slammed the critics and provided the perfect answer to those who said they have no chance in the First Division, when they started the campaign with a 1-0 win at mighty Arsenal. The big match build-up was all for Arsenal, with City being led on like lambs to the slaughter. It was to be Arsenal's and Malcolm MacDonald's carnival day, but the reverse was the case, as the Gunners star-studded team, which included seven Internationals, was cut down to size. City outplayed them and were so much on target with their shooting that only goalkeeper Jimmy Rimmer, England's newest recruit, lived up to his reputation, and saved Arsenal from a rout. It might have been four or five to City, with nothing for Arsenal. Only once did MacDonald make something for himself with a quick turn and venomous drive which cleared the bar, the ball being lost in the crowd. Arsenal, bitterly disappointed, took their humiliation well.

Manager Terry Neil said: "We were bad right through. Bristol played it better and deserved to win. They wanted to do it more than our lads did and, if they keep up this standard, they will make a future for themselves. We were choked at losing, and I am concerned about it but not worried". MacDonald, signed from Newcastle for £330,000 and committed to score 30 goals for his new club, chipped in saying: "I am bitterly disappointed. I didn't play well, neither did the team, but you have got to give it to Bristol City, and every credit for their win".

Any other result than a win for City would have been an injustice, and the goal which did the trick - and which just had to come - was from one of a number of class movements which taunted Arsenal. It came in the 65th minute. Ray Cashley hit a long ball up to Paul Cheesley, who flicked it on to Tom Ritchie, who forced his way past Peter Simpson and darted for goal, but played the ball too wide. Ritchie then did the next best thing, pushing the ball back to Clive Whitehead, who played his centre perfectly for the strong running **Cheesley** to ram home an eight-yard header past Rimmer.

Arsenal occasionally displayed neat touches in midfield but made nothing for MacDonald and all the scoring attempts came from City. Cheesley made a chance for Ritchie who steered the ball across the face of an open net. Cheesley headed against the foot of a post, while Rimmer brought off two wonderful saves, first from Jimmy Mann, and then from Trevor Tainton. In the second-half, Rimmer again fisted away from Cheesley who powered in a header from an extremely difficult position. Rimmer beat out another stinging drive by Cheesley before the City striker stunned the large crowd with his brilliantly taken goal.

City: *Cashley; Sweeney, Drysdale, Gow, Collier, Merrick, Tainton, Ritchie, Mann, Cheesley, Whitehead.*

Arsenal: *Rimmer; Rice, Nelson, Ross, O'Leary, Simpson, Ball, Armstrong, MacDonald, Radford, Cropley (Storey 74 minutes).*

Referee: G.C. Kew (Amersham)
Attendance: 41,082 (£31,643.33)
(Source: Western Daily Press, Monday, 23rd August, 1976)

A Hot Start

A great start on the Club's return to the top flight after an absence of sixty-five years saw a tremendous winning performance on the opening day of the 1976-77 campaign. A 1-0 scoreline did scant justice to the Robins superiority over Arsenal at Highbury on August 21st when again, as in 1906, the weather was extremely hot. After four games, of which two were won, the City were in second place with an undefeated record, but the loss of centre-forward Paul Cheesley following an injury in the first home League match of the season against Stoke City had it's effect, and the campaign eventually developed into a battle to preserve the Club's newly won status. With two games left the City were looking doomed but a 2-1 home success over Liverpool, who were to win the European Champions Cup as well as retain the Championship, set up the side for a do-or-die battle against fellow strugglers Coventry City at Highfield Road on Thursday, May 19th.

Tom Ritchie scores, and Gerry Gow joins in the celebrations in the November 1975 victory over York City. Gow went on to make 368 League appearances for City, and Ritchie 401.

What A Night!

Tottenham Hotspur and Stoke City were already doomed to relegation, but on this vital night Sunderland - the other club involved in the fight to keep away from the third relegation place - were also playing their last game, at Everton. Coventry, Sunderland and the City were all tied with the same number of points but with Coventry having an inferior goal difference, this being the first campaign of the change from goal average, the Robins only required a point to be safe whilst the 'Sky Blues' needed the security of two as insurance against the possibility of Sunderland winning. This situation conspired to produce an electric atmosphere at Highfield Road, and such was the interest in the fixture the start was delayed for five minutes to allow time for all 36,903 spectators to gain admittance.

Coventry went ahead after fifteen minutes through Tommy Hutchison, their Scottish International left-winger, and when he struck again seven minutes into the second-half to put his side 2-0 in front things looked all up for the Robins. However a goal was pulled back within a couple of minutes when Gerry Gow scored from twelve yards, and then with only eleven minutes left Donnie Gillies put the ball into the far corner from ten yards to level matters. This situation, which obviously posed a serious threat to Coventry's prospects of First Division survival, lead to a battle royal until about four minutes from time.

On the instructions of Jimmy Hill who was Managing Director of the Sky Blues, the electronic scoreboard flashed the match result from Goodison Park as Everton 2 Sunderland 0. This produced cheering from the crowd who realised that a draw was now sufficient to enable both clubs to retain their status, and with this message soon being picked up by the players the game became a farce, the heart pounding action coming to a halt with the Robins keeping possession in their own half, the only danger being the prospect of a backpass going astray. So passed a bizarre last four minutes, or so, until the bemused referee blew for time with both sets of supporters deliriously happy.

Coventry City: Sealey; Oakey, McDonald, Yorath, Holton, Coop, Beck, Wallace, Ferguson, Powell, Hutchison.
City: Shaw; Gillies, Sweeney, Gow, Collier, Hunter, Tainton, Ritchie, Garland, Mann, Whitehead (Cormack).

Charmed Left Foot

Whilst City's survival was due to a great team effort, one particular signing was the most significant in helping to bring about this situation. This was the capture of Norman Hunter from Leeds United in October 1976, a so called 'hard man' who revealed himself to be a supreme footballer who was able to charm the birds out of the trees with his cultured left foot. He became an idol at Ashton Gate, his passing and positional play was impeccable, and without doubt he ranks among the best ever signings for the Robins. His leaving at the end of the 1978-79 campaign to become Player-coach with Barnsley was a major factor in City's relegation the following season.

The Beginning Of The End

City's survival though was to be the seed that eventually brought about the formation of Bristol City (1982) Plc. Chairman Robert Hobbs realised that if the Robins were to make any real impression on the First Division an influx of money was required, and so he announced that potential Directors could buy themselves vacancies on the Board for £25,000. This news stirred the other four Directors into action and Hobbs was deposed on May 23rd, Stephen Kew succeeding him with the full backing of Bill Garland, Graham Griffiths, and Norman Jones. This change lead to a lengthy fight, costing the Club money it could ill afford, with unsuccessful attempts at reinstatement, and the legacy of this was to bring the Club to the brink of extinction.

New Badge

City's return to the First Division brought change to the Club badge, this new one, which is still currently in use, consisting of a robin on a ball surmounted by the Clifton Suspension Bridge, which was adopted on July 22nd, 1976. Up until the summer of 1972 the Club's badge had always been the Coat of Arms of the City and County of Bristol (though a robin had been worn on the players shirts in 1949-50), but with increasing marketing of the Club's products and the problems of pirating, a competition was held to design an official badge. This resulted in a badge that depicted a robin in front of a five bar gate being officially adopted, though the Bristol Coat of Arms continued to be worn on the players shirts until the end of 1975-76. This Coat of Arms was restored to the shirts in place of the robin for the 1994-95 season, provoking much debate amongst the supporters, but the official badge remains the well known association of bird, ball and bridge.

Another Song

First Division life also brought forth another official Club song, this rendering by The Wurzels entitled *'One For the Bristol City'*, was released on record in 1977:-

> *One for the Bristol City*
> *Two for the boys in red*
> *Three for the fans down Ashton Gate*
> *We'll follow till we're dead me boys*
> *Follow till we're dead.*
>
> *Down at Ashton Gate there's Alan Dicks*
> *And the red, red robins too*
> *If they win or if they lose*
> *We'll follow them through and through.*
>
> *I spend a little time on a Saturday*
> *I'm ready for anything*
> *Spend an hour or two in a bloddy girt queue*
> *To get in the ground and sing.*
>
> *One for the Bristol City*
> *Two for the boys in red*
> *Three for the fans down Ashton Gate*
> *We'll follow till we're dead me boys*
> *Follow till we're dead.*
>
> *They are the best from way down west*
> *And we think they are grand*
> *Now they're in the groove*
> *Pretty soon they'll prove the finest in the land.*
>
> *They come on combine harvesters, by bus, train and car*
> *And in every ground*
> *You will hear the sound as we shout*
> *Ooh ar ooh ar.*
>
> *One for the Bristol City*
> *Two for the boys in red*
> *Three for the fans down Ashton Gate*
> *We'll follow till we're dead me boys*
> *Follow till we're dead.*

Above chorus repeated three more times.

Cup Shocks

Season 1977-78 showed up the basic lack of ability in the side as Third Division Wrexham were played three times during the course of the campaign - once in the Football League Cup and twice in the F.A. Cup - with City being humiliated by their supposedly inferior opponents who won 1-0 and 3-0 at the Racecourse Ground as well as achieving a well merited 4-4 draw at Ashton Gate. This trend also displayed itself the following season when City were beaten in both cup competitions by Second Division Crystal Palace, going down 2-1 at Ashton Gate in the Football League Cup, and succumbing at Selhurst Park 3-0 in the F.A. Cup. In the League in these two campaigns the Robins finished seventeenth and thirteenth respectively, and such was their form at one stage in 1978-79, that the chance of a place in European competitions seemed a distinct possibility. The Anglo-Scottish Cup was won in 1977-78, when St. Mirren were beaten over two legs in the Final, by 2-1 at Love Street and then a rather fortunate 1-1 draw at Ashton Gate.

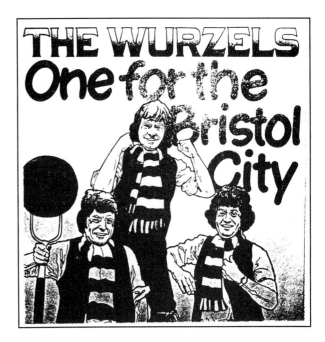

Rapid Decline

Relegation was City's fate at the end of 1979-80 when they finished third from bottom, despite being as high as sixth early on. Although they only suffered four defeats in the opening fourteen League matches, the warnings signs were apparent as the team was not playing well. Complacency and lack of ambition were undoubtably the major causes of the Club's decline, and it was unfortunate that a more vigorous 'buy and sell' policy wasn't pursued instead of giving lengthy contracts to existing players, many of whom were not of sufficient ability to be able to raise the stature of the Robins from a struggling, to a successful, First Division side. Such lack of ambition was amply demonstrated in the Football League Cup at Nottingham Forest on November 14th when the playing of a purely defensive game brought a deserved 3-0 defeat, this loss appearing to have such an effect on morale that only one League win was achieved during the intervening period to February 19th, this poor form causing City to drop to twentieth place. Salvation though was still a possibility when Norwich City came to Ashton Gate for the last home match of the campaign on April 26th, but in rather unluckily losing 3-2 to one of their bogey teams relegation became almost inevitable with two away fixtures left. Defeat at the Dell by 5-2 against Southampton on the following Thursday made demotion a fact, but a good performance at White Hart Lane on May 3rd produced a 0-0 draw with Tottenham Hotspur. This served to improve the Robins position by one place to twentieth, a placing that until the advent of three-up and three down seven years previously would have guaranteed survival.

Another Final

Limited success was achieved in the F.A. Cup this campaign as City suddenly found some form to beat fellow strugglers Derby County 6-2 in the Third Round on January 5th, but they found high fliers Ipswich Town a much more difficult proposition in going down 2-1 in the Fourth Round on January 26th. The Anglo-Scottish Cup though saw the Robins win through to the Final for the second time and finding themselves facing St. Mirren yet again. This time though the Scottish side gained revenge for losing the Final of two years previously as the men from Paisley won the 1st leg as Ashton Gate 2-0 and the return at Love Street 3-1.

Dismissal of Alan Dicks

Back in the Second Division for 1980-81 the Robins were quoted at 12-1 to make a quick return to the top flight, but such optimism was not shared by supporters or the local newspapers. The selling of Joe Royle - who had been signed from Manchester City and scored four goals on his Robins' debut against Middlesbrough at Ashton Gate on November

26th, 1977 - to Norwich City, was a prime factor in the side's poor start. This brought about the dismissal of Alan Dicks who at that time was the longest serving one-club Manager in the Football League. Assistant Manager Tony Collins and Coach Ken Wimshurst then took over the temporary running of the Club whilst the task of finding a new Manager was undertaken. This led to an approach to Norman Hunter who was assistant to Allan Clarke at Barnsley, but he turned the offer down on September 17th. City then turned their attention to Bob Houghton who had been in charge of Swedish club Malmo when they had reached the Final of the European Champions Cup in 1978-79, and he accepted the position. Houghton left the Greek club Ethnikos to start at Ashton Gate on September 29th.

Bristol Rovers At Ashton Gate

The new Manager couldn't however arrest the Club's slide, and the end of a campaign of perpetual struggle - that also saw the fight to reinstate Robert Hobbs flare up again - brought a further relegation in consequence of a final next to bottom placing. The Club beneath was Bristol Rovers, and this produced the first ever case of two teams from the same provincial city being relegated from the same division together, a fact which had it's own additional irony as, in consequence of the South Stand fire at Eastville Stadium, the Rovers shared the use of Ashton Gate early on in the campaign. This was the second such occasion that the Rovers had made use of facilities at Ashton Gate, the first in 1939-40 when the following Regional League fixtures were played:-

October 28th	Bristol Rovers 2 Newport County 3	1,186
November 25th	Bristol Rovers 1 Plymouth Argyle 2	1,311
December 9th	Bristol Rovers 1 Swansea Town 3	773
December 23rd	Bristol Rovers 2 Torquay United 2	704

The Rovers played five matches at Ashton Gate in 1980, three in the League and two in the Football League Cup, and these resulted as follows:-

August 30th	Bristol Rovers 2 Grimsby Town 2	4,461
September 3rd	Bristol Rovers 1 York City 0	3,047
(Football League Cup, 2nd Round, 2nd Leg - after extra time)		
September 16th	Bristol Rovers 0 Oldham Athletic 0	3,808
September 23rd	Bristol Rovers 0 Portsmouth 0	6,982
(Football League Cup, 3rd Round, 1st Leg)		
September 27th	Bristol Rovers 0 Newcastle United 0	5,171

Since 1980 the Rovers made one further use of Ashton Gate for a home fixture, on April 11th 1987, when they were beaten 4-3 by Swindon Town in a Third Division match watched by 8,196 spectators.

Cricket at Ashton Gate

The 1980-81 campaign also brought a return of cricket to Ashton Gate for the first time since the Bedminster Club vacated the ground. On September 17th, the second floodlit cricket match to be played in England took place when a crowd of 7,925 were in attendance to see a Rest of the World XI beat an England XI. This fixture helped to bring about the first Floodlit Cricket Championships, and Ashton Gate was the venue for the South West Zone matches that were played in terrible weather exactly twelve months later. On this latter evening Somerset beat Hampshire in the Zone Final, after disposing of Gloucestershire in the Semi-Final, in front of a disappointing small gathering of 1,539.

Lacrosse at Ashton Gate

Three years previously, on October 14th 1978, early arrivals at Ashton Gate for the game against Nottingham Forest had the opportunity to view yet another sport being played on the ground when they were treated to a special forty minute exhibition of Lacrosse. The English Women beat a Scottish & Welsh Womens side 15-3, this encounter adding to the many various events that have been staged at the venue. Included have been, 'All In The Game' in 1974, 1976 & 1977 (a competition devised by Bristol City and shown on I.T.V.), Athletic Meetings, Boxing Tournaments, Evangelical Meetings, Fairs, Gymnastic Displays, Pop Concerts as well as the playing of Rugby and Baseball that have been previously detailed.

Unenviable Task for Archie Gooch

The Boardroom battle that flared up again at Ashton Gate was brought about by a group of rebel shareholders lead by Lionel Amos and supported by Leslie Kew, Frederick Matthews, D. Squires and J. Drinkwater. But at a Shareholders Meeting held in the Supporters Club on December 22nd 1980, the rebels realised that they couldn't win, and withdrew their challenge. However nine days later, Stephen Kew, who had been Chairman for the three and a half years since the overthrow of Robert Hobbs, stood down from this position, though he remained on the Board. The new man at the helm, at what was to prove to be the most difficult period the Club had ever faced was Archie Gooch, a long standing City supporter who had been on the Board for less than a year. He was though President of the 'National Federation of Football Supporters Clubs', and it was hoped that this would bring about an improvement in public relations, this factor being a long standing problem with Bristol City, as with so many other clubs.

An Unenviable Record

With City finding themselves back in the Third Division for the first time in sixteen years, it was generally felt that the Club would now have the opportunity to stabilise itself and possibly make a bid for promotion - especially as Mike Harford was signed from Newcastle United just prior to the start of the campaign. Relegation therefore at the end of a season that saw the introduction of three points for a win came as another blow to the long suffering Robins supporters. Especially significant since relegation meant that Bristol City suffered the indignity of being the first club to tumble from the First to the Fourth Divisions in successive campaigns (this unenviable record since equalled by Wolverhampton Wanderers between 1982-86). Harford performed wonders at centre-forward without getting much support, and it was no surprise to the Ashton Gate faithful that when he went on to perform with other clubs and better players he was eventually selected for England.

The Ashton Gate Eight

However, not withstanding the poor performances on the field, the real drama of the campaign was the Robins worsening financial position which lead to the general public being informed on October 21st, 1981, that the Club was in debt by a figure in excess of £700,000. Following this announcement various funds, such as 'Friends of Bristol City', were set up, and a number of rescue packages discussed, but towards the end of January the situation was so bad that closure appeared imminent. Indeed many supporters went to see their favourites at Newport County on January 30th convinced that this would be the Club's last match, despite the attempts of Deryn Coller and Ken Sage to save the rather long in the tooth 'Bristol Babe'. Their plan in effect meant the re-birth of the Club, involving the start of a new organisation known as Bristol City (1982) Plc, to take over the running of the Club. This takeover was initially dependant on the acceptance of redundancy by eight players ('The Ashton Gate Eight'), who were on high wages and long contracts.

These players eventually agreed, an hour before the midday deadline on February 2nd, to accept an improved redundancy offer, this being the only way the Club could be saved from being compulsory wound up, and so cleared the path for the new organisation to take over in a temporary capacity the following day. This therefore brought to a premature close the Bristol City career of 'The Ashton Gate Eight', these being Peter Aitken, Chris Garland (who did however return and play on a match-by-match basis in 1982-83), Jimmy Mann, Julian Marshall, Geoff Merrick, David Rodgers, Gerry Sweeney and Trevor Tainton. These players all found other clubs to play out the season; Aitken to York City, Garland and Merrick to Hong Kong side Carolina Hill, Mann to Barnsley, Marshall to Blackburn Rovers, Rodgers to Torquay United and then onto Lincoln City, Tainton to Torquay United, plus Sweeney who had a brief stay at Trowbridge Town before joining York City. After the eventual winding up of the old Club these players shared £82,500, such money included the proceeds of a special match between Ipswich Town and Southampton played at Ashton Gate on Wednesday, March 24th, 1982, when 6,200 spectators saw the 'Saints' win 2-1. The others creditors of the Club were hopeful of receiving approximately 70p. in the pound.

In the Balance

The fate of the new organisation was, however, still in the balance as everything depended on the outcome of the share issue in April 1982. This only proved successful at the last, due to the injection of money from local businessmen, Bob Boyd, Bob Marshall, John Pontin and David Russe, which together with further investment from the Board members eventually ensured the survival of the fledgling Bristol City (1982) Plc. The new organisation now took over completely, and on Friday May 7th, the Company purchased the Ashton Gate ground from the old Club for £565,000.

Directors

The interim Directors had been:- Deryn Coller, Les Kew, Ken Sage, Ivor Williams and Olivier Newland, but following the first A.G.M. that was held at the Colston Hall, Bristol on Monday 21st June 1982, the Board that started the 1982-83 campaign comprised:- Des Williams (Chairman), Les Kew (Vice-Chairman), Bob Boyd, Deryn Coller, Bob Marshall, Olivier Newland, Ken Sage and Ivor Williams.

Financial Restraints

In consequence of the financial restraints incumbent on the new organisation, and the lack of players, the Reserve team resigned from the Football Combination on February 10th, 1982, their record of P18 W4 D4 L10 F21 A30 being expunged from the table. The players remaining at the Club had their registrations retained by the old company, even though it was the new organisation that paid their wages.

Apart from Swedish International goalkeeper Jan Moller, Welsh International defender Terry Boyle, ace goalscorer Mike Harford, and goalkeeper John Shaw, the remaining players were mainly untried youngsters. This led to the team being once again called 'The Babes', after a lapse of over thirty years, with the local press applauding them for achieving a deserved draw with promotion-chasing Fulham, in the first match of Bristol City (1982) PLC. Roy Hodgson, the Caretaker Manager who took over when Bob Houghton resigned following a 3-1 home defeat by Wimbledon on January 2nd 1982, was left with an unenviable task, but not daunted he signed on loan and short term transfers Aidan McCaffery from Bristol Rovers, Ray Gooding from Coventry City and Les Carter from Crystal Palace. Unfortunately the Football League would not allow the monthly contracts to be renewed and McCaffery and Gooding soon returned to their Clubs, a situation which together with the loss of Jan Moller on

(Above) The Evening Post of 5th February 1982 heralds the arrival of the 'new' Babes. (Below) Benefit match for the 'Ashton Gate Eight' (24th March).

IPSWICH
VERSUS
SOUTHAMPTON
TESTIMONIAL MATCH

WEDNESDAY 24th MARCH ASHTON GATE
7·30 KICK OFF · OFFICIAL PROGRAMME 30p

March 13th and Mick Harford on March 25th (sold by the old Company for £85,000 and £125,000 to Toronto Blizzards and Birmingham City respectively), resulted in no real surprise when relegation was the ultimate outcome.

Gerry Sharpe Interlude

Roy Hodgson, who had been Bob Houghton's assistant, was dismissed on April 30th when the new Company officially took over, and Gerry Sharpe, the ex-City player whose career had been cut short by injury and who was the Club's Youth Team Manager, took over for the remainder of the season. The team did well under his charge, only losing once in six outings, three games being won and two drawn. This record though didn't impress the Directors and rather than give Gerry Sharpe the opportunity he wished, they selected Terry Cooper as Player-Manager on May 19th.

Shirt Advertising

Before leave is taken of the traumatic 1981-82 Season it is worth noting that it also heralded the dubious benefits of shirt advertising. November 18th saw City appear with a sponsor's name emblazoned across the front of their shirts for the first time, this sponsorship by Park Furnishers lasting until the 23rd January 1982. The birth of Bristol City (1982) Plc brought forth new sponsors, and from March 27th the shirts carried the word 'Hirerite', and continued until the start of 1990-91, when 'Thorn' took over for three seasons.

City then brought their first century to a close bearing the legend 'Dry Blackthorn Cider', but started their 101st campaign with 'Auto Windscreens' as the sponsor.

Rolling Stones

The close season of 1982 brought forth a 35,123 crowd to Ashton Gate, but not for football, for the attraction on June 26th was a concert by the 'Rolling Stones'. It was only this event, together with 'Billy Graham's Crusade' when almost 250,000 attended the eight days from May 12th,

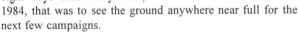

Jimmy Mann   &   Clive Whitehead
Long periods with the Club (1975-82 and 1973-81 respectively)

1984, that was to see the ground anywhere near full for the next few campaigns.

Rock Bottom

In the Fourth Division for the first time, in 1982-83, the Robins' early form did little to encourage the missing fans. Losing 7-1 at Northampton on September 19th was a shock to the faithful, but this was made worse when a 1-0 defeat at Rochdale on December 4th saw rock bottom being reached. City remained bottom of the pile until drawing 2-2 at Bury two weeks later, and an improvement over the rest of the season brought an eventual finishing position of fourteenth.

Promotion

Hopeful that the Club's decline had now been arrested a more optimistic atmosphere prevailed prior to the start of the 1983-84 campaign, and this was borne out by seven wins being gained in the opening eleven League matches, to put the Robins at the head of affairs. Unfortunately a reaction then set in and the next four games were lost, but only five more defeats during the remainder of the season brought City the final promotion spot behind York City (Champions), Doncaster Rovers and Reading. This success increased gate receipts from £144,144 to £265,645, including season tickets which increased from £35,739 to £40,076, and at the A.G.M. held on December 13th 1984, a profit of £32,089 was announced.

Strong Bid

A strong bid was made for promotion from the Third Division in 1984-85, but a negative approach in the local derby against the Rovers at Eastville Stadium on April 13th, following on from a 1-0 defeat in their previous away match at Plymouth, cost the ultimate prize. The Rovers game was played in a gale force wind, and City electing to play against it in the first-half, gave their rivals an indication of their lack of belief. It was no surprise therefore that all three points were lost, even though the players mistakenly thought they were there for the taking when the interval was reached with their goal intact. However, a good campaign saw the Robins finish in fifth place, and this led to them being installed as second favourites to Derby County for promotion in 1985-86.

Success at Wembley

A terrible start with five successive defeats, including one in the Football League Cup, deposited City at the bottom of the table, but the team recovered to claim ninth position at the season's conclusion. The highlight of the campaign was the progress of the Robins to reach the Final of the 'Freight Rover Trophy' a competition for Third and Fourth Division Clubs. Saturday May 24th 1986, found the City at 'Wembley Stadium' for the first time to face the famous 'Trotters' of Bolton Wanderers, who were making their sixth appearance at this venue. City were the favourites by virtue of their higher League placing, and they were also considered to be Bolton's bogey side. Not wishing to dispel the notion of being a jinx side to the Trotters, the Robins took the trophy winning 3-0. However, this scoreline does not do justice to the endeavours of Bolton in what was a fine entertaining game, which reflected great credit - not only on the players - but also to the supporters of both sides, a great day being had by all.

This success, coupled with the signing of centre-half John McPhail from York City and winger Gordon Owen from Barnsley in the close-season, made City the bookmakers favourites for promotion in 1986-87. This campaign was the first to involve a promotion play-off system, the first change since the implementation of three-up and three-down between the First, Second and Third Divisions in 1973-74. However, the Robins only flattered to deceive, just doing enough to keep the supporters hopes alive for a promotion play-off position, thanks to a good home record that saw only three defeats.

A Near Miss

Away from home though it was a different story - a reasonable return of seventeen points prior to the turn of the year, followed by poor form and only a further ten points in the remaining twelve fixtures. An unexpected home defeat by a well organised Brentford team on April 28th looked to have destroyed all hopes of City taking part in the play-offs, but slip-ups by other contenders enabled the Robins to reach the final day of the League season in fifth place. With home advantage over Swindon Town it was confidently expected that the requisite win would be achieved. After taking an early lead City were unable to put the game beyond the visitors reach and sloppy defensive work allowed the Wiltshire Club to draw level mid-way through the second-half. The City kept up the pressure and thirteen minutes from time they were presented with a golden opportunity - a penalty being awarded after Jordan was tripped. Owen stepped up to take the kick, after a long delay occasioned by Swindon's protests, and as City fans held their breath, the ball was driven wide of the post at the covered end. This failure, coupled with Gillingham's win over Bolton, sent the City down to sixth place, and prevented them from taking part in these historic play-offs.

Match to Remember

Bristol City 3 Hereford United 0
Freight Rover Trophy Southern Area Final 2nd Leg
Friday, 9th May 1986.

After an hour of this match, the Robins looked unable to make any impression on Hereford's 2-0 lead from the 1st Leg three days earlier. The chances of the homesters reaching the National Final at Wembley Stadium appeared remote in the extreme, but an error by the visitors goalkeeper Kevin Rose, who up to then had performed heroics, let a tame header by **Glyn Riley** slip through his hands after sixty-two minutes. This brought the City renewed hope.

The City started the game in determined mood, and having bombarded the Hereford goal without success in the first-half it was beginning to look as though they were never destined to score. Then their luck changed with a vengeance, and two minutes after taking the lead the Robins levelled the aggregate scores. Howard Pritchard, after receiving a pass from skipper Bobby Hutchinson, sent over a fierce cross shot that was deflected into the net off the unfortunate **Mel Pejic**.

United however were not dismayed and they were unfortunate when a great shot by Ian Wells hit the crossbar after seventy minutes, and then two minutes from the end of normal time Chris Price went close to snatching a Wembley place for them, but his shot went inches wide.

During the first period of extra-time, the Robins lost the ever dangerous Pritchard who had to hobble off with calf-trouble (being replaced by Gary Marshall). It seemed Hereford might snatch the victory, when three minutes before the end Paul Maddy found himself unmarked inside the penalty area with the goal at his mercy, and it certainly appeared all up for the homesters. But Keith Waugh in goal stood his ground and then dived to the left to parry a powerful shot, to keep the tie perfectly balanced, and a penalty shoot out seemingly inevitable.

However, the City were not yet done, and in the dying seconds Steve Neville scored a superbly taken goal at the Covered End, Alan Walsh crossing from the left and Hutchinson heading down for **Neville** to calmly control the ball before steering in his 25th goal of the season. This took the Robins to Wembley for the first time with an aggregate score of 3-2. An emotional exciting game that will live long in the memory but in the midst of the euphoria of the moment it was impossible not to feel sympathy for a Hereford side whose neat football always threatened on the break.

City: Waugh; Newman, Williams, Curle, Moyes, Riley, Pritchard (Marshall 101 minutes), Hutchinson, Harle (Llewellyn 60 minutes), Walsh, Neville.

United: Rose; Price, Dalziel, Pejic, Cegielski, Delve, Harvey, Maddy, Wells (Beacock 105 minutes), Kearns, Carter.

Referee: Ray Lewis (Surrey) Attendance: 11,558
(Source: Bristol Evening Post, Saturday, 10th May, 1986.)

Another Costly Penalty Failure

The supporters looked for solace in the Freight Rover Trophy as the Robins had won through to 'Wembley' for the second year running, but in this they were to be cruelly disappointed. With the Final being played on a Sunday on this occasion, the match with Mansfield Town took place on the same date as the previous year, and City were again hot favourites. However the hand of fate decried that this time the outcome would be different, even though City were given a reprieve by obtaining a late equaliser (Glyn Riley 86 minutes) against a superior Mansfield combination. After the playing of extra-time in which both sides had opportunities to win in front of a new record Freight Rover crowd of 58,586, the contest went to the first ever penalty shoot-out to decide a Wembley Final. Fate had the last laugh, as another failure by Gordon Owen prevented what would have been a rather fortunate success. City started the penalty competition, and were successful with their first four through Brian Williams, Rob Newman, John McPhail and Keith Curle. Meanwhile Mansfield only notched three by Kearney, Stringfellow and Pollard (Cassells having their second saved by Keigh Waugh), and City had the opportunity to win when Owen strode up to take his side's last kick in the best of 'five' shoot-out. He decided to blast the ball which was heading for the middle of the goal, hit goalkeeper Hitchcock's feet, and was deflected over the bar.

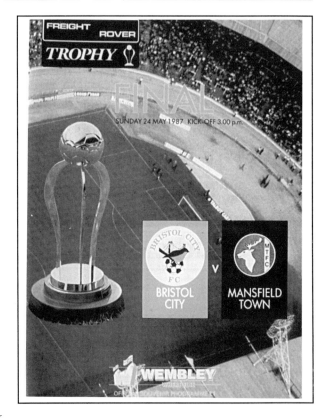

Mansfield then made use of their reprieve to tie up the first part of the penalty competition at 4-4 when Kevin Kent duly dispatched his kick to take the contest into sudden death. This didn't take long as David Moyes had his effort saved by Hitchcock, leaving Tony Kenworthy to secure the trophy for the 'Stags', an honour that their better football had deserved.

City: Waugh; Newman, Williams, Moyes, McPhail, Llewellyn (Fitzpatrick 105 mins), Owen, Walsh (Curle 70 mins), Riley, Marshall, Jordan.

Mansfield: Hitchcock; Graham, Garner, Lowery, Foster, Kenworthy, Kent, Danskin (Pollard 90 mins), Whatmore (Stringfellow 66 mins), Cassells, Kearney.

Referee: Allan Gunn (Burgess Hill, Sussex).

Attendance: 58,586 (£324,592).

Supporters Player of the Year

This award had been instigated in 1970-71 when Gerry Sharpe was the first recipient, and other winners have been:-

1971-72 Geoff Merrick	1972-73 John Emanuel
1973-74 Gerry Gow	1974-75 Gary Collier
1976-76 The Whole Team	1976-77 Norman Hunter
1977-78 Norman Hunter	1978-79 Gerry Gow
1979-80 Geoff Merrick	1980-81 Kevin Mabbutt
1981-82 No Award	1982-83 Glyn Riley
1984-85 Alan Walsh	1985-86 Bobby Hutchinson
1986-87 Rob Newman	1987-88 Alan Walsh
1988-89 Keith Waugh	1989-90 Bob Taylor
1990-91 Andy Llewellyn	1991-92 Martin Scott
1992-93 Keith Welch	1993-94 Wayne Allison

Two of the early recipients

The Junior Reds also have their own award. Winners have included Alan Walsh, 1987-88, Keigh Waugh, 1988-89, Dave Smith in 1989-90 & 1990-91, Jacki Dziekanowski in 1991-92, Keith Welch in 1992-93 and Wayne Allison in 1993-94.

Farewell Terry Cooper

Strongly fancied for promotion in 1987-88 the City had a chance for quick revenge over Mansfield, where they opened the new campaign. The Stags however proved their performance at Wembley was no fluke as they won 2-0, and completed the double at Ashton Gate later in the season by inflicting a 2-1 defeat. Not deterred by this initial setback, the Robins attained top place in the Third Division table on September 29th after a run of nine League games without this experience being repeated. But more fluctuating form throughout the rest of the season brought a decline from an automatic promotion slot, though a place was secured in the play-offs. Poor form brought Terry Cooper's reign as Manager to an end on March 15th, the decision to sack him amazing the majority of City supporters who were beginning to think that the job was his for as long as he wanted it. He was popular with most of the fans who enjoyed his appearances for the team during his first three years in charge when he was Player-manager, and he created a bit of football history when he became Britain's first Player-director. He was appointed as Manager of Exeter City on May 9th, 1988, guiding them to the Fourth Division Championship in 1989-90, and resigned in August 1991 when he took over at Birmingham City. At St. Andrews he secured promotion as Third Division Runners-up in 1991-92, but being unable to achieve much success in the higher reaches of the Football League he resigned in November 1993 and re-joined Exeter later in the season.

Into the Play-Offs

Joe Jordan the Assistant Manager took over on a temporary basis, but in breathing new fire into the team got them into the play-offs with only two defeats in the eleven games up to the end of the League season; he was confirmed as Player-manager on May 10th. The Semi-final of the play-offs brought City into two-legged confrontation with Second Division Sheffield United, and a well earned 1-0 victory at Ashton Gate on May 15th set the scene for a difficult encounter at Bramall Lane three days later. A battling performance and a first-half goal from Carl Shutt gained City a 1-1 draw, to progress into the Final to face a Walsall side that had drawn both League encounters with the Robins during the course of the season. Ashton Gate was the venue for the 1st leg on May 25th when two late goals by David Kelly, who so often had been a thorn in the Robins side, gave the Saddlers an unexpected 3-1 success, and left most City supporters thinking that their favourites were out of it. The Manager and players though had different thoughts, and in winning the 2nd leg 2-0 at Fellow Park on May 28th the scene was set for a deciding match. Another penalty shoot-out gave the Saddlers ground advantage for the replay on May 30th, and whilst City were confident prior to the game, they found themselves unable to cope in the first-half.

The End of a Dream

In the space of eight minutes, three goals flew into the Robins nest. David Kelly struck twice - after eleven minutes and again on seventeen - followed by a strike from Phil Hawker soon after, to put the Saddlers firmly in control. City made some isolated attempts to come back either side of the interval, but that man again, David Kelly, settled the issue with a fine run and cross shot into the Hillary Street goal after sixty-four minutes, to give the Saddlers a 4-0 win and clinch the promotion prize, in front of 13,007 spectators.

Walsall: Barber; Taylor, Dornan (M.Jones 55 mins), Shakespeare, Forbes, Goodwin (Sanderson 71 mins), Hawker, Hart, Christie, Kelly, Naughton.

City: Waugh, Llewellyn, Newman, Humphries, Pender, McClaren, Milne, Galliers, Shutt, Walsh, Jordan.

Referee: George Courtney (Spennymoor).

Marathon Tie

Joe Jordan's first full season in charge brought disappointment in the League with City only managing eleventh place, but much interest was aroused by performances in the two major cup competitions. The F.A. Cup saw the Robins engaged in a marathon contest with Aldershot in the Second Round, this going to three replays before City squeezed through by 1-0, only to lose by the same score at Hartlepool in the next round.

Record Run

It was the Football League Cup though that provided the highlights, as City progressed through to the Semi-Finals for the second time, creating a record in the process as the Robins were the first club to win seven successive games to reach this stage of the competition.

The 1st leg of the Semi-Final saw the City take a sixty-fifth minute lead through Paul Mardon at Nottingham Forest, but an own goal by Paul Pender set up an interesting contest for the 2nd leg at Ashton Gate on February 26th. A crowd of 28,084 paying record receipts of £97,097 were present on this wet and windy day to see a dour contest that City could have won right at the end of normal time, when a shot from Alan Walsh hit the left hand post of the Covered End goal. This escape for Forest took the game into extra-time, and the visitors in scoring through Gary Parker six minutes from the end prevented yet another penalty shoot-out.

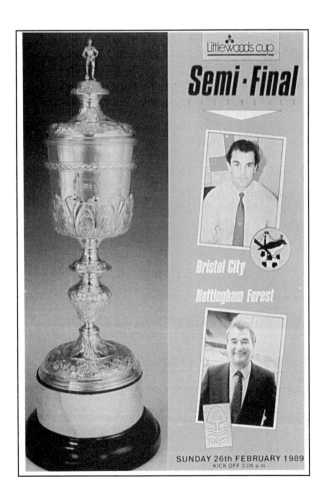

SUNDAY 26th FEBRUARY 1989
KICK OFF 3.06 p.m.

Promotion at Last

The 1989-90 season brought promotion at last when City put together many great performances to reach a grand total of ninety-one points. This should have been enough to secure the Championship, but on this occasion the one club to have secured more points in the whole Football League was in the same division, so the Robins had to be content with the Runners-up spot. Unfortunately the 'other' club happened to be Bristol Rovers, a fact that made missing out on the Championship more frustrating than would normally have been the case! City however had only themselves to blame as the Championship appeared all sown up when they beat Fulham 5-1 on April 16th, but only one win in the remaining five games gave an opportunity for the Rovers to take over. A gutless performance at Twerton Park, when City succumbed to a 3-0 defeat on May 2nd, took Rovers to pole position. This particularly annoyed a section of Robins' fans, who looked as though they would bring disgrace on the Club, until Joe Jordan did a great job in helping restore order.

Great Win

The F.A. Cup brought a great 3-1 win over Chelsea in the Fourth Round, and presented the City with a home tie against Fourth Division Cambridge United. Unfortunately Cambridge surprised the majority of the 20,676 crowd at Ashton Gate on February 17th, with the quality of their football, and in gaining a deserved draw the stage was set for another marathon, though this time it was only to involve two more meetings. The first replay took place four days later, when a goal from Bob Taylor gained City a 1-1 draw after the playing of extra-time, but in the second replay, also at Cambridge, the Robins were annihilated 5-1.

Death of Dean Horrix

The season was saddened by the unfortunate death of Dean Horrix, a player City had signed from Millwall only a few weeks before. Returning as a passenger in a car driven by his wife from an evening with friends in celebration of his move, the vehicle went out of control on a bend on the A340 near his home at Tadley, in the early hours of March 11th. He died instantly when the car hit a tree, and firemen took forty-five minutes to free Mrs. Horrix, who sustained a badly damaged hand. A collection at Ashton Gate on March 17th raised £6,772 for his widow, this sum being added to the proceeds from a Benefit Match that took place at Millwall on May 9th.

Lack of Ambition

Back in the Second Division for 1990-91, City opened in fine form, not suffering their first defeat until going down 2-1 at West Bromwich Albion on September 15th. However events in the first part of the campaign were overshadowed by the resignation of Manager Joe Jordan, only a month after signing a new three year contract. This shock news was announced on September 19th, and many thought his move to Scottish club Heart of Midlothian was in consequence of lack of ambition by the Directors of Bristol City Football Club. Jordan's assistant, Jimmy Lumsden, was appointed Acting Manager, and the team responded with three successive wins, including a fine 1-0 victory at Sunderland in the Football League Cup.

Defeat to Bristol Rovers by 2-3 at Twerton Park on 21st December 1991.

Lumsden was confirmed in the role as manager on October 8th, the day before City suffered their record Football League Cup defeat when they succumbed 6-1 at Ashton Gate to Sunderland in the 2nd leg of their Second Round tie.

Death of Des Williams

In the League the team performed quite well, and they were in the running for a place in the play-offs throughout the campaign, but eventually had to settle for a commendable ninth place. The season though was marred by the sudden death of Chairman Des Williams on February 23rd. He was sixty-six years of age and had suffered a heart attack whilst getting ready to attend City's home game with Oxford United that day. He was succeeded by Leslie Kew, another who had done much to save the Club from oblivion in 1982.

Goodbye Jimmy Lumsden

After starting 1991-92 with only one defeat in the first eight League games, form declined to such an extent that the City were later in serious danger of relegation. In consequence Manager Jimmy Lumsden was dismissed, together with his assistant Tony Taylor, on February 24th, and senior players Mark Aizlewood, Russell Osman and Gary Shelton were put in temporary charge whilst a new manager was sought. This search resulted in ex-Sunderland boss Denis Smith being appointed on March 9th, and it was due to

Joe Jordan

Rob Newman left City in 1991, after 10 years and 387 League appearances.

his astute dealings in the transfer market, obtaining the services of Leroy Rosenior from Fulham and Andy Cole on loan from Arsenal, that survival was achieved with an end of season placing of seventeenth. Unfortunately some of his other transfer acquisitions, in Ray Atteveld from Everton on March 25th for a new Club record fee of £250,000, David Thompson from Millwall in exchange for Andy May on June 18th, and Brian Mitchell from Bradford City on July 2nd, were less successful. This factor, which together with the implementation of a defensive formation that the players seemingly didn't have the ability to operate, was to produce problems reminiscent of the split camp era of 1959-60. He did however appreciate the worth of Andy Cole, and pulled off a great coup in persuading Arsenal to part with this talented player on July 14th, when he had to raise the Club record fee to £500,000.

Premier League

The 1992-93 season brought a real upheaval to the structure of English Football with the Football League being supplanted at the pinnacle of the game by the F.A. Premier League. The formation of this - in many people's eyes - totally unnecessary 'new' League could have been stopped if the Football Association had refused to sanction it, or made it operate at the base of the football 'pyramid'. It can be seen that such a move would have denied the greedy clubs, who were the instigators in the formation

Kenilworth Road, 22nd August 1992 (a 3-0 victory).
City's Leroy Rosenior challenges Luton's Julian James.

of this League, entry in European competition and exemption from the early stages of the F.A. Cup. Unfortunately the F.A. chose to side with the rebel clubs, a situation which to many supporters minds, was akin to 'bringing the game into disrepute'.

False Status

This new structure brought a change to the Football League, with the loss of their top twenty-two clubs, and the rest of the competition was restructured. The remaining three divisions had their status enhanced, and all the clubs became full members, this honour only being previously accorded to those in the top two divisions. Bristol City therefore found themselves a First Division Club once again, but now the goal was to gain promotion to the Premier League.

Farewell Denis Smith

Apart from a brilliant display in the 5-1 success over Cardiff City in the Football League Cup on August 25th, and the entertainment offered in a 3-3 draw with Portsmouth on the opening day of the League campaign, there was little to enthuse over during 1992-93. Heavy consecutive defeats at home to West Ham United and away to Newcastle, just after City gained a fortuitous 4-3 win at Derby, heralded the problems to come, and it wasn't long before the Robins were descending into the relegation zone. Another poor performance at Twerton Park brought a 4-0 defeat versus the 'old enemy' on December 13th, this being the third match in a sequence of twelve without a win, and by the time of the Third Round of the F.A. Cup on January 19th, the pressure was really on Manager Denis Smith. Unfortunately the away tie with Luton Town brought a further disaster with the

sending off of Martin Scott contributing to a 2-0 defeat. Within two days Denis Smith was dismissed, having only completed ten months of a three year contract, and to the surprise of most, his assistant in the failures of the season took over in a temporary capacity. Russell Osman though took the opportunity presented, and in steering the Club to safety - despite being obliged to sale Andy Cole - he reaped the reward of a 3 year managerial contract, which he signed on May 1st.

Farewell 'King Cole'

The selling of Andy Cole gave a further indication to many Bristol City supporters of the Club's apparent lack of ambition and poor business acumen. Newcastle had been after Cole for some time, a fact which together with the exciting potential of the player and the upward movement of transfer fees served to make the Club record fee of £1¾ million that was agreed, being well below what should have been collected.

This poor judgement was made even worse when it was later revealed that the full payment would not be made for twelve months. The timing of the transfer was also poorly arranged with no thought as to City's status, letting him move on the day prior to a crucial relegation battle at Birmingham City, and given the fact that Newcastle were not playing that weekend, appeared foolhardy in the extreme. As luck would have it though a 1-0 win was achieved at St. Andrews on March 13th, thanks to a strike by Nicky Morgan, and the Directors were therefore spared any embarrassing questions in this regard.

European Competition

The campaign saw the Robins engaged in European competition for the first time, in the Anglo-Italian Cup. This competition which had operated in the early 1970's was resurrected and revamped this season to take over from the Full Members (Zenith Data Systems) Cup. City qualified for the International stage of the tournament but disappointed in their matches with Italian Second Division clubs; both home games were lost, and a 2-2 draw at Cremonese was the best result.

Boardroom Conflict

The close season of 1993 hardly filled the fans with much optimism for the campaign ahead, the signings of Ian Baird from Heart of Midlothian and Liam Robinson from Bury doing little to suggest that the goalscoring void created by the departure of Andy Cole was going to be filled. More importantly though indications of Boardroom conflict were coming to light following on from the resignation of Ivor Williams who then sold his 5% holding of 'foundation shares' to the Supporters Club for £35,000. Apparently a bitter power battle had been waging for the best part of eighteen months, and with the Football Association having announced on May 18th that they would be holding an Inquiry into the Club's actions in respect of monies claimed from the Football Trust for ground improvements it was apparent that the rebels were just awaiting their opportunity.

The Reform Group

These rebels, calling themselves the 'Reform Group', officially announced their bid for power on September 30th and issued their blueprint for the future, 'The Way To Win!' five days later. The Reform Group consisted Mike Fricker (a member of the existing Board), Deryn Coller (a recent member of the Board), Peter Burchill, John Clapp and David Russe. It was revealed that Deryn Coller had resigned from the Board in March 1993 because (according to Reform Group literature) he was unable to accept the financial irregularities that were taking place, and because he was unable to change things due to the block vote of the four Directors they were seeking to remove. His resignation following the advice of a leading Barrister who, having seen the evidence of the financial irregularities in question, stated to him quite clearly that to stay on the Board would make him as guilty as those persons who had actually committed or sanctioned them. However, Mr. Fricker felt that he had a duty to stay, feeling that he should protect those who had brought to his attention the matters that had led to the Inquiry. The Board sought to make an issue over Mr. Coller's resignation, questioning his commitment as he had also resigned in 1983, after being a member of the original Board of the new Club. But many supporters remembered the huge amount of work put in by Mr. Coller to save the Club in 1982.

Extraordinary General Meeting

However this particular issue didn't apparently concern the 2,200 small shareholders of the Club (accounting for 30% of the vote) of whom about 1,000 crowded into Whitchurch Sports Centre, Bristol, on the evening of Friday, November 12th, for an Extraordinary General Meeting to decide the fate of the opposing parties. A substantial number of those present did not appear to be impressed by the case for either faction,

and there was obvious concern over the fact that the Reform Group had no proposals for the injection of cash into the Club. Decisions had to be made however, and in the end it appeared that, apart from the commitment in respect of the Club's future progress, the issue the Reform Group had used to make their bid for power was the overriding factor. Earlier in the day the Football Association announced the result of their Inquiry into City's use of grants from the Football Trust, and the fact that a guilty verdict was passed made it unlikely that the Board would be able to retain control.

F.A. Inquiry

This F.A. Inquiry had culminated in a seven hour hearing at the Park Hotel, London, on November 9th when the three man commission, headed by Southampton Vice-Chairman Keith Wiseman, and supported by Alan Turvey, a divisional member from Hayes, and Barry Bright of the Kent F.A., interviewed City Chairman Leslie Kew, as well as taking evidence from Commercial Manager John Cox, Secretary Jean Harrison, Stadium Manager Dave Lewis, and Dave Fear who represented the Company that carried out the floodlighting work at Ashton Gate. Following the guilty verdict a five hour disciplinary hearing was held at 'Lancaster Gate' on November 26th, and this resulted in Mr. Kew being banned from soccer for nine months, and the Club being fined £40,000 (£30,000 suspended for two years) for cash irregularities.

The Reform Group Take Over

As was expected the Reform Group won the battle for power, the results being announced on Monday, November 15th as follows:-

To remove Leslie Kew:	For 19,880 against 14,690
To remove Oliver Newland:	For 19,806 against 14,753
To remove Peter Manning:	For 19,771 against 14,773
To remove Ken Sage:	For 19,872 against 14,678
To re-elect Mike Fricker:	For 19,991 against 14,439
To elect Peter Burchill:	For 19,819 against 14,562
To elect John Clapp:	For 19,888 against 14,494
To elect Deryn Coller:	For 19,845 against 14,572
To elect David Russe:	For 19,856 against 14,497.

New Board

The new Board met on the same afternoon as the results were announced. David Russe being elected Chairman, with Mike Fricker as his deputy, and Supporters Club Chairman Gary Williams being co-opted to the body. A statement was then issued in which it said that *"We must now start the task of rebuilding bridges which have been broken. We must start the task of uniting this great club, it's staff and it's supporters, so that we can now surge forward to one common goal"*. A laudable statement, but a pity that despite such intent the new Board felt compelled to ban Leslie Kew from Ashton Gate in order to avoid breaching the F.A.'s suspension order. However, a ruling by the F.A. allowed the board to revoke the ban.

Only Thirteenth

The City were in eighth position in the table when the new Board took over, and their declared ambitions for the progress of the Club in the time scale proposed by themselves was, on the face of it, looking decidedly optimistic with a slump to thirteenth place at the campaign's end. This bland statement of the bare facts does however conceal developments that hopefully will auger well for the future. In all 1st team competitions a Club record of thirty-eight players made appearances, amongst them a number of youngsters who seized the unexpected early opportunity and impressed many with their potential.

Firm and Decisive

Manager Russell Osman found himself placed in an unenviable situation during the Boardroom conflict, but he impressed all with the way he got on with his job, and whilst many of his decisions were unpopular with the fans he has shown with his firm and decisive manner, that he had the attributes to make a success in the role.

Cup Success at Anfield

It was in the F.A. Cup that the Robins demonstrated their potential, and whilst their run came to a disappointing halt in a Fifth Round Replay at the 'Valley', where they lost 2-0 to Charlton Athletic (another bogey team), the magnificent performance in beating Liverpool at Anfield in a Third Round Replay suggests the catalyst for change that was ignited by City's other previous cup success of this magnitude, when they beat Leeds in 1974, could well operate again.

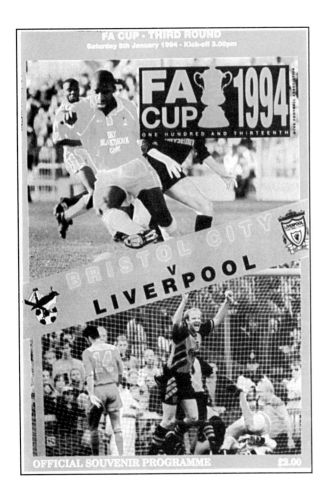

Football Council

The new Board were busy behind the scenes, and as promised in their blueprint for the future they implemented greater supporters' involvement in the Club by forming the Bristol City Football Council. This new body was set up in January and it consisted of representatives from all organisations affiliated to the Club, and selected representatives from various sections of the ground. Among the items discussed by this Council have been stadium facilities, spectator behaviour, reduced prices for children, the unemployed, improvements to the inadequate match programme etc. This helped bring about more 'Quid-A-Kid' days - against Oxford United, Grimsby Town, Watford and Luton Town - following on from the initial one when Wolverhampton Wanderers were the visitors on December 18th.

New Stand

Work on the new stand at the 'Open (Park) End' was due to have commenced on September 13th, but planning delays and the Boardroom changes meant that a start wasn't made until six months later on March 14th. The terrace at this end was last used for the match with Derby County on March 5th, and this meant that for the rest of the season the away supporters were accommodated in Blocks A & B of the Dolman Stand. Originally it was suggested that this new structure was just going to be called the 'North Stand', but eventually, on April 26th, came the news that City supporters wanted to hear. The Stand was to be named in memory of John Atyeo who had died from a heart attack, at the age of 61, on June 8th, 1993. A fitting tribute to a man who became a legend during his time as a player at Ashton Gate.

Hundred Up!

The Club ended their first hundred years of existence by beating Grimsby Town 1-0 at Ashton Gate on April 9th, thanks to Martin Scott registering with a last kick penalty, and then started activities for their second hundred years by gaining a rather fortuitous 2-2 draw with Birmingham City at St. Andrews seven days later. All this unfortunately passed by without any acknowledgement from the present custodians of Bristol City Football Club, of the significance of their April 12th birthdate, and the credit that is due to the founders of the Club a hundred years ago.

Tour of Zimbabwe

The conclusion of the hundredth campaign saw the team off on a three match eleven day tour of Zimbabwe, where a 2-1 win was achieved over Zimbabwean League Champions Highlanders on May 22nd, before a 2-1 victory and a scoreless draw was accomplished against a Select XI on May 27th and Dynamos two days later respectively.

The Shape of Things to Come?

At Ashton Gate the campaign had ended on May 9th when defender Andy Llewellyn had his Benefit Match. Swindon Town provided the opposition, but the real attraction for the 5,032 spectators was seeing Andy Cole, Jacki Dziekanowski and Joe Jordan appearing in City shirts again. An entertaining

Dynamos (Zimbabwe) 2 Bristol City 2 - 30th May 1994.
Chunga is sandwiched between Robinson (no. 8) and Munro.

Andy Llewellyn

3-3 draw was played out, but early arrivals were treated to the skills of womens soccer, and who knows perhaps this is where the future of the game lies, given the ever increasing salaries paid out to the many second rate players that inhabit the modern game.

Womens Soccer

The womens match saw a Bristol City side, that had been adopted by the Club the previous season, easily beat a Bristol Rovers team 6-0.

This was the second such game between the two at Ashton Gate, the first having taken place on May 16th the year before, when City won 2-0 in front of more than 1,000 fans. City's link up with womens football wasn't very successful in the initial season as the team, after a good start, ended up being relegated from Division One of the South West Regional League, but 1993-94 was crowned with honours.

The team won all of their twelve League games, scoring a massive total of 104 goals, and conceding only 8, on their way to taking the Second Division Championship. They also won the Division Two League Cup, and their Reserves reached the Final of the Division Three League Cup.

Midsummer's Dream

It is pleasant to dream that the male players might emulate some of this success next season, especially as Bristol City have not won a Championship for almost forty years, but despite the promise of the youngsters it appears unlikely that much advancement will be made without major investment in the transfer market. Hope however springs eternal for the supporters of the 'Bristol Babe' who has always proved a lusty infant, and it is anticipated that a satisfactory addition will be made to the substantial contribution the Club has already made to the history of football, as embarkation is made on their 101st campaign.

****

BEDMINSTER PARK: (Southville A.F.C. 1887-1889)

Southville's home was a public park and today it is known as Greville Smyth Park. It is situated on Ashton Road, directly opposite the present Ashton Gate Stadium. Other names by which this venue has been known include Peoples Park and Ashton Park.

****

GREENWAY BUSH-LANE: (Bedminster A.F.C. 1889-1896)

When Southville became the football section of Bedminster Cricket Club in 1889, they changed their name and moved to the cricket ground in Greenway Bush Lane, Southville. Also known as the Coronation Road Ground, it was situated on the right-hand side of the lane when approached from North Street, on an area of land between Greenway Bush Lane and Raleigh Road, and on which was later built a factory for the tobacco firm of Messrs. W.D. & H.O. Wills.

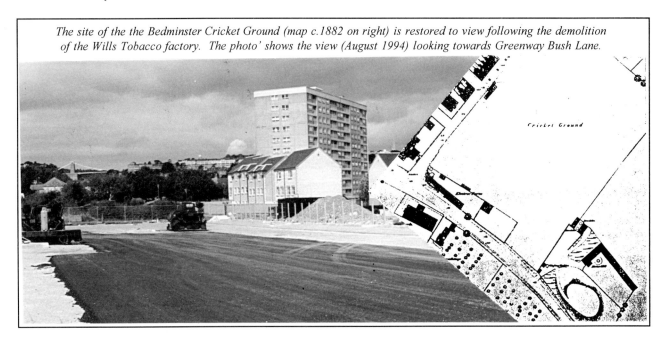

The site of the the Bedminster Cricket Ground (map c.1882 on right) is restored to view following the demolition of the Wills Tobacco factory. The photo' shows the view (August 1994) looking towards Greenway Bush Lane.

This move allowed the footballers to take gate-money, but there was a considerable drawback. Each February the best playing area had to be vacated so that it could be made ready for the cricket season, and this meant that the footballers had to conclude their season at the far end of the ground where the field had a considerable slope.

Initially spectators facilities were limited, but for important matches a temporary grandstand was erected. In 1894 it was decided to build a permanent structure and on December the 22nd when Bedminster Reserves lost 1-0 to Warmley Reserves in the Semi-Final of the Gloucestershire Junior Cup it was in use for the first time. Other facilities at this venue included tennis courts and a miniature bowling green.

****

ST. JOHN'S LANE:
(Bristol South End/Bristol City A.F.C. 1894-1904)

This ground, which was leased from the Trustees of the Ashton Court Estate, was little more than an enclosed field in it's early days, but gradually it was developed and by the 1897-98 campaign a grandstand to seat five hundred spectators had been erected on the south-west side of the ground. At this time there was also banking behind both goals, and during the following season further improvements were made, these included the enclosing of the pitch with white painted wooden railings.

The 1899 close season saw the banking at the ends of the ground increased, the fitting of glass to the sides of the grandstand to protect patrons from the wind, installation of hot-baths in the dressing-rooms, and the erection of a flag-pole on a corner of the Grandstand so that a silk flag in the Club's colours (a gift of Chairman W.P. Kingston) could be flown.

In the early days at St. John's Lane, revenue was lost to the Club when spectators climbed what was known as Mutton Hill at one end of the ground and enjoyed a free view. This vantage point on what is now known as Windmill Hill was dubbed 'scroungers gallery', and the Club responded by blocking out the view with canvas sheets hoisted on a number of 30ft high poles on match days. The sheets themselves then became a source of additional revenue when they were used as advertising hoardings.

Bristol City only held a short lease on St. John's Lane and with the need to improve the standard of accommodation, an approach was made to the Ashton Court Estate Trustees during the 1903-04 campaign for an extension of the lease for another ten years. Mr. H.B. Napier, the Steward of the Trustees, held out no hope and suggested the possibility of moving to Ashton Gate where fourteen games had been played in 1900-01, following the amalgamation with Bedminster. The Directors being therefore unable to improve on a lease that contained a clause whereby the Trustees could, on giving six months notice, take away one-third of the ground - such area including where the Grandstand was sited - felt unable to justify any further outlay at this venue. In consequence it was decided to act upon Mr. Napier's suggestion, and meetings were held with the Bedminster Athletic Ground Company, with whom agreement was reached

Advert from the 'Bristol Times and Mirror' (an early match for the 'new' Bristol City - 20 September 1897)

for the Football Club to take over the lease on 1st May 1904. The Trustees were happy for City to vacate St. John's Lane at the same time, and accordingly the last Bristol City match on the ground took place on April 30th, when the First Team beat the Reserves - who had just won the Bristol Charity League and the Western League Division Two titles - 3-2.

Above: ('Bristol Observer') A view of the St. John's Lane Grandstand during the City v. Notts County match, 12 February 1898
Below: c.1902 map of the St.John's Lane ground

This did not, however, see the end of St. John's Lane as a sporting venue. Bristol Rugby Union Football Club played two trial matches there at the start of the following season, and today this venue is known as the Robinson Athletic Sports Ground, where the works team stages Somerset Senior League football. Even Bristol City made further use of the ground, holding the Club's Annual Sports there on September 10th, 1904, this being the sixth such event, the first being held on August 12th, 1899, and the Bristol City Wednesday team played at this venue between 1908 and 1912. Originally the pitch ran lengthways from St. John's Lane, but now two pitches are accommodated which run parallel with the road.

When Bristol South End and Bristol City used St. John's Lane the facilities included provision for the playing of lawn tennis and bowls, and just outside the ground, running parallel with the south west side, was a rifle range. The record of the 274 Bristol South End - City First Team matches played at St. John's Lane is:- 187 won, 31 drawn, and 56 lost, with 784 goals for and 391 against, such details not including the home fixture which was lost 3-2 against Street on March 9th, 1895, as this match was brought off on the ground of the Waverley Club, behind the Talbot public House on the Wells Road in the Bristol district of Knowle.

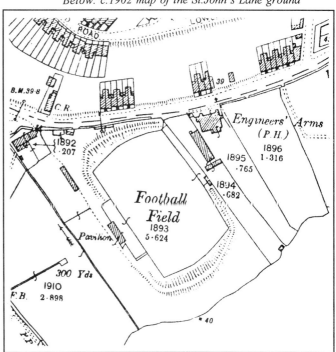

ASHTON GATE: (Bedminster A.F.C. 1896-1900 & BRISTOL CITY A.F.C. 1904 to date)

Ashton Gate, since 1904 the home of Bristol City Football Club, was first used by the Bedminster Club who moved there at the start of 1896-97, when the venue was known as 'Bedminster Athletic Ground'. The opening match was a Friendly against Staple Hill on September 12th when Bedminster achieved an entertaining 4-2 victory.

On that occasion only a portion of the ground was open to accommodate spectators, but two weeks later, for the official opening of the ground when Warmley were the visitors for a Western League match, all was prepared except the dressing rooms and grandstand which were awaiting completion.

In those days the football pitch was laid out in the same direction as it is today, running lengthways towards Ashton Road, but it wasn't in the same location as now. With the requirement of the ground for

(Left) Cup action during the second season at Ashton Gate ('Bedminster Guardian')

(Below) c.1900 the layout of the 'Athletic Ground' (Ashton Gate) located very close to the current ground.

the playing of cricket as well as football, the needs of the soccer fraternity were met in the south-east corner of the complex, such area corresponding to where the 'Bristol Bowling Club' green is located today.

The 'Western Daily Press' in commenting in it's issue of September 28th in regard to the new ground confidentially predicted that when all the work was completed it would.... *"undoubtably rank as one of the finest athletic grounds in the West of England"*. By the time that England met Wales on March 20th, 1899, in the first international to be played in Bristol, Ashton Gate was well equipped to host such an event, and a sketch in the Bristol Observer five days later shows the completed grandstand on the right-hand side of the ground, when looking towards the Clifton Suspension Bridge. This stand gave excellent service for after being moved when the football pitch was re-located in 1904, it lasted until the summer of 1966, when after being deemed unsafe it was demolished.

When Bristol City made their permanent move to Ashton Gate in 1904 it was felt they required to increase the spectator accommodation. Agreement was therefore made with the Directors of the Bedminster Athletic Ground Company to take over the whole arena, which comprised an area of 6 acres, 1½ roods. This extension enabled a soccer pitch - 120 yards by 80 yards - to run directly down the centre of the site, with a 10 yard border all round. Bedminster Cricket Club (as tenants of the City Club) were given plenty of room for the playing of their matches when they took over the ground for four months in the summer - this border being fenced in with 3ft 9ins. high iron railings.

On March 5th, the Western Daily Press reproduced a sketch on how it was hoped the ground would eventually look. It was an ambitious plan, as it showed all four sides under cover, something that is only now - in the summer of 1994 - coming to fruition with the building of a grandstand at the Park End of the ground.

On August 27th, 1904, when the First Team beat the Possibles 9-0 in the first public practice game on the ground, a Western Daily Press report described Ashton Gate as having two Grandstands (Numbers One and Two), each of which seated 1,200 people. Admission to Number One Stand on the east side of the ground was one shilling, and for Number Two on the opposite side the cost was only ninepence. There was covered accommodation for approximately 8,000 at the south end, and the other (Park) end was open.

In 1916 the Covered End was badly damaged by gales, and in December of the following year it was demolished due to it's unsafe condition. It was not until summer 1928 that the cover was replaced, paid for by money which City had received from the transfers of Albert Keating and Clarrie Bourton, who had been sold to Blackburn Rovers for a combined fee of £3,650. The structure that went up in the wake of their departure is still there, known simply as the Covered End or Winterstoke Road End, and most commonly (for some unknown reason) as the East End. Originally it was affectionately referred to as the Keating Stand, and given that the two stands on the sides of the pitch are named after Club Directors, and that the new stand being erected at the Park End is being named after John Atyeo, one of the Club's greatest players, it would be nice for parity to be achieved by officially naming this structure after Albert Keating, or perhaps honouring the memory of City's greatest player by calling it the 'Billy Wedlock Stand'. During the 1986-87 campaign the roof of this stand was renewed, it being sheeted in red, and the close season of 1991 brought about the installation of seats, this latter event bringing forth much protest from standing patrons. Further protest was then made towards the end of the 1993-94 season when it was announced that in consequence of the Grandstand being built at the Open (Park) End the Away Supporters Enclosure which had been situated on the Dolman Stand side of this terrace, would in the following campaign be located on the Des Williams Stand side of the Covered End. This would include the area allocated as the Family Enclosure, a move that would deprive many of their favoured place in this popular part of the ground.

(Left) The Number Two Grandstand was partly burnt-out in August 1929....
(Right) .... and the Number One Grandstand was a casualty of air raids in early January 1941.

The Number One Grandstand was quite an imposing structure, and it was unfortunate that the German bombs that destroyed this building during an air raid on the night of January 3rd/4th, 1941, chose to land on this side of the ground rather than rid the Club of what had become known as the Cow Shed on the opposite side, though this Number Two Grandstand also had a close shave three months later as bombs fell on the pitch during the night of April 11th/12th. This bombing brought about the switching of the home match with Cardiff City on January 11th to Ninian Park, the closure of Ashton Gate until February 22nd, and cancellation of the home fixture with Bath City on April 12th.

Building restrictions in post-war Britain meant that it was 1951 before a permit was issued for the Club to build a new Grandstand. Work began in the summer of that year, when the first half of the new Stand, nearest to the Covered End, was completed. A steel shortage and lack of funds delayed completion until 1953, when the Supporters Club made a donation of £3,000 towards it's cost. The City Directors in return leasing the Supporters Club space beneath the stand for their first permanent home.

This was, incidently, City's fourth supporters club, and was formed on October 9th 1949. The first was founded in the Club's St. John's Lane days but did not survive long, after opposition from some Board members. The second came into being on April 25th, 1919, but how long it lasted is unclear, though it had obviously lapsed by October 16th, 1936, when at a meeting convened by Mr. A.H. Wookey, held at the Ford Memorial Hall, Bedminster, the third such organisation was born. Again it is unclear as to how long this body remained in existence, though it is likely that problems occasioned by the Second World War hastened its demise.

STEEL FINGERS — The framework of Bristol City's new grandstand going up. The workman is climbing the tiered steps as they will be placed inside the stand.

(Above) A Reserve local derby match in the 1950's - with a good view of the Number Two Stand.
(Below) The Stand was demolished during the 1966 close season.

The 1953 Grandstand (which was named the Des Williams Grandstand on June 4th, 1992, in memory of City's late Chairman) has altered much in subsequent years, though until the summer of 1991 none of these changes much effected the appearance inside the ground. Apart from such things as erecting the Press Box at the back of the stand in 1969, and a new Directors Box in 1973, the alterations have been inside the stand or to the frontage. These alterations include the opening of the Robins Club in 1964-65, the enlargement of the Supporters Club premises by extending the 1st floor level out over the officials car park in 1965, enlargement of Club Offices 1976, new Turnstile blocks the same year, Sportsmans Suite (1991), and the brickwork pillars to the main entrance one year later. It was the installation of seats at the Covered End in 1991 that produced the major change, as the roof of this Grandstand was joined up with the Covered End and extended out over the enclosure in order that the provision of seats could be made in these areas as well. Unfortunately this extension meant additional stanchions being erected, which from the writer's viewpoint ruined the best seat in the ground. Seat 10, Row S, Block D, in the back row of the Grandstand -from where the Ashton Gate scene had been surveyed for twenty-five seasons - being rendered unsuitable by a stanchion blocking the Covered End goal.

Bristol City became one of the pioneers of floodlit football in the 1950's and it was Club Chairman Harry Dolman who designed and produced the first lights at Ashton Gate. By modern day standards it was an antiquated system, consisting of fourteen 40ft high metal pylons, seven on each side of the pitch (this later augmented by six more, three at each end), each pylon having a cluster of three lamps. On January 27th, 1953, Wolverhampton Wanderers became the first visitors for a floodlit match at Ashton Gate, this fixture having been postponed a week earlier due to fog. A crowd of 24,008 turned up to see the First Division club win 4-2.

Floodlit Football League and F.A. Cup games were not permitted at that time, so the first competitive match under City's lights was a Football Combination fixture against Swansea Town Reserves on February 24th, 1953, when 4,315 saw City's second string win 2-1. These lights remained in operation until the end of 1964-65, when they were sold to Southern League club Burton Albion for £2,000.

City then invested £27,000 in a system of four 160ft high pylons, one at each corner of the ground. At that time the angled heads had forty-eight lamps on each, and Wolverhampton Wanderers were again the visitors to 'switch-on' the lights. This time however it was for a Second Division game on December 28th, 1965, when 36,183 spectators saw the Midlands Club escape with a 1-0 win. Later, due to problems of shadow caused by the building of the Dolman Stand, additional lights were fitted to the front of this stand. Following modern technical improvements in regard to illumination, the number of lamps on each pylon was able to be reduced over the years.

These 'lights were last used in 1991, for on November 5th that year a new system which consisted of floodlights fitted to gantries on the roof of each of the two Grandstands, was fully in use. A crowd of 7,735 was present to witness the first match, a 2-0 success over Plymouth Argyle in a Second Division clash. These new lights though had been in partial use two weeks previously, when City lost 2-1 to Southampton in a Full Members (Zenith Data Systems) Cup match on October 22nd, the lights fitted to the main Grandstand (Des Williams Stand) having been switched on. The unwanted pylons were given to Wigan Athletic, on the basis that they made arrangements to collect them, and with these pylons coming down on June 8th, 1992, part of the character of Ashton Gate was lost.

The Number Two Grandstand was condemned as unsafe, and demolished in the close season on 1966, but it had a fortunate escape much earlier in it's seventy year life. On the evening of August 31st, 1929, it was partially destroyed by fire, and it was only thanks to the action of a policeman on duty at Ashton Bridge at 9.40 p.m., and the prompt turn out of the Fire Brigade that the blaze was brought under control. During the 1½ hours that battle was waged against the fire, approximately 120ft of the structure nearest the Park End was destroyed, but fortunately the refreshment room underneath was saved. Work on the damaged portion was carried out relatively quickly, and it was not long before it was looking as before.

Unfortunately the removal of this eyesore Number Two Grandstand did little to improve the look of Ashton Gate for some considerable time, as it wasn't until four years later that the Dolman Stand, which incorporates greens for indoor bowls, was built, this being opened at the commencement of the 1970-71 campaign. There are now plans afoot to provide twenty-three luxury boxes at the back of this stand and cover up the unsightly wall at the front, by installing seats to the edge of the pitch.

The Open (Park) End of Ashton Gate had changed little over the years, although with the destruction of the Number One Grandstand in 1941, the various outbuildings in this area of the ground were used as offices and dressing-rooms for over a decade. However with the requirement of all-seater stadiums in consequence of the 'Taylor Report', this end now boasts the John Atyeo Stand. The standing terrace was last used on March 5th, 1994, when a 0-0 draw was played out with Derby County, and work started in preparation for the erection of the Stand on March 14th. This new Stand cost £1.5 million and it offers the same uninterrupted view of the pitch as does the Dolman Stand. It seats 4,100 people, in a single tier, maximum height 33ft and 295ft wide. Originally it was hoped to be a double decker of some 48ft in height, but protests by the residents of houses close by at the back of the Stand brought about modification. This new John Atyeo Stand, which incorporates dressing-rooms, gymnasium, players lounge, treatment-rooms, club shop, and offices, was opened early in the Club's 101st (1994-95) season.

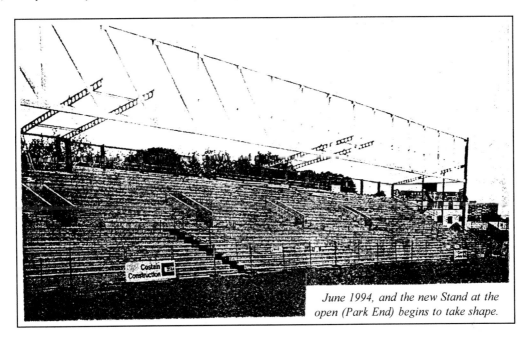

June 1994, and the new Stand at the open (Park End) begins to take shape.

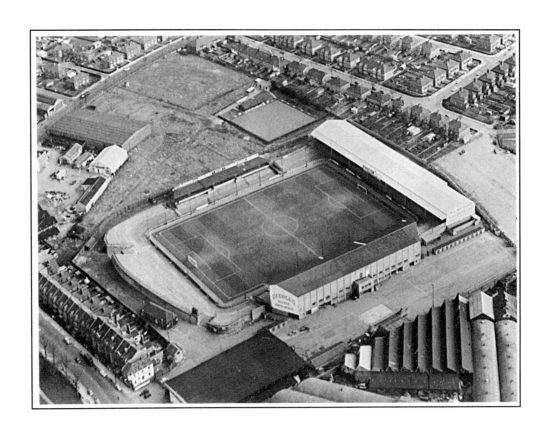

Ashton Gate
(Above) in the late 1950's, and (Below) 7th May 1977 (the home 1-1 match with Manchester United)

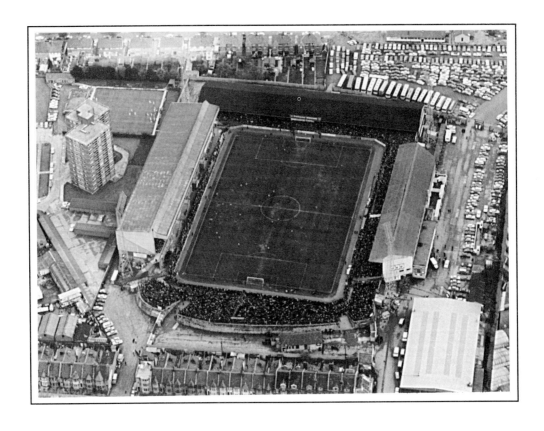

(Above) 20th March 1899 - England v. Wales International at Ashton Gate.

The view, looking North, shows the No.2 Grandstand that was demolished in 1966.

(Right) 11th July 1968 - Ashton Road.

The floods that Summer destroyed many of the Bristol City F.C. records. This photograph was taken, just outside Ashton Gate. Note, on the left is Greville Smyth Park, the home ground of Southville F.C.

(Left) St.John's Lane - September 1994.

The view looking towards Lane End. The present playing pitch, used by Robinsons in the Somerset Senior League, runs left to right, whereas when used by City, it ran at right angles.

CHAPTER THIRTEEN - PROGRAMME NOTES

PART 1: THE POST-WAR BRISTOL CITY PROGRAMME

When Football League action returned after the war the continuing shortage of paper allowed for little improvement over the single sheet wartime issues. Throughout 1946-47 City issued a four page programme measuring 8½ inches x 5½ inches. The front cover featuring a large advertisement for 'Georges Beer' beneath the Club Name, whilst the centre pages provided team line-ups surrounded by advertisements and, occasionally, a fixture list. Another advertisement filled the back cover. This issue cost 2d. and the only variety during the season was provided by occasional changes in the colour of the paper.

1947-48 brought a doubling to eight pages though the price remained stable. The Georges Beer advertisement remained a feature of the front cover, though it was reduced in size. The cover with a red background, a 'Welcome to our visitors' slogan, and match details made the programme look much brighter and interesting. The centre pages again featured the team line-ups surrounded by advertisements, and generally advertising accounted for about 50% of content. A fixture list was now a regular feature, along with League tables, half-time scoreboard, and Club Chatter. This design was the basis of the City programme for the next three years as, apart from the inclusion during October 1948 of an F.A. warning about crowd behaviour (who said hooliganism was a modern phenomenon?), the publications were virtually unchanged throughout 1947-48 and through to much of 1949-50. November 1949 however saw the price increase to 3d., but an extra four pages gave scope for a longer Club Chatter which began to include regular pen pictures of the opponents, a 'Know the Laws' feature explaining different aspects of the laws of the game each week, and pen pictures together with photographs of City players. Small cartoons also made frequent appearances, reflecting perhaps the popularity of such inclusions in the Bristol Rovers programmes of this time. The eight page issues appeared again though, for a short while in 1950-51, and a single sheet programme was produced for the League game with Southend United, but otherwise there were no changes until the Festival of Britain match with Dinamo Zagreb on May 15th, 1951, the smaller programme on sale this day being the model for what was to come.

Making its debut on the same day as John Atyeo made his first League appearance for the City, the new programme measured 7 inches x 5 inches, contained eight pages, and cost 3d. The cover featured the Club name and badge, a drawing of a player and the Number Two Grandstand, match details, together with the usual Georges' advertisement, all on a red background. Advertising content remained close to 50% and the traditional centre page spread was continued, leaving room only for Club Chatter, fixture list (and at times League tables), together with some action photographs, and details of Supporters Club trips to away games. This style was continued throughout 1951-52, 1952-53 and 1953-54 although, in December 1953, the size increased, and the colouring of the cover changes slightly.

During 1953-54 Supporters Club notes and Club information generally became more extensive but this was achieved largely by the exclusion of the fixture list. A rather unusual feature of the programme at this time was the appearance, usually following a Friendly match, of a whole page of reproduced autographs of recent opponents. The widening horizons of English football and the supporters is very much in evidence in the programmes of the 1951-54 period. Not only were Supporters Club trips more widely advertised (in pre-inflation and pre-motorway days 12s.0d. for the journey which started at 7 a.m. were the norm for games in London), but in the Club Chatter column efforts were made to drum up support for trips abroad - twenty-nine guineas for a trip to Milan for an Italy v England game.

At the same time as travel was becoming easier, City installed their first set of floodlights, and a special programme was issued for the official switch-on. City attracted leading clubs from home and abroad to play floodlit matches at Ashton Gate, teams such as Cardiff City, East Fife, Fener Bache, Chelsea, Hajduk Split, Arsenal, Rheims, Linz A.S.K., Frankfurt, Stuttgart Kickers, Nice, Radnicki, Shelbourne, Tottenham Hotspur, Singen and Bordeaux providing attractive opposition throughout the 1950's. Programmes were produced for all these Friendly matches, normally the same size and design as the regular League issue, or a smaller and less elaborate eight page publication featuring a photograph of a floodlit Ashton Gate on the cover. In either case the content consisted primarily of the history of that evening's opponents and pen pictures of their players. The exception was the programme for the game against Arsenal on March 30th, 1954, when a large, glossy, special souvenir edition costing 6d. was produced. Possibly encouraged by the income from the sales of this programme, a similar programme was issued by the Club at the end of the season when Gloucestershire Cup battle was engaged with the Rovers.

These large format programmes sized 9½ inches x 7 inches became standard issue in 1954-55 and 1955-56, but were produced on cheaper paper in order that they could be sold at the regular price of 3d. The advertising content of this eight page programme remained at a little under 50% and it regularly contained fixture lists, League tables, quizzes, and a '25 Years Ago feature'. In addition three traditional items were retained, the front cover Georges' advertisement (underneath the Club name and crest, and a small photograph), the centre spread team line-ups, and the Club Chatter.

Throughout the late 1940's and much of the 1950's this Club Chatter (which was mainly written by the Rev. F.C. Vyvyan-Jones) provided the bulk, and sometimes the only, reading matter in the programme. It was in essence the equivalent of the modern day club news, national round-up, managers notes, visitors pen pictures, and editorial column all rolled into one, varying in topic and length from week to week. At its worst the column would be no more than a routine statement of Club policy, or a view on a relatively minor matter, together with brief pen pictures on the opponents of the day, or comment on City's recent performances (the tendency towards this type of content becoming more pronounced during the late fifties and early sixties when a separate page was frequently devoted to short pen pictures). At best the column provided, and still provides, a fascinating commentary on a whole variety of football topics and controversies.

As previously mentioned increasing opportunity for travel, coupled with the growing potential for evening Friendlies that the introduction of floodlights provided, brought about a much greater interest in continental football, and this was often reflected in the Club Chatter. Such information would include interviews with the officials of the visiting European clubs, articles by, and about, Alec Eisentrager (City's German winger) and German football. On the home front the issues of the maximum wage, and the pros and cons of floodlit football were among the controversies of the time that were given an airing in the column.

Season 1956-57 brought the arrival of the programme that was to become the hallmark of the Club for the next ten years. Measuring 7 inches x 4½ inches, and costing 4d., the cover featured the Club name and crest, an action photograph, and the match details, all on a red background between two advertisements (one of course for a certain beer!). Advertising content within the sixteen pages was generally about one third, and the remainder of the programme was given over to a fairly traditional mixture of statistics (fixtures, tables, half-time scoreboard), line-ups on the centre page, introduction of the opposition, together with Club notes and news. The programme remained much the same until the end of 1965-66, but on the cover there were a number of changes to the action photograph, and the takeover of Georges Brewery by Courage in 1962-63 saw the departure of this familiar name. The price increased to 6d in 1964-65, and the following season saw the disappearance of information on opponents and the date from the front cover. Internally there were minor variations, such as occasional cartoons, looking back features, and (a sign of things to come) a brief appearance during 1960-61 of a Manager's Column. The main change though was the gradual polarisation of the longer and more general Club Notes into separate and distinct features. A regular new players feature appeared in 1962-63, a separate page - sometimes two - of opponents pen pictures was common by 1960-61, and the Supporters Club, together with commercial activities, received more extensive coverage. The Supporters Club were now advertising trips to most away matches and, in 1959-60, even offered a 8/6d. steamer trip to the game at Cardiff City.

Season 1960-61 saw the start of the Football League Cup and the City, unlike many clubs, issued normal programmes for their matches in this competition. Thinking they might gain entry to European competition the City took part, after an absence of twenty four years, in the Welsh Cup in 1962, and whilst only a single sheet issue, on a par with the Reserve programmes, was produced for the game with Merthyr Tydfil, the usual 1st team effort was on sale for the Cardiff game.

The 1966-67 programme measured 8½ inches x 5½ inches, contained sixteen pages, and cost 6d. For the first time since the single sheet wartime issues there were no advertisements on the front cover, which instead gave details of opponents and the match date beside a full page sketch of two players (one being Brian Clark), on a white background. Team line-ups remained on the centre pages, but were now simply listed 1 to 11, rather than being shown in formation. Although the size of the programme remained unaltered during the next eight years there were considerable developments in regard to the content and production. A growing awareness of the importance of the Club's commercial activities was reflected in the programme itself. The need to increase the money making potential of the product brought about a change to the cover

design every season (except 1970-71), and the issue of high quality gloss paper together with the incorporation of the Football League Review, both for 1968-69, enabled the Club to justify a doubling of the price to 1s. One use to which City put the income generated by it's commercial activities was towards the building of the Dolman Stand, and the progress of it's construction is charted in photographs and articles throughout the 1968-69 and 1969-70 campaigns, culminating in the efforts to sell the first season tickets for this stand at £9.10s.0d. for it's opening at the start of 1970-71.

Endeavours to make the programme a more attractive product continued with the appearance of a variety of new and different articles each season, 'Personality of the Week', 'The Young Ones', '2nd Division Survey', 'Down Memory Lane', all made their first regular appearance during the early seventies. Finally the financial potential of the programme was further exploited with the production of a number of special issues. These started with a twenty-four page publication costing 1s. for the 1967 F.A. Cup match with Southampton, and then continued with larger sized and differently designed issues for the 1968 F.A. Cup game with Bristol Rovers (1s.), the 1970 Football League Cup Semi-Final against Tottenham Hotspur (same price), and the 1974 F.A. Cup ties with Leeds United and Liverpool which each cost 10p. The 1973-74 campaign also saw a 'power strike emergency edition programme' being produced for the League game with Millwall on February 26th, this issue only consisting of four pages (plus the Football League Review). The Football League Review was the best thing that happened to football programmes at this time, and it was unfortunate that the publication was stopped at the end of 1973-74. Another unusual programme was produced on December 18th, 1967, when Ashton Gate was used as a neutral venue for an F.A. Cup 1st Round, 2nd Replay, between Nuneaton Borough and Exeter City. A four page issue with red print (and two red tinted players photographs) on white paper costing 6d. was produced. A development of this period was the increasing use of articles by 'Personalities'. At first City seemed unsure as to who the personality should be, the 1966-67 programme sometimes carried a Manager's column by Fred Ford, and at other times an article by a guest writer, as well as a regular page by John Atyeo. By 1967-68 the programme had settled (as had many clubs at this time) on the manager as the public personality, and the A.D. column, by City Manager Alan Dicks, became as much a part of the programme as the team line-ups.

Having held the price at 1s. and then the equivalent 5p. (on decimalisation in February 1971), it was increased to 7p. in 1973-74 and 10p. for the following season. Throughout the Football League the mid-seventies was the time of larger, more adventurous programmes, and City were no exception. The 1974-75 issue measured 9 inches x 7 inches and the front cover featured an aerial view of Ashton Gate with 'City' in large red lettering. A third of the content was advertising and the remainder of the twenty four pages were given over to the traditional mix of club news, statistics, photographs, Supporters Club, and Manager's notes. In addition three pages were devoted to information on the visitors, and Jim Evans (City's Promotions Manager) had a page on the Club's fund-raising activities. Other features of this, and the subsequent four seasons, included players profiles, articles by backroom staff, and in 1975-76 a weekly City-girl photograph.

During these years however it was the design of the programme which varied more than the actual content. In marked contrast to the tendencies of other clubs, the 1975-76 issue only measured 7½ inches x 4 inches, and cost 12p. for twenty four pages. The larger size, this time with action photographs on the cover, returned in 1976-77, but the Club's return to the top division of the English game after an absence of sixty-five years was marked by a price increase to 15p. Season 1978-79 brought a slight reduction in the size while the price went up to 20p. to allow for the fact that colour photographs now began to appear regularly inside. The programme was named the 'City News', and a different colour photograph was shown on the cover of each issue.

Variation in programmes issued occurred for City's games in the Anglo-Scottish Cup when small four page editions often appeared (this design also serving for a number of Friendly matches) costing 5p. or 10p. Exceptions though were the production of a single duplicated sheet for the 1975-76 game with Norwich City, an eight page issue against St. Mirren in 1978-79, and a standard format for the clashes with Hibernian and St. Mirren in 1977-78.

Season 1979-80 was a disappointing one for the Club in regard to playing performance, but it proved the highpoint in the history of the City programme. Undoubtably the best programme ever issued by the Club, only marred by the incorrect season (1978-79) being shown above the Reserve results throughout the campaign. This programme (together with an almost identical one produced by Norwich City) were arguably one of the best ever produced regularly throughout the Football League, and it was a deserved winner of the 'Programme of the Year' award. The programme was called 'The Robin' and the cover consisted of a drawing of a robin on a colour photograph that changed with each issue. The thirty-two page programmes, size 8½ inches x 6 inches, cost 30p., and with less than 10% advertising content it was good value for money. On the inside imaginative use was made of colourful backgrounds, lettering and many photographs (including a regular competition for readers to supply a caption), together with the traditional mix of contents. These contents included extensive statistics, 'Club Diary', 'Junior Reds Column', 'letters', 'Robins Nest' (article and photograph on a players family), 'Youth Team Notes', 'Flashback features', 'ABC History of the Club', at least two articles by City staff, newspaper reporters or supporters, a Topic feature dealing with a subject of current interest, and even small ads. No doubt exhausted by their efforts, the Club could only manage a sixteen page issue for the Football League Cup game with Rotherham United, and as little as eight pages for the clash with Peterborough United. Additionally two League fixtures, against Everton and Norwich City, were reduced to sixteen pages. The Anglo-Scottish Cup matches began with a four page programme when Fulham were the visitors on August 11th, but this was reduced to two pages for the next game against Partick Thistle on October 23rd. Then the horror of the single duplicated sheet which was issued versus Morton on November 6th, this then serving for the remainder of City's home games in the competition, both for that season and the next.

From 1980-81 City's programme began to reflect the Club's declining fortunes on the field. The campaign began hopefully with a twenty four page issue measuring some 9½ inches x 6¾ inches, almost devoid of advertisements and costing 30p.

By October however the new manager, Bob Houghton, was writing his column in a sixteen page programme which had lost most of it's more unusual and imaginative features (information of the Club's trophies and articles by the Club Physiotherapist). A Topic page remained though, and this was something of a throwback to the 1950's 'Club Chatter'. Despite these cutbacks, and to the surprise of most City fans, the programme, which was still named 'The Robin', was thought good enough to win an award, being voted the best in the Second Division by the Football Commercial Managers Association.

By 1981-82 The Robin had reduced to eight pages (plus a nationally produced insert), and even to four pages for the Football League Cup game with Walsall on September 1st. The programme only provided the bare minimum, a couple of photographs, line-ups, statistics, club news, visitors pen pictures, and the manager's page. The latter article was an unusual feature of the programmes for the first half of the season in that it appeared on the front cover. This was moved inside from January 23rd when a coloured match action photograph gave the programme a more professional look. The Club's financial problems were highlighted by the use of a programme printed for the postponed game with Exeter City on Boxing Day being used for the fixture with Wimbledon on January the 2nd., a duplicated insert being deemed sufficient to induce the public to part with 30p. when attending this hastily rearranged game. The match had previously been postponed in consequence of City winning through to the 3rd Round of the F.A. Cup. In the latter part of the season much of the editorial content of the programme was largely given over to appeals for financial help by the new company that had taken over the Club, and an indication of the support they received can be gauged by the supporters apparent willingness to continue to pay 30p. for a production with less content than at any time since 1947.

The 1982-83 campaign saw the programme, still called The Robin, reduced in size to 8¼ inches x 5¾ inches, but this sixteen page issue only lasted until the Colchester United game on November the 27th as the next home game, against Port Vale on December the 27th, brought forth change. This saw a change of name to 'The Robins', use of better quality paper, and an increase to twenty-four pages which allowed for better articles and more extensive information on the visitors, all for the same 35p. price tag that had been in force since the start of the campaign. Among the regular features were 'Press Gang', 'Remember' (articles from the past by Geoff Rose), 'Captain's Corner', 'Where Are They Now', 'Profile', 'Supporters Letters', 'Guest Spot', 'Commercially Speaking by Brian White', 'Meet Our Visitors' by David M. Woods, and the Manager's page under the banner of 'T.C. Speaking'. The statistics section, entitled 'Where, When and Who', was also greatly improved, and it included details of all the Club's teams operating in the Western League, the Bristol & Suburban League, and the seniors in the Football League.

Season 1983-84 saw a very similar programme to that of the previous campaign, but the price was raised to 40p. and the name 'The Robins' disappeared. Content was much the same, though Herbie Gillam (ex Sports Editor of the Western Daily Press) was now writing 'Looking Back' articles, and the match action photographs were included under the heading of John Kellands Action Parade. The most interesting development though was the start of 'Robins Through The Years' by David M. Woods on October 8th.

This was a season-by-season account of the doings of the City from 1894, which continued to appear until the end of 1985-86, when having reached the 1934-35 campaign, it was dropped by the Club without any explanation being given. There were a few changes in the number of pages during 1983-84, a twelve page issue being produced for the F.A. Cup 3rd Round Replay with Notts County on January 10th, but prior to this it consisted of twenty-four, apart from the game with Corinthian Casuals in the F.A. Cup on November 23rd, when eight pages appeared at a cost of 20p. The fixture with Wrexham on January 21st brought an increase to twenty eight-pages, and thus it remained until the concluding match when the adding of a further four pages saw a thirty- two page issue appearing for the game against Swindon Town on May 5th.

1984-85 again saw a very similar programme, priced at 40p., for thirty-two pages at the outset, but the production of a thirty six-page edition costing 50p. for the clash with Bristol Rovers on November 10th gave excuse for the increased price to remain, even though the number of pages reverted to thirty-two. The cover of the 1985-86 programme was unusual in that it featured a close up picture of a City Shirt, but hitherto in the period from 1982-83 they consisted of an assortment of match action photographs. The biggest disappointment in the 1985-86 programme was the discontinuing of the extensive historical information in regard to the visitors, but apart from this it was similar to what had gone before.

The overriding impression of the programme in this period following the Club's fall from the pinnacle of the game is the importance of City's fund-raising and commercial activities. Although content improved after the 1981-82 programme, it was generally a fairly unimaginative collection of traditional features, enlivened only by historical articles. Many printing errors occurred which even extended to the misspelling of the opponents name on the front cover. This served to create the feeling that the Club sought to produce no more than an adequate programme, with the minimum of effort, an impression that is still gained from current issues, even though the problems of spelling appear to have been overcome. To a certain extent the Club's League and financial positions necessitated this attitude, and they were certainly not alone among the Third and Fourth Division teams in this respect. Nevertheless other clubs did show an effort could still be made even within strict financial limits. As an example contrast the difference between City and Darlington in 1983.

On January 1st, City issued a programme for the match with Swindon that contained editorial comment and statistics that referred to nothing after December 4th, but the 'Quakers' by contrast in their programme for the visit of City two days after the Swindon game, were able to include full coverage of all matches up to New Years Day. The commercial nature of the programmes was also reflected in the growing space given over to both advertising content (up to 35%), and Commercial News, this little more than advertising for the lottery, City Society etc. By 1986-87 up to seven pages were used in this way, making almost 50% of the programme containing advertising of one sort or another, very poor value in a product that had been reduced to twenty-eight pages. For a Club that had ended the previous campaign by winning the Associate Members (Freight Rover) Trophy at Wembley Stadium this programme produced by the wealthiest organisation in the lower divisions was a truly awful publication that made one wonder if the City had any interest at all in what they chose to put in front of their own supporters.

Despite the complaints a similar poor quality product on the same thick paper was issued for 1987-88 and 1988-89, both these seasons seeing a twenty-four page programme selling at 50p. For the promotion campaign of 1989-90 a significant improvement was made, and a much more professional looking programme was produced. The supporters had to pay 70p. for this larger sized (9½ inches x 6½ inches), twenty-four page programme which resurrected the idea of the shirt cover design of 1985-86, though now with a view of a players' legs as well.

City's return to the Second Division, after an absence of nine seasons, saw the improvement being maintained, but the price was increased to £1.00. However poor presentation again betrayed itself in regard to the cover where five different photographs were used during the course of the campaign. Four of these photographs had been used by February 2nd, when repeats were started, but March 5th brought the fifth, which lasted through to the last match of the season on May 4th. At this time, the picture that was first used between December 8th and January 12th, and was repeated on February 23rd, appeared yet again. 1991-92 brought better use of the cover with a changed photograph being used for every match, and the £1.00 price being maintained for the same sized (9½ inches x 6½ inches) twenty-four pages as before. This represented reasonable value, even if the concept of what should be produced in a programme remained beyond the desire of the Club to provide it.

This style and size has subsequently remained, and whilst it is praiseworthy that the price has stayed stable for League issues, it is seen as regrettable by many supporters that the Club's one hundredth campaign was not celebrated by the production of a programme fitting for such a season. Special programmes were however issued during this 1993-94 season for the F.A. Cup games with Charlton Athletic and Liverpool. The abandoned match with Liverpool, and the tie with Charlton, brought out the same awkward size (11¾ inches x 8¼ inches) that had appeared for the Football League Cup Semi-Final clash with Nottingham Forest in 1989 when twenty four pages were produced for £1.00. This time though the content was not so good, and with the price being increased to £2.00 these twenty-four page issues were considered to represent poor value for money. The re-arranged game with Liverpool saw £1.50 being charged for a programme on a par with normal League issues, but on this occasion it is only fair to mention that the Club greatly reduced the admission cost as a gesture in recognition of the inconvenience caused by the floodlight failure which brought proceedings to a premature halt before.

To conclude the history of the programme, brief mention needs to be made in regard to Reserve Team issues, which during the inter-war period were the same as those produced for 1st team games. After the War they became single sheet issues (8½ inches x 5½ inches) printed on both sides, the programme produced for 1947-48 having the same front cover as that of 1st team matches. The use of the 1st team cover was soon discontinued, but these single sheet programmes with printing on both sides were the normal issue throughout the 1950's and into the 1960's. Eventually though, with declining Reserve Team attendances, they were replaced with the large (11½ inches x 8¼ inches) single duplicated sheet that have remained until this day, except for the first half of 1984-85. This short four month period saw proper sixteen page programmes sized 8¼ inches x 5¾ inches being issued at a cost of 20p. for Western League games, and it was a great pity that the innovation was not continued after the turn of the year.

Part 2
PROGRAMME PARADE
50 programme covers
from 100 years of
BRISTOL CITY

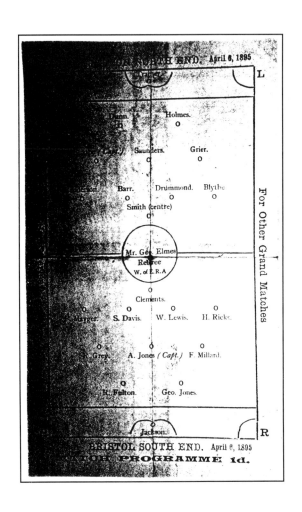

(Above, left): Probably the oldest surviving example - a Bristol South End publication of the 1894/95 season. This copy once belonged to Frank Mayger, who played on the left wing in this prestigious match against Preston North End.

(Above, right): 11th March 1899, the oldest known City 'away' fixture programme - a Southern League match at Southampton.

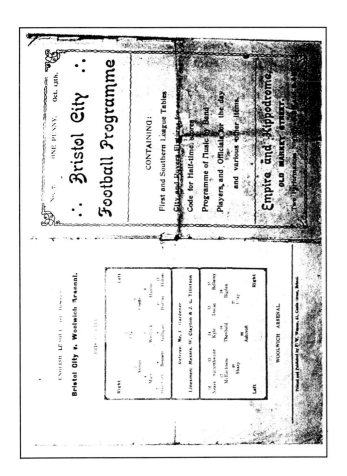

(Above, left) On gaining promotion to the First Division, City resurrected the issuing of an elaborate programme. The number 7 indicates that issues were also produced for Reserve games.

(Above, right) The Babes beat Bolton Wanderers 2-0 on 18th April 1908.

(Right) The F.A.Cup Final (souvenir) programme on 24th April 1909 between the City and Manchester United.

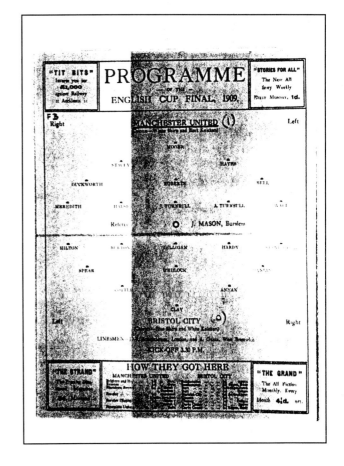

(Above, left)   15th April 1911, a new record Division One win - 5-1 versus Nottingham Forest.

(Above, right)   The Babes drew   1-1 with Birmingham on the 3rd January 1920.

(Left) The opening match of the 1920/21 season, a 1-0 defeat at home to Notts County.

(Above left) A similar cover to the previous campaign, but devoid of date and even season (1921/22).

(Above right) On the 17th January 1931, City were defeated 1-0 by Bradford City.

(Right) Another home defeat, this time to Luton Town on the 13th February 1937.

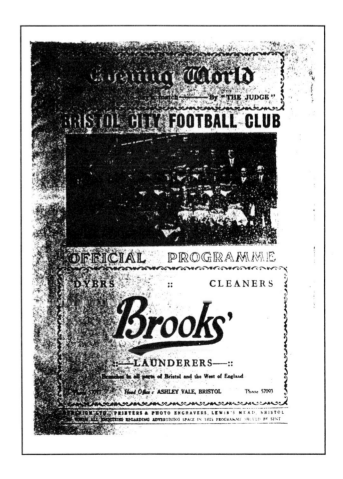

Bristol City Official Programme

NEXT HOME MATCH

ALDERSHOT

Saturday, October 26th.

City play team away Saturday, October 12th.
This Match should be a good guide as
to the result of the home match

A GAME WELL WORTH SEEING

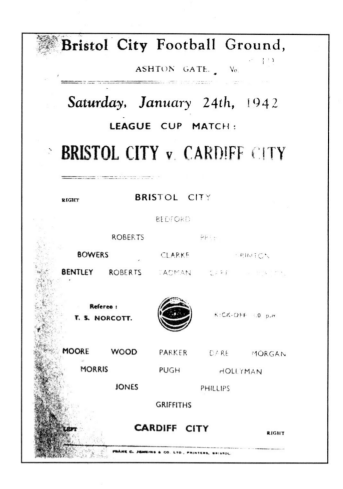

Bristol City Football Ground,

ASHTON GATE.

Saturday, January 24th, 1942

LEAGUE CUP MATCH:

BRISTOL CITY v. CARDIFF CITY

| | | BRISTOL CITY | | |

RIGHT

BEDFORD

ROBERTS

BOWERS   CLARKE

BENTLEY   ROBERTS   CADMAN

Referee :
T. S. NORCOTT.

KICK-OFF 3.0 p.m

MOORE   WOOD   PARKER   DARE   MORGAN

MORRIS   PUGH   HOLLYMAN

JONES   PHILLIPS

GRIFFITHS

LEFT   **CARDIFF CITY**   RIGHT

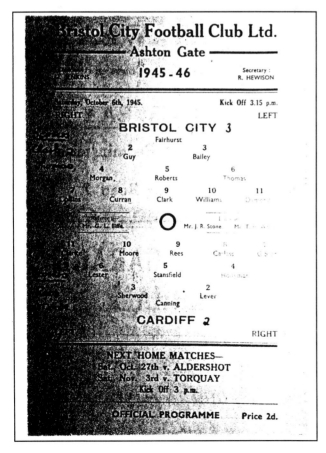

Bristol City Football Club Ltd.
Ashton Gate

1945 - 46

Secretary :
R. HEWISON

Saturday, October 6th, 1945.   Kick Off 3.15 p.m.

RIGHT   LEFT

BRISTOL CITY 3

Fairhurst

2   3
Guy   Bailey

4   5   6
Morgan   Roberts   Thomas

8   9   10   11
Curran   Clark   Williams

O   Mr. J. R. Stone

10   9
Moore   Rees   Carless

5   4
Stansfield   Horniman

3   2
Sherwood   Lever

Canning

CARDIFF 2

RIGHT

NEXT HOME MATCHES—
Sat. Oct. 27th v. ALDERSHOT
Sat. Nov. 3rd v. TORQUAY
Kick Off 3 p.m.

OFFICIAL PROGRAMME   Price 2d.

(Above left) A simple programme in the early years of the war (Cardiff City were beaten 1-0 on the 5th October 1940).

(Above right) Even more basic the following season - 1941/42 - when Cardiff City were the visitors again. 3,312 spectators had value for money, a 8-3 home win.

(Left) A 'hat-trick' of Cardiff visits - a 3-2 victory during the 1945/46 season (the attendance was 18,721)

(Above left) Although nothing to identify the match on the cover, this game produced the City's record League victory - 9-0 versus Aldershot on the 28th December 1946.

(Above right) Walsall were the visitors on the 26th March 1948.

(Right) A completely revised programme cover by the 1952/53 season.

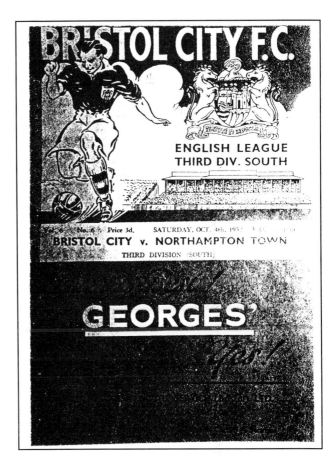

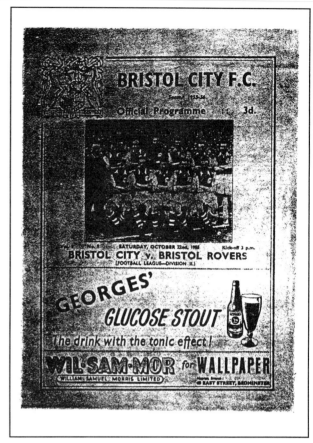

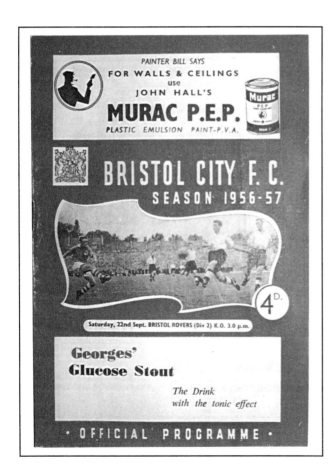

(Above left) A special 'souvenir' programme for the County Cup Final match - 1953/54 season.

(Above right) Another local derby match, this time in the League. 1955/56 season.

(Left)   Rovers were the opponents again, for this 1956/57 season programme.

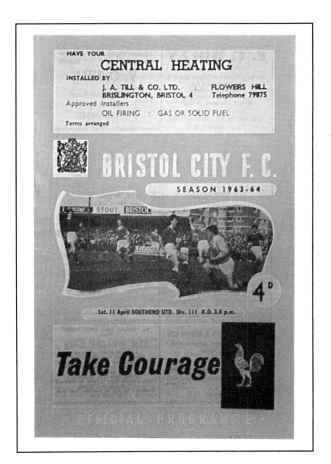

(Above left) Middlesbrough were the Second Division visitors for this 1959/60 fixture.

(Above right) By the 1963/64 season, the programme cover had changed very little.

(Right) A special was issued for the switch-on of City's new floodlights in 1965.

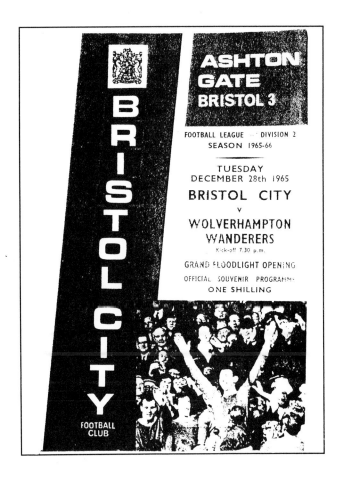

(Above left) John Atyeo's testimonial, when Leeds United were the visitors on the 10th October 1966.

(Above right) A radical change in design for standard issues of the 1967/68 season.

(Left) Another new cover (1968/69 season), and the programme now included the 'Football League Review'.

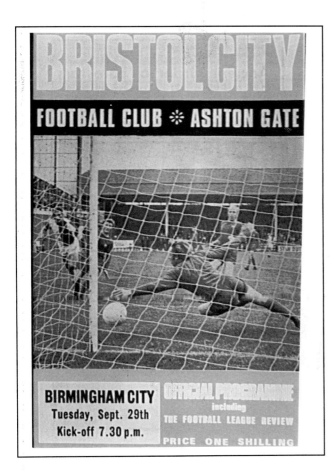

(Above left)   The
Robins beat Birming-
ham City 2-1 on the
29th September 1970.

(Above right)   The
1971/72 season was the
first with decimal-
isation, 5p being the
same as the previous
one shilling.

(Right)   Something
special for the juniors
team - the Final (sec-
ond leg) of the 1972/73
season F.A. Youth Cup.

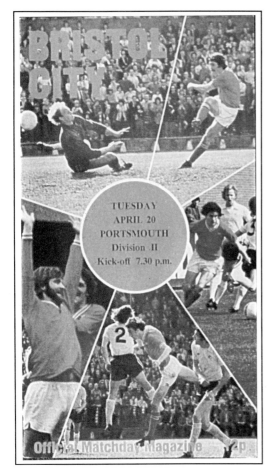

(Above left) A typical issue for the 1973/74 season in the Second Division.

(Above right) And a radical change in design for the following season.

(Left) Not only a change of design, but also shape for the 1975/76 season - City clinch promotion from the Second Division with victory over Portsmouth.

(Above left) City's first home match back in the top flight after 65 years. 25,316 were present to see a 1-1 draw.

(Above right) A 1-0 defeat to Manchester United in the 1977/78 League clash.

(Right) But Bolton Wanderers were beaten 4-1 on the 11th November 1978.

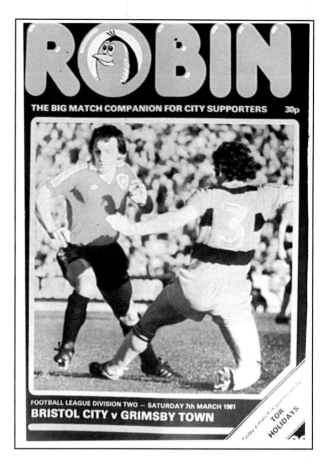

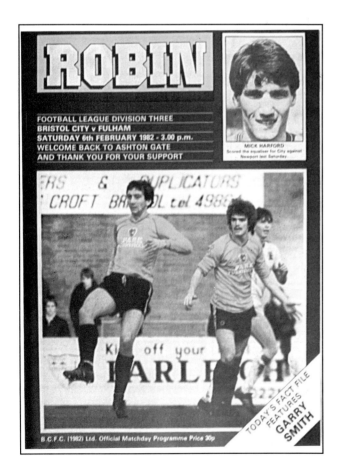

(Above left) **Not** a standard issue for this special 1979/80 season Christmas edition.

(Above right) Back to Division Two fare for the 1980/81 season.

(Left) The slide continues - Fulham were the visitors in this 1981/82 Third Division encounter.

(Above left) The lowest ebb - the 1982/83 campaign, and Fourth Division football.

(Above right) For the 1983/84 season, 'The Robin' was no longer a major feature on the cover

(Right) The 1984/85 season saw 'The City' continue as the principal name feature.

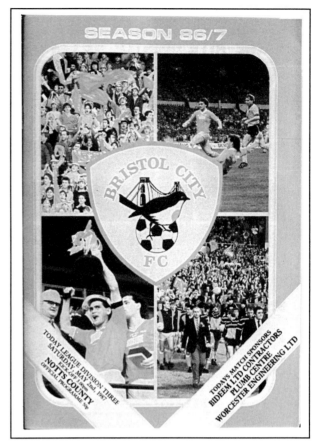

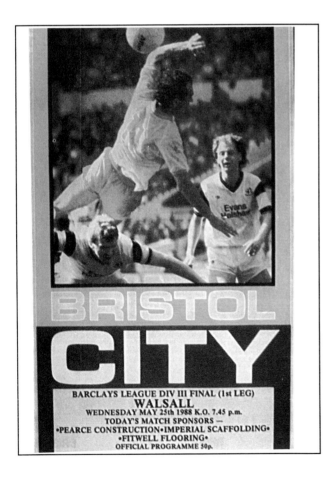

(Above left) 1985/86 season. Hardly the most imaginative of designs -but City were at this time one step away from Wembley.

(Above right) The 1986/87 campaign draws to an end - the match versus Notts County on the 2nd May.

(Left) The programme design continues to change dramatically each season. (1987/88 nearly produced a return to the Second Division)

(Above left) The cover design for 1988/89 dispensed with all nicknames and badges.

(Above right) And the following season saw the removal of a match action photograph, but on the field a return to a higher Division.

(Right) Back in the Second Division for the 1990/91 season - and live action on the cover.

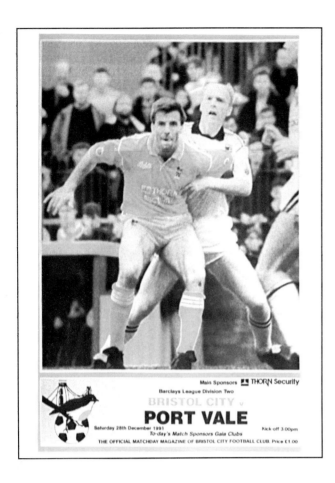

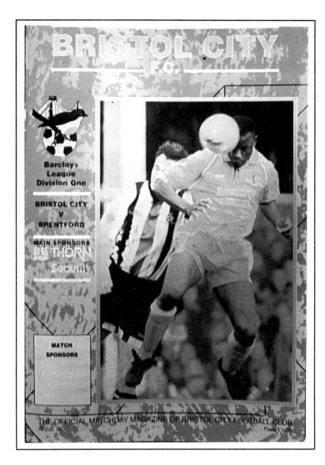

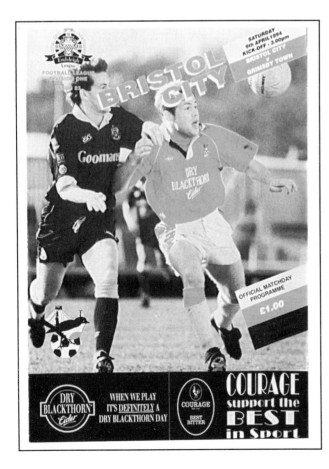

(Above left) By 1991/92 the 'programme' had become established as a 'Matchday Magazine'.

(Above right) This - undated - programme was in fact the last League game of the 1992/93 season - and the victory ensured the relegation of Brentford.

(Left) The programme for City's last match before their 100th birthday. Grimsby were beaten in the match on the 9th April 1994.

The earliest local soccer annual was J.A. Steven's Official Soccer Guide, the first being produced for 1892-93 to coincide with the commencement of the Bristol & District League, this competition changing it's name to the Western League in 1895-96. This annual was still being published in 1899-1900, but the date of it's eventual discontinuation is unknown. Also being produced at the turn of the century were the Western Football Handbook, and Burleigh's Football Guide. Copies of the Western Football Handbook exist for 1898-99 and 1900-01, while those of Burleigh's Football Guides - published by Burleigh Limited, Narrow Lewins Mead, Bristol - that have survived include 1900-01, 1901-02, 1902-03 & 1904-05.

In 1907-08 Weaver's Football Guide was published from 41, Castle Street, Bristol, but the most famous local sports annual came on the scene two years earlier. This was the 'Bristol Evening Times Football Annual', which was issued for every season (except for 1915-16 to 1918-19), up to and including 1931-32, when the twenty third and final edition was produced. This annual, which had changed name to the Bristol Evening Times & Echo Football Annual in 1910-11, was printed and published by the proprietors of the newspaper whose name it carried at their premises in St. Stephen's Street, Bristol.

It would appear that the void left by this demise was not filled until after the Second World War when the proprietors of the Bristol Evening Post and the Bristol Evening World brought out their own publications, the Green 'Un Football Guide and the Pink 'Un Sports Annual respectively. These annuals continued to be published separately until 1957-58 when they combined to become the West of England Football Annual. This latter title lasted until the closure of the Evening World in 1962 brought about a new name - the Evening Post Football Annual - for the final edition of 1962-63. In the late 1940's Pink 'Un Speedway, and Cricket Annuals were also produced.

EARLY BRISTOL NEWSPAPERS

Prior to the appearance of the Sports Times in 1909, followed by the Sports News in 1919, the local evening newspapers produced late Saturday editions that carried match reports of the local soccer and rugby clubs together with results of the principal games throughout the country. These newspapers were the Bristol Evening News - which was Bristol's first evening paper, being founded on May 29th, 1877, the Bristol Echo, the first edition coming out on October 26th, 1901, The Bristol Evening Times - which had hit the streets on October 3rd, 1904 - and the Bristol Evening Express. This latter newspaper was a short-lived venture, first appearing on December 4th, 1899 (printed on pink paper until March 21st 1900). It only lasted until April 27th 1900, but the amalgamation of the Evening Times with the Echo on December 1st 1909 ensured the survival of a rival to the Evening News.

The local morning press also gave excellent coverage to the sporting scene, the principal newspapers being the Western Daily Press (founded on June 1st, 1858), and the Bristol Times & Mirror which, as a daily paper, had commenced life on January 5th, 1865, as a result of an amalgamation of the Bristol Times & Journal (which first saw the light of day on March 2nd, 1839, when it was called the Bristol Times & Bath Advocate) with the Bristol Mirror (a name adopted on January

19th, 1811). The Bristol Mirror started life as Bonner & Middleton's Bristol Journal in August 1774, but the merger of the Bristol Times with Felix Farley's Bristol Journal on April 2nd, 1853 provides a link that takes the roots back still further - to April 25th, 1752 when Felix Farley's publication first appeared on the streets of Bristol. This was almost fifty years after the very first newspaper to be published in the provinces, the Bristol Post Boy, made it's debut.

Amongst the weekly press was the Bristol Observer (published by the proprietors of the Western Daily Press), and the Bristol Guardian. The latter publication was called the Bedminster Guardian and South Bristol Advertiser when it made its initial appearance on June 5th, 1897, and it wasn't until December 4th, 1897 that a change of name was effected. Both of these included a football column, and that in the Bristol Guardian was particularly extensive for the period up to the conclusion of the 1899-1900 campaign. The Bristol Observer continues to this day, but is now a free publication produced, in consequence of take over of the Western Daily Press in 1960, by the proprietors of the Bristol Evening Post. It still includes a modicum of sports coverage, as does the other free paper circulating locally, the Bristol Journal, but it is a pale shadow on what was provided in pre- 1st World War days.

BRISTOL CITY PUBLICATIONS

Handbooks have been published intermittently by the Club over the years. The oldest known to still exist is that for their very first professional campaign of 1897-98, when it was called the Bristol City Football Annual. This was priced at 3d., but another early edition, that of 1899-1900 - despite being of larger size - only cost 2d., being then known as the Bristol City Football Club Ltd., Annual Handbook. Both of these annuals were printed by F.H. Webb of Bedminster.

During 1965 a Club newspaper called the Robin was produced on good quality paper, this ran to two issues - on February 13th and April 24th - and in 1978 two editions of the Bristol City Soccer Special were produced on poor quality paper.

The Independent Voice
of Bristol City

Smith unhappy about Watford injuries

Issue 5   Still only 50p

The late 1980's brought forth a new football phenomenon, when fanzines began appearing throughout the Football League. These were produced by fans of the clubs concerned, mainly in response to the sterile content of match programmes, and the frustration felt over the lack of interest exhibited by footballing authorities over the concerns of the genuine supporters of the game.

It didn't take long for Robins' fans to follow the trend, and this resulted in five such fanzines having been offered for sale during the intervening years - Over the Gate, Take Your Seats, One Team In Bristol, The Bountyhunter, and Ultra. The last two publications have given excellent value for money, The Bountyhunter establishing a much improved content for fanzines when it came onto the market, and Ultra went a step further by introducing a glossy image. The Scandinavian Supporters Club of Bristol City also publish a regular magazine (the June 1994 edition was numbered 18), and the contents - with pages varying from 24 to 36 - are packed with information on the Robins.

SPORTS PAPERS

The signing of the armistice on the 11th November 1918 brought an end to hostilities, and the return of men to England thereafter produced an increase in attendances during the final wartime season. This growth of interest in Bristol brought about the birth of a Saturday night sports paper to rival the 'Sports Times - Green 'Un' which had changed from white to green paper on March 24th, 1917. This alternative, the 'Sports News', was published for the first time on the 5th April 1919, becoming 'Sports News - Pink 'Un' on the 25th March 1922 from which time it was printed on pink paper. These sports papers were to be a familiar sight on the streets of Bristol, until falling victim of the newspaper war that developed when the 'Bristol Evening World' commenced publication on

October 1st, 1929. The final edition of the 'Sports News - Pink 'Un' was on March 22nd the following year and the 'Sports Times - Green 'Un' breathed it's last in 1932 on the 23rd January. The 'Sports Times' was published by the proprietors of 'The Bristol Times & Mirror' and the 'Evening Times & Echo' which were last published in 1932 (January 29th), after which the morning paper was absorbed into 'The Western Daily Press' and the evening paper by the 'Bristol Evening World'. The 'Sports News' was produced by the proprietors of 'The Western Daily Press' and the 'Bristol Evening News' who stopped producing the evening paper on March 27th, 1930, though the Western Daily Press' continues to the present.

The principal soccer writers in the 'Sports Times - Green 'Un' were H.J. Slater-Stone ('Half-back') and Bill Pinnell ('The Traveller). In the 'Sports News - Pink 'Un' soccer was covered by Phil Barnes ('Quip') and Tom Gray Smith ('Scribe'). The 'Bristol Evening World' started their rival sports paper in 1929, on October 5th, calling this the 'Sports World'. It later became the 'Sports Blue' until the adoption of the 'Pink 'Un' title at the commencement of the 1937-38 campaign being then produced on pink paper from this time until - apart from the war years - it's demise on the 27th January 1962. This date also marking the death of the 'Bristol Evening World' itself, which was absorbed by the 'Bristol Evening Post'. Among the reporters engaged on the 'Pink 'Un' were J.G. Ure ('Judge'), Phil Barnes ('Quip'), Bill Andrews, George Baker, Peter Barnes, Don Burland, J.G. Coates, Ronnie Dix, David Foot, Bob Hatsell, Pat Kavanagh, Stanley Manning, Charlie Murphy, Bruce Perry, Jack Pugsley, John Sanders, Ian Todd and Sam Tucker. Prior to World War 2, the principal cartoonists were Geary followed by by Arthur Potts ('Spot'). Jim Neal ('Speed') took up the role in the post war years.

The mantle of the 'Green 'Un' was taken on by the proprietors of the 'Bristol Evening Post', a newspaper that first saw the light of day on Monday the 18th April 1932. They started a sports paper on the following Saturday, when it was printed on green paper and called the 'Bristol Sports Post', becoming the 'Bristol Evening Post Special Sports' for one issue on February 11th, 1933. It was thereafter known as the 'Bristol Evening Post Sports' until becoming the 'Green-'Un' at the start of the 1937-38 season.

This name endured, despite the fact that the use of green paper was discontinued from the 8th December 1962 issue, until the last edition of this much loved sports paper in 1979 (May 12th). The fact that the successful 'Bristol United Press Group' saw fit to let this popular and much needed sports paper die produced much public protest at the time and much comment subsequently, especially as other cities and towns have managed to carry on producing their sports editions. Numbered among the reporters who wrote for the 'Green 'Un' were H.J. Slater-Stone ('Half-back'), Bill Pinnell ('The Traveller'), Arthur J. Spurll ('Reservist'), Bill Andrews, John Barber, Jeremy Brien, John Coe, Bob Cooper, John Donaldson, Chris Ducker, Peter Godsiff, Chris Hewitt, John Mason, Charlie Murphy, Robin Perry, Tony Reed, Arthur Smith, Stan Vickery and Brian Woosey. The main cartoonist was Bob Bennett.

Following the finish of the 'Green 'Un' there has been one attempt to fill the void, with the production of the 'Sports Sketch' on February 23rd, 1986. This was a valiant attempt by a private individual, Jonathan Morgan, to produce a sports paper in the Saturday night tradition, even though it was aimed at the Sunday market, but unable to obtain financial backing he was not able to continue with the enterprise. Other efforts to fill the various gaps in the local sporting scene have resulted in weekly publications such as 'The Bristol Sporting Progress' (1980), 'Avon Soccerworld (1985), 'Avon Sportsworld' (1987), 'The Bristol Sport' (1991), and 'Bristol Soccerworld' (1992).

(Right) From the front page of the the first 'Evening Post', and the first Bob bennett football cartoon.
(18th April 1932)

(Below) The last issues of the 'Pink 'Un' (27 January 1962), and the 'Green 'Un' (12 May 1979).

Bedminster 1892 - 1900

FRED W. KEENAN: Fred Keenan, one of the founders of Bristol South End, was a Yorkshireman, though his early days were spent in London where he commenced his sporting life. he became associated with the Shaftesbury Institute in Lavender Hill, and not only was he actively engaged on behalf of its cricket and football, but he founded a library (books and drama always having a particular fascination for him). Sport though was a major interest, and he proposed a dark blue jersey with a badge labelled 'S.I.' for adoption by the soccer team, but was no doubt amused when instead of being interpreted as the 'Shaftesbury Institute', the labelling on the badge was popularly construed as meaning 'Silly Idiots'! Mr Keenan played for the Institute, and then for Clapham Pilgrims who were turning out rugger and soccer teams. He was well acquainted with Clapham Rovers when they won the F.A. Cup in 1880, and he was a spectator at many Cup Finals at this time, especially when Blackburn Rovers were at the top of the tree.

Mr Keenan came to Bristol in 1889 and soon got involved with the Bedminster Club, working for them with great zest until the rift within brought about the formation of Bristol South End in 1894. Full of energy and good temper, though somewhat original and fearless in his methods, he plunged headlong into work on behalf of the new Club, always up to something that he thought would be of benefit. He was a particular friend of the press.

BOB KELSO: The first captain of the professional Bedminster Club, was one of the great names of Victorian football. He was born in Renton in 1867 and played for his home town club when they were a powerful force in Scottish football, winning Scottish F.A. Cup winners medals with them in 1885 and 1888. The Scot moved to Newcastle West End in the close season of 1888 and played one game for Everton in the Football League's first season of 1888-89. He was a member of the Preston North End team that retained the League Championship the following season and after signing permanently for Everton, he appeared for them in the Cup Final of 1893 as well as being a member of their side that finished as runners-up in the League in 1894-95. Joined Dundee in 1896 and two years later won his seventh Scottish Cap - ten years after he had picked up his sixth; in those days the Scottish selectors did not consider those Scots who were playing with English Clubs.

In 1888 he had played in the Renton team that defeated West Bromwich Albion in what was billed as a 'World Championship Match', a contest between the English and Scottish Cup holders. When he left Everton he was presented with an illuminated address, and when he moved to Bedminster, in 1898, Dundee supporters game him a handsome gold watch. His signature was considered a great coup for the Bedminster Club even though he only played for one season. He died on August 10th, 1942, at the age of 75.

S.J. MILNE: Known as Scottie, he was Bedminster's most popular player, and recalled by those who remembered his playing as possessing a big heart and a wonderful zest for the game, always in the thick of the fray and never stopping until the final whistle. He had one of the hardest shots in local soccer and made his mark straight away on joining the 'Minsters', in 1892-93, making 25 appearances and scoring 7 goals in his first season. He remained with the Club until the end of the 1896-97 campaign by which time he had played in almost a hundred games for Bedminster. During World War One he saw action at Salonica. He was still active and well when he and his wife celebrated their Golden Wedding on February 18th, 1943. They lived in Chatterton Square, Temple, Bristol. Scottie made one appearance for Bristol South End, against Warmley on April 4th, 1896. He played for the Western League Representative XI, including the match that was won 2-0 against Aston Villa in 1896.

JIMMY WHITEHOUSE: Born in Birmingham in 1873 and played for Albion Swifts and Birmingham St. George before joining Grimsby Town in May, 1892. Stayed with the 'Mariners' for four years before moving to Aston Villa for £200. At Perry Barr he was a member of the famous Villa team which won the League and F.A. Cup double in 1896-97, and many people felt that if he could have kept his temperament in check he would have also played for England. He moved to Bedminster for the 1897-98 season, and whilst with the Club he became known as a goalkeeper who, whilst excelling in the air and able to clear his lines with huge kicks, was suspect in dealing with low shots. Nevertheless, he was a popular figure at Bedminster and there was regret at his leaving in May 1899 to join Grimsby again. He moved on in December 1900 to Newton Heath, then Manchester City in February 1903, Third Lanark in September of the same year, Hull City in July 1904, and finally to Southend in the close season of 1905. He died on February 7th, 1934.

Bristol City: 1897-1915

ALEX CAIE

Alex Caie was one of the stars of the first Bristol City professional side, a versatile player who was a high scoring forward able to perform with equal skill in defence. He was born in Aberdeen in 1878, and his first club was Victoria United, a local side from that City. Caie eventually moved to Woolwich Arsenal and played eight Second Division games for the Gunners in 1896-97, scoring four goals. The following season he joined Bristol City and continued his scoring exploits, playing 142 first team games in various competitions, obtaining 77 goals. In March 1900, Caie moved to Millwall, and then transferred to Newcastle United in May 1901. He appeared 31 times in the Magpies First Division side, by now playing almost exclusively in the half-back line, before being on the move again, to Brentford in the close season of 1903. Caie eventually emigrated to Canada, playing initially for the Westmount Club, and then the Sons of Scotland. He was still turning out for that Club when his body was found beside the railway at Lowell, Massachusetts, in December 1914. His death was recorded as murder, given that all his money was missing, and he was buried in Montreal.

PETER CHAMBERS

Sam Hollis maintained that Peter Chambers was the cleverest left-half in the Southern League, and he was certainly a skilful player who helped Bristol City make the transformation to the Football League. Born in Workington in 1878, he played for local club, Black Diamonds, who he helped secure the Cumberland League Championship and Cup. He joined Blackburn Rovers in 1897 and made 33 League appearances for the Ewood Park Club as well as playing for them in the Lancashire Cup Final against Newton Heath before signing on for Bedminster in 1899. After one season with the Southern League Club, Chambers made the short journey to St. Johns' Lane following Bedminster's amalgamation with Bristol City in 1900, and a season later he was a member of the Babes first Football League team. He made a valuable contribution to the endeavours of the Club for six seasons, and his efforts culminated with a Second Division Championship medal in 1905-06, before moving to Swindon Town in 1907. On retiring from the game he remained in the Wiltshire town, where he became landlord of the Red Lion in Moredon. Chambers was 5ft 10ins. tall, and weighed 11st. 10lbs. He died in Swindon in 1952 at the age of 74.

WILLIAM DEMMERY

This local goalkeeper was born in Kingswood, Bristol, in 1877 and he died at the age of 78 on December 28th, 1955. He first came to public notice with his displays for the Warmley Club in 1894, and he helped them secure the Western League Championship in 1895-96 &

1896-97, after being a member of their Reserve side that annexed the Western League Second Division Championship and the Gloucestershire Junior Cup in 1894-95. William also gained winners medals for the Gloucestershire Senior Cup in 1896 and 1897, and the Bristol Charity Cup in 1897 whilst with Warmley, before moving to Staple Hill in 1897-98. He didn't stay long though with the Hillians and the following

season he returned to Warmley for what turned out to be the Club's last campaign. Upon the demise of the famous White Shirts he teamed up with the newly formed Bristol East, a club that was created to keep alive the interest that Warmley had fostered in the district.

Demmery played on many occasions for the Gloucestershire Representative side, and also turned out for J.A. Stevens Bristol City XI. He signed on at St. Johns' Lane in 1902, but for most of his time he was reserve to Harry Clay. In 1906-07 however he earned a Football League Championship Runners-Up medal by appearing in thirty League games. He joined Bristol Rovers in 1908, and for the Stapleton Road Club he made eight Southern League appearances. He was acknowledged as being the best amateur goalkeeper in the locality, though at times he had appeared in outfield positions as centre-forward for Warmley and at half-back for Bristol East. Whilst at Bristol City he weighed 11st. and stood 5ft. 10ins. tall.

ALBERT FISHER

Albert Fisher's two seasons with Bristol City saw him score 21 goals in 50 League games, and although he never made the very top bracket - First Division Aston Villa released him after only one campaign - he proved a good player in the lower division. Fisher was born in Glasgow during June, 1879, and first came to prominence with the Birmingham Club, Ashbury Richmond, in 1900-01 when they won the Handsworth & District League.

During 1901-02 he moved to Soho Caledonians, whom he helped to the Small Heath & District League title, and in 1902-03 to Aston Villa. He managed only one League appearance for Villa, and in the 1903 close season signed for Bristol City. After two campaigns of Second Division football Fisher joined Brighton & Hove Albion, then onto Manchester City in June 1906, followed by Bradford Park Avenue in 1907, before bringing his playing career to a close by performing on the non-League scene in Scotland.

He moved south in 1912 when he became Manager of Merthyr Town, and a year later took on the role of Secretary/Manager with Notts County, a post he held until 1927. Besides being a useful footballer, Fisher was also a keen cricketer whose bowling was of good club standard. In addition he was fond of swimming, and was a good sprinter who won the Aston Villa players 150 yards Challenge Cup. Fisher died at the age of 58 on December 4th, 1937.

WILLIAM JONES

Half-back Billy Jones was the first player to win International recognition whilst on Bristol City's books. He was capped for England in a 3-0 win over Ireland at The Dell on March 9th, 1901. He was also the first player connected with the Club to be awarded a benefit match when he pocketed £102.6s.6d. from a game against Third Lanark in 1902-03.

Jones was born in Brighton on March 6th, 1876, but started his football career with the Derbyshire Club Long Eaton Rangers. He moved to Wellington Athletic, and then Loughborough Town for whom he was top scorer in their 1896-97 Second

Division campaign. In 1897 he became the first player signed by City Manager, Sam Hollis, and his career spanned the Babes election to the Football League and their subsequent promotion season of 1905-06.

He was a consistent performer, a dashing player who overcame several injuries in his early days at the Club. Following nine seasons of valuable service he moved to Tottenham Hotspur in the summer of 1906, and a year later signed on for Swindon Town with whom he ended his career. After retiring from football he became landlord of the Barley Mow in Bristol, living until the age of 83 when he died on September 25th, 1959, at the Snowdon Road Hospital, Bristol. In his prime Billy weighed in at 12 stones and stood 5ft. 10ins. tall.

ALBERT EDWARD (TALBOT) LEWIS

Was born in Bedminster on January 20th, 1877, and as well as being a goalkeeper of note, he was an accomplished cricketer, playing for Somerset from 1899 until his premature retirement, due to injury, in 1912. He was a fine all-rounder, being a reliable batsman and a top class right-arm bowler. He topped the Somerset averages for both batting and bowling in 1910 & 1911, and was their leading bowler in 1907, 1908 & 1909. With the bat he made nine centuries, and his highest score came in his benefit match against Kent when he made 201 not out. Talbot took 513 wickets, and scored almost 8,000 runs, as well as holding over a hundred catches in his first-class career with Somerset.

On the football field he also had a remarkable career after signing professional forms for Bristol City in 1898 when he was looked upon as one of the most promising of local players. He joined Everton for the 1898-99 season, but returned to St. Johns' Lane the following campaign, before being off on his travels once again. Between 1902 and 1904 he played twenty three League games for Sheffield United, and turned out on four occasions for Sunderland in 1904-05. Next port of call saw him at Leicester Fosse for whom he made thirty eight League appearances in 1906-07 before joining up with Bristol City once more. At Ashton Gate he made twenty-one Football League and two F.A. Cup appearances in 1907-08, to add to the games he played for the Club previously, before bringing to an end his football career that had commenced with Bedminster in 1895-96.

Talbot was also a brilliant billiards player, and he was still performing at this game right up to a few weeks before his death at his home in Manor Park, Redland, Bristol on February 22nd, 1956, at the age of 79. On his retiring from cricket he ran a sports shop in Taunton, had four years employment as a cricket coach to an Indian Prince, and between the Wars kept a Billiards Saloon in Castle Street, Bristol. In his prime he stood 6ft. tall and weighed 12st. 7lbs. In all competitions, including Friendlies, Talbot made forty nine appearances for Bristol City, and sixteen for Bedminster for whom he also obtained two goals.

HUGH MONTEITH

One of the most popular goalkeepers to play for Bristol City, Hugh Monteith was born at New Cumnock, Ayrshire, in 1875, and he played his early football in Glasgow with Parkhead Juniors before joining Celtic. After only one season though he moved to Loughborough Town, then a Second Division club,

and in the summer of 1897 he signed for Bristol City. Monteith had few peers in the Southern League, and he did much to help the fledgling professional City Club get established in their new environment. One critic, comparing his goalkeeping to that of Bedminster keepers Whitehouse and Toone, as well as Gray of Bristol Rovers, said that whilst the others were brilliant individuals, Monteith's great strength was his consistency, it being difficult to single out even a single bad performance. He was a fearless, but never reckless, goalkeeper who, if he could not reach the ball with his hands, would not think twice about using his head or feet. After three seasons at St. Johns' Lane he joined West Ham United in 1900 and made 60 Southern League and F.A. Cup appearances for the Hammers before he returned to the Football League scene when he signed for Bury in the close season of 1902. He remained at Gigg Lane until 1906, appearing in the Shakers F.A. Cup Final team of 1903 when Derby County were beaten by a record 6-0 scoreline to enable Bury to win the Cup without conceding a goal in the competition.

PADDY O'BRIEN

Inside-forward Paddy O'Brien was one of the pluckiest and trickiest little players that ever stepped on to a football pitch. He was the absolute terror of goalkeepers and was never satisfied until he had the ball in the net. Although on the slight side, weighing barely 10st and standing only 5ft. 5ins. tall, he possessed great endurance and kept going until the final whistle of every game, never seeming to accept defeat. One writer said of him: *"It matters not how many times they knock him down, he always comes up smiling"*. O'Brien was born in 1873 and began his career with the Scottish Club Elm Park, and then made his name with Glasgow Northern before joining Woolwich Arsenal in the close season of 1893. He rarely missed a game in four seasons with the Gunners, and proved himself to be one of the best inside-lefts in the Second Division of the Football League. O'Brien moved to Bristol City (though the Club was still called Bristol South End at the time of his singing) in the close season of 1897, and he went on to give five valuable season of service at St. Johns' Lane before moving to Swindon Town in the summer of 1902. He scored forty-four goals in various League competitions during his career with the Babes, two of these ensuring that the Club's Football League debut at Blackpool on September 7th, 1901, was celebrated with a win. On retiring from the game he took over a Newsagents in East Street, Bedminster, where he and his wife - who was a teacher at Boot Lane School - remained until taking over the tenancy of the Avon Packet Public House in 1924. O'Brien died at Sunny Patch, Long Ashton, Bristol, on October 2nd, 1950, when he was 76 years of age.

FRED STANIFORTH

Outside-right Fred Staniforth was a member of City's only F.A. Cup Final team, playing in the 1-0 defeat by Manchester United at the Crystal Palace in 1909. He was described as *"an often brilliant player who is clean, clever and brainy"*. He was born at Kilnhurst, near Rotherham, in 1884 and played for Kilnhurst Town, Rotherham Main, and Mexborough Town, before signing for Bristol City in the close season of 1906. He was a regular during his time at Ashton Gate and although his strike rate of 14 goals in 134 League games was nothing special, he could lay on goals for others. His days with the Babes were spent exclusively in the First Division as he signed for City immediately after promotion had been achieved, and left at the end of their relegation season. Staniforth signed for Grimsby Town in 1911, then moved to Liverpool in 1913 where he only made three League appearances. He returned to Bristol to live after retiring from the game, and died there at the age of 70 on May 23rd 1955.

GEORGE TOONE:
English International goalkeeper George Toone was another of the experienced footballers who found their way to the West Country towards the end of the last century. He was born in Nottingham in 1868 and played with several local teams before joining up with Notts County, helping them to the Second Division title in 1896-97. It was while with County that he won his two England Caps, against Scotland and Wales in 1892 when he was on the winning side both times.

He also won an F.A. Cup Winners Medal in 1894 when County beat Bolton Wanderers, this making up for the disappointment of missing the 1891 Final through injury. He moved to Bedminster in 1899, and when they amalgamated with Bristol City in 1900 he made the short journey to St. Johns' Lane. He had been Bedminster's regular keeper, and in his one season with City he didn't miss a game. Toone returned to Notts County in the close season of 1901, and he put in two more campaigns with the Magpies before retiring at the end of the 1902-03 season when he became a publican in the city of his birth. He died on September 1st, 1943, at the age of 75. During his time in Bristol he created a big impression, and the Bristol Observer once described him as being *"without doubt one of the best conducted professional players in the West"*.

The Inter-war Years

ERNIE BRINTON: Born in Bristol on May 26th, 1908, Ernie made his Bristol City debut in his favourite left-half position on March 1st, 1930, when Blackpool beat City 1-0 at Ashton Gate. He represented Bristol Boys whilst at Avonmouth School, and he later played for the Avonmouth Club in the Bristol & Suburban League, as well as performing for the Gloucestershire F.A. XI. For seven seasons Brinton was a regular member of City's 1st team and clocked up exactly 250 League appearances, if one cares to count an abandoned game against Crystal Palace in 1935-36.

At the end of the following season he was transferred to Newport County where he played a leading part in the Somerton Park Club winning the Third Division (South) Championship in 1938-39. Newport had to wait seven years to take their place in Division Two, and during the War Brinton returned to guest for City, making 107 League and Cup appearances between 1940-41 and 1945-46. When peacetime soccer resumed in August 1946, Brinton was 38 years old, and instead of rejoining Newport he signed for Aldershot, for whom he played one season before retiring after 12 League appearances.

CLIFF MORGAN: Clifford Ivor Morgan was born in Bristol on September 26th 1923. He first played soccer at St. George School, and after being spotted playing in the Boys Brigade League began his long career with Bristol City when he signed as an amateur on September 1st, 1930. Made his 1st team debut in a 2-1 defeat at Tottenham Hotspur on March 12th, 1932 playing at inside-right, but his career really blossomed when he switched to the half-back line. Was a regular in the Robins side from early 1934 through to his retirement in 1949, making 248 League appearances, scoring 11 goals, and became skipper of the team. Unfortunately, like many others, his career was blighted by the War which covered the period when he was at the pinnacle of his game. In Wartime competitions during the period 1939-46, Cliff made a further 203 appearances, obtaining 15 goals, and when added to F.A. Cup, Welsh Cup, Division Three (South) Cup, Gloucestershire Cup, Minor Cups and Friendly matches produces a grand total of 537 games and 36 goals for the Club.

He was an expert dead-ball kicker, and it was appropriate that he should score the only goal of the League match against Bournemouth & Boscombe Athletic on October 12th, 1946 as this was his 2nd Benefit. His 1st Benefit had been a joint affair with Cyril Bridge when Torquay United were beaten 2-0 in a League fixture on April 16th, 1938. Cliff became chief scout at Ashton Gate and he went on to give such good service in this role that he was the recipient of another Benefit on May 5th, 1975, when Leicester City beat the City 4-2 in a Friendly in front of 1,796 fans who paid receipts of £1,019. Unfortunately Cliff was rather ill at this time and he died two months later, at Frenchay Hospital on July 31st, aged 61.

BERT NEESAM: Bert Neesam's long career with Bristol City spanned the 1st World War, otherwise he would probably have made nearer 400 League appearances for the Club. He was born at Brompton, Yorkshire, on June 2nd, 1892, and played as a forward for his village club in the Northallerton League. He was Brompton's leading scorer and gained three winners medals before switching to Grangetown Athletic in the Northern League, before joining the City in 1913.

He made his debut in a 1-1 draw at Glossop on March 10th, 1914, and before the Great War brought League football to a halt at the end of the following campaign he had added a further 19 games (2 goals) in the League and 2 F.A. Cup appearances. During the Wartime period he remained at Ashton Gate and played in 104 games, scoring 76 goals, and was in fine form for the resumption of the League programme in August 1919. During the early post-war years he switched to wing half, and it was in that position that Neesam enjoyed the greater part of his career. He saw plenty of variation with City, missing only one game when the Babes finished bottom of Division Two in 1921-22, and was a regular member of the side that took the Division Three (South) title the following season. He played only ten games as City went straight back down again in 1923-24, but in 1926-27 only missed two games when the Club again took the Division Three (South) Championship. In 1928 Neesam left Bristol City for Bath City with whom he brought his footballing career to a close. He was also a keen cricketer and played for the Long Ashton Club for many years. He died at Northallerton on July 6th 1969.

DENNIS ROBERTS: Born in Bretton, South Yorkshire, on the 5th February 1918, he first came to prominence playing in school's soccer in Huddersfield. He gained representative honours before signing amateur forms for Huddersfield Town. At the age of 17, he moved to Notts County he played in defence in the reserve team, although learning much from 'Dixie' Dean and Hughie Gallacher who were both with that Club at the time. After not being retained by Notts County, he was recommended to City by Joe Riley, playing first in the reserve team at right-back before moving to centre-half after the retirement of Joe Pearce. As with Cliff Morgan, and others, Roberts played for much of his career during WW2. A magnificent defender, he earned rave notices in the Press, and was often lauded by the opposition players and officials. He pefected the sliding tackle, and he had many duels with Tommy Lawton, and had few peers with his ability at heading. Despite interest shown by Aston Villa, Chelsea, and others, he remained loyal to the Club that he served from 1938 to 1954. He played in 306 League matches, during which he scored 2 goals, including a brilliant equaliser at Ashton Gate in a game versus Plymouth Argyle. Following a bad leg injury, Dennis captained the reserves in the Football Combination, where he became the side's penalty ace. He retired from football in 1954, and became 'mine host' at the Avon Packet, then at the newly built Ship Inn at Cathay. Prior to his full retirement he worked as a fork lift driver at G.K.N. Bedminster. On the death of his wife, Dennis moved back to his roots, to the Emley area of Yorkshire.

ALF ROWLES: Although he only played 24 times for Bristol City in League Football, Alf Rowles was the scoring sensation of the 1937-38 season. He set a Football League record by finding the net in six consecutive games, from his debut against Exeter City on January 15th when he notched a hat-trick. He ended the campaign with a remarkable tally of 18 goals, including two more hat-tricks - from only 14 games - but he was to be one of the briefest shooting stars to appear at Ashton Gate. Early in the following season, in the match with Notts County on September 7th, Rowles collided with the visiting goalkeeper and sustained a knee ligament injury which effectively ended his career. He made a few attempts at a comeback but was eventually forced to give up the game on medical advice, his last appearance being in a Friendly against Bristol Rovers on September 16th 1939.

Alf was born on May 6th, 1916, and played for South Bristol Central School, then for St. Pancras in the Bristol & District League, and Weston-super-Mare in the Somerset League before City scout, Sam Poople, brought him to Ashton Gate for a trial. After his playing retirement he failed, due to his injury, to gain entry into the Wartime Services, so he returned to his trade as a fitter, working for Messrs. Brecknell, Dolman & Rodgers. He kept in close contact with the City though by looking after the Youth team and acting as trainer to the United side for more than sixteen years.

FRANK VALLIS: Born in Bristol on April 5th, 1896, Frank was regarded as the best locally produced goalkeeper. He was City's answer to the brilliant Bristol Rovers keeper, Jesse Whatley, who had learnt his art at Trowbridge. Vallis first turned out for City in a Friendly against the Rovers on April 5th, 1919, after catching the eye whilst playing for Horfield United in the Bristol & Suburban League. He impressed

straight away and he played four more games in this last season before League football resumed and signed profcssional forms.

Frank was City's first-choice for over six seasons, sharing in all the ups and downs of this period. He was an ever-present in his first two campaigns, saw the Babes relegated in 1921-22, and then won a Third Division (South) Championship medal the following season. Midway through the 1925-26 campaign he lost his place to Billy Coggins, and moved on to Merthyr Town (who were then in the Third Division South), on June 16th, 1926. In the 1921-22 season Frank was injured in the first match at Notts County on August 27th and after the goalkeeping duties were taken on for a short spell by Joseph Hughes, another member of the Vallis clan took over on September 5th. This was Frank's brother Jack, who held the fort until November 19th. Jack had been signed from Dundee during the close season of 1921, and his presence at Ashton Gate together with that of another brother, Arthur, (who moved to Halifax Town in the Summer of 1922) ensured plenty of family solidarity.

THOMAS (TOT) WALSH: A native of Bolton, born on February 12th, 1900, Tot was spotted by Bolton Wanderers when he was playing in local football. The Burnden Park Club snapped him up and he spent three seasons with them, playing mainly in the Reserve team for whom he scored 77 goals. He made his League debut in 1923-24 but played in only two First Division games before joining Bristol City on January 16th 1924.

As Ashton Gate his career finally blossomed and he scored 91 goals in 150 League & F.A. Cup appearances, his totals being raised to exactly 100 goals in 161 games when appearances for the Club in all types of matches are taken into consideration. He won a Third Division (South) Championship medal with the Babes in 1926-27 when he obtained nearly a goal a game to help City finish two points ahead of Plymouth Argyle. Highlight was his notching of 6 goals in the League match against Gillingham at Ashton Gate on January 15th, 1927 when he helped City achieve a 9-4 success.

This little goalscoring hero - he stood just 5ft 7in. tall - moved to Crystal Palace on May 11th, 1928, and he died at the age of 50 on November 22nd 1950.

ALBERT (BERTIE) WILLIAMS: Born in Merthyr on March 4th, 1907, this tricky, brainy, player earned rave reviews for his performance for City in an F.A. Cup game at Derby County in January 1930. He joined the Babes from Merthyr Town, and made his debut on Christmas Eve 1927 in a 3-1 success at South Shields. He remained with City for almost five seasons, most of which were spent in a struggling side, and in January 1932 - midway through a campaign in which City were relegated - he was transferred to Sheffield United, where he remained until the end of 1936-37. Bertie played in one International for Wales, winning his cap in the side that was defeated 7-0 by Northern Ireland in Belfast during February 1930. Whilst at Ashton Gate he made 109 appearances in League & F.A. Cup, obtaining 29 goals in the process.

Post-Second World War

BRIAN CLARK: The son of former City hero Don Clark, Brian turned into a goalscoring hero in his own right, a dedicated professional who had a magnificent career with six different clubs. Bristol born (on January 13th, 1943), whilst a pupil at Bristol Technical School of Engineering he played for Bristol Boys when they secured the English Schools Trophy .

He joined City as an amateur, turning out for the United team in the Premier Combination, but he soon progressed to the Colts side that performed in the Western League, and was knocking on the door of the 1st Team after good displays for the Reserves in the Football Combination. Brian's senior debut, in tandem with Lou Peters, came in the concluding match of the 1960-61 campaign when Brentford were beaten 3-0 in what was Tommy Burden's final game of an illustrious career. Clark soon formed an effective and skilful inside-trio alongside John Atyeo and 'Shadow' Williams, and many Third Division defences suffered during the early 1960's.

Clark hit twelve goals in the first eight games of 1964-65 to put City on course for the Second Division, and his goal in the final game against Oldham Athletic capped a tremendous season. Two seasons later, goals were temporarily less easy to come by and he moved to Huddersfield Town in a deal that saw City receive £2,500 as well as obtaining the services of John Quigley. Eighteen months later, in February 1968, Brian went to Cardiff City where he formed a feared partnership with John Toshack. The goals continued to come in subsequent moves to Bournemouth, Millwall, Cardiff again, and Newport County. He appeared in more than 600 Football League games, scoring 217 goals, and given the early problems he had with his stamina, which necessitated a nose and throat operation, it is a record that says much for his fitness.

Clark has often been described as the model professional, and his Millwall team mate Eamon Dunphy, in his book 'Only A Game', wrote of him: *"He is a much respected player in the Second Division. He has been around a lot of clubs: Huddersfield, Bristol City, Bournemouth, and he always does a good honest job. Very skilled, good in the air. He is the kind of pro other pros really respect and like"*. On leaving the Football League, Brian became Player/Manager of Bridgend Town, combining this with the coaching of the Welsh Federation of Boys Clubs (under 14) side. Had a spell with Maesteg but returned to Bridgend in 1992.

JACK CONNOR. Jack Connor joined City in October 1960 when John McCann moved in the opposite direction. Born in Maryport, Cumberland, on July 25th, 1934, Connor was to be the centre-half anchor of the City side throughout the 1960's. Standing 6ft 1in Connor was strong in the air, wholehearted on the ground, and his inspiring influence spread right through the team, 'Jovial Jack' though put football in the right perspective, as while no one would strive harder on the pitch it was rare to catch him without a huge smile on his face. A swashbuckling, larger than life figure he lifted the spirits of team-mates and supporters alike.

At Huddersfield, where he had also played as a wing-half and centre-forward, he played 85 League games, scoring 10 goals in the period following his signing for them in October 1952. At Ashton Gate he again managed to obtain 10 League goals, though this time he made 354 + 1 substitute appearances in the League, and this added to games played in the F.A. and the League Cup gave him a Bristol City record of 404 appearances and 12 goals when he retired at the end of the 1970-71 campaign. He was granted a testimonial, and on the 15th March 1971, 7,800 spectators paying receipts of approximately £2,000 turned out for his Benefit match when Wolverhampton Wanderers beat the City 2-1.

He then took up coaching, firstly with City and then at Everton. He now has a job outside the game and lives in the North-west.

TONY COOK: Tony Cook - height 6ft 1in, weight 11st 2lbs - was one of a long line of brilliant goalkeepers that have performed for Bristol City over the years. He started his career by playing as a winger for Durdham Down Adult School, but he took over in goal when the regular custodian was unable to play. After winning various medals with the Adult School he moved on to Clifton St. Vincent with whom he came to the notice of the City. Following a trial with the Reserves, when he saved a penalty in a 1-0 defeat against Southampton at the Dell on December 26th, 1949, the Manager Bob Wright was waiting at Ashton Gate on the players' return to secure his signature on professional forms.

It wasn't until almost three years later though that he made his senior debut, taking his place between the sticks for the 4-2 win over Swindon Town at Ashton Gate on November 8th 1952. Throughout his career saving penalties was to be his forte. In the 1958-59 campaign he saved six out of the nine spot-kicks he faced, and in one game that season, at Scunthorpe on the 11th April, he twice saved Brownsword's efforts but both were ordered to be retaken, before Donnelly scored at the third attempt. Cook missed the run-in to the 1954-55 Championship Season with a broken arm, losing his place to Bob Anderson.

Another broken arm, in 1962-63, ended a regular run when he was at the peak of his form. Mike Gibson then took over, and Cook left on a free transfer. He played at Southern League Worcester City for two seasons before putting in another brace with Cinderford Town. A local man, born on October 8th, 1929, Tony appeared for only one Football League Club, though Bristol Rovers were keen to secure his services in April 1963 when the 'Soccer Bribes Scandal' broke and deprived the Eastville Club of their 'keeper Esmond Million.

Tony brought his footballing career to a close by returning to the local scene and playing in the Downs League with Manor Farm Boys Club, plus a short spell with Sneyd Park. He also started a new career as a prison officer, a position from which he retired in 1994.

This extrovert 'keeper played in almost 350 games for Bristol City in the major competitions, but he was often tense before games needing to indulge in a puff on his Woodbines to calm his nerves. He was strong and brave, well able to take care of himself in an era when goalkeepers were not mollycoddled by referees, and he was an acrobatic shot-stopper who displayed tremendous confidence in claiming crosses.

Tony acknowledges that Bristol City were always his favourite Club when a schoolboy at Anglesea Place School, Blackboy Hill, Bristol, and that the player he most admired was the great Frank Swift of Manchester City and England fame.

DERMOT CURTIS: This effective centre-forward, born in Dublin on August 26th, 1932, was the leading scorer in the Republic of Ireland when he signed for Bristol City in November 1956, a transfer fee of £5,000 being paid to Shelbourne to secure his services. At this time Dermot was already an established International whilst still working as a panel-beater in a Dublin garage. Taking up full-time soccer on joining the Robins, he held his place to play on the opposite side to City's John Atyeo in the World Cup Qualifying matches against England. The matches were played at Wembley on May 8th, 1957 (when Curtis scored in a 5-1 defeat), and at Dalymont Park eleven days later, when Atyeo headed a goal in the dying seconds to secure a rather fortunate point that gained England passage to the final stages of the World Cup in Sweden in 1958.

Dermot had a distinguished international career making seventeen appearances for his country, five whilst at Ashton Gate, but despite scoring 16 times in 27 League appearances, he was allowed to leave for Ipswich Town on August 7th 1958. At Portman Road though he only turned out on 41 occasions in the League side (17 goals), and he moved on to Exeter City in August 1963. Dermot had two successful spells at St. James Park, making a total of 162 + 3 substitute appearances and notching 33 goals, before retiring in 1969. Between his two periods at Exeter he appeared for Torquay United, playing in 12 League matches and scoring just 1 goal. In his prime, Dermot was 5ft 11ins tall and weighed 11st. He remained in Exeter after his retirement from the game, and he currently works there as a roofer.

JANTZEN DERRICK: Winger Jantzen Derrick was the youngest player to appear in a League game for Bristol City when he turned out at Sincil Bank against Lincoln City on November 28th, 1959, at an age of 16 years and 324 days. Derrick was the star of the England Schoolboys team and it was considered quite a coup when City persuaded him to join his local team in the face of much competition from the major clubs.

He served the Robins well, yet he was an enigmatic character, and despite his impressive array of skills he sometimes appeared to lack the motivation necessary for success at the very top. This had the effect of his talents not always being reflected in his play, a situation that caused much frustration among the fans. Many thought that his best position was in a more midfield role, rather than being isolated on the wing, and it is a fact that when he switched positions he was often seen to better effect.

After twelve seasons at Ashton Gate he went on loan to Mansfield Town in March 1971, but he only made two League appearances for the Stags. Returning to the City Derrick found himself not retained at the end of the 1970-71 campaign, and he then went abroad to play in France for Paris St-Germain, and on his return played for Bath City then Keynsham Town He still lives in Bristol, and is Chairman of the Bristol City Old Players Association.

ALEC EISENTRAGER: Alois Bernhard Eisentrager was born in Hamburg on July 20th, 1927, and he came to Britain as a prisoner of war in February 1945. He attended Llangenforde and Schaudingsveg Schools in Hamburg, and was on the books of S.V. Hamburg from 1940 to 1944. He enlisted in the Luftwaffe in October 1944 at the age of 17.

Alec remained in England and played for Trowbridge Town with whom he scored over 200 goals before joining Bristol City in January 1950. He was a ball artist whose smooth control, deft flicks and a touch of showmanship endured him to the Ashton Gate crowd who took this diminutive - yet muscular - forward to their hearts. His version of the bicycle-kick, then something of a novelty in the British game, adding a new dimension to the City attack.

His best position was probably as a deep-lying schemer, but being most often employed on the wing he was able to utilise his dribbling and crossing skills to splendid effect, but his lack of pace was sometimes a handicap. He was a firm tackler, and had a fierce long range shooting ability that he used to excellent effect. Alec made 240 appearances in League and Cup for the City, scoring 47 goals, before signing for a brief stay with Southern League Merthyr Tydfil in July 1958. He then played for local club Westbury Park in the Downs League before hanging up his boots, and is a printer by trade.

MIKE GIBSON: Mike Gibson, in the eyes of many City supporters, ranks as a goalkeeper without equal in the annals of the Club. Given the number of great keepers to have performed for the Robins - with the likes of Hugh Monteith, George Toone, Harry Clay, Frank Vallis, Billy Coggins, Tony Cook and Bob Anderson - this speaks volumes for the impression that this signing from Shrewsbury Town created during his long reign between the sticks at Ashton Gate. He was born in Derby on July 15th 1939 and played non-League football for Gresley Rovers and Nuneaton Borough before he moved to Gay Meadow in March 1960.

Gibson made 76 Third Division appearances (including a brilliant display against the City on December 23rd 1961) in three seasons with Shrewsbury before moving to Ashton Gate in April 1963. His early form though was disappointing, but after replacing Tony Cook for the fourth game of 1963-64 this former England Youth International never looked back. His form over the following eight years was exceptional, and he rarely missed a game. Had he been taller - he stood 5ft 9ins - then he might have attracted the big clubs, and his career may have reached even greater heights. He had exceptional talent and those of us who witnessed his displays for the Club at this time felt that he was deserving of international recognition. Bristol City were fortunate in being able to enjoy his skills for so long.

In July 1972, he moved to Gillingham and played 80 League games for the Medway Club before retiring at the conclusion of the 1973-74 campaign. Gibson returned to Bristol, where he now works as a postman, and he is also employed on a part-time basis at Ashton Gate.

GERRY GOW: Gerry Gow was tough, aggressive and dynamic, following in the tradition of John Quigley and Bobby Kellard, making plenty of enemies in the ranks of opposition fans with his biting tackles. Born in Glasgow on May 29th 1952, he played for Glasgow Schools Under 13's and it was a sign of City's increasing prestige that they were able to sign a Scot like Gow when he left school in June 1969.

He was only 17 when he made his City debut, turning out against Charlton Athletic in the concluding game of the 1969-70 campaign when they lost 2-1 at the Valley. The following season saw him established as a regular in the side, and he made the midfield role his own, until moving on to Manchester City following relegation from the top flight in 1980. Gow won a Scottish Under-23 cap in March 1973, coming on as substitute against England at Newcastle and was seen as a candidate for full honours, though he was not a prolific goalscorer unlike his rival John Wark of Ipswich Town. He was an ever-present in the promotion side of 1975-76 and adjusted easily to the higher demands of the First Division.

In October 1980 he moved to John Bond's Manchester City, and while his erstwhile colleagues were facing up to relegation to the Third Division, Gow was appearing in the F.A. Cup Final. The next season was him move to Rotherham United, and then to Burnley in August 1983. Later he tried his hand at management, ending a two-year stint at Yeovil by resigning on January 2nd, 1987. Gow played in a total of 460 League games for his four clubs, notching 56 goals in the process, a fine record for a fine player.

ERNIE JONES: Ernest George Jones was born in St. Philips, Bristol, on May 12th, 1919, and attended St. Silas School. He was a member of the Bristol Boys XI for three years, playing in the same side as Harry Bamford (who went on to find fame with Bristol Rovers). Ernie had two unsuccessful trials for the English Schoolboys team, and from 1933 to 1936 he played for Victoria Athletic before joining the City.

Ernie didn't appear in the 1st team until the first wartime season when he was in the side that lost 7-2 at Swindon Town on December 23rd 1939. During the war he served with distinction with the 6th Airborne Division, being wounded and taken prisoner at Arnhem in 1944. Returning to Ashton Gate at the conclusion of hostilities he claimed a spot in the side that drew 0-0 with the Rovers at Eastville on March 23rd, 1946, and went on to make a total of six appearances by the end of the campaign. At the return to normal League football in 1946-47, Ernie was a virtual ever-present for the first half of the season, and the following season he made five appearances before becoming Player/Manager of Wells City in the Western League, where he remained until 1958. From 1958 to 1983 he was involved with local football, becoming team manager of Downs League Club Avon St. Philips Athletic, and serving as Manager of the Downs League representative XI for many years. In 1947 Ernie weighed 11st and his height was given as 5ft 10ins.

GEORGE LOWRIE: George Lowrie was born in Tonypandy on December 19th 1919 and he started his twenty year career in soccer when he signed as an amateur for Swansea Town in August 1936. He turned professional with the Swans five months later, but in November 1937 moved on to Preston North End. In June 1939 he was transferred to Coventry City, assisting the Club right through the period of the Second World War, and he remained at Highfield Road until March 1948 when Newcastle United paid £18,000 for his services.

A brawl with Sammy Smyth in a game with Wolverhampton Wanderers brought about his move to Ashton Gate in September 1949, when City paid a new club record fee of £10,000. With the Robins, George used to thrill the fans with his great vision and dynamic shooting, but following a broken leg sustained against Nottingham Forest on November 17th, 1950, his confidence appeared to suffer after a lengthy lay-off. He made his return to 1st XI action on October 27th, 1951, but four months later was on his way back to Coventry after the Robins received a £2,750 fee. However, he only put in one season back with the Bantems, and in July 1953 he joined Lovells Athletic with whom he played out his career before retiring in 1956.

George made thirteen Welsh International appearances, including nine wartime games, one of which saw him notching a hat trick against England at Wembley but still having the misfortune of being on the losing side, England winning 5-3. He returned to Bristol on his retirement to work for Messrs. Douglas in Kingswood, and retained his interest in the game by coaching the works team. George died in Kingswood, Bristol, on May 3rd 1989.

NICKY MORGAN: Nicky Morgan must rank as one of Joe Jordan's best buys as the capture of this extremely gifted player for £30,000 from Stoke City on March 23rd, 1990, proved to be a brilliant piece of business. Nicky was born in East Ham on 30th October, 1959, and started his career with West Ham, where he made 22 League and Cup appearances (7 as substitute) for the Hammers, and scoring two goals before moving to Portsmouth for £50,000 in March 1983. At Fratton Park he played in over 100 games, notching 35 goals in all competitions before teaming up with Stoke in December 1986, when £30,000 was paid for his services. Again he gave good value for he obtained 26 goals from 104 games, before coming to Ashton Gate, where he proved to be a revelation.

With Bristol City it wasn't his goalscoring prowess that took the eye, though his tally of 29 from 88 games (5 as substitute) is a good enough record, it was his skill that really impressed. His ability on the ball, and vision of his play marked him out to be a player much better than most that the Ashton Gate faithful have had to endure over the years. Indeed it can be said that he was the best all-round player to have played for the Robins since the Club was reconstituted in 1982. Nicky moved to Exeter City for a short spell in 1993-94, but the end of the campaign found him with Southern League Dorchester Town.

ROB NEWMAN: Rob Newman, born in Bradford-on-Avon on December 13th, 1963, was Bristol City's very own 'Captain Marvel', being able to play in all outfield positions. A tall, talented, wholehearted performer, he came early into League football due to the crisis which threatened the Club's very existence in 1982. He made his debut in the match immediately after the departure of the 'Ashton Gate Eight', helping the City to a 0-0 draw with Fulham on the 6th February that year.

His ability to adapt to almost any position made him especially useful, and it was apparent that if he remained at Ashton Gate then it was likely that he would surpass John Atyeo's club appearance record. Unfortunately he was allowed to leave the Robins during the close season of 1991, when the Club directors appeared to be almost forcing him to move to Norwich City, after accepting a bid of £600,000. This was a new record transfer fee that the Club had received (since beaten by the £1.75 million for Andy Cole in March 1993), but as so often at Ashton Gate, it represented poor business acumen. Newman was clearly worth a fee far in excess of this figure, but the real loss was the ability of the player on the park, a void that hasn't been satisfactory filled since his departure.

During his career at Ashton Gate, Newman (known as 'Biff') appeared in a total of 456 games (including 13 as substitute), and obtained 54 goals in the major competitions. He notched a particularly fine goal against Newport County at Ashton Gate on March 14th 1987, his effort bringing the house down. At Norwich he adapted well to the demands of higher division football, and being retained at Carrow Road in the close season of 1994 he has high hopes of adding to the 91 games and 11 goals he has obtained for the Canaries in League competition.

Shortly before leaving Ashton Gate Newman had a Benefit match, when a crowd of 11,739 turned up on August 20th, 1990, to witness the Robins 2-0 success over Aston Villa.

DAVID NOAKE: Even though this nippy, tenacious winger didn't remain long at Ashton Gate he made sufficient impact on many supporters of Bristol City to be worthy of mention. He was born in Dorchester on June 9th, 1940, and joined Luton Town from the local Town Club in November 1959. For the Hatters he made 17 League appearances before his £750 transfer to Ashton Gate in the close season of 1961. Although appearing for just one campaign, the decision by Fred Ford to release him produced much protest by supporters and an outcrop of 'Noake Must Stay' graffiti in the area of Ashton Gate. He joined Southern League Trowbridge Town and many years later was still playing the game at Western League level. Noake made 2 F.A. Cup appearances for the City, including the brilliant team performance when Hereford United were beaten 5-2 at Edgar Street on November 8th 1961. In the League he managed 11 games and notched 3 goals. David weighed in at 11st 8lbs and stood 5ft 9ins tall.

ERNIE PEACOCK: Ernie 'Ginger' Peacock was born in Bristol on December 11th, 1924, but he arrived at Ashton Gate from Notts County in October 1946 after playing as a guest for Bath City. 'Ginger' was an excellent clubman whose temperament off the pitch was in direct contrast to his attitude on it, where he showed a fiery commitment, and a temper that sometimes matched his red hair. He played soccer for his school - Barleyfields - but later, during the 1944-45 season, when turning out for Syston he came to the notice of the Meadow Lane Club. He was to eventually enjoy thirteen seasons at Ashton Gate.

A tireless and popular wing-half of the 'old school', never happier than when he was in the thick of the action, 'Ginger' won a Third Division (South) Championship medal in 1954-55 when he only missed two games. In League and Cup matches, Peacock made a total of 357 appearances for the Robins - securing 8 goals - before moving to Weymouth in June 1959. He later became a car salesman, but heart trouble brought his premature death in the Bristol General Hospital on February 12th, 1973, when he was only 48 years of age. He is still fondly remembered by many older supporters, who considered that no one wore the City shirt with greater pride than good old Ginger.

JOHN QUIGLEY: John Quigley must rank as one of the most skilful and tenacious players to have appeared in Bristol City's colours, despite a somewhat disappointing debut at Northampton Town in November 1966. He was born in Glasgow on June 28th 1935 and after being released by Celtic played for Ashfield Juniors before joining Nottingham Forest in the close season of 1957. Quigley stayed with Forest for almost eight years, winning an F.A. Cup winners medal in 1959 when Luton Town were beaten 2-1. After 236 League appearances (51 goals) for Forest he moved to Huddersfield Town in February 1965. He appeared in 69 League games for the Leeds Road Club (one as substitute) and scored five goals before being transferred to Bristol City as part of the deal which also saw Huddersfield part with £2,500 to enable Brian Clark to move in the opposite direction.

Quigley became a great favourite the Ashton Gate, and it was a surprise when he was allowed to move the Mansfield Town for £3,000 in July 1968, especially as the City then paid out a Club record fee of £33,500 to obtain the services of Bobby Kellard from Portsmouth as his replacement. At Field Mill he brought his playing career to a close, scoring two goals in 104 games before being appointed assistant to Manager Jock Basford in November 1970. Unfortunately the sacking of Mr Basford 12 months later also brought Quigley's stay at Field Mill to an end, and he chose to coach in the Middle East. For the Robins, Quigley made a total of 82 1st team appearances made up as follows:- League 66 (7 goals); F.A. Cup 9; Gloucestershire Cup 2; Friendship Cup 1; Friendlies 4.

ALEX TAIT: Alex Tait was Fred Ford's first signing for Bristol City, and alongside that of Jack Connor, Mike Gibson and John Quigley, it ranks as his best. Tait came to Ashton Gate on the 22nd June, 1960, when City paid Newcastle United £5,000. Born at Bedlington, Northumberland, on the 28th November, 1933, Tait joined the Magpies in September 1952 and his eight years at St. James Park might have been much more successful had he decided to concentrate on full-time soccer instead of qualifying as a schoolteacher. He made only 34 appearances for Newcastle and scored ten goals, three of them coming in a memorable match against local rivals Sunderland in 1956.

Red-haired Tait was a great favourite as Ashton Gate where the supporters appreciated his speed and skill. Those who were present are undoubtably able to recall a particularly fine goal against Hereford United in an F.A. Cup First Round Replay in November 1961 when he found the net from an apparently impossible angle.

Alex moved on to Doncaster Rovers in June 1964 and scored seven goals in 19 League appearances for them before joining Southern League Burton Albion, where he eventually replaced Peter Taylor as manager. Following his departure from Burton he returned to teaching and recently retired as Deputy Headmaster of a Comprehensive School in Burton-on-Trent. He lives in Tutbury, near Burton.

BOB TAYLOR: Bob Taylor became an idol at Ashton Gate during his short spell with the Robins. He was signed for £225,000 from Leeds United in March 1989 and the City certainly got value for money from this Elland Road reserve player. Bob was a gem beyond the wildest dreams of the Ashton gate faithful, and as with Andy Cole three years later they found the Club had acquired a man obsessed with scoring goals. In the promotion campaign of 1989-90 Bob indulged freely in his passion, and the dashing North-Easterner became the first City marksman, since the days of John Atyeo, to find the net thirty times in a campaign.

It wasn't only the number of goals he scored that enraptured the audience, but the quality, as Bob would habitually lash the ball home from outside the box, and his aerial work was often inspired. There is little doubt that the Robins would have secured the Third Division Championship in 1989-90 if they hadn't lost the services of Taylor, due to the injury sustained shortly after completing his hat trick in the game with Crewe Alexandra on the 10th April. The loss of his talents for all but the match at Bolton on April 28th brought about a stuttering conclusion to the campaign, and the City had to settle for the Runners-up spot behind old rivals Bristol Rovers. His 27 League goals though made him the top marksman in the Third Division and this added to 5 goals in the F.A. Cup, 2 in the League Cup, and 1 in the Gloucestershire Cup gave Bob a haul of 35, to become the second highest seasonal scorer in the history of the Robins.

Unfortunately though he found things much harder in the higher division, and being a player whose confidence was affected by lack of goals, his deft touches, powers of control and distribution deserted him. After obtaining only 15 goals in 57 Second Division appearances, he was transferred to Third Division West Bromwich Albion for £300,000 on the 31st January 1992, a move that upset a great number of Ashton Gate fans. At the Hawthorns his old confidence came back, helping the Baggies to promotion in 1992-93 he showed that he could perform at the higher level by continuing to do the necessary for them in 1993-94, and he is now valued in the couple of million class. Bob was born in Horden on February 3rd 1967, and after playing for his local side he signed professional forms for Leeds United in March 1986. At Elland Road he made 52 appearances in all competitions (including 11 as substitute) and scoring 13 goals, before joining City, where he became one of the most popular players to have performed at Ashton Gate.

BERT TINDILL: Bert Tindill signed for City from Doncaster Rovers on February 3rd, 1958, and he formed an effective partnership with John Atyeo to save the Robins from the jaws of relegation at the expense of his old club. All action inside-forward Bert Tindill made his name with the Yorkshire Club, joining them during World War Two, and going on to make 402 League appearances and scoring 122 goals for Rovers.

At Ashton gate his 10 goals in 14 games were a major contribution in pulling the Club to safety in 1958, for when he joined in February they looked doomed for the drop. Bert was a Yorkshireman through and through, and could not settle in the West County. He made several requests for a transfer and was eventually allowed to return 'home' in the summer of 1959, after playing in all of City's games in 1958-59. He joined Barnsley - in an exchange deal that saw City paying a new record club fee of £14,500 to obtain the services of Malcolm Graham and John McCann - and at Oakwell he made 98 appearances and scored 29 goals in two seasons to produce a career total of 556 League games and 180 goals. Bert was born in South Hindley, Yorkshire, on the 31st December, 1926, and met an untimely death from a heart attack, in the same locality, on the 10th July, 1973, at the age of only only forty-six.

Bert Tindill was extremely popular at Ashton Gate, ranking alongside later heroes from the North such as Norman Hunter and Bob Taylor, producing a long-lasting rapport with the Ashton Gate crowd, and he was much applauded on his returns with Barnsley.

ALAN WALSH: Alan Walsh was an outstanding player during his career at Ashton Gate, and there is little doubt that the Robins benefited from a bargain deal when the Football League Tribunal set the fee for his transfer from Darlington at a ridiculously low figure of £18,000. The Quakers had every reason to feel aggrieved at losing a player who had scored 100 goals for them in 278 games in the three major competitions.

Despite his apparently casual approach, Walsh consistently underlined the bargain that the City bought, and his hard and accurate shooting produced many fine goals, often from dead-ball kicks. Many fans felt though that he should have adopted a more forward role, but his long-ball passing from deep positions gave an added dimension to City's play.

Unfortunately the Robins lost his services when he accepted a lucrative offer to join Turkish Club Besiktas in 1989, where he remained for two seasons. Since returning to England, he has played for Walsall (1991-92), local side Imperial United, as well as Southern League Clevedon Town, and Western League Taunton Town. He performed for the latter at Wembley Stadium in last season's F.A. Vase Final. On Wednesday September 14th, 1994, Alan returned to his roots when he joined Third Division Hartlepool United as Player/Coach, helping them three days later to achieve a 2-0 success over Gillingham at the Victoria Ground when he scored with an 89th minute penalty.

Walsh was born in Hartlepool on the 9th December 1956, and he started his footballing career with Horden, then moved to Middlesbrough in December 1976 (for whom he made three substitute appearances in 1977-78), before moving to Darlington in October 1978. At Ashton Gate, Alan played in 257 games (including 3 as substitute) and notched 90 goals in the principal competitions. It is something of a mystery to West County fans that this gem of a player has spent his entire English career in the relative obscurity of the lower reaches of the League, for without doubt he had the talent to have graced the top level.

JOHNNY WATKINS: John Vincent Watkins, 5ft 11ins, 11st 10lbs, was born in Bristol on April 9th 1933. A pupil at Portway School, he played for Bristol Boys and had trials for England Schoolboys. On leaving school he worked for Mardons, and later did his National Service in the R.A.F. Played for Coombe Dingle Boys Club before joining Clifton St. Vincent in the Downs League. John signed for Bristol City in June 1951, gaining four England Youth caps, but it wasn't until September 30th, 1953, that he made his 1st Team debut when Norwich City were beaten 3-1 at Ashton Gate. He held his place for the next game, a 5-0 defeat at Swindon, but it wasn't until November 24th, 1956, that he again appeared for the seniors, scoring in a 2-1 defeat by Stoke City at Ashton Gate. Thereafter he was a regular and he played a significant part in the famous F.A. Cup Fifth Round game against Bristol Rovers on February 15th, 1958, when he opened the scoring with a rare headed goal but then missed a penalty just before half-time as Rovers went on to win 4-3. In the close season of 1959 he was sold to Cardiff City for £2,500, a move that the Robins Manager Peter Doherty probably regretted, for Watkins went on to star in the Bluebirds Second Division promotion side in 1959-60, while his erstwhile colleagues were relegated.

For Cardiff City John made 65 League appearances and scored 17 goals, before joining Bristol Rovers in February 1961. He only played in 23 League games for the Eastville Club before bringing his career to a close with spells at Bath City and Welton Rovers. A fine cricketer, he was associated with Stoke Bishop C.C. for many years, but lately his main hobby is bowls with the National Smelting Club.

Watkins was a very confident left-wing raider with a cannonball shot, such a shot against Ipswich Town at Ashton Gate on March 27th 1959 breaking the net.

His best goal though was thought to be his strike against Barnsley at Oakwell on August 27th 1958. Taking a pass from Mike Thresher, he lobbed the ball over Short's head, and then volleyed home a missile-like shot from about 40 yards.

ALAN WILLIAMS: Centre-half Alan Williams was regarded as one of Bristol City's most outstanding post-war discoveries, but the traumatic events of the 1959-60 campaign caused his early form to desert him and it took a transfer to Oldham Athletic in June 1961 to revive his career. He was born in Bristol on June 3rd, 1938, and made his League debut in a 3-1 defeat at Blackburn Rovers on February 9th 1957. He was a regular thereafter but relegation to the Third Division took its toll and after making only 11 League appearances in 1960-61 he moved to Boundary Park. In four seasons with Oldham he made 172 appearances and scored nine goals before joining Watford in July 1965.

At Vicarage Road Alan put in 43 appearances, and further moves to Newport County in November 1966 (63 appearances, 3 goals), and Swansea Town in October 1968 (146 appearances - 4 as substitute - 7 goals) led to his retirement in 1971, by which time he had amassed a grand total of 559 League appearances during the process of which he obtained 21 goals.

Alan played for the R.A.F. during his National Service days, and he was robbed of an England Under-23 cap when the game against Scotland in 1959 was cancelled because of bad weather. Following his retirement he returned to Bristol and became the landlord of the White Horse in West Street, Bedminster, and later mine host of The Horse and Groom in St.George's Road. His son Gary followed in his footsteps, playing for Bristol City (1980-84), Swansea (1985), Oldham (1985-92), and Hearts, and is now landlord of the Pineapple Inn which is also in St. George's Road.

Ernie Brinton

Mike Gibson

Ernie Peacock

John Quigley

Jack Connor

APPENDIX

WHO?

How Many ?

How Often ?

WHEN ?

How Much ?

NAME	Born	Died	From	To	Pos.	Apps. League	Cup	Goals League	Cup
AFFLECK D.R.	Coylton 26.7.1912	Stoke-s-Hambdon 11.8.1984	Notts.County cs1932	Clapton O. cs1934	HB	3	.	.	.
AITKEN P.G.	Cardiff 30.6.1954		Bristol Rov. Nov.1980	York City Feb.1982	M	41 *	14	1	.
AIZLEWOOD M.	Newport 1.10.1959		Bradford C. 8.8.1990	Cardiff C. Oct.1993	D	99(2)	13(1)	3	.
ALLEN P.M.	Bristol 8.10.1934		Local cs1953	Local cs1955	HB	1	.	.	.
ALLEN R.H.A.	Shepton Mallet 5.12.1916		Notts.County Nov.1946	Bridgewater T. cs1947	FB	1	.	.	.
ALLEN T.S.			cs1912	cs1913	F	1	.	.	.
ALLISON W.	Huddersfield 16.10.1968		Watford 9.8.1990	Current player	F	112(46)	14(6)	35	8
ALLWRIGHT C.R.S.	Brentford 1886	Wallingford 1966	Brentford cs1919	Swindon T. cs1920	F	11	.	.	.
ANDERSON F.	Scotland 1888		Shields Ath. cs1911	cs1912	G	7	.	.	.
ANDERSON J.R.	Newcast-U-Tyne 9.11.1924		Bristol R. Apr.1954	Retired cs1961	G	107	6	.	.
ANDREWS			Local cs1896	Local cs1897	F	1	.	.	.
ANDREWS F.E.	Kings Norton, Jul.1886		Burton All S. 11.1.24	Burton A.Saints Sep.24	F	1	.	.	.
ANNAN W.A.	Bathgate 1879		Sheff.U. 28.4.1905	Burslem P.V July 1911	FB	143	18	.	.
ARMSTRONG R.J.	Scotswood, 31.8.1909	Nottingham 10.3.1969	Nottm.Forest 8.5.1935	Mar.1944	F	115	3	19	.
ARTUS K.G.			Local cs1942	Bristol Rov. cs1946	F	.	1	.	1
ATTEVELD R.	Amsterdam 8.9.1966		Everton Mar.1992		M	9(5)	.	1	.
ATYEO P.J.W.	Dilton Marsh, Wilts. 7.2.1932	Warminster 8.6.1993	Portsmouth (A)14.6.51	Retired cs1966	F	597	48	315	35
BACH P.	Ludlow late 1872	Middlesbrough 30.12.1937	Middlesbrough cs1900	Retired cs1904	FB	42	3	.	.
BADDELEY K.	Swindon 12.3.1962		Apprentice Mar.1980	Swindon T. Jun.1981	D	1	.	.	.
BAILEY E.J.	Bristol 17.6.1921	Bristol 31.12.1986	B.A.C. 23.12.1944	Trowbridge T. 15.7.58	FB	348	33	.	.
BAILEY J.A.	Liverpool 1.4.1957		Newcastl.U. 7.12.1988	Retired cs1991	D	79(1)	20	1	.
BAILIFF W.E.	Ruabon,N.Wales. 19.3.1882	Aberdare,S.Wales 12.4.1972	Treharris May 1910	Treharris Oct.1911	G	7	1	.	.
BAILLIE J.	Dumfries 26.2.1929		Wolv.Wands. Jun.1956	Leicest. C. Jun.1957	FB	10	.	.	.
BAIN D.	Rutherglen 5.8.1900		Everton Nov.1928	Halifax T. cs1930	HB	50	2	2	.
BAIN J.	Falkirk 23.6.1957		Apprentice Jul.1974	Portland Timbers 1979	M	5(1)	.	.	.
BAIRD I.	Rotherham 1.4.1964		Heart O.Mid. 6.7.1993	Current player	F	16(3)	2	5	.
BAKER J.E.	Trethomas 5.5.1904	Coventry 2.3.1979	Coventry C. cs1935	Colchest.U. Jun.1937	HB	10	.	.	.
BALL C.G.	Leek, Staffs. 31.10.1906	Great Barr, B'ham. 1.2.1987	Bristol Rov. cs1931	Walsall Feb.1932	F	3	.	.	.
BALL H.			Bristol C.Wed. 1911	cs1912	F	2	1	1	.
BANFIELD A.J.	Bristol 5.5.1912	Bristol 1970	St.Ph.Marsh AS s1933	York City cs 1935	F	38	4	8	.
BANFIELD L.	Paulton,Somerset 11.11.1889	Paulton,Somerset 11.9.1979	Paulton R. cs1911	Ilfracombe T. 1925-26	FB	259	18	6	.
BANKS H.E.	Coventry 1874	1947	Aston Villa Nov.1901	Watford cs1903	F	43	2	17	3
BARBER S.	Wallsend 28.5.1908	18.4.1984	Newcastl.U. 13.6.1928	Exeter C. Aug.1930	HB	23	.	1	.
BARCLAY D.R.	Bristol 5.9.1976		St.Geo.School(YTS)93	Current player	M	2	.	.	.
BARKER G.			Everton cs1898	Bedminster Nov.1899	FB	33	3	.	.
BARNES C.E.	Chesham 1879		Reading cs1902	Watford cs1904	F	23	.	5	.
BARNEY V.C.	London 3.4.1922		Reading 15.10.1948	Grimsby T. 20.6.1949	F	28	3	4	1
BARTLETT E.			cs1900	cs1901	F	3	.	1	.
BARTLEY D.R.	Paulton,Somerset 3.10.1947		Apprentice Oct.1964	Swansea C. Aug.1973	F	93(8)	3	7	.
BATEY T.	Brancepeth 18.10.1894		Esh Winning 3.5.1913	Norwich C. cs1915	F	7	.	1	.
BATTEN H.G.	Bristol 11.5.1896	Chelsea, London 15.5.1956	Paulton R. cs1920	Plymouth A. 16.5.1921	F	7	.	.	.
BATTY W.	Killamarsh, Sheff. 13.7.1886		Sheff. U. 6.4.1910	Lincoln C. cs1911	F	5	.	.	.
BEAK C.G.	Bristol 22.12.1902		Hanham Ath.22.6.1928	cs1930	F	1	.	.	.
BEARE G.	STONEHAM, 2.10.1888	Cardiff Jan. 1970	Cardiff C.. 3.11.1921	Cardiff C. cs 1922	F	14	.	2	.
BEASLEY A.E.	Stourbridge 27.7.1913	Taunton 3.3.1986	Fulham 19.7.1950	Retired cs1952	HB	66	7	5	.
BENNETT W.	Mexborough, 17.4.1874	Denaby 6.4.1908	Sheffield U. Apr.1905	Denaby U. cs1907	F	48	1	22	.
BENNETT W.R.	Sheffield 17.4.1901	Sheffield Aug. 1988	Gains.Trin. 1.5.1928	Ballymena June 1930	HB	20	.	.	.
BENT J.	Huddersfield 1.3.1970		Hudders.T. 22.3.1990	Current Player	F	52(26)	9(4)	9	1
BENTLEY R.T.F.	Bristol 17.5.1924		Bristol R.(A) cs1939	Newcast.U. 14.6.1947	F	.	6	.	1
BEVAN B.E.	Exeter 20.3.1937		Bridgwater T.Feb.56	Carlisle U. Mar.1960	F	2	.	.	.
BICKNELL R.	Edlington, Doncaster 19.2.26		Charlton A. 10.6.1949	Colchest.U. Jun.1952	HB	21	1	.	.
BILLINGHAM J.	Daventry 3.12.1914	Nottingham 7.10.1981	Northampton T. cs1937	Burnley Jun.1938	F	7	.	.	.
BINDING			Local cs1896	Local cs1897	HB	1	.	.	.
BIRKS L.	Stoke-on-Trent 6.10.1896	Bristol 22.3.1975	Plymouth A. 13.9.1933	Yeovil & Pet.U.1.8.34	FB	30	4	.	.
BLAKE H.E.	Bristol 26.8.1894	Bristol 21.1.1958	Fishponds 31.1.1919	Mid-Rhondda cs1919	G	1	.	.	.
BLAKEMORE C.	Stourbridge 8.12.1897	Stourbridge 15.9.1963	Crystal P. May 1927	Brentford 2.5.1929	F	42	.	20	.
BLESSINGTON J.	Linlithgow 28.2.1874	Newton Abbot 18.4.1939	Derby C. Oct.1899	Luton T. Aug.1900	F	33	2	8	1
BOND L.A.	Ilminster 12.2.1954		Apprentice Sep.1971	Brentford Aug.1977	G	31	7	.	.
BOOTH L.	Merthyr		Bangor C. cs1936	Retired cs1946	F	65	2	22	.
BORROWS B.	Liverpool 20.12.1960		Coventry C.(L)Sep.93	Coventry C.Oct.1993	D	6	.	.	.
BORTHWICK G.W.	Poplar, London 1897		cs 1921	Hartlepools U.cs1922	F	1	.	.	.
BOUCHER T.	West Bromwich 1874		Bristol Rov. cs1901	New Brompton cs1903	F	51	3	14	1
BOURTON C.F.T.	Clutton 30.9.1908	Bath 20.4.1981	Paulton Rov. Jan.1927	Blackburn R.May 1928	F	61	.	15	.
			Plymouth A. 25.1.1938	Retired cs1944					
BOWEN E.C.	Darfield,Barnsley 1.7.1903		Northampton T.cs1932	cs1934	F	55	4	33	4
BOWN A.J.W.	Highworth, Wilts. 1882	Southampton 19.8.1958	Swindon T. cs1919	Weymouth T. Aug.1922	F	35	3	5	1
BOWYER S.	Northwich 12.10.1887	11.4.1967	Liverpool Feb.1912	S.Liverpool cs1913	F	49	1	14	.
BOXLEY J.	Cradley Heath 31.5.1931		Stourbridge Oct.1950	Coventry C. Dec.1956	F	205	8	34	1
			Coventry C. 1960	Chippenham T. cs1961					
BOXSHALL D.	Bradford 2.4.1920		Q.P.R. May 1948	Bourne. & BA Jul.50	F	52	3	10	1
BOYD J.	Massachussets USA 10.9.26		Gloucester C. cs1950	Bath City 15.8.1952	FB	31	.	6	.
BOYLE T.D.J.	Ammanford 29.10.1958		Crystal P. Oct.1981	Newport C. Oct.1982	D	36(1)	9	.	2
BRACE T.F.	Bristol 8.3.1908	Taunton 1983	cs1929	cs1930	F	1	.	.	.
BRADBURY J.J.L.	South Bank 1878		Barnsley cs1901	New Brompton cs1902	F	31	4	4	1
BRADFORD J.	Peggs Grn, Leics. 22.1.1901	Birmingham 6.9.1980	Birmingham May 1935	Retired cs1936	F	5	.	1	.
BRAIN J.	Ebbw Vale. 28.1.1910	Norwich 15.3.1981	Swansea T. 1.6.1937	Watford WWII	F	32	3	9	1

NAME	Born	Died	From	To	Pos.	Apps. League	Cup	Goals League	Cup
BRAND R.A.	Scotland 1888		Motherwell cs1911	cs1912	F	8	.	.	.
BRAY W.S.	Bristol 17.11.1964		Apprentice Nov.1981	Weston-S-Mare cs1984	M	28(1)	2(1)	2	.
BREAKER			Local cs1896	Local cs1897	FB	1	.	.	.
BREWSTER G.W.	Barnburgh 19.10.1925		Retford T. Sep.1949	Grave.& North. cs1951	F	13	1	3	.
BRIDGE C.A.V.	Bristol 28.8.1909	Bristol 27.1.1988	St.Ph.Marsh PH cs32	Retired 1939	FB	155	12	.	.
BRIGGS A.M.	Sheffield 21.6.1939		Soundwell Apr.1957	Retired cs1970	FB	350(2)	43	1	.
BRINTON E.J.	Bristol 26.5.1908	Bristol 17.9.1981	Avonmouth cs1929	Newport C. 8.6.1937	HB	250	18	7	2
BRINTON J.V.	Bristol 11.7.1916		Newport C. Aug.1935	Derby C. Jan.1938	F	12	.	1	.
BRITTON P.	Bristol approx. 1873		Warmley cs1898	Bristol East cs1899	HB	18	2	1	.
BROAD T.H.	Stalybridge 31.7.1887		Oldham A. 10.5.1912	Man. C. Mar 1919	F	106	5	8	.
BROLLY M.J.	Kilmarnock 6.10.1954		Chelsea 16.5.1974	Grimsby T. Sep.1976	F	27(3)	3	2	1
BROMAGE R.	Stoke-on-Trent 9.11.1959		Port Vale 13.8.1987	Brighton & HA 24.8.90	D	44(2)	7	1	.
BROOK R.	Nottingham Jul.1912		Southend U. 12.6.1937	Sep.1939	FB	74	1	1	.
BROOKSBANK C.	Halifax 1890		Exeter City cs1914	cs1915	F	10	.	7	.
BROOMFIELD I.L.	Bristol 17.12.1950		Local Aug.1968	Stockport C. Dec.1972	F	18(3)	4(3)	2	.
BROUGH J.	Burslem 9.11.1886	5.10.1968	Liverpool Jan.1912	Burslem P.V. cs1913	F	22	.	11	.
BROWN I.	Ipswich 11.9.1965		Chel'ford C. Apr.1993	Current player	F	5(6)	1	1	.
BROWN J.			Local cs1896	Local cs1897	F	3	.	1	.
BROWN J.R.	South Bank Nov.1887		Middlesbrough cs1908	Middlesbrough cs1909	F	3	.	.	.
BROWN T.H.	Kilmarnock		Cardiff City cs1922	South Shields cs1923	F	8	.	.	.
BROWN W.Y.	Dysart, Fife		Chelsea cs1913	Swansea T. Sep.1919	F	62	4	23	.
BROWN W.	Southampton 14.1.1977		Bashley Apr.1994	Current player	G	1	.	.	.
BRUTON D.E.	Gloucester 31.10.1952		Apprentice Jul.1971	Swansea C. Aug.1973	D	16(1)	-(1)	.	.
BRYANT M.	Bristol 21.9.1970		Trainee 1.7.1989	Current player	D	133(1)	13	4	.
BRYANT R.J.	Bristol 20.6.1963		Robinsons cs1985	cs1986	D	2	.	1	.
BUCKLAND W.A.	Shipston-on-Stour 1900		Cinderford T. cs1924	cs1925	HB	1	.	.	.
BUNGAY R.H.	Reading 5.2.1911	Plymouth Oct. 1986	Plymouth A. cs1935	Mansfield T. cs1936	F	9	.	3	.
BURDEN T.D.	Andover 21.2.1924		Leeds U. Oct.1954	Retired cs1961	HB	231	12	20	1
BURNSIDE D.G.	Bristol 10.12.1939		Plymouth A. Dec.1971	Colchest.U. Mar.1972	F	1	.	.	.
BURROWS L.G.	Exeter 1906		Taunton T. Apr.1929	Torquay U. cs1930	F	1	.	.	.
BURTON A.D.	Lochgelly 1884		Motherwell cs1905	Everton cs1911	F	192	19	45	3
BURTON E.	Dunston, Gateshead 1893	Killed in Action Aug.1916	Shildon Ath. 5.5.1913		F	18	1	5	2
BUSH T.D.	Ingoldsthorpe, Norf. 29.1.43		Junior Feb.1960	Ret.due to inj.cs1970	F	147(15)	17(1)	43	2
BUTCHER C.			Bristol Rov. 7.11.1935	cs1936	F	1	.	.	.
BUTLER J.T.	Scotland 1889		Motherwell cs1911	Newport C. cs1913	F	43	1	12	.
CAESAR G.	London 5.3.1966		Cambridge U. cs1991	Airdrieonians 31.1.1992	D	9(1)	2	.	.
CAIE A.	Aberdeen 1878	Lowell, U.S.A. Dec.1914	Woolwich cs1897	Millwall Ath. Mar.1899	F	97	8	55	4
CAINEY W.P.	Bristol 12.12.1914	Bristol 10.3.66	Wesley Rangers cs1932	Bradford PA 27.5.1936	F	77	12	12	1
CAIRNS T.	Merryton, 30.10.1890	Dec. 1967	Larkhall Thistle cs1911	Peebles Rovers cs1912	F	11	.	1	.
CALDWELL A.	Salford 21.3.1958		Bolton Wand. 9.7.1987	Grimsby T. 8.9.1988	F	9(9)	1(1)	3	1
CALDWELL R.	South Kirby 1909		Doncaster R. May.1936	Bristol Rovers Jul.1939	HB	39	1	3	.
CALLAGHAN P.J.	Longbridge, Ireland 1904		Aberdare A. 17.6.1927	Aberdare Ath. cs1928	F	12	.	1	.
CAPES A.J.	Burton-on-Trent 23.2.1875	Burton-on-Trent 26.2.1945	Stoke cs1904	Swindon T. cs1905	F	29	5	7	.
CARNELLY A.	Nottingham 29.12.1870	Nottingham Aug. 1920	Leicest. Fosse cs1897	Ilkeston Town cs1898	F	52	3	34	5
			Ilkeston T. Nov.1898	Thames Ironwk.cs1899					
CARTER L.A.	Farnborough 24.10.1960		Crystal P. Feb.1982	cs 1982	F	16	.	.	.
CARTER T.D.	Bristol 5.10.1967		Sunderland (L) 15.9.88	Sunderland 27.9.1988	G	3	.	.	.
CASEY T.	Culmer, N.Ireland 11.3.30		Portsmouth Mar.1959	Gloucester C. cs1963	HB	122	10	9	.
CASHLEY A.R.	Bristol 23.10.1951		Junior Sep.1970	Bristol Rov. Aug.1982	G	227	20	1	.
CAVANAGH T.H.	Liverpool 29.6.1928		Doncast.R. Jul.1959	Carlisle U. Jun.1960	F	24	1	6	1
CHAMBERS P.	Workington 1878	Swindon 1952	Bedminster cs1900	Swindon Town cs1906	HB	175	18	10	.
CHANDLER R.D.	Bristol 26.9.1961		Apprentice Oct.1978	Bath City cs1983	F	57(4)	6(1)	13	2
CHAPMAN A.T.	Bristol 1871	Chatham 1929	Chatham cs1907	Maidstone cs1912	HB	7	.	1	.
CHAPPLE F.J.	Bristol		Brentford cs1913	Douglas F.C. cs1919	F	20	2	10	.
CHEESLEY P.M.	Bristol 20.10.1953		Norwich City Dec.1973	Retired cs1977	F	61(3)	6	20	1
CHERRETT P.A.M.	Bournemouth 12.9.1899		Crystal P. May.1927	B'mouth & BA Jul.28	F	25	1	15	.
CHILCOTT K.	Rhondda 17.3.1920		Eastville U.cs1937	Bridgwater T.cs1949	F	46	9	6	4
CLACK E.C.	Cirencester 4.6.1900		Sunderland 17.5.1923	cs1924	F	2	.	.	.
CLACK F.E.	Witney, Oxon. 30.3.1912		Brentford 15.5.1947	Guildford C. cs1949	G	67	6	.	.
CLARK R.D.	Bristol 13.1.1943		Juniors Mar.1960	Hud'field T. Oct.1966	F	100	20	04	0
CLARK D.F.	Bristol 25.10.1917		N.Bristol O.B. cs1937	Retired cs1951	F	117	19	67	15
CLARK E.C.			cs1923	cs1924	F	2	.	.	.
CLARK W.B.	Airdrie 1880	Bristol 17.3.1937	Sunderland Oct.1910	Leices.Foss Aug.1911	F	24	1	1	.
CLARKE M.M.G.	Clydebank 29.6.1944		Cardiff C. Jul 1969	Hartlepool U. Jul.1970	M	2(1)	1	.	.
CLAY H.A.	Kimberley, Notts.29.1.1881	Bristol 9.8.1964	Kimberley SJ Nov.1901	Retired cs1913	G	311	22	.	.
CLAYTON R.	East Retford 1916		Manchest.C. 10.6.1938	Lincoln City Jul.1939	F	13	.	3	.
CLEAK A.			Local cs1894	Local cs1897	F	3	.	.	.
CLEGG J.	Sheffield 1889		cs 1908	Barnsley cs1911	G	13	3	.	.
CLEMENTS H.H.	Bristol Aug.1884	Nailsea,Bristol 29.3.1910	Bedminster cs1894	Bedminster cs1898	HB	16	10	1	4
CLIPSON R.	Newark 18.4.1909	Seaford 6.9.1970	Bury cs1934	Dartford 4.10.1935	FB	17	2	.	.
COCKERILL H.L.	Ryhope 14.1.1894	1960	Mid-Rhondda cs1921	Reading cs1923	HB	16	.	.	.
COGGINS P.R.F.	Bristol 10.7.1940		Local Oct.1958	Bristol Rov. Jun 1960	F	4	.	.	.
COGGINS W.H.	Bristol 16.9.1901		Bristol St.G. Sep.1925	Everton 15.3.1930	G	171	6	.	.
COLE A.A.	Nottingham 15.10.1971		Arsenal Mar.1992	Newcastle U.Mar 1993	F	41	4	20	4
COLLIER G.B.	Bristol 4.2.1955		Apprentice Nov.1972	Coventry C. Jul.1979	D	194	22	3	.

NAME	Born	Died	From	To	Pos.	Apps. League	Apps. Cup	Goals League	Goals Cup
COLLINS R.D.	Bristol 13.1.1923		Local cs1943	Torquay U. cs1948	F	14	2	2	.
COLLINSON R.	Rawmarsh 5.12.1940	approx. 1992	Doncast.R. Oct.1958	Stockport C. Jul 1961	FB	50	6	1	.
COLQUHOUN D.M.	Motherwell 9.1.1906	Motherwell 3.6.1983	Blantyre V. cs1937	Southport Jun.1938	F	3	.	.	.
COMPTON T.D.	Bristol 28.11.1931	Bristol 6.10.1991	Phildown R. Dec.1948	Salisbury C. cs1958	HB	45	3	.	.
COMPTON W.A.	Bristol 5.4.1897		Brist.Motor W.cs1919	Exeter City cs1924	F	14	.	.	.
CONNELLY F.H.			Rotherham M. cs1906	cs1908	F	13	.	6	.
CONNER J.	Glasgow 27.12.1896		Newport C 16.12.1924	Millwall 12.6.1925	F	16	.	3	.
CONNOR J.F.	Maryport 25.7.1934		Hudders.T. Oct.1960	Retired cs1971	HB	355(1)	50	10	2
CONNOR M.J.	Lochee,Ireland 14.7.1880	Scotland 2.8.1934	Walsall cs1901	Woolwich A. cs1902	F	26	3	10	1
CONNOR T.	Leeds 9.11.1962		Swansea C. 21.9.1991	Yeovil T. cs1993	F	11(5)	1	1	1
COOK A.	Bristol 8.10.1929		Clifton St.V.Dec.1949	Worcster C. cs1964	G	320	27	.	.
COOK C.I.	Cheltenham 28.1.1937		Gloucester C.Feb.1957	cs1958	FB	2	.	.	.
COOK W.			cs1911	cs1912	F	3	.	.	.
COOKSON W.S.	Preston 1881		Nelson cs1901	Blackpool cs1902	F	17	3	6	3
COOMBE M.A.	Torquay 17.9.1968		A.F.C.Bourne. cs1987	Carlisle United cs1988	G	.	1	.	.
COOMBS F.H.	East Ham,London 24.4.1925		Dartford 3.6.1949	Southend U. Jun 1950	G	24	1	.	.
COOPER T.	Castleford 12.7.1944		Middlesbrough Jul.1978	Bristol R. Aug.1979	D	49(22)	4(5)	1	.
			Doncast. R. May 1982	Retired Oct. 1984					
COPESTAKE L.	London 1885		Blackpool cs1907	Exeter City cs1908	F	43	1	6	.
			Exeter City cs1910	cs1913					
CORBETT F.	West Ham, London Dec.1881	Brentford, London 15.4.1924	Bristol Rov. cs1903	Bristol Rov. Apr.1905	F	49	4	14	1
CORBETT W.	Wolverhamtpon 29.7.1920		Doncaster R. Jun.1948	Bath City 1949	FB	1	.	.	.
CORMACK P.B.	Edinburgh 17.7.1946		Liverpool Nov.1976	Hibernian cs1980	F	60(8)	5(1)	15	1
COTTLE J.R.	Bristol 1886	Bristol 3.2.1958	Dolphins cs1905	Bristol Rov. cs1911	FB	204	19	.	.
COTTRELL A.T.	Bristol 1913		Dockland Sett. cs1933	Northampton T. cs1935	HB	4	.	.	.
COUSINS K.F.	Bristol 6.6.1922		Local cs1940	Bath City cs1948	G	3	3	.	.
COWELL J.	Blyth 9.6.1887		Rother'm.T. 22.4.1909	Sunderland Oct.1910	F	37	.	20	.
COX E.			Nunhead cs1932	cs1933	HB	1	.	.	.
CRAIG E.	Stewarton 9.2.1903		Fulham Aug.1930	Halifax T. Aug.1932	F	47	3	4	.
CRAWFORD A.	Glasgow		Clyde cs1899	cs1900	F	37	1	6	.
CRAWFORD A.P.	Rotherham 30.10.1953		Chesterfield Aug.1982	Exeter City cs1985	F	85(7)	13	26	2
CRIDLAND C.H.			Local cs1894	Local cs1895	HB	.	1	.	.
CROWE C.	Newcast-U-Tyne 11.6.1939		Nottingham F.Jan.1967	Walsall Sep.1969	F	66(1)	11	13	3
CRUMLEY J.B.	Dundee 17.7.1898	1981	Swansea T. 8.8.1923	Darlington cs1924	G	2	.	.	.
CUNNINGHAM E.	Jarrow 20.9.1919		Luton Amateurs cs1939	Luton Town cs1947	F	1	.	.	.
CURLE K.	Bristol 14.11.1963		Torquay U. Mar 1984	Reading 23.10.1987	M	113(8)	12(1)	1	.
CURRAN F.	Royton-on-Tyne 31.5.17		Bristol Rov. cs1939	Bristol Rov. May1946	F	3	3	1	2
CURTIS D.P.	Dublin 26.8.1932		Shelbourne Nov.1956	Ipswich T. 7.8.1958	F	27	3	16	3
DARKE T.W.			cs1904	cs1905	F	3	.	2	.
DATE M.			Frome Town cs1910	Local cs1911	F	1	. ,	.	.
DAVIES F.P.	Swansea 1.8.1903	Northampton 1.1.1970	Swansea Town cs1923	Charlton A. 14.10.1926	HB	54	1	.	.
DAVIES J.W.	Denbigh 14.11.1916		Plymouth A. May 1948	cs1949	HB	30	3	1	.
DAVIES R.H.	Bolton 1876		Bedminster cs1900	Bolton Wands. cs1903	FB	78	8	2	.
DAVIS E.	Bristol 1892	Bristol 6.3.1954	Blackburn R. May 1925	Bath City Nov.1926	G	3	.	.	.
DAVIS F.S.			Local cs1894	Local cs1896	HB	.	3	.	.
DAVIS K.E.	Romsey 6.2.1933		Junior May 1952	Minehead 7.1.1954	F	1	.	.	.
DAVIS R.F.	Plymouth 14.11.1943		Southampton Jul.1965	Barrow Mar. 1969	FB	8	.	.	.
DAVIS W.			cs1911	cs1912	G	1	.	.	.
DAVY H.	Padiham, Lancs. 1872		Leicest.Fosse cs1897	Retired cs1899	FB	53	6	1	.
DAWSON E.	South Pelaw 16.1.1913		Man.City May.1936	Gateshead Mar.1944	G	69	4	.	.
DEAN A.	West Bromwich 2.1.1877	Wolverhampton 1.1.1959	Grimsby T. Apr. 1902	Swindon T. cs1905	F	84	11	35	2
DEMMERY W.	Kingswood, Bristol 1877	Bristol 28.12.1955	Bristol East cs1902	Bristol Rov. cs1908	G	38	2	.	.
DENT F.	Sheffield 24.1.1896	Leeds 11.7.1983	Mid-Rhondda 11.5.1925	Exeter City Jun.1926	F	12	.	1	.
DERRICK J.S.	Bristol 10.1.1943		Juniors Jan.1960	Paris St-Ger. cs1971	F	254(6)	38(1)	32	4
DEVINE P.	Blackburn 25.5.1960		Vancouver.W. Jul.1981	Blackburn R. cs1982	F	19(2)	6(1)	1	.
DICKIE J.	Montrose 22.9.1903	25.6.1960	New Brighton 1.12.28	Chester Aug.1930	F	48	.	4	.
DIMMER H.	Scotstown 14.3.1924		Aldershot 4.6.1947	cs1948	F	1	.	.	.
DOLAN E.	Dagenham 20.9.1967		West Ham U.(L) Feb.89	West Ham.U. Feb.1989	F	3	.	.	.
DOLMAN H.W.	Bloxwich 30.8.1903		Chesterfield 25.5.1934	Luton Town 12.3.1936	G	62	10	.	.
DONALDSON J.	Glasgow 1909	Glasgow (murdered) 22.2.39	Kilsythe Rang. cs1931	cs1932	F	4	.	.	.
DONOWA L.	Ipswich 24.9.1964		Ipswich T. 10.8.1990	B'ham C. 30.8.1991	F	11(13)	1(1)	3	.
DOWN D.F.	Bristol 7.7.1948		Apprentice Sep.1965	Bradford PA 2.10.1967	F	6(1)	3	3	2
DOWN W.F.	Bristol 8.11.1963		Apprentice Oct.1981	Bristol Manor F.cs1982	D	1	.	.	.
DOWNIE A.L.B.	Dunoon 1878	Withington 9.12.1977	Third Lanark cs1903	Swindon Town cs1908	HB	41	2	2	.
DOYLE I.P.	Torquay 27.2.1959		Barnstaple T. Dec.78	Gloucester C. cs1981	F	2(1)	1(1)	.	.
DRANSFIELD E.W.	Sheffield 1901		Worksop T. Dec.1927	Merthyr T. cs1928	F	2	.	.	.
DRINNAN J.M.K.	Harthill 28.5.1906	1936	Larkhall Thistle cs1923	Aberaman cs1924	F	2	1	.	.
DRUMMOND R.C.	Dalmeny 1898		Pembroke Dock cs1926	B'mouth & BA cs1927	F	2	1	1	.
DRURY C.	Darlaston 4.7.1937		West Brom.A. Jun.64	Bradford PA Mar.1968	HB	51	2	2	.
DRYDEN J.G.	Broomhill 21.8.1908	Ashington 16.9.1975	Sheffield U. Jul.1936	Burnley Jun.1938	F	63	4	13	.
DRYSDALE B.	Wingate 24.2.1943		Hartlepool U.May 1969	Oxford U. Jul.1977	D	281(2)	41	3	.
DUNN E.	1909		Trowbridge T.22.6.32	cs1934	HB	27	.	1	.
DURRELL J.T.	London 15.3.1953		West Ham U. Jul.1973	Gillingham Nov.1975	F	5(3)	2	.	.
DYER R.E.	Bristol 18.4.1900	Harlow Jan.1990	Ashton City Oct.1921	Fulham May 1925	FB	49	3	.	.
DYMOND W.H.	Kenton, Devon 13.2.1920		Exeter City cs1946	Exeter City 4.6.1947	F	8	.	1	.

NAME	Born	Died	From	To	Pos.	Apps. League	Apps. Cup	Goals League	Goals Cup
DZIEKANOWSKI D.P.	Warsaw, Poland 30.9.1962		Celtic 17.1.1992	Aachen 1993-94	F	40(3)	5(1)	7	2
EATON J.	Bristol 29.1.1969		Trowbridge T.23.3.89	Gloucest.City Nov.1990	F	6(7)	1(2)	1	.
ECONOMOU J.	Kingston-On-Thames 25.10.61		Apprentice Oct. 1979	Devizes Town cs1984	M	62(3)	7	3	.
EDDOLLS J.D.	Bristol 19.8.1919		Peasdown M.W cs1945	Bristol Rov. Aug.1948	G	6	5	.	.
EDWARDS A.		Killed in Action 1918	Aston Villa Oct.1912	Newport C. cs1913	HB	4	.	.	.
EDWARDS A.R.			Local cs1896	Local cs1897	HB	5	.	.	.
EDWARDS C.I.	Cannock 8.3.1921		West.B.Albion Jun.1948	Gravesend & N. Jul.50	HB	33	1	3	.
EDWARDS R.	Kendal 1.7.1973		Carlisle U. Mar.1991	Current player	D	57(20)	12(1)	3	.
EISENTRAGER A.B.	Hamburg,Germany 20.7.1927		Trowbridge T. cs1949	Merthyr T. Jul.1958	F	229	11	47	.
ELLIOTT S.D.	Sunderland 1908		Chelsea 21.7.1930	Notts C. 16.3.1932	F	50	4	24	4
EMANUEL W.J.	Treherbert 5.4.1948		Ferndale A. May 1971	Newport C. Jan 1976	M	125(4)	8(2)	10	.
EMERY T.G.	Bristol 8.9.1936		Feb.1957	cs1958	F	11	2	.	.
EMMANUEL J.G.	Swansea 1.2.1954		Swindon Town cs1985	Swansea C. Aug.1985	M	2	1	.	.
ETHERIDGE R.J.	Gloucester 25.3.1934	Gloucester 4.4.1988	Gloucest.C. Sep.1956	Cheltenham T. cs1965	HB	260	30	43	7
EVELEIGH G.E.	Lymington 26.7.1922		Guildford C. May 1948	Guildford C. cs1949	F	2	.	.	.
FAGAN S.	Attercliffe 28.10.1886		Plymouth A. cs1910	Stockport C. cs1912	FB	34	.	.	.
FAIRCLOUGH A.	St.Helens 4.10.1891	Stockport 5.11.1958	Southend U. 15.3.1921	Derby County 4.7.1924	F	91	3	44	3
FAIRHURST W.G.	St. Helens 23.4.19??		Bury Sep. 1941	cs1946	G	.	1	.	.
FARR F.E.	Bristol	Bristol 27.7.1981	Local cs1931	Bath City cs1934	HB	0	.	.	.
FEAR K.W.	Bristol 8.5.1952		Junior Jun. 1969	Plymouth A. Feb 1978	F	127(25)	16(3)	32	3
FENTON F.	1880		West.B.Albion cs1904	Swindon T. cs1907	F	36	1	1	.
FERGUSON A.	Lochore 4.8.1904		Newport C. May 1946	Swindon T. Sep.1947	G	32	1	.	.
FERGUSON I.			Heart O.M (L) Sep.90	Heart O.M. May 1990	F	8(3)	.	2	.
FIELDING A.			Gloucester cs1896	cs1897	F	7	5	4	2
FIELDING F.B.			Gloucester cs1896	cs1897	F	10	6	5	2
FINNERHAN F.P.			Liverpool cs1898	cs1899	F	33	4	13	3
FISH I.	Cardiff 1913		G.W.R.Inst. 27.3.1934	cs1936	F	7	.	1	.
FISHER J.A.	Glasgow Jun.1879	4.12.1937	Aston Villa cs1903	Bri'ton & HA Aug.1905	F	50	8	21	1
FITZPATRICK A.C.	Glasgow 3.3.1956		St.Mirren 20.7.1979	St.Mirren cs1981	M	75	13	1	.
FITZPATRICK P.J.	Liverpool 5.10.1965		Bolton W. 20.8.1986	Carlisle U. 1.10.1988	M	40(4)	8(1)	7	.
FLYNN J.	1875		Walsall cs1901	Reading cs1903	F	31	2	1	.
FORBES J.	Scotland 1892		Dundee Violet cs1911	cs1912	F	27	1	5	.
FORD A.M.	Thornbury 26.11.1944		Apprentice Nov.1961	Bristol Rov. Dec.1969	FB	170(1)	13	10	2
FOSTER A.	Rawmarsh		Rotherham T. cs1909	Watford cs1911	F	13	.	1	.
FOSTER J.T.F.	Southwick, S'land 21.3.1903		Grimsby T. Jun.1926	Brentford May 1929	F	47	4	4	1
FOWLER J.	Bristol 20.8.1974		Trainee	Current player	M	-(2)	.	.	.
FOX R.V.	Bristol 28.1.1921		St.Adhelm's cs1938	Bath City cs1950	FB	23	.	.	.
FOY T.G.	Croydon 1911		Scarborough 10.3.1934	Barrow cs1935	F	10	.	2	.
FREEMAN D.R.	Dartford 29.8.1921		Charlton A. May 1949	Southend U. Aug.1950	HB	8	.	.	.
FRITH A.P.			Local cs1896	Local cs1897	FB	6	3	.	.
FRY G.			Local cs1894	Local cs1895	F	.	1	.	.
FUGE T.	St. George, Bristol	Sep. 1944	Llannelly cs1913	cs1914	F	6	.	3	.
FULTON W.	Alva, Scotland		Sunderland cs1900	Derby County cs1901	F	35	3	18	1
GADSBY E.	New Whittington 1888		Barnsley cs1910	Castleford T.cs1911	F	10	1	1	.
GALE T.	Falkirk		Rotherham M. cs1906	Grimsby T. cs1908	FB	3	.	.	.
GALLACHER F.	Paisley		Barnsley 11.3.1938	Sep.1939	F	23	1	6	.
GALLEY J.E.	Clowne 7.5.1944		Rotherham U. 5.12.67	Nottm.Forest Dec.1972	F	172	23	84	7
GALLIERS S.	Fulwood 21.8.1957		Wimbledon 21.8.1985	Maidstone U.8.8.1989	M	79(3)	15(1)	5	.
GANE G.B.H.	Midsomer Norton		Bradford City cs1914	Douglas F.C. cs1920	HB	2	.	.	.
GARA A.	Ireland Aug.1875		Nottm.For. 31.10.1902	Ashton Town cs1904	F	18	3	6	.
GARD			cs1898	cs1899	F	2	.	2	.
GARLAND C.S.	Bristol 24.4.1949		Apprentice May 1966	Chelsea Sep.1971	F	196(12)	27(2)	42	8
			Leicester C. Dec 1976	Retired Feb.1983					
GARLAND G.E.	Bristol 1898		Kingswood AFC cs1927	cs1930	HB	7	.	2	.
GAVIN M.	Baillieston 10.12.1963		Hearts 4.10.1988	Watford 9.8.1990	F	96(14)	25(1)	7	1
			Watford 6.12.1991	Exeter City Feb.1994					
GECHERN P.			cs1911	cs1912	FB	4	.	1	.
GEDDES A.J.	West Bromwich Apr.1871	Bristol Oct.1927	Bedminster cs1900	Bristol Rov. cs1901	F	24	2	4	.
GEDDES J.	Stane Shotts 1902	Scotland Oct.1937	Albion Rov. 21.6.1926	Greenock M. Jun.1929	HB	5	3	1	.
GIBSON			cs1897	cs1898	FB	7	.	.	.
GIBSON M.J.	Derby 15.7.1939		Shrews.T. 4.4.1963	Gillingham Jul.1972	G	332	44	.	.
GILDEA H.	Falkirk		Grimsby T. cs1910	cs1911	F	1	.	.	.
GILES J.E.	Bristol 7.11.1947		Apprentice Jun.1965	Exeter C. May 1969	F	3	.	1	.
GILHESPY T.W.C.	Fence Hse, D'ham 18.2.1898		Liverpool May 1925	Blackburn R. 9.6.1929	F.	117	1	25	.
GILLIES D.G.	Fort William 20.6.1951		Morton Mar.1973	Bristol Rov. Jun.1980	F	184(17)	20(5)	26	2
GILLIGAN S.A.	Dundee 1882		Celtic May 1904	Liverpool cs1910	F	188	23	78	9
GILSON A.T.	Waddesdon 1881		Brentford cs1903	cs1905	FB	47	5	1	.
GLENN E.	Redditch 12.4.1902	Coventry 25.2.1965	Willenhall T. May.1923	Retired cs1931	FB	276	12	.	.
GODDARD R.J.	Bristol 22.11.1898		Charles Hill cs1921	Reading Aug.1925	G	21	.	.	.
GODSMAN A.	Inverness		Inverness cs1899	Feb.1900	FB	17	.	.	.
GOLDIE E.			Reading Mar.1900	cs1900	F	10	.	.	.
GOLLEDGE L.H.	Chipping Sodbury 3.8.1911	Bristol 28.7.1989	Kingswood AFC cs1928	Bristol Rov. cs1935	F	25	2	3	.
GOOD M.W.	Airdrie 1877		Preston N.E cs1902	Reading cs1903	HB	32	2	5	.
GOODING R.	Hartlepool 16.2.1959		Covent.C.(L)Mar.1982	Coventry C. Mar.1982	M	3	.	.	.
GORDON C.K.	Stourbridge 17.1.1963		Reading (L) Mar.1988	Reading May 1988	F	10	.	4	.

NAME	Born	Died	From	To	Pos.	Apps. League	Apps. Cup	Goals League	Goals Cup
GOULD C.			cs1911	cs1913	F	27	1	·	·
GOULD R.A.	Coventry 12.6.1946		West.B.Alb. Dec.1972	West Ham U. Nov.1973	F	36	7	15	4
GOW R.G.	Drumchapel, Glasgow 29.5.52		Apprentice Jun.1969	Manchester C.Oct 1980	M	368(7)	44(2)	48	5
GRAHAM M.	Hall Green 26.1.1934		Barnsley May 1959	Leyton O. Jun.1960	F	14	·	8	·
GRAY A.D.	Glasgow 1899		Kilmarnock 19.5.1926	Queen O.South 1927	F	8	3	3	·
GREEN H.	Sheffield 1908		Leeds U. 14.5.1934	York City 25.6.1935	F	12	·	1	·
GREY R.			Local cs1894	Local cs1897	HB	·	4	·	·
GRIFFIN K.R.	Plymouth 5.10.1953		Apprentice Sep.1971	Bath City cs1975	F	5(3)	1(1)	·	·
GRINDLEY			Local cs1895	Local cs1896	F	·	1	·	1
GUY I.	Hambrook, Bristol 27.2.1926	Frenchay, Bristol 2.9.1986	Hambrook Villa cs1944	Bath City 2.8.1957	FB	404	30	2	1
GUY S.W.			Liverpool cs1936	cs1937	F	1	·	·	·
HALES W.H.			cs1903	Bristol Rov.12.5.1904	HB	1	·	·	·
HALL B.	Newburn 1903		Norwich City cs1932	cs1933	HB	2	1	·	·
HALL G.W.E.	Worksop 1912		Newport C. 6.5.1937	cs1939	HB	13	3	·	·
HALL C.T.	Wolverhampton 2.2.1948		Bradford C. Jul.1972	Chelmsford C. cs1973	F	-(1)	-(1)	·	·
HALLIDAY B.	Sunderland 3.1.1961		Bury Aug.1983	Hereford U. May 1985	D	52(1)	11	·	1
HAMILTON A.J.	Ayr 1872	Bristol late Oct.1931	Loughborough T.cs1897	Leic. Fosse Sep.1900	HB	119	9	5	·
HAMLIN			Local cs1895	Local cs1896	F	·	1	·	·
HAMPSHIRE J.C.	Goldthorpe 5.10.1913		Man.City 15.4.1936	Bath City 29.7.1938	HB	21	·	·	·
HAMSON g.	Nottingham 24.8.1959		Leeds U. cs1986	Port Vale 12.12.1986	M	12	4	2	·
HANLIN P.	West Calder		Everton cs1905	cs1911	HB	162	6	3	·
HARDING			cs1900	cs1901	F	1	·	·	·
HARDING S.J.	Bristol 23.7.1956		Apprentice Dec.1974	Bristol Rov. Jun. 1977	D	2	·	·	·
HARDY R.W.	South Bank 16.6.1885		South Bank 4.5.1908	cs1911	F	74	11	13	2
HARFORD M.G.	Sunderland 12.2.1959		Newcastle U. Aug.1981	B'ham City Mar 1982	F	30	10	11	3
HARGETT A.	Bristol		Army cs1903	Bath City cs1905	F	16	·	3	·
HARGETT G.H.	Bristol		Bristol Rov. cs1904	cs1905	FB	3	·	·	·
HARGREAVES J.	Rotherham 1.5.1915	Bristol 22.12.1978	Leeds U. May 1942	Yeovil Town cs1947	F	26	7	9	3
HARLE D.	Denaby 15.8.1963		Leeds U. 28.3.1986	Scunthorpe U.27.11.86	M	23	4	2	·
HARRIOTT M.	Dulwich, London 20.4.1974		Barnsley 1993-94	Current player	D	17	·	·	·
HARRIS J.	Glasgow		Burnley 16.5.1912	Leeds U. 28.7.1922	F	205	13	26	2
HARRIS W.H.	Plymouth Jul.1904		Scotswood 16.6.1929	Loughboro. C. cs1930	F	26	·	15	·
HARRISON F.	Bristol 1881		cs1913	cs1914	F	15	·	5	·
HARRISON G.	London 15.4.1972		Watford cs1991	Cardiff City	D	25(13)	3(2)	1	·
HARSTON E.	Monk Bretton 27.2.1907		Reading May.1934	Mansfield T. 17.10.35	F	28	8	17	3
HART A.	Scotland		Port Glasgow 16.6.22	cs1923	F	2	·	·	·
HARVEY J.	Lurgan 2.5.1958		Hereford U. 27.3.1987	Tranmere R. 8.10.1987	M	2(1)	·	·	·
HARVEY J.H.	Maiden Law 6.4.1915		Bradford P.A. 6.5.1937	Newport C. Jun.1938	F	2	·	·	·
HAWKINS B.W.	Bristol 29.9.1923		Bristol Rov. 23.5.1949	Bath City cs.1950	F	8	·	4	·
HAWKINS N.	Bristol 7.9.1968		Apprentice cs.1986	Blackpool 24.10.1989	F	8(10)	3(2)	2	1
HAWLEY F.W.		May 1954	Swindon T. 15.3.1923	Brghtn & HA Aug.1925	HB	75	6	1	·
HAY A.B.	Dunfermline 28.11.1958		Bolton W. Jul.1978	York City Aug.1982	D	72(2)	9(2)	1	·
HAYCOX J.	Cheltenham 1913		Newport C. 22.5.1936	Torquay U. 16.2.1938	F	43	3	25	2
HEALE J.A.	Bristol 19.9.1914		S.Bristol Cent. cs.1931	Man.City 24.1.1934	F	26	7	8	2
HENRY T.	South Bank		South Bank cs1913	cs1915	HB	3	·	·	·
HEWLETT M.	Bristol 25.2.1976		Trainee	Current player		11(1)	·	·	·
HICK J.	Birmingham 1912		Birmingham Aug.1934	Ipswich T. cs.1939	FB	84	5	·	·
HICK W.M.	West Felton 13.2.1903	Chelmsford 1972	Southend Utd. cs1928	Exeter C. 24.1.1929	F	10	1	1	·
HIGGINS W.	Smethwick 1872		Grimsby T. May 1897	Newcast.U. May 1898	HB	32	2	8	3
HILL A.G.	Glasgow 25.4.1934		Dundee Nov.1959	Stirling Alb. Mar.1960	F	3	·	·	·
HILL B.W.	Bedworth 31.7.1941		Coventry C.(L) Mar.71	Coventry C. May 1971	M	7	·	·	·
HILTON F.	Barnsley 1884		Doncast.St.J. cs1905	cs1910	F	116	9	21	1
HINSHELWOOD W.A.A.	Battersea, London 27.10.29		Reading Feb.1956	Millwall Jun.1960	F	149	10	16	3
HIRST M.P.	Batley 26.10.1961		Bath City Oct.1983	Cont.Cancelled Jan.86	M	36(5)	8	1	1
HOCKIN G.E.			Local cs1894	Local cs.1897	HB	10	4	·	·
HODGE J.R.	Plymouth		Plymouth A. 27.7.1934	Luton Town 14.3.1936	F	62	10	8	4
HOMER S.	Bloxwich 14.1.1903	Walsall 22.1.83	Bristol Rov.8.11.1929	Worcester C. Aug.1934	F	179	7	18	·
HONOR C.R.	Bristol 5.6.1968		Apprentice 4.7.1986	Airdrieonians 14.8.1991	M	44(16)	7(1)	1	·
HOOPER M.D.	Bristol 10.2.1964		Mangotsfield U.8.11.83	Wrexham 8.2.1985	G	1	1	·	·
HOOPER P.J.	Teignmouth 2.2.1933		Cardiff City Jul.1963	Worcester C. cs1966	F	55	8	15	3
HOPKINS I.M.	Merthyr 11.10.1910		Brentford May 1947	Retired cs.1948	F	24	3	·	·
HOPKINSON G.	Sheffield 19.6.1933		Doncast.Rov. Jul.1958	Margate cs1961	FB	67	7	1	·
HORRIX D.	Taplow 21.11.1961	Berkshire 11.3.1990	Millwall 2.3.1990	Deceased (Car Accid.)	M	3	·	·	·
HOSIE J.	Glasgow 1876		Stockport C. cs.1903	Retired cs.1903	HB	53	6	10	2
HOWARTH J.T.	Rochdale 15.4.1890	Newport 2.11.1946	Army Jan.1914	Leeds U. 10.3.1921	F	52	5	17	5
HOWLING E.	Stockton 1888		South Bank 1.5.1913	Bradford P.A cs.1915	G	55	2	·	·
HOWSON G.S.	Blackburn		cs1925	N.Brighton 29.5.1927	FB	3	·	·	·
HOYLAND J.W.	Sheffield 23.1.1966		Sheffield U.(L) 4.3.94	Sheffield U.4.4.1994	M	6	·	·	·
HUGHES J.	Porth		Porth Athletic cs.1921	cs1922	G	3	·	·	·
HUGHES J.H.	Birmingham		Birmingham May.1934	cs1935	HB	10	·	·	·
HUGHES L.			cs1914	Bristol Rov. cs.1919	HB	5	·	·	·
			Bristol Rov. Dec.1919	Reinstat.Amat.1.6.1921					
HUGHES M.	Port Talbot 3.2.1962		Swansea C. 7.2.1985	Tranmere Rov. 19.9.85	D	21(1)	1	·	·
HUGHES R.G.	Sunderland 2.8.1902		Sunderland 6.9.1920	Exeter City 19.8.1932	FB	268	12	·	·
HUMPHRIES G.	Kingston-U-Hull 11.8.1964		Doncaster.R. 23.10.1987	Scunthorpe U.7.3.1991	D	86(4)	15	·	·

NAME	Born	Died	From	To	Pos.	Apps. League	Apps. Cup	Goals League	Goals Cup
HUMPISH A.E.	Bury 3.4.1902		Arsenal 12.12.1930	Stockport C. Aug.1932	HB	36	4	1	.
HUNT R.P.	Swindon 17.3.1943		Coventry C. Dec.1973	Atherstone T.Nov.1974	F	9(3)	4	2	.
HUNTER N.	Eighton Banks 29.10.1943		Leeds United Oct.1976	Barnsley Jun.1979	D	109	5	4	.
HUTCHINSON R.	Glasgow 19.6.1953		Tranmere R. cs1984	Walsall 3.2.1986	M	89(3)	13	10	2
INGHAM W.E.			Aberdare cs1905		FB	1	.	.	.
IRVING S.J.	Belfast 28.8.1893	Dundee 18.1.1969	Shildon Ath. Dec.1913	Dundee cs1919	F	18	.	4	.
JACKSON A.			Local cs1894	Local cs1896	G	.	4	.	.
JACKSON N.E.	Bradford 6.7.1925		Sheffield W. 19.6.1954	Oldham Ath. 29.6.1954	FB	8	1	.	.
JACOBS F.A.	Bristol 22.4.1940		May 1958	Cheltenham T. cs1961	HB	5	1	.	.
JACOBS T.F.	Bristol 28.11.1946		Apprentice Jul.1965	Bristol Rov. May 1973	FB	130(1)	15	3	.
JANTUNEN P.K.	Finland 26.6.1952		Eskilstuna Mar.1979	cs1981	M	7(1)	3(1)	1	1
JARVIS M.J.	Bristol 20.10.1924		Douglas AFC May 1948	cs1949	F	4	.	.	.
JAY J.	Kingswood, Bristol	Bristol Mar.1927	Bristol East cs1901	Brentford cs1903	HB	22	2	4	.
JENKINS E.J.	Cardiff 16.7.1909		Cardiff City Jun.1934	Newport C. cs1935	FB	10	.	.	.
JENNINGS W.H.	Bristol 1.4.1909	Bristol 4.11.1993	S.Bristol Cent.cs1928	Cardiff C. Jun.1934	HB	122	4	1	.
JOHNSON A.	Atherstone Jan.1904		Birmingham May 1928	Coventry City cs1931	F	60	2	7	.
JOHNSON J.A.	Grimsby 4.4.1911		Scunthorpe U.8.5.1931	Stoke City Apr.1932	F	7	.	.	.
JOHNSON P.E.	Harrogate 5.10.1958		Newcast.U. (L) Sep.82	Newcast.U. Jan.1983	D	20	1	.	1
JOHNSON S.A.	Liverpool 23.6.1957		Wigan Ath. 27.3.1985	Chester C. 17.3.1986	F	14(7)	1(1)	3	2
JONES A.			Bedminster cs1894	Local cs1897	HB	1	4	.	.
JONES A.M.	Wrexham 9.1.1963		Charlton A.(L)30.11.89	Charlton A. 30.12.1989	F	2(2)	.	1	.
JONES E.	Tyldesley 1894	Birmingham Nov. 1953	Exeter City Feb.1910	Bristol Rov. cs1923	FB	107	2	4	.
JONES E.G.	Bristol 12.5.1919		Victoria Ath. 3.2.1938	Wells City cs1948	HB	27	2	1	.
JONES G.			Bedminster cs1894	Local cs1895	FB	.	1	.	.
JONES J.	Wolverhampton 1887	Wolverhampton Mar.1944	Wellington T. cs1913	Wolv. Wand. Aug 1919	FB	19	2	.	.
JONES M.G.	Bristol 2.12.1965		Apprentice cs1982	Weston-s-Mare cs1983	M	-(1)	.	.	.
JONES S.			Aberdare cs1901	cs1902	F	5	3	2	2
JONES T.E.	Cardiff		Aug. 1919	Southend U. 20.6.1921	HB	10	.	.	.
JONES W.E.A.	Cwbwria,Swansea 12.11.20		Southampton Nov.1951	Rhyl Mar.1954	F	50	2	7	.
JONES W.M.	Brighton 6.3.1876	Bristol 25.9.1959	Loughborough T.cs1897	Tottenham Hot. cs1906	F	290	26	44	4
JORDAN J.	Carluke 15.12.1951		Southampton Feb.1987	Retired cs1990	F	40(22)	8(1)	8	.
KAMARA A.	10.2.1974		Southampton cs1993	cs1994		-(1)	.	.	.
KEARNEY S.F.	Liverpool 28.3.1917	Chelsea, London 1982	Accrington S.4.1.1947	Stonehouse cs1950	HB	65	.	5	.
KEARNS J.	Brownhills, Staffs.		Aston Villa cs1912	cs1916	FB	93	3	1	.
KEATING A.E.	Swillington Com. 28.6.1902	Newcast-U-Tyne 18.10.1984	Newcastle Nov.1925	Blackburn R. May 1928	F	100	4	33	1
			Cardiff City Nov.1932	North Shields Jul.1933					
KEEN J.F.	Walker-on-Tyne 25.11.1897	Darlington 1980	Walker Celtic cs1920	Newcastle U.May 1922	F	9	2	1	.
KELLARD R.S.W.	Edmonton, London 1.3.1943		Portsmouth Jul.1968	Leicester C. Aug.1970	F	77	7	6	2
KELLY E.E.	St.Vincent, W.Indies.8.4.58		Lincoln City Mar.1983	Coventry C. Aug.1983	F	4(1)	.	.	.
KELLY L.	Bellshill 19.11.1911	Aldershot 11.2.1979	Southend U.cs1936	Aldershot 1937	FB	5	.	.	.
KELLY N.	Coventry 14.2.1966		Junior cs1982	R.C. Warwick cs1983	F	2(4)	-(1)	.	.
KENYON R.N.	Blackpool 4.1.1949		Vancouver White.Oct.79	Vancouver W. Feb.1980	D	4	1	.	.
KERR J.	Birkenhead 23.11.1959		Tranmere R. Aug.1983	Stockport C. Jan.1984	F	13(1)	4	4	.
KIRBY H.H.	Barry 22.7.1903		Barry Town Nov.1924	Charlton Ath. Jan.1926	F	5	.	.	.
KIRK H.	Sheffield 22.4.1899		Sherwood R. Mar.1920	Plymouth Arg. cs1921	F	17	.	7	.
KIRK R.H.	Clydebank 22.2.1899		Albion Rov. Jul.1924	Exeter City cs1927	F	54	.	5	.
KNOX W.	Bathgate		Luton Town Aug.1932	cs1933	FB	19	.	1	.
KRISTENSEN B.	Malling, Denmark 10.10.1963		Newcastle.U.(L) 20.11.92	Newcastle U. 20.12.92	D	4	.	.	.
KURILLA J.	Glasgow 10.4.1941		Hamilton Steels.Aug.63	Northampton T. Nov.63	HB	6	.	.	.
LAIDMAN F.	New Elvert,Durham 20.6.13		Everton Jun.1938	Darlington cs1939	F	10	.	.	.
LAMBERTON J.			cs1902	cs1903	FB	3	.	.	.
LANCELEY F.J.	Bristol 13.9.1908	Bristol 1963	Bath City 16.9.1932	cs1933	G	5	.	.	.
LANDELLS J.	Gateshead 11.11.1904	Durham 1960	West Ham U. cs1934	Carlisle Utd. 5.6.1935	F	21	9	2	2
LANE W.H.C.	Ledbury 28.10.1904	Chelmsford Nov.1985	Watford cs1935	Clapton O. cs1937	F	30	.	11	.
LANGHAM W.	Nottingham		Notts.County cs1898	Leices.Fosse Nov.1900	F	74	6	28	3
LATHAM F.			Bristol Rov. cs1908	cs1909	F	1	.	.	.
LAWRENCE G.H.	Ilkeston 10.3.1889		Derby County 9.9.1924	Lincoln City 20.8.1925	G	14	.	.	.
LEANING A.J.	York 18.5.1962		Sheffield U. 27.9.88	Lincoln City Mar.1994	G	75	24	.	.
LEIGH I.R.	Ilfracombe 11.6.1962		AFC Bourne.(L) Jan.85	AFC Bourne. Feb.1985	G	1	.	.	.
LEIGH W.	Smethwick		Grimsby Town cs1902	New Brompton cs1903	F	30	3	5	1
LEWIS G.	Chasetown 1876		Notts.County cs1902	Stourbridge cs1903	FB	30	3	1	.
LEWIS G.	Abertillery 3.7.1921		Crystal P. Jul.1948	Llanelly cs1950	F	18	.	.	.
LEWIS W.			Local cs1894	Local cs1897	F	3	4	.	1
LLEWELLYN A.D.	Bristol 26.2.1966		Apprentice Mar.1984	Current player	FB	301(12)	43	3	.
LOFTUS J.L.	Ferryhill 24.1.1906		Notts.Forest 3.6.1932	Gillingham Aug.1935	F	93	10	29	5
LOGAN A.T.	Barrhead 1883		Aston Villa 10.11.1910	cs1912	F	37	.	9	.
LOW G.A.	Aberdeen 11.7.1940		Hudders.T. Mar.1961	Stockport C. 20.7.1968	HB	204(2)	21	12	2
LOWRIE G.	Tonypandy 19.12.1919	Bristol 3.5.1989	Newcastle.U. Sep.1949	Coventry C. Feb.1952	F	48	2	21	.
LYONS M.C.	Winterbourne 31.1.1932		Winterb.AFC Jun.1950	Bristol Rov. cs1953	F	2	.	.	.
LYTHGOE D.	Bolton 5.5.1933		Norwich City Aug.1962	Kings Lynn cs1964	F	13	.	2	.
MABBUTT K.R.	Bristol 5.12.1958		Apprentice Jan.1976	Crystal P. Oct.1981	F	112(17)	20	29	10
McCAFFREY A.	Newcastle-U-Tyne 30.8.1957		Bristol Rov.(L) Feb.82	Bristol Rov. Mar.1982	D	6	.	1	.
McCALL P.	West Ham, 11.9.1936		Kings Lynn Apr.1955	Oldham Ath. May 1962	HB	78	6	1	.
McCANN J.	Govan, Glasgow 23.7.1934		Barnsley May 1959	Hudders. T. Oct.1960	F	30	.	.	.
McCARTHY J.F.	Cork 22.1.1922		Dartford Jul.1949	cs1950	F	3	.	.	.

NAME	Born	Died	From	To	Pos.	Apps. League	Apps. Cup	Goals League	Goals Cup
McCLAREN S.	Fulford 3.5.1961		Derby C. 19.2.1988	Oxford U. 25.8.1989	M	66(1)	13	2	1
McDONALD A.	Glasgow 1871		Clyde cs1899	Clyde cs1900	FB	38	2	.	.
McDOUGALL D.	Irvine		Partick Thistle cs1900	Glasgow R. cs1901	F	23	1	4	.
McFARLANE A.B.			Bedminster cs1895	Local cs1896	F	.	3	.	.
McGARVEY S.T.	Glasgow 22.4.1963		Grimsby T. 8.9.1988	Oldham Ath. cs1989	F	20(6)	6	9	1
McGOVERN J.T.	Glasgow		Clydebank Jun.1924	Merthyr T. cs1925	F	3	.	1	.
McGURK F.R.	Eddlewood 15.1.1909	2.3.1978	Birmingham Jun.1933	Whitt.Ellis.FC cs1936	F	3	.	.	.
McILMOYLE H.	Cambuslang 29.1.1940		Wolv.Wand. 1.3.1967	Carlisle U. 22.9.1967	F	20	1	4	.
McINTYRE J.	Dumbarton 24.5.1972		Duntocher Boys	Exeter City	F	1	.	.	.
McKOP H.	Bulawayo, Zimbabwe 8.7.67		Bonner F.C. 1993-94	Current player	D	2(2)	.	.	.
McLEAN J.C.	Port Glasgow 22.5.1872		Grimsby T. May 1898	Bristol Rov. cs1902	HB	158	13	10	.
McLEAN J.S.	Clydebank		Vale of Leven 19.6.25	cs1926	HB	1	.	.	.
McMURTRIE A.	Scotland 1907		Motherwell 23.5.1929	cs1930	F	10	.	1	.
McNEILL B.	Newcast-U-Tyne 1.4.1956		Apprentice Oct.1974	Plymouth A. Dec.1978	D	-(3)	.	.	.
McPHAIL J.	Dundee 7.12.1955		York City 18.7.1986	Sunderland 31.7.1987	D	26	5	1	.
MAHONEY M.J.	Bristol 25.10.1950		Apprentice Aug.1968	Torquay U. Aug.1970	G	4	.	.	.
MANN G.W.	1873		Manchester C. cs1897	Retired cs1899	HB	41	3	13	.
MANN J.A.	Goole 15.12.1952		Leeds U. 26.4.1974	Barnsley Feb.1982	M	205(26)	25(2)	31	6
MARDON H.J.	Cardiff 8.6.1914	Bristol 1981	Bour.& BA 10.11.1938	cs1943	F	13	1	3	1
MARDON P.	Bristol 14.9.1969		Trainee 29.1.1988	Birmingham C. 1.8.91	D	29(13)	3(3)	1	.
MARKS			cs1899	cs1900	F	1	.	.	.
MARKS G.W.	Figheldean 9.4.1915		Blackburn R. Aug.1948	Reading Oct.1948	G	9	.	.	.
MARR C.R.	Doncaster 1884	Bristol 5.3.1961	Mexborough cs1906	Retired cs1920	HB	178	16	11	.
MARRISON T.	Sheffield		Oldham Ath. cs1912	cs1913	F	13	1	1	.
MARSH R.			cs1900	cs1901	FB	2	.	.	.
MARSHALL G.	Bristol 20.4.1964		Shepton Mallet cs1983	Carlisle U. 13.7.1988	M	48(21)	6(7)	7	2
MARSHALL J.P.	Swansea 6.7.1957		Hereford U. Aug.1980	Blackburn R. Feb.1982	D	29	6	.	.
MARTIN D.	East Ham, 25.4.1963		Southend U. Jul.1993	Current player	M	33(1)	6	1	.
MARTIN J.C.	Stoke-on-Trent		Aberdare Ath. 13.5.26	Blackpool 13.2.1928	F	40	3	16	2
MASON S.R.			cs1910	cs1911	HB	3	1	.	.
MASTERS G.J.	Bristol 13.8.1931		Dorset H.O.B.Aug.1948	Glastonbury 8.7.1954	F	9	1	1	.
MATTHEWS A.W.	Bristol 28.4.1901		Parson St.OB Dec.1920	Exeter City cs1925	F	1	.	.	.
MATTHEWS R.W.	Plas Bennion 14.4.1897	Wrexham 18.12.1987	Liverpool 2.3.1922	Wrexham 1.11.1923	HB	42	2	1	.
MAY A.	Bury 26.2.1964		Hudders.T. 7.8.1990	Millwall 18.6.1992	M	88(2)	9	4	1
MAYS A.W.	Yngshir 12.3.1902	Derby 3.11.1959	Watts Town Sep.1923	Plymouth A. Jun.1926	F	19	.	4	.
MAXWELL W.S.	Arbroath 21.9.1876	Bristol 1940	Millwall cs1905	Leopold FC cs1909	F	120	5	58	3
MAYGER F.E.	Bristol 16.10.1873	Bristol 7.1.1960	Bedminster cs1894	cs1896	F	.	3	.	2
MEIJER G.	Holland 15.3.1951		Ajax Amster. Mar.1979	Sparta Rott.25.2.1980	F	12(3)	1(1)	2	.
MELLON M.	Paisley 18.3.1972		Heart O.Mid.6.12.1989	West Brom.Alb.11.2.93	M	26(9)	4(1)	1	.
MENMUIR W.F.	Glasgow 3.2.1952		Jun.1969	Heart of Mid. cs1971	M	1(1)	.	.	.
MERCER A.S.	St. Helens		Connahs Quay Jul.1930	Chester 23.10.1931	F	31	1	8	.
MERRICK G.	Bristol 29.4.1951		Apprentice Aug.1968	Carolina Hills Feb.82	D	363(6)	46(1)	10	3
MEYER B.J.	Bournemouth 21.8.1932		Newport C. 5.9.1961	Hereford U. 1.7.1963	F	11	.	8	.
MICHAEL W.	1875		Heart O.Mid. cs1900	cs1901	F	20	2	15	.
MICKLEWRIGHT A.A.J.	Birmingham 31.1.1931		Bristol Rov. May 1953	Swindon T. Sep.1955	F	39	.	17	3
MILLAR A.	Coaltown 1915		Bristol Rov. cs1939	cs1940	FB	3	.	.	.
MILLARD F.	1873	Bristol 26.1.1952	Bedminster cs1895	cs1897	HB	1	4	.	.
MILLER P.A.	Bisley 31.1.1968		Wimbledon (L) 11.1.90	Wimbledon 11.2.1990	F	-(3)	.	.	.
MILLIGAN A.	Glasgow 1877		1st Scots.G.Oct.1897	Third Lanark cs1902	FB	35	1	1	.
MILNE R.	Dundee 13.5.1961		Charlton A. 25.2.1988	Man.United 11.11.1988	F	34(1)	3(1)	6	3
MILSOM P.J.	Bristol 5.10.1974		Trainee	Current player	F	1(2)	.	.	.
MILTON C.A.	Bristol 10.3.1928		Arsenal 16.2.1955	Retired cs1955	F	14	.	3	.
MITCHELL B.	Stonehaven 16.7.1963		Bradford C. 2.7.1992		D	15(1)	4	.	.
MITCHELSON K.G.	Edmonton,London 16.5.1928		Charlton A. 15.7.1949	Bath City 2.7.1954	FB	28	1	.	.
MOLES W.	London 1879		Tottenham H. cs1901	cs1902	G	6	.	.	.
MOLLER J.B.	Sweden 17.9.1953		Malmo F.F. Dec.1980	Toronto Bliz. Mar.1982	G	48	13	.	.
MOLLOY W.			Swansea T. 11.9.1933	cs1934	F	7	.	2	.
MOLYNEUX F.			Stoke cs1899	Luton T. cs1900	F	5	.	.	.
MONTEITH H.	New Cumnock, Ayrshire 1875		Loughborough T.cs1897	West Ham U. cs1900	G	120	9	.	.
MOONEY J.	Glasgow 1898		Glasgow Pe.FC 13.6.21	Cowdenbeath cs1923	F	2	.	.	.
MOORE G.	Greenock 27.6.1968		Non Contract cs1985	cs1987	M	-(1)	.	.	.
MORGAN C.I.	Bristol 26.9.1913	Bristol 31.7.1975	Bristol Boys 1.9.1930	Retired cs1949	HB	249	27	11	2
MORGAN J.	Bristol 1904		Doncast. Rov. cs1930	Barrow 11.6.1931	HB	1	.	.	.
MORGAN M.	Mountain Ash 1914		Plymouth A. Jul.1938	cs1940	F	2	.	.	.
MORGAN N.	East Ham, 30.10.1959		Stoke City 23.3.1990	Exeter City Feb.1994	F	75(5)	8	23	6
MORGAN S.S.	Bristol 1.8.1926		Farmer AFC Dec.1947	Millwall Mar.1958	G	71	2	.	.
MORGAN T.	Bristol		Fishponds C. cs1912	Caerphilly T. cs1913	HB	2	.	.	.
MORGAN T.J.	Forest Gate, 30.9.1956		AFC Bourne. Mar.1984	Exeter C. Nov.1984	F	51	5	15	3
			Bristol Rov. 23.1.86	Bolton Wands.25.6.87					
MORRIS J.J.	Liscard, Cheshire 11.2.1878		Notts.County cs1903	New Brompton cs1904	F	29	3	11	1
MORTON J.	Leith		Barnsley Apr.1914	cs1915	F	12	.	7	.
MOSELEY H.C.	Lewisham, London		Millwall Aug.1934	cs1935	F	4	.	.	.
MOSS A.J.	Crewe		Aston Villa cs1912	Retired cs1919	HB	85	5	.	.
MOULSON C.	Clogheen, Ireland 3.9.1906	Lincoln 27.10.1989	Grimsby T. 8.5.1931	Lincoln City Apr.1932	HB	11	.	1	.
MOYES D.W.	Blythswood 25.4.1963		Camb. U. 10.10.85	Shrewsbury T.30.10.87	D	83	11	6	.

NAME	Born	Died	From	To	Pos.	Apps. League	Apps. Cup	Goals League	Goals Cup
MULLEN J.W.	Larne, Ireland 10.1.1921		Crystal P. Feb.1949	Barrow Sep.1950	F	17	.	2	.
MUNRO S.D.	Falkirk 15.9.1962		Blackburn R. 4.2.1993	Current player	D	59(1)	8	.	.
MUNROE W.J.	Dublin 28.11.1933		Ards Dec.1957	Scunthorpe U. Jul.1958	F	1	.	.	.
MURPHY J.			cs1898	cs1899	F	17	1	6	.
MURRAY D.J.	Wyneberg, S. Africa 1902		Everton 26.10.1926	Bristol R. 1.11.1928	HB	16	.	.	.
MUSKER R.	Teignmouth 10.7.1962		Apprentice Aug.1979	Gillingham Nov.1983	M	44(2)	9	1	.
NEAL R.G.	Blackpool 1914		Yeovil & PU May.1936	Southport Jun.1937	F	9	.	.	.
NEAL R.M.	Rotherham 14.1.1906	Fence 26.12.1986	Southampton May1937	Acc.Stanley June 1938	F	6	2	.	.
NEATE T.			Chippenham T. cs1924	cs1925	F	2	.	.	.
NEESAM H.	Brompton, Yorks. 2.6.1892	Northallerton 6.7.1969	Grangetown A.3.9.1913	Bath City cs1928	HB	282	16	18	1
NESBITT W.	Burnley		Burnley May.1923	Retired cs1924	F	26	4	.	.
NEVILLE S.F.	Walthamstow 18.9.1957		Exeter City Dec.1984	Exeter City 26.7.1988	F	130(6)	11(3)	40	6
NEWLANDS G.	Cambeltown 14.1.1906	17.2.1969	Shotts B'field cs1927	Belfast Dist. Nov.1932	G	90	3	.	.
NEWMAN R.N.	Bradford-on-Avon 13.12.1963		Apprentice 5.10.1981	Norwich C. 15.7.1991	M	387(12)	56(1)	47	7
NICHOL D.	Arbroath		Millwall cs1900	cs1901	F	8	.	.	.
NICHOL W.D.	Newcastle-U-Tyne		Celtic cs1912	cs1913	F	3	.	.	.
NICHOLLS			cs1900	cs1901	HB	1	.	.	.
NICHOLLS A.	Plymouth 10.2.1963		Apprentice Feb.1980	Retired inj. cs1984	D	70	5	5	.
NICHOLLS R.B.	Sharpness 4.12.1933	23.7.1994	Cardiff C. Jul.1961	Cheltenham T.Jul.1965	G	39	5	.	.
NICHOLSON C.H.	Carlisle 25.1.1932		Leyton O. Jul.1960	Poole Town 10.7.1961	O	1	.	.	.
NICHOLSON J.A.	1889	Weston-super-Mare Jun.1970	Glasgow Ash. cs1911	Glasgow Rang. cs1921	HB	196	10	4	.
NIXON J.	Bathgate 1885		Hibernian cs1907	cs1908	F	7	.	.	.
NOAKE D.J.	Dorchester 9.6.1940		Luton Town Jun.1961	Trowbridge T. cs1962	F	11	2	3	.
NOBLE W.	Ayr 1898		Cumnock Jnrs 6.7.20	cs1921	F	6	.	.	.
NORRIS R.G.	Bristol 17.7.1922	Bristol 30.5.1972	Bminster Down May.47	Gloucester C. cs1948	HB	3	.	.	.
O'BRIEN P.	Glasgow 1873	Long Ashton, 2.10.1950	W.Arsenal cs1897	Swindon T. cs1902	F	106	7	44	2
ORAM D.G.	Knowle, Bristol 14.1.1920		St.Pancras cs1946	cs1947	FB	3	.	.	.
OSBORNE A.E.	Bristol 1886	Bristol 1940	Bristol Rov.Aug.1910	cs1912	HB	2	.	.	.
OSBORNE R.			cs1899	cs1900	F	4	.	.	.
OSMAN H.J.	Alton, Hampshire 1911		Millwall 1.10.1947	Dartford Aug.1948	F	18	3	1	.
OSMAN R.	Repton 14.2.1959		South'ton 10.10.1991	Current Player/Manager	D	67(3)	6(2)	3	.
OWEN G.	Barnsley 14.6.1959		Barnsley 21.8.1986	Mansfield T. 13.1.1988	F	51(2)	9	11	4
OWERS E.H.	Leytonstone 21.10.1888		Chesterfield cs1910	Darlington cs1911	F	62	2	32	.
			Darlington Mar.1912	Clyde Mar.1913					
PADFIELD W.	Paulton		cs1910	cs1911	FB	4	.	.	.
PALMER G.	Barnsley 12.11.1940		Doncaster R. Aug.1958	Gloucester C. cs1962	FB	1	.	.	.
PALMER J.N.	Bristol 1.7.1958		Weston-s-Mare Mar.83	Weston-S-Mare cs1984	M	2(6)	.	.	.
PANES S.M.	Almondsbury 22.2.1960		Melksham T. Aug.1982	Mangotsfield U. cs1983	F	2(2)	.	.	.
PARKER G.	Eccles		11.6.1931	cs1932	F	3	.	.	.
PARKER T.A.	Bristol 1910		Man.United May 1932	Carlisle U. cs1934	HB	54	3	1	.
PARR G.J.	Bristol 6.12.1938		Junior Feb.1957	Waterford cs1972	HB	282(6)	39	4	.
PARTRIDGE S.	Leicester 13.10.1974		Bradford C. 1993-94	Current player	F	7(2)	.	4	.
PAUL J.C.	Scotland 29.1.1904	Somerset 20.1.1979	Port Glasgow Aug.1922	Taunton T. 8.11.1930	F	206	13	49	2
PEACOCK E.G.	Bristol 11.12.1924	Bristol 12.2.1973	Notts.County Oct.1946	Weymouth T. Jun.1959	HB	343	14	7	1
PEARCE J.G.	Chirk, N.Wales.		Army Aug.1934	Rochdale 19.5.1939	HB	149	14	2	.
PEARSON H.	Tamworth 6.4.1907		Newport C. 24.9.1938	cs1939	G	16	.	.	.
PENDER J.P.	Luton 19.11.1963		Charlton A.30.10.1987	Burnley 18.10.1990	D	88	19	3	.
PENMAN T.	1887		Crook Town cs1908	cs1909	HB	1	.	.	.
PENN T.	Heath Common, Wakefield		Altofts Colliery cs1925	Darlington cs1927	FB	6	.	.	.
PENNYFATHER G.	Billericay 11.2.1963		Ipswich T. 12.3.1993	cs1994	M	21(5)	2(1)	1	.
PERRY H.	Manchester 1911		Bridgwater T. 8.5.1929	Bath City 5.2.1931	F	1	.	.	.
PETERS F.R.	Birmingham 26.2.1910		Swindon T. 5.5.1936	cs1939	F	113	5	22	.
PETERS R.D.	Cheltenham 5.3.1944		Apprentice Mar.1961	Bourn.& BA Jun.1968	F	158	18	25	2
PHILLIPSON-MASTERS F.E.	Bournemouth 14.11.1965		Plymouth A. Nov.1982	Yeovil T. 3.6.1985	D	94	10	4	.
PICKEN J.	Hurlford	Plymouth 1952	Burnley 6.10.1913	Retired cs1915	F	51	3	13	1
PICKETT T.A.	Merthyr 5.2.1909		Q.P.R. 8.6.1932	Yeovil & Pet.U. cs1933	G	6	3	*	.
POCOCK W.T.	Bristol 24.2.1884	Bristol 4.2.1959	St. Francis Jun.1919	St.Johnstone 13.7.26	F	238	17	46	2
POLLOCK R.			cs1899	Kettering cs1900	FB	13	1	1	.
POOL A.	Annan, Scotland		Blackburn R. May 1925	Exeter City cs1926	HB	12	.	.	.
PORTER H.			Staple Hill cs1896	Staple Hill cs1897	F	8	5	3	.
POTTER A.	Nottingham 1878		Notts County cs1898	cs1900	F/G	44	1	11	.
POULTON A.	Wolverhampton 1890		Middlesb'. 28.9.1921	Reading 1.11.1922	F	28	.	9	.
PRESLEY D.C.	Warminster 8.3.1930		Warminster T.Mar.1950	Bristol Rov. May 1952	HB	9	.	.	.
PRICE A.H.			cs1904	cs1905	HB	3	.	.	.
PRICE J.C.			cs1923	cs1924	HB	3	.	.	.
PRITCHARD H.K.	Cardiff 18.10.1958		Apprentice Aug.1976	Swindon T. Aug.1981	F	148(9)	24(1)	24	5
			Swindon T. Aug.1983	Gillingham 11.8.1986					
PRUDOE M.			Walsall (L) 6.11.1987	Walsall 11.12.1987	G	3	.	.	.
PUGSLEY J.	Grange Town 1.4.1900	Neath 1.8.1976	Grimsby T. May 1927	Charlton A. 11.5.1928	HB	16	1	.	.
PULLAN R.L.	Tyneside 19.2.1898	1983	Dawdon FC 8.7.1920	Exeter City cs1924	HB	18	3	1	.
PYLE W.D.	Trowbridge 19.12.1936		Bristol Rov. Jul.1962	Trowbridge T. cs1963	HB	8	.	.	.
QUIGLEY J.	Glasgow 28.6.1935		Huddersf. T. Oct.1966	Mansfield T.19.7.1968	F	66	9	7	.
QUINLAN J.			Bedminster cs1894	Local cs1897	F	11	5	2	1
QUINLAN M.	Platts Common, 4.12.1941		Doncast.R. Mar.1959	Welton Rovers cs1961	HB	2	.	.	.
RADFORD J.T.	Bristol		Salisbury C. cs1908	Treharris Dec.1911	F	1	.	.	.
RAE I.J.	Grangemouth 19.1.1933		Falkirk Oct.1957	cs1958	FB	12	1	.	.
RAE J.	Blackmill 1912		Partick Thistle cs1937	B.A.C. cs1939	F	2	.	.	.

NAME	Born	Died	From	To	Pos.	Apps. League	Cup	Goals League	Cup
RANDALL J.	Guide Post 12.12.1904		Derby C. May.1936	Ashington 13.7.1936	F	19	.	.	.
RANKIN A.	Glasgow 30.4.1904	Yeovil 1.11.1962	Dykehead FC Aug.1926	Charlton A. Jul.1929	F	70	4	12	.
READER A.R.	Derby 3.6.1894		Derby County Jun.1914	Luton Town 19.6.1922	F	51	5	4	.
REED G.	Spennymoor 6.5.1913		Everton Apr.1932	Newport`C. 9.2.1934	F	12	2	4	2
REES J.	Ebbw Vale		Ebbw Vale cs1930	Southampton cs1931	G	1	.	.	.
REGAN D.J.T.	Stoke-in-Ham, 3.6.1922		Exeter City Dec.1952	Weymouth T. cs1956	F	39	.	11	.
REGAN J.	Hemsworth 7.12.1927		Rotherham U. Jun.1953	Coventry C. 1.3.1956	HB	51	3	1	.
REID N.S.	Ormston 30.10.1960		Blackb.Rov.(L) 17.9.92	Blackburn R.17.10.92	D	3(1)	.	.	.
RENNIE D.	Edinburgh 29.8.1964		Leeds U. 31.7.1989	B'ham City 20.2.1992	M	101(3)	17	8	.
RILEY G.	Barnsley 24.7.1958		Barnsley Aug.1982	Aldershot 23.10.1987	F	184(15)	27	61	8
RILEY J.	Sheffield 1908		Bristol Rov. 25.5.1933	Bourn.& BA May 1935	F	59	11	21	2
RIPPON W.	Beighton 15.5.1886	1956	Kilnhurst T. cs1907	W.Arsenal 9.7.1910	F	36	9	13	6
RITCHIE S.K.	Glasgow 17.2.1954		Apprentice Sep.1971	Morton cs1973	D	1	.	.	.
RITCHIE T.G.	Edinburgh 2.1.1952		Bridgend This.Jul.1969	Sunderland Jan.1981	F	401(14)	51(3)	102	11
			Sunderland Jun.1982	Yeovil T. Dec.1984					
ROBERTS D.	Bretton, Yorks. 5.2.1918		Notts C. 12.5.1938	Retired cs1954	HB	306	25	2	.
ROBERTS W.S.	Bargoed 12.7.1908	Bristol 22.2.1976	Tottenham H. Sep.1933	Newport C. Jul.1938	FB	136	15	7	.
ROBERTSON J.S.	1873		New Brompton cs1901	Acc.Stanley cs1902	G/FB	12	4	.	.
ROBINSON L.	Bradford 29.12.1965		Bury Aug.1993	Burnley 26.7.1994	F	31(9)	8	4	1
ROBSON C.	High Wheatley 19.10.1900	County Durham Oct.1972	Connahs Q. May.1930	Chester 23.10.1931	F	25	1	2	.
ROBSON D.J.			Wellingborough cs1899	Brentford cs1901	FB	40	.	1	.
ROBSON E.			Local cs1895	Local cs1896	FB	10	5	.	.
RODGERS A.W.	Wickersley, 5.12.1923	Bristol 5.10.1993	Hudders. T. Oct.1949	Shrewsbury T.Jun.56	F	195	9	106	5
RODGERS D.M.	Bristol 28.2.1952		Junior Jul.1969	Torquay U. Feb.1982	D	191(2)	30(1)	15	3
ROGERS J.R.	Wednesday,Staffs.31.12.29		Wolv.Wands. May 1950	Coventry C. Dec.1956	F	270	18	102	6
			Coventry C. Dec.1958	Cinderford T. cs1962					
ROGERS L.M.			Apprentice 21.12.1984	Exeter C. 24.6.1988	D	30	6	.	.
ROOKS R.	Sunderland 29.5.1940		Middlesb'. Jun.1969	Retired, injury cs.1972	D	96	14	4	1
ROSE L.A.			cs1913	cs1914	F	4	.	.	.
ROSENIOR L.	Clapton,London 24.3.1964		West Ham U.19.3.92	Current player	F	35(15)	4(2)	12	1
ROSS J.S.			Local cs1895	Local cs1897	HB	9	6	2	1
ROWLES A.	Bristol 6.5.1916		Weston-s-Mare cs1937	Retired inj.Sep.1939	F	24	.	20	.
ROYLE J.	Liverpool 8.4.1949		Man.City Nov.1977	Norwich C. Aug.1980	F	100(1)	10(1)	18	2
RUDKIN T.W.	Worksop 17.6.1919		Southampton May 49	Hastings cs1951	F	34	3	4	.
RUSSELL A.C.	Bristol 17.4.1925		Local Nov.1947	Bridgwater T. cs1949	F	3	.	.	.
RUSSELL J.	Carstairs 1873		W.Arsenal cs1897	Blackburn R. cs1900	F	92	7	30	1
RYAN J.J.	Alloa 16.10.1930		Newcastle.U. 6.7.1960	Retired cs1961	F	3	1	.	.
SARGEANT C.	Cornsay, Lanchester 2.2.09		Norwich C. 19.6.1931	Hull City 20.5.1932	F	27	.	10	.
SAVINO R.J.	Norwich 16.11.1938		Norwich C. Jul.1962	Kings Lynn cs1968	F	75	5	2	1
SCATTERGOOD K.	Riddings 6.4.1912		Sheffield W. Aug.1933	Stoke C. May 1934	G	39	4	.	.
SCOTT M.	Sheffield 7.1.1968		Rotherham U.Dec.1990	Current player	D	153	19	12	1
SCOTT T.	Newcast.-U-Tyne 6.4.1904	Bootle 24.12.1979	Liverpool 25.10.1928	Preston NE 11.6.1930	F	35	.	6	.
SCRIVEN A.	Cleobury Mortimer 7.7.1904		Bradford C. 23.5.1932	Worcester C. Jul.1934	F	54	5	12	1
SEARLE F.B.	Hednesford 30.1.1906	Waltham Forest 16.6.1977	Willenhall T.10.12.26	Charlton Ath. cs1928	HB	1	.	.	.
SHAIL M.	Sandviken, Sweden 15.10.66		Yeovil T. Mar.1993	Current player	D	38(2)	8	2	1
SHARP A.A.	Nottingham 1908		Carlisle Utd. 30.6.1932	Aldershot May 1933	F	28	.	9	.
SHARPE G.R.	Gloucester 17.3.1946		Apprentice Mar.1964	Retired inj. cs1971	F	149(4)	25	48	6
SHARPE J.			Local cs1896	Local cs1897	F	1	.	.	.
SHAW J.K.	Stirling 4.2.1954		Leeds U. May 1974	Exeter City cs1985	G	296	35	.	.
SHEARMAN B.	Sheffield 1888		Rother'm T. 22.4.1909	W.Brom.Alb. 15.6.1911	F	60	4	4	.
SHELTON G.	Nottingham 21.3.1958		Oxford U. Aug.1989	Chester City cs1994	M	149(1)	19	24	.
SHEPHERD A.			Celtic (L) 30.12.1988	Celtic 30.1.1989	F	2(1)	2	.	.
SHERLAW D.D.	Penicuik 17.9.1901		Bathgate 29.5.1925	Charlton Ath. cs1926	F	20	1	6	.
SHOWELL G.W.	Bilston 9.2.1934		Wolv.Wands. May 1965	Wrexham Nov.1966	HB	9(3)	.	.	.
SHUTT C.S.	Sheffield 10.10.1961		Sheff.Wed. 30.10.1987	Leeds U. 23.3.1989	F	43(8)	12(3)	13	8
SINCLAIR J.F.	Glasgow 1873		W.Arsenal cs1897	cs1898	FB	11	2	.	.
SINCLAIR R.	Stirling 19.11.1964		Leeds U. 1.9.1989	Stoke City 9.1.1992	G	44	8	.	.
SINDEN			Local cs1896	Local cs1897	FB	12	5	.	.
SKELDING			Local cs1896	Local cs1897	FB	3	4	.	.
SKIRTON A.F.G.	Bath 23.1.1939		Blackpool Nov.1968	Torquay U. Jul.1971	F	75(3)	15	14	4
SLIMAN A.M.	Busby 27.2.1906	1945	Arthurlie Jun. 26.9.28	Chesterfield 4.3.1932	HB	136	6	1	.
SMAILES A.	Radcliffe,Nor'land 21.5.1896	Cardiff Autumn 1978	Wednesday 18.10.23	Rotherham U. 23.8.29	HB	162	7	14	1
SMITH D.	Sidcup 25.6.1971		Gillingham 3.8.1989	Plymouth A. 19.12.91	F	94(3)	16	10	4
SMITH D.B.	Dundee 22.9.1933		Bright. & HA Jun.62	Burnley cs.1963	FB	3	.	.	.
SMITH D.R.	Bristol 5.10.1934		Junior Apr.1953	Millwall Sep.1959	F	21	2	1	.
SMITH G.			Gainsb.Trinity cs1906	Crystal P. cs1907	F	11	.	2	.
SMITH G.A.	Trowbridge 12.11.1962		Apprentice Nov.1979	Bath City cs1981	F	7(7)	.	.	.
SMITH H.A.	Ettingshall 10.10.1932		Torquay U. Jul.1961	Dorchester T. cs1962	FB*	1	.	.	.
SMITH J.R.	Bristol		Victoria Albions cs1921	Plymouth A. Feb.1924	F	27	.	12	.
SMITH M.	Redruth 21.9.1963		Apprentice Sep.1981	Exmouth Town cs1982	M	1(4)	.	.	.
SMITH N.K.	Bath 12.1.1966		Apprentice Jan.1984	Cheltenham T. cs1985	M	2	.	.	.
SMITH R.G.	Westbury 1916		Trowbridge T. Mar.35	cs1937	F	7	.	1	.
SMITH W.			Local cs1896	Local cs1897	F	13	2	6	2
SOMMERVILLE G.D.L.	Dalziel 21.12.1900		Burnley 29.8.1932	Burton Town cs.1934	G	34	.	.	.
SOUTHWAY L.F.	Bristol 22.7.1893	Bristol 21.4.1982	Local cs1913	Exeter City cs1922	FB	27	1	.	.

NAME	Born	Died	From	To	Pos.	Apps. League	Apps. Cup	Goals League	Goals Cup
SPALDING W.	Glasgow 24.11.1926		Ballymena 3.1.1950	cs1951	F	10	2	.	.
SPEAR A.T.	Bristol 1883	Bath 12.12.1946	Local cs1904	cs1911	HB	136	15	1	.
SPECK G.			Gloucester cs1896	cs1897	G	15	6	.	.
SPIRING G.	1921		Local cs1937	Glastonbury cs1948	F	4	.	1	.
SPIRING P.J.	Glastonbury 13.12.1950		Junior Jun.1968	Liverpool Mar.1973	F	59(5)	5(2)	16	1
STACEY S.D.	Bristol 27.8.1944		Sneyd Park Nov.1961	Wrexham 25.2.1966	F	9	.	.	.
			Ipswich T. Sep.1970	Exeter C. Jul.1971	D				
STANIFORTH F.W.	Kilnhurst 1884	Bristol 23.5.1955	Mexboro.T. cs1906	Grimsby T. cs1911	F	134	15	14	1
STANLEY G.E.	Burton-on-Trent 4.3.1954		Wichita,Canada cs88	Gosport Boro. cs1989	M	8(2)	2(2)	.	.
STEEDS C.	Bristol 11.1.1929		Bed.Down B.C.Mar.47	Bristol Rov.May 1952	F	9	.	.	.
STEELE R.	Ferryhill 13.3.1930		Ferryhill A. Jun.1953	York City Jul.1956	FB	3	.	.	.
STEVENS C.			cs1905	cs1906	F	1	.	.	.
STEVENS P.D.	Bristol 4.4.1960		Apprentice Apr.1978	Bath City Jul.1985	D	146(1)	12	3	.
STEVENSON A.	1906		Sheff.U. May 1930	cs1931	F	5	.	1	.
STEVENSON J.			Newcastle.U. cs1898	Clyde cs1901	F	47	1	17	.
STEWART W.S.	Arbroath		Everton cs1898	cs1900	FB	51	1	.	.
STOLZ W.			Bed.St.Francis cs1904	Bed.St.Francis cs1905	F	1	.	.	.
STONE F.W.	Bristol 5.7.1925		Oldland C. AFC Feb.47	Chippenham T. cs1953	FB	64	.	3	.
STOUT P.W.	20.11.1875	9.10.1937	Gloucester cs1894	cs1897	F	.	1	.	1
STROUD K.A.	London 1.12.1953		Swindon T. Oct.1983	Retired cs1985	M	68(1)	.	4	.
SULLIVAN C.H.	Bristol 22.8.1928		Horfield O.B May.1949	Arsenal 3.2.1954	G	73	5	.	.
SUTHERLAND C.	Scotland		Millwall 18.8.1922	Merthyr T. 18.5.1926	F	103	4	23	.
SWEENEY G.	Renfrew,Glasgow 10.7.1945		Morton cs1971	York City Feb.1982	D	398(1)	50	22	5
SWEET F.G.			St.Mich's AFC cs1910	cs1921	HB	4	.	1	.
TAINTON T.K.	Bristol 8.6.1948		Apprentice Sep.1965	Torquay U.Feb.1982	M	458(30)	66(3)	24	2
TAIT A.	Bedlington 28.11.1933		Newcast.U. 22.6.1960	Doncast.R. Jun.1964	F	117	17	38	6
TALBOT-LEWIS A.E.	Bristol 20.1.1877	Bristol 22.2.1956	Bedminster cs1898	Everton cs1899	G/FB	34	3	.	.
			Everton cs1899	Walsall 1901					
			Leics.Fosse cs1907	Retired cs1908					
TANNER M.W.	Bristol 28.10.1964		cs1985	Bath City cs1988	D	16(3)	3	1	1
TASKER R.H.			cs1913	cs1914	F	1	.	.	.
TAYLOR A.			Local cs1894	Local cs1897	FB	2	3	.	.
TAYLOR A.M.	Dunscroft, Doncast.7.11.39		Doncast.R. May 1958	Barnsley Jul.1961	F	12	.	2	.
TAYLOR J.S.	Cowdenbeath 17.8.1909	Bristol 7.3.1964	Raith Rovers cs1927	Halifax T. May 1934	HB	148	10	.	.
TAYLOR R.	Horden 3.2.1967		Leeds U. Mar.1989	W.Brom.Alb. 31.1.1992	F	96(10)	15(2)	50	7
TERRIS J.	Chippenham 25.7.1933		Chippenham T.Oct.1955	Carlisle U.30.4.1959	FB	4	.	.	.
TERRY J.C.	Scotland 1909		Man.City 16.6.1931	Yeovil & Pet.U.21.7.32	FB	5	.	.	.
THICKETT H.	Hexthorpe 1873	Trowbridge 15.11.1920	Sheffield U. May.1904	Retired cs1905	FB	14	4	.	.
THOMAS D.S.	Machynlleth 12.11.1919		Fulham 14.6.1950	Retired cs1951	F	13	.	1	.
THOMAS E.			Local cs1894	Local cs1895	FB	.	1	.	.
THOMAS W.G.	Derby 18.11.1918		B.A.C. cs1943	Stonehouse Jul.1950	F	77	13	18	2
THOMPSON D.	Dundee 10.8.1891		St.Johnstone cs1925	Bourne. & BA 6.7.1926	F	6	.	.	.
THOMPSON D.	Ashington 15.4.1969		Millwall Jun.1992	Brentford	D	17	4	.	.
THOMPSON J.L.	1895		Sheffield U. 10.11.20	Retired cs1922	F	29	.	1	.
THOMPSON S.J.	Plymouth 12.1.1963		Junior Jun.1981	Torquay U. cs1982	M	10(2)	3(1)	1	.
THOMPSON W.			Local cs1896	Local cs1897	F	11	4	.	3
THOMPSON W.			cs1899	cs1900	F	2	.	.	.
THORLEY E.C.	Denaby 12.11.1909		Cheltenham T. 11.3.38	Retired 1.3.39	F	14	.	3	.
THRESHER T.M.J.	Cullompton 9.3.1931		Chard Town 27.1.1954	Bath City Jul.1965	FB	381	36	1	.
TINDILL H.	South Hindley 31.12.1926	South Hindley 10.7.1973	Doncast.R. 3.2.1958	Barnsley cs1959	F	56	3	29	2
TINNION B.	Stanley, Durham 23.2.1968		Bradford C. 22.3.1993	Current player	M	51(1)	8	7	2
TOMAN M.	Whitehaven 15.12.1913	Burma during W.W.II	Preston NE 12.5.1938	cs1939	F	2	.	.	.
TOMLINSON J.	Horwich 17.5.1910		Bolton White H.cs1934	cs1935	F	1	.	.	.
TONG D.J.	Blackpool 21.9.1955		Cardiff City cs1985	Merthyr T. cs1986	M	19	3	.	.
TONNER S.	Glasgow 30.8.1894		Clapton O. cs1919	Crystal P. cs1926	FB	6	.	1	.
TOONE G.	Nottingham 10.6.1868	Nottingham 1.9.1943	Bedminster cs1900	Notts.County cs1901	G	47	3	.	.
TORRANCE A.	Glasgow 29.9.1901	Bristol (air raid) 14.4.1941	Renfrew Jun. 13.6.21	Bath City 13.7.1928	HB	167	8	10	.
TOWNROW F.A.	West Ham, London 1903		Dundee Jun.1930	Bristol Rov. cs1931	F	22	.	5	.
TOWNSEND L.F.	Brentford 31.8.1917		Brentford Jun.1947	Millwall Jul.1949	F	74	6	45	5
TOVEY R.A.	Bristol 24.9.1930		Southmead S. 8.1.1952	Chippenham T. cs1954	F	12	.	3	.
TOVEY W.J.	Bristol 18.10.1931		Junior Dec.1948	Retired cs1953	HB	57	3	2	.
TREASURE C.J.	Farrington Gurney 1.9.1895	Taunton Jun.1985	Paulton R. cs1919	Halifax T. 11.6.1922	FB	63	6	.	.
TUFT W.	Wolverhampton 1874		Walsall cs1901	Retired cs1907	FB	138	15	.	.
TURNER A.			Plymouth A. May.1932	York City May 1934	FB	16	.	.	.
TURNER A.D.			cs1904	cs1905	F	1	.	.	.
TURNER H.	1916		Chesterfield Jun.1935	Retired 2.9.1936	F	7	.	1	.
TURNER J.K.	Wednesbury 1915		Mansfield T. 26.5.1939	Sep.1939	F	3	.	1	.
TURNER J.T.	Wednesbury 1915		Chester 22.10.37	Clapton Orient cs1939	FB	23	.	.	.
TURNER R.	Peterlee 18.9.1966		Wimbledon 27.1.1989	Plymouth A. 23.7.1990	F	45(7)	7	12	3
UNDERHILL G.	Bristol 10.4.1968		Apprentice cs1985	cs1987	M	1	.	.	.
VALLIS A.G.	Bristol 1898	Torquay 17.12.1962	Horfield U. Nov.1919	Halifax T. cs1922	F	6	.	.	.
VALLIS F.	Bristol 5.5.1896		Horfield U. cs1919	Merthyr T. 16.6.1926	G	219	17	.	.
VALLIS J.	Bristol		Dundee cs1921	cs1922	G	10	.	.	.
VAUGHAN J.	Isleworth 26.6.1964		West Ham U.(L) 4.3.86	West Ham U. 4.4.1986	G	5	.	.	.
			Fulham (L) 21.1.1988	Fulham 21.2.1988					

NAME	Born	Died	From	To	Pos.	Apps. League	Apps. Cup	Goals League	Goals Cup
VIALS P.A.	Market Harb. 31.1.1908	1983	Market Har. Oct.1928	Middlesb. 14.5.1932	F	75	5	36	1
VICKERSTAFFE E.B.	Hanley		Eastville A. cs1901	Leicest.O.B. cs1902	F	1	.	.	.
VIDLER H.J.	Portsmouth 13.6.1905	6.4.1953	Plymouth A. cs1939	cs1940	F	3	.	.	.
VIRGIN D.E.	South Petherton 10.12.1934		S.Petherton 10.8.1953	Bath City cs1961	F	21	1	4	.
WADLEY H.E.			cs1904	cs1905	F	1	.	.	.
WADSWORTH W.	Bootle Oct.1890	Bristol 6.10.1951	Liverpool 14.5.1926	Flint Town 2.6.1928	HB	67	1	1	.
WALKER G.W.	Sunderland 30.5.1034		Chippenham T.Jul.57	Carlisle U. Mar.1959	F	15	2	5	.
WALKER W.B.	Lanemark, Ayrshire 1895		Merthyr T. 12.10.1922	The Wed'day 18.10.23	F	37	2	7	1
WALLIS G.H.	Sawley 1910		Birmingham Aug.1934	Bath City Aug.1937	F	42	2	14	.
WALSH A.	Hartlepool 9.12.1956		Darlington cs1984	Besiktas(Turkey)cs1989	F	220(3)	39	79	11
WALSH J.	Blackburn 11.2.1901	Bristol 12.6.1965	Aberdare A. Dec.1926	Millwall 15.3.1932	FB	164	3	1	.
WALSH T.	Bolton 12.2.1900	22.11.1950	Bolton Wand.16.1.1924	Crystal P. 11.5.1928	F	142	8	88	3
WARE T.	Bristol	Killed in action Jun.1915	cs1911		G	51	4	.	.
WATERHOUSE K.	Ormskirk 23.1.1930		Rotherham U. 5.4.1963	Darlington Aug.1964	HB	16	1	1	.
WATKIN C.	Stoke-on-Trent		Stoke City Jul.1952	Leek Town Mar.1954	FB	3	.	.	.
WATKINS J.V.	Bristol 9.4.1933		Clifton St.V. Jun.1951	Cardiff C. 29.6.1959	F	96	8	19	2
WATLING B.J.	Walthamstow 16.7.1946		Orient Jul.1965	Notts County 8.6.1969	G	2	.	.	.
WATTS J.			cs1899	cs1900	G	4	.	.	.
WAUGH K.	Sunderland 27.10.1956		Sheff. U. Dec.1984	Coventry C.18.8.1989	G	175	30	.	.
WEAVER R.S.	Ponkey 1912		Luton T. 31.5.1933	cs1934	F	3	.	.	.
WEBBER G.W.			cs1934	cs1935	HB	1	.	.	.
WEDLOCK W.J.	Bristol 28.10.1880	Bristol 25.1.1965	Arlington R. cs1900	Aberdare cs1901	HB	364	29	17	.
			Aberdare cs1905	Retired cs1921					
WELCH K.	Bolton 3.10.1968		Rochdale 25.7.1991	Current player	G	116	15	.	.
WHELAN M.	Middlesbrough		Bedminster cs1900	cs 1901	F	28	3	5	.
WHITE A.S.	Bristol 25.7.1924		Soundwell Mar.1947	Millwall 7.8.1951	F	82	1	12	.
WHITE J.	Doncaster 17.3.1924		Aldershot Mar.1952	Cambridge C. Jul.58	HB	217	11	11	.
WHITE W.T.	Kircaldy 1911		Newport C. 8.5.1935	Lincoln C. 30.12.1936	F	51	2	15	.
WHITEHEAD C.R.	Birmingham 24.11.1955		Northfield Jun. Mar.73	W.Brom.Alb. 4.11.1981	F/D	210(20)	24(3)	10	4
WHITELAW D.L.	Calder 1910		Calder United cs1930	Southend U. cs1931	G	12	.	.	.
WILCOX J.C.	Coleford, Somerset 1896		Abertillery cs1919	Bradford PA 8.9.1922	F	59	3	20	.
WILLIAMS Adrian D.	Bristol 4.8.1943		Apprentice 1.7.1960	Exeter City Jul.1963	F	4	3	.	4
WILLIAMS Alan	Bristol 3.6.1938		Junior Sep.1955	Oldham A. 10.6.1961	HB	135	10	2	.
WILLIAMS Albert	Merthyr 4.3.1907		Merthyr T. cs1927	Sheff. U. Jan.1932	F	103	6	26	3
WILLIAMS B.	South Alford 5.11.1955		Bristol Rov. cs1985	Shrews.T. 28.7.1987	D	77	9(1)	3	.
WILLIAMS C.E.	Bristol 17.11.1921		Local cs1938	W.Brom.Alb. Jun.1948	F	296	22	69	8
			W.Brom.Alb. Aug.1951	Chippenham T. cs1958					
WILLIAMS G.A.	Bristol 8.6.1963		Apprentice Aug.1980	Oldham Ath. cs1984	D	98(2)	17	1	.
WILLIAMS P.S.	Newton Abbot 20.2.1965		Ottery St.M. Mar.1983	Saltash cs1984	F	16(3)	1(2)	1	.
WILLIAMS R.G.	Bristol 17.2.1940		Junior May 1958	Rotherham U.Feb.1965	F	188	26	76	5
WILLIAMS S.F.	Bristol 21.12.1919		Local cs1937	Stonehouse Jan.1952	F	100	8	11	1
WILLIAMS T.H.	Rhyhope 25.3.1899	Easington 14.12.1960	Bristol Rov. 19.6.1928	Merthyr T. 4.2.1929	F	8	.	4	.
WILLSHAW G.J.	London 18.10.1912		Southend U. cs1938	Clapton Orient cs1939	F	34	.	9	.
WILSON H.	Mauchline, Ayrs. 18.3.1869	7.4.1940	Bedminster cs1900	Third Lanark cs1901	HB/F	46	6	13	5
WILSON J.E.	Leeds 1909		Bradford PA Aug.1934	Bristol Rov. 2.6.1938	G	67	1	.	.
WILSON J.T.	Leadgate 8.3.1897		Man. United May.1932	cs1933	HB	18	3	.	.
WILSON L.J.	Manchester 10.7.1947		Wolv.Wands. Mar.1971	Norwich C. Sep.1973	M	42(1)	2	1	1
WILSON P.			cs 1911	cs1912	F	10	.	.	.
WILSON R.J.	Birmingham 23.5.1943		Cardiff C.(L)Oct.1969	Cardiff C. Nov.1969	G	1	.	.	.
WIMBLETON P.	Havant 13.11.1964		Cardiff C. 26.5.1989	Shrewsb. T.18.1.1990	M	10(6)	3	2	2
WIMSHURST K.P.	South Shields 23.3.1938		Southampton Oct.1967	Retired cs1972	M	146(3)	19	9	1
WITHEY G.A.	Bristol 11.6.1960		Bath City cs1986	Cheltenham T. cs1987	F	1(1)	.(1)	1	.
WOMBWELL R.	Nottingham		Derby C. cs1902	Man.United Mar 1905	F	92	11	19	3
WOODS E.	Ton Pentre 29.7.1951		Ferndale A. Sep.1971	Newport C. Sep.1974	F	1(1)	1(1)	.	.
WOODS T.	Atherton		Plymouth A. 15.6.1937	cs1938	HB	7	.	.	.
WORLOCK C.S.R.	Bristol 24.12.1895	Bristol 17.2.1973	St.P.Marsh A.S Aug.22	Bradford PA 19.5.1925	F	73	.	9	.
WREN J.E.	Bristol	Bristol 30.7.1948	Millwall cs 1919	Notts County 5.8.1922	HB	104	8	1	.
WYATT M.J.	Yate, Bristol 12.9.1974			Current player	F	8(2)	.	.	.
WYLLIE T.G.	Maybole, Ayrshire 1872		Bury cs1897	Retired cs1898	F	26	3	12	4
YOUNG R.K.	Guardbridge 1886		Dundee Violet cs1907	cs1920	FB	168	4	.	.
UNKNOWN SCORERS	1896 - 1898							6	.
OPPOSITION OWN GOALS	1897 - 1994							95	5

* Played his one game for the City at outside-right.

NOTE: (i)   Figures in brackets are additional substitute appearances.

(ii)   The above details (which include abandoned matches plus the three games played at the start of the aborted 1939-40 Football League Season), are missing ten of the team for the Western League fixture against Bedminster on April 16th 1897 as the only certainty is that H. Porter played.

(iii)   The details in the League column include all games played as League matches by Bristol South End/Bristol City in the Western, Southern, United, Southern District Combination, and the Football League from 1896-97 to 1993-94 inclusive. It does not include the emergency wartime competitions in either the First or the Second World Wars, but does allow for the five play-off matches played 1988.

(iv)   The details in the Cup column include all games played by Bristol South End/Bristol City in the F.A. Cup, Football League Cup, and the F.A. Amateur Cup from 1894-95 to 1993-94 inclusive.

KEY: G - Goal   FB - Full-back   HB - Half-back   F - Forward   Variations from 1966:   D - Defender   M - Midfield

BEDMINSTER - PLAYERS WHO'S WHO

NAME	Born	Died	From	To	Pos.	Apps.		Goals	
						League	Cup	League	Cup
AYRE			cs1899	cs1900	HB	6	·	·	·
BARKER G.			Bristol C. Nov.1899	cs1900	FB	25	1	·	·
BAYNON			cs1899	cs1900	F	2	·	·	·
BECTON F.	Preston		Sheff.U. cs1899	Swindon T. cs1900	F	13	2	2	2
BELL			cs1898	cs1899	F	13	5	·	2
BOUCHER T.	West Bromwich 1874		Notts County cs1899	Bristol Rov. cs1900	F	27	2	11	2
BRAMLEY			cs1899	cs1900	HB	4	1	·	·
BROOKS G.			cs1898	cs1899	FB	7	2	·	·
CALLENDER			Local cs1897	Local cs1899	F	1	·	1	·
CHAMBERS P.	Workington 1878	Swindon 1952	Blackburn R. cs1899	Bristol C. cs1900	HB	24	3	·	·
CLAPP A.			Bedminster St.F.cs1899	Bedminster St.F.cs1900	G	1	·	·	·
CLEMENTS H.H.	Bristol Aug.1884	Nailsea, Bristol 29.3.1910	Bristol C. cs1897	Local cs1898	F	·	1	·	·
COPELAND D.	Ayr 2.4.1875	Birmingham 16.11.1931	Walsall cs1898	Tottenham Hot.cs1899	F	35	5	11	1
COX W.			cs1898	cs1899	G	3	·	·	·
CRONE R.			Notts County cs1898	cs1900	FB	55	7	1	·
DAVIES R.H.	Bolton 1876		Bolton Wands. cs1899	Bristol C. cs1900	FB	34	3	6	·
DAVIES W.H.	Blakeley 1877		Bolton Wands. cs1899	Bristol R. cs1900	HB	27	1	·	·
DRAYCOTT W.			Newton Heath cs1899	cs1900	HB	33	3	·	·
FLEWITT A.	Nottingham 1873		West Brom.Alb.cs1899	cs1900	F	27	3	9	1
GEDDES A.J.	West Bromwich Apr.1871	Bristol Oct.1927	Millwall cs1899	Bristol C. cs1900	F	33	2	9	1
GRAY			cs1898	cs1899	F	29	1	8	1
KELSO R.	Renton 2.10.1865	10.8.1942	Dundee cs1898	cs1899	FB	28	5	1	·
LAMONT J.			cs1898	cs1899	HB	33	5	·	1
LEONARD			cs1898	cs1899	F	32	2	7	·
LIVESEY			cs1898	cs1899	F	2	1	3	·
McDONALD A.			cs1898	cs1899	HB	28	2	·	·
McVEAN M.			cs1898	cs1899	F	33	4	7	3
MASSIE			cs1898	cs1899	F	12	2	3	·
NORTH A.E.			cs1898	cs1899	F	1	·	·	·
PROUDFOOT J.			cs1898	cs1899	HB	28	1	1	·
SAXTON A.			Sunderland cs1898	cs1899	F	23	1	5	·
STEWART			cs1899	cs1900	F	32	5	7	1
STOLZ W.	1880		Bedminster St.F.cs1899	Bedminster St.F.cs1900	F	4	·	·	·
TOONE G.	Nottingham 10.6.1868	Nottingham 1.9.1943	Notts.C. cs1899	Bristol C. cs1900	G	36	3	·	·
WHELAN M.	Middlesbrough		Sheffield U. cs1899	Bristol C. cs1900	F	35	3	5	·
WHITEHOUSE J.	Birmingham 1873	7.2.1934	Aston Villa cs1897	Grimsby T. May 1899	G	32	5	·	·
WHITTLE			cs1898	cs1899	F	2	4	·	1
WILSON H.	Mauchline 18.3.1869	7.4.1940	Sunderland cs1899	Bristol C. cs1900	HB/F	32	3	9	5
UNKNOWN SCORERS								4	·
OPPONENTS OWN GOALS								7	·

NOTE: The above is the complete record of the players for Bedminster in the Southern League and the F.A. Cup during their period as a professional club. These details include the games with disbanded clubs, as well as the match against New Brompton on October 21st 1899 that was abandoned.

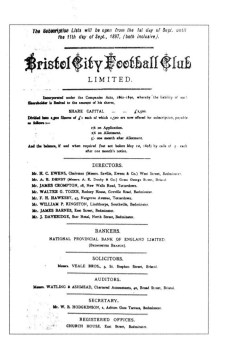

BRISTOL CITY PROFIT/(LOSS): 1897 - 1993

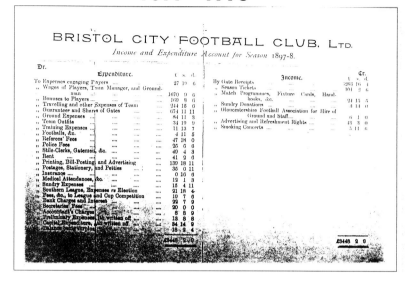

	Profit/(Loss) £	Season Tickets	Annual General Meeting
1897-98	18.2.4	101.2.6	Temperance Hall, East Street, July 5th 1898
1898-99	(182.10.3)	131.11.2	
1899-00	(1,163.16.11)		
1900-01	(974.5.11)	132.16.10	
1901-02	39.14.9	75.3.9	June 17th 1902
1902-03	360.10.10	117.19.4	
1903-04	(366.17.1)	200.6.0	
1904-05	71.5.0	272.2.11	
1905-06	425.19.0	250.10.4	
1906-07	3,048.12.6	464.16.9	Temperance Hall, East Street, June 24th 1907
1907-08	757.18.10	429.3.11	
1908-09	3,133.18.11	430.0.10	Temperance Hall, East Street, June 30th 1909
1909-10	(78.0.10)	327.3.6	
1910-11	(3,842.5.4)	359.11.8	Temperance Hall, East Street, June 30th 1911
1911-12	(817.0.0)	199.15.6	Temperance Hall, East Street, June 26th 1912
1912-13	(987.2.7)	318.1.8	Ford Memorial Hall, Mill Lane, June 26th 1913
1913-14	(968.17.1)	280.3.6	Ford Memorial Hall, Mill Lane, June 29th 1914
1914-15	(1,417.6.4)	79.9.0	Ford Memorial Hall, Mill Lane, June 30th 1915
1915-16	(809.6.7)		Ford Memorial Hall, Mill Lane, June 28th 1916
1916-17	(537.17.9)		Ford Memorial Hall, Mill Lane, June 29th 1917
1917-18	(555.8.2)		Ashton Gate, July 3rd, 1918
1918-19	264.4.10		Ford Memorial Hall, Mill Lane, June 30th 1919
1919-20	3,155.7.2	295.5.0	Ford Memorial Hall, Mill Lane, June 30th 1920
1920-21	1,737.15.7	1,036.15.7	Grand Hotel, Broad Street, July 8th 1921
1921-22	(3,642.16.1)	1,281.19.6	Ford Memorial Hall, Mill Lane, June 16th 1922
1922-23	1,116.15.9	924.6.0	Ford Memorial Hall, Mill Lane, July 19th 1923
1923-24	(2,251.12.11)	1,466.13.3	Ford Memorial Hall, Mill Lane, June 26th 1924
1924-25	43.1.5	915.3.1	Ford Memorial Hall, Mill Lane, June 25th 1925
1925-26	(651.12.10)	1,169.18.2	Ford Memorial Hall, Mill Lane, June 24th 1926
1926-27	1,913.1.9	1,078.13.9	Ford Memorial Hall, Mill Lane, June 30th 1927
1927-28	2,179.17.3	1,999.5.7	Ford Memorial Hall, Mill Lane, July 5th 1928
1928-29	(5,109.9.3)	956 Number	Ford Memorial Hall, Mill Lane, June 27th 1929
1929-30	444.19.4	791	Ford Memorial Hall, Mill Lane, June 26th 1930
1930-31	37.19.10	848	Ford Memorial Hall, Mill Lane, June 25th 1931
1931-32	1,092.12.0	713	Ford Memorial Hall, Mill Lane, June 23rd 1932
1932-33	(4,352.1.0)	656	Provident Hall, Prewett Street, May 5th 1933
1933-34	3,649.12.7	866	Provident Hall, Prewett Street, June 29th 1934
1934-35	935.7.6	1,201.17.2	Provident Hall, Prewett Street, July 12th 1935
1935-36	(2,631.7.8)	1,431.3.9	Provident Hall, Prewett Street, June 26th 1936
1936-37	(1,237.8.10)	1,184.6.0	Provident Hall, Prewett Street, July 9th 1937

Year	Profit/(Loss)	Attendance/Number	Venue
1937-38	3,494.13.2	1,264.2.0	Provident Hall, Prewett Street, June 29th 1938
1938-39	(4,418.16.5)	1,903.18.9	Provident Hall, Prewett Street, June 20th 1939
1939-40	(2,971.11.3)	733 Number	Ashton Gate, October 28th, 1940
1940-41	(330.5.5)		Ashton Gate, January 7th, 1942
1941-42	35.18.7		Ashton Gate, March 31st, 1943
1942-43	1,331.18.11		Ashton Gate, May 12th, 1944
1943-44	163.14.11		Ashton Gate, November 8th, 1944
1944-45	2,453.11.8		Ashton Gate, October 24th, 1945
1945-46	4,313.13.8		Ashton Gate, December 17th, 1946
1946-47	5,450.2.5	383.3.6	Ashton Gate, February 10th, 1948
1947-48	(2,222.11.4)	2,493.15.0	Grand Hotel, Broad Street, March 15th 1949
1948-49	(12,055.4.1)	2,402.5.2	Grand Hotel, Broad Street, April 4th 1950
1949-50	(24,328.13.7)	1,407 Number	Grand Hotel, Broad Street, August 10th 1951
1950-51	(483.13.4)	4,484.10.10	Grand Hotel, Broad Street, May 13th 1952
1951-52	2,228.3.6	5,265.19.0	Grand Hotel, Broad Street, April 20th 1953
1952-53	(2,346.7.9)	5,159.15.0	Grand Hotel, Broad Street, March 15th 1954
1953-54	8,041.12.5	8,419.18.0	Grand Hotel, Broad Street, December 20th 1954
1954-55	4,289	9,095	Royal Hotel, College Green, December 30th 1955
1955-56	7,699	16,869	Royal Hotel, College Green, April 2nd 1957
1956-57	1,233	17,031	Brecknell, Dolman & Rogers, April 15th 1958
1957-58	4,839	2,838 Number	Brecknell, Dolman & Rogers, April 20th 1959
1958-59	(13,050).	3,014 Number	Brecknell, Dolman & Rogers, January 26th 1960
1959-60	43,009*	17,350	Brecknell, Dolman & Rogers, March 7th 1961
1960-61	(10,075)	10,744	Brecknell, Dolman & Rogers, March 5th 1962
1961-62	4,512.	1,562 Number	Brecknell, Dolman & Rogers, December 4th 1962
1962-63	(25,000)	1,052 Number	Brecknell, Dolman & Rogers, December 23rd 1963
1963-64	(3,860)	1,191 Number	Brecknell, Dolman & Rogers, December 1st 1964
1964-65	13,917	7,613	Brecknell, Dolman & Rogers, June 2nd 1966
1965-66	22,701	14,178	51 Club, Ashton Gate, February 16th 1967
1966-67	(26,890)	13,000	51 Club, Ashton Gate, November 13th 1967
1967-68	(25,599)		51 Club, Ashton Gate, March 10th 1969
1968-69	(20,252)	20,802	51 Club, Ashton Gate, March 10th 1970
1969-70	3,856		Indoor Bowls Club, Dolman Stand, July 19th 1971
1970-71	15,172	37,000	Indoor Bowls Club, Dolman Stand, December 10th 1971
1971-72	64,637		Indoor Bowls Club, Dolman Stand, August 8th 1972
1972-73	(20,912)	42,139	Indoor Bowls Club, Dolman Stand, August 14th 1973
1973-74	(26,447)	46,128	Indoor Bowls Club, Dolman Stand, August 14th 1974
1974-75	(68,456)	51,488	Indoor Bowls Club, Dolman Stand, November 11th 1975
1975-76	(5,900)	68,942	Patrons Bar, Dolman Stand, August 19th 1976
1976-77	(113,039)	177,571	Patrons Bar, Dolman Stand, August 18th 1977
1977-78	161,944	237,255	Supporters Club, Ashton Gate, November 16th 1978
1978-79	56,730	236,058	Supporters Club, Ashton Gate, November 22nd 1979
1979-80	(161,223)	230,896	Supporters Club, Ashton Gate, December 22nd 1980
1980-81	(461,969)	101,146	Supporters Club, Ashton Gate, November 19th 1981
1981-82	(60,672)**	}	Supporters Club, Ashton Gate, December 1st 1983
1982-83	2,391	36,739. }	
1983-84	31,089	40,076	Supporters Club, Ashton Gate, December 13th 1984
1984-85	46,156	65,452	Supporters Club, Ashton Gate, December 12th 1985
1985-86	72,937	78,885	Supporters Club, Ashton Gate, December 11th 1986
1986-87	156,925	83,806	Supporters Club, Ashton Gate, December 10th 1987
1987-88	106,877	90,725	Supporters Club, Ashton Gate, December 15th 1988
1988-89	(185,354)	102,219	Supporters Club, Ashton Gate, December 14th 1989
1989-90	68,550	122,165	Ashton Suite, Ashton Gate, December 10th 1990
1990-91	424,172	250,235	Sportsmans Suite, Ashton Gate, December 11th 1991
1991-92	(659,284)	311,452	Sportsmans Suite, Ashton Gate, December 3rd 1992
1992-93	517,481	325,799	Sportsmans Suite, Ashton Gate, December 8th 1993

*   This profit was due to the gift of shares by Chairman Harry Dolman, otherwise a loss of £6,649.

**   These, the first set of accounts by the new Company Bristol City (1982) Plc., include cost of share issue £43,649. Unable to ascertain figures for 1981-82 in respect of the old company.

Notes   The above details are from newspaper reports, except for 1897-98, 1906-07, 1934-35 and the period from 1977-78 where shareholders reports have been to hand. The 1st A.G.M. of Bristol City (1982) Plc took place at the Colston Hall Bristol on June 21st, 1982.

BRISTOL CITY A.F.C. - RÉSUMÉ

Founded: April 12th 1894 as Bristol South End.

Changed name to Bristol City on joining the Southern League and adopting professionalism in 1897.

Amalgamated with Bedminster at the end of the 1899-1900 Season.

Club reconstituted in February 1982.

Present Ground: Ashton Gate, Bedminster, Bristol, BS3 2EJ.

(Permanent home from, and including, the 1904-05 Season, though 14 matches were played here in 1900-01. Was home of Bedminster A.F.C., from 1896-97 to 1899-1900).

Record Attendance: 43,335 (£3,209) v Preston North End, F.A. Cup 5th Round, February 16th 1935. (0-0)

Record Receipts: £155,482 (20,612) v Liverpool, F.A.Cup 3rd Round, January 8th 1994. (1-1 abandoned)

Principal Record Attendances and/or Record Receipts:

F.A.Cup:

8,000	(£214)	v Blackpool, January 14th 1905 (2-1)
10,000	(£299)	v Woolwich Arsenal, February 8th 1905 (1-0)
19,371	(£742)	v Preston North End, February 18th 1905 (0-0)
20,000	(£670)	v Southampton, January 16th 1909 (1-1)
24,000	(£817)	v Bury, February 6th 1909 (2-2)
24,009	(£868)	v Norwich City, February 20th 1909 (2-0)
25,900	(£2,031)	v The Arsenal, January 31st 1920 (1-0)
32,432	(£3,551)	v Cardiff City, February 21st 1920 (2-1)
32,972	(£2,202)	v Derby County, February 3rd 1923 (0-3)
36,260	(£2,442)	v Tottenham Hotspur, January 14th 1928 (1-2)
42,885	(£2,570)	v Portsmouth, January 30th 1935 (2-0)
35,648	(£2,732)	v Brentford, January 26th 1946 (2-1)
36,454	(£4,252)	v Chelsea, January 8th 1949 (1-3)
32,196	(£4,341)	v Accrington Stanley, January 7th 1958 (3-1)
39,160	(£5,439)	v Bristol Rovers, February 15th 1958 (3-4)
42,594	(£5,570)	v Blackpool, January 24th 1959 (1-1)
22,176	(£6,174)	v Aston Villa, January 16th 1963 (1-1)
38,017	(£8,879)	v Southampton, February 18th 1967 (1-0)
37,237	(£9,954)	v Bristol Rovers, January 27th 1968 (0-0)
37,141	(£28,111)	v Leeds United, February 16th 1974 (1-1)
37,671	(£28,826)	v Liverpool, March 9th 1974 (0-1)
20,079	(£45,000)	v Aston Villa, January 23rd 1982 (0-1)
19,367	(£45,300)	v Bristol Rovers, December 8th 1984 (1-3)
24,535	(£97,780)	v Chelsea, January 27th 1990 (3-1)

F.L.Cup:

9,229	(£1,350)	v Aldershot, October 25th 1960 (3-0)
22,054	(£4,960)	v Everton, September 13th 1967 (0-5)
23,228	(£7,985)	v Fulham, November 24th 1970 (1-0)
30,022	(£13,931)	v Tottenham Hotspur, December 16th 1970 (1-1)
25,695	(£43,000)	v Nottingham Forest, October 30th 1979 (1-1)
28,084	(£97,097)	v Nottingham Forest, February 26th 1989 (0-1)

Football League:

14,000	(£300)	v Bolton Wanderers, Division Two, September 3rd 1904 (3-4)
18,000	(£335)	v Manchester United, Division Two, January 7th 1905 (1-1)
19,000	(£726)	v Manchester United, Division Two, December 30th 1905 (1-1)
21,000	(£485)	v Manchester United, Division One, September 1st 1906 (1-2)
22,000	(£622)	v Woolwich Arsenal, Division One, October 13th 1906 (1-3)
23,000	(£660)	v Bradford City, Division One, December 26th 1908 (0-1)
20,000	(£780)	v Manchester United, Division One, April 12th 1909 (0-0)
21,000	(£1,150)	v Fulham, Division Two, October 4th 1919 (0-3)
26,022	(£1,500)	v Clapton Orient, Division Two, October 30th 1920 (2-0)
34,710	(£2,039)	v Port Vale, Division Two, December 27th 1920 (3-0)
33,672	(£2,091)	v Cardiff City, Division Two, January 15th 1921 (0-0)
36,985	(£2,080)	v Everton, Division Two, April 3rd 1931 (0-1)
38,953	(£2,330)	v Cardiff City, Division Three (South), March 5th 1938 (0-1)
32,878	(£2,685)	v Nottingham Forest, Division Three (South) November 11th 1950 (0-3)
30,332	(£3,429)	v Southend United, Division Three (South), December 26th 1952 (5-0)
35,606	(£4,089)	v Bristol Rovers, Division Three (South), February 7th 1953 (0-0)
39,583	(£4,503)	v Bristol Rovers, Division Two, October 22nd 1955 (1-1)
36,183	(£7,303)	v Wolverhampton Wanderers, Division Two, December 28th 1965 (0-1)
25,904	(£10,990)	v Oxford United, Division Two, March 2nd 1974 (0-0)
28,104	(£12,992)	v Manchester United, Division Two, November 9th 1974 (1-0)
28,953	(£13,450)	v Bristol Rovers, Division Two, April 1st 1975 (1-1)
38,688	(£23,881)	v Liverpool, Division One, May 16th 1977 (2-1)
29,122	(£25,272)	v Tottenham Hotspur, Division One, January 13th 1979 (0-0)
20,183	(£107,775)	v Bristol Rovers, Division Two, September 4th 1991 (1-0)
20,725	(£134,142)	v Nottingham Forest, Division One, December 28th 1993 (1-4)

Southern League:
10,000 (£245)	v Tottenham Hotspur, Division One, September 22nd 1900 (1-1)
15,500 (£380)	v Bristol Rovers, Division One, October 20th 1900 (1-0)

Western League:
8,000 (£200)	v Bristol Rovers, Professional Section, April 5th 1901 (3-0)

Gloucestershire Cup:
300	v Bristol East, April 3rd 1905 (5-1)
3,916 (£110)	v Bristol Rovers, April 28th 1905 (1-3)
8,836 (£248)	v Bristol Rovers, April 16th 1906 (4-0)
8,966 (£252)	v Bristol Rovers, February 3rd 1912 (1-0)
11,994 (£711)	v Bristol Rovers, September 29th 1920 (1-0)
11,434 (£768)	v Bristol Rovers, June 7th 1947 (2-0)
15,727 (£1,027)	v Bristol Rovers, May 8th 1948 (1-2)
16,560 (£1,150)	v Bristol Rovers, May 13th 1950 (2-0)
16,214 (£1,672)	v Bristol Rovers, May 10th 1952 (2-1)
13,668 (£1,816)	v Bristol Rovers, May 3rd 1954 (2-2)
10,278 (£7,877)	v Bristol Rovers, May 4th 1976 (3-2)
6,153 (£21,000)	v Bristol Rovers, August 8th 1989 (1-2)
6,796 (£35,000)	v Bristol Rovers, August 7th 1991 (3-2)
6,698 (£40,000)	v Bristol Rovers, August 5th 1993 (1-1)

Welsh Cup:
800 (£53)	v Newport County, February 1st 1933 (3-4)
900 (£51)	v Cardiff City, February 26th 1934 (1-0)
2,000	v New Brighton, March 21st 1934 (2-1)
2,000 (£117)	v Swansea Town, March 3rd 1937 (1-2)
3,134	v Merthyr Tydfil, January 23rd 1962 (4-2)
13,579	v Cardiff City, February 20th 1962 (0-2)

Division Three South Cup:
1,150	v Gillingham, September 30th 1936 (0-2)
1,337 (£76)	v Torquay United, October 6th 1937 (3-0)
2,130	v Cardiff City, November 10th 1937 (2-1)

Associate Members Cup:
1,421	v Torquay United, August 17th 1982 (1-0)
2,226	v Newport County, August 21st 1982 (1-4)
3,446	v Hereford United, February 20th 1985 (1-0)
3,635	v Port Vale, March 18th 1985 (2-1)
5,707	v Gillingham, April 16th 1986 (3-0)
11,558	v Hereford United, May 9th 1986 (3-0)
16,371 (£45,000)	v Aldershot, April 14th 1987 (2-0)

Full Members Cup:
5,672	v Southampton, October 22nd 1991 (1-2)

Anglo-Scottish Cup:
3,823	v Norwich City, August 9th 1975 (4-1)
4,941	v West Bromwich Albion, August 7th 1976 (1-0)
5,503	v Bristol Rovers, August 6th 1977 (3-1)
6,072	v Hibernian, November 1st 1977 (5-3)
16,110	v St. Mirren, December 5th 1977 (1-1)

Anglo-Italian Cup:
3,588	v Watford, September 2nd 1992 (1-0)
3,644	v Cosenza, November 11th 1992 (0-2)

South West Combination:
2,000	v Cardiff City, April 8th 1916 (2-0)
4,000	v Bristol Rovers, April 24th 1916 (0-2)

Bristol County Combination:
3,000 (£85)	v Bristol Rovers, December 26th 1918 (2-3)

Second World War Regional Leagues:
6,545 (£334)	v Cardiff City, October 21st 1939 (1-1)
7,455 (£488)	v Bath City, October 21st 1944 (2-0)
10,609 (£759)	v Bristol Rovers, September 1st 1945 (3-0)
13,660 (£967)	v Crystal Palace, September 8th 1945 (1-2)
18,727 (£1,344)	v Cardiff City, October 6th 1945 (3-2)

Second World War Cup Competitions:
3,175 (£187)	v Reading, February 22nd 1941 (1-2)
3,312 (£179)	v Cardiff City, January 24th 1942 (8-3)
3,857 (£199)	v Swansea Town, February 14th 1942 (1-1)
7,448 (£390)	v Northampton Town, April 6th 1942 (3-1)
14,236 (£803)	v Bath City, March 27th 1943 (2-1)
24,649 (£1,606)	v Aston Villa, April 3rd 1943 (0-0)
21,371 (£1,646)	v West Bromwich Albion, March 24th 1945 (5-2)

Friendlies:

500		v Queens Park Rangers, September 26th 1900 (0-0)
3,000		v Leicester Fosse, February 23rd 1901 (1-0)
5,000		v Bristol Rovers, September 5th 1904 (4-2)
7,000		v Bristol Rovers, December 25th 1905 (2-0)
7,321	(£290)	v Bristol Rovers, April 18th 1919 (1-5)
7,500		v Bradford Park Avenue Reserves, April 22nd 1919 (4-0)
20,000		v German Prisoner of War XI, May 19th 1947 (4-0)
23,866	(£2,969)	v Wolverhampton Wanderers, January 27th 1953 (1-4)
26,560	(£3,312)	v East Fife, March 10th 1953 (0-2)
28,991	(£3,821)	v Arsenal, March 30th 1954 (3-1)

Record Reserve XI Attendances:
London Combination:
    9,500 (£275)   v Arsenal Reserves, March 30th 1934 (2-0)
Football Combination:
    7,287   v Arsenal Reserves, December 26th 1947 (1-2)
Football Combination Cup:
    5,400   v Bournemouth & Boscombe Ath. Res., September 19th 1953 (0-1)
    5,566   v Bournemouth & Boscombe Ath. Res., September 28th 1954 (3-2)
    5,603   v Cardiff City Reserves, October 2nd 1954 (4-2)
    5,700   v Swansea Town Reserves, October 9th 1954 (2-2)
South Eastern League:
    4,000   v Brighton & Hove Albion Reserves, October 5th 1912 (2-1)
Western League:
    5,000   v Bristol Rovers Reserves, March 2nd 1907 (2-0)
Southern League:
    7,000   v Bristol Rovers Reserves, April 2nd 1923 (1-0)
Bristol Charity League:
    2,000   v Bristol East, April 16th 1904 (3-0)
    4,000   v Bristol Rovers Reserves, November 3rd 1906 (3-1)
South West Counties League:
    1,500   v Merthyr Tydfil Reserves, April 9th 1991 (15-0)
South West Counties League Cup:
    800   v Exeter City Reserves, August 11th 1987 (2-2)
Somerset Premier Cup:
    2,500   v Weston-super-Mare, April 29th 1991 (2-1)

Record Youth XI Attendances:
F.A. Youth Cup:
    1,000   v Briggs Sports, January 31st 1953 (2-1)
    4,012 (£228)   v Arsenal Youth, March 14th 1956 (4-3)
    6,385   v Chesterfield Youth, April 24th 1956 (1-1)
    13,686   v West Ham United Youth,March 22nd 1960 (3-2)
    18,181   v Chelsea Youth, April 5th 1960 (0-3)
Wessex Youth League:
    1,694   v Bristol Rovers Youth, September 30th 1961 (4-1)

Previous Ground: St. John's Lane, Bedminster, Bristol.

Record Attendance and Receipts:
    17,909 (£754)   v Sheffield United, F.A. Cup 1st Round Proper, February 6th 1904 (1-3)

Principal Record Attendances and/or Record Receipts:
F.A.Cup: 1,000   v Slough, October 5th 1895 (5-1)
    2,000   v Great Marlow, October 12th 1895 (0-1)
    4,500   v Bedminster, October 10th 1896 (2-4)
    6,000   v Reading, December 10th 1898 (3-2)
    16,945 (£524)   v Sunderland, January 28th 1899 (2-4)
Football League:
    7,000   v Stockport County, September 14th 1901 (3-0)
    8,000   v Lincoln City, October 12th 1901 (1-1)
    10,500 (£267)   v Woolwich Arsenal, October 26th 1901 (0-3)
    14,175 (£331)   v West Bromwich Albion, February 15th 1902 (1-2)
    14,000 (£408)   v Woolwich Arsenal, September 26th 1903 (0-4)
Southern League:
    4,000   v Wolverton L.N.W.R., September 11th 1897 (7-4)
    12,170 (£380)   v Southampton, January 15th 1898 (5-2)
    13,000 (£440)   v Southampton, April 29th 1899 (3-4)

Western League:
2,300   v St. George, November 28th 1896 (2-1)
3,500   v Bedminster, April 16th 1897 (1-3)
4,500   v Reading, November 20th 1897 (4-2)
10,000 (£265) v Warmley, April 8th 1898 (3-2)
United League:
4,000   v Kettering, September 10th 1898 (3-0)
8,000   v Tottenham Hotspur, October 15th 1898 (0-1)
Southern District Combination:
3,000   v Tottenham Hotspur, November 15th 1899 (3-3)
6,000   v Millwall Athletic, December 25th 1899 (1-3)
F.A. Amateur Cup:
800   v Hereford Thistle, November 10th 1894 (2-4)
1,500   v Bedminster, November 14th 1896 (2-1)
1,700   v Old Carthusians, January 30th 1897 (0-10)
Gloucestershire Cup:
6,400 (£170) v Eastville Rovers, February 26th 1898 (2-0)
10,537 (£296) v Bristol Rovers, April 4th 1904 (2-1)
Bristol Charity Cup:
2,000 (£22)   v Eastville Wanderers, March 20th 1897 (4-1)
Friendlies:
3,500   v Swindon Town, September 1st 1894 (2-4)
4,000   v Hereford Thistle, April 12th 1895 (1-4)
4,500   v Middleton, December 25th 1897 (5-1)
5,000   v Corinthians, April 12th 1898 (1-3)
7,000   v Bristol Rovers, December 26th 1901 (3-1)

COLOURS: 1894-95 to 1896-97 inclusive: Red shirts, navy blue shorts.
1897-98 to 1964-65 inclusive: Red shirts, white shorts.
1965-66 to 1970-71 inclusive: Red shirts, red shorts.
1971-72 to 1980-81 inclusive: Red shirts, white shorts.
1981-82 only: Red shirts, black shorts.
1982-83 to 1993-94 inclusive: Red shirts, white shorts.
(NOTE: City's shirts were reported as being Crimson in 1932-33 and Maroon in 1945-46)

Change Colours:

As far as can be reasonably determined it would appear that the Club's original change of colours was an all white strip. This remained until the adoption of blue shirts and white shorts c.1905, until the 1930's when white shirts and black shorts were also used. After the Second World War blue and white still held sway but during the early 1950's white and black became the Club's accepted change strip, and remained so until the adoption of all yellow at the start of the 1984-85 Season. This in turn was superseded for the 1992-93 season when the current change kit of purple and green was introduced.

MANAGERS:

Samuel W. Hollis 1897-1899

Robert Campbell 1899-1901

Samuel W. Hollis 1901-1905

Henry Thickett 1905-1910

Frank Bacon (Caretaker) 1910-1911

Samuel W. Hollis 1911-1913

George A. Hedley 1913-1915

A. John Hamilton 1915-1919

Joseph Palmer 1919-1921

Archie Annan & C.H. Hancock (Caretakers) 1921

Alexander G. Raisbeck 1921-1929

Joseph H. Bradshaw 1929-1932

Robert Hewison 1932-1938

Clarence F.T. Bourton 1938-1939 *

Robert Hewison 1939-1949

Robert C. A. Wright 1949-1950

Albert Beasley 1950-1958 (Player/Manager 1950-1952)

Leslie Bardsley (Caretaker) 1958

James Seed (Caretaker) 1958

Peter D. Doherty 1958-1960

Leslie Bardsley (Caretaker) 1960

Frederick G.L. Ford 1960-1967

Leslie Bardsley (Caretaker) 1967

Alan V. Dicks 1967-1980

Anthony Collins & Kenneth Wimshurst(Caretakers) 1980)

Robert Houghton 1980-1982

Roy Hodgson (Caretaker) 1982

Gerald R. Sharpe (Caretaker) 1982

Terry Cooper 1982-1988 (Player/Manager 1982-1984)

Joe Jordan 1988-1990 (Player/Manager 1988-1989)

James Lumsden 1990-1992

Mark Aizlewood, Russell Osman & Gary Shelton (Caretakers) 1992

Denis Smith 1992-1993

Russell Osman (Caretaker) Jan-Mar 1993

Russell Osman (Player/Manager March 12th 1993-

* (Player/Manager during period of Hewison's suspension by the F.A.)

HONOURS

Football League:

Championship Runners-up 1906-07

Division Two Champions 1905-06; Runners-up 1975-76

Division Three (South) Champions 1922-23, 1926-27 & 1954-55; Runners-up 1937-38.

Division Three Runners-up 1964-65 & 1989-90.

Division Four Promotion (4th place) 1983-84

Division Three Play-Off's Runners-up 1987-88

Southern League:

Championship Runners-up 1897-98, 1898-99 & 1900-01

English Section Champions 1922-23; Runners-up 1921-22

Western Section Champions 1927-28; Runners-up 1925-26 & 1926-27

Western League:

Champions 1897-98, 1910-11, 1920-21, 1925-26, 1926-27, 1937-38, 1942-43, 1961-62 & 1962-63.

Runners-up 1896-97, 1909-10 & 1963-64

Division One Champions 1983-84

Division Two Champions 1903-04, 1907-08 & 1908-09; Runners-up 1904-05, 1905-06 & 1953-54

Bristol Charity League:

Champions 1903-04, 1908-09, 1927-28, 1928-29, 1931-32, 1936-37 & 1941-42;

Shared (after indecisive p/off) 1905-06 & 1906-07; Run/up 1904-05, 1909-10, 1934-35 & 1940-41

South Eastern League:

Championship Runners-up 1914-15 (lost Championship on goal average)

Football Combination:

Championship Runners-up 1954-55. Division Two Champions 1967-68

South West Counties League:

Champions 1986-87, 1990-91 & 1991-92

Bristol County Combination:

Champions 1917-18; Runners-up 1918-19

South Bristol & District League:

Champions 1895-96

Somerset League:

Champions 1954-55; Division Two Champions 1951-52

Bristol & Suburban League:

Champions 1942-43, 1944-45 & 1954-55; Runners-up 1943-44, 1953-54 & 1956-57.

Division Two Champions 1952-53; Division Three Champions 1951-52 & 1956-57.

Division Four Champions 1954-55; Division Six Champions 1953-54.

Junior Section Runners-up 1951-52 & 1952-53

Bristol Wednesday League:

Champions 1908-09, 1909-10, 1910-11, 1911-12 & 1928-29; Runners-up 1927-28.

Division Two Champions 1949-50

Wessex Youth League:

Champions 1961-62, 1964-65, 1965-66 & 1966-67; Runners-up 1960-61, 1962-63 & 1967-68.

South East Counties League:

Division Two Runners-up 1992-93

F.A. Cup: Finalists 1908-09; Semi-Finalists 1919-20; Quarter-Finalists 1973-74

F.L. Cup: Semi-Finalists 1970-71 & 1988-89

Welsh Cup: Winners 1933-34

Anglo-Scottish Cup: Winners 1977-78; Finalists 1979-80

Division Three (South) Cup: Finalists 1937-38

Freight Rover Trophy (Associate Members Cup): Winners 1985-86. Finalists 1986-87 (Southern Area Winners)

Somerset Professional Cup: Winners 1963-64, 1970-71, 1971-72, 1974-75 & 1990-91; Shared 1956-57

(Premier Cup from 1975-76) Finalists 1961-62, 1962-63, 1969-70 & 1973-74

Western League Cup: Winners 1961-62

Alan Young Cup: Winners 1963-64; Finalists 1962-63 & 1964-65

Bristol Charity Cup: Finalists 1896-97

West Regional Cup: Winners 1940-41; Finalists 1944-45

Football Combination Cup: Semi-Finalists 1967-68

Allen Palmer Cup: Winners 1925-26; Shared 1924-25; Finalists 1926-27

International Fayre Cup: Winners 1978-79

Berkley Hunt Charity Cup: Winners 1936-37, 1937-38 & 1938-39

Berkley Hospital Cup: Winners 1947-48

Bath Coronation Cup: Winners 1938-39, 1945-46 & 1947-48

James Howell Challenge Cup: Winners 1949-50; Finalists 1948-49

Warminster Challenge Cup: Winners 1951-52, 1953-54 & 1954-55 (Shared 1952-53, Finalists 1955-56)
Chippenham Sportsmen & Traders Trophy: Winners 1953-54 & 1954-55
Friendship Cup: Finalists 1966-67
Gloucestershire Senior Amateur Cup: Winners 1943-44; Finalists 1944-45, 1953-54 & 1954-55
Gloucestershire Intermediate Cup: Finalists 1956-57
South West Counties League Cup: Winners 1989-90 & 1990-91; Finalists 1987-88
Bristol Wednesday League Cup: Winners 1908-09, 1909-10, 1910-11 & 1911-12
F.A. Youth Cup: Finalists 1972-73; Semi-Finalists 1955-56, 1959-60 & 1969-70
Gloucestershire Youth Shield: Winners 1951-52, 1952-53 & 1953-54; Finalists 1949-50
Wessex Youth League Cup: Winners 1965-66
Alf Bosley Cup: Winners 1956-57
Tilberg Youth Tournament: Winners 1971, 1972, 1973 & 1974
Blau-Wit Youth Tournament: Winners 1973 & 1976
Coup Henri Cicquel Youth Tournament: Winners 1983, 1984 & 1985
Bordeaux Etudiantes Youth Tournament: Winners 1973
Orsay Youth Tournament: Winners 1983 & 1984
Rotterdam Youth Tournament: Winners 1991
A.S.Line Sixes Cup: Winners 1956-57
Pontins Sixes: Finalists 1976
Pontins Fives: Winners 1975
St.Dunstan's Charity Cup: Winners 1951-52
Gloucestershire Senior Professional Cup: Winners 53 times; Shared 7 times; Runners-up 27 times
South West Counties Youth League Cup: Finalists 1993-94
Mangotsfield Sixes: Winners 1961-62
Gloucester Youth Sixes: Winners 1963-64
Bristol City Women: South West Womens League Division Two: Champions 1993-94
                                              Division Two League Cup: Winners 1993-94

Best Football League Position: Runners-up Division One 1906-07

Worst Football League Position: 14th Division Four 1982-83

Most Points: (Two for a win)
70 out of a possible 92, 1954-55. Equals record for Division Three (South)
66 out of 76, 1905-06. This was a new record for Division Two
62 out of 84, 1927-28. This was a new record for Division Three (South)
        (Three for a win)
91 out of 138, 1989-90 Division Three; 82 out of 138, 1983-84 Division Four

Least Points: (Two for a win)
23 out of 84, 1931-32 Division Two
            (Three for a win)
46 out of 138, 1981-82 Division Three

Most Goals Scored :   1926-27, 104 goals in 42 Division Three (South) matches
Least Goals Scored: 1980-81, 29 goals in 42 Division Two matches
Least Goals Conceded: 1905-06, 28 goals in 38 Division Two matches
                         1920-21, 29 goals in 42 Division Two matches
Most Goals Conceded: 1959-60, 97 goals in 42 Division Two matches

Highest Goalscorer (Season)   Don Clark with 41 (36 League, 5 F.A. Cup) in 1946-47
Highest League Goalscorer (Season):   Don Clark with 36 in 1946-47 (top Division Three South goalscorer)
                                          Len Townsend with 31 goals 1947-48 (top Div.Three South goalscorer).
Overall Top Goalscorer: 350 by John Atyeo (315 League, 30 F.A. Cup, 5 Football League Cup) 1951-66.
Most Goals in a Match: 8 - Chapman 1920-21 v Army Supply Corps (White City, Bristol) Friendly, Ashton Gate, April 29th 1916.
Most Goals (Competitive Fixture): 6 - 'Tot' Walsh v Gillingham, Division Three (South), Ashton Gate, January 15th 1927.
Most International Goals: 5 - John Atyeo for England 1955-57.

Most Appearances: 645 by John Atyeo (597 League, 42 F.A. Cup, 6 Football League Cup) 1951-66.
Most International Appearances: 26 by Billy Wedlock for England 1907-1914 (2 goals)

Record Transfer Fee - Paid: £500,000 to Arsenal for Andrew Cole in July 1992
Records Transfer Fee - Received: £1,750,000 from Newcastle United for Andrew Cole in March 1993

Record Victory: 20-1 v Army Supply Corps (White City, Bristol), Friendly, Ashton Gate, April 29th 1916
Record Victory - Competitive Match: 14-1 v Eastleigh, Western League (Prof.Sect.), St. John's Lane, January 26th 1898
Record Victory - Football League: 9-0 v Aldershot, Division Three (South), Ashton Gate, December 28th 1946
Record Victory - F.A.Cup: 11-0 v Chichester City, F.A.Cup 1st Round, Ashton Gate, November 5th 1960
Record Away Victory - Competitive Match: 8-2 v Walsall, Division Three (South), February 26th 1938
Record Away Victory - F.A.Cup: 7-1 v Kingstonians, F.A. Cup 1st Round, November 25th 1933
Record Defeat: 0-10 v Old Carthusians, F.A. Amateur Cup 1st Round Proper, St. John's Lane, January 30th 1897
Record Defeat - Football League: 0-9 v Coventry City, Division Three (South), Highfield Road, April 28th 1934.
Record Defeat - Football League (Home): 0-8 v Derby County, Division Two, September 29th 1923
Record Defeat - F.A.Cup: 1-6 v Sunderland, Fourth Round, Roker Park, January 25th 1964
Record Defeat - Football League Cup: 1-6 v West Ham United, Second Round, 2nd Leg, Upton Park, October 9th 1984
                                                                    1-6 v Sunderland, Second Round, 2nd Leg, Ashton Gate, October 8th 1990

Largest Attendances at Bristol City Matches:
71,409 at The Crystal Palace, 0-1 v. Manchester United (F.A.Cup Final), April 24th 1909
63,099 at Villa Park, 1-2 v Aston Villa (F.A. Cup 5th round), February 16th 1957
58,586 at Wembley Stadium, 1-1 v Mansfield Town (Freight Rover Trophy Final), May 24th 1987
54,610 at White Hart Lane, 0-2 v Tottenham Hotspur (F.A. Cup 5th round), March 11th 1967
54,502 at Wembley Stadium, 3-0 v Bolton Wanderers (Freight Rover Trophy Final), May 24th 1986

Football League Records:
1905-06: Equalled record set by Manchester United (1904-05) - won 14 consecutive League matches (included in an unbeaten sequence of 24 League games). Since equalled by Preston North End (1950-51).
1905-06: First Football League club to win 30 matches in a season, and a new points record with 66.
1954-55: Equalled points record for Division Three (South) - 70. (Also Nottingham Forest 1950-51)
Most Championships of Division Three (South) - 3.
1936-37: Scoring in consucutive matches by debutant - Alf Rowles with six (12 goals in total).

Unusual Records:
1962-63: Scored 100 goals in 46 league games but only finished in 14th place in Division Three,
(lowest position in any Division for a team scoring a century of goals)
1980-81: (Before the introduction of 3 points for a win) gained more points (30), than goals (29).
1958-59: Post-war League record at start of season - 13 goals in the first two matches.

Nicknames:
The Club's first nickname appears to have been the 'Garibaldians' and in the early days they were also known as the 'Red Shirts', 'Reds' and the 'Citizens'. However, following their rapid rise to prominence they were soon christened the 'Babes', a nickname that lasted until the early 1950's when their present popular name of the 'Robins' - which had also been in use in the inter-war years - came to the fore.

Representative Honours gained by players whilst playing for the club:
Full Internationals:
England: W. Wedlock (26), J. Atyeo (6), J. Cottle (1), W. Jones (1)
Wales: M. Aizlewood (21), J.Emanuel (2 subs), R. Matthews (1), B. Williams (1), H.Pritchard (1 sub).
Eire: D. Curtis (5)
Sierra Leone: L. Rosenior (1)

'B' Internationals:
England: J. Atyeo (3)   Wales: R. Edwards (2)

Under 23's & Under 21's:
England: J. Atyeo (2), A. Cole (1), C. Garland (1 sub)
Scotland: D. Gillies (1), G. Gow (1 sub)
Wales: R. Edwards (9)

Youth Internationals:
England: D.R. Bartley, D.R. Barton, G. Burgess, D. Church, A. Ford, P.J. Glover, R. Hewlett, J. Knight, A. Llewellyn, K.Mabbutt, D.Mogg, B. Munday, R. Roberts, M. Rogers, D.R. Smith, P.J. Spiring, J.V. Watkins, C. Whitehead, Adrian Williams.
Wales: H.Pritchard
Football League XI: W. Wedlock (3), J. Atyeo (2), J. Dziekanowski (1), F. Hilton (1), A. Cole (1 sub).
Football Combination XI: J. Atyeo (1)
F.A. XI: J. Atyeo (5), J. Boxley (3), W. Hinshelwood (1), C.J.Treasure, J. White (1).

Full International matches played at Ashton Gate:

March 20th, 1899	England	4(2)	Wales	0	6,000	(£320)
March 17th, 1913	England	4(3)	Wales	3(1)	9,000	(£393)

Under 23 Internationals played at Ashton Gate:

October 17th, 1956	England	0	France	0	25,817	(£4,610)
Novem. 13th, 1963	England	1(1)	Wales	1(1)	16,841	
October 1st, 1969	England	2(0)	Wales	0	22,286	
March 22nd, 1972	England	0	E.Germany	1(1)	20,230	(£8,500)
January 16th,1974	England	0	Wales	0	3,117	

Under 21 Internationals played at Ashton Gate:

October 15th, 1985	England	3(1)	Turkey	0	3,826

Football League Representative match played at Ashton Gate:

October 21st, 1992	Football League XI	3(2)	Italian Seria 'B'	1(0)	3,360

Schoolboys International matches played at Ashton Gate:

April 9th, 1932	England	1(0)	Wales	0	9,800	
May 12th, 1956	England	3(1)	Wales	2(1)	17,400	(£2,400)
May 7th, 1966	England	3(2)	Wales	1(1)	6,068	(£1,134.15s.0d.)

International Trial at Ashton Gate:

February 13th, 1905	South	1(0)	North	3(1)	7,500	(£230)

Other Sports - Major matches at Ashton Gate:

Rugby Union International:	January 18th 1908	England	18(8)	Wales 28(15)	21,000 (£1,600)
Rugby League:	December 20th 1911	West of England & S.Wales 3(0)		Australians 23(15)	
Baseball:	July 13th 1918	U.S.America	6	Canada 5	2,000
Lacrosse:	October 14th 1978	English Women	15	Scottish & Welsh 3	

(Note: This special 40 minutes exhibition match was played prior to the start of the City v Nottm. F. match).

Cricket: (Floodlit) September 17th 1980. Rest of the World XI beat an England XI before a crowd of 7,925.

This was only the second floodlit cricket match held in England.

From 1896 to 1906 Bedminster Cricket had use of the ground during the summer months.

Association Football matches at Ashton Gate involving other teams:

Exhibition Games:

April 21st, 1897	Derby County	2(0)	West Bromwich Albion	1(0)	5,000	(£123.13s.6d.)
May 5th, 1932	Bath City	1(1)	Blackburn Rovers	1(1)	2,000	(Bath ground flooded)
March 24th, 1982	Southampton	2(2)	Ipswich Town	1(0)	6,020	

F.A. Cup:

November 27th, 1911	Merthyr Town	2(1)	Exeter City	0	2,000	(£48) (2nd Qual,2nd replay)
February 28th, 1921	Chelsea	2(0)	Plymouth Argyle	1(0)	26,007	(£1,600) (3rd Round,2nd replay)
January 16th, 1922	Swansea Town	1(0)	West Ham United	0	8,976	(£568)(1st Round,2nd replay,a.e.t.)
December 8th, 1924	Exeter City	1(1)	Newport County	0	5,000	(5th Qual.,2nd replay)
December 7th, 1925	Reading	2(1)	Torquay United	0	3,765	(£263.16s.4d.)(1st Round,2nd replay)
November 5th, 1928	Yeovil & P. Utd.	3(0)	Barry Town	1(1)	650	(£42) (4th Qual,2nd replay)
December 5th, 1932	Torquay United	3(2)	Bournemouth & B.A.	2(1)	2,000	(1st Round,2nd replay)
January 2nd, 1952	Swindon Town	3(2)	Torquay United	1(1)	12,241	(£1,497) (2nd Round,2nd replay)
December 18th, 1967	Exeter City	1(0)	Nuneaton Borough	0	5,071	(£1,297) (1st Round 2nd replay)

Bristol Rovers 'Home' matches:

1939-40 season Regional League South West Division - 4 fixtures.

1980-81 season Football League Division Two - 3 fixtures. (plus 2 League Cup)

1986-87 season Football League Division Three - 1 fixture.

F.A. XI Matches:

November 22nd, 1941	F A XI	2(1)	R A F XI	7(5)	9,854	(£695 17 10)
January 22nd, 1944	F.A.XI	2(0)	R.A.F. XI	4(2)	17,821	(£1,391)
March 2nd, 1954	F.A.XI	4(3)	Western League XI	0	5,089	

(Western League Diamond Jubilee Match - Abandoned after 65 minutes)

March 22nd, 1955	F.A. XI	3(2)	Western League XI	0	4,278

Western League Diamond Jubilee Match Replay

October 8th, 1958	F.A. XI	1(0)	R.A.F. XI	4(1)	14,457

Schoolboys International Trials:

April 4th, 1923	South	4(1)	North	2(2)	4,000
April 2nd, 1949	England	2(0)	The Rest	0	10,500

Bristol R.F.C. (Rugby Union)

1920-21 - 2 fixtures. 1956-57 - 2 fixtures. 1957-58, 1958-59, 1959-60 - 1 fixture each season.

Other Events at Ashton Gate:

These have included Boxing Tournaments, Athletics Meetings, Pop Concerts, Gymnastic Displays, Fairs, Evangelical Meetings, and three competitions of 'All in The Game' in 1974, 1976 and 1977, these being transmitted on I.T.V. In the Dolman Stand there are indoor bowling rinks which are in use every day, and the Grandstand (Des Williams Stand) Car Park is utilised for a Sunday Market. The F.A. Cup run of 1993-94 brought three 16 foot x 12 foot video screens to Ashton Gate on February 9th for more than 2,000 fans to view City's 4-0 win at Stockport. This screening followed the success of that of the Liverpool match on January 25th when similar facilities were provided at the Colston Hall (1,000) and Whitchurch Sports Centre (500).

Opening of the Ashton Gate floodlights:

1st Set: January 27th, 1953:   Bristol City 1(1)   Wolverhampton W.4(2)   23,866 (£2,960) (Friendly0
(Note: These floodlights were sold to Burton Albion in 1966).
2nd Set: December 28th, 1965:   Bristol City 0   Wolverhampton W.1(0)   36,183 (£7,302) (Div.2)
(Note: These floodlights were given to Wigan Athletic in the summer of 1992)
3rd Set: November 5th, 1991:   Bristol City 2(2)   Plymouth Argyle   0   7,735 (Div.2)

First Bristol City match under floodlights:

April 2nd, 1951   Swindon Town 2(1)   Bristol City   1(1)   3,171 (Friendly)

First Football League match played under floodlights by Bristol City:

February 20th, 1957   Bristol City 3   Notts. County   0   19,042 (Football League Div.Two)

First Bristol City competitive match under floodlights:

February 24th, 1953   Bristol City Res. 2(0)   Swansea Town Res. 1(1) 4,315 (Football Comb. Div.2)

Association Football matches at St.Johns' Lane involving other teams:

Mock International:
October 9th, 1899   English Players 2(2)   Scottish Players 1(0)   1,911 (In aid of West.League Funds)
F.A. Cup:
October 28th, 1898   Warmley   2(1)   Bedminster   1(1)   1,000 (2nd Qual.Round,2nd replay)
Bristol Rovers 'Home' match:
October 17th, 1903   Bristol Rovers 1(0)   Tottenham H.   0   8,000 (Southern League Division One)

Rugby Union at St. Johns' Lane:

September 13th, 1902   Bristol   11   Lydney   0
September 3rd, 1904   Stripes   24(8)   Whites   3(0)   (Bristol R.F.C. Trial match)
September 7th, 1904   Stripes   23   Whites   0   (Bristol R.F.C. Trial match)

First Bristol City Programmes:

It would appear that Bristol City first published a substantial programme in 1906-07, but prior to this it is clear that at least a team sheet was produced from the outset. However, the Club Handbook for 1899-1900 refers to editorial comment being included in the Club programme, so it is clear that by this time it had grown to become something more than just a team sheet. The oldest team sheet that is known to have survived is that for the Bristol South End v Preston North End match at St. John's Lane on April 6th 1895.

Football League Election: Was achieved in 1901 when the voting went as follows:-

Bristol City 23 (elected), Burton Swifts 23 (re-elected), Doncaster Rovers 16, Stockport County 16, Stalybridge Rovers 7, Walsall 7, Crewe Alexandra 5, Darwen 0. This was Bristol City's second attempt to gain election to the Football League. In 1898 they finished bottom of the poll:- Lincoln 21 (re-elected), Burslem Port Vale 18 (elected), Loughborough Town 16 (re-elected), Darwen 15, New Brighton Tower 13, Nelson 3, Bristol City 1. (The membership of the League was later increased, but Bristol City did not feature in the election of the additional member clubs).

BEDMINSTER ASSOCIATION FOOTBALL & CRICKET CLUB RÉSUMÉ

Founded: Football section as Southville in 1887, became Bedminster when joined forces with the Cricket Club in 1889.
The Cricket Club was formed in 1847, and is still operating today.
Bedminster A.F.C. amalgamated with Bristol City at the end of the 1899-1900 Season.

Ground: Ashton Gate, Bedminster, Bristol, from and including the 1896-97 Season.

Record Attendance: 7000 v Bristol City, Southern League, 4th March 1899 (1-0)

Lowest Attendance: 100 v Queens Park Rangers, Southern League, 25th April, 1900 (4-1)

Previous Grounds: Bedminster Park, Bedminster, Bristol, 1887-1889.
Greenway Bush Lane, off Coronation Road, Bedminster, Bristol, 1889-1896.
(Record Attendance, at Greenway Bush Lane: 5000 v Mr. J.A. Stevens Bristol XI, 6-3, 14th Sept. 1895)

Colours: Maroon and Old Gold Shirts.

Managers: Harry Smith 1898-99; Samuel W. Hollis 1899-1900.

Honours: Western League (Amateur Section) Champions 1897-98.
Western League Runners-up 1899-1900.
Gloucestershire Senior Cup Winners 1890-91 & 1899-1900.
Gloucestershire Senior Cup Finalists 1891-92 & 1896-97.
Gloucestershire Junior Cup Winners 1896-97.
Bristol Charity Cup Winners 1898-99 & 1899-1900.
Bristol Charity Cup (Amateur Section) Winners 1897-98.
Final Qualifying Round of the F.A. Cup 1899-1900.
4th Qualifying Round of the F.A. Amateur Cup 1897-98.

Southern League - Positions: Season 1898-99 - 8th; 1899-1900 - 6th.

Western League - Positions: Season 1892-93 - 4th; 1893-94 - 4th; 1894-95 - 9th; 1895-96 - 8th; 1896-97 - 3rd; 1897-98 - 1st; 1898-99 - Bottom; 1899-1900 - 2nd.

First match:	Southville	1 Criterion 0 (Friendly)	15th October, 1887.
First match (As Bedminster):	Clevedon	6 Bedminster 0 (Friendly)	12th October, 1889.
First Home match (As Bedminster):	Bedminster	4 St. Agnes 1 (Friendly)	2nd November, 1889.
First Western League match:	Wells	2 Bedminster 2	22nd October, 1892.
First Western League home match:	Bedminster	4 Trowbridge Town 0	5th November, 1892.
First F.A. Cup match:	Bedminster	1 Luton Town 4	14th November, 1891.
First F.A. Amateur Cup match:	Bedminster	0 Home Park (Plymouth) 3	4th November, 1893.
First Southern League match:	Tottenham Hotspur 1 Bedminster 1		10th, September, 1898.
First Southern League Home match:	Bedminster	1 Brighton United 1	14th September, 1898.
Last match at Greenway Bush Lane:	Bedminster	2 Eastville Rovers 1 (Friendly) 11th April, 1896.
First match at Ashton Gate:	Bedminster	4 Staple Hill 2 (Friendly)	12th September, 1896.
Official Opening:	Bedminster	1 Warmley 1 (Western Lge.)	26th September, 1896.
Last match at Ashton Gate:	Bedminster	4 Queens Park Rangers 1 (Southern League) 25th April, 1900.
Last F.A. Cup match:	Bedminster	1 Portsmouth 2	9th December, 1899.
Last Western League match:	Bristol Rovers	0 Bedminster 2	16th April, 1900.
Last Southern League match:	Reading	0 Bedminster 0	28th April, 1900.
Last match:	Bedminster 3 Bristol City 1 (Glos.Sen.Cup Final at Stapleton Road) 30th April 1900.

BEDMINSTER RESERVES

Summary (including Southville 1887 -1889):

South Bristol & District League:

	P	W	D	L	F	A	Pts	Pos
1893/94 Division 2	18	6	3	9	35	43	15	6
1894/95	20	8	1	11	36	39	17	6

Western League:

	P	W	D	L	F	A	Pts	Pos
1895/96 Division 2	18	6	1	11	35	39	13	8
1896/97	12	6	1	5	19	20	13	5
1897/98 Amateur Division 2	10	1	0	9	10	34	2	6

Gloucestershire Junior Cup:

	P	W	D	L	F	A	Pts	Pos
1889/90	1	0	0	1	1	5		1st round
1892/93	2	1	0	1	6	5		2nd round
1893/94	3	2	0	1	8	4		Semi-final
1894/95	4	3	0	1	9	4		Semi-final
1895/96	1	0	0	1	0	4		1st round
1896/97	4	4	0	0	18	3		Winners
1897/98	1	0	0	1	0	3		1st round

Bristol Charity Cup Amateur Section:

	P	W	D	L	F	A	Pts	Pos
1897/98 Division 2	1	1	0	0	4	2		2nd round *

Warminster Six-A-Side Tournament:

	P	W	D	L	F	A	Pts	Pos
1897/98	2	1	0	1	10	12		2nd round

Friendlies:

	P	W	D	L	F	A
1888/89	8	2	2	4	3	12
1889/90	6	1	2	3	3	16
1890/91	6	3	0	3	9	23
1891/92	8	3	3	2	17	22
1892/93	13	9	2	2	43	19
1893/94	4	3	0	1	20	11
1894/95	2	1	0	1	4	8
1895/96	6	3	1	2	25	9
1896/97	5	2	3	0	12	8

* Drawn away to the Royal Artillery (Horfield) in the 2nd round, but result not traced.

FOOTBALL LEAGUE RESULTS SUMMARY
1901-02 to 1993-94 inclusive

Bristol City have played 101 clubs in the Football League since 1901-02. Below is their record against each club which includes the three matches played in the abandoned 1939-40 season. Some clubs changed their names (e.g. Small Heath became Birmingham, then Birmingham City) and some clubs modified their titles (e.g. Leicester Fosse became Leicester City). In all cases the last name used by each club also covers games under previous names.

	HOME						AWAY					
	P	W	D	L	F	A	P	W	D	L	F	A
Aberdare Athletic	4	2	1	1	3	2	4	3	1	0	13	7
A.F.C. Bournemouth	27	20	5	2	49	22	27	4	9	14	19	53
Aldershot	20	12	7	1	46	14	21	7	7	7	21	20
Arsenal	14	3	2	9	10	23	14	3	4	7	13	23
Aston Villa	16	5	6	5	14	18	16	3	3	10	19	27
Barnsley	31	23	4	4	75	25	31	5	9	17	39	71
Birmingham City	22	11	5	6	29	18	22	4	8	10	23	36
Blackburn Rovers	17	10	6	1	30	13	17	5	3	9	23	39
Blackpool	31	16	8	7	49	25	31	9	6	16	37	53
Bolton Wanderers	23	13	8	2	44	24	23	7	6	10	28	29
Bradford City	12	4	1	7	9	12	12	3	3	6	11	21
Bradford P.A.	10	7	3	0	17	3	10	2	0	8	16	27
Brentford	18	9	4	5	32	18	18	7	2	9	20	30
Brighton & H.A.	29	15	7	7	56	36	28	5	9	14	20	46
Bristol Rovers	39	19	13	7	64	37	39	10	14	15	47	55
Burnley	13	5	3	5	20	19	13	5	5	3	20	21
Burton United	5	4	0	1	16	3	5	3	1	1	9	6
Bury	28	20	4	4	59	33	28	8	6	14	32	57
Cambridge United	4	1	1	2	4	3	4	1	1	2	5	6
Cardiff City	28	15	6	7	37	25	28	11	6	11	40	40
Carlisle United	14	8	4	2	25	11	14	4	3	7	17	25
Charlton Athletic	24	10	5	9	44	27	24	4	4	16	23	47
Chelsea	12	6	6	0	16	7	12	0	5	7	9	25
Chester City	7	4	2	1	9	5	7	3	1	3	8	5
Chesterfield	13	10	3	0	28	9	13	4	2	7	14	16
Colchester United	11	7	1	3	26	11	11	4	3	4	13	15
Coventry City	22	11	8	3	33	17	22	2	9	11	28	52
Crewe Alexandra	4	3	1	0	9	4	4	1	1	2	4	8
Crystal Palace	30	15	10	5	51	24	30	5	6	19	33	64
Darlington	4	2	2	0	5	3	4	1	3	0	4	3
Derby County	22	7	8	7	29	31	22	4	1	17	21	54
Doncaster Rovers	12	9	2	1	35	11	12	2	4	6	12	19
Everton	10	4	1	5	13	14	10	1	2	7	9	20
Exeter City	22	14	6	2	44	20	22	6	8	8	17	27
Fulham	24	10	6	8	33	27	24	5	6	13	22	42
Gainsborough Trinity	6	5	1	0	12	2	6	2	0	4	9	14
Gateshead	5	3	1	1	9	5	5	2	2	1	6	4
Gillingham	22	15	4	3	52	26	22	5	9	8	25	34
Glossop	9	7	2	0	24	7	9	4	2	3	14	12
Grimsby Town	21	14	6	1	47	13	21	5	3	13	26	39
Halifax Town	5	4	1	0	15	7	5	3	1	1	14	10
Hartlepool United	2	2	0	0	4	0	2	0	1	1	3	5
Hereford United	2	1	1	0	2	1	2	2	0	0	5	1
Huddersfield Town	18	7	5	6	26	22	18	6	1	11	17	40
Hull City	32	20	8	4	66	31	32	6	8	18	35	61
Ipswich Town	21	14	2	5	49	27	21	2	6	13	14	35
Leeds City	5	3	2	0	9	3	5	0	3	2	4	7
Leeds United	10	2	4	4	7	10	10	3	2	5	10	13
Leicester City	24	11	6	7	29	18	24	3	8	13	18	44
Leyton Orient	41	28	10	3	86	26	41	11	9	21	39	71
Lincoln City	18	14	2	2	42	11	18	5	6	7	24	26
Liverpool	15	8	2	5	19	16	15	3	1	11	20	36
Luton Town	19	11	3	5	38	18	19	4	6	9	20	31

	HOME						AWAY					
	P	W	D	L	F	A	P	W	D	L	F	A
Manchester City	11	8	3	0	18	8	11	2	3	6	12	23
Manchester United	17	5	7	5	21	17	17	5	3	9	18	30
Mansfield Town	11	6	3	2	23	11	11	3	2	6	14	22
Merthyr Town	4	4	0	0	9	1	4	2	1	1	7	6
Middlesbrough	28	12	12	4	44	24	28	2	5	21	16	52
Millwall	36	16	14	6	69	45	36	8	9	19	41	66
Nelson	1	1	0	0	1	0	1	0	0	1	1	2
Newcastle United	11	5	4	2	16	13	11	1	4	6	4	19
Newport County	25	17	4	4	52	20	25	6	9	10	27	34
Northampton Town	28	18	5	5	58	34	28	9	4	15	38	58
Norwich City	28	9	5	14	40	36	27	3	10	14	26	52
Nottingham Forest	28	9	7	12	36	44	28	4	12	12	22	43
Notts County	39	23	8	8	69	41	39	9	9	21	36	64
Oldham Athletic	13	8	3	2	24	13	13	3	2	8	17	27
Oxford United	13	6	4	3	20	13	13	1	4	8	7	22
Peterborough United	8	4	1	3	13	8	8	3	1	4	12	18
Plymouth Argyle	19	13	5	1	39	18	19	4	2	13	21	46
Port Vale	33	20	8	5	65	26	33	8	5	20	35	65
Portsmouth	19	11	4	4	34	22	19	6	6	7	19	26
Preston North End	29	17	9	3	52	24	29	3	11	15	29	60
Queens Park Rangers	30	15	8	7	54	35	30	7	6	17	28	56
Reading	34	20	5	9	71	40	34	9	10	15	52	57
Rochdale	2	0	2	0	1	1	2	1	0	1	1	1
Rotherham United	16	7	1	8	28	22	16	4	4	8	19	33
Scunthorpe United	4	0	1	3	2	7	4	0	3	1	7	10
Sheffield United	13	4	4	5	21	21	13	2	3	8	17	30
Sheffield Wednesday	17	7	4	6	23	20	17	2	2	13	21	37
Shrewsbury Town	11	7	3	1	24	10	11	4	2	5	19	22
Southampton	13	7	3	3	19	9	13	1	2	10	14	33
Southend United	31	22	3	6	88	36	31	9	5	17	30	58
Stockport County	13	11	1	1	51	10	13	5	6	2	17	16
Stoke City	18	6	7	5	28	19	18	3	3	12	17	37
Sunderland	18	11	4	3	35	17	18	4	7	7	22	30
Swansea City	19	10	5	4	30	20	19	3	6	10	21	43
Swindon Town	35	19	12	4	74	41	35	10	11	14	41	49
Torquay United	20	10	5	5	41	21	20	8	5	7	32	37
Tottenham Hotspur	10	4	3	3	9	10	10	1	2	7	9	18
Tranmere Rovers	7	3	2	2	10	9	7	0	3	4	8	20
Walsall	21	12	5	4	51	24	21	7	6	8	34	38
Watford	33	20	8	5	65	33	33	10	11	12	42	49
West Bromwich Albion	16	7	4	5	19	16	16	3	6	7	14	23
West Ham United	11	3	6	2	13	14	11	1	0	10	5	26
Wigan Athletic	6	5	0	1	12	3	6	2	3	1	9	9
Wimbledon	2	1	0	1	5	5	2	0	1	1	1	2
Wolverhampton Wand.	23	11	3	9	30	26	23	2	9	12	20	42
Workington	1	1	0	0	5	0	1	0	0	1	0	1
Wrexham	4	2	0	2	6	5	4	0	1	3	3	7
York City	8	5	3	0	16	7	8	3	3	2	10	8
	1734	945	427	362	3133	1736	1733	400	451	882	1907	3099

PLAY-OFFS

Sheffield United	1	1	0	0	1	0	1	0	1	0	1	1
Walsall	1	0	0	1	1	3	2	1	0	1	2	4

STATISTICAL NOTES

The seasonal statistical pages that follow have been designed for easy reference, and are generally self explanatory, however the following notes are added to avoid confusion:

Left hand column: Provides the match numbers of the particular competition (e.g. Football League, Friendly, etc.), or the round number in a Cup Competition (INT = intermediate round, PR = preliminary round, Q = qualifying round, R = round proper - e.g. 1R = 1st round proper, Rr = round replay - e.g. 2Rr = 2nd round replay, R2r = round 2nd replay, R1 = round 1st leg, R2 = round 2nd leg, SF = Semi-final, F = Final). GM = Group match (Southern Section) in Associate Members (and subsequently sponsors' named) Cup.
Second column: Provides the date (Months abbreviated)
Third column: Provides the opposition ('Home' matches in upper case - capital letters)
Fourth column: Is the position in the League table (where applicable), after the playing of that match.
Fifth column: Is the final score. Sixth column: The half-time score. Seventh column: The attendance (where known).
Eighth column: The goalscorers. These are as given in the local newspapers, and the contemporary records of the Club kept by Thomas Bowden (1897 to 1915). These details are not always in accord with accepted records, but are considered a more accurate record from previously published details. The order of goalscorers is arranged alphabetically and not the time order in which the goals were scored. O.G. indicates a goal scored by an opposition player (whilst the identity of such goalscorers is generally known, these have been omitted due to space, conformity, and for clarity reasons). Unknown, denotes an untraceable goalscorer (name), a numeral following indicates the number of goals by unknown scorers.

In the appearance charts, where full line-ups have not been traced, the use of a P, denotes that that player appeared in the line-up (as gleaned from match reports). The numbers used in the charts refer to the normally accepted position for that period (numbered shirts did not appear until the 1939-40 season), e.g. 1 = goalkeeper, 2 = right-back .... 10 = inside-left, 11 = left-winger. Substitutes (n.b. only where they made an actual appearance in that match) are included, i.e. 12 and/or 14. 12 replaced the asterisked suffixed player (e.g. 4*), and 14 replaced the inverted comma suffixed player (e.g. 6"). The somewhat unnecessary numbering of the goalkeeper (1) has only become necessary since the 1993-94 season when some Clubs adopted the squad numbering system, however in the case of Bristol City, they chose to continue with the 1 to 11 (plus 12 and 14) numbering method for this, the last season contained in these records.

The team line-ups have only been included for Friendly matches and minor Cup competitions up to the entry of the Club into the Football League, plus one 1st World War season - when only such fixtures were played. Whilst the Author has researched and has details of the majority of these 'missing' line-ups (including 90% of the Friendly fixtures), they have been omitted from the latter years for space considerations and in view of the non-Football League/major Cup players used in such games which would require additional columns in the players tables. With regard to Friendly and minor Cup games there have been some changes from those included in the Author's previous work. Further research in compiling a full list of Reserve team matches, has revealed that some matches previously detailed as First team fixtures were in fact played by the Reserve team.

'Home' attendances for the period 1925-26 to 1965-66 inclusive (except the war years) are as per figures kept by the Football League (such information is not available pre-1925-26), and use of the work undertaken by many Authors has been made to ascertain 'Away' crowd numbers where they themselves have made use of these Football League records. Prior to 1925-26, the majority of attendances have been taken from newspaper estimates. In the Resume, the receipt details have been rounded to the nearest pound (£), and it should be noted that in the early years, the comparison of various match receipts compared to attendances as given, suggest the likelihood that many of these estimated crowd figures were widely inaccurate.

The line-up details for the 1919-20 season differ from previously recorded sources, due to the confusion caused by the inclusion of the two Jones' in the line-ups. This record can now be considered as accurate due to the fortunate discovery of official records kept by the Club at that time. Similarly the confusion caused by the inclusion of 'C.I.Morgan' and 'J.Morgan' for seasons 1930-31 to 1932-33 has been clarified from records kept by the Football League. The appearances made by Cyril and Sid Williams during the 1939-40 and 1940-41 seasons have also been corrected. The former assumption that 'Johnson' (1928-29 to 1931-32) was one and the same player has been corrected (Arthur Johnson was 'replaced' by A.J.[Joey] Johnson for the 1931-32 season). Printer's errors within the Author's previous work have been corrected.

Hopefully the vast majority of previously published errors have been corrected in this book, but given the nature of the work, further errors are possible, and the Author would welcome any information (backed up by documentary evidence) which contradicts any of the facts herein.

SEASON 1887-88   SOUTHVILLE

FRIENDLIES

No.	Date	Opposition	Pos.	Res.	H.T.	Att.	Goalscorers	Gyles C.E.	Gyles F.W.	Morris H.	Harris S.J.	McCarthy J.F.	Fox W.H.	Griffiths W.G.	Brown A.	Parker V.	Latham A.	Burland W.H.	Lewis R.	Bucknell J.	Green C.A.	Merchant F.	Morris B.	Harris H.G.
1	15 Oct	CRITERION		1-0	0-0		McCarthy	P	P	P	P	P	P	P	P									
2	22	CRITERION																					
3	29	NORTH ROVERS																					
4	5 Nov	St. Agnes		0-1	0-1			P															
5	26	Warmley Res.																					
6	10 Dec	NORTH ROVERS		4-0	1-0		Fox(2), Griffiths, McCarthy		P				P	P	P									
7	17	ST. SIMONS		2-0	1-0		Fox, McCarthy							P	P									
8	24	CRITERION																					
9	31	Bristol East																					
10	7 Jan	WARMLEY RES.																					
11	14	BRISTOL EAST		5-0	1-0		Fox, Griffiths, McCarthy, Morris, Parker		P			P	P	P	P	P	P							
12	21	ST. MICHAELS		0-0	0-0			P															
13	28	St. Simons		0-0	0-0																		
14	4 Feb	GLOBE		0-0	0-0			P	P	P	P												
15	11	Warmley Hearts of Oak*		2-0	1-0		McCarthy(2)	P	P			P						P						
16	18	ST. AGNES																					
17	25	North Rovers		2-0			Unknown(2)																
18	3 Mar	CLIFTON RES.		1-0	0-0		Fox									P	P						
						Apps.		5	5	3	2	5	5	4	2	1	1						
						Goals				1		6	5	2		1							

GLOUCESTERSHIRE CUP

								Gyles C.E.	Gyles F.W.	Morris H.	Harris S.J.	McCarthy J.F.	Fox W.H.	Griffiths W.G.	Brown A.	Parker V.	Latham A.
1R	12 Nov	Globe		1-1			Unknown	P		P			P				
1Rr	19	GLOBE		0-0	0-0			P	P	P			P				
1Rrr	3 Dec	GLOBE		0-1	0-0												

* Southville turned up 2 players short, so an opponent switched sides to even the numbers.   Note: Additional players names are those taken from the 'Half-Backs' details on Bedminster.

SEASON 1888-89

FRIENDLIES

No.	Date	Opposition	Pos.	Res.	H.T.	Att.	Goalscorers	Gyles C.E.	Harris E.T.	McCarthy J.F.	Griffiths W.G.	Hemmens T.	Morris H.	Brown A.	Gyles F.W.	Bendall S.	Harris S.J.	Gerish G.	Hanover R.	Morris B.	Harris H.G.	Fox W.H.	Beard G.
1	6 Oct	Q.E.H. OLD BOYS		0-2	0-1			P	P	P	P												
2	20	St. Simons		2-0			Unknown					P											
3	27	OLDLAND																					
4	3 Nov	Kingswood Congregat.		0-0	0-0																		
5	10	ST. ANGNES		0-1	0-0			P															
6	17	SOUTHVILLE RES.																					
7	24	EASTVILLE ROVERS																					
8	1 Dec	BEAUFORT		4-0			McCarthy(3), Brown			P				P	P								
9	8	Warmley		1-3	0-0		Hanover	1	7		10		5	11	2	3	4	6	8	9			
10	15	Q.E.H. OLD BOYS		0-1	0-1			1	7	9	10	3	4	11	2		5				6	8	
11	22	ST. SIMONS																					
12	29	St. Agnes																					
13	5 Jan	SOUTHVILLE RES.																					
14	12	St. Simons		1-0	0-0		Griffiths						P								P		
15	19	Eastville Rovers		0-1	0-1																		
16	26	Oldland																					
17	2 Feb	KINGSWOOD CONGRE.		0-1	0-1			1	5	7	9	3	10	11	2		4				8	6	10
18	16	St. George		1-5			Unknown																
19	23	NORTH ROVERS		9-1			Unknown																
20	2 Mar	Q.E.H. OLD BOYS		4-1	0-0		Griffiths(3), H.Harris	1	11	7	9	3	4		2		5				8	6	10
21	9	WARMLEY																					
22	16	Wick & Doynton																					
23	23	St. Agnes		1-2			Unknown																
						Apps.		6	5	5	6	4	5	4	4	1	4	1	1	1	4	3	1
						Goals				3	4			1					1		1		

GLOUCESTERSHIRE CUP

1R	24 Feb	Warmley		1-2	0-1		Griffiths	1	5	7	9	3	10	11	2		4				8	6	

SEASON 1889-90   BEDMINSTER
FRIENDLIES

No.	Date	Opposition	Pos.	Res.s	H.T.	Att.	Goalscorers	Gyles C.E.	Gyles F.W.	Connelly F.	Parker V.	Harris S.J.	Harris H.G.	Harris E.T.	McCarthy J.F.	Griffiths W.G.	Brown B.	Hemmens T.	Pearce T.	Morris H.	Dawes S.	Murdock E.G.	Harris F.J.	Bass J.	Woodford	Morris F.	Ferris F.	Burland W.H.	Welham J.W.	Burgess F.	Perrin W.	Cox
1	12 Oct	Clevedon*		0-0	0-2			1	?	3	4	5	6	7	8	9	10															
2	26	Graigmore College		1-4			Unknown	1	9			6	5	10	8	7	11	2	3	4												
3	2 Nov	ST. AGNES		4-1			Dawes(3), Unknown	1	9			5		11	8	10	6	2	3	4	7											
4	16	St. Agnes**		10-2			Unknown (10)																									
5	23	GRAIGMORE COLLEGE		1-1	0-1		Unknown															P										
6	30	Warmley		0-4	0-2			1	5			3	6	10	7	11		2		4	8	9										
7	7 Dec	Kingswood																															
8	14	ST. SIMONS		8-0			Unknown (8)	1	5			3	6	11	7	9		2		4	8		10									
9	21	CLIFTON		1-5	1-3		Unknown		5			2	4	11	7	9		3		6	8		10	1								
10	28	WICK & DOYNTON																														
11	4 Jan	Bath		1-4			H.Harris		9	4		2	11	10	8			1	5	6	7				3							
12	11	St. George		1-7	1-4		F.Gyles		8	4		3	9		7	10		2		6				5		1	11					
13	18	EASTVILLE ROVERS																															
14	25	BEDMINSTER RES.					Cancelled due to Gloucestershire Cup Match																									
15	1 Feb	CLEVEDON		5-3	4-1		H.Harris(2), McCarthy(2), F.Harris		4			5	8		7	9		2	6	11			10					1	3			
16	8	Clifton		0-3	0-1			1	5	6		8	4	7	9			2					11					3	10			
17	15	Q.E.H. OLD BOYS		5-0			Unknown (5)																									
18	22	CLIFTON		3-2	1-2		Griffiths, F.Harris, H.Harris	1	5	6		4	10		11	9		2					7					3		8		
19	1 Mar	BATH																															
20	8	KINGSWOOD																															
21	15	ST. SIMONS		4-0			Unknown (4)																									
22	22	WARMLEY		7-0	4-0		Griffiths(3),E.Harris,F.Harris,S.Harris,McCarthy	1	6	5		4	8	11	7	9		3					10					2				
23	29	ST. GEORGE		0-4	0-1			1	4	6		5	8	11	7	9		2										3				10
		Apps.						9	12	8	1	12	12	10	13	12	3	13	4	8	5	1	6	2	1	1	1	1	5	1	1	1
		Goals							1			1	4	1	3	4					3		3									

GLOUCESTERSHIRE CUP

1R	25 Jan	GRAIGMORE COLLEGE		0-2			

* Bedminster only fielded 10 players.

** This score is from the 'Western Daily Press', but it should be noted that the 'Bristol Times & Mirror' records Bedminster winning 10-0.

SEASON 1890-91
FRIENDLIES

No.	Date	Opposition	Pos.	Res.	H.T.	Att.	Goalscorers	Gyles C.E.	Hemmens T.	Welham J.W.	Hunt F.	Harris S.J.	Burland W.H.	Griffiths W.G.	Morris H.	Gyles F.W.	Harris E.T.	Harris F.J.	Marshall H.A.	Connelly F.	McCarthy J.F.	Waring	Batchelor H.J.	Dodderall	Gee	Skeates F.E.	Jones G.E.	Burt	Dowling W.	Tay or W.	Gillam S.	Horton
1	27 Sep	CLIFTON		1-3	1-2		F.Harris	1	2	3	4	5	6	7	8	9	10	11														
2	11 Oct	EASTVILLE ROVERS		4-2	1-2		F.Harris(2), Griffiths, McCarthy	1		3		5		9		2	11	10	4	6	7	8										
3	18	BETHESDA		4-0			Unknown (4)	1		3		5		8		2		10	4	6	7		9	11								
4	25	ST. GEORGE		3-3	1-1		Griffiths, F.Harris, McCarthy	1		2		5	9	8		3	11	10	4	6	7											
5	1 Nov	CLIFTON		2-2	2-0		E.Harris(2)	1		2		5	9	8		3	11	10	4	6	7											
6	8	Q.E.H. Old Boys		4-0	2-0		Burland, E.Harris, F.Harris, McCarthy	1		3		5	9	8		2	11	10	4		7				6							
7	15	BETHESDA		9-0			Grffths(2),E.Harrs(2),Mrshll(2),Batchlr,Brlnd,OG	1		3		5	10	8		2	11		4	6	7		9									
8	22	Clevedon		6-1	6-0		Batchelor(2), Griffiths(2), E.Harris, F.Harris	1		2		5		8		3	11	10	4	6	7		9									
9	29	Fishponds		3-1			Unknown (3)																									
10	6 Dec	Graigmore College		6-1	1-1		Batchlr,Grffths,F.Harrs,McCrthy,Marshll,Uknwn	1		3		5		8		2	10	11	4	6	7		9									
11	13	EASTVILLE ROVERS		4-1	2-1	300	Batchelor(2), F.Harris, McCarthy	1		3		5		8		2	11	10	4	6	7		9									
12	20	ST. SIMONS																													
13	27	Bath																													
14	3 Jan	Wells		0-2																												
15	10	FISHPONDS																													
16	17	BRISTOL NOMADS																													
17	24	Q.E.H. Old Boys																													
18	7 Feb	St. Simons		3-0			F.Harris, McCarthy, Marshall		2	3		5	1			8	11	10	9	6	7					4						
19	14	CLIFTON		4-0	1-0		F.Gyles(2), Batchelor, McCarthy		2			5	1			11	10		6	4	7		9	8		3						
20	28	Warmley		1-0	0-0		Unknown	1		3		5				8	11		4		7		9	8		6	2	10				
21	7 Mar	CLEVEDON		1-1	1-0		Unknown		7	3		5	1			8					6		9			4	2		10	11		
22	14	BAPTIST COLLEGE																													
23	21	Trowbridge Town		1-2	1-1		Unknown			3		5	8			9	11	10	4							6	2				1	7
24	30	CLIFTON		5-1	4-0		Batchelor(3), McCarthy(2)		4	2		5	1			11	10		8		7		9			6	3					
25	4 Apr	EASTVILLE ROVERS																													
		Apps.						11	4	16	1	16	10	10	1	16	14	11	14	11	13	1	9	2	1	6	4	1	1	1	1	1
		Goals										2	7			2	6	9	4		9		10									

GLOUCESTERSHIRE CUP

	Date	Opposition	Pos.	Res.	H.T.	Att.	Goalscorers	Gyles C.E.	Hemmens T.	Welham J.W.	Hunt F.	Harris S.J.	Burland W.H.	Griffiths W.G.	Morris H.	Gyles F.W.	Harris E.T.	Harris F.J.	Marshall H.A.	Connelly F.	McCarthy J.F.	Waring	Batchelor H.J.	Dodderall	Gee
1R	31 Jan	Eastville Rovers		3-2	2-2		Batchelor, Griffiths, E.Harris	1		3		5		8		2	11	10	4	6	7		9		
SF	21 Feb	GRAIGMORE COLLEGE		12-0	2-0	500	Btchlr(4),McCrthy(3),Dddrll(2),Cnnlly,Grffths,E.H	1	3	2				8		5	11			6	4	7	9	10	
F	28 Mar	Warmley*		2-0	0-0	2,500	Batchelor, Griffiths	1		3		5		8		2	11	10	4		7		9	6	

* Played on the St. George Ground

SEASON 1891-92 BEDMINSTER

FRIENDLIES

Player columns (left to right): Gyles C.E., Welham J.W., Jones G.E., Marshall H.A., Gyles F.W., Skeates F.E., McCarthy J.F., Dowling W., Batchelor H.J., Rich G., Harris H.G., Harris S.J., Merchant F., Harris E.T., Mackay J., Miles E.G., Burland W.H., Jones A., Taylor W., Griffiths W.G., Brown W.M., Coutice D.L., Wright J., Latham S., Owen M.L., Gutteridge J.M., Uffer A.D., Francis H.H., Byswater, Curtis G., Bucknall A., Thomas H., Bucknell B., Macfarlane A.B., Hurston W., Fagan J.J., Wallace J.W., Batten F.J., Jenkins C.

No.	Date	Opposition	Pos.	Res.	H.T.	Att.	Goalscorers
1	26 Sep	CLIFTON		2-3			Unknown (2)
2	10 Oct	WARMLEY		1-2	0-2		Skeates
3	17	Eastville Rovers		2-1			Unknown (2)
4	31	Clifton		0-4	0-1		
5	7 Nov	Swindon Town		0-13	0-4		
6	21	TROWBRIDGE TOWN		3-1	1-1	800	Batchelor, F.Gyles, Rich
7	28	St.George *		0-2	0-0		
8	5 Dec	CRAIGMORE COLLEGE		7-0	4-0		Batchl'r(3),E.Har's,G.Jones,Miles,U'k'n
9	12	Chippenham Town		2-1	2-0		Byswater, Francis
10	19	KINGSWOOD		6-0			Mackay(2),Miles(2),A.Jones, Unknown
11	28	Mangotsfield		1-6	1-1		Unknown
12	2 Jan	SWINDON TOWN		5-2	3-0	1000	Batchelor,McCarthy,Miles,Unknown(2)
13	9	Wells					
14	16	CLIFTON					
15	23	Warmley		2-1	1-1	500	Hurston, A.Jones
16	6 Feb	ST.GEORGE		1-2	0-2	400	Batchelor
17	13	Clevedon		3-1	1-0		McCarthy (2), Unknown
18	20	TROWBRIDGE TOWN					
19	5 Mar	CHIPPENHAM TOWN **		1-0			Macfarlane
20	19	WELLS		5-1	3-0	1000	Wallace(2),Mac'lane,Wes'ke,Wel'm
21	26	Trowbridge Town		2-3	2-1		A,Jones, Miles
22	2 Apr	CLEVEDON		4-1	2-0		Batchelor (2), Taylor, Wallace
23	9	MANGOTSFIELD		4-8	0-8	600	G.Jones, Macfarlane, Taylor, Wallace
24	16	St.George		0-2	0-0	300	
25	18	SHEFFIELD		1-6	1-4		Taylor

Apps. 4 16 17 16 10 6 16 2 12 14 1 8 1 4 5 14 2 8 5 1 1 9 3 2 3 1 1 1 1 1 1 9 1 3 7 1 2
Goals 1 2 1 1 3 8 1 1 2 5 3 3 1 1 3 1 4

* Bedminster only fielded 10 players. ** Abandoned after 15 mins. (Dr.Brown of Chippenham broke his leg)
Other players: Westlake A.(20/5,22/5,25/4), Drewett W.J.(21/3), Plaister (21/6), Laurie A.(21/8,22/7,24/10), Stone (23/5), Belcher (23/9), Nelmes F.J.(24/5)

F.A.CUP

	Date	Opposition	Res.	H.T.	Goalscorers
2Q.	24 Oct	93rd HIGHLANDERS			Walkover (opponents military duties)
3Q	14 Nov	LUTON TOWN	1-4	0-3	Batchelor

Other player - Harris F.J. 8/3Q)

GLOUCESTERSHIRE CUP

	Date	Opposition	Res.	H.T.	Att.	Goalscorers
1R	30 Jan	KINGSWOOD	3-1	1-1	200	Mackay (2), Macfarlane
SF	27 Feb	ST.GEORGE	1-0	0-0	1300	Unknown
F	12 Mar	Warmley +	1-2	1-2	6000	Macfarlane

+ Played at Kingwood Athletic Ground

SEASON 1892-93

BRISTOL & DISTRICT LEAGUE

Player columns (left to right): Gyles C.E., Jones G.E., Wallace J.W., Skeates F.E., Rich G., Andrews, McCarthy J.F., Griffiths W.G., Milne S.J., Macfarlane A.B., Mayger F.E., Marshall H.A., Harris S.J., Jones A., Wright A.T., Burland W.H., Harris E.T., Harris F.J., Gyles F.W., Farr-Smith C., Drewett W.J., King A., Olds J., Westlake A., Batten F.J., Davis W.H., Cooke J., Miles E.G., Thomas H.J.

No.	Date	Opposition	Pos.	Res.	H.T.	Att.	Goalscorers
1	22 Oct	Wells	7	2-2	2-1		Milne, Unknown
2	5 Nov	TROWBRIDGE TOWN	5	4-0	4-0		McCarthy(2), Griffiths, Milne
3	12	St. George	6	1-3	1-0	1500	Mayger
4	19	Warmley*		0-9	0-6	250	
5	3 Dec	EASTVILLE ROVERS	5	5-0	3-0	1000	Griffiths(2), McCarthy(2), Macfarlane
6	10	Clevedon	4	3-2	2-0		Unknown (3)
7	17	MANGOTSFIELD**	4	3-1	0-1	1000	Griffiths, Unknown (2)
8	21 Jan	WARMLEY	4	2-0	1-0	3000	Macfarlane, Mayger
9	11 Feb	Clifton	4	0-4	0-1		
10	18	WELLS ***	4	1-1	1-1		O.G.
11	4 Mar	Trowbridge Town	4	0-4	0-1		
12	11	CLIFTON	4	1-1	1-1	1000	Griffiths
13	18	ST. GEORGE	4	1-1	0-0	2000	McCarthy(pen)
14	25	Eastville Rovers	5	2-5	2-1		Griffiths, Milne
15	4 Apr	CLEVEDON	5	1-1	0-1	800	Mayger
16	8	Mangotsfield	4	4-0	2-0		Mayger(2), Griffiths, Macfarlane

Apps. 13 13 16 10 3 1 15 15 15 15 9 1 1 2 3 3 2 2 1 1 6 2 1 1
Goals 5 7 3 3 5

	P	W	D	L	F	A
Home	8	4	4	0	18	5
Away	8	2	1	5	12	20

(Final fourth)

F.A. CUP

	Date	Opposition	Res.	H.T.	Att.	Goalscorers
1Q	15 Oct	Uxbridge	1-7	1-3	800	McCarthy

GLOUCESTERSHIRE CUP

	Date	Opposition	Res.	H.T.	Att.	Goalscorers
1R	28 Jan	CRAIGMORE COLLEGE	5-0			Mayger(5)
SF	25 Feb	GLOUCESTER	0-5	0-2	2000	

FRIENDLIES

No.	Date	Opposition	Res.	H.T.	Att.	Goalscorers
1	24 Sep	SWINDON ST. MARKS	2-1	1-0	600	McCarthy, Milne
2	1 Oct	Swindon Athletic	2-7	1-1		Griffiths, Milne
3	8	SWINDON ATHLETIC	4-4			Unknown (4)
4	29	WESTON-SUPER-MARE	8-0	4-0		Macfarlane(4), Griffiths(2), Marshall, Milne
5	26 Nov	CRAIGMORE COLLEGE +	6-1			Marshall, Unknown (5)
6	24 Dec	Weston-super-Mare				
7	26	SWINDON ATHLETIC	1-1	1-0	1500	Milne
8	27	SOUTH BRISTOL XI	3-2	1-1		Burland, F.Gyles, Macfarlane
9	31	Swindon St. Marks				
10	4 Feb	EASTVILLE ROVERS	0-0	0-0	600	
11	3 Apr	ST. GEORGE	0-0	0-0	800	

* Fielded only 10 men 1st half, Mayger arrived after the interval but Skeates didn't turn up for 2nd half which lasted only 35 mins.(failing light) ** Only 80 mins.played (due to Mangotsfield player injury) + Only 30 mins. each ½. *** Wells - 10 men.

Player columns (left to right): Gyles C.E., Jones G.E., Beverley W.G., Millard F., Jores A., Skeates F.E., McCarthy J.F., Milne S.J., Clements H.H., Wallace J.W., Mayger F.E., King A., Griffiths W.G., Carey F., Gyles F.W., Gold A., Philips J.D., Burland W.H., Harris H.G., Farr-Smith C., Drewett W.J., Lewis W., Smith H.E., Paterson H., Hardy, Jenkins, Wright A.T., Olds J., Popham G.

No.	Date	Opposition	Pos.	Res.	H.T.	Att.	Goalscorers
1	00 Sep	GLOUCESTER		0-2	2-0		Milne(2), O.G.
2	7 Oct	EASTVILLE ROVERS	1	2-0	0-0		Mayger, O.G.
3	28	Staple Hill	1	5-0	3-0		Mayger(2), Griffiths, McCarthy, Wallace
4	18 Nov	WARMLEY	3	0-1	0-1	300	Abandoned at half-time due to blizzard
5	25	Clevedon	2	1-1	1-1		Unknown(pen)
6	2 Dec	TROWBRIDGE TOWN	2	3-1	1-1	1000	Griffiths(2), Mayger
7	9	Mangotsfield	1	2-0	2-0		Clements, Griffiths
8	16	Clifton	1	3-1	3-0		Clements(2), Griffiths
9	13 Jan	STAPLE HILL	2	0-1	0-0	1500	
10	20	ST. GEORGE	2	3-0	3-0	2000	Beverley, Burland, Unknown
11	3 Feb	CLEVEDON	1	5-1	4-0		Burland(2), Griffiths, Unknown (2)
*	10	St. George	1	2-2	2-1	1500	Griffiths, Skeates
12	17	CLIFTON	2	0-3	0-2		
13	3 Mar	Eastville Rovers	2	3-3	1-2		Griffiths, Mayger, Unknown
14	17	Trowbridge Town*	3	1-5	1-4		Beverley
15	24	MANGOTSFIELD	3	7-2	4-0		McCarthy(2), Phillips(2), Unknown (3)
16	26	WARMLEY	3	0-2	0-1	3500	
17	31	Gloucester	3	2-5	2-0		Burland, Lewis
18	7 Apr	Warmley	4	0-3	0-2		
19	9	St.George	4	1-6	0-2		Unknown

* Subsequent to recording results this match was in fact a Friendly (Match no. 8)

	P	W	D	L	F	A	
Home	9	6	0	3	23	12	
Away	9	3	2	4	18	24	(Final - Fourth)

Apps. 16 1 11 11 7 11 11 1 11 14 15 7 11 1 1 8 8 3 1 4 2 2   1 1 1
Goals   2   1 3 2 3 1 5   7   2 4   1

F.A. CUP

1Q	14 Oct	UXBRIDGE		2-6	0-2	750	Clements(2)

F.A. AMATEUR CUP

2Q	21 Nov	HOME PARK (Plymouth)		0-3	0-2	600	

GLOUCESTERSHIRE CUP

1R	27 Jan	Waverley		5-1	3-0	700	Mayger(4), McCarthy
SF	24 Feb	ST. GEORGE		2-2	0-1	4000	Griffiths, Mayger
SFR	10 Mar	St. George		1-3	0-1	3000	Griffiths

FRIENDLIES

1	16 Sep	Staple Hill		0-2	0-1	400	
2	21 Oct	St. George		0-2	0-0	700	
3	11 Nov	CLIFTON		2-0	0-0		McCarthy, Mayger
4	26 Dec	SWINDON ATHLETIC		3-1	2-1	1500	Clements, Mayger, Wallace
5	27	STH BRISTOL & DIS. XI		4-1	1-0	800	Phillips, Unknown (3)
6	28	LEINSTER NOMADS		1-0	1-0		King
7	30	OLD MANNAMEDIANS		4-0	1-0		Clements, Skeates, Unknown (2)
9	27 Mar	SR&DL XI					
10	14 Apr	SWINDON ATHLETIC		1-0			Unknown

* Bedminster only fielded 10 players (McCarthy missed the train).

BEDMINSTER A.F.C. 1892/93 Season (J.F.McCarthy appeared to make a habit of being late - he arrived after the photo' was taken!)
(Players only L.to R.) Middle: A.King, G.Jones, C.Gyles, J.Wallace, F.Skeates, F.Gyles, W.Griffiths.
Front: A.Jones, S.Milne, Rev.A.MacFarlane, F.Mayger.

SEASON 1894-95 BEDMINSTER
BRISTOL & DISTRICT LEAGUE DIVISION 1

No.	Date	Opposition	Pos.	Res.	H.T.	Att.	Goalscorers
1	6 Oct	CLEVEDON	5	3-1	0-0	1500	Smith(2), Milne
2	13	Trowbridge Town	9	0-7	0-3		
3	3 Nov	SWINDON WANDERERS	8	5-1	3-1	700	Griffiths, E.Harris, Unknown(3)
4	10	Clevedon	5	8-2	5-0		Phillips(2),Smith(2),Skeates, Unk'n(3)
5	17	WARMLEY	4	2-1	2-0	3000	Milne, Patterson
6	8 Dec	STAPLE HILL	4	2-1	1-0	900	Milne(pen), Millard
7	15	Eastville Rovers	6	2-4	2-1	600	Smith(2)
8	5 Jan	Hereford Thistle	7	0-4	0-1	400	
9	19	St.George *	7	0-7	0-2	1000	
10	26	CLIFTON	6	5-1	1-1		Smith(2), Phillips, Popham, Thomas
11	16 Feb	ST. GEORGE	7	0-3	0-2	2000	
12	2 Mar	Gloucester	8	0-3	0-1		
13	9	Mangotsfield **	6	1-0			Unknown
14	16	Swindon Wanderers	7	1-6	0-3		Milne(pen)
15	30	TROWBRIDGE TOWN	7	0-5	0-1		
16	6 Apr	GLOUCESTER	9	3-5	0-4		McCarthy, Phillips, Popham
17	8	St.George	9	0-9	0-1	400	
18	12	Staple Hill	9	1-4	1-3		Unknown
19	13	HEREFORD THISTLE	9	1-4	0-4	800	Osborne
20	15	MANGOTSFIELD	9	2-4	0-3	300	Britton, Thayer
21	20	EASTVILLE ROVERS	9	1-4	0-2		Popham
22	22	Warmley	9	***	.		
23	27	Clifton	0	0-1	0-0		Unknown(2)

Player columns (appearances / shirt numbers by match), in header order:
Gyles F.W., Popham G., Drewett W.J., Millard F., Milne S.J., Skeates F.E., Smith H.E, Phillips J.D., Wallace J.W., Patterson H., Griffiths W.G., Lawton E., Harris E.T., Batten F.J., Davis W., Yates F.A., Hale W., Gyles G., Berry W., Hemmens G.H., Hunt F., Thomas H.J., Beverley W.G., Murdock E.G., Francombe, Britton T., McCarthy J.F., Slade H., Osborne, Thayer C., Burland W.H., Wright A.T., Ormiston J.P., Monckton, Cranfield M., Woodcock H.C., Chambers, Winstone, Grindley W.H.

Apps: 13, 12, 2, 10, 19, 8, 17, 15, 17, 9, 11, 1, 5, 8, 7, 1, 1, 5, 3, 9, 10, 3, 1, 2, 1, 2, 5, 2, 2, 1, 1, 1

Goals: 3 · · 1 · 4 · 1 · 8 · 4 · 1 · · 1 · 1 · 1 · · · · · · · · 1 · · 1 · 1 · · 1 · 1

* Abandoned (failing light) ** Mangotsfield only fielded two men (offside rule did not prevent a goal - scored from a corner) *** Bedminster unable to raise a team (points awarded to Warmley)

	P.	W.	D.	L.	F.	A.
Home	11	5	0	6	24	30	
Away	11	2	0	9	15	43	(Final - Ninth)

F.A. AMATEUR CUP

No.	Date	Opposition	Res.	H.T.	Att.	Goalscorers
1Q	27 Oct	OLD WEYMOUTHIANS	2-3	1-3	300	Griffiths, Skeates

GLOUCESTERSHIRE CUP

No.	Date	Opposition	Res.	H.T.	Att.	Goalscorers
2R	23 Feb	Warmley	1-10	0-4	700	Unknown

FRIENDLIES

No.	Date	Opposition	Res.	H.T.	Att.	Goalscorers
1	15 Sep	Staple Hill	3-1	3-0		Monckton(2), Phillips
2	22	WARMLEY *	0-3	0-0	600	
3	29	StGeorge	2-2	1-2	700	Griffiths, Unknown
4	20 Oct	NEWPORT	9-0	4-0		Milne(3),Grif'ths(2),Pop'm(2),Davis,Mil'd
5	24 Nov	Staple Hill	1-2			Unknown
6	24 Dec	CLIFTON	2-4			Unknown(2) Unemployed Ironworkers Benefit
7	26	ROYAL MARINE ARTILLERY XI	2-2	1-1	2000	Millard, Unknown
8	27	BRISTOL SOUTH LEAGUE XI	6-3	1-0		Chambers(3), Phillips(3)
9	28	CORSHAM	3-5	3-0		Unknown(3)
10	29	LEINSTER NOMADS	0-3	0-1	1500	
11	2 Jan	OLD MANNAMEDIANS	3-2	1-1		Chambers, Grindley, Winstone
12	23 Mar	BRISTOL SOUTH END	0-2	0-2	4000	
13	17 Apr	SOUTH BRISTOL & DIST.LGE XI	2-3	1-0		Farr-Smith, Unknown

* Warmley arrived late (and with only 10 men) - match duration only 40 minutes.

Friendly Matches - other players (all in last game): Bosanquet (1), Farr-Smith C. (4), Peglar (6), 'A.N.Other'(7), Harding (8), Baugh D. (9), Mann (11)

SEASON 1895-96 BEDMINSTER
WESTERN LEAGUE DIVISION ONE

Player columns (left to right): McCarthy J.F., Milne S.J., Wright A.T., Skeates F.E., Hammens G.H., Harris E.T., Asprey, Walters R., Mayall, Baugh D., Rhodes E., Sevier, Dickenson, Wallace J.W., Matthews, Smith H.E., Phillips J.D., Popham G., Gyles F.W., Thayer C., Drury W., Welham J.W., Nicholls H., Daniells T.C., Burke D., Talbot-Lewis A.E., Thomas H.J., Gyles C.E., Clements H.H., McMillan, Burland W.H., Slade H., McAuliffe O., Llewellyn, Britton T., Brooks G., Marsh D., Ross J.S., Berry W.

No.	Date	Opposition	Pos.	Res.	H.T.	Att.	Goalscorers
1	21 Sep	Mangotsfield		2-4	1-4		McCarthy, Milne
2	28	Swindon Wanderers	12	2-6	1-3		Mayall, Rhodes
3	19 Oct	STAPLE HILL	12	0-2	0-2	800	
4	26	EASTVILLE ROVERS	12	1-3	1-2	900	Popham
5	9 Nov	St. George	11	3-1	0-1		Popham, Rhodes, O.G.
6	16	SWINDON WANDERERS	9	1-0	1-0	2000	Rhodes
7	30	TROWBRIDGE TOWN	9	1-2	0-0	2500	Unknown
8	7 Dec	St. Pauls	10	1-3	0-1		Unknown
9	14	CLIFTON	9	5-2	3-7		Milne(2), Baugh, Harris, Walters
10	21	GLOUCESTER *	7	0-0	0-0		
11	26	CARDIFF		·			(Cardiff failed to turn up) **
12	4 Jan	Warmley	8	1-4	1-1	1000	Nicholls
13	11	ST. PAULS	6	3-0	1-0		Hemmens, Unknown(2)
14	18	ST. GEORGE	7	1-2	1-2	2000	Baugh(pen)
15	1 Feb	Clifton	8	2-4	0-3		Daniells, Unknown
16	8	Eastville Rovers	8	2-1	0-0		Baugh, Thomas
17	15	WARMLEY	8	0-1	0-1	3500	
18	22	Staple Hill	9	2-3	2-1		Harris, Rhodes
19	7 Mar	Trowbridge Town	8	2-4	1-0		Smith, Walters
20	21	MANGOTSFIELD	7	7-0	5-0		Rhodes(3), Harris(2), Baugh, Smith

* Bedminster started with 8 players, later full team, although McCartney retired with injury.
The away fixture with Gloucester was adjudicated a 0-0 draw (smallpox epidemic).

** Cardiff expelled from League

	P.	W.	D.	L.	F.	A.	
Home	10	4	1	5	19	12	
Away	10	2	1	7	17	30	(Final · Eighth)

F.A. CUP

			Res.	H.T.		Goalscorers
1Q	12 Oct	WEYMOUTH	2-2	1-0		Baugh(2)
1Qr	16	Weymouth	1-3			Unknown

F.A. AMATEUR CUP

			Res.	H.T.		
1Q	5 Oct	ST. GEORGE	0-3	0-3		

GLOUCESTERSHIRE CUP

			Res.	H.T.		Goalscorers
PR	25 Jan	ST PAULS	5-1	1-1	1500	Drury(3), Harris, Slade
1R	29 Feb	STAPLE HILL	2-1	1-0	2500	Daniells, Harris
SF	28 Mar	EASTVILLE ROVERS	0-1	0-0	4000	

FRIENDLIES

No.	Date	Opposition	Res.	H.T.	Att.	Goalscorers
1	11 Sep	ST PAULS	0-1	0-0	500	
2	14	MR.J.A.STEVENS BRISTOL XI	6-3	2-1	5000	Mayall(3), Rhodes, Walters, Unknown
3	2 Nov	85th KINGS LIGHT INF.(Portland)	4-1	1-1		Hemmens, Milne, Rhodes, Unknown
4	23	ROYAL ARTILLERY (Plymouth)	6-2	2-1	1800	Rhodes(3), Popham(2), Baugh
5	27 Dec	GLOUCESTER	0-2	0-0	1000	
6	28	BRISTOL SOUTH END	2-1	0-0	3000	Unknown(2)
7	14 Mar	HEREFORD TOWN	2-3	0-2	1500	Popham(2)
8	7 Apr	Bristol South End	1-2	1-2	2500	Burland
9	11	EASTVILLE ROVERS	2-1	0-0		Burland, Marsh

League Apps: 12, 15, 1, 1, 15, 10, 2, 9, 1, 16, 15, 2, 2, 1, 3, 9, 1, 5, 12, 2, 12, 9, 10, 1, 2, 2, 1, 1
League Goals: 1, 3, 1, 4, 2, 1, 4, 7, 2, 2, 1, 1, 1

SEASON 1896-97 BEDMINSTER

WESTERN LEAGUE DIVISION ONE

No.	Date	Opposition	Pos.	Res.	H.T.	Att.	Goalscorers	Berry W.	Brooks G.	Hemmens G.H.	Baugh D.	Milne S.J.	McAuliffe O.	McCarthy J.F.	Harris E.T.	Pearson G.A.	Cottle G.	Burley W.	Talbot-Lewis A.E.	Roberts F.J.	Fudge	Bennett	Curry	Harris F.J.	Hargett A.	Thomas F.H.	Popham G.	Harrison W.	Jordan C.	Wiggins	Fussell	Burke D.	Morris H.	Ellis	Gyles F.W.	Elmes H.	Salter A.F.	Sage	Peglar	Sutton	Cranfield M.	Osborne R.	Mahoney	Young	Weston	Brown W.S.A.
1	19 Sep	Eastville Rovers		1-0	1-0	4000	Cottle	1	2	3	4	5	6	7	8	9	10	11																												
2	26	WARMLEY	3	1-1	1-0	3000	E.Harris	1	3	2	4	5	6	11	10	8	9	7																												
3	3 Oct	STAPLE HILL	5	0-1	0-1			1	3	2	4	5	6	7	8	10	9	11																												
4	17	St. Pauls	5	2-3	1-1		Baugh(pen), Burley		2	3	4		5	7	8	6	10	11	1	9																										
5	24	ST.GEORGE	4	2-1	2-1		McAuliffe, O.G.		3	2	6	9	5	7	8	4	10	11	1	1																										
6	28 Nov	Trowbridge Town	6	0-0	0-0			1		3		4	5		7	6	10	11			2	8	9																						
7	12 Dec	ST. PAULS	4	1-0	1-0		McAuliffe	P					P																																
8	19	CLIFTON	2	5-0	3-0		Pearson(2), Cottle, E.Harris, McAuliffe	1	2	3	4		5		8	10	11				6				7	9																					
9	26	BRISTOL SOUTH END	3	0-1	0-0			1	2		3		5		7	6	10	11				4	9		8																				
10	29	Warmley	3	0-2	0-2	3000		1	2	3		6	5			11						10	9	7	8	4																			
11	2 Jan	EASTVILLE ROVERS	4	1-2	0-2		McAuliffe	1	3	2	4		5		8	6	10	11						9	7																					
12	23	St. George	5	2-2	1-0	800	McAuliffe, Popham	1	3	2			5		4	10	11				6				7	8	9																				
13	6 Mar	Staple Hill	3	3-0	1-0		Harrison, McAuliffe, Unknown	1	2				5		7	4	10	11	3		6						8		9																		
14	3 Apr	TROWBRIDGE TOWN	5	4-0	1-0	800	Cottle(2), Harrison, Lewis	1	3				5		7	6	10	11	2		4						8		9																		
15	12	Clifton	4	7-1	1-0		Cot'le,Har't,E.Harris,McAu'fe,Wig's,Unk'n(2)	1	2				5		7	6	10		3								8					4	9	11												
16	16	Bristol South End	3	3-1		3500	Unknown(3)																																							
				Apps.			**Goals**	13	13	10	8	6	15	5	12	13	14	11	5	1	5	3	4	4	7	1	1	2	1	1															
							Goals			1			7		3	2	5	1	1				1		1		2	1																	

		P.	W.	D.	L.	F.	A.
Home		8	4	1	3	14	6
Away		8	4	1	3	18	10	(Final - Third)

F.A. CUP

	Date	Opposition	Res.	H.T.	Att.	Goalscorers	Berry	Brooks	Hemmens	Baugh	Milne	McAuliffe	McCarthy	Harris E.T.	Pearson	Cottle	Burley	Talbot-Lewis	Roberts	Fudge	Bennett	Curry	Harris F.J.	Hargett
1Q	10 Oct	Bristol South End	4-2	3-2	4500	Curry(2), Cottle, McCarthy		3	2	4		6	7	8	5	10	11	1				9		
2Q	31	FREEMANTLE	2-0	2-0		Burley, Curry	1		3	4		5		7	6	10	11			2	8	9		
2Q	21 Nov	READING AMATEURS	0-5	0-4	1000		1		3	4		5			6	10	11			2	8	9	7	

F.A. AMATEUR CUP

2Q	7 Nov	BRISTOL SOUTH END	3-3	2-3	2500	Burley, McAuliffe, Unknown	1		3	4		5		7	6	10	11			2	8	9		
2Qr	14	Bristol South End	1-2	0-1	1500	Unknown	1		3	4		5		7	6	10				2	8	9	11	

GLOUCESTERSHIRE CUP

1R	6 Feb	Staple Hill	2-0	0-0		E.Harris, Unknown	1	2	3	4		5		7		10	11	6						8		9
2R	27	Mangotsfield	1-0	1-0		Hargett	1	3	2			5		7		10	11	6						8		9	4
SF	27 Mar	FISHPONDS	2-1	1-0	2000	Cottle, Lewis(pen)	1	4				5		7	6	10	11	3						8		9		2
F	19 Apr	Warmley	0-2	0-2	6705	(Played at St.George) (£191.15.5)	1	3				5				10	11	2						7	8	9	4			6

BRISTOL CHARITY CUP

PR	13 Feb	Trowbridge Town	2-2	0-2		Cottle, Harrison	1	2	3			5		7		10	11	6		4				8		9
PRr	17 Mar	TROWBRIDGE TOWN	1-0	1-0	500	Cottle (£10.4.11)	1	2				7	6	10	11	3		5						8		9	4
1R	10 Apr	Eastville Rovers	2-0	0-0	1500	Fudge, Unknown	1	3				5			6	8		2		4				10		11	7	9
SF	27	WARMLEY	1-2	0-1	1800	Cottle (£27.7.6)	1	3				5		7	4	10				6				8		9	11		2

FRIENDLIES

1	5 Sep	Bristol South End	0-1	0-0	3000			3	4	5	6	2	7		10	9	11																	1	8
2	12	STAPLE HILL	4-2	1-2		Burley, Cottle, E.Harris, Pearson		3	4	5	6	7	8	10	9	11																	1		2
3	28 Dec	STH.BRISTOL & DIST.LGE.XI	3-2	0-2		Cranfield, Ellis, Unknown						2						8			3			4			10	1			3	6	7	9	11
4	9 Jan	WELLS	6-0	3-0		Young(3), Burley, E.Harris, Mahoney			P			P		P			P																	P	P
5	16	BRISTOL SOUTH END	1-3	0-0		McAuliffe	1	2	3			5		7		6	11				8	4																			9	10
6	30	Staple Hill *	3-1	1-0		Cottle(2), Harrison	1	2	3			5			10	11	6			7	8			9	4															
7	13 Mar	63rd ROYAL ARTILLERY(Horfield)	3-0	1-0		Hargett, Harrison, Pearson							P							P						P															
8	20	Eastville Rovers	0-2	0-0			1	2				5		7	6	10	11	3			8			9	4															
9	17 Apr	EASTVILLE ROVERS	1-6			Unknown																																	

* Scheduled as a Gloucestershire Cup match - pitch unfit - played as a Friendly

SEASON 1897-98 BEDMINSTER

WESTERN LEAGUE DIV. ONE (AMAT. SECT.)

Player columns (left→right): Cranfield M., Cottle G., Berry W., Brooks G., Robson E., McBain H., McAuliffe O., Gretton, Harris E.T., Hargett A., Brown W.S.A., Smith, Clements H.H., Parsons, Daniells T.C., Stone, Dymock W.G., McCarthy J.F., Heyward H., Bidwell, Callender, Mayo L., Gytes C.E., Trestrail A.E.Y., Tolman A., Wilkinson, Wyatt, O'Brien J., Thomas, Pearson G.A., Taylor C.J.

No.	Date	Opposition	Pos.	Res.	H.T.	Att.	Goalscorers
1	18 Sep	BARTON HILL		2-0	1-0		Cranfield(2)
2	2 Oct	Staple Hill		3-1	1-0		Cottle, Unknown(2)
3	9	MANGOTSFIELD	1	6-0	4-0	2000	Brown(3), Cottle, Hargett, McAuliffe
4	6 Nov	EASTVILLE WANDERERS	1	3-1	3-0		Hargett(2), Cottle
5	27	Radstock	1	4-0	2-0		Cottle(2), Brown, Stone
6	4 Dec	STAPLE HILL	1	2-1	0-0		Dymock, Hargett
7	1 Jan	MIDSOMER NORTON	1	10-1	5-1		Br'n(3), Gret'n(2), Har't(2), Bid'l, Cal'der, Unk'n
8	8	ST. PAULS	1	7-1	2-1		Gret'n(2), Har't, McAuliffe, McBain, Mayo, Unk'n
9	15	Fishponds	1	5-0	2-0		Callender(2), Gretton, Unknown(2)
10	22	St. Pauls	1	3-2	2-1		Brown, Unknown
11	19 Feb	Mangotsfield	1	2-0	0-0		Unknown(2)
12	19 Mar	FISHPONDS	1	7-0	3-0		Bidwell(2), Har't(2), Callender, Dymock, McAu'fe
13	26	Barton Hill	1	3-1	3-0		Unknown(3)
14	2 Apr	RADSTOCK	1	5-0	1-0		Brown, Cottle, Dymock, Hargett, Unknown
15	9	Eastville Wanderers	1	1-0	0-0		McAuliffe
16	23	Midsomer Norton	1	2-3	1-2		Clements, Unknown

Apps. 2 5 6 6 2 4 7 4 2 8 9 1 6 1 1 2 3 1 3 2 5 2 1 1 1

Goals 2 6 _ _ 1 4 5 _ _ 10 9 _ 1 _ _ 1 3 _ _ 3 4 1

	P.	W.	D.	L.	F.	A.
Home	8	8	0	0	42	4
Away	8	7	0	1	23	7 (Final - Champions)

F.A. CUP

No.	Date	Opposition	Res.	H.T.	Att.	Goalscorers
1Q	25 Sep	Newbury	3-1	0-1	600	Cranfield(2), Hargett
2Q	16 Oct	Eastville Rovers	2-3	0-2		Hargett(2)

F.A. AMATEUR CUP

No.	Date	Opposition	Res.	H.T.	Goalscorers
2Q	30 Oct	YEOVIL CASUALS	1-0	0-0	Brown
3Q	20 Nov	OLD WEYMOUTHIANS	3-1	2-1	Harris(2), Wilkinson
4Q	11 Dec	STREET	1-4	1-1	O.G.

GLOUCESTERSHIRE CUP

No.	Date	Opposition	Res.	H.T.	Att.	Goalscorers
1R	29 Jan	FISHPONDS	3-0	2-0		Bidwell, Cottle, Wyatt
2R	5 Mar	Warmley	3-4	1-2	1000	Callender(2), Gretton

BRISTOL CHARITY CUP (AMATEUR SECTION)

No.	Date	Opposition	Res.	H.T.	Att.	Goalscorers
1Q	23 Oct	MANGOTSFIELD	2-1	1-0	500	Cottle, Unknown
SF/Q	13 Nov	CLIFTON	3-1	3-0		Brown, Cottle, Hargett
F/Q	18 Dec	STAPLE HILL	4-1	2-1		Dymock(2), Hargett(2)
F	25	BARTON HILL	5-1	1-1		Gretton, Hargett, McAuliffe, Stone, O.G.

BRISTOL CHARITY CUP (PROFESSIONAL SECTION)

No.	Date	Opposition	Res.	H.T.	Att.
1R	17 Jan	Warmley	0-4	0-1	1000

FRIENDLIES

No.	Date	Opposition	Res.	H.T.	Att.	Goalscorers
1	1 Dec	WARMLEY	0-3	0-1	600	
2	5 Feb	SWINDON AMATEURS	9-0	7-0	500	Har't(3), Bid'l(2), Brown(2), Cottle, Gr'tn
3	9	Bristol City	2-9	0-5	2000	Gretton, Hargett
4	26	Trowbridge Town	4-1	2-0	500	Callender(2), Gretton, Unknown
5	31 Mar	Bath Banks & District XI	2-0	1-0	800	Cottle, Taylor
6	27 Apr	DERBY COUNTY	1-4	1-0	1000	Hargett

SEASON 1898-99 — BEDMINSTER

SOUTHERN LEAGUE DIVISION ONE

No.	Date	Opposition	Pos.	Res.	H.T.	Att.	Goalscorers	Whitehouse J.	Stewart	Crone R.	Lamont J.	Proudfoot J.	McDonald A.	McVean M.	Bell	Leonard	Copeland D.	Gray	Cox W.	Kelso R.	Brooks G.	Whittle	Callender	Massie	Livesey	North A.E.	Clements H.H.
1	10 Sep	Tottenham Hotspur		1-1	0-1	5500	Proudfoot	1	2	3	4	5	6	7	8	9	10	11									
2	14	BRIGHTON UNITED		1-2	0-1	1000	Stewart(pen)		2	3	4	5	6	7	9	8	10	11	1								
3	8 Oct	Reading	11	0-4	0-0	4000		1	4	3	5		6	8	9	7	11	10		2							
4	22	New Brompton	11	2-5	1-3	3000	Callender, McVean	1	4	6	5			8	10					2			3	7	11		
5	5 Nov	Sheppey United	12	2-2	1-1	1000	Crone, Kelso	1	10	3	4	5	6	8		7	9	11		2							
6	12	NEW BROMPTON	12	4-1	4-0	3000	Stewart(2), Copeland, McVean	1	9	3	4	5	6	8		7	10	11		2							
7	19	Chatham	8	1-0	0-0	5000	McVean	1	9	3	4	5	6	8		7	10	11		2							
8	26	SHEPPEY UNITED	8	3-1	2-0	1000	Gray, Leonard, Stewart	1	9	3	4	5	6	8		7	10	11		2				2			
9	30	Brighton United	8	2-0	1-0	1560	Leonard, Stewart	1	9	3	4	5	6	8		7	10	11		2				2			
10	3 Dec	Gravesend United	7	1-1	1-1	1500	O.G.	1	9	3	4	5		8	6	7	10	11		2				2			
11	17	Bristol City	8	2-5	1-1	10250	McVean, Leonard	1	9	3	4	5		8	6	7	10	11		2							
12	26	Warmley*	8	2-3	1-2	4000	Copeland, Gray	1	9	3	4	5	6	8		7	10	11		2							
13	31	Southampton	8	0-1	0-1	2000		1	9	3	4	5	6	8		7	10	11		2							
14	7 Jan	CHATHAM	9	0-0	0-0	3000		1	9	3	4	5	6	8		7	10	11		2							
15	14	Swindon Town	10	3-4	3-0	3000	Gray, Stewart, O.G.		9		4	5	6	8		7	10	11	1	2	3						
16	21	GRAVESEND UNITED	9	4-1	3-1	1000	Copeland, Gray, Leonard, McVean	1	9	3	4	5	6	8		7	10	11		2							
17	4 Feb	MILLWALL ATHLETIC	9	1-4	0-2		Leonard	1	9	3	4	5	6	8		7	10	11		2							
18	4 Mar	BRISTOL CITY	9	1-0	0-0	7000	Leonard	1	6	3	4	5		9		7	10	11		2				8			
19	11	Millwall Athletic	9	0-3	0-1	6000		1		3	4	5	6	9		7	10	11		2				8			
20	31	ROYAL ARTILLERY(Pompey)	10	0-1	0-0	2000		1	6	3	4	5		9		7	10	11		2				8			
21	1 Apr	SWINDON TOWN	10	0-1	0-0			1	5	3	4		6	9	11	7			6	2				8			
22	4	SOUTHAMPTON	10	2-1	0-0	3000	Copeland, Leonard	1	5	3	4		6	7		9	10	11		2				8			
23	8	Royal Artillery (Pompey)	9	2-0	0-0		Copeland, Gray	1	5	3	4		6	7		9	10	11		2				8			
24	15	TOTTENHAM HOTSPUR	8	1-0	0-0	2000	Gray	1	5	3	4		6	7		9	10	11		2				8			
25	29	READING	8	2-1	2-0		Copeland, Gray	1	6	3	4	5		9		7	10	11		2				8			
		Apps.						23	24	24	25	19	19	25	7	24	25	23	2	20	5	1	1	8		1	1
		Goals							6	1		1		5		7	6	7				1				1	

	P	W	D	L	F	A
Home	12	7	1	4	19	13
Away	12	3	3	6	16	26

(Final · Eighth)

WESTERN LEAGUE (PROFESSIONAL SECTION)   (Fifth)

No.	Date	Opposition	Pos.	Res.	H.T.	Att.	Goalscorers	Whitehouse J.	Stewart	Crone R.	Lamont J.	Proudfoot J.	McDonald A.	McVean M.	Bell	Leonard	Copeland D.	Gray	Cox W.	Kelso R.	Brooks G.	Whittle	Callender	Massie	Livesey	North A.E.	Clements H.H.
1	7 Sep	Trowbridge Town*		4-1	2-0		Livesey(3), Copeland	1	4	3		5	6	7	8		10	11		2					9		
2	17	SOUTHAMPTON		2-1	2-1	2500	Copeland, Massie	1	4	3	6	5				10	7	11		2		9		8			
3	10 Oct	BRISTOL ST. GEORGE	4	1-4	0-2	1250	Copeland	1		3	4	5	6	8	10	7	11			2					9		
4	26	TROWBRIDGE TOWN*	4	3-1	1-0		Massie(2), Copeland	1		3	4	5	6	7	8		10			2				9			11
5	24 Dec	BRSTL E/VILLE ROVERS	2	1-0	0-0	6000	Gray	1	9	3	4	5	6	8		7	10	11		2							
6	28 Jan	Bristol Eastville Rovers	4	2-2	2-0	3500	Copeland, McVean	1	9	3	4	5	6	8		7	10	11		2							
7	11 Feb	Bristol St. George	4	2-3	1-1	3000	Stewart(pen), O.G.	1	9	3	4	5	6		8	7	10	11		2							
8	22	Southampton	4	0-3	0-1			1	9	3	4	5	6	8		7	10	11		2							
9	6 Mar	SWINDON TOWN	5	0-0	0-0	1000		1	6	3	4			5	9		7	10	11		2			8			
10	22 Apr	Swindon Town	5	1-3	0-0	3000	McVean		4	3		5	6	8	7		10	11	1	2				9			

* Clubs disbanded during the season, Trowbridge in October 1898, and Warmley in January 1899. In both instances their records were expunged.

F.A. CUP

Rd	Date	Opposition		Res.	H.T.	Att.	Goalscorers	Whitehouse J.	Stewart	Crone R.	Lamont J.	Proudfoot J.	McDonald A.	McVean M.	Bell	Leonard	Copeland D.	Gray	Cox W.	Kelso R.	Brooks G.	Whittle	Callender	Massie	Livesey	North A.E.	Clements H.H.
P	24 Sep	Newbury		3-0	1-0		Bell, Lamont, Whittle	1	4	3	6	5				10	7	11		2		9		8			
1Q	1 Oct	RYDE		3-1	2-0	1000	Bell, Gray, McVean	1	4	3	5		6	8	10	7	9	11		2							
2Q	15	Warmley		1-1	0-1	1500	Stewart	1	4	6	5			8	10			11		2		3	7	9			
2Qr	19	WARMLEY		2-2	2-0	500	Copeland, McVean	1	5	3	6		4	8	10		9			2			7				11
2Q2r	24	Warmley		1-2	1-1	1000	McVean (Played at St. John's Lane)	1	4	6	5			8	10			11		2		3	7	9			

GLOUCESTERSHIRE CUP

Rd	Date	Opposition		Res.	H.T.	Att.	Goalscorers	Whitehouse J.	Stewart	Crone R.	Lamont J.	Proudfoot J.	McDonald A.	McVean M.	Bell	Leonard	Copeland D.	Gray	Cox W.	Kelso R.	Brooks G.	Whittle	Callender	Massie	Livesey	North A.E.	Clements H.H.
1R	27 Feb	BRISTOL ST. GEORGE		3-2	1-0	1000	McVean(2), Copeland	1	6	3	4	5		9		7	10	11		2				8			
SF	25 Mar	Bristol Rovers		0-1	0-1	3000		1	4	2	6	5		9		8	10	11		3				7			

BRISTOL CHARITY CUP

Rd	Date	Opposition		Res.	H.T.	Att.	Goalscorers	Whitehouse J.	Stewart	Crone R.	Lamont J.	Proudfoot J.	McDonald A.	McVean M.	Bell	Leonard	Copeland D.	Gray	Cox W.	Kelso R.	Brooks G.	Whittle	Callender	Massie	Livesey	North A.E.	Clements H.H.
SF	17 Apr	SWINDON TOWN		2-0	1-0		Copeland, McVean	1	5	3	4		6	7		9	10	11		2				8			
F	24	Reading		3-2	0-1	1911	Gray(2), McDonald (Played at St.Johns' Lane)	1	5	3	4		6	7		9	10	11		2				8			

FRIENDLIES

No.	Date	Opposition		Res.	H.T.	Att.	Goalscorers	Whitehouse J.	Stewart	Crone R.	Lamont J.	Proudfoot J.	McDonald A.	McVean M.	Bell	Leonard	Copeland D.	Gray	Cox W.	Kelso R.	Brooks G.	Whittle	Callender	Massie	Livesey	North A.E.	Clements H.H.
1	1 Sep	SOUTHAMPTON		1-2	1-1		Copeland	1	4			5	6	7	8	9	10	11		2	3						
2	3	WARMLEY		2-0	1-0	2000	Unknown (2)	1	4			5	6	7	8	9	10	11		2	3						
3	29 Oct	BLACKPOOL		1-1	1-1	600	Callender	1	4	3		5	6				9			2		7	10	8		11	
4	10 Dec	Swindon Town		0-2	0-2	1000																					
5	27	SWINDON TOWN		3-0	2-0	2000	Copeland(3)	1	8	3	4	5	6			7	10	9	11	2							
6	2 Jan	Ryde		2-2	2-1		McVean(2)					P		P													
7	25 Feb	BRISTOL AMATEURS		9-2	5-2		Leonard(2),Bell,Lamont,McVean,Massie,Unknown(3)		0	0	4	0		0	10	7				1	9			11		9	
8	18 Mar	GLOSSOP NORTH END		4-2	0-0	1000	Copeland(3), Massie			3	4	5	6			9	7	10	11	1	2			8			

BEDMINSTER 1898/99
(L.toR.) Back: Mountford(Trainer), Whitehouse, Cox, H.Smith(Manager)
Middle: Brooks, Lamont, Proudfoot, Kelso, McDonald, Stewart, Gray.
Front: McVean, Crone, Leonard, Copeland, Bell.

1899/1900 Season

BEDMINSTER.

Photo by T. Burchill, Redcliff Hill.

MOUNTFORD (Trainer). CRONE. TOONE. R. H. DAVIS. S. W. HOLLIS (Sec. and Manager).
BRAMLEY. W. H. DAVIS. DRAYCOTT WILSON. CHAMBERS. AYRE.
W. H. BURLAND (Fin. Sec.) WHEELAN. FLEWITT. BOUCHER. BECTON. GEDDES. SAXTON.

SEASON 1899-1900   BEDMINSTER

SOUTHERN LEAGUE DIVISION ONE

No.	Date	Opposition	Pos.	Res.	H.T.	Att.	Goalscorers	Toone G.	Crone R.	Davies R.H.	Draycott W.	Davies W.H.	Chambers P.	Whelan M.	Flewitt A.	Boucher T.	Wilson H.	Geddes A.	Saxton 'A.	Becton F.	Barker G.	Bramley	Stoltz P.W.	Ayre	Baynon	Clapp A.
1	2 Sep	Sheppey United		2-0	1-0	2000	Flewitt, Wilson	1	2	3	4	5	6	7	8	9	10	11								
2	9	BRIGHTON UNITED*	2	3-1	1-1	3000	Boucher, Geddes, Saxton	1	2	3		5	6	7	8	9	4	11	10							
3	23	Bristol Rovers	3	3-0	1-0	6000	Flewitt(2), Boucher	1	3	2	6	5		7	8	9	4	10	11							
4	7 Oct	Thames Ironworks	6	0-1	0-1	5000		1	3	2	4		6	7	9		5	11	10	8						
5	14	TOTTENHAM HOTSPUR	5	2-1	1-1	5000	Boucher, Flewitt	1	2	3	4		6	7	8	9	5	11		10						
6	21	New Brompton	6	0-1	0-1	2500	Abandoned after 50 minutes due to fog	1	2	3	4		6	7	8	9	5		11	10						
7	4 Nov	Swindon Town	8	1-2	1-1	3000	Wilson	1	2	3	4	5	6	7	8	9	10	11								
8	11	BRISTOL CITY	8	1-1	1-0	5500	O.G.	1	2	3	4		6	7	8	9	5	11		10						
9	25	SOUTHAMPTON	9	0-2	0-2	4000		1	2	3	4		6	7	8	9	5		11	10						
10	2 Dec	Millwall Athletic	8	2-1	1-1	5000	Becton, Wilson	1		3	4		6	7	8	9	5		11	10	2					
11	16	Chatham	8	0-3	0-1	1500		1	6	3	8	4		7		9	5	11	10		2					
12	18	New Brompton	8	0-5	0-4	1500		1	6	3	4	5		7		9		11	10	8	2					
13	23	READING	8	1-0	0-0	2000	Saxton	1		3	4		6	7	8		5	11	10	9	2					
14	26	Portsmouth	8	0-2	0-1	11000		1		3	4		6	7	9		5	11	10	8	2					
15	6 Jan	Brighton United*	6	4-1	1-1	1500	R.Davies, Flewitt, Geddes, Unknown	1	3	8		5		7	9		6	11	10		2	4				
16	20	BRISTOL ROVERS	10	2-5	1-2	4000	Whelan, O.G.	1		3	5			7	10		6	11	9		2	4	8			
17	3 Feb	PORTSMOUTH	9	2-0	1-0	500	R.Davies, Boucher	1	3	10	4	5		7	8	9	6	11			2					
18	10	THAMES IRONWORKS	6	3-1	1-1	2000	R.Davies, Flewitt, Geddes	1	3	10	4	5		7	8	9	6	11			2					
19	12	SHEPPEY UNITED	4	4-2	2-1	1000	Boucher, Saxton, Whelan, Wilson	1	3		4	5		7		9	8	11	10		2			6		
20	17	Tottenham Hotspur	4	2-5	1-4	7000	Flewitt(2)	1		3	4	5		7	8	9		11	10		2					
21	24	NEW BROMPTON	4	3-1	3-1	1000	Boucher, Whelan, Wilson	1		3	4	5	6	7	8	9	10	11			2					
22	3 Mar	Gravesend United	5	2-3	1-2	2000	Geddes, Wilson	1		3	4	5	6	7	8	9	10	11			2					
23	10	SWINDON TOWN	4	2-1	1-0	3000	Boucher, Saxton	1		2	4	5		7		9	10	11	8		2			6		
24	17	Bristol City	4	2-0	2-0	5000	Geddes, Saxton	1		3	4	5	6	7		9	10	11	8		2					
25	31	Southampton	7	2-3	0-3	4000	R.Davies, Wilson	1		3		5	6		8	9	10	11		7	2			4		
26	7 Apr	MILLWALL ATHLETIC	5	2-0	1-0	4000	Boucher, Wilson	1		3	4	5	6	7		9	8	11	10		2					
27	14	Queens Park Rangers	7	1-2	1-1	3000	Geddes	1		3	4	5	6	7	8	9	10	11			2					
28	17	GRAVESEND UNITED	6	1-2	0-0	3000	Geddes	1	3	8	4	5	6	7			10	11	9		2					
29	21	CHATHAM	7	0-1	0-0	2000		1		3	4	5	6	7	8	9		11	10		2					
30	25	QUEENS PK RANGERS	6	4-1	2-0	100	Boucher, R.Davies, Geddes, Whelan	1	3	10	4	5	6	7		9		11			2		8			
31	28	Reading	6	0-0	0-0	2000		1		3	4	5	6	7	10	9		11			2		8			
							Apps.	31	17	30	28	22	21	30	23	24	28	28	19	10	22	2	3	3		
							Goals			5				4	8	9	8	8	5	1						

```
          P  W  D  L  F  A
Home    14  9  1  4  27 18
Away    14  4  1  9  17 27   (Final - Sixth)
```

WESTERN LEAGUE (PROFESSIONAL SECTION)   (Runners-up)

1	30 Sep	BRISTOL ROVERS	2	1-1	1-1	2000	Boucher	1	2	3	4	5			8	9	6		11	10					7	
2	15 Nov	SWINDON TOWN	3	1-2	0-0		Becton	1	2		4	5	6	7	8	9		11		10			3			
3	6 Dec	Bristol City	4	1-8	1-3	2000	Geddess		3		5		8				10	11	9		4	7	2	6	1	
4	17 Jan	Swindon Town	4	1-0	0-0		Wilson	1		8	5			7	10		6	11	9		2	4		3		
5	7 Mar	BRISTOL CITY	3	4-1	2-1	4000	Boucher, Flewitt, Whelan, O.G.	1		3	4	5	6	7	8	9	10	11			2					
6	16 Apr	Bristol Rovers	1	2-0	2-0	6000	R.Davies, O.G.	1	3	8	4	5	6	7			10	11			2					

F.A. CUP

3Q	28 Oct	Weymouth		6-0	4-0		Wilson(3), Boucher(2), Flewitt	1	2	3	4		6	7	8	9	10	11				5				
4Q	18 Nov	BRISTOL EAST		4-1	3-1	400	Wilson(2), Becton, Geddes	1	2	3	4	5	6	7	9		10	11		8						
5Q	9 Dec	PORTSMOUTH		1-2	1-1	6000	Becton	1		3	4		6	7	8	9	5		11	10	2					

GLOUCESTERSHIRE CUP

| SF | 28 Mar | STAPLE HILL | | 2-0 | 2-0 | | Saxton(2) | 1 | | 3 | | 6 | 5 | 7 | | 9 | 10 | 11 | 8 | | 2 | | | 4 | | |
| F | 30 Apr | Bristol City | | 3-1 | 2-0 | 1975 | Geddes(2), Boucher (Played at Eastville) | 1 | | 3 | 4 | 5 | 6 | 7 | 8 | 9 | 10 | 11 | | | 2 | | | | | |

BRISTOL CHARITY CUP

SF	13 Jan	BRISTOL CITY		1-1	1-1	4200	Flewitt	1	3	8	4	5		7	10	9	6	11			2					
SFr	21 Feb	Bristol City		6-0	3-0	2000	Flewitt(2), Wilson(2,1 pen), Boucher, Geddes	1		3	4	5	6	7	8	9	10	11			2					
F	24 Mar	BRISTOL ROVERS		4-1	1-1	6034	Bouchr,Gedds,Sxtn,Wilsn (At - St.John's Ln)	1		3	4	5	6	7		9	10	11	8		2					

FRIENDLIES

1	1 Sep	Swindon Town		2-0	0-0	3000	Whelan(2)	1	2	3	4		6	7	8	9	5	11		10						
2	16	LLANDUDNO SWIFTS		7-0	1-0		Boucher(2), Saxton(2), Wilson(2), Becton	1	2	3	4	5	6			8	9	10		11	7					
3	30 Dec	STOCKPORT COUNTY		3-2	0-2	1000	Becton, Draycott, Saxton	1	2	3	4					9		5	11	10	8			7	6	
4	27 Jan	Woolwich Arsenal		0-3	0-1	2000		1		3	4	5		7	8	9	6	11	10		2					

* Brighton United disbanded in March 1900, record expunged.

Note: Bedminster amalgamated with Bristol City at the end of the season.

BRISTOL SOUTH

SEASON 1891-92
FRIENDLIES

No.	Date	Opposition	Pos.	Res
1	3 Oct	ST. JOHNS		1-3
2	10	REDCLIFFE		0-3
3	7 Nov	FISHPONDS		
4	14	Bedminster Zion		
5	21	EASTVILLE ROVERS RES.		
6	28	BITTON		
7	5 Dec	Maudlin Street		
8	12	St. Johns		
9	19	Bedminster Res.		
10	26	BARTON HILL		
11	2 Jan	Warmley Church		1-3
12	9	Bedminster Res.		
13	16	Brislington		
14	23	BARTON HILL		1-1
15	30	ST. JOHNS		1-2
16	6 Feb	Clarence		
17	13	Bitton		2-1
18	20	UNITED PRESS		
19	27	Warmley Res.		
20	5 Mar	Brislington		3-1
21	12	MAUDLIN STREET		
22	19	Redcliffe		3-1
23	26	Fishponds		
24	2 Apr	St. Pauls		3-0
25	9	BEDMINSTER RES.		4-0

SEASON 1892-93
FRIENDLIES

No.	Date	Opposition	Pos.	Res
1	1 Oct	Barton Hill		1-5
2	15	Bitton		
3	5 Nov	MANGOTSFIELD RES.		
4	12	AVONDALE		
5	3 Dec	WAVERLEY		1-3
6	10	ST. PAULS		2-2
7	17	St. George Res.		
8	31	Mangotsfield Res.		
9	7 Jan	BITTON		
10	14	CLIFTON RES.		
11	28	BARTON HILL		
12	11 Feb	MANGOTSFIELD		
13	18	St. Johns		1-2
14	25	WAVERLEY RES.*		2-2
15	11 Mar	St. Pauls		
16	18	BRISLINGTON		
17	1 Apr	Warmley Res.		

GLOUCESTERSHIRE JUNIOR CUP

1R	22 Oct	Willsbridge**		1-2
1Rr	29	Willsbridge		2-3

* Combined Bristol South & St. Johns XI opposed Waverley Res.

** Unable to ascertain why the match was replayed.

SEASON 1893-94
SOUTH BRISTOL & DISTRICT LEAGUE (Champions)

No.	Date	Opposition	Pos.	Res
1	7 Oct	RADSTOCK		3-1
2	14	W.D. & H.O. Wills		6-0
3	28	BRISLINGTON		7-4
4	11 Nov	Bradford-on-Avon*		3-2
5	18	WILLSBRIDGE (Postponed)		
6	25	FRENCHAY		0-2
7	16 Dec	REDCLIFFE		2-0
8	30	W.D. & H.O. WILLS		2-1
9	13 Jan	BRADFORD-ON-AVON		8-0
10	20	Brislington		2-2
11	3 Feb	Radstock		3-2
12	10	WILLSBRIDGE		2-2
13	24	Bradford-on-Avon		3-3
14	3 Mar	Frenchay**		3-1
15	10	Redcliffe		3-0
16	17	Willsbridge		0-5
17	24	Frenchay#		

FRIENDLIES

1	4 Nov	ST. JOHNS		2-2
2	2 Dec	Wotton-u-Edge & Kingswood XI		
3	26	Melrose		
4	26 Mar	MELROSE		
5	31	ASHTON COURT ESTATE		1-1

* Abandoned due to poor light.   ** Ordered to be replayed.   # Adjudicated win.

SEASON 1894-95 BRISTOL SOUTH END

FRIENDLIES

No.	Date	Opposition	Pos.	Res.	H.T.	Att.	Goalscorers
1	1 Sep	SWINDON TOWN		2-4	2-2	3500	Fry, Unknown
2	8	SWINDON WANDERERS		11-0	2-0	1500	Fry(4), Lewis(4), Mayger, Walters, Unk'n
3	15	St. George		0-2	0-2	800	
4	22	EASTVILLE ROVERS		2-1	2-0		Clements, Mayger
5	29	MANGOTSFIELD		4-1	2-1	1500	Clements(2), Lewis, Quinlan
6	6 Oct	Swindon Athletic		2-1	0-0	300	Clements, Unknown
7	13	WELLS		4-0	1-0	1300	Clements(2), Mayger, Walters
8	20	CARDIFF		2-0	2-0		Lewis, Walters
9	27	Street		2-2	1-1	250	Hollister, Lewis
10	3 Nov	CALNE		3-0	2-0	1200	Cleak, Clements, Lewis
11	17	Burnham		1-0	0-0		Luffman
12	1 Dec	GLOUCESTERSHIRE XI		2-0	1-0	1000	Clements, A.Jones
13	8	SWINDON ATHLETIC		1-0	1-0	700	Walters
14	15	CLIFTON		2-4	2-3		Clements, Mayger
15	22	TROWBRIDGE TOWN		0-1			
16	26	GLOUCESTER		3-3	1-2	1200	Clements, Mayger, Unknown
17	27	ST. GEORGE		2-2	2-1	3500	Clements, Mayger
18	29	WARMLEY *		4-0	2-0	900	Binding(2), Clements, Stout
19	5 Jan	Cardiff		1-3	0-2	500	Lewis
20	26	Clevedon **		1-3	0-2	100	Unknown
21	23 Feb	Wells		3-2	2-2	200	Binding, Fry, Luffman
22	2 Mar	EASTVILLE ROVERS		2-5	0-3	600	Lewis(2)
23	9	STREET ***		2-3	2-2		Clements(2)
24	16	Calne		2-2	1-0		Hollister, Lewis
25	23	Bedminster		2-0	2-0	4000	Clements, Luffman
26	30	Staple Hill		2-1	0-1		Clements, Grey
27	6 Apr	PRESTON NORTH END		1-6	1-3	3500	Clements
28	10	STH.BRISTOL & DIST.LGE.XI		2-2	1-2		Clements, Davis
29	12	HEREFORD THISTLE		1-4	1-2	4000	Clements
30	13	LONDON WELSH		1-3	0-0	2000	Ricks
31	15	1st SCOTS GUARDS		0-1	0-1		
32	16	TOTTENHAM HOTSPUR		0-7	0-1	2000	
33	20	Cardiff		0-3	0-3		
34	27	EASTVILLE ROVERS		2-3	0-3		Davis, Unknown
35	29	BRISTOL & DIST.LGE. XI +		4-1	1-0	800	Mayger(2), Cleak, Lewis

Other Players - Friendlies: Chambers 20/9. Fulton R. 26/3, 27/3, 29/2, 30/2, 33/3, 34/3.
Millard F. 26/6, 27 to 31/4, 33 to 35/4. Vowles V.H. 29/6, 30/3. Dickenson 29/12†, 34/1. Calder 32/5. Cresswell 32/6. Crabbe 32/10. Elmes H. 33/2. Mercer 35/1   † Jackson injured, Dickenson allowed as substitute
* Warmley only fielded 10 players. ** South End only fielded 10 players. *** Played on Waverley ground (Knowle district of Bristol). + Benefit match for trainer J.Pavey

	P	W	D	L	F	A
Home	26	11	3	12	59	55
Away	9	4	2	3	14	15

F.A. AMATEUR CUP

2Q	10 Nov	HEREFORD THISTLE		2-4	1-2	800	Clements, Lewis

GLOUCESTERSHIRE CUP

1R	19 Jan	Mangotsfield		0-2	0-0	500	

BRISTOL SOUTH END 1894/95 Season. The side that met Swindon Town in the Club's first match - 1 September 1894.
(Players only L.toR.) Back: Taylor, Trestrail, Welham. Middle: Davis, A.Jones, G.E.Jones.
Front: Walters, Fry, Lewis, Clements, Mayger.

SEASON 1895-96 BRISTOL SOUTH END

FRIENDLIES

No.	Date	Opposition	Pos.	Res.	H.T.	Att.	Goalscorers
1	4 Sep	ST. PAULS		3-1	1-0		Grindley(2), Towle
2	7	SWINDON WANDERERS		4-1	2-0		Grindley(4)
3	14	Warmley		0-4	0-4		
4	21	HEREFORD TOWN		4-4	1-2	2000	Clements, Lewis, Unknown(2)
5	28	MANGOTSFIELD		5-0	1-0	1500	Macfarlane,(3), Clements, Lewis
6	19 Oct	EASTVILLE ROVERS		1-1	0-1	2000	Davis
7	26	CLIFTON		6-4	1-0	1200	Clements,Lewis,Macfarlane,Unk'n(3)
8	9 Nov	ROYAL ART.(Port'mth)		0-0	0-0	2000	
9	23	FREEMANTLE		0 1	0-0		
10	30	SWINDON WANDERERS		2-0	1-0	1200	Clements, Lewis
11	7 Dec	SEAFORTH HIGHLANDERS		4-3	2-1	1200	Welham(3), Binding
12	14	WELLS		5-2	1-2	500	Lewis(2), Clements, Grey, Macfarlane
13	21	ST. PAULS		5-0	3-0	1000	Clements(2), Mayger(2), Macfarlane
14	26	GLOUCESTER		4-1	4-1	500	Binding, Grindley, A.Jones, Millard
15	27	St. George		2-2	1-2	700	Clements, Davis
16	28	Bedminster		1-2	0-0	3000	Grindley
17	4 Jan	Eastville Rovers		0-3	0-1	2000	
18	11	BERWICK RANG'S.(Worcs.)		3-3	2-0	1700	Macfarlane(2), Millard
19	18	STAPLE HILL		1-0	0-0	1500	Macfarlane
20	1 Feb	SWINDON TOWN RES.		2-2	1-0	2000	Clements, Elmes
21	15 *	SOUTH END WEDS.		6-3	1-2		Binding, Hollister, Unknown(4)
22	22	READING AMATEURS		5-3	1-2		Binding(2), Millard, Unknown(2)
23	29	TROWBRIDGE TOWN		4-1	3-1	1500	Lewis(2), Elmes, Osborne
24	4 Mar	Clevedon **		0-4			
25	7	Midsomer Norton		1-0			Unknown
26	7	CLIFTON		3-1	1-1		Elmes, Lewis, Unknown
27	14	SMALL HEATH RES.		0-3	0-1	2000	
28	21	St. Pauls		3-0	0-0		Clayton(2), Welham
29	28	Trowbridge Town		0-0	0-0	800	
30	3 Apr	1st SCOTS GUARDS		0-3		3000	
31	4	WARMLEY		3-2	2-1	2000	Clements, Elmes, Unknown
32	7	BEDMINSTER		2-1	2-1	2500	Clements, O.G.
33	8	HEREFORD THISTLE		1-2	0-0	600	Adams
34	11	ST GEORGE		0-3	0-2	1000	
35	18	EASTVILLE ROVERS		1-0	0-0		Adams
36	25	MIDSOMER NORTON		1-2	0-1		Ford
37	30	SOUTH END ATHLETIC		***			

* Only 10 players each side. ** Score as given in the Bristol Evening News, but later doubts, allied to the club's seasonal record, suggests that this was not a South End match.

*** No record of score, seasonal summary suggests match did not take place.

	P	W	D	L	F	A
Home	28	17	5	6	75	47
Away	8	2	2	4	7	15

F.A. CUP

	Date		Res.	H.T.	Att.	Goalscorers
PR	5 Oct	SLOUGH	5-1	4-1	1000	Clements(3), Grindley, Mayger
1Q	12	GREAT MARLOW	0-1	0-1	2000	

F.A.AMATEUR CUP

	Date		Res.	H.T.		Goalscorers
2Q	2 Nov	Old Weymouthians	1-3	1-2		Mayger

GLOUCESTERSHIRE CUP

	Date		Res.	H.T.	Att.	
PR	25 Jan	Eastville Rovers	0-4	0-0	2000	

SEASON 1896-97 BRISTOL SOUTH END

WESTERN LEAGUE DIVISION ONE

No.	Date	Opposition	Pos.	Res.	H.T.	Att.	Goalscorers	Speck G.	Skelding	Sinden	Clements H.H.	Ross J.S.	Grey R.	Quinlan J.	Sharpe J.	Porter H.	Fielding F.B.	Smith W.	Cleak A.	Binding	Fielding A.	Robson E.	Hockin G.E.	Thompson W.	Frith A.P.	Millard F.	Lewis W.	Breaker	Andrews	Jones A.	Edwards A.R.	Taylor A.	Brown J.	Stout P.W.	Tucker	Painter	Fulton
1	19 Sep	STAPLE HILL		3-1	1-0		Clements, F.Fielding, Porter	1	2	3	4	5	6	7	8	9	10	11																			
2	26	Eastville Rovers	1	2-0	1-0	3000	Porter, Ross	1	2	3	4	5	6	7		8	10	11	9																		
3	24 Oct	TROWBRIDGE TOWN	1	3-0	1-0		A.Fielding, F.Fielding, Quinlan	1	2	3	8	5	6	7			10			9	4	11															
4	28 Nov	ST. GEORGE	2	2-1	0-1	2300	Smith, Unknown	1		3	4	5				9	11				10	2	6	7													
5	26 Dec	Bedminster	2	1-0	0-0		Smith	1		9	5			8				11			10	2	6	7	3	4											
6	28	Warmley	2	0-4	0-1	4464		1		6	4	5		8		9	11				10	2		7	3												
7	2 Jan	ST. PAULS	2	3-2	1-1		Ross, Unknown (2)	1		3	4	5	6			10	11	9				2		7			8										
8	9	EASTVILLE ROVERS	3	1-3	0-3		A.Fielding	1			4	5				10	11				9	2	6	7	3		8										
9	23	St. Pauls	2	4-1	3-1	500	Smith(2), A.Fielding, Quinlan	1			4	5		8		9		11			10		6		3				2	7							
10	6 Feb	St. George	3	1-2	1-2	1500	F.Fielding	1		9	4			7			10	11				2	6	8	3					5							
11	20	Clifton	2	3-1	2-1	1000	F.Fielding(2), A.Fielding	1		3	4			9				11			10	2	6	7		8				5							
12	6 Mar	Trowbridge Town	2	2-1	2-1		F.Fielding, Porter	1		4	9					8	10	11				2	6	7						5	3						
13	27	Staple Hill	2	1-0	1-0	600	Brown	1			4					8		9				2	6	7						5	3	10					
14	3 Apr	CLIFTON	2	1-0	1-0	2000	F.Fielding	1		3	4					8	10	11				2	6	7						5		9					
15	16	BEDMINSTER	2	1-3	1-0	3500	Unknown										P																				
16	24	WARMLEY	2	0-3	0-0	2500		1		2	4	9		8				11					6	7	3						5		10				
							Apps.	15	3	12	15	9	4	11	1	8	10	13	1	3	7	10	10	11	6	1	3	1	1	1	5	2	3				
							Goals			1	2	2		2		3	5	6			4												1				

Home 8 5 0 3 14 13
Away 8 6 0 2 14 9   (Final - Runners-up)

F.A. CUP

No.	Date	Opposition		Res.	H.T.	Att.	Goalscorers																														
1Q	10 Oct	BEDMINSTER		2-4	2-3	4500	A.Fielding, Smith	1	2	3	4	5	6	7		8	9	11			10																

F.A. AMATEUR CUP

No.	Date	Opposition		Res.	H.T.	Att.	Goalscorers																														
2Q	7 Nov	Bedminster		3-3	3-2	2500	F.Fielding, Ross, Stout	1		6	4	5				8	11				10	2		7	3									9			
2Qr	14	BEDMINSTER		2-1	1-0	1500	Smith, Thompson	1		3	4	5		8		9	10	11				2	6	7													
3Q	21	TROWBRIDGE TOWN		3-0	1-0		Thompson(2), Quinlan	1		3	4	5		8		9	11				10	2	6	7													
FQ	12 Dec	St. George		2-0	2-0		A.Fielding, F.Fielding	1		9	4	5		8			10				11	3	6		2	7											
1R	30 Jan	OLD CARTHUSIANS		0-10	0-2	1700		1			4	5		8		9	11				10	2	6	7	3												

GLOUCESTERSHIRE CUP

No.	Date	Opposition		Res.	H.T.	Att.	Goalscorers																														
2R	27 Feb	Fishponds		1-3	1-3	600	O.G.	1		3	4	5		9				11				10	6	7	2									8			

BRISTOL CHARITY CUP

No.	Date	Opposition		Res.	H.T.	Att.	Goalscorers																														
1R	20 Mar	EASTVILLE WANDERERS		4-1	1-1	2000	Quinlan(2), Brown, Thompson (£21-17-7)	1		3	9	4		8				11					6	7							5	2	10				
SF	20 Apr	ST. PAULS		2-1	1-0	1500	Brown, Thompson (£24)	1		3	4	5		8				11					8	7	2							9		10			
F	30	Warmley		1-2	0-1	2000	Unknown (£25) (played at Stapleton Road)	1		3	2	5		8		9		11					6	7	4							10					

FRIENDLIES

No.	Date	Opposition		Res.	H.T.	Att.	Goalscorers																														
1	5 Sep	BEDMINSTER		1-0	0-0	3000	Porter	1	2	3	10	5	4	6	8	9		11																7			
2	12	St. Pauls		1-2	0-2		Unknown	P																													
3	3 Oct	HORFIELD GARRISON		3-1	2-1		F.Fielding (2), A.Fielding	1	2	3	4	5	6	7		9	11		8	10																	
4	31	2nd GRENADIER GUARDS		1-1	1-1		A.Fielding	1		3	4	5		7		10	9		6	11	2		8														
5	5 Dec	Staple Hill		2-1	1-1		Porter, Quinlan	1		3	4	5		8		9		11			10	2	6	7													
6	19	KINGS OWN LANCASTER REG.		4-0	2-0		Thompson (2), A.Fielding, F.Fielding	1		9		5		8			11				10	2	6	7	3												4
7	16 Jan	Bedminster		3-1	0-0		Davis (2), Smith	1		2	4	5				9		11					6		3		8										
8	13 Feb	STAPLE HILL *		3-1	1-1		Niblett, Smith, Thompson	1													10		6	7		4	8				3						
9	13 Mar	1st SCOTS GUARDS		4-3	1-3	2500	Quinlan, Brown, Edwards	1		9	4			8				11					2	6	7						5	3	10				
10	10 Apr	GLOUCESTERSHIRE REG.		3-3	3-1		F.Fielding, Quinlan, Unknown	1		3	4	5		8			10	11					6	7													
11	17	VAMPIRES		0-2	0-1	1000		1		2	5			7			10	11		8			6		3	4							9				
12	19	BARKING WOODVILLE		1-0	1-0	2000	Porter	1		3	4	5		8		9		11					6	7			2						10				

* South End only fielded 10 players.

Additional players (Friendlies): Davis A. (7/7 & 10/9), Young (7/10), Barrett (8/2), Thompson A.(8/5), Niblett (8/9), Davis F.S. (10/2)

SEASON 1897-98 BRISTOL CITY

SOUTHERN LEAGUE DIVISION ONE

No.	Date	Opposition	Pos.	Res.	H.T.	Att.	Goalscorers	Monteith H.	Davy H.	Sinclair J.F.	Mann G.W.	Higgins W.	Hamilton A.J.	Wyllie T.G.	Carnelly A.	Caie A.	O'Brien P.	Russell J.	Jones W.	Talbot-Lewis A.E.	Clements H.H.	Milligan A.	Gibson	Callender	O'Brien J.	Smith W.
1	11 Sep	WOLVERTON & LNWR		7-1	6-1	4000	Caie(2), Carnelly(3), Higgins, Russell	1	2	3	4	5	6	7	8	9	10	11								
2	18	Millwall Athletic	2	6-2	2-1	6000	O'Brien(4), Caie, Carnelly	1	2	3	4	5	6	7	8	9	10	11								
3	2 Oct	Gravesend United	4	2-2	2-1	3000	Higgins(2)	1	2		4	5	6	7	8	3	10	11	9							
4	9	New Brompton	3	2-1	0-1	5000	Davy, Higgins	1	2		8	5	6	7		9	10	11		3	4					
5	23	NORTHFLEET	2	3-2	2-1	4000	Carnelly(2), Mann	1	2		4	5	6	7	8	9	10	11				3				
6	6 Nov	Chatham	3	0-0	0-0	5000		1	2		4	5	6	7	8	9	10	11				3				
7	13	Tottenham Hotspur	4	2-2	2-1	8000	Jones, O'Brien	1	2		4	5	6	7	8		10	11	9			3				
8	27	TOTTENHAM HOTSPUR	3	3-1	0-0	4000	Caie, Mann, O'Brien	1	2		4	5	6	7	8	9	10	11				3				
9	4 Dec	SHEPPEY UNITED	1	7-0	2-0	4000	Caie(3), Carnelly, Mann, Russell, Wyllie	1	2		4	5	6	7	8	9	10	11				3				
10	18	Swindon Town	2	2-2	1-0	4000	Caie, Russell	1	2		4	5	6	7	8	9	10	11				3				
11	1 Jan	Southampton	3	0-4	0-2	8000		1	2	3	6	5		7	9	4	10	11	8							
12	8	Reading	2	2-2	0-2	8000	Jones, Wyllie	1	2		4	5	6	7		9	10	11	8			3				
13	15	SOUTHAMPTON	1	5-2	1-1	12170	Caie(2), Carnelly, Russell, Wyllie	1	2		4	5	6	7	8	9	10	11				3				
14	22	CHATHAM	1	6-1	3-1	4500	Carnelly(4), Caie(2)	1		2	4	5	6	7	8	9	10	11				3				
15	5 Feb	Wolverton & LNWR	1	3-0	1-0	3000	Carnelly, Mann, Russell	1	2		4	5	6	7	8	9	10	11				3				
16	19	SWINDON TOWN	1	4-1	2-1	4000	Caie, Hamilton, Higgins, Mann	1	2		4	5	6	7	8	9	10	11				3				
17	5 Mar	Northfleet	1	4-1	1-1	1000	Mann(3), O'Brien	1			4	5	6		8	9	10	11	2	7		3				
18	12	READING	1	3-2	1-0	6000	Caie(2), Carnelly	1	4		7	5	6		8	9	10	11				3	2			
19	19	MILLWALL ATHLETIC	1	1-1	1-0	2100	Caie	1	2		7	5	6		8	9	10	11	4			3				
20	9 Apr	Sheppey United	2	0-2	0-1	1000		1	5	4	8		6		11	9		10		3		7	2			
21	16	NEW BROMPTON	2	1-1	1-1	4000	Carnelly	1	2	6	7	10	5		8	9		11	4			3				
22	20	GRAVESEND UNITED	2	4-0	0-0	2000	Caie, Carnelly, Higgins, Russell	1	2	6	8	7	5		10	9		11	4				3			
							Apps.	22	20	7	22	21	21	16	20	21	19	22	8	3	1	16	3			
							Goals		1		8	6	1	3	15	18	7	6	2							

	P.	W.	D.	L.	F.	A.	
Home	11	9	2	0	44	15	
Away	11	4	5	2	23	18	(Final - Runners-up)

WESTERN LEAGUE (PROFESSIONAL SECTION) (Champions)

No.	Date	Opposition	Pos.	Res.	H.T.	Att.	Goalscorers	Monteith H.	Davy H.	Sinclair J.F.	Mann G.W.	Higgins W.	Hamilton A.J.	Wyllie T.G.	Carnelly A.	Caie A.	O'Brien P.	Russell J.	Jones W.	Talbot-Lewis A.E.	Clements H.H.	Milligan A.	Gibson	Callender	O'Brien J.	Smith W.
1	6 Oct	SWINDON TOWN		3-3	3-2	1500	Wyllie(2), Caie	1	2		4	5	6	7	8	9		11	10	3						
2	13	EASTVILLE ROVERS		4-0	1-0	3000	Carnelly(2), Caie, Wyllie	1	2		4	5	6	7	8	9	10	11		3						
3	27	Bristol St. George	2	2-0	0-0	3000	Caie, Russell	1	2	3	8	5	6	7		9	10	11				4				
4	20 Nov	READING	2	4-2	1-1	4500	Caie, Hamilton, Wyllie, O.G.	1	2		4	5	6	7	8	9	10	11				3				
5	11 Dec	Reading	2	1-2	1-0	4000	Wyllie	1	2		4	5	6	7	8	9	10	11				3				
6	27	Warmley	2	5-2	3-0	7000	Hamilton, Jones, O'Brien, Russell, Wyllie	1	2		6		5	7	9	4	10	11	8			3				
7	5 Jan	BRISTOL ST. GEORGE	1	3-0	1-0	1000	O'Brien(2), Caie	1	2		6	3	5	7	4	9	10	11	8							
8	26	EASTLEIGH	1	14-1	8-1	1000	Jons(4),Crnlly(2),Hggngs(2),Wlle(2),Caie,Hmltn,Rssll,OG	1			4	5	6	7	8	9		11	10	3		2				
9	2 Mar	Eastleigh	1				Opponents scratched, City awarded points.																			
10	16	Eastville Rovers	1	3-2	1-1	4000	O'Brien, Russell, Wyllie	1		2			6	7	8	9	10	11	4			3	5			
11	6 Apr	Trowbridge Town	1	5-1	5-0	2000	O'Brien(2), Caie, Jones, Mann	1	2	4	7	5	6			9	10	11	8				3			
12	8	WARMLEY	1	3-2	3-0	10000	Carnelly, Higgins, Wyllie	1	2			5	6	7	8	9	10	11	4				3			
13	13	Swindon Town	1	0-1	0-1	2000		1	5		8	10	6			9		11	4	2		7	3			
14	18	TROWBRIDGE TOWN	1	4-0	1-0	2000	Carnelly(2), Mann, Milligan	1	2	6	8	7	5		10	9		11	4			3				

F.A. CUP

Rd.	Date	Opposition		Res.	H.T.	Att.	Goalscorers	Monteith H.	Davy H.	Sinclair J.F.	Mann G.W.	Higgins W.	Hamilton A.J.	Wyllie T.G.	Carnelly A.	Caie A.	O'Brien P.	Russell J.	Jones W.	Talbot-Lewis A.E.	Clements H.H.	Milligan A.	Gibson	Callender	O'Brien J.	Smith W.
1Q	25 Sep	CLIFTON		9-1	5-1	1000	Carnelly(4), Wyllie(4), O'Brien	1	2	3	4	5	6	7	8	9	10	11								
2Q	16 Oct	Trowbridge Town		5-2	3-2	2000	Higgins(3), Caie, Carnelly	1	2		4	5	6	7	8	9	10	11		3						
3Q	30	Southampton		0-2	0-1	10000		1	5	3	4		6	7	9	2	10	11						8		

GLOUCESTERSHIRE CUP

Rd.	Date	Opposition		Res.	H.T.	Att.	Goalscorers	Monteith H.	Davy H.	Sinclair J.F.	Mann G.W.	Higgins W.	Hamilton A.J.	Wyllie T.G.	Carnelly A.	Caie A.	O'Brien P.	Russell J.	Jones W.	Talbot-Lewis A.E.	Clements H.H.	Milligan A.	Gibson	Callender	O'Brien J.	Smith W.
2R	26 Feb	EASTVILLE ROVERS		2-0	2-0	6400	Jones, Russell (£170)	1	2		4	5	6		8	9	10	11	7			3				
SF	26 Mar	Bristol St. George		1-1	1-0	3500	Carnelly (Played at The Chequers) (£68)	1	2	6		7	5		8	9	10	11	4			3				
SFr	31	Bristol St. George		2-0	1-0	2000	Caie, Mann(pen) (At Ashton Gate) (£40)	1	2	6	7		5		8	9	10	11	4			3				
F	11 Apr	Warmley		2-1	2-0	11186	Caie, Higgins (At Stapleton Road) (£348.6.3)	1	2	6	7	8	5		10	9		11	4			3				

BRISTOL CHARITY CUP

Rd.	Date	Opposition		Res.	H.T.	Att.	Goalscorers	Monteith H.	Davy H.	Sinclair J.F.	Mann G.W.	Higgins W.	Hamilton A.J.	Wyllie T.G.	Carnelly A.	Caie A.	O'Brien P.	Russell J.	Jones W.	Talbot-Lewis A.E.	Clements H.H.	Milligan A.	Gibson	Callender	O'Brien J.	Smith W.
1R	15 Dec	EASTLEIGH		10-3	4-1	800	Wyllie(3),Caie(2),Carnelly(2),O'Brien(2),Russell	1	2		4	5	6	7	8	9	10	11				3				
2R	21 Feb	WARMLEY		0-1	0-1	500		1	2		4	5	6	7	8	3	10	11	9							

FRIENDLIES

No.	Date	Opposition		Res.	H.T.	Att.	Goalscorers	Monteith H.	Davy H.	Sinclair J.F.	Mann G.W.	Higgins W.	Hamilton A.J.	Wyllie T.G.	Carnelly A.	Caie A.	O'Brien P.	Russell J.	Jones W.	Talbot-Lewis A.E.	Clements H.H.	Milligan A.	Gibson	Callender	O'Brien J.	Smith W.
1	1 Sep	SOUTHAMPTON		3-1	3-0	600	Caie, Carnelly, Higgins	1	2	3	4	5	6	7	8	9	10	11								
2	4	SWINDON TOWN		3-1	1-1	4000	O'Brien(2), Carnelly	1	2	3	4	5	6	7	8	9	10	11								
3	6	CHORLEY		6-2	3-2	2000	Caie(2), Wyllie(2), Mann, Russell	1		3	4	5	6	7	8	9	10	11		2						
4	20	BURTON SWIFTS		2-2	1-0	1500	Carnelly, Wyllie	1	2	5			6	7	8	9	10	11		3	4					
5	29	1ST SCOTS GUARDS		7-0	7-0	100	Carnelly(3), Caie, Callender, Hamilton,Wyllie	1	2		5		6	7	8	9		11		3	4			10		
6	15 Nov	WOOLWICH ARSENAL		4-2	2-1	3000	Carnelly, O'Brien, Russell, Wyllie	1	2		4	5	6	7	8	9	10	11				3				
7	20 Dec	LUTON TOWN		3-2	2-1	1000	Caie, Carnelly, Wyllie	1	2	4	11	5	6	7	8	9			10			3				
8	25	MIDDLETON		5-1	4-0	4500	Caie(2), Higgins, O'Brien, Wyllie		6	2		5	4	7	8	9	10	11		1		3				
9	29 Jan	LOUGHBOROUGH TWN		6-1	2-0	2000	O'Brien(3), Higgins, Mann, O.G.	1			4	5	6	7	9	2	10	11	8			3				
10	9 Feb	BEDMINSTER		9-2	5-0	2000	Carnelly(4), Caie(2), O'Brien(2), Wyllie	1	2		4	5	6	7	8	9	10	11				3				
11	12	NOTTS COUNTY		2-2	1-1	4000	Mann, Unknown	1			4	5	6	7	9	2	10	11	8			3				
12	21 Mar	Woolwich Arsenal		1-3	1-1	5000	Higgins	1	2	4	7	11	6		8	9		10				3	5			
13	28	Luton Town		1-5	0-4	1000	Mann		2	3	7		5		10	9			4	1			6		8	11
14	2 Apr	DARWEN		5-1	2-0	3000	O'Brien(3), Caie, Mann	1	5		7		6			9	10	11	4	3			2		8	
15	12	CORINTHIANS		1-3	0-1	5000	Carnelly	1		6	5	10			8	9		11	4	2		7	3			
16	23	WEST BROMWICH ALBIO		1-1	1-0	3000	Mann(pen)	1		6	8	7	5		10	9		11	4			3	2			
17	30	BURSLEM PORT VALE		2-0	1-0	1500	Higgins, Mann	1	2		9	5	6		8	7	10	11	4			3				

DAVEY.   HOLLIS (trainer).   MONTEITH.   [Photo, G. H. Wick.
MANN.   HIGGINS (capt.)   SINCLAIR,   HAMILTON.
WYLLIE,   CARNELLY,   CAIE,   O'BRIEN,   RUSSELL.

BRISTOL CITY 1897/98 Season
(Prior to the opening Southern League match v. Wolverton 11 September 1897.

New Photo by Taylor & Co., Baldwin Street, special for "Magpie."   [Copyright.]

Batten.   Britton.   Davey.   Monteith.   Hollies.   Caie.   Stewart.   Mann.
Potter.   Barker.   Jones.   McLean.   Hamilton.   Murphy.
Langham.   Carnelly.   Finnerham.   Stevenson.   O'Brien.   Russell.

1898/99 Season

SEASON 1898-99 BRISTOL CITY
SOUTHERN LEAGUE DIVISION ONE

Player columns (left to right): Monteith H., Baker G., Davy H., Jones W., Hamilton A.J., Stewart W.S., Langham W., Finnerhan F.P., Caie A., O'Brien P., Russell J., McLean J.C, Mann G.W., Murphy J., Potter A., Milligan A., Carnelly A., Stevenson J., Britton P., Gard, Giddings

No.	Date	Opposition	Pos.	Res.	H.T.	Att.	Goalscorers
1	17 Sep	Millwall Athletic		1-1	0-1	10000	Caie
2	8 Oct	WARMLEY*	9	4-2	1-0	5000	Caie, Finnerhan, Russell, O.G.
3	22	CHATHAM	8	2-1	2-1	4000	Finnerhan, Mann
4	5 Nov	SWINDON TOWN	7	4-2	3-1	4000	Caie(2), Langham, Russell
5	26	Reading	6	1-0	0-0	4000	Finnerhan
6	3 Dec	TOTTENHAM HOTSPUR	5	2-1	1-1	6000	Langham, Russell
7	17	BEDMINSTER	4	5-2	1-1	10250	Carnelly(2), Finnerhan, Russell, O.G.
8	24	Gravesend United	4	2-2	1-1	1500	Russell, O.G.
9	7 Jan	New Brompton	4	1-0	1-0	3000	Russell
10	11	Brighton United	4	1-2	0-2	800	Langham
11	14	MILLWALL ATHLETIC	4	2-1	1-0	5000	Carnelly, Langham
12	21	Chatham	4	0-2	0-1	3000	
13	1 Feb	SHEPPEY UNITED	4	4-1	3-0	1500	Carnelly, Finnerhan, Langham, Potter
14	4	Swindon Town	4	2-2	1-1	3000	Langham(2)
15	11	GRAVESEND UNITED	2	5-2	3-2	4000	Carnelly, Finnerhan, Langham, Potter, Russell
16	18	Tottenham Hotspur	2	2-3	0-1	8000	Caie(pen), Finnerhan
17	4 Mar	Bedminster	4	0-1	0-0	7000	
18	11	Southampton	4	1-4	0-1	6000	Langham
19	18	Royal Artillery (Portsmouth)	4	3-0	0-0	4000	Carnelly, Finnerhan, Murphy
20	25	READING	3	1-0	1-0	4000	O'Brien
21	8 Apr	BRIGHTON UNITED	3	3-1	1-1	3000	McLean, O'Brien, Stevenson
22	12	ROYAL ART.(PORTSM'TH)	2	6-1	4-1	1000	Stevenson(4), Carnelly(2)
23	15	Sheppy United	2	2-0	1-0	1000	Hamilton, Langham
24	22	NEW BROMPTON	1	2-0	1-0	6000	Carnelly, O'Brien
25	29	SOUTHAMPTON	2	3-4	2-0	13000	Langham(2), Caie

Apps. 23 19 13 23 24 19 24 22 18 9 24 21 3 5 6 1 15 5 1
Goals 1 12 8 6 3 7 1 1 1 2 9 5

	P.	W.	D.	L.	F.	A.	
Home	13	12	0	1	43	18	
Away	12	4	3	5	16	17	(Final - Runners-up)

UNITED LEAGUE (Fifth)

No.	Date	Opposition	Pos.	Res.	H.T.	Att.	Goalscorers
1	10 Sep	KETTERING		3-0	0-0	4000	Finnerhan, Langham, Mann
2	21	BRIGHTON UNITED		4-0	2-0	2000	Caie(2), Finnerhan, O'Brien
3	28	Reading	1	2-1	0-0	1500	Caie, Potter
4	1 Oct	WELLINGBOROUGH	1	2-1	2-1	4000	Caie, Russell
5	15	TOTTENHAM HOTSPUR	2	0-1	0-1	8000	
6	26	Brighton United	2	1-2	0-1	2000	McLean
7	9 Nov	WOOLWICH ARSENAL	5	1-2	1-1	2250	Langham
8	12	Tottenham Hotspur	5	1-2	1-2	8000	Finnerhan
9	30	LUTON TOWN	4	6-0	0-0	1000	Russell(2), Caie, Finnerhan, Mann, Murphy
10	12 Dec	Woolwich Arsenal	5	3-1	2-1	3000	Caie, Finnerhan, Murphy
11	4 Jan	Southampton	5	0-6	0-4	3000	
12	16	Wellingborough	6	0-3	0-3	5000	
13	8 Feb	RUSHDEN	6	3-0	0-0	1000	Caie, Jones, O'Brien
14	22	MILLWALL ATHLETIC	6	2-3	1-3	2000	Gard, Russell
15	27	Luton Town	6	3-1	1-0	500	Murphy(2), Gard
16	8 Mar	READING	4	5-1	3-0	1500	Potter(3), Carnelly, Murphy
17	16	Millwall Athletic	5	1-4	0-1	3000	Carnelly
18	1 Apr	Kettering	6	3-0	1-0	1000	Stevenson(3)
19	19	SOUTHAMPTON	4	2-1	2-0	3000	Caie(2)
20	24	Rushden	5	1-2	0-0	500	Carnelly

F.A. CUP

	Date	Opposition		Res.	H.T.	Att.	Goalscorers
3Q	29 Oct	Cowes		5-0	2-0	2000	Caie, Finnerhan, Langham, O'Brien, Russell
4Q	19 Nov	Bristol St. George		1-0	1-0	11228	Finnerhan (£347.5.6)
5Q	10 Dec	READING		3-2	2-1	6000	Caie(2,1pen), Langham
1R	28 Jan	SUNDERLAND		2-4	2-3	16945	Finnerhan, Langham (£524.1.6)

GLOUCESTERSHIRE CUP

	Date	Opposition		Res.	H.T.	Att.	Goalscorers
1R	20 Feb	BRISTOL AMATEURS		7-3	1-2	1000	O'Brien(4), Caie, Carnelly, Langham
SF	22 Mar	FISHPONDS		8-1	3-0	1500	Carnelly(2), O'Brien(2), Russell(2), Jones, Murphy
F	3 Apr	Bristol Rovers		2-1	0-0	11433	Langham, Murphy (AOt Bell Hill) (£356.1.9)

FRIENDLIES

	Date	Opposition		Res.	H.T.	Att.	Goalscorers
1	1 Sep	Eastville Rovers		0-1	0-0	3500	
2	3	West Norwood		4-3	0-1		Mann(2), Jones, O'Brien
3	7	NEW BRIGHTON TOWER		4-0	0-0	1000	Hamilton, Mann, O'Brien, Potter
4	24	BRISTOL ST. GEORGE		2-1	2-0	5000	Caie, Murphy
5	31 Oct	Ryde		3-1	2-1		Caie, Langham, Potter
6	10 Nov	Corinthians **		1-1	1-0	1500	O'Brien (Played at Queens Club)
7	26 Dec	Notts County		4-2	2-0	8000	Carnelly, Finnerhan, Murphy, Russell
8	27	Bristol St. George		1-9	1-4	3500	Caie
9	31	BRSTL EASTVILLE ROVERS		2-3	1-0	5000	Murphy, O'Brien
10	25 Feb	BURNLEY		2-1	2-1	5000	Carnelly, McLean
11	31 Mar	STOCKTON		3-0	1-0	5000	O'Brien(2), Potter
12	4 Apr	CORINTHIANS #		4-3	1-3	4000	Russell(2), O'Brien, Stevenson

* Warmley disbanded in January 1899 and their record was expunged.

** Abandoned after 75 minutes due to failing light and mist.

\# Only 40 minutes each way played.

Note: Bristol Rovers commenced the season as 'Eastville Rovers', changing to Bristol Eastville Rovers early on in the campaign and finally adopting their current title on February 18th 1899.

SEASON 1899-1900   BRISTOL CITY
SOUTHERN LEAGUE DIVISION ONE

Player columns (left to right): Monteith H., Milligan A., Stewart W.S., Jones W., McLean J.C., Hamilton A.J., Langham W., Molyneux F., Caie A., Downie A.L.B., Crawford A., Godsman A., O'Brien P., Russell J., McDonald A., Britton P., Potter A., Watts J., Thompson W., Robson D.J., Blessington J., Pollock R., Goldie E., Talbot-Lewis A.E., Leslie H., Osborne R., Marks, O'Brien J.

No.	Date	Opposition	Pos.	Res.	H.T.	Att.	Goalscorers
1	2 Sep	SWINDON TOWN		3-2	3-1	6000	Caie(2), Downie
2	16	Cowes*	5	5-1	2-0	1500	Crawford(2), O'Brien(2), Caie
3	23	SOUTHAMPTON	7	1-3	0-2	6000	Caie(pen)
4	30	Millwall	9	1-3	0-2	6000	Langham
5	7 Oct	QUEENS PARK RANGERS	9	5-3	3-1	7500	Caie(2), Langham(2), Russell
6	14	Chatham	8	2-2	2-2	4000	Caie, Langham
7	21	READING	7	1-2	1-0	5000	Jones
8	28	Sheppey United	7	0-0	0-0	1200	
9	4 Nov	BRIGHTON UNITED*	5	3-2	2-1	2000	Caie(2), Potter
10	11	Bedminster	6	1-1	0-1	5500	O.G.
11	18	COWES*	3	5-0	3-0	2000	Blessington(3), Caie, Langham
12	25	Portsmouth	7	0-2	0-1	6000	
13	2 Dec	THAMES IRONWORKS	5	2-0	1-0	5000	Blessington, Caie
14	9	Tottenham Hotspur	3	2-2	0-1	6000	Crawford, Russell
15	16	NEW BROMPTON	3	2-1	1-0	3500	Crawford, Jones
16	23	Gravesend United	5	2-2	2-2	2000	Blessington, Langham
17	26	BRISTOL ROVERS	4	1-0	0-0	7000	Britton
18	30	Swindon Town	4	1-2	0-2	2500	Jones
19	3 Feb	MILLWALL	10	0-2	0-2	2000	
20	17	CHATHAM	10	4-1	3-1	2000	Blessington, Jones, Langham, O'Brien
21	24	Reading	12	0-3	0-1	3000	
22	3 Mar	SHEPPEY UNITED	10	5-1	2-0	2500	Jones(4), Potter
23	5	Queens Park Rangers	8	1-1	0-1	1000	O'Brien
24	10	Brighton United*	7	1-0	1-0	1200	Jones
25	17	BEDMINSTER	8	0-2	0-2	5000	
26	31	PORTSMOUTH	10	3-6	1-4	4000	Jones(2), Blessington
27	7 Apr	Thames Ironworks	8	0-0	0-0	5000	
28	13	Bristol Rovers	10	0-1	0-1	10000	
29	14	TOTTENHAM HOTSPUR	8	3-0	1-0	5000	Jones, Langham, O'Brien
30	21	New Brompton	11	0-1	0-0	1200	
31	23	Southampton	12	1-4	0-2	200	Jones
32	28	GRAVESEND UNITED	9	3-0	1-0	2000	Jones(2), O'Brien

Apps. 30 2 4 31 30 31 29 3 16 23 25 8 11 9 23 7 10 1 2 22 21 7 6 1
Goals 15 8 11 1 4 6 2 1 2 7

```
                P.  W.  D.  L.  F.  A.
Home           14   9   0   5  33  23
Away           14   0   7   7  11  24   (Final- Ninth)
```

* Clubs disbanded during the season, Cowes in December 1899 and Brighton United in March 1900. In both instances their records were expunged.

SOUTHERN DISTRICT COMBINATION (Sixth)

No.	Date	Opposition	Pos.	Res.	H.T.	Att.	Goalscorers
1	13 Sep	Reading		4-2	2-1	1500	Caie(3), Crawford
2	4 Oct	CHATHAM	2	5-1	2-0	1000	O'Brien(2), Downie, Langham, Russell
3	30	Woolwich Arsenal	5	0-3	0-0	3000	
4	15 Nov	TOTTENHAM HOTSPUR	5	3-3	2-2	3000	Langham(2), Jones
5	22	Southampton		1-5	0-2	2000	Langham
6	29	PORTSMOUTH	6	1-3	0-1	1000	Crawford
7	25 Dec	MILLWALL		1-3	0-2	6000	Caie(pen)
8	10 Jan	WOOLWICH ARSENAL	7	1-3	0-1	2000	Russell
9	17	Chatham	8	0-3	0-0	500	
10	28 Feb	SOUTHAMPTON	7	4-1	3-1	1000	Jones, Langham, O'Brien, Robson
11	12 Mar	Tottenham Hotspur	8	0-2	0-1	3000	
12	21	READING	6	3-1	3-1	1000	Jones(2), Pollock
13	26	Queens Park Rangers	6	0-0	0-0	500	
14	28	Portsmouth	6	0-0	0-0	1000	
15	4 Apr	QUEENS PARK RANGERS	6	2-1	2-0	1000	O'Brien, Potter
16	16	Millwall	6	0-1	0-1	5000	

WESTERN LEAGUE (PROFESSIONAL SECTION) (Fourth)

No.	Date	Opposition	Pos.	Res.	H.T.	Att.	Goalscorers
1	20 Sep	Swindon Town	4	0-1	0-1		
2	1 Nov	Bristol Rovers	4	0-2	0-0		
3	6 Dec	BEDMINSTER	3	8-1	3-1	2000	Russell(5), Jones(2), Blessington
4	13	SWINDON TOWN	1	3-1	2-0		Potter(2), Jones
5	7 Mar	Bedminster	4	1-4	1-2	4000	Langham
6	25 Apr	BRISTOL ROVERS	4	0-3	0-2	4000	

F.A. CUP

	Date	Opposition		Res.	H.T.	Att.	Goalscorers
1R	27 Jan	STALYBRIDGE ROVERS		2-1	2-1	5000	Blessington, Jones (£131)
2R	10 Feb	Aston Villa		1-5	1-3	16000	Jones (£533)

GLOUCESTERSHIRE CUP

	Date	Opposition		Res.	H.T.	Att.	Goalscorers
SF	2 Apr	Bristol Rovers		1-1	1-0	3000	O'Brien
SFr	9	BRISTOL ROVERS		2-1	2-1	2000	Blessington, O'Brien
F	30	Bedminster		1-3	0-2	1975	Russell (Played at Stapleton Road) (£61.9.3)

BRISTOL CHARITY CUP

	Date	Opposition		Res.	H.T.	Att.	Goalscorers
SF	13 Jan	Bedminster		1-1	1-1	4200	McLean (£110)
SFr	21 Feb	BEDMINSTER		0-6	0-3	2000	

FRIENDLIES

No.	Date	Opposition		Res.	H.T.	Att.	Goalscorers
1	6 Sep	BRISTOL ROVERS		0-2	0-1		
2	9	DEVON COUNTY XI		3-1	1-0		Langham(3)
3	23 Nov	Ryde		1-0			Jones
4	1 Jan	KAFFIRS		6-5	3-1	3000	Unknown (6)
5	6	BRISTOL ROVERS		2-0	0-0		Jones, Potter
6	24 Mar	Corinthians		0-3	0-2	1000	(Played at Queens Club)
7	17 Apr	CORINTHIANS		2-1	1-0	1000	Crawford, Goldie

SEASON 1900-01
SOUTHERN LEAGUE DIVISION ONE

No.	Date	Opposition	Pos.	Res.	H.T.	Att.	Goalscorers	Tcone G.	Bach P.	Davies R.H.	Jones W.	Wilson H.	Chambers P.	Whelan M.	Stevenson J.	Michael W.	Fulton W.	Nichol D.	O'Brien P.	McDougall D.	McLean J.C.	Robson D.J.	Geddes A.J.	Wadlock W.J.	Nicholls	Bartlett E.	Harding	Marsh R.	Brooks
1	1 Sep	Swindon Town		1-0	0-0	4000	Whelan	1	2	3	4	5	6	7	8	9	10	11											
2	8	WATFORD	1	6-1	3-0	7000	Michael(5,2pens), Fulton	1	2	3	4	5	6			8	9	10	11	7									
3	15	Luton Town	6	0-2	0-0	3000		1	2	3	4	5	6			8	9	10	7		11								
4	22	TOTTENHAM HOTSPUR *	6	1-1	0-0	10000	Michael(pen)	1	2	3	4	5	6	7	8	9	10	11											
5	29	West Ham United	3	2-1	1-0	5000	Fulton, Michael	1	2	3	4	8	6	7		9	10	11			5								
6	6 Oct	PORTSMOUTH	2	3-2	3-1	6000	Fulton, Michael, Wilson	1	2	3	4	8	6	7		9	10	11			5								
7	13	New Brompton	2	1-1	0-0	2500	Wilson	1	2	3	4	8	6	7		9	10	11			5								
8	20	BRISTOL ROVERS *	2	1-0	0-0	15500	Michael	1	2	3	4	8	6	7		9	10	11			5								
9	27	Reading	2	1-0	0-0	3000	Jones	1	2	3	4	11	6	7	8	9	10				5								
10	7 Nov	KETTERING TOWN *	1	6-0	3-0	2000	Michael(2), Fulton, Stevenson, Whelan, Wilson	1	2		4	11	6	7	8	9	10				5	3							
11	10	Gravesend United	1	3-1	2-1	1000	Michael(2), McLean	1	2	3	4	11	6	7	8	9	10				5								
12	17	MILLWALL *	1	7-1	4-1	6000	O'Brien(3), Stevenson(2), McLean, Whelan	1	2	3		4	6	7	8		9		10		5		11						
13	24	Southampton	1	1-2	1-1	8000	McLean	1	2	3		4	6	7	8		9		10		5		11						
14	1 Dec	CHATHAM **	1	4-0	3-0	4000	Fulton, Michael, Stevenson, Wilson	1	2	6	4	7				8	9	10			5	3	11						
15	8	Chatham **	1	4-1	2-1	1500	Geddes(3), McLean	1	2	3	4	8	6	7		9	10				5		11						
16	15	SWINDON TOWN *	1	2-0	1-0	5000	Fulton, Wilson	1	2	3	4	8	6	7		9	10				5		11						
17	22	Watford	1	0-0	0-0	2000	(Abandoned after 75 minutes due to fog)	1	2	3	4	8	6	7		9	10				5		11						
18	29	LUTON TOWN	1	1-0	0-0	4000	Stevenson	1	2	3	4	10	6	7	8	9					5		11						
19	12 Jan	WEST HAM UNITED *	1	1-0	0-0	2500	Michael	1		3	4	7	6			8	9	10			11	5	2						
20	19	Portsmouth	2	0-4	0-2	7500		1	2	3	4	7	6			8	9	10			11	5							
21	9 Feb	QUEENS PARK RANGERS *	2	2-0	1-0	5000	Fulton, O'Brien	1	2	3	4	7	6			8	9		10		5		11						
22	16	READING	2	1-0	0-0	7000	Geddes	1	2	3	4	7	6			8	9		10		5		11						
23	27	NEW BROMPTON *	2	2-0	2-0	1500	Stevenson, Wilson	1	2	3	4	10	6			8	9				7	5	11						
24	2 Mar	GRAVESEND UNITED	1	6-0	3-0	4000	Wilson(3), McLean(2), O'Brien	1	2	3	4	9	6	7	8				10	11	5								
25	9	Millwall	2	0-4	0-2	3000		1	2	3		9	6	7	8				10	11	4		5						
26	16	SOUTHAMPTON *	2	1-1	0-0	10500	Whelan	1	2	3	4	11	6	7	8		9		10		5								
27	23	Queens Park Rangers	2	0-2	0-2	5000		1	2	3	4	10	6	7	8		9			11				5					
28	6 Apr	Tottenham Hotspur	3	0-1	0-0	4500		1	2	3	4	9	6			8			10	7	5		11						
29	8	Bristol Rovers	2	1-1	0-1	10000	McDougall	1		3	4	2	6			9			10	7	5		11			8			
30	17	Watford	2	3-1	2-1	2000	Bartlett, McDougall, Stevenson	1	2	3	4	6				9			8	7	5		11				10		
31	22	Kettering Town	2	1-1	1-0	2000	Fulton	1	2	3	4	9	6			8		10			7	5	11						
							Apps.	31	29	30	28	31	29	19	24	18	25	8	11	11	26	3	14	1		1	2		
							Goals				1	9		4	7	15	8		5	2	6		4			1			

```
          P.  W.  D.  L.  F.  A.
Home     14  12   2   0  40   6
Away     14   5   3   6  14  21   (Final - Runners-up)
```

** Chatham disbanded on December 20th 1900 and their record was expunged.

WESTERN LEAGUE (PROFESSIONAL SECTION) (Fifth)

No.	Date	Opposition	Pos.	Res.	H.T.	Att.	Goalscorers	Tcone G.	Bach P.	Davies R.H.	Jones W.	Wilson H.	Chambers P.	Whelan M.	Stevenson J.	Michael W.	Fulton W.	Nichol D.	O'Brien P.	McDougall D.	McLean J.C.	Robson D.J.	Geddes A.J.	Wadlock W.J.	Nicholls	Bartlett E.	Harding	Marsh R.	Brooks
1	14 Nov	SOUTHAMPTON		4-1	2-0	5000	Fulton(2), O'Brien, Stevenson	1	2	3		4	6	7	8		9		10	11	5								
2	26	Tottenham Hotspur	2	1-4	0-1	3000	Fulton	1	2	6		4		7	8		9		10		5	3	11						
3	25 Dec	READING*	5	0-1	0-0	5000		1	2		4		6	7	8	9			10	11	5	3							
4	26	Bristol Rovers	5	1-1	0-0	10000	McLean	1	2	3	4	10	6	7	8	9					5		11						
5	26 Jan	PORTSMOUTH	6	2-2	0-2	2000	Jones, Wilson(pen)	1		3	9	4	6	7	8				10	11	5	2							
6	13 Feb	Portsmouth	7	0-3	0-0	2000		1	2	3	4	7	6			8	9		10		5		11						
7	18	Queens Park Rangers	5	2-0	1-0	1000	Fulton(2)	1		3		2	6			8	9		10	7	4		11	5					
8	27 Mar	TOTTENHAM HOTSPUR	6	4-1	1-0		Wilson(3), Fulton	1	2	3	4	9	6	7	8		10			11	5								
9	30	SWINDON TOWN	4	4-0	3-0	2500	Fulton, McDougall, O'Brien, Whelan	1		3	4	2	6	7	8		9		10	11	5								
10	1 Apr	Southampton	5	1-2	0-2		Fulton	1		3	4	2	6	7	8		9		10	11	5								
11	5	BRISTOL ROVERS*	4	3-0	3-0	8000	Jones, O'Brien, Stevenson	1	2	3	4	9	6	7	8				10		5		11						
12	9	QUEENS PARK RANGERS	4	2-2	1-2		McDougall, O'Brien	1		3	4	2	6			9			10	7	5		11			8			
13	13	Reading	4	2-2	1-1	200	Fulton, Jones	1			4	2	6			8	9		10	7	5		11					3	
14	20	MILLWALL*	5	0-1	0-1			1	2		4	6				9			8	7	5		11				10	3	
15	24	Swindon Town	5	1-0	1-0		Fulton	1	2		4	3	6			9		10		8	7	5	11						
16	27	Millwall	5	0-4	0-3	5000		1	2		4	3	6			8		9		10	7	5	11						

F.A. CUP

Rd	Date	Opposition		Res.	H.T.	Att.	Goalscorers	Tcone G.	Bach P.	Davies R.H.	Jones W.	Wilson H.	Chambers P.	Whelan M.	Stevenson J.	Michael W.	Fulton W.	Nichol D.	O'Brien P.	McDougall D.	McLean J.C.	Robson D.J.	Geddes A.J.
1R	5 Jan	Reading		1-1	1-1	8000	Fulton (£219)	1	2	3	4	10	6	7	8		9				5		11
1Rr	9	READING		0-0	0-0	3000	(Extra time, stopped after 110 mins, bad light)	1	2	3	4	8	6	7		9	10				5		11
1R2r	14	Reading		1-2	1-2	5000	Michael (At County Ground, Swindon) (£112)	1	2	3	4	8	6	7		9	10			11	5		

GLOUCESTERSHIRE CUP FINAL

	Date	Opposition		Res.	H.T.	Att.	Goalscorers	Tcone G.	Bach P.	Davies R.H.	Jones W.	Wilson H.	Chambers P.	Michael W.	Fulton W.	McDougall D.	McLean J.C.	Robson D.J.	Geddes A.J.
	29 Apr	BRISTOL ROVERS		4-0	2-0	2800	Fulton(2), McDougall, Wilson (£84.5.4.)	1	2	3	4	10	6		9	8	7	5	11

FRIENDLIES

No.	Date	Opposition		Res.	H.T.	Att.	Goalscorers	Tcone G.	Bach P.	Davies R.H.	Jones W.	Wilson H.	Chambers P.	Whelan M.	Stevenson J.	Michael W.	Fulton W.	Nichol D.	O'Brien P.	McDougall D.	McLean J.C.	Robson D.J.	Geddes A.J.	Wadlock W.J.	Nicholls	Bartlett E.	Harding	Marsh R.	Brooks
1	5 Sep	BRISTOL ROVERS		3-0	1-0	3000	Michael, Nichol, Whelan	1	2	3	4	5	6	7	8	9	10	11											
2	26	QUEENS PARK RANGERS *		0-0	0-0	500		11	2		4	6				8	9	10	11		7	5	3						
3	24 Oct	Queens Park Rangers		2-1	1-0		O'Brien, Stevenson	1	2			4	6	7	8				10	11	5	3							
4	31	SOUTHAMPTON		0-0	0-0			1		3	4	7	6			8	9	10			11	5	2						
5	3 Nov	SMALL HEATH		2-0	2-0	5000	Fulton, Geddes	1		3	4	10	6	7	8		9				5	2	11						
6	23 Feb	LEICESTER FOSSE *		1-0	1-0	3000	Davies(pen)	1	2	3			6			8	9		10	7	4	11		5					
7	4 Mar	Aberdare		4-0	2-0	1000	McDougall(2), O'Brien, Stevenson	1	2	3	4	9	6			8			10	11	5								7

* Matches played at Ashton Gate (others at St.Johns' Lane)

SEASON 1901-02
FOOTBALL LEAGUE DIVISION TWO

No.	Date	Opposition	Pos.	Res.	H.T.	Att.	Goalscorers
1	7 Sep	Blackpool		2-0	1-0	3000	O'Brien(2)
2	9	Burslem Port Vale		0-3	0-1	5000	
3	14	STOCKPORT COUNTY	4	3-0	2-0	7000	Connor, S.Jones, O'Brien
4	21	Newton Heath	9	0-1	0-0	5000	
5	28	GLOSSOP	5	2-0	1-0	6000	Connor, O.G.
6	5 Oct	Doncaster Rovers	10	0-3	0-1	1500	
7	12	LINCOLN CITY	8	1-1	1-1	8000	O'Brien
8	19	West Bromwich Albion	9	2-2	1-1	7829	Boucher, Connor
9	26	WOOLWICH ARSENAL	11	0-3	0-1	10500	
10	9 Nov	LEICESTER FOSSE	8	2-1	1-0	5000	Davies(pen), O'Brien
11	30	Preston North End	11	0-0	0-0	1000	
12	7 Dec	CHESTERFIELD	8	5-2	2-1	4000	Banks(2), Connor(2), Chambers
13	14	GAINSBOROUGH TRINITY	8	2-1	2-1	4000	Cnnr,Cksn (Aband. h/t bad light. Opp. 1hr late)
14	21	MIDDLESBROUGH	8	1-0	1-0	6000	Banks
15	25	Barnsley	6	2-2	0-1	3000	Connor, Davies
16	28	Burton United	7	2-2	0-2	2000	Connor, O.G.
17	4 Jan	BLACKPOOL	7	3-0	0-0	2000	Boucher(2), Connor
18	11	Stockport County	6	1-1	1-0	1000	Banks
19	18	NEWTON HEATH	6	4-0	3-0	7500	Boucher(2), Banks, Flynn
20	25	GAINSBOROUGH TRINITY	4	4-0	2-0	4000	Boucher, Bradbury, Jay, McLean
21	1 Feb	DONCASTER ROVERS	4	3-0	2-0	4000	Banks, Boucher, Cookson
22	15	WEST BROMWICH ALBION	5	1-2	0-1	14175	Bradbury
23	22	Woolwich Arsenal	5	0-2	0-2	8000	
24	1 Mar	BARNSLEY	5	3-1	3-1	4000	Bradbury, Connor, Cookson
25	4	Glossop	5	2-1	0-1	2500	O'Brien(2)
26	8	Leicester Fosse	5	1-0	1-0	4000	S.Jones
27	15	PRESTON NORTH END	5	2-0	0-0	8000	Boucher, Cookson
28	22	Burnley	4	1-0	1-0	1000	Cookson
29	29	BURSLEM PORT VALE	5	4-0	3-0	5000	Banks(2), Bradbury, Cookson
30	2 Apr	Gainsborough Trinity	5	0-2	0-1	2000	
31	5	Chesterfield	5	0-1	0-1	1000	
32	12	BURNLEY	5	1-0	0-0	4000	Banks
33	19	Middlesbrough	5	0-2	0-0	12000	
34	21	Lincoln City	5	0-1	0-1	3000	
35	26	BURTON UNITED	6	0-2	0-1	4000	

Appearances / Goals grid

No.	Moles W.	Tuff W.	Davies R.H.	W.Jones W.	McLean J.C.	Chambers P.	Bradbury J.J.L.	Connor M.J.	Boucher T.	O'Brien P.	Flynn J.	S.Jones S.	Robertson J.S.	Jay J.	Banks H.E.	Clay H.A.	Cookson W.S.	Wickerstaffe E.B.
1	1	2	3	4	5	6	7	8	0	10	11							
2	1	2	3	4	5	6	7	8	9	10	11							
3	1	2	3	4	5	6	7			10	11	9						
4	1		3	10	4	5	6	7	8			11	9	2				
5	1		3	10	4	5	6	7	8	9		11		2				
6	1		3	10	4	5	6	7	8			11		2				
7		2	3	4	5	6	7	8	9	10	11		1					
8		2	3	4	5	6	7	8		10		9	1					
9		2	3	4	5	6	7	8		10		9	1					
10		2	3	4	5	6	7	8	9	10			1	11				
11		2	3	4	5	6	7	8	9				1	11	10			
12		2	3	4	5	6	7	8				9		11	10	1		
13		2	3	4	5	6	7	8						11	10	1	9	
14		2	3	4	5	6	7	8				11			10	1	9	
15		2	3	4	5	6		8	9		7			11	10	1		
16		2	3	4	5			7	8	9		11		6	10	1		
17		2	3	4	5			8	9			11		6	10	1	7	
18		2	3	4	5			7	8	9		11		6	10	1		
19		2	3	4	5			7	8	9		11		6	10	1		
20		2	3	4	5		6	8		9		10			11			7
21		2	3	4	5	6	7		9		11		1		10		8	
22		2	3	4	5	6	7	8	9		11				10	1		
23		2		4	5	6		8			8				10	1	7	
24		2	3	4	5			7	8	10	11			6		1	9	
25		2	3	4	5			7	8	10	11			6		1	9	
26		2	3	4	5	6	7	8		10	11					1	9	
27		2	3	4	5	6	7		8		11				10	1	9	
28		2	3	4	5	6	7		8		11				10	1	9	
29		2	3	4	5	6	7		8		11				10	1	9	
30		2	3	4	5	6	7		8		11				10	1	9	
31		2	3	4	5	6		8	9		11				10	1	7	
32		2	3	4	5	6	7		8		11				10	1	9	
33		2		4	5	6	7	8			11		3		10	1		
34		2		4	5	6	7	8			11		3		10	1		
35		3		4	5	6	7	8			11		2		10	1		9
Apps	6	35	32	35	35	29	31	26	26	8	31	5	12	12	21	23	17	1
Goals			2	1	1		4	10	8	7	1	2		1	9		6	

F.A. CUP

No.	Date	Opposition		Res.	H.T.	Att.	Goalscorers	Tuff	Davies	W.Jones	McLean	Chambers	Bradbury	Connor	Boucher	O'Brien	Flynn	S.Jones	Robertson	Banks
3Q	2 Nov	BRISTOL EAST		5-1	2-1	2000	Cookson(2), S.Jones(2), W.Jones(pen)	2	3	4	5	6	7			10		11 9 1		8
4Q	16	Bristol Rovers		0-2	0-2	8900	(Abandoned after 80 mins. due to fog) (£290)	2	3	4	5	6	7	8	9	10	11		1	
4Q	23	Bristol Rovers		1-1	1-1	9900	Bradbury (bad light, 116 mins played) (£283)	2	3	9	5	6	7	10			11	4 1		8
4Qr	27	BRISTOL ROVERS		2-3	1-0	5000	Connor, Cookson (£143)	2	3	9	5	6	7	10			11	4 1		8

GLOUCESTERSHIRE CUP

	Date	Opposition		Res.	H.T.	Att.	Goalscorers
SF	10 Mar	BRISTOL EAST		2-1	1-0	1000	Banks, Connor
F	31	Bristol Rovers		0-0	0-0	13835	(£416.14.9.)
Fr	23 Apr	BRISTOL ROVERS		0-0	0-0	4223	(118.13.0.)

FRIENDLIES

	Date	Opposition		Res.	H.T.	Att.	Goalscorers
1	2 Sep	Bristol Rovers		1-0	1-0	4000	Boucher
2	16	BRIDGEWATER*		11-1	6-0	100	Connor(5),Cookson(2),S.Jnes(2),Chmbrs,Rbrtson
3	26 Dec	BRISTOL ROVERS		3-1	1-1	7000	Banks, Connor, McLean
4	5 Feb	Devon County XI		6-1	2-0	3000	Boucher(3),Bnks,Flynn,OG.(played at Devonport)
5	6	Cornwall County XI		5-0	1-0	1000	Banks(2),Boucher,Flynn,W.Jnes(played at Truro)
6	17 Mar	Aberdare		2-0	1-0	1500	Banks, Wickerstaffe
7	28	CLAPTON		2-0	0-0	3000	Flynn, Wickerstaffe
8	16 Apr	ASTON VILLA		0-1	0-1	4000	

* Only 35 minutes each way played.

FINAL LEAGUE TABLE

1	West Bromwich	34	25	5	4	82:29	55
2	Middlesbrough	34	23	5	6	90:24	51
3	Preston	34	18	6	10	71:32	42
4	Woolwich Arsenal	34	18	6	10	50:26	42
5	Lincoln	34	14	13	7	45:35	41
6	Bristol C	34	17	6	11	52:35	40
7	Doncaster	34	13	8	13	49:58	34
8	Glossop	34	10	12	12	36:40	32
9	Burnley	34	10	10	14	41:45	30
10	Burton U.	34	11	8	15	46:54	30
11	Barnsley	34	12	6	16	51:63	30
12	Burslem P Vale	34	10	9	15	43:59	29
13	Blackpool	34	11	7	16	40:56	29
14	Leicester Fosse	34	12	5	17	38:56	29
15	Newton Heath	34	11	6	17	38:53	28
16	Chesterfield	34	11	6	17	47:68	28
17	Stockport	34	8	7	19	36:72	23
18	Gainsborough	34	4	11	19	30:80	19

W. Jones. Robertson. Moles. Tuft. Chambers. Davies.

(Trainer). Bradbury. Connor. Boucher. O'Brien. Flynn. S. W. Hollis (Manager)
Cookson. McLean. S. Jones.

1901/02 Season

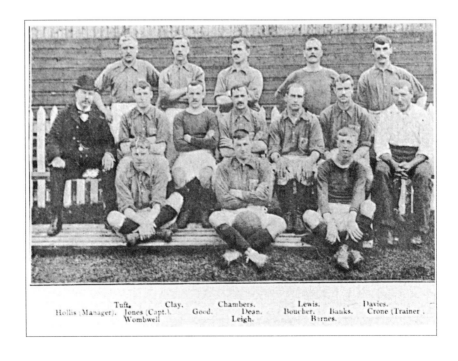

Tuft. Clay. Chambers. Lewis. Davies.
Hollis (Manager). Jones (Capt.) Good. Dean. Boucher. Banks. Crone (Trainer).
Wombwell Leigh. Barnes.

1902/03 Season

SEASON 1902-03
FOOTBALL LEAGUE DIVISION TWO

No.	Date	Opposition	Pos.	Res.	H.T.	Att.	Goalscorers	Clay H.A.	Tuft W.	Lewis G.	Jones W.	Good M.W	Chambers P.	Dean A.	Wombwell R.	Leigh W.	Banks H.E.	Barnes C.E.	Boucher T.	Gara A.	Davies R.H.	Jay J.	Lamberton J.
1	6 Sep	CHESTERFIELD		2-1	2-0	5000	Dean, Wombwell	1	2	3	4	5	6	7	8	9	10	11					
2	13	Glossop	2	2-0	0-0	1000	Dean, Wombwell	1	2	3	4	5	6	7	8	9	11		10				
3	20	MANCHESTER UNITED	1	3-1	2-0	8000	Dean(2,1pen), Good	1	2	3	4	5	6	7	8	9	11		10				
4	27	Stockport County	1	1-0	1-0	4000	Dean	1	2	3	4	5	6	7	8	9	11		10				
5	4 Oct	WOOLWICH ARSENAL	1	1-0	0-0	12024	Leigh	1	2	3	4	5	6	7	8	9		11	10				
6	11	Woolwich Arsenal	2	1-2	0-1	12000	Wombwell	1	2	3	4	5	6	7	8	9	11		10				
7	18	DONCASTER ROVERS	1	4-2	3-0	7000	Dean(pen), Good, Jones, Wombwell	1	2	3	4	5	6	7	8	9	11		10				
8	25	Lincoln City	1	1-1	0-0	4000	Leigh	1	2	3	4	5	6	7	11	9	10		8				
9	1 Nov	SMALL HEATH	1	1-1	1-0	11000	Boucher	1	2	3	4	5	6	7	11	9	10		8				
10	8	Leicester Fosse	2	2-2	0-1	5000	Boucher, Gara	1	2	3	4	5	6	7	11	9	10		8	10			
11	15	MANCHESTER CITY	1	3-2	2-1	13000	Wombwell(2), Good	1	2	3	4	5	6	7	11	8	10			9			
12	22	Burnley	3	0-0	0-0	1250		1	2	3	4	5	6	7	11	8			10	9			
13	29	PRESTON NORTH END	3	2-1	0-1	5000	Boucher, Dean	1	2	3	4	5	6	7	11	8			9	10			
14	6 Dec	Burslem Port Vale	4	0-2	0-0	2000		1	2	3	4	5	6	7	11	8			10	9			
15	20	Gainsborough Trinity	4	1-2	1-0	3000	Boucher	1	2	3	4		6	7	11	8			10	9	5		
16	25	BARNSLEY	3	3-3	2-3	6000	Banks, Boucher, Wombwell	1	2		4	5	6	7	11		10		8	9	3		
17	27	BURTON UNITED	3	3-1	2-0	7000	Banks(2), Gara	1	2	3	4	5		7	11		10		8	9		6	
18	1 Jan	Blackpool	3	1-0	1-0	4000	Dean	1	2	3	4	5	6	7	11	8			10	9			
19	3	Chesterfield	4	0-3	0-1	5000		1	2		4	9	6	7	11	8				10	3	5	
20	10	GLOSSOP	4	1-1	0-1	6000	Lewis(pen)	1		3	4	5		7	8		10	11		9	2		
21	17	Manchester United	4	2-1	1-0	12000	Good, Leigh	1	2	3	4	9	6		11	8	10				7	5	
22	24	STOCKPORT COUNTY	4	7-1	3-0	3000	Jay(3), Banks(2), Barnes, Jones	1	2	3	4	5	6		11	8	10	7				9	
23	31	BLACKPOOL	4	0-1	0-0	1600		1	2		4	5	6	7	11	8	10				8	J	
24	14 Feb	Doncaster Rovers	4	0-0	0-0	2500		1	2	3	4	5	6	7		8	11	10	9				
25	28	Small Heath	4	0-2	0-2	8000		1	2	3	4	5	6	7	11		10		8	9			
26	7 Mar	LEICESTER FOSSE	4	6-1	3-1	5000	Gara(2), Leigh(2), Banks, Barnes	1	2	3	4	5	6		11	8	10	7		9			
27	14	Manchester City	4	2-2	0-1	25000	Wombwell(2)	1	2	3	4	5	6		11	8		7	10	9			
28	21	BURNLEY	4	3-0	1-0	5000	Gara(2), Good	1	2	3		5	6		11	8		7	10	9		4	
29	28	Preston North End	4	0-1	0-0	3000		1	2	3		5	6		11	8		7	10	9			
30	30	LINCOLN CITY	4	0-2	0-0	5000		1	2	3	4	5		7	11	8	10			9		6	
31	4 Apr	BURSLEM PORT VALE	4	3-0	2-0	2000	Dean(2,1pen), Wombwell	1	2	3		6	9		11	9	10	7	8				
32	11	Barnsley	4	0-2	0-1	4000		1	2	3	4	5		7	11	8	10		9			6	
33	18	GAINSBOROUGH TRINITY	4	1-0	1-0	4000	Banks	1	3		4	5			11	8	10	7	9			6	2
34	25	Burton United	4	3-0	1-0	2000	Banks, Boucher, Wombwell	1	2	3		5		7	11	8	10		9			6	4
							Apps.	34	33	30	32	32	29	25	34	30	22	12	25	18	5	10	3
							Goals			1	2	5		10	11	5	8	2	6	6		3	

F.A. CUP

	Date		Res.	H.T.	Att.	Goalscorers	Clay	Tuft	Lewis	Jones		Chambers	Dean	Wombwell	Leigh	Banks			Boucher	Gara	Davies	
INT	13 Dec	MIDDLESBROUGH	3-1	2-1	10500	Boucher, Leigh, Wombwell (£268-0-3)	1	2	3	4		6	7	11	8				10	9	5	
1R	7 Feb	Bolton Wanderers	5-0	3-0	7750	Banks(3), Dean, Wombwell (£295)	1	2	3	4	5	6	7	11	8	10			9			
2R	21	Tottenham Hotspur	0-1	0-1	18750	(£1386)	1	2	3	4	5	6	7	11	8	10			9			

GLOUCESTERSHIRE CUP FINAL

	Date		Res.	H.T.	Att.	
1R	13 Apr	Bristol Rovers	0-0	0-0	11790	(£355.3.6.)
1Rr	20	BRISTOL ROVERS	1-1	0-1	4044	Banks (£113.12.6.)
1R2r	29	BRISTOL ROVERS	2-4	1-3	4985	Banks(2) (£140.1.8)

FRIENDLIES

	Date		Res.	H.T.	Att.	Goalscorers
1	1 Sep	BRISTOL ROVERS	2-4	1-2	6000	Dean(2,1pen)
2	20 Oct	Aberaman	2-3	1-1		Boucher, Leigh
3	26 Dec	Bristol Rovers	1-2	0-2	10000	Banks
4	19 Mar	Somerset XI*	10-0	4-0	500	Leigh(4), Lewis(2), Wombwell(2), Gara, Jones
5	10 Apr	Southport Central	0-1	0-0	5000	
6	14	THIRD LANARK	1-1	0-0	7000	Leigh (Billy Jones Benefit)
7	22	WOOLWICH ARSENAL	1-2	0-0	500	Boucher
8	27	THE WEDNESDAY	2-2	1-2		Lewis(pen),Wombwell (35 mins each way played)

* Played at Weston-super-Mare.

FINAL LEAGUE TABLE

1	Manchester C.	34	25	4	5	95:29 54
2	Small Heath	34	24	3	7	74:36 51
3	Woolwich Arsenal	34	20	8	6	66:30 48
4	Bristol C.	34	17	8	9	59:38 42
5	Manchester U.	34	15	8	11	53:38 38
6	Chesterfield	34	14	9	11	67:40 37
7	Preston	34	13	10	11	56:40 36
8	Barnsley	34	13	8	13	55:51 34
9	Burslem P. Vale	34	13	8	13	57:62 34
10	Lincoln	34	12	6	16	46:53 30
11	Glossop	34	11	7	16	43:58 29
12	Gainsborough	34	11	7	16	41:59 29
13	Burton U.	34	11	7	16	39:59 29
14	Blackpool	34	9	10	15	44:59 28
15	Leicester Fosse	34	10	8	16	41:65 28
16	Doncaster	34	9	7	18	35:72 25
17	Stockport	34	7	6	21	39:74 20
18	Burnley	34	6	8	20	30:77 20

SEASON 1903-04
FOOTBALL LEAGUE DIVISION TWO

No.	Date	Opposition	Pos.	Res.	H.T.	Att.	Goalscorers	Clay H.A.	Gilson A.T.	Tuft W.	Jones W.	Hosie J.	Chambers P.	Dean A.	Fisher A.	Corbett F.	Morris J.J.	Wombwell R.	Bach P.	Hargett A.	Barnes C.E.	Hales W.H.
1	5 Sep	Manchester United		2-2	0-0	40000	Chambers, Fisher	1	2	3	4	5	6	7	8	9	10	11				
2	12	GLOSSOP	5	5-0	2-0	10000	Corbett, Fisher, Hosie, Jones, Morris	1		3	4	5	6	7	8	9	10	11	2			
3	19	Bradford City	10	0-1	0-0	12000		1		2	4	5	6	7	8	9	10	11		3		
4	26	WOOLWICH ARSENAL	11	0-4	0-2	14000		1		2	4	5	6	7	8	9	10	11		3		
5	3 Oct	Barnsley	12	0-2	0-1	4000		1	2	3	4	5	6	7	8	9	10	11				
6	10	LINCOLN CITY	10	3-1	2-1	7000	Barnes, Dean, Wombwell	1	3	2	4	5	6	7	8	9		10			11	
7	17	Stockport County	10	1-1	0-0	5000	Wombwell	1	2	3	4		6	7	8	9		11		5	10	
8	24	CHESTERFIELD	8	3-2	1-1	5000	Dean, Morris, Wombwell	1	2	3	4		6	7		9	8	11		5	10	
9	31	Bolton Wanderers	8	1-1	0-1	9000	Morris	1	2	3	4	5	6	7		9	8	10			11	
10	7 Nov	BURNLEY	6	6-0	4-0	6000	Dean(3,1pen), Corbett, Morris, Wombwell	1	2	3	4	5	6	7		9	8	10			11	
11	14	Preston North End	6	0-3	0-1	9000		1	2	3	4	5	6	7		9	8	10			11	
12	21	GRIMSBY TOWN	4	4-0	3-0	8000	Barnes(2), Chambers, Dean	1	2	3	4	5	6	7		9	8	10			11	
13	5 Dec	BLACKPOOL	4	5-0	3-0	5000	Cambers, Corbett, Fisher, Morris, O.G.	1	2	3	4	5	6	7	10	9	8	11				
14	19	BURTON UNITED	3	4-0	2-0	5000	Morris(2), Chambers, Corbett	1	2	3	4	5	6	7	10	9	8	11				
15	26	Burslem Port Vale	4	1-3	0-3	4000	Dean(pen)	1	2	3	4	5	6	7	10	9	8	11				
16	2 Jan	MANCHESTER UNITED	5	1-1	1-0	8000	Morris	1	2	3	4	5	6	7	10	9	8	11				
17	9	Glossop	5	1-1	0-0	800	Corbett	1	2	3	4	5	6	7	10	9	8	11				
18	16	BRADFORD CITY	6	1-1	0-1	6000	Fisher	1	2	3		5	6	7	10	9	8	11		4		
19	30	BARNSLEY	6	2-0	2-0	2500	Fisher(2)	1	2	3	4	5	6	7	10	8		9			11	
20	13 Feb	STOCKPORT COUNTY	6	6-0	4-0	1700	Corbett(4), Jones, Morris	1		3	4	5	6	7	10	8	9	11	2			
21	20	Chesterfield	6	0-1	0-1	4000		1		3	4	5	6	7	10	8	9	11	2			
22	25	Leicester Fosse	6	0-1	0-1	3000		1	2	3	4	5	6	7	10	8	9	11				
23	27	BOLTON WANDERERS	5	2-0	2-0	6000	Corbett, Dean	1	2	3	4	5	6	7	10	8	9	11				
24	5 Mar	Burnley	5	3-2	1-1	4000	Hargett(2), Chambers	1	2	3	4	5	6	7		10	8	11		9		
25	7	Lincoln City	4	6-2	2-1	4000	Chambers,Dean(pen),Hargett,Hosie,Jones,Morris	1	2	3	4	5	6	7		10	8	11		9		
26	12	PRESTON NORTH END	3	3-1	2-1	10000	Chambers, Hosie, Morris	1	2	3	4	5	6	7		10	8	11		9		
27	14	Woolwich Arsenal	3	0-2	0-2	10000		1	2	3	4	5	6	7		10	8	11		9		
28	19	Grimsby Town	4	0-2	0-1	4000		1	2	3	4	5	6	7		10	8	11		9		
29	26	LEICESTER FOSSE	3	4-0	2-0	5000	Corbett(2), Dean Hosie	1	2	3		5	6	7	8	10		11		9		4
30	1 Apr	Gainsborough Trinity	4	1-3	0-2	3000	Dean	1	2	3	4	5	6	7	8	10		11		9		
31	2	Blackpool	4	1-0	1-0	2000	Jones	1	2	3	4	5	6	7	8	10		11		9		
32	9	GAINSBOROUGH TRINITY	4	2-1	0-0	4000	Corbett, Wombwell	1	2	3	4	5	6		8	10	9	11			7	
33	16	Burton United	4	3-2	0-2	2000	Dean(2), Fisher	1	2		4	5	6	7	8		9	11		3	10	
34	23	BURSLEM PORT VALE	4	2-1	0-0	4000	Fisher, Hosie	1	2		4	5			3	8	10	9	11		6	7
							Apps.	34	29	32	32	32	33	32	24	33	29	34	3	15	11	1
							Goals				4	5	7	13	8	13	11	5		3	3	

F.A. CUP

	Date	Opposition		Res.	H.T.	Att.	Goalscorers	Clay	Gilson	Tuft	Jones	Hosie	Chambers	Dean	Fisher	Corbett	Morris	Wombwell
INT	12 Dec	New Brompton		1-1	1-0	8000	Wombwell	1	2	3	4	5	6	7	8	9	10	11
INT/r	16	NEW BROMPTON		5-2	0-1	5000	Corbett, Fisher, Hosie, Morris, O.G.	1	2	3	4	5	6	7	10	9	8	11
1R	6 Feb	SHEFFIELD UNITED		1-3	1-2	17909	Hosie (£754.11.9)	1	2	3	4	5	6	7	10	8	9	11

GLOUCESTERSHIRE CUP

	Date	Opposition	Res.	H.T.	Att.	Goalscorers
SF	23 Mar	Bristol East	4-0	0-0	500	Fisher(2), Morris, Wombwell (At Stapleton Road)
F	4 Apr	BRISTOL ROVERS	2-1	2-0	10537	Corbett, Jones (£296.2.1)

FRIENDLIES

	Date	Opposition	Res.	H.T.	Att.	Goalscorers
1	2 Sep	Bristol Rovers	1-0	1-0		Dean(pen)
2	11 Nov	OXFORD UNIVERSITY	3-1	2-0	2000	Fisher(2), Barnes(pen)
3	28	Clapton Orient	2-1	2-1	1000	Dean, Fisher
4	25 Dec	BRISTOL ROVERS	5-3	3-1	7000	Hargett(2), Dean, Fisher, Jones
5	8 Feb	Oxford University	0-3	0-2		
6	5 Apr	HIBERNIANS	3-1	2-1		Corbett, Dean(pen), O.G.
7	20	Weymouth	3-0	2-0		Barnes(pen), Jones, Morris
8	30	BRISTOL CITY RES.	3-2	2-1		Corbett(2), Fisher

FINAL LEAGUE TABLE

1	Preston	34	20	10	4	62:24	50
2	Woolwich Arsenal	34	21	7	6	91:22	49
3	Manchester U	34	20	8	6	65:33	48
4	Bristol C.	34	18	6	10	73:41	42
5	Burnley	34	15	9	10	50:55	39
6	Grimsby	34	14	8	12	50:49	36
7	Bolton	34	12	10	12	59:41	34
8	Barnsley	34	11	10	13	38:57	32
9	Gainsborough	34	14	3	17	53:60	31
10	Bradford C.	34	12	7	15	45:59	31
11	Chesterfield	34	11	8	15	37:45	30
12	Lincoln	34	11	8	15	41:58	30
13	Burslem P. Vale	34	10	9	15	54:52	29
14	Burton U.	34	11	7	16	45:61	29
15	Blackpool	34	11	5	18	40:67	27
16	Stockport	34	8	11	15	40:72	27
17	Glossop	34	10	6	18	57:64	26
18	Leicester Fosse	34	6	10	18	42:82	22

1903/04 Season
(L.to R.) Back: Gilson, Tuft, Clay, Bach. Middle: Hollis (Manager), Barnes, Jones, Hosie, Chambers, Batten (Trainer).
Front: Dean, Fisher, Corbett, Morris, Wombwell.

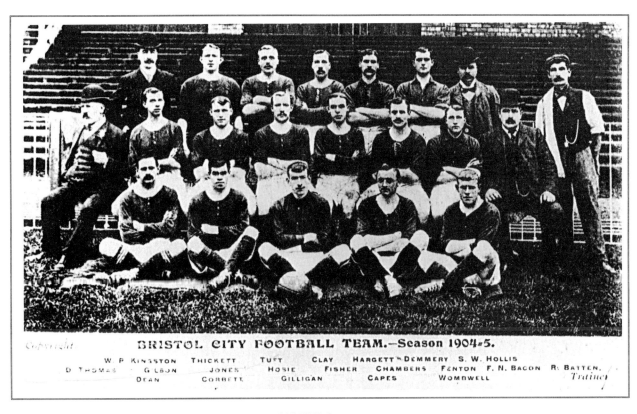

BRISTOL CITY FOOTBALL TEAM.—Season 1904=5.

W. P. KINGSTON   THICKETT   TUFT   CLAY   HARGETT DEMMERY S. W. HOLLIS
D. THOMAS   GILSON   JONES   HOSIE   FISHER   CHAMBERS   FENTON F. N. BACON R. BATTEN,
DEAN   CORBETT   GILLIGAN   CAPES   WOMBWELL   Trainer

1904/05 Season

SEASON 1904-05
FOOTBALL LEAGUE DIVISION TWO

No.	Date	Opposition	Pos.	Res.	H.T.	Att.	Goalscorers
1	0 Sep	BOLTON WANDERERS		3-1	2-2	14000	Dean, Gilligan, Wombwell
2	10	Manchester United		1-4	1-1	18000	Wombwell
3	17	GLOSSOP	15	2-0	1-0	7000	Gilligan(2)
4	24	Chesterfield	10	3-0	1-0	4000	Dean(2), Hosie
5	1 Oct	BRADFORD CITY	4	1-0	1-0	8000	O.G.
6	8	Lincoln City	3	3-1	3-1	7000	Dean(pen), Gilligan, Hosie
7	15	LEICESTER FOSSE	3	0-0	0-0	9000	Gilligan(2), O.G.
8	22	Barnsley	6	0-1	0-1	4000	
9	29	WEST BROMWICH ALBION	5	2-1	1-0	10795	Fisher, Gilligan
10	5 Nov	Burnley	4	3-2	1-1	3000	Dean(2,1pen), Chambers
11	12	GRIMSBY TOWN	4	5-0	2-0	10000	Capes(2), Fisher(2), Gilligan
12	19	Blackpool	4	4-2	2-2	4000	Capes(2), Chambers, Fisher
13	26	DONCASTER ROVERS	3	4-1	0-1	5000	Capes, Gilligan, Jones, Wombwell
14	3 Dec	Gainsborough Trinity	4	1-4	1-1	3000	Jones
15	10	BURTON UNITED	4	5-0	2-0	4000	Dean(2,1pen), Capes, Fisher, Hosie
16	17	Liverpool	4	1-3	1-2	12000	Hosie
17	24	BURSLEM PORT VALE	4	4-2	2-1	6000	Corbett, Dean(pen), Hosie, Jones
18	27	Glossop	4	1-0	0-0	1500	Gilligan
19	31	Bolton Wanderers	4	1-3	1-2	16000	Gilligan
20	7 Jan	MANCHESTER UNITED	4	1-1	1-1	18000	Fisher
21	21	CHESTERFIELD	4	2-1	1-0	5000	Darke, Fisher (Peter Chambers Benefit)
22	28	Bradford City	4	3-2	0-1	14000	Dean(pen), Fisher, Gilligan
23	11 Feb	Leicester Fosse	4	1-2	1-1	6000	Gilson
24	25	West Bromwich Albion	4	0-0	0-0	4172	
25	4 Mar	BURNLEY	4	0-0	0-0	4000	
26	11	Grimsby Town	4	0-4	0-1	4000	
27	18	BLACKPOOL	4	2-0	1-0	7000	Capes, Fisher
28	25	Doncaster Rovers	4	2-0	1-0	1600	Dean(pen), Fenton
29	29	BARNSLEY	4	3-0	1-0	3000	Fisher(2), Gilligan
30	1 Apr	GAINSBOROUGH TRINITY	4	1-1	1-1	6000	Dean
31	8	Burton United	4	0-2	0-2	2000	
32	15	LIVERPOOL	4	0-1	0-0	10000	
33	22	Burslem Port Vale	4	2-3	2-2	2000	Fisher, Gilligan
34	25	LINCOLN CITY	4	2-0	0-0	4000	Darke, Fisher

Player appearances (shirt numbers by match):

No.	Clay H.A.	Gilson A.T.	Tuft W.	Jones W.	Hosie J.	Chambers P.	Dean A.	Corbett F.	Gilligan S.A.	Capes A.J.	Wombwell R.	Fenton F.	Thickett H.	Fisher A.	Spear A.T.	Hargett G.H.	Darke T.W.	Turner A.D.	Price A.H.	Hargett A.	Stolz W.	Bennett W.	Wadley H.E.
1	1	2	3	4	5	6	7	8	9	10	11												
2	1	2	3	4		6	7	8	9	5	11	10											
3	1	3	2	4					9	8	10	11											
4	1		3	4	5	6	7	8	9	10	11	2											
5	1		3	4	5	6	7	8	9	10	11	2											
6	1		3	4	5	6	7	8	9	10	11	2											
7	1		3	4	5	6	7	8	9	10	11	2											
8	1		3	4	5	6	7	8	9	10	11	2											
9	1		3	4	5	6	7		9	10	11	2		8									
10	1	5	3	4		6	7		9	10	11	2		8									
11	1	5	3	4		6	7		9	10	11	2		8									
12	1	5	3	4		6			9	10	7	11	2	8									
13	1	5	3	4		6			9	10	7	11	2	8									
14	1		3	4	5	6	7		9	10	11	2		8									
15	1	2	3	4	5	6	7		9	10		11		8									
16	1	3	2	4	5	6	7		9		8	11		10									
17	1	5	2	4			6	3	10	9		7	11	8									
18	1		3	4	5			2	10	9		7	11	8	6								
19	1		3	4	5			2	10	9		7	11	8	6								
20	1	2	3	4	5			7	10	9	6	11		8									
21	1			4					9	6	7	11	2	8	5	3	10						
22	1		3	4			7		10	9	6	11	2	8	5								
23	1	5	3					9		4	7	8		10	6	2		11					
24	1	2	3	4	5				9	10	11	7		8					6				
25	1	2	3	4	5				9	10	11			8					6				
26	1	5	3	4			6	7	9			10	11	2	8								
27	1	3	2	4			6	7	9			10		11	8	5							
28	1	2	3	4		6		7	9			10	11	8	5								
29	1	2	3	4		6		7	9			10	11	8	5								
30	1		2	4		6		7	9			11		8	5		10		3				
31	1		3	4		6			9			10	11	8	5	2				7			
32	1		3	4	5	6	2		9			10	11	8							7		
33	1		3	4		6	2		9			10	11	8	5						7		
34	1					5	2					11		8	4		9	6			7		10
Apps.	34	18	33	32	21	21	27	16	30	29	24	21	14	26	12	3	3	1	3	1	1	3	1
Goals		1		3	5	2	12	1	14	7	3	1		13			2						

F.A. CUP

	Date	Opposition	Res.	H.T.	Att.	Goalscorers	Clay H.A.	Gilson A.T.	Tuft W.	Jones W.	Hosie J.	Chambers P.	Dean A.	Corbett F.	Gilligan S.A.	Capes A.J.	Wombwell R.	Fenton F.	Thickett H.	Fisher A.
INT	14 Jan	BLACKPOOL *	2-1	2-1	8000	Gilligan, Jones (£214)	1		3	4	5			2	10	9	6	7	11	8
1R	4 Feb	Woolwich Arsenal	0-0	0-0	26197	(£718)	1		3	4	5	6	7		9	10	11		2	8
1Rr	8	WOOLWICH ARSENAL	1-0	0-0	12024	Dean (£298-19-3)	1		3	4	5	6	7		9	10	11		2	8
2R	18	PRESTON NORTH END	0-0	0-0	19371	(£742)	1	5	3	4		6	7		9	10	11		2	8
2Rr	23	Preston North End	0-1	0-0	15000	(£466)	1	5	3	4		6	7		9	10	11		2	8

City paid Blackpool £200 to switch match to Ashton Gate.

GLOUCESTERSHIRE CUP

	Date	Opposition	Res.	H.T.	Att.	Goalscorers
SF	3 Apr	BRISTOL EAST	5-1	1-1	300	Gilligan(2), Dean, Fisher, Hosie
F	24	Bristol Rovers	2-2	2-1	10610	Capes, Fenton (£306.9.0)
Fr	28	BRISTOL ROVERS	1-3	1-1	3916	Fisher (£110.0.10)

FRIENDLIES

	Date	Opposition	Res.	H.T.	Att.	Goalscorers
1	1 Sep	Woolwich Arsenal	2-3	2-2	6000	Capes, Gilligan
2	5	BRISTOL ROVERS	4-2	2-2	5000	Chambers, Corbett, Dean, Gilligan
3	9 Nov	OXFORD UNIVERSITY	6-1	3-1	300	Corbett(2), Rowlands(2), Fisher, Spear
4	26 Dec	Bristol Rovers	2-5	1-2	14000	Corbett, Darke
5	27 Apr	Aberdare	1-0	1-0		Fisher
6	29	CORINTHIANS	0-1	0-1	2000	

FINAL LEAGUE TABLE

1	Liverpool	34	27	4	3	93:25	58
2	Bolton	34	27	2	5	87:32	56
3	Manchester U.	34	24	5	5	81:30	53
4	Bristol C.	34	19	4	11	66:45	42
5	Chesterfield Town	34	14	11	9	44:35	39
6	Gainsborough	34	14	8	12	61:58	36
7	Barnsley	34	14	5	15	38:56	33
8	Bradford C.	34	12	8	14	45:49	32
9	Lincoln	34	12	7	15	42:40	31
10	West Bromwich	34	13	4	17	56:48	30
11	Burnley	34	12	6	16	43:52	30
12	Glossop	34	10	10	14	37:46	30
13	Grimsby	34	11	8	15	33:46	30
14	Leicester Fosse	34	11	7	16	40:55	29
15	Blackpool	34	9	10	15	36:48	28
16	Burslem P. Vale	34	10	7	17	47:72	27
17	Burton U.	34	8	4	22	30:84	20
18	Doncaster	34	3	2	29	23:81	8

SEASON 1905-06
FOOTBALL LEAGUE DIVISION TWO

No.	Date	Opposition	Pos.	Res.	H.T.	Att.	Goalscorers	Clay H.A.	Annan W.A.	Tuft W.	Jones W.	Wedlock W.J.	Chambers P.	Bennett W.	Maxwell W.S.	Gilligan S.A.	Burton A.D.	Fenton F.	Spear A.T.	Cottle J.R.	Hanlin P.	Ingham W.E.	Hilton F.	Demmery W.	Stevens C.
1	2 Sep	Manchester United		1-5	0-2	25000	Maxwell	1	2	3	4	5	6	7	8	9	10	11							
2	9	GLOSSOP		2-1	1-0	4000	Bennett, Maxwell	1	2	3	4	5	6	7	8	9	10	11							
3	16	Stockport County	9	3-2	2-1	7000	Bennett, Gilligan, Maxwell	1	2	3	4	5	6	7	8	9	10	11							
4	20	BRADFORD CiTY	3	1-0	0-0	5000	Gilligan	1	2	3	4	5	6	7	8	9	10	11							
5	23	BLACKPOOL	2	2-1	1-0	9000	Bennett(pen), Burton	1	2	3	4	5	6	7	8	9	10	11							
6	30	Bradford City	2	2-1	1-1	16000	Bennett, Gilligan	1	2		4	5		7	8	9	10	11	3	4					
7	7 Oct	WEST BROMWICH ALBION		1-0	0-0	10000	Gilligan	1	2		4	5	6	7	8	9	10	11	3						
8	14	Leicester Fosse	1	2-1	1-1	7000	Bennett(2,1pen)	1	2		4	5	6	7	8	9	10	11	3						
9	21	HULL CITY	1	2-1	1-1	10000	Bennett, Maxwell	1	2		4	5	6	7		9	10	11	3			8			
10	28	Lincoln city	2	3-0	1-0	3000	Bennett(2,1pen), Maxwell	1	2		4	5	6	7	8	9	10		3				11		
11	4 Nov	CHESTERFIELD	2	3-1	1-0	10000	Maxwell(2), Bennett	1	2		4	5	6	7	8	9	10		3				11		
12	11	Burslem Port Vale	1	1-0	0-0	3000	Maxwell	1	2		4	5	6	7	8	9	10		3				11		
13	18	BARNSLEY	1	3-0	1-0	10000	Maxwell, Wedlock, O.G.	1	2		4	5	6	7	8	9	10		3				11		
14	25	Clapton Orient	1	2-0	2-0	7000	Bennett(pen), Maxwell	1	2		4	5	6	7	8	9	10		3				11		
15	2 Dec	BURNLEY	1	2-0	1-0	8000	Maxwell, O.G.	1	2		4	5	6		8	9	10	7	3				11		
16	9	Leeds City	1	1-1	1-0	15000	Maxwell	1	2		4	5		7	8	9	10	6	3				11		
17	16	BURTON UNITED	1	4-0	3-0	8000	Maxwell(3), Burton	1	2			5	6	7	8	9	10		3	4			11		
18	23	Chelsea	1	0-0	0-0	25000		1	2			5	6	7	8	9	10		3	4			11		
19	26	Gainsborough Trinity	1	3-1	1-1	5000	Burton(2), Bennett	1	2			5	6	7	8	9	10		3	4			11		
20	27	Grimsby Town	1	1-1		6000	Gilligan	1	2		4	5	6	7	8	9	10		3				11		
21	30	MANCHESTER UNITED	1	1-1	0-0	19000	Gilligan		2			5	6	7	8	9	10		3	4			11	1	
22	6 Jan	Glossop	1	5-1	3-0	2000	Gilligan(4), Bennett(pen)		2		4	5	6	7	8	9	10		3				11	1	
23	20	STOCKPORT COUNTY	1	7-0	4-0	7000	Gilligan(4), Maxwell(3)	1	2			5	6	7	8	9		11	3	4					10
24	27	Blackpool	1	3-1	3-0	4000	Maxwell(2), Gilligan	1	2			5	6	7	8	9	10		3	4			11		
25	10 Feb	West Bromwich Albion	1	3-1	2-0	6400	Bennett, Gilligan, Maxwell	1	2			5	6	7	8	9	10		3	4			11		
26	17	LEICESTER FOSSE	1	1-2	0-2	8000	Gilligan	1	2			5	6	7	8	9	10		3	4			11		
27	24	Hull City	1	3-0	1-0	8000	Bennett(pen), Hilton, Maxwell	1	2			5	6	7	8	9	10		3	4			11		
28	3 Mar	LINCOLN CITY	1	1-0	1-0	10000	Hilton	1	2			5		7	8	9	10		3	4	6		11		
29	10	Chesterfield	1	2-1	0-1	4000	Burton, Maxwell	1	2			5		7	8	9	10		3	4	6		11		
30	17	BURSLEM PORT VALE	1	4-0	2-0	10000	Bennett(3,1pen), Gilligan	1	2			5		7	8	9	10		3	4	6		11		
31	24	Barnsley	1	2-2	1-1	6000	Bennett(pen), Maxwell	1	2			5		7	8	9	10		3	4	6		11		
32	31	CLAPTON ORIENT	1	1-0	0-0	8000	Hilton	1	2			5		7	8	9	10		3	4	6		11		
33	7 Apr	Burnley	1	2-2	0-0	10000	Burton, Gilligan	1	2			5		7	8	9	10		3	4	6		11		
34	13	GAINSBOROUGH TRINITY	1	2-0	2-0	11000	Bennett, Burton	1	2			5		7	8	9	10	11	3	4	6				
35	14	LEEDS CITY	1	2-0	0-0	13000	Spear, Wedlock	1	2			5		7	8	9	10	11	3	4	6				
36	17	GRIMSBY TOWN	1	2-0	1-0	7000	Hilton, Maxwell	1	2			5		7	8	9	10		3	4	6		11		
37	21	Burton United	1	1-0	1-0	5000	Hilton	1	2			5		7	8	9	10		3	4	6		11		
38	28	CHELSEA	1	2-1	1-0	14000	Burton, Gilligan	1	2			5		7	8	9	10		3	4	6		11		
							Apps.	36	38	5	18	38	20	37	38	37	37	13	24	33	14	1	26	2	1
							Goals					2		20	25	20	8		1				5		

F.A. CUP

	Date	Opposition		Res.	H.T.	Att.	Goalscorers	Clay	Annan		Jones	Wedlock	Chambers	Bennett	Maxwell	Gilligan	Burton		Spear				Hilton		
1R	13 Jan	Brentford		1-2	1-0	10112	Maxwell (£333)	1	2		4	5	6	7	8	9	10		3				11		

GLOUCESTERSHIRE CUP FINAL

	Date	Opposition	Res.		Att.	Goalscorers
	16 Apr	BRISTOL ROVERS	4-0	2	8836	Bennett(pen), Burton, Gilligan, Wedlock (£248.5.11)

FRIENDLIES

No	Date	Opposition		Res.	H.T.	Att.	Goalscorers
1	6 Sep	Bristol Rovers		6-0	1-0	5000	Maxwell(3), Bennett, Burton, Gilligan
2	18 Oct	Plymouth Argyle		3-1	1-1	3000	Burton, Gilligan, Ingham
3	25 Dec	BRISTOL ROVERS		2-0	0-0	7000	McKay, Stevens
4	3 Feb	BRISTOL ROVERS		0-3	0-2	4000	

FINAL LEAGUE TABLE

		P	W	D	L	F	A	Pts
1	Bristol C.	38	30	6	2	83	28	66
2	Manchester U.	38	28	6	4	90	28	62
3	Chelsea	38	22	9	7	90	37	53
4	West Bromwich	38	22	8	8	79	36	52
5	Hull	38	19	6	13	67	54	44
6	Leeds C.	38	17	9	12	59	47	43
7	Leicester Fosse	38	15	12	11	53	48	42
8	Grimsby	38	15	10	13	46	46	40
9	Burnley	38	15	8	15	42	53	38
10	Stockport	38	13	9	16	44	56	35
11	Bradford C.	38	13	8	17	46	60	34
12	Barnsley	38	12	9	17	60	62	33
13	Lincoln	38	12	6	20	69	72	30
14	Blackpool	38	10	9	19	37	62	29
15	Gainsborough	38	12	4	22	44	57	28
16	Glossop	38	10	8	20	49	71	28
17	Burslem P. Vale	38	12	4	22	49	82	28
18	Chesterfield Town	38	10	8	20	40	72	28
19	Burton U.	38	10	6	22	34	67	26
20	Clapton Orient	38	7	7	24	35	78	21

1905/06 Season - Second Division Champions
(L.toR.) Back: Harry Thickett(Manager), Jones, Tuft, Annan, Spear, Clay, Cottle, Demmery (?), Hanlin, Batten (Trainer).
Front: Gilligan, Bennett, Maxwell, Chambers, Burton, Hilton, Ingham, Stevens. On ground: Wedlock, Fenton.

1906/07 Season - with Gloucestershire Cup and Second Division Shield (from previous season).
(L.to R.) Back: E.J.Locke (Hon.Sec.), F.N.Bacon (Director), W.P.Kingston(Director), W.H.Burland (Vice-Chair.), J.Daveridge (Director).
Middle: Thickett (Manager), Tuft, Gale, Annan, Clay, Demmery, Cottle, Marr, F.V.Larway (Director), Batten (Trainer).
Front: Bennett, Maxwell, Gilligan, Chambers, Burton, Hilton, Wedlock. On ground: Spear, Ingham, Staniforth, Connelly.

SEASON 1906-07
FOOTBALL LEAGUE DIVISION ONE

No.	Date	Opposition	Pos.	Res.	H.T.	Att.	Goalscorers
1	1 Sep	MANCHESTER UNITED		1-2	1-2	21000	Bennett(pen)
2	3	Birmingham		2-2	1-0	10000	Gilligan, O.G.
3	8	Stoke	10	3-0	1-0	8000	Benett, Gilligan, Maxwell
4	15	BLACKBURN ROVERS	8	3-0	0-0	18000	Burton, Hilton, Maxwell
5	22	Sunderland	6	3-3	1-1	28000	Maxwell(2), Burton
6	29	BIRMINGHAM	7	0-0	0-0	17000	
7	6 Oct	Everton	9	0-2	0-2	20000	
8	13	WOOLWICH ARSENAL	11	1-3	0-2	22000	Wedlock
9	20	The Wednesday	14	0-3	0-1	20000	
10	27	BURY	10	2-0	1-0	12000	Burton, Maxwell
11	3 Nov	Manchester City	10	1-0	1-0	16000	Maxwell
12	10	MIDDLESBROUGH	9	3-0	2-0	14000	Gilligan, Hanlin, Smith
13	17	Preston North End	9	1-3	0-2	6000	Maxwell
14	24	NEWCASTLE UNITED	8	2-1	1-1	20000	Burton, Wedlock
15	1 Dec	Aston Villa	10	2-3	0-2	27000	Burton, Gilligan (J.Bache Benefit)
16	8	LIVERPOOL	8	3-1	0-1	18000	Burton(2), Gilligan
17	15	DERBY COUNTY	6	3-0	1-0	12000	Burton(2), Gilligan
18	22	Notts County	6	3-2	1-1	10000	Hilton, Maxwell, Staniforth
19	24	SHEFFIELD UNITED	6	3-3	2-2	17500	Burton(2), Gilligan
20	29	Manchester United	6	0-0	0-0	16000	
21	31	Sheffield United	6	1-1	0-1	10873	Maxwell
22	5 Jan	STOKE	6	4-0	2-0	12000	Gilligan, Hilton, Marr, Maxwell
23	19	Blackburn Rovers	4	1-0	0-0	15000	Gilligan
24	26	SUNDERLAND	5	1-1	1-1	14000	Gilligan
25	9 Feb	EVERTON	5	2-1	2-0	20000	Gilligan, Maxwell
26	16	Woolwich Arsenal	4	2-1	1-0	18000	Hilton, Marr
27	2 Mar	Bury	5	1-1	0-0	11000	Smith
28	9	MANCHESTER CITY	4	2-0	0-0	12000	Hanlin, Staniforth
29	16	Middlesbrough	4	0-1	0-1	10000	
30	23	PRESTON NORTH END	3	1-0	1-0	15000	Staniforth
31	29	Bolton Wanderers	3	2-1	1-1	20000	Burton, Maxwell
32	30	Newcastle United	4	0-3	0-0	40000	
33	2 Apr	BOLTON WANDERERS	4	1-2	1-0	14000	Maxwell
34	6	ASTON VILLA	6	2-4	0-2	18000	Burton, Maxwell(pen)
35	13	Liverpool	5	4-2	2-1	12000	Maxwell(2), Connelly, Gilligan
36	20	Derby County	3	3-1	2-1	6000	Gilligan, Hanlin, Maxwell
37	24	THE WEDNESDAY	2	2-0	0-0	16000	Connelly, Gilligan
38	27	NOTTS COUNTY	2	1-0	0-0	12000	Gilligan

Appearances / Goals grid

No.	Clay H.A.	Annan W.A.	Cottle J.	Spear A.	Wedlock W.J.	Hanlin P.	Bennett W.	Maxwell W.S.	Gilligan S.A.	Burton A.	Hilton F.	Marr C.R.	Staniforth F.W.	Denney W.	Smith G.	Fenton F.	Connelly F.H.	Gale T.
1	1	2	3	4	5	6	7	8	9	10	11							
2	1	2	3		5	6	7	8	9	10	11	4						
3	1	2	3		5	6	7	8	9	10	11	4						
4	1	2	3		5	6	7	8	9	10	11	4						
5	1	2	3		5	6	7	8	9	10	11	4						
6	1	2	3		5	6	7	8	9	10	11	4						
7	1	2	3	4	5	6		8	9	10	11		7					
8	1	2	3		5	6		8	9	10	11	4	7					
9		2	3		5	6	7	8	9	10	11	4		1				
10		2	3		5	6	7	8		10	11	4		1	9			
11		2	3		5	6		8	9	10	11	4		1	7			
12		2	3		5	6		8	9	10		4		1	7	11		
13		2	3		5	6		8	9	10	11	4		1	7			
14		2	3		5	6		8	9	10	11	4		1	7			
15		2	3		5	6		8	9	10	11	4		1	7			
16		2	3		5	6		8	9	10	11	4		1	7			
17		2	3		5	6		8	9	10	11	4	7	1				
18		2	3		5	6		8	9	10	11	4	7	1				
19		2	3		5	6		8	9	10	11	4	7	1				
20		2	3		5	6		8	9	10	11	4	7	1				
21		2	3	6	5			8	9	10	11	4	7	1				
22		2	3	6	5			8	9	10	11	4	7	1				
23		2	3		5	6		8	9	10	11	4	7	1				
24		2	3		5	6		8	9	10	11	4	7	1				
25		2	3	4	5	6		8	9	10	11		7	1				
26		2	3	5		6		8	9	10	11	4	7	1				
27		2	3	4	5	6			9	10	11		7	1	8			
28		2	3		5	6		8	9	10	11	4	7	1				
29		2	3		5	6		8	9	10		4	7	1			11	
30		2	3	6	5			8	9	10	11	4	7	1				
31		2	3	4	5	6		8	9	10			7	1			11	
32		2	3	4	5	6		8	9	10			7	1			11	
33		2	3	5		6		8	9	10		4	7	1			11	
34		2	3	5		6		8	9	10	11	4	7	1				
35		2	3		5	6		8	9		11	4	7	1			10	
36		2	3		5	6		8	9		11	4	7	1			10	3
37		2	3	4	5	6		8	9		11		7	1			10	
38		2	3	4	5	6		8	9		11		7	1			10	
Apps	8	38	37	15	34	36	8	37	37	34	32	30	24	30	11	2	4	1
Goals					2	3	2	17	15	13	4	2	3		2		2	

F.A. CUP

Rd	Date	Opposition	Res.	H.T.	Att.	Goalscorers	Annan	Cottle	Spear	Wedlock	Hanlin	Maxwell	Gilligan	Burton	Hilton	Marr	Staniforth	Denney
1R	12 Jan	LEEDS CITY	4-1	3-0	14324	Gilligan(2), Maxwell(2) (£427-0-9)	2	3		5	6	8	9	10	11	4	7	1
2R	2 Feb	Woolwich Arsenal	1-2	0-1	31300	Gilligan (£1066)	2	3	4	5	6	8	9	10	11		7	1

GLOUCESTERSHIRE CUP FINAL

	Date	Opposition	Res.	H.T.	Att.	Goalscorers
	1 Apr	Bristol Rovers	2-0	1-0	12629	Gilligan(2) (£318)

FRIENDLIES

No.	Date	Opposition	Res.	H.T.	Att.	Goalscorers
1	10 Dec	Southampton	1-2	0-1	3000	Bennett (Harrison Benefit)
2	23 Feb	BIRMINGHAM	3-2	3-1	6000	Gilligan(2), Connelly
3	25	SOUTHAMPTON	2-4	0-1	2000	Connelly,Fenton(£140,14,0)(William Tuft Benefit)

FINAL LEAGUE TABLE

		P	W	D	L	F	A	Pts
1	Newcastle	38	22	7	9	74	46	51
2	Bristol C.	38	20	8	10	66	47	48
3	Everton	38	20	5	13	70	46	45
4	Sheffield U	38	17	11	10	57	55	45
5	Aston Villa	38	19	6	13	78	52	44
6	Bolton	38	18	8	12	59	47	44
7	Woolwich Arsenal	38	20	4	14	66	59	44
8	Manchester U.	38	17	8	13	53	56	42
9	Birmingham	38	15	8	15	52	52	38
10	Sunderland	38	14	9	15	65	66	37
11	Middlesbrough	38	15	6	17	56	63	36
12	Blackburn	38	14	7	17	56	59	35
13	The Wednesday	38	12	11	15	49	60	35
14	Preston	38	14	7	17	44	57	35
15	Liverpool	38	13	7	18	64	65	33
16	Bury	38	13	6	19	58	68	32
17	Manchester C.	38	10	12	16	53	77	32
18	Notts Co.	38	8	15	15	46	50	31
19	Derby	38	9	9	20	41	59	27
20	Stoke	38	8	10	20	41	64	26

SEASON 1907-08 BRISTOL CITY
FOOTBALL LEAGUE DIVISION ONE

No.	Date	Opposition	Pos.	Res.	H.T.	Att.	Goalscorers	Demmery W.	Annan W.A.	Cottle J.	Marr C.R.	Wedlock W.J.	Hanlin P.	Staniforth F.W.	Maxwell W.S.	Gilligan S.A.	Burton A.	Hilton F.	Gale T.	Connelly F.H.	Young R.K.	Clay H.A.	Copestake L.	Spear A.	Rippon W.	Talbot-Lewis A.E.	Nixon J.	Chapman A.T.
1	2 Sep	EVERTON		3-2	2-2	14000	Gilligan, Maxwell, Staniforth	1	2	3	4	5	6	7	8	9	10	11										
2	7	Woolwich Arsenal	4	4-0	1-0	17000	Connelly(2), Maxwell(2)	1		3	4	5	6	7	8	9		11		2	10							
3	14	THE WEDNESDAY	5	0-2	0-0	20000		1		3	4	5	6	7	8	9	10	11		2								
4	21	NEWCASTLE UNITED	8	1-1	1-1	20000	Hilton	1		3	4	5	6	7	8	9		11		2	10							
5	23	The Wednesday	9	3-5	0-1	12000	Connelly, Maxwell, O.G.	1		3	4	5	6	7	8	9		11		2	10							
6	28	Notts County	13	1-3	1-1	14000	Gilligan			3	4	5	6	7	8	9	10			2		1	11					
7	5 Oct	MANCHESTER CITY	12	2-1	2-0	15000	Hilton, Staniforth			3	4	5		7		9	10	11		2		1		6	8			
8	12	Preston North End	14	0-3	0-1	8000				3	4	5	11	7		9	10			2		1		6	8			
9	19	BURY	12	1-1	1-0	12000	Rippon			3	4	5		7	8		10	11		2		1		6	9			
10	26	Aston Villa	10	4-4	1-3	22000	Gilligan, Hilton, Maxwell, Wedlock			3	4	5	6	7	8	9	10	11		2		1						
11	2 Nov	LIVERPOOL	8	2-0	1-0	12000	Gilligan, Wedlock			3	4	5	6	7	8	9	10	11		2		1						
12	9	Middlesbrough	7	2-0	0-0	18000	Maxwell, Staniforth			3	4	5	6	7	8	9	10	11		2		1						
13	16	SHEFFIELD UNITED	6	3-2	2-1	14000	Burton, Gilligan, Maxwell			3	4	5	6	7	8	9	10	11		2		1						
14	23	Chelsea	7	1-4	0-3	40000	Burton			3	4	5	6	7	8	9	10	11		2		1						
15	30	NOTTINGHAM FOREST	4	3-0	3-0	15000	Burton, Hilton, Maxwll(pen) (Harry Clay benefit)		2	3	4	5	6	7	8	9	10	11								1		
16	7 Dec	Manchester United	5	1-2	1-1	30000	Hilton		2	3		5	6	7	8	9	10	11			4					1		
17	14	BLACKBURN ROVERS	7	2-2	2-0	12000	Burton, Maxwell		2	3		5		7	8	9	10	11			4			6		1		
18	21	Bolton Wanderers	5	2-1	0-1	10000	Burton(2)		2	3	4	5		7	8	9		11			10			6		1		
19	25	Sunderland	5	3-3	3-2	10000	Gilligan, Maxwell, Staniforth		2	3		5	6	7	8	9		11			10			4		1		
20	26	Everton	5	0-0	0-0	30000			2	3		5	6	7	8	9	10				4					1	11	
21	28	BIRMINGHAM	5	0-0	0-0	12000			2	3		5	6	7	8	9	10				4					1	11	
22	4 Jan	WOOLWICH ARSENAL	7	1-2	0-1	15000	Gilligan		2	3		5	6	7	8	9	10				4					1	11	
23	18	Newcastle United	7	0-2	0-1	30000				3	4	5	6	7	8	9	10	11		2						1		
24	25	NOTTS COUNTY	6	2-1	2-0	12000	Gilligan(2)			3	4	5	6	7	8	9	10	11		2						1		
25	8 Feb	PRESTON NORTH END	9	1-3	1-2	10000	Maxwell	1		3	4		6	7	8	9	10	11		2								5
26	15	Bury	9	1-1	0-1	10000	Gilligan			3	4		6	7	8	9	10	11		2	1				5			
27	29	Liverpool	13	1-3	0-2	15000	Gilligan			3	4		6	7	8	9	10	11		2	1				5			
28	7 Mar	MIDDLESBROUGH	14	0-1	0-1	10000			2	3		5	6	7	8	9	10	11			4					1		
29	11	ASTON VILLA	11	2-2	2-1	10000	Connelly, Copestake		2	3		5	6	7		9	10			8	4		11			1		
30	14	Sheffield United	14	0-2	0-1	14000			2	3		5	6	7	8	9	10	11			4					1		
31	21	CHELSEA	16	0-0	0-0	15000			2	3		5	6		8	9	10	11			4	1		7				
32	28	Nottingham Forest	17	1-3	1-2	15000	Gilligan		2	3		5	6	7	8	9	10	11			4	1						
33	4 Apr	MANCHESTER UNITED	17	1-1	0-1	15000	Maxwell		2	3		5	6	7	8		10	11			4	1			9			
34	11	Blackburn Rovers	19	1-4	1-2	8000	Gilligan		2	3		5	6	7	8	9	10	11			4	1						
35	18	BOLTON WANDERERS	17	2-0	0-0	10000	Gilligan(2)		2	3		5	6		8	9	10	11			4	1		7				
36	20	SUNDERLAND	17	3-0	2-0	19500	Burton, Gilligan, Maxwell		2	3		5	6		8	9	10	11			4	1		7				
37	21	Manchester City	17	0-0	0-0	2500			2	3		5	6		8	9	10	11			4	1		7				
38	25	Birmingham	10	4-0	1-0	4000	Burton(2), Rippon, O.G.		2	3		5	6	7	8		10	11			4	1			9			
							Apps.	6	13	36	24	34	34	35	34	33	32	30	2	9	24	11	2	23	7	21	7	1
							Goals					2		4	13	16	9	5		4			1		2			

		P.	W.	D.	L.	F.	A.
Home		19	8	7	4	29	21
Away		19	4	5	10	29	40

F.A. CUP

No.	Date	Opposition		Res.	H.T.	Att.	Goalscorers	Demmery W.	Annan W.A.	Cottle J.	Marr C.R.	Wedlock W.J.	Hanlin P.	Staniforth F.W.	Maxwell W.S.	Gilligan S.A.	Burton A.	Hilton F.	Gale T.	Connelly F.H.	Young R.K.	Clay H.A.	Copestake L.	Spear A.	Rippon W.	Talbot-Lewis A.E.	Nixon J.	Chapman A.T.
1R	11 Jan	GRIMSBY TOWN		0-0	0-0	11000	(£350)		2	3	4	5	6	7	8	9	10	11								1		
1Rr	15	Grimsby Town		1-2	1-2	6000	Hilton (£203)		2	3		5	6	7	8	9	10	11			4					1		

GLOUCESTERSHIRE CUP FINAL

	Date	Opposition	Res.	H.T.	Att.	Goalscorers
	29 Apr	BRISTOL ROVERS	2-0	2-0	8186	Burton, Maxwell (£230)

FRIENDLIES

No.	Date	Opposition	Res.	H.T.	Att.	Goalscorers
1	1 Feb	Brentford	3-1	1-0	4000	Gilligan(2), Maxwell
2	2 Apr	Swansea Town	3-2	1-2		Gould(2), Connelly
3	30	Aberdare	1-0	1-0		Staniforth

FINAL LEAGUE TABLE

		P	W	D	L	F	A	Pts
1	Manchester U.	38	23	6	9	81	48	52
2	Aston Villa	38	17	9	12	77	59	43
3	Manchester C.	38	16	11	11	62	54	43
4	Newcastle	38	15	12	11	65	54	42
5	The Wednesday	38	19	4	15	73	64	42
6	Middlesbrough	38	17	7	14	54	45	41
7	Bury	38	14	11	13	58	61	39
8	Liverpool	38	16	6	16	68	61	38
9	Nottingham F.	38	13	11	14	59	62	37
10	Bristol C.	38	12	12	14	58	61	36
11	Everton	38	15	6	17	58	64	36
12	Preston	38	12	12	14	47	53	36
13	Chelsea	38	14	8	16	53	62	36
14	Blackburn	38	12	12	14	51	63	36
14	Woolwich Arsenal	38	12	12	14	51	63	36
16	Sunderland	38	16	3	19	78	75	35
17	Sheffield U.	38	12	11	15	52	58	35
18	Notts Co.	38	13	8	17	39	51	34
19	Bolton	38	14	5	19	52	58	33
20	Birmingham	38	9	12	17	40	60	30

1907/08 season
(L.to R.) Back: Batten (Trainer), Gale, Rippon, Young, Demmery, Spear, F.N.Bacon (Dir.), H.Thickett (Manager).
Middle: Marr, Staniforth, Maxwell, Gilligan, Connelly, Hanlin, Cottle, J.Daveridge (Dir.). Front: Wedlock, Hilton.

Hardy   The Cup Final side of 1909.   Marr
H.Thickett (Manager)   F.W.Bacon (Director)   Annan   Young   Clay   Cottle   Rippon   Batten
Spear   Staniforth   Gilligan   Maxwell   Burton   Hilton   Wedlock   Hanlin

SEASON 1908-09
FOOTBALL LEAGUE DIVISION ONE

No.	Date	Opposition	Pos.	Res.	H.T.	Att.	Goalscorers	Clay H.A.	Young R.K.	Cottle J.	Spear A.	Wedlock W.J.	Hanlin P.	Staniforth F.W.	Maxwell W.S.	Gilligan S.A.	Burton A.	Hilton F.	Marr C.R.	Rippon W.	Hardy R.W.	Annan W.A.	Penman T.	Latham F.	Radford J.T.	Brown J.R.	Clegg J.	Cowell J.
1	1 Sep	Blackburn Rovers		1-1	0-0	15000	Maxwell	1	2	3	4	5	6	7	8	9	10	11										
2	5	EVERTON		0-2	0-1	15000		1	2	3	4	5	6	7	8	9	10	11										
3	9	Newcastle United	18	1-2	1-0	22000	Gilligan	1	2	3		5	6	7		9	10	11	4		8							
4	12	Leicester Fosse		1-1	1-1	17000	Burton	1	2	3		5	6	7		9	10	11	4		8							
5	19	WOOLWICH ARSENAL	13	2-1	1-0	16000	Gilligan, Hilton	1	2	3	4	5	6	7		9	10	11			8							
6	26	Notts County	9	1-0	0-0	13000	Burton	1	2	3		5	6	7		9	10	11	4		8							
7	3 Oct	NEWCASTLE UNITED	8	3-3	1-0	16000	Gilligan(2), Burton	1	2	3		5	6	7		9	10	11	4		8							
8	10	The Wednesday	11	0-2	0-2	15000		1	4	3	6			7		9	10	11			8		2	5				
9	17	Preston North End	15	1-2	0-2	6000	Burton	1	2	3	4	5	6	7		9	10	11			8							
10	24	MIDDLESBROUGH	15	1-1	1-0	12000	Hardy (Bill Demmery's Benefit)	1	2	3	4	5	6	7		9	10	11			8							
11	31	Manchester City	17	1-5	0-1	30000	Wedlock	1	2	3	4	5	6	7	8	9	10	11										
12	7 Nov	LIVERPOOL	15	1-0	0-0	14000	Burton	1		3	6	5		7		8	10			4			11	2	9			
13	14	Bury	12	2-1	0-1	8000	Burton, Rippon	1	2	3	6	5		7		8	10				9		11	2				
14	21	SHEFFIELD UNITED	12	1-1	1-0	12000	Gilligan	1		3	6	5		7		9	10			4	8		11	2				
15	28	Aston Villa	11	1-1	1-0	20000	Gilligan	1		3	6	5		7		9	10			4	8		11	2				
16	5 Dec	NOTTINGHAM FOREST	9	2-1	1-0	12000	Hilton(2)	1		3	6	5		7		9	10	11	4		8			2				
17	12	Sunderland	8	2-0	1-0	12000	Hilton, Rippon	1		3	6	5		7	8		10	11	4	9				2				
18	19	CHELSEA	5	1-0	1-0	12000	Hilton	1		3	6	5		7	8		10	11	4	9				2				
19	25	Bradford City	5	1-0	1-0	35000	Hilton	1		3	6	5		7			10	11	4	9				2		8		
20	26	BRADFORD CITY	5	0-1	0-0	23000		1		3	6	5		7	8		10		4	9	11			2				
21	2 Jan	Everton	9	2-5	1-4	18000	Rippon, Staniforth	1		3	6	5		7	8		10		11	4	9			2		7		
22	9	LEICESTER FOSSE	10	1-1	0-0	12000	Gilligan	1		3	6	5	4			9	10	11			8			2				
23	23	Woolwich Arsenal	7	1-1	1-1	10000	Rippon	1		3	6	5	4	7		8	10				9		11	2				
24	30	NOTTS COUNTY	7	1-0	1-0	10000	Staniforth	1		3	6	5	4	7		8	10				9		11	2				
25	13 Feb	THE WEDNESDAY	6	1-1	0-0	10000	Burton	1				5	6	7		8	10	11	4	9				2		3		
26	27	Middlesbrough	10	0-4	0-2	10000		1			6	5		7	8		10	11	4	9				2		3		
27	13 Mar	Liverpool	9	2-1	1-0	8000	Rippon(2,1pen)	1	2	3	5		6	7		8	10			4	9		11					
28	17	PRESTON NORTH END	10	2-3	1-2	6000	Gilligan, Hardy	1	2	3	5		6	7		8	10			4	9		11					
29	20	BURY	8	4-2	3-1	10000	Hardy, Maxwell, Rippon, Staniforth	1	6	3		5		7	8		10			4	9		11	2				
30	3 Apr	ASTON VILLA	12	0-0	0-0	16000		1		3	5		6	7	8		10			4	9		11	2				
31	5	Sheffield United	13	1-3	1-1	5000	Maxwell		4	3	5		6	7	10			11		9	8		2				1	
32	9	Manchester United	8	1-0	1-0	18000	Burton	1		3	6	5	4	7	8	9	10						11	2				
33	10	Nottingham Forest	7	1-1	0-1	10000	Gilligan	1		3	6	5	4	7		9	10	11			8			2				
34	12	MANCHESTER UNITED	6	0-0	0-0	20000		1	4	3	6	5			8		10	11		9			7	2				
35	13	BLACKBURN ROVERS	8	1-4	0-1	8000	Hardy	1	4	3	6	5			8		10	11		9			7	2				
36	17	SUNDERLAND	12	2-4	2-0	7000	Gilligan, Hilton	1	4	3	6	5			8	9	10	11					7	2				
37	26	Chelsea	15	1-3	0-2	12000	Staniforth	1	4	3	6	5	8	7			10	11					9	2				
38	28	MANCHESTER CITY	8	1-0	0-0	5000	O.G.	1	4	3	6	5		7	8		10	11						2				9
		Apps.						37	21	36	33	32	22	34	11	29	35	27	18	23	26	1	1	1	3	1	1	1
		Goals										1		4	3	10	8	7		7	4							

F.A. CUP

Round	Date	Opposition		Res.	H.T.	Att.	Goalscorers	Clay H.A.	Young R.K.	Cottle J.	Spear A.	Wedlock W.J.	Hanlin P.	Staniforth F.W.	Maxwell W.S.	Gilligan S.A.	Burton A.	Hilton F.	Marr C.R.	Rippon W.	Hardy R.W.	Annan W.A.	Penman T.	Latham F.
1R	16 Jan	SOUTHAMPTON		1-1	1-1	20000	Rippon (£670)	1		3	6	5		7		8	10			4	9		11	2
1Rr	20	Southampton		2-0	1-0	18800	Hardy, Rippon(pen) (£962)	1		3	6	5		7		8	10			4	9		11	2
2R	6 Feb	BURY		2-2	2-0	24000	Burton, Gilligan (£817-4-4)	1		3	6	5		7		9	10	11	4		8			2
2Rr	10	Bury		1-0	1-0	9895	Gilligan (£353)	1		3	6	5		7		8	10	11	4	9				2
3R	20	NORWICH CITY		2-0	1-0	24009	Burton, Rippon (£868-0-9)	1		3	6	5		7		8	10	11	4	9				2
4R	6 Mar	Glossop		0-0	0-0	4500	(£238)	1		3	6	5		7		8	10			4	9		11	2
4Rr	10	GLOSSOP		1-0	0-0	15932	Gilligan (£586)	1		3	6	5		7		8	10			4	9		11	2
SF	27	Derby County		1-1	0-0	33878	Rippon(pen) (At Stamford Bridge) (£2056)	1		3	6	5		7		8	10			4	9		11	2
SFr	31	Derby County		2-1	1-0	27600	(At St. Andrew's) (£962-8-6)	1		3	6	5		7		8	10			4	9		11	2
F	24 Apr	Manchester United		0-1	0-1	71401	(At The Crystal Palace) (£6434)	1		3	6	5	4	7		9	10	11			8			2

N.B. Gloucestershire Cup Final held over to 1909-10 season.

FINAL LEAGUE TABLE

1	Newcastle	38	24	5	9	65:41	53
2	Everton	38	18	10	10	82:57	46
3	Sunderland	38	21	2	15	78:63	44
4	Blackburn	38	14	13	11	61:50	41
5	The Wednesday	38	17	6	15	67:61	40
6	Woolwich Arsenal	38	14	10	14	52:49	38
7	Aston Villa	38	14	10	14	58:56	38
8	Bristol C.	38	13	12	13	45:58	38
9	Middlesbrough	38	14	9	15	59:53	37
10	Preston	38	13	11	14	48:44	37
11	Chelsea	38	14	9	15	56:61	37
12	Sheffield U.	38	14	9	15	51:59	37
13	Manchester U.	38	15	7	16	58:68	37
14	Nottingham F.	38	14	8	16	66:57	36
15	Notts C.	38	14	8	16	51:48	36
16	Liverpool	38	15	6	17	57:65	36
17	Bury	38	14	8	16	63:77	36
18	Bradford C.	38	12	10	16	47:47	34
19	Manchester C.	38	15	4	19	67:69	34
20	Leicester Fosse	38	8	9	21	54:102	25

SEASON 1909-10
FOOTBALL LEAGUE DIVISION ONE

No.	Date	Opposition	Pos.	Res.	H.T.	Att.	Goalscorers	Clay H.A.	Annan W.A.	Cottle J.R.	Marr C.R.	Wedlock W.J.	Spear A.T.	Staniforth F.W.	Gilligan S.A.	Rippon W.	Foster A.	Shearman B.	Hanlin P.	Cowell J.	Hardy R.W.	Burton A.D.	Hilton F.	Clegg J.	Young R.K.	Chapman A.T.	Batty W.
1	4 Sep	Bradford City		1-3	0-3	24000	Rippon	1	2	3	4	5	6	7	8	9	10	11									
2	8	BURY		1-1	0-0	7000	Cowell	1	2	3	4	5		7	8		10	11	6	9							
3	11	THE WEDNESDAY	14	1-1	1-1	10000	Cowell	1	2	3	4	5		7	8		10	11	6	9							
4	13	Blackburn Rovers	15	2-5	1-3	8000	Foster, Shearman	1	2	3	4	5		7	8		10	11	6	9							
5	18	MIDDLESBROUGH	13	4-1	2-0	12000	Cowell(3), Staniforth	1	2	3		5	4	7				11	6	9	8	10					
6	25	Bury	11	2-1	0-1	12000	Cowell, Hardy	1	2	3		5	4	7				11	6	9	8	10					
7	2 Oct	TOTTENHAM HOTSPUR	11	0-0	0-0	18000		1	2	3		5	4	7				11	6	9	8	10					
8	9	Preston North End	13	0-3	0-1	11000		1	2	3	4	5		7				11	6	9	8	10					
9	16	NOTTS COUNTY	11	3-1	1-1	12000	Hardy(2), Cowell	1	2	3	4	5	6	7				11		9	8	10					
10	23	Newcastle United	12	1-3	0-1	10000	Cowell	1	2	3	4	5	6	7						9	8	10	11				
11	30	LIVERPOOL	13	0-1	0-0	12000		1	2	3	4	5	6	7	8					9	11	10					
12	6 Nov	Aston Villa	15	0-1	0-1	25000		1	2	3	4	5	6	7				11		9	8	10					
13	13	SHEFFIELD UNITED	15	0-2	0-1	10000		1	2	3		5	6	7			10	11	4	9	8						
14	20	Woolwich Arsenal	13	2-2	2-1	8000	Rippon(2)	1	2	3		5	6		8	9		11	4		7	10					
15	27	BOLTON WANDERERS	14	1-0	0-0	8000	Burton	1	2	3	4	5	6		8	9		11			7	10					
16	4 Dec	Chelsea	14	1-4	0-0	20000	Rippon(pen)		2	3	4	5	6		8	9		11			7	10		1			
17	11	BLACKBURN ROVERS	14	2-2	1-1	4000	Hardy, Marr		2	3	4	5	6		8	9		11			7	10		1			
18	18	Nottingham Forest	13	0-0	0-0	8000			2	3	4	5	6		8			11		9	7	10		1			
19	25	EVERTON	13	3-1	1-0	15000	Cowell, Gilligan, Staniforth		2	3		5	6	7	8			11	4	9		10		1			
20	27	Everton	13	0-1	0-1	30000			2	3		5	6	7	8			11	4	9		10		1			
21	28	SUNDERLAND	13	2-3	0-0	20000	Cowell(2pens)		2	3		5	6	7	8			11	4	9		10		1			
22	1 Jan	Sunderland	15	0-4	0-0	20000			2	3	4	5	6		8			11		9	7	10		1			
23	8	Bradford City	14	2-0	1-0	8000	Burton(2)		2	3	4	5	6		8			11		9	7	10		1			
24	22	The Wednesday	15	0-2	0-2	6000			2	3	4	5	6		8			11		9	7	10		1			
25	12 Feb	Tottenham Hotspur	16	2-3	1-2	25000	Gilligan, Marr	1	2	3	9		6	7	8			11	4			10			5		
26	19	PRESTON NORTH END	15	2-0	1-0	10000	Cowell, Shearman	1		3	4	5			8			11	6	9	7	10			2		
27	26	Notts County	15	2-0	0-0	8000	Cowell(2)	1		3	4	5			8			11	6	9	7	10			2		
28	12 Mar	Liverpool	15	1-0	0-0	20000	Gilligan	1		3	4	5	6		8			11		9	7	10			2		
29	19	ASTON VILLA	15	0-0	0-0	16000	(Sammy Gilligan's Benefit)	1		3	4	5	6		8			11		9	7	10			2		
30	25	Manchester United	15	1-2	0-1	50000	Staniforth	1		3		5	6	7				11	4	9	8	10			2		
31	26	Sheffield United	15	0-4	0-2	12000		1		3		5	6	7				11	4	9	8	10			2		
32	28	MANCHESTER UNITED	14	2-1	1-1	18000	Cowell, Wedlock	1		3	4	5		7	8			11	6	9		10			2		
33	2 Apr	WOOLWICH ARSENAL	15	0-1	0-1	8000		1		3	4			7	8			11	6	9		10			2	5	
34	9	Bolton Wanderers	18	2-4	2-3	5000	Cowell, Hardy	1	2	3		5					10	11	6	9	7				4		8
35	16	CHELSEA	17	1-0	1-0	16000	Marr	1		3	4	5						11	6	9	7	10			2		8
36	20	Middlesbrough	17	0-0	0-0	12000		1	2	3		5						11	6	9	7	10			4		8
37	25	NEWCASTLE UNITED	17	0-3	0-1	5000		1		3	4	5						11	6	9	7	10			2		8
38	30	NOTTINGHAM FOREST	16	4-0	1-0	11000	Cowell(4,1pen)	1	2	3		5		7				11	6	9	8	10			4		
							Apps.	29	28	38	25	35	26	22	22	6	7	35	24	31	28	33	1	9	14	1	4
							Goals				3	1		3	3	4	1	2		20	5	3					

F.A. CUP

				Res.	H.T.	Att.	Goalscorers	Annan	Cottle	Marr	Wedlock	Spear	Staniforth	Gilligan	Shearman	Hardy	Burton	Clegg
1R	15 Jan	LIVERPOOL		2-0	1-0	16000	Burton, Rippon (£552)	2	3	4	5	6		8	11	7	10	1
2R	5 Feb	WEST BROMWICH ALBION		1-1	1-1	16885	Gilligan (£576)	2	3	4	5	6		8	11	7	10	1
2Rr	9	West Bromwich Albion		2-4	1-2	14870	Gilligan, Staniforth (£560)	2	3	4	5	6	7	9	11	8	10	1

GLOUCESTERSHIRE CUP FINAL(S)

			Res.	H.T.	Att.	Goalscorers
	1 Sep	Bristol Rovers *	1-1	1-1	9521	Burton (£275)
r	13 Oct	BRISTOL ROVERS *	1-1	1-0	3000	Cowell
2r	26	Bristol Rovers *	2-1	2-0	2000	Cowell, Radford
	6 Apr	BRISTOL ROVERS	2-0	1-0	1175	Foster(2) (£33)

* Season 1908-09

FRIENDLIES

			Res.	H.T.	Att.	Goalscorers
1	6 Oct	THE BUTTERFLIES	7-2	3-0		Stock(3),Cottle(2),Spear(2) (Unemployed Benefit)
2	3 Nov	Exeter City	1-4	1-2	3000	Gilligan
3	17	Cardiff City	7-0	3-0	2000	Rippon(3), Hardy(2), Shearman, Wedlock
4	5 Mar	Plymouth Argyle	1-1	1-1	6000	Hardy

FINAL LEAGUE TABLE

1	Aston Villa	38	23	7	8	84:42	53
2	Liverpool	38	21	6	11	78:57	48
3	Blackburn	38	18	9	11	73:55	45
4	Newcastle	38	19	7	12	70:56	45
5	Manchester U.	38	19	7	12	69:61	45
6	Sheffield U.	38	16	10	12	62:41	42
7	Bradford C.	38	17	8	13	64:47	42
8	Sunderland	38	18	5	15	66:51	41
9	Notts Co.	38	15	10	13	67:59	40
10	Everton	38	16	8	14	51:56	40
11	The Wednesday	38	15	9	14	60:63	39
12	Preston	38	15	5	18	52:58	35
13	Bury	38	12	9	17	62:66	33
14	Nottingham F.	38	11	11	16	54:72	33
15	Tottenham	38	11	10	17	53:69	32
16	Bristol C.	38	12	8	18	45:60	32
17	Middlesbrough	38	11	9	18	56:73	31
18	Woolwich Arsenal	38	11	9	18	37:67	31
19	Chelsea	38	11	7	20	47:70	29
20	Bolton	38	9	6	23	44:71	24

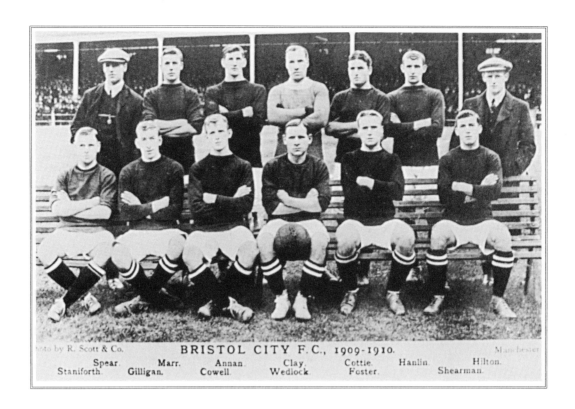

Photo by R. Scott & Co.   BRISTOL CITY F.C., 1909-1910.   Manchester

Spear.   Marr.   Annan.   Clay.   Cottle.   Hanlin.   Hilton.
Staniforth. Gilligan.   Cowell.   Wedlock.   Foster.   Shearman.

1909/10 Season

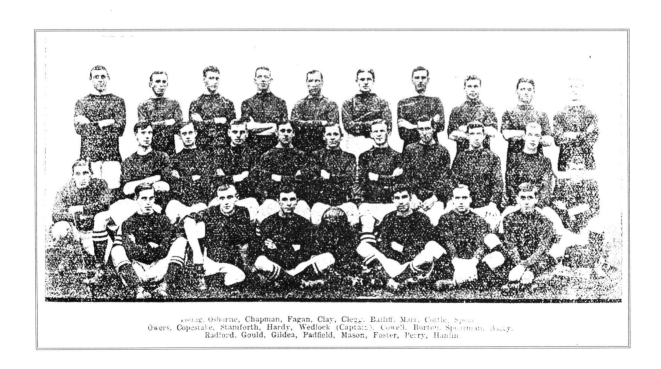

Young, Osborne, Chapman, Fagan, Clay, Clegg, Bailiff, Marr, Cottle, Spear.
Owers, Copestake, Stamforth, Hardy, Wedlock (Captain), Cowell, Burton, Spearman, Batty.
Radford, Gould, Gildea, Padfield, Mason, Foster, Perry, Hanlin.

1910/11 Season

SEASON 1910-11
FOOTBALL LEAGUE DIVISION ONE

No.	Date	Opposition	Pos.	Res.	H.T.	Att.	Goalscorers	Clegg J.	Young R.K	Cottle J.R.	Marr C.R.	Wedlock W.J	Hanlin P.	Staniforth F.W.	Hardy R.W.	Cowell J.	Burton A.D.	Shearman B.	Clay H.A.	Owers E.H.	Foster A.	Fagan S.	Mason S.R.	Clark W.B.	Osborne A.T.	Date M.	Logan A.T.	Gadsby E.	Bailiff W.E.	Spear A.T.	Padfield W.	Sweet F.G.	Jones E.	Gildea H.	Batty W.	Chapman A.T.	Copestake L.
1	3 Sep	Newcastle United		1-0	0-0	26000	Hardy	1	2	3	4	5	6	7	8	9	10	11																			
2	10	TOTTENHAM HOTSPUR		0-2	0-0	18000		1	2	3	4	5	6	7	8	9	10	11																			
3	17	Middlesbrough	17	0-3	0-1	26000		1	2	3	4	5	6	7	8	9	10	11																			
4	24	PRESTON NORTH END	18	0-0	0-0	15000			2	3	4	5	6	7	8		10	11	1	9																	
5	1 Oct	Notts County	20	0-2	0-1	14000			2	3	4	5	6		7	8	9	11	1			10															
6	8	MANCHESTER UNITED	20	0-1	0-1	20000	(Billy Wedlock's Benefit)			3		5	6		7	8	10			1	9		11	2	4												
7	15	Liverpool	20	0-4	0-1	15000			2	3		5	6	7	8			11	1	9	10		4														
8	22	BURY	19	2-0	1-0	12000	Burton, Owers		2	3	4	5	6		8			10	11	1	9				7												
9	29	Sheffield United	18	4-0	1-0	10000	Hardy(2), Burton, Owers		2	3	4	5	6		8			10	11	1	9				7												
10	5 Nov	ASTON VILLA	18	1-2	1-2	18000	Owers (Andy Burton's Benefit)		5	3	4		6		8			10	11	1	9			2	7												
11	12	Sunderland	19	1-3	0-2	15000	Owers		5	3	4		6		8			10	11	1	9			2	7												
12	19	WOOLWICH ARSENAL	20	0-1	0-0	8000			2	3	4	5	6		8			10	11	1	9				7												
13	26	Bradford City	20	1-3	1-3	15000	Owers			3	4	5		7				11	1	9	10	2			8	6											
14	3 Dec	BLACKBURN ROVERS	20	1-0	1-0	5000	Burton		2	3	4	5	6		11		10		1	9					7		8										
15	10	Nottingham Forrest	20	3-3	2-1	8000	Owers(2), Logan		2	3	4	5	6		8				11	1	9				7		10										
16	17	MANCHESTER CITY	18	2-1	1-1	10000	Logan, Wedlock		2	3	4	5	6						11	1	9				7		10	8									
17	24	Everton	20	3-4	1-1	8000	Logan, Owers, Wedlock		2	3	4	5	6						11	1	9				7		10	8									
18	26	THE WEDNESDAY	20	2-2	2-1	20000	Gadsby(pen), Shearman		2	3	4	5							11		9				7		10	8	1	6							
19	27	OLDHAM ATHLETIC	18	3-2	2-1	16500	Owers, Shearman, Wedlock		2	3	4	5		7					11		9		3				10	8	1								
20	31	NEWCASTLE UNITED	14	1-0	1-0	15000	Logan		2	6		5		7					11		9		3				10	8	1	4							
21	2 Jan	The Wednesday	16	1-2	0-2	5000	Logan		2	6		5		7					11		9		3	4			10	8	1								
22	7	Tottenham Hotspur	18	2-3	1-2	20000	Owers(2)		2	6		5							11		9		3		7		10	8	1	4							
23	21	MIDDLESBROUGH	19	3-2	1-2	8000	Owers(3)		4		5					11																						
24	28	Preston North End	18	0-4	0-1	12000			4	3		5	6	8		11					9		2		7		10		1								
25	4 Feb	NOTTS COUNTY	15	1-0	0-0	6000	Owers		4			5	6	8		11				1	9		3		7		10				2						
26	11	Manchester United	17	1-3	0-2	17000	Sweet		2		4		6		8			11	1	9				7		10					3	5					
27	18	LIVERPOOL	18	1-1	1-1	10000	Hardy		2		4	5	6		8			11	1					7		9	10					3					
28	25	Bury	18	1-2	1-1	7000	Owers		2		4	5	6					11	1	9				7		8	10					3					
29	4 Mar	SHEFFIELD UNITED	18	0-2	0-1	7000			2		4	5	6	8	11				1	9			3		7		10										
30	11	Aston Villa	20	0-2	0-2	20000			2		4	5	6				10		1	9	11	3		7		8										
31	18	SUNDERLAND	20	1-1	0-1	5000	Logan(pen)		2		4	5	6	7			10		1	9	11					8					3					
32	25	Woolwich Arsenal	20	0-3	0-3	10977			2		4	5	6	7			10	11	1	9				8							3				
33	1 Apr	BRADFORD CITY	20	0-2	0-0	8000			2		4		6	7			10	11	1	9						8						5	3			
34	8	Blackburn Rovers	20	0-2	0-0	7000			2		4	5	6				11		1	9		3		7									8	10		
35	14	Oldham Athletic	20	0-1	1-2	12000			2		4	5	6				10		1		3	7			8									9	11
36	15	NOTTINGHAM FOREST	20	5-1	1-1	5000	Burton, Chapman, Clark, Marr(pen), O.G.		2		4	5	6	7			10		1		3	8												9	11
37	22	Manchester City	19	2-1	1-1	34000	Logan(pen),Marr(pen) (G.Dorsett Benefit)		2		4	5	6	7			10		1	9		3				8									11
38	29	EVERTON	19	0-1	0-1	10000	(Joint benefit for A.Annan/A.Spear)		2		4	5	6	7			10		1	9		3				8									11
						Apps.		3	36	24	30	34	32	19	20	5	21	25	28	31	6	18	3	24	1	1	20	10	7	3	4	2	3	1	1	2	4
						Goals			2	3					4		4	2		16				1			7	1			1				1	1

	P.	W	D	L	F	A
Home	19	8	4	7	23	21
Away	19	3	1	15	20	45

F.A. CUP

				Res.	H.T.	Att.				Young R.K	Cottle J.R		Wedlock W.J	Hanlin P.				Burton A.D		Clay H.A	Owers E.H	Foster A								Bailiff W.E		Padfield W				
1R	14 Jan	CREWE ALEXANDRA		0-3	0-1	11600	(£370)			2	3		5	6				10		11		9			4	7				8	1				

GLOUCESTERSHIRE CUP FINAL

	Date	Opposition		Res.	H.T.	Att.	Goalscorers
	19 Apr	Bristol Rovers		1-0	1-0	4466	Foster (£129)

FINAL LEAGUE TABLE

1	Manchester U.	38	22	8	8	72:40	52
2	Aston Villa	38	22	7	9	69:41	51
3	Sunderland	38	15	15	8	67:48	45
4	Everton	38	19	7	12	50:36	45
5	Bradford C.	38	20	5	13	51:42	45
6	The Wednesday	38	17	8	13	47:48	42
7	Oldham	38	16	9	13	44:41	41
8	Newcastle	38	15	10	13	61:43	40
9	Sheffield U.	38	15	8	15	49:43	38
10	Woolwich Arsenal	38	13	12	13	41:49	38
11	Notts Co.	38	14	10	14	37:45	38
12	Blackburn	38	13	11	14	62:54	37
13	Liverpool	38	15	7	16	53:53	37
14	Preston	38	12	11	15	40:49	35
15	Tottenham	38	13	6	19	52:63	32
16	Middlesbrough	38	11	10	17	49:63	32
17	Manchester C.	38	9	13	16	43:58	31
18	Bury	38	9	11	18	43:71	29
19	Bristol C.	38	11	5	22	43:66	27
20	Nottingham F.	38	9	7	22	55:75	25

SEASON 1911-12
FOOTBALL LEAGUE DIVISION TWO

No.	Date	Opposition	Pos.	Res.	H.T.	Att.	Goalscorers
1	2 Sep	FULHAM		1-0	1-0	14000	Butler
2	4	Wolverhampton Wanderers		1-3	1-2	8000	Cairns
3	9	Derby County	17	0-3	0-0	8000	
4	16	STOCKPORT COUNTY	11	2-1	2-1	10000	Butler, Marr(pen)
5	23	Leeds City	15	1-3	1-1	12000	Logan
6	30	WOLVERHAMPTON WNDRS	16	0-3	0-0	10000	
7	7 Oct	Leicester Fosse	17	0-2	0-2	12000	
8	14	GAINSBROUGH TRINITY	15	2-0	1-0	7000	Copestake, Forbes
9	21	Grimsby Town	17	0-3	0-2	6000	
10	28	NOTTINGHAM FORREST	16	2-2	1-0	8000	Forbes(2)
11	4 Nov	Chelsea	18	2-2	1-2	25000	Logan, Wedlock
12	11	CLAPTON ORIENT	16	1-0	1-0	6000	Wedlock
13	18	Burnley	16	2-4	1-2	11000	Copestake(2)
14	25	Birmingham	15	0-0	0-0	12000	
15	2 Dec	HUDDERSFIELD TOWN	13	3-2	1-1	5000	Butler(3)
16	9	Blackpool	14	0-1	0-0	2400	
17	16	GLOSSOP	13	2-0	1-0	5000	Copestake, Forbes
18	23	Hull City	14	0-3	0-1	9000	
19	25	Barnsley	14	1-4	0-0	12000	Gechern
20	26	BARNSLEY	14	0-1	0-0	6000	
21	30	Fulham	15	1-2	0-1	10000	Forbes
22	6 Jan	DERBY COUNTY	14	1-1	0-1	4000	Ball
23	20	Stockport County	14	0-1	0-1	5000	
24	27	LEEDS CITY	14	4-1	3-1	8000	Butler(2), Brough, Wedlock
25	10 Feb	LEICESTER FOSSE	17	0-1	0-0	6000	
26	17	Gainsborough Trinity	16	3-2	1-0	5000	Bowyer, Butler, Marr
27	24	GRIMSBY TOWN	15	3-0	2-0	6000	Bowyer, Butler, Copestake
28	2 Mar	Nottingham Forest	16	0-2	0-1	7000	
29	9	CHELSEA	17	1-1	0-1	10000	Bowyer
30	16	Clapton Orient	17	0-4	0-2	8000	
31	23	BURNLEY	17	0-3	0-2	10000	
32	30	BIRMINGHAM	17	2-1	2-0	8000	Butler, Marr(pen)
33	5 Apr	Bradford Park Avenue	17	1-0	1-0	8000	Owers
34	6	Huddersfield Town	16	2-1	2-1	2000	Bowyer, Owers
35	8	BRADFORD PARK AVENUE	12	1-0	0-0	9000	Owers
36	13	BLACKPOOL	10	2-0	0-0	10000	Bowyer, Butler
37	20	Glossop	13	0-3	0-2	3000	
38	27	HULL CITY	13	0-0	0-0	6000	

Appearances / Goals summary

	Anderson F.	Young R.K.	Jones E.	Marr C.R.	Wedlock W.J.	Nicholson J.A.	Brand R.A.	Cams T.	Butler J.T.	Logan A.T.	Forbes J.	Fagan S.	Gould C.	Cley H.A.	Gechern P.	Osborne A.E.	Wilson P.	Copestake L.	Davis W.	Ware T.	Cook W.	Sweet F.G.	Ball H.	Brough J.	Bowyer S.	Chapman A.T.	Owers E.	Banfield L.
Apps.	7	27	31	33	35	37	8	11	28	17	27	16	26	25	4	1	10	29	1	5	3	2	2	8	13	3	8	1
Goals				3	3			1	11	2	5				1			5					1	1	5		3	

F.A. CUP

			Res.	H.T.			
1R	13 Jan	Northampton Town	0-1	0-0	16000	(£529)	

GLOUCESTERSHIRE CUP FINAL

			Res.	H.T.		
	3 Feb	BRISTOL ROVERS	1-0	1-0	8966	Copestake (£251-16-3)

FRIENDLIES

	Date		Res.	H.T.	Att.	Goalscorers
1	1 Jan	Cardiff City	0-2	0-2		
2	4 May	BRISTOL ROVERS *	3-1	1-1	1500	Gould, Owers, Wedlock

* Titanic Disaster Fund.

FINAL LEAGUE TABLE

		P	W	D	L	F	A	Pts
1	Derby	38	23	8	7	74	28	54
2	Chelsea	38	24	6	8	64	34	54
3	Burnley	38	22	8	8	77	41	52
4	Clapton Orient	38	21	3	14	61	44	45
5	Wolverhampton	38	16	10	12	57	33	42
6	Barnsley	38	15	12	11	45	42	42
7	Hull	38	17	8	13	54	51	42
8	Fulham	38	16	7	15	66	58	39
9	Grimsby	38	15	9	14	48	55	39
10	Leicester Fosse	38	15	7	16	49	66	37
11	Bradford P A	38	13	9	16	44	45	35
12	Birmingham	38	14	6	18	55	59	34
13	Bristol C	38	14	6	18	41	60	34
14	Blackpool	38	13	8	17	32	52	34
15	Nottingham F	38	13	7	18	46	48	33
16	Stockport	38	11	11	16	47	54	33
17	Huddersfield	38	13	6	19	50	64	32
18	Glossop	38	8	12	18	42	56	28
19	Leeds C	38	10	8	20	50	78	28
20	Gainsborough	38	5	13	20	30	64	23

SEASON 1912-13
FOOTBALL LEAGUE DIVISION TWO

No.	Date	Opposition	Pos.	Res.	H.T.	Att.	Goalscorers	Clay H.A.	Kearns J.	Jones E.	Marr C.R.	Wedlock W.J.	Nicholson J.A.	Broad T.H.	Marrison T.	Owers E.	Bowyer S.	Harris J.	Banfield L.	Butler J.T.	Copestake L.	Nichol W.D.	Moss A.J.	Brough J.	Ware T.	Edwards A.	Morgan T.	Gould C.	Young R.K.	Allen T.S.
1	4 Sep	BRADFORD PARK AVENUE		0-0	0-0	8000		1	2	3	4	5	6	7	8	9	10	11												
2	7	Wolverhampton Wanderers		1-1	1-0	14000	Owers	1	2	3	4	5	6	7	8	9	10	11												
3	14	LEICESTER FOSSE	7	1-0	1-0	13000	Owers	1	2	3	4	5	6	7	8	9	10	11												
4	21	Stockport County	2	1-0	0-0	7000	Bowyer	1	2	3	4	5	6	7	8	9	10	11												
5	28	PRESTON NORTH END	3	1-1	0-0	12000	Owers	1	2	3	4	5	6	7	8	9	10	11												
6	5 Oct	Burnley	5	2-2	1-0	15000	Boyer, Owers	1	2		4	5	6	7	8	9	10	11	3											
7	12	HULL CITY	5	1-1	0-0	20000	Marr(pen)	1	2	3	4	5	6	7	8	9	10			11										
8	19	Glossop	9	1-3	1-2	3000	Wedlock	1	2	3	4	5	6	7	8	9			10		11									
9	26	CLAPTON ORIENT	8	1-0	1-0	11000	Owers	1	2	3	4	5	6	7		8	10	11					9							
10	2 Nov	Lincoln City	10	0-2	0-1	10500		1	2	3		5	6	7		9	10	11						8	4					
11	9	NOTTINGHAM FOREST	12	1-2	1-0	12000	Marrison	1	2	3		5	6	7	8		10	11						9	4					
12	16	BLACKPOOL	10	0-0	0-0	10000		1	2	3		5	6	7		9	10	11						4	8					
13	23	Birmingham	11	0-3	0-2	20000			2	3		5	6	7	8		10	11	9							1	4			
14	30	HUDDERSFIELD TOWN	13	0-0	0-0	6000			2	3		5	6	7	8		10		9							1	4			
15	7 Dec	Leeds City	12	1-1	1-1	16000	Brough		2			5	6	7			10	11	3					9	8	1	4			
16	14	GRIMSBY TOWN	12	2-2	1-0	6000	Bowyer(2)		2			5	6				10	11	3					9	8	1	4		7	
17	21	Bury	11	1-0	1-0	7000	Owers		2			5	6	7		9	10	11	3						8	1			4	
18	25	FULHAM	10	2-1	0-0	10000	Brough, Owers		2			5	6	7		9	10	11	3						8	1			4	
19	28	WOLVERHAMPTON WNDRS	8	3-1	2-0	8000	Brough(3)		2				6	7		9	10	11	3					5	8	1			4	
20	1 Jan	Bradford Park Avenue	10	1-4	0-2	10000	Brough		2				6	7		9	10		3		11			5	8	1			4	
21	4	Leicester Fosse	11	1-3	1-1	3000			2				6	7		9	10	11	3					5	8	1			4	
22	18	STOCKPORT COUNTY	8	7-2	2-1	5000	Owers(4), Bowyer(2), Broad		2				6	7	8	9	10	11	3					5		1			4	
23	25	Preston North End	10	1-6	1-0	10000	Owers		2				6	7		9	10	11	3					5	8	1			4	
24	8 Feb	BURNLEY	10	3-3	2-1	11000	Brough, Harris, Owers (Reuben Marr Benefit)		2				6	7		9	10	11	3					5	8	1			4	
25	15	Hull City	11	1-3	1-1	7000	Jones(pen)		2	6				7	8	9	10	11	3					5		1			4	
26	22	GLOSSOP	10	3-3	2-2	4000	Allen, Broad, Jones(pen)		2	6				7		9	8	11	3					5		1			4	10
27	1 Mar	Clapton Orient	11	0-0	0-0	10000			2				6	7		9	10	11	3					5	8	1			4	
28	8	LINCOLN CITY	10	2-0	1-0	5000	Brough, Harris		2				6	7			10	11	3			9		5	8	1			4	
29	15	Nottingham Forest	11	1-4	0-1	7000	Brough		2				6	7			10	11	3			9		5	8	1			4	
30	21	Barnsley	12	1-7	0-4	8000	Butler		2				6	7			10	11	3			9		5	8	1			4	
31	22	Blackpool	12	1-1	0-0	4000	Jones		2				6	7	8			11	10			3		9	5	1			4	
32	24	BARNSLEY	12	3-0	1-0	15000	Bowyer(2), Jones		2				6	7			10	11	10			3		8	9	1			4	
33	29	BIRMINGHAM	13	0-3	0-3	6000			2	5			6	7				11	10			3		8	9	1			4	
34	5 Apr	Huddersfield Town	15	0-5	0-3	7000			2	5			6	7				11	10			3		8	9	1			4	
35	7	Fulham	15	0-0	0-0	2000			2	5			6	7				11	10			3		8	9	1			4	
36	12	LEEDS CITY	13	1-1	0-1	5000	Broad		2	5			6	7				11	10			3		8	9	1			4	
37	19	Grimsby Town	15	0-3	0-2	4000			2				6	7				11	10			3		5	9	1	8		4	
38	26	BURY	16	1-5	0-3	4000	Bowyer		2			5	6	7				11	10			3		9					4	
							Apps.	12	36	25	9	23	33	37	13	23	36	32	25	15	8	3	18	14	26	4	2	1	22	1
							Goals		4	1	1			3	1	13	9	2		1				10						1

F.A. CUP

	Date	Opposition		Res.	H.T.	Att.		Kearns			Nicholson	Broad	Marrison	Owers	Bowyer	Harris	Banfield					Ware	Edwards			Young
1R	15 Jan	Liverpool		0-3	0-2	14000	(£357)	2			6	7	8	9	10	11	3					5	1			4

GLOUCESTERSHIRE CUP FINAL

	Date	Opposition	Res.	H.T.	Att.	
	25 Mar	Bristol Rovers	0-1	0-0	9590	(£277)

FRIENDLIES

	Date	Opposition	Res.	H.T.	Att.	Goalscorers
1	23 Sep	Wycombe Wanderers	10-2	4-1	1000	Brough(4), Nichol(3), Butler, Copestake, Marrison
2	1 Feb	Exeter City	1-2	1-0		Harris

FINAL LEAGUE TABLE

		P	W	D	L	F	A	Pts
1	Preston	38	19	15	4	56	33	53
2	Burnley	38	21	8	9	88	53	50
3	Birmingham	38	18	10	10	59	44	46
4	Barnsley	38	19	7	12	57	47	45
5	Huddersfield	38	17	9	12	66	40	43
6	Leeds C	38	15	10	13	70	64	40
7	Grimsby	38	15	10	13	51	50	40
8	Lincoln	38	15	10	13	50	52	40
9	Fulham	38	17	5	16	65	55	39
10	Wolverhampton	38	14	10	14	56	54	38
11	Bury	38	15	8	15	53	57	38
12	Hull	38	15	6	17	60	56	36
13	Bradford P.A.	38	14	8	16	60	60	36
14	Clapton Orient	38	10	14	14	34	47	34
15	Leicester Fosse	38	13	7	18	50	65	33
16	Bristol C.	38	9	15	14	46	72	33
17	Nottingham F.	38	12	8	18	58	59	32
18	Glossop	38	12	8	18	49	68	32
19	Stockport	38	8	10	20	56	78	26
20	Blackpool	38	9	8	21	39	69	26

No.	Date	Opposition	Pos.	Res.	H.T.	Att	Goalscorers
1	0 Oup	OLOOOOP		1·1	0·1	10000	Droad, Fuge, Harris, O.G.
2	6	STOCKPORT COUNTY	1	5-0	5-0	12000	Chapple(3), Broad, Fuge
3	13	Bradford Park Avenue	5	3-4	0-2	15000	Harrison(2), Burton
4	20	NOTTS COUNTY	6	1-1	0-1	14000	Chapple(pen)
5	27	Leicester Fosse	11	0-3	0-1	16000	
6	4 Oct	WOLVERHAMPTON WNDRS	11	0-0	0-0	10000	
7	11	Hull City	7	1-0	0-0	10000	Fuge
8	18	BARNSLEY	9	1-1	1-0	15000	Chapple
9	25	Bury	11	1-3	0-2	12800	Harris
10	1 Nov	HUDDERSFIELD TOWN	10	1-0	0-0	10000	Picken
11	8	Lincoln City	12	1-2	1-1	7000	Picken
12	15	BLACKPOOL	10	1-0	0-0	8000	Harrison
13	22	Nottingham Forest	9	1-1	1-1	6000	Harrison
14	29	WOOLWICH ARSENAL	10	1-1	0-1	15000	Harrison
15	6 Dec	Grimsby Town	11	0-1	0-1	9000	
16	13	BIRMINGHAM	12	1-2	0-1	10000	Brown
17	20	Fulham	13	1-3	0-1	10000	Chapple(pen)
18	25	Clapton Orient	14	2-5	2-0	18000	Brown(2)
19	26	CLAPTON ORIENT	12	3-0	2-0	14000	Chapple(2), Brown
20	27	Stockport County	13	1-5	0-3	5000	Brown
21	3 Jan	BRADFORD PARK AVENUE	13	2-0	1-0	10000	Chapple, Kearns
22	17	Notts County	14	0-4	0-1	10000	
23	24	LEICESTER FOSSE	13	1-0	0-0	7000	Broad
24	7 Feb	Wolverhampton Wanderers	11	2-0	0-0	10000	Howarth, Picken
25	14	HULL CITY	11	2-1	1-1	10000	Brown, Howarth
26	21	Barnsley	12	0-3	0-1	8000	
27	28	BURY	12	2-0	1-0	10000	Picken(2)
28	7 Mar	Huddersfield Town	11	2-1	2-0	5000	Irving(2)
29	10	Glossop	11	1-1	0-1	1000	Picken
30	14	LINCOLN CITY	8	4-1	1-0	6000	Harris(2), Brown, Picken
31	21	Blackpool	9	1-0	0-0	4000	Irving
32	28	NOTTINGHAM FOREST	7	1-0	0-0	12000	Wedlock
33	4 Apr	The Arsenal *	7	1-1	1-1	20000	Brown
34	10	LEEDS CITY	6	1-1	1-1	18000	Brown
35	11	GRIMSBY TOWN	5	1-0	1-0	12000	Morton
36	13	Leeds City	7	0-1	0-1	12000	
37	18	Birmingham	8	2-2	0-2	17000	Brown, Harris
38	25	FULHAM	8	0-1	0-1	10000	

Player appearances grid (shirt numbers):

No.	Howling E.	Kearns J.	Banfield L.	Young R.K.	Wedlock W.J.	Nicholson J.A.	Broad T.H.	Fuge F.	Harrison F.	Tasker R.H.	Harris J.	Chapple F.J.	Burton E.	Moss A.J.	Rose L.A.	Picken J.	Jones E.	Henry T.	Jones J.	Brown W.Y.	Irving S.J.	Ware T.	Howarth J.T.	Neesam H.	Morton J.
1	1	2	3	4	5	6	7	8	9	10	11														
2	1	2	3	4	5	6	7	8	9			10	11												
3	1	2	3	4		6	7	8	9			10	11			5									
4	1	2	3	4		6	7	8	9			10	11			5									
5	1	2	3	4	5	6	7	8	9			10	11												
6	1	2	3	4	5	6	7		8			10	9				11								
7	1	2	3	4	5	6	7	8	9		11	10													
8	1	2	3	4	5		7		9			11		8	10	6									
9	1		3	4	5		7		9			11		8	10	6	2								
10	1	2	3	4	5		7		9			11		8	10	6									
11	1	2				6	7		9			11		8	5	10	3	4							
12	1		3			6	7		9			11		8	5	10	2	4							
13	1		3	2	5	6	7		11					4		10				8	9				
14	1	2	3	4		6	7		10		11		5							9					
15	1	2	3	4			7				5			6	11	10				9	8				
16	1	2	3	4	5		7							6	11	9				10	8				
17	1	2	3	4	5		7				11	9		6		10				8					
18	1	2		4	5		7				11	9		6		10	3			8					
19		2		4	5		7				11	9		6		10	3			8		1			
20		2		4	5		7				11	9		6			3			8	10	1			
21		2		4	5		7				11	9		6		10	3			8		1			
22		2	3	4	5		7				11			6						8	10	1	9		
23		2	3	4	5		7				11			6		9				8	10	1			
24		2	3	4	5		7				11			6		10				8		1	9		
25		2	3	4	5		7				11			6		10				8		1	9		
26		2	3	4	5		7				11			6		10				8		1	9		
27		2	3	4	5		7				11			6		10				8		1	9		
28		2	3	4	5		7				11			6		10				8		1	9		
29		2	3	4			7				11			5		10				8	6	1		9	
30		2	3	4		6	7				11			5		10				9	8	1			
31		2	3	4	5		7				11			6		10				8	9	1			
32		2	3	4	5		7				11			6		10				8	9	1			
33		2	3	4	5		7				11			6		10				8	9	1			
34		2	3	4	5		7				11			6		10				8	9	1			
35		2		4	5		7				11			6		10	3			8		1			9
36		2		4	5		7				11			6			3			8	10	1			9
37		2		4	5		7				11			6		10	3			8		1			9
38		2	3	4	5		7				11			6		10				8		1			9
Apps.	18	37	28	17	30	31	38	6	15	1	31	16	5	33	4	27	9	2	1	24	14	20	6	1	4
Goals		1			1		3	3	5		5	9	1			7				10	3		2		1

* Approval for Woolwich Arsenal
name change to 'The Arsenal' ·
3rd April 1914

F.A. CUP

	Date	Opposition	Res.	H.T.	Att	Goalscorers	Howling	Kearns	Banfield	Young	Wedlock	Nicholson	Broad	Fuge	Harrison	Tasker	Harris	Chapple	Moss	Picken	Brown	Ware
1R	10 Jan	Queens Park Rangers	2-2	1-1	20000	Picken, O.G. (£624-17-6)		2	3	4	5		7				11	9	6	10	8	1
1Rr	14	QUEENS PARK RANGERS	0-2	0-0	14000	(£470-2-3) (after extra time)		2	3		5	4	7				11	9	6	10	8	1

GLOUCESTERSHIRE CUP FINAL

	Date	Opposition	Res.	H.T.	Att	Goalscorers
	14 Apr	BRISTOL ROVERS	2-0	1-0	8501	Brown, Picken (£238-15-4)

FRIENDLY

	Date	Opposition	Res.	H.T.	Att	Goalscorers
	31 Jan	Bristol Rovers	1-0	0-0	4000	Howarth

FINAL LEAGUE TABLE (TOP POSITIONS)

1	Notts Co	38	23	7	8	77 36	53
2	Bradford P A	38	23	3	12	71 47	49
3	The Arsenal	38	20	9	9	54 38	49
4	Leeds C	38	20	7	11	76 46	47
5	Barnsley	38	19	7	12	51 45	45
6	Clapton Orient	38	16	11	11	47 35	43
7	Hull	38	16	9	13	53 37	41
8	Bristol C	38	16	9	13	52 50	41
9	Wolverhampton	38	18	5	15	51 52	41
10	Bury	38	15	10	13	39 40	40

Back: F.N.Bacon(Dir.), Harris, Broad, Young, Ware, J.Jones, Howling, Moss, Kearns, E.Jones, Batten(Asst.Trainer),
G.H.Bacon(Dir.). Middle: W.Pont(Vice-Chair.), G.Hedley(Manager), Shortt, Harrison, Fuge, Wedlock,
Tasker, Chapple, Nicholson, Palmer(Trainer), E.Murdock(Chair.). Front: Henry, Irving, Burton, Batey.

SEASON 1914-15
FOOTBALL LEAGUE DIVISION TWO

No.	Date	Opposition	Pos.	Res.	H.T.	Att.	Goalscorers	Howling E.	Kearns J.	Banfield L.	Nicholson J.A.	Wedlock W.J.	Moss A.J.	Broad T.H.	Brown W.Y.	Brooksbank C.	Picken J.	Harris J.	Morton J.	Jones J.	Chapple F.J.	Irving S.J.	Neesam H.	Blake H.E.	Burton E.	Hughes L.	Jones E.	Batey T.	Gane G.B.H.	Young R.K.	Reader R.	Henry T.
1	2 Sep	BLACKPOOL		2-1	1-1	3000	Brooksbank(2,1pen)	1	2	3	4	5	6	7	8	9	10	11														
2	5	Bury	6	1-2	0-0	6500	Brooksbank	1	2	3	4	5	6	7	8	9	10	11														
3	12	PRESTON NORTH END	5	4-0	2-0	5000	Morton(2), Brown, Harris	1	2	3	4	5	6	7	8		10	11	9													
4	19	Nottingham Forest	3	1-0	0-0	8000	Brown	1	2	3	4	5	6	7	8		10	11	9													
5	26	LEICESTER FOSSE	2	1-0	1-0	10000	Morton	1		3	4	5	6	7	8		10	11	9	2												
6	3 Oct	Barnsley	6	1-2	1-2	5000	Picken	1		3	4	5	6	7	8		10	11	9	2												
7	10	GLOSSOP	4	3-1	1-0	10000	Broad, Chapple(pen), O.G.	1		3	4	5	6	7	8		10	11		2	9											
8	17	Wolverhampton Wanderers	3	2-2	1-0	8000	Irving, Wedlock	1		3	4	5	6	7	8		10	11		2		9										
9	24	FULHAM	4	0-0	0-0	8000		1		3	4	5	6	7	8		10	11		2		9										
10	31	Stockport County	4	2-2	0-1	5000	Brown, Picken	1		3	4	5	6	7	8		10	11		2												
11	7 Nov	HULL CITY	2	5-2	3-1	10000	Brooksbank(3), Brown, Harris	1		3	4	5	6	7	8	9	10	11		2												
12	14	Leeds City	4	1-1	1-1	8000	Picken	1		3	4	5	6	7	8	9	10	11		2												
13	21	CLAPTON ORIENT	3	3-0	1-0	8000	Brooksbank, Brown, Picken	1		3	4	5	6	7	8	9	10	11		2												
14	28	The Arsenal	4	0-3	0-1	7000		1		3	4	5	6	7	8	9	10	11		2												
15	5 Dec	DERBY COUNTY	5	2-2	2-2	5000	Brown(2)	1		3	4	5	6	7	8	9	10	11		2												
16	12	Lincoln City	5	1-3	0-2	5000	Neesam	1		3	4	5	6	7	8		10	11		2			9									
17	19	BIRMINGHAM	9	2-3	0-3	4000	Harris, Nicholson			3	4	5	6	7	8		10	11		2			9	1								
18	25	Grimsby Town	9	3-2	2-1	8000	Neesam(3)	1		3	4	5	6	7	8			11		2			9		10							
19	26	GRIMSBY TOWN	5	7-0	7-0	11000	Brown(2), Harris(2), Neesam(2), Burton	1		3	4	5	6	7	8			11		2			9		10							
20	1 Jan	Blackpool	9	0-2	0-1	4000		1		3	4		6	7	8			11		2	5		10		9							
21	2	BURY	5	1-0	1-0	6000	Neesam	1		3	4	5		7	8					2	6		10		9	11						
22	23	NOTTINGHAM FOREST	7	1-2	0-1	5000	Burton	1		3	4	5	6	7	8			11		2			9		10							
23	6 Feb	BARNSLEY	8	3-1	0-1	4000	Picken(2,1pen), Neesam	1	2	3		5		7	8		10						9			4		11				
24	11	Preston North End	6	1-4	1-2	5000	Brown	1	2	3	4	5		7	8		10	11				6	9									
25	13	Glossop	8	1-2	1-0	5000	Harris	1	2	3	4	5		7	8		10	11				4	9									
26	20	WOLVERHAMPTON WNDRS	10	0-1	0-1	5000		1	2	3		5		7	8		10	11					9				4		6			
27	27	Fulham	10	2-1	1-1	8000	Burton, Harris	1	2	3	4	5	6		8			9							9	10		7				
28	6 Mar	STOCKPORT COUNTY	10	0-2	0-1	4000		1	2	3	4	5	6		8							9	11			10		7				
29	13	Hull City	10	1-1	1-1	5000	Neesam	1	2	3	4	5	6		8						9				7	10		11				
30	20	LEEDS CITY	10	1-0	1-0	5000	Neesam	1	2	3	4	5	6		8								7		9	10		11				
31	25	Leicester Fosse	7	3-1	1-1	3000	Brown(2), Batey	1	2	3	4	5	6		8								7		9	10		11				
32	27	Clapton Orient	9	0-2	0-1	6000		1	2	3	6	5			8								7		9	10		11		4		
33	3 Apr	THE ARSENAL	9	1-1	1-1	7000	Neesam	1	2	3	4	5	6	7	8			11					9			10						
34	5	HUDDERSFIELD TOWN	12	0-0	0-0	12000		1	2	3		5	6	7	8		10	11					9							4		
35	6	Huddersfield Town	12	3-5	2-2	5500	Morton(3)	1	2	3		5	6	7	8			11	10				9							4		
36	10	Derby County	12	0-1	0-1	7000		1	2	3	6	5			8			11	10				9							4	7	
37	17	LINCOLN CITY	12	2-1	1-0	4000	Broad, Harris	1	2	3		5		7	8	9		11	10											4		6
38	24	Birmingham	13	1-1	1-0	5000	Brown	1	2	3	6	5		7	8	9		11	10													
		Apps.						37	20	38	33	32	34	31	38	10	24	35	8	18	4	4	19	1	13	2	1	7	1	6	1	1
		Goals									1	1		2	13	7	6	9	6		1	1	10		4			1				

F.A. CUP

Rd	Date	Opposition		Res.	H.T.	Att.	Notes	Howling E.	Banfield L.	Nicholson J.A.	Wedlock W.J.	Moss A.J.	Broad T.H.	Brown W.Y.	Picken J.	Harris J.	Jones J.	Neesam H.	Burton E.
1R	9 Jan	CARDIFF CITY		2-0	0-0	17000	Burton(2), (£488-9-0)	1	3	4	5	6	7	8		11	2	9	10
2R	30	Everton		0-4	0-2	24500	(£770)	1	3	4	5	6	7	8	10	11	2	9	

FRIENDLY

No.	Date	Opposition		Res.			Goalscorers
1	20 Jan	REMOUNT LEAGUE XI		4-1			Neesam(3), Stevens

FINAL LEAGUE TABLE

		P	W	D	L	F:A	Pts
1	Derby	38	23	7	8	71:33	53
2	Preston	38	20	10	8	61:42	50
3	Barnsley	38	22	3	13	51:51	47
4	Wolverhampton	38	19	7	12	77:52	45
5	The Arsenal	38	19	5	14	69:41	43
6	Birmingham	38	17	9	12	62:39	43
7	Hull	38	19	5	14	65:54	43
8	Huddersfield	38	17	8	13	61:42	42
9	Clapton Orient	38	16	9	13	50:48	41
10	Blackpool	38	17	5	16	58:57	39
11	Bury	38	15	8	15	61:56	38
12	Fulham	38	15	7	16	53:47	37
13	Bristol C.	38	15	7	16	62:56	37
14	Stockport	38	15	7	16	54:60	37
15	Leeds C.	38	14	4	20	65:64	32
16	Lincoln	38	11	9	18	46:65	31
17	Grimsby	38	11	9	18	48:76	31
18	Nottingham F.	38	10	9	19	43:77	29
19	Leicester Fosse	38	10	4	24	47:88	24
20	Glossop	38	6	6	26	31:87	18

SEASON 1915-16
SOUTH WEST COMBINATION

No.	Date	Opposition	Pos.	Res.	H.T.	Att.	Goalscorers	Davis E.	Treasure C.J.	Kearns J.	Young R.K.	Southway L.F.	Gane G.B.H.	Reader A.R.	Allen T.	Chapple F.	Neesam H.	Kelson H.	Banfield L.	Hayes V.	Wedlock W.J.	Kerswell	Martin H.J.	Williams R.	Leslie W.	Cross W.	Ketford T.	Norris T.	Ies A.	Nash	Wilson P.	Wall T.	Stevens C.	Simmons C.	Slade C.	Packer B.	Welch	Simmonds W.
1	1 Jan	NEWPORT COUNTY	1	2-0	0-0	500	Chapple(2)	1	2	3	4	5	6	7	8	9	10	11																				
2	8	Southampton	4	1-2	1-0	2000	Southway	1	2		4	5	6	7	8		10	11	3	9																		
3	15	SOUTHAMPTON	2	4-0	2-0		Chapple(2), Allen, Neesam	1	2		4	5		7	8	9	10	11	3		6																	
4	22	Cardiff City	2	0-1	0-0	2000		1	2			5	6	7	8	9	10		3	11			4															
5	29	PORTSMOUTH	4	0-1	0-1			1	2		4	5		7	8	9		11	3	10	6																	
6	5 Feb	Newport County	5	0-4	0-1																			1	2	3	4	5	6	7	8	9	10	11				
7	12	SWINDON TOWN	3	1-0	1-0		Allen	1	2		4	5	6	7	9			11		10	5			3									8					
8	4 Mar	Portsmouth	4	0-3	0-2			1	2				6	7	4	9		11	3	10													8					
9	8 Apr	CARDIFF CITY	4	2-0	0-0	2000	Neesam, Slade		2		4		6	7			10	11	3		5	1													9		8	
10	15	Swindon Town	4	2-1	1-0		Neesam, Slade	1	2		4	5		7	8		10	11	3																9	6		
11	21	Bristol Rovers	4	1-1	0-0	4000	Chapple	1	2		4				8	9	10	11	3		5					6												7
12	24	BRISTOL ROVERS	5	0-2	0-1	4000		1			4				8		10	11	3		5					2									9			7
		Apps.						9	10	1	8	7	7	9	7	6	9	9	9	5	6	1	3	5	1	4	1	1	1	1	1	1	1	1	4	1	1	2
		Goals										1			2	5	3																		2			

	P	W	D	L	F	A	
Home	6	4	0	2	9	3	
Away	6	1	1	4	4	12	(Final - Fifth)

FRIENDLIES

	Date	Opposition	Res.	H.T.	Att.	Goalscorers
1	4 Sep	R.A.S.C.MOTOR TRANS.(352 Co.)	4-1	2-0	2000	Slade(2), Hayes, Reader
2	11	Cardiff City	0-1	0-1	3500	
3	18	CARDIFF CITY	1-1	1-1	2000	Slade
4	25	Portsmouth	2-4	0-1	4000	Neesam(2, 1 pen.)
5	2 Oct	NEWPORT COUNTY	8-0	3-0	1000	Slade(3), Batey(2), Hayes(2), Sweet
6	9	Southampton	3-2	2-1	4000	Hayes(2), Clarke
7	16	PORTSMOUTH	5-1	2-0	1000	Clarke(2), Slade(2), Neesam
8	23	Newport County	3-1	1-0		Allen(2), Neesam
9	30	READING	3-0	0-0	1500	Clarke(2), Slade
10	6 Nov	Swindon Town	1-1	0-0	500	Slade
11	13	SWINDON TOWN	2-2	1-2	1000	Hayes, Neesam
12	20	Reading	3-1	3-0		Reader(3)
13	27	SOUTHAMPTON	2-1	2-0	1000	Slade, Wedlock
14	4 Dec	Barry District	0-0	0-0		
15	11	BARRY DISTRICT	3-0	0-0	1000	Chapple(2), Banfield(pen)
16	18	RASC MOTOR TRANS.(259Co.Wells)	5-2	1-1		Hayes(3), Allen. Southway
17	27	BRISTOL ROVERS	0-0	0-0	3000	
18	5 Feb	Bristol Rovers	0-0	0-0	3000	
19	11 Mar	ROYAL GLOS.HUSSARS (Gloucester)	7-0	5-0		Allen(2), Hayes(2), Neesam(2), Gane
20	18	Barry District	2-5	1-4		Kelson, Wichard
21	25	BARRY DISTRICT	1-0	1-0		Slade
22	1 Apr	ROYAL ENGINEERS (Tewkesbury)	2-2	1-1		Allen(2)
23	22	Portsmouth	0-2	0-0	3000	
24	29	RASC (WHITE CITY BRISTOL)	20-1	10-0		Chap'n(8),R'der(5),Neesam(3),Slade(3),Cross
25	6 May	3rd OFFICER CADET (Bris.Univ.)	6-3	3-2		Chap'n(2),Kelson,Mann'g,Neesam,R'der

SEASON 1916-17

FRIENDLIES

No.	Date	Opposition	Pos.	Res.	H.T.	Att.	Goalscorers
1	9 Sep	Bristol Rovers		0-2	0-0		
2	16	BARRY DISTRICT		2-2	1-1		Southway(2)
3	23	Portsmouth		0-4	0-2	2000	
4	30	BRISTOL ROVERS		3-1	2-1	1500	Chapman(pen), Scott, Smith(pen)
5	7 Oct	Barry District		0-3	0-1		
6	14	SWINDON TOWN		5-0	0-0		Ball(2), Packer, Reader, Stevens
7	21	3rd OFFICER CADET BATT.		6-0	2-0	261	Southway(2),Stevens(2),Reader,Wilcox
8	28	BATH CITY		4-1	2-1		Chapman, Cross, Southway, Wilcox
9	4 Nov	Bristol Rovers		5-1	3-1	2000	Wilcox(3), Chapman, Neesam
10	11	MOTOR TRACTOR DEP.(A'mouth)		8-1	4-0		Wilcox(6), Reader, Southway
11	18	Bath City *		4-0	1-0		Neesam(2), Chapman. Wilcox
12	25	BRISTOL ROVERS		3-1	2-0		Wilcox(2), Reader
13	2 Dec	3rd OFFICER CADET BATT.		5-2			Wilcox(4), Neesam
14	9	FOOTBALLERS BATTALION		2-0	0-0		Chapman(pen), Southway
15	23	LONDON RIFLE REG.(Warm'ster)		7-0	5-0		Willcox(4), Stevens(2), Reader
16	25	Bristol Rovers		0-3	0-1	2000	
17	26	BRISTOL ROVERS		0-1	0-1		
18	30	2/6th LONDON REGIMENT		3-4	2-1		Critchley, Neesam, Stevens
19	6 Jan	MIDDLESEX REGIMENT		3-1	0-1		Muckian(3)
20	13	ROYAL GARR.ARTIL.(Ash.Gate)			1-0		Wedlock
21	20	REMOUNT LEAGUE XI		4-1	1-0		Neesam(3), Stevens
22	27	ROYAL ARMY ORD. CORP.		2-1	1-0		Reader, Southway
23	3 Feb	BRISTOL ROVERS		1-0	1-0	1000	Wilcox
24	17	30th MIDDLESEX REG.		11-1	4-0		Wilcox(5),Neesam(2),Stevens(2),Tho'ton,Rea'r
25	24	Bristol Rovers		2-0	1-0		Neesam, Wilcox
26	3 Mar	Remount League XI		2-1	1-1	1200	Bramley, Wilcox
27	17	BRISTOL ROVERS		1-2	1-1		Neesam
28	24	BRISTOL DOCKERS		2-0	1-0		Stevens(2)
29	31	BARRY DISTRICT		2-0	1-0	2000	Green, Neesam(pen)
30	6 Apr	Bristol Rovers		1-1	0-0	2000	O.G.
31	7	R.F.A. (Frome)		0-4			(Played at Frome)
32	9	BRISTOL ROVERS		1-0	0-0	2000	Wilcox
33	14	R.A.S.C.(AVONMOUTH)		4-1	0-0		Neesam(2), Green, Wilcox
34	21	Barry District		1-4	1-2		Wilcox
35	28	Bristol Rovers		0-0	0-0		

Appearances and Goals (player columns)

Player columns, left to right: Giblett R., Treasure C.J., Banfield L., Cross W., Wedlock W.J., Williams R., Reader A.R., Southway L.F., Chapman A., Lord, Neesam H., Marr C.R., Holt A., Sweet F.G., Wakefield A., Packer B., Roberts E.D., Martin H.J., Smith Pte., Scott, Wakley, Ball H., Stevens C., Cottle J., Young R.K., Wilcox J.C., King J., Balacombe, Barber, Wilcox John, Kelson H., Roost F.W., Critchley W., Muckian, Burrell, Jones E., Farnham, Cecchini W., Birks

	Giblett	Treasure	Banfield	Cross	Wedlock	Williams	Reader	Southway	Chapman	Lord	Neesam	Marr	Holt	Sweet	Wakefield	Packer	Roberts	Martin	Smith	Scott	Wakley	Ball	Stevens	Cottle	Young	Wilcox J.C.	King	Balacombe	Barber	Wilcox J.	Kelson	Roost	Critchley	Muckian	Burrell	Jones	Farnham	Cecchini	Birks
App.	4	2	32	18	24	24	28	35	15	2	25	1		20	1	2	1	26	7	1	1	2	24	2	5	24	3	1	1	1	1	1	3	1	1	1	1	1	1
Goals				1	1		7	8	5		15					1			1	1		2	11			33							1	3					

* Due to fading light short time played in second half.

	P	W	D	L	F	A
Home	23	19	1	3	80	20
Away	12	4	2	6	15	23

Other Players: Russell H. 22/1, Appleyard 23/6, Williams F. 24/1, Smith Sgt. 24/2, Thornton D. 24/11, May 25/6 & 26/4, Stone G. 25/10, Burton J. 26/6,29/4,31/4 & 35/8, Bramley 26/8, Winterbottom 27/4, 28/4, 33/6, 33 & 34/6, 35/4, White A. 27/7, Wickham 27/11, 28/11, Brown W. 28/7, Norris T. 29/6, Morley-Green 29 & 30/10, 32-35/10, Farrier-Brown 30/2, 31/6, 32-35/2, Cox 30/6 & 35/6, Templar A.31/1, 33/1, Witcombe 31/2, Hawley 31/10.

SEASON 1917-18
BRISTOL COUNTY COMBINATION

No.	Date	Opposition	Pos.	Res.	H.T.	Att.	Goalscorers	Martin H.J.	Southway L.F.	Perkins A.	Roberts E.D.	Wedlock W.J.	Sweet F.G.	Challender H.	Whitchurch R.	Reader A.R.	Kelson H.	Watt W.	Cross W.	Young R.K.	Stevens F.	Morley-Green	Critchley	Lewis W.	Hamilton A.J.	Neesam H.	Watkins J.	Jones E.	Cecchini W.	Merryweather P.	Morgan J.	Southway P.	Walker	Hunt A.S.	King A.
1	19 Jan	H.M.FACTORY(Avonmouth)*	1	2-0	1-0		Kelson, Reader	1	2	3	4	5	6	7	8	9	10	11																	
2	2 Feb	BRISTOL DOCKERS	1	3-0	1-0		Reader(3)	1	2		10	5		7		8	11			3	4	6	9												
3	9	Bristol Rovers	2	0-2	0-2			1	2			5	6	7		8	11			3	4			9	10										
4	16	R.F.C. (FILTON)	2	2-1	1-1		Lewis, Neesam(pen)		2	3		5	6	7		8					4			10	1	9	11								
5	23	ROYAL ENGINEERS(Portbury)	2	4-0	2-0		Reader(2, 1 pen), Roberts, Wedlock	1	2		10	9	5			8	11	6			4								3	7					
6	2 Mar	BRISTOL DOCKERS	2	1-0			Roberts	1	2		6	5	3	7		9	10				4					8	11								
7	9	BRISTOL ROVERS	1	1-0	0-0		Morgan	1	2		6	5	3	7		8	11				4						10				9				
8	30	ROYAL ENGINEERS(Portbury)	2	7-1	2-1		Morgan(4), Green, Neesam, Reader	1	2					7			11				4	9				8					10	3	5	6	
9	6 Apr	ROYAL ENGINEERS(WhiteCity)	2	1-2	1-2		Neesam	1	2		10	5				8	11				4					9				7		3		5	6
10	13	RAF (FILTON)		14-2	5-1		Nee'm(4),Kel'n(3),Rea'r(3,1p)Chal'r,Hu't,Rob',Sw't	1	2		10		5	7		8	11				4					9								3	6
11	20	ROYAL ENGINEERS(WhiteCity)	1	3-0	2-0		Reader(2,1pen), Roberts	1	2		9	5		7		8	11				4										10			6	3
		Apps.						10	11	2	8	8	8	8	1	11	10	1		3	10	2	1	2	1	5	1	1	2	2	3	3	1	4	1
		Goals									4	1	1	1		12	4					1		1		7					5			1	

* Later resigned from Combination, record expunged

	P	W	D	L	F	A	
Home	9	8	0	1	36	6	
Away	1	0	0	1	0	2	(Final · Champions)

FRIENDLIES

No.	Date	Opposition	Res.	H.T.	Att.	Goalscorers
1	8 Sep	Bristol Rovers	2-1	1-1		Green, Reader
2	15	DOUGLAS BROS.	7-0	3-0		Green(2),Reader(2),Chal'der,South'y,Wed'k
3	22	BRISTOL DOCKERS	6-0	3-0		Neesam(2),Wilcox(2),Green,Wedlock
4	29	BRISTOL ROVERS	2-0	1-0		Needam, Wilcox
5	6 Oct	Portsmouth	0-4	0-2	2000	
6	13	ROYAL ENGINEERS(WhiteCity)	3-2	3-1		Templar, Wedlock, Wilcox
7	20	6th RESERVE CAVALRY	2-2	2-1		Wilcox(2)
8	27	Bristol Rovers	1-3	1-1		Wilcox
9	3 Nov	ROYAL ENGINEERS (Henbury)	4-1	1-1		Neesam, Smith, Wilcox, O.G.
10	10	R.F.C. (FILTON)	13-0	5-0		Wil'x(5),Reader(4),Neesam(2),Smith,Wed'k(pen)
11	17	BRISTOL ROVERS	0-0	0-0	1000	
12	24	ROYAL ENGINEERS(WhiteCity)*	1-1	0-1		Roberts
13	1 Dec	6th RESERVE CAVALRY	2-1	1-1		Neesam, Reader
14	8	Southampton	1-2	0-1		Reader
15	15	Artillery Cadets (Exeter)	1-2	1-2		Watkins
16	22	DOUGLAS BROS.	2-1	2-0		Arrowsmith, Neesam
17	25	Bristol Rovers	2-1	2-0	2000	Kelson, Neesam
18	26	BRISTOL ROVERS	0-3	0-2	1000	
19	5 Jan	H.M.FACTORY (AVONMOUTH)	1-0	0-0		Reader
20	12	RASC TRACTOR(Avonmouth)	1-0	0-0		Morecroft
21	26	FISHPONDS CITY	0-1	0-0		
22	16 Mar	R.A.O.C. (DIDCOT)	3-0	0-0		Hunt, Kelson, Reader(pen)
23	23	R.F.A. (LARKHILL	7-0	3-0		Neesam(3),Morgan(2),Kelson,Reader
24	29	BRISTOL ROVERS	2-0	2-0	2000	Kelson, Morgan
25	1 Apr	Bristol Rovers	1-0	1-0	2500	Morgan

* Second half only 37 minutes played (failing light)

SEASON 1918-19
BRISTOL COUNTY COMBINATION

No.	Date	Opposition	Pos.	Res.	H.T.	Att.	Goalscorers
1	12 Oct	ROYAL ENGINEERS(White City) *	3	4-0	0-0		Morgan(3), Reader
2	19	ROYAL ENGINEERS(Portbury)*	2	2-1	1-1		Morgan(pen), Ratcliffe
3	2 Nov	TRACTOR DEPOT(Avonmouth)*	3	7-0	4-0		Morgan(3),Lock,Merry'er,Neesam,O.G.
4	9	RAF (FILTON) *	1	3-2	2-1		Morgan, Ratcliffe, Wedlock
5	16	BRISTOL DOCKERS	1	1-0	1-0		Neesam
6	7 Dec	ROYAL ENGINEERS(Portbury)*	1	4-1	2-0		Hayes(2), Morgan, Neesam
7	26	BRISTOL ROVERS	1	2-3	2-3	3000	Neesam(2)
8	8 Feb	R.A.V.C.	2	3-0	1-0		Green, Harris
9	15	BRISTOL DOCKERS **	2	6-0	1-0	200	Neesam(3,1pen), Morgan(2), Harris
10	29 Mar	R.A.V.C.	2	4-0	2-0	1000	Nunn(3,2 pens.), Stephens
11	21 Apr	Bristol Rovers	2	1-1	0-0	11053	Jones(pen)

Player appearance grid (shirt numbers by match):

No.	Martin H.G.	Southway L.E.	Copeland W.F.	Stevens F.	Sweet F.G.	Southway P.	Challender H.	Reader A.R.	Morgan J.H.	Morgan T.	Kelson H.	Hunt A.S.	Ratcliffe F.	Henry T.	Lock A.	Jarman G.	Neesam H.	Merryweather P.	Burnham W.	Wedlock W.J.	Dyke	Girling	Hayes V.	Jeffries H.	Harris J.	Burchill	Giblett R.	Jones E.	Phinally H.G.	Morley-Green	Steer J.H.	Banfield L.	Mitchell W.	Exton	Treasure C.J.	Hardman P.	Lloyd H.	Nunn L.C.	Dark A.
1	1	2	3	4	5	6	7	8	9	10	11																												
2	1	2		4	5	3	7	8	9		11	6	10																										
3	1	2		6	5				9					3	4	7	8	10	11																				
4	1	2		4	5	3		8	10		11						7	6	9																				
5	1	2		4	5	3		8			11		6				10			9		7																	
6	1	2				6		9			11	3					10	4					5		7	8													
7		2				5	3		9	6	11	4					10						1	7	8														
8		2		4		6	7	9			11												8		1	3	5	10											
9				4			7		10		11	6					9						8	1								2	3	5					
10					5		7							11														2							1	3	4	6	8	9
11				4	5		7		10		11	6																3					2						
Apps.	6	8	1	8	8	7	4	4	10	2	9	4	5	1	1	1	5	4	1	3	1	1	1	3	1	2	2	1	1	2	2	1	1	1	1	1	1	1	1
Goals								1	11				2		1		8	1		1			2		2			1		2									

Other players: Stephens W. 10/10, Vallis F. 11/1, Peet 11/8, Bailey V.S. 11/9

* Resigned during season, records expunged.

** Abandoned after 85 minutes, Crowd encroachment on pitch, result allowed to stand.

	P	W	D	L	F	A	
Home	5	4	0	1	16	3	
Away	1	0	0	1	1	1	(Final - Runners-up)

FRIENDLIES

No.	Date	Opposition	Res.	H.T.	Att.	Goalscorers
1	7 Sep	FED.DISCHARGED SOLDIERS ††	13-0	8-0		Rea'r(4),Spear(4),Nee'm(2),Chal'er,Kelson,O.G
2	14	Bristol Rovers	2-5	1-2		Reader(2,1 pen)
3	21	DOUGLAS BROS.	3-0	1-0		Morgan, Neesam, Reader
4	28	RAF (Reading)	1-3	0-2		Morgan (Played at Reading)
5	5 Oct	BRISTOL ROVERS	4-2	1-1		Morgan(2), Kelson, Neesam(pen)
6	26	Bristol Rovers	0-1	0-0	2000	
7	23 Nov	RAF (YATE)	4-3	3-1		Kelson, Morgan, Neesam, Reader
8	30	BRISTOL ROVERS	0-0	0-0		
9	14 Dec	TIMSBURY ATHLETIC	2-0	0-0		Hunt, Morgan
10	21	DOUGLAS BROS.	2-0	0-0		Morgan(2)
11	25	Bristol Rovers	2-2	0-2	3000	Harris, Morgan
12	28	RAF CADETS (EXETER)	1-1	1-0		Bailey
13	4 Jan	STAPLE HILL EX-SERVICEMEN	5-0	1-0		Harris(3), Morgan(2)
14	11	BRITISH COLONIAL AERO.CO.	6-1	2-1		Harris(3), Neesam(3,1 pen)
15	18	FISHPONDS CITY	5-3	3-0		Harris(2), Needam(2), Morgan
16	25	WEDLOCK'S XI	4-1	0-1		Harris(2), Kelson, Neesam(pen)
17	1 Feb	BRISTOL ROVERS	2-2	0-1		Morgan, Neesam(pen)
18	1 Mar	HORFIELD UNITED	1-1	0-1		Hunt
19	8	BRISTOL ROVERS	1-0	1-0	4000	Morgan
20	15	WEDLOCK'S XI	1-2	0-0		Southway
21	22	BRISTOL DOCKERS	3-3	2-0		Neesam(2), Kelson
22	29	Ebbw Vale	4-2	1-2	5000	Neesam(3), Wedlock(pen)
23	5 Apr	Bristol Rovers	0-2	0-1	6431	
24	12	WEST HAM UNITED RES.	4-0	0-0	5591	Howarth(2), Neesam, Pocock
25	18	Bristol Rovers	1-5	1-3	7321	Mitchell
26	19	COVENTRY CITY RES.	1-0	0-0	6000	Neesam
27	22	BRADFORD P.A. RES.	4-0	1-0	7500	Howarth(2), J.Harris, N.Harris
28	26	THE ARSENAL RES.	5-1	4-0		Howarth(3), Pocock(2)
29	3 May	3rd STH.MIDLAND FIELD AMB. †	0-0	0-0	1073	
30	10	Bristol Rovers	1-4	1-2	7450	Kelson
31	24	Bristol Rovers *	2-1	2-1	4044	Morgan, Neesam

* Match billed as "Ellis Crompton's XI v. Billy Wedlock's XI".

† Full name, "3rd South Midland Field Ambulance 48th Division R.A.M.C."

†† Full name, "Federation of Discharged Soldiers and Sailors".

SEASON 1919-20
FOOTBALL LEAGUE DIVISION TWO

Player columns (left to right): Vallis F., Southway L.F., Banfield L., Wren J.E., Wedlock W.J., Nicholson J.A., Allwright C.R.S, Neesam H, Howarth J.T., Pocock W.T., Harris J., Wilcox J.C., Gane G.B.H., Reader A.R., Young R.K., Treasure C.J., Jones E., Marr C.R., Vallis A.G., Compton W.A., Hughes L., Bown A.J.W., Kirk H., Jones T.E.

No.	Date	Opposition	Pos.	Res.	H.T.	Att.	Goalscorers
1	30 Aug	BURY		1-0	0-0	10000	Howarth
2	1 Sep	Nottingham Forest		2-1	2-1	6000	Neesam, Wilcox
3	6	Bury	2	1-0	0-0	12000	Howarth
4	8	NOTTINGHAM FOREST	2	0-0	0-0	15000	
5	13	Lincoln City	3	0-0	0-0	6000	
6	20	LINCOLN CITY	2	6-0	3-0	14000	Howarth(2,1pen), Pocock(2), Neesam, Nicholson
7	4 Oct	FULHAM	4	0-3	0-2	21000	
8	11	Rotherham County	7	2-2	0-2	10000	Neesam(pen), Reader
9	13	Fulham	5	1-1	0-0	9000	Pocock
10	18	ROTHERHAM COUNTY	4	2-1	1-0	16500	Howarth(2)
11	25	Coventry City	3	0-0	0-0	17500	
12	1 Nov	COVENTRY CITY	3	1-0	0-0	12000	Wren
13	15	STOKE	8	1-2	1-2	17000	Harris
14	17	Stoke	8	0-2	0-0	10000	
15	22	Huddersfield Town	9	0-1	0-1	7897	
16	29	HUDDERSFIELD TOWN	8	2-1	1-0	10000	Pocock, Reader
17	6 Dec	GRIMSBY TOWN	8	3-1	2-1	15000	Harris(2), Howarth
18	13	Grimsby Town	7	2-2	0-1	4000	Nicholson, Pocock
19	20	BLACKPOOL	7	0-0	0-0	20000	
20	25	West Ham United	9	0-2	0-2	20000	
21	26	WEST HAM UNITED	8	0-0	0-0	12000	
22	27	Blackpool	10	0-0	0-0	8000	
23	3 Jan	BIRMINGHAM	9	1-1	0-1	14000	Pocock
24	17	Birmingham	9	0-1	0-1	29500	
25	24	PORT VALE	9	1-1	1-1	12000	Howarth
26	26	Port Vale	9	1-3	1-1	7000	Harris
27	7 Feb	CLAPTON ORIENT	11	1-1	0-1	12000	Reader
28	14	Clapton Orient	12	0-0	0-0	14960	
29	25	TOTTENHAM HOTSPUR	13	1-2	0-0	19000	Pocock
30	28	Tottenham Hotspur	13	0-2	0-1	38000	
31	10 Mar	South Sheilds	14	2-0	1-0	10000	Harris, Howarth
32	13	SOUTH SHIELDS	12	3-1	2-1	10000	Howarth, Neesam, Pocock
33	20	WOLVERHAMPTON WNDRS	12	1-1	0-0	16000	Pocock
34	2 Apr	Barnsley	15	0-0	0-0	13000	
35	3	Hull City	14	0-0	0-0	9000	
36	5	LEICESTER CITY	12	0-0	0-0	20000	
37	6	Leicester City	13	1-2	1-0	23000	Wilcox
38	10	HULL CITY	13	2-2	1-1	11000	Kirk(2) (Robert Young Benefit)
39	17	Stockport County	10	3-2	2-0	5000	Neesam(2), Howarth
40	19	Wolverhampton Wanderers	10	1-3	0-3	10000	Howarth
41	24	STOCKPORT COUNTY	8	1-0	0-0	15000	Banfield(pen)
42	1 May	BARNSLEY	8	3-1	1-1	14000	Howarth(2), Pocock

Apps. 42 13 40 37 30 28 11 35 36 39 35 8 1 28 1 33 10 9 6 3 3 4 6 4
Goals 1 1 2 6 14 10 5 2 3 2

	P.	W.	D.	L.	F.	A.
Home	21	9	9	3	30	18
Away	21	4	8	9	16	25

F.A. CUP

			Res	HT	Att	Goalscorers
1R	10 Jan	Grimsby Town	2-1	1-0	7000	Howarth(2) (£525)
2R	31	THE ARSENAL	1-0	1-0	25900	Howarth (£2031.7.0)
3R	21 Feb	CARDIFF CITY	2-1	1-1	32432	Howarth, Neesam (£3551.7.6)
4R	6 Mar	BRADFORD CITY	2-0	1-0	26443	Harris(2) (£2891)
SF	27	Huddersfield Town	1-2	0-0	35863	Howarth (£4643.12.9) (at Stamford Bridge)

GLOUCESTERSHIRE CUP FINAL

	24 Sep	Bristol Rovers	4-0	3-0	7000	Howarth(2), Neesam(2)

FRIENDLIES

	Date	Opposition	Res	HT	Att	Goalscorers
1	22 Apr	Bath City	5-2	4-2	4500	Howarth(3), Bown, Neesam
2	26	Pontypridd	2-3			Howarth, Neesam
3	27	Cardiff City	3-1	2-1	7000	Kirk(2), Allwright (£450) (J.Evans Benefit)
4	3 May	Cardiff City	0-2			
5	5	CARDIFF CITY	3-0	2-0	5000	Hwrth(2),Reader (£270) (Lord Mayor's Hosp Fund)

FINAL LEAGUE TABLE (TOP POSITIONS)

1	Tottenham	42	32	6	4	102	32	70
2	Huddersfield	42	28	8	6	97	38	64
3	Birmingham	42	24	8	10	85	34	56
4	Blackpool	42	21	10	11	65	47	52
5	Bury	42	20	8	14	60	44	48
6	Fulham	42	19	9	14	61	50	47
7	West Ham	42	19	9	14	47	40	47
8	Bristol C	42	13	17	12	46	43	43
9	South Shields	42	15	12	15	58	48	42
10	Stoke	42	18	6	18	60	54	42
11	Hull	42	18	6	18	78	72	42

Back: Treasure, Wren, Vallis, Banfield, Harris, Nicholson.
Front: Reader, Neesam, Wedlock, Howarth, Pocock.

F.A.Cup Semi-Final at Stamford Bridge (Prior to match with Huddersfield Town) 27 March 1920.

SEASON 1920-21
FOOTBALL LEAGUE DIVISION TWO

No.	Date	Opposition	Pos.	Res.	H.T.	Att.	Goalscorers
1	28 Aug	NOTTS COUNTY		0-1	0-0	25600	
2	30	Blackpool		2-1	1-0	15000	Pocock(2)
3	4 Sep	Notts County	9	2-2	0-0	20000	Wilcox(2)
4	8	BLACKPOOL	10	1-1	0-0	20000	Banfield(pen)
5	11	Hull City	11	0-2	0-0	14000	
6	18	HULL CITY	11	2-1	1-1	17000	Howarth, Wilcox
7	20	Rotherham County	10	0-0	0-0	10000	
8	25	Wolverhampton Wanderers	12	0-0	0-0	25000	
9	2 Oct	WOLVERHAMPTON WNDRS	9	2-0	1-0	15000	Pocock, Wilcox
10	9	Stockport County	6	2-0	0-0	9000	Kirk, Wilcox
11	16	STOCKPORT COUNTY	4	5-1	2-1	15000	Harris(2), Kirk(2), Pocock
12	23	Clapton Orient	4	0-0	0-0	25000	
13	30	CLAPTON ORIENT	3	2-0	2-0	26022	Kirk, Reader
14	6 Nov	Bury	3	0-2	0-1	15000	
15	13	BURY	3	1-0	0-0	22000	Pocock
16	20	NOTTINGHAM FOREST	3	1-0	1-0	22000	Pocock
17	27	Nottingham Forest	2	1-0	1-0	9000	Kirk
18	4 Dec	BARNSLEY	1	1-0	1-0	18000	Pocock
19	11	Barnsley	2	1-1	1-1	8000	Pocock
20	25	Port Vale	2	2-0	0-0	16000	Pocock, Wilcox
21	27	PORT VALE	1	3-0	2-0	34710	Bown, Nicholson, Wilcox (Banfield Benefit)
22	1 Jan	ROTHERHAM COUNTY	1	2-4	1-2	15000	Wilcox(2)
23	15	CARDIFF CITY	2	0-0	0-0	33672	
24	22	Cardiff City	3	0-1	0-1	43000	
25	29	LEICESTER CITY	3	1-0	0-0	15000	Bown
26	5 Feb	Leicester City	2	0-0	0-0	20000	
27	12	FULHAM	2	2-0	1-0	16000	Pocock, Wilcox
28	26	WEST HAM UNITED	2	1-0	1-0	20000	Pocock(pen)
29	28	Fulham	3	0-3	0-0	11000	
30	5 Mar	West Ham United	4	0-1	0-1	25000	
31	12	BIRMINGHAM CITY	4	0-0	0-0	26000	(Edwin Jones Benefit)
32	19	Birmingham	4	0-0	0-0	35000	
33	25	South Shields	4	0-0	0-0	15000	
34	26	Leeds United	3	1-0	0-0	16000	Fairclough
35	28	SOUTH SHIELDS	3	4-2	2-0	25000	Fairclough(2), Pocock, Wilcox
36	2 Apr	LEEDS UNITED	3	0-0	0-0	25000	
37	9	Coventry City	4	1-2	1-1	12000	Fairclough
38	16	COVENTRY CITY	3	2-0	1-0	20000	Fairclough, Pocock
39	23	Stoke	3	0-0	0-0	10000	
40	30	STOKE	3	5-0	2-0	14000	Wilcox(3), Bown, Thompson
41	2 May	The Wednesday	3	2-2	0-2	14000	Bown, Pocock
42	7	THE WEDNESDAY	3	0-1	0-0	12000	

Apps.: Vallis 42, Treasure 29, Banfield 22, Wren 38, Wedlock 5, Nicholson 34, Reader 13, Noble 6, Howarth 10, Pocock 40, Harris 42, Neesam 36, Wilcox 38, Bown 15, Batten 7, Kirk 11, Thompson 26, Jones T.E. 6, Jones E. 20, Southway 8, Fairclough 8, Hughes 5, Keen 1

Goals: Banfield 1, Howarth 1, Reader 1, Harris 1, Pocock 14, Wilcox 14, Bown 4, Kirk 5, Fairclough 1, Thompson 5

F.A. CUP

1R	8 Jan	Aston Villa		0-2	0-2	49734	(£2963)

GLOUCESTERSHIRE CUP FINAL

	29 Sep	BRISTOL ROVERS		1-0	0-0	11994	Banfield (£710.8.6.)

FRIENDLIES

1	22 Sep	CARDIFF CITY		0-0	0-0	6000	(Jock Nicholson Benefit)
2	15 Dec	Army XI (At Portsmouth)		3-2	3-1	3000	Kirk, Wedlock, Wilcox
3	18	West Ham United		0-2	0-2	4000	
4	28	Bristol Rovers		1-3	1-1	12000	Batten

FINAL LEAGUE TABLE

1	Birmingham	42	24	10	8	79:38	58
2	Cardiff	42	24	10	8	59:32	58
3	Bristol C.	42	19	13	10	49:29	51
4	Blackpool	42	20	10	12	54:42	50
5	West Ham	42	19	10	13	51:30	48
6	Notts Co.	42	18	11	13	55:40	47
7	Clapton Orient	42	16	13	13	43:42	45
8	South Shields	42	17	10	15	61:46	44
9	Fulham	42	16	10	16	43:47	42
10	The Wednesday	42	15	11	16	48:48	41
11	Bury	42	15	10	17	45:49	40
12	Leicester	42	12	16	14	39:46	40
13	Hull	42	10	20	12	43:53	40
14	Leeds	42	14	10	18	40:45	38
15	Wolverhampton	42	16	6	20	49:66	38
16	Barnsley	42	10	16	16	48:50	36
17	Port Vale	42	11	14	17	43:49	36
18	Nottingham F	42	12	12	18	48:55	36
19	Rotherham Co.	42	12	12	18	37:53	36
20	Stoke	42	12	11	19	46:56	35
21	Coventry	42	12	11	19	39:70	35
22	Stockport	42	9	12	21	42:75	30

SEASON 1921-22
FOOTBALL LEAGUE DIVISION TWO

Player columns (left to right): Vellis F., Treasure C.J., Banfield L., Neesam H., Wren T.J.E., Bown A.J.W., Reader A.R., Wilcox J.C., Fairclough A., Pocock W.T., Harris J., Hughes J., Jones E., Scuthway L.F., Smith J.R., Hughes R.G., Poulton A., Torrance A., Matthews A.W., Keen J.F., Beare G., Mooney J., Pullan R.L., Dyer R.E., Thompson J.L., Borthwick G.W., Cockerill H.L., Matthews R.W., Goddard R.J., Compton W.A., Vellis J.

No.	Date	Opposition	Pos.	Res.	H.T.	Att.	Goalscorers
1	27 Aug	Notts County		2-0	2-0	18000	Wilcox(?)
2	29	LEEDS UNITED		0-0	0-0	20000	
3	3 Sep	NOTTS COUNTY	4	2-2	2-2	17000	Harris, Fairclough
4	5	Leeds United	10	0-3	0-2	18000	
5	10	Derby County	15	1-5	1-3	10000	Fairclough
6	17	DERBY COUNTY	19	1-2	1-1	18000	Harris
7	24	Leicester City	20	1-4	1-2	16000	Pocock
8	1 Oct	LEICESTER CITY	21	1-1	1-0	14000	Wilcox
9	8	West Ham United	21	0-3	0-0	18000	
10	15	WEST HAM UNITED	21	0-1	0-0	11000	
11	22	Hull City	21	0-1	0-0	6000	
12	29	HULL CITY	21	1-0	0-0	12000	Fairclough
13	5 Nov	PORT VALE	20	2-1	1-1	15000	Fairclough(2)
14	12	Port Vale	21	1-3	0-2	8000	Beare
15	19	South Shields	21	0-2	0-1	9000	
16	26	SOUTH SHIELDS	21	0-1	0-0	12000	
17	3 Dec	Bury	21	0-5	0-2	10000	
18	10	BURY	21	2-0	1-0	12000	Beare, Fairclough
19	17	Nottingham Forest	21	0-1	0-0	8000	
20	24	NOTTINGHAM FOREST	21	0-1	0-0	10000	
21	26	Barnsley	21	1-1	0-1	10000	Harris
22	27	BARNSLEY	21	3-0	1-0	25000	Bown, Fairclough, Torrance
23	31	WOLVERHAMPTON WNDRS	19	2-0	1-0	18000	Banfield(pen), Fairclough
24	14 Jan	Wolverhampton Wanderers	18	2-2	1-0	8862	Keen, Pocock
25	21	Crystal Palace	18	1-1	0-1	7000	Fairclough
26	8 Feb	CRYSTAL PALACE	20	1-2	1-1	10000	Wilcox
27	11	ROTHERHAM COUNTY	21	1-2	1-0	8000	Fairclough
28	18	The Wednesday	22	0-1	0-0	25000	
29	20	Rotherham County	22	0-0	0-0	7000	
30	25	THE WEDNESDAY	20	3-1	2-0	15000	Fairclough, Poulton, Torrance
31	4 Mar	Fulham	21	0-0	0-0	20000	
32	11	FULHAM	19	1-0	0-0	20000	Fairclough
33	18	BLACKPOOL	20	0-1	0-1	16000	
34	25	Blackpool	22	0-2	0-2	9000	
35	8 Apr	Bradford Park Avenue	22	1-2	1-1	7000	Poulton
36	11	BRADFORD PARK AVENUE	22	1-0	0-0	7000	Smith
37	15	CLAPTON ORIENT	20	2-1	2-0	14000	Pocock, Smith
38	17	COVENTRY CITY	22	0-2	0-1	18912	
39	18	Coventry City	22	1-1	1-1	12000	Smith
40	22	Clapton Orient*	22	1-0	0-0	10000	Poulton
41	29	STOKE	21	2-0	1-0	18000	Poulton(2)
42	6 May	Stoke	22	0-3	0-2	19250	

Apps: 22, 1, 42, 41, 29, 16, 9, 13, 38, 40, 30, 3, 6, 6, 10, 36, 20, 30, 1, 8, 14, 1, 1, 1, 3, 1, 3, 12, 7, 8, 10
Goals: 1, 1, 4, 12, 3, 3, 3, 5, 2, 1, 2

* The Duke of York, the future King George VI, was present at this match.

F.A. CUP

	Date	Opposition	Res.	H.T.	Att.	Goalscorers
1R	7 Jan	NOTTINGHAM FOREST	0-0	0-0	25000	(£1800)
1Rr	11	Nottingham Forest	1-3	0-3	17300	Bown (£1425)

GLOUCESTERSHIRE CUP FINAL

	Date	Opposition	Res.	H.T.	Att.	Goalscorers
	1 May	Bristol Rovers	2-0	1-0	9000	Fairclough, Pocock

FRIENDLIES

	Date	Opposition	Res.	H.T.	Att.	Goalscorers
1	31 Oct	Cardiff City	2-2	0-2		Keen, Smith (Fred Keenor Benefit)
2	28 Jan	BIRMINGHAM	3-3	1-0	4000	Fairclough(2), Poulton
3	9 May	GLOUCESTERSHIRE F.A. XI	2-1	1-0		Figgures, Smith (G.F.A. Benevolent Fund)

FINAL LEAGUE TABLE

1	Nottingham F	42	22	12	8	51	30	56
2	Stoke	42	18	16	8	60	44	52
3	Barnsley	42	22	8	12	67	52	52
4	West Ham	42	20	8	14	52	39	48
5	Hull	42	19	10	13	51	41	48
6	South Shields	42	17	12	13	43	38	46
7	Fulham	42	18	9	15	57	38	45
8	Leeds	42	16	13	13	48	38	45
9	Leicester	42	14	17	11	39	34	45
10	The Wednesday	42	15	14	13	47	50	44
11	Bury	42	15	10	17	54	55	40
12	Derby	42	15	9	18	60	64	39
13	Notts Co	42	12	15	15	47	51	39
14	Crystal Palace	42	13	13	16	45	51	39
15	Clapton Orient	42	15	9	18	43	50	39
16	Rotherham Co	42	14	11	17	32	43	39
17	Wolverhampton	42	13	11	18	44	49	37
18	Port Vale	42	14	8	20	43	57	36
19	Blackpool	42	15	5	22	44	57	35
20	Coventry	42	12	10	20	51	60	34
21	Bradford P A	42	12	9	21	46	62	33
22	Bristol C	42	12	9	21	37	58	33

SEASON 1922-23
FOOTBALL LEAGUE DIVISION THREE (SOUTH)

Player columns (left to right): Goddard R.J., Jones E., Banfield L., Neesam H., Matthews R.W., Torrance A., Hart A., Poulton A., Fairclough A., Pocock W.T., Brown T.H., Vallis F., Hughes R.G., Sutherland C., Cockerill H.L., Smith J.R., Mooney J., Worlock C.S.R., Dyer R.E., Walker W.B., Paul J.C., Pullan R.L., Hawley F.

No.	Date	Opposition	Pos.	Res.	H.T.	Att.	Goalscorers
1	26 Aug	READING		2-1	1-1	14000	Poulton(2)
2	28	Plymouth Argyle		1-5	0-1	17000	Fairclough
3	2 Sep	Reading	11	0-0	0-0	11000	
4	4	PLYMOUTH ARGYLE	5	2-0	1-0	14620	Smith(2)
5	9	NEWPORT COUNTY	5	2-0	2-0	11000	Banfield(pen), Smith
6	16	Newport County	5	1-0	1-0	9500	Smith
7	23	BRISTOL ROVERS	6	0-1	0-1	28000	
8	30	Bristol Rovers	4	2-1	1-1	25000	Fairclough, Poulton
9	7 Oct	Swansea Town	8	1-4	1-3	21000	Poulton
10	14	SWANSEA TOWN	6	1-0	1-0	15000	Fairclough (Bert Neesam Benefit)
11	21	SOUTHEND UNITED	5	5-0	4-0	11000	Fairclough(2,1pen), Neesam, Sutherland, Walker
12	28	Southend United	4	3-0	1-0	5800	Fairclough(3)
13	4 Nov	PORTSMOUTH	3	2-1	0-0	17500	Fairclough(2)
14	11	Portsmouth	2	2-1	1-0	13790	Pocock, Sutherland
15	18	MILLWALL	2	1-1	1-0	22000	Walker
16	25	Millwall	4	1-1	0-0	20000	Sutherland
17	2 Dec	Luton Town	2	1-1	1-1	12000	Matthews
18	9	LUTON TOWN	2	1-0	0-0	15000	Fairclough
19	16	Queens Park Rangers	1	2-1	2-0	12000	Fairclough(2,1pen)
20	23	QUEENS PARK RANGERS	1	3-2	1-1	15000	Fairclough, Sutherland, Worlock
21	26	SWINDON TOWN	1	3-1	3-1	28500*	Sutherland(2), Fairclough
22	27	Swindon Town	1	1-0	1-0	7309	Worlock
23	30	Gillingham	1	1-1	0-1	8000	Torrance
24	6 Jan	GILLINGHAM	1	2-1	2-1	12000	Fairclough, Sutherland
25	20	Brighton & Hove Albion	1	1-2	0-1	7200	Fairclough
26	27	BRIGHTON & HOVE ALBN	1	3-1	1-0	16000	Walker(2), Pocock
27	10 Feb	Merthyr Town	1	1-0	0-0	6000	Worlock
28	14	MERTHYR TOWN	1	3-0	2-0	8000	Smith(2), Sutherland
29	17	EXETER CITY	1	1-1	1-0	14000	Smith
30	24	Exeter City	1	0-0	0-0	7000	
31	3 Mar	NORTHAMPTON TOWN	1	1-0	1-0	15000	Sutherland
32	10	Northampton Town	1	1-2	0-0	12000	Banfield(pen)
33	17	Norwich City	1	2-2	2-1	9000	Pocock(2)
34	24	NORWICH CITY	1	4-0	2-0	15000	Pocock(2), Fairclough, Pullan
35	30	ABERDARE ATHLETIC	1	0-0	0-0	23000	
36	31	Brentford	1	0-4	0-1	10000	
37	2 Apr	Aberdare Athletic	1	1-0	0-0	16350	Fairclough
38	7	BRENTFORD	1	1-1	0-1	16000	Pocock
39	14	Watford	1	1-1	0-1	7000	Walker(pen)
40	21	WATFORD	1	3-1	2-1	16000	Walker(2,1pen), Smith
41	28	Charlton Athletic	1	0-1	0-1	7000	
42	5 May	CHARLTON ATHLETIC	1	3-1	2-0	11000	Paul, Smith, Torrance

Apps: 4, 2, 34, 31, 29, 35, 2, 8, 31, 40, 8, 38, 29, 36, 13, 11, 1, 35, 17, 32, 6, 10, 10
Goals: 2, 1, 1, 2, 4, 19, 7, 9, 9, 3, 7, 1, 1

* Offical paid attendance, but as at least 4000 people broke in,
the actual figure was in the region of 32500.

F.A. CUP

	Date	Opposition		Res.	H.T.	Att.	Goalscorers
1R	13 Jan	WREXHAM		5-1	2-1	23000	Fairclough(3), Paul, Walker (£1350)
2R	3 Feb	DERBY COUNTY		0-3	0-2	32972	(£2202)

GLOUCESTERSHIRE CUP FINAL

	Date	Opposition		Res.	H.T.	Att.	Notes
	16 Apr	BRISTOL ROVERS		3-1	1-1	7838	Smith,Walkr,Wolck (Aban.80 mins fail.light) (£453)
	7 May	BRISTOL ROVERS		1-0	0-0	4991	Smith (extra time played) (£288.9.2.)

FRIENDLIES

	Date	Opposition		Res.	H.T.	Att.	Notes
1	30 Apr	Plymouth Argyle		1-2			Smith (T.Gallogley's Benefit)
2	2 May	SWANSEA TOWN		0-0	0-0	2123	(Edwin Jones Benefit)

FINAL LEAGUE TABLE

		P	W	D	L	F	A	Pts
1	Bristol C.	42	24	11	7	66	40	59
2	Plymouth	42	23	7	12	61	29	53
3	Swansea	42	22	9	11	78	45	53
4	Brighton	42	20	11	11	52	34	51
5	Luton	42	21	7	14	68	49	49
6	Millwall Athletic	42	14	18	10	45	40	46
7	Portsmouth	42	19	8	15	58	52	46
8	Northampton	42	17	11	14	54	44	45
9	Swindon	42	17	11	14	62	56	45
10	Watford	42	17	10	15	57	54	44
11	QPR	42	16	10	16	54	49	42
12	Charlton	42	14	14	14	55	51	42
13	Bristol R.	42	13	16	13	35	36	42
14	Brentford	42	13	12	17	41	51	38
15	Southend	42	12	13	17	49	54	37
16	Gillingham	42	15	7	20	51	59	37
17	Merthyr Town	42	11	14	17	39	48	36
18	Norwich	42	13	10	19	51	71	36
19	Reading	42	10	14	18	36	55	34
20	Exeter	42	13	7	22	47	84	33
21	Aberdare	42	9	11	22	42	70	29
22	Newport	42	8	11	23	40	70	27

Player columns (left to right): Vallis F. | Hughes R.G. | Banfield L. | Neesam H. | Hawley F. | Torrance A. | Worlock C.S.R. | Walker W.B. | Fairclough A. | Sutherland C. | Pocock W.T. | Price J.C. | Dyer R.E. | Paul J.C. | Cack E.C. | Goddard R.J. | Dinnan J.M.K. | Compton W.A. | Pullan R.L. | Nesbitt W. | Smith J.R. | Crumley J.B. | Matthews R.W. | Smailes A. | Davies F.P. | Glenn E. | Mays A.W. | Walsh T. | Andrews F.E.

No.	Date	Opposition	Pos.	Res.	H.T.	Att.	Goalscorers
1	25 Aug	MANCHESTER UNITED		1-2	0-2	25000	Pocock
2	27	Barnsley		1-3	1-2	12000	Fairclough
3	1 Sep	Manchester United	22	1-2	1-2	21000	Banfield(pen)
4	3	BARNSLEY	20	1-1	0-1	20000	Fairclough
5	8	Coventry City	19	1-1	1-0	16000	Hawley
6	15	COVENTRY CITY	21	2-2	0-0	18000	Fairclough(2)
7	22	Derby County	19	3-2	2-0	12000	Fairclough(2), O.G.
8	29	DERBY COUNTY	22	0-8	0-4	20000	
9	6 Oct	Southampton	22	0-1	0-1	13000	
10	13	SOUTHAMPTON	22	1-1	0-0	14000	Sutherland
11	20	FULHAM	22	0-1	0-1	13000	
12	27	Fulham	22	1-1	1-1	15000	Torrance(pen)
13	3 Nov	Blackpool	22	0-2	0-1	9500	
14	10	BLACKPOOL	22	1-1	0-0	10000	Torrance(pen)
15	17	NELSON	22	1-0	1-0	8000	Torrance(pen)
16	24	Nelson	22	1-2	1-1	8000	Torrance(pen)
17	1 Dec	BURY	21	4-1	3-1	7000	Smailes(2), Fairclough, Pocock
18	8	Bury	22	0-6	0-5	9000	
19	15	HULL CITY	21	1-0	1-0	8000	Fairclough
20	22	Hull City	22	0-5	0-2	9000	
21	25	CRYSTAL PALACE	22	0-0	0-0	10000	
22	26	Crystal Palace	22	0-1	0-1	10000	
23	29	STOKE	21	1-1	1-1	12000	Paul
24	5 Jan	Stoke	22	0-3	0-2	10000	
25	19	BRADFORD CITY	22	0-1	0-1	11000	(Laurence Banfield Benefit)
26	26	Bradford City	22	1-1	1-1	10000	Pocock
27	9 Feb	Port Vale	22	2-0	1-0	6000	Smailes, Walsh
28	13	PORT VALE	22	0-0	0-0	10000	
29	16	LEEDS UNITED	22	0-1	0-0	14000	
30	1 Mar	LEICESTER CITY	22	0-1	0-1	11000	
31	8	Leicester City	22	1-5	1-2	22000	Smailes
32	15	Clapton Orient	22	0-2	0-0	16000	
33	19	Leeds United	22	0-0	0-0	8000	
34	22	CLAPTON ORIENT	22	0-2	0-1	10000	
35	29	Stockport County	22	0-0	0-0	9000	
36	5 Apr	STOCKPORT COUNTY	22	3-0	0-0	8000	Mays, Pocock, Smailes
37	12	Oldham Athletic	22	0-0	0-0	5870	
38	18	THE WEDNESDAY	22	2-3	0-1	16000	Smailes, Walsh
39	19	OLDHAM ATHLETIC	22	0-0	0-0	10000	
40	21	The Wednesday	22	0-1	0-0	8000	
41	26	South Shields	22	1-1	1-1	4000	Smailes
42	3 May	SOUTH SHIELDS	22	1-0	0-0	6000	Pocock

Apps. 30 15 28 10 28 38 14 5 14 22 40 3 17 31 2 10 2 3 7 26 6 2 1 30 24 24 12 17 1

Goals: Banfield 1, Hawley 1, Torrance 4, Fairclough 8, Sutherland 1, Pocock 5, Paul 1, Smailes 7, Mays 1, Walsh 2

F.A. CUP

			Res.	H.T.	Att.	Goalscorers
1R	12 Jan	Norwich City	1-0	0-0	11349	Smailes (£815)
2R	2 Feb	The Wednesday	1-1	0-1	38868	Pocock (£2964)
2Rr	6	THE WEDNESDAY	2-0	2-0	22754	Walsh(2) (£1488.15.0)
3R	23	Cardiff City	0-3	0-1	50000	(£2950)

GLOUCESTERSHIRE CUP FINAL

			Res.	H.T.	Att.	Goalscorers
	30 Apr	Bristol Rovers	1-1	1-1	7396	Walsh (£418)
r	5 May	BRISTOL ROVERS	2-0	0-0	6091	Torrance, Walsh (£352)

FINAL LEAGUE TABLE (BOTTOM POSITIONS)

9	South Shields	42	17	10	15	49	50	44
10	Clapton Orient	42	14	15	13	40	36	43
11	Barnsley	42	16	11	15	57	61	43
12	Leicester	42	17	8	17	64	54	42
13	Stockport	42	13	16	13	44	52	42
14	Manchester U.	42	13	14	15	52	44	40
15	Crystal Palace	42	13	13	16	53	65	39
16	Port Vale	42	13	12	17	50	66	38
17	Hull	42	10	17	15	46	51	37
18	Bradford C.	42	11	15	16	35	48	37
19	Coventry	42	11	13	18	52	68	35
20	Fulham	42	10	14	18	45	56	34
21	Nelson	42	10	13	19	40	74	33
22	Bristol C.	42	7	15	20	32	65	29

Back: Nesbitt, Glenn, Pullan , Vallis, Smailes, Banfield.
Front: Walsh, Torrance, Pocock, Paul, Hawley.

SEASON 1924-25
FOOTBALL LEAGUE DIVISION THREE (SOUTH)

No.	Date	Opposition	Pos.	Res.	H.T.	Att.	Goalscorers	Vallis F.	Hughes R.G.	Glenn E.	Paul J.C.	Hawley F.	Torrance A.	Worlock C.S.R.	Mays A.W.	Walsh T.	Smailes A.	Pocock W.T.	Banfield L.	Kirk R.H.	Dyer R.E.	McGovern J.	Sutherland C.	Lawrence G.H.	Davies F.P.	Neate T.	Neesam H.	Buckland W.A.	Conner J.	Kirby H.H.
1	30 Aug	Aberdare Athletic		2-1	2-0	13000	Walsh, Worlock	1	2	3	4	5	6	7	8	9	10	11												
2	1 Sep	EXETER CITY		0-1	0-0	15000		1	2		4	5	6	7	8	9	10		3	11										
3	6	NORWICH CITY	6	2-0	0-0	12000	McGovern, Smailes	1			4	5	6	7		9	10			11	3	8								
4	10	Exeter City	4	2-0	1-0	9000	Walsh(2)	1		2	4	5	6	7		9	10			11	3	8								
5	13	Brentford	5	0-1	0-0	9000		1		2	4	5	6	7		9	10			11	3	8								
6	17	SWINDON TOWN	3	0-0	0-0	7000		1	2		4	5	6	7		9	10			11	3		8							
7	20	MILLWALL	3	4-1	2-0	5000	Mays, Sutherland, Worlock, O.G.		3	2	4		6	7	8		9			11			10	1	5					
8	24	CHARLTON ATHLETIC	3	1-1	0-1	7000	Worlock(pen)		3	2	4		6	7	8		9						10	1	5	11				
9	27	Luton Town	5	0-3	0-1	11000			3	2	8	5	6	7			9						10	1	4	11				
10	4 Oct	GILLINGHAM	4	2-1	1-1	12000	Sutherland, Worlock		3	2	8	5		7		9	6	11					10	1	4					
11	11	Bournemouth & B. A.	2	3-1	1-1	5000	Walsh(2), Worlock		3	2	8	5		7		9	6	11					10	1		4				
12	18	BRIGHTON & HOVE ALB.	3	2-1	0-1	12000	Paul, Walsh		3	2	8	5		7		9	6	11					10	1		4				
13	25	Bristol Rovers	2	0-0	0-0	30000			3	2	8	5		7		9	6	11					10	1		4				
14	1 Nov	NEWPORT COUNTY	2	2-0	1-0	8000	Paul, Walsh		3	2	8	5		7		9	6	11					10	1		4				
15	8	Southend United	3	0-2	0-1	8000			3	2	8	5		7		9	6	11					10	1		4				
16	15	WATFORD	4	1-1	1-0	12000	Walsh		3	2	7	5	8			9	6	11					10	1		4				
17	22	Northampton Town	1	2-1	0-0	8000	Sutherland, Walsh		3	2	7	5	8			9	6			11			10	1		4				
18	6 Dec	Queens Park Rangers	3	0-3	0-2	6000			3	2	7	5	8			9	6			11			10	1		4				
19	13	MERTHYR TOWN	2	1-0	0-0	7000	Sutherland (Frank Vallis Benefit)	1	3	2	7	5	6			9	8	11					10			4				
20	20	Reading	1	1-0	1-0	3000	Conner	1	3	2		5		7			8	11					10			4	6	9		
21	25	Swansea Town	1	1-1	1-0	20000	Conner	1		2		5		7		9	6	11			3		10			4		8		
22	26	SWANSEA TOWN	2	0-0	0-0	28566		1		2		5		7		9	6	11			3		10			4		8		
23	27	ABERDARE ATHLETIC	3	0-1	0-1	7000		1		2	4			7	8	9	6	11			3				5			10		
24	3 Jan	Norwich City	1	0-0	0-0	7000		1	2		4		6	7		9	10	11			3				5			8		
25	17	BRENTFORD	1	3-0	2-0	9000	Smailes, Walsh, Worlock(pen)	1	2			5	6	7		9	8	11			3		10			4				
26	24	Millwall	3	1-3	0-1	18000	Pocock	1	2			5	6	7		9	10	11			3					4		8		
27	7 Feb	Gillingham	6	1-1	1-1	5000	Pocock	1		2	8	5				9	6	11			3		10			4		7		
28	14	BOURNEMOUTH & B. A.	6	2-1	2-1	8000	Paul, Sutherland	1		2	8	5				9	6	11			3		10			4		7		
29	21	Brighton & Hove Albion	7	0-1	0-0	7570		1	2		8					9	6			11	3		10	5		4		7		
30	28	BRISTOL ROVERS	6	2-0	1-0	15370	Paul, Walsh	1	2		8	5				9	6			11	3		10			4				7
31	4 Mar	LUTON TOWN	3	2-0	1-0	6000	Walsh(2) (Billy Pocock Benefit)	1	3	2	8	5				9	6			11			10			4				7
32	7	Newport County	3	2-0	1-0	11800	Kirk, Paul	1	3	2	8	5				9	6			11			10			4		7		
33	14	SOUTHEND UNITED	1	5-0	1-0	9000	Paul(2), Sutherland(2), Walsh	1	3	2	8	5				9	6			11			10			4		7		
34	21	Watford	3	0-1	0-0	4800		1	3	2	8	5				9	6			11			10			4		7		
35	28	NORTHAMPTON TOWN	3	1-0	1-0	11000	Paul	1	3	2	8	5				9	6			11			10			4				
36	4 Apr	Charlton Athletic	2	1-0	1-0	6000	Smailes	1	3	2	8	5		7		9	6			11			10			4				
37	10	Plymouth Argyle	3	1-7	0-3	22000	Sutherland	1	3	2	8	5		7		9	6			11			10			4				
38	11	QUEENS PARK RANGERS	3	5-0	2-0	8000	Sutherland(2), Walsh(2), Conner		3	2	8	5				9	6			11			10	1		4		7		
39	13	PLYMOUTH ARGYLE	3	2-2	2-0	23600	Paul, Sutherland		3	2	8	5				9	6			11			10	1		4		7		
40	18	Merthyr Town	3	3-2	1-1	2000	Walsh(2), Paul	1	3	2	8	5				9	6			11			10			4				7
41	25	READING	3	3-0	3-0	10000	Walsh(2), Paul	1	3	2	8	5				9	6			11			10			4				7
42	2 May	Swindon Town	3	0-3	0-2	8361		1	3	2		5				9	6			11			10			4		8	7	
		Apps.						28	34	35	36	37	16	24	5	38	42	18	1	22	14	3	34	14	7	2	30	1	16	5
		Goals									11			6	1	20	3	2		1		1	11					3		

F.A. CUP

No.	Date	Opposition		Res.	H.T.	Att.	Goalscorers	Vallis F.	Hughes R.G.	Glenn E.	Paul J.C.	Hawley F.	Torrance A.	Worlock C.S.R.	Mays A.W.	Walsh T.	Smailes A.	Pocock W.T.	Banfield L.	Kirk R.H.	Dyer R.E.	McGovern J.	Sutherland C.	Lawrence G.H.	Davies F.P.	Neate T.	Neesam H.	Buckland W.A.	Conner J.	Kirby H.H.
1R	10 Jan	Bristol Rovers		1-0	1-0	31500	Walsh (£1950)	1	2			5	6	7		9	8	11			3		10			4				
2R	31	LIVERPOOL		0-1	0-0	29363	(£2035.8.8)	1	2		8	5		7		9	6	11			3		10			4				

GLOUCESTERSHIRE CUP FINAL

	Date	Opposition		Res.	H.T.	Att.	Goalscorers
	27 Apr	BRISTOL ROVERS		1-1	0-0	5102	Walsh(pen) (£289.15.0)
r	29	Bristol Rovers		0-2	0-2	4335	(£245)

ALLEN PALMER CUP FINAL

	Date	Opposition		Res.	H.T.	Att.	Goalscorers
	5 May	Trowbridge Town		1-1	1-1	1700	Gutteridge (aet 1-1 90 mins)

FRIENDLIES

No.	Date	Opposition		Res.	H.T.		Goalscorers
1	2 Oct	Ilfracombe Town		4-1			Walsh(2), McGovern, Sutherland
2	29 Nov	Brighton & Hove Albion		1-2	0-2		Worlock

FINAL LEAGUE TABLE

		P	W	D	L	F	A	Pts
1	Swansea	42	23	11	8	68	35	57
2	Plymouth	42	23	10	9	77	38	56
3	Bristol C	42	22	9	11	60	41	53
4	Swindon	42	20	11	11	66	38	51
5	Millwall Athletic	42	18	13	11	58	38	49
6	Newport	42	20	9	13	62	42	49
7	Exeter	42	19	9	14	59	48	47
8	Brighton	42	19	8	15	59	45	46
9	Northampton	42	20	6	16	51	44	46
10	Southend	42	19	5	18	51	61	43
11	Watford	42	17	9	16	38	47	43
12	Norwich	42	14	13	15	53	51	41
13	Gillingham	42	13	14	15	35	44	40
14	Reading	42	14	10	18	37	38	38
15	Charlton	42	13	12	17	46	48	38
16	Luton	42	10	17	15	49	57	37
17	Bristol R.	42	12	13	17	42	49	37
18	Aberdare	42	14	9	19	54	67	37
19	QPR	42	14	8	20	42	63	36
20	Bournemouth	42	13	8	21	40	58	34
21	Brentford	42	9	7	26	38	91	25
22	Merthyr Town	42	8	5	29	35	77	21

BRISTOL CITY.

Back Row (Left to Right)—Paul, Hughes, Worlock, Vallis, Smailes, Hawley.
Middle Row—Kirk, Davies, Glenn, Torrance, McGovern.
Front Row—Dyer, Connor (in circle), Walsh.

1924/25 Season.

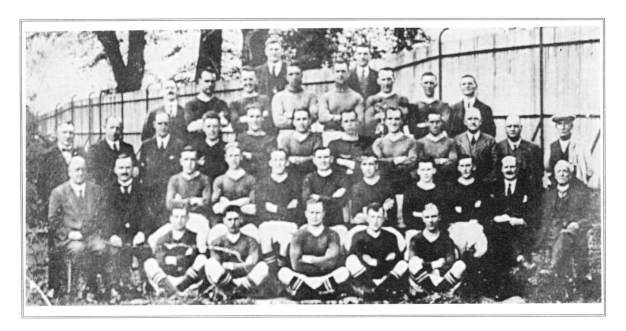

1925/26 Season

Back: Annan(Coach), Hanlon(Trainer). 4th Row: Tanner(Dir.), Glenn, MacLean, Vallis, E.Davis, Smailes, Pocock, J.A.Hooper(Dir.). 3rd Row: A.R.P.Bray(Dir.), F.J.Humphries(Dir.), F.Widgery(Dir.), Gilhespy, Perry, Penn, Mays, Dent, Pool, F.Drewett(Dir.), A.Wise(Dir.), Batten(Asst.Trainer). 2nd Row: P.O.Daniell(Dir.), G.Jenkins(Chair.), Sherlaw, Bell, Paul, Tonner, F.P.Davies, Kirby, Kirk, A.Raisbeck (Sec/Man.), W.H.Roberts(Dir.). Front: Neesam, Hughes, Walsh, Sutherland, Torrance.

FOOTBALL LEAGUE DIVISION THREE (SOUTH)

No.	Date	Opposition	Pos.	Res.	H.T.	Att.	Goalscorers	Vallis F.	Tonner S.	Hughes R.G.	Neesam H.	Pool A.	Smailes A.	Gilhespy T.W.C.	Paul J.C.	Walsh T.	Sutherland C.	Kirk R.H.	Penn T.	Glenn E.	Sherlaw D.D.	Dent F.	Davis E.	Torrance A.	Davies F.P.	Pocock W.T.	Keating A.E.	Coggins W.H.	Thompson D.	Mays A.W.	Howson G.S.	McLean J.S.
1	29 Aug	NORWICH CITY		0-1	0-0	17517		1	2	3	4	5	6	7	8	9	10	11														
2	31	Swindon Town		3-1	0-1	11960	Walsh(2), Smailes	1			4	5	6	7		9		11	2	3	8	10										
3	5 Sep	Millwall	14	0-3	0-1	23000		1		2	4	5	6	7		9		11		3	8	10										
4	9	SWINDON TOWN	9	5-1	0-0	12362	Sherlaw(3), Gilhespy, Kirk			2	4	5	6	7	8			11		3	9	10	1									
5	12	NORTHAMPTON TOWN	9	1-1	1-1	14954	Sherlaw			2	4	5		7	8			11		3	9	10	1	6								
6	19	Aberdare Athletic	11	3-3	3-1	3000	Dent, Neesam, Paul			2	4	5			8	9		11		3	7	10	1	6								
7	23	Crystal Palace	15	2-5	1-3	8078	Paul, Sutherland	1		2	4	5	6	7	8		10	11		3	9											
8	26	BRIGHTON & HOVE ALB.	12	1-0	1-0	10531	Paul	1		2	4	5	6	7	8	9	10	11		3												
9	3 Oct	Watford	11	2-2	0-0	8000	Paul, Walsh	1		3	6	5	4	11	10	9	8	7		2												
10	7	CRYSTAL PALACE	7	2-0	0-0	6144	Paul	1		2	4			7	8		10	11		3	9			6	5							
11	10	BRENTFORD	4	3-0	1-0	11095	Kirk, Sherlaw, Tonner(pen)	1	2		4		6	7	8			11		3	9				5	10						
12	17	Exeter City	4	1-1	0-0	8000	Pocock	1	2		4		6	7		8		11		3	9				5	10						
13	24	READING	4	0-1	0-0	10858		1	2		4		6	7		8		11		3	9				5	10						
14	31	Queens Park Rangers	4	2-0	0-0	15000	Walsh(2)	1		2	4			7		9		11		3	8			6	5	10						
15	7 Nov	BRISTOL ROVERS	3	2-0	0-0	18816		1		2	4			7		9				3	8	10		6	5	11						
16	14	Gillingham	3	1-0	0-0	6779	Gilhespy	1			4			7		9			2	3	8	10		6	5	11						
17	21	MERTHYR TOWN	3	2-1	1-1	10058	Sherlaw, Walsh	1			4			7		9			2	3	8	10		6	5	11						
18	5 Dec	LUTON TOWN	3	5-1	2-0	10208	Keating(2), Kirk, Pocock, Walsh	1		2	4			7		9		11		3				6	5	10	8					
19	19	CHARLTON ATHLETIC	2	4-0	2-0	10708	Walsh(2), Keating, Pocock	1		2	4					9		11		3	7			6	5	10	8					
20	25	SOUTHEND UNITED	4	1-4	0-3	13841	Keating	1		2	4					9		11		3	7			6	5	10	8					
21	26	Southend United	3	2-1	1-1	13438	Keating, Walsh			2	4					9		11		3	7			6	5	10	8	1				
22	28	Newport County	3	0-1	0-0	4593				2	4					9		11		3	7	10		6	5		8	1				
23	2 Jan	Norwich City	3	3-1	3-0	6000	Walsh(2), Pocock			2	4		10			9				3	7			6	5	11	8	1				
24	13	Bournemouth & B.A.	3	1-1	1-0	6000	Smailes			2	4		10	7		9				3				6	5	11	8	1				
25	16	MILLWALL	3	1-1	0-0	9296	Walsh			2	4					9	10	11		3	7			6	5		8	1				
26	23	Northampton Town	3	2-1	1-1	7000	Gilhespy, Keating			2	4			7		9		11		3				6	5	10	8	1				
27	30	ABERDARE ATHLETIC	3	1-0	0-0	8833	Pocock (Bob Hughes Benefit)			2	4			7		9		11		3				6	5	10	8	1				
28	6 Feb	Brighton & Hove Albion		0-0	0-0	9890				2	4			7		9		11		3				6	5	10	8	1				
29	13	WATFORD	1	1-0	1-0	14628	Walsh			2	4			7		9		11		3				6	5	10	8	1				
30	20	Brentford	3	1-2	1-0	11500	Walsh			2	4			7		9		11		3				6	5	10	8	1				
31	27	EXETER CITY	2	1-0	1-0	13140	Walsh			2	4			7	8	9				3				6	5	10		1	11			
32	6 Mar	Reading	3	1-1	1-1	24334	Keating			2	4		5	7	8	9				3				6			10	1	11			
33	13	QUEENS PARK RANGERS	1	3-1	0-1	12193	Gilhespy, Keating, Walsh(pen)			2	4		5	7	8	9				3				6			10	1	11			
34	20	Bristol Rovers	1	0-3	0-0	27000				2	4		5	7	8	9				3				6			10	1	11			
35	27	GILLINGHAM	2	4-0	1-0	10569	Paul(2), Sutherland, Walsh			3	4		5	7	8	9	10			2				6				1	11			
36	2 Apr	Plymouth Argyle	3	1-3	0-3	30000	Mays			3	4		5	7	8					2				6		10		1	11	9		
37	3	Merthyr Town	4	2-3	2-1	6000	Gilhespy, Mays			3	4		5	7	8			11		2				6		10		1		9		
38	5	PLYMOUTH ARGYLE	4	1-2	0-0	20079	Walsh(2)			2	4		5	7	8	9		11						6		10		1			3	
39	10	NEWPORT COUNTY	4	1-2	0-0	9802	Walsh (Bert Neesam Benefit)			2	4		5	7		9	10	11				8		6				1			3	
40	17	Luton Town	4	1-4	0-2	6000	Walsh			2			5	7	8	9		11						6		10		1			3	4
41	24	BOURNEMOUTH & B.A.	4	5-0	4-0	5559	Walsh(2), Gilhespy, Paul, Torrance		3	2	4		5	7	8	9		11						6		10		1				
42	1 May	Charlton Athletic	4	1-3	0-3	6000	Kirk		3	2	4		5	7	8	9		11						6		10		1				
							Apps.	17	6	36	26	12	24	35	29	33	11	30	6	33	20	12	3	32	23	21	19	22	6	2	3	1
							Goals		1		1		2	6	8	25	2	4			6	1		1		5	8			2		

F.A. CUP

	Date	Opposition		Res.	H.T.	Att.	Goalscorers	Vallis F.	Tonner S.	Hughes R.G.	Neesam H.	Pool A.	Smailes A.	Gilhespy T.W.C.	Paul J.C.	Walsh T.	Sutherland C.	Kirk R.H.	Penn T.	Glenn E.	Sherlaw D.D.	Dent F.	Davis E.	Torrance A.	Davies F.P.	Pocock W.T.	Keating A.E.
3R	9 Jan	West Bromwich Albion		1-4	1-2	33295	Pocock (£1920)	1		2	4		10			9				3	7			6	5	11	8

GLOUCESTERSHIRE CUP FINAL

	Date	Opposition		Res.	H.T.	Att.	Goalscorers
	19 Apr	Bristol Rovers		4-1	4-1	4123	Keating(2), Paul, Walsh (£233)

ALLEN PALMER CUP FINAL

	Date	Opposition		Res.	H.T.	Att.	Goalscorers
	3 May	Trowbridge Town		5-1	3-1	1181	Unknown (5)

FRIENDLIES

No.	Date	Opposition		Res.	H.T.	Att.	Goalscorers
1	30 Sep	CARDIFF CITY		2-1	1-0	3328	Gil'py(pen), Sherlaw (Benefit-family late Ted Hanlon)
2	28 Nov	Wolverhampton Wanderers		2-4	1-2	3000	Gilhespy, Walsh
3	12 Dec	Exeter City		3-5	1-4	4000	Keating(2), Walsh

FINAL LEAGUE TABLE

1	Reading	42	23	11	8	77:52	57
2	Plymouth	42	24	8	10	107:67	56
3	Millwall	42	21	11	10	73:39	53
4	Bristol C.	42	21	9	12	72:51	51
5	Brighton	42	19	9	14	84:73	47
6	Swindon	42	20	6	16	69:64	46
7	Luton	42	18	7	17	80:75	43
8	Bournemouth	42	17	9	16	75:91	43
9	Aberdare	42	17	8	17	74:66	42
10	Gillingham	42	17	8	17	53:49	42
11	Southend	42	19	4	19	78:73	42
12	Northampton	42	17	7	18	82:80	41
13	Crystal Palace	42	19	3	20	75:79	41
14	Merthyr Town	42	14	11	17	69:75	39
15	Watford	42	15	9	18	73:89	39
16	Norwich	42	15	9	18	58:73	39
17	Newport	42	14	10	18	64:74	38
18	Brentford	42	16	6	20	69:94	38
19	Bristol R.	42	15	6	21	66:69	36
20	Exeter	42	15	5	22	72:70	35
21	Charlton	42	11	13	18	48:68	35
22	QPR	42	6	9	27	37:84	21

SEASON 1926-27
FOOTBALL LEAGUE DIVISION THREE (SOUTH)

No.	Date	Opposition	Pos.	Res.	H.T.	Att.	Goalscorers	Coggins W.H.	Hughes R.G.	Glenn E.	Neesam H.	Wadsworth W.	Torrance A.	Gilhespy T.W.C.	Paul J.C.	Walsh T.	Keating A.E.	Rankin A.	Smailes A.	Gray A.D.	Geddes J.	Foster J.T.F.	Martin J.C.	Drummond R.C.	Kirk R.H.	Walsh J.	Murray D.J.	Taylor J.S.
1	28 Aug	Gillingham		1-1	0-0	9118	Paul	1	2	3	4	5	6	7	8	9	10	11										
2	1 Sep	NEWPORT COUNTY		4-1	3-1	13478	Gilhespy, Keating, Paul, Walsh	1	2	3	4	5	6	7	8	9	10	11										
3	4	WATFORD	1	5-0	3-0	14962	Walsh(4), Keating	1	2	3	4	5	6	7	8	9	10	11										
4	9	Newport County	1	0-0	0-0	7888		1	2	3	4	5	6	7	8	9	10	11										
5	11	Crystal Palace	7	2-4	0-2	16902	Keating, Torrance	1	2	3	4	5	6	7	8	9	10	11										
6	18	COVENTRY CITY	6	3-0	2-0	13454	Paul, Walsh, O.G.	1	2	3	4	5	6	7	8	9	10	11										
7	22	PLYMOUTH ARGYLE	3	4-2	2-0	19346	Paul(3), Keating	1	2	3	4	5	6	7	8	9	10	11										
8	25	Queens Park Rangers	2	2-1	1-0	12000	Keating, Rankin	1	2	3	4	5	6	7	8	9	10	11										
9	2 Oct	CHARLTON ATHLETIC	1	4-1	3-0	14965	Paul(2), Rankin, O.G.	1	2	3	4	5		7	8	9	10	11	6									
10	9	Bristol Rovers	1	5-0	2-0	28731	Walsh(2,1pen), Keating, Paul, Rankin	1	2	3	4	5		7	8	9	10	11	6									
11	16	EXETER CITY	1	3-2	1-1	16617	Paul, Rankin, Smailes	1	2	3	4	5		7	8	9	10	11	6									
12	23	Swindon Town	1	2-2	0-2	20057	Gilhespy, Paul	1	2	3	4	5		7	8	9	10	11	6									
13	30	MILLWALL	1	4-1	1-1	18012	Rankin(2), Keating, Walsh	1	2	3	4	5		7	8	9	10	11	6									
14	6 Nov	Brentford	2	0-3	0-2	10000		1	2	3	4	5		7	8	9	10	11	6									
15	13	NORTHAMPTON TOWN	2	4-3	1-2	8280	Walsh(2,1pen), Gray, Paul	1	2	3	4	5		7	8	9		11	6	10								
16	20	Birghton & Hove Albion	2	0-3	0-2	9958		1	2	3	4			7	8	9	10	11	5	6								
17	4 Dec	Luton Town	2	0-0	0-0	9000		1	2	3	4				8	9		11	6	5	7	10						
18	18	Merthyr Town	3	1-1	0-1	1500	Keating	1	2	3	4	5		7	8		10		6					9	11			
19	25	Aberdare Athletic	3	7-3	3-2	6000	Walsh(3), Martin(2), Keating, Rankin	1	2	3	4	5		7		9	10	11	6				8					
20	27	ABERDARE ATHLETIC	3	2-1	2-0	23634	Smailes, Walsh	1	2	3	4	5		7		9	10	11	6				8					
21	15 Jan	GILLINGHAM *	4	9-4	2-2	11081	Walsh(6,1pen), Gilhespy, Keating, Martin	1	2	3	4	5		7		9	10	11	6				8					
22	22	Watford	3	1-0	0-0	4000	Rankin	1		3	4	5		7		9	10	11	6				8			2		
23	29	CRYSTAL PALACE	2	5-4	5-1	11938	Keating(3), Drummond, Gilhespy	1		3	4	5		7			10	11	6				8	9		2		
24	5 Feb	Coventry City	2	5-2	3-1	11500	Walsh(2), Gilhespy, Keating, Martin	1		3	4	5		7		9	10	11	6				8			2		
25	9	NORWICH CITY	1	1-0	0-0	9121	Keating	1		3	4	5		7		9	10	11	6				8			2		
26	12	QUEENS PARK RANGERS	1	1-0	1-0	12029	Keating	1		3		5		7		9	10	11	6		4		8			2		
27	19	Charlton Athletic	1	1-0	0-0	8000	Gilhespy	1		3	4	5		7		9	10	11	6				8			2		
28	23	SOUTHEND UNITED	1	5-1	2-1	8533	Keating(2), Martin(2), Walsh	1		3	4	5		7		9	10	11	6				8			2		
29	26	BRISTOL ROVERS	1	3-1	1-1	28696	Walsh(2), Gray	1		3	4	5		7		9	10	11	6	8						2		
30	5 Mar	Exeter City	1	1-1	1-0	8000	Gray	1		3	4	5		7		9	10	11	6	8						2		
31	12	SWINDON TOWN	1	2-0	1-0	31417	Martin, Walsh	1		3	4	5		7		9	10	11	6				8			2		
32	19	Millwall	1	1-0	0-0	25000	Martin	1		3	4	5		7		9		11	6	10			8			2		
33	26	BRENTFORD	1	1-0	1-0	14062	Rankin	1		3	4	5	9					11	6	10			8		7	2		
34	2 Apr	Northampton Town	1	0-2	0-2	7191		1		3	4	5		7		9		11	6	10			8			2		
35	9	BRIGHTON & HOVE ALB.	1	0-2	0-1	21905		1		3	4	5		7		9		11	6				8			2	10	
36	15	BOURNEMOUTH & B. A.	1	2-0	0-0	24644	Keating, Walsh(pen)	1		3	4	5		7		9	10	11	6				8			2		
37	16	Norwich City	1	1-1	0-1	10000	Walsh(pen)	1		3	4	5		7		9	10	11	6				8			2		
38	18	Bournemouth & B. A.	1	0-2	0-1	12000		1		3	4	5	10	7		9		11	6				8			2		
39	23	LUTON TOWN	1	6-0	4-0	12826	Keating(3), Walsh(2), Martin	1		3	4	5		7		9	10	11	6				8			2		
40	30	Southend United	1	1-0	0-0	6608	Walsh	1		3	4	5		7		9	10	11	0				0			2		
41	4 May	Plymouth Argyle	1	2-4	1-0	15800	Gilhespy, Martin	1		3		5		7		9	10	11	6		4		8			2		
42	7	MERTHYR TOWN	1	3-0	1-0	14563	Gilhespy, Keating, Martin	1		3	4	5	6	7		9	10	11					8			2		
							Apps.	42	26	37	40	40	11	40	18	39	35	41	32	8	3	1	23	2	2	21	1	
							Goals						1	8	12	32	23	9	2	3			11	1				

* Sandy Torrance Benefit

F.A. CUP

	Date	Opposition	Res.	H.T.	Att.	Goalscorers	Coggins	Hughes	Glenn	Neesam				Paul	Walsh		Rankin	Smailes	Gray	Geddes	Foster	Martin	Drummond	Kirk	Walsh J.		Taylor
1R	27 Nov	Merthyr Town	2-0	1-0	6410	Foster, Paul (£341)	1	2	3	4				8	9		11		6	5	7	10					
2R	11 Dec	BOURNEMOUTH & B. A.	1-1	1-1	20297	Martin (£1267)	1	2	3	4				8	9		11		6	5	7	10					
2Rr	15	Bournemouth & B. A.	0-2	0-2	8849	(£571)	1	2	3	4							11		10	5	7			9			6

GLOUCESTERSHIRE CUP FINAL

	Date	Opposition	Res.	H.T.	Att.	Goalscorers
1	Jan	BRISTOL ROVERS	4-0	1-0	9601	Walsh(2,1pen), Keating, Martin (£547)

ALLEN PALMER CUP FINAL (At Trowbridge)

	Date	Opposition	Res.	H.T.	Att.	
	9 May	Bristol Rovers	0-1	0-1	4000	

FRIENDLIES

	Date	Opposition	Res.	H.T.		Goalscorers
1	8 Jan	Crystal Palace	3-7	2-3		Gray, Walsh, O.G.
2	5 May	Truro	1-0			Unknown

FINAL LEAGUE TABLE

1	Bristol C.	42	27	8	7	104-54	62
2	Plymouth	42	25	10	7	95-61	60
3	Millwall	42	23	10	9	89-51	56
4	Brighton	42	21	11	10	79-50	53
5	Swindon	42	21	9	12	100-85	51
6	Crystal Palace	42	18	9	15	84-81	45
7	Bournemouth	42	18	8	16	78-66	44
8	Luton	42	15	14	13	68-66	44
9	Newport	42	19	6	17	57-71	44
10	Bristol R.	42	16	9	17	78-80	41
11	Brentford	42	13	14	15	70-61	40
12	Exeter	42	15	10	17	76-73	40
13	Charlton	42	16	8	18	60-61	40
14	QPR	42	15	9	18	65-71	39
15	Coventry	42	15	7	20	71-86	37
16	Norwich	42	12	11	19	59-71	35
17	Merthyr Town	42	13	9	20	63-80	35
18	Northampton	42	15	5	22	59-87	35
19	Southend	42	14	6	22	64-77	34
20	Gillingham	42	11	10	21	54-72	32
21	Watford	42	12	8	22	57-87	32
22	Aberdare	42	9	7	26	62-101	25

1926/27 Season - Third Division South Champions.
Back: Neesam, Nicholson(Trainer), Glenn, G.Jenkins(Chair.), Coggins, Hughes, Drummond, Smailes.
Front: Gilhespy, Martin, Wadsworth, T.Walsh, Keating, Rankin.

1927/28 season
Back: Batten(Asst.Ground.), Annan(Scout), Southway(Asst.Trainer).
4th Row: F.J.Widgery(Dir.), Murray, Pugsley, Neesam, Keating, Blakemore, Coggins, Geddes, I.Walsh,
Holbrook, Smailes, A.R.P.Bray(Dir.), J.A.Hooper(Dir.).
3rd Row: F.Drewitt(Dir.), Paul, Gilhespy, Foster, J.Walsh, Williams, Callaghan, Newlands,
Good, Bourton, Glenn, W.H.Roberts(Dir.), J.Matthews(Dir.).
2nd Row: P.O.Daniell(Vice.Chair.), Garland, Searle, Torrance, Taylor, Martin, G.Jenkins(Chair.),
Wadsworth, Rankin, Cherrett, Hughes, Brain, A.Raisbeck(Sec/Manager).
Front: Nicholson(Trainer), C.H.Hancock (Asst.Sec.).

SEASON 1927-28
FOOTBALL LEAGUE DIVISION TWO

No.	Date	Opposition	Pos.	Res.	H.T.	Att.	Goalscorers	Coggins W.H.	Walsh J.	Glenn E.	Neesam H.	Wadworth W.	Smailes A.	Gilhespy T.W.C.	Martin J.C.	Walsh T.	Blakemore C.	Rankin A.	Paul J.C.	Pugsley J.	Cherrett P.A.M.	Callaghan P.J.	Keating A.E.	Foster J.T.F.	Newlands G.	Murray D.J.	Williams A.	Hughes R.G.	Geddes J.	Dransfield E.W.	Torrance A.	Garland G.E.	Searle F.B.	Taylor J.S.	Bourton C.F.T.
1	27 Aug	Notts County		2-1	1-1	15300	Blakemore, Gilhespy	1	2	3	4	5	6	7	8	9	10	11																	
2	31	PORT VALE		4-0	1-0	20305	Martin(2), Gilhespy, T.Walsh	1	2	3	4	5	6	7	8	9	10	11																	
3	3 Sep	OLDHAM ATHLETIC	1	2-1	2-1	23694	Gilhespy, T.Walsh	1	2	3	4	5	6	7	8	9	10	11																	
4	10	Grimsby Town	2	3-1	1-0	13006	Gilhespy(2), Martin, T.Walsh	1	2	3	4	5	6	7	8	9	10	11																	
5	17	READING	2	4-1	2-0	22480	T.Walsh(2), Gilhespy, Martin	1	2	3	4	5	6	7	8	9	10	11																	
6	19	Port Vale	2	1-5	0-3	11319	Blakemore	1	2	3	4	5	6	7	8	9	10	11																	
7	24	Blackpool	4	2-6	0-2	12509	Rankin, T.Walsh	1	2	3	4	5	6	7	8	9	10	11																	
8	1 Oct	CHELSEA	5	1-1	1-1	24005	Blakemore	1	2	3		5		7		9	10	11	4	6	8														
9	8	Clapton Orient	8	2-4	2-3	21202	Blakemore, Cherrett	1	2	3		5		7		9	10		4	6	8	11													
10	15	WEST BROMWICH ALBION	10	0-1	0-0	24442		1	2	3				5	7	8		10		4	6	9	11												
11	22	FULHAM	8	3-0	2-0	7701	Gilhespy, Martin, Wadsworth	1	2	3		5	8	7	8				11	4		9		10											
12	29	Barnsley	5	3-2	2-0	10500	Cherrett(2), Foster	1	2	3		5	6		8					4		9	11	10	7										
13	5 Nov	WOLVERHAMPTON WNDRS	3	4-1	4-0	14384	Cherrett(2), Foster, Keating	1	2	3		5	6		8					4		9	11	10	7										
14	12	Swansea Town	3	1-1	0-1	12000	Callaghan		2	3		5	6		8					4		9	11	10	7	1									
15	19	PRESTON NORTH END	7	1-3	0-2	9932	Cherrett	1	2	3		5			8					4	6	9	11	10	7										
16	26	Nottingham Forest	8	1-1	0-1	10082	Cherrett	1	2	3		5			8			10	11	4	6	9			7										
17	3 Dec	MANCHESTER CITY	6	2-0	2-0	23114	Blakemore, Keating	1	2	3		5		7				10	11	4	6	9		8											
18	10	Hull City	5	1-1	0-1	6716	Paul	1	2	3		5		7	8			10	11	4	6	9													
19	17	LEEDS UNITED	8	1-2	1-0	17199	Blakemore	1	2	3					8			10	11	4	6	9			7		5								
20	24	South Shields	7	3-1	2-1	5000	Keating(2), Cherrett	1	2	3									11	4	6	9		10	7		5	8							
21	26	SOUTHAMPTON	5	3-0	1-0	17072	Keating(2), Cherrett	1	2	3										4	6	9	11	10	7		5	8							
22	27	Southampton	6	2-3	1-2	10132	Cherrett, Williams	1	2	3										4	6	9	11	10	7		5	8							
23	31	NOTTS COUNTY	6	1-2	1-2	6476	Keating	1		3	4					8				6	9	11	10	7		5		2							
24	7 Jan	Oldham Athletic	8	1-4	1-1	12168	Geddes	1	2	3					9				6		11	10	7		5	8		4							
25	21	GRIMSBY TOWN	9	0-0	0-0	11690		1	2	3			5		8			10	11	4	6	9	11	10	7										
26	28	Leeds United	9	2-3	0-2	15632	Blakemore(pen), Cherrett	1	2	3						10		4	6	9	11		7		5			8						
27	4 Feb	BLACKPOOL	9	2-2	1-1	11395	Cherrett, Keating	1	2	3										4	6	9	11	10	7		5			8					
28	11	Chelsea	10	2-5	2-2	31949	Cherrett, Paul	1	2	3	4	5						10		8		9			7						6	11			
29	15	Reading	10	2-3	1-2	6000	Paul, Rankin	1	2	3	4	5						10	11	8		9			7						6				
30	18	CLAPTON ORIENT	9	5-1	3-0	15432	Keating(3),T.Walsh(2,1pen) (Johnny Paul Benefit)	1	2	3	4				9				11	8				10	7		5				6				
31	25	West Bromwich Albion	9	0-0	0-0	32115		1	2	3	4				9				11	8				10	7		5				6				
32	3 Mar	Fulham	11	0-5	0-3	23000		1	2	3					9				11	8				10	7		5				6		4		
33	10	BARNSLEY	10	2-0	1-0	12662	T.Walsh, Williams	1	2	3			6		9				11	4				10	7		5	8							
34	17	Wolverhampton Wanderers	11	2-5	0-3	15492	Keating, Rankin	1	2	3			6		9				11	4				10	7		5	8							
35	24	SWANSEA TOWN	8	2-1	1-0	17123	Cherrett, Williams	1	2	3		5	6						11	4		9		10	7			8							
36	31	Preston North End	11	1-5	1-2	10000	Keating	1	2	3		5	6						11	4		9		10	7			8							
37	6 Apr	STOKE CITY	10	4-0	1-0	21503	Keating(2), Cherrett, Foster	1	2	3		5	6						11	4		9		10	7			8							
38	7	NOTTINGHAM FOREST	10	0-0	0-0	14575		1		3		5	6						11	4		9		10	7			8	2						
39	9	Stoke City	10	0-5	0-0	15000		1										10	11	4					7		5	8	2	6				3	9
40	14	Manchester City	12	2-4	1-2	30000	Bourton, Keating	1		3			6						11	4				10	7		5	8						2	9
41	21	HULL CITY	12	0-1	0-1	10198		1	2	3		5	6	7						4				10	11			8							9
42	5 May	SOUTH SHIELDS	12	1-1	1-0	5607	Williams	1	2	3		5	6							4				10	7			8							9
		Apps.						41	38	41	12	27	20	14	17	15	19	28	33	16	25	12	25	29	1		15	14	3	2	2	5	1	1	2	4
		Goals												1			7	5	9	7	3	3			15	1	16	3			4		1			1

F.A. CUP

3R	14 Jan	TOTTENHAM HOTSPUR		1-2	0-2	36260	Martin (£2442)	1	2	3		5		7	10			11	4	6	9		8												

GLOUCESTERSHIRE CUP FINAL

	10 Apr	Bristol Rovers		0-1	0-0	7600	(£439.10.1)

FRIENDLIES

1	19 Oct	Bristol Rovers		3-3	3-1	3000	T.Walsh(2), Williams (J.Haydon's Benefit)
2	3 Nov	Newport County		2-2			Garland, Gilhespy (J.Nairn's Benefit)

FINAL LEAGUE TABLE

		P	W	D	L	F	A	Pts
1	Manchester C	42	25	9	8	100	59	59
2	Leeds	42	25	7	10	98	49	57
3	Chelsea	42	23	8	11	75	45	54
4	Preston	42	22	9	11	100	66	53
5	Stoke	42	22	8	12	78	59	52
6	Swansea	42	18	12	12	75	63	48
7	Oldham	42	19	8	15	75	51	46
8	West Bromwich	42	17	12	13	90	70	46
9	Port Vale	42	18	8	16	68	57	44
10	Nottingham F.	42	15	10	17	83	84	40
11	Grimsby	42	14	12	16	69	83	40
12	Bristol C.	42	15	9	18	76	79	39
13	Barnsley	42	14	11	17	65	85	39
14	Hull	42	12	15	15	41	54	39
15	Notts Co.	42	13	12	17	68	74	38
16	Wolverhampton	42	13	10	19	63	91	36
17	Southampton	42	14	7	21	68	77	35
18	Reading	42	11	13	18	53	75	35
19	Blackpool	42	13	8	21	83	101	34
20	Clapton Orient	42	11	12	19	55	85	34
21	Fulham	42	13	7	22	68	89	33
22	South Shields	42	7	9	26	56	111	23

SEASON 1928-29
FOOTBALL LEAGUE DIVISION TWO

No.	Date	Opposition	Pos.	Res.	H.T.	Att.	Goalscorers	Coggins W.H.	Walsh J.	Glenn E.	Paul J.C.	Bennett W.R.	Smailes A.	Foster J.T.F.	Williams T.H.	Hick W.M.	Blakemore C.	Johnson A.	Hughes R.G.	Barber S.	Wiliams A.	Rankin A.	Taylor J.S.	Gilhespy T.W.C.	Sliman A.M.	Scott T.	Garland G.E.	Vails P.A.	Bain D.	Dickie J.	Newlands G.
1	25 Aug	GRIMSBY TOWN		2-2	1-1	16083	Blakemore, Hick	1	2	3	4	5	6	7	8	9	10	11													
2	27	Stoke City		0-2	0-0	15000		1		3	4	5	6	7	8	9	10	11	2												
3	1 Sep	Bradford Park Avenue	18	2-3	2-2	20157	Blakemore, T.Williams	1	2	3	4	5	6	7	8	9	10	11													
4	5	STOKE CITY	18	1-1	1-0	12481	T.Williams	1		3	4	5	6	7	8	9	10	11	2												
5	8	SWANSEA TOWN	8	2-1	0-1	15608	Blakemore, Foster	1		3	4		6	7		9	10	11	2	5	8										
6	15	Blackpool	14	1-2	1-2	14135	Blakemore	1		3	4		6	7		9	10	11	2	5	8										
7	22	CHELSEA	15	0-0	0-0	24748		1		3	4		6	7		9	10		2	5	8	11									
8	29	Barnsley	18	2-4	2-3	7000	Gilhespy, T.Williams	1	2		4		6			9	10	11		5	8		3	7							
9	6 Oct	SOUTHAMPTON	19	1-1	1-1	17190	Blakemore	1	2	3	8		6			9	10	11		4				7	5						
10	13	NOTTINGHAM FOREST	19	2-5	1-1	14039	Blakemore, Paul	1	2	3	8		6			9	10	11		4				7	5						
11	20	Wolverhampton Wanderers	20	1-2	0-2	14690	T.Williams	1		3	4		6	7	8	9	10	11	2	5				7							
12	27	NOTTS COUNTY	20	0-4	0-1	8496		1		3	4					9	10	11	2	5				6	7	8					
13	3 Nov	Millwall	20	1-3	1-1	25000	Blakemore	1		3	4		5				9	11	2					6	7		8	10			
14	10	OLDHAM ATHLETIC	20	6-0	4-0	9845	Gilhespy(2), Vails(2), Barber, Scott	1		3	4		5				11		2	6				7		8	10	9			
15	17	Hull City	20	1-5	0-2	8545	Garland	1		3	4		5				11		2	6				7		8	10	9			
16	24	TOTTENHAM HOTSPUR	20	2-1	1-1	13937	Blakemore(pen), Gilhespy (Ernie Glenn Benefit)	1	2	3	4					11			10	6				7		8		9	5		
17	1 Dec	Reading	21	1-2	0-1	10533	Vials	1	2	3	4						10			6				7		8		9	5	11	
18	8	PRESTON NORTH END	21	1-0	0-0	15747	Vials	1	2	3	4						10			6				7		8		9	5	11	
19	15	Middlesbrough	21	1-3	0-1	9541	Blakemore	1	2	3	4						10			6				7	5	8		9		11	
20	22	PORT VALE	21	2-1	0-0	10459	Blakemore, Vials	1	2	3	4						10			6				7	5	8		9		11	
21	25	West Bromwich Albion	21	1-1	1-1	11303	Vials	1	2	3	4				7				10	6					5	8		9		11	
22	26	WEST BROMWICH ALBION	21	2-3	1-1	21070	Blakemore, Dickie	1	2	3	4				7				10	6	8				5			9		11	
23	29	Grimsby Town	21	0-0	0-0	8618	Blakemore, Garland	1	2	3	4			7			8	10		6				9			5		11		
24	5 Jan	BRADFORD PARK AVENUE	20	1-0	1-0	10956	O.G.	1	2	3	8									6				7	5			10	9	4	11
25	19	Swansea Town	20	2-0	2-0	8000	Paul, Scott	1	2	3	10	4		7						6					5	8			9	11	
26	26	BLACKPOOL	18	3-2	1-0	13748	Vials(2), Scott	1	2	3	10			7						6					5	8		9	4	11	
27	2 Feb	Chelsea	20	0-3	0-0	24000		1		3	10			7					2					6	5	8		9	4	11	
28	9	BARNSLEY	18	3-1	0-0	11035	Paul, Scott, Vials	1		3	10								2					6	5	8		9	4	11	
29	16	Southampton	18	1-2	1-2	10095	Blakemore(pen)	1		3		4					10		2		8			6	7	5		9		11	
30	23	Nottingham Forest	18	1-1	1-1	8296	Paul	1	2	3	10	4							2					6	7	5	8	9		11	
31	2 Mar	WOLVERHAMPTON WNDRS	17	3-2	1-1	12981	Paul, Scott, Vials	1	2	3	10	4							2					6	7	5	8	9		11	
32	9	Notts County	18	0-2	0-0	13100		1	2	3	10	4												6	7	5	8	9		11	
33	16	MILLWALL	17	5-0	3-0	13448	Dickie(2), Paul(2), Scott	1		3	10								2					6	7	5	8	9	4	11	
34	23	Oldham Athletic	19	0-1	0-0	14243		1		3	10								2					6	7	5	8	9	4	11	
35	29	Clapton Orient	18	1-0	1-0	12454	Paul	1		3	10								2					6	7	5	8	9	4	11	
36	30	HULL CITY	18	0-0	0-0	15426				3	10								2					6	7	5	8	9	4	11	1
37	1 Apr	CLAPTON ORIENT	17	1-0	1-0	15695	Vials			3	8						10	11	2					6	7	5		9	4		1
38	6	Tottenham Hotspur	15	1-1	0-1	23000	Vials	1		3	10	4							2					6	7	5		9		11	
39	13	READING	15	0-0	0-0	10561		1		3	10	4							2	8				6	7	5		9		11	
40	20	Preston North End	16	2-2	1-0	9000	Bain, Vails	1		3	10	4							2					6	7	5		8	9	11	
41	27	MIDDLESBROUGH	17	0-1	0-1	18234		1		3	10	4							2					6	7	5		9	8	11	
42	4 May	Port Vale	20	0-5	0-2	3307		1	2	3	10	4										7		6	5			9	8	11	
					Apps			40	20	41	40	14	14	17	8	10	23	12	22	19	8	1	21	28	26	22	5	27	17	25	2
					Goals						8			1	4	1	13			1				4		6	2	13	1	3	

F.A. CUP

				Res.	H.T.	Att.		Coggins	Walsh	Glenn	Paul			Foster		Hick		Johnson		Barber			Taylor	Gilhespy		Scott				Dickie	
3R	12 Jan	LIVERPOOL		0-2	0-0	28544	(£1942.2.3)	1	2	3	10			7		9		11		8			6			5				4	

GLOUCESTERSHIRE CUP FINAL

	Date			Res.	H.T.	Att.	
	19 Sep	BRISTOL ROVERS		2-0	2-0	6923	Barber, B.Williams (£382.8.7)

FRIENDLIES

No.	Date			Res.	H.T.	Att.	
1	10 Apr	CARDIFF CITY		1-1	1-0	3000	B.Williams (Andy Smailes Benefit)
2	25	Taunton Town		3-2	0-2	3000	Gilhespy, Sliman, B.Williams

FINAL LEAGUE TABLE (BOTTOM POSITIONS)

13	Preston	42	15	9	18	78·79	39
14	Millwall	42	16	7	19	71·86	39
15	Reading	42	15	9	18	63·86	39
16	Barnsley	42	16	6	20	69·66	38
17	Wolverhampton	42	15	7	20	77·81	37
18	Oldham	42	16	5	21	54·75	37
19	Swansea	42	13	10	19	62·75	36
20	Bristol C.	42	13	10	19	58·72	36
21	Port Vale	42	15	4	23	71·86	34
22	Clapton Orient	42	12	8	22	45·72	32

(Names reading from Left to Right.) [Veale & Co., Bristol.

Back Row.—J. Nicholson (Trainer), W. Jennings, W. Hick, E. Glenn, L. Southway (Asst. Trainer), Mr. J. Matthews (Director), A. Annan (Scout). 2nd Row.—A. Johnson, A. Jennings, C. Blakemore, H. Garrett, W. Coggins, A. Smailes, G. Smith, C. Beak. 3rd Row—Mr. W. H. Roberts (Director), Mr. P. J. Humphries (Director), Mr. F. Drewett (Director), W. Bennett, C. Gilhespy, D. Murray, G. Newlands, J. Walsh, S. Barber, W. Holbrook, Mr. J. A. Hooper (Director), Mr. A. G. Wise (Director), C. H. Hancock (Asst. Secretary). Sitting 4th Row.—Mr. P. O. Daniell (Vice-Chairman), G. Garland, J. Taylor, T. Williams, Mr. G. Jenkins (Chairman), J. Paul, J. Geddes, A. Rankin, R. Hughes, Mr. A. G. Raisbeck (Secretary-Manager). Front Row.—B. Williams, W. Dransfield, H. King, J. Foster.

SEASON 1929-30
FOOTBALL LEAGUE DIVISION TWO

Player columns (in order): Coggins W.H., Walsh J., Glenn E., Bain D., Sliman A.M., Taylor J.S., Williams A., Paul J.C., Burrows' L.G., Harris W.H., Dickie J., Bennett W.R., McMurtie A., Johnson A., Jennings W.H., Scott T., Vials P.A., Newlands G., Barber S., Hughes R.G., Homer S., Beak C.G., Garland G.E., Perry H., Britton E.J., Brace T.F.

No.	Date	Opposition	Pos.	Res.	H.T.	Att.	Goalscorers
1	31 Aug	Notts County		1-3	1-1	12000	Harris
2	2 Sep	Swansea Town		1-1	0-1	16000	
3	7	READING	11	5-3	2-1	15248	Paul(3), Sliman, Williams
4	11	SWANSEA TOWN	8	2-1	0-0	12935	Harris(2)
5	14	Charlton Athletic	13	1-3	0-1	20000	Walsh
6	18	PRESTON NORTH END	10	2-2	2-1	11129	McMurtie, Williams
7	21	HULL CITY	4	4-0	2-0	13154	Harris(2,1pen), Johnson(2)
8	28	Stoke City	12	2-6	2-3	8000	Harris, Williams
9	5 Oct	WOLVERHAMPTON WNDRS	14	1-2	1-2	8185	Vials
10	12	Bradford City	17	0-3	0-1	16584	
11	19	BURY	17	1-2	0-1	13438	Harris
12	26	Blackpool	17	1-7	1-2	11192	Harris
13	2 Nov	BARNSLEY	17	2-1	2-1	8531	Vials, Williams
14	9	Bradford Park Avenue	17	1-3	0-2	9845	Johnson
15	16	WEST BROMWICH ALBION	17	2-1	1-0	10040	Bain, Harris
16	23	Tottenham Hotspur	17	1-2	0-2	11863	Harris
17	30	SOUTHAMPTON	16	3-1	2-0	11926	Harris(2), Johnson
18	7 Dec	Millwall	18	1-1	0-1	12000	Harris
19	14	OLDHAM ATHLETIC	19	0-4	0-2	10307	
20	21	Nottingham Forest	19	2-5	1-3	6904	Williams(2)
21	25	CARDIFF CITY	19	2-0	1-0	17140	Johnson, Williams
22	26	Cardiff City	19	1-1	1-0	27000	Vials
23	28	NOTTS COUNTY	19	0-0	0-0	8520	
24	4 Jan	Reading	15	6-1	2-0	8132	Vials(2), Homer, Johnson, Paul, Williams
25	18	CHARLTON ATHLETIC	16	1-1	0-0	12276	Williams
26	1 Feb	STOKE CITY	19	2-6	1-1	9197	Harris, Paul
27	8	Wolverhampton Wanderers	20	0-1	0-0	12776	
28	22	Bury	22	0-2	0-2	8792	
29	26	BRADFORD CITY	22	1-3	1-1	6100	Vials
30	1 Mar	BLACKPOOL	22	0-1	0-0	11925	
31	8	Barnsley	22	1-3	1-2	5000	Johnson
32	15	BRADFORD PARK AVENUE	22	0-0	0-0	5961	
33	22	West Bromwich Albion	22	0-2	0-1	5060	
34	29	TOTTENHAM HOTSPUR	22	1-0	0-0	10935	Williams
35	5 Apr	Southampton	22	0-3	0-2	9788	
36	12	MILLWALL	22	1-0	0-0	8406	Homer(pen)
37	18	Chelsea	22	1-2	1-0	40000	Vials
38	19	Oldham Athletic	22	2-2	0-0	12667	Homer, Vials
39	21	CHELSEA	22	2-1	0-1	17488	Homer, Williams
40	26	NOTTINGHAM FOREST	22	4-1	2-1	12381	Williams(3), Dickie
41	1 May	Hull City	20	1-0	0-0	10348	Williams
42	3	Preston North End	20	2-2	1-0	9000	Vials, Williams

Apps. Coggins 26, Walsh 26, Glenn 39, Bain 33, Sliman 40, Taylor 33, Williams 36, Paul 13, Burrows 1, Harris 26, Dickie 23, Bennett 6, McMurtie 10, Johnson 33, Jennings 7, Scott 13, Vials 20, Newlands 16, Barber 4, Hughes 18, Homer 28, Beak 1, Garland 1, Perry 1, Britton 7, Brace 1

Goals Walsh 1, Bain 1, Sliman 1, Williams 16, Paul 5, Harris 15, Dickie 1, McMurtie 1, Johnson 7, Vials 9, Homer 4

F.A. CUP

	Date	Opposition		Res.	H.T.	Att.	Goalscorers
3R	11 Jan	Derby County		1-5	1-3	21559	Williams (£1790)

GLOUCESTERSHIRE CUP FINAL

	Date	Opposition		Res.	H.T.	Att.	Goalscorers
	30 Sep	Bristol Rovers		0-0	0-0	3000	
r	22 Apr	BRISTOL ROVERS		4-1	1-0	3500	Vials(2), Homer, Johnson

FRIENDLY

	Date	Opposition		Res.	H.T.	Att.	Goalscorers
1	25 Jan	Northampton Town		2-4	1-1	4000	Vials(2)

FINAL LEAGUE TABLE

1	Blackpool	42	27	4	11	98:67	58
2	Chelsea	42	22	11	9	74:46	55
3	Oldham	42	21	11	10	90:51	53
4	Bradford P.A.	42	19	12	11	91:70	50
5	Bury	42	22	5	15	78:67	49
6	West Bromwich	42	21	5	16	105:73	47
7	Southampton	42	17	11	14	77:76	45
8	Cardiff	42	18	8	16	61:59	44
9	Wolverhampton	42	16	9	17	77:79	41
10	Nottingham F.	42	13	15	14	55:69	41
11	Stoke	42	16	8	18	74:72	40
12	Tottenham	42	15	9	18	59:61	39
13	Charlton	42	14	11	17	59:63	39
14	Millwall	42	12	15	15	57:73	39
15	Swansea	42	14	9	19	57:61	37
16	Preston	42	13	11	18	65:80	37
17	Barnsley	42	14	8	20	56:71	36
18	Bradford C.	42	12	12	18	60:77	36
19	Reading	42	12	11	19	54:67	35
20	Bristol C.	42	13	9	20	61:83	35
21	Hull	42	14	7	21	51:78	35
22	Notts Co.	42	9	15	18	54:70	33

SEASON 1930-31
FOOTBALL LEAGUE DIVISION TWO

No.	Date	Opposition	Pos.	Res.	H.T.	Att.	Goalscorers
1	30 Aug	West Bromwich Albion		0-3	0-3	11037	
2	3 Sep	PLYMOUTH ARGYLE		2-1	1-0	19225	Stevenson, Vials
3	6	PORT VALE	13	1-1	1-1	13206	Vials
4	10	Bury	16	0-6	0-5	8844	
5	13	Bradford City	17	1-1	0-0	11837	Elliott
6	17	BURY	14	4-2	2-1	8990	Townrow(3), Elliott
7	20	CHARLTON ATHLETIC	7	3-0	2-0	10312	Elliott(2), Homer
8	27	Barnsley	13	0-1	0-1	7000	
9	4 Oct	NOTTINGHAM FOREST	15	1-4	0-1	15472	Mercer
10	11	CARDIFF CITY	12	1-0	1-0	19447	Elliott
11	18	Millwall	14	0-2	0-2	16000	
12	25	OLDHAM ATHLETIC	11	1-0	0-0	12589	Elliott
13	1 Nov	Burnley	14	2-4	1-2	10207	Mercer(2)
14	8	SOUTHAMPTON	11	2-1	1-1	14398	Mercer, O.G.
15	15	Bradford Park Avenue		2-5	1-2	8000	Elliott, Townrow
16	22	WOLVERHAMPTON WNDRS	14	0-3	0-0	8609	
17	29	Reading	14	1-4	0-1	5698	Mercer
18	6 Dec	STOKE CITY	14	1-1	1-0	9538	Townrow
19	13	Tottenham Hotspur	17	1-4	1-3	21464	O.G.
20	20	PRESTON NORTH END	16	1-1	1-0	11169	Vials
21	25	Swansea Town	17	2-5	1-5	15000	Mercer, Vials
22	26	SWANSEA TOWN	16	2-1	1-1	17950	Vials(2)
23	27	WEST BROMWICH ALBION	15	1-1	0-1	17705	Vials
24	3 Jan	Port Vale	18	0-1	0-0	7411	
25	17	BRADFORD CITY	19	0-1	0-1	8815	
26	24	Charlton Athletic	20	0-0	0-0	10000	
27	31	BARNSLEY	17	2-1	1-0	6222	Elliott(2)
28	7 Feb	Nottingham Forest	20	1-6	0-2	7395	Elliott
29	14	Cardiff City	17	1-0	1-0	16000	Williams
30	21	MILLWALL	18	1-2	1-0	10757	Elliott
31	28	Oldham Athletic	17	3-1	2-0	4436	Vials(2), Robson
32	7 Mar	BURNLEY	17	1-0	1-0	8940	Williams
33	14	Southampton	19	1-5	0-0	10463	Vials
34	21	BRADFORD PARK AVENUE	18	2-0	0-0	8719	Vials, Williams
35	28	Wolverhampton Wanderers	16	1-0	1-0	10141	Vials
36	3 Apr	EVERTON	17	0-1	0-1	36985	
37	4	READING	16	1-0	0-0	12055	Homer
38	6	Everton	16	3-1	2-1	23058	Mercer(2), Elliott
39	11	Stoke City	16	1-3	0-1	7000	Robson
40	18	TOTTENHAM HOTSPUR	16	2-1	0-0	15149	Craig, Homer
41	25	Preston North End	16	2-2	1-1	7000	Brinton, Elliott
42	2 May	Plymouth Argyle	16	3-5	1-3	19423	Elliott(2), Homer

Player appearances (shirt numbers by match)

No.	Newlands G.	Walsh J.	Glenn E.	Jennings W.H.	Sliman A.M.	Taylor J.S.	Homer S.	Mercer A.S.	Vials P.A.	Williams A.	Johnson A.	Stevenson A.	Townrow F.A.	Elliott S.D.	Robson C.	Brinton E.	Hughes R.G.	Craig E.	Whitelaw D.L.	Morgan J.	Humpish A.E.	Rees J.
1	1	2	3	4	5	6	7	8	9	10	11											
2	1	2	3	4	5	6	7	8	9	10		11										
3	1	2	3	4	5	6	7	8	9				11	10								
4	1	2	3	4	5	6	7	8						10	9	11						
5	1	2	3	4	5		7	8						10	9	11	6					
6	1	2	3	4	5		7	8						10	9	11	6					
7	1	2	3	4	5		7	8						10	9	11	6					
8	1		3	4	5		7	8						10	9	11	6	2				
9	1	2	3	4	5		7	8				10			9	11	6					
10	1	2	3	4	5		7	8						10	9	11	6					
11	1	2	3	4	5		7							10	9	11	6		8			
12	1	2	3	4	5		7	8						10	9	11	6					
13	1		3	4	5		7	8					11	10	9		6	2				
14	1		3	4	5		7	8			11			10	9		6	2				
15	1		3	4	5		7	8			11			10	9		6	2				
16	1	2	3	4	5		7	8					11	10	9		6					
17		2			5		3	7	8				11		9		6		10	1	4	
18		2	3	4	5		7	8	9		11		10				6		1			
19		2		4	5		7	8	9		11		10			6		3	1			
20		2	3		5	6	7	8	9		11		10						1		4	
21		2	3		5	6	7	8	9	11			10						1		4	
22		2	3		5	6		8	9	11			10		7				1		4	
23		2	3		5			8	9	11			10		7	6			1		4	
24		2	3		5	4		8	9	11			10		7	6			1			
25		2	3		5	6		8	9	11				10	7				1			
26	1	2	3	4	5		7	8					10	11		9	6					
27	1	2	3	4	5		7					8	10	11		9	6					
28	1	2	3	4			5	7				8	10	11		9	6					
29	1	2		4	5			7		8			10	11		9	6	3				
30	1	2		4	5			7		8			10	11		9	6	3				
31	1	2			5				9	10	11				7	6	3	8			4	
32	1	2			5				9	10	11				7	6	3	8			4	
33	1	2			5		7		9	10						11	6	3	8		4	
34	1	2		5	4		7		9	10						11	6	3	8			
35	1	2		4	5		7		9	8	11					6	3	10				
36	1	2		4	5		7		9	8	11					6	3	10				
37		2		4	5		7		9	8						11	6	3	10	1		
38		2		4	5		7	8						9		11	6	3	10	1		
39		2		4	5		7	8						9		11	6	3	10	1		
40	1	2		4	6		7				8			9		11	6	3	10			
41	1	2		4	5		7	8						9		11	6	3	10			
42		2		4	5		7			8				9		6	3	10				1
Apps	29	38	26	21	40	23	36	30	18	22	15	5	22	25	23	34	19	14	12	1	8	1
Goals							4	8	12	3		1	5	15	2	1		1				

F.A. CUP

Rd	Date	Opposition		Res.	H.T.	Att.	Goalscorers	Walsh	Glenn	Sliman	Taylor	Mercer	Vials	Johnson	Townrow	Robson	Whitelaw	Humpish
3R	10 Jan	Barnsley		1-4	0-4	12932	Vials (£708)	2	3	5	6	8	9	11	10	7	1	4

GLOUCESTERSHIRE CUP FINAL

Date	Opposition	Res.	H.T.	Att.	Goalscorers
1 Oct	BRISTOL ROVERS	3-1	1-1	5026	Elliott, Homer, Townrow

FINAL LEAGUE TABLE

		P	W	D	L	F:A	Pts
1	Everton	42	28	5	9	121:66	61
2	West Bromwich	42	22	10	10	83:49	54
3	Tottenham	42	22	7	13	88:55	51
4	Wolverhampton	42	21	5	16	84:67	47
5	Port Vale	42	21	5	16	67:61	47
6	Bradford P.A.	42	18	10	14	97:66	46
7	Preston	42	17	11	14	83:64	45
8	Burnley	42	17	11	14	81:77	45
9	Southampton	42	19	6	17	74:62	44
10	Bradford C.	42	17	10	15	61:63	44
11	Stoke	42	17	10	15	64:71	44
12	Oldham	42	16	10	16	61:72	42
13	Bury	42	19	3	20	75:82	41
14	Millwall	42	16	7	19	71:80	39
15	Charlton	42	15	9	18	59:86	39
16	Bristol C.	42	15	8	19	54:82	38
17	Nottingham F.	42	14	9	19	80:85	37
18	Plymouth	42	14	8	20	76:84	36
19	Barnsley	42	13	9	20	59:79	35
20	Swansea	42	12	10	20	51:74	34
21	Reading	42	12	6	24	72:96	30
22	Cardiff	42	8	9	25	47:87	25

(Back Row): Jennings, Nicholson (Trainer), Sliman, Newlands, Hughes, Craig, Taylor.
(Front Row): Homer, Mercer, Vials, Walsh, Williams, Elliot.

1930/31 Season

1932/33 season

Back: Pickett, Southway(Asst.Trainer), Young.
3rd Row: Mellors(Trainer), Sharp, Jennings, Taylor, Coombs, Turner, Bowen, Brinton,
Bob Hewison(Manager), C.H.Hancock(Secretary)
2nd Row: A.P.R.Bray(Dir.), F.J.Humphries(Dir.), Hall, Reed, Parker, Donaldson,
Dunn, Heale, F.Drewett(Dir.), G.Jenkins(Chair.)
Front: Joyce, Cainey, Wren, Bridge, Homer, Wilson, Scriven, Loftus, Knox, Morgan, Farr.

SEASON 1931-32
FOOTBALL LEAGUE DIVISION TWO

Player columns (left to right): Newlands G., Walsh J., Hughes R.G., Jennings W.H., Sliman A.M., Brinton E.J., Homer S., Mercer A.S., Elliott S.D., Craig E., Sargeant C., Williams A., Moulson C., Humpish A.E., Taylor J.S., Robson C., Johnson J.A., Parker G., Vials P.A., Heale J.A., Ball C.G., Golledge L.H., Morgan C.I., Terry J.C., Donaldson J., Reed G., Farr F.E.

No.	Date	Opposition	Pos.	Res.	H.T.	Att.	Goalscorers
1	29 Aug	BURY		1-3	0-2	15584	Elliott
2	2 Sep	NOTTS COUNTY		3-2	1-1	8552	Sargeant(2), Elliott
3	5	Port Vale	17	2-4	0-4	10770	Homer, Sargeant
4	12	MILLWALL	22	1-4	1-4	10167	Moulson
5	16	Plymouth Argyle	22	1-2	0-2	16276	Elliott
6	19	Bradford City	22	0-3	0-2	12284	
7	23	PLYMOUTH ARGYLE	22	0-2	0-0	7021	
8	26	LEEDS UNITED	22	0-2	0-1	9157	
9	3 Oct	Swansea Town	22	0-2	0-2	20000	
10	10	BARNSLEY	21	4-0	2-0	8056	Elliott(2), Craig, Williams
11	17	CHESTERFIELD	21	1-1	1-1	8919	Elliott
12	24	Nottingham Forest	21	1-3	1-3	7808	Humpish
13	31	TOTTENHAM HOTSPUR	21	1-1	0-0	9129	Elliott
14	7 Nov	Preston North End	21	1-1		8000	O.G.
15	14	BRADFORD PARK AVENUE	21	0-0	0-0	8213	
16	21	Wolverhampton Wanderers	22	2-4	1-3	16503	Sargeant, Vials
17	28	CHARLTON ATHLETIC	22	1-2	1-1	5956	Williams
18	5 Dec	Stoke City	22	1-1		8000	Sargeant
19	12	SOUTHAMPTON	22	0-1	0-1	7844	
20	19	Manchester United	22	1-0	1-0	4697	Elliott
21	25	OLDHAM ATHLETIC	22	1-1	1-1	12370	Craig
22	26	Oldham Athletic	22	1-2	0-0	10523	Williams
23	2 Jan	Bury	22	1-2	0-1	3753	Vials(pen)
24	16	PORT VALE	22	0-2	0-1	8690	
25	25	Millwall	22	0-0	0-0	15000	
26	30	BRADFORD CITY	22	0-1	0-1	7215	
27	6 Feb	Leeds United	22	0-1	0-0	12000	
28	13	SWANSEA TOWN	22	1-1	1-0	6547	Sargeant
29	20	Barnsley	22	1-1	1-1	4000	Sargeant
30	27	Chesterfield	22	1-3	0-2	8100	Elliott
31	5 Mar	NOTTINGHAM FOREST	22	1-1	0-1	5365	Golledge
32	12	Tottenham Hotspur	22	1-2	1-0	15178	Sargeant
33	19	PRESTON NORTH END	22	4-2	2-1	5473	Homer(2), Golledge, Sargeant
34	25	Burnley	22	2-1	1-1	7297	Craig, Homer
35	26	Bradford Park Avenue	22	0-2	0-0	10000	
36	28	BURNLEY	22	1-6	0-0	8129	Morgan
37	2 Apr	WOLVERHAMPTON WNDRS	22	0-4	0-2	7433	
38	9	Charlton Athletic	22	0-2	0-0	10000	
39	16	STOKE CITY	22	0-0	0-0	3590	
40	23	Southampton	22	1-1	1-1	6322	Sargeant
41	30	MANCHESTER UNITED	22	2-1	0-1	5874	Morgan, Reed
42	7 May	Notts County	22	0-3	0-1	5000	

Apps. 42 21 25 26 30 39 38 1 25 33 27 23 11 28 33 2 7 3 8 9 3 9 7 5 4 2 1

Goals 4 9 3 10 3 1 1 2 2 2 1

F.A. CUP

	Date	Opposition		Res.	H.T.	Att.	Goalscorers
3R	9 Jan	Notts County		2-2	1-1	22761	Elliott(2) (£1410)
3Rr	13	NOTTS COUNTY		3-2	1-1	16065	Williams(2), Elliott (£1036)
4R	23	Watford		1-2	0-2	19369	Elliott (£1319)

GLOUCESTERSHIRE CUP FINAL

	Date	Opposition	Res.	H.T.	Att.	Goalscorers
	9 Sep	Bristol Rovers	1-0	0-0	10862	Elliott (£600)

FRIENDLIES

	Date	Opposition	Res.	H.T.	Att.	Goalscorers
1	20 Apr	Swindon Town	1-3	1-0	1338	Donaldson (Harry Morris Bnefit)
2	27	Birstol Rovers	2-1	2-1	5000	Dnldsn,Iles (Charity, Bridgewater Rugby Club)
3	4 May	NICHOLSON'S XI	4-4	3-2	3000	Donaldson,Homer,Vials,O.G. (J.Nicholson Benefit)

FINAL LEAGUE TABLE

1	Wolverhampton	42	24	8	10	115:49	56
2	Leeds	42	22	10	10	78:54	54
3	Stoke	42	19	14	9	69:48	52
4	Plymouth	42	20	9	13	100:66	49
5	Bury	42	21	7	14	70:58	49
6	Bradford P.A.	42	21	7	14	72:63	49
7	Bradford C.	42	16	13	13	80:61	45
8	Tottenham	42	16	11	15	87:78	43
9	Millwall	42	17	9	16	61:61	43
10	Charlton	42	17	9	16	61:66	43
11	Nottingham F.	42	16	10	16	77:72	42
12	Manchester U.	42	17	8	17	71:72	42
13	Preston	42	16	10	16	75:77	42
14	Southampton	42	17	7	18	66:77	41
15	Swansea	42	16	7	19	73:75	39
16	Notts Co.	42	13	12	17	75:75	38
17	Chesterfield	42	13	11	18	64:86	37
18	Oldham	42	13	10	19	62:84	36
19	Burnley	42	13	9	20	59:87	35
20	Port Vale	42	13	7	22	58:89	33
21	Barnsley	42	12	9	21	55:91	33
22	Bristol C.	42	6	11	25	39:78	23

SEASON 1932-33
FOOTBALL LEAGUE DIVISION THREE (SOUTH)

No.	Date	Opposition	Pos.	Res.	H.T.	Att.	Goalscorers
1	27 Aug	Exeter City		0-2	0-1	9500	
2	31	TORQUAY UNITED	13	2-0	1-0	8762	Bowen, Loftus
3	3 Sep	LUTON TOWN	5	5-2	2-1	9044	Bowen, Homer, Loftus, Morgan, O.G.
4	7	Torquay United	4	0-0	0-0	6000	
5	10	Newport County	5	1-1	0-1	6025	Scriven
6	17	BOURNEMOUTH & B.A.	5	1-1	1-1	9009	Scriven
7	24	Swindon Town	5	4-1	2-0	7507	Sharp(2), Homer, Jennings
8	1 Oct	CLAPTON ORIENT	2	3-0	0-0	7520	Bowen, Homer, Sharp
9	8	Northampton Town	4	1-2	1-2	9000	Bowen
10	15	BRISTOL ROVERS	3	3-1	2-0	25501	Bowen, Knox, Loftus
11	22	Aldershot	5	0-1	0-1	4866	
12	29	QUEENS PARK RANGERS	9	2-3	2-2	7126	Bowen, Sharp
13	5 Nov	Southend United	10	1-3	0-2	7017	Bowen
14	12	CRYSTAL PALACE	9	3-3	2-2	7804	Bowen(2), Scriven
15	19	Gillingham	14	2-4	2-3	4553	Loftus, Parker
16	3 Dec	Cardiff City	13	1-1	0-0	6000	Keating
17	17	Norwich City	15	0-3	0-0	8840	
18	24	BRIGHTON & HOVE ALB.	17	3-4	2-3	6992	Loftus(3)
19	26	COVENTRY CITY	18	5-3	3-1	13485	Loftus(2), Bowen, Homer, Scriven
20	27	Coventry City	18	0-6	0-3	17000	
21	31	EXETER CITY	18	0-1	0-0	6000	
22	7 Jan	Luton Town	18	4-5	2-3	6000	Scriven(2), Homer, Sharp
23	21	NEWPORT COUNTY	19	3-2	3-0	4800	Bowen(2), Loftus
24	25	WATFORD	19	2-3	2-2	2402	Loftus(2)
25	28	Bournemouth & Bos. Ath.	19	1-6	0-2	2000	Loftus
26	4 Feb	SWINDON TOWN	18	5-1	1-1	4353	Bowen(2,1pen), Cainey, Dunn, Sharp
27	11	Clapton Orient	18	2-2	2-2	5497	Bowen(2,1pen)
28	18	NORTHAMPTON TOWN	17	5-4	3-2	6334	Cainey(2), Keating(2), Sharp
29	3 Mar	ALDERSHOT	18	2-2	1-0	8643	Cainey, Keating
30	11	Queens Park Rangers	16	1-1	1-0	6305	Bowen (at the White City Stadium)
31	18	SOUTHEND UNITED	15	5-1	4-0	7467	Bowen(2), Keating(2), Loftus
32	25	Crystal Palace	16	2-2	0-2	9641	Bowen(2)
33	29	Bristol Rovers	14	1-1	1-1	23447	Bowen
34	1 Apr	GILLINGHAM	15	1-1	0-0	7309	Cainey
35	8	Watford	16	0-1	0-1	6000	
36	14	BRENTFORD	18	1-2	0-1	19326	Cainey
37	15	CARDIFF CITY	17	3-1	2-0	7176	Bowen(3)
38	17	Brentford	17	1-2	0-0	21000	Sharp
39	22	Reading	16	2-2	1-0	4777	Scriven(2)
40	26	READING	15	4-1	4-0	4500	Bowen(3), Sharp
41	29	NORWICH CITY	15	1-1	1-1	6423	Heale
42	6 May	Brighton & Hove Albion	15	0-7	0-2	3645	

Player appearances

No.	Pickett T.A.	Knox W.	Taylor J.S.	Jennings W.H.	Parker T.A.	Wilson J.T.	Homer S.	Sharp A.A.	Bowen E.C.	Loftus J.L.	Scriven A.	Sommerville G.D.L.	Morgan C.I.	Bridge C.A.V.	Goledge L.H.	Keating A.E.	Hal B.	Brinton E.J.	Reed G.	Dunn E.	Lanceley F.J.	Turner A.	Cainey W.P.	Cox E.	Heale J.A.
1	1	2	3	4	5	6	7	8	9	10	11														
2		2	3	4	5	6	7		9	10	11	1		8											
3		2	3	4	5	6	7		9	10	11	1		8											
4		2	3	4	5	6	7		9	10	11	1		8											
5		2	3	4	5	6	7	8	9	10	11														
6		2	3	4	5	6	7	8	9	10	11														
7		2	3	4	5	6	7	8	9	10	11														
8		2	3	4	5	6	7	8	9	10	11														
9		2	3	4	5	6	7	8	9	10	11	1													
10		2	3	4	5	6	7	8	9	10	11	1													
11		2	3	4	5	6	7	8	9	10	11	1													
12		2	3	4	5	6	7	8	9	10	11	1													
13		2	3	4	5	6	7	8	9	10	11														
14			3	4	5	6	7		9	10	11	2		8											
15			3	4	5		7		9	10	11	2		8											
16	1		3		5		7			10	11	2		8	4	6									
17	1		3		5		7			10	11	2		8	4	6	9								
18	1		3	4	5		7		9	10	11	2		8		6	9								
19	1		3		5	4	7		9	10	11	2		8		6									
20	1	2	3		5		7		9	10	11			8		6									
21		2	3		5		7		9	10	11	1		8		6				4					
22		2	3		5		7	8	9	10	11	1				6				4					
23		2			5	4	7	8	9	10	11		3			6					4	1			
24					5		7	8	9	10	11		3			6					4	1			
25					5		7	8		10	11		3							6	9	4	1		
26		2			5		7	8	9									10		6	4	11	3		
27		2			5		7	8	9									10		6	4	11	3		
28		2			5		7	8	9			1						10		6		11	3		
29		2			5		7	8	9			1						10		6		11	3		
30		2			5		7	8	9			1						10		6		11	3		
31		2			5		7		9	10		1						8		6		11	3		
32		2					7		9	10		1						8		6		11	3	5	
33		2			5		7		9			1						8		6	4	11	3		10
34		2			5		7	8	9			1						10		6		11	3		
35		2			5		7	8	9			1						10		6	4	11	3		
36		2			5		7	8	9			1						10		6		11	3		
37		2			5		7	8	9			1			4			10		6		11	3		
38		3			5		7	8	9		11	1			4			10		6					
39		3			5	6	7	8	9		11	1			4			10		6					
40		3			5		7	8	9	10	11	1			2	4				6					
41		3			5		7	8	9		11	1			2	4				6					10
42		3			5		7	8	9	10	11	1			4					6					
Apps.	6	19	27	33	41	18	42	28	39	29	30	31	3	9	7	21	2	23	3	19	5	12	12	1	2
Goals	1		1	1			5	9	28	14	8		1			6				1			6		1

F.A. CUP

			Res.	H.T.	Att.	Goalscorers
1R	26 Nov	ROMFORD	4-0	4-0	8930	Bowen(3), Loftus
2R	10 Dec	TRANMERE ROVERS	2-2	0-0	9295	Keating, Loftus (£530)
2Rr	14	Tranmere Rovers	2-3	1-2	6793	Bowen, Loftus (£368)

F.A. Cup appearances:
- 1R: Pickett 1, Taylor 3, Parker 5, Wilson 6, Homer 7, Bowen 9, Loftus 10, Scriven 11, Morgan 2, Bridge 8, Goledge 4
- 2R: Pickett 1, Taylor 3, Parker 5, Wilson 4, Homer 7, Bowen 9, Loftus 10, Scriven 11, Morgan 2, Bridge 8, Goledge 6
- 2Rr: Pickett 1, Taylor 3, Parker 5, Wilson 4, Homer 7, Bowen 9, Loftus 10, Scriven 11, Morgan 2, Bridge 8, Goledge 6

WELSH CUP

			Res.	H.T.	Att.	Goalscorers
7R	1 Feb	NEWPORT COUNTY	3-4	2-2	800	Bowen, Homer, Scriven

GLOUCESTERSHIRE CUP FINAL

	Date		Res.	H.T.	Att.	Goalscorers
	14 Sep	BRISTOL ROVERS	3-3	0-2	6929	Homer(2), Bowen (£393)
r	24 Apr	Bristol Rovers	4-3	2-1	5809	Scriven(2), Bowen, Loftus (£296)

FRIENDLIES

	Date		Res.	H.T.	Att.	Goalscorers
1	14 Jan	Brentford	2-8	2-4	3000	Bowen, Sharp(pen)
2	1 May	Bath City	1-3	0-1	3000	Scriven
3	4	Yeovil & Petters United	5-5	2-2		Bowen(2), Loftus, Sharp, O.G. (A.Rankin's Benefit)

FINAL LEAGUE TABLE

		P	W	D	L	F:A	Pts
1	Brentford	42	26	10	6	90:49	62
2	Exeter	42	24	10	8	88:48	58
3	Norwich	42	22	13	7	88:55	57
4	Reading	42	19	13	10	103:71	51
5	Crystal Palace	42	19	8	15	78:64	46
6	Coventry	42	19	6	17	106:77	44
7	Gillingham	42	18	8	16	72:61	44
8	Northampton	42	18	8	16	76:66	44
9	Bristol R.	42	15	14	13	61:56	44
10	Torquay	42	16	12	14	72:67	44
11	Watford	42	16	12	14	66:63	44
12	Brighton	42	17	8	17	66:65	42
13	Southend	42	15	11	16	65:82	41
14	Luton	42	13	13	16	78:78	39
15	Bristol C.	42	12	13	17	83:90	37
16	QPR	42	13	11	18	72:87	37
17	Aldershot	42	13	10	19	61:72	36
18	Bournemouth	42	12	12	18	60:81	36
19	Cardiff	42	12	7	23	69:99	31
20	Clapton Orient	42	8	13	21	59:93	29
21	Newport	42	11	7	24	61:105	29
22	Swindon	42	9	11	22	60:105	29

SEASON 1933-34
FOOTBALL LEAGUE DIVISION THREE (SOUTH)

Player columns (left to right): Sommerville G.D., Jennings W.H., Turner A., Dunn E., Parker T.A., Brinton E.J., Homer S., Riley J., Bowen E.C., Loftus J.L., Scriven A., Golledge L.H., Taylor J.S., Farr F.E., Scattergood K., Reed G., Cainey W.P., Roberts W.S., Birks L., Heale J.A., Weaver R.S., Molloy W., Morgan C.I., Banfield A.J., Foy T.G., Cottrell A.T.

No.	Date	Opposition	Pos.	Res.	H.T.	Att.	Goalscorers
1	26 Aug	BRISTOL ROVERS		0-3	0-2	26218	
2	28	Norwich City	22	2-7	0-2	11354	Riley, Scriven
3	2 Sep	Clapton Orient	22	0-4	0-3	10920	
4	6	NORWICH CITY	22	0-1	0-1	7798	
5	9	SWINDON TOWN	22	2-2	1-0	9863	Loftus, Reed
6	16	Brighton & Hove Albion	22	1-5	0-0	7308	Bowen
7	23	ALDERSHOT	22	1-0	0-0	6830	Bowen
8	30	Luton Town	22	0-3	0-2	10000	
9	7 Oct	NORTHAMPTON TOWN	22	2-3	1-2	8598	Bowen, Scriven
10	14	Torquay United	22	2-2	1-0	4000	Bowen, Heale
11	21	CRYSTAL PALACE	22	2-2	2-2	8919	Heale(2)
12	28	Gillingham	22	1-2	1-2	6238	Loftus
13	4 Nov	EXETER CITY	22	1-1	1-1	10143	Cainey
14	11	Cardiff City	22	5-1	3-1	7000	Reed(2), Heale, Homer, Loftus
15	18	BOURNEMOUTH & B.A.	22	3-1	1-1	10070	Heale(2), Riley(pen)
16	2 Dec	WATFORD	21	1-0	0-0	7744	Brinton
17	16	COVENTRY CITY	20	0-0	0-0	7007	
18	23	Southend United	21	0-3	0-2	4549	
19	25	Newport County	21	2-2	2-1	8039	Bowen, Loftus
20	26	NEWPORT COUNTY	21	1-1	1-0	16836	Loftus
21	30	Bristol Rovers	22	1-5	0-2	23907	Riley(pen)
22	6 Jan	CLAPTON ORIENT	21	3-0	0-0	7512	Brinton, Heale, Scriven
23	20	Swindon Town	22	2-4	1-2	7000	Loftus(2)
24	3 Feb	Aldershot	21	2-2	1-2	4000	Banfield(2)
25	7	BRIGHTON & HOVE ALB.	20	5-0	4-0	4556	Riley(5)
26	10	LUTON TOWN	20	0-0	0-0	8697	
27	22	Northampton Town	19	3-2	1-2	3000	Loftus(2), Scriven
28	24	TORQUAY UNITED	17	2-0	1-0	7124	Banfield, Golledge
29	3 Mar	Crystal Palace	16	1-0	1-0	10947	O.G.
30	10	GILLINGHAM	16	1-1	0-0	6890	Riley
31	17	Exeter City	17	0-2	0-0	4000	
32	24	CARDIFF CITY	14	3-0	0-0	7186	Riley(2), Foy
33	30	Queens Park Rangers	16	0-1	0-0	15000	
34	31	Bournemouth & Bos. Ath.	17	0-5	0-3	5000	
35	2 Apr	QUEENS PARK RANGERS	18	0-2	0-2	11441	
36	7	CHARLTON ATHLETIC	19	0-1	0-1	7230	
37	14	Watford	18	1-1	1-0	2500	Riley
38	18	Reading	18	1-1	0-0	5000	Riley
39	21	READING	19	1-2	0-1	7032	Roberts
40	23	Charlton Athletic	19	1-2	1-1	4833	Loftus
41	28	Coventry City	20	0-9	0-5	7035	
42	5 May	SOUTHEND UNITED	19	5-1	3-0	4323	Molloy(2), Banfield, Brinton, Loftus

Apps. 3 35 4 8 13 39 35 34 16 39 24 8 9 8 39 7 12 35 30 15 3 7 14 18 6 1
Goals: 3 1 13 5 11 4 1 — 3 1 1 — 7 — 2 — 4 1

FINAL LEAGUE TABLE

1	Norwich	42	25	11	6	88	49	61
2	Coventry	42	21	12	9	100	54	54
3	Reading	42	21	12	9	82	50	54
4	QPR	42	24	6	12	70	51	54
5	Charlton	42	22	8	12	83	56	52
6	Luton	42	21	10	11	83	61	52
7	Bristol R.	42	20	11	11	77	47	51
8	Swindon	42	17	11	14	64	68	45
9	Exeter	42	16	11	15	68	57	43
10	Brighton	42	15	13	14	68	60	43
11	Clapton Orient	42	16	10	16	75	69	42
12	Crystal Palace	42	16	9	17	71	67	41
13	Northampton	42	14	12	16	71	78	40
14	Aldershot	42	13	12	17	52	71	38
15	Watford	42	15	7	20	71	63	37
16	Southend	42	12	10	20	51	74	34
17	Gillingham	42	11	11	20	75	96	33
18	Newport	42	8	17	17	49	70	33
19	Bristol C.	42	10	13	19	58	85	33
20	Torquay	42	13	7	22	53	93	33
21	Bournemouth	42	9	9	24	60	102	27
22	Cardiff	42	9	6	27	57	105	24

SEASON 1934-35
FOOTBALL LEAGUE DIVISION THREE (SOUTH)

Player columns (left to right): Dolman H.W., Roberts W.S., Clipson R., Morgan C.J., Affleck D.R., Brinton E.J., Green H., Moseley H.C., Riley J., Loftus J.L., Hodge J.R., Hughes J.H., Harston E., Wallis G.H., Cainey W.P., Pearce J.G., Bridge C.A.V., Lardells J., Golledge L.H., Banfield A.J., Hick J., Cottrell A.T., Fish I., Jenkins E.J., Wilson J.E., Tomlinson J., Webber G.W., Foy T.G.

No.	Date	Opposition	Pos.	Res.	H.T.	Att.	Goalscorers
1	25 Aug	WATFORD		3-1	1-0	14041	Brinton(pen), Hodge, Riley
2	29	Reading	8	0-2	0-2	10000	
3	1 Sep	Newport County	14	0-2	0-1	10978	
4	5	READING	11	1-0	0-0	9032	Riley
5	8	EXETER CITY	7	2-0	0-0	10872	Riley(2)
6	15	Bristol Rovers	9	2-2	1-2	24568	Green, Wallis
7	22	Millwall	7	1-0	1-0	12000	Brinton
8	29	COVENTRY CITY	11	0-2	0-1	8920	
9	6 Oct	Clapton Orient	14	0-4	0-1	8665	
10	13	GILLINGHAM	8	3-1	0-1	9862	Riley(2), Loftus
11	20	SOUTHEND UNITED	7	2-0	0-0	10235	Morgan, Riley
12	27	Luton Town	6	1-1	0-0	9000	Cainey
13	3 Nov	CRYSTAL PALACE	8	0-1	0-0	11289	
14	10	Charlton Athletic	13	1-4	0-2	3000	Hodge
15	17	ALDERSHOT	10	2-0	0-0	9239	Loftus, Pearce
16	1 Dec	TORQUAY UNITED	8	1-0	0-0	8251	Hodge
17	15	BRIGHTON & HOVE ALB.	7	1-0	0-0	9981	Hodge
18	22	Cardiff City	7	3-3	2-0	6000	Harston(2), Loftus
19	25	NORTHAMPTON TOWN	7	1-1	1-1	11914	Cainey
20	26	Northampton Town	7	2-2	1-1	18000	Harston, Hodge
21	29	Watford	8	0-4	0-2	8367	
22	1 Jan	Queens Park Rangers	8	1-4	1-2	4000	Harston
23	5	NEWPORT COUNTY	8	2-1	1-0	8968	Landells, Wallis
24	19	Exeter City	11	0-3	0-2	5000	
25	2 Feb	MILLWALL	10	4-2	2-2	11384	Banfield(2), Harston, Wallis
26	6	BRISTOL ROVERS	8	1-1	1-1	7911	Harston
27	9	Coventry City	9	1-1	1-0	14000	Riley
28	23	Gillingham	11	0-1	0-1	4713	
29	2 Mar	Southend United	12	0-6	0-4	6581	
30	9	LUTON TOWN	14	0-2	0-1	6749	
31	13	CLAPTON ORIENT	13	0-0	0-0	3428	
32	16	Crystal Palace	14	1-3	0-1	10357	Cainey
33	23	CHARLTON ATHLETIC	16	1-4	1-3	8150	Harston
34	30	Aldershot	17	0-1	0-0	3000	
35	6 Apr	SWINDON TOWN	15	2-0	1-0	5900	Harston(2)
36	10	Swindon Town	17	0-1	0-1	3452	
37	13	Torquay United	17	1-3	1-3	3000	Harston
38	19	BOURNEMOUTH & B.A.	14	2-1	1-0	8916	Harston, O.G.
39	20	QUEENS PARK RANGERS	14	5-1	3-0	5868	Harston(2), Banfield, Foy, Landells
40	22	Bournemouth & Bos. Ath.	14	1-1	0-0	8000	Harston
41	27	Brighton & Hove Albion	15	0-2	0-1	3873	
42	4 May	CARDIFF CITY	15	4-0	3-0	5558	Banfield, Brinton, Harston, Loftus

Apps. 41 29 17 29 3 35 12 4 25 25 32 10 22 17 31 29 27 21 1 20 11 3 1 10 1 1 1 4

Goals — Morgan 1, Brinton 3, Green 1, Riley 8, Loftus 4, Hodge 5, Harston 15, Wallis 3, Cainey 3, Pearce 1, Lardells 2, Foy 1

F.A. CUP

Rd	Date	Opposition	Res.	H.T.	Att.	Goalscorers
1R	24 Nov	GILLINGHAM	2-0	0-0	10558	Landells(2) (£604)
2R	8 Dec	Rotherham United	2-1	2-0	11223	Loftus(2) (£611.11.0)
3R	12 Jan	BURY	1-1	0-1	23300	Harston (£1465)
3Rr	16	Bury	2-2	1-0	14069	Harston, Hodge (£872.18.3) (aet)
3R2r	21	Bury	2-1	0-0	10300	Hodge(2) (£656.18.0) (at Villa Park)
4R	26	Portsmouth	0-0	0-0	29239	(£2062.4.0)
4Rr	30	PORTSMOUTH	2-0	0-0	42885	Harston, Hodge (£2570) *
5R	16 Feb	PRESTON NORTH END	0-0	0-0	43335	(£3208.18.0)
5Rr	25	Preston North End	0-5	0-4	19889	(£1365.15.1)

* Official attendance. Break-in by crowd, unofficial estimates put the number at over 50000.

FOOTBALL LEAGUE DIVISION THREE (SOUTH) CUP

Rd	Date	Opposition	Res.	H.T.	Att.	Goalscorers
2R	24 Oct	Watford	1-4	0-3	1623	Harston

GLOUCESTERSHIRE CUP FINAL

Date	Opposition	Res.	H.T.	Att.	Goalscorers
26 Sep	BRISTOL ROVERS	1-2	1-1	5216	Riley

FRIENDLIES

No	Date	Opposition	Res.	H.T.	Att.	Goalscorers
1	1 Oct	Yeovil & Petters United	3-2	1-1		Morgan, Riley, Wallis
2	1 Apr	Rhymney Valley League	3-2		7000	Landells, Pearce, Riley
3	29	Stoke City	2-3	2-0	2382	Harston, Landells (Ernest Brinton's Benefit)
4	2 May	Plymouth Argyle	1-3	0-2	2000	Loftus (Tommy Haynes' Benefit)

FINAL LEAGUE TABLE

		P	W	D	L	F:A	Pts
1	Charlton	42	27	7	8	103:52	61
2	Reading	42	21	11	10	89:65	53
3	Coventry	42	21	9	12	86:50	51
4	Luton	42	19	12	11	92:60	50
5	Crystal Palace	42	19	10	13	86:64	48
6	Watford	42	19	9	14	76:49	47
7	Northampton	42	19	9	14	65:67	46
8	Bristol R.	42	17	10	15	73:77	44
9	Brighton	42	17	9	16	69:62	43
10	Torquay	42	18	6	18	81:75	42
11	Exeter	42	16	9	17	70:75	41
12	Millwall	42	17	7	18	57:62	41
13	QPR	42	16	9	17	63:72	41
14	Clapton Orient	42	15	10	17	65:65	40
15	Bristol C.	42	15	9	18	52:68	39
16	Swindon	42	13	12	17	67:78	38
17	Bournemouth	42	15	7	20	54:71	37
18	Aldershot	42	13	10	19	50:75	36
19	Cardiff	42	13	9	20	62:82	35
20	Gillingham	42	11	13	18	55:75	35
21	Southend	42	11	9	22	65:78	31
22	Newport	42	10	5	27	54:112	25

1934/35 Season

Back: Hick, Pearce. 3rd Row: Phipps, Roberts, Dolman, Clipson, Wilson, Webber, Cottrell.
2nd Row: Mellors(Trainer), Harston, Riley, Bridge, Hughes, Affleck, Morgan, Jenkins, Davies, Southway(Asst.Trainer).
Front: Bob Hewison(Manager), Cainey, Banfield, Green, Brinton, Loftus, Wallis, Foy, Fish, Moseley, C H Hancock(Sec.).
On ground: Hodge. (N.B. Trophies are the Gloucestershire and the Welsh Cups).

1935/36 Season.
Back: Wilson, Hodge, Turner, Dolman.
3rd Row: Simms, Mosley, Hick, Pearce, Baker, Cottrell, McGurk.
2nd Row: Mellors(Trainer), Berry, Bridge, Armstrong, Morgan, Bradford,
Randall, J.V.Brinton, Smith, Southway(Asst.Trainer).
Front: Roberts, Harston, Cainey, White, Bob Hewison(Manager), Wallis, E.Brinton, Fawkes, Bungay.

SEASON 1935-36
FOOTBALL LEAGUE DIVISION THREE (SOUTH)

Player columns (left to right): Dolman H.W., Roberts W.S., Bridge C.A.V., Armstrong R.J., Pearce J.G., Brinton E.J., Hodge J.R., Bradford J., Turner H., Bungay R.H., Randall J., White W.T., Harston E., Baker J.E., Morgan C.I., Wallis G.H., Hick J., Caney W.P., Smith R.G., McGurk F.R., Butcher C., Wilson J.E., Lane W.H.C., Fisn I., Brinton J.V., Hampshire J.G.

No.	Date	Opposition	Pos.	Res.	H.T.	Att.	Goalscorers
1	31 Aug	Watford		2-0	0-0	11201	Bradford, Bungay
2	4 Sep	NEWPORT COUNTY	9	1-2	0-1	14933	Bungay
3	7	BRISTOL ROVERS	16	0-2	0-2	25039	
4	9	Newport County	17	0-2	0-0	7885	
5	14	MILLWALL	14	4-1	2-0	10389	Harston(2), Armstrong, Hodge
6	18	Exeter City	11	1-0	0-0	6000	Wallis
7	21	Torquay United	15	0-2	0-2	5000	
8	28	ALDERSHOT	12	1-0	1-0	9038	Cainey
9	5 Oct	Swindon Town	12	1-1	1-0	11945	Smith
10	12	COVENTRY CITY	10	0-0	0-0	15206	
11	19	Clapton Orient	19	0-2	0-0	8983	
12	26	SOUTHEND UNITED	12	2-1	1-0	8891	Armstrong, Hodge
13	2 Nov	Northampton Town	8	2-0	2-0	5000	Armstrong, Cainey
14	9	NOTTS COUNTY	8	1-1	1-1	12343	White
15	16	Reading	10	2-5	2-2	10000	Wallis, White
16	23	CARDIFF CITY	15	0-2	0-1	10350	
17	7 Dec	BOURNEMOUTH & B.A.	14	1-0	0-0	7223	Bungay
18	14 Dec	Luton Town	14	0-1	0-0	9000	
19	21	CRYSTAL PALACE	14	1-1	0-0	3442	Turner (Abandoned after 83 mins. due to fog)
20	25	Brighton & Hove Albion	15	0-3	0-1	8634	
21	26	BRIGHTON & HOVE ALB.	17	0-3	0-1	13175	
22	4 Jan	Bristol Rovers	17	1-1	0-0	18459	Hodge
23	11	Gillingham	17	1-2	1-2	7587	Armstrong
24	18	Millwall	20	1-1	1-1	10000	White
25	25	TORQUAY UNITED	15	2-0	1-0	7662	Lane, White
26	1 Feb	Aldershot	16	0-0	0-0	3000	
27	8	SWINDON TOWN	14	5-0	2-0	8304	Armstrong(2), White(2), Lane
28	15	Coventry City	15	1-3	0-2	16000	Lane
29	22	CLAPTON ORIENT	13	2-0	2-0	4865	Armstrong, White
30	29	Notts County	14	1-1	1-0	3154	Lane
31	7 Mar	LUTON TOWN	16	1-2	0-1	8173	Lane
32	14	Southend United	13	1-0	1-0	6233	Armstrong
33	21	READING	14	1-1	0-1	10066	Lane
34	28	Cardiff City	17	0-1	0-1	7000	
35	1 Apr	WATFORD	17	2-2	2-0	3412	Fish, White
36	4	GILLINGHAM	14	2-1	2-1	6065	Armstrong, J.V. Brinton
37	10	Queens Park Rangers	15	1-4	0-0	14000	Lane
38	11	Bournemouth & Bos. Ath.	16	0-3	0-0	6000	
39	13	QUEENS PARK RANGERS	14	0-0	0-0	10838	
40	18	NORTHAMPTON TOWN	14	3-2	2-1	6463	Wallis(2), Armstrong
41	25	Crystal Palace	16	1-6	1-1	6244	Armstrong
42	29	CRYSTAL PALACE	14	2-0	0-0	5099	Lane, Wallis
43	2 May	EXETER CITY	13	2-1	1-0	5564	Lane, Wallis

Apps: 21, 36, 29, 36, 41, 41, 30, 5, 7, 9, 19, 36, 6, 5, 35, 12, 21, 22, 6, 3, 1, 22, 20, 6, 2, 2
Goals: 11, 3, 1, 1, 3, 8, 2, 6, 2, 1, 9, 1, 1

F.A. CUP

			Res.	H.T.	Att.	
1R	30 Nov	CRYSTAL PALACE	0-1	0-0	13997	(£859)

FOOTBALL LEAGUE DIVISION THREE (SOUTH) CUP

			Res.	H.T.	Att.	Goalscorers
1R	2 Oct	Bristol Rovers	4-2	2-1	2100	White(2), Cainey, Smith
2R	30	Bournemouth & Bos. Ath.	0-1	0-0	2261	

WELSH CUP

			Res.	H.T.	Att.	
6R	29 Jan	Cardiff City	1-2	1-1	1000	Turner

GLOUCESTERSHIRE CUP FINAL

			Res.	H.T.	Att.	
	25 Sep	Bristol Rovers	1-3	0-2	6293	Bradford

FINAL LEAGUE TABLE

		P	W	D	L	F	A	Pts
1	Coventry	42	24	9	9	102	45	57
2	Luton	42	22	12	8	81	45	56
3	Reading	42	26	2	14	87	62	54
4	QPR	42	22	9	11	84	53	53
5	Watford	42	20	9	13	80	54	49
6	Crystal Palace	42	22	5	15	96	74	49
7	Brighton	42	18	8	16	70	63	44
8	Bournemouth	42	16	11	15	60	56	43
9	Notts Co.	42	15	12	15	60	57	42
10	Torquay	42	16	9	17	62	62	41
11	Aldershot	42	14	12	16	53	61	40
12	Millwall	42	14	12	16	58	71	40
13	Bristol C.	42	15	10	17	48	59	40
14	Clapton Orient	42	16	6	20	55	61	38
15	Northampton	42	15	8	19	62	90	38
16	Gillingham	42	14	9	19	66	77	37
17	Bristol R.	42	14	9	19	69	95	37
18	Southend	42	13	10	19	61	62	36
19	Swindon	42	14	8	20	64	73	36
20	Cardiff	42	13	10	19	60	73	36
21	Newport	42	11	9	22	60	111	31
22	Exeter	42	8	11	23	59	93	27

SEASON 1936-37
FOOTBALL LEAGUE DIVISION THREE (SOUTH)

No.	Date	Opposition	Pos.	Res.	H.T.	Att.	Goalscorers
1	29 Aug	QUEENS PARK RANGERS		3-2	1-2	13689	Caldwell, Dryden, Lane
2	2 Sep	Reading	11	1-2	0-0	10000	Lane
3	5	Bristol Rovers	15	1-3	0-1	25638	Roberts
4	12	Torquay United	20	2-5	1-2	5000	White(2)
5	14	Cardiff City	20	1-3	1-3	24100	White
6	19	NOTTS COUNTY	20	1-1	0-1	10329	White
7	23	READING	19	1-2	1-1	7246	Haycock
8	26	Clapton Orient	19	0-0	0-0	8747	
9	3 Oct	WALSALL	21	0-0	0-0	9460	
10	10	Luton Town	21	0-4	0-1	15000	
11	17	MILLWALL	21	2-0	1-0	12072	Peters, White
12	24	Swindon Town	19	1-0	1-0	13121	Armstrong
13	31	ALDERSHOT	19	3-0	1-0	12414	Dryden, Roberts(pen), White
14	7 Nov	Gillingham	18	2-2	2-2	4023	Armstrong, Peters, White
15	14	NEWPORT COUNTY	17	3-1	2-1	14467	Roberts(3)
16	21	Southend United	18	0-3	0-2	7069	
17	5 Dec	Brighton & Hove Albion	18	0-2	0-0	8101	
18	19	Northampton Town	18	1-5	1-3	7143	Wallis
19	25	CRYSTAL PALACE	18	1-0	1-0	13346	Roberts
20	26	Queens Park Rangers	19	0-5	0-2	12000	
21	28	Crystal Palace	19	0-1	0-1	4195	
22	2 Jan	BRISTOL ROVERS	19	4-1	2-1	13863	Peters(2), Haycox, Morgan
23	9	TORQUAY UNITED	17	4-1	2-0	8591	Haycox(2), Armstrong, Peters
24	16	WATFORD	16	2-2	2-2	7653	Haycox, Wallis
25	23	Notts County	18	0-1	0-0	9000	
26	27	BOURNEMOUTH & B.A.	17	4-1	1-1	3785	Peters(2), Haycox, Wallis
27	30	CLAPTON ORIENT	14	4-0	0-0	4565	Haycox(2), Dryden, Peters
28	6 Feb	Walsall	13	5-1	5-0	4762	Wallis(2), Dryden, Haycox, Peters
29	13	LUTON TOWN	14	2-3	2-2	17193	Haycox(2)
30	22	Millwall	16	1-3	0-0	7000	Haycox
31	6 Mar	Aldershot	16	0-3	0-1	3000	
32	13	GILLINGHAM	16	2-0	2-0	7803	Haycox(2)
33	20	Newport County	15	0-0	0-0	8749	
34	26	EXETER CITY	14	2-1	0-0	13348	Booth, Haycox
35	27	SOUTHEND UNITED	14	0-1	0-0	10130	
36	29	Exeter City	16	0-3	0-2	8342	
37	3 Apr	Watford	16	0-1	0-1	6000	
38	10	BRIGHTON & HOVE ALB.	15	1-0	1-0	8817	Haycox
39	17	Bournemouth & Bos. Ath.	16	0-0	0-0	5000	
40	24	NORTHAMPTON TOWN	17	0-1	0-1	6729	
41	28	SWINDON TOWN	17	1-2	0-0	3537	Armstrong
42	1 May	CARDIFF CITY	16	2-1	2-1	4360	Armstrong, Haycox

Player appearances (shirt numbers)

No.	Wilson J.E.	Roberts W.S.	Bridge C.A.V.	Morgan C.I.	Pearce J.G.	Brinton E.J.	Peters F.R.	Caldwell R.	Lane W.H.C.	Neal R.G.	Dryden J.G.	Baker J.E.	White W.T.	Haycox J.	Hick J.	Wallis G.H.	Guy S.W.	Armstrong R.J.	Booth L.	Hampshire J.G.	Brinton J.V.	Smith R.G.	Kelly L.	Dawson E.
1	1	2	3	4	5	6	7	8	9	10	11													
2	1	2	3	4	5	6	7	8	9	10	11													
3	1	2	3	4		6	7	8	9				11	5	10									
4	1	2	3	4	5	6	7	8					11		10	9								
5	1	2	3	4		6	7	8					11	5	10	9								
6	1	2	3	4	5	6	7	8					11	10										
7	1	2	3	4	5	6	7	8					11	10	9									
8	1	2	3	4	5		7		9	8	11				6	10								
9	1	2	3	4	5			8		9	10	11			6		7							
10	1	2	3	4	5		7				11			10	9			8						
11	1	9	2	4	5	6	7				11			10	3			8						
12	1	9	2	4	5	6	7				11			10	3			8						
13	1	9	2	4	5	6	7				11			10	3			8						
14	1		2	4	5	6	7				11		9	10	3			8						
15	1	9	2	4	5		7				11	6		10	3			8						
16	1		2	4	5		7				11	6		10	9	3		8						
17	1		2	4		6	7			9	11			10				8	5					
18	1		2	4	5	6	7				11			10	3	9		8						
19	1	2	3	4		6	7			9	11				10			8	5					
20	1	2	3	4		6	7			9	11				10			8	5					
21	1	2	3	4		6	7				11			10	9			8	5					
22	1	2		4		6	7				11			10	3	9		8	5					
23	1	2		4		6	9							10	3	8		7	5	6	11			
24	1	2		4		6	9							10	3	8		7	5		11			
25	1	2					7	4						9	3	10	6	8	5		11			
26	1	2				6	7	4			11			9	3	10		8	5					
27	1	2				6	9	4			11			10	3	8		7	5					
28	1	2				6	7	4			11			9	3	10		8	5					
29	1	2				6	7	4			11			9	3	10		8	5					
30	1	2	3			6	7	4						9				8	10	5	11			
31	1	2	3			6	7	4		10				9				8	5					
32	1	2				6	7	4		10				9	3			8	5	11				
33	1	2		5		6	9	4		10	7				3			8		11				
34	1	2				6	7	4		10				9	3			8		11				
35	1	2	6	5			4			10	11			9	3			8				7		
36	1	2		4	5		7			10					6			8	9		11		3	
37	1	2	3	4	5		9				10				6			8	7		11			
38	1	2	3	4	5		10							8	6			9	7		11			
39	1	2	3	4	5		7				11			9	6			10	8					
40	1	2	3	4	5	6	7				11			9				10	8					
41		2		4		6	7				11			9	3			10	8	5				1
42	1		2	4	5	6	9	7			11			10	3			8						
Apps	41	36	29	32	24	32	40	19	10	9	35	5	15	24	28	13	1	21	19	16	10	1	1	1
Goals		6		1			9	1	2		4		7	17		5		5	1					

F.A. CUP

				Res.	H.T.	Att.																	
1R	28 Nov	Newport County		0-3	0-1	11165	(£650)

Players: Wilson 1, Roberts 9, Bridge 2, Morgan 4, Pearce 5, Brinton E.J. 6, Peters 7, Dryden 11, Haycox 10, Hick 3, Armstrong 8

WELSH CUP

6R	3 Mar	SWANSEA TOWN		1-2	0-1	2000	Haycox

FOOTBALL LEAGUE DIVISION THREE (SOUTH) CUP

1R	30 Sep	GILLINGHAM		0-2	0-0	1150	

GLOUCESTERSHIRE CUP FINAL

	9 Sep	BRISTOL ROVERS		1-0	1-0	5100	Haycox

BERKELEY HUNT CHARITY CUP FINAL (At Thornbury)

	19 Apr	Thornbury		5-1		3000	Haycox(2), Morgan, Peters, Roberts

FRIENDLIES

1	22 Apr	Cheddar & District XI		5-3		1000	Unknown(5) (Pat Bolger's Benefit)
2	26	Bristol Rovers		4-2	1-2	4000	Booth(2), Bourton, Taylor (W.H. Pickering's Benefit)

FINAL LEAGUE TABLE

		P	W	D	L	F:A	Pts
1	Luton	42	27	4	11	103:53	58
2	Notts Co.	42	23	10	9	74:52	56
3	Brighton	42	24	5	13	74:43	53
4	Watford	42	19	11	12	85:60	49
5	Reading	42	19	11	12	76:60	49
6	Bournemouth	42	20	9	13	65:59	49
7	Northampton	42	20	6	16	85:68	46
8	Millwall	42	18	10	14	64:54	46
9	QPR	42	18	9	15	73:52	45
10	Southend	42	17	11	14	78:67	45
11	Gillingham	42	18	8	16	52:66	44
12	Clapton Orient	42	14	15	13	52:52	43
13	Swindon	42	14	11	17	75:73	39
14	Crystal Palace	42	13	12	17	62:61	38
15	Bristol R.	42	16	4	22	71:80	36
16	Bristol C.	42	15	6	21	58:70	36
17	Walsall	42	13	10	19	62:84	36
18	Cardiff	42	14	7	21	54:87	35
19	Newport	42	12	10	20	67:98	34
20	Torquay	42	11	10	21	57:80	32
21	Exeter	42	10	12	20	59:88	32
22	Aldershot	42	7	9	26	50:89	23

SEASON 1937-38
FOOTBALL LEAGUE DIVISION THREE (SOUTH)

No.	Date	Opposition	Pos.	Res.	H.T.	Att.	Goalscorers	Wilson J.E.	Brook R.	Bridge C.A.V.	Morgan C.I.	Hampshire J.G.	Woods T.	Peters F.R.	Brain J.	Haycox J.	Booth L.	Dryden J.G.	Hick J.	Pearce J.G.	Billingham J.	Dawson E.	Hall G.W.E.	Armstrong R.J.	Harvey J.H.	Neal R.M.	Colquhoun D.M.	Turner J.T.	Caldwell R.	Rae J.	Chilcott K.	Rowles A.	Bourton C.F.T.	Thorley E.C.	Gallacher F.
1	28 Aug	GILLINGHAM		3-1	2-0	14134	Booth, Dryden, Haycox	1	2	3	4	5	6	7	8	9	10	11																	
2	1 Sep	Watford		1-3	1-1	7000	Dryden	1	2	3	4	5	6	7	8	9	10	11																	
3	4	Exeter City	14	2-3	0-1	7000	Booth(2)	1	2	3	4	5	6	7	8	9	10	11																	
4	8	WATFORD	10	3-1	0-1	10259	Booth, Dryden(pen), Haycox		2		4		6		8	9	10	11	3	5	7	1													
5	11	SWINDON TOWN	13	1-1	0-0	15969	Haycox		2		4		6		8	9	10	11	3	5	7	1													
6	18	Aldershot	13	1-1	0-1	5000	Brain		2		4		6		10	9	8	11		5	7	1	3												
7	22	Notts County	13	0-2	0-1	10937			2	3	4				10	9	8	11		5	7	1		6											
8	25	MILLWALL	14	0-0	0-0	12784			2	3	4				10	9	8	11		5	7	1		6											
9	2 Oct	Reading	12	1-0	1-0	8527	Peters			3	4			7		9	8	11	2	5		1		6		10									
10	9	CRYSTAL PALACE	12	0-0	0-0	13262				3	4			7		9	8	11	2	5		1		6		10									
11	16	WALSALL	8	3-1	1-0	11051	Dryden(2,1pen), Haycox			3	4			7		9	8	11	2	5		1		6		10									
12	23	Cardiff City	10	0-0	0-0	16844				3	4			7		9	8	11	2	5		1		6		10									
13	30	BOURNEMOUTH & B.A.	8	2-1	1-0	10371	Haycox(2)			3	4			7		9	8	11	2	5		1		6		10									
14	6 Nov	Brighton & Hove Albion	8	1-1	1-1	8256	Dryden			3	4			7		9	8	11	2	5		1		6		10									
15	13	QUEENS PARK RANGERS	6	2-0	0-0	17343	Brain, Haycox			3	4			7	10	9	8	11	2	5		1		6											
16	20	Southend United	8	0-5	0-3	6682				3	4			7	10	9	8		2	5		1		6				11							
17	4 Dec	Torquay United	6	3-1	1-0	2000	Brain(2), Haycox			3	4			7	8	9		11	2	5		1		6				10							
18	27	NORTHAMPTON TOWN	6	1-0	1-0	20135	Booth		2				6	7	10	9	8	11		5		1						3	4						
19	28	Bristol Rovers	8	0-1	0-0	26300			2	3	4			7	10			11		5		1		6			8				9				
20	1 Jan	Gillingham	10	0-1	0-0	5126			2	3	4			7	10			11		5		1		6			8				9			
21	8	CLAPTON ORIENT	8	2-0	1-0	7775	Brain, Morgan		2	3	4			7	10	9	8	11		5		1		6											
22	15	EXETER CITY	6	4-1	1-0	8312	Rowles(3), Pearce		2		4			7	10		8			5		1		6						3		9			
23	29	ALDERSHOT	7	3-1	2-0	13449	Rowles(2), Brain		2		4			7	10			11		5		1		6						3		9	8		
24	5 Feb	Millwall	6	3-0	0-0	23235	Rowles(2), Dryden		2		4			7	10			11		5		1		6						3		9	8		
25	12	READING	4	1-0	1-0	25189	Rowles		2		4			7	10					5		1		6				11		3		9	8		
26	19	Crystal Palace	4	1-1	0-1	16129	Rowles		2		4			7	10					5		1		6				11		3		9	8		
27	26	Walsall	3	8-2	4-1	4368	Rowles(3), Peters (2), Bourton, Brain, Brook		2		4			7	10			11		5		1		6						3		9	8		
28	5 Mar	CARDIFF CITY	3	0-1	0-1	38953			2		4			7	10			11		5		1		6						3		9	8		
29	12	Bournemouth & Bos. Ath.	4	0-0	0-0	10873			2		4			7	10					5		1		6						3		9	8		11
30	19	BRIGHTON & HOVE ALB.	5	1-1	1-0	20127	Peters		2		4			7	10					5		1		8						3		9			11
31	26	Queens Park Rangers	5	2-0	1-0	23242	Rowles, Thorley		2		4			7								1	5	6						3		9	8	11	10
32	2 Apr	SOUTHEND UNITED	4	4-2	2-1	19632	Gallacher, Morgan, Rowles, Thorley		2		4			7								1	5	6						3		9	8	11	10
33	9	Clapton Orient	5	0-0	0-0	8760			2		4			7						5		1		6						3		9	8	11	10
34	15	NEWPORT COUNTY	5	0-0	0-0	26907			2		4			7						5		1		6						3		9	8	11	10
35	16	TORQUAY UNITED	5	2-0	0-0	17167	Brain, Gallacher		2		4			7	9					5		1		6						3		8		11	10
36	18	Newport County	5	0-0	0-0	17008			2		4			7	9					5		1		6						3		8		11	10
37	22	Northampton Town	5	0-1	0-1	8901			2		4			7	9					5		1		6						3		8		11	10
38	23	Mansfield Town	5	5-3	3-0	7233	Rowles(3), Gallacher, Thorley		2		4			7						5		1		6						3		9	8	11	10
39	27	MANSFIELD TOWN	4	2-1	2-0	15231	Bourton, Dryden		2		4							11		5	7	1		6						3		9	8		10
40	30	BRISTOL ROVERS	4	0-0	0-0	23424			2		4			7	9						6	5		1						3			8	11	10
41	4 May	Swindon Town	3	3-2	2-1	10532	Booth, Bourton, Peters		2		4			7			8	11		5		1								3	6				10
42	7	NOTTS COUNTY	2	3-1	2-0	13781	Dryden, Gallacher, Rowles		2		4					8		11		5	7	1								3	6	9			10
							Apps.	3	30	20	41	3	7	35	29	19	21	28	12	37	7	39	12	23	2	6	3	22	3	2	1	15	19	11	12
							Goals		1		2			5	8	8	6	9		1												18	3	3	4

F.A. CUP

	Date	Opposition		Res.	H.T.	Att.	Goalscorers	Bridge	Morgan	Peters	Brain	Haycox	Booth	Dryden	Hick	Pearce	Dawson	Armstrong	Neal
1R	27 Nov	ENFIELD		3-0	1-0	9333	Haycox(2), O.G. (£526)	3	4	7	10	9	8	11	2	5	1	6	
2R	11 Dec	Cardiff City		1-1	0-1	25472	Brain(pen) (£1,450.15.3)	3	4	7	8	9		11	2	5	1	6	10
2Rr	15	CARDIFF CITY		0-2	0-2	23050	(£1,431)	3	4	7	8	9		11	2	5	1	6	10

WELSH CUP

	Date	Opposition		Res.	H.T.	Att.	Goalscorers
6R	10 Feb	Newport County		2-6	1-2	1095	Colquhoun, Neal

FOOTBALL LEAGUE DIVISION THREE (SOUTH) CUP

	Date	Opposition		Res.	H.T.	Att.	Goalscorers
1R	6 Oct	TORQUAY UNITED		3-0	0-0	1337	Dryden(2,1 pen) Haycox
2R	10 Nov	CARDIFF CITY		2-1	0-0	2130	Brain, Haycox
3R	10 Jan	Walsall		2-1	0-1	526	Brain, Colquhoun
SF	30 Mar	MILLWALL		2-0	1-0	1513	Booth, Brain

GLOUCESTERSHIRE CUP FINAL

	Date	Opposition		Res.	H.T.	Att.	Goalscorers
	27 Sep	Bristol Rovers		1-2	1-0	3648	Brain

FRIENDLY

	Date	Opposition		Res.	H.T.	Att.	Goalscorers
	22 Jan	Plymouth Argyle		1-2	0-2	4500	Rae

FINAL LEAGUE TABLE

1	Millwall	42	23	10	9	83:37	56
2	Bristol C.	42	21	13	8	68:40	55
3	QPR	42	22	9	11	80:47	53
4	Watford	42	21	11	10	73:43	53
5	Brighton	42	21	9	12	64:44	51
6	Reading	42	20	11	11	71:63	51
7	Crystal Palace	42	18	12	12	67:47	48
8	Swindon	42	17	10	15	49:49	44
9	Northampton	42	17	9	16	51:57	43
10	Cardiff	42	15	12	15	67:54	42
11	Notts Co	42	16	9	17	50:50	41
12	Southend	42	15	10	17	70:68	40
13	Bournemouth	42	14	12	16	56:57	40
14	Mansfield	42	15	9	18	62:67	39
15	Bristol R.	42	13	13	16	46:61	39
16	Newport	42	11	16	15	43:52	38
17	Exeter	42	13	12	17	57:70	38
18	Aldershot	42	15	5	22	39:59	35
19	Clapton Orient	42	13	7	22	42:61	33
20	Torquay	42	9	12	21	38:73	30
21	Walsall	42	11	7	24	52:88	29
22	Gillingham	42	10	6	26	36:77	26

SEASON 1938-39
FOOTBALL LEAGUE DIVISION THREE (SOUTH)

No.	Date	Opposition	Pos.	Res.	H.T.	Att.	Goalscorers	Dawson E.	Brook R.	Bridge C.A.V.	Morgan C.I.	Pearce J.G.	Armstrong R.J.	Peters F.R.	Bourton C.F.T.	Rowles A.	Laidman F.	Willshaw G.J.	Clayton R.	Hall G.W.E.	Hick J.	Caldwell R.	Roberts D.	Gallacher F.	Morgan M.	Pearson H.	Thorley E.C.	Brain J.	Chilcott K.	Mardon H.J.	Booth L.	Turner J.T.	Clark D.F.	Toman M.	Spiring G.
1	27 Aug	Watford		2-2	1-2	10000	Peters, Willshaw	1	2	3	4	5	6	7	8	9	10	11																	
2	31	Aldershot	7	1-0	1-0	6400	Bourton	1	2	3	4	5	6	7	8	9	10	11																	
3	3 Sep	PORT VALE	4	5-1	2-0	16975	Peters(2), Rowles(2), Bourton	1	2	3	4	5	6	7	8	9	10	11																	
4	7	NOTTS COUNTY	2	2-1	0-1	17038	Bourton(pen), Willshaw	1	2	3	4	5	6	7	8	9	10	11																	
5	10	Swindon Town	3	0-1	0-1	17769		1	2	3	4	5	6	7	8		10	11	9																
6	17	TORQUAY UNITED	9	1-2	1-0	12695	Clayton	1	2	3		5	6	7	8		10	11	9	4															
7	24	Clapton Orient	10	1-1	0-0	8918	Clayton	1	2				6	7	8			11	9	3	4	5	10												
8	1 Oct	NEWPORT COUNTY	12	0-2	0-0	14497		1	2	3	4	5	6		8		10	11	9					7											
9	8	Northampton Town	11	2-2	1-0	10309	Caldwell, Laidman		2	3		5	6		8		10	7	9			4				1	11								
10	15	Bournemouth & Bos. Ath.	16	0-4		5000			2	3		5	6		8	9	10	7				4					11								
11	22	BRISTOL ROVERS	13	2-1	1-0	17105	Willshaw(2)		2	3		5	6	7	8			11	9			4						10							
12	29	Mansfield Town	16	2-3	1-2	7398	Brain, Chilcott		2	3		5	6	7				11	9			4						10	8						
13	5 Nov	QUEENS PARK RANGERS	16	2-2	1-2	11386	Clayton, Peters	1	2	3			6	7			10	11	9				5						8						
14	12	Southend United	19	0-2	0-1	5957		1	2	3	4		6	7			10	11					5						8	9					
15	19	EXETER CITY	14	4-1	1-0	8302	Mardon(2), Booth, Willshaw	1	2	3			6	7				11				4	5	10						9	8				
16	3 Dec	IPSWICH TOWN	10	3-2	2-1	9105	Booth, Bourton, Peters	1	2	3				7	8			11			6	4	5							9	10				
17	10	Reading	10	2-2	1-1	7524	Booth, Bourton	1	2	3				7	8			11			6	4	5							9	10				
18	17	WALSALL	8	2-1	2-1	7526	Mardon, Peters	1	2	3				7	8			11			6	4	5							9	10				
19	24	WATFORD	8	2-0		7127	Bourton, Gallacher	1	2	3		5		7	8			11			6	4		10						9					
20	26	BRIGHTON & HOVE ALB.	7	2-0	2-0	9958	Caldwell, Peters	1	2	3		5		7	8			11			6	4		10						9					
21	27	Brighton & Hove Albion	8	0-1	0-1	12071		1	2	3		5		7	8			11			6	4		10						9					
22	31	Port Vale	10	0-4	0-3	4957		1	2	3		5		7	8			11			6	4		10						9					
23	11 Jan	Cardiff City	10	1-2	0-0	9000	Booth		2			5		7	8			11	9		6	4									10		3		
24	14	SWINDON TOWN	10	1-1	1-1	10111	Willshaw		2	3		5			8			11	9		6	4	7	1							10				
25	21	Torquay United	12	1-3	1-2	4000	Booth		2	3	4	5	6	7			10	9								1		11			8				
26	28	CLAPTON ORIENT	11	3-1	2-0	7731	Booth(2), O.G.		2	3	4		6	7	8			11	9				5					1			10				
27	4 Feb	Newport County	9	2-0	1-0	12436	Booth(2)		2	3	4		6	7				11	9				5					1		8	10				
28	11	NORTHAMPTON TOWN	8	0-0	0-0	10549			2	3	4		6	7				11					5			8		1		9	10				
29	18	BOURNEMOUTH & B.A.	8	2-0	2-0	10131	Booth(2)		2	3	4		6	7		9		11					5					1			10				
30	25	Bristol Rovers	7	1-1	0-0	14824	Booth		2	3	4		6	7		9		11					5					1			10				
31	4 Mar	MANSFIELD TOWN	6	2-0	2-0	8270	Armstrong, Bourton		2	3	4		6	7	8			11					5					1			10	9			
32	11	Queens Park Rangers	8	1-3	1-2	7000	O.G.		2	3	4		6	7	8								5					1			10	9		11	
33	18	SOUTHEND UNITED	7	1-0	0-0	7747	Spiring		2	3	4		6	7	8								5					1			10	9			11
34	25	Exeter City	7	1-1	0-0	4847			2	3	4		6	7	8	9							5					1			10				11
35	1 Apr	CARDIFF CITY	7	1-1	1-1	10003	Armstrong		2	3	4		6	7		9							5	10				1			8				11
36	7	Crystal Palace	9	2-3	1-2	21913	Bourton(2,1pen)		2	3			6	7		9						4	5					1	8		10				11
37	8	Ipswich Town	10	0-4		12834			2	3				8				11	9		6	4	5					1	7		10				
38	10	CRYSTAL PALACE	10	1-0	0-0	11055	Bourton	1	2	3			6	7	8			11				4	5								10				
39	15	READNG	9	5-1	2-0	7420	Willshaw(3), Booth, Peters	1	2	3			6	7	8			11					5	9							10		4		
40	22	Walsall	10	0-5	0-4	5149		1	2	3			6	7	8			11					5	9							10		4		
41	29	ALDERSHOT	8	1-0	0-0	4355	Booth	1	2	3				7	8								5				6				10		4	11	
42	6 May	Notts County	8	0-0	0-0	5000		1	2	3			6	7		9		11					5						8		10		4		
							Apps.	26	41	41	19	18	32	38	35	9	10	34	13	1	12	17	24	10	2	16	3	3	8	13	23	1	7	2	4
							Goals						2	8	10	2	1	9	3			2		1				1	1	3	15				1

F.A. CUP

	Date	Opposition		Res.	H.T.	Att.	Goalscorers	Dawson	Brook	Bridge			Armstrong	Peters				Willshaw				Caldwell	Roberts	Gallacher						Mardon	Booth				
1R	26 Nov	Bournemouth & Bos. Ath.		1-2	1-1	10207	Mardon (£675)	1	2	3			6	7				11				4	5	10						9	8				

FOOTBALL LEAGUE DIVISION THREE (SOUTH) CUP

	Date	Opposition		Res.	H.T.	Att.	Goalscorers
F1	28 Sep	Reading		1-6	1-3	1097	Willshaw (Season 1937-38 Final, 1st leg)
F2	12 Oct	READING		1-0	1-0	718	Brain (Season 1937-38 Final, 2nd leg)
2R	16 Nov	CARDIFF CITY		6-0	2-0	670	Mardon(2), M.Morgan(2), Gallacher, C.Morgan
3R	22 Mar	TORQUAY UNITED		0-1	0-0	200	

Additional player: P.Clarke 2/3rd round.

GLOUCESTERSHIRE CUP FINAL

	Date	Opposition	Res.	H.T.	Att.	Goalscorers
	21 Sep	BRISTOL ROVERS	3-0	3-0	2465	Clayton(2), Gallacher

BATH CORONATION CUP FINAL

	Date	Opposition	Res.	H.T.	Att.	Goalscorers
	1 May	Swindon Town	2-0	1-0	806	Booth, Willshaw (at Twerton Park, Bath)

FOOTBALL LEAGUE JUBILEE MATCH

	Date	Opposition	Res.	H.T.	Att.	Goalscorers
	20 Aug	BRISTOL ROVERS	1-3	0-2	8259	Willshaw

FRIENDLY

	Date	Opposition	Res.	H.T.	Att.	Goalscorers
1	3 May	BRISTOL ROVERS	6-3	2-2	993	Gallacher(4), C.Williams(2) *

* Bristol Rugby Football Club's Jubilee Fund

FINAL LEAGUE TABLE

1	Newport	42	22	11	9	58	45	55
2	Crystal Palace	42	20	12	10	71	52	52
3	Brighton	42	19	11	12	68	49	49
4	Watford	42	17	12	13	62	51	46
5	Reading	42	16	14	12	69	59	46
6	QPR	42	15	14	13	68	49	44
7	Ipswich	42	16	12	14	62	52	44
8	Bristol C.	42	16	12	14	61	63	44
9	Swindon	42	18	8	16	72	77	44
10	Aldershot	42	16	12	14	53	66	44
11	Notts Co.	42	17	9	16	59	54	43
12	Southend	42	16	9	17	61	64	41
13	Cardiff	42	15	11	16	61	65	41
14	Exeter	42	13	14	15	65	82	40
15	Bournemouth	42	13	13	16	52	58	39
16	Mansfield	42	12	15	15	44	62	39
17	Northampton	42	15	8	19	51	58	38
18	Port Vale	42	14	9	19	52	58	37
19	Torquay	42	14	9	19	54	70	37
20	Clapton Orient	42	11	13	18	53	55	35
21	Walsall	42	11	11	20	68	69	33
22	Bristol R.	42	10	13	19	55	61	33

(Standing) G.Jenkins(Chair.), Morgan, Mellors(Trainer), Brain, Peters, Dawson, Armstrong, Brook. (Sitting) Bourton, Bridge, Booth, Hick, Rowles. (Front) Pearce

'Spot' in the 'Pink 'Un' on August 20th, depicts the players in Victorian kit.

SEASON 1939-40
FOOTBALL LEAGUE DIV. THREE (SOUTH)

No.	Date	Opposition	Pos.	Res.	H.T.	Att.	Goalscorers
1	26 Aug	Aldershot		1-0	0-0	6000	Turner
2	30	NORWICH CITY		1-2	0-1	11544	Bourton
3	2 Sep	BRIGHTON & HOVE ALB.	9	3-3	2-3	7694	Armstrong, Curran, Gallacher

Competition abandoned due to outbreak of World War II.

	P.	W.	D.	L.	F.	A.
Home	2	0	1	1	4	5
Away	1	1	0	0	1	0

REGIONAL LEAGUE SOUTH WEST DIVISION

No.	Date	Opposition	Pos.	Res.	H.T.	Att.	Goalscorers
1	21 Oct	CARDIFF CITY		1-1	1-0	6545	C.Williams
2	28	Plymouth Argyle	7	0-6	0-1	3635	
3	4 Nov	SWINDON TOWN	8	2-6	1-1	2787	Dix, Vidler
4	11	BRISTOL ROVERS	8	0-3	0-1	2817	
5	25	Torquay United	8	3-3	0-1	600	Dix(pen), Milsom, C.Williams
6	2 Dec	SWANSEA TOWN	7	3-1	2-1	2022	Bourton, Dix, C.Williams
7	9	Cardiff City	8	3-7	2-3	1195	Dix(pen), Milsom, C.Williams
8	16	PLYMOUTH ARGYLE	8	1-0	0-0	1478	Milsom(pen)
9	23	Swindon Town	8	2-7	1-2	2027	Dix, Milsom
10	25	Newport County*	8	1-1		2001	Dix
11	26	NEWPORT COUNTY	8	1-3	0-2	2763	Vidler
12	30	Bristol Rovers	8	2-4	2-2	1966	Bourton, Dix
13	13 Jan	TORQUAY UNITED	8	1-3	0-1	1156	C.Williams
14	3 Feb	Plymouth Argyle	8	3-10	2-5	896	Armstrong(2), Booth
15	10	SWINDON TOWN	8	5-1	2-0	1261	Dix(3), Bourton, Vidler
16	24	NEWPORT COUNTY	8	6-2	2-1	1799	Bourton(3), Armstrong(2),
17	2 Mar	Torquay United	8	0-3	0-2	1200	
18	9	Bristol Rovers**	8	4-4	2-2	2153	Armstrong(2), Booth(2)
19	16	Cardiff City	8	2-3	1-1	4000	Armstrong, Clark
20	22	CARDIFF CITY	8	3-2	2-1	3343	Armstrong, Booth, Bourton
21	23	PLYMOUTH ARGYLE	8	3-4	2-3	2840	Bourton(2), Armstrong
22	25	SWANSEA TOWN	8	2-0	2-0	2719	Bourton, Dix(pen)
23	30	Swindon Town	6	3-1	1-1	3006	Bourton, Morgan(pen), Vidler
24	6 Apr	BRISTOL ROVERS		0-1	0-0	3358	
25	4 May	Newport County		1-4	0-3	2000	Booth
26	13	Swansea Town		2-6		3000	C.Williams, S.Williams
27	18	TORQUAY UNITED		2-2	1-2	2000	Bourton(2)
28	8 Jun	Swansea Town	8	1-4		300	C.Williams

	P.	W.	D.	L.	F.	A.
Home	14	6	2	6	30	29
Away	14	1	3	10	27	63	(Final - Eight)

* Played at Rodney Parade
** Played at the Aero Engines Ground

WAR LEAGUE CUP

	Date	Opposition	Res.	H.T.	Att.	Goalscorers
P	13 Apr	Bournemouth & Bos. Ath.	1-5	1-1	5000	Bourton

FOOTBALL LEAGUE JUBILEE MATCH

	Date	Opposition	Res.	H.T.	Att.	
	19 Aug	Bristol Rovers	0-4	0-2	5393	(£291.4.5)

FRIENDLIES

No.	Date	Opposition	Res.	H.T.	Att.	Goalscorers
1	16 Sep	Bristol Rovers	2-3	1-2	1775	Curran, Spiring
2	23	Plymouth Argyle	1-7	0-3	3000	C.Williams
3	30	PLYMOUTH ARGYLE	1-5	1-3	2210	O.G.
4	7 Oct	BRISTOL ROVERS	5-5	1-4	1409	Milsom(3), Bourton, C.Williams
5	14	Portsmouth	1-5	0-3	2088	Curran
6	18 Nov	NOTTINGHAM FOREST	3-9	1-4	1362	Milsom(2), Vilder
7	27 Apr	Swindon Town	2-5	1-2	1000	Armstrong, Bourton

Back: Bridge, Brook, Morgan, Meacock. 3rd Row: Brooks(Groundsman), Vidler, Gallacher, Henderson, Millar, Cunningham, Southway(Asst.Trainer).
2nd Row: Mellors(Trainer), Bob Hewison(Manager), Booth, Armstrong, Brain, Roberts, Clark, Chilcott, A.S.Sperring(Dir.), C.H.Hancock(Sec.).
Front: A.J.Garland(Dir.), J.A.Hooper(Dir.), G.Jenkins(Chair.), Rowles, Spiring, Peters, Bourton, Mardon, Curran, Turner,
A.R.P.Bray(Vice.Chair.), E.V.J.Bence(Dir.), H.J.Dolman(Dir.).
On ground: Caple, Pearson, Watts, Dawson.

SEASON 1940-41
SOUTH REGIONAL LEGUE

Players (column headers, left to right): Maggs P., Roberts D., Preece J.C., Clark D.F., Low N.H., Brinton E.J., Morgan C.I., Bourton C.F.T., Iles A.K., Carr L.L., Whitfield W., King E.T., Mizen R.V., Bentley R.T.F., Williams C.E., O'Mahoney M.T., Tadman G.H., Armstrong R.., Gregg I., Robinson T.W., Paisley R., Gibson C.H., Quick E., Kingston, Warren R.R., Lewis J.W., Shankley R., McPherson A., Roberts E., Lownie G., Mitchell W., Bowers C.H., Cousins K.F., Dix R.W., Prescott J.R., Booth L., Collis R., Goddard R., English J.

No.	Date	Opposition	Pos.	Res.	H.T.	Att.	Goalscorers
1	31 Aug	SWANSEA TOWN		1-1	1-0	2312	Iles
2	7 Sep	Bournemouth & Bos. Ath.		2-5	1-2	2000	Carr, Williams
3	14	WALSALL*		2-0		1886	Clark, Tadman
4	21	Walsall		1-4	1-1	1546	Carr
5	28	Cardiff City	25	2-2	0-1	3500	Quick, Williams
6	5 Oct	CARDIFF CITY	25	1-0	0-0	1582	Lewis(pen)
7	12	Aldershot		1-5	1-4	3500	Carr
8	19	Swansea Town		1-0	0-0	4000	Williams
9	26	ALDERSHOT		6-0	4-0	1780	Bentley(2),Tadman(2), Carr, E.Roberts
10	2 Nov	SWANSEA TOWN		4-1	2-0	520	Carr(2), E.Roberts, Williams
11	9	Swansea Town		1-2	1-2	100	E.Roberts
12	23	CARDIFF CITY	11	4-1	2-1	2500	Williams(2), Dix, E.Roberts
13	30	Cardiff City		1-5	0-0	2000	Prescott
14	7 Dec	SOUTHAMPTON		6-2	5-1	778	E.Roberts(4), Bentley, Gregg
15	14	BOURNEMOUTH & B.A.	11	3-0	1-0	340	Carr, E.Roberts, Williams
16	25	Bournemouth & Bos. Ath.		1-7		600	Bowers
17	28	SOUTHAMPTON		5-0	3-0	823	Bourton(3), Bowers, Dix
18	11 Jan	Cardiff City		2-5	0-3	2000	Bowers, E.Roberts
19	8 Feb	Cardiff City		4-7	1-4	1500	E.Roberts(3), Talbot
20	8 Mar	SWANSEA TOWN**	16	7-1	3-1	753	Bourton(3,2pens),E.Roberts(3),Will'ms

Apps. 17 13 15 16 2 2 17 5 2 14 4 2 18 19 4 4 1 3 5 1 1 3 1 1 2 3 10 1 10 5 3 3 1 2 1 1

Goals 1 6 1 7 3 8 3 1 1 1 16 3 2 1

	P.	W.	D.	L.	F.	A.
Home	10	9	1	0	39	8
Away	10	1	1	8	16	42	(Final - Sixteenth)

Additional South Reg.League players: Southway (18/2), Talbot L. (19/8, 1 goal)

WESTERN REGIONAL LEAGUE

No	Date	Opposition	Pos	Res	HT	Att	Goalscorers
1	15 Mar	Aberaman	1	2-1			Bentley, Williams
2	22	ABERAMAN		2-4		984	Jones, E.Roberts
3	29	Lovells Athletic		2-7			Bourton, Bowers
4	5 Apr	LOVELLS ATHLETIC		2-2	2-0	369	Clark, Williams
5	14	Bath City		1-2			Bourton
6	19	Cardiff Corinthians	4	2-0			Bowers, Williams
7	26	CARDIFF CORINTHIANS		7-1		356	Bour'n(2),Carr(2),Ben'y,Bowers,Will'ms
8	24 May	Bath City		3-2	1-1		Bowers, Carr, Williams

Additional West. Reg.Lge. players: Fitz D.(1/2,3/3), Roberts J.H.(1/4,4/5), Mills (1/10), Jones E.G.(2/2), Anthony (4/7), Smith (5/2), Carnwell (8/5)

WAR LEAGUE CUP

	Date	Opposition		Res	HT	Att	Goalscorers
1/1L	15 Feb	Reading		2-3	0-1	3385	E.Roberts, Williams (£195.4.5)
1/2L	22	READING		1-2	0-0	3175	E.Roberts (£187.9.10)

WESTERN REGIONAL LEAGUE CUP FINAL

	Date	Opposition		Res	HT	Att	Goalscorers
	17 May	Bath City		4-0	1-0	2476	Morgan(2 pens), Bowers, Clark

Additional Reg. League Cup Final player: Carnwell (5)

FRIENDLIES

1	21 Dec	R.A.F. XI		4-1	2-0	357	Dix(3,1pen), Williams
2	3 May	RAY WARREN'S ARMY XI		3-3	2-2		Bowers(2), Williams
3	10	R.A.F. XI		4-1			Bourton(3), Unknown (At Barnstaple)

* Only 32 minutes played due to air raid warning. Result allowed to stand.

** This result also counted in the Western Regional League, until Swansea Town resigned from this competition on March 20th.

SEASON 1941-42

SOUTH REGIONAL LEAGUE

No.	Date	Opposition	Pos.	Res.	H.T.	Att.	Goalscorers
1	30 Aug	WOLVERHAMPTON W.		4-2	1-0	5964	Tadman(2), Carr, E.Roberts
2	6 Sep	Wolverhampton W.	1	2-1	2-0	6892	Bentley, E.Roberts
3	13	Bournemouth & Bos. Ath.		1-2	0-2	2000	E.Roberts
4	20	BOURNEMOUTH & B.A..	3	2-1	2-1	2943	Bentley, E.Roberts
5	27	SWANSEA TOWN	2	6-3	3-1	2904	Tadman(3), E.Roberts(2), Carr(pen)
6	4 Oct	Swansea Town	1	2-1	0-1	1500	Carr, C.Williams
7	11	SWANSEA TOWN	1	8-1	5-1	1632	Tadman(4),E.Roberts(2), Bentley, Carr
8	8 Nov	Northampton Town	3	2-5	2-1	2000	Carr, Mitchell
9	15	NORTHAMPTON TOWN	2	5-1	3-1	2744	Tadman(4), E.Roberts
10	22	Walsall	4	0-5	0-2	2000	
11	29	WALSALL	3	4-2	2-1	2547	Tadman(2), E.Roberts, Warren
12	6 Dec	Cardiff City	4	2-8	2-4	3000	Bourton, O.G.
13	13	CARDIFF CITY		2-6	1-3	3022	E.Roberts, Tadman
14	20	SOUTHAMPTON		4-2	3-1	2500	Tadman(3), Carr
15	25	Southampton	6	2-5		2250	Gallagher, Bourton

No.	Maggs P.	Brown W.H.	Preece J.C.	Clark D.F.	Roberts D.	Mitchell W.	Bentley R.T.F.	Tadman G.H.	Roberts E.	Carr L.L.	Perry C.	Cousins K.F.	Morgan C.I.	Bourton C.F.T.	Fairhurst W.G.	Bowers C.H.	Williams C.E.	Brinton E.J.	Hall	Warren R.R.	Arnold J.	Rogers A.	Charles R.	Fisher K.W.	Messom G.	Aldersea	McNess	Gallagher	Perrett R.F.	Chaney L.	Waterman	Bedford J.E.	Williams G.E.	Mills M.	Rew R.W.	Pickwick	Dumble H.E.	Britton H.	Hesford
1	1	2	3	4	5	6	7	8	9	10	11																												
2		2	3	8	5	6	7		9	11		1	4	10																									
3			3	4	2	6	7		9	11			5	10	1	8																							
4			3	4	2	6	7	9	8	10			5		1		11																						
5	1		3	4	2		7	9	8	11			5					6	10																				
6			3	8	2	4	7			10		1	5	9			11	6																					
7			3	5	2	4	7	9	8	11		1		10				6																					
8			3		2	4	7	9		11		1	5	10			8	6																					
9			3	6	2		8	9	10			1	5	11		7				4																			
10			3		2	4		9	8			1	5			10		6			7	11																	
11			3		2	4	7	9	8			1	5	11				6		10																			
12			3	8	2	4	7	9				1	5	11		10		6																					
13			3		2	4	7	9	8			1	5	10			11	6																					
14	1	2	3	8	5		7	9	10	11			4					6																					
15			3											9									1	2	4	5	6	7	8	10	11								
Apps.	3	3	15	10	14	11	13	11	11	9	1	9	12	10	2	4	4	9	1	2	1	1	1	1	1	1	1	1	1	1	1								
Goals						1	3	19	11	6				2			1			1								1											

	P.	W.	D.	L.	F.	A.	
Home	8	7	0	1	35	18	
Away	7	2	0	5	11	27	(Final - Sixth)

WAR LEAGUE CUP QUALIFYING COMPETITION (Seventh)

No.	Date	Opposition	Pos.	Res.	H.T.	Att.	Goalscorers
1	27 Dec	SWANSEA TOWN		1-1	1-0	2210	Tadman
2	3 Jan	Swansea Town		3-1	1-1	4500	Tadman(2), Bentley
3	10	BOURNEMOUTH & B.A.		5-0	2-0	2753	Bentley(2), Tadman(2), Mills
4	17	Bournemouth & B.A.	5	2-2	1-2	1500	Bentley(pen), Dumble
5	24	CARDIFF CITY	2	8-3	5-0	3312	Tadman(5), Bentley, Carr, E.Roberts
6	31	Cardiff City	1	2-0	1-0	6000	Bentley(2)
7	7 Feb	Swansea City	2	1-2	0-2	5000	Bentley
8	14	SWANSEA TOWN		1-1	0-1	3857	Tadman
9	21 Mar	SOUTHAMPTON		5-1	3-1	3402	Tadman(2), Bentley, Carr, Garrett
10	28	Southampton	7	1-5	0-4	3000	Garrett

No.	Maggs P.	Brown W.H.	Preece J.C.	Clark D.F.	Roberts D.	Mitchell W.	Bentley R.T.F.	Tadman G.H.	Roberts E.	Carr L.L.	Perry C.	Cousins K.F.	Morgan C.I.	Bourton C.F.T.	Fairhurst W.G.	Bowers C.H.	Williams C.E.	Brinton E.J.	Hall	Warren R.R.	Arnold J.	Rogers A.	Charles R.	Fisher K.W.	Messom G.	Aldersea	McNess	Gallagher	Perrett R.F.	Chaney L.	Waterman	Bedford J.E.	Williams G.E.	Mills M.	Rew R.W.	Pickwick	Dumble H.E.	Britton H.	Hesford
1	1		3	4	2		7	9	8	10			5	11				6																					
2			3		2		8	9		10				5		7		6														1	4	11					
3			3	4	2		8	9		10			6	5		7																1		11					
4			3	5	2		9		10							7																1		6	4	8	11		
5			3	5	2		7	9	8	10				11		4		6														1							
6			3	5	2		7	9		10				8		6		4														1					11		
7			3	5	2		7	9					4	10		6																1						8	11
8			3	5	2		7	9	8	10			4			6		11														1							
9			3	5		4	7	9		10			2			11		6														1							
10			3	5		4	8			10			2			11		6														1							

Additional players in Lge.Cup Qual. Comp.: Garrett A. (9/8, 10/9), Harris T. (10/7)

LEAGUE CHAMPIONSHIP (Twenty-seventh) *

No.	Date	Opposition	Pos.	Res.	H.T.	Att.	Goalscorers
1	7 Mar	LUTON TOWN		2-3	2-1	2519	Garrett, Tadman
2	14	SWANSEA TOWN		10-0	4-0	1872	Tadman(4),Gar'tt(3),Bentley,Brin'n,Carr
3	11 Apr	LUTON TOWN		7-0	5-0	2887	Bentley(2),Gar'tt(2),Tadman(2),Bowers
4	23 May	Leicester City		1-5	0-3	2000	Bentley
5	30	LEICESTER CITY	27	3-1	2-1	1800	Bowers, Garrett, Tadman

No.	Maggs P.	Brown W.H.	Preece J.C.	Clark D.F.	Roberts D.	Mitchell W.	Bentley R.T.F.	Tadman G.H.	Roberts E.	Carr L.L.	Perry C.	Cousins K.F.	Morgan C.I.	Bourton C.F.T.	Fairhurst W.G.	Bowers C.H.	Williams C.E.	Brinton E.J.	Hall	Warren R.R.	Arnold J.	Rogers A.	Charles R.	Fisher K.W.	Messom G.	Aldersea	McNess	Gallagher	Perrett R.F.	Chaney L.	Waterman	Bedford J.E.	Williams G.E.	Mills M.	Rew R.W.	Pickwick	Dumble H.E.	Britton H.	Hesford
1			3	5	2	4	7	9		11			6																			1							
2			3	5		4	7	9		10			2				11	6														1							
3		2	3			4	8	9					5			7		6														1							
4			3	8	5	6	7						2			4					9																		
5			3	2	5	4	8	9								7				6																			

Additonal Lge. Championship players: Garrett A. (1/8, 2/8, 3/10, 5/10), Painter E.G. (1/10), Jeffries J.T. (3/11), Graham D.R. (4/1), Billington F. (4/10), Hargreaves J. (4/11, 5/11), Mardon W.J. (5/1)

WAR LEAGUE CUP COMPETITION PROPER

No.	Date	Opposition	Pos.	Res.	H.T.	Att.	Goalscorers
1/1L	4 Apr	Northampton Town		0-3	0-2	5000	(£271)
1/2L	6	NORTHAMPTON TOWN		3-1	2-0	7448	Duns(2), Tadman (£390.8.0)

No.	Maggs P.	Brown W.H.	Preece J.C.	Clark D.F.	Roberts D.	Mitchell W.	Bentley R.T.F.	Tadman G.H.	Roberts E.	Carr L.L.	Perry C.	Cousins K.F.	Morgan C.I.	Bourton C.F.T.	Fairhurst W.G.	Bowers C.H.	Williams C.E.	Brinton E.J.	Hall	Warren R.R.	Arnold J.	Rogers A.	Charles R.	Fisher K.W.	Messom G.	Aldersea	McNess	Gallagher	Perrett R.F.	Chaney L.	Waterman	Bedford J.E.	Williams G.E.	Mills M.	Rew R.W.	Pickwick	Dumble H.E.	Britton H.	Hesford
1/1L			3	5		4	7	9		10			2			11		6														1							
1/2L		2	3	5		4	7	9					6																			1							

* The final League Championship table included all the matches played in the League Cup, as well as the Championship.

Additonal War Lge.Cup Comp.Proper players: Garrett A. (1/8, 2/8), Billingtom F. (2/10), Duns L. (2/11)

FRIENDLIES

No.	Date	Opposition	Pos.	Res.	H.T.	Att.	Goalscorers
1	18 Oct	Army XI		2-1	2-1	1500	Bourton, Carr (At Warminster)
2	25	ARMY XI		6-1	3-1	1506	Rogers(3), Carr(2), Bourton
3	1 Nov	R.A.F. XI (home)		9-2	3-2	858	Bentley(3,2pens),E.Roberts(3), Tadman(2), Rogers
4	21 Feb	R.A.F. XI		1-6	1-3	888	Carr (At Weston-super-Mare)
5	28	R.A.F. XI		2-2	2-2		Dumble, Harris (At Chippenham)
6	25 May	FOOTBALL LEAGUE XI		1-2	1-1	907	Tadman
7	6 Jun	FOOTBALL LEAGUE XI		3-8	1-3	1036	Warren(2), Bentley

SEASON 1942-43
WEST REGIONAL LEAGUE

Player columns (left to right): Mardon W.J. · Fitz D. · Preece J.C. · Clark D.F. · Roberts D. · Brinton E.J. · Bentley R.T.F. · Garrett A. · Bourton C.F.T. · Chilcott K. · Hargreaves J · Mitchell W. · Bowers C.H. · Tadman G.H. · Roberts E. · Morgan C.I. · Benjamin J. · Kelso J.P. · Davis · Williams C.E. · Maggs P. · Hayward D.S. · Beckett H · Warren R.R. · Mardon H.J. · Lambert C. · Ford V. · Scott W.J. · Fox D. · Carney S. · Bradshaw G.F. · Dumble H.E. · Hobbs H.H.F. · McLaren A. · Butterworth A.G. · Newman · Miller A. · Moore J.F.B. · McDonald J.C.

No.	Date	Opposition	Pos.	Res.	H.T.	Att.	Goalscorers
1	29 Aug	Swansea Town		2-2	1-0	5000	Chicott, Hargreaves
2	5 Sep	SWANSEA TOWN		6-1	3-1	1700	Tadman(4), Hargreaves, Bentley
3	12	CARDIFF CITY		9-1	4-0	2743	Harg'ves(4),Bo'n(2),E.Rob's(2),Bentley
4	19	Cardiff City		0-0	0-0	2500	
5	26	ABERAMAN	2	7-1	3-1	2376	Bentley(3), Tadman(3), Hargeaves
6	3 Oct	Aberaman	1	6-2	2-0	1200	Bentley(2),Tad'n(2),Benjamin,Harg'ves
7	10	LOVELLS ATHLETIC	2	2-3	1-0	3264	Bentley, E.Roberts
8	17	Lovells Athletic	3	1-3	1-2	3000	E.Roberts
9	24	BATH CITY		2-3	1-0	2208	Harvreaves, Tadman
10	31	Bath City		2-5	0-1	3720	Bentley (2 pens)
11	7 Nov	Aberaman	4	5-2	2-0	500	E.Roberts(2), Tadman(2), Bentley
12	21	Swansea Town	4	1-3	1-2	1000	Hargreaves
13	28	SWANSEA TOWN	4	4-0	2-0	1512	Clark(2), Tadman(2)
14	5 Dec	Cardiff City	4	3-4	1-2	3000	Bourton, Clark, Warren
15	12	CARDIFF CITY	4	5-0	3-0	1800	Hayward(2), Tadman(2), E.Roberts
16	19	LOVELLS ATHLETIC	4	2-2	0-2	1500	E.Roberts (2 pens)
17	25	Bath City	4	2-5		4762	Mardon, Tadman

Apps. — Mardon W.J. 10, Fitz 5, Preece 15, Clark 14, Roberts D. 17, Brinton 13, Bentley 11, Garrett 1, Bourton 11, Chilcott 1, Hargreaves 14, Mitchell 14, Bowers 2, Tadman 15, Roberts E. 12, Morgan 11, Benjamin 3, Kelso 1, Davis 1, Williams 1, Maggs 7, Hayward 3, Beckett 1, Warren 3, Mardon H.J. 1

Goals — Clark 3, Bentley 11, Bourton 3, Chilcott 1, Hargreaves 10, Tadman 17, Roberts E. 9, Benjamin 1, Hayward 2, Warren 1, Mardon H.J. 1

	P.	W.	D.	L.	F.	A.	
Home	8	5	1	2	37	11	
Away	9	2	2	5	22	26	(Final - Fourth)

WAR LEAGUE CUP NORTH QUALIFYING COMPETITION (Seventeenth) *

No.	Date	Opposition	Pos.	Res.	H.T.	Att.	Goalscorers
1	26 Dec	BATH CITY		4-2	2-1	6576	Tadman(2), Beckett, Clark
2	2 Jan	Lovells Athletic		0-8	0-5	2000	
3	9	SWANSEA TOWN	18	3-0	2-0	2042	Tadman(2), Hargreaves
4	16	Swansea Town	14	4-3	2-3	1500	Tadman(2), Bourton(pen), Dumble
5	23	ABERAMAN		8-1	3-1	2890	Bourton(3), E.Roberts(3),
6	30	Aberaman		1-2	1-2	300	Bentley
7	6 Feb	Cardiff City		3-0	2-0	3000	Hargreaves, E.Roberts, O.G.
8	13	CARDIFF CITY		1-1	1-1	3000	C.Williams
9	20	Bath City		1-3	1-1	4500	Bentley
10	27	LOVELLS ATHLETIC	17	1-1	0-1	5673	Bourton

WAR LEAGUE CUP NORTH COMPETITION PROPER

No.	Date	Opposition	Pos.	Res.	H.T.	Att.	Goalscorers
1/1L	6 Mar	Aberaman		3-1	2-1	2500	E.Roberts(2), Morre
1/2L	13	ABERAMAN		1-2	0-0	5047	Bourton (ex-time played, 0-2 at 90min)
2/1L	20	Bath City		2-2	2-1	9085	Bentley (2) (£540)
2/2L	27	BATH CITY		2-1	0-0	14236	Hayward, Moore (£803)
3/1L	3 Apr	ASTON VILLA		0-0	0-0	24649	(£1,606.7.1)
3/2L	10	Aston Villa		1-2	1-1	28000	Bourton (£2,440)

Additional players Cup Comp. proper players: Mather H.(2/6, 3/6), Hyslop A (4/2,5/2,6/2).

WEST REGIONAL LEAGUE CUP

No.	Date	Opposition	Pos.	Res.	H.T.	Att.	Goalscorers
1	17 Apr	Swansea Town		1-1	1-1	3500	R.Williams
2	24	BATH CITY		3-3	0-1	3779	Chilcott(2), R.Williams (£214)

Additional Reg. League Cup players: Hyslop A.(1/2,2/2), Artus K.G.(1/9,2/9), Williams R.B.(1/10,2/10), Jefferies J.T.(2/11)

NORTH LEAGUE (SECOND CHAMPIONSHIP)**

No.	Date	Opposition	Pos.	Res.	H.T.	Att.	Goalscorers
1	1 May	CARDIFF CITY	16	3-0	1-0	2500	Buchan, Hargreaves, McLaren

Additional Second Championship players: Southcombe(1/4), Buchan W.(1/8)

* Top 32 qualified for the Competition Proper.

** Final record in the North League (Second Championship) included results from all competitions played from and including December 26th.

FRIENDLY

No.	Date	Opposition	Res.	H.T.	Goalscorers
1	15 May	Bath City ***	1-5	1-3	Bourton

*** 'Wings For Victory' match, played at Corsham.

SEASON 1943-44
WEST REGIONAL LEAGUE

No.	Date	Opposition	Pos.	Res.	H.T.	Att.	Goalscorers
1	28 Aug	Swansea Town		3-1	3-0	2500	Clark(2), Hargreaves
2	4 Sep	SWANSEA TOWN	1	6-0	3-0	3300	Bourton(3), Milton, Morgan(pen), O.G.
3	11	Cardiff City		1-4	0-2	3000	Morgan
4	18	CARDIFF CITY		2-1		3310	Chilcott, Morgan
5	25	LOVELLS ATHLETIC	1	3-2	2-2	4500	Bourton, Carter, Hargreaves
6	2 Oct	Lovells Athletic	1	0-6	0-1	3000	
7	9	BATH CITY	4	2-4	0-2	4425	Hargreaves(2)
8	16	Bath City	4	0-1	0-1	5500	
9	23	ABERAMAN	3	2-1	2-1	2797	Chilcott, Milton
10	30	Aberaman	4	2-2	0-2	800	
11	6 Nov	Cardiff City	5	0-1	0-0	3000	
12	13	CARDIFF CITY	5	1-1	1-1	4000	Bentley
13	20	SWANSEA TOWN		3-2	3-1	3000	Edwards, Hargreaves, Mitchell
14	27	Swansea Town	5	0-3	0-1	1200	
15	4 Dec	Aberaman	5	1-2	1-1	800	Holmes
16	11	ABERAMAN		3-1	3-0	1500	Bourton, Chilcott, Holmes
17	18	Bath City	5	2-3	1-1	3000	Bourton, Mitchell
18	25	BATH CITY	5	3-1	1-1	3390	Bentley, Holmes, Morgan(pen

	P.	W.	D.	L.	F.	A.	
Home	9	7	1	1	25	13	
Away	9	1	0	8	7	23	(Final - Fifth)

WAR LEAGUE CUP NORTH QUALIFYING COMPETITION (Twenty-first) *

No.	Date	Opposition	Pos.	Res.	H.T.	Att.	Goalscorers
1	27 Dec	Swansea Town		1-1	0-0	5000	Morgan
2	1 Jan	SWANSEA TOWN		2-1	2-0	3316	Hargreaves, Norcott
3	8	Lovells Athletic		3-3	3-1	3000	Chilcott, Hargreaves, Jennings
4	15	LOVELLS ATHLETIC	12	1-0	1-0	6000	Holmes
5	22	Bath City		0-3	0-1	3500	
6	29	BATH CITY		2-2	0-1	5000	Hargreaves, E.Roberts
7	5 Feb	Cardiff City	31	0-2	0-1	5000	
8	12	CARDIFF CITY	27	2-0	1-0	4000	Hargreaves, E.Roberts
9	19	ABERAMAN		2-0	1-0	3000	Hargreaves, Norcott
10	26	Aberaman	21	4-4	2-3	400	Chilcott(2), Clark, Garrett

* Top 32 qualified for the Competition Proper.
Additional League Cup Qual. Comp. players: McPhee J.(7/3), Rich L.(7/8, 8/8), Stuart R.W.(8/3), Artus K.G.(8/7), Garrett A.(10/10)

WAR LEAGUE CUP NORTH COMPETITION PROPER

No.	Date	Opposition	Res.	H.T.	Att.	Goalscorers
1/1L	4 Mar	Bath City	1-2	0-2	10000	Brinton(pen)
1/2L	11	BATH CITY	1-2	0-1	10444	D.Roberts

Additional League Cup Proper platers: Stuart R.W.(1/2, 2/3), Armstrong R.J.(2/9)

NORTH LEAGUE (SECOND CHAMPIONSHIP) (Thirty-eighth)

No.	Date	Opposition	Pos.	Res.	H.T.	Att.	Goalscorers
1	18 Mar	Swansea Town		4-5	3-2	3000	Collins(2), Dumble, Mitchell
2	25	SWANSEA TOWN		3-3		2408	Bentley, Brinton, Mitchell
3	1 Apr	Cardiff City		2-6	1-2	1000	Clark, Thomas
4	8	CARDIFF CITY		1-2	0-1	2000	Thomas
5	10	ABERAMAN		5-0	3-0	2476	Hargreaves(2), Thomas(2), Clark
6	15	Aberaman		1-3	0-3	2000	Hargreaves
7	22	LOVELLS ATHLETIC		2-1	1-1	2376	Clark, Thomas
8	29	Lovells Athletic	38	1-2	0-2	1200	Collins

* Final record in the North League (Second Championship) includes results from all the competitions played from and including December 27th.
Additional Second Champ. players: Green A.C. (1/1), Collis R.(1/3,5/3,8/6), Britton H.(1/8), Collins R.D. (1/9,2/9,4/9,6/8,7/8,8/8),
Thomas W.(All games at '10'), Dumble H.E.(1/11,2/11), Dawson E.(2/1), Bishop G.T.(5/8), Phillips R.(6/7), Jones (6/9), Cochrane W.(8/7), Haydon T.J.(8/9)

FRIENDLY

No.	Date	Opposition	Res.	Goalscorers
1	20 May	Bath City	1-5	Unknown(at Peasedown in aid of local comforts)

SEASON 1944-45
WEST REGIONAL LEAGUE

Player columns (left to right): Ferguson A., Preece J.C., McPhee J., Mitchell W., Roberts D., Brinton E.J., Collins R.D., Stock A.W.A., Owen W., Thomas W.G., Hargreaves J., Reilly L.H., Clark D.F., Chilcott K., Morgan C.I., Williams C.E., Guy I., Bentley R.F.T., Fox G.R., Scrimshaw, Hayward D.S., Bailey E.J., Fitz O., Nutt I., Jenkins C.

No.	Date	Opposition	Pos.	Res.	H.T.	Att.	Goalscorers
1	26 Aug	Cardiff City		1-4	0-3	6600	Hargreaves
2	2 Sep	CARDIFF CITY	3	3-0	0-0	3930	Thomas(2), Collins
3	9	ABERAMAN		5-2	4-2	3800	Chilcott(2), Collins, Hargreaves, Thomas
4	16	Aberaman		4-0	2-0	400	Owen(2), Collins, Thomas
5	23	LOVELLS ATHLETIC		1-3	1-2	6000	Clark
6	30	Lovells Athletic		0-2	0-1	4000	
7	7 Oct	SWANSEA TOWN	4	6-1	4-1	3400	Collins(2), Hargreaves(2), Owen, Williams
8	14	Swansea Town		2-0	2-0	5000	Morgan, Thomas
9	21	BATH CITY		2-0	2-0	7455	Hargreaves, Thomas
10	28	Bath City		2-2	2-2	5000	Clark, Hargreaves
11	4 Nov	SWANSEA TOWN		4-2	2-2	3801	Hargreaves(2,1pen), Clark, Thomas
12	11	Swansea Town		4-3	3-1	3000	Bentley, Morgan, Owen, Thomas
13	18	Aberaman	1	5-1	4-1	500	Collins(2), Clark, Owen, O.G.
14	25	ABERAMAN	1	4-2	0-0	4448	Clark(2), Chilcott, Owen
15	2 Dec	Lovells Athletic		2-3	2-3	4000	Owen(2)
16	9	LOVELLS ATHLETIC		5-1	3-1	5792	Hargreaves(2), Morgan, Owen, Thomas
17	16	Bath City		5-1	1-1	6000	Hargreaves(3), Clark, Thomas
18	23	BATH CITY	2	4-3	2-1	6171	Clark(2), Hargreaves, Owen

Apps: Ferguson 18, Preece 16, McPhee 1, Mitchell 7, Roberts 18, Brinton 13, Collins 17, Stock 1, Owen 17, Thomas 17, Hargreaves 16, Reilly 4, Clark 14, Chilcott 11, Morgan 14, Williams 1, Guy 11, Bentley 1, Fox 1

Goals: Collins 7, Owen 10, Thomas 10, Hargreaves 14, Clark 9, Chilcott 3, Morgan 3, Williams 1, Bentley 1

	P	W	D	L	F	A	
Home	9	8	0	1	34	14	
Away	9	5	1	3	25	16	(Final - Runners-up)

WAR LEAGUE CUP NORTH QUALIFYING COMPETITION (Third)

No.	Date	Opposition	Pos.	Res.	H.T.	Att.	Goalscorers
1	25 Dec	BATH CITY		2-1	0-0	4141	Thomas(2)
2	30	Bath City		2-0	0-0	4000	Clark, Owen
3	6 Jan	Swansea Town	4	2-1	0-1	3500	Clark, Morgan
4	13	SWANSEA TOWN	2	3-1	1-0	4752	Collins(2), Clark
5	20	ABERAMAN	1	10-0	4-0	3778	Clark(4), Collins(2), Thomas(2), Bentley, Hargreaves
6	3 Feb	LOVELLS ATHLETIC		2-1	1-1	7755	Hargreaves, Owen
7	10	Lovells Athletic		1-2	1-2	5000	Thomas
8	17	Cardiff City		2-4	2-2	11500	Clark(2) (£913)
9	24	CARDIFF CITY		1-0	0-0	11657	Thomas
10	3 Mar	Aberaman	3	2-0	1-0	500	Clark, Thomas

NORTH LEAGUE (SECOND CHAMPIONSHIP) (Eleventh) **

No.	Date	Opposition	Pos.	Res.	H.T.	Att.	Goalscorers
1	10 Mar	BATH CITY		4-1	2-0	6210	Thomas(2), Chilcott, Clark
2	17	Bath City		0-1	0-0	3000	
3	2 Apr	Cardiff City		2-3	0-1	14000	Clark(2)
4	21	ABERAMAN		2-1	2-1	3547	Clark(2)
5	5 May	SWANSEA TOWN	11	4-2	1-1	1456	Hargreaves(2), Chilcott, Clark

WAR LEAGUE CUP NORTH COMPETITION PROPER

No.	Date	Opposition	Res.	H.T.	Att.	Goalscorers
1/1L	24 Mar	WEST BROMWICH ALBION	5-2	1-0	21371	Clark(3), Collins, Hargreaves (£1,645.17.2)
1/2L	31	West Bromwich Albion	3-3	2-2	18306	Clark(2), Brinton (£1,416)
2/1L	7 Apr	CARDIFF CITY	1-2	1-0	20714	Morgan (£1,599)
2/2L	14	Cardiff City#	2-2	1-1	23161	Hargreaves, Thomas (a.e.t., 2-1 at end 90 mins)

WAR LEAGUE CUP WEST

No.	Date	Opposition	Res.	H.T.	Att.	Goalscorers
	28 Apr	Swansea Town	2-2	1-1	4000	Hargreaves, Thomas
	12 May	PLYMOUTH ARGYLE	3-1	1-1	4484	Thomas(3)
F/1L	19	Bath City	0-1	0-1	5000	
F/2L	26	BATH CITY	3-4		6400	Hargreaves, Thomas, Williams

GLOUCESTERSHIRE CUP FINAL

Date	Opposition	Res.	H.T.	Att.	Goalscorers
26 Dec	Bristol Rovers	5-0	1-0	9048	Clark(4), Owen (£800.16.3)

* Top 32 qualified for the Competition Proper.

** Final record in the North League (Second Championship) included results from all competitions, except the Gloucestershire Cup Final and the War League Cup West match v. Plymouth Argyle, played from December 25th to May 26th (inclusive). For League purposes the 2-1 score at the end of normal-time in the game with Cardiff City on April 14th was used.

\# 3 hours 22 minutes played (before result of two-legged tie was decided).

SEASON 1945-46
DIVISION THREE SOUTH (SOUTH REGION)

Player columns (left to right): Fairhurst W. | Guy I. | Bailey E.J. | Morgan C.I. | Roberts D. | Preece J.C. | Chilcott K. | Hayward D. | Clark D.F. | Thomas W.G. | Hargreaves J. | Bentley R.F.T. | Williams C.E. | Edcolls J.D. | Silcocks L. | Curran F. | Colins R.D. | Brinton E.J. | Dymond W.H. | Gadsby K.J. | Artus K.G. | Hancock G. | Cousins K.F. | Booth L. | Howarth S. | Spring G. | Carter J. | Lovering W. | Ashton E. | Jones E.G.

No.	Date	Opposition	Pos.	Res.	H.T	Att.	Goalscorers	Fairhurst W.	Guy I.	Bailey E.J.	Morgan C.I.	Roberts D.	Preece J.C.	Chilcott K.	Hayward D.	Clark D.F.	Thomas W.G.	Hargreaves J.	Bentley R.F.T.	Williams C.E.	Edcolls J.D.	Silcocks L.	Curran F.	Colins R.D.	Brinton E.J.	Dymond W.H.	Gadsby K.J.	Artus K.G.	Hancock G.	Cousins K.F.	Booth L.	Howarth S.	Spring G.	Carter J.	Lovering W.	Ashton E.	Jones E.G.
1	25 Aug	Bristol Rovers		3-0	1-0	14906	Hayward(2), Hargreaves(pen)	1	2	3	4	5	6	7	8	9	10	11																			
2	1 Sep	BRISTOL ROVERS	1	3-0	1-0	10609	Clark(2), Bentley	1	2	3	4	5	6		8	9		11	7	10																	
3	5	BRIGHTON & HOVE ALB.	1	3-1	1-0	7793	Clark(2,1pen), Thomas		2	3	4	5	6		8	9	10	11	7		1																
4	8	CRYSTAL PALACE		1-2	0-2	13660	Bentley		2	3	4	5	6		8	9	10	11	7			1															
5	12	Reading		2-6	2-2	4172	Curran(2)		2	3	4	5	6			9		11	7	10		1	8														
6	15	Crystal Palace		1-0	1-0	12000	Collins			3	4	5	2			6		11	9	10		1	8	7													
7	19	Brighton & Hove Albion		3-4	0-2	2787	Clark, Curran, D.Roberts			3	4	5	2			9		11		10		1	8	7	6												
8	22	Bournemouth & B. A.		1-8	1-3	7000	Curran		2	3	4	5	6	11		9				10		1	8	7													
9	29	BOURNEMOUTH & B. A.		1-1	0-0	11162	Clark(pen)	1	2	3	4	5				9	6			10			8	11		7											
10	6 Oct	CARDIFF CITY		3-2	1-2	18727	Clark(2), Thomas	1	2	3	4	5				9	6			10			8	7		11											
11	13	Cardiff City		4-2	3-1	22621	Clark(pen), Collins, Guy, Williams	1	2	3	4	5			8	9	6			10				7		11											
12	20	Aldershot		1-2	1-0	4000	Williams		2	3		5	4			9	6	11	8	10	1			7													
13	27	ALDERSHOT		3-0	1-0	11172	Curran(2), Chilcott		2	3	4	5		11		9	6			10	1		8	7													
14	3 Nov	TORQUAY UNITED	2	6-2	2-2	9101	Clark(4,2pens), Collins, Curran		2	3	4	5		11		9	6			10	1		8	7													
15	10	Torquay United	2	1-0	1-0	4000	Williams		2	3	4	5		11		9	6			10	1		8	7													
16	1 Dec	Exeter City		0-1	0-0	9000		1	2		4	5		6						8	10			9	11			3	7								
17	25	Swindon Town		3-4	1-3	9470	Chilcott(2), Hargreaves	1		3	4	5	2	8			6	11		10				9	7												
18	26	SWINDON TOWN		4-1	4-0	14364	Bentley, Clark, Hargreaves, Williams		2	3	4	5			7		9	6	11	8	10	1															
19	27	EXETER CITY		5-1	1-0	7481	Clark(3), Collins, O.G.		2		4	5			6		9		11		10	1		8	7					3							
20	29	READING	3	3-3	1-0	12184	Collins, Curran(pen), Hargreaves		2	3	4	5	6	8	10			11						9	7							1					
		Apps.						7	17	18	19	20	11	10	6	17	12	12	8	16	7	5	13	14	1	3		1	1	1		1					
		Goals						1			1			3	2	17	2	4	3	4			8	5													

```
                          P.  W.  D.  L.   F.   A.
Home       10   7   2   1   32  13
Away       10   4   0   6   19  27   (Final - Third)
```

DIVISION THREE SOUTH (SOUTH REGION) CUP QUALIFYING COMPETITION (Sixth) *

No.	Date	Opposition	Pos.	Res.	H.T	Att.	Goalscorers	Fairhurst W.	Guy I.	Bailey E.J.	Morgan C.I.	Roberts D.	Preece J.C.	Chilcott K.	Hayward D.	Clark D.F.	Thomas W.G.	Hargreaves J.	Bentley R.F.T.	Williams C.E.	Edcolls J.D.	Silcocks L.	Curran F.	Colins R.D.	Brinton E.J.	Dymond W.H.	Gadsby K.J.	Artus K.G.	Hancock G.	Cousins K.F.	Booth L.	Howarth S.	Spring G.	Carter J.	Lovering W.	Ashton E.	Jones E.G.
1	12 Jan	Swindon Town		1-1	0-1	10353	Clark(pen) (£789)		2	3	4	5		7		9	6	11		10										1	8						
2	19	SWINDON TOWN		2-1	1-1	8791	Curran(2)		2	3		5		7	8		6	11		10			9							1		4					
3	2 Feb	QUEENS PARK RANGERS		2-0	1-0	10800	Clark(2) (£722)		2	3		5		4	7	9	6	11		10										1			8				
4	9	Exeter City		0-3	0-1	8000			2	3		5				6	11	7	10			9							1			8	4			
5	16	EXETER CITY	3	3-0	3-0	12891	Chilcott, Lovering, Thomas		2	3	4	5		7		6	11	8	10										1						9		
6	23	Torquay United	6	2-4	1-1	4000	Lovering, Thomas		2	3	4	5		7		6		8	10										1				11		9	1	
7	2 Mar	TORQUAY UNITED	3	5-1	4-0	10820	Lovering(2), Williams(2), Bentley		2	3	4	5		7		6	11	8	10										1						9	1	
8	9	CARDIFF CITY	2	3-2	2-0	17375	Chilcott, Hargreaves, Williams(pen)		2	3	4	5		7		9	11	8	10										1		6					1	
9	16	Cardiff City	3	2-3	2-2	19000	Bentley, Hargreaves		2	3	4	5			9	10	11	8		1									1			7					
10	23	Bristol Rovers	4	0-0	0-0	20598			2	3	4	5		7	8	10	11													1							6
11	30	BRISTOL ROVERS		1-2	0-0	18199	Williams (£1,325)		2	3	4	5		7			11	8	10											1							6
12	6 Apr	Crystal Palace		2-1	1-0	15000	Bentley, Hargreaves		2	3	4	5		7			8	11	9	10										1							6
13	13	CRYSTAL PALACE		2-2	1-0	16264	Thomas, Williams	7	2	3	4	5		9			8	11		10					7					1							6
14	19	Queens Park Rangers		2-4	1-0	17500	Chilcott, Hargreaves		2	3	4	5		7	9			11	8	10										1							6
15	20	Bournemouth & B. A.	6	2-3	2-2	12863	Bentley, Clark		2	3	4	5		7	9			11	8	10										1							6
16	22	BOURNEMOUTH & B. A.	6	1-0	0-0	11632	Williams (£807)		2	3	4	5		7		6		11	9	10	1												8				

* Top two teams in each section qualified for the Semi-finals.
Additional Qualifying Cup players: Wedlock D.(9/6), Sutton J.B.(10/9,11/9)

F.A. CUP

	Rd	Date	Opposition	Res.	H.T	Att.	Goalscorers	Fairhurst W.	Guy I.	Bailey E.J.	Morgan C.I.	Roberts D.	Preece J.C.	Chilcott K.	Hayward D.	Clark D.F.	Thomas W.G.	Hargreaves J.	Bentley R.F.T.	Williams C.E.	Edcolls J.D.	Silcocks L.	Curran F.	Colins R.D.	Brinton E.J.	Dymond W.H.	Gadsby K.J.	Artus K.G.	Hancock G.	Cousins K.F.	Booth L.	Howarth S.	Spring G.	Carter J.	Lovering W.	Ashton E.	Jones E.G.
1R1	17 Nov		Yeovil & Petters United	2-2	1-0	7690	Artus, Curran (£654.5.0.)		2	3	4	5		11		9	6			10	1		8				7										
1R2	24		YEOVIL & PETTERS UTD	3-0	1-0	13469	Chilcott(2), Curran (£965)		2	3	4	5		11		9	6		7	10	1		8														
2R1	8 Dec		BRISTOL ROVERS	4-2	3-0	19295	Morgan(2), Clark, Williams (£1,501.12.0)		2	3	4	5		11		9	6		8	10	1					7											
2R2	15		Bristol Rovers	2-0	1-0	21045	Clark, Thomas (£1,842.18.0)		2	3	4	5		7		9	6	11	8	10	1																
3R1	5 Jan		SWANSEA TOWN	5-1	1-0	26551	Clark(3), Bentley, Chilcott (£2,015.12.3.)		2	3	4	5		7		9	6	11	8	10									1								
3R2	10		Swansea Town	2-2	1-0	18400	Chilcott, Williams (£1,450)		2	3	4	5		7		9	6	11		10		8							1								
4R1	26		BRENTFORD	2-1	1-0	35648	Hargreaves, Williams (£2,732.3.3.)		2	3	4	5				9	6	11	8	10		7							1								
4R2	31		Brentford	0-5	0-1	18000	(£1,469)	1	2	3	4	5		7		9	6	11	8	10																	

GLOUCESTERSHIRE CUP FINAL

	Date	Opposition	Res.	H.T	Att.	Goalscorers
	24 Sep	BRISTOL ROVERS	3-1	1-1	7962	Clark, Collins, Curran (£559.11.4.)

BATH CORONATION CUP FINAL (At 'Twerton Park')

	Date	Opposition	Res.	H.T	Att.	Goalscorers
	4 May	Bath City	2-1	1-1	10000	Bentley(2)

BOLTON DISASTER FUND

	Date	Opposition	Res.	H.T	Att.	Goalscorers
	11 May	Bristol Rovers	7-1	1-0	9859	Clark(2),Bentley,Hargrves,Morgn,Thmas,C.Wlliams

FRIENDLIES

	Date	Opposition	Res.	H.T	Att.	Goalscorers
1	22 Dec	Queens Park Rangers	2-1	2-0		Chilcott, Clark
2	27 Apr	Crystal Palace	4-4	2-2	3000	Bentley(2), Thomas, Williams
3	30	Avonmouth/Shirehampton	7-4			Hargreaves(3), Williams(3), Thomas
4	1 Jun	Randers Freja	4-6		5000	Bentley, Hargreaves, Thomas, Williams
5	2	Aalborg Byhold	3-1	3-1	5500	Bentley, Hargreaves, Morgan
6	5	Jutland State XI	2-1	1-0	3000	Bentley, Hargreaves (Played at Aarhus)

The City side in Denmark, 1946, shortly before Roy Bentley was transferred to Newcastle. Back row (left to right): Ernie Jones, Ken Cousins, Ivor Guy, Don Clark, Roy Bentley, Denis Roberts, Lemo Southway. Front row: Cyril Williams, Cliff Morgan, Bill Thomas, Jack Bailey, Jack Hargreaves.

1946-47 Season - F.A. Cup, 1st round side that beat Hayes 9-3.
Back: Thomas, Spiring (reserve), Chilcott, Jones, Ferguson, Roberts, Guy.
Front: Bailey, Clark, Morgan, Cyril Williams, Hargreaves.

SEASON 1946-47
FOOTBALL LEAGUE DIVISION THREE (SOUTH)

No.	Date	Opposition	Pos.	Res.	H.T.	Att.	Goalscorers	Ferguson A.	Guy I.	Bailey E.J.	Morgan C.I.	Roberts D.	Jones E.G.	Dymond W.H.	Thomas W.G.	Clark D.F.	Williams C.E.	Hargreaves J.	Chilcott K.	Oram D.G.	Peacock E.G.	Fox R.V.	Cunningham E.	Eddolls J.D.	Allen R.H.A.	Cousins K.F.	Kearney S.F.	Williams S.F.	Collins R.D.	White A.S.	Clack F.E.
1	31 Aug	Aldershot		3-4	0-1	7000	Clark, Thomas, O.G.	1	2	3	4	5	6	7	8	9	10	11													
2	4 Sep	NORWICH CITY		2-1	0-1	12033	Clark, Hargreaves	1	2	3	4	5	6	7	8	9	10	11													
3	7	BRIGHTON & HOVE ALB.	11	0-0	0-0	21316		1	2	3	4	5	6	7	8	9	10	11													
4	11	Notts County	5	3-0	2-0	25000	Chilcott, Clark, Thomas	1	2	3	4	5	6		8	9	10	11	7												
5	14	Exeter City	3	3-1	2-1	13100	Clark(3)	1	2	3	4	5	6		8	9	10	11	7												
6	18	Norwich City	4	2-2	0-1	11038	Clark(2)	1	2	3	4	5	6		8	9	10	11	7												
7	21	PORT VALE	3	3-0	2-0	21284	C.Williams(2), Clark(pen)	1	2	3	4	5	6		8	9	10	11	7												
8	28	Bristol Rovers	2	3-0	3-0	25578	Clark, Hargreaves, C.Williams	1	2	3	4	5	6		8	9	10	11	7												
9	5 Oct	Swindon Town	3	1-1	1-0	25007	Thomas	1	2	3	4	5	6		8	9	10	11	7												
10	12	BOURNEMOUTH & B.A.	3	1-0	1-0	22336	Morgan	1		3	4	5	6		8	9	10	11	7		2										
11	19	MANSFIELD TOWN	2	5-2	3-2	17357	Clark(3), Thomas, C.Williams	1	2	3	4	5	6		8	9	10	11	7												
12	26	Torquay United	2	3-2	2-0	7700	Chilcott(2), Morgan	1	2	3	4	5	6		8	9	10	11	7												
13	2 Nov	CRYSTAL PALACE	2	3-0	1-0	26418	Clark(2), C.Williams	1	2	3	4	5	6		8	9	10	11	7												
14	9	Reading	2	5-2	3-1	16105	C.Williams(2), Clark, Hargreaves, Thomas	1	2	3	4	5	6		8	9	10	11	7												
15	16	WALSALL	3	1-2	1-0	26424	Peacock	1		3	4	5			8	9	10	11	7		2	6									
16	23	Watford	3	3-2	2-2	11364	Hargreaves(2), C.Williams	1		3	4	5			8	9	10	11	7		2	6									
17	7 Dec	Leyton Orient	3	1-4	1-2	7600	C.Williams	1	2	3	4	5			8	9	10	11	7												
18	21	Southend United	3	1-4	1-2	8007	Clark			3	4	5	6		8	9	10		7		2		11	1							
19	25	Northampton Town	3	2-2	1-1	13501	Hargreaves, C.Williams			3	4	5	6		8	9	10	11	7		2			1							
20	26	NORTHAMPTON TOWN	4	2-3	2-1	23109	Clark, Thomas				4	5	6		8	9	10	11	7	3	2			1							
21	28	ALDERSHOT	3	9-0	6-0	17690	Clark(4,1pen), Hargreaves(3), Jones, C.Williams					5	6		8	9	10	11	7	3	2	4			1						
22	4 Jan	Brighton & Hove Albion	3	1-1	1-0	9527	Thomas					5	6		8	9	10	11	7	3	2	4		1							
23	11	IPSWICH TOWN	3	1-2	1-2	16894	Thomas					5	6		8	9	10	11	7		2	4		1		3					
24	18	EXETER CITY	3	2-2	1-1	20415	Clark, C.Williams		2			5			8	9	10	11	7			4		1		3					
25	1 Feb	BRISTOL ROVERS	3	4-0	2-0	17450	Clark(2), Thomas(2)					5			8	9	10		7		2	4		1				6	11		
26	8	SWINDON TOWN	3	3-1	0-0	13502	C.Williams(2), Thomas					5			8	9	10		7		2	4		1				6	11		
27	15	Bournemouth & Bos. Ath.	3	0-0	0-0	9436		1				5			8	9	10		7		2	4						6	11		
28	17	Port Vale	3	1-2	0-2	8264	Clark	1				5			8	9	10		7		2	4						6	11		
29	1 Mar	TORQUAY UNITED	3	5-0	2-0	20596	Clark(4,1pen), O.G.	1	2	3		5			8	9	10		7			4						6			
30	15	READING	3	5-2	3-0	10140	Clark(2), Thomas(2), Chilcott	1	2	3		5			8	9	10	11	7			4						6			
31	22	Walsall	3	0-3	0-1	11592		1	2	3		5			8	9	10	11	7			4						6			
32	29	WATFORD	3	1-2	0-1	13651	Clark	1	2	3	4	5			8	9	10	11	7									6			
33	4 Apr	CARDIFF CITY	3	2-1	1-0	32535	Clark, Collins	1	2	3	4	5			8	9	10											6	11	7	
34	5	Ipswich Town	3	2-3	2-2	16022	Collins, Thomas	1	2	3	4	5			8	9	10											6	11	7	
35	7	Cardiff City	3	1-1	1-0	51621	S.Williams	1	2	3						9	10											6	11	7	8
36	12	LEYTON ORIENT	3	3-0	1-0	16751	Clark(2), S.Williams	1	2	3	4	5				9	10											6	11	7	8
37	19	Queens Park Rangers	3	0-1	0-1	22000		1	2	3	4	5				9	10											6	11	7	8
38	26	SOUTHEND UNITED	3	2-0	0-0	12816	Dymond, S.Williams	1	2	3	4	5		9			10											6	11	7	8
39	3 May	NOTTS COUNTY	3	1-1	1-0	12210	Kearney	1	2	3	4	5		9	10												6	11	7	8	
40	10	QUEENS PARK RANGERS	3	1-1	0-0	20861	Kearney(pen)	1	2	3	4	5		7			10										9	6	11	8	
41	17	Mansfield Town	3	3-1	3-1	7012	C.Williams(3)	1	2	3	4	5		7			10	11									9	6		8	
42	24	Crystal Palace	3	0-0	0-0	11634			2		4	5		7		9	10	11						3				6		8	1
							Apps.	32	32	34	32	42	22	8	35	37	41	26	31	3	16	12	1	6	1	3	16	13	10	8	1
							Goals				2		1	1	14	36	17	9	4		1						2	3	2		

F.A. CUP

	Date	Opposition		Res.	H.T.	Att.	Goalscorers	Ferguson	Bailey	Morgan	Roberts	Jones	Thomas	Clark	WilliamsCE	Hargreaves	Chilcott	Eddolls	Guy
1R	30 Nov	HAYES ATHLETIC		9-3	4-2	21610	Clrk(4),Hargrves(2),Chlctt,Thoms,C.Wllms(£1480)	1	3	4	5	6	8	9	10	11	7	2	
2R	14 Dec	GILLINGHAM		1-2	0-0	21623	Clark		3	4	5	6	8	9	10	11	7		2

GLOUCESTERSHIRE CUP FINAL

	Date	Opposition		Res.	H.T.	Att.	Goalscorers
	26 May	Bristol Rovers		2-2	1-1	17151	Clark, Collins
r	7 Jun	BRISTOL ROVERS		2-0	0-0	11434	Thomas, S.Williams

FRIENDLIES

	Date	Opposition		Res.	H.T.	Att.	Goalscorers
1	24 Aug	Plymouth Argyle		6-3	3-2	16988	Clark(4), Hargreaves, Morgan
2	29 May	GERMAN P.O.W. XI		4-0	3-0	20000	Clark, Kearney, Thomas, C.Williams
3	2 Jun	Yatton & District XI		6-1	2-1	1000	Clark(2), Morgan(2), Chilcott, C.Williams
4	11	Weston St. Johns		5-0		2000	Clark(3), Collins, Fox

FINAL LEAGUE TABLE

1	Cardiff	42	30	6	6	93 30	66
2	QPR	42	23	11	8	74 40	57
3	Bristol C.	42	20	11	11	94 56	51
4	Swindon	42	19	11	12	84 73	49
5	Walsall	42	17	12	13	74 59	46
6	Ipswich	42	16	14	12	61 53	46
7	Bournemouth	42	18	8	16	72 54	44
8	Southend	42	17	10	15	71 60	44
9	Reading	42	16	11	15	83 74	43
10	Port Vale	42	17	9	16	68 63	43
11	Torquay	42	15	12	15	52 61	42
12	Notts Co.	42	15	10	17	63 63	40
13	Northampton	42	15	10	17	72 75	40
14	Bristol R	42	16	8	18	59 69	40
15	Exeter	42	15	9	18	60 69	39
16	Watford	42	17	5	20	61 76	39
17	Brighton	42	13	12	17	54 72	38
18	Crystal Palace	42	13	11	18	49 62	37
19	Leyton Orient	42	12	8	22	54 75	32
20	Aldershot	42	10	12	20	48 78	32
21	Norwich	42	10	8	24	64 100	28
22	Mansfield	42	9	10	23	48 96	28

SEASON 1947-48
FOOTBALL LEAGUE DIVISION THREE (SOUTH)

No.	Date	Opposition	Pos.	Res.	H.T.	Att.	Goalscorers	Clack F.E.	Guy I.	Bailey E.J.	Morgan C.I.	Roberts D.	Kearney S.F.	Hopkins I.M.	Townsend L.F.	Clark D.F.	Williams C.E.	Williams S.F.	Thomas W.G.	Jones E.G.	White A.S.	Peacock E.G.	Chilcott K.	Osman H.J.	Norris R.G.	Collins R.D.	Stone F.W.	Fox R.V.	Dimmer H.	Russell A.C.
1	23 Aug	SOUTHEND UNITED		6-0	3-0	23874	Townsend(3), Clark(2), C.Williams	1	2	3	4	5	6	7	8	9	10	11												
2	28	Newport County		0-1	0-1	16584		1	2	3	4	5	6	7	8	9	10	11												
3	30	Notts County	13	1-3	0-1	18950	Townsend	1	2	3	4	5	6	7	8	9	10	11												
4	3 Sep	NEWPORT COUNTY	8	1-0	1-0	25706	Townsend	1	2	3	4	5	6	7	8	9	10	11												
5	6	SWANSEA TOWN	6	3-2	1-2	28068	Clark, Thomas, C.Williams	1	2	3	4	5		7		9	10	11	8	6										
6	11	Leyton Orient	4	2-0	1-0	10888	Clark, S.Williams	1	2	3	4	5		7		9	10	11		6	8									
7	13	Bournemouth & Bos. Ath.	7	0-2	0-0	18984		1	2	3	4	5		7	8	9	10	11		6										
8	17	LEYTON ORIENT	5	6-0	5-0	16788	Clark(2), Townsend(2), C.Williams(2)	1	2	3		5		7	8	9	10	11		6	4									
9	20	IPSWICH TOWN	4	4-0	1-0	23483	Townsend(2), Clark, C.Williams	1	2	3		5		7	8	9	10	11		6	4									
10	27	Bristol Rovers	3	2-0	0-0	34188	Chilcott, Clark	1	2	3		5	6	7	8	9	10						4	11						
11	4 Oct	Reading	2	7-2	3-2	17529	Clark(4), Kearney(2), Townsend	1	2	3		5	6	7	8	9	10						4	11						
12	11	NORWICH CITY	2	6-0	2-0	27896	Townsend(4), Osman, C.Williams	1	2	3		5	6	7	8	9	10						4	11						
13	18	Brighton & Hove Albion	2	2-0	1-0	11820	Clark, Townsend	1	2	3		5	6	7	8	9	10						4	11						
14	25	WATFORD	2	1-2	1-0	31624	Guy	1	2	3		5	6	7	8	9	10					4		11						
15	1 Nov	Queens Park Rangers	3	0-2	0-1	28205		1	2	3		5	6	7	8	9	10					4		11						
16	8	PORT VALE	3	2-1	1-0	27740	Townsend, C.Williams	1	2	3			6	7	8	9	10					4		11	5					
17	15	Swindon Town	3	2-2	1-1	26401	Clark, Townsend	1	2	3			6	7	8	9	10					4		11	5					
18	22	TORQUAY UNITED	4	1-2	0-1	18368	Townsend(pen)	1	2	3			6	7	8	9	10					4		11	5					
19	20 Dec	Southend United	5	0-4	0-1	7717		1	2	3	4	5			8	9	10	11	6				7							
20	26	Exeter City	7	1-3	0-2	12627	Townsend	1	2	3	4	5			8	9	10	11	6											
21	27	EXETER CITY	6	1-1	1-0	11620	Thomas	1	2	3				7	8	9		11	6			10	4							
22	3 Jan	NOTTS COUNTY	6	1-0	1-0	35287	Townsend	1	2	3	4	5			8	9		11	6			10				7				
23	17	Swansea Town	8	1-0	1-1	15000	White	1	2	3	4	5			8	9		11	6		10					7				
24	24	Northampton Town	7	4-0	3-0	7450	Clark, Kearney, Townsend, C.Williams	1	2	3		5	6	7	8	9	10					4		11						
25	31	BOURNEMOUTH & B.A.	7	0-4	0-3	23287		1	2	3		5	6	7	8	9	10					4		11						
26	7 Feb	Ipswich Town	9	0-1	0-0	10862		1	2	3		5	6		8	9	10					4		11		7				
27	14	BRISTOL ROVERS	8	5-2	3-1	26386	Clark(3), Townsend, C.Williams	1	2	3		5	6	7	8	9	10					4		11						
28	21	READING	8	0-2	0-0	12542		1	2	3		5	6	7	8	9	10					4		11						
29	28	Norwich City	8	3-2	0-1	23643	Clark, Townsend, O.G.	1	2	3	4	5	6		8	9	10	11					7							
30	6 Mar	BRIGHTON & HOVE ALB.	8	1-2	0-1	13383	Clark	1	2	3	4	5			8	9	10	11	6				7							
31	13	Watford	9	1-1	1-0	14000	Townsend(pen)	1	2	3					8	9	10	7	4	6				11						
32	20	QUEENS PARK RANGERS	8	2-1	2-1	21184	Townsend(2)	1	2	3					8	9	10	7	4					11						
33	26	WALSALL	8	0-0	0-0	24998		1	2	3		5				9	10	7	4	6	8			11						
34	27	Port Vale	8	0-1	0-1	12541		1	2	3	4	5			8	9	10	7	6					11						
35	29	Walsall	9	0-2	0-0	12743		1	2	3	4	5			8	9	10	7			6			11						
36	3 Apr	SWINDON TOWN	9	2-2	1-1	16859	Townsend(pen), White	1		3	4	5	6		9			11	10	7	8							2		
37	5	Crystal Palace	9	0-4	0-3	13405		1		3	4	5	6		9			11	10	7								2	8	
38	10	Torquay United	9	3-2	0-1	6097	Stone, Townsend, S.Williams	1		3		5	6		8	9	10	11						4			7	2		
39	17	CRYSTAL PALACE	6	2-0	2-0	12560	Townsend, C.Williams	1	2	3		5	6		8	9	10	11						4			7			
40	24	Aldershot	7	1-1	1-0	4500	Clark	1	2	3		5	6		8	9		11						4			7			10
41	26	ALDERSHOT	7	2-4	1-2	9936	Clark, Townsend	1	2	3	4	5	6		8	9		11									7			10
42	1 May	NORTHAMPTON TOWN	7	1-1	0-0	9714	Townsend	1		3		5			8	9	10	11	4								7	2		
							Apps.	42	38	42	19	38	26	24	39	40	37	28	30	5	6	6	4	18	3	4	4	6	1	2
							Goals		1				3		31	22	10	2	2		2		1	1			1			

F.A. CUP

			Res.	H.T.	Att.		Clack F.E.	Guy I.	Bailey E.J.	Morgan C.I.	Roberts D.	Kearney S.F.	Hopkins I.M.	Townsend L.F.	Clark D.F.	Williams C.E.	Williams S.F.	Thomas W.G.	Jones E.G.	White A.S.	Peacock E.G.	Chilcott K.	Osman H.J.
1R	29 Nov	Dartford	0-0	0-0	7540	(extra-time played)	1	2	3	4	5		7	8	9	10		6					11
1Rr	6 Dec	DARTFORD	9-2	5-1	19785	Clark(3), Townsend(3), C.Williams(3) (£1,533)	1	2	3	4	5		7	8	9	10		6					11
2R	13	CRYSTAL PALACE	0-1	0-0	22327	(extra-time played) (£1,569)	1	2	3	4	5		7	8	9	10		6					11

GLOUCESTERSHIRE CUP FINAL

			Res.	H.T.	Att.	
	8 May	BRISTOL ROVERS	1-2	0-2	15727	Clark

BATH CORONATION CUP FINAL

			Res.	H.T.	Att.	
	29 Apr	Bath City	3-2	1-2	3000	Moon(2), White (at Twerton Park)

FRIENDLIES

			Res.	H.T.	
1	15 Apr	Yeovil Town	0-3	0-0	
2	5 May	Dursley & District XI	5-1	2-0	Coles(3), Clark, Thomas

FINAL LEAGUE TABLE

		P	W	D	L	F	A	Pts
1	QPR	42	26	9	7	74	37	61
2	Bournemouth	42	24	9	9	76	35	57
3	Walsall	42	21	9	12	70	40	51
4	Ipswich	42	23	3	16	67	61	49
5	Swansea	42	18	12	12	70	52	48
6	Notts Co.	42	19	8	15	68	59	46
7	Bristol C.	42	18	7	17	77	65	43
8	Port Vale	42	16	11	15	63	54	43
9	Southend	42	15	13	14	51	58	43
10	Reading	42	15	11	16	56	58	41
11	Exeter	42	15	11	16	55	63	41
12	Newport	42	14	13	15	61	73	41
13	Crystal Palace	42	13	13	16	49	49	39
14	Northampton	42	14	11	17	58	72	39
15	Watford	42	14	10	18	57	79	38
16	Swindon	42	10	16	16	41	46	36
17	Leyton Orient	42	13	10	19	51	73	36
18	Torquay	42	11	13	18	63	62	35
19	Aldershot	42	10	15	17	45	67	35
20	Bristol R	42	13	8	21	71	75	34
21	Norwich	42	13	8	21	61	76	34
22	Brighton	42	11	12	19	43	73	34

1947-48 Season
Back: Thomas, Guy, Clack, Roberts (Captain), Kearney, Bailey.
Front: Hopkins, Townsend, Clark, Cyril Williams, Osman.

1948-49 Season
Back: Clark, Guy, Roberts, Marks, Davies, Bailey.
Front: Townsend, Sid Williams, Edwards, Lewis, Boxshall

SEASON 1948-49
FOOTBALL LEAGUE DIVISION THREE (SOUTH)

No.	Date	Opposition	Pos.	Res.	H.T.	Att.	Goalscorers
1	21 Aug	Southend United		0-1	0-1	14000	
2	25	BRIGHTON & HOVE ALB.		1-1	0-0	24432	Clark
3	28	NORTHAMPTON TOWN	9	3-0	0-0	22663	Townsend(2), Thomas
4	1 Sep	Brighton & Hove Albion	9	0-0	0-0	17483	
5	4	Norwich City	16	0-4	0-2	22667	
6	8	MILLWALL	14	0-0	0-0	16126	
7	11	EXETER CITY	11	1-0	1-0	17055	Boxshall
8	13	Millwall	12	1-4	1-3	18941	Boxshall
9	18	Bristol Rovers	19	1-3	0-2	30003	Clark
10	25	Swindon Town	20	1-2	1-2	22932	Clark
11	2 Oct	LEYTON ORIENT	19	3-0	2-0	13414	Boxshall, Morgan, O.G.
12	9	TORQUAY UNITED	20	0-2	0-1	15134	
13	16	Walsall	20	1-0	0-0	13979	Clark
14	23	CRYSTAL PALACE	17	2-0	1-0	14913	Davies, Morgan
15	30	Reading	18	1-2	1-1	17579	Clark
16	6 Nov	BOURNEMOUTH & B.A.	16	2-1	2-0	21414	Boxshall, Townsend
17	13	Watford	16	1-1	0-1	12500	Barney
18	20	NOTTS COUNTY	12	3-1	2-0	29663	Barney, Clark, Williams
19	18 Dec	SOUTHEND UNITED	11	2-1	1-1	13900	Boxshall, Townsend
20	25	Aldershot	11	0-0	0-0	4500	
21	27	ALDERSHOT	10	1-1	0-0	19541	Townsend
22	1 Jan	Northampton Town	12	1-3	0-1	6900	Townsend
23	15	NORWICH CITY	13	1-6	0-1	10969	Barney
24	22	Exeter City	13	1-1	0-1	9762	Clark
25	29	Ipswich Town	14	0-2	0-0	11190	
26	5 Feb	BRISTOL ROVERS	13	1-1	0-0	27543	Clark
27	19	SWINDON TOWN	15	1-3	0-0	15728	Townsend(pen)
28	26	Leyton Orient	17	1-3	0-2	8989	Barney
29	5 Mar	Torquay United	13	2-0	1-0	5200	Townsend(2)
30	12	WALSALL	15	2-2	1-2	12263	Townsend(2)
31	19	Crystal Palace	17	0-4	0-1	11840	
32	26	READING	18	0-2	0-1	11622	
33	2 Apr	Bournemouth & Bos. Ath.	17	0-0	0-0	14190	
34	7	Newport County	16	2-0	0-0	10278	Mullen(2)
35	9	WATFORD	16	1-1	1-1	12459	Boxshall
36	15	Port Vale	16	2-4	0-2	13571	Guy, Townsend(pen)
37	16	Notts County	16	1-2	0-0	27313	Townsend
38	18	PORT VALE	16	1-1	1-1	11094	Stone
39	23	IPSWICH TOWN	16	2-0	0-0	10229	Boxshall(2)
40	27	SWANSEA TOWN	15	0-0	0-0	14054	
41	30	Swansea Town	15	0-2	0-1	32000	
42	7 May	NEWPORT COUNTY	16	1-1	1-0	12757	Townsend

Appearances / Goals (player grid)

Players (shirt numbers per match): Marks G.W., Guy I., Bailey E.J., Edwards C.I., Roberts D., Davies J.W., Boxshall D., Townsend L.F., Clark D.F., Lewis G., Williams S.F., Kearney S.F., Thomas W.G., White A.S., Chilcott K., Jarvis M.J., Russell A.C., Clack F.E., Corbett W., Morgan C.I., Fox R.V., Barney V.C., Peacock E.G., Eveleigh G.E., Mullen J.W., Stone F.W., Tovey W.J., Morgan S.S.

No.	Mks	Guy	Bai	Edw	Rob	Dav	Box	Tow	Cla	Lew	Wil	Kea	Tho	Whi	Chi	Jar	Rus	Clk	Cor	MoC	Fox	Bar	Pea	Eve	Mul	Sto	Tov	MoS
1	1	2	3	4	5	6	7	8	9	10	11																	
2	1	2	3	4	5	6	7	8	9	10	11																	
3	1	2	3	4	5		7	8	9				11	6	10													
4	1	2	3	4	5		7	8	9					6	10													
5	1	2	3	4	5	6	7		9		11			8	10													
6	1	2	3	4	5	6		8	9	7								10		11								
7	1	2	3	4	5	6	7	8	9									10		11								
8	1	2	3	4	5	6	10	9						8						11	7							
9	1	2	3	4	5	6	11		9	7				10				8										
10		2		4	5	6	10		9	7		11		8				1			3							
11		2	3		5		10	7		9	11			8				1				4	6					
12		2	3		5		10	7		9	11			8				1				4	6					
13		2	3		5	6		8	9	11	7							1		4		10						
14		2	3		5	6		8	9	11	7							1		4		10						
15		2	3		5	6		8	9	11	7							1		4		10						
16		2	3		5	6	7	8	9		11							1		4		10						
17		2	3		5	6	7	8	9		11							1		4		10						
18		2	3		5	6	7	8	9		11							1		4		10						
19		2	3		5		7	8	9		11	6						1		4		10						
20		2	3		5		7	8	9	11		6						1		4		10						
21		2	3		5		7	8	9	11		6						1		4		10						
22		2	3	4		6	7	8	9		11							1				10						5
23		2	3		5	6		8			7					11	1				1	10						
24		2	3		5	6		8	9		7							1				10	4	11				
25		2	3		5			8	9	7								1			6	10	4	11				
26		2	3		5			7	9	11								1		4		10	6		8			
27		2	3		5	6		8	9									1		4		10	7		11			
28			3		5	6		8	9									1				10		4	2	11		
29			3		5	6		8						7				1				10	9	4	2	11	1	
30			3		5	6		8						7				1				10	9	4	2	11	1	
31			3		5	6		9		7				8				1				10		4		7	3	
32	2	11		5			9				6			8				1				10	4		7	3		
33	2	11		5	6	9	8				4							1				10			7	3		
34	2	11		5	6	9	8				4							1				10			7	3		
35	2	7		5	6	9	8				4							1				10			11	3		
36	9	3	4	5	6	7	8															10			11	2		1
37	9	3		5	6	7	8				4	10													11	2		1
38	9	3		5	6	7	8				4	10							11						2			1
39	9	3		5		7					4		8						6	10					11	2		1
40	2	9		5		7					4		8						6	10					11	3		1
41		3	6	5		7	9				4		8							10					11	2		1
42		3	6	5		7	9				4		8							10					11	2		1
Apps.	9	36	41	14	41	30	28	35	27	18	13	15	6	15	2	4	1	24	1	15	5	28	8	2	16	15	4	9
Goals		1				1	8	14	8		1		1							2		4			2	1		

F.A. CUP

Round	Date	Opposition	Res.	H.T.	Att.	Goalscorers
1R	27 Nov	Crystal Palace	1-0	0-0	16700	Townsend (a.e.t.) (£1,450)
2R	11 Dec	SWANSEA TOWN	3-1	2-1	22136	Barney, Boxshall, Townsend (£1,610)
3R	8 Jan	CHELSEA	1-3	1-0	36454	Clark (£4,252.1.9.)

F.A. Cup line-ups (all three rounds): Guy 2, Bailey 3, Roberts 5, Davies 6, Boxshall 7, Townsend 8, Clark 9, Williams 11, Clack 1, Morgan C. 4, Barney 10.

GLOUCESTERSHIRE CUP FINAL

Date	Opposition	Res.	H.T.	Att.
14 May	Bristol Rovers	0-2	0-2	15111

JAMES HOWELL CHALLENGE CUP FINAL

Date	Opposition	Res.	H.T.	Att.
2 May	Cardiff City	0-1	0-0	8000

FRIENDLIES

No.	Date	Opposition	Res.	H.T.	Att.	Goalscorers
1	12 Feb	Merthyr Tydfil	5-5	1-5	6000	Townsend(3), Clark, O.G.

FINAL LEAGUE TABLE

		P	W	D	L	F	A	Pts
1	Swansea	42	27	8	7	87	34	62
2	Reading	42	25	5	12	77	50	55
3	Bournemouth	42	22	8	12	69	48	52
4	Swindon	42	18	15	9	64	56	51
5	Bristol R	42	18	10	13	61	51	48
6	Brighton	42	15	18	9	55	55	48
7	Ipswich	42	18	9	15	78	77	45
8	Millwall	42	17	11	14	63	64	45
9	Torquay	42	17	11	14	65	70	45
10	Norwich	42	16	12	14	67	49	44
11	Notts Co	42	19	5	18	102	68	43
12	Exeter	42	15	10	17	63	76	40
13	Port Vale	42	14	11	17	51	54	39
14	Walsall	42	15	8	19	56	64	38
15	Newport	42	14	9	19	68	92	37
16	Bristol C	42	11	14	17	44	62	36
17	Watford	42	10	15	17	41	54	35
18	Southend	42	9	16	17	41	46	34
19	Leyton Orient	42	11	12	19	58	80	34
20	Northampton	42	12	9	21	51	62	33
21	Aldershot	42	11	11	20	48	59	33
22	Crystal Palace	42	8	11	23	38	76	27

SEASON 1949-50
FOOTBALL LEAGUE DIVISION THREE (SOUTH)

Player columns (left → right):
Coombs F.H. · Stone F.W. · Baley E.J. · Freeman D.R. · Roberts D. · Edwards C.I. · Williams S.F. · White A.S. · Clark D.F. · Eisentrager A.B. · Rudkin T.W. · McCarthy J.F. · Mullen J.W. · Kearney S.F. · Boxshall D. · Hawkins B.W. · Lowrie G. · Mitchelson K.G. · Thomas W.G. · Bicknell R. · Guy I. · Rodgers A.W. · Brewster G.W. · Morgan S.S. · Peacock E.G. · Spalding W. · Steeds C.

No.	Date	Opposition	Pos.	Res.	H.T.	Att.	Goalscorers
1	20 Aug	NORTHAMPTON TOWN		3-1	2-0	27463	Edwards, White, Williams
2	24	Nottingham Forest	14	0-3	0-1	27061	
3	27	Norwich City	18	0-3	0-2	26551	
4	30	NOTTINGHAM FOREST	19	0-2	0-0	25924	
5	3 Sep	NEWPORT COUNTY	14	6-0	3-0	20007	Eisentrager(4), Hawkins, White *
6	10	Bristol Rovers	13	3-2	1-0	34463	Hawkins, Lowrie, Rudkin
7	13	SWINDON TOWN	10	1-0	1-0	27255	Eisentrager
8	17	Brighton & Hove Albion	11	1-2	1-1	16687	Lowrie(pen)
9	21	Bournemouth & Bos. Ath.	11	1-3	0-0	8836	Stone
10	24	WALSALL	10	2-1	1-0	21691	Hawkins, Rudkin
11	1 Oct	Millwall	11	1-3	1-2	23875	Hawkins
12	8	SOUTHEND UNITED	12	1-1	0-0	20221	Eisentrager
13	15	Notts County	12	1-4	0-3	37978	Rodgers
14	22	PORT VALE	11	2-0	1-0	19855	Rodgers, Rudkin
15	29	Ipswich Town	12	0-0	0-0	12717	
16	5 Nov	EXETER CITY	11	1-0	1-0	21568	Rodgers
17	12	Leyton Orient	11	0-1	0-1	9289	
18	19	READING	12	2-2	0-0	19507	Brewster, Rodgers
19	3 Dec	CRYSTAL PALACE	12	2-0	0-0	15304	Lowrie, Rodgers
20	17	Northampton Town	12	2-4	2-2	11125	Edwards, Eisentrager
21	24	NORWICH CITY	12	1-2	0-1	23780	Rodgers
22	26	TORQUAY UNITED	12	0-0	0-0	24162	
23	27	Torquay United	11	3-3	1-2	13000	Boxshall, Eisentrager, Rodgers
24	31	Newport County	11	4-6	1-2	13208	Rodgers(2), Edwards, Thomas
25	14 Jan	BRISTOL ROVERS	14	1-2	1-2	36550	Lowrie
26	21	BRIGHTON & HOVE ALB.	17	1-2	1-0	14811	Rodgers
27	4 Feb	Walsall	16	1-2	0-0	9060	White
28	18	MILLWALL	16	2-1	1-1	19021	Lowrie, Rodgers
29	25	Southend United	16	0-2	0-2	9000	
30	4 Mar	NOTTS COUNTY	16	4-0	1-0	32491	Eisentrager(2), Lowrie, Rodgers
31	11	Port Vale	16	2-0	1-0	11444	Rodgers, White
32	18	IPSWICH TOWN	14	4-2	2-0	15963	Eisentrager, Lowrie, Rodgers, Williams
33	25	Exeter City	15	0-0	0-0	10937	
34	1 Apr	LEYTON ORIENT	14	0-0	0-0	16908	
35	7	ALDERSHOT	14	2-0	1-0	21592	Williams, Rodgers
36	8	Reading	14	0-1	0-0	14828	
37	10	Aldershot	14	1-0	0-0	6500	Rodgers
38	15	WATFORD	14	0-1	0-1	15066	
39	20	Watford	14	0-2	0-2	8799	
40	22	Crystal Palace	14	1-1	1-0	17198	Boxshall
41	29	BOURNEMOUTH & B.A.	15	3-2	1-0	11350	Rodgers(2), Peacock
42	6 May	Swindon Town	15	1-1	0-1	10401	Lowrie(pen)

Appearances / Goals (per player column):

Player	Apps	Goals
Coombs F.H.	24	
Stone F.W.	23	1
Baley E.J.	14	
Freeman D.R.	8	
Roberts D.	39	
Edwards C.I.	19	3
Williams S.F.	17	3
White A.S.	32	4
Clark D.F.	1	
Eisentrager A.B.	37	11
Rudkin T.W.	27	3
McCarthy J.F.	3	
Mullen J.W.	1	
Kearney S.F.	8	
Boxshall D.	24	2
Hawkins B.W.	26	4
Lowrie G.	19	8
Mitchelson K.G.	6	
Thomas W.G.	17	1
Bicknell R.	28	
Guy I.		
Rodgers A.W.	28	18
Brewster G.W.	6	1
Morgan S.S.	18	
Peacock E.G.	16	1
Spalding W.	9	
Steeds C.	4	

* Dennis Roberts Benefit

F.A. CUP

	Date	Opposition	Res.	H.T.	Att.	
1R	26 Nov	Nottingham Forest	0-1	0-0	15567	(£1,685.16.2)

GLOUCESTERSHIRE CUP FINAL

	Date	Opposition	Res.	H.T.	Att.	Goalscorers
	13 May	BRISTOL ROVERS	2-0	2-0	16560	Williams(2) (£1,150)

JAMES HOWELL CHALLENGE CUP FINAL

	Date	Opposition	Res.	H.T.	Att.	Goalscorers
	10 May	CARDIFF CITY	2-0	0-0	8250	Lowrie(2,1pen) (£692.6.6)

FRIENDLIES

	Date	Opposition	Res.	H.T.	Att.	Goalscorers
1	28 Sep	Trowbridge Town	2-1	1-1	5516	Boxshall, White
2	10 Dec	Halifax Town	1-1	0-1	3000	Rodgers
3	7 Jan	HALIFAX TOWN	4-0	2-0	11894	Lowrie(2), Eisentrager, Rudkin
4	12 Apr	Cleve, Yatton & Clevedon XI	4-3	3-0	2000	Clark, Eisentrager, Hall, Leslie Lowrie *
5	3 May	BRENTFORD	4-1	2-1	4500	Boxshall(3,1pen), O.G. (Maurice Roberts Benefit)
6	20	Wuppertal	0-0	0-0	8000	
7	21	Hamborn 07	2-3	0-3	15000	Eisentrager, Lowrie
8	27	Alemannia	5-2	1-0		Lowrie(3), Eisentrager(2)
9	28	Borussia Monchengladbach	3-1		5000	Brewster(2), Williams

* Norman Stockham Benefit, played at Cleve.

FINAL LEAGUE TABLE

		P	W	D	L	F	A	Pts
1	Notts Co	42	25	8	9	95	50	58
2	Northampton	42	20	11	11	72	50	51
3	Southend	42	19	13	10	66	48	51
4	Nottingham F	42	20	9	13	67	39	49
5	Torquay	42	19	10	13	66	63	48
6	Watford	42	16	13	13	45	35	45
7	Crystal Palace	42	15	14	13	55	54	44
8	Brighton	42	16	12	14	57	69	44
9	Bristol R	42	19	5	18	51	51	43
10	Reading	42	17	8	17	70	64	42
11	Norwich	42	16	10	16	65	63	42
12	Bournemouth	42	16	10	16	57	56	42
13	Port Vale	42	15	11	16	47	42	41
14	Swindon	42	15	11	16	59	62	41
15	Bristol C	42	15	10	17	60	61	40
16	Exeter	42	14	11	17	63	75	39
17	Ipswich	42	12	11	19	57	86	35
18	Leyton Orient	42	12	11	19	53	85	35
19	Walsall	42	9	16	17	61	62	34
20	Aldershot	42	13	8	21	48	60	34
21	Newport	42	13	8	21	67	98	34
22	Millwall	42	14	4	24	55	63	32

1949-50 Season.
Back: Freeman, Stone, Coombs, Roberts (Captain), Edwards, Bailey.
Front: Sid Williams, White, Clark, Eisentrager, Rudkin.

1950-51 Season
Back: Roberts, Guy, White, Sullivan, Peacock, Bailey.
Front: Sid Williams, Eisentrager, Clark, Beasley (Player/Manager), Rodgers, Rudkin.

SEASON 1950-51
FOOTBALL LEAGUE DIVISION THREE (SOUTH)

No.	Date	Opposition	Pos.	Res.	H.T.	Att.	Goalscorers
1	19 Aug	Bournemouth & Bos. Ath.		0-1	0-0	21430	
2	23	EXETER CITY	11	3-1	0-0	23598	Lowrie(2), O.G.
3	26	GILLINGHAM	6	2-0	2-0	21531	Beasley, Rodgers
4	30	Exeter City	7	0-1	0-1	9546	
5	2 Sep	BRISTOL ROVERS	6	1-0	0-0	29916	Lowrie
6	6	CRYSTAL PALACE	3	2-0	0-0	13422	Rodgers, Williams
7	9	Millwall	8	3-5	1-2	22659	Beasley, Lowrie, Thomas
8	13	Crystal Palace	10	0-1	0-0	12937	
9	16	WATFORD	9	3-0	2-0	19383	Lowrie(2,1pen), Brewster
10	23	Walsall	11	1-3	1-0	8593	Brewster
11	30	LEYTON ORIENT	7	4-1	2-0	16286	Lowrie(2), Eisentrager, White
12	7 Oct	Brighton & Hove Albion	7	1-1	0-1	11557	Peacock
13	14	NEWPORT COUNTY	7	2-1	2-1	22930	Lowrie(pen), White
14	21	Norwich City	6	0-0	0-0	27114	
15	28	NORTHAMPTON TOWN	7	1-0	0-0	20798	Lowrie(pen)
16	4 Nov	Port Vale	6	3-1	2-0	11603	Boxley, Lowrie, Rodgers
17	11	NOTTINGHAM FOREST	7	0-3	0-0	32878	
18	18	Torquay United	9	1-4	0-2	7500	Rodgers
19	2 Dec	Swindon Town	9	0-1	0-0	13079	
20	16	BOURNEMOUTH & B.A.	9	2-0	0-0	15438	Clark, Rodgers
21	23	Gillingham	6	2-1	1-1	8579	Boyd, Rodgers
22	25	PLYMOUTH ARGYLE	5	1-0	0-0	21158	Boyd
23	26	Plymouth Argyle	8	0-2	0-1	26306	
24	30	Bristol Rovers	9	1-2	0-1	31578	Rodgers
25	13 Jan	MILLWALL	9	2-1	1-1	21723	Rodgers, Rudkin
26	17	SOUTHEND UNITED	10	0-3	0-2	7745	
27	20	Watford	7	2-1	0-1	8678	Boyd, White
28	31	Southend United	7	1-1	1-1	5500	Rodgers
29	3 Feb	WALSALL	8	3-3	2-2	15508	Boyd(2), Williams
30	24	BRIGHTON & HOVE ALB.	8	2-0	1-0	12748	Rodgers(2)
31	3 Mar	Newport County	8	1-0	1-0	11494	Rogers
32	10	NORWICH CITY	9	2-2	1-2	22079	Rodgers(2)
33	17	Northampton Town	8	2-2	1-0	8010	Eisentrager, White
34	23	Reading	9	2-4	1-0	19875	Eisentrager, Rodgers
35	24	PORT VALE	9	3-1	2-0	17301	Rodgers(2), White
36	26	READING	9	3-3	1-2	23778	Boyd, Rodgers, White
37	31	Nottingham Forest	8	0-0	0-0	16733	
38	4 Apr	ALDERSHOT	8	1-1	0-0	11369	Rogers
39	7	TORQUAY UNITED	9	0-2	0-1	13975	
40	14	Aldershot	9	0-0	0-0	6800	
41	18	IPSWICH TOWN	8	2-1	2-1	12026	Beasley, Rodgers
42	21	SWINDON TOWN	8	2-0	2-0	16129	Rodgers(2)
43	25	COLCHESTER UNITED	8	0-2	0-0	12802	
44	28	Colchester United	10	1-1	1-1	7202	Eisentrager
45	3 May	Leyton Orient	7	2-0	0-0	6479	Boxley, Eisentrager
46	5	Ipswich Town	10	0-2	0-1	10728	

Appearances and Goals

Player	Apps	Goals
Morgan S.S.	26	
Guy I.	46	
Bailey E.J.	39	
Peacock E.G.	44	1
Roberts D.	41	
Beasley A.E.	43	3
Thomas D.S.	13	1
Eisentrager A.B.	42	5
Rodgers A.W.	39	20
Lowrie G.	16	11
Rudkin T.W.	7	1
Williams S.F.	25	2
Bicknell R.	4	
White A.S.	21	6
Brewster G.W.	7	2
Boxley J.	23	2
Rogers J.R.	8	2
Spalding W.	1	
Sullivan C.H.	20	
Boyd J.	24	6
Clark D.F.	5	1
Stone F.W.	7	
Lyons M.C.	1	
Presley D.C.	4	

F.A. CUP

Round	Date	Opposition	Res.	H.T.	Att.	Goalscorers
1R	25 Nov	GLOUCESTER CITY	4-0	2-0	17058	Guy, Peacock, Rodgers, Rogers (£1580.11.9)
2R	9 Dec	WREXHAM	2-1	0-1	18514	Rogers, Williams (£1670.3.3)
3R	6 Jan	BLACKBURN ROVERS	2-1	2-1	23245	Rodgers(2) (£2149.3.0)
4R	27	BRIGHTON & HOVE ALB.	1-0	0-0	28763	Clark(pen) (£2593.1.8)
5R	10 Feb	Birmingham City	0-2	0-1	47831	(£4241.19.3)

GLOUCESTERSHIRE CUP FINAL

Date	Opposition	Res.	H.T.	Att.	Goalscorers
12 May	Bristol Rovers	1-1	1-0	16673	Boxley

FRIENDLIES

No.	Date	Opposition	Res.	H.T.	Att.	Goalscorers
1	2 Apr	Swindon Town	1-2	1-1	3171	Brewster
2	9 May	HAMBORN 07	1-0	0-0	7701	Rodgers (Festival of Britain Fund)
3	15	DINAMO ZAGREB	2-1	1-0	15353	Beasley, Rogers (Festival of Britain Fund)
4	18	Helston Athletic	2-0	1-0		Beasley, Rodgers
5	19	Truro	7-1	6-0	2500	Beasley(3), Rodgers(2), Boyd, Rogers

FINAL LEAGUE TABLE

		P	W	D	L	F	A	Pts
1	Nottingham F	46	30	10	6	110	40	70
2	Norwich	46	25	14	7	82	45	64
3	Reading	46	21	15	10	88	53	57
4	Plymouth	46	24	9	13	85	55	57
5	Millwall	46	23	10	13	80	57	56
6	Bristol R	46	20	15	11	64	42	55
7	Southend	46	21	10	15	92	69	52
8	Ipswich	46	23	6	17	69	58	52
9	Bournemouth	46	22	7	17	65	57	51
10	Bristol C	46	20	11	15	64	59	51
11	Newport	46	19	9	18	77	70	47
12	Port Vale	46	16	13	17	60	65	45
13	Brighton	46	13	17	16	71	79	43
14	Exeter	46	18	6	22	62	85	42
15	Walsall	46	15	10	21	52	62	40
16	Colchester	46	14	12	20	63	76	40
17	Swindon	46	18	4	24	55	67	40
18	Aldershot	46	15	10	21	56	88	40
19	Leyton Orient	46	15	8	23	53	75	38
20	Torquay	46	14	9	23	64	81	37
21	Northampton	46	10	16	20	55	67	36
22	Gillingham	46	13	9	24	69	101	35
23	Watford	46	9	11	26	54	88	29
24	Crystal Palace	46	8	11	27	33	84	27

SEASON 1951-52
FOOTBALL LEAGUE DIVISION THREE (SOUTH)

No.	Date	Opposition	Pos.	Res.	H.T.	Att.	Goalscorers	Sullivan C.H.	Guy I.	Stone F.W.	Peacock E.G.	Roberts D.	Beasley A.E.	Eisentrager A.B.	Williams C.E.	Atyeo P.J.W.	Rodgers A.W.	Boxley J.	Presley D.C.	Bailey E.J.	Boyd J.	Tovey W.J.	Steeds C.	Rogers J.R.	Lowrie G.	Williams S.F.	Jones W.E.A.	Masters G.J.	Compton T.C.	Lyons M.C.
1	18 Aug	NEWPORT COUNTY		3-1	3-1	30048	Atyeo, Rodgers, C.Williams	1	2	3	4	5	6	7	8	9	10	11												
2	22	Bournemouth & Bos. Ath.	6	0-0	0-0	16659		1	2	3		5	6	7	8	9	10	11	4											
3	25	Reading	14	0-3	0-1	21890		1	2	3		5	6	7	8	9	10	11	4											
4	28	BOURNEMOUTH & B.A.	3	1-0	1-0	19750	Boxley	1	2			5	6	7	8	9	10	11	4	3										
5	1 Sep	Northampton Town	3	2-1	2-0	15580	Beasley(pen), C.Williams	1	2			5	6	7	8	9	10	11	4	3										
6	8	Port Vale	11	0-1	0-1	14472		1		2		5	6	7	8	9	10	11	4	3										
7	11	MILLWALL	5	2-1	1-0	20602	Atyeo, Eisentrager	1		2	4	5	6	7	8	9	10	11		3										
8	15	BRISTOL ROVERS	9	1-1	0-0	31497	Atyeo	1		2	4	5	6	7	8	9	10	11		3										
9	19	Millwall	10	2-3	1-1	14570	Atyeo, Eisentrager	1		2	4	5	6	7	8	9	10	11		3										
10	22	IPSWICH TOWN	12	0-2	0-0	20664		1	2		4	5	6	7	8	9	10			3	11									
11	29	Torquay United	13	2-1	1-1	8305	Atyeo, Eisentrager	1	2			5	6	7	8	9	10			3	11	4								
12	6 Oct	Norwich City	15	0-1	0-1	28532		1	2		4	5	6	7	8	9	10			3	11									
13	13	EXETER CITY	15	1-1	1-1	19053	Rodgers	1	2		4	5	6		8	9	10	11		3	7									
14	20	Colchester United	15	1-4	0-2	9552	C.Williams	1	2			5	10	7	8		9	11		3		4	6							
15	27	CRYSTAL PALACE	14	2-0	0-0	18857	Atyeo, Lowrie	1	2		4	5	6	11	8	9				3					7	10				
16	3 Nov	Swindon Town	13	0-0	0-0	16296		1	2			5	6	8	4	9				3					7	10	11			
17	10	LEYTON ORIENT	13	1-1	1-1	19607	Atyeo	1	2		4	5	6	7	8	9				3					11	10				
18	17	Walsall	14	0-2	0-1	6549		1	2			5	6	7	4	9	8			3						10		11		
19	1 Dec	Aldershot	15	0-1	0-0	6781		1	2			5	6	8	10	9				3	11	4					7			
20	8	WATFORD	17	1-3	0-1	10228	Jones	1	2			5	6	8		9	10			3	4						7	11		
21	22	READING	20	1-3	0-0	14680	Eisentrager	1	2		4	5		8		9	10			3	6						7	11		
22	25	Plymouth Argyle	19	2-2	2-2	17498	Atyeo, Rodgers	1	2		4	5		8	10	9				3	6				11		7			
23	26	PLYMOUTH ARGYLE	17	1-1	0-0	27092	Roberts	1	2		4	5		8	10	9				3	6				11		7			
24	29	NORTHAMPTON TOWN	16	2-0	1-0	18733	Eisentrager(pen), Rodgers	1	2		4	5		8	10	9				3	6				11				7	
25	5 Jan	PORT VALE	15	1-0	1-0	17598	Rodgers	1	2		4	5		8	10	9				3	6				11			7		
26	12	GILLINGHAM	14	3-2	2-1	13567	Eisentrager(pen), Tovey, C.Williams	1	2		4	5		8	10	9				3	6				11		7			
27	19	Bristol Rovers	15	0-2	0-1	34504		1	2		4	5		8	10	9				3	6				11		7			
28	26	Ipswich Town	15	1-1	1-0	9136	Atyeo	1	2		4	5	6		8	9	10			3					11		7			
29	6 Feb	SOUTHEND UNITED	13	6-0	1-0	8638	Rodgers(2), Atyeo, Jones, Lowrie, Rogers	1	2		4	5				9	8			3	6				11	10	7			
30	9	TORQUAY UNITED	14	2-2	2-1	19787	Rodgers(2)	1	2		4	5				9	8			3	6				11	10	7			
31	16	NORWICH CITY	14	2-5	2-2	19825	Beasley, Rodgers	1		2	4	5	10			9	8			3	6				11			7		
32	27	Southend United	14	1-5	0-1	3806	Rodgers	1	2		4	5		8		9	10			3				6	11			7		
33	1 Mar	Exeter City	14	0-0	0-0	8204		1	2		4	5	6	7		9	10			3	11		8							
34	8	COLCHESTER UNITED	14	2-0	2-0	14373	Rodgers, C.Williams	1	2		4	5			8	9	10			3			6	7		11				
35	15	Crystal Palace	15	1-2	1-0	13285	Rodgers	1	2		4	5			6	9	10			3				8		11	7			
36	22	SWINDON TOWN	11	2-1	0-1	14823	Atyeo, Rodgers(pen)	1			4	2			6	9	10			3	11			8			7		5	
37	5 Apr	WALSALL	13	2-0	1-0	8558	Rodgers, Rodgers	1	2		4	5			6	9	10			3				8			7	11		
38	11	BRIGHTON & HOVE ALB.	11	4-1	2-0	18915	Masters, Rodgers, Rodgers, C.Williams	1	2		4	5			6	9	10			3				8			7	11		
39	12	Shrewsbury Town	11	0-2	0-1	11419		1	2		4	5			8	9	10			3	6						7	11		
40	14	Brighton & Hove Albion	12	1-1	1-0	17518	Eisentrager	1	2		4	5		8	6	9	10			3						11	7			
41	19	ALDERSHOT	13	1-1	0-0	12540	Rodgers	1	2		4	5		8	6	9	10	11		3							7			
42	22	SHREWSBURY TOWN	10	3-0	2-0	9502	Atyeo, Jones, Rogers	1	2		4	5			6	9	10	11		3				8			7			
43	26	Watford	12	1-3	0-0	5795	Rodgers	1	2		4	5			6	9	10			3	4		8			7				
44	28	Newport County	13	0-1	0-1	7714		1	2		4	5		10	6		9	11		3			8			7				
45	1 May	Leyton Orient	14	0-2	0-1	7000		1	2		4	5		8	6	9	10	11		3						7				
46	3	Gillingham	15	0-5	0-2	12017		1	2		4	5			6	9	10			3	11		8			7				
								46	36	12	34	46	23	32	39	44	36	16	5	43	7	17	5	22	6	4	22	9	1	1
					Apps.					1		2	7	6	12	12	1					1		10	2		3	1		
					Goals																									

F.A. CUP

	Date	Opposition		Res.	H.T.	Att.	Goalscorers	Sullivan C.H.	Guy I.	Stone F.W.	Peacock E.G.	Roberts D.	Beasley A.E.	Eisentrager A.B.	Williams C.E.	Atyeo P.J.W.	Rodgers A.W.	Boxley J.	Presley D.C.	Bailey E.J.	Boyd J.	Tovey W.J.	Steeds C.	Rogers J.R.	Lowrie G.	Williams S.F.	Jones W.E.A.
1R	24 Nov	Brighton & Hove Albion		2-1	2-1	17740	Atyeo(2) (£1910.7.9)	1	2			5	6	7	8	9				3	11	4			10		
2R	15 Dec	Colchester United		1-2	0-2	9988	Rodgers (£913.10.6)	1	2			5	6	8		9	10			3		4				7	11

GLOUCESTERSHIRE CUP FINAL

	Date	Opposition		Res.	H.T.	Att.	Goalscorers
	10 May	BRISTOL ROVERS		2-1	2-1	16214	Rogers, C.Williams (£1672)

ST. DUNSTAN'S CHARITY CUP

	Date	Opposition		Res.	H.T.	Att.	Goalscorers
	7 May	Chippenham Town		9-1	4-0	2531	Norman(3), Atyeo(2), Beasley(2), Evans, Jones

FRIENDLIES

	Date	Opposition		Res.	H.T.	Att.	Goalscorers
1	31 Oct	Cheltenham Town		4-1	3-1	3500	Lowrie(3), C.Williams
2	2 Feb	CHARLTON ATHLETIC		3-5	1-3	13728	Rodgers(2), Jones
3	23	Bury		1-4	1-1	5024	S.Williams
4	24 Apr	Westbury United		2-0	1-0	2000	Atyeo(2,1pen)
5	30	OVERSEAS XI		2-4	1-2	3013	Beasley, Rodgers (D.Clark & F.Peacock's Benefit)

FINAL LEAGUE TABLE

1	Plymouth	46	29	8	9	107	53	66
2	Reading	46	29	3	14	112	60	61
3	Norwich	46	26	9	11	89	50	61
4	Millwall	46	23	12	11	74	53	58
5	Brighton	46	24	10	12	87	63	58
6	Newport	46	21	12	13	77	76	54
7	Bristol R.	46	20	12	14	89	53	52
8	Northampton	46	22	5	19	93	74	49
9	Southend	46	19	10	17	75	66	48
10	Colchester	46	17	12	17	56	77	46
11	Torquay	46	17	10	19	86	98	44
12	Aldershot	46	18	8	20	78	89	44
13	Port Vale	46	14	15	17	50	66	43
14	Bournemouth	46	16	10	20	69	75	42
15	Bristol C.	46	16	12	10	60	60	42
16	Swindon	46	14	14	18	51	68	42
17	Ipswich	46	16	9	21	53	74	41
18	Leyton Orient	46	16	9	21	55	68	41
19	Crystal Palace	46	15	9	22	61	80	39
20	Shrewsbury	46	13	10	23	62	86	36
21	Watford	46	13	10	23	57	81	36
22	Gillingham	46	11	13	22	71	81	35
23	Exeter	46	13	9	24	65	86	35
24	Walsall	46	13	5	28	55	94	31

1951-52 Season
(Back) Prentice, Steeds, Lowrie, Hague, Rogers, Cook, Morgan, Presley, Tovey, Mitchelson, Bailey, B.Mitchell (Coach)
(Middle) E.Nash (Trainer), D.Clark (Asst.Sec.), Sullivan, Atyeo, C.Williams, Rodgers, Stone, Guy, Roberts, Woodfield,
Compton, Peacock, L.Southway (Asst.Trainer), S.Webb (Office), S.Hawkins (Sec.).
(Front) Boyd, S.Williams, Rev.F.C.Vyvyan Jones (Dir.), A.J.Amor (Dir.), N.B.Jones (Dir.), C.W.Crawford (Vice-Chair.), H.J.Dolman (Chairman),
P.Beasley (Player/Manager), W.J.Kew (Dir.), G.J.Jones (Dir.), W.G.Garland (Dir.), P.Bennett (Dir.), F.C.Chambers (Dir.), Eisentrager.

1952-53 Season
Back: Nash (Trainer), Guy, Peacock, Cook, Tovey, Atyeo, Bailey
Front: Jones, Rodgers, White (Captain), Cyril Williams, Boxley.

SEASON 1952-53
FOOTBALL DIVISION THREE (SOUTH)

No.	Date	Opposition	Pos.	Res.	H.T.	Att.	Goalscorers
1	23 Aug	Watford		1-4	1-2	21651	Williams
2	26	MILLWALL	15	0-0	0-0	20975	
3	30	BRIGHTON & HOVE ALB.	19	2-2	0-1	17352	Boxley, Rodgers
4	3 Sep	Millwall	16	1-1	0-0	18407	Atyeo
5	6	Newport County	18	3-4	1-3	9573	Rodgers(2), Roberts(pen)
6	9	IPSWICH TOWN	15	4-2	2-1	7622	Williams(2), Eisentrager, Rodgers
7	13	CRYSTAL PALACE	12	5-0	3-0	17163	Williams(3), Atyeo, Rodgers
8	17	Ipswich Town	13	0-1	0-1	7118	
9	20	Bristol Rovers	14	0-0	0-0	29880	
10	23	COLCHESTER UNITED	11	3-2	3-2	13464	Rodgers(2), Rogers
11	27	Torquay United	11	2-1	2-0	7005	Rodgers(2)
12	2 Oct	Leyton Orient	8	3-1	2-1	7300	Rodgers(2), Boxley
13	4	NORTHAMPTON TOWN	10	2-3	1-1	21795	Atyeo, Eisentrager
14	11	Gillingham	7	4-0	2-0	19755	Eisentrager(2), Jones, Rodgers
15	18	Walsall	6	3-3	1-2	7229	Boxley, Eisentrager, Jones
16	25	SHREWSBURY TOWN	5	3-2	2-1	19998	Boxley, Eisentrager, Rodgers
17	1 Nov	Queens Park Rangers	6	1-2	1-2	14661	Eisentrager
18	8	SWINDON TOWN	4	4-2	3-1	21266	Eisentrager, Rodgers, Rogers, Williams
19	15	Aldershot	4	2-1	0-1	5857	Rodgers(2)
20	29	Norwich City	4	0-0	0-0	20088	
21	6 Dec	EXETER CITY	4	4-1	2-1	18594	Rodgers(2), Eisentrager(pen), O.G.
22	13	Exeter City	4	1-1	0-1	10597	Rodgers
23	20	WATFORD	4	5-1	2-0	12744	Rodgers(2), Eisentrager, Williams
24	26	SOUTHEND UNITED	3	5-0	2-0	30332	Peacock, Regan, Rodgers, W.Tovey, Williams
25	3 Jan	Brighton & Hove Albion	3	1-0	1-0	15905	Williams
26	10	READING	3	1-1	0-1	22676	Atyeo
27	17	Newport County	4	2-0	1-0	20756	Rodgers, Williams
28	24	Crystal Palace	2	3-1	0-1	12143	Williams(2), Rodgers
29	31	Reading	4	0-4	0-2	11088	
30	7 Feb	BRISTOL ROVERS	4	0-0	0-0	35606	
31	14	TORQUAY UNITED	4	4-4	1-2	15138	Atyeo, Eisentrager, Regan, Williams
32	21	Northampton Town	2	2-0	1-0	15241	Regan(2,1pen)
33	28	Gillingham	2	1-0	1-0	10500	Atyeo
34	7 Mar	WALSALL	2	6-1	4-0	16864	Atyeo(2), Regan(2,1pen), Rodgers, Williams
35	14	Shrewsbury Town	2	1-0	0-0	11093	Rogers
36	21	QUEENS PARK RANGERS	2	4-4	1-3	20052	Atyeo, Rogers, White, Williams
37	28	Swindon Town	2	0-0	0-0	10026	
38	3 Apr	BOURNEMOUTH & B.A.	2	1-1	1-2	25403	Atyeo
39	4	ALDERSHOT	2	0-0	0-0	16177	
40	6	Bournemouth & Bos. Ath.	4	1-4	0-2	13884	R.Tovey
41	11	Colchester United	5	1-3	0-0	7519	R.Tovey
42	18	NORWICH CITY	5	0-1	0-1	17650	
43	21	LEYTON ORIENT	5	2-1	0-1	9527	Jones, White
44	25	Coventry City	6	2-2	1-0	11110	R.Tovey, White
45	28	COVENTRY CITY	5	1-0	1-0	10562	White
46	29	Southend United	4	4-0	2-0	7500	Atyeo, Eisentrager, Regan, Williams

Player appearances (shirt numbers)

Column key: Sul = Sullivan C.H.; Mit = Mitchelson K.G.; Bai = Bailey E.J.; Pea = Peacock E.G.; Rob = Roberts D.; Wil = Williams C.E.; Jon = Jones W.E.A.; Rog = Rogers J.R.; Aty = Atyeo P.J.W.; Rod = Rodgers A.W.; Box = Boxley J.; Mor = Morgan S.S.; Eis = Eisentrager A.; ToW = Tovey W.J.; Guy = Guy I.; Com = Compton T.D.; Sto = Stone F.W.; Whi = White J.; Coo = Cook A.; Wat = Watkin C.; Reg = Regan D.J.T.; Dav = Davis K.E.; ToR = Tovey R.A.

No.	Sul	Mit	Bai	Pea	Rob	Wil	Jon	Rog	Aty	Rod	Box	Mor	Eis	ToW	Guy	Com	Sto	Whi	Coo	Wat	Reg	Dav	ToR
1	1	2	3	4	5	6	7	8	9	10	11												
2		2	3	4	5	6	7	8	9	10	11	1											
3		2	3	4	5	6	7	8	9	10	11	1											
4		2	3	4	5	6		7	8	9		1	10	11									
5		2	3	4	5	6		7	8	9		1	10	11									
6	1	2	3	4	5	10		8	9	6	11		7										
7	1		3	4	5	10		8	9	6	11		7		2								
8	1		3	4	5	10		8	9	6	11		7		2								
9	1		3	4	5	10		8	9	6	11		7		2								
10			3	4	5	10		8	9	6	11	1	7		2								
11			3	4	5	10		8	9	6	11	1	7		2								
12			3	4	5	10		8	9	6	11	1	7		2								
13			3	4	5	10		8	9	6	11	1	7		2								
14			3	4	5	10	11	8	9	6		1	7		2								
15			3	4	5	10	11	8	9	6		1	7		2								
16	1		3	4	5	10	11	8	9	6			7		2								
17	1		3	4	5	10	11	8	9	6			7		2								
18			3	4		10	11	8	9	6			7		2			5	1				
19			3	4		10	11	8	9	6			7		2			5	1				
20			3	4		10	11	8	9	6			7		2			5	1				
21			3	4		10	11	8	9	6			7		2			5	1				
22			3	4		10	11	8	9	6			7		2			5	1				
23			3	4		10		8	9	6			7		2			5	1		11		
24			3	4		10		8	9	6			7		2			5	1		11		
25			3	4		10		8	9	6			7		2			5	1		11		
26			3	4		10		8	9	6					2	7		5	1		11		
27			3	4		10		8	9	6			7		2			5	1		11		
28			3	4		10		8	9	6			7		2			5	1		11		
29			3	4		10			9	6			7		2			5	1	8	11		
30			3	4		10		8	9	6			7		2			5	1		11		
31			3	4		10		8	9	6			7		2			5	1		11		
32			3	4		10		8	9	6			7		2			5	1		11		
33			3	4		10		8	9	6			7		2			5	1		11		
34			3	4		10		8	9	6			7		2			5	1		11		
35			3	4		10		8	9	6			7		2			5	1		11		
36			3	4		10		8	9	6			7		2			5	1		11		
37			3	4		10		8	9	6			7		2			5	1		11		
38			3	4		10		8	9	6			7		2			5	1		11		
39		2	3	4		10		8	9	6			7					5	1		11		
40			3	4		10			9	6			7		2			5	1		11		8
41			3	4		10		8		6	11		7		2		5	5	1		11		9
42			3	4		10		8		6			7		2			5	1		11		9
43			3	4		10	7	8		6	11				2			5	1				9
44			3	4		10	7	8		6	11							5	1				9
45			3	4		10	7	8		6	11							5	1				9
46			3	4		10		8	9	6			7		2			5	1		11		
Apps	7	9	41	46	17	42	17	18	33	33	25	10	38	36	37	1	3	33	29	3	21	1	6
Goals				1	1	17	3	4	11	26	4		12	1				4			7		3

F.A. CUP

	Date	Opposition		Res.	H.T.	Att.	
1R	22 Nov	Coventry City		0-2	0-1	17062	(£2195.14.3)

Team: Bailey 3, Peacock 4, White 5, Rodgers 6, Eisentrager 7, Rogers 8, Atyeo 9, Williams 10, Jones 11, Cook 1, Guy 2

GLOUCESTERSHIRE CUP FINAL

	Date	Opposition		Res.	H.T.	Att.	Goalscorers
	8 May	Bristol Rovers		2-0	2-0	19194	Atyeo, Eisentrager (£2000)

FRIENDLIES

No.	Date	Opposition		Res.	H.T.	Att.	Goalscorers
1	27 Jan	WOLVERHAMPTON WNDRS		1-4	1-2	23866	Rodgers
2	17 Feb	CARDIFF CITY		0-2	0-1	14580	
3	10 Mar	EAST FIFE		0-2	0-1	26562	
4	1 May	Torquay United		2-0	1-0	2684	Atyeo, Boxley (Sammy Collins Benefit)
5	4	Penzance		6-1	3-0		Atyeo(2), Boxley, Rodgers, R.Tovey, O.G.
6	5	Newquay		9-1			Atyeo(4), Rodgers(3), Boxley, O.G.

FINAL LEAGUE TABLE

		P	W	D	L	F	A	Pts
1	Bristol R	46	26	12	8	92	46	64
2	Millwall	46	24	14	8	82	44	62
3	Northampton	46	26	10	10	109	70	62
4	Norwich	46	25	10	11	99	55	60
5	Bristol C.	46	22	15	9	95	61	59
6	Coventry	46	19	12	15	77	62	50
7	Brighton	46	19	12	15	81	75	50
8	Southend	46	18	13	15	69	74	49
9	Bournemouth	46	19	9	18	74	69	47
10	Watford	46	15	17	14	62	63	47
11	Reading	46	19	8	19	69	64	46
12	Torquay	46	18	9	19	87	88	45
13	Crystal Palace	46	15	13	18	66	82	43
14	Leyton Orient	46	16	10	20	68	73	42
15	Newport	46	16	10	20	70	82	42
16	Ipswich	46	13	15	18	60	69	41
17	Exeter	46	13	14	19	61	71	40
18	Swindon	46	14	12	20	64	79	40
19	Aldershot	46	12	15	19	61	77	39
20	QPR	46	12	15	19	61	82	39
21	Gillingham	46	12	15	19	55	74	39
22	Colchester	46	12	14	20	59	76	38
23	Shrewsbury	46	12	12	22	68	91	36
24	Walsall	46	7	10	29	56	118	24

FOOTBALL LEAGUE DIVISION THREE (SOUTH)

No.	Date	Opposition	Pos.	Res.	H.T.	Att.	Goalscorers	Cook A.	Guy I.	Bailey E.J.	Regan J.	Peacock E.G.	White J.	Eisentrager A.B.	Atyeo P.J.W.	Rodgers A.W.	Williams C.E.	Regan D.J.T.	Roberts D.	Tovey R.A.	Boxley J.	Jones W.E.A.	Micklewright A.	Rogers J.R.	Watkins J.V.	Steele R.	Compton T.D.	Morgan S.S.
1	19 Aug	GILLINGHAM		1-1	0-1	19506	Atyeo	1	2	3	4	5	6	7	8	9	10	11										
2	22	QUEENS PARK RANGERS		1-2	0-1	20819	Rodgers	1	2	3	4		6	7	8	9			5				10	11				
3	27	Walsall	15	0-0	0-0	15158		1	2	3	4	5	7	8	9	6							10	11				
4	29	Southampton	20	2-4	2-2	17832	Micklewright(2)	1	2	3	4	5			8	9	6				11	7	10					
5	1 Sep	WALSALL	11	4-1	1-1	14708	Boxley(2,1pen), Rodgers(2)	1	2	3	4	5			8	9	6				11	7	10					
6	5	COLCHESTER UNITED	11	3-0	1-0	17424	Rodgers(2), Boxley	1	2	3	4				8	9	6	7	5		11		10					
7	9	Exeter City	8	1-0	1-0	10310	Boxley	1	2	3	4				8	9	6	7	5		11		10					
8	12	Crystal Palace	6	2-1	0-1	18545	Atyeo, Rodgers	1	2		4	3			8	9	6	7	5		11		10					
9	15	EXETER CITY	5	5-1	0-0	15529	D.Regan(2), Rodgers(2), Atyeo	1	2		4	3			8	9	6	7	5		11		10					
10	19	Leyton Orient	7	1-4	0-3	13125	Rodgers	1	2		4	3			8	9	6	11	5				10	7				
11	23	Norwich City	7	1-1	1-0	20833	Rodgers	1			4	3			8	9	6		5		10	11		7				
12	26	ALDERSHOT	6	4-0	1-0	19949	Atyeo(2), Peacock, Rogers	1	2	3	4	5			8	9	6				10	11		7				
13	30	NORWICH CITY	5	3-1	1-1	18706	Micklewright(2), Atyeo	1			4	3		9			6		5		10		8	7	11			
14	3 Oct	Swindon Town	5	0-5	0-2	15481		1	2	3	4		8			6			5		10		9	7	11			
15	10	IPSWICH TOWN	8	2-3	1-1	22711	Boxley(2,1pen)	1	2		4	3		9			6		5		10	11	8	7				
16	17	Bournemouth & Bos. Ath.	9	2-5	2-2	10061	Atyeo(2)	1	2		4	6			8	9	10		5		11			7		3		
17	24	COVENTRY CITY	6	1-0	1-0	16395	Micklewright	1	2	3	4		7	9			6	11	5		10		8					
18	31	Gillingham	7	2-2	1-1	10958	Atyeo(2)	1	2	3	4		7	8	9	6			5		11		10					
19	7 Nov	NORTHAMPTON TOWN	6	2-1	0-0	17380	Atyeo, Rodgers	1	2	3	4		7	8	9	6			5		11		10					
20	14	Torquay United	7	0-4	0-2	7574		1	2	3	4		7	8		6			5	9	11		10					
21	28	Brighton & Hove Albion	12	1-2	1-0	19294	Williams	1	2	3		4	6		8		10	11			9	7				5		
22	5 Dec	SOUTHEND UNITED	9	4-1	2-1	14543	Boxley(2,1pen), Rogers, Williams	1	2	3		4	6		8		10				11	9	7			5		
23	19	Queens Park Rangers	8	1-0	1-0	8052	Boxley	1	2	3	4		6		8		10				11	9	7			5		
24	25	Newport County	10	2-3	1-1	14800	Micklewright, Rogers	1	2	3	4		6		8		10				11	9	7			5		
25	26	NEWPORT COUNTY	8	3-0	2-0	24607	Atyeo(2), Williams	1	2	3	4		6		8		10				11	9	7			5		
26	2 Jan	SOUTHAMPTON	8	1-0	1-0	21693	Atyeo	1	2	3	4		6		8		10				11	9	7			5		
27	16	Colchester United	5	2-0	1-0	7931	Boxley, Micklewright	1	2	3	4		6		8		10				11	7	9			5		
28	23	CRYSTAL PALACE	4	4-0	1-0	17552	Jones, Micklewright, J.Regan, White	1	2	3	4		6		8		10				11	7	9			5		
29	30	Shrewsbury Town	4	3-4	1-4	6500	Micklewright(2), Atyeo	1	2	3	4		6		8		10				11	7	9			5		
30	6 Feb	LEYTON ORIENT	4	1-0	0-0	15846	Micklewright	1	2	3	4		6		8		10				11	7	9			5		
31	13	Aldershot	4	5-2	1-0	6038	Atyeo(2), Micklewright(2), White	1	2	3	4		6		8		10				11	7	9			5		
32	20	SWINDON TOWN	4	5-1	3-1	23749	Atyeo(3), Micklewright(2)	1	2	3	4		6	10	8						11	7	9			5		
33	27	Ipswich Town	4	1-2	0-1	14182	Williams	1	2	3	4		6		8		10				11	7	9			5		
34	6 Mar	BOURNEMOUTH & B.A.	4	1-1	0-0	16821	White	1	2	3	4		6		8		10				11	7	9			5		
35	13	Watford	6	0-2	0-1	12318		1	2	3	4		6		8		10	11				7	9			5		
36	20	BRIGHTON & HOVE ALB.	6	1-1	0-0	22138	D.Regan	1	2	3	4	5	6	7	8		10	11					9					
37	27	Northampton Town	8	0-3	0-1	8283		1	2	3	4	5	6		8		10	11			7		9					
38	3 Apr	TORQUAY UNITED	5	3-0	2-0	14246	Atyeo, Boxley, Eisentrager	1	2	3	4	5	6	10	8	9					11		7					
39	7	Reading	5	2-0	1-0	6778	Eisentrager, Micklewright		2	3	4	5	6	10	8	9					11		7					1
40	10	Southend United	3	1-0	0-0	10000	O.G.		2	3	4	5	6	10	8	9					11		7					1
41	16	Millwall	3	0-1	0-1	17374			2	3	4	5	6	10	8	9					11		7					1
42	17	READING	3	3-1	1-1	16701	Rodgers(2), Eisentrager		2	3	4	5	6	7	8	9	10				11							1
43	19	MILLWALL	3	2-1	2-1	14618	Atyeo, O.G.		2	3	4	5	6	7	8	9	10				11							1
44	24	Coventry City	3	0-3	0-0	7439			2	3	4	5	6	7	8		10				11		9					1
45	27	Watford	3	2-1	1-0	10941	Boxley, Rodgers		2	3	4	5	6	7	8	9	10				11							1
46	29	SHREWSBURY TOWN	3	3-1	2-0	8129	Boxley(2,1pen), D.Regan		2	3	4	5	6	10	8	9		7			11							1
		Apps.						38	46	39	25	32	40	19	45	23	39	12	15	6	41	11	36	13	2	1	15	8
		Goals									1	1	3	3	22	14	4	4			14	1	16	3				1

F.A. CUP

	Date	Opposition		Res.	H.T.	Att.	Goalscorers	Cook	Guy	Bailey	Regan J	Peacock	White	Eisen	Atyeo	Rodgers	Williams	Regan D	Roberts	Tovey	Boxley	Jones	Micklewright	Rogers	Watkins	Steele	Compton	Morgan
1R	21 Nov	Torquay United		3-1	2-1	10042	Micklewright(2), Atyeo (£1,130.0.9)	1	2	3		4	6		8		10				11	9	7			5		
2R	12 Dec	Rhyl		3-0	2-0	9000	Atyeo, Micklewright, Williams (£1,504.17.6)	1	2	3	4		6		8		10				11	9	7			5		
3R	9 Jan	ROTHERHAM UNITED		1-3	0-0	29216	Atyeo (£3,856.8.3)	1	2	3	4		6		8		10				11	9	7			5		

GLOUCESTERSHIRE CUP FINAL

	Date	Opposition		Res.	H.T.	Att.	Goalscorers
	3 May	BRISTOL ROVERS		2-2	1-1	13668	Eisentrager, Williams (£1816)

CHIPPENHAM SPORTSMENS & TRADERS TROPHY (at Chippenham United F.C.)

	Date	Opposition		Res.	H.T.	Att.	Goalscorers
	27 Apr	Swindon Town		2-0	0-0		Rogers(pen), Smith

FRIENDLIES

	Date	Opposition		Res.	H.T.	Att.	Goalscorers
1	13 Oct	FENER BACHE		7-4	3-2	14266	Wllms(2), Atyo, Mcklwrght, Pcock, D.Rgan(p), Rogers
2	3 Nov	EAST FIFE		4-3	2-2	13323	Atyeo, Eisentrager, Micklewright, Williams
3	1 Dec	CHELSEA		2-5	1-3	18040	Atyeo, Micklewright
4	20 Jan	HAJDUK SPLIT		1-1	0-1	17981	Boxley(pen)
5	30 Mar	ARSENAL		3-1	1-1	28991	Rodgers(2), Atyeo

FINAL LEAGUE TABLE

1	Ipswich	46	27	10	9	82	51	64
2	Brighton	46	26	9	11	86	61	61
3	Bristol C	46	25	6	15	88	68	56
4	Watford	46	21	10	15	85	69	52
5	Northampton	46	20	11	15	82	55	51
6	Southampton	46	22	7	17	76	63	51
7	Norwich	46	20	11	15	73	66	51
8	Reading	46	20	9	17	86	73	49
9	Exeter	46	20	8	18	68	58	48
10	Gillingham	46	19	10	17	61	66	48
11	Leyton Orient	46	18	11	17	79	73	47
12	Millwall	46	19	9	18	74	77	47
13	Torquay	46	17	12	17	81	88	46
14	Coventry	46	18	9	19	61	56	45
15	Newport	46	19	6	21	61	81	44
16	Southend	46	18	7	21	69	71	43
17	Aldershot	46	17	9	20	74	86	43
18	QPR	46	16	10	20	60	68	42
19	Bournemouth	46	16	8	22	67	70	40
19	Swindon	46	15	10	21	67	70	40
21	Shrewsbury	46	14	12	20	65	76	40
22	Crystal Palace	46	14	12	20	60	86	40
23	Colchester	46	10	10	26	50	78	30
24	Walsall	46	9	8	29	40	87	26

Football League Di.3.South BRISTOL CITY FOOTBALL CLUB 1953-4
Peacock Guy Cook Bailey Williams.C
Eisentrager Atyeo Rodgers Tovey.R Boxley White

BRISTOL CITY'S PROMOTION SIDE. Front row, left to right, E. Peacock, J. Rogers, J. White capt., T. Burden, J. Boxley; back row, W. Copping, trainer, A. Milton, I. Guy, B. Anderson, J. Ateyo, C. Williams, M. Thresher.

- 1954-55 -

SEASON 1954-55
FOOTBALL LEAGUE DIVISION THREE (SOUTH)

Player columns (left to right): Cook A., Jackson N.E., Bailey E.J., Regan J., Peacock E.G., White J., Eisentrager A.B., Atyeo P.J.W., Rodgers A.W., Williams C.E., Boxley J., Guy I., Rogers J.R., Allen P.M., Mcklewright A., Burden T.D., Regan D.J.T., Anderson J.R., Thresher T.M.J., Milton C.A.

No.	Date	Opposition	Pos	Res	H.T.	Att	Goalscorers	Cook	Jackson	Bailey	Regan J	Peacock	White	Eisentr.	Atyeo	Rodgers	Williams	Boxley	Guy	Rogers JR	Allen	Mcklew.	Burden	Regan DJT	Anderson	Thresher	Milton
1	21 Aug	Gillingham		1-1	0-1	14434	Atyeo	1	2	3	4	5	6	7	8	9	10	11									
2	25	Torquay United		2-2	0-1	10432	White, O.G.	1		3	4	5	6	7	8	9	10	11	2								
3	28	LEYTON ORIENT	4	5-0	2-0	19715	Rodgers(2), Boxley(pen), Williams, O.G.	1		3	4	5			8	9	10	11	2	7							
4	31	TORQUAY UNITED	4	1-1	0-1	18773	Rogers	1		3	4	5	6		8	9	10	11	2	7							
5	4 Sep	Millwall	2	3-1	2-1	15566	Boxley, Rogers, Williams	1		3	4	5	6		8	9	10	11	2	7							
6	9	Colchester United	2	2-0	1-0	8522	Rodgers(2)	1		3	4	5	6		8	9	10	11	2	7							
7	11	SOUTHAMPTON	2	2-0	1-0	24809	Atyeo, Williams	1		3	4	5	6		8	9	10	11	2	7							
8	14	COLCHESTER UNITED	1	4-0	3-0	18710	Rodgers(3), Atyeo	1		3	4	5	6		8	9	10	11	2	7							
9	18	Coventry City	1	3-1	3-1	29865	Atyeo(2), Rogers	1		3	4	5	6		8	9	10	11	2	7							
10	21	WALSALL	1	5-3	2-0	20394	Boxley(2), Atyeo, Rogers, O.G.	1		3	4		6		8	9	10	11	2	7		5					
11	25	BRENTFORD	1	2-1	2-0	28980	Rodgers(2)	1		3	4	5	6		8	9	10	11	2	7							
12	30	Walsall	1	3-1	3-0	8911	Atyeo(2), Rodgers	1		3	4	5	6		8	9	10	11	2	7							
13	2 Oct	Brighton & Hove Albion	1	1-0	1-0	21581	Rogers	1		3	4	5	6		8	9	10	11	2	7							
14	9	Southend United	1	2-3	1-1	12291	Atyeo, Boxley	1		3	4	5	6		8	9	10	11	2	7							
15	16	ALDERSHOT	1	6-1	2-0	21875	Atyeo(2), Rogers(2), Williams, O.G.	1		3	4	5	6		8	9	10	11	2	7							
16	23	Swindon Town	1	2-2	0-2	19880	Boxley(pen), Rogers	1		3	4	5		10	8	9		11	2	7							
17	30	EXETER CITY	1	2-0	0-0	26449	Atyeo, Mickwright	1		3	4	5			8	9		11	2	7		10					
18	6 Nov	Northampton Town	1	0-2	0-1	11408		1		3	4	5	6		8	9		11	2	7					10		
19	13	WATFORD	1	1-0	0-0	21910	Boxley	1	3		4	5	6		8	9	10	11	2	7							
20	27	QUEENS PARK RANGERS	1	1-1	0-1	17657	Rogers	1	3			5	6		8	9		11	2	7		10	4				
21	4 Dec	Newport County	1	2-2	0-2	10886	Atyeo, Burden	1	3		4	5	6		8	9		11	2	7			10				
22	11	Shrewsbury Town	1	2-0	1-0	8121	Rodgers(2)	1	3			5	6		8	9	10	11	2	7			4				
23	18	GILLINGHAM	2	1-4	1-1	17880	Atyeo	1	3			5	6		8	9	10		2	7			4	11			
24	25	READING	1	2-1	2-0	16800	Eisentrager, Rogers		3			5	6	10	8	9			2	7			4	11	1		
25	27	Reading	1	2-0	1-0	18850	Atyeo, Rogers				4	5	6	10	8	9			2	7				11	1	3	
26	1 Jan	Leyton Orient	1	1-4	1-2	20347	Boxley					5	6	10	8	9		11	2	7			4		1	3	
27	8	NORWICH CITY	2	0-1	0-0	16332					4	5	6		8	9		11	2	7			10		1	3	
28	22	Southampton	2	1-2	0-1	18334	Atyeo				4	5	6		8	9		11	2	7			10		1	3	
29	29	Norwich City	2	1-0	1-0	24183	Burden				4	5	6	7	8			11	2	9			10		1	3	
30	5 Feb	COVENTRY CITY	2	2-0	1-0	21758	Rogers, White				4	5	6	7	8			11	2	9			10		1	3	
31	12	Brentford	2	2-2	1-2	11400	Atyeo, Eisentrager				4	5	6	7	8			11	2	9			10		1	3	
32	19	BRIGHTON & HOVE ALB.	2	3-2	2-1	24649	Rogers(2), Atyeo(pen)				4	5	6		8			11	2	9			10		1	3	7
33	26	SOUTHEND UNITED	1	3-2	1-2	20837	Rogers(2), Atyeo				4	5	6		8			11	2	9			10		1	3	7
34	5 Mar	Aldershot	1	2-0	1-0	6832	Burden, Rogers				4	5	6		8			11	2	9			10		1	3	7
35	9	MILLWALL	1	5-1	2-0	13264	Atyeo(2,1pen), Rogers(2), Boxley				4	5	6		8			11	2	9			10		1	3	7
36	12	SWINDON TOWN	1	3-0	1-0	24390	Burden(2), Boxley				4	5	6		8			11	2	9			10		1	3	7
37	19	Exeter City	1	1-0	0-0	12111	Rogers				4	5	6		8			11	2	9			10		1	3	7
38	26	NORTHAMPTON TOWN	1	5-1	2-1	20955	Rogers(2), Atyeo, Boxley, Milton				4	5	6		8			11	2	9			10		1	3	7
39	2 Apr	Watford	1	2-0	1-0	14632	Atyeo, Milton				4	5	6		8			11	2	9			10		1	3	7
40	9	BOURNEMOUTH & D.A.	1	2-2	2-2	33302	Atyeo(2,1pen)				4	5	6		8			11	2	9			10		1	3	7
41	11	SHREWSBURY TOWN	1	4-1	2-0	26208	Burden(2), Atyeo(pen), Rogers				4	5	6		8			11	2	9			10		1	3	7
42	16	Queens Park Rangers	1	1-1	0-0	12456	Rogers				4	5	6		8			11	2	9			10		1	3	7
43	19	CRYSTAL PALACE	1	3-0	2-0	27657	Atyeo(2), Rogers				4	5	6		8			11	2	9			10		1	3	7
44	23	NEWPORT COUNTY	1	0-0	0-0	27726					4	5	6		8			11	2	9			10		1	3	7
45	27	Bournemouth & Bos. Ath.	1	1-0	1-0	9688	Milton				4	5	6		8			11	2	9			10		1	3	7
46	30	Crystal Palace	1	2-1	1-1	14425	Burden, Rogers				4	5	6	7	8			11	2	9			10		1	3	
		Apps.						23	7	18	22	44	46	10	46	26	39	43	45	44	1	3	27	3	23	22	14
		Goals											2	2	28	13	4	11		25		1	8				3

F.A. CUP

	Date	Opposition	Res	H.T.	Att	Goalscorers	Cook	Bailey	Peacock	White	Eisentr.	Atyeo	Rodgers	Williams	Boxley	Guy	Rogers JR
1R	20 Nov	SOUTHEND UNITED	1-2	1-0	20594	Rodgers (£2,774.1.3)	1	3	4	5	6	8	9	10	11	2	7

GLOUCESTERSHIRE CUP FINAL

	Date	Opposition	Res	H.T.	Att	Goalscorers
	2 May	Bristol Rovers	1-2	0-1	20097	Atyeo

FRIENDLIES

	Date	Opposition	Res	H.T.	Att	Goalscorers
1	19 Oct	RHEIMS F.C.	5-2	3-2	15552	Eisentrager, White, J.Regan, Rodgers, Rogers
2	1 Feb	LINZ A.S.K.	3-1	1-1	10582	Burden, Nelson, White
3	6 May	St. Blazey	1-0		3000	Rogers
4	7	Helston Athletic	5-1			Rogers(2), Boxley, Rodgers, White
5	22	Hamborn 07	5-1	3-1	7000	D.Regan(2), Rogers(2), White
6	25	Augsburgh	0-0	0-0	2000	
7	26	Linz A.S.K.	1-2	0-1		Mickwright
8	30	Stuggart Kickers	1-0	0-0	6500	Atyeo
9	1 Jun	Singen	3-2	2-2	4000	Atyeo, Boxley, Rogers

FINAL LEAGUE TABLE

		P	W	D	L	F:A	Pts
1	Bristol C	46	30	10	6	101:47	70
2	Leyton Orient	46	26	9	11	89:47	61
3	Southampton	46	24	11	11	75:51	59
4	Gillingham	46	20	15	11	77:66	55
5	Millwall	46	20	11	15	72:68	51
6	Brighton	46	20	10	16	76:63	50
7	Watford	46	18	14	14	71:62	50
8	Torquay	46	18	12	16	82:82	48
9	Coventry	46	18	11	17	67:59	47
10	Southend	46	17	12	17	83:80	46
11	Brentford	46	16	14	16	82:82	46
11	Norwich	46	18	10	18	60:60	46
13	Northampton	46	19	8	19	73:81	46
14	Aldershot	46	16	13	17	75:71	45
15	QPR	46	15	14	17	69:75	44
16	Shrewsbury	46	16	10	20	70:78	42
17	Bournemouth	46	12	18	16	57:65	42
18	Reading	46	13	15	18	65:73	41
19	Newport	46	11	16	19	60:73	38
20	Crystal Palace	46	11	16	19	52:80	38
21	Swindon	46	11	15	20	46:64	37
22	Exeter	46	11	15	20	47:73	37
23	Walsall	46	10	14	22	75:86	34
24	Colchester	46	9	13	24	53:91	31

SEASON 1955-56
FOOTBALL LEAGUE DIVISION TWO

No.	Date	Opposition	Pos.	Res.	H.T.	Att.	Goalscorers	Anderson J.R.	Guy I.	Thresher T.M.J.	White J.	Peacock E.G.	Williams C.E.	Regan D.J.T.	Atyeo P.J.W.	Rogers J.R.	Burden T.D.	Boxley J.	Eisentrager A.B.	Smith D.R.	Cook A.	Rodgers A.W.	Regan J.	Compton T.D.	Virgin D.E.	Bailey E.J.	Jackson N.E.	Hinshelwood W.	Steel R.
1	20 Aug	SWANSEA TOWN		2-1	1-0	31618	Rogers, Williams	1	2	3	4	5	6	7	8	9	10	11											
2	22	Rotherham United		3-1	1-0	15112	Atyeo, Eisentrager, Rogers	1	2	3	4	5	6	7	8	9		11	10										
3	27	Notts County	9	2-3	1-2	15000	Atyeo(pen), Williams	1	2	3	4	5	6	7	8	9	10	11											
4	30	ROTHERHAM UNITED	4	5-2	5-1	27142	Rogers(2), Atyeo, Eisentrager, White	1	2	3	4	5	6		8	9	10	11	7										
5	3 Sep	LEEDS UNITED	6	0-1	0-0	31060		1	2	3	4	5	6			9	10	11	8	7									
6	6	WEST HAM UNITED	3	3-1	2-0	25993	Atyeo, Rodgers, O.G.		2	3	4	5	6		8		10	11	7			1	9						
7	10	Fulham	8	0-3	0-1	26847			2	3	4	5	6		8		10	11	7			1	9						
8	17	BURY	8	3-1	2-0	22949	Atyeo(3,1pen)		2	3	4	5	6		8		10	11	7			1	9						
9	24	Barnsley	9	0-0	0-0	19447			2	3	4	5	6		8		10	11	7			1	9						
10	1 Oct	MIDDLESBROUGH	7	2-0	1-0	28788	Atyeo, Rodgers		2	3	4	5	6		8		10	11	7			1	9						
11	8	LIVERPOOL	4	2-1	0-1	25496	Atyeo(2)		2	3	4	5	6		8	9	10	11	7			1							
12	15	Leicester City	4	2-2	1-2	28254	Atyeo, Rogers		2	3	4	5	6		8	9	10	11	7			1							
13	22	BRISTOL ROVERS	5	1-1	0-0	39583	Rogers		2	3	4	5	6		8	9	10	11	7			1							
14	29	Blackburn Rovers	2	6-4	4-2	24695	Atyeo(2), Boxley, Burden, Eisentrager, Rogers		2	3	4	5	6		8	9	10	11	7			1							
15	5 Nov	HULL CITY	2	5-2	2-1	22776	Rogers(2), Atyeo, Eisentrager, Peacock		2	3	4	5	6		8	9	10	11	7			1							
16	12	Nottingham Forest	2	2-0	1-0	14145	Atyeo, O.G.		2	3	4	5			8	9	10	11	7			1		6					
17	19	SHEFFIELD WEDNESDAY	1	3-2	2-1	32731	Rogers(2), Atyeo		2	3	4	5	6		8	9	10	11	7			1							
18	26	Doncaster Rovers	1	2-3	0-0	11144	Burden, Rogers		2	3	4	5	6		8	9	10	11	7			1							
19	3 Dec	LINCOLN CITY	1	5-1	3-0	26329	Atyeo(3), Rogers, Williams		2	3	4				8	9	10	11	7			1		5					
20	10	Stoke City	1	2-4	1-3	17039	Atyeo(pen), Rogers		2	3	4	5	6		8	9	10	11	7			1							
21	17	Swansea Town	1	1-2	1-2	23000	Eisentrager		2	3	4	5	6		8	9	10	11	7			1							
22	24	NOTTS COUNTY	0	1-3	1-0	24075	Rogers		2	3	4	5	6		8	9	10	11	7			1							
23	26	Plymouth Argyle	4	0-5	0-2	22096			2	3	4	5				9	10	11	8	7	1		6						
24	27	PLYMOUTH ARGYLE	2	6-0	3-0	27716	Rogers(3), Atyeo(2), Burden	1	2	3	4	5			8	9	10	11						6		7			
25	31	Leeds United	5	1-2	0-2	31751	Rogers	1	2	3	4	5			8	9	10	11	8					6		7			
26	14 Jan	FULHAM	3	2-1	0-0	27798	Atyeo, Eisentrager	1	2	3	4		6		8	9	10	11	7					5					
27	21	Bury	2	1-1	0-0	13832	Rogers	1	2	3	4	5	6		8	9	10	11	7										
28	4 Feb	BARNSLEY	3	2-0	1-0	19581	Atyeo, Boxley	1	2	3	4	5	6		8	9	10	11	7										
29	11	Middlesbrough	3	1-2	1-1	15412	Burden	1	2		4	5	6		8	9	10	11	7							3			
30	18	Sheffield Wednesday	5	1-2	1-1	22539	Burden	1		3	4	5	6		8	9	10	11									2	7	
31	25	LEICESTER CITY	4	1-1	1-1	27654	Burden	1	2	3	4	5	6		8	9	10	11										7	
32	3 Mar	Bristol Rovers	3	3-0	1-0	35324	Atyeo(2), Rogers	1	2	3	4	5	6		8	9	10	11										7	
33	10	STOKE CITY	4	0-1	0-1	28275		1	2	3	4	5	6		8	9	10	11										7	
34	17	Hull City	4	3-1	1-0	11174	Atyeo, Hinshelwood, Rodgers	1	2	3	4	5	6		8		10				11		9					7	
35	24	NOTTINGHAM FOREST	4	0-0	0-0	22824		1	2	3	4	5	6		8		10	11					9					7	
36	30	Port Vale	6	0-2	0-1	24900		1	2	3	4	5	6		8		10	11					9					7	
37	31	Liverpool	7	1-2	1-0	46713	Atyeo	1	2		3	5	6		8	9	4	11	10									7	
38	2 Apr	PORT VALE	8	0-0	0-0	24348		1	2			5	6		8	9	4	11	10						3			7	
39	7	DONCASTER ROVERS	5	4-1	1-0	20777	Rogers(3), Atyeo	1	2		4	5			8	7	6	11	10				9		3				
40	14	Lincoln City	8	0-2	0-1	10311		1	2		4	5			8	7	6		10				9		3		11		
41	21	BLACKBURN ROVERS	7	2-0	2-0	20554	Burden, Rogers		6		4				8	9	10	11	7		1				5	3			2
42	28	West Ham United	8	0-3	0-1	13000			6		4				8	9	10	11	7		1				5	3			2
							Apps.	22	39	35	41	40	34	3	39	34	41	40	32	3	20	10	4	4	2	6	1	10	2
							Goals				1	1	3		30	25	6	2	6			3						1	

F.A. CUP

3R	7 Jan	Everton		1-3	0-1	46493	Atyeo (£6488.17.6)	1	2	3	4	5	6		8	9	10	11						7					

GLOUCESTERSHIRE CUP FINAL

	30 Apr	BRISTOL ROVERS		0-1	0-1	11952	(£1711)

FRIENDLIES

1	27 Sep	FRANKFURT		3-3	1-2	13713	Atyeo(2), Burden
2	8 Nov	STUTTGART KICKERS		3-1	1-0	9391	Burden(2), Eisentrager
3	6 Dec	NICE		1-1	1-1	12039	Rogers
4	25 Jan	HUDDERSFIELD TOWN		2-2	0-1	10188	Atyeo, Fitzgerald
5	6 Feb	Bridgwater Town		6-3	4-1	2500	Burden(2), Rogers(2), Atyeo, Eisentrager
6	23 Apr	Chippenham Town		7-1	5-0	1500	Atyeo(2), Eisentrager(2), Rogers(2), Watkins
7	4 May	Newquay		6-2	3-0		Hinshelwood(2), Rogers(2), C.Williams(2)
8	5	Helston Athletic		5-1			Rogers(2), Boxley, White, C.Williams
9	27	Nice		3-1	1-0	2500	Rogers(2), C.Williams

FINAL LEAGUE TABLE

1	Sheffield W.	42	21	13	8	101·62	55
2	Leeds	42	23	6	13	80·60	52
3	Liverpool	42	21	6	15	85·63	48
4	Blackburn	42	21	6	15	84·65	48
5	Leicester	42	21	6	15	94·78	48
6	Bristol R.	42	21	6	15	84·70	48
7	Nottingham F.	42	19	9	14	68·63	47
8	Lincoln	42	18	10	14	79·65	46
9	Fulham	42	20	6	16	89·79	46
10	Swansea	42	20	6	16	83·81	46
11	Bristol C.	42	19	7	16	80·64	45
12	Port Vale	42	16	13	13	60·58	45
13	Stoke	42	20	4	18	71·62	44
14	Middlesbrough	42	16	8	18	76·78	40
15	Bury	42	16	8	18	86·90	40
16	West Ham	42	14	11	17	74·69	39
17	Doncaster	42	12	11	19	69·96	35
18	Barnsley	42	11	12	19	47·84	34
19	Rotherham	42	12	9	21	56·75	33
20	Notts Co.	42	11	9	22	55·82	31
21	Plymouth	42	10	8	24	54·87	28
22	Hull	42	10	6	26	53·97	26

1955-56 Season
Back: J.Regan, Watkins, Steel, Morgan Guy, Anderson, Atyeo, Cook, Woodfield, Compton.
Middle: Bailey, Rawlings, Eisentrager, Thresher, White, Rogers, Rodgers, Wilshire, Nelson.
Front: Gerrish, Cyril Williams, Jackson, Peacock, M.Smith, Micklewright, Boxley, Knight, D.Regan.

BRISTOL CITY, 1956-57 : Back (left to right)—A. Williams, J. Atyeo, I. Guy, R. Anderson, J. Bailey, T. Burden. Front (left to right—W. Hinshelwood, C. Williams, J. White, R. Etheridge, J. Watkins.

SEASON 1956-57
FOOTBALL LEAGUE DIVISION TWO

The match-by-match record below is followed by the player line-up grid. The player columns, in order, are:

Cook A., Baillie J., Thresher T.M.J., White J., Peacock E.G., Williams C.E., Hinshelwood W., Eisentrager A.B., Atyeo P.J.W., Burden T.D., Boxley J., Rogers J.R., Smith D.R., Compton T.D., Anderson J.R., Guy I., Bailey E.J., Walker G.W., Watkins J.V., Curtis D.P., Etheridge R.J., Williams Alan, Cook C.I., Terris J., Emery T.G.

No.	Date	Opposition	Pos.	Res.	H.T.	Att.	Goalscorers
1	18 Aug	Lincoln City		1-1	0-0	12842	Atyeo
2	21	NOTTINGHAM FOREST		1-5	0-2	27898	Atyeo
3	25	ROTHERHAM UNITED	12	2-1	2-0	21241	Atyeo(2)
4	30	Nottingham Forest	14	2-2	1-1	22032	Atyeo, Smith
5	1 Sep	Port Vale	17	1-3	0-2	17645	Rogers
6	4	FULHAM	18	0-3	0-3	22675	
7	8	BARNSLEY	20	1-2	1-1	19863	Atyeo
8	12	Fulham	20	1-2	1-1	15019	Hinshelwood
9	15	Sheffield United	20	1-1	0-0	22962	Atyeo
10	22	BRISTOL ROVERS	18	5-3	1-1	37207	Atyeo(2), C.Williams(2), Hinshelwood
11	29	BLACKBURN ROVERS	15	3-0	1-0	23323	Rogers(2), Atyeo
12	6 Oct	Notts County	13	1-1	1-1	12000	C.Williams
13	13	LIVERPOOL	12	2-1	1-1	26263	Rogers, C.Williams
14	20	Middlesbrough	14	1-4	0-1	23824	Rogers
15	27	HUDDERSFIELD TOWN	12	2-1	1-1	25111	Atyeo, Burden
16	3 Nov	Bury	11	3-2	1-2	9641	Hinshelwood(2), C.Williams
17	10	GRIMSBY TOWN	15	0-2	0-1	19202	
18	17	Doncaster Rovers	15	1-4	1-1	12472	White(pen)
19	24	STOKE CITY	16	1-2	0-2	18022	Watkins
20	1 Dec	Leyton Orient	16	2-2	2-1	17573	Hinshelwood, Walker
21	8	LEICESTER CITY	16	0-2	0-1	24757	
22	15	LINCOLN CITY	16	4-2	1-1	12772	Hinshelwood(?), Atyeo, Curtis, Watkins
23	22	Rotherham United	19	1-6	1-2	4453	Peacock
24	26	Swansea Town	19	0-5	0-1	18000	
25	29	PORT VALE	19	3-3	3-2	18561	Burden, Curtis, Etheridge
26	12 Jan	Barnsley	19	0-3	0-1	13439	
27	19	SHEFFIELD UNITED	19	5-1	3-1	19968	Atyeo(3), Etheridge, C.Williams
28	2 Feb	Bristol Rovers	19	0-0	0-0	32055	
29	9	Blackburn Rovers	19	1-3	1-1	25986	C.Williams
30	20	NOTTS COUNTY	18	3-0	3-0	19288	Atyeo, Watkins(pen), C.Williams
31	23	Liverpool	18	1-0	1-0	17492	Etheridge (Aband. half-time, waterlogged pitch)
32	2 Mar	MIDDLESBROUGH	18	2-1	2-1	22402	Etheridge, Watkins(pen)
33	9	Huddersfield Town	18	1-2	1-0	14218	Atyeo
34	16	BURY	18	2-0	1-0	15167	Atyeo(2)
35	23	Grimsby Town	16	3-0	1-0	12692	Curtis(2), O.G.
36	30	DONCASTER ROVERS	16	4-0	4-0	18848	Etheridge(2), Atyeo, Curtis
37	6 Apr	Stoke City	15	2-0	0-0	13397	Atyeo, Watkins
38	13	LEYTON ORIENT	14	4-2	1-1	19350	Curtis(2), Atyeo, Etheridge
39	19	WEST HAM UNITED	14	1-0	0-1	24731	Curtis
40	20	Leicester City	14	1-1	1-1	32653	Curtis
41	22	West Ham United	15	1-3	1-1	9500	Atyeo
42	27	SWANSEA TOWN	13	3-1	1-0	19344	Curtis(3)
43	1 May	Liverpool	13	1-2	0-1	15108	Curtis

Appearances and Goals

	Cook A.	Baillie	Thresher	White	Peacock	Williams C.E.	Hinshelwood	Eisentrager	Atyeo	Burden	Boxley	Rogers	Smith	Compton	Anderson	Guy	Bailey	Walker	Watkins	Curtis	Etheridge	Williams A.	Cook C.I.	Terris	Emery
Apps	21	10	37	37	19	22	41	11	37	40	5	16	15	21	22	21	19	2	24	16	22	12	1	1	1
Goals				1	1	8	7		23	2		5	1					1	5	13	7				

F.A. CUP

	Date	Opposition	Res.	H.T.	Att.	Goalscorers
3R	5 Jan	ROTHERHAM UNITED	4-1	2-1	25048	Atyeo(2), Curtis, Hinshelwood (£3586)
4R	26	RHYL	3-0	2-0	29438	Atyeo(2), Etheridge (£4112.7.6)
5R	16 Feb	Aston Villa	1-2	1-1	63099	Atyeo

GLOUCESTERSHIRE CUP FINAL

	Date	Opposition	Res.	H.T.	Att.	Goalscorers
	29 Apr	Bristol Rovers	2-1	1-1	14648	Atyeo, Curtis

FRIENDLIES

	Date	Opposition	Res.	H.T.	Att.	Goalscorers
1	15 Oct	Gloucester City	1-1	0-0		Boxley
2	12 Nov	MANAGERS XI	4-2	3-1	7820	Boxley, Smith, Walker, White
3	4 Dec	RADNICKI	2-0	1-0	12207	Etheridge, Watkins
4	12 Mar	SHELBOURNE	3-1	2-0	8989	Atyeo, Burden, O.G.
5	17 May	Shelbourne Select	6-1	2-0		Etheridge(2), Watkins(2), Hinshelwood, Williams

FINAL LEAGUE TABLE

	Team	P	W	D	L	F:A	Pts
1	Leicester	42	25	11	6	109:67	61
2	Nottingham F.	42	22	10	10	94:55	54
3	Liverpool	42	21	11	10	82:54	53
4	Blackburn	42	21	10	11	83:75	52
5	Stoke	42	20	8	14	83:58	48
6	Middlesbrough	42	19	10	13	84:60	48
7	Sheffield U.	42	19	8	15	87:76	46
8	West Ham	42	19	8	15	59:63	46
9	Bristol R.	42	18	9	15	81:67	45
10	Swansea	42	19	7	16	90:90	45
11	Fulham	42	19	4	19	84:76	42
12	Huddersfield	42	18	6	18	68:74	42
13	Bristol C.	42	16	9	17	74:79	41
14	Doncaster	42	15	10	17	77:77	40
15	Leyton Orient	42	15	10	17	66:84	40
16	Grimsby	42	17	5	20	61:62	39
17	Rotherham	42	13	11	18	74:75	37
18	Lincoln	42	14	6	22	54:80	34
19	Barnsley	42	12	10	20	59:89	34
20	Notts Co.	42	9	12	21	58:86	30
21	Bury	42	8	9	25	60:96	25
22	Port Vale	42	8	6	28	57:101	22

SEASON 1957-58
FOOTBALL LEAGUE DIVISION TWO

No.	Date	Opposition	Pos.	Res.	H.T.	Att.	Goalscorers
1	24 Aug	LIVERPOOL		1-2	1-0	28431	Watkins
2	26	Stoke City		0-3	0-2	23001	
3	31	Middlesbrough	19	0-0	0-0	21834	
4	3 Sep	STOKE CITY	14	2-1	2-1	25817	Atyeo, Burden
5	7	LEYTON ORIENT	16	2-2	0-2	23283	Etheridge, Hinshelwood
6	10	GRIMSBY TOWN	13	3-2	2-1	20127	Atyeo(2), Watkins(pen)
7	14	Charlton Athletic	17	0-1	0-1	22354	
8	17	Grimsby Town	15	1-1	0-0	11970	Atyeo
9	21	DONCASTER ROVERS	17	2-2	1-2	21476	Atyeo(2)
10	28	Rotherham United	18	1-4	0-1	8715	Etheridge
11	5 Oct	HUDDERSFIELD TOWN	19	1-3	1-1	21636	Watkins(pen)
12	12	BRISTOL ROVERS	18	3-2	1-0	33746	Atyeo(2), Walker
13	26	NOTTS COUNTY	15	3-1	2-1	18394	Atyeo(2), Watkins(pen)
14	2 Nov	Ipswich Town	17	2-4	1-3	17683	Atyeo, Eisentrager
15	9	BLACKBURN ROVERS	18	0-0	0-0	23276	
16	16	Sheffield United	15	3-0	1-0	15278	Atyeo(3)
17	23	WEST HAM UNITED	15	1-1	1-0	22305	Walker
18	30	Barnsley	17	1-4	1-1	13449	Atyeo
19	7 Dec	FULHAM	18	0-5	0-4	16983	
20	14	Swansea Town	20	1-5	0-3	10200	Curtis
21	21	Liverpool	21	3-4	0-2	38051	Burden, Curtis, Watkins
22	25	DERBY COUNTY	18	2-1	1-0	17090	Atyeo(2)
23	26	Derby County	19	2-5	1-2	25630	Atyeo, Curtis
24	28	MIDDLESBROUGH	18	0-0	0-0	23124	
25	11 Jan	Leyton Orient	20	0-4	0-1	15862	
26	18	CHARLTON ATHLETIC	20	1-2	1-0	19526	Atyeo
27	1 Feb	Doncaster Rovers	21	1-2	1-1	9752	Walker
28	8	ROTHERHAM UNITED	21	0-1	0-0	25639	
29	19	Huddersfield Town	21	0-0	0-0	5971	
30	22	West Ham United	21	2-3	1-2	21616	Hinshelwood, Tindill
31	1 Mar	LINCOLN CITY	20	4-0	3-0	20041	Etheridge(2), Watkins(2,1pen)
32	8	Notts County	19	1-0	0-0	9942	Tindill
33	15	IPSWICH TOWN	18	1-0	0-0	20101	Tindill
34	24	Blackburn Rovers	18	0-5	0-0	8825	
35	29	SHEFFIELD UNITED	18	1-4	0-2	20215	Atyeo
36	4 Apr	Cardiff City	18	3-2	2-2	20000	Atyeo, Etheridge, Tindill
37	5	Bristol Rovers	17	3-3	3-3	24782	Etheridge, Hinshelwood, O.G.
38	7	CARDIFF CITY	17	2-0	0-0	25726	Atyeo, Etheridge
39	12	BARNSLEY	17	5-0	3-0	18249	Tindill(3), Watkins(2,1pen)
40	19	Fulham	17	4-3	4-0	27200	Tindill(3), Atyeo
41	23	Lincoln City	17	0-4	0-3	11001	
42	26	SWANSEA TOWN	17	1-2	1-1	18029	Walker

Player appearances (shirt numbers). Column legend:
1 Anderson J.R., 2 Bailey E.J., 3 Thresher T.M.J., 4 Burden T.D., 5 White J., 6 Williams Alan, 7 Hinshelwood W., 8 Atyeo P.J.W., 9 Curtis D.P., 10 Etheridge R.J., 11 Watkins J.V., 12 Peacock E.G., 13 Compton T.D., 14 Williams C.E., 15 Eisentrager A.B., 16 Cook C.I., 17 Walker G.W., 18 Rae J., 19 Cook A., 20 Parr G., 21 Munroe W.J., 22 Smith D.R., 23 Emery T.G., 24 Terris J., 25 Tindill H., 26 Briggs A.M., 27 McCall P., 28 Virgir D.E., 29 Bevan B.E.

Apps.	35	12	41	38	20	34	38	42	11	31	40	30	3	3	8	1	12	12	7	2	1	1	10	3	14	4	7	1	1
Goals		2					3	23	3	7	9				1		4								10				

F.A. CUP

Rnd	Date	Opposition	Res.	H.T.	Att.	Goalscorers
3R	4 Jan	Accrington Stanley	2-2	1-1	12278	Curtis, Hinshelwood
3Rr	7	ACCRINGTON STANLEY	3-1	1-1	32196	Atyeo(2), Curtis (£4340.10.0)
4R	25	Notts County	2-1	0-0	18395	Etheridge, Hinshelwood (£2545)
5R	15 Feb	BRISTOL ROVERS	3-4	1-3	39160	Burden, Etheridge, Watkins (£5439.1.0)

GLOUCESTERSHIRE CUP FINAL

Date	Opposition	Res.	H.T.	Att.	Goalscorers
29 Apr	BRISTOL ROVERS	4-1	2-1	10590	Etheridge(2), Atyeo, Curtis

FRIENDLIES

No.	Date	Opposition	Res.	H.T.	Att.	Goalscorers
1	22 Oct	NICE	4-2	2-0	9516	Hinshelwood(2), Walker, Watkins
2	6 Nov	TOTTENHAM HOTSPUR	4-3	3-2	13089	Atyeo(2), Hinshelwood, Walker
3	12	SINGEN	4-2	2-1	6402	Atyeo, Etheridge, Hinshelwood, Walker
4	25	Reading	1-2	0-2	3902	Watkins
5	15 May	Nice	0-3	0-1	5000	
6	21	Bordeaux	2-1	1-1		Hinshelwood, Watkins
7	22	Ruffec	4-3	4-1		Tindill(3), Bevan

FINAL LEAGUE TABLE

		P	W	D	L	F	A	Pts
1	West Ham	42	23	11	8	101	54	57
2	Blackburn	42	22	12	8	93	57	56
3	Charlton	42	24	7	11	107	69	55
4	Liverpool	42	22	10	10	79	54	54
5	Fulham	42	20	12	10	97	59	52
6	Sheffield U.	42	21	10	11	75	50	52
7	Middlesbrough	42	19	7	16	83	74	45
8	Ipswich	42	16	12	14	68	69	44
9	Huddersfield	42	14	16	12	63	66	44
10	Bristol R.	42	17	8	17	85	80	42
11	Stoke	42	18	6	18	75	73	42
12	Leyton Orient	42	18	5	19	77	79	41
13	Grimsby	42	17	6	19	86	83	40
14	Barnsley	42	14	12	16	70	74	40
15	Cardiff	42	14	9	19	63	77	37
16	Derby	42	14	8	20	60	81	36
17	Bristol C.	42	13	9	20	63	88	35
18	Rotherham	42	14	5	23	65	101	33
19	Swansea	42	11	9	22	72	99	31
20	Lincoln	42	11	9	22	55	82	31
21	Notts Co.	42	12	6	24	44	80	30
22	Doncaster	42	8	11	23	56	88	27

1957-58 Season
Back: Terris, Walker, Atyeo, Anderson, Emery, Alan Williams.
Front: Hinshelwood, Thresher, Burden, Etheridge, Tindill.

BRISTOL CITY FOOTBALL CLUB 1958-9
A.Williams, J.Atyeo, A.Cook, M.Thresher, P.McCall.
W.Hinshelwood, G.Hopkinson, B.Tindill, T.Burden, R.Etheridge, J.Watkins.

SEASON 1958-59
FOOTBALL LEAGUE DIVISION TWO

No.	Date	Opposition	Pos.	Res.	H.T.	Att.	Goalscorers	Anderson J.R.	Peacock E.G.	Thresher T.M.J.	McCall P.	Williams Alan	Burden T.D.	Hinshelwood W.	Tindill H.	Atyeo P.J.W.	Etheridge R.J.	Watkins J.V.	Cook A.	Hopkinson G.	Virgin D.E.	Rogers J.R.	Walker G.W.	Smith D.R.	Casey T.	Williams R.G.
1	23 Aug	ROTHERHAM UNITED		6-1	1-1	25253	Hinshelwood(2), Tindill(2), Atyeo, Etheridge	1	2	3	4	5	6	7	8	9	10	11								
2	27	Barnsley		7-4	2-1	14187	Atyeo(3), Tindill(2), Etheridge, Watkins	1	2	3	4	5	6	7	8	9	10	11								
3	30	Sheffield United	5	0-4	0-2	23170		1	2	3	4	5	6	7	8	9	10	11								
4	2 Sep	BARNSLEY	2	3-1	1-1	28530	Atyeo, Tindill, Watkins	1	2	3	4	5	6	7	8	9	10	11								
5	6	BRIGHTON & HOVE ALB.	2	3-0	2-0	23661	Atyeo, Etheridge, McCall	1	2	3	4	5	6	7	8	9	10	11								
6	9	Huddersfield Town	2	1-0	1-0	13884	Atyeo		2	3	4	5	6	7	8	9	10	11	1							
7	13	Grimsby Town	3	0-2	0-2	15606			2	3	4	5	6	7	8	9	10	11	1							
8	16	HUDDERSFIELD TOWN	2	2-1	2-0	29428	Tindill, Watkins		2	3	4	5	6	7	8	9	10	11	1							
9	20	LIVERPOOL	3	1-3	1-1	27162	O.G.			3	4	5	6	7	8	9	10	11	1	2						
10	27	Middlesbrough	3	0-0	0-0	29275				3	4	5	6	7	8	9	10	11	1	2						
11	4 Oct	CHARLTON ATHLETIC	5	2-4	1-1	23831	Etheridge, Tindill			3	4	5	6	7	8	9	10	11	1	2						
12	11	SWANSEA TOWN	5	4-0	1-0	24309	Atyeo(3), Watkins			3	4	5	6	7	8	9	10	11	1	2						
13	18	Stoke City	5	1-2	0-0	22657	Etheridge			3	4	5	6	7	8	9	10	11	1	2						
14	25	SUNDERLAND	4	4-1	3-1	25510	Virgin(2), Atyeo, Tindill			3	4	5	6		8	9	10	11	1	2	7					
15	1 Nov	Bristol Rovers	4	2-1	0-0	32104	Atyeo, Tindill			3	4	5	6		8	9	10	11	1	2	7					
16	8	FULHAM	3	1-1	1-1	32378	Etheridge(pen)			3	4	5	6	7	8	9	10	11	1	2						
17	15	Sheffield Wednesday	3	3-2	1-2	30164	Atyeo, Tindill, A.Williams			3	4	5	6	7	8	9	10	11	1	2						
18	22	SCUNTHORPE UNITED	3	0-1	0-0	20306				3	4	5	6	7	8	9	10	11	1	2						
19	29	Leyton Orient	4	2-4	0-1	9591	Atyeo, Etheridge			3	4	5	6	7	8	9	10	11	1	2						
20	6 Dec	DERBY COUNTY	6	1-3	0-1	20312	Etheridge			3	4	5	6	7	11	8	10		1	2		9				
21	13	Lincoln City	5	2-0	2-0	7040	Hopkinson, Tindill			3	4	5	6	7	8		10	11	1	2		9				
22	20	Rotherham United	5	2-1	1-0	6551	Atyeo, Hinshelwood			3	4	5	6	7	9	8	10	11	1	2						
23	26	CARDIFF CITY	6	2-3	1-1	27570	Atyeo, Etheridge			3	4	5	6	7	8	9	10	11	1	2						
24	27	Cardiff City	6	0-1	0-1	30000				3	4	5	6	7	9		10	11	1	2			8			
25	3 Jan	SHEFFIELD UNITED	6	3-1	2-0	20834	Tindill(2), Atyeo			3	4	5	6	7	8	9	10		1	2				11		
26	17	Brighton & Hove Albion	6	2-2	1-0	18166	Tindill(2)			3	4	5	6	7	8	9	10		1	2				11		
27	7 Feb	Liverpool	9	2-3	1-2	34091	Atyeo, Tindill			3	4	5	6	7	8	9	10		1	2			11			
28	14	MIDDLESBROUGH	8	2-2	1-0	18336	Atyeo, Etheridge			3	4	5	6	7	8	9	10		1	2			11			
29	21	Charlton Athletic	10	1-4	0-1	11146	Tindill			3	4	5	6	7	8	9	10		1	2			11			
30	24	GRIMSBY TOWN	8	1-0	1-0	15440	Atyeo			3	4	5	6	7	8	9	10		1	2			11			
31	28	Fulham	9	0-1	0-1	27000				3	4	5	6	7	8	9	10		1	2			11			
32	7 Mar	STOKE CITY	8	2-1	1-0	15945	Burden, Tindill			3	4	5	6	7	8	9	10		1	2	11					
33	14	Sunderland	9	1-3	1-0	24094	Atyeo			3	4	5	6	7	8	9	10		1	2	11					
34	21	BRISTOL ROVERS	10	1-1	0-1	27140	Atyeo				4	5	3	7	8	9	10	11	1	2					6	
35	27	IPSWICH TOWN	8	3-0	1-0	20117	Etheridge(2,1pen), Watkins			3		5	4	7	8	9	10	11	1	2					6	
36	28	Swansea Town	8	0-1	0-0	14000				3	4		5	7	8	9	10	11	1	2					6	
37	30	Ipswich Town	8	1-1	1-0	13652	Atyeo			3	4		5	7	8	9	10	11	1	2					6	
38	4 Apr	SHEFFIELD WEDNESDAY	10	1-2	1-2	21495	Tindill			3		5	4	7	8	9	10	11	1	2					6	
39	11	Scunthorpe United	8	3-3	2-1	11101	Atyeo(2), Etheridge(pen)			3	4		5	7	8	9	10	11	1	2					6	
40	18	LEYTON ORIENT	12	0-1	0-0	14708				3		5	4	7	8	9		11	1	2					6	10
41	21	LINCOLN CITY	8	1-0	1-0	10369	Atyeo			3		5	4	7	8	9	10		1	2			11		6	
42	25	Derby County	10	1-4	0-2	12034	R.Williams			3	4	5		7	8	9	6		1	2			11			10
		Apps.						5	8	41	38	39	41	40	42	40	42	40	41	30	37	34	4	9	1	2	8	2
		Goals									1	1	1	3	19	26	13	5			1	2					1

F.A. CUP

3R	19 Jan	Doncaster Rovers		2-0	1-0	8432	Tindill, Watkins (£1142)			3	4	5	6	7	8	9	10	11	1	2						
4R	24	BLACKPOOL		1-1	1-0	42594	Tindill (£5569.15.6)			3	4	5	6	7	8	9	10	11	1	2						
4Rr	28	Blackpool		0-1	0-0	25933				3	4	5	6	7	10	9	8	11	1	2						

GLOUCESTERSHIRE CUP FINAL

| | 4 May | Bristol Rovers | | 1-1 | 0-1 | 11022 | Tindill |

FRIENDLIES

| 1 | 21 Oct | BORDEAUX | | 2-0 | 2-0 | 7118 | Atyeo(2) |
| 2 | 10 Nov | ALL STAR MANAGERS XI | | 6-5 | 2-0 | 5503 | Atyeo(4), Etheridge, James |

FINAL LEAGUE TABLE

		P	W	D	L	F	A	Pts
1	Sheffield W	42	28	6	8	106	48	62
2	Fulham	42	27	6	9	96	61	60
3	Sheffield U.	42	23	7	12	82	48	53
4	Liverpool	42	24	5	13	87	62	53
5	Stoke	42	21	7	14	72	58	49
6	Bristol R.	42	18	12	12	80	64	48
7	Derby	42	20	8	14	74	71	48
8	Charlton	42	18	7	17	92	90	43
9	Cardiff	42	18	7	17	65	65	43
10	Bristol C.	42	17	7	18	74	70	41
11	Swansea	42	16	9	17	79	81	41
12	Brighton	42	15	11	16	74	90	41
13	Middlesbrough	42	15	10	17	87	71	40
14	Huddersfield	42	16	8	18	62	55	40
15	Sunderland	42	16	8	18	64	75	40
16	Ipswich	42	17	6	19	62	77	40
17	Leyton Orient	42	14	8	20	71	78	36
18	Scunthorpe	42	12	9	21	55	84	33
19	Lincoln	42	11	7	24	63	93	29
20	Rotherham	42	10	9	23	42	82	29
21	Grimsby	42	9	10	23	62	90	28
22	Barnsley	42	10	7	25	55	91	27

SEASON 1959-60
FOOTBALL LEAGUE DIVISION TWO

No.	Date	Opposition	Pos.	Res.	H.T.	Att.	Goalscorers	Cook A.	Collinson R.	Thresher T.M.J.	Burden T.D.	Williams Alan	Casey T.	Hinshelwood W.	Cavanagh T.H.	Atyeo P.J.W.	Rogers J.R.	McCann J.	Hopkinson G.	McCall P.	Etheridge R.J.	Briggs A.M.	Taylor A.M.	Williams R.G.	Virgin D.E.	Jacobs F.A.	Coggins P.R.F.	Graham M.	Hill A.G.	Derrick J.S.	Bevan B.E.
1	22 Aug	Scunthrope United		1-1	0-1	10862	Rogers	1	2	3	4	5	6	7	8	9	10	11													
2	26	Liverpool		2-4	1-2	33071	Atyeo, Rogers	1		3		5	6	7	8	9	10	11	2	4											
3	29	ROTHERHAM UNITED	18	2-3	0-1	20407	Cavanagh(pen), Hinshelwood	1		3	4		6	7	8	9	10	11	2		5										
4	1 Sep	LIVERPOOL	14	1-0	1-0	22766	Rogers	1		3	4	5	6	7		9	8	11	2		10										
5	5	Cardiff City	18	2-4	1-4	22545	Atyeo, Hinshelwood	1		3	4	5	6	7		9	8	11	2		10										
6	9	Charlton Athletic	20	2-4	0-2	13461	Taylor, R.Williams	1			4	5	6	7		9		11	2				3	8	10						
7	12	HULL CITY	22	0-1	0-0	16427		1			4	5	6	7		9		11	2				3	8	10						
8	15	CHARLTON ATHLETIC	22	1-2	1-0	19717	Etheridge	1		3	5	4	6			8	7	11	2		10					9					
9	19	Sheffield United	22	2-5	1-2	17739	Rogers, Virgin	1		3		4	6			8	7	11	2	5	10					9					
10	26	MIDDLESBROUGH	18	2-0	1-0	21640	Rogers, A.Williams	1		3	4	9	6			8	7	11	2	5	10										
11	3 Oct	Derby County	20	0-3	0-2	16270		1		3	4	9	6			8	7	11	2	5	10										
12	10	BRISTOL ROVERS	20	2-1	0-0	26253	Atyeo(2)	1		3	4		6	7	8	9		11	2	5	10										
13	24	BRIGHTON & HOVE ALB.	20	0-1	0-0	18093		1		3	4		6	7	8	9		11	2	5	10										
14	31	Stoke City	20	3-1	1-1	14439	Graham(2), Atyeo	1	2	3		5	4			9		11			8						6	7	10		
15	7 Nov	PORTSMOUTH	18	2-0		21298	Atyeo, Graham	1	2	3		5	4			9		11			8						6	7	10		
16	14	Sunderland	20	2-3	1-1	21035	Graham, O.G.	1	2	3		5	4			9		11			8						6	7	10		
17	21	ASTON VILLA	21	0-5	0-2	29985		1	2	3		5	4			8		11									6	7	10	9	
18	28	Lincoln City	22	1-3	0-0	10671	Cavanagh	1	2	3		5	6	7	4	8	9				10									11	
19	5 Dec	LEYTON ORIENT	21	1-1	1-1	14126	Etheridge	1	2	3		5	6	7	4	8	9	11			10										
20	12	Huddersfield Town	22	1-6	0-5	10705	Rogers	1	2	3		5	6	7	4	8	9	11			10										
21	19	SCUNTHORPE UNITED	22	0-2	0-1	9099		1	2	3	6	5		7	4	8	9	11			10										
22	26	Plymouth Argyle	21	1-1	0-1	19277	Atyeo(2), Rogers, R.Williams	1	2	3	6	5			8	9	7	11		4				10							
23	28	PLYMOUTH ARGYLE	21	2-1	2-0	22644	Atyeo, Rogers	1	2	3	6	5			8	9	7			4				10						11	
24	2 Jan	Rotherham United	21	1-3	1-2	13594	Cavanagh	1	2	3	6	5			8	9	7			4				10							11
25	16	CARDIFF CITY	21	0-3	0-1	18184		1	2	3	6	5		7	8	9				4	10									11	
26	23	Hull City	21	1-1	1-1	12605	Atyeo	1	2	3	6	5	10	11	8	9				4							7				
27	6 Feb	SHEFFIELD UNITED	21	2-2	2-1	16248	Cavanagh, Graham	1	2	3	6	5		11	8	9				4							10	7			
28	13	Middlesbrough	21	3-6	1-3	17643	Cavanagh(pen), Graham, Rogers	1	2	3	5	6		11	8	9	7				4		16				10				
29	20	DERBY COUNTY	21	0-1	0-1	14055		1	2	3	6	5		11	8	9	7			4							10				
30	27	Bristol Rovers	21	1-2	1-2	27048	Graham	1	2	3	6	5			8	9	7	11		4							10				
31	5 Mar	SWANSEA TOWN	21	2-2	1-1	14368	Rogers(2)	1	2	3	6	5		11	8	9	7			4							10				
32	12	Brighton & Hove Albion	21	1-5	0-1	15962	Cavanagh	1	2	3	5	6		11	10	9	7			4							8				
33	19	LINCOLN CITY	21	1-0	1-0	16221	Rogers	1	2	3	10	6			9		7			5	4						8			11	
34	26	Portsmouth	21	0-2	0-2	15697		1	2	3	10	6			9		7	11		5	4						8				
35	2 Apr	SUNDERLAND	21	1-0	1-0	13437	Atyeo	1	2	3	8	6			9		7	11			4						10				
36	9	Aston Villa	21	1-2	1-2	38556	Collinson	1	2	3	8	5	6		9		7	11			4						10				
37	15	Ipswich Town	21	3-1	0-0	13050	Atyeo(2), Rogers	1	2	3	8	5	6		9		7				4			11			10				
38	16	HUDDERSFIELD TOWN	21	2-3	1-1	17722	Atyeo, O.G.	1	2	3	8	5	6		9		7				4			11			10				
39	18	IPSWICH TOWN	21	5-1	2-1	11140	Atyeo(2), Rogers(2), R.Williams	1	2	3	8	5	6		9		7				4			10	11						
40	23	Leyton Orient	22	1-3	1-2	9153	R.Williams	1	2	3	8	5	6		9		7				4			10						11	
41	26	Swansea Town	22	1-6	1-3	7920	Graham	1	2		5	6			9		7	11			4	2		8			10				
42	30	STOKE CITY	22	1-2	0-2	9013	Rogers	1			5	6			9		7				4	2		10						11	
							Apps.	42	29	40	30	39	25	20	24	42	31	26	12	20	27	4	2	9	8	4	4	14	3	6	1
							Goals		1			1		2	6	16	16				2		1	4	1			8			

F.A. CUP

| 3R | 9 Jan | CHARLTON ATHLETIC | | 2-3 | 2-0 | 18400 | Atyeo, Cavanagh (£2972.17.3) | 1 | 2 | 3 | 6 | 5 | | | 8 | 9 | 7 | | | 4 | 10 | | | | | | | | | 11 | |

GLOUCESTERSHIRE CUP FINAL

| | 2 May | BRISTOL ROVERS | | 3-2 | 0-1 | 7195 | Atyeo(2), Rogers |

FINAL LEAGUE TABLE

		P	W	D	L	F:A	Pts
1	Aston Villa	42	25	9	8	89:43	59
2	Cardiff	42	23	12	7	90:62	58
3	Liverpool	42	20	10	12	90:66	50
4	Sheffield U.	42	19	12	11	68:51	50
5	Middlesbrough	42	19	10	13	90:64	48
6	Huddersfield	42	19	9	14	73:52	47
7	Charlton	42	17	13	12	90:87	47
8	Rotherham	42	17	13	12	61:60	47
9	Bristol R.	42	18	11	13	72:78	47
10	Leyton Orient	42	15	14	13	76:61	44
11	Ipswich	42	19	6	17	78:68	44
12	Swansea	42	15	10	17	82:84	40
13	Lincoln	42	16	7	19	75:78	39
14	Brighton	42	13	12	17	67:76	38
15	Scunthorpe	42	13	10	19	57:71	36
16	Sunderland	42	12	12	18	52:65	36
17	Stoke	42	14	7	21	66:83	35
18	Derby	42	14	7	21	61:77	35
19	Plymouth	42	13	9	20	61:89	35
20	Portsmouth	42	10	12	20	59:77	32
21	Hull	42	10	10	22	48:76	30
22	Bristol C	42	11	5	26	60:97	27

1959-60 Season
Back: Hopkinson, Rogers, Etheridge, Cook, Cavanagh, Casey.
Front: Hinshelwood, Atyeo, Burden, Thresher, McCann.

Bristol City before the start of the 1960-61 season. Back row (left to right): Hopkinson, Derrick, McCall. Middle: Casey, Alan Williams, Etheridge, Cook, Anderson, Burden, Collinson, Thresher. Seated: Ryan, Rogers, Atyeo, Tait, McCann.

SEASON 1960-61
FOOTBALL LEAGUE DIVISION THREE

Player columns (left to right): Cook A., Collinson R., Thresher T.M.J., Burden T.D., Williams Alan, Casey T., Taylor A.M., Atyeo P.J.W., Virgin D.E., Ryan J.J., Derrick J.S., Williams R.G., Etheridge R.J., Rogers J.R., Tait A., McCann J., Boxley J., Hopkinson G., McCall P., Quinlan M., Briggs A.M., Connor J.F., Williams Adrian, Nicholson G.H., Jacobs F.A., Low G.A., Bush T.D., Peters R.D., Clark B.D.

No.	Date	Opposition	Pos.	Res.	H.T.	Att.	Goalscorers
1	20 Aug	Bradford City		0-2	0-0	11034	
2	23	BOURNEMOUTH & B.A.		1-0	0-0	14455	Derrick
3	27	BARNSLEY	5	4-0	1-0	8495	Casey, Rogers, Taylor, R.Williams
4	31	Bournemouth & Bos. Ath.	8	2-2	1-2	9642	Burden, Rogers
5	3 Sep	Newport County	15	1-4	0-2	8543	R.Williams
6	6	SWINDON TOWN	12	1-1	0-1	16550	Rogers
7	10	COLCHESTER UNITED	6	5-0	3-0	11842	Derrick, Casey, Etheridge, Rogers Tait
8	17	Grimsby Town	13	2-5	1-4	11839	Tait(2)
9	20	NOTTS COUNTY	9	2-1	2-1	14839	Atyeo(2)
10	24	HULL CITY	13	1-2	1-2	14899	Atyeo
11	29	Notts County	15	0-3	0-1	14230	
12	1 Oct	Reading	16	1-1	0-0	7265	R.Williams
13	4	COVENTRY CITY	13	2-0	1-0	14108	Casey, Etheridge
14	8	PORT VALE	16	3-4	2-2	8803	Atyeo(2), Tait
15	15	Southend United	16	0-1	0-0	8848	
16	19	Swindon Town	16	1-3	0-1	16618	Atyeo
17	22	CHESTERFIELD	16	3-0	2-0	7796	Derrick, Rogers, Tait
18	29	Bury	16	0-1	0-1	10856	
19	12 Nov	Shrewsbury Town	17	2-4	1-4	7968	Tait, R.Williams
20	19	HALIFAX TOWN	15	3-2	0-0	10910	Atyeo, Casey, R.Williams
21	10 Dec	Brentford	17	0-2	0-0	5200	
22	17	BRADFORD CITY	18	1-2	0-1	7833	Connor
23	26	QUEENS PARK RANGERS	18	1-1	1-0	10794	Tait
24	27	Queens Park Rangers	18	1-1	1-0	15391	Tait
25	31	Barnsley	19	0-2	0-1	7939	
26	14 Jan	NEWPORT COUNTY	19	3-0	2-0	12172	Tait(2), Casey
27	21	Colchester United	18	1-0	1-0	5099	Atyeo
28	4 Feb	GRIMSBY TOWN	18	2-1	2-1	11141	Atyeo(2,1pen)
29	13	Hull City	16	3-3	2-2	7077	Derrick(2), Atyeo
30	18	READING	14	2-0	1-0	11606	Rogers, Tait
31	21	WALSALL	12	2-0	2-0	12029	Atyeo(2)
32	25	Watford	12	1-0	0-0	7595	O.G.
33	27	Tranmere Rovers	13	2-3	1-0	11477	Rogers, R.Williams
34	4 Mar	SOUTHEND UNITED	13	2-0	1-0	11379	Tait, R.Williams
35	11	Chesterfield	14	0-3	0-0	4458	
36	14	WATFORD	10	4-1	1-0	12141	Atyeo, Etheridge, Rogers, Tait
37	18	BURY	11	1-2	1-2	12764	O.G.
38	25	Walsall	14	0-4	0-1	10115	
39	31	TORQUAY UNITED	13	2-2	2-1	13713	Bush(2)
40	1 Apr	SHREWSBURY TOWN	13	0-0	0-0	8805	
41	3	Torquay United	13	0-0	0-0	6766	
42	8	Halifax Town	15	1-2	0-1	4659	Virgin
43	15	TRANMERE ROVERS	14	2-0	0-0	8504	Atyeo, Tait
44	22	Port Vale	13	1-1	1-1	4068	Tait
45	24	Coventry City	15	1-2	0-1	8328	Atyeo
46	29	BRENTFORD	14	3-0	2-0	8656	Atyeo(3,1pen)

Apps. Cook 45, Collinson 21, Thresher 41, Burden 14, Williams Alan 11, Casey 36, Taylor 10, Atyeo 37, Virgin 6, Ryan 3, Derrick 32, Williams R.G. 36, Etheridge 38, Rogers 37, Tait 35, McCann 4, Boxley 12, Hopkinson 21, McCall 11, Quinlan 2, Briggs 9, Connor 28, Williams Adrian 4, Nicholson 1, Jacobs 1, Low 7, Bush 2, Peters 1, Clark 1

Goals Collinson 1, Casey 5, Taylor 1, Atyeo 19, Virgin 1, Derrick 5, Williams R.G. 7, Etheridge 3, Rogers 8, Tait 15, Connor 1, Bush 2

F.A. CUP

	Date	Opposition	Res.	H.T.	Att.	Goalscorers
1R	5 Nov	CHICHESTER CITY*	11-0	8-0	12588	Aty(5), Ad.Wllms(3), Tait, R.Wllms, OG (£2074.10.0)
2R	26	Kings Lynn	2-2	2-0	6762	Atyeo, Rogers
2Rr	29	KINGS LYNN	3-0	2-0	14471	Rogers(2), Atyeo (£2228.14.6)
3R	7 Jan	Plymouth Argyle	1-0	1-0	13087	R.Williams
4R	28	Leicester City	0-0	0-0	26109	(Aband. half-time, waterlogged pitch) (£5900)
4R	31	Leicester City	1-5	1-5	27710	O.G. (£5600)

* Chichester forfeited home advantage to play at Ashton Gate.

F.L. CUP

	Date	Opposition	Res.	H.T.	Att.	Goalscorers
2R	10 Oct	Aldershot	1-1	1-0	5700	Boxley
2Rr	25	ALDERSHOT	3-0	2-0	9229	Atyeo(2), Adrian Williams (£1349.12.0)
3R	15 Nov	Nottingham Forest	1-2	0-1	3690	Atyeo

GLOUCESTERSHIRE CUP FINAL

	Date	Opposition	Res.	H.T.	Att.	Goalscorers
	1 May	Bristol Rovers	3-1	0-0	12109	Atyeo(2), Derrick

FINAL LEAGUE TABLE

		P	W	D	L	F	A	Pts
1	Bury	46	30	8	8	108	45	68
2	Walsall	46	28	6	12	98	60	62
3	QPR	46	25	10	11	93	60	60
4	Watford	46	20	12	14	85	72	52
5	Notts Co.	46	21	9	16	82	77	51
6	Grimsby	46	20	10	16	77	69	50
7	Port Vale	46	17	15	14	96	79	49
8	Barnsley	46	21	7	18	83	80	49
9	Halifax	46	16	17	13	71	78	49
10	Shrewsbury	46	15	16	15	83	75	46
11	Hull	46	17	12	17	73	73	46
12	Torquay	46	14	17	15	75	83	45
13	Newport	46	17	11	18	81	90	45
14	Bristol C.	46	17	10	19	70	68	44
15	Coventry	46	16	12	18	80	83	44
16	Swindon	46	14	15	17	62	55	43
17	Brentford	46	13	17	16	56	70	43
18	Reading	46	14	12	20	72	83	40
19	Bournemouth	46	15	10	21	58	76	40
20	Southend	46	14	11	21	60	76	39
21	Tranmere	46	15	8	23	79	115	38
22	Bradford C.	46	11	14	21	65	87	36
23	Colchester	46	11	11	24	68	101	33
24	Chesterfield	46	10	12	24	67	87	32

SEASON 1961-62
FOOTBALL LEAGUE DIVISION THREE

Match Results

No.	Date	Opposition	Pos.	Res.	H.T.	Att.	Goalscorers
1	19 Aug	Notts County		0-1	0-0	10203	
2	22	NORTHAMPTON TOWN		1-0	0-0	14415	Atyeo
3	26	SHREWSBURY TOWN	18	1-3	0-0	12033	
4	29	Northampton Town	12	1-0	0-0	12832	Williams
5	2 Sep	Peterborough United	10	4-3	3-2	14758	Williams(2), Etheridge, Low
6	5	NEWPORT COUNTY	11	1-2	0-0	15915	Williams
7	9	PORT VALE	17	0-1	0-0	10670	
8	16	Lincoln City	16	1-1	0-0	3973	Williams
9	18	Southend United	18	0-1	0-1	9316	
10	23	Bradford Park Avenue	19	0-2	0-1	10432	
11	26	SOUTHEND UNITED	17	3-2	2-1	10679	Meyer(pen), Williams, O.G.
12	29	GRIMSBY TOWN	13	3-0	1-0	11256	Atyeo(3)
13	3 Oct	BRENTFORD	10	3-0	0-0	10717	Williams(2), Etheridge
14	7	HULL CITY	10	1-1	0-1	10088	Atyeo
15	10	Brentford	7	2-0	2-0	8500	Tait, Williams
16	14	Watford	8	1-1	0-1	11852	Tait
17	16	Newport County	9	1-3	0-1	7006	Atyeo
18	21	SWINDON TOWN	7	5-3	3-2	13158	Williams(2), Atyeo, Noake, Tait
19	28	Torquay United	5	3-1	1-0	4599	Atyeo, Casey(pen), Rogers
20	11 Nov	Barnsley	9	3-7	1-4	5548	Conner, Tait, Williams
21	18	QUEENS PARK RANGERS	8	2-0	0-0	10892	Williams(2)
22	2 Dec	BOURNEMOUTH & B.A.	6	2-1	0-1	14285	Atyeo(2)
23	9	Crystal Palace	5	3-2	1-2	17365	Atyeo(2), Derrick
24	16	NOTTS COUNTY	3	6-0	3-0	12805	Atyeo(4), Tait(2)
25	23	Shrewsbury Town	4	2-2	1-0	4408	Derrick, Tait
26	26	Reading	4	2-2	1-1	11304	Atyeo, Etheridge
27	13 Jan	PETERBOROUGH UNITED	7	1-2	1-1	17123	Atyeo
28	20	Port Vale	6	2-0	0-0	7262	Rogers, Williams
29	27	Halifax Town	3	4-3	2-3	5521	Conner, Etheridge, Tait, O.G.
30	3 Feb	LINCOLN CITY	3	2-1	1-0	12910	Williams, O.G.
31	6	READING	3	5-0	3-0	18590	Atyeo, Casey, Derrick, Tait, Williams
32	10	BRADFORD PARK AVENUE	2	6-1	6-1	16217	Williams(2), Atyeo, Casey(pen), Rogers, Tait
33	17	Grimsby Town	3	0-1	0-1	11662	
34	24	Hull City	3	2-3	1-1	3876	Connor, O.G.
35	3 Mar	WATFORD	3	2-1	0-0	11983	Atyeo, Casey
36	6	PORTSMOUTH	3	0-4	0-3	22124	
37	10	Swindon Town	3	4-0	0-0	12936	Atyeo(3), Tait
38	17	TORQUAY UNITED	3	4-1	0-0	11946	Derrick, Rogers, Tait, Williams
39	24	Portsmouth	3	0-5	0-2	20584	
40	31	BARNSLEY	3	0-0	0-0	8606	
41	7 Apr	Queens Park Rangers	5	1-4	0-2	11364	Noake
42	14	HALIFAX TOWN	4	4-3	2-1	6807	Atyeo, Conner, Noake, Tait
43	21	Bournemouth & Bos. Ath.	6	1-2	0-1	12916	Connor
44	23	Coventry City	6	1-1	0-1	5965	Atyeo
45	24	COVENTRY CITY	6	3-2	1-0	6674	Clark(2), Williams
46	28	CRYSTAL PALACE	6	2-2	1-1	7199	Etheridge, Peters

Appearances and Goals

	Cook A.	Briggs A.M.	Thresher T.M.J.	Etheridge R.J.	Connor J.F.	Low G.A.	Rogers J.R.	Clark B.D.	Atyeo P.J.W.	Williams R.G.	Peters R.D.	Derrick J.S.	Nicholls R.B.	Casey T.	Tait A.	Smith H.A.	Meyer B.J.	Noake D.J.	Ford A.M.	Palmer G.	McCall P.	Bush T.D.	Stacey S.D.
Apps.	40	46	37	46	46	10	38	8	42	45	13	26	6	40	34	1	5	11	8	1	2	1	
Goals				5	5	1	4	2	26	21	1	4		4	13		1	3					

F.A. CUP

	Date	Opposition	Res.	H.T.	Att.	Goalscorers
1R	4 Nov	HEREFORD UNITED	1-1	0-1	14518	Tait (£2349.15.6)
1Rr	8	Hereford United	5-2	2-0	11222	Atyeo(2), Etheridge, Tait, Williams (£1362.8.0)
2R	25	DARTFORD	8-2	4-0	13086	Tait(3), Derrick(2), Atyeo, Connor, Rgrs (£2100.3.6)
3R	6 Jan	WALSALL	0-0	0-0	22535	(£3647.11.6)
3Rr	9	Walsall	1-4	0-1	15420	Derrick (£2481.3.6)

F.L. CUP

	Date	Opposition	Res.	H.T.	Att.
1R	13 Sep	York City	0-3	0-0	8379

WELSH CUP

	Date	Opposition	Res.	H.T.	Att.	Goalscorers
5R	23 Jan	MERTHYR TYDFIL	4-2	4-2	3134	Atyeo, Briggs, Stacey, Williams
6R	20 Feb	CARDIFF CITY	0-2	0-1	13579	

GLOUCESTERSHIRE CUP FINAL

	Date	Opposition	Res.	H.T.	Att.	Goalscorers
	1 May	BRISTOL ROVERS	3-1	0-1	9201	Clark(3)

FRIENDLY

	Date	Opposition	Res.	H.T.	Att.
	10 Apr	HAMBORN 07	0-1	0-0	3142

FINAL LEAGUE TABLE

		P	W	D	L	F	A	Pts
1	Portsmouth	46	27	11	8	87	47	65
2	Grimsby	46	28	6	12	80	56	62
3	Bournemouth	46	21	17	8	69	45	59
4	QPR	46	24	11	11	111	73	59
5	Peterborough	46	26	6	14	107	82	58
6	Bristol C	46	23	8	15	94	72	54
7	Reading	46	22	9	15	77	66	53
8	Northampton	46	20	11	15	85	57	51
9	Swindon	46	17	15	14	78	71	49
10	Hull	46	20	8	18	67	54	48
11	Bradford P.A.	46	20	7	19	80	78	47
12	Port Vale	46	17	11	18	65	58	45
13	Notts County	46	17	9	20	67	74	43
14	Coventry	46	16	11	19	64	71	43
15	Crystal Palace	46	14	14	18	83	80	42
16	Southend	46	13	16	17	57	69	42
17	Watford	46	14	13	19	63	74	41
18	Halifax	46	15	10	21	62	84	40
19	Shrewsbury	46	13	12	21	73	84	38
20	Barnsley	46	13	12	21	71	95	38
21	Torquay	46	15	6	25	76	100	36
22	Lincoln	46	9	17	20	57	87	35
23	Brentford	46	13	8	25	53	93	34
24	Newport	46	7	8	31	46	102	22

1961-62 Season. F.A. Cup replay side that lost 4-1 to Walsall on Jan. 9th.
Back: Casey, Connor, Briggs, Cook, Etheridge, Thresher.
Front: Rogers, Tait, Atyeo, Williams, Derrick.

1962-63 Season
Back: Proudler (Coach), Ford, Casey, Briggs.
Middle: Bardsley (Trainer), Etheridge, Cook, Thresher, Connor, Ford (Manager).
Front: Peters, Clark, Atyeo, Tait, Bobby Williams, Derrick.

SEASON 1962-63
FOOTBALL LEAGUE DIVISION THREE

No.	Date	Opposition	Pos.	Res.	H.T.	Att.	Goalscorers	Cook A.M.	Briggs A.M.	Thresher T.M.J	Connor J.F.	Pyle W.D.	Low G.A.	Savino R.J.	Atyeo P.J.W.	Tait A.	Lythgoe D.	Derrick J.S.	Etheridge R.J.	Williams R.G.	Clark B.D.	Parr G.J.	Nicholls R.B.	Casey T.	Peters R.D.	Bush T.D.	Ford A.M.	Meyer B.J.	Smith D.B.	Waterhouse K.	Gibson M.J.
1	18 Aug	MILLWALL		2-2	1-2	14049	Atyeo(2)	1	2	3	4	5	6	7	8	9	10	11													
2	20	Colchester United		0-1	0-1	6824		1	2	3	4	5		7		9	10	11	6	8											
3	25	Shrewsbury Town	17	3-3	1-1	6097	Atyeo(2), Lythgoe	1	2	3	4	5		7	8	9	10	11	6												
4	28	COLCHESTER UNITED	20	1-2	1-1	12508	Etheridge(pen)	1	2	3	4	5		7	8	9	10	11	6												
5	1 Sep	PORT VALE	14	2-0	1-0	9626	Atyeo, Clark	1	2	3		5		7	9		10	11	6		8	4									
6	5	Bournemouth & Bos. Ath.	13	1-1	1-0	11655	Atyeo	1	2	3		5		7	9		10	11	6		8	4									
7	8	Reading	10	3-0	0-0	6746	Atyeo(2), Clark		2	3		5			9	7		11	6	10	8	4	1								
8	11	BOURNEMOUTH & B.A.	8	1-0	1-0	13283	Atyeo		2	3		5			9	7		11	6	10	8	4	1								
9	15	Bristol Rovers	3	2-1	0-0	20708	Clark, Etheridge(pen)		2	3		5			9	7		11	6	10	8	4	1								
10	20	Notts County	8	2-3	2-2	5993	Atyeo, Tait		2	3		5			9	7		11	6	10	8	4	1								
11	22	WATFORD	7	3-3	1-0	13426	Atyeo, Williams, O.G.		2	3		5			9	7		11	6	10	8	4	1								
12	29	Bradford Park Avenue	4	5-2	3-1	8917	Clark(2), Derrick(2), Tait		2	3		5			9	7		11	6	10	8	4	1								
13	2 Oct	COVENTRY CITY	5	1-1	1-1	13433	Derrick		2	3		5			9	7		11	6	10	8	4	1								
14	5	Carlisle United	3	5-2	3-2	8229	Williams(2), Clark, Derrick, Peters	1	2	3		5			9			11		10	8	4		6	7						
15	13	SWINDON TOWN	6	2-2	0-2	21864	Atyeo, Williams	1	2	3		5			9			11		10	8	4		6	7						
16	20	Peterborough United	7	1-3	1-0	12760	Etheridge(pen)	1	2	3		5			9			11		10	8	4		6	7						
17	23	Coventry City	8	2-4	2-3	11390	Atyeo(2)	1	2	3		5			9			11		10	8	4		6	7						
18	27	BARNSLEY	6	5-2	3-2	10034	Clark(2), Atyeo, Etheridge(pen), Williams	1	2	3		5			9			11		10	8	4		6	7						
19	10 Nov	QUEENS PARK RANGERS	13	2-4	1-1	13262	Bush, Williams	1	2	3		5						11		10	8	4		6	7	9					
20	17	Hull City	14	0-4	0-2	7367			2	3		5						11		10	8	4	1	6		9					
21	1 Dec	Wrexham	14	1-2	1-2	10773	Meyer		2			5	6	7							4		1				11	2	9		
22	8	HALIFAX TOWN	15	2-2	1-2	6244	Clark, Meyer		2			5	6			7					4		1				11	2	9		
23	15	Millwall	15	2-4	2-2	8151	Meyer(2)		2			5	6			9		7	4		8		1				11		10	3	
24	22	SHREWSBURY TOWN	14	3-1	0-0	6656	Clark(2), Peters		2			5			9				11	4	8		1	6	7				10	3	
25	26	BRIGHTON & HOVE ALB.	14	1-2	0-2	9096	Clark		2			5				9				4	8		1	6	11				10	3	
26	16 Feb	BRADFORD PARK AVENUE	14	4-2	3-0	7805	Derrick, Etheridge, Tait, Williams		2	3		5			9	7		11	6	10	8	4	1								
27	23	CARLISLE UNITED	14	2-2	0-0	8413	Clark, Peters		2	3		5			9	7			6	10	8	4	1		11						
28	2 Mar	Swindon Town	15	2-3	1-0	16778	Clark, Williams		2	3		5			9	7		11	6	10	8	4	1								
29	9	PETERBOROUGH UNITED	14	1-1	1-0	7347	Tait		2	3		5			9	7		11	6	10	8	4	1								
30	16	Barnsley	14	1-1	1-0	6077	Clark		2	3		5			9	7		11		10	8	4	1		6						
31	19	Brighton & Hove Albion	15	0-1	0-1	5391			2	3		5			9	7		11		10	8	4	1		6						
32	23	NORTHAMPTON TOWN	14	3-1	1-1	9642	Clark, Tait, Williams		2	3		5			9	7		11		10	8	4	1		6						
33	26	Watford	11	4-1	3-0	5992	Clark(3,1pen), Williams		2	3		5			9	7		11		10	8	4	1		6						
34	30	Queens Park Rangers	13	1-3	1-1	5683	Tait		2	3			5		9	7		11		10	8	4	1		6						
35	6 Apr	HULL CITY	12	3-1	2-1	8794	Clark(3,2pens)		2	3			5		9	7		11		10	8	4	1		6						
36	8	Northampton Town	12	1-5	1-2	12366	O.G.		2	3			5		9	7		11		10	8	4	1		6						
37	13	Crystal Palace	13	2-3	1-0	14645	Savino, Tait		2	3			5	7		9		11	4	10	8		1							6	
38	15	Southend United	14	2-2	0-1	12570	Derrick(2)		2	3			5	7		9		11	4	10	8		1							6	
39	16	SOUTHEND UNITED	12	6-3	4-1	9815	Meyer(3), Williams(3)		2	3			5	7		9		11	4	10			1					8		6	
40	23	BRISTOL ROVERS	12	4-1	3-0	22739	Clark, Derrick, Waterhouse, Williams		2	3			5	7		9		11	4	10	8		1							6	
41	27	Halifax Town	12	5-2	1-2	2109	Williams(4), Tait		2	3			5	7		9		11	4	10	8		1							6	
42	30	NOTTS COUNTY	12	1-1	1-0	12197	Derrick	1	2	3			5	7		9		11	4	10	8									6	
43	3 May	Wrexham	13	0-2	0-1	9795		1	2	3			5	7		9		11	4	10	8									6	
44	7	CRYSTAL PALACE	12	1-1	1-1	8732	Williams		2	3			5	7		9		11	4	10	8									6	1
45	11	Port Vale	14	1-3	0-2	5337	Etheridge		2	3			5	7		9		11	4	10	8									6	1
46	18	READING	14	4-2	1-1	7043	Tait(2), Atyeo, Derrick	1	2	3			5		9	7		11	4	10	8									6	
		Apps						15	46	41	29	8	17	15	30	37	6	35	45	38	42	16	29	13	19	2	2	6	3	10	2
		Goals												1	16	10	1	10	6	19	23				3	1		7		1	

F.A. CUP

	Date	Opposition		Res.	H.T.	Att.	Goalscorers	Cook	Briggs	Thresher	Connor	Pyle	Low	Savino	Atyeo	Tait	Lythgoe	Derrick	Etheridge	Williams	Clark	Parr	Nicholls	Casey	Peters	Bush	Ford	Meyer	Smith	Waterhouse	Gibson
1R	3 Nov	WELLINGTON TOWN		4-2	1-1	9379	Atyeo(2), Derrick, Etheridge(pen) (£1620.7.6)	1	2	3		5			9			11	4	10	8			6	7						
2R	24	WIMBLEDON		2-1	2-0	13778	Clark(2) (£2454.6.6)		2	3		5			6			11	4	10	8		1	7	9						
3R	16 Jan	ASTON VILLA		1-1	1-0	22176	Clark (£6173.13.6)		2	3		5			9	7		11	6	10	8	4	1								
3Rr	7 Mar	Aston Villa		2-3	2-1	23718	Etheridge, Williams (£4489.11.0)		2	3		5			9	7		11	6	10	8	4	1								

F.L. CUP

	Date	Opposition		Res.	H.T.	Att.	Goalscorers	Cook	Briggs	Thresher	Connor	Pyle	Low	Savino	Atyeo	Tait	Lythgoe	Derrick	Etheridge	Williams	Clark	Parr	Nicholls	Casey	Peters	Bush	Ford	Meyer	Smith	Waterhouse	Gibson
2R	25 Sep	ROTHERHAM UNITED		1-2	0-0	7469	Etheridge(pen) (£1263.9.0)		2	3		5			9			11	6	10	8	4	1		7						

GLOUCESTERSHIRE CUP FINAL

	Date	Opposition		Res.	H.T.	Att.	Goalscorers
	23 May	Bristol Rovers		1-2	0-1	8018	Derrick

FINAL LEAGUE TABLE

1	Northampton	46	26	10	10	109:60	62
2	Swindon	46	22	14	10	87:56	58
3	Port Vale	46	23	8	15	72:58	54
4	Coventry	46	18	17	11	83:69	53
5	Bournemouth	46	18	16	12	63:46	52
6	Peterborough	46	20	11	15	93:75	51
7	Notts Co.	46	19	13	14	73:74	51
8	Southend	46	19	12	15	75:77	50
9	Wrexham	46	20	9	17	84:83	49
10	Hull	46	19	10	17	74:69	48
11	Crystal Palace	46	17	13	16	68:58	47
12	Colchester	46	18	11	17	73:93	47
13	QPR	46	17	11	18	85:76	45
14	Bristol C.	46	16	13	17	100:92	45
15	Shrewsbury	46	16	12	18	83:81	44
16	Millwall	46	15	13	18	82:87	43
17	Watford	46	17	8	21	82:85	42
18	Barnsley	46	15	11	20	63:74	41
19	Bristol R.	46	15	11	20	70:88	41
20	Reading	46	16	8	22	74:78	40
21	Bradford P.A.	46	14	12	20	79:97	40
22	Brighton	46	12	12	22	58:84	36
23	Carlisle	46	13	9	24	61:89	35
24	Halifax	46	9	12	25	64:106	30

SEASON 1963-64
FOOTBALL LEAGUE DIVISION THREE

No.	Date	Opposition	Pos	Res	H.T.	Att	Goalscorers	Cook A.	Briggs A.M.	Thresher T.M.J.	Etheridge R.J.	Connor J.F.	Waterhouse K.	Derrick J.S.	Clark B.D.	Atyeo P.J.W.	Williams R.G.	Hooper P.J.	Lythgoe D.	Tait A.	Gibson M.J.	Kurilla J.	Ford A.M.	Parr G.J.	Low G.A.	Nicholls R.B.	Bush T.D.	Savino R.J.
1	24 Aug	BRISTOL ROVERS		3-0	1-0	20697	Atyeo, Derrick, Hooper	1	2	3	4	5	6	7	8	9	10	11										
2	27	Brentford		2-1	0-0	16800	Atyeo, Lythgoe	1	2	3	4	5	6	7	8	9	10		11									
3	31	Port Vale	9	1-4	0-1	10363	Clark	1	2	3	4	5	6		8	9	10		11	7								
4	7 Sep	NOTTS COUNTY	6	2-0	1-0	9440	Atyeo(2)		2	3	4	5			8	9	10	11			1		7	6				
5	10	BRENTORD	5	3-3	3-2	12689	Atyeo, Clark, Hooper		2	3	4	5			8	9		11	10		1		7	6				
6	14	Crewe Alexandra	9	0-2	0-1	5841			2	3	4	5			8	9		11	10		1		7	6				
7	18	Shrewsbury Town	13	0-2	0-1	7152			2	3	4	5	6	7	8	9	10	11			1							
8	21	CRYSTAL PALACE	14	1-1	0-0	9782	Williams		2	3	4	5	6	11	8	9	10			7	1							
9	28	Walsall	15	1-0	0-0	6312	Atyeo			3				11	8	9			10	7	1	2	4		6			
10	1 Oct	SHREWSBURY TOWN	14	2-2	0-2	9247	Atyeo, Derrick			3		5		7	8	9		11	10		1	2	4		6			
11	5	READING	16	0-2	0-1	7585				3		5		7	8	9		11	10		1	2	4		6			
12	8	Coventry City	17	1-2	0-2	23884	Hooper			3		5		7	8	9	10	11			1	2	4	6				
13	11	PETERBOROUGH UNITED	16	3-1	1-1	10770	Williams(2), Derrick			3		5		7	8	9	10	11			1	2	4	6				
14	15	COVENTRY CITY	18	0-1	0-1	13582			2	3		5		7	8	9	10	11			1		4	6				
15	19	Bournemouth & Bos. Ath.	17	1-0	0-0	11454	Atyeo		2	3		5		7	8	9	10			11	1		4	6				
16	23	Luton Town	15	4-1	1-0	5207	Atyeo, Clark, Derrick, O.G.		2	3		5		7	8	9	10			11	1		4	6				
17	26	HULL CITY	11	1-0	0-0	10568	Williams		2	3		5		7	8	9	10			11	1		4	6				
18	29	LUTON TOWN	9	5-1	3-0	10269	Williams(2), Atyeo, Clark, Hooper		2	3		5		7	8	9	10	11			1		4	6				
19	2 Nov	Barnsley	7	4-2	2-1	5950	Clark(2), Atyeo, Williams		2	3		5		7	8	9	10	11			1		4	6				
20	9	MILLWALL	8	1-1	0-0	10332			2	3		5		7	8	9	10	11			1		4	6				
21	23	WATFORD	6	2-0	0-0	9962	Atyeo, Clark(pen)		2	3		5		7	8	9	10	11			1		4	6				
22	30	Southend United	6	1-1	0-0	6930	Thresher		2	3		5		7	8	9	10	11			1		4	6				
23	14 Dec	Bristol Rovers	7	0-4	0-3	18451			2	3		5		7	8	9	10	11			1		4	6				
24	21	PORT VALE	8	0-0	0-0	6021			2	3		5		7	8	9	10	11			1		4	6				
25	26	QUEENS PARK RANGERS	8	3-0	3-0	10681	Clark, Derrick, Hooper(pen) (Aband. h-t due to fog)		2	3		5		7	8	9	10	11			1		4	6				
26	28	Queens Park Rangers	8	2-0	1-0	6917	Low, Williams		2	3		5		7	8	9	10	11			1		4	6				
27	11 Jan	Notts County	8	1-1	1-0	5824	Williams		2	3		5		7	8	9	10	11			1		4	6				
28	18	CREWE ALEXANDRA	10	1-1	0-1	8117	Clark			3	2	5	6	7	8	9	10			11	1							
29	1 Feb	Crystal Palace	10	0-1	0-0	16539			2	3		5		7	8	9	10	11			1		4	6				
30	8	WALSALL	9	5-1	1-1	7503	Atyeo(3), Clark, Williams		2	3		5		7	8	9	10	11			1		4	6				
31	11	WREXHAM	8	4-0	1-0	8905	Clark(2), Atyeo, Hooper		2	3		5		7	8	9	10	11			1		4	6				
32	15	Reading	8	1-1	0-1	9711	Atyeo		2	3		5		7	8	9	10	11			1		4	6				
33	22	Peterborough United	8	2-4	1-2	7400	Hooper, Williams		2	3		5		7	8	9	10	11			1		4	6				
34	24	Colchester United	7	1-0	0-0	4803	Atyeo		2	3		5		7	8	9	10	11			1		4	6				
35	29	OLDHAM ATHLETIC	6	3-1	2-0	9900	Clark, Williams, O.G.		2	3		5		7	8	9	10	11			1		4	6				
36	7 Mar	Hull City	5	4-4	1-3	4726	Williams(2), Clark, Hooper(pen)		2	3		5		7	8	9	10	11			1		4	6				
37	10	QUEENS PARK RANGERS	5	2-1	1-1	8869	Hooper, Parr		2	3		5		7	8	9	10	11					4	6		1		
38	14	BARNSLEY	5	5-2	2-1	6950	Atyeo(2), Clark, Hooper(pen), Williams		2	3		5		7	8	9	10	11					4	6		1		
39	21	Oldham Athletic	5	2-1	2-0	7546	Low, Williams			3					8	9	10	11		7		2	4	6		1		
40	27	MANSFIELD TOWN	5	2-3	0-3	13914	Clark, Hooper			3					8	9	10	11				2	4	6		1		7
41	28	COLCHESTER UNITED	5	3-1	1-0	7779	Atyeo, Clark, Williams						3		8	9	10	11			1	2	4	5			6	7
42	30	Mansfield Town	5	0-4	0-3	8741				3					8	9	10	11			1	2	4	5			6	7
43	4 Apr	Watford	5	2-2	1-1	9907	Hooper, Williams			3					8	9	10	11			1	2	4	5			6	7
44	11	SOUTHEND UNITED	5	2-0	0-0	7314	Bush, Williams			3					8	9	10	11			1	2	4	5			6	7
45	18	Wrexham	5	1-1	0-1	2808	Clark			3					8	9	10	11			1	2	4	5			6	7
46	20	Millwall	5	1-0	0-0	12123	Hooper(pen)			3					8	9	10	11			1	2	4	5			6	7
47	25	BOURNEMOUTH & B.A.	5	3-1	3-0	7787	Clark, Parr, Williams			3					8	9	10	11			1	2	4	5			6	7
							Apps.	3	39	39	10	40	6	34	47	47	42	39	7	11	40	6	14	39	33	4	9	8
							Goals		1					5	19	21	20	13	1				2	2			1	

F.A. CUP

	Date			Res	H.T.	Att	Goalscorers																				
1R	16 Nov	Corby Town		3-1	2-1	4904	Clark, Low, Williams (£858.11.0)		2	3		5		7	8	9	10	11			1		4	6				
2R	7 Dec	Exeter City		2-0	1-0	15077	Atyeo(2) (£2430.1.0)		2	3		5		7	8	9	10	11			1		4	6				
3R	4 Jan	Doncaster Rovers		2-2	1-1	18050	Atyeo, Clark (£2722.17.6)		2	3		5		7	8	9	10	11			1		4	6				
3Rr	7	DONCASTER ROVERS		2-0	1-0	20269	Atyeo, Hooper(pen) (£3599.5.6)		2	3		5		7	8	9	10	11			1		4	6				
4R	25	Sunderland		1-6	1-3	46201	Hooper (£9008.1.0)		2	3		5		7	8	9	10	11			1		4	6				

F.L. CUP

	Date			Res	H.T.	Att	Goalscorers																				
1R	4 Sep	Gillingham		2-4	0-2	5940	Atyeo(2)	1	2	3	4	5	6		8	9	10	11		7								

GLOUCESTERSHIRE CUP FINAL

	Date			Res	H.T.	Att	Goalscorers
	28 Apr	BRISTOL ROVERS		2-2	1-0	7693	Low, Williams

FRIENDLIES

	Date			Res	H.T.	Att	Goalscorers
1	17 Aug	Portsmouth		2-3	0-1	4127	Atyeo, Derrick
2	8 May	Cork Hibernians		5-2	4-0	2000	Hooper(2), Bush, Clark, Williams
3	10	Limerick		5-0	1-0	3000	Williams(3), Bush, Clark

FINAL LEAGUE TABLE

		P	W	D	L	F:A	Pts
1	Coventry	46	22	16	8	98:61	60
2	Crystal Palace	46	23	14	9	73:51	60
3	Watford	46	23	12	11	79:59	58
4	Bournemouth	46	24	8	14	79:58	56
5	Bristol C.	46	20	16	10	84:64	56
6	Reading	46	21	10	15	79:62	52
7	Mansfield	46	20	11	15	76:62	51
8	Hull	46	16	17	13	73:68	49
9	Oldham	46	20	8	18	73:70	48
10	Peterborough	46	18	11	17	75:70	47
11	Shrewsbury	46	18	11	17	73:80	47
12	Bristol R.	46	19	8	19	91:79	46
13	Port Vale	46	16	14	16	53:49	46
14	Southend	46	15	15	16	77:78	45
15	QPR	46	18	9	19	76:78	45
16	Brentford	46	15	14	17	87:80	44
17	Colchester	46	12	19	15	70:68	43
18	Luton	46	16	10	20	64:80	42
19	Walsall	46	13	14	19	59:76	40
20	Barnsley	46	12	15	19	68:94	39
21	Millwall	46	14	10	22	53:67	38
22	Crewe	46	11	12	23	50:77	34
23	Wrexham	46	13	6	27	75:107	32
24	Notts Co.	46	9	9	28	45:92	27

1963-64 Season
Back: Parr, Tony Ford, Gibson, Low, Briggs, Kurilla.
Front: Tait, Clark, Atyeo, Lythgoe, Derrick, Connor.

1964-65 Season
Back: Briggs, Parr, Connor, Gibson, Tony Ford, Low, Drury.
Middle: Bush (Secretary), Sharpe, Derrick, Hooper, Atyeo, Fred Ford (Manager), Bush, Clark,
Peters, Savino, Bardsley (Trainer)
Front, Directors: G.W.Young, G.Whittock, A.J.Amor, L.Smart (Vice Chairman), H.J.Dolman (Chairman),
N.B.Jones, W.G.Garland, S.F.Kew, R.T.Poeton.

FOOTBALL LEAGUE DIVISION THREE

No.	Date	Opposition	Pos.	Res.	H.T.	Att.	Goalscorers	Gibson M.J.	Ford A.M.	Thresher T.M.J.	Parr G.J.	Low G.A.	Bush T.D.	Savino R.J.	Clark B.D.	Atyeo P.J.W.	Williams R.G.	Peters R.D.	Drury C.	Connor J.F.	Briggs A.M.	Derrick J.S.	Hooper P.J.	Sharpe G.R.
1	22 Aug	Scunthorpe United		2-5	1-1	5522	Clark(2)	1	2	3	4	5	6	7	8	9	10	11						
2	25	BARNSLEY		5-1	4-0	10491	Clark(3), O.G.(2)	1	2	3	4	5		7	8	9	10	11	6					
3	29	WALSALL	7	5-1	2-0	9478	Atyeo(3), Clark, Ford(pen)	1	2	3	4	5	6	7	8	9	10	11						
4	5 Sep	Watford	10	2-2	1-2	9418	Peters, Williams	1	2	3	4		6	7	8	9	10	11	5					
5	8	SOUTHEND UNITED	3	4-0	1-0	11737	Atyeo(3), Williams	1	2	3	4		6	7	8	9	10	11	5					
6	12	WORKINGTON	4	5-0	1-0	10536	Clark(3), Bush(2)	1	2	3	4		6	7	8	9	10	11	5					
7	14	Southend United	1	4-0	1-0	8675	Clark(2), Bush, Williams	1	2		4		6	7	8	9	10	11	5	3				
8	19	Hull City	4	2-3	1-1	7485	Clark, Williams	1	2		4		6		8	9	10	11	5	3	7			
9	26	GILLINGHAM	8	1-2	0-1	11556	Bush	1	2		4		6	7	8	9	10		5	3			11	
10	29	READING	4	2-0	0-0	11981	Bush, Low	1	2		4		6	7	8	9	10	11	5	3				
11	3 Oct	Bristol Rovers	7	1-1	1-1	25370	Bush	1	2		4		6	7	8	9	10	11	5	3				
12	7	Reading	6	1-1	1-0	11120	Parr	1	2		4		6	7	8	9	10	11	5	3				
13	10	COLCHESTER UNITED	6	1-1	1-1	9983	Atyeo	1	2		4		6	7	8	9	10	11	5	3				
14	13	QUEENS PARK RANGERS	3	2-0	0-0	11133	Atyeo(2)	1	2		4		6	7	8	9	10	11	5	3				
15	17	Port Vale	4	2-1	1-1	5564	Atyeo, Savino	1	2		4		6	7	8	9	10		5	3				11
16	19	Queens Park Rangers	4	0-1	0-1	5578		1	2		4		6	7	8	9	10		5	3				11
17	23	CARLISLE UNITED	4	1-2	0-1	10303	Atyeo	1	2		4		6	7	8	9			5	3			11	10
18	28	Oldham Athletic	11	3-7	2-3	8013	Sharpe(2), Clark	1	2		4	5	6	7	8	9			11	3				10
19	31	Luton Town	8			5385		1	2		4	5	6		8	9			11	3				10
20	3 Nov	Barnsley	6	2-1	0-1	3768	Clark, Sharpe	1	2		4	5	6		8	9			11	3	7			10
21	7	MANSFIELD TOWN	6	1-1	0-0	9653	Hooper	1	2		4	5	6		8	9				3	7		11	10
22	21	PETERBOROUGH UNITED	5	3-1	1-0	9222	Atyeo, Ford(pen), O.G.	1	2		4	5	6	7	8	9			11	3				10
23	28	Bournemouth & Bos. Ath.		2-1	1-0	9171	Clark, Peters	1	2		4	5	6	7	8	9			11	3				10
24	12 Dec	SCUNTHORPE UNITED	4	2-2	1-1	8387	Atyeo, Bush	1	2		4	5	6	7	8	9			11	3				10
25	19	Walsall	3	4-2	2-1	5213	Sharpe(2), Bush, Clark	1	2		4	5	6	7	8	9			11	3				10
26	26	Brentford	7	1-2	1-1	16065	Sharpe	1	2		4	5	6	7	8	9			11	3				10
27	2 Jan	WATFORD	7	1-1	0-0	10758	Atyeo	1	2		4	5	6	7	8	9			11	3				10
28	15	Workington	8	0-1	0-0	3380		1	2	3	4	5	6	7	8	9		10	11					
29	23	HULL CITY	8	1-2	0-0	14131	Peters	1	2		4	5	6	7	10	9			11	3	8			
30	30	EXETER CITY	7	1-1	0-0	8450	Clark	1	2		4	5	6	7	10	9			11	3	8			
31	6 Feb	Gillingham	9	0-2	0-2	10972		1	2			5	6	9	8			10	11	3	4			7
32	13	BRISTOL ROVERS	7	2-1	0-0	23053	Bush, Clark	1	2			5	6	9	10	8			11	3	4			7
33	20	Colchester United	7	3-2	1-0	2898	Atyeo, Clark, Ford(pen)	1	2			5	6	9	10	8			11	3	4			7
34	27	PORT VALE	7	3-0	1-0	8552	Peters(2), Bush	1	2			5	6	9	10	8			11	3	4			7
35	2 Mar	BRENTFORD	6	3-2	1-1	11152	Bush(2), Ford(pen)	1	2			5	6	9	7	10	8		11	3	4			
36	6	Exeter City	4	1-0	0-0	7359	Clark	1	2			5	6	9	7	10	8		11	3	4			
37	9	Grimsby Town	4	2-0	1-0	5748	Bush, Drury	1	2			5	6	9		10	8		7	3	4			11
38	13	LUTON TOWN	3	1-0	0-0	11001	Ford(pen)	1	2		4	5	6	9	7	10	8			3			11	
39	20	Mansfield Town	6	0-3	0-0	9434		1	2			5	6	9	7	10	8		11	3	4			
40	26	GRIMSBY TOWN	3	4-0	2-0	11464	Atyeo(2), Clark, Peters	1	2			5	6	9	7	10	8		11	3	4			
41	3 Apr	Peterborough United	5	1-0	1-0	8156	Bush	1	2			5	6	9	7	10	8		11	3	4			
42	9	BOURNEMOUTH & B.A.	4	0-0	0-0	12861		1	2			5	6	9	7	10	8		11	3	4			
43	16	Carlisle United	5	1-1	0-0	16069	Bush	1	2			5	6	9	7	10	8		11	3	4			
44	19	Shrewsbury Town		5-1	1-1	5857	Atyeo(4), Clark	1	2			5	6	9		10	8		7	3	4			11
45	20	SHREWSBURY TOWN	2	3-0	3-0	16423	Atyeo, Bush, Clark	1	2			5	6	9		10	8		11	3	4	7		
46	24	OLDHAM ATHLETIC	2	2-0	1-0	28248	Atyeo, Clark	1	2			5	6	9		10	8		11	3	4			7
		Apps.						46	46	7	21	46	37	34	46	38	16	40	16	43	39	11	7	13
		Goals							5		1	1	16	1	24	23	4	6	1				1	6

F.A. CUP

Rnd	Date	Opposition	Pos.	Res.	H.T.	Att.	Goalscorers	Gibson	Ford	Thresher	Parr	Low	Bush	Savino	Clark	Atyeo	Williams	Peters	Drury	Connor	Briggs	Derrick	Hooper	Sharpe
1R	14 Nov	BRIGHTON & HOVE ALB.		1-0	0-0	12618	Savino (£2786)	1	2				6	4	7	8	9		11		5	3		10
2R	5 Dec	Bournemouth & Bos. Ath.		3-0	3-0	10592	Sharpe(2), Clark	1	2				6	4	7	8	9		11		5	3		10
3R	9 Jan	SHEFFIELD UNITED		1-1	0-1	20091	Ford(pen) (£4599)	1	2				6	4	7	8	9	10	11		5	3		10
3Rr	11	Sheffield United		0-3	0-2	27688		1	2				6	4	7	8	9	10			5	3	11	

F.L. CUP

Rnd	Date	Opposition	Pos.	Res.	H.T.	Att.	Goalscorers	Gibson	Ford	Thresher	Parr	Low	Bush	Savino	Clark	Atyeo	Williams	Peters	Drury	Connor	Briggs	Derrick	Hooper	Sharpe
2R	23 Sep	Carlisle United		1-4	1-4	10055	Hooper	1	2		4		6	9		8			10		5	3	7	11

GLOUCESTERHIRE CUP FINAL

Date	Opposition		Res.	H.T.	Att.	Goalscorers
26 Apr	Bristol Rovers		2-3	1-1	8907	Bush, Clark

FRIENDLIES

No.	Date	Opposition		Res.	H.T.	Att.	Goalscorers
1	12 Aug	SWINDON TOWN		1-0	1-1	6001	Atyeo (Bristol Cathedral Restoration Appeal)
2	15	Torquay United		3-1	1-0	2610	Bush, Clark, Peters
3	1 May	Sligo Rovers		5-1	2-0	1500	Bartley, Bush, Clark, Ford, Low
4	4	Derry City		3-2	3-1	5000	Bush, Derrick, Sharpe

FINAL LEAGUE TABLE

		P	W	D	L	F	A	Pts
1	Carlisle	46	25	10	11	76	53	60
2	Bristol C.	46	24	11	11	92	55	59
3	Mansfield	46	24	11	11	95	61	59
4	Hull	46	23	12	11	91	57	58
5	Brentford	46	24	9	13	83	55	57
6	Bristol R.	46	20	15	11	82	58	55
7	Gillingham	46	23	9	14	70	50	55
8	Peterborough	46	22	7	17	85	74	51
9	Watford	46	17	16	13	71	64	50
10	Grimsby	46	16	17	13	68	67	49
11	Bournemouth	46	18	11	17	72	63	47
12	Southend	46	19	8	19	78	71	46
13	Reading	46	16	14	16	70	70	46
14	QPR	46	17	12	17	72	80	46
15	Workington	46	17	12	17	58	69	46
16	Shrewsbury	46	15	12	19	76	84	42
17	Exeter	46	12	17	17	51	52	41
18	Scunthorpe	46	14	12	20	65	72	40
19	Walsall	46	15	7	24	55	80	37
20	Oldham	46	13	10	23	61	83	36
21	Luton	46	11	11	24	51	94	33
22	Port Vale	46	9	14	23	41	76	32
23	Colchester	46	10	10	26	50	89	30
24	Barnsley	46	9	11	26	54	90	29

SEASON 1965-66
FOOTBALL LEAGUE DIVISION TWO

No.	Date	Opposition	Pos.	Res.	H.T.	Att.	Goalscorers	Gibson M.J.	Ford A.M.	Briggs A.M.	Drury C.	Connor J.F.	Low G.A.	Peters R.D.	Atyeo P.J.W.	Bush T.D.	Clark B.D.	Hooper P.J.	Showell G.W.	Sharpe G.R.	Derrick J.S.	Parr G.J.	Savino R.J.	Bartley D.R.
1	21 Aug	ROTHERHAM UNITED		2-1	1-1	16801	Atyeo, Hooper	1	2	3	4	5	6	7	8	9	10	11						
2	25	Norwich City		0-0	0-0	17315		1	2	3	4	5	6	7	8	9	10	11						
3	28	Manchester City	7	2-2	2-0	19349	Atyeo, Drury	1	2	3	4	5	6	7	8*	9	10	11	12					
4	31	NORWICH CITY	7	0-0	0-0	15737		1	2	3	4	5	6	7		9	10	11			8			
5	4 Sep	HUDDERSFIELD TOWN	4	2-1	1-1	15704	Bush, Peters	1	2*	3	4	5	6	7		9	10	11	12	8				
6	7	Bury	3	2-1	0-0	6331	Sharpe(2)	1		3	4	5	6	7		9	10	11	2	8				
7	11	COVENTRY CITY	2	1-1	1-0	19887	Bush	1		3	4	5	6	7		9*	10	11	2	8	12			
8	17	Carlisle United	6	0-5	0-1	10694		1	2	3	4		6	11	9		8			5	10	7		
9	25	CARDIFF CITY	9	1-1	0-0	15299	Atyeo	1	2	3	4	5	6	7	9		10	11		8				
10	2 Oct	Derby County	10	1-2	0-1	11012	Peters	1	2	3	6		5	11	9		8			10	7	4		
11	9	Crystal Palace	13	1-2	1-0	16356	Clark	1	2	3	4	5	6*	11	9	12	8			10	7			
12	16	PRESTON NORTH END	10	1-0	0-0	15583	Bush	1	2	3	4	5	6	11	8	9	10				7			
13	23	Charlton Athletic	8	4-1	0-0	11315	Clark(2), Atyeo, Peters	1	2	3	4	5	6	11	8	9	10				7			
14	30	PLYMOUTH ARGYLE	8	0-0	0-0	17533		1	2	3	4	5	6	11	8	9	10				7			
15	6 Nov	Portsmouth	6	4-2	2-1	15748	Atyeo(2), Bush, Ford(pen)	1	2	3	4	5	6	11	8	9	10				7			
16	13	BOLTON WANDERERS	7	2-2	1-1	19912	Atyeo, Clark	1	2	3	4*	5	6	11	8	9	10			12	7			
17	20	Ipswich Town	6	0-0	0-0	8935		1	2	3		5	6	11	8	9	10				7	4		
18	27	BIRMINGHAM CITY	7	2-0	0-0	13727	Low, Peters	1	2	3		5	6	11	8	9	10				7	4		
19	4 Dec	Leyton Orient	5	4-0	2-0	5559	Clark(3), Atyeo	1	2	3		5	6	11	8	9	10				7	4		
20	11	MIDDLESBROUGH	6	2-2	0-0	16086	Clark, Low	1	2	3		5	6	11	8	9	10				7	4		
21	18	Preston North End	5	1-1	0-0	10776	Atyeo	1	2	3		5	6	11	8	9	10				7	4		
22	27	Wolverhampton Wanderers	6	1-1	0-0	32526	Atyeo	1	2	3		5	6	11	8	9	10					4	7	
23	28	WOLVERHAMPTON WNDRS	6	0-1	0-0	36184		1	2			5	6	11	8	9	10		3	7		4*		12
24	1 Jan	CRYSTAL PALACE		1-1	1-1	16428	Clark	1	2		4	5	6	11	8	9	10		3	7				
25	8	Bolton Wanderers	5	2-1	0-0	10256	Atyeo, Peters	1	2	3	4	5	6	11	8	9	10				7			
26	29	Rotherham United	5	2-1	2-0	10405	Clark, Derrick	1	2	3	4	5	6	11	8		10			9		7		
27	5 Feb	MANCHESTER CITY	6	1-1	1-1	25723	Clark	1	2	3	4	5*	6	11	8		10		12	9		7		
28	11	BURY	4	2-1	1-0	18363	Atyeo, Peters	1	2	3	4		6	11	8		10		5	9*	12	7		
29	19	Huddersfield Town	6	0-3	0-3	18544		1	2	3	4		6	11	8		10		5	9		7		
30	26	Coventry City	6	2-2	1-1	30062	Atyeo(2)	1	2	3	4		10	11	9		8		5			6	7	
31	5 Mar	Middlesbrough	6	2-4	0-3	13744	Atyeo(2)	1	2	3	4		10	11	9		8		5			6	7	
32	12	CARLISLE UNITED	5	2-0	1-0	14724	Clark, Sharpe	1	2	3	4	5	6	7	9		8			10				11
33	18	Cardiff City	5	1-2	0-2	13587	Clark	1	2	3	4	5	6	7	9		8			10				11
34	25	DERBY COUNTY	4	1-1	1-1	13614	Atyeo	1	2	3	4	5	6	11	9		8				10	7		
35	2 Apr	PORTSMOUTH	5	1-0	1-0	11804	O.G.	1	2	3		5	6		9		8	11		10	7	4		
36	8	SOUTHAMPTON	6	0-1	0-1	25106		1	2	3		5	6	11	9		8			10	7	4		
37	9	Plymouth Argyle	5	2-0	1-0	15396	Bush, Clark	1	2	3	4	5	6		9	8	8			10			7	11
38	11	Southampton	5	2-2	1-1	23120	Ford(pen), Sharpe	1	2	3		5	6		9		8			10	7	4		11
39	22	Birmingham City	6	3-1	2-0	11677	Sharpe(2), Clark	1	2	3		5	6			8	9			10	7	4		11
40	30	LEYTON ORIENT		2-0	0-0	10849	Bush(2)	1	2	3		5	6			8	9			10	7	4		11
41	3 May	CHARLTON ATHLETIC	6	0-0	0-0	10478		1	2	3		5	6		9	8	10				7	4		11
42	10	IPSWICH TOWN	5	4-1	1-1	13893	Atyeo(2), Bush, Parr	1	2	3		5	6		9	8	10				7	4		11
		Apps.						42	40	40	28	36	42	35	35	26	42	9	9	18	27	17	8	8
		Subs.															1		3	1	1	1		1
		Goals							2		1		2	6	19	8	15	1		6	1	1		

F.A. CUP

	Rnd	Date	Opposition		Res.	H.T.	Att.	Goalscorers	Gibson	Ford	Briggs	Drury	Connor	Low	Peters	Atyeo	Bush	Clark	Derrick
	3R	22 Jan	Birmingham City		2-3	1-1	24340	Bush, Low	1	2	3	4	5	6	11	8	9	10	7

F.L. CUP

	Rnd	Date	Opposition		Res.	H.T.	Att.	Goalscorers	Gibson	Ford	Briggs	Drury	Connor	Low	Peters	Bush	Clark	Sharpe	Derrick
	2R	22 Sep	Shrewsbury Town		0-1	0-1	7158		1	2	3	4	5	6	11	9	8	10	7

GLOUCESTERSHIRE CUP FINAL

	Date	Opposition		Res.	H.T.	Att.	
	12 May	BRISTOL ROVERS		0-1	0-1	9431	

FRIENDLIES

No.	Date	Opposition		Res.	H.T.	Att.	Goalscorers
1	10 Aug	Swindon Town		3-0	2-0	6003	Atyeo, Bush, Peters
2	14	SWINDON TOWN		4-3	2-1	4404	Bush(3), Derrick
3	18	F.C. HAKA		4-1	2-1	3060	Bush(2), Clark, Sharpe
4	22 May	Waterford		2-2	1-1	2500	Clark, Low
5	25	Drumcondra Select XI		6-2	1-1		Connor(3), Clark, Derrick, Peters

FINAL LEAGUE TABLE

1	Manchester C.	42	22	15	5	76:44	59
2	Southampton	42	22	10	10	85:56	54
3	Coventry	42	20	13	9	73:53	53
4	Huddersfield	42	19	13	10	62:36	51
5	Bristol C.	42	17	17	8	63:48	51
6	Wolverhampton	42	20	10	12	87:61	50
7	Rotherham	42	16	14	12	75:74	46
8	Derby	42	16	11	15	71:68	43
9	Bolton	42	16	9	17	62:59	41
10	Birmingham	42	16	9	17	70:75	41
11	Crystal Palace	42	14	13	15	47:52	41
12	Portsmouth	42	16	8	18	74:78	40
13	Norwich	42	12	15	15	52:52	39
14	Carlisle	42	17	5	20	60:63	39
15	Ipswich	42	15	9	18	58:66	39
16	Charlton	42	12	14	16	61:70	38
17	Preston	42	11	15	16	62:70	37
18	Plymouth	42	12	13	17	54:63	37
19	Bury	42	14	7	21	62:76	35
20	Cardiff	42	12	10	20	71:91	34
21	Middlesbrough	42	10	13	19	58:86	33
22	Leyton Orient	42	5	13	24	38:80	23

1965-66 Season - John Atyeo's last League game 10th May.
Back: Connor, Ford, Parr, Gibson, Briggs, Low.
Front: Derrick, Sharpe, Clark, Atyeo, Bush, Bartley.

1966-67 Season
Back: Drury, Parr, Clark, Connor, Gibson, Tony Ford, Low, Briggs, Showell, Ford (Manager)
Front: Savino, Bush, Derrick, Sharpe, Peters, Bartley.

SEASON 1966-67
FOOTBALL LEAGUE DIVISION TWO

Player columns (left to right): Gibson M.J., Ford A.M., Briggs A.M., Parr G.J., Connor J.F., Low G.A., Derrick J.S., Clark B.D., Bush T.D., Sharpe G.R., Bartley D.R., Peters R.D., Down D.F., Savino R.J., Giles J.E., Quigley J., Drury C., Jacobs T.F., Garland C.S., Crowe C., McIlmoyle H.

No.	Date	Opposition	Pos.	Res.	H.T.	Att.	Goalscorers
1	20 Aug	Huddersfield Town		0-2	0-2	10241	
2	23	CRYSTAL PALACE		0-1	0-0	13365	
3	27	CARDIFF CITY	22	1-2	1-1	11911	Low
4	31	Crystal Palace	22	1-2	0-1	16477	Clark
5	3 Sep	Wolverhampton Wanderers	20	1-1	0-0	17952	Peters
6	6	CHARLTON ATHLETIC	18	4-0	1-0	11182	Bush, Ford, Sharpe, O.G.
7	10	IPSWICH TOWN	18	1-1	0-1	12971	Low
8	17	Coventry City	20	0-1	0-0	21082	
9	24	Carlisle United	22	1-2	0-1	9948	Sharpe
10	27	Charlton Athletic	22	0-5	0-1	10463	
11	1 Oct	BLACKBURN ROVERS	21	2-2	1-1	12824	Ford(pen), Peters
12	8	NORWICH CITY	19	1-0	0-0	11008	Sharpe
13	15	Birmingham City	19	0-4	0-1	15358	
14	21	PORTSMOUTH	19	3-3	3-2	16404	Bartley, Down, Giles
15	29	Hull City	19	2-0	2-0	26630	Derrick, Down
16	5 Nov	PLYMOUTH ARGYLE	19	1-0	0-0	19375	Down
17	12	Northampton Town	20	1-2	0-1	10004	Sharpe
18	19	MILLWALL	20	1-1	1-1	11771	Sharpe
19	26	Rotherham United	20	3-3	0-3	8534	Bartley, Low, Sharpe
20	3 Dec	PRESTON NORTH END	17	2-0	1-0	10815	Bush, Quigley
21	10	Bury	19	1-2	0-2	4433	Low
22	17	HUDDERSFIELD TOWN	18	1-1	1-0	11299	O.G.
23	26	BOLTON WANDERERS	18	1-1	0-1	16735	Low
24	31	Cardiff City	19	1-5	0-2	12460	Sharpe
25	7 Jan	WOLVERHAMPTON WNDRS	18	1-0	0-0	17699	Quigley
26	14	Ipswich Town	19	0-0	0-0	13883	
27	21	COVENTRY CITY	18	2-2	2-2	21600	Bush, Crowe
28	4 Feb	CARLISLE UNITED	17	3-0	1-0	23206	Bush, Crowe, Derrick
29	11	Blackburn Rovers	18	0-1	0-1	12089	
30	25	Norwich City	18	0-1	0-0	28147	
31	4 Mar	HULL CITY	18	2-1	2-0	23496	McIlmoyle, Peters
32	18	Portsmouth	15	1-1	1-1	14649	Peters
33	25	BIRMINGHAM CITY	15	3-1	1-1	20579	Crowe, Peters, Quigley
34	27	Derby County	16	0-2	0-0	15491	
35	28	DERBY COUNTY	14	4-1	2-0	20137	Crowe(2), Derrick, Peters
36	1 Apr	Plymouth Argyle	14	2-1	2-1	12223	Derrick, Quigley
37	7	NORTHAMPTON TOWN	14	1-0	1-0	23752	Peters
38	15	Millwall	14	2-3	0-2	11343	McIlmoyle, Quigley
39	19	Bolton Wanderers	13	0-0	0-0	8491	
40	22	ROTHERHAM UNITED	14	1-2	0-1	16888	Crowe
41	29	Preston North End	15	2-2	2-1	9439	Peters, Sharpe
42	6 May	BURY	16	3-3	2-2	12614	Ford(pen), Low, Peters

Apps. 42 40 42 38 42 41 33 10 21 25 20 28 5 7 3 25 7 2 1 18 12
Subs. 1
Goals 3 6 4 1 4 8 2 9 3 1 5 6 2

F.A. CUP

				Res.	H.T.	Att.	Goalscorers
3R	28 Jan	Halifax Town		1-1	0-0	15591	Peters
3Rr	31	HALIFAX TOWN		4-1	2-0	23188	Crowe(2), Down, Peters
4R	18 Feb	SOUTHAMPTON		1-0	1-0	38017	Bush (£8879)
5R	11 Mar	Tottenham Hotspur		0-2	0-1	54610	

F.L. CUP

				Res.	H.T.	Att.	Goalscorers
2R	13 Sep	SWANSEA TOWN		1-1	0-1	6952	Ford
2Rr	19	Swansea Town		1-2	1-0	5466	Down (extra-time played)

GLOUCESTERSHIRE CUP FINAL

				Res.	H.T.	Att.	Goalscorers
	9 May	Bristol Rovers		3-0	1-0	17433	Crowe, Ford(pen), Peters

FRIENDSHIP CUP

				Res.	H.T.	Att.	Goalscorers
	16 Nov	HANOVER 96		2-3	1-1	4599	Bartley, Giles
	23 May	Hanover 96		1-2	1-1	12000	Ford(pen)

FRIENDLIES

				Res.	H.T.	Att.	Goalscorers
1	8 Aug	Oxford United		4-1	1-1	2164	Clark(2), Peters, O.G.
2	10	Swindon Town		2-1	1-1	2057	Bush, O.G.
3	13	SOUTHAMPTON		1-1	1-1	6903	Sharpe
4	10 Oct	LEEDS UNITED		2-4	0-3	17425	Derrick, Sharpe (John Ayteo's Benefit)

FINAL LEAGUE TABLE

1	Coventry	42	23	13	6	74	43	59
2	Wolverhampton	42	25	8	9	88	48	58
3	Carlisle	42	23	6	13	71	54	52
4	Blackburn	42	19	13	10	56	46	51
5	Ipswich	42	17	16	9	70	54	50
6	Huddersfield	42	20	9	13	58	46	49
7	Crystal Palace	42	19	10	13	61	55	48
8	Millwall	42	18	9	15	49	58	45
9	Bolton	42	14	14	14	64	58	42
10	Birmingham	42	16	8	18	70	66	40
11	Norwich	42	13	14	15	49	55	40
12	Hull	42	16	7	19	77	72	39
13	Preston	42	16	7	19	65	67	39
14	Portsmouth	42	13	13	16	59	70	39
15	Bristol C.	42	12	14	16	56	62	38
16	Plymouth	42	14	9	19	59	58	37
17	Derby	42	12	12	18	68	72	36
18	Rotherham	42	13	10	19	61	70	36
19	Charlton	42	13	9	20	49	53	35
20	Cardiff	42	12	9	21	61	87	33
21	Northampton	42	12	6	24	47	84	30
22	Bury	42	11	6	25	49	83	28

SEASON 1967-68
FOOTBALL LEAGUE DIVISION TWO

No.	Date	Opposition	Pos.	Res.	H.T.	Att.	Goalscorers	Gibson	Ford	Briggs	Parr	Connor	Low	Derrick	Crowe	McIlmoyle	Quigley	Peters	Savino	Bush	Jacobs	Tainton	Bartley	Down	Garland	Sharpe	Davis	Wimshurst	Galley	Watling	Merrick	Mahoney
1	19 Aug	HUDDERSFIELD		2-3	1-1	18148	Crowe, McIlmoyle	1	2	3	4	5	6	7	8	9	10	11														
2	22	QUEENS PARK RANGERS		0-2	0-1	20228		1	2	3	4	5	6	7	8	9	10	11														
3	26	Ipswich Town	21	0-5	0-2	13541		1	2	3	4	5	6		8	9	10	11		7												
4	29	Queens Park Rangers	21	1-3	1-0	15448	McIlmoyle	1	2	3	4	5	6			9	10	11		7	8											
5	2 Sep	CARLISLE UNITED	20	1-0	1-0	13736	Jacobs	1		3		5	6		8	9	4	7			2	10*	11	12								
6	5	MIDDLESBROUGH	19	0-0	0-0	13216		1		3	5*	6		8	9	4	11	7	12	2	10											
7	9	Blackburn Rovers	21	0-2	0-0	14621		1		3	4	5	7	10	9	8	11			2	6											
8	16	BLACKPOOL	22	2-4	1-2	13193	Derrick, Quigley	1		3	4	5	6	7	8	9	8	11		2												
9	23	Millwall	21	1-1	1-1	12121	Crowe	1	12	3		5		9	7		4	11*	6	2			10	8								
10	30	HULL CITY	21	3-3	3-3	11635	Bush, Garland, Sharpe	1	2	3	6	5		11	7		4		9			8	10									
11	7 Oct	Crystal Palace	22	0-2	0-0	19938		1	2	3	6	5			7		4		9	11		8	10									
12	14	CARDIFF CITY	20	1-1	0-1	15609	Crowe	1	2	3	6	5		8	7		4	10	9		11											
13	21	Portsmouth	21	0-2	0-1	21278		1	2	3	6	5	12	7			4	11	9				10*	8								
14	4 Nov	Rotherham United	21	0-1	0-0	5706		1		2	6	5		7	8		10				11	9*	12	3	4							
15	10	DERBY COUNTY	21	1-0	0-0	15919	Garland	1		2	6	5		7	8		10				11	9		3	4							
16	18	Plymouth Argyle	20	1-0	1-0	11179	Connor	1		2	6	5		7	8		10				11	9		3	4							
17	25	CHARLTON ATHLETIC	21	0-2	0-0	12590		1		2	6	5		7	8		10				11	9		3	4							
18	2 Dec	Preston North End	20	1-0	1-0	10127	Garland	1		2	6	5			7		10			12	11	9	8	3*	4							
19	5	NORWICH CITY	20	0-2	0-1	13444		1			2	5	12			7	10		6		11	9	8*	3	4							
20	16	Huddersfield Town	20	3-0	1-0	12071	Galley(3)	1		3	2	5			7		10		6		11			8	4	9						
21	22	IPSWICH TOWN	20	1-1	1-0	17628	Galley	1		3	2	5			7		10		6		11			8	4	9						
22	20	Birmingham City	20	1-1	0-1	10420	Wimshurst	1		3	2	5		12	7*		10	11	6					8	4	9						
23	30	BIRMINGHAM CITY	20	3-1	1-0	23493	Galley(2), Crowe	1		3	2	5		7	8		10	11	6					8	4	9						
24	6 Jan	Carlisle United	20	0-0	0-0	8261		1		3	2	5		7	8		10	11	6						4	9						
25	13	BLACKBURN ROVERS	19	0-0	0-0	19900		1			3	5		7	8		10	11	6	2					4	9						
26	20	Blackpool	19	1-1	0-1	13032	Galley	1			3	5		7	8		10	11	6	2*				12	4	9						
27	3 Feb	MILLWALL	20	0-2	0-2	14673		1		3	2	5			8		10	11	6					7	4	9						
28	10	Hull City	20	2-4	1-0	12596	Galley(2)	1		3	2	5		7	11		10	11	6					8	4	9						
29	24	CRYSTAL PALACE	19	2-1	2-0	13082	Galley, Wimshurst	1		3	6	5		7	11		10			2				8	4	9						
30	27	ASTON VILLA	19	0-0	0-0	17133		1		3	6	5		7	11		10			2				8	4	9						
31	2 Mar	Cardiff City	19	1-0	0-0	15356	Galley	1		3	4	5			8		10	11		2				8	6	9						
32	16	PORTSMOUTH	18	3-0	1-0	16085	Galley, Garland, O.G.	1		3	6	5			7		10	11		2				8	4	9						
33	23	Norwich City	19	2-3	1-1	14298	Garland, Quigley	1		3	6	5			7		10	11		2				8	4	9						
34	29	ROTHERHAM UNITED	19	0-1	0-1	19783		1		3	6	5			7		10	11*	12	2				8	4	9						
35	2 Apr	BOLTON WANDERERS	19	1-1	1-0	11047	O.G.	1		3	6	5		10	7			11*	12	2				8	4	9						
36	6	Derby County	19	1-3	0-1	15938	Briggs	1		3	6	5			7		11		10*	2	12			8	4	9						
37	13	PLYMOUTH ARGYLE	20	2-0	0-0	17076	Galley(2)	1		3	6	5		7	12		11		10*	2				8	4	9						
38	17	Bolton Wanderers	20	0-1	0-1	7105		1		3	6	5		7	10		11			2				8	4	9						
39	20	Charlton Athletic	20	2-1	2-0	11756	Crowe, Galley	1		3		5		7	10		11		6	2				8	4	9						
40	27	PRESTON NORTH END	19	4-1	2-1	16858	Crowe, Galley, Garland, Wimshurst	1		3		5		7	10		11		6	2				8	4	9						
41	4 May	Aston Villa	19	4-2	3-2	14732	Bush, Crowe, Derrick, Garland			3		5		7	8		10		12	2		11		9*	4					1	6	
42	11	Middlesbrough	19	1-2	0-1	12684	Garland			3		5		7	8		10		2			11		9	4							1
		Apps.						40	8	39	36	41	8	27	38	8	41	22	3	20	21	4	12	1	29	5	6	29	21	1	1	1
		Subs.						1						2	1					5			1	1	1	1						
		Goals							1		1			2	7	2	2			2	1				8	1		3	16			

F.A. CUP

No.	Date	Opposition		Res.	H.T.	Att.	(fee)	Goalscorers	Gibson	Briggs	Parr	Connor	Derrick	Crowe	Quigley	Peters	Savino	Bush	Garland	Sharpe	Wimshurst	Galley
3R	27 Jan	BRISTOL ROVERS		0-0	0-0	37237	(£9954)		1	3	2	5	7	8	10	11		6			4	9
3Rr	30	Bristol Rovers		2-1	2-1	30157	(£6600)	Crowe, Galley	1	3	2	5	7*	8	10	11		6		12	4	9
4R	17 Feb	Middlesbrough		1-1	1-1	29086	Garland (£7913.9.6)		1	3	6	5	7	11	10			2	8		4	9
4Rr	20	MIDDLESBROUGH		2-1	2-0	21771	Connor, Galley (£5743.10.0)		1	3	6	5	7		10	11		2	8		4	9
5	9 Mar	Leeds United		0-2	0-2	45227	(£15250)		1	3	6	5		11	10			2	8	7	4	9

F.L. CUP

No.	Date	Opposition		Res.	H.T.	Att.	(fee)	Gibson	Briggs	Parr	Connor	Derrick	Crowe	McIlmoyle	Peters	Bush	Jacobs	Garland
2R	13 Sep	EVERTON		0-5	0-2	22054	(£4959.12.1)	1	3	4	5	7	8	9	11	6	2	10

GLOUCESTERSHIRE CUP FINAL

	Date	Opposition		Res.	H.T.	Att.	Goalscorers
	14 May	BRISTOL ROVERS		1-1	1-1	11375	Sharpe

FRIENDLIES

No.	Date	Opposition		Res.	H.T.	Att.	Goalscorers
1	3 Aug	SWINDON TOWN		1-0	1-0		Bush
2	7	WEST BROMWICH ALB.		1-4	0-1	7719	Crowe
3	9	Swindon Town		2-2	1-2	6727	Bush, McIlmoyle, Williams
4	11	COVENTRY CITY*		2-0	1-0	5222	Crowe, McIlmoyle
5	6 May	Cheltenham Town		2-1	1-1	2378	Crowe, Peters

* Only 40 minutes each way played.

FINAL LEAGUE TABLE

1	Ipswich	42	22	15	5	79:44	59
2	QPR	42	25	8	9	67:36	58
3	Blackpool	42	24	10	8	71:43	58
4	Birmingham	42	19	14	9	83:51	52
5	Portsmouth	42	18	13	11	68:55	49
6	Middlesbrough	42	17	12	13	60:54	46
7	Millwall	42	14	17	11	62:50	45
8	Blackburn	42	16	11	15	56:49	43
9	Norwich	42	16	11	15	60:65	43
10	Carlisle	42	14	13	15	58:52	41
11	Crystal Palace	42	14	11	17	56:56	39
12	Bolton	42	13	13	16	60:63	39
13	Cardiff	42	13	12	17	60:66	38
14	Huddersfield	42	13	12	17	46:61	38
15	Charlton	42	12	13	17	63:68	37
16	Aston Villa	42	15	7	20	54:64	37
17	Hull	42	12	13	17	58:73	37
18	Derby	42	13	10	19	71:78	36
19	Bristol C.	42	13	10	19	48:62	36
20	Preston	42	12	11	19	43:65	35
21	Rotherham	42	10	11	21	42:76	31
22	Plymouth	42	9	9	24	38:72	27

Back row, left to right: Alec Briggs, Trevor Jacobs, Gordon Parr, Mike Gibson, Gordon Low, Trevor Tainton, Terry Bush. Front: Jantzen Derrick, John Quigley, Hugh McIlmoyle, Chris Crowe, Roger Peters. (Prov. 1.)

1967-68 Season

1968-69 Season
Back: Derrick, Galley, Connor, Gibson, Parr, Briggs, Bush.
Front: Jacobs, Garland, Sharpe, Kellard, Wimshurst.

SEASON 1968-69
FOOTBALL LEAGUE DIVISION TWO

Player columns (left to right): Gibson M.J. · Jacobs T.F. · Briggs A.M. · Wimshurst K.P. · Connor J.F. · Parr G.J. · Crowe C. · Garland C.S. · Galley J.E. · Kellard R.S.W. · Bartley D.R. · Merrick G. · Derrick J.S. · Sharpe G.R. · Bush T.D. · Tainton T.K. · Ford A.M. · Skirton A.F.G. · Davis R.F. · Broomfield I.L. · Watling B.J.

No.	Date	Opposition	Pos.	Res.	H.T.	Att.	Goalscorers	Gib	Jac	Bri	Wim	Con	Par	Cro	Gar	Gal	Kel	Bar	Mer	Der	Sha	Bus	Tai	For	Ski	Dav	Bro	Wat
1	10 Aug	Fulham		0-1	0-1	15537		1	2	3	4	5	6	7	8	9	10	11										
2	17	SHEFFIELD UNITED		1-1	0-0	19280	Galley	1		2	4	5	6	7	8	9	10		3	11								
3	20	BOLTON WANDERERS	13	2-2	1-1	17353	Galley, Garland	1	2	12	4	5	6	7	8	9	10		3*	11								
4	24	Blackpool	15	2-2	2-1	15767	Garland, Kellard	1	2	3	4	5	6	7	8	9	10			11								
5	26	Aston Villa	16	0-1	0-0	17679		1	2	3	4	5	6	7*	8	9	10					11	12					
6	31	BLACKBURN ROVERS	16	1-0		19740	Galley	1	2	3	4	5	6	7	8	9	10					11						
7	7 Sep	Hull City	16	1-1		12309	Galley	1	2	3	4	5	6		7	9	10					11	12	8*				
8	14	DERBY COUNTY	16	0-0	0-0	15850		1	2	3	4	5	6	7	8	9	10					11						
9	16	Millwall	16	2-2	1-1	12331	Garland, Wimshurst	1	2	3	4	5	6		8	9	10				7	11						
10	21	Oxford United	16	0-0	0-0	13043		1	2	3	4	5	6		8	9	10					11	7					
11	28	CARDIFF CITY	17	0-3	0-0	20630		1	2	3	4	5	6		8	9	10				12	11	7*					
12	5 Oct	Charlton Athletic	18	0-0	0-0	15394		1	2	3	4	5	6		8		10					11	7	9				
13	8	ASTON VILLA	17	1-0	0-0	15203	Kellard	1	2	3	4	5	6		8	9	10					11	7					
14	12	BIRMINGHAM CITY	17	1-0	0-0	19478		1	2*	3	4	5	6		8	9	10					11	7	12				
15	19	Crystal Palace	17	1-2	1-0	15033	Sharpe	1		3	4	5	6			9	10				11	8		7	2			
16	26	PORTSMOUTH	16	2-2	0-1	16071	Galley, Sharpe	1		3	4	5	6			9	10				11	8		7	2			
17	9 Nov	HUDDERSFIELD TOWN	17	0-1	0-1	13738		1		3	4	5	6		8	9	10				11	7			2			
18	16	Preston North End	19	0-1	0-0	12325		1	2	3*	4	5	6		10	9	11			12	7	8						
19	23	NORWICH CITY	18	0-1		13822		1		3		5	6			9	10				11	8	4*	12	2	7		
20	30	Carlisle United	20	0-3	0-0	9263		1	2		4	5	6			9	10				11	8			7	3		
21	3 Dec	Middlesbrough	21	1-4	0-2	18042	Sharpe	1	2		4*	5	6			9	11				8		10	12	7	3		
22	7	BURY	20	2-1	1-0	9664	Galley, Skirton	1	2	3	4	5	6			9	10	11			8				7			
23	14	Birmingham city	20	0-2	0-2	18749		1	2	3	4	5	6			9	10	12		11*	8				7			
24	26	CHARLTON ATHLETIC	19	2-0	0-0	17431	Sharpe, Skirton	1	2	3	4	5	6			9	10	11			8				7			
25	28	Portsmouth	20	1-1	1-0	19529	Galley	1	2	3	4	5	6			9	10	11		12	8*				7			
26	11 Jan	MIDDLESBROUGH	19	3-0	1-0	13696	Galley(2), Sharpe	1	2	3	4	5	6		8	9	10				11				7			
27	18	Huddersfield Town	20	1-4	0-4	9059	Galley	1	2	3	4	5	6		8	9	10				11				7			
28	25	Cardiff City	20	0-3	0-2	26235		1	2	3	4*	5	6		8	9	10				11	12			7			
29	1 Feb	PRESTON NORTH END	19	2-1	0-0	13419	Galley, Sharpe	1	2	3	4	5	6		8	9	10				11				7			
30	15	CARLISLE UNITED	19	3-0	1-0	13785	Garland(2), Sharpe	1	2	3	4	5	6		8	9	10				11				7			
31	25	CRYSTAL PALACE	19	1-1		14698	Connor	1	2	3	4	5	6		8	9	10				11				7			
32	1 Mar	FULHAM	17	6-0	4-0	15715	Garland(2), Galley, Sharpe, Skirton, O.G.	1	2	3	4	5	6		8	9	10				11				7			
33	8	Sheffield United	19	1-2	0-1	14887	Sharpe	1	2	3	4	5	6		8		10				11				7		9	
34	15	BLACKPOOL	18	1-1	1-0	16079	Galley	1	2	3	4	5	6		8	9	10				11				7			
35	22	Blackburn Rovers	17	3-1	1-1	7566	Galley(2), Derrick	1	2	3	4	5	6		8	9	10	12		11					7*			
36	26	Norwich City	17	1-1		10152	Kellard(pen)	1	2	3	4	5	6		8	9	10			7	11							
37	29	HULL CITY	15	1-1		13105	Connor	1	2	3	4	5	6		8	9	10			7	11							
38	7 Apr	Bolton Wanderers	17	0-1	0-0	7984		1	2	3	4	5	6	7	8	9	10*			11			12					
39	8	MILLWALL	18	0-0	0-0	14385		1	2	3	4	5	6	7	8	9	10				11							
40	12	OXFORD UNITED	17	2-0		11457	Galley(2)	1		3	4	5	6		8	9	10				11				2	7		
41	15	Bury	14	2-1	1-1	6020	Galley, Sharpe	1	2	3	12	5	6		8	9	4	11*			10				7			1
42	19	Derby County	16	0-5	0-3	31664		1	2	3	4	5	6		8		10	9			11				7			
		Apps.						41	37	38	40	42	42	10	31	39	42	6	2	16	36	7	3	5	21	2	1	1
		Subs.							1	1									2		3	4	3		3			
		Goals								1	2				6	19	3			1	10				3			

F.A. CUP

Rd	Date	Opposition	Res.	H.T.	Att.	Goalscorers	Players
3R	4 Jan	West Ham United	2-3	1-1	32526	Galley, Skirton	Gibson 1, Jacobs 2, Briggs 3, Wimshurst 4, Connor 5, Parr 6, Garland 8, Galley 9, Kellard 10, Sharpe 11, Skirton 7

F.L. CUP

Rd	Date	Opposition	Res.	H.T.	Att.	Goalscorers	Players
1R	14 Aug	NEWPORT COUNTY	2-0	1-0	9778	Galley, Garland	Gibson 1, Jacobs 2, Briggs 3, Wimshurst 4, Connor 5, Parr 6, Garland 8*, Galley 9, Kellard 10, Bartley 11, Sharpe 7, Tainton 12
2R	4 Sep	MIDDLESBROUGH	1-0	0-0	14218	Galley	Gibson 1, Jacobs 2, Briggs 3, Wimshurst 4, Connor 5, Parr 6, Crowe 7, Garland 8, Galley 9, Kellard 10, Bush 11
3R	25	Leeds United	1-2	0-1	16359	Garland	Gibson 1, Jacobs 2, Briggs 3*, Wimshurst 4, Connor 5, Parr 6, Crowe 10, Garland 8, Galley 9, Kellard 11, Tainton 12, Skirton 7

GLOUCESTERSHIRE CUP FINAL

Date	Opposition	Res.	H.T.	Att.	Goalscorers
28 Apr	Bristol Rovers	5-0	0-0	14735	Galley, Garland, Kellard, Sharpe, Skirton

FRIENDLIES

No.	Date	Opposition	Res.	H.T.	Att.	Goalscorers
1	27 Jul	SOUTHAMPTON	5-3	2-3	7862	Bartley, Galley, Garland, Kellard, Sharpe
2	30	Bournemouth & B.A.	1-3	0-2	2498	Galley
3	1 Aug	Hereford United	1-1	1-1		Wimshurst(pen)
4	3	Torquay United	0-1	0-0	4912	
5	4 Nov	Morton	4-2	3-1	2300	Connor, Derrick, Galley, Sharpe

FINAL LEAGUE TABLE

		P	W	D	L	F:A	Pts
1	Derby	42	26	11	5	65:32	63
2	Crystal Palace	42	22	12	8	70:47	56
3	Charlton	42	18	14	10	61:52	50
4	Middlesbrough	42	19	11	12	58:49	49
5	Cardiff	42	20	7	15	67:54	47
6	Huddersfield	42	17	12	13	53:46	46
7	Birmingham	42	18	8	16	73:59	44
8	Blackpool	42	14	15	13	51:41	43
9	Sheffield U.	42	16	11	15	61:50	43
10	Millwall	42	17	9	16	57:49	43
11	Hull	42	13	16	13	59:52	42
12	Carlisle	42	16	10	16	46:49	42
13	Norwich	42	15	10	17	53:56	40
14	Preston	42	12	15	15	38:44	39
15	Portsmouth	42	12	14	16	58:58	38
16	Bristol C.	42	11	16	15	46:53	38
17	Bolton	42	12	14	16	55:67	38
18	Aston Villa	42	12	14	16	37:48	38
19	Blackburn	42	13	11	18	52:63	37
20	Oxford	42	12	9	21	34:55	33
21	Bury	42	11	8	23	51:80	30
22	Fulham	42	7	11	24	40:81	25

SEASON 1969-70
FOOTBALL LEAGUE DIVISION TWO

Player columns (left to right): Gibson M.J., Jacobs T.F., Drysdale B., Clarke M.M.G., Rooks R., Parr G.J., Skirton A.F.G., Garland C.S., Galley J.E., Kellard R.S.W., Sharpe G.R., Derrick J.S., Bush T.D., Merrick G., Connor J.F., Tainton T.K., Briggs A.M., Menmuir W.F., Ford A.M., Bartley D.R., Wimshurst K.P., Spiring P.J., Broomfield I.L., Wilson R.J., Mahoney M.J., Gow R.G.

No.	Date	Opposition	Pos.	Res.	H.T.	Att.	Goalscorers
1	9 Aug	WATFORD		1-0	1-0	19346	Galley
2	16	Hull City		0-2	0-0	10170	
3	23	CARDIFF CITY	18	0-2	0-0	23237	
4	26	Sheffield United	19	1-2	1-2	15539	Tainton
5	30	Huddersfield United	20	0-3	0-2	10206	
6	6 Sep	PRESTON NORTH END	20	0-0	0-0	13740	
7	13	Middlesbrough	21	0-2	0-2	14513	
8	20	NORWICH CITY	21	4-0	1-0	11879	Galley(2), Bartley, Skirton
9	23	CHARLTON ATHLETIC	18	6-0	2-0	15098	Galley(3), Skirton(2), Bartley
10	27	Millwall	18	1-1	1-1	11406	O.G.
11	4 Oct	BIRMINGHAM CITY	15	2-0	0-0	18706	Galley, Garland
12	7	HULL CITY	12	3-1	1-0	18132	Galley, Garland, Skirton
13	11	Portsmouth	11	0-0	0-0	14890	
14	18	Leicester City	15	0-2	0-1	25954	
15	25	CARLISLE UNITED	15	0-0	0-0	15161	
16	1 Nov	Bolton Wanderers	15	1-3	0-1	6450	Sharpe
17	8	ASTON VILLA	13	1-0	1-0	16065	Skirton
18	11	OXFORD UNITED	12	2-0	1-0	10698	Bartley, Garland
19	15	QUEENS PARK RANGERS	10	2-0	1-0	18893	Bush, Garland
20	22	Blackburn Rovers	11	3-3	1-1	13307	Sharpe(2), Bush
21	29	BLACKPOOL	9	2-1	1-0	14818	Rooks, Sharpe
22	6 Dec	Swindon Town	9	1-1	1-0	23289	O.G.
23	13	MIDDLESBROUGH	10	0-0	0-0	15290	
24	27	HUDDERSFIELD TOWN	11	1-2	1-1	20541	Skirton
25	29	Cardiff City	11	0-1	0-0	18496	
26	10 Jan	Norwich City	11	1-4	0-1	7746	Garland
27	17	MILLWALL	11	1-1	1-1	13133	Bush
28	24	Preston North End	11	1-0	1-0	10994	Sharpe
29	31	Birmingham City	11	2-2	1-1	20421	Bush, Skirton
30	7 Feb	PORTSMOUTH	9	3-0	1-0	13931	Bush(2), Sharpe
31	14	Watford	11	0-2	0-1	12744	
32	21	Aston Villa	11	2-0	0-0	26830	Connor, Sharpe
33	28	LEICESTER CITY	11	0-0	0-0	17044	
34	7 Mar	BLACKBURN ROVERS	10	4-0	2-0	12683	Bush(2), Kellard, Sharpe
35	14	Blackpool	10	0-1	0-0	13657	
36	18	Oxford United	11	0-2	0-1	9233	
37	21	SWINDON TOWN	11	3-3	0-1	24905	Galley, Kellard(pen), Sharpe
38	27	BOLTON WANDERERS	11	2-2	1-0	17298	Kellard(pen), Sharpe
39	28	Queens Park Rangers	10	2-2	1-0	11017	Bush, Jacobs
40	31	Carlisle United	11	1-2	1-2	6219	Jacobs
41	4 Apr	SHEFFIELD UNITED	13	0-1	0-1	11159	
42	14	Charlton Athletic	14	1-2	0-1	14997	Garland

Apps: 38 31 42 2 38 38 34 39 20 35 28 6 22 3 5 25 4 1 7 16 18 4 1 1 3 1
Subs: 1 1 2 1 4 1 1 4 1 1 2
Goals: 2 1 7 6 9 3 10 9 1 1 3

F.A. CUP

3R	3 Jan	Chester		1-2	0-1	10030	Skirton

F.L. CUP

1R	13 Aug	Exeter City		1-1	0-0	8003	Kellard
1Rr	19	EXETER CITY		3-2	2-0	10915	Kellard, Rooks, Sharpe
2R	2 Sep	Leicester City		0-0	0-0	15883	
2Rr	10	Leicester City		0-0	0-0	20797	(Extra time played)
2R2r	15	Leicester City		1-3	1-1	12600	Galley (at Leicester)

GLOUCESTERSHIRE CUP FINAL

	22 Apr	BRISTOL ROVERS		2-1	0-0	12004	Kellard(2,1pen)

FRIENDLIES

1	26 Jul	CHELSEA		1-1	0-1	11502	Galley
2	30	WOLVERHAMPTON W.		1-1	1-0	9200	Sharpe
3	31	Swansea Town		2-2	1-0		Bush, Ford
4	2 Aug	Canterbury City		5-0	2-0	300	Bush(3), Bartley, Fear
5	28 Oct	Bordeaux		0-1	0-1	5000	
6	2 Dec	VEJLE BOLOKLUB		4-0	1-0	2813	Galley(2), Garland, Parr
7	17 Feb	BORDEAUX		3-2	1-1	3785	Garland, Kellard, Spiring
8	17 Apr	Weymouth Town		3-1	1-0		Bush, Garland, Gow (John Clarke Benefit)
9	19	Taunton Town		1-1	0-1	1750	Fear (Ground Development Fund - £200)
10	5 May	JUVENTUS		2-1	2-1	6736	Parr, Skirton

FINAL LEAGUE TABLE

1	Huddersfield	42	24	12	6	68 37	60
2	Blackpool	42	20	13	9	56 45	53
3	Leicester	42	19	13	10	64 50	51
4	Middlesbrough	42	20	10	12	55 45	50
5	Swindon	42	17	16	9	57 47	50
6	Sheffield U.	42	22	5	15	73 38	49
7	Cardiff	42	18	13	11	61 41	49
8	Blackburn	42	20	7	15	54 50	47
9	QPR	42	17	11	14	66 57	45
10	Millwall	42	15	14	13	56 56	44
11	Norwich	42	16	11	15	49 46	43
12	Carlisle	42	14	13	15	58 56	41
13	Hull	42	15	11	16	72 70	41
14	Bristol C.	42	13	13	16	54 50	39
15	Oxford	42	12	15	15	35 42	39
16	Bolton	42	12	12	18	54 61	36
17	Portsmouth	42	13	9	20	66 80	35
18	Birmingham	42	11	11	20	51 78	33
19	Watford	42	9	13	20	44 57	31
20	Charlton	42	7	17	18	35 76	31
21	Aston Villa	42	8	13	21	36 62	29
22	Preston	42	8	12	22	43 63	28

(Photograph by courtesy of Bristol Evening Post)
Back row: Alec Briggs, Tony Ford, Jack Connor, Mike Gibson, John Galley, Terry Bush, Ken Wimshurst; Middle row: Gordon Parr, Bobby Kelland, Gerry Sharpe, Trevor Jacobs, Jantzen Derrick, Alan Skirton; Front row: Chris Garland, Dickie Rooks, Brian Drysdale, Malcolm Clarke.

1970-71 Season
(Back) Jacobs, Derrick, Skirton, Parr, Gibson, Connor, Galley, Garland, Wimshurst.
(Front) Bartley, Tainton, Sharpe, Rooks, Drysdale, Merrick, Gow.

SEASON 1970-71
FOOTBALL LEAGUE DIVISION TWO

No.	Date	Opposition	Pos.	Res.	H.T.	Att.	Goalscorers	Gibson M.J.	Jacobs T.F.	Drysdale B.	Wimshurst K.P.	Rooks R.	Parr G.J.	Skirton A.F.G.	Garland C.S.	Galley J.E.	Gow R.G.	Sharpe G.R.	Tainton T.K.	Stacey S.D.	Connor J.F.	Broomfield I.L.	Merrick G.	Fear K.W.	Rodgers D.M.	Bartley D.R.	Spiring P.J.	Derrick J.S.	Cashley A.R.	Hill B.W.	Wilson L.J.	Bond L.A.	Merrnuir W.F.
1	19 Aug	SUNDERLAND		4-3	2-1	17984	Sharpe(2), Skirton, Wimshurst	1	2	3	4	5	6	7	8	9	10	11															
2	22	Charlton Athletic		1-1	0-1	10422	Galley	1	2	3	4	5	6	7	8	9	10	11															
3	29	CARDIFF CITY	3	1-0	0-0	24920	Sharpe	1	2	3	4	5	6	7	8*	9	10	11	12														
4	2 Sep	Leicester City	10	0-4	0-4	20228		1	2	3	4	5	6	7		9	10	11	8														
5	5	Sheffield United	8	3-3	1-0	15097	Galley(2), Gow	1		3	4	5	6	7	8	9	10	11		2													
6	12	HULL CITY	8	3-3	2-1	12978	Skirton(2), Garland	1		3	4		6	7	8	9	10	11		2	5												
7	19	Queens Park Rangers	12	1-2	0-0	13367	Garland	1		3	4		6	7	8	9	10	11		2	5												
8	26	BLACKBURN ROVERS	13	1-1	0-0	14012	Skirton	1		3	4	5	6	7	8	9	10	11		2													
9	29	BIRMINGHAM CITY	8	2-1	0-0	15973	Galley, Sharpe	1		3	4	5	6	7	8	9	10	11		2													
10	3 Oct	Luton Town	12	0-3	0-2	15992		1		3	4*	5	6	7	8		10	11	12	2		9											
11	10	OXFORD UNITED	14	0-4	0-1	16027		1		3		5	6	7	8		10	11	4	2		9											
12	17	Sunderland	17	0-1	0-1	17226		1		3	4	5	6	7	8	9	10*	11	12	2													
13	20	Middlesbrough	19	0-1	0-0	16651		1		3	4	5	6		8	9		11	10	2*				12	7								
14	24	Bolton Wanderers	21	0-1	0-0	7459		1		2	4	5	6	7	8	9		11				9			3								
15	31	SHEFFIELD WEDNESDAY	21	1-2	0-0	13093	Broomfield	1		2	4		6	7		9*	12	11	10			5	8	3									
16	7 Nov	Swindon Town	20	1-2	0-0	16453	Galley	1		2	4	5			7	9		11	10				8	3		6							
17	14	WATFORD	20	3-0	2-0	11100	Broomfield, Sharpe, Wimshurst	1		2	4	5			7	9		11	10				8	3		6							
18	21	Millwall	20	0-2	0-2	9158		1		2		5	12		7	9	10	11	4				8	3		6*							
19	28	CARLISLE UNITED	19	2-1	0-0	13526	Galley, Gow	1	2	3		5			9	4	7	10					8	12		6*	11						
20	5 Dec	Orient	19	1-1	0-1	6250	Sharpe	1	2	3	4	5	6	7	8*	9	10	11	12														
21	12	NORWICH CITY	19	0-1	0-0	10637		1	2*	3	4	5	6	7	8	9	10	11	12														
22	19	CHARLTON ATHLETIC	20	2-2	0-2	10187	Rooks, Sharpe(pen)	1	2	3	4	5	6*	7	8	9	10	11	12														
23	9 Jan	Birmingham City	20	0-2	0-2	15292		1	2*	3	4	5	6	7	9		10	11	12						8								
24	16	MIDDLESBROUGH	20	0-2	0-1	10335		1		2		6	7	8	9	4	11					12	3		5			10*				
25	30	Carlisle United	20	1-2	1-1	7764	Galley		2	3	4	5	6		11*	9	8		12				10	7				1				
26	6 Feb	ORIENT	21	0-0	0-0	11423			3	4	5	6		8	9	10		2					11			7		1				
27	13	Norwich City	21	2-3	2-0	11007	Fear, Galley		3	4	5	6		8*	9			2				12	10	11		7		1				
28	20	MILLWALL	19	3-2	2-0	10578	Fear, Gow, Wimshurst		3	4	5	6		8		10		2				9		11		7		1				
29	27	Sheffield Wednesday	20	0-2	0-2	12481			3	4*	5	6		8		10		2				9	12	11		7		1				
30	6 Mar	BOLTON WANDERERS	19	1-1	1-1	10550	Garland	1		3	4	5	6	7	8	9		10				2			11							
31	10	Portsmouth	19	1-1	1-0	8676	Garland	1	2	3	4		5		8	9		10				11							6	7		
32	13	Watford	19	3-0	0-0	12268	Galley, Garland, Gow	1	2	3	4		6		8	9		10				7			5	11						
33	20	SWINDON TOWN	19	2-1	0-0	17310	Galley, Gow	1	2	3	10		5		8	9		11				7							6	4		
34	27	SHEFFIELD UNITED	19	0-1	0-1	14999		1	2	3	10*	4			8	9		11				7				12			5	6		
35	3 Apr	Cardiff City	19	0-1	0-1	24687		1	2	3	10	5			8	9		11				7							6	4		
36	9	LUTON TOWN	19	3-2	0-1	18846	Garland(2), Rooks		2	3	10	5			8	9		11				7			12				1	6*	4	
37	10	PORTSMOUTH	18	2-0	1-0	14663	Garland, Tainton		2	3	10	5			8	9*		11	4			7			6	12			1		7	
38	12	Hull City	18	0-1	0-0	22178			2	3	10	5			8	9*		11	7						6				1		4	
39	17	Oxford United	19	0-1	0-0	9048			2	3		5	8*			9		10	7						6	11		12	1		4	
40	24	QUEENS PARK RANGERS	19	0-0	0-0	12522				3		5		12	8	9*		11				2			10	7			1	6	4	
41	27	LEICESTER CITY	19	0-1	0-0	16103			2	3		5		12	9			11	7						6	10		8*	1		4	
42	1 May	Blackburn Rovers	19	2-2	2-0	3971	Galley(2)		2	3		5			8*	9		11	4						10	7				6		1	12
		Apps.						30	21	42	34	34	31	20	38	35	37	24	26	9	3	10	13	10	7	2	6	1	11	7	10	1	
		Subs.									2		2				1		8			2	4	2		1							1
		Goals								3	2			4	8	12	5	7	1			2		2								

F.A. CUP

				Res.	H.T.	Att.					Wimshurst K.P.	Rooks R.	Parr G.J.		Garland C.S.			Sharpe G.R.				Broomfield I.L.		Fear K.W.	Rodgers D.M.				Cashley A.R.			
3R	11 Jan	Southampton		0-3	0-0	24131				3	4*	5	2		8			10	11	7			9	12		6				1			

F.L. CUP

	Date	Opposition		Res.	H.T.	Att.	Goalscorers	Gibson M.J.	Jacobs T.F.	Drysdale B.	Wimshurst K.P.	Rooks R.	Parr G.J.	Skirton A.F.G.	Garland C.S.	Galley J.E.	Gow R.G.	Sharpe G.R.	Tainton T.K.	Stacey S.D.	Connor J.F.	Broomfield I.L.	Merrick G.	Fear K.W.	Rodgers D.M.	Bartley D.R.		Derrick J.S.					
2R	8 Sep	Rotherham United		0-0	0-0	6384		1	2	3	4		6	7	8	9	10	11*	12		5						
2Rr	15	ROTHERHAM UNITED		4-0	1-0	9403	Garland(2), Gow, Skirton	1	2*	3	4		6	7	8	9	10	11	12		5						
3R	7 Oct	Blackpool		1-0	1-0	10877	Sharpe	1		3		5	6	7	8	9*	10	11	4	2		12					
4R	28	Leicester City		2-2	1-1	21577	Garland, Sharpe	1	2	4	5	6	7	8*		12	11	10			9	3					
4Rr	3 Nov	LEICESTER CITY		2-1	1-0	16575	Rodgers, Wimshurst (Extra time played)	1		2	4		6	7*		9	12	11	10			8	3		5		
5R	17	Fulham		0-0	0-0	16281		1		2	4	5			7	9		11	10			8	3		6		
5Rr	24	FULHAM		1-0	1-0	23228	Sharpe(pen) (£7984.9.2)	1		2	4	5	6	7	8*	9	4	11	10			12	3				
SF1	16 Dec	TOTTENHAM HOTSPUR		1-1	0-0	30022	Skirton (£13931)	1	2	3	4	5	6	7	8	9	10	11									
SF2	23	Tottenham Hotspur		0-2	0-0	29982	(Extra time played)	1	2	3	4	5	6	7*	8		10	9	12							11	

GLOUCESTERSHIRE CUP FINAL

				Res.	H.T.	Att.	
	4 May	Bristol Rovers		1-1	0-0	12256	Fear

FRIENDLIES

	Date	Opposition		Res.	H.T.	Att.	Goalscorers
1	29 Jul	Holstein Kiel		2-0	1-0	2200	Garland(2)
2	1 Aug	Go Ahead Deventer		1-1	0-0	10000	Sharpe
3	2	Veendam		2-1	1-1	1200	Garland, Tainton
4	5	WEST HAM UNITED		1-0	0-0	9655	Garland
5	8	GO AHEAD DEVENTER		2-0	1-0	3686	Garland(2,1pen)
6	22 Jan	Plymouth Argyle		2-1	2-1	2657	Galley, O.G.
7	15 Mar	WOLVERHAMPTON W.		1-2	0-0	7800	Spiring (Jack Connor's Benefit)
8	13 May	Espanol		1-3	1-1	11000	Tainton
9	20	Calella		2-1	1-1		Drysdale, Fear

FINAL LEAGUE TABLE

1	Leicester	42	23	13	6	57 30	59
2	Sheffield U	42	21	14	7	73 39	56
3	Cardiff	42	20	13	9	64 41	53
4	Carlisle	42	20	13	9	65 43	53
5	Hull	42	19	13	10	54 41	51
6	Luton	42	18	13	11	62 43	49
7	Middlesbrough	42	17	14	11	60 43	48
8	Millwall	42	19	9	14	59 42	47
9	Birmingham	42	17	12	13	58 48	46
10	Norwich	42	15	14	13	54 52	44
11	QPR	42	16	11	15	58 53	43
12	Swindon	42	15	12	15	61 51	42
13	Sunderland	42	15	12	15	52 54	42
14	Oxford	42	14	14	14	41 48	42
15	Sheffield W	42	12	12	18	51 69	36
16	Portsmouth	42	10	14	18	46 61	34
17	Orient	42	9	16	17	29 51	34
18	Watford	42	10	13	19	38 60	33
19	Bristol C	42	10	11	21	46 64	31
20	Charlton	42	8	14	20	41 65	30
21	Blackburn	42	6	15	21	37 69	27
22	Bolton	42	7	10	25	35 74	24

SEASON 1971-72
FOOTBALL LEAGUE DIVISION TWO

No.	Date	Opposition	Pos.	Res.	H.T.	Att.	Goalscorers	Cashley A.R.	Wimshurst K.P.	Drysdale B.	Emanuel W.J.	Rooks R.	Merrick G.	Tainton T.K.	Garland C.S.	Galley J.E.	Sweeney G.	Gow R.G.	Fear K.W.	Spiring P.J.	Gibson M.J.	Jacobs T.F.	Parr G.J.	Bruton D.E.	Broomfield I.L.	Wilson L.J.	Griffin K.R.	Burnside D.G.	Bartley D.R.	Bond L.A.	Rodgers D.M.
1	14 Aug	MILLWALL		3-3	2-2	12612	Garland, Gow, Sweeney	1	2	3	4	5	6	7	8*	9	10	11	12												
2	21	Sheffield Wednesday		5-1	3-0	12738	Galley(3), Emanuel, Garland	1	2	3	4	5	6	7	8*	9	10	11	12												
3	28	MIDDLESBROUGH	2	2-1	2-0	16474	Garland(pen), Wimshurst	1	2	3	4	5	6	7	8*	9	10	11													
4	31	CARDIFF CITY	1	2-0	1-0	23560	Galley, Gow	1	2	3	4	5	6	7	8	9	10	11													
5	4 Sep	Burnley	2	1-1	0-0	13593	Galley	1	2	3	4	5	6	7		9	10	11*	8	12											
6	11	HULL CITY	1	4-0	2-0	16659	Galley(2), Fear(pen), Gow	1	2	3	4	5	6	7		9	10	11	8												
7	18	Birmingham City	2	0-1	0-1	28745		1	2	3	4*	5	6	7		9	10	11	8	12											
8	25	NORWICH CITY	4	0-1	0-1	18768		1	2	3	4*	5	6	7		9	10	11	8	12											
9	28	BLACKPOOL	2	4-0	1-0	20352	Galley, Gow(pen), Tainton, Wimshurst	1	2	3	4	5	6	7		9	10	11		8											
10	2 Oct	Swindon Town	2	1-0	1-0	21383	Spiring	1	2	3	4	5	6	7		9	10	11		8											
11	9	WATFORD	2	2-1	1-0	18100	Galley, Spiring	1	2	3	4	5	6	7		9	10	11		8											
12	16	Millwall	3	1-3	1-1	14039	Spiring	1	2	3	4	5	6	7*		9	10	11	12	8											
13	20	Portsmouth	3	1-1	0-0	12575	Spiring	1	2	3	4	5	6	7		9	10	11		8											
14	23	ORIENT	3	5-3	1-3	17772	Galley(2), Rooks, Spiring, Tainton	1	2	3	4	5	6	7		9	10	11		8											
15	30	Charlton Athletic	4	0-2	0-1	10074		1	2	3	4*	5	6	7		9	10	11	12	8											
16	6 Nov	FULHAM	5	1-1	0-2	17295	Galley		2	3	4*	5	6	7		9	10	11		8	1	12									
17	13	Queens Park Rangers	7	0-3	0-1	14898			2	3	4	5	6	7		9	10	11		8	1										
18	19	CARLISLE UNITED	8	1-4	1-3	13123	Gow		8	3	4	5	6	7				10	11	9*			1	2	12						
19	27	Sunderland	9	1-1	0-1	15655	Wilson		2	3	4*		6	7				10		11	1	12			5	8	9				
20	4 Dec	LUTON TOWN	10			12921			2	3		5	6	7				10		11*		12	1		9	8					
21	11	Oxford United	9	0-0	0-0	8056			2	3		5	6	7				10			1	4			9	8			11		
22	18	BURNLEY	11	0-2	0-0	12909			2	3		6	9	7				10	4		1				5	8	12		11*		
23	27	Preston North End	11	0-1	0-1	19738				3			6	7				10	11	9	1	4									
24	1 Jan	BIRMINGHAM CITY	10	1-0	1-0	17457	Galley		2	3			6	7		9		10		11	1	8			5	4					
25	8	Middlesbrough	11	0-1	0-0	13117			2	3			6	7		9		10		11	1	8			5	4					
26	22	Blackpool	15	0-1	0-1	9923				3			6	7		9	12	10		8*	1			2					11		5
27	29	PORTSMOUTH	14			10949	Galley			3			6	7		9		10	4	8	1			2					11		5
28	12 Feb	Orient	18	0-2	0-1	13112				3	4		6	7		9		10		11*	1	12		2		8					5
29	19	CHARLTON ATHLETIC	16	2-0	2-0	10207	Galley, Tainton	1		3	4	5	6	7		9	10			8				2					11		
30	26	Fulham	17	0-2	0-0	9276		1		3		5	6	7		9	10			8				2		4			11		
31	4 Mar	QUEENS PARK RANGERS	15	2-0	0-0	11105	Galley, Rodgers	1		3	4		6	7		9		10		8				2					11		5
32	11	Watford	11	2-0	1-0	5384	Bartley, Galley	1		3	4		6	7		9		10		8				2					11		5
33	18	SHEFFIELD WEDNESDAY	10	1-0	1-0	12568	Spiring	1		3	4		6	7		9		10		8				2					11		5
34	25	Hull City	10	1-1	0-1	11700	Tainton	1		3	4		6	7*		9	12	10		8				2					11		5
35	31	SWINDON TOWN	8	1-0	0-0	21496	Galley	1		3	4		6	7		9		10		8				2					11		5
36	1 Apr	PRESTON NORTH END	7	4-1	1-1	12962	Emanuel, Galley, Spiring, Tainton	1		3	4		6	7		9		10		8				2					11		5
37	4	Norwich City	7	2-2	0-1	35076	Gow(pen), Sweeney	1		3	4		6	7		9	12	10		8				2					11		5*
38	8	Carlisle United	9	0-2	0-1	6596		1		3	4		6	7*		9	12	10		8				2					11		5
39	15	SUNDERLAND	8	3-1	0-1	12178	Drysdale, Galley, Gow(pen)	1		3	4		6	7		9	12	10		8				2*					11		5
40	22	Luton Town	10	0-0	0-0	8329		1		3	4		6	7		9		10		8									11	2	5
41	26	Cardiff City	8	3-2	2-1	17249	Spiring(2), Gow(pen)	1		3	4		6	7		9		10		8									11	2	5
42	29	OXFORD UNITED	8	4-2	2-1	10793	Galley(2), Gow(pen), Sweeney	1		3	4		6	7		9		10		8									11	2	5
							Apps.	29	25	42	33	24	42	41	4	37	33	39	5	28	11	15	2	10	3	11	1	1	16	2	8
							Subs.										1			4	4	3	1	3	1		1				1
							Goals		2	1	2	1		5	3	22	3	9	1	9						1			1		1

F.A. CUP

Rd	Date	Opposition		Res.	H.T.	Att.	Goalscorers	Cashley A.R.	Wimshurst K.P.	Drysdale B.	Emanuel W.J.	Rooks R.	Merrick G.	Tainton T.K.	Garland C.S.	Galley J.E.	Sweeney G.	Gow R.G.	Fear K.W.	Spiring P.J.	Gibson M.J.	Jacobs T.F.	Parr G.J.	Bruton D.E.	Broomfield I.L.	Wilson L.J.
3R	15 Jan	Preston North End		2-4	2-1	13619	Spiring, Wilson		2	3		5*	6	7		9	10	11		8	1	12				4

F.L. CUP

Rd	Date	Opposition		Res.	H.T.	Att.	Goalscorers	Cashley A.R.	Wimshurst K.P.	Drysdale B.	Emanuel W.J.	Rooks R.	Merrick G.	Tainton T.K.	Garland C.S.	Galley J.E.	Sweeney G.	Gow R.G.	Fear K.W.	Spiring P.J.
1R	17 Aug	Plymouth Argyle		0-1	0-0	11248		1	2	3	4*	5	6	7		9	10	11	8	12

GLOUCESTERSHIRE CUP FINAL

Date	Opposition	Res.	H.T.	Att.	Goalscorers
9 May	BRISTOL ROVERS	1-1	0-0	13137	Emanuel

Rovers were awarded the Cup (4-2 in penalty shoot out competition - a new innovation). Score at 90 minutes - 1-1.

FRIENDLIES

No.	Date	Opposition	Res.	H.T.	Att.	Goalscorers
1	29 Jul	Newport County	2-1	1-1	1901	Fear(2)
2	31	BRISTOL ROVERS	1-3	0-3	8067	Gow (Bush & Ford joint Benefit)
3	2 Aug	WOLVERHAMPTON W.	0-1	0-1	4816	
4	4	Torquay United	0-1	0-1	2893	
5	7	Port Vale	1-1	1-1	2365	Tainton
6	30 Nov	WEST BROMWICH ALB.	0-0	0-0	4884	(Terry Bush Benefit)
7	4 Feb	Southend United	1-0	0-0	2488	Fear(pen)
8	1 May	MORTON	1-1	0-1	1700	Gow(pen)
9	10	Ferndale Athletic				
10	28	Teheran Select XI	2-0	0-0	12000	Fear, Spiring
11	30	Persepolis	1-0			Spiring
12	3 Jun	Appollo Limasol	1-0	0-0		Gow
13	4	Famagusta	3-1			Fear, Galley, Spiring

FINAL LEAGUE TABLE

		P	W	D	L	F	A	Pts
1	Norwich	42	21	15	6	60	36	57
2	Birmingham	42	19	18	5	60	31	56
3	Millwall	42	19	17	6	64	46	55
4	QPR	42	20	14	8	57	28	54
5	Sunderland	42	17	16	9	67	57	50
6	Blackpool	42	20	7	15	70	50	47
7	Burnley	42	20	6	16	70	55	46
8	Bristol C	42	18	10	14	61	49	46
9	Middlesbrough	42	19	8	15	50	48	46
10	Carlisle	42	17	9	16	61	57	43
11	Swindon	42	15	12	15	47	47	42
12	Hull	42	14	10	18	49	53	38
13	Luton	42	10	18	14	43	48	38
14	Sheffield W	42	13	12	17	51	58	38
15	Oxford	42	12	14	16	43	55	38
16	Portsmouth	42	12	13	17	59	68	37
17	Orient	42	14	9	19	50	61	37
18	Preston	42	12	12	18	52	58	36
19	Cardiff	42	10	14	18	56	69	34
20	Fulham	42	12	10	20	45	68	34
21	Charlton	42	12	9	21	55	77	33
22	Watford	42	5	9	28	24	75	19

1971-72 Season
Back: Fear, Bartley, Spring, Merrick, Tainton.
Centre: Rooks, Garland, Gibson, Galley, Cashley, Parr, Merrington.
Front: Sweeney, Gow, Jacobs, Drysdale, Wimshurst.

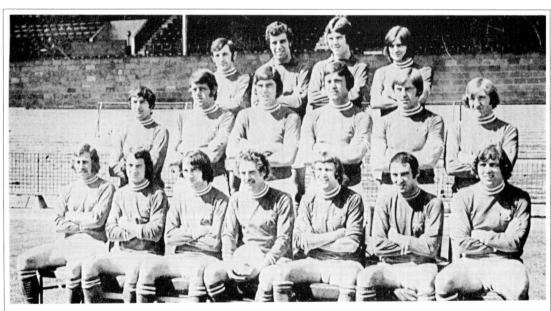

Bristol City 1972-73. Back row (left to right): Trevor Tainton, Ray Cashley, Len Bond, Keith Fear. Centre: Gerry Sweeney, John Galley, David Bruton, David Rodgers, David Merrington, John Emanuel. Front: Brian Drysdale, Peter Spiring, Gerry Gow, Geoff Merrick (captain), Les Wilson, Danny Bartley, Trevor Jacobs.

No.	Date	Opposition	Pos.	Res.	H.T.	Att.	Goalscorers	Cashley A.R.	Wilson L.J.	Drysdale B.	Emanuel W.J.	Rodgers D.M.	Merrick G.	Tainton T.K.	Spring P.J.	Galley J.E.	Gow R.G.	Bartley D.R.	Ritchie T.G.	Sweeney G.	Broomfield I.L.	Bruton D.E.	Fear K.W.	Ritchie S.K.	Jacobs T.F.	Bond L.A.	Gould R.A.	Hall C.	Woods E.	Gillies D.G.	Collier G.B.
1	12 Aug	Brighton & Hove Albion		1-1	1-1	16839	Bartley	1	2	3	4		5	6	7	8	9	10	11												
2	19	MILLWALL	9	2-2	1-1	15648	Gow, Spring	1	2	3			5	6	7	8	9*	10	11	12											
3	26	Swindon Town	16	1-2	1-1	15034	Spring	1	2	3			5	6	7	8	9	10	11	4											
4	29	Hull City	19	0-2	0-1	8867		1		3			5	6	7	8*	9	10	11	4	2		12								
5	2 Sep	SHEFFIELD WEDNESDAY	22	1-2	0-1	12373	Gow	1		3	4		5	6	7	8*	9	10	11	12	2										
6	9	Orient	18	2-0	1-0	4482	Galley, Spring	1	2				6	7	8	9	10	11	4	3		5									
7	16	MIDDLESBROUGH	17	1-1	1-0	12185	Spring	1	2				5	6	7	8	9	10	11	4	3										
8	19	Queens Park Rangers	16	1-1	1-0	11586	Spring	1	2		4		5	6	7	8	10		11	3			9								
9	23	Cardiff City	13	3-1	2-1	14204	Drysdale, Galley, Gow(pen)	1	2	3	4		5	6	7		9	11		10		8									
10	26	FULHAM	13	1-1	0-1	14210	Gow	1	2	3	4		5	6	7		9			12	11		8*								
11	30	HUDDERSFIELD TOWN	14	0-0	0-0	12406		1	2	3	4		5	6	7*	8	9	11		12	10										
12	7 Oct	Portsmouth	10	3-0	1-0	9375	Sweeney(2), Emanuel	1	2	3	4		5	6	7	8*	9	10		12	11										
13	14	NOTTINGHAM FOREST	11	1-1	0-0	13861	Gow	1	2	3	4		5	6	7		9	11*	12	8	10										
14	21	Oxford United	9	2-0	1-0	9936	Galley, Gow(pen)	1	2	3	4		5	6	7*		9	11	12		10										
15	28	LUTON TOWN	11	0-1	0-1	13562		1	2		4*				8	9	10	11	7	3		5	12								
16	4 Nov	Fulham	13	1-5	1-2	8982	Galley	1	2				5	6*	7	9		4	10	12	3										
17	11	QUEENS PARK RANGERS	14	1-2	1-2	12570	Galley	1		3	12		5	6	7	8*	9	10	11	4					2						
18	14	Huddersfield Town	13	1-0	0-0	5692	Fear	1		3			4	5	6	7	9	10		11	8				2						
19	18	Blackpool	14	0-3	0-2	8341		1		3			4	5	6	7	9	11		10	8				2						
20	25	SUNDERLAND	12	1-0		10666	Galley		2	3	4	5*	6	7	12	9	11			10			8			1					
21	2 Dec	Carlisle United	10	2-1	1-0	6526	Fear, Spring			3	4		6	7	10	9	11			2	5		8			1					
22	16	BURNLEY	12	0-1	0-1	15334		12		3	4		6	7	8*		10			2	5		11			1	9				
23	23	Preston North End		3-0	2-0	7700	Gould, T.Ritchie, Tainton		2	3	4*		6	7			10		12				8			1	9				
24	26	CARDIFF CITY	11	1-0	0-0	20490	Gow(pen)	1	2	3			5	6	7		10		4		11		8				9				
25	30	Millwall	13	0-3	0-2	9707		1	2	3		5*	6	7	12		10		4		11		8				9				
26	6 Jan	SWINDON TOWN	10	3-0		12481	Emanuel, Fear, Gould			3	4	5	6	7	8		10			2			11*			1	9		12		
27	20	Sheffield Wednesday		0-0		11195	(aband. after 55 mins due to snow and ice)			3	4	5	6	7	8			11		2			9			1	10				
28	27	ORIENT	11	2-2	0-1	11766	Gow, Merrick			3	4	5	6	7	8		10	11		2						1	9				
29	10 Feb	Middlesbrough	12	1-2		8511	Emanuel	1		3	4		6	7	8		10	11*	12	2		5					9				
30	17	BRIGHTON & H.A.		3-1	1-1	11116	T.Ritchie, Spring, Tainton	1		3	4		6	7	8		10*	11	12	2		5					9				
31	24	Burnley	10	1-1	0-1	13588	T.Ritchie			3	4	5	6	7			10			8	2		11			1	9				
32	3 Mar	PORTSMOUTH	11	3-1	2-0	10977	Gow(2), Fear			3	4	5	6	7			10			8	2		11			1	9				
33	10	Nottingham Forest	10	0-1	0-1	8680				3	4	5*	6	7			10			8	2		11			1	9		12		
34	14	Sheffield Wednesday	12	2-3	0-0	13819	Gould, T.Ritchie			3	4	5	6	7*			10			8	2		12				9			11	
35	17	OXFORD UNITED	12	0-0		11177		1		3	4	5	6	7			10			8	2						9			11	
36	24	Luton Town	11	3-1		7102	Fear, Gillies, Gow	1		3	4	5					10			8	2		7				9			11	6
37	27	ASTON VILLA	10	3-0		15654	Gould(2), Gillies	1		3	4	5	6				10			8	2		7				9			11	
38	31	Sunderland	8	2-2	0-1	33255	Emanuel, Merrick	1		3	4	5	6				10			8	2		7				9			11	
39	7 Apr	CARLISLE UNITED	7	4-1	3-1	10530	Gould, Gow(pen), Rodgers, O.G.	1		3	4	5	6	12			10			8	2		7				9*			11	
40	14	Aston Villa	9	0-1	0-0	19545		1		3	4	5*	6	12			10			8	2		7				9			11	
41	21	BLACKPOOL	8	3-0	2-0	11537	Emanuel, Fear, Gould	1		3	4	5*	6	12			10			8	2		7				9			11	
42	23	PRESTON NORTH END	7	2-1		10799	Fear, Merrick	1		3	4		6	12			10			8	2		7				9			11	5
43	28	HULL CITY	5	2-1	0-0	11066	Gould, O.G.	1		3	4		6	12			10			8	2		7				9			11	5*
							Apps.	32	21	35	34	35	42	34	21	20	42	13	24	40	3	6	21	1	3	11	20	1		11	3
							Subs.		1		1			4	2				2	7	1	1				3			1	1	
							Goals		1	5	1	3	2	7	6	12	1	4	2			7					8			2	

F.A. CUP

								Cashley	Wilson	Drysdale	Emanuel	Rodgers	Merrick	Tainton	Spring	Galley	Gow	Bartley	RitchieTG	Sweeney	Broomfield	Bruton	Fear	RitchieSK	Jacobs	Bond	Gould	Hall	Woods	Gillies	Collier
3R	13 Jan	Portsmouth		1-1	0-0	15177	Gould			3	4	5	6	7	8		10			2			11*			1	9			12	
3Rr	16	PORTSMOUTH		4-1	1-0	16699	Gould, Gow(pen), Sweeney, Tainton			3	4	5	6	7	8		10	11		2						1	9				
4R	3 Feb	Wolverhampton Wndrs		0-1	0-1	30849		1		3	4	5*	6	7	8		10	11	12	2							9				

F.L. CUP

								Cashley	Wilson	Drysdale	Emanuel	Rodgers	Merrick	Tainton	Spring	Galley	Gow	Bartley	RitchieTG	Sweeney	Broomfield
2R	6 Sep	West Ham United		1-2	0-1	17688	Galley	1	2	3		5*	6	7	8	9	10			11	4

GLOUCESTERSHIRE CUP FINAL

	1 May	Bristol Rovers		2-2	0-0	12350	Gow(2)

City were awarded the Cup (after penalty shoot-out competition 5-3). Score at 90 minutes - 1-1.

FRIENDLIES

No.	Date	Opposition	Res.	H.T.	Att.	Goalscorers
1	27 Jul	Newport County	2-1	2-1		T.Ritchie, Spring
2	29	LEICESTER CITY	5-1	3-1	3122	Broomfield, Galley, Gow, T.Ritchie, O.G.
3	1 Aug	COVENTRY CITY	1-2	1-0	3611	Tainton
4	3	ITALIAN YOUTH XI	3-0	1-0	651	T.Ritchie(2,1pen), O.G.
5	5	Port Vale	4-0	3-0		Broomfield(3), Tainton
6	17 Oct	CHELSEA	2-1	2-0	12783	Fear, O.G. (Gordon Parr Benefit)
7	23	Morton	1-0	1-0	2000	Sweeney (Floodlight opening)
8	10 Apr	ALL STAR XI	5-3	5-2	6726	Galley(2), Gould, Gow, O.G.
9	16 May	Baltimore Bays	1-2	1-0	5500	Fear
10	23	Cincinatti Comets	4-1		2500	Fear, Gould, Gow, T.Ritchie

FINAL LEAGUE TABLE

		P	W	D	L	F	A	Pts
1	Burnley	42	24	14	4	72	35	62
2	QPR	42	24	13	5	81	37	61
3	Aston Villa	42	18	14	10	51	47	50
4	Middlesbrough	42	17	13	12	46	43	47
5	Bristol C.	42	17	12	13	63	51	46
6	Sunderland	42	17	12	13	59	49	46
7	Blackpool	42	18	10	14	56	51	46
8	Oxford	42	19	7	16	52	43	45
9	Fulham	42	16	12	14	58	49	44
10	Sheffield W.	42	17	10	15	59	55	44
11	Millwall	42	16	10	16	55	47	42
12	Luton	42	15	11	16	44	53	41
13	Hull	42	14	12	16	64	59	40
14	Nottingham F	42	14	12	16	47	52	40
15	Orient	42	12	13	17	49	53	36
16	Swindon	42	10	16	16	46	60	36
17	Portsmouth	42	12	11	19	42	59	35
18	Carlisle	42	11	12	19	50	52	34
19	Preston	42	11	12	19	37	64	34
20	Cardiff	42	11	11	20	43	58	33
21	Huddersfield	42	8	17	17	36	56	33
22	Brighton	42	8	13	21	46	83	29

SEASON 1973-74
FOOTBALL LEAGUE DIVISION TWO

No.	Date	Opposition	Pos.	Res.	H.T.	Att.	Goalscorers
1	25 Aug	BOLTON WANDERERS		1-0	1-0	13288	Gould
2	1 Sep	Orient	2	1-0	0-0	7216	Rodgers
3	8	LUTON TOWN	9	1-3	1-2	12208	Gould(pen)
4	11	Swindon Town	2	1-0	1-0	13991	Gould
5	15	Preston North End	4	1-1	0-1	10790	Fear
6	18	HULL CITY	1	3-1	0-1	10711	Cashley, Gould, Ritchie
7	22	SHEFFIELD WEDNESDAY	1	2-0	1-0	13829	Fear, Gould
8	29	Middlesbrough	2	0-2	0-0	17049	
9	2 Oct	Hull City	4	1-2	0-2	7235	Rodgers
10	6	WEST BROMWICH ALB.	5	1-1	1-1	14326	Gould
11	13	Millwall	4	2-0	0-0	7592	Gould, Whitehead
12	20	Aston Villa	3	2-2	2-1	26918	Fear, Ritchie
13	23	SWINDON TOWN	2	1-0	1-0	14474	Fear
14	27	BLACKPOOL	4	0-1	0-0	13896	
15	3 Nov	Fulham	5	1-2	0-0	9613	Tainton
16	10	CRYSTAL PALACE	9	0-1	0-1	15488	
17	17	SUNDERLAND	8	2-0	0-0	14965	Gillies, Sweeney
18	24	Carlisle United	9	1-2	1-1	6000	Ritchie
19	1 Dec	NOTTS COUNTY	10	2-2	1-1	10436	Fear, Gillies
20	8	Portsmouth	11	0-1	0-0	13178	
21	15	Cardiff City	9	1-0	0-0	9388	Gillies
22	22	MIDDLESBROUGH	9	1-1	0-1	13116	Gillies
23	26	Oxford United	13	0-5	0-2	7493	
24	29	Luton Town	13	0-1	0-1	11398	
25	1 Jan	ORIENT	14	0-2	0-0	19126	
26	12	PRESTON NORTH END	13	0-0	0-0	11450	
27	20	Bolton Wanderers	15	1-2	1-2	23315	Hunt
28	2 Feb	CARDIFF CITY	13	3-2	1-2	24487	Sweeney(2,1pen), Tainton
29	10	Sheffield Wednesday	15	1-3	1-1	15888	Ritchie
30	23	West Bromwich Albion	16	2-2	1-1	17653	Hunt, Tainton
31	26	MILLWALL	12	5-2	2-1	9605	Fear(3), Tainton, O.G.
32	2 Mar	OXFORD UNITED	14	0-0	0-0	25904	
33	16	ASTON VILLA	16	0-1	0-0	12405	
34	19	Blackpool	16	2-2	2-1	7710	Emanuel, Gow
35	23	Crystal Palace	16	1-3	0-0	16690	Whitehead
36	30	FULHAM	16	0-1	0-0	10946	
37	6 Apr	CARLISLE UNITED	16	2-0	1-0	9570	Cheesley, Gillies
38	12	NOTTINGHAM FOREST	16	1-0	1-0	13125	Cheesley
39	13	Sunderland	16	2-1	1-1	28884	Emanuel, Ritchie
40	16	Nottingham Forest	15	1-1	0-0	12756	Ritchie
41	20	PORTSMOUTH	16	0-2	0-1	11143	
42	27	Notts County	16	1-2	0-2	6991	Gillies

Apps. 27 42 40 24 26 31 42 39 16 41 32 28 32 15 9 2 9 7
Subs. 2 2 3 8 2 3 2 2 1
Goals 1 3 2 1 5 6 7 1 8 6 2 2 2

F.A. CUP

	Date	Opposition		Res.	H.T.	Att.	Goalscorers
3R	5 Jan	Hull City		1-1	1-1	8968	Merrick
3Rr	8	Hull City		1-0	0-0	5340	Tainton
4R	26	Hereford United		1-0	1-0	17431	Merrick
5R	16 Feb	LEEDS UNITED		1-1	0-1	37141	Fear (£28111)
5Rr	19	Leeds United		1-0	0-0	47182	Gillies (£32283)
6R	9 Mar	LIVERPOOL		0-1	0-0	37671	(£28826)

F.L. CUP

	Date	Opposition		Res.	H.T.	Att.	Goalscorers
2R	9 Oct	Scunthorpe United		0-0	0-0	4418	
2Rr	16	SCUNTHORPE UNITED		2-1	0-1	7837	Fear, Sweeney
3R	30	COVENTRY CITY		2-2	1-1	19129	Gould(2)
3Rr	6 Nov	Coventry City		1-2	1-2	13049	Whitehead

WATNEY CUP

	Date	Opposition		Res.	H.T.	Att.	Goalscorers
1R	11 Aug	Peterborough United		2-1	0-1	9138	Gould(2)
SF	15	Stoke City		1-4	1-2	13812	Ritchie

GLOUCESTERSHIRE CUP FINAL

	Date	Opposition		Res.	H.T.	Att.
	29 Apr	BRISTOL ROVERS		0-2	0-1	15986

FRIENDLIES

	Date	Opposition		Res.	H.T.	Att.	Goalscorers
1	2 Aug	Merthyr Tydfil		1-2	1-1		Sweeney
2	4	Swansea City		2-0	0-0		Gould, Gow
3	7	Newport County		3-1	2-0		Gould(2), Ritchie
4	3 Dec	DERBY COUNTY		0-1	0-0	3607	(Gerry Sharpe Benefit)
5	23 Apr	Hereford United		1-0	0-0	3061	Whitehead (Alan Jones Benefit)
6	9 May	Mangotsfield United		3-2	0-1		Fear, Ritchie, O.G., (Clubhouse opening)
7	12	Imperial Athletic		6-1			Ritchie(3),Gow(2),Cashley(pen) (Hos. Benefit)

FINAL LEAGUE TABLE

1	Middlesbrough	42	27	11	4	77:30	65
2	Luton	42	19	12	11	64:51	50
3	Carlisle	42	20	9	13	61:48	49
4	Orient	42	15	18	9	55:42	48
5	Blackpool	42	17	13	12	57:40	47
6	Sunderland	42	19	9	14	58:44	47
7	Nottingham F	42	15	15	12	57:43	45
8	West Bromwich	42	14	16	12	48:45	44
9	Hull	42	13	17	12	46:47	43
10	Notts Co.	42	15	13	14	55:60	43
11	Bolton	42	15	12	15	44:40	42
12	Millwall	42	14	14	14	51:51	42
13	Fulham	42	16	10	16	39:43	42
14	Aston Villa	42	13	15	14	48:45	41
15	Portsmouth	42	14	12	16	45:62	40
16	Bristol C.	42	14	10	18	47:54	38
17	Cardiff	42	10	16	16	49:62	36
18	Oxford	42	10	16	16	35:46	36
19	Sheffield W.	42	12	11	19	51:63	35
20	Crystal Palace	42	11	12	19	43:56	34
21	Preston	42	9	14	19	40:62	31
22	Swindon	42	7	11	24	36:72	25

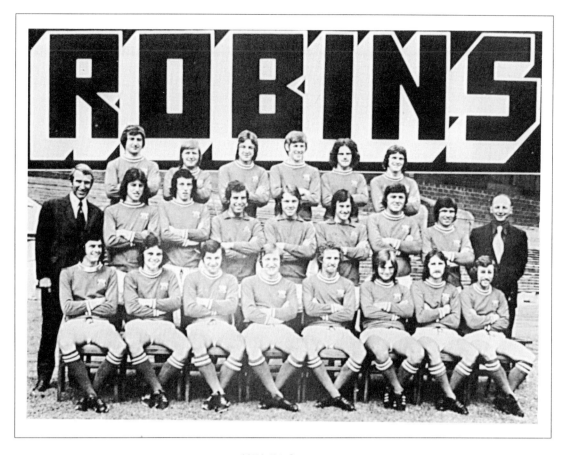

1973-74 Season
Back: Sweeney, Durrell, Rogers, Crowley, Whitehead, Gillies.
Middle: Dicks (Manager), Collier, Ritchie, Cashley, Bond, Wardle, Rodgers, Gould, Sillet (Chief Coach).
Front: Woods, Griffin, Tainton, Emanuel, Merrick, Fear, Gow, Drysdale.

1974-75 Season
Back: Wimshurst, Emanuel, Gillies, Cheesley, Bond, Shaw, Cashley, Rodgers, Collier, Ritchie, Bardsley (Physiotherapist).
Front: Fear, Brolly, Hunt, Tainton, Merrick, Dicks (Manager), Drysdale, Mann, Sweeney, Gow, Whitehead.

SEASON 1974-75
FOOTBALL LEAGUE DIVISION TWO

No.	Date	Opposition	Pos.	Res.	H.T.	Att.	Goalscorers	Cashley A.R.	Sweeney G.	Drysdale B.	Gow R.G.	Rodgers D.M.	Merrick G.	Tanton T.K.	Mann J.A.	Gillies D.G.	Cheesley P.M.	Whitehead C.R.	Collier G.B.	Ritchie T.G.	Hunt R.P.	Fear K.W.	Erranuel W.J.	Brolly M.J.	Griffin K.R.	Durrell J.T.
1	17 Aug	Nottingham Forest		0-0	0-0	11339		1	2	3	4	5	6	7	8	9	10	11								
2	24	ORIENT	11	0-0	0-0	10985		1	2	3	4		6	7	12	9	10	11	5	8*						
3	31	Oldham Athletic	21	0-2	0-0	9860		1	2	3	4		6	7		9	10	11*	5	8	12					
4	7 Sep	BOLTON WANDERERS	14	2-1	1-1	9263	Drysdale, Gillies	1	2	3	4		6	7		9			5	8		10	11			
5	14	Cardiff City	10	1-0	0-0	8856	Fear	1	2	3	4		6			9		7	5	8		10	11			
6	21	SOUTHAMPTON	7	2-0	1-0	15708	Merrick, Sweeney	1	2	3	4		6			9		7	5	8		10	11			
7	24	YORK CITY	7	0-0	0-0	11867		1	2	3	4		6			9		7	5	8		10	11			
8	28	Millwall	13	0-1	0-0	5750		1	2	3	4		6			9*		7	5	8		10	11	12		
9	5 Oct	Sheffield Wednesday	13	1-1	0-0	10088	Merrick	1	2	3	4		6	7		9			5	8		10	11			
10	12	SUNDERLAND	11	1-1	1-0	13084	Gow	1	2	3	4		6	7		9*		12	5	8		10	11			
11	19	Fulham	11	1-1	1-1	8960	Fear	1	2	3	4		6	7				10	5	8		9	11			
12	23	Oxford United	15	0-2		5590		1	2	3	4		6	7	10				5	8		9	11			
13	26	NOTTS COUNTY	10	3-0	0-0	10343	Cheesley, Mann, Sweeney(pen)	1	2	3			6	7	4		10		5	8		9	11			
14	2 Nov	Portsmouth	6	1-0	0-0	9590	Gow	1	2	3	10		6	7	4				5	8		9	11			
15	5	OXFORD UNITED	5	3-0	0-0	10036	Mann, Merrick, Ritchie	1	2	3	4		6	7	10				5	8		9	11			
16	9	MANCHESTER UNITED	4	1-0	0-0	28104	Emanuel	1	2	3*	10		6	7	4			12	5	8		9	11			
17	16	West Bromwich Albion		0-1	0-1	12145		1	2	3	4		6	7*	10			12	5	8			11	9		
18	23	BLACKPOOL	7	0-1	0-1	11584		1	2	3	4		6	7				12	5	8		10*	11	9		
19	30	Hull City	8	0-1	0-1	9612		1	2	3	4	5	6	7	10			12		8		9*	11			
20	7 Dec	ASTON VILLA	8	1-0	1-0	13399	Mann	1	2	3	4*		6	7	10		12	11	5	8				9		
21	14	NOTTINGHAM FOREST	7	1-0	1-0	10006	Cheesley	1	2	3	4	5	6	7			10	11		8				9		
22	21	Norwich City	8	2-3	2-1	17439	Mann, Ritchie	1	4	3		5	6	7	2	9		11		8					10*	12
23	26	CARDIFF CITY	8	0-0		12485		1	2	3			6	7	4	9			5	8		10				11
24	28	Bristol Rovers	5	4-1		20933	Fear(2), Mann, Tainton	1	2	3			6	7	4	9			5	8		10				11
25	11 Jan	Aston Villa	6	0-2		21762		1	2	3			6	7	4	9*	12		5	8		10				11
26	18	HULL CITY	6	2-0		10423	Collier, Gillies	1	2	3			6	7	8	10			5			9	4	11		
27	1 Feb	Manchester United	5	1-0	0-0	47118	Gillies	1	2	3			6	7	4	10			5	8		9		11		
28	8	PORTSMOUTH	5	3-1		13802	Gillies, Sweeney, O.G.	1	2	3			6	7	8	9			5			10	4	11		
29	15	Blackpool	6	0-2	0-2	8687		1	2	3			6	7	8	9	10		5				4	11		
30	22	WEST BROMWICH ALB.	5	2-1	0-1	14180	Fear, Sweeney(pen)	1	2	3			6	7	8	9			5			10	4	11		
31	1 Mar	OLDHAM ATHLETIC	5	3-1	2-0	12461	Brolly, Fear, O.G.	1	2	3			6	7	8	9			5			10	4	11		
32	8	York City	6	0-1	0-1	6994		1	2	3			6	7	8	9*			5	12		10	4	11		
33	15	MILLWALL	5	2-1	1-0	12393	Fear, Mann	1	2	3			6	7	8	9			5			10	4	11		
34	22	Bolton Wanderers	5	2-0		11066	Gillies, Ritchie	1	2	3			6	7	10	9			5	8			4	11		
35	28	Southampton	3	1-0		21019	Gillies	1	2	3			6	7	8	9			5	10			4	11		
36	29	NORWICH CITY	5	0-1		22204	Sweeney	1	2	3	12		6	7	8	9			5			10	4*	11		
37	1 Apr	BRISTOL ROVERS	5	1-1		28953	Sweeney	1	2	3	12		6	7	8	9			5	10			4*	11		
38	5	Notts County	4	2-1	1-1	7227	Gillies(2)	1	2	3	11		6	7	10	9			5	8			4			
39	12	SHEFFIELD WEDNESDAY	5	1-0	0-0	11976	Fear	1	2	3	4		6	7	10*	9			5	8		12	11			
40	15	Orient	5	0-1		6487		1	2	3	4		6	7	8	9			5	10		12	11*			
41	19	Sunderland	5	0-3		30530		1	2	3			6	7	8	9			5	8		11*	4	12		
42	26	FULHAM	5	3-1	0-1	11538	Gillies, Ritchie, Sweeney(pen)	1	2	3	4		6	7		9		11	5	8		10				

			Apps.	42	42	38	22	5	42	38	29	28	13	10	41	32		29	31	13	4	3
			Subs.		2						1	1	2	4				1	1	2		2		1
			Goals	6	1	2			3	1	6	9	2			1	4		8	1	1		

F.A. CUP

Rd	Date	Opposition		Res.	H.T.	Att.	Goalscorers	Cashley	Sweeney	Drysdale	Merrick	Tanton	Mann	Cheesley	Collier	Ritchie	Fear	Brolly	Griffin	Durrell
3R	4 Jan	Sheffield United		0-2	0-1	20163		1	2	3	6	7	4	10	5	8	9*		12	11

F.L. CUP

Rd	Date	Opposition		Res.	H.T.	Att.	Goalscorers
1R	19 Aug	CARDIFF CITY		2-1	1-0	8813	Merrick, Sweeney
2R	10 Sep	Crystal Palace		4-1	0-1	16263	Gillies, Gow, Sweeney(pen), Whitehead
3R	8 Oct	LIVERPOOL		0-0	0-0	25573	
3Rr	16	Liverpool		0-4	0-1	23694	

GLOUCESTERSHIRE CUP FINAL

	Date	Opposition		Res.	H.T.	Att.	Goalscorers
	29 Apr	Bristol Rovers		1-2	0-0	11408	Collier

Extra-time played following score of 1-1 at end of ninety minutes.

FRIENDLIES

No.	Date	Opposition	Res.	H.T.	Att.	Goalscorers
1	3 Aug	VEENDAM	5-0	1-0	2271	Cheesley(2), Gow, Sweeney(pen), Whitehead
2	10	COVENTRY CITY	2-1	0-0	3237	Gillies, Rodgers
3	12	Wolverhampton Wndrs	1-1	1-1	5247	Gillies
4	13 Jan	Falmouth Town*	8-0	3-0		Fear(2), Gillies(2), Brlly, Chsley(p), Emnuel, Mrrick
5	24	MANCHESTER CITY	2-2	2-0	5466	Gillies, Penny
6	5 May	LEICESTER CITY	2-4	0-0	1796	Mabbutt, Steele (Cliff Morgan Benefit)
7	17	Molde S.C.	2-0	1-0	3500	Durrell, Ritchie
8	19	Bodo-Glimt	1-0	1-0	3500	Ritchie
9	21	Mjolner F.C. of Narvik	5-2		2000	Ritchie(2), Durrell, Gow, Mann
10	23	Mo	10-0	3-0	2500	Gillies(3), Ritchie(3), Merrick(2), Cheesley, Fear

* Floodlight opening

FINAL LEAGUE TABLE

		P	W	D	L	F:A	Pts
1	Manchester U	42	26	9	7	66:30	61
2	Aston Villa	42	25	8	9	69:32	58
3	Norwich	42	20	13	9	58:37	53
4	Sunderland	42	19	13	10	65:35	51
5	Bristol C.	42	21	8	13	47:33	50
6	West Bromwich	42	18	9	15	54:42	45
7	Blackpool	42	14	17	11	38:33	45
8	Hull	42	15	14	13	40:53	44
9	Fulham	42	13	16	13	44:39	42
10	Bolton	42	15	12	15	45:41	42
11	Oxford	42	15	12	15	41:51	42
12	Orient	42	11	20	11	28:39	42
13	Southampton	42	15	11	16	53:54	41
14	Notts Co.	42	12	16	14	49:59	40
15	York	42	14	10	18	51:55	38
16	Nottingham F.	42	12	14	16	43:55	38
17	Portsmouth	42	12	13	17	44:54	37
18	Oldham	42	10	15	17	40:48	35
19	Bristol R.	42	12	11	19	42:64	35
20	Millwall	42	10	12	20	44:56	32
21	Cardiff	42	9	14	19	36:62	32
22	Sheffield W.	42	5	11	26	29:64	21

SEASON 1975-76
FOOTBALL LEAGUE DIVISION TWO

No.	Date	Opposition	Pos.	Res.	H.T.	Att.	Goalscorers	Cashley A.R.	Sweeney G.	Drysdale B.	Gow R.G.	Collier G.B.	Merrick G.	Tainton T.K.	Ritchie T.G.	Cheesley P.M.	Mann J.A.	Brolly M.J.	Emanuel W.J.	Gillies D.G.	Harding S.J.	Whitehead C.R.	Fear K.W.	McNeill B.	Shaw J.K.
1	16 Aug	BOLTON WANDERERS		1-0	0-0	10510	Sweeney(pen)	1	2	3	4	5	6	7	8	9	10	11							
2	19	SUNDERLAND	1	3-0	2-0	12199	Mann(2), Brolly	1	2		4	5	6	7	8	10	9	11	3						
3	23	Hull City	3	1-3	0-2	5076	Ritchie	1	2		4	5	6	7	8	10	9	11	3						
4	26	Southampton	7	1-3	0-2	16833	Gow	1	2		4	5	6	7	8	10	9	11*	3	12					
5	30	BRISTOL ROVERS	6	1-1	1-1	17918	Cheesley	1	2	3	4	5	6	7	8	10	9	11							
6	6 Sep	Blackburn Rovers	5	2-1	0-0	10281	Mann, Sweeney(pen)	1	2	3	4	5	6	7	8	10	9	11							
7	12	OXFORD UNITED	1	4-1	1-0	10373	Cheesley(2), Ritchie(2)	1	2*	3	4		6	7	8	10		11	12	9	5				
8	20	Chelsea	4	1-1	1-1	17661	Cheesley	1		3	4	5	6	7	8	9	10	11	2						
9	27	BLACKPOOL	4	2-0	2-0	10240	Cheesley, Gow(pen)	1		3	4	5	6	7	8	10*	9	11	2			12			
10	4 Oct	Notts County	5	1-0	0-0	10802	Mann	1		3	4	5	6	7	8	9	10	11	2						
11	7	Oldham Athletic	2	4-2	1-1	9572	Cheesley, Gillies, Mann, Whitehead	1		3	4	5	6	7	8	10	9	11*	2			12			
12	11	CHARLTON ATHLETIC	2	4-0	2-0	12701	Cheesley(2), Gow(pen), Whitehead	1		3	4	5	6	7	8	9	10		2			11			
13	18	York City	2	4-1	3-0	4661	Cheesley(3,1pen), Ritchie	1		3	4	5	6	7	8	10	9		2			11			
14	25	WEST BROMWICH ALB.	2	0-2	0-0	19132		1	12	3	4	5	6	7	8	9	10		2*			11			
15	1 Nov	Luton Town	2	0-0	0-0	11446		1		3	4	5	6	7	8	9	10		2			11			
16	7	ORIENT	3	0-0	0-0	14553		1		3	4	5	6	7	8	10	9		2			11*	12		
17	15	Nottingham Forest	3	0-1	0-1	11583		1	12	3	4	5	6	7	8	10	9		2			11*			
18	22	YORK CITY	3	4-1	2-1	11228	Ritchie(3), Merrick	1	2	3	4	5	6	7	8	10*	9					11	12		
19	29	Fulham	2	2-1	0-0	11400	Ritchie(2)	1	2	3*	4		6	7	8	10	9			5		11	12		
20	6 Dec	CARLISLE UNITED	3	0-0	0-0	12446		1	2	3	4	5	6	7	8	10	9					11			
21	13	HULL CITY	3	3-0	1-0	10796	Cheesley, Mann, Ritchie	1	2	3	4	5	6	7	8	10	9					11			
22	20	Bolton Wanderers	3	0-1	0-0	18503		1	2	3	4	5	6	7	8	10*	9		12			11			
23	26	PLYMOUTH ARGYLE	3	1-1	1-1	11471	Bullon, Merrick	1	2	3	4	5	6	7	8	10*	9					12	11		
24	27	Portsmouth	3	1-0	1-0	14315	Ritchie	1	2	3	4	5	6	7	8		9	10				11			
25	10 Jan	Oxford United	3	1-1	1-0	7355	Cheesley	1	2	3	4	5	6	7	8	10	9					11			
26	17	BLACKBURN ROVERS	2	1-0	1-0	12168	Mann	1	2	3	4	5	6	7	8		9	11					10		
27	24	Plymouth Argyle	2	0-0	0-0	17887		1	2	3	4	5	6	7	8		9	11					10		
28	7 Feb	SOUTHAMPTON	2	1-1	1-1	23316	Ritchie	1	2	3	4	5	6	7	8	10	9					11			
29	14	Orient	1	1-0	0-0	5785	Ritchie	1	2	3	4	5	6	7	8	10*	9			12		11			
30	21	NOTTINGHAM FOREST	3	0-2	0-1	15302		1	2	3	4	5	6	7	8	10	9			12		11*			
31	24	OLDHAM ATHLETIC	1	1-0	1-0	14361	Cheesley	1	2	3	4	5	6	7	8	10	9					11			
32	6 Mar	LUTON TOWN	1	3-0	1-0	15870	Ritchie(2), Cheesley	1	9	3	4	5	6	7	8	10			2			11			
33	12	Charlton Athletic	1	2-2	0-0	12683	Gow, Sweeney	1	2	3	4	5	6	7	8	10*			9			11		12	
34	17	West Bromwich Albion	1	1-0	0-0	26640	Sweeney	1	2	3	4	5	6	7	8	10	12		9			11*			
35	20	FULHAM	1	0-0	0-0	19935		1	10	2	4	5	6	7	8	9			3			11			
36	23	Sunderland	1	1-1	0-0	38395	Sweeney	1	10	3	4	5	6	7	8	9*	12		2			11			
37	27	Carlisle United	1	1-0	1-0	7593	Gow(pen)	1	10	3	4	5	6	7	8				2			11	9*		
38	3 Apr	Blackpool	1	1-2	1-1	8273	Ritchie	1	10	3	4	5	6	7	8	9*	12		2			11			
39	10	CHELSEA	2	2-2	1-1	24710	Ritchie(2)	1	7	3	4	5	6	8	9	10	12		2			11*			
40	16	Bristol Rovers	1	0-0	0-0	26430		1	2	3	4	5	6	7	8	10				9		11			
41	20	PORTSMOUTH	2	1-0	1-0	27394	Whitehead	1	2	3	4	5	6	7	8	10				9		11			
42	24	NOTTS COUNTY	2	1-2	0-1	24614	Whitehead	1	10	3	4	5	6	7	8	9	12		2*			11			
		Apps.						42	32	39	42	40	42	42	42	38	30	14	3	22	2	19	13		
		Subs.							2								6	1	1	3		3	2	2	
		Goals							5		5	1	2		18	15	7	1		1		4			

F.A. CUP

	Date	Opposition		Res.	H.T.	Att.	Goalscorers																		
3R	3 Jan	Coventry City		1-2	0-1	15653	Brolly	1	2	3	4	5	6	7	8		9	10					11		

F.L. CUP

	Date	Opposition		Res.	H.T.	Att.	Goalscorers																		
2R	9 Sep	West Ham United		0-0	0-0	19837		1	2	3	4	5	6	7	8	10	9	11*		12					
2Rr	24	WEST HAM UNITED		1-3	1-0	19643	Cheesley	1	2	3	4	5	6	7	8	10	9	11*		12					

ANGLO SCOTTISH CUP

	Date	Opposition		Res.	H.T.	Att.	Goalscorers																		
GM	2 Aug	Chelsea	4	0-1	0-0	7515		1	2	3	4	5	6	7	8	10	12	11		9*					
GM	5	Fulham	3	2-2	0-1	4200	Mann, Sweeney(pen)	1"	2	3	4	5	6	7	8	10	9	11							14
GM	9	NORWICH CITY	2	4-1	2-0	3823	Mann(2), Drysdale, Ritchie	1"	2	3	4	5	6	7	8*	10	9			12		11			14

GLOUCESTERSHIRE CUP FINAL

	Date	Opposition		Res.	H.T.	Att.	Goalscorers
	4 May	BRISTOL ROVERS		3-2	1-1	10278	Mann(2), Cheesley (£7877)

Extra-time played following score of 2-2 at end of ninety minutes.

FRIENDLIES

	Date	Opposition	Res.	H.T.	Att.	Goalscorers
1	30 Jul	Cardiff City	1-0	0-0	1700	Cheesley
2	11 Aug	Hereford United	1-4		1271	Cheesley
3	28 Oct	STOKE CITY	2-1	1-1	1900	Cheesley, Gow
4	18 Nov	Taunton Town*	3-1	0-0	1100	Cheesley(2), Whitehead
5	25	HALMSTADS	4-0	1-0	1074	Bain(2 pens), Fear, Mann
6	27 Apr	HEREFORD UNITED	1-1	1-1	3151	Cheesley (Brian Drysdale Benefit)
7	29	Yeovil Town	5-0	1-0	1552	Mann(2), Ritchie, Tainton, Whitehead
8	30	Chelmsford City	2-1		831	Bain, Gillies
9	11 May	Cardiff City	2-1	0-0	5867	Cheesley, Tainton
10	29	Orhuela Deportiva	1-1			Cheesley

* Floodlight opening

FINAL LEAGUE TABLE

1	Sunderland	42	24	8	10	67	36	56
2	Bristol C.	42	19	15	8	59	35	53
3	West Bromwich	42	20	13	9	50	33	53
4	Bolton	42	20	12	10	64	38	52
5	Notts Co.	42	19	11	12	60	41	49
6	Southampton	42	21	7	14	66	50	49
7	Luton	42	19	10	13	61	51	48
8	Nottingham F.	42	17	12	13	55	40	46
9	Charlton	42	15	12	15	61	72	42
10	Blackpool	42	14	14	14	40	49	42
11	Chelsea	42	12	14	16	53	54	40
12	Fulham	42	13	14	15	45	47	40
13	Orient	42	13	14	15	37	39	40
14	Hull	42	14	11	17	45	49	39
15	Blackburn	42	12	14	16	45	50	38
16	Plymouth	42	13	12	17	48	54	38
17	Oldham	42	13	12	17	57	68	38
18	Bristol R.	42	11	16	15	38	50	38
19	Carlisle	42	12	13	17	45	59	37
20	Oxford	42	11	11	20	39	59	33
21	York	42	10	8	24	39	71	28
22	Portsmouth	42	9	7	26	32	61	25

1975-76 Season
Back: Fear, Durrell, Bond, Cashley, Shaw, Brolly, Whitehead.
Middle: Wimshurst (Chief Coach), Emanuel, Gillies, Rodgers, Collier, Ritchie, Cheesley, Bardsley (Physiotherapist).
Front: Tainton, Drysdale, Merrick, Dicks (Manager), Gow, Sweeney, Mann.

Back Row: Left to Right: Donnie Gillies, Ray Cashley, John Shaw, Clive Whitehead. Centre Row: Left to Right: Alan Dicks (Manager), Paul Cheesley, David Rodgers, Tom Ritchie, Gary Collier, Ken Wimshurst (Chief Coach), Les Bardsley (Physiotherapist). Front Row: Left to Right: Michael Brolly, Jimmy Mann, Brian Drysdale, Geoff Merrick (Captain), Trevor Tainton, Gerry Sweeney, Gerry Gow.

1976-77 Season

SEASON 1976-77
FOOTBALL LEAGUE DIVISION ONE

No.	Date	Opposition	Pos.	Res.	H.T.	Att.	Goalscorers	Cashley A.R.	Sweeney G.	Drysdale B.	Gow R.G.	Collier G.B.	Merrick G.	Tainton T.K.	Ritchie T.G.	Mann J.A.	Cheesley P.M.	Whitehead C.R.	Gillies D.G.	Fear K.W.	Bond L.A.	Bain J.	McNeill B.	Rodgers D.M.	Shaw J.K.	Hunter N.	Cormack P.B.	Garland C.S.
1	21 Aug	Arsenal		1-0	0-0	41082	Cheesley	1	2	3	4	5	6	7	8	9	10	11										
2	24	STOKE CITY		1-1	0-0	25316*	Gillies	1	2	3	4	5	6	7	8	9	10*	11	12									
3	28	Newcastle United	8	0-0	0-0	31357		1	2	3	4	5	6	7	8		10		11	9								
4	4 Sep	SUNDERLAND	2	4-1	3-1	20593	Gillies, Mann, Ritchie, Tainton	1	2	3	4	5	6	7	8*	9		11	10	12								
5	11	Manchester City	7	1-2	0-2	35891	Fear	1	2	3	4	5	6	7	8*	9		11	10	12								
6	18	WEST HAM UNITED	6	1-1	1-0	28932	Fear	1	2	3	4	5	6	7		9		11	10	8								
7	25	Everton	10	0-2	0-0	25761		1	2	3	4	5	6	7	8	9		11	10									
8	2 Oct	IPSWICH TOWN	16	1-2	0-1	21114	Tainton	1	2	3	4	5	6	7	8	9		11	10*	12								
9	16	LEICESTER CITY	19	0-1	0-0	20102			2	3		5	6*	7	8	9		11	10	12	1	4						
10	23	Aston Villa	20	1-3	1-0	37094	Ritchie		2	3	4*	5		7	8	9		11	10		1		12			6		
11	26	BIRMINGHAM CITY	20			21927			4	3		5	6	7	8	9		11	10					2	1			
12	30	Derby County	20	0-2	0-1	22252			2			5	3	7	8	9		11	10			4			1	6		
13	6 Nov	COVENTRY CITY	20	0-0	0-0	17172			4			5	3	7	8	9		11	2	10					1	6		
14	13	Tottenham Hotspur	19	1-0	0-0	28795	Fear		4			5	3	7	8	9		11	2	10					1	6		
15	20	NORWICH CITY	17	3-1	2-0	19641	Cormack, Ritchie, Sweeney(pen)		4			5	3*	7	8	9		11	2	12					1	6	10	
16	27	Liverpool	19	1-2	1-1	44323	Ritchie		4			5	3	7	8	9*		11	2	12					1	6	10	
17	4 Dec	LEEDS UNITED	19	0-0	0-0	31400	(Abandoned at half-time due to fog)		4			5	3	7	8			11	2						1	6	10	9
18	18	MIDDLESBROUGH	19	1-2	0-1	15074	Merrick		4			5*	3	7	8			11	2	12					1	6	10	9
19	27	West Bromwich Albion	19	1-1	0-0	30444	Ritchie		4			5	3	7	8			11	2	12					1	6	10	9*
20	19 Jan	Manchester United	20	1-2	1-0	43051	Fear		4			5	3	7	8			11	2	12					1	6	10*	9
21	22	ARSENAL	20	2-0	1-0	26282	Cormack(2)		4			5	3	7	8			11	2						1	6	10	9
22	5 Feb	NEWCASTLE UNITED	20	1-1	0-0		Garland		4			5	3	7	8			11*	2	12					1	6	10	9
23	11	Sunderland	20	0-1	0-0	21407			4			5	3	7	8			11	2						1	6	9	10
24	19	MANCHESTER CITY	18	1-0	0-0	27601	Garland		4			5	3*	7	8			11	2	12					1	6	9	10
25	26	West Ham United	20	0-2	0-0	29713			4			5	3	7	8			11	2	12					1	6	10	9*
26	5 Mar	EVERTON	21	1-2	1-1	21588	Cormack(pen)		4			5	3	7	8			11	2	12					1	6	10*	9
27	12	Ipswich Town	22	0-1	0-0	24547			4			5	3	7	8			11	2	10					1	6	9	
28	15	DERBY COUNTY	22	2-2	0-2	18507	Fear, Sweeney		4		10	5	3	7	8			11	2	12					1	6		9*
29	19	QUEENS PARK RANGERS	20	1-0	0-0	22441	Collier		4		10	5	3		8			11	2	9					1	6		
30	26	Leicester City	19	0-0	0-0	16454			4		10	5	3		8			11	2	9					1	6		
31	2 Apr	ASTON VILLA	20	0-0	0-0	27958			4		10	5	3	7	8			11	2	9*					1	6		12
32	5	WEST BROMWICH ALB.	20	1-2	0-1	23752	Fear(pen)		2		4	5	3	7				11	10	9					1	6		
33	9	Birmingham City	22	0-3	0-2	19626			4		10	5	3	7	8*			11	2	9					1	6		12
34	12	TOTTENHAM HOTSPUR	22	1-0	0-0	28101	Cormack(pen)		2		4	5	3	7	8			11		12					1	6	10	9*
35	16	Norwich City	22	1-2	1-1	18434	Cormack		2		4	5	3	7	8			11		12					1	6	10	9*
36	20	Stoke City	22	2-2	1-0	12277	Garland, Ritchie		2		4	5	3	7	8*			11		12					1	6	10	9
37	26	Queens Park Rangers	22	1-0	0-0	14576	Ritchie		2		4	5	3	7	8			11							1	6	10	9
38	30	Leeds United	22	0-2	0-1	21461			2		4	5	3	7	8			11		12					1	6	9*	10
39	7 Mar	MANCHESTER UNITED	22	1-1	1-0	27800+	Garland		2		4	5	3	7	8*			11	10	12					1	6		9
40	10	LEEDS UNITED	21	1-0	0-0	23587	Garland		2		4	5	3	7	8			11	10						1	6		9
41	14	Middlesbrough	22	0-0	0-0	14849			2		4	5	3*	7	8			11	10	12					1	6		9
42	16	LIVERPOOL	19	2-1	1-1	38688	Garland(2)		3		4	5		7	8			11	2	10					1	6		9
43	19	Coventry City	18	2-2	0-1	36903	Gillies, Gow		3		4	5		7	8			11*	2	10					1	6	12	9
Apps.								8	43	11	27	43	40	37	30	25	3	42	37	17	2	2		1	33	32	20	20
Subs.									3				2	1		5			1	9			1				1	2
Goals									2		1	1	1	2	7	1	1		3	6							6	7

* The attendance was originally given as 32537, but within 24 hours was reduced.
\+ All ticket match, number of tickets sold totalled 32166.

F.A. CUP

	Date	Opposition		Res.	H.T.	Att.	Goalscorers	Cashley	Sweeney	Drysdale	Gow	Collier	Merrick	Tainton	Ritchie	Mann	Cheesley	Whitehead	Gillies	Fear	Bond	Bain	McNeill	Rodgers	Shaw	Hunter	Cormack	Garland
3R	8 Jan	Ipswich Town		1-4	0-3	25139	Fear		4			5	3	7	8			11	2	9					1	6	10	

F.L. CUP

	Date	Opposition		Res.	H.T.	Att.		Cashley	Sweeney	Drysdale	Gow	Collier	Merrick	Tainton	Ritchie	Mann	Cheesley	Whitehead	Gillies
2R	31 Aug	COVENTRY CITY		0-1	0-1	13878		1	2	3	4	5	6	7	8	9		11	10

ANGLO SCOTTISH CUP

	Date	Opposition		Res.	H.T.	Att.	Goalscorers	Cashley	Sweeney	Drysdale	Gow	Collier	Merrick	Tainton	Ritchie	Mann	Cheesley	Whitehead	Gillies	Fear
GM	7 Aug	WEST BROMWICH ALB.	1	1-0	0-0	4941	Ritchie	1	2	3	4	5	6	7	8			11	10	9
GM	10	NOTTS COUNTY	1	2-0	1-0	3272	Mann, Ritchie	1	2	3	4	5	6	7	8			11	10	9*
GM	14	Nottingham Forest	2	2-4	1-3	8527	Mann, Tainton	1	2	3	4	5	6	7	8	9		11	10	

GM = Group Match

GLOUCESTERSHIRE CUP FINAL

	Date	Opposition		Res.	H.T.	Att.	Goalscorers
	24 May	Bristol Rovers		1-0	0-0	10432	Mann

FRIENDLIES

	Date	Opposition		Res.	H.T.	Att.	Goalscorers
1	31 Jul	Cambridge United		3-2	1-0		Cheesley(2), Ritchie
2	1 Aug	Crediton United					
3	4	Reading		0-2	0-0	1800	
4	8 Oct	WOLVERHAMPTON W.		0-0	0-0	1506	
5	30 Nov	BRISTOL ROVERS		2-1	1-0	5554	Garland(2) (Trevor Tainton Benefit) (£4000)
6	27 Jan	Liskeard Athletic **		8-1	3-0	850	Chsly(2),Fear(2),Whitehd(2,1p),Cshley,Mbbutt
7	28	Plymouth Argyle		1-1	0-0	3808	Fear
8	5 Jun	Andraitx		9-1			Unknown(9)

** Floodlight opening

DAILY EXPRESS FIVE-A-SIDE TOURNAMENT

	Date	Opposition		Res.			
1R	3 Nov	Wolverhampton Wndrs		0-3			(At the Empire Pool, Wembley)

FINAL LEAGUE TABLE

		P	W	D	L	F	A	Pts
1	Liverpool	42	23	11	8	62	33	57
2	Manchester C.	42	21	14	7	60	34	56
3	Ipswich	42	22	8	12	66	39	56
4	Aston Villa	42	22	7	13	76	50	51
5	Newcastle	42	18	13	11	64	49	49
6	Manchester U.	42	18	11	13	71	62	47
7	West Bromwich	42	16	13	13	62	56	45
8	Arsenal	42	16	11	15	64	59	43
9	Everton	42	14	14	14	62	64	42
10	Leeds	42	15	12	15	48	51	42
11	Leicester	42	12	18	12	47	60	42
12	Middlesbrough	42	14	13	15	40	45	41
13	Birmingham	42	13	12	17	63	61	38
14	QPR	42	13	12	17	47	52	38
15	Derby	42	9	19	14	50	55	37
16	Norwich	42	14	9	19	47	64	37
17	West Ham	42	11	14	17	46	65	36
18	Bristol C.	42	11	13	18	38	48	35
19	Coventry	42	10	15	17	48	59	35
20	Sunderland	42	11	12	19	46	54	34
21	Stoke	42	10	14	18	28	51	34
22	Tottenham	42	12	9	21	48	72	33

SEASON 1977-78
FOOTBALL LEAGUE DIVISION ONE

No.	Date	Opposition	Pos.	Res.	H.T.	Att.	Goalscorers	Shaw J.K.	Gillies D.G.	Merrick G.	Gow R.G.	Collier G.B.	Hunter N.	Tainton T.K.	Ritchie T.G.	Cormack P.B.	Garland C.S.	Whitehead C.R.	Sweeney G.	Mann J.A.	Mabbutt K.R.	Royle J.	Rodgers D.M.	Stevens P.D.	Fear K.W.	Bain J.	McNeill B.	Cashley A.R.	Pritchard H.K.
1	20 Aug	WOLVERHAMPTON W.		2-3	1-1	25136	Cormack(2pens)	1	2	3	4	5	6	7	8	9	10	11											
2	23	Nottingham Forest		0-1	0-0	21743		1		3*	4	5	6	7	8		10			2	11	9	12						
3	27	Leicester City	18	0-0	0-0	17011		1		3*	4	5	6	7	8		10			2	11	9							
4	3 Sep	ASTON VILLA	17	1-1	0-1	22200	Mabbutt	1		3	4	5	6	7	8*		10			2	11	9	12						
5	10	Norwich City		1-1	0-1	13940		1		3	4	5	6	7	10	8*				2	11	9							
6	17	WEST HAM UNITED	17	3-2	2-1	21180	Ritchie(2), Mabbutt	1	2		4	5	6	7	8		10			3	11	9							
7	24	Manchester City	18	0-2	0-1	41897		1	2		4	5	6	7	8	10*				3	11	9	12						
8	1 Oct	QUEENS PARK RANGERS	18	2-2	1-2	20947	Cormack(pen), Tainton	1	2			5	6	7	8	10				3	11	9	4						
9	8	LEEDS UNITED	17	3-2	1-1	26215	Hunter, Mabbutt, Ritchie	1	2			5	6	7	8	10				3	11	9	4						
10	15	Everton	18	0-1	0-1	39230		1	2			12	5	6	7	8	10			3	11*	9	4						
11	22	ARSENAL	18	0-2	0-1	25497		1	2	6	4	5		7	8					3	11	9	10						
12	29	Chelsea	20	0-3	0-1	22313		1	9	3	4*	5	6	7	8	10				12	2	11							
13	5 Nov	Newcastle United	20	1-1	0-0	23316	Gillies	1	10	3	4	5	6	7	8					12	2	11	9*						
14	12	DERBY COUNTY	19	3-1	2-1	20051	Ritchie(2), Gillies	1	10	3	4	5	6	7	8					11	2	9							
15	19	Liverpool	19	1-1	1-1	41053	Gow	1	11	3	4	5	6	7	8					2	10	9							
16	26	MIDDLESBROUGH	18	4-1	2-1	20565	Royle(4)	1	10	3	4	5	6	7	8	12				11*	2	9							
17	3 Dec	Coventry City	17	1-1	0-1	22322	Ritchie	1	10	3		5	6	7	8	4				11	2	9							
18	10	IPSWICH TOWN	14	2-0	1-0	24701	Gillies, Tainton	1	10	3	4	5	6	7	8					11	2	9*	12						
19	17	Derby County		2-1	0-1	21802		1	9	3	4	5	6	7	8					11	2	10							
20	26	WEST BROMWICH ALB.	15	3-1	0-1	28879	Ritchie(2), Gow	1	10	3	4	5	6	7	8					11*	2	9	12						
21	27	Birmingham City	16	0-3	0-0	24110		1	2	6	4	5		7	8	11					3	9	10						
22	31	NOTTINGHAM FOREST	16	1-3	0-2	31990	Mabbutt	1	10*	3	4	5	6	7	8					2	11	9	12						
23	2 Jan	Wolverhampton Wndrs	18	0-0	0-0	25283		1	3	6	4	5		7	8					2	11	9	10						
24	14	LEICESTER CITY	17	0-0	0-0	19704		1		3	4	5	6	7	8					11	2	9	10						
25	28	Aston Villa	18	0-1	0-0	29676		1	10*	3	4	5	6	7	8					11	2	12	9						
26	4 Feb	NORWICH CITY	17	3-0	3-0	16929	Ritchie, Royle, Whitehead	1		3	4	5	6		8	10		11		2	7	9							
27	8	Manchester United	15	1-1	1-1	43560	Cormack	1		3	4	5*	6	12	8	10		11		2	7	9							
28	11	West Ham United	14	2-1	1-1	19934	Mann, Royle	1		3	4		6	7	8	10		11		2	7	9	5						
29	17	MANCHESTER CITY	12	2-2	2-1	25834	Royle(2)	1		3	4*		6	12	8	10		11		2	7	9	5						
30	25	Queens Park Rangers	13	2-2	0-1	17051	Gow, Sweeney	1		3	4		6	7	8			11		2	10	9	5						
31	4 Mar	Leeds United	11	2-0	0-0	24830	Gillies, Ritchie	1	12	3	4		6	7	8			11*		2	10	9	5						
32	11	EVERTON	12	0-1	0-1	25986		1	12	3	4		6	7	8			11*		2	10	9	5						
33	18	Arsenal	13	1-4	1-4	28463	Tainton	1		3	4		6	7	8			11		2	10	9	5						
34	21	CHELSEA	11	3-0	2-0	19961	Cormack(pen), Gow, Rodgers	1	12	3	4		6	7	8	10				2	11	9*	5						
35	25	BIRMINGHAM CITY	12	0-1	0-1	21884		1	9	3	4		6		8	10		11*		2	7	12	5						
36	27	West Bromwich Albion	13	1-2	1-0	23898	Hunter	1	2	3	4		6	7	8	10					11	12	9*	5					
37	1 Apr	NEWCASTLE UNITED	14	3-1	1-0	17344	Hunter, Ritchie, O.G.	1		3	4		6	7	8	10				2	11	9	5						
38	8	Middlesbrough	15	0-2	0-1	14667		1	3	6	4			8	10	7*				11	12	9	5	2					
39	15	LIVERPOOL	15	1-1	0-1	31471	Cormack	1	2	3	4		6	7*	8	10				11	12	9	5						
40	22	Ipswich Town	16	0-1	0-0	22535		1		3	4		6	7	8	10*				2	11	12	9	5					
41	25	MANCHESTER UNITED	16	0-1	0-0	25858		1		3			6	7	8	10*		11		2	4	12	9	5					
42	29	COVENTRY CITY	15	1-1	0-0	21045	Royle	1		3	4		6	7	8			11*		2	10	12	9	5					
		Apps.						42	24	37	37	27	38	36	41	25	2	31	38	26	16	26	15	1					
		Subs.							3			1						2			1	2	5	10					
		Goals							4		4		3	3	11	6		2	1	1	4	8	1					

F.A. CUP

Rnd	Date	Opposition		Res.	H.T.	Att.	Goalscorers	Shaw	Gillies	Merrick	Gow	Collier	Hunter	Tainton	Ritchie	Cormack	Garland	Whitehead	Sweeney	Mann	Mabbutt	Royle	Rodgers
3R	7 Jan	WREXHAM		4-4	2-2	19644	Mabbutt(2), Cormack, Ritchie	1	3*	6	4	5		7	8	12				2	11	9	10
3Rr	9	Wrexham		0-3	0-3	15614		1	3	6	4	5		7	8	11				2		9	10

F.L. CUP

Rnd	Date	Opposition		Res.	H.T.	Att.	Goalscorers	Shaw	Gillies	Merrick	Gow	Collier	Hunter	Tainton	Ritchie	Cormack	Garland	Whitehead	Sweeney	Mann	Mabbutt	Royle	Rodgers	Fear	Bain
2R	29 Aug	STOKE CITY		1-0	1-0	11877	Mabbutt	1	12	3	4*	5	6	7	8	10				2	11	9			
3R	26 Oct	Wrexham		0-1	0-0	10183		1	2	6	4	5		7	8					3	11	10		9*	12

ANGLO SCOTTISH CUP

Rnd	Date	Opposition		Res.	H.T.	Att.	Goalscorers	Shaw	Gillies	Merrick	Gow	Collier	Hunter	Tainton	Ritchie	Cormack	Garland	Whitehead	Sweeney	Mann	Mabbutt	Royle	Rodgers	Stevens	Fear	Bain	McNeill	Cashley	Pritchard
GM	6 Aug	BRISTOL ROVERS	1	3-1	2-0	5503	Ritchie(3)	1	2	6		5		7	8	10	9*	11	3	4	12								
GM	9	Plymouth Argyle	1	2-0		4648	Cormack, Mabbutt	1"		6	4	5		7	8	10		11*	3	12	9					2	14		
GM	12	Birmingham City	1	0-1	0-1	9512		1	2		4		6	7	8		10	9		3	11	8	5						
QF1	13 Sep	Partick Thistle		0-2	0-1	4000		1		3	4	5	6	7	8	10		11	2							12			9*
QF2	27	PARTICK THISTLE		3-0	1-0	5400	Mann(2), Whitehead	1	2	3	4	5	6	7	8			11	3	10	9								
SF1	19 Oct	Hibernian		1-1	1-0		Gillies	1	9	3	4	5	6	7	8	10			2	11									
SF2	1 Nov	HIBERNIAN		5-3	3-1	6072	Mabbutt(2), Ritchie, Sweeney(pen), Tainton	1	2	6	4*	5		7	8			11	3	10	9					12			
F1	23	St. Mirren		2-1	1-0	7800	Cormack, Mabbutt	1	3	6	4	5		7	8	10			2	11	9								
F2	5 Dec	ST. MIRREN		1-1	0-0	16110	Mabbutt	1	2	6	4	5		7	8				3	10	9								

GLOUCESTERSHIRE CUP FINAL

	Date	Opposition		Res.	H.T.	Att.	Goalscorers
	2 May	BRISTOL ROVERS		3-0	2-0	10178	Mabbutt(2), Mann

FRIENDLIES

No.	Date	Opposition		Res.	H.T.	Att.	Goalscorers
1	21 Jul	Hacken-Gais		1-0	1-0	3000	Bain
2	23	Ockero IF		1-0	0-0	2500	Gillies
3	25	Kungsbacka BIK		5-0			Cormack(2), Whitehead(2), Ritchie
4	27	Gislaved XI		9-1	2-1		Mnn(2),Crmck,Mbbtt,McNl,Rtch,Swny,Tntn,Whthd
5	28	Hudiksvall		3-1			Garland(2), Cormack
6	29	Lysekil AIK		6-0			Mabbutt(3), Bain(2), Ritchie
7	10 Aug	Minehead		2-0	2-0		Mabbutt, Rodgers
8	20 Sep	ENGLAND XI		4-6	2-4	6426	Bain(pen),Fear,Gray,Mabbutt (T.Collins Benefit)
9	28 Feb	BOBBY CHARLTON'S XI*		1-2	1-1	3200	Gow (Les Bardsley Benefit) (£3000)
10	17 Apr	Newport County		2-2	0-0	1700	Mabbutt, Penny (Bobby Woodruff Benefit)
11	1 Jun	Portland Timbers		1-0	1-0	8038	Mabbutt

* Score in 'Western Daily Press' and the 'Evening Post' given as 1-3, but incorrect (1 opposition goal disallowed).

FINAL LEAGUE TABLE

1	Nottingham F.	42	25	14	3	69:24 64
2	Liverpool	42	24	9	9	65:34 57
3	Everton	42	22	11	9	76:45 55
4	Manchester C.	42	20	12	10	74:51 52
5	Arsenal	42	21	10	11	60:37 52
6	West Bromwich	42	18	14	10	62:53 50
7	Coventry	42	18	12	12	75:62 48
8	Aston Villa	42	18	10	14	57:42 46
9	Leeds	42	18	10	14	63:53 46
10	Manchester U.	42	16	10	16	67:63 42
11	Birmingham	42	16	9	17	55:60 41
12	Derby	42	14	13	15	54:59 41
13	Norwich	42	11	18	13	52:66 40
14	Middlesbrough	42	12	15	15	42:54 39
15	Wolverhampton	42	12	12	18	51:64 36
16	Chelsea	42	11	14	17	46:69 36
17	Bristol C.	42	11	13	18	49:53 35
18	Ipswich	42	11	13	18	47:61 35
19	QPR	42	9	15	18	47:64 33
20	West Ham	42	12	8	22	52:69 32
21	Newcastle	42	6	10	26	42:78 22
22	Leicester	42	5	12	25	26:70 22

BRISTOL CITY : 1977-78

Back: KEVIN MABBUTT, DONNIE GILLIES, RAY CASHLEY, NORMAN HUNTER, JOHN SHAW, CLIVE WHITEHEAD, HOWARD PRITCHARD

Middle: KEN WIMSHURST (*Chief Coach*), PAUL CHEESLEY, TOM RITCHIE, DAVID RODGERS, GARY COLLIER, CHRIS GARLAND, BRIAN McNEILL, LES BARDSLEY (*Physiotherapist*)

Front: ALAN DICKS (*Manager*), JIMMY MANN, JOHN BAIN, TREVOR TAINTON, GEOFF MERRICK, GERRY SWEENEY, GERRY GOW, KEITH FEAR, TONY COLLINS (*Asst. Manager*)

1978-79

Back: Pritchard, Ritchie, Shaw, Rodgers, Collier, Royle.
Middle: Heather (Physio), Mann, Hunter, Cormack, Cashley, Garland, Hay, Whitehead, Wimshurst (Coach).
Front: Mabbutt, Tainton, Merrick, Dicks (Manager), Gow, Sweeney.Gillies. (Inset) Cooper.

SEASON 1978-79
FOOTBALL LEAGUE DIVISION ONE

No.	Date	Opposition	Pos.	Res.	H.T.	Att.	Goalscorers	Shaw J.K.	Sweeney G.	Cooper T.	Tainton T.K.	Rodgers D.M.	Hunter N.	Garland C.S.	Ritchie T.G.	Royle J.	Cormack P.B.	Mann J.A.	Whitehead C.R.	Gillies D.G.	Pritchard H.K.	Gow R.G.	Mabbutt K.R.	Bain J.	Collier G.3.	Cashley A.R.	Meijer G.	Jantunen P.K.	McNeill B
1	19 Aug	Bolton Wanderers		2-1	0-1	21355	Mann, Ritchie	1	2	3	4	5	6	7	8	9	10	11											
2	22	NORWICH CITY		1-1	0-1	19274	Cormack(pen)	1	2	3		5	6	11*	8	9	10	4	12										
3	26	ASTON VILLA	5	1-0	0-0	23493	Rodgers	1	11		7	5	6		8	9		10	3	2	4								
4	2 Sep	Wolverhamton Wndrs	7	0-2	0-1	16121		1	2		7	5	6		8	9*	12	10	11	3		4							
5	9	Tottenham Hotspur	12	0-1		34035		1	2		7	5	6		8	9		4	11	3		10							
6	16	SOUTHAMPTON	8	3-1	1-1	21420	Ritchie(2), Rodgers	1	2		7	5	6		8	9*	10	12		3		4	11						
7	23	Ipswich Town	6	1-0	0-0	20168	Ritchie(pen)	1	2		7	5	6		8	9		10		3		4	11						
8	30	EVERTON	5	2-2	2-1	22331	Gow, Hunter	1	3		7	5	6		8	9		10		2		4	11						
9	7 Oct	Queens Park Rangers	9	0-1	0-0	15707		1	2		7	5	6		8	9		10	11	3		4							
10	14	NOTTINGHAM FOREST	11	1-3	1-2	26953	Ritchie(pen)	1	2		7	5	6		8	9		10	12	3*		4	11						
11	21	Manchester United	9	3-1	1-0	47211	Mabbutt(3)	1	2		7	5	6		8	9		10		3		4	11						
12	28	ARSENAL	11	1-3	1-2	27016	Rodgers	1	2		7	5	6		8			10*	9	3		4	11	12					
13	4 Nov	Middlesbrough	11	0-0	0-0	20471		1	2		7	5	6		8	9				3		4	11	10					
14	11	BOLTON WANDERERS	10	4-1	1-1	18168	Royle(2), Ritchie, Rodgers	1	2		7	5	6		8	9			12	3		4	11	10*					
15	18	Aston Villa	12	0-2	0-0	27621		1	2		7	5	6		8	9			12	3		4	11	10*					
16	21	WOLVERHAMPTON W.	12	0-1	0-0	17421		1	2		7	5	6					12	10*	11	3	4		9					
17	25	Birmingham City	13	1-1	1-0	21552	Mabbutt	1	3		7	5	6		8	9		10		2		4	11						
18	2 Dec	DERBY COUNTY	11	1-0	0-0	17487	Gillies	1	2		7	5	6		8	9		10		3		4	11						
19	9	Leeds United	11	1-1	1-1	22529	Royle	1	2			5	6		8	9		10	7	3		4	11						
20	16	LIVERPOOL	11	0-2	0-1	28722	Royle	1	2		7	5	6		8	9		10	11*	12	3	4							
21	23	Chelsea	10	0-0	0-0	19093		1	2		7	5	6		8	9		10			11	3	4						
22	26	COVENTRY CITY	7	5-0	2-0	22324	Royle(3), Cormack, Ritchie	1	2		7	5	6		8	9		10			11	3	4						
23	30	MANCHESTER CITY	7	1-1	1-0	25253	Ritchie	1	2		7	5	6*		8	9		10	12		11	3	4						
24	1 Jan	West Bromwich Albion	7	1-3	1-2	31593	Cormack(pen)	1	2		7	5			8	9*		10	12		11	3	4			6			
25	13	TOTTENHAM HOTSPUR	7	0-0	0-0	29122		1	2		7	5	6		8	9		10			11		4						
26	3 Feb	IPSWICH TOWN	7	3-1	2-0	17025	Gow, Tainton, Whitehead	1	2	3	7	5			9	10		11				4	8		6				
27	10	Everton	7	1-4	1-1	29166	Whitehead	1	2	3	7	5	6		8	9		10			11		4						
28	20	Southampton	7	0-2	0-2	19845		1	2	3	7	5	6		8*	9		10			11		4	12					
29	24	Nottingham Forest	7	0-2	0-0	28008			2	3	7	5			8	9	10*	12				4	11		6	1			
30	3 Mar	MANCHESTER UNITED	10	1-2	1-0	24784	Gow		3		7		6	8		9		10	11	2		4		5	1				
31	10	Arsenal	13	0-2	0-2	24408		1	2		7		6	8	12	9		10	11	3		4*		5					
32	17	MIDDLESBROUGH	14	1-1	1-0	12319	Gow	1	2		7	5	6		8	9			11	3		4	10						
33	24	Norwich City	14	0-3	0-3	14507		1	2		7	5	6		8	9*	12		11	3		4	10						
34	31	BIRMINGHAM CITY	14	2-1	1-0	15584	Garland, Meijer	1	2	3		5	6	12	8	9*		7				4	10				11		
35	3 Apr	QUEENS PARK RANGERS	14	2-0	0-0	15687	Mabbutt(2)	1	2	3	7	5	6		8	9		4					10				11		
36	7	Derby County	9	1-0	0-0	17090	Ritchie	1	2	3		5	6		8	9		7	12			4	10*				11		
37	10	CHELSEA	7	3-1	0-0	18645	Mabbutt, Meijer, Rodgers	1	2	3		5	6		8	9		7*	12			4	10				11		
38	13	Coventry City	8	2-3	0-3	17812	Gow, Mabbutt	1	2	3		5*	6		8	9		4	12				10				11		
39	17	WEST BROMWICH ALB.	9	1-0	0-0	29914	Mabbutt	1	2			6			8	9			3			4	10				11		
40	21	Liverpool	9	0-1	0-1	43191		1	2		7		6		8	9			3			4*	10				11	12	
41	28	LEEDS UNITED	11	0-0	0-0	25388		1	2		7		6		8	9			3			4	10				11		
42	5 May	Manchester City	12	0-2	0-1	29739		1	2		7		6		8	9			12	3		4	10*				11		
							Apps.	40	42	11	37	36	39	4	39	40	14	23	22	27	1	38	26	3	9	2	9		
							Subs.								1		1	3	5	8			1	1				1	
							Goals			1	5	1	1	9	7	3	1	2	1			5	9				2		

F.A. CUP

								Shaw J.K.	Sweeney G.	Cooper T.	Tainton T.K.	Rodgers D.M.	Hunter N.	Garland C.S.	Ritchie T.G.	Royle J.	Cormack P.B.	Mann J.A.	Whitehead C.R.	Gillies D.G.	Pritchard H.K.	Gow R.G.	Mabbutt K.R.	Bain J.
3R	9 Jan	BOLTON WANDERERS		3-1	0-0	17392	Gow, Ritchie, Rodgers	1	2		7	5	6		8	9	10			11	3	4		
4R	29	Crystal Palace		0-3	0-1	21463		1	2		7	5	6		8	9	10*	12	11	3		4		

F.L. CUP

								Shaw J.K.	Sweeney G.		Tainton T.K.	Rodgers D.M.	Hunter N.	Garland C.S.	Ritchie T.G.	Royle J.		Mann J.A.	Whitehead C.R.	Gillies D.G.	Gow R.G.
2R	29 Aug	CRYSTAL PALACE		1-2	0-1	10433	Ritchie	1	2		7	5	6	12	8	9*		4	11	3	10

ANGLO SCOTTISH CUP

								Shaw J.K.	Sweeney G.	Cooper T.	Tainton T.K.	Rodgers D.M.	Hunter N.	Garland C.S.	Ritchie T.G.	Royle J.	Cormack P.B.	Mann J.A.	Whitehead C.R.	Gillies D.G.	Pritchard H.K.	Gow R.G.	Mabbutt K.R.	Bain J.	Collier	Cashley	Meijer	Jantunen	McNeill
GM	5 Aug	BRISTOL ROVERS	1	6-1	1-1	9874	Ritchie(6),Cormack(p),Grland,Taintn,Whtehead	1	2	3	7	5	6	11	8	9	10	4*	12										
GM	8	CARDIFF CITY	1	1-0	0-0	6916	Hunter		2	3	7	5	6	11	8	9*	10	4	12							1			
GM	12	Fulham	1	3-0	1-0	4324	Mann, Royle, O.G.	1	2		5*	6	11	8	9		10	4		3	12								
QF1L	12 Sep	ST. MIRREN		1-2	0-1	5572	Ritchie		2		7	5	6		8	9	12		11*			4	10			1			3
QF2L	26	St. Mirren		2-2	1-1	10000	Garland, Mann	1	2		7*	5	6	8	9			11		3		4	10	12					

GLOUCESTERSHIRE CUP FINAL

	15 May	BRISTOL ROVERS		2-0	0-0	6661	Gow, Mann

FRIENDLIES

				Res.	H.T.	Att.	Goalscorers
1	20 Jul	Vasteras SK		2-1	2-1		Cormack, Ritchie
2	23	Edsbro IF		2-0	2-0		Mabbutt, Mann
3	25	Enkopnings		4-0	2-0		Cormack(pen), Mann, Royle, Tainton
4	27	IFK Eskilstuna		2-1	1-1		Cormack, Royle
5	15 Aug	Bath City		2-1	1-0		Gillies, Mabbutt
6	27	Crediton United					
7	10 Oct	Plymouth Argyle		3-0	2-0	3267	Antic, Ritchie, Royle
8	17	Vojudina		3-1	1-1		Gillies, Gow, Royle (Int. Fayre Cup)
9	7 Nov	Bristol Rovers		2-0	0-0	5610	O.G., O.G. (Frankie Prince Benefit)
10	14	MOSCOW DYNAMO		0-0	0-0	6373	
11	27	NORWICH CITY		3-6	1-3	2676	Chsley(p),Greenhoff,Mbbtt(Cheesley Benefit)
12	27 Feb	MALMO		0-1	0-0	1942	
13	14 Mar	Malmo		0-0	0-0	3000	
14	1 May	Hungerford Town		5-0			Unknown(5) (Oland Cup)
15	2	Torquay United		2-3			Unknown(2) (Jimmy Dunne Benefit)
16	18	Yeovil Town		4-3	1-1	465	Mbbtt(2),Crmck(p),OG(Cottle/Harrison Benefit)
17	24	Seattle Sounders		1-0		3700	Mabbutt
18	26	Vancouver Whitecaps		1-1	0-1	13000	Jantunen
19	28	Vancouver Island		8-3	5-1	1400	Ritchie(4), Mabbutt(2), Penny(2,1pen)
20	30	Portland Timbers		1-2	0-2	6000	Pritchard

FINAL LEAGUE TABLE

1. Liverpool	42	30	8	4	85:16	68
2. Nottingham F.	42	21	18	3	61:26	60
3. West Bromwich	42	24	11	7	72:35	59
4. Everton	42	17	17	8	52:40	51
5. Leeds	42	18	14	10	70:52	50
6. Ipswich	42	20	9	13	63:49	49
7. Arsenal	42	17	14	11	61:48	48
8. Aston Villa	42	15	16	11	59:49	46
9. Manchester U.	42	15	15	12	60:63	45
10. Coventry	42	14	16	12	58:68	44
11. Tottenham	42	13	15	14	48:61	41
12. Middlesbrough	42	15	10	17	57:50	40
13. Bristol C.	42	15	10	17	47:51	40
14. Southampton	42	12	16	14	47:53	40
15. Manchester C.	42	13	13	16	58:56	39
16. Norwich	42	7	23	12	51:57	37
17. Bolton	42	12	11	19	54:75	35
18. Wolverhampton	42	13	8	21	44:68	34
19. Derby	42	10	11	21	44:71	31
20. QPR†	42	6	13	23	45:73	25
21. Birmingham	42	6	10	26	37:64	22
22. Chelsea	42	5	10	27	44:92	20

SEASON 1979-80

FOOTBALL LEAGUE DIVISION ONE

No.	Date	Opposition	Pos.	Res.	H.T.	Att.	Goalscorers	Shaw J.K.	Sweeney G.	Whitehead C.R.	Gow R.G.	Rodgers D.M.	Merrick G.	Fitzpatrick A.C.	Ritchie T.G.	Mabbutt K.R.	Jantunen P.K.	Meijer G.	Tainton T.K.	Mann J.A.	Royle J.	Cormack P.B.	Hay A.B.	Gillies D.G.	Kenyon R.N.	Pritchard H.K.	Garland C.S.	Doyle I.P.	Cashley A.R.	Stevens P.D.	Baddeley K.	Smith G.A.
1	18 Aug	LEEDS UNITED		2-2	1-1	22845	Jantunen, Ritchie(pen)	1	2	3	4	5	6	7	8	9	10	11													
2	21	Coventry City		1-3	1-1	19293	Ritchen(pen)	1	2	3	4	5*	6	7	8	9	10	11	12												
3	25	Aston Villa	11	2-0	1-0	25526	Mabbutt, Ritchie(pen)	1	5	3	4		6	7	8	9*	10		2	12	11										
4	1 Sep	WOLVERHAMPTON W.	6	2-0	1-0	18835	Gow, Royle	1	5	3	4		6	7	8	11	10		2		9										
5	8	Ipswich Town	10	0-1	0-0	16915		1	5	3	4		6	7	8	11	10*		2		9	12									
6	15	STOKE CITY	10	0-0	0-0	16662		1	5	3	4		6	7	8	11		12	2	10	9*										
7	22	NOTTINGHAM FOREST	10	1-1	1-0	22759	Mann	1	5	3	4		6	7	8*	9			2	10	12	11									
8	29	Everton	8	0-0	0-0	24733		1	5	3	4		6	7	8*	11			2	10	9		12								
9	6 Oct	Liverpool	12	0-4	0-3	38213		1	5	3			6	7	8	11	10*		2		9	12		4							
10	9	COVENTRY CITY	10	1-0	0-0	14853	Ritchie	1	2	3	4	5	6	7	8				11	10	9										
11	13	MANCHESTER UNITED	11	1-1	1-1	28783	Rodgers	1	2	3	4	5*	6	7	8	12			11	10	9										
12	20	Crystal Palace	13	1-1	0-0	27333	Royle	1	2	3	4*	5	6	7	8	12			11	10	9										
13	27	ARSENAL	16	0-1	0-0	23029		1	2	3		5	6	7	8	4			11	10	9										
14	3 Nov	Leeds United	11	3-1	1-1	17376	Mabbutt(2), Merrick	1	2	3			6	7	8	4			11	10	9		5								
15	10	DERBY COUNTY	15	0-2	0-2	16401		1	2				6	7	8	4		12	11	10	9		5*		3						
16	17	Middlesbrough	16	0-1	0-0	14517		1	2			5	6	7	8	9*			4	10				3		12	11				
17	24	MANCHESTER CITY	14	1-0	1-0	18296	Rodgers	1	2	3	4	5	6	7	12				8*	10	9						11				
18	1 Dec	Bolton Wanderers	14	1-1	0-0	12074	Rodgers	1	2	3	4	5	6	7					8	10	9						11				
19	8	TOTTENHAM HOTSPUR	17	1-3	0-1	20593	Ritchie(pen)	1	2	3	4	5	6	7	12			11*	8		9						10				
20	15	Norwich City	19	0-2	0-1	12473		1	2	3	4	5*	6	7	10				8		9	12					11				
21	21	SOUTHAMPTON	19	0-1	0-0	12489		1	2	3	4		6	7	10	12			8	11*	9				5						
22	26	West Bromwich Albion	20	0-3	0-0	19564		1	2	3	4		6	7		10		12	8	11*	9				5						
23	29	ASTON VILLA	20	1-3	0-0	18221	Gow(pen)	1	2	3	4	5	6			9			8	10						7	11				
24	1 Jan	BRIGHTON & HOVE ALB.	20	2-2	1-0	19259	Gow(2pens)	1		3	4	5	6	8	12	9*			2	10						7	11				
25	12	Wolverhampton Wndrs	20	0-3	0-1	18835		1	12	3	4	5	6	8*	9				2	10						7	11				
26	19	IPSWICH TOWN	20	0-3	0-1	14218		1	6	3	4	5		8			10		2		9					7	11				
27	2 Feb	Stoke City	20	0-1	0-0	14510		1	10	3		5		8	9*				4					2	6	7	11	12			
28	9	Nottingham Forest	20	0-0	0-0	23421			2	3		5	6	7	8				4		9					10		11	1			
29	19	EVERTON	20	2-1	0-1	15119	Ritchie, Rodgers		2	3	4	5	6	8	10				11		9					7			1			
30	23	Manchester United	20	0-4	0-3	43329			2	3	4	5	6	8	10	12			11		9*					7			1			
31	1 Mar	CRYSTAL PALACE	20	0-2	0-0	15947			2	3	4	5	6	8	10*	12			11		9					7			1			
32	11	Arsenal	20	0-0	0-0	21559			2	3			6	8	10	7			11	4	9			5					1			
33	15	LIVERPOOL	21	1-3	0-1	27187	Mabbutt		2	3			6	8	10	7			11	4	9			5					1			
34	22	Derby County	21	3-3	2-1	17020	Ritchie(2,1pen), Mann		2	3			6	7	8	10			11	4	9			5					1			
35	5 Apr	WEST BROMWICH ALB.	21	0-0	0-0	15677			2	3*	4	5	6	7	8	10			12	11	9								1			
36	7	Brighton & Hove Albion	21	1-0	0-0	23171	Ritchie		2	3	4	5	6	7	8					10	9					11			1			
37	12	BOLTON WANDERERS	21	2-1	1-0	13584	Mann, Ritchie(pen)		2	3	4	5	6	7	8				12	10	9					11*			1			
38	19	Manchester City	21	1-3	0-3	32745	Rodgers		2	3	4	5	6	7	8				12	10	9					11*			1			
39	22	MIDDLESBROUGH	20	3-1	1-1	10837	Ritchie(2), Royle		2	3		5	6	8	10				11	4	9					7			1			
40	26	NORWICH CITY	21	2-3	0-1	16123	Ritchie, Rodgers		2	3	4	5	6*	7	8				12	10	9					11			1			
41	29	Southampton	21	2-5	0-0	16309	Mabbutt(2)		2	3	4			7	8*	12			6	10	9			5		11			1			
42	3 May	Tottenham Hotspur	20	0-0	0-0	23585		1	2	3	4		6	7*	8	11				10	9		5	12								
							Apps.	28	40	40	31	26	39	41	35	21	7	3	34	28	34	1	3	7	4	15	10	1	14			
							Subs.		1						3	6		3	5	1	1	3	1	1		1		1				
							Goals				4	6	1		13	6	1			3	3												

F.A. CUP

Rd	Date	Opposition	Pos.	Res.	H.T.	Att.	Goalscorers	Shaw J.K.	Sweeney G.	Whitehead C.R.	Gow R.G.	Rodgers D.M.	Merrick G.	Fitzpatrick A.C.	Ritchie T.G.	Mabbutt K.R.	Jantunen P.K.	Meijer G.	Tainton T.K.	Mann J.A.	Royle J.	Cormack P.B.	Hay A.B.	Gillies D.G.	Kenyon R.N.	Pritchard H.K.	Garland C.S.	Doyle I.P.	Cashley A.R.	Stevens P.D.	Baddeley K.	Smith G.A.
3R	5 Jan	DERBY COUNTY		6-2	3-0	13384	Garland(2), Pritchard(2), Mann, Whitehead	1		3	4	5	6	8	9				2	10						7	11				
4R	26	IPSWICH TOWN		1-2	1-1	19608	Whitehead	1	3	11	4	5	6*	8		9			2							7	10	12			

F.L. CUP

Rd	Date	Opposition	Pos.	Res.	H.T.	Att.	Goalscorers	Shaw J.K.	Sweeney G.	Whitehead C.R.	Gow R.G.	Rodgers D.M.	Merrick G.	Fitzpatrick A.C.	Ritchie T.G.	Mabbutt K.R.	Jantunen P.K.	Meijer G.	Tainton T.K.	Mann J.A.	Royle J.	Cormack P.B.	Hay A.B.	Gillies D.G.	Kenyon R.N.	Pritchard H.K.	Garland C.S.	Doyle I.P.	Cashley A.R.	Stevens P.D.	Baddeley K.	Smith G.A.
2R1	28 Aug	ROTHERHAM UNITED		1-0	1-0	6981	Ritchie(pen)	1	5	3	4		6	7	8		10	11	2		9										
2R2	4 Sep	Rotherham United		1-1	0-1	7327	Mabbutt	1	5	3	4		6	7	8	11	10		2		9										
3R	26	Peterborough United		1-1	0-1	7067	Gow	1	5	3	4		6	7	8	9			2	10	12	11*									
3Rr	2 Oct	PETERBOROUGH UNITED		4-0	3-0	9125	Royle(2), Jantunen, Mabbutt	1	2	3	4*		6	7		11	10	12	8		9		5								
4R	30	NOTTINGHAM FOREST		1-1	0-1	25695	Sweeney (£4300)	1	2	3		5*	6	7	8	4			11	10	9		12								
4Rr	14 Nov	Nottingham Forest		0-3	0-2	20462		1	2				6	7	8	4			11	10	9*		5	12	3						

ANGLO SCOTTISH CUP

Rd	Date	Opposition	Pos.	Res.	H.T.	Att.	Goalscorers	Shaw J.K.	Sweeney G.	Whitehead C.R.	Gow R.G.	Rodgers D.M.	Merrick G.	Fitzpatrick A.C.	Ritchie T.G.	Mabbutt K.R.	Jantunen P.K.	Meijer G.	Tainton T.K.	Mann J.A.	Royle J.	Cormack P.B.	Hay A.B.	Gillies D.G.	Kenyon R.N.	Pritchard H.K.	Garland C.S.	Doyle I.P.	Cashley A.R.	Stevens P.D.	Baddeley K.	Smith G.A.
GM	4 Aug	Birmingham City	1	4-0	3-0	7691	Mabbutt(2), Ritchie(2)	1	5	3*	4		6	7	8	9	10	11	2			12									
GM	8	Plymouth Argyle	1	0-0	0-0	2848		1	5	3	4		6	7	8*	9	10	11	2		12										
GM	11	FULHAM	1	1-0	1-0	6116	Ritchie	1	6	3	4	5		7	8	9	10*	11	2		12										
QF1	18 Sep	Partick Thistle		1-1	1-0	4000	Ritchie	1	5				6	7	8	9		11	2	10		4	3								
QF2	23 Oct	PARTICK THISTLE		2-0	1-0	5015	Gillies, Ritchie	1	2	3				7	8			11	4	10			6	5			9				
SF1	6 Nov	MORTON		2-2	1-0	4399	Garland, Mabbutt	1	2					7		4			10	8			6	3	5	11	9				
SF2	15Jan	Morton		1-0	0-0	8500	Pritchard	1	5	3	4			8			10		2		9		6*	12		7	11				
F1	25 Mar	ST. MIRREN		0-2	0-1	3731			2	3			6	8	10	7			11	4*	9			5		12			1			
F2	16 Apr	St. Mirren		1-3	0-0	12300	Stevens	1	2							9	11		7	10			3	5				12		4	6	8*

GLOUCESTERSHIRE CUP FINAL

	6 May	BRISTOL ROVERS		1-0	0-0	5584	Pritchard

FRIENDLIES

1	23 Jul	Gefle IF	0-1		3500	
2	25	IK Brage	1-0	0-0		Royle
3	26	IFK Vasteras	4-2	1-1		Gow, Mabbutt, Pritchard, Ritchie
4	28	Bergs IK	4-0	2-0		Mabbutt(3), Pritchard
5	30	IFK Eskilstuna	3-0	2-0		Jantunen, Mabbutt, Meijer
6	12 Feb	Newport County	0-0	0-0	1300	
7	7 Mar	VANCOUVER WHITECAPS	0-0	0-0		
8	12 May	DEREK DOUGAN'S XI	1-3	0-2	1586	Garland (Geoff Merrick Benefit) (£1086)
9	15	South West League	1-3	0-3		Royle (at St. Blazey) (£400)

FINAL LEAGUE TABLE

1	Liverpool	42	25	10	7	81:30	60
2	Manchester U	42	24	10	8	65:35	58
3	Ipswich	42	22	9	11	68:39	53
4	Arsenal	42	18	16	8	52:36	52
5	Nottingham F.	42	20	8	14	63:43	48
6	Wolverhampton	42	19	9	14	58:47	47
7	Aston Villa	42	16	14	12	51:50	46
8	Southampton	42	18	9	15	65:53	45
9	Middlesbrough	42	16	12	14	50:44	44
10	West Bromwich	42	11	19	12	54:50	41
11	Leeds	42	13	14	15	46:50	40
12	Norwich	42	13	14	15	58:66	40
13	Crystal Palace	42	12	16	14	41:50	40
14	Tottenham	42	15	10	17	52:62	40
15	Coventry	42	16	7	19	56:66	39
16	Brighton	42	11	15	16	47:57	37
17	Manchester C	42	12	13	17	43:66	37
18	Stoke	42	13	10	19	44:58	36
19	Everton	42	9	17	16	43:51	35
20	Bristol C.	42	9	13	20	37:66	31
21	Derby	42	11	8	23	47:67	30
22	Bolton	42	5	15	22	38:73	25

Back Row: (l to r): Donnie Gillies, Clive Whitehead, Geert Meijer, John Shaw, Tom Ritchie, Ray Cashley, David Rodgers, Joe Royle, Howard Pritchard. **Front Row:** Jimmy Mann, Pertti Jantunen, Kevin Mabbutt, Geoff Merrick, Gerry Gow, Gerry Sweeny, Trevor Tainton, Chris Garland, Peter Cormack.

1979-80 Season

1980-81 Season
Back: Jantunen, Garland, Ritchie, Cashley, Rodgers, Shaw, Doyle, Hay, Pritchard.
Front: Whitehead, Tainton, Mann, Gow, Mabbutt, Merrick, Sweeney, Fitzpatrick.

SEASON 1980-81
FOOTBALL LEAGUE DIVISION TWO

No.	Date	Opposition	Pos.	Res.	H.T.	Att.	Goalscorers
1	16 Aug	Preston North End		1-1	0-0	6058	Mann
2	19	WEST HAM UNITED		1-1	1-1	13554	Ritchie
3	23	BRISTOL ROVERS	12	0-0	0-0	16937	
4	30	Watford	18	0-1	0-0	10450	
5	6 Sep	SWANSEA CITY	21	0-1	0-1	9528	
6	13	Sheffield Wednesday	22	1-2	1-1	15054	Ritchie
7	20	NOTTS COUNTY	22	0-0	0-0	7485	
8	27	Queens Park Rangers	22	0-4	0-2	8551	
9	4 Oct	Grimsby Town	22	0-1	0-0	8781	
10	7	LUTON TOWN	21	2-1	0-1	7014	Mabbutt, Ritchie(pen)
11	11	NEWCASTLE UNITED	21	2-0	0-0	10539	Ritchie(2,1pen)
12	18	Bolton Wanderers	21	1-1	1-1	8988	Mabbutt
13	21	Wrexham	21	0-1	0-0	4179	
14	25	DERBY COUNTY	21	2-2	1-0	12020	Mabbutt(2)
15	1 Nov	Orient	21	1-3	0-1	4698	Mabbutt
16	8	BLACKBURN ROVERS	20	2-0	0-0	8773	Garland, Tainton
17	11	West Ham United	21	0-5	0-2	25210	
18	15	PRESTON NORTH END	21	0-0	0-0	8042	
19	22	Cambridge United	21	1-2	0-2	4922	Mann
20	29	OLDHAM ATHLETIC	21	1-1	0-1	8037	Fitzpatrick
21	6 Dec	Shrewsbury Town	21	0-4	0-1	4435	
22	13	BOLTON WANDERERS	21	3-1	1-1	7384	Mabbutt(2), Aitken
23	20	Newcastle United	21	0-0	0-0	14100	
24	26	CARDIFF CITY	21	0-0	0-0	14921	
25	27	Chelsea	21	0-0	0-0	18514	
26	10 Jan	CAMBRIDGE UNITED	21	0-1	0-1	9727	
27	17	WATFORD	21	0-0	0-0	8746	
28	31	Bristol Rovers	21	0-0	0-0	10087	
29	7 Feb	SHEFFIELD WEDNESDAY	21	1-0	0-0	11639	Pritchard
30	21	QUEENS PARK RANGERS	21	0-1	0-0	10988	
31	28	Notts County	21	1-2	1-2	7609	Nicholls
32	10 Mar	GRIMSBY TOWN	21	1-1	0-1	5881	Tainton
33	14	Luton Town	21	1-3	1-2	8745	Pritchard
34	17	Swansea City	21	0-0	0-0	10832	
35	21	WREXHAM	21	0-2	0-1	6677	
36	28	Derby County	21	0-1	0-0	15008	
37	4 Apr	ORIENT	21	3-1	0-0	5803	Hay, Mabbutt, Mann
38	11	Blackburn Rovers	21	0-1	0-0	9970	
39	18	CHELSEA	21	0-0	0-0	9764	
40	20	Cardiff City	21	3-2	1-1	5579	Mann(2), Mabbutt
41	25	SHREWSBURY TOWN	21	1-1	1-0	5698	Mann
42	2 May	Oldham Athletic	21	0-2	0-0	4785	

Player appearances (shirt numbers):

No.	Cashley A.R.	Sweeney G.	Hay A.B.	Tainton T.K.	Rodgers D.M.	Merrick G.	Whitehead C.R.	Fitzpatrick A.C.	Mabbutt K.R.	Ritchie T.G.	Mann J.A.	Garland C.S.	Baddeley K.	Gow R.G.	Pritchard H.K.	Doyle I.P.	Smith G.A.	Marshall J.P.	Shaw J.K.	Aitken P.G.	Moller J.B.	Chandler R.D.	Stevens P.D.	Nicholls A.	Musker R.	Williams G.A.	Jantunen P.K.
1	1	2	3	4	5	6*	7	8	9	10	11	12															
2	1	2		4	5*	6	11	7	8	9	10	12	3														
3	1	2		4		6	3	7	8	9	10			5	11												
4	1	2	5			6	3		9	8	10	12					4	11*									
5	1	2	5	3		6	7		9	8					11*		4	12	10								
6	1	2	3	4	5	6	9	7	11	10		8															
7	1	2	3	4	5	6	9	11	10	7		8															
8	1	3	2			6	5	8	9	10	7						4	11*	12								
9	1	2	3	7	5*	6	11	8	10	9	12						4										
10	1	2	3	7		6	5	8	9	10							4	11									
11	1	2	3	7		6	5	8	9	10							4	11									
12	1	2	3	7		6	5	8	9	10							4	11									
13	1	2	3	7		6	5	8	9	10	12						4	11*									
14	1	2	3	7		6	5	8	9	10				4*	11		12										
15	1	2	3	7		6	5	8	9	10				4	11												
16	1	2	3	7			5	8	9*	10				4	11		12		6								
17	1	2	3	7*		6	9	8	10					4	11		12		5								
18	1	2	3	7	12	6		8*	10					4	9		11		5								
19	1	2	3	7		6		8	10					4	9		11		5								
20	1	2	3	7	5	6*	4	8	9	10							11	12									
21		2	3	7	5		11	8	9	10									6	1	4						
22		2	3	7	5		11*	8	9	10							12		6	1	4						
23		2	3	7	5			8	9	10					11*		12		6	1	4						
24		2	3	7	5			8	9	10					11				6	4	1						
25		2	3	7	5			8	10					9*	11		12		6	4	1						
26		2	3	7	5			8	9	10					11				6	4	1						
27		2	3	7	5			8	9	10*					11				6	1	4		12				
28		2	3	7	5*		11	8	9			12			10				6	1	4						
29	3		7				11	9	8						10		5			4	1			2	6		
30	3		7				11	8	9						10*		12		5	4	1			2	6		
31	3		7				11	8	9						10		5			4	1			2	6		
32	3		7				11	8							10*		12	5		4	1			2	6		
33	3		7*			6		8	9			12			10		11	5		4	1			2			
34		6	3	7			11	8	9						10		5			4	1			2			
35		6	3	7			11	8	9						10		5			4	1			2			
36		6	3	7				8*	9			12			11		5			4	1		10	2			
37		6	3	7				9	8						11		5			4	1		10	2			
38		6	3	7				8	9						10		5			4	1		11	2			
39		6	3					8	9						10		5			4	1		11	2		7	
40		6	3	12				8	9						10		5			4	1		11	2		7*	
41		6	8		3*				9						10		12	5		4	1		11	2		7	3
42		6	7		3*				9						10*		12	5		4	1		11	2		8	3
Apps.	20	38	36	40	14	17	31	34	38	27	22	10	1	11	15	1	7	26	5	22	17	7	14	4	4	1	
Subs.		1			1							3		5		6		7		1							
Goals			1	2				1	9	5	6	1			2					1				1			

F.A. CUP

Rd	Date	Opposition	Res.	H.T.	Att.	Goalscorers
3R	3 Jan	Derby County	0-0	0-0	19071	
3Rr	7	DERBY COUNTY	2-0	1-0	13649	Mabbutt, Ritchie
4R	24	Carlisle United	1-1	0-1	10057	Mabbutt
4Rr	28	CARLISLE UNITED	5-0	0-0	12801	Mabbutt(2), Ritchie(2,1pen), Mann
5R	14 Feb	Nottingham Forest	1-2	1-0	26732	Mabbutt

F.A. Cup player appearances:

Rd	Swe	Hay	Tai	Rod	Fit	Mab	Rit	Man	Pri	Smi	Sha	Ait	Mol	Nic	Mus	Cas
3R	2	3	7	5	8	9	10		11		6	1	4			
3Rr	2	3	7	5	8	9	10		11		6	1	4			
4R	2	3	7	5	8	9	10*	11		12	6	4	1			
4Rr	2	3	7*	5	8	9	10	11		12	6	4	1			
5R		7			8	9		11	10	5		4	1	2	6	3

F.L. CUP

Rd	Date	Opposition	Res.	H.T.	Att.	Goalscorers
2R1	26 Aug	Birmingham City	1-2	0-1	12163	Ritchie
2R2	2 Sep	BIRMINGHAM CITY	0-0	0-0	6958	

F.L. Cup player appearances:

Rd	Cas	Swe	Hay	Tai	Mer	Whi	Fit	Mab	Rit	Man	Gow	Pri	Smi	Mar	Jan
2R1	1	2	12	4	6	3	7*	9	8	10	5	11			
2R2	1	2	5	3	6	7		9	8			11	4	10*	12

ANGLO SCOTTISH CUP

Rd	Date	Opposition	Pos.	Res.	H.T.	Att.	Goalscorers
GM	2 Aug	FULHAM	1	2-0	1-0	1929	Gow, Ritchie(pen)
GM	6	NOTTS COUNTY	1	1-1	0-0	1678	Gow
GM	9	Orient	2	0-1	0-0	1999	

Anglo Scottish Cup player appearances:

Rd	Cas	Swe	Hay	Tai	Rod	Mer	Whi	Fit	Mab	Rit	Man	Gar	Gow	Pri	Doy	Smi
GM	1	2	3	7	5*	6	8	11	9	12	10"		4		14	
GM	1		3	7	5*	6	8	11"	9			10	2	4	14	12
GM	1	2	12	7	5	6	3		9	8"	10		12	11*	14	

GLOUCESTERSHIRE CUP FINAL

Date	Opposition	Res.	H.T.	Att.	
5 May	Bristol Rovers	1-0	0-0	2558	(Extra-time played)

FRIENDLIES

No.	Date	Opposition	Res.	H.T.	Att.	Goalscorers
1	28 Jul	Poole Town	1-1	0-1		Fitzpatrick (Centenary Match)
2	30	Barnstaple Town	1-0	0-0		Ritchie
3	4 Aug	Swindon Town	1-1	1-1	2261	Fitzpatrick

FINAL LEAGUE TABLE

		P	W	D	L	F:A	Pts
1	West Ham	42	28	10	4	79:29	66
2	Notts Co.	42	18	17	7	49:38	53
3	Swansea	42	18	14	10	64:44	50
4	Blackburn	42	16	18	8	42:29	50
5	Luton	42	18	12	12	61:46	48
6	Derby	42	15	15	12	57:52	45
7	Grimsby	42	15	15	12	44:42	45
8	QPR	42	15	13	14	56:46	43
9	Watford	42	16	11	15	50:45	43
10	Sheffield W	42	17	8	17	53:51	42
11	Newcastle	42	14	14	14	30:45	42
12	Chelsea	42	14	12	16	46:41	40
13	Cambridge	42	17	6	17	53:65	40
14	Shrewsbury	42	11	17	14	46:47	39
15	Oldham	42	12	15	15	39:48	39
16	Wrexham	42	12	14	16	43:45	38
17	Orient	42	13	12	17	52:56	38
18	Bolton	42	14	10	18	61:66	38
19	Cardiff	42	12	12	18	44:60	36
20	Preston	42	11	14	17	41:62	36
21	Bristol C.	42	7	16	19	29:51	30
22	Bristol R.	42	5	13	24	34:65	23

SEASON 1981-82
FOOTBALL LEAGUE DIVISION THREE

Player columns (left to right): Moller J.B., Stevens P.D., Merrick G., Mann J.A., Rodgers D.M., Marshall J.P., Tainton T.K., Musker R., Mabbutt K.R., Harford M.G., Devine P., Hay A.B., Sweeney G., Aitken P.G., Nicholls A., Whitehead C.R., Williams G.A., Boyle T.D.J., Chandler R.D., Garland C.S., Newman R.N., Smith M., Bray W., Economou J., McCaffery A., Carter L.A., Gooding R., Shaw J.K., Down W.F., Thompson S.J.

No.	Date	Opposition	Pos.	Res.	H.T.	Att.	Goalscorers	Moller	Stevens	Merrick	Mann	Rodgers	Marshall	Tainton	Musker	Mabbutt	Harford	Devine	Hay	Sweeney	Aitken	Nicholls	Whitehead	Williams	Boyle	Chandler	Garland	Newman	Smith	Bray	Economou	McCaffery	Carter	Gooding	Shaw	Down	Thompson
1	29 Aug	Carlisle United		2-2	0-2	3930	Harford, Mann	1	2	3	4	5	0	7	0	0	10	11																			
2	5 Sep	DONCASTER ROVERS		2-2	2-0	6586	Harford, Mabbutt	1	2	3	4	5	6	7	8	9	10	11																			
3	12	Fulham	19	1-2	1-0	4196	Mann	1	2	6	4	5		7	8	10	9	11	3																		
4	19	NEWPORT COUNTY	13	2-1	0-1	7552	Mann(2)	1	2		8	5	6	7		9	10		11	3	4																
5	22	PLYMOUTH ARGYLE	6	3-2	1-2	7371	Harford, Mann, Nicholls	1	2		8	5*		7	12	9	10			11	3	4	6														
6	26	Portsmouth	13	0-2	0-1	10203		1	2		8	5		7		9	10			11	3	4	6														
7	29	Gillingham	15	1-1	0-0	3887	Harford	1	2		8	5		7	11	9	10			3		4	6														
8	3 Oct	WALSALL	19	0-1	0-0	6033		1	2		8	5		7	11	9	10			3		4		6													
9	10	PRESTON NORTH END	18	0-0	0-0	5389		1	2		8	5			7	9	10			3	4	6			11												
10	17	Oxford United	20	0-1	0-1	3906		1	2		8	5			9	10	7			3	6	4			11												
11	20	READING	17	2-0	0-0	5006	Devine, Tainton	1	2		8	5		7			9	10	3	6	4				11												
12	24	Lincoln City	16	2-1	2-0	3683	Harford(2)	1	2		8	5		3		9	10	7			6	4			11												
13	31	CHESTERFIELD	15	0-0	0-0	8442		1	2		8	5		7		9	10			4		11	3	6													
14	3 Nov	Millwall	17	0-2	0-1	5002		1	2		8	5		7		9	10			4			3	6	11												
15	7	Brentford	14	1-0	0-0	6760	Harford	1	2		8	5		7		9	10			'4			3	6	11												
16	14	SOUTHEND UNITED	17	0-2	0-0	6381		1	2		8*	5		7	11	9	10			12	4		3	6													
17	28	BURNLEY	19	2-3	1-1	4862	Garland, Mann(pen)	1	2		8	5			•11	9	7			4			3	6		10											
18	5 Dec	Swindon Town	20	0-0	0-0	6949		1	2		8			11		10	7			4	6		3	5	9												
19	29	Bristol Rovers	21	0-1	0-1	12355		1	2		8	5		7			10	11		4			3	5	9												
20	2 Jan	WIMBLEDON	21	1-3	1-1	4660	Stevens	1	2		8			7			10	11*			12	4	6	3	5	9											
21	16	HUDDERSFIELD TOWN	22	0-0	0-0	4921		1	2		8			7	11		10				4		6	3	5	9*	12										
22	30	Newport County	22	1-1	1-1	5927	Harford	1	2		8			7	11		10			12	6	4		3	5*	9											
23	6 Feb	FULHAM	22	0-0	0-0	9228		1	2					7			10			3			6	5		9	4*	12	8	11							
24	9	Plymouth Argyle	22	1-2	0-1	5260	Chandler	1	2					7			10			3			6	5		9	4		8	11							
25	13	Walsall	22	1-0	1-0	4020	Newman	1	2					7			10			3			6	5		9	4	12	8	11*							
26	20	PORTSMOUTH	22	0-1	0-0	9397		1	2					7			10			11			6	3		9	4				5	8				
27	23	EXETER CITY	22	3-2	2-1	6612	Harford(2), Chandler	1	2					7			10			11			5	3		9	4*			12	6	8				
28	27	Preston North End	18	3-1	1-1	6411	Bray, Harford, McCaffery	1	2					7*			10			11			6	3		9	12		4		5	8				
29	6 Mar	OXFORD UNITED	21	0-2	0-1	8155		1	2								10			11			6	3		9			4		5	8	7		
30	10	Reading	21	1-3	0-0	3107	O.G.	1	2					7						11			6	3		9	12		4		5	8	10*		
31	13	LINCOLN CITY	22	0-1	0-1	6341		1	2											3			6	5		9	4		7	11	5	8	10		
32	20	Chesterfield	22	0-1	0-0	4230			2					7		10				3			6	5			4		8	11		9	1		
33	27	BRENTFORD	22	0-1	0-0	5997			2					7						3			5		6	12	9	4*	8	11		10	1		
34	3 Apr	Southend United	22	0-3	0-1	3133			2					4						11			6	3	5	9	12		8	7*		10	1		
35	6	CARLISLE UNITED	22	1-1	0-1	4329	Chandler		2					4						11			6	3	5	8	9		7			10	1		
36	10	Exeter City	22	0-4	0-2	4580			2					4						11			6	3	5	8	9		7	12		10*	1		
37	12	BRISTOL ROVERS	22	1-2	0-1	10791	Bray		2					4				12	11				6	3	5	8	9*		7	10			1		
38	17	SWINDON TOWN	23	0-3	0-1	6524			2					4				7*	3				6	5	9		12	8	11		10	1		
39	21	Chester	22	0-0	0-0	1034			2					4				12	3			6	7	5	9		8*	11		10	1		
40	24	Burnley	22	0-2	0-0	7039			2					4				8	3			6	7	5	9	12			11	10*		1		
41	1 May	GILLINGHAM	23	2-1	1-0	3931	Economou, Williams	10						4				8	3			6	2	5	9				7	11	1		
42	4	Huddersfield Town	23	0-5	0-3	3468		10						4				8	3			6	2	5	9		12		7	11*	1		
43	8	Wimbledon	23	0-0	0-0	2114			2					4				8	3			5		9	10	7	11		1		
44	12	MILLWALL	23	4-1	2-1	2696	Chandler(2), Newman(2,1pen)	3						5					4			7	2	6	9	10	12	8*	11	1		
45	15	CHESTER	23	1-0	1-0	3934	Chandler	8						4				3				6	2*	5	9	10	11	8*	7	1		
46	18	Doncaster Rovers	23	2-2	0-2	4252	Chandler, Thompson	2						4					6				5	9	10	11	8*	7		1	3	12

	Moller	Stevens	Merrick	Mann	Rodgers	Marshall	Tainton	Musker	Mabbutt	Harford	Devine	Hay	Sweeney	Aitken	Nicholls	Whitehead	Williams	Boyle	Chandler	Garland	Newman	Smith	Bray	Economou	McCaffery	Carter	Gooding	Shaw	Down	Thompson
Apps.	31	46	3	22	18	3		19	32	11	30	19	33	8	19	27	6	33	22	30	1	15	1	19	17	6	16	3	15	1
Subs.				1								2	1	2					1			1	6	4		2			1	
Goals	1		6				1			11	1				1				7	1	3		2	1		1				1

F.A. CUP

No.	Date	Opposition	Res.	H.T.	Att.	Goalscorers	Moller	Stevens	Mann	Rodgers	Tainton	Musker	Mabbutt	Harford	Devine	Aitken	Nicholls	Boyle	Chandler	Garland	Bray	Economou
1R	20 Nov	TORQUAY UNITED	0-0	0-0	5221		1	2	8	5	7		9	10		4		3	6	11		
1Rr	25	Torquay United	2-1	0-0	4334	Mann(2)	1	2	8	5	7	11	9	10		4		3	6			
2R	15 Dec	NORTHAMPTON TOWN	3-0	1-0	2901	Harford(2), Tainton	1	2	8	5	7		10	11		4		3	6	9		
3R	6 Jan	Peterborough United	1-0	0-0	6811	Chandler	1	2	8		7	11	10			4	6	3	5	9		
4R	23	ASTON VILLA	0-1	0-0	20079	(£45000)	1	2	8		7	11	10			6	4	3	5	12	9*	

F.L. CUP

No.	Date	Opposition	Res.	H.T.	Att.	Goalscorers	Moller	Stevens	Merrick	Mann	Rodgers	Marshall	Tainton	Musker	Mabbutt	Harford	Devine	Hay	Sweeney	Aitken	Nicholls	Whitehead	Boyle	Chandler
1R1	1 Sep	WALSALL	2-0	2-0	3906	Harford, Mann	1	2	3	4	5	6	7	8	9	10	11							
1R2	15	Walsall	0-1	0-0	2830		1	2	6*	8	5		7	9	10	12	11	3	4					
2R1	6 Oct	Carlisle United	0-0	0-0	4111		1	2	8	5		11	9	10	3	6	4	7					
2R2	27	CARLISLE UNITED	2-1	0-1	5220	Mann(pen), Rodgers	1	2	8	5	3	9	10	7	6	4	11						
3R	10 Nov	Queens Park Rangers	0-3	0-2	9215		1	2	8	5		7	11	9	10	4	3	6					

GLOUCESTERSHIRE CUP FINAL

	Date	Opposition	Res.	H.T.	Att.	
	8 Sep	BRISTOL ROVERS	0-1	0-0	4022	

FRIENDLIES

No.	Date	Opposition	Res.	H.T.	Att.	Goalscorers
1	26 Jul	Veberod	1-0	1-0		Rodgers
2	28	Angelholm	3-1	2-0		Aitken, Marshall, Musker
3	30	Tideholm	4-0			Devine(2), Chandler, Rodgers
4	1 Aug	Molmlycka	6-0			Chandler(2), Mabbutt, Mann, Merrick, O.G.
5	15	CHARLTON ATHLETIC	0-0	0-0	1264	
6	18	CRYSTAL PALACE	1-0	1-0	1220	Chandler
7	24	Torquay United	2-1	1-1		Harford, Mabbutt

FINAL LEAGUE TABLE

	Team	P	W	D	L	F	A	Pts
1	Burnley	46	21	17	8	66	49	80
2	Carlisle	46	23	11	12	65	50	80
3	Fulham	46	21	15	10	77	51	78
4	Lincoln	46	21	14	11	66	40	77
5	Oxford	46	19	14	13	63	49	71
6	Gillingham	46	20	11	15	64	56	71
7	Southend	46	18	15	13	63	51	69
8	Brentford	46	19	11	16	56	47	68
9	Millwall	46	18	13	15	62	62	67
10	Plymouth	46	18	11	17	64	56	65
11	Chesterfield	46	18	10	18	67	58	64
12	Reading	46	17	11	18	67	75	62
13	Portsmouth	46	14	19	13	56	51	61
14	Preston	46	16	13	17	50	56	61
15	Bristol Rovers	46	18	9	19	58	65	61
16	Newport	46	14	16	16	54	54	58
17	Huddersfield	46	15	12	19	64	59	57
18	Exeter	46	16	9	21	71	84	57
19	Doncaster	46	13	17	16	55	68	56
20	Walsall	46	13	14	19	51	55	53
21	Wimbledon	46	14	11	21	61	75	53
22	Swindon	46	13	13	20	55	71	52
23	Bristol City	46	11	13	22	40	65	46
24	Chester	46	7	11	28	36	78	32

1981-82 Season
Back: Chandler, Aitken, Harford, Moller, Rodgers, Nicholls, Boyle (Captain).
Front: Tainton, Stevens, Sweeney, Musker, Devine, Mann, Williams.

1982-83 Season
Back: Thompson, Williams, Shaw, Musker, Crawford.
Middle: Lockhart (Physiotherapist), Stevens, Economou, Garry Smith, Bray, Cooper (Player/Manager).
Front: Chandler, Nicholls, Boyle, Ritchie, Newman, Riley.

SEASON 1982-83
FOOTBALL LEAGUE DIVISION FOUR

Player columns (left to right): Shaw J.K., Stevens P.D., Williams G.A., Newman R.N., Boyle T.D.J., Riley G., Economou J., Musker R., Cooper T., Ritchie T.G., Crawford A.P., Bray W., Thompson S.J, Chandler R.D., Nicholls A., Panes S.M., Johnson P.E., Phillipson-Masters, Kelly E.E., Llewellyn A.D., Garland C.S., Smith N.K., Williams P.S., Palmer J.N., Jones M.G., Kelly N.

No.	Date	Opposition	Pos.	Res.	H.T.	Att.	Goalscorers
1	28 Aug	HULL CITY		2-1	1-0	4877	Musker, Riley
2	4 Sep	Tranmere Rovers	4	2-2	0-2	1534	Ritchie(2)
3	7	Crewe Alexandra	14	1-4	0-1	1409	Ritchie(pen)
4	11	BLACKPOOL	15	0-0	0-0	4681	
5	19	Northampton Town	17	1-7	0-3	3017	Riley
6	25	SCUNTHORPE UNITED	21	0-2	0-0	3890	
7	28	TORQUAY UNITED	22	0-1	0-1	3041	
8	2 Oct	Peterborough United	23	0-3	0-2	2739	
9	9	YORK CITY	22	2-2	1-1	3680	Chandler, Crawford
10	16	Hartlepool United	23	1-3	1-2	1449	Riley
11	19	Halifax Town	23	2-2	1-2	1465	Newman, Ritchie
12	23	WIMBLEDON	22	4-2	3-0	4723	Riley(3), Nicholls
13	30	Aldershot	23	0-0	0-0	2826	
14	2 Nov	CHESTER	21	0-0	0-0	3942	
15	6	STOCKPORT COUNTY	21	2-2	0-0	4645	Chandler, Riley
16	13	Mansfield Town	22	1-1	1-0	1979	Riley
17	27	COLCHESTER UNITED	23	0-2	0-1	4310	
18	4 Dec	Rochdale	24	0-1	0-0	1307	
19	11	Chester	24	0-1	0-0	1163	
20	18	Bury	23	2-2	0-0	2196	Chandler, Crawford
21	27	PORT VALE	23	1-3	0-1	6729	Phillipson-Masters
22	28	Hereford United	23	3-1	3-1	3548	Chandler(2), N.Kelly
23	1 Jan	SWINDON TOWN	22	1-1	0-0	9002	Riley
24	3	Darlington	22	2-2	2-2	1425	Chandler, Garland
25	15	Hull City	23	0-1	0-0	7035	
26	18	TRANMERE ROVERS	21	1-0	0-0	3344	Riley
27	22	NORTHAMPTON TOWN	21	1-3	1-2	4855	Ritchie(pen)
28	5 Feb	Scunthorpe United	23	1-1	0-0	3624	Nicholls
29	12	PETERBOROUGH UNITED	21	1-0	1-0	3959	Ritchie(pen)
30	15	HALIFAX TOWN	18	3-0	2-0	3169	Cooper, Economou, Ritchie
31	19	York City	20	0-3	0-0	2879	
32	26	HARTLEPOOL UNITED	17	2-0	1-0	4194	Economou, Ritchie(pen)
33	5 Mar	Wimbledon	20	1-2	0-2	2541	E.Kelly
34	12	ALDERSHOT	20	2-0	1-0	4329	Crawford, Riley
35	18	Stockport County	21	2-2	1-1	2036	Riley, Ritchie
36	20	Torquay United	17	2-0	1-0	3096	Crawford, Riley
37	26	MANSFIELD TOWN	15	3-1	0-1	4919	Crawford, Riley, P.Williams
38	2 Apr	HEREFORD UNITED	15	1-1	1-1	6264	Ritchie
39	4	Port Vale	15	1-1	1-1	6573	Riley
40	9	ROCHDALE	15	0-0	0-0	4772	
41	16	Blackpool	14	4-1	1-1	2209	Crawford, Riley, Ritchie(pen), O.G.
42	23	BURY	15	2-1	0-0	5298	Nicholls, O.G.
43	29	Colchester United	15	1-3	1-2	2196	Ritchie(pen)
44	2 May	DARLINGTON	15	2-2	1-2	4788	Crawford, Phillipson-Masters
45	7	CREWE ALEXANDRA	14	2-1	0-0	4700	Newman(2)
46	14	Swindon Town	14	0-2	0-1	5103	

Apps. 46, 10, 35, 42, 14, 43, 34, 6, 37, 37, 44, 9, 10, 20, 39, 2, 20, 25, 4, 5, 7, 2, 11, 2, , 2
Subs. , 1, 1, , 1, , , , , , , , 1, 1, 1, 3, , 2, , 1, 2, 2, , 6, 1, 4
Goals , , 3, , , 16, 2, 1, 1, 12, 7, , , 6, 3, , 2, 1, , 1, 1, , 1, , , 1

F.A. CUP

| 1R | 20 Nov | Orient | | 1-4 | 1-3 | 2772 | Johnson |

F.L. (MILK) CUP

1R1	31 Aug	Swindon Town		1-2	0-1	3736	Boyle
1R2	14 Sep	SWINDON TOWN		2-0	2-0	3786	Boyle, Ritchie
2R1	4 Oct	SHEFFIELD WEDNESDAY		1-2	0-2	4486	Newman
2R2	26	Sheffield Wednesday		1-1	0-0	7920	Chandler (Extra-time, 1-0 end of 90 mins.)

F.L. TROPHY

GM	14 Aug	Exeter City	3	1-2	1-0	1040	Economou
GM	17	TORQUAY UNITED	2	1-0	0-0	1421	Ritchie
GM	21	NEWPORT COUNTY	3	1-4	1-2	2226	Chandler

GLOUCESTERSHIRE CUP FINAL

| | 21 Sep | Bristol Rovers | | 1-2 | 0-1 | 4369 | G.Williams |

FRIENDLIES

1	7 Aug	Bridport		5-1	2-0		Ritchie(3), Chandler, Musker
2	10	Cheltenham Town		1-0	0-0		Chandler
3	23	ALL STAR XI		4-3	2-1	3404	Chndler, Cper, Nwman, Rley (C.Garland Ben.)
4	25	Ledbury Town		8-1			Chandler(3), Riley(3) Thompson(2)
5	17 Apr	ROGER QUINTIN'S XI		4-4		800	Unknown(4) (Bristol Childrens Hospital)
6	10 May	Bridgwater Town		1-0	1-0	300	Bray
7	15	Shepton Mallet		1-1			Ritchie

FINAL LEAGUE TABLE

1	Wimbledon	46	29	11	6	96	45	98
2	Hull	46	25	15	6	75	34	90
3	Port Vale	46	26	10	10	67	34	88
4	Scunthorpe	46	23	14	9	71	42	83
5	Bury	46	24	12	11	76	44	81
6	Colchester	46	24	9	13	75	55	81
7	York	46	22	13	11	88	58	79
8	Swindon	46	19	11	16	61	54	68
9	Peterborough	46	17	13	16	58	52	64
10	Mansfield	46	16	13	17	61	70	61
11	Halifax	46	16	12	18	59	66	60
12	Torquay	46	17	7	22	56	65	58
13	Chester	46	15	11	20	55	60	56
14	Bristol City	46	13	17	16	59	70	56
15	Northampton	46	14	12	20	67	75	54
16	Stockport	46	14	12	20	60	79	54
17	Darlington	46	13	13	20	61	71	52
18	Aldershot	46	12	15	19	61	82	51
19	Tranmere	46	13	11	22	49	71	50
20	Rochdale	46	11	16	19	55	73	49
21	Blackpool	46	13	12	21	55	74	49
22	Hartlepool	46	13	9	24	46	76	48
23	Crewe	46	11	8	27	53	71	41
24	Hereford	46	11	8	27	43	79	41

SEASON 1983-84
FOOTBALL (CANON) LEAGUE DIVISION FOUR

No.	Date	Opposition	Pos.	Res.	H.T.	Att.	Goalscorers	Shaw J.K.	Stevens P.D.	Williams G.A.	Phillipson-Masters	Halliday B.	Riley G.	Pritchard H.K.	Ritchie T.G.	Kerr J.	Musker R.	Crawford A.P.	Williams P.S.	Newman R.N.	Economou J.	Cooper T.	Stroud K.A.	Hirst M.P.	Marshall G.	Morgan T.J.	Curle K.	Hooper M.D.	Llewellyn A.D.
1	27 Aug	MANSFIELD TOWN		4-0	2-0	5758	Crawford(2), Riley(2)	1	2	3	4	5	6	7	8	9*	10	11	12										
2	3 Sep	Bury	9	1-2	1-2	2015	Kerr	1	2	3	4	5	6	7	8	9*	10	11	12										
3	6	Colchester United	7	0-0	0-0	2120		1	10	3	4	5	6*	7	8			11	12	2									
4	10	HARTLEPOOL UNITED	7	2-0	0-0	5390	Pritchard, Riley	1	12	3*	4	5	10	7	8	9		11				2	6						
5	16	Wrexham	10	1-3	0-1	1731	Crawford	1	8	3	5	4	6	7			12	11	9*	2	10								
6	24	TORQUAY UNITED	6	5-0	1-0	5268	Crawford(3), Riley, Ritchie(pen)	1	2	3	5	4	6	7	8	9		11				10							
7	27	READING	4	3-1	1-0	6322	Pritchard(2), Ritchie	1	2	3	5	4	6	7	8	9*		11				10		12					
8	1 Oct	Hereford United	2	2-0	1-0	5875	Kerr, Ritchie	1	2	3	5	4	6	7	8	9		11				10							
9	8	HALIFAX TOWN	2	3-0	3-0	6739	Crawford, Kerr, Riley	1	2	3	5	4	6	7	8	9		11				10*		12					
10	14	Tranmere Rovers	2	0-2		2518		1	2	3	5	4	6	7	8	9		11				10*		12					
11	18	YORK CITY	1	1-0	1-0	10827	Stevens	1	2	3	5	4*	6	7	8	9		11				10		12					
12	22	Aldershot	1	0-1	0-1	3195		1	2	3	5		6	7	8	9*		11			4	10		12					
13	29	PETERBOROUGH UNITED	2			7380		1	2	3	5	4	6	7	8			11				12	10*		9				
14	1 Nov	Blackpool	6	0-1	0-1	4344		1	2	12	5	4	6*	7	8			11	10	3			9						
15	5	DONCASTER ROVERS	7	1-2	1-1	5963	Stroud	1	2	3	5	4*	6	7	8			11	10			12	9						
16	12	Darlington	5	1-0	0-0	1888	Kerr	1	2	3	5	4	6*	7	8	12		11				10	9						
17	26	CHESTERFIELD	4	2-0		5797	Pritchard, Ritchie(pen)	1	2	3	4		6	7	8	10		11*	5			9	6	12					
18	3 Dec	Northampton Town	7	0-1	0-1	2823		1	2	3	4	11*	7	8	10							5	12	9	6				
19	17	Rochdale	7	1-0	0-0	1496	Pritchard	1	2	3	5		10	7	8			11*				4	12	9	6				
20	26	STOCKPORT COUNTY	4	3-1	2-0	8888	Crawford, Riley, Stroud	1	2	3	5	4	10	7	8*			11				12	6	9					
21	28	Crewe Alexandra	4	2-2	1-2	3457	Pritchard, Ritchie(pen)	1	2	3	5	4	9	7	8			11				12	6	9*					
22	31	CHESTER CITY	3	4-2	0-1	7293	Crawford, Riley, Ritchie, Stevens	1	2	3	5	4	6	7	8			11				12	10	9*					
23	21 Jan	WREXHAM	6	2-1	1-0	6441	Crawford, Ritchie(pen)	1	2	3	5	4	10	7	8			11				12	6	9*					
24	24	Swindon Town	4	1-1		6493	Riley	1	2	3	5	4	9	7	8			11				12	6	10*					
25	28	Hartlepool United	4	2-2	1-2	1881	Pritchard, Riley	1	2	3	5	4	9	7	8			11*				12	6	10					
26	31	BURY	3	3-2	1-0	7759	Crawford, Riley, Ritchie(pen)	1	2	3	5		10	7	8			11			4		6	9					
27	4 Feb	HEREFORD UNITED	3	1-0	1-0	7184	Crawford	1	2	3	5		10	7	8			11			4	12	6	9*					
28	11	Torquay United	3	0-1	0-0	4188		1	2	3	5			7	8			11*			9	12	6	10					
29	14	BLACKPOOL	3	1-1	0-1	7413	Stroud	1	2	3	5			7	8			11			10	12	6	9*					
30	18	Peterborough United	5	1-4	1-1	3356	Crawford	1	2	3	5			7	8			11*			9	12	6	10					
31	25	ALDERSHOT	4	2-1	2-1	6849	Riley, Ritchie(pen)	1	2		5	4	9	7	8			11					3	6		12			
32	3 Mar	York City	3	1-1	1-1	5096	Morgan	1	2		5	4	9	7	8								3	6		10	11		
33	6	Doncaster Rovers	3	0-1	0-1	4954		1	2		5	4	10*	7	8								3	6	12	9	11		
34	10	DARLINGTON	5	1-0	1-0	6579	Morgan	1	2		5	4	9	7	8								3	6		10	11		
35	13	ROCHDALE	4	1-1	0-1	6996	Riley	1	2		5	4	9	7	8								3	6	12	10	11*		
36	17	Halifax Town	4	2-1	0-0	1204	Pritchard, Riley	1	2		5	4	10	7	8								3	6		9	11		
37	24	TRANMERE ROVERS	4	1-1	0-0	6548	Morgan	1	2		5	4	9	7	8								3	12	6*	11	10		
38	27	Mansfield Town	3	1-0	0-0	1826	Newman	1	2		5	4	9	7	8								3	6		11	10		
39	31	COLCHESTER UNITED	2	4-1	1-0	6504	Riley(2), Ritchie(2,1pen)	1	2		5	4	9	7	8								3	6		11	10		
40	7 Apr	Reading	2	0-2	0-2	8528		1	2		5	4	9	7	8								3	12	6	11*	10		
41	14	NORTHAMPTON TOWN	2	4-1	1-0	6602	Crawford(2), Riley, Ritchie(pen)	1	2		5	4	9	7	8			11*					3	12	6		10		
42	17	CREWE ALEXANDRA	2	2-1	2-0	8139	Hirst, Pritchard	1	2			9		7	8			11					3	6	4		10		
43	21	Stockport County	2	0-0	0-0	2645		1	2		5	4	9	7	8								3	6		11	10		
44	28	Chesterfield	3	1-1	0-0	2975	Phillipson-Masters	1	2		5	4	9*	7	8								3	6		11	10	12	
45	5 May	SWINDON TOWN	3	1-0	0-0	12786	Pritchard	1	2		5	4	9	7	8			11					3	6			10		
46	7	Chester City	3	2-1	1-0	3900	Morgan(2)	1	2		5	4	9	7	8			11					3	6			10		
		Apps						46	45	29	44	41	42	46	45	13	2	31	5	29	11	1	34	22		15	5		
		Subs							1	1						1	1			3	1	1	20		2	1		1	
		Goals						2	1				16	10	12	4		15		1			3	1		5			

F.A. CUP

No.	Date	Opposition		Res.	H.T.	Att.	Goalscorers	Shaw	Stevens	Williams G	P-M	Halliday	Riley	Pritchard	Ritchie	Kerr	Musker	Crawford	Williams P	Newman	Economou	Cooper	Stroud	Hirst	Marshall	Morgan	Curle	Hooper	Llewellyn
1R	19 Nov	Corinthian Casuals		0-0	0-0	2118	(Played on Dulwich Hamlet ground)	1	2	3		4		7	8	6			9	5	10*	12		11					
1Rr	23	CORINTHIAN CASUALS		4-0	2-0	5339	Pritchard(3), Riley	1	2	3		4	9	7	8	10			5	6*	12	11							
2R	10 Dec	Bristol Rovers		2-1	0-0	14396	Hirst, Ritchie	1	2	3	5	4	10	7	8			11*				12	6	9					
3R	8 Jan	Notts County		2-2	1-1	11042	Crawford, Ritchie	1	2	3	5	4	6	7	8			11*				12	9	10					
3Rr	10	NOTTS COUNTY		0-2	0-0	16107		1	2	3	5	4	6	7	8			11*				12	9	10					

F.L. (MILK) CUP

No.	Date	Opposition		Res.	H.T.	Att.	Goalscorers	Shaw	Stevens	Williams G	P-M	Halliday	Riley	Pritchard	Ritchie	Kerr	Musker	Crawford	Williams P	Newman	Economou	Cooper	Stroud	Hirst					
1R1	31 Aug	Oxford United		1-1	0-1	3924	Riley	1	2	3	5	4	6	7	8	9*	10	11	12										
1R2	12 Sep	OXFORD UNITED		0-1	0-1	5233		1		3	5	4	6	7	8*	9		11	12	2		10							

ASSOCIATE MEMBERS CUP

No.	Date	Opposition		Res.	H.T.	Att.	Goalscorers	Shaw	Stevens	Williams G	P-M	Halliday	Riley	Pritchard	Ritchie	Kerr	Musker	Crawford	Williams P	Newman	Economou	Cooper	Stroud	Hirst	Marshall	Morgan	Curle	Hooper	Llewellyn
1R	22 Feb	Exeter City		1-3	0-1	1754	Ritchie(pen)		2	12	5	4*		7"	8							9	3	6	11		10	1	14

GLOUCESTERSHIRE CUP FINAL

	Date	Opposition		Res.	H.T.	Att.	Goalscorers
	20 Sep	BRISTOL ROVERS		2-3	0-1	6538	Pritchard, Riley (Extra-time, 1-1 90 mins)

FRIENDLIES

No.	Date	Opposition		Res.	H.T.	Att.	Goalscorers
1	4 Aug	Coleford Athletic		8-0		1000	Crawford(2), Rtchie(2), Kerr, Meacck, Muskr, OG
2	6	A.F.C. BOURNEMOUTH		2-3		1054	Kerr, Ritchie(pen)
3	10	Cheltenham Town		2-2	0-0		Riley(2)
4	13	Walsall		3-3			Musker, Newman, Riley
5	16	BARNSLEY		3-1	2-0	1183	Crawford, Economou, Riley
6	20	BRENTFORD		1-0	1-0	1111	Musker
7	20 May	Backwell United		5-0			Halliday, Morgan, Pritchard, Riley, Shaw(pen)
8	22	Bridgwater Town		0-0	0-0		

FINAL LEAGUE TABLE

1	York	46	31	8	7	96	39	101
2	Doncaster	46	24	13	9	82	54	85
3	Reading	46	22	10	8	84	56	82
4	Bristol City	46	24	10	12	70	44	82
5	Aldershot	46	22	9	15	76	69	75
6	Blackpool	46	21	9	16	70	52	72
7	Peterborough	46	18	14	14	72	48	68
8	Colchester	46	17	16	13	69	53	67
9	Torquay	46	18	13	15	59	64	67
10	Tranmere	46	17	15	14	53	53	66
11	Hereford	46	16	15	15	54	53	63
12	Stockport	46	17	11	18	60	64	62
13	Chesterfield	46	15	15	16	59	61	60
14	Darlington	46	17	8	21	49	50	59
15	Bury	46	15	14	17	61	64	59
16	Crewe	46	16	11	19	56	57	59
17	Swindon	46	15	13	18	58	56	58
18	Northampton	46	13	13	20	53	78	52
19	Mansfield	46	13	13	20	66	70	52
20	Wrexham	46	11	15	20	59	74	48
21	Halifax	46	12	12	22	55	89	48
22	Rochdale	46	11	13	22	52	80	46
23	Hartlepool	46	10	16	26	47	85	40
24	Chester	46	7	13	26	45	82	34

1983-84 Season
Back: Stevens, Meacock, Musker, Paul Williams, Gary Williams.
Middle: Middlemass (Coach), Newman, Nicholls, Shaw, Phillipson-Masters, Palmer, Lockhart (Physiotherapist).
Front: Economou, Crawford, Ritchie, Cooper (Player/Manager), Pritchard, Bray, Riley.

BRISTOL CITY F.C.: 1984/85 SQUAD PHOTO

Back row — Gary Marshall, Howard Pritchard, Tom Ritchie, Bruce Halliday, Nigel Smith;
Middle row — Rob Newman, Trevor Morgan (now Exeter City), Alan Walsh, John Shaw, Keith
Curle, Forbes Phillipson-Masters, Alan Nicholls; — Front row: Paul Stevens, Bob Hutchinson,
Alan Crawford, Terry Cooper (Manager), Andy Llewellyn, Martin Hirst, Glyn Riley.

SEASON 1984-85
FOOTBALL (CANON) LEAGUE DIVISION THREE

No.	Date	Opposition	Pos.	Res.	H.T.	Att.	Goalscorers	Shaw J.K.	Stevens P.D.	Newman R.N.	Rogers L.M.	Phillipson-Masters	Hirst M.P.	Pritchard H.K.	Riley G.	Morgan T.J.	Walsh A.	Crawford A.P.	Curle K.	Halliday B.	Ritchie T.G.	Cooper T.	Stroud K.A.	Llewellyn A.D.	Hutchinson R.	Hooper M.D.	Neville S.F.	Waugh K.	Leigh I.R.	Hughes M.	Marshall G.	Johnson S.
1	25 Aug	WIGAN ATHLETIC		2-0	0-0	7840	Riley(2)	1	2	3	4	5	6	7	8	9	10	11														
2	1 Sep	Newport County	6	0-0	0-0	5079		1	2	3	4	5	6	7	8	9*	10	11	12													
3	8	SWANSEA CITY	10	2-2	1-2	8464	Crawford, Walsh(pen)	1	2	3	4		6	7	8*	9	10	11	12	5												
4	15	Cambridge United	7	3-2	1-1	2444	Crawford, Newman, Walsh	1	2	3	4		6	7	8	9	10	11		5												
5	19	Derby County	7	0-1	0-1	11314		1	2	3		5	6	7	8*	9	10	11	12	4												
6	22	ORIENT	7	3-2	1-1	6941	Crawford, Newman, Walsh	1	2	3		5	6	7	8	9	10	11		4												
7	29	Walsall	10	1-4	0-1	4754	Walsh	1	2	3		5	6	7	8	9	10	11		4												
8	2 Oct	ROTHERHAM UNITED	11	0-1	0-1	6586		1	2	3		5	6	7	8	9	10	11	4													
9	6	York City	9	2-0	1-0	4890	Morgan, Walsh	1	2	3		5	6*	7	11	9	10		4			8	12									
10	13	GILLINGHAM	7	2-0	1-0	7088	Morgan, Riley	1	2	3		5		7	6	9	10	11	4			8										
11	20	Bradford City	5	1-1	0-1	4485	Pritchard	1	2	3		5		7	6*	9	10	12	4			8		11								
12	23	BOLTON WANDERERS	4	3-2	2-2	7715	Walsh(2,1pen), Pritchard	1	2	3		4		7		9	10	11	5			8		6								
13	27	Millwall	6	1-1	0-0	7024	Morgan	1		3		5		7	6	9	10		4			8		11	2							
14	3 Nov	BRENTFORD	7	1-1	0-0	7874	Walsh	1		3		5		7	6	9	10		4			8		11	2							
15	6	Doncaster Rovers	5	1-1	0-0	3947	Walsh	1		3*		5		7	6	9	10		4			8		11	2	12						
16	10	BRISTOL ROVERS	4	3-0	1-0	18672	Riley(2), Stroud	1				4		7	6	9	10		5	3		8		11	2							
17	24	Preston North End	8	2-3	1-1	3902	Phillipson-Masters, Riley	1				5		7	6	9	10		4	3		8		11	2*	12						
18	1 Dec	LINCOLN CITY	6	2-1	2-1	7270	Ritchie, Walsh					4			6		10	12	5	3	8*			11	2	9	1	7				
19	15	A.F.C. Bournemouth	8	1-2	1-1	4987	Riley	1				5		7	6		10		4	3				11	2	9		8				
20	22	Reading	10	0-1	0-0	3878		1			3	5		7	6		10		4					11	2	9		8				
21	26	PLYMOUTH ARGYLE	8	4-3	3-2	10399	Hutchinson(2), Walsh(2,1pen)				3	4			6	10		9					5	8	2	7		11	1			
22	29	BURNLEY	7	1-0	0-0	8282	Pritchard		2			5		7	6		10		4			12		11	3	9		8*	1			
23	1 Jan	Hull City	8	1-2	1-1	9753	Riley		3			5		7	6		10	12	4					11	2	9*		8	1			
24	26	CAMBRIDGE UNITED	7	3-0	1-0	6557	Pritchard, Riley, Walsh	1	2*			5		7	6		10	12	4					11	3	9		8				
25	2 Feb	WALSALL	9	1-2	0-1	7240	Walsh		2			5*		7	6		10	12	4					11	3	9		8	1			
26	9	Orient	8	1-0	0-0	2869	Walsh	1	3			5		7	6		10		4					11	2	9		8				
27	16	Rotherham United	8	1-2	1-1	4901	Riley	1	3			5	7*		6		10		4					11	2	9		8		12		
28	23	Brentford	7	2-1	2-1	4526	Neville(2)	1	2	3				7	6		10		4					11		9		8		5		
29	26	DERBY COUNTY	6	3-0	2-0	8728	Crawford, Marshall, Riley	1	2	3					6*		10	12	4					11		9		8		5	7	
30	2 Mar	MILLWALL	6	0-1	0-0	10875		1	2	3				7	6*		10		4					11		9		8		5	12	
31	5	Bolton Wanderers	5	4-1	3-0	3774	Neville(3), Riley	1	2	3				7	6		10		4					11		9		8		5		
32	9	Bradford City	5	2-0	1-0	9222	Pritchard, Walsh	1	2	3				7	6*		10		4					11		9		8		5	12	
33	16	Gillingham	5	3-1	1-0	6369	Hutchinson(2), Neville	1	2	3				7	6		10		4					11		9		8		5		
34	23	YORK CITY	4	1-0	1-0	8655	Walsh	1	2	3				7	6		10		4					11		9		8		5		
35	30	DONCASTER ROVERS	4	1-0	0-0	7965	Riley	1	2	3				7	6		10		4					11		9		8*		5		12
36	5 Apr	Plymouth Argyle	5	0-1	0-0	9959		1	2	3				7	6*		10		4					11		9		8		5		12
37	8	HULL CITY	4	2-0	0-0	11952	Johnson, Pritchard	1	2	3				7	6		10		4					11		9		8		5		8
38	13	Bristol Rovers	5	0-1	0-0	12957		1	2	3				7	6*		10		4					11		9		12		5		8
39	20	PRESTON NORTH END	5	4-0	2-0	6937	Riley(2), Walsh(2,1pen)	1	2	3				7*	6		10		4					11		9		12		5		8
40	23	Wigan Athletic	5	2-2	1-0	2423	Johnson, Walsh(pen)	1		3				11	7		10		4						2	9		6		5		8
41	27	Lincoln City	4	1-1	0-1	1908	Johnson	1		3					6		10		4					11	2	9		7		5		8
42	30	NEWPORT COUNTY	4	2-1	1-1	5952	Newman, Riley	1		3					12		6		10		4				11	2	9		7		5		8*
43	4 May	A.F.C. BOURNEMOUTH	4	2-0	1-0	7083	Marshall, Riley	1		3					12		6		10		4				11*	2	9		7		5	8	
44	6	Burnley	4	1-0	0-0	4460	Neville	1		3					7		6				4	12			11	2	9		8		5	10*
45	11	READING	4	2-3	2-1	7038	Neville, Riley	1		3					7		6		12		10*			4	11	2	9		8		5	
46	17	Swansea City	5	0-0	0-0	10709		1		3					11	7*	6		10			4			12	2	9		8		5	
					Apps.			41	30	34	6	25	13	39	44	17	45	10	37	11	10		34	22	29	1	26	3	1	19	3	6
					Subs.										3					6	3	1	1	1	1		2		2		1	2	2
					Goals				3			1		6	18	3	20	4			1		1		4		4				2	3

F.A. CUP

								Shaw	Stevens	Newman	Rogers	Phillipson-Masters	Hirst	Pritchard	Riley	Morgan	Walsh	Crawford	Curle	Halliday	Ritchie	Cooper	Stroud	Llewellyn	Hutchinson	Hooper	Neville	Waugh	Leigh	Hughes	Marshall	Johnson
1R	17 Nov	Fisher Athletic		1-0	1-0	2000	Riley	1				5		7	6	9	10		4	3		8		11	2							
2R	8 Dec	BRISTOL ROVERS		1-3	1-3	19367	Halliday (£45300)					5	8*	7	6		10		4	3	12			11	2	9	1					

F.L. (MILK) CUP

								Shaw	Stevens	Newman	Rogers	Phillipson-Masters	Hirst	Pritchard	Riley	Morgan	Walsh	Crawford	Curle	Halliday	Ritchie
1R1	28 Aug	NEWPORT COUNTY		2-1	1-1	5424	Crawford, Riley	1	2	3	4	5	6	7	8	9	10	11			
1R2	4 Sep	Newport County		3-0	2-0	3276	Morgan(2), Riley	1	2	3	4	5	6	7	8	9*	10	11	12		
2R1	25	WEST HAM UNITED		2-2	2-2	15894	Morgan, Walsh	1	2	3		5	6	7	8	9	10	11		4	
2R2	9 Oct	West Ham United		1-6	1-1	11376	Walsh(pen)	1	2	3		4		7	6	9	10	11	5		8

ASSOCIATE MEMBERS (FREIGHT ROVER) TROPHY

								Shaw	Stevens	Newman	Rogers	Phillipson-Masters	Hirst	Pritchard	Riley	Morgan	Walsh	Crawford	Curle	Halliday	Ritchie	Cooper	Stroud	Llewellyn	Hutchinson	Hooper	Neville	Waugh	Leigh	Hughes	Marshall
1R1	6 Feb	Hereford United		1-1	1-0	2690	Walsh	1	2			5		7	6		10		4					11	3	9		8			
1R2	20	HEREFORD UNITED		1-0	0-0	3446	Riley	1	2	3			7		6		10	12	4					11		9		8*		5	
2R	18 Mar	PORT VALE		2-1	1-1	3635	Walsh(2,1pen)	1	2	3				7	6		10		4					11		9		8		5	
SQF	25 Apr	NEWPORT COUNTY		1-2	0-0	3167	Walsh(pen)	1		3				7*	6		10		4	12				11	2	9		8		5	

GLOUCESTERSHIRE CUP FINAL

	21 May	Bristol Rovers		1-3	0-1	4033	Walsh(pen) (Extra-time, 1-1 at end 90 mins)

FRIENDLIES

1	28 Jul	Bristol Manor Farm		2-1	1-0	500	Riley, Wiffill (St. Peter's Hospice Benefit)
2	1 Aug	Exeter City		0-0	0-0		
3	4	Hereford United		3-3	1-2		Riley(2), Morgan
4	7	CHELSEA		1-0	1-0	4400	Pritchard
5	11	Cheltenham Town		6-2	2-1		Walsh(2), Cooper, Curle, Morgan, O.G.
6	15	NOTTS COUNTY		2-2	2-2	2000	Op de Beeck, Pritchard
7	18	Torquay United		1-0	0-0	540	Morgan
8	13 May	WEST BROMWICH ALB.		2-4	1-0	1950	Hughes, Walsh (John Shaw Benefit)

FINAL LEAGUE TABLE

1	Bradford	46	28	10	8	77	45	94
2	Millwall	46	26	12	8	83	42	90
3	Hull City	46	25	12	9	88	49	87
4	Gillingham	46	25	8	13	80	62	83
5	Bristol City	46	24	9	13	74	47	81
6	Bristol Rovers	46	21	12	13	66	48	75
7	Derby	46	19	13	14	65	54	70
8	York	46	20	9	17	70	57	69
9	Reading	46	19	12	15	68	62	69
10	Bournemouth	46	19	11	16	57	46	68
11	Walsall	46	18	13	15	58	52	67
12	Rotherham	46	18	11	17	55	55	65
13	Brentford	46	16	14	16	62	64	62
14	Doncaster	46	17	8	21	72	74	59
15	Plymouth	46	15	14	17	62	65	59
16	Wigan	46	15	14	17	60	64	59
17	Bolton	46	16	6	24	69	75	54
18	Newport	46	13	13	20	55	67	52
19	Lincoln	46	11	18	17	50	51	51
20	Swansea	46	12	11	23	53	80	47
21	Burnley	46	11	13	22	60	73	46
22	Orient	46	11	13	22	51	76	46
23	Preston	46	13	7	26	51	100	46
24	Cambridge	46	4	9	33	37	95	21

SEASON 1985-86
FOOTBALL (CANON) LEAGUE DIVISION THREE

No.	Date	Opposition	Pos.	Res.	H.T.	Att.	Goalscorers	Weugh K.	Llewellyn A.D.	Williams B.	Curle K.	Hughes M.	Riley G.	Marshall G.	Huchinson R.	Emmanuel J.G.	Neville S.F.	Walsh A.	Johnsons S.	Newman R.N.	Rogers L.M.	Pritchard H.K.	Hirst M.P.	Moyes D.W.	Tong D.J.	Tanner M.W.	Bryant R.J.	Vaughan J.	Underhill G.S.	Hale D.	Moore G.	Honor C.R.
1	17 Aug	WALSALL		2-3	1-1	7196	Neville, Walsh(pen)	1	2	3	4	5	6	7*	8	9	10	11	12													
2	24	A.F.C. Bournemouth	24	0-5	0-4	4969		1	2	8	4	5		6	7		11	10	9	3												
3	26	GILLINGHAM	24	1-2	1-0	6052	Hutchinson	1	2	8	4		12	6			11*	10	9	3		5 7										
4	31	Rotherham United	24	0-2	0-1	3134		1	2		4		12		8		11	10	9	3	5	7	6*									
5	7 Sep	WIGAN ATHLETIC	23	1-0	0-0	5673	Pritchard	1	2	6	4		12		8		10*	11	9	3	5	7										
6	14	Cardiff City	20	3-1	1-0	4412	Walsh(2), Pritchard	1	2	6	4		12		8		11	10	9*	3	5	7										
7	17	DERBY COUNTY	20	1-1	1-0	7750	Newman	1	2	6	4		9	12	8		11*	10		3	5	7										
8	21	York City	19	1-1	0-1	3904	Pritchard	1	2	6	4		9*	12	8		11	10		3	5	7										
9	28	BLACKPOOL	16	2-1	1-1	6570	Neville, Pritchard	1	2	6	4		9*		8		11	10	12	3	5	7										
10	1 Oct	Newport County	18	1-3	0-0	3776	Neville	1	2	6	4		12		8		11	10	9*	3	5	7										
11	5	CHESTERFIELD	18	0-0	0-0	6416		1	2*	6	4		12		8		11	10	9	3	5	7										
12	12	Notts County	19	0-4	0-2	4332		1		6	4		12		8		11	10	9*	3	2	7		5								
13	19	DARLINGTON	17	1-0	1-0	5878	Walsh	1		6	4		9		8		11	10		3	2	7		5								
14	22	Bury	18	3-6	0-1	2460	Neville, Riley, Walsh(pen)	1		6	4		9		8		11	10	12	3*	2	7		5								
15	26	WOLVERHAMPTON W.	16	3-0	2-0	7138	Hutchinson, Riley, Walsh(pen)	1	2		4				8		11	10		3	5	7		9								
16	2 Nov	Doncaster Rovers	14	1-1	1-0	2871	Riley	1	2		4		6		8		11	10		3	5	7		9								
17	6	Lincoln City	15	1-1	1-1	1379	Neville	1	2		4		6		8		11	10		3	5	7		9								
18	9	BRENTFORD	16	0-0	0-0	6596		1	2		4		6		8		11	10*	12	3	5	7		9								
19	23	Swansea City	14	3-1	2-1	4414	Hutchinson(2), Walsh	1	2		4		6		8		11	10		3	5	7		9								
20	30	BOLTON WANDERERS	12	2-0	1-0	6253	Neville, Riley	1	2		4		6		8		11	10		3	5	7		9								
21	14 Dec	Reading	13	0-1	0-0	5565		1	2		4		6		8		11	10		3	5			9	7							
22	21	A.F.C. BOURNEMOUTH	13	1-3	0-1	5691	Hutchinson	1	2		4		6		8		11	10		3	5	7		9								
23	26	PLYMOUTH ARGYLE	12	2-0	2-0	8298	Neville, Walsh(pen)	1	2		4		6		8		11	10		3		7		9	5							
24	28	Gillingham	12	1-1	0-0	4672	Newman	1			4		6		8		11	10		2	6	7		9	5							
25	7 Jan	DONCASTER ROVERS	12	4-1	0-0	5385	Walsh(2,1pen), Neville, Pritchard	1		3	4		6		8		11	10		2		7		9	5							
26	11	ROTHERHAM UNITED	12	3-1	2-0	6672	Neville, Walsh, Williams	1		3	4		6		8		11	10		2		7		9	5							
27	18	Walsall	12	1-2	1-0	4952	Neville	1		3	4	12	6		8		11	10		2		7*		9	5							
28	25	CARDIFF CITY	12	2-1	2-1	7541	Marshall, Neville	1		3	4		6	7	8		11	10		2				9	5							
29	1 Feb	Wigan Athletic	10	1-1	0-1	3402	Newman	1	7	3	4		6			12	11	10		2				9	5	8*						
30	4	BURY	9	4-1	1-0	5074	Riley(2), Neville, Walsh	1		3	4		6	7			11	10		2				9	5							
31	22	YORK CITY	9	2-2	1-1	6409	Moyes, Neville	1	2	3	4		6		8		11	10						9	5							
32	1 Mar	Blackpool	10	1-2	0-1	3366	Bryant	1*	2	3	4		6	12	8		11	10						9	5		7					
33	4	NEWPORT COUNTY	8	3-1	1-0	4395	Curle, Neville, Walsh		2	3	4		6	7	8*		11	10	12					9	5			1				
34	8	Chesterfield	9	0-0		2547			2	3	4		6	7	8		11	10		9					5			1				
35	15	NOTTS COUNTY	7	3-0	1-0	5701	Moyes, Riley, Walsh	1	2	3	4		6	7	8		11	10						9	5							
36	19	Derby County	7	0-2	0-2	11113		1	2	3	4		6	7*	8		11	10			12			9	5							
37	22	Wolverhampton Wndrs	10	1-2	0-0	3696	Walsh	1	2	3			6	7	8		11*	10			12			9	5			4				
38	29	BRISTOL ROVERS	9	2-0	1-0	12171	Neville, Walsh	1	2	3			6		8		11	10			12	7			5				9*			
39	5 Apr	LINCOLN CITY	10	1-1	0-1	5395	Neville	1	2	3	4		6	10	8		11					7			5					9		
40	13	Brentford	9	2-1	2-1	3702	Pritchard, Riley	1	2	3	4		6	10*	8		11				12	7			5					9		
41	19	SWANSEA CITY	11	1-1	0-0	6013		1	2	3	4		6*		8		11	10				7			5					9	12	
42	22	Bristol Rovers	10	1-1	0-0	9926	Neville	1	2	3	4		6		8		11	10				7			5					9		
43	26	Bolton Wanderers	9	4-0	1-0	4493	Neville(2), Llewellyn, Riley	1	2	3	4		6		8		11	10		8		7			5					9		
44	29	Plymouth Argyle	9	0-4	0-1	19990		1	2	3	4		6				11	10		8		7			5					9		
45	3 May	READING	9	3-0	3-0	7814	Walsh(2pens), Neville	1	2	3	4		6		8		11	10		4		7			5					9		
46	15	Darlington	9	1-1	0-1	1615	Riley	1	2	3	4		12	7			11*	10		8					5	9						6
		Apps						44	38	36	44	2	33	14	42	2	46	44	8	37	21	32	1	27	19	2	2	2	1	8		1
		Subs.																	8	5				5	2	2						1	
		Goals							1	1	1		10	2	5		19	18		3		6	2	2			1					

F.A. CUP

	Date	Opposition	Res.	H.T.	Att.	Goalscorers	Weugh	Llewellyn	Williams	Curle	Hughes	Riley	Marshall	Huchinson	Emmanuel	Neville	Walsh	Johnsons	Newman	Rogers	Pritchard	Moyes
1R	17 Nov	Swindon Town	0-0	0-0	10468		1	2		4		6		8		11	10		3	5	7	9
1Rr	20	SWINDON TOWN	4-2	1-0	8979	Neville(3), Riley	1	2	3			10		7		11	9		5	4	6	8
2R	7 Dec	EXETER CITY	1-2	1-1	8052	Walsh(pen)	1	2*	12	4		6		8		11	10		3	5	7	9

F.L. (MILK) CUP

	Date	Opposition	Res.	H.T.	Att.	Goalscorers	Weugh	Llewellyn	Williams	Curle	Hughes	Riley	Marshall	Huchinson	Emmanuel	Neville	Walsh	Johnsons	Newman	Rogers	Pritchard
1R1	21 Aug	Hereford United	1-5	0-3	2449	Johnson	1	2	3	4	5	6	7*	8	9	10	11	12			
1R2	3 Sep	HEREFORD UNITED	2-0	1-0	2373	Hutchinson, Johnson	1	2	6*	4		12		8		11	10	9	3	5	7

ASSOCIATE MEMBERS (FREIGHT ROVER) TROPHY

	Date	Opposition	Pos.	Res.	H.T.	Att.	Goalscorers	Weugh	Llewellyn	Williams	Curle	Hughes	Riley	Marshall	Huchinson	Emmanuel	Neville	Walsh	Johnsons	Newman	Rogers	Pritchard	Moyes	Tong	Underhill
GM	14 Jan	PLYMOUTH ARGYLE	1	0-0	0-0	2402		1		3	4	12	6		8		11	10		2		7*	9	5	
GM	28	Walsall	1	2-1	2-1	2625	Walsh, O.G.	1	7	3	4		6		8		11*	10		2	12		9	5	
SQF	27 Mar	NORTHAMPTON TOWN		3-2	1-1	3038	Hutchinson, Neville, Riley	1	2	3	4		6	7*	8		11	10			9		9	5	
SSF	16 Apr	GILLINGHAM		3-0	0-0	5707	Neville, Riley, Walsh(pen)	1	2	3	4		6		8		11	10				7		5	9
SF1	6 May	Hereford United		0-2	0-2	7608		1	2	3	4		6*		8		11	10				7	10	5	9
SF2	9	HEREFORD UNITED		3-0	0-0	11558	Neville, Riley, O.G. (Extra-time played)	1	12	3	4		6	14	8		11	10		2		7*		5	9*
F	24	Bolton Wanderers		3-0	1-0	54502	Riley(2), Pritchard (at Wembley Stadium)	1		3	4		6		8		11	10		2		7		5	9

GLOUCESTERSHIRE CUP FINAL

	Date	Opposition	Res.	H.T.	Att.	Goalscorers
	9 Sep	BRISTOL ROVERS	1-0	0-0	4894	Johnson(pen)

FRIENDLIES

	Date	Opposition	Res.	H.T.	Att.	Goalscorers
1	25 Jul	Coleford United	11-0			Marshall(3), Walsh(3), Lane(2), Hirst, Neville, Smith
2	27	Hereford United	0-3	0-2	1000	
3	30	Bath City	2-2	2-0		Hughes, Walsh(pen)
4	3 Aug	MANCHESTER UNITED	0-1	0-0	6707	
5	6	Cheltenham Town	1-3	0-0		Smith
6	7	WIMBLEDON	2-2	2-0	861	Hutchinson, Neville
7	10	LIVERPOOL	3-3	1-3	8182	Neville(2), O.G.
8	12	Torquay United	0-2	0-1		
9	26 Nov	Bristol Manor Farm*	3-2	3-0	500	Neville, Riley, Walsh

* Dennis Thorne Memorial Match/Floodlight opening

FINAL LEAGUE TABLE (TOP POSITIONS)

		P	W	D	L	F	A	Pts
1	Reading	46	29	7	10	67	50	94
2	Plymouth	46	26	9	11	88	53	87
3	Derby	46	23	15	8	80	41	84
4	Wigan	46	23	14	9	82	48	83
5	Gillingham	46	22	13	11	81	54	79
6	Walsall	46	22	9	15	90	64	75
7	York	46	20	11	15	77	58	71
8	Notts County	46	19	14	13	71	60	71
9	Bristol City	46	18	14	14	69	60	68
10	Brentford	46	18	14	14	58	61	68
11	Doncaster	46	16	16	14	45	52	64
12	Blackpool	46	17	12	17	66	55	63
13	Darlington	46	15	13	18	61	78	58
14	Rotherham	46	15	12	19	61	59	57
15	Bournemouth	46	15	9	22	65	72	54
16	Bristol Rovers	46	14	12	20	51	75	54
17	Chesterfield	46	13	14	19	61	64	53
18	Bolton	46	15	8	23	54	68	53
19	Newport	46	11	18	17	52	65	51

1985-86 Season
Back: Lee Rogers, Newman, Hughes, Johnson, Pritchard, Curle.
Middle: Lockhart (Physiotherapist), Marshall, Walsh, Waugh, West, N.Smith.
Front: Neville, Llewellyn, Hutchinson, Hirst, Brian Williams.

1986-87 squad with the Freight Rover Trophy won the previous season.
Back: Fitzpatrick, Curle, McPhail, Lee Rogers.
Middle: Neville, Marshall, Tanner, Moyes, Waugh, Newman, Walsh, Honor, Underhill.
Front: Owen, Llewellyn, Harle, Hutchinson, Brian Williams, Riley, Hamson, Moore.

SEASON 1986-87

FOOTBALL (TODAY) LEAGUE DIVISION THREE

No.	Date	Opposition	Pos.	Res.	H.T.	Att.	Goalscorers	Waugh K.	Llewellyn A.D.	Newman R.N.	Curle K.	Moyes D.W.	Riley G.	Owen G.	Hutchinson R.	Harle D.	Walsh A.	Neville S.F.	Hamson G.	Fitzpatrick P.J.	Williams B.	Marshall G.	Rogers L.M.	MacPhail J.	Withey G.	Morgan T.J.	Jordan J.	Tanner M.W.	Galliers S.	Honor C.R.	Harvey J.	Moore G.
1	23 Aug	BURY		2-2	2-2	8238	Hutchinson, Moyes	1	2	3	4	5	6	7	8	9	10	11														
2	30	Gillingham		1-1	1-1	4049	Hamson	1	3	2	4	5	6	7	8	9	10		11													
3	6 Sep	WIGAN ATHLETIC	9	2-1	1-1	6729	Moyes, Walsh	1	2	3	4	5	6	7	8*	9	10		11	12												
4	13	Chesterfield	2	3-0	1-0	2605	Harle, Newman, Owen	1	2	3	4	5	6	7	8	9	10		11													
5	17	Doncaster Rovers	7	0-1	0-0	2265		1	2	3	4	5	6	7	8	9	10	12	11*													
6	20	CARLISLE UNITED	5	3-0	2-0	7040	Walsh(2), Moyes	1	2	12	4	5	6	7	8	9*	10	11			3											
7	27	A.F.C. Bournemouth	7	0-2	0-0	5975		1	2		4	5	6	7	8	9	10	11			3											
8	30	DARLINGTON	9	1-1	0-0	6677	Newman	1	2	12	4	5	6*	7	8	9	10	11			3											
9	4 Oct	Chester City	7	3-0	1-0	2796	Hamson, Harle, Neville	1		2	4	5		7	8	9	10	11	6		3											
10	11	YORK CITY	5	3-0	0-0	7951	Walsh(2), Neville	1	2	5	4			7	8*	9	10	11	6		3	12										
11	25	MIDDLESBROUGH	9	2-2	2-2	8800	Walsh(2,1pen)	1		2			12	7*		9	10	11	6		3	8	4	5								
12	1 Nov	Blackpool	10	0-1	0-0	4370		1	7	2			12			9	10	11	6		3	8*	4	5								
13	4	MANSFIELD TOWN	10	0-0	0-0	6407		1		2			6			9	10	11	8		3	7*	4	5	12							
14	8	Fulham	8	3-0	2-0	4453	Neville(2), Walsh(pen)	1		2		4	6		8	9	10	11	7		3			5								
15	22	ROTHERHAM UNITED	9	0-1	0-1	6756		1		2		4	6	12	8	9*	10				3	7		5	11							
16	29	Notts County	11	0-2	0-2	3987		1		2		4		7	8		10	11	6	9	3			5								
17	2 Dec	Newport County	9	1-0	1-0	3205	Neville	1		2		4		7	8		10	11	6	9	3			5								
18	14	Swindon Town	7	2-1	0-1	7637	Neville(2)	1		2		4	12	7*	8		10	11		9	3	6		5								
19	20	BOLTON WANDERERS	6	4-1	2-1	8208	Neville, Newman, Riley, Walsh	1	12	2		4	6		8*		10	11		9	3	7		5								
20	26	Port Vale	7	0-0	0-0	4118		1		2		4	7		8		10	11		9	3	6		5								
21	27	WALSALL	7	2-1	0-1	10193	Fitzpatrick, MacPhail(pen)	1		2	8	4	6				10	11		9	3	7		5								
22	1 Jan	BRISTOL ROVERS	7	0-1	0-0	17122		1		2	8	4	7*		12		10	11		9	3	6		5								
23	3	Rotherham United	7	0-2	0-0	3270		1		2	7	4	6		8		10	11		9*	3	12		5								
24	24	Wigan Athletic	8	1-3	1-2	3092	Walsh	1		2	8	4	12				10	11*		6	3	7		5		9						
25	31	CHESTERFIELD	8	1-0	0-0	6426	Walsh	1		6	2	4	12	11			10			9	3	7		5*		8						
26	7 Feb	DONCASTER ROVERS	7	5-0	2-0	8782	Walsh(3), Newman, Owen,	1		2	6	4		7			10			8*	3			5		9	11	12				
27	14	Carlisle United	5	2-1	2-0	2500	Jordan, Morgan	1	2	11	4	5		7			10			9	3					6	8					
28	21	A.F.C. BOURNEMOUTH	4	2-0	1-0	14539	Owen(pen), O.G.	1	5	2	4	6		7			10				3					9	11		8			
29	28	Darlington	7	0-0	0-0	2044		1	5	2	6	4		7			10			8	3					9	11					
30	3 Mar	BLACKPOOL	5	3-1	3-1	10769	Fitzpatrick, Newman, Walsh	1	5	2	6	4		7			10			8	3					9	11					
31	7	Middlesbrough	5	0-1	0-1	10220		1	5	2	6	4	12	7			10			8*	3					9	11					
32	14	NEWPORT COUNTY	5	4-0	2-0	9137	Jordon, Morgan, Newman, Williams(pen)	1	5	2	6	4		7			10*				3	12				9	11	8				
33	17	Brentford	6	1-1	1-0	4051	Owen	1	5	2	6	4		7			10				3					9	11	8				
34	21	York City	6	1-1	0-1	2863	Tanner	1	5	2	6*	4	11	7			10				3	12				9		8				
35	28	CHESTER CITY	6	1-0	0-0	8230	Morgan	1	5	2		4	11	7			10			6	3					9		8				
36	31	Bury	5	2-1	2-1	2200	Morgan, Owen	1	5	2		4		7*			10			6	3	12				9	11			8		
37	4 Apr	FULHAM	5	0-0	0-0	8551		1	5	2				7			10			6*	3			4		9	11			12	8	
38	11	Mansfield Town	7	0-2	0-0	2884		1	6	2		4		7			10				3			5		9	11				8	
39	18	Bristol Rovers	7	0-0	0-0	4695		1	6	2		4					10				3	7		5		9	11		8			
40	20	PORT VALE	7	1-0	1-0	8482	Walsh	1	6	2		4	9	7			10*				3	12		5			11		8			
41	22	GILLINGHAM	6	2-0	2-0	10260	Marshall, Williams(pen)	1	6	2		4	9	7							3	10		5			11		8			
42	25	Bolton Wanderers	6	0-0	0-0	4414		1	6	2	12	4	9	7*							3	10		5			11		8			
43	28	BRENTFORD	7	0-2	0-0	9050		1	6	2	12	4	9				10*				3	7		5			11		8			
44	2 May	NOTTS COUNTY	5	3-1	1-1	9189	Jordon, Marshall, Morgan	1	6	2		4		7							3	10		5		9	11		8			
45	4	Walsall	5	1-1	0-0	7684	Morgan	1	6	2	12	4		7							3	10*		5		9	11		8			
46	9	SWINDON TOWN	6	1-1	1-0	19201	Morgan	1	6	2	12	4		7							3*	10		5		9	11		8			
							Apps.	46	30	43	24	41	22	34	18	15	41	19	12	18	41	18	3	26	1	19	19	4	9	1	2	
							Subs.		1	2	4		6	1	1			1		1		6			1			1		1		
							Goals			6		3	1	5	1	2	16	8	2	2	2	2		1		7	3	1				

F.A. CUP

Rd	Date	Opposition	Pos.	Res.	H.T.	Att.	Goalscorers	Waugh K.	Llewellyn A.D.	Newman R.N.	Curle K.	Moyes D.W.	Riley G.	Owen G.	Hutchinson R.	Harle D.	Walsh A.	Neville S.F.	Hamson G.	Fitzpatrick P.J.	Williams B.	Marshall G.	Rogers L.M.	MacPhail J.	Withey G.	Morgan T.J.	Jordan J.	Tanner M.W.	Galliers S.	Honor C.R.	Harvey J.	Moore G.
1R	15 Nov	V.S. RUGBY		3-1	0-0	7069	Hutchinson, Marshall, Walsh	1		2		4	6		8	9	10		7*		3	12		5	11							
2R	6 Dec	BATH CITY		1-1	0-0	10053	Neville (Switched to Ashton Gate)	1		2		4		7	8		10	11		9	3	6		5								
2Rr	9	BATH CITY		3-0	1-0	9058	Owen(2,1pen), Neville	1		2		4		7	8		10	11		9	3	6		5								
3R	10 Jan	PLYMOUTH ARGYLE		1-1	0-0	16943	Riley	1	8	2		4	7				10	11		9	3	6		5								
3Rr	19	Plymouth Argyle		1-3	0-0	14142	Marshall (Extra-time played, 0-0 at 90 mins)	1	8	2		4	7				10	11		9	3	12		5				6*				

F.L. (LITTLEWOODS) CUP

Rd	Date	Opposition	Pos.	Res.	H.T.	Att.	Goalscorers	Waugh K.	Llewellyn A.D.	Newman R.N.	Curle K.	Moyes D.W.	Riley G.	Owen G.	Hutchinson R.	Harle D.	Walsh A.	Neville S.F.	Hamson G.	Fitzpatrick P.J.	Williams B.	Marshall G.	Rogers L.M.	MacPhail J.	Withey G.	Morgan T.J.	Jordan J.	Tanner M.W.	Galliers S.	Honor C.R.	Harvey J.	Moore G.
1R1	26 Aug	A.F.C. Bournemouth		1-0	0-0	2631	Walsh	1	2	3	4	5	6	7	8	9	10		11													
1R2	2 Sep	A.F.C. BOURNEMOUTH		1-1	0-0	4776	Riley (Extra-time played, 0-1 at 90 mins)	1	2	3	4	5	6	7	8	9*	10		11"	12		14										
2R1	23	SHEFFIELD UNITED		2-2	1-2	8366	Neville, Walsh(pen)	1	2		4	5	6*	7	8		10	9		11	3	12										
2R2	7 Oct	Sheffield United		0-3	0-1	5587		1	2	12	4	5		7	8*	9	10	11"	6		3				14							

ASSOCIATE MEMBERS (FREIGHT ROVER) TROPHY

Rd	Date	Opposition	Pos.	Res.	H.T.	Att.	Goalscorers	Waugh K.	Llewellyn A.D.	Newman R.N.	Curle K.	Moyes D.W.	Riley G.	Owen G.	Hutchinson R.	Harle D.	Walsh A.	Neville S.F.	Hamson G.	Fitzpatrick P.J.	Williams B.	Marshall G.	Rogers L.M.	MacPhail J.	Withey G.	Morgan T.J.	Jordan J.	Tanner M.W.	Galliers S.	Honor C.R.	Harvey J.	Moore G.
GM	26 Nov	Exeter City		1-1	0-1	1338	Moyes	1		2		4		7	8		10	11	6	9	3			5								
GM	16 Dec	BRISTOL ROVERS		3-0	1-0	6903	Moyes, Newman, Walsh	1		2		4	7		8		10	11*		9	3	6		5								12
1R	27 Jan	SOUTHEND UNITED		1-0	1-0	4195	Moyes	1		2	6	4	8				10			9	3	7	11	5								
SQF	10 Feb	BRENTFORD		3-0	0-0	7425	Jordon(2), Riley	1	5	2	6	4	9	7			10			8	3						11					
SSF	10 Mar	GILLINGHAM		2-0	2-0	10508	Moyes, Tanner	1	5	2	6	4	9	7			10				3	12					11	8*				
SF1	8 Apr	Aldershot		2-1	2-1	5000	Jordon, Newman	1	6	2		4	9	7			10				3			5			11		8			
SF2	14	ALDERSHOT		2-0	2-0	16371	Jordan, Walsh (£45000)	1	6	2		4	9	7"			10				3	14		5*			11	12	8			
F	24 May	Mansfield Town*		1-1	0-0	58586	Riley (£324592)	1	6*	2	14	4	9	7			8"			12	3	10		5			11					

* Final at Wembley Stadium (Lost penalty shoot-out 5-4 after extra-time. Score after 90 minutes, 1-1).

GLOUCESTERSHIRE CUP FINAL

Held over to 1987-88 Season

FRIENDLIES

No.	Date	Opposition	Res.	H.T.	Att.	Goalscorers
1	23 Jul	R.A.F. Hullavington	5-0			Unknown(5)
2	27	Midsomer Norton Select	10-0			Newman(2), Unknown(8)
3	29	Bath City	2-0	0-0		Neville, O.G.
4	30	Torrington	3-1	3-0		Moyes, Newman, Riley
5	31	Coleford United	5-0			Walsh(3), Neville(2)
6	2 Aug	Cheltenham Town	2-3	2-1		Neville(2)
7	6	Brighton & Hove Albion	0-3	0-0		
8	9	WEST BROMWICH ALB.	1-0	1-0	2227	Walsh
9	12	BIRMINGHAM CITY	0-1	0-0	1755	
10	15	Swansea City	0-0	0-0		
11	15 Feb	Merthyr Tydfil	4-1	3-0		Riley(2), Underhill, Walsh

FINAL LEAGUE TABLE (TOP POSITIONS)

1	Bournemouth	46	29	10	7	76	40	97
2	Middlesborough	46	28	10	8	67	30	94
3	Swindon	46	25	12	9	77	47	87
4	Wigan	46	25	10	11	83	60	85
5	Gillingham	46	23	9	14	65	48	78
6	Bristol City	46	21	14	11	63	36	77
7	Notts County	46	21	13	12	77	56	76
8	Walsall	46	22	9	15	80	67	75
9	Blackpool	46	16	16	14	74	59	64
10	Mansfield	46	15	16	15	52	55	61
11	Brentford	46	15	15	16	64	66	60
12	Port Vale	46	15	12	19	76	70	57
13	Doncaster	46	14	15	17	56	62	57
14	Rotherham	46	15	12	19	48	57	57
15	Chester	46	13	17	16	61	59	56
16	Bury	46	14	13	19	54	60	55
17	Chesterfield	46	13	15	18	56	69	54
18	Fulham	46	12	17	17	59	77	53
19	Bristol Rovers	46	13	12	21	49	75	51

SEASON 1987-88
FOOTBALL (BARCLAYS) LEAGUE DIV. THREE

No.	Date	Opposition	Pos.	Res.	H.T.	Att.	Goalscorers	Waugh K.	Llewellyn A.D.	Bromage R.	Moyes D.W.	Newman R.N.	Tanner M.W.	Marshall G.	Fitzpatrick P.J.	Caldwell A.	Walsh A.	Jordan J.	Owen G.	Harvey J.	Neville S.F.	Galliers S.	Curle K.	Humphries G.	Honor C.R.	Pender J.P.	Shutt C.S.	Prudoe M.	Mardon P.	Hawkins N.	Vaughan J.	Milne R.	McClaren S.	Gordon C.K.	Coombe M.	Rogers L.M.
1	15 Aug	Mansfield Town		0-2	0-2	5441		1	2	3	4	5	6	7	8"	9*	10	11	12	14																
2	22	PRESTON NORTH END	12	3-1	1-0	7655	Owen(2), Walsh(pen)	1	2	3	4	5	6	7	8		10	11	9																	
3	29	Brentford	7	2-0	0-0	4328	Newman(pen), Owen	1	2	3	4	5	6		8		10	11	9		7															
4	31	PORT VALE	3	1-0	0-0	8716	Neville	1	2	3	4	5	6	7"	8	14	10*	11	9		12															
5	5 Sep	Bury	4	1-1	1-1	2376	Neville	1	2	3	4	5	6		8	9	10	11			7															
6	12	BRISTOL ROVERS	7	3-3	1-1	14746	Fitzpatrick, Moyes, Walsh	1	2	3	4	5		7	8		10	11			9	6														
7	15	Walsall	7	1-1	0-0	6425	Llewellyn	1	2	3	4	5			8		10	11	7		9	6														
8	19	Notts County	5	1-0	0-0	5705	Newman(pen)	1	2	3	4	5			8		10	11	7		9	6														
9	26	GILLINGHAM	6	3-3	1-2	10070	Owen(2), Fitzpatrick	1	2	3	4	5			8	14	10	11"	9		7	6														
10	29	CHESTERFIELD	1	2-1	1-0	9088	Newman, Owen	1	2	3	4	5			8		10	11	9"		7	6														
11	3 Oct	Northampton Town	5	0-3	0-1	6234		1	2	3	4	5		12	8	14	10	11*	9"		7	6														
12	10	SOUTHEND UNITED	3	3-2	1-1	8606	Newman(2,1pen), Fitzpatrick	1	14	3	4	5		7*	8		10*	11	9		12	6	2													
13	17	Grimsby Town	3	4-1	4-0	3100	Newman(2), Jordan, Neville	1	2	3	4	5	6	7*			12	11	9		10		8													
14	20	SUNDERLAND	3	0-1	0-1	15109		1	2	3	4	5	14				12	10*	11		9	7	6"	8												
15	24	Rotherham United	6	1-4	1-3	3397	Caldwell	1	2	3	4	5	7"		8*	10	12	11	9				6	14												
16	3 Nov	Blackpool	8	2-4	1-1	3140	Shutt(2)	1		3		2		10	8			11	7			6		4		5	9									
17	7	Aldershot	14	1-2	0-1	4324	Shutt		2	3		8		10"			14		7		11	6		4		5	9	1								
18	21	CHESTER CITY	12	2-2	1-2	8103	Newman, Shutt		2	3		5		11	8			14	7"		10	6		4			9	1								
19	28	Wigan Athletic	13	1-1	1-0	2879	Walsh		2	3		7			8		10	11				6		4		5	9	1								
20	12 Dec	YORK CITY	12	3-2	2-1	6238	Galliers(2), Fitzpatrick	1				3			8		10"	14	7		11	6		4		2	5	9								
21	15	FULHAM	7	4-0	3-0	6150	Shutt(4)	1	14			3			8"		10		7		11	6		4		2	5	9								
22	19	Doncaster Rovers	5	2-1	1-0	1819	Shutt, Walsh	1	14			3	7		8"		10				11	6		4		2	5	9								
23	26	Gillingham	5	1-1	1-0	6457	Newman(pen)	1	14			3	8"		7		10	12			11"	6		4		2	5	9								
24	28	BRIGHTON & HOVE ALB.	4	5-2	3-0	16058	Fitzpatrick, Jordan, Newman, Pender, Walsh	1	14			3		7*	8		10	12			11	6		4		2"	5	9								
25	1 Jan	BRENTFORD		2-3	0-3	12877	Galliers, Shutt	1				3	8	7*			10	12			11	6		4			5	9								
26	9	Preston North End	8	0-2	0-1	5229		1	2	3		8	14				10	12			11"	6		4			9		5	7*						
27	16	NOTTS COUNTY	8	2-1	0-1	9558	Jordan, Walsh	1	14	3		8		7*			10	12			11	6				2	5	9	4"							
28	6 Feb	BURY	8	3-2	0-1	9158	Galliers, Milne, Walsh		2	3		8					10				11	6				2	5	9	4		1	7				
29	9	WALSALL	7	0-0	0-0	8454			2	3		8				14	10				11"	6*				12	5	9	4		1	7				
30	13	Brighton & Hove Albion	7	2-3	0-1	8781	Caldwell, Walsh		2	3		8				14	10				11					6	5	9"	4		1	7				
31	20	MANSFIELD TOWN	8	1-2	1-2	9528	O.G.	1		3		8		14		9	10				11"					2	5		4			7	6			
32	27	NORTHAMPTON TOWN	9	2-2	1-2	8578	Walsh, O.G.	1	2			8			12		9	10			11*					4	5					7	6			
33	1 Mar	Chesterfield	8	4-1	2-1	1657	Caldwell, Milne, Pender, Walsh	1	2			8					9	10				11		4		3	5					7	6			
34	5	GRIMSBY TOWN	8	1-1	0-0	8343	Walsh	1	2			3					9	10			14	11*		4		12	5	8"				7	6			
35	11	Southend United	8	0-2	0-1	3664		1	2			3		14	12	9					11*	8		4		10	5					7"	6			
36	19	Fulham	8	0-0	0-0	4896		1	2					9	12	10*					11	8				3	5		4			7	6			
37	26	ROTHERHAM UNITED	7	2-0	0-0	7517	Gordon(pen), Neville	1	2					12			10				11	8		4		3	5					7	6	9*		
38	2 Apr	ALDERSHOT	7	2-0	1-0	8712	Milne, Walsh	1	2	14							10				11	8		4			5	12				7"	6	9*		
39	4	Chester City	7	0-1	0-1	2849		1	2			3					10				11"8			4			5	12				7	6	9		
40	9	BLACKPOOL	7	2-1	1-0	6460	Gordon(pen), McClaren	1	2			3					10				11"8			4			5					7	6	9		
41	12	Bristol Rovers	7	2-1	1-0	5947		1	2			3					10	12			11"8			4			5					7*	6	9		
42	18	Port Vale	8	1-1	0-0	2671	Newman	1	2	3		11					10				8			4				12	5			7	6	9		
43	23	Sunderland	8	1-0	1-0	18225	Gordon	1	2	14		3					10				11"8			4			5	12				7	6	9*		
44	30	WIGAN ATHLETIC	7	4-1	2-1	7340	Galliers, Jordan, Marshall, Neville	1	2	3		4		14			10"	12			11*8						5	9				7	6			
45	2 May	York City	6	1-0	0-0	2616	Milne	1	2	3		4		10	14			12			11"8			4			5	9*				7	6			
46	7	DONCASTER ROVERS	5	1-0	0-0	18373	Gordon	1	2			3					10	12			11*8			4			5					7	6	9		
		Apps.						40	36	28	15	44	10	13	22	8	39	17	17		37	35	3	24		14	28	18	3	8	1	3	19	16	8		
		Subs.							6	2			2	6	2	8		11	1		1	3					3		4									
		Goals						1			1	11		1	5	3	12	4	6		5	5					2	10					4	1	4		

PROMOTION PLAY-OFFS

	Date			Res.	H.T.	Att.	Goalscorers	Waugh	Llewellyn			Newman		Marshall			Walsh	Jordan			Neville					Pender	Shutt					Milne	McClaren	Gordon	
SF1	15 May	SHEFFIELD UNITED		1-0	1-0	25335	Walsh	1	2			3					10	12			11*8			4			5	14					7	6	9"	
SF2	18	Sheffield United		1-1	1-0	19066	Shutt	1	2			3		14			10	12			8			4			5	11"					7	6	9*	
F1	25	WALSALL		1-3	1-0	25128	Walsh	1	2			3					10	12			11*8			4			5	9					7	6		
F2	28	Walsall*		2-0	1-0	13941	Newman, Shutt	1	2			3			12		10	11			8			4			5	9*					7	6		
F2r	30	Walsall		0-4	0-3	13007		1	2			3					10	11			8			4			5	9					7	6		

* Walsall won penalty shoot-out for right to stage the replay.

F.A. CUP

	Date			Res.	H.T.	Att.	Goalscorers	Waugh	Llewellyn			Newman		Marshall			Walsh	Jordan			Neville					Pender	Shutt					Milne	McClaren	Gordon		Rogers
1R	14 Nov	AYLESBURY UNITED		1-0	0-0	8263	Caldwell		2	3		8		12		11	10*		7			6		4			5	9									1
2R	5 Dec	TORQUAY UNITED		0-1	0-0	9027		1		3		8		14	7"		10	11*			12	6		4		2	5	9									

F.L. (LITTLEWOODS) CUP

	Date			Res.	H.T.	Att.	Goalscorers	Waugh	Llewellyn	Bromage	Moyes	Newman	Tanner	Marshall	Fitzpatrick	Caldwell	Walsh	Jordan	Owen		Neville	Galliers														
1R1	18 Aug	Swindon Town		0-3	0-0	6807		1	2	3	4	5	6	7*	8		10	11	9		12															
1R2	25	SWINDON TOWN		3-2	3-1	7013	Owen(2), Tanner	1	2	3	4	5	6	7"	8	14	10	11*	9		12															

ASSOCIATE MEMBERS (SHERPA VAN) TROPHY

	Date			Res.	H.T.	Att.	Goalscorers	Waugh	Llewellyn	Bromage	Moyes	Newman		Marshall		Caldwell	Walsh	Jordan	Owen	Harvey	Neville	Galliers					Shutt								Coombe
GM	10 Nov	SWANSEA CITY	1	2-0	2-0	5037	Shutt, Walsh		2	3		4			8	12	10		7		11*	6					5	9	1								
GM	24	Wolverhampton Wndrs	2	1-3	0-2	5174	Shutt		2	3		5		7	8	11	10					6					9	1									4
1D	19 Jan	Aldershot		0-1	0-0	8088	(Extra time played)	1	2	3		8		7"	11		10	12				11				0"	5	9		4							

GLOUCESTERSHIRE CUP FINAL

	Date			Res.	H.T.	Att.	Goalscorers
	2 Dec	Bristol Rovers		2-1	1-0	1376	Fitzpatrick(p),Tanner (1986-87 final held over)
	15 Mar	BRISTOL ROVERS		3-1	3-0	2278	Fitzpatrick, Galliers, Pender

FRIENDLIES

	Date			Res.	H.T.	Att.	Goalscorers
1	25 Jul	Swansea City		1-2	0-1	1508	Caldwell
2	29	SOUTHAMPTON		2-4	0-1	2815	Hawkins, Newman
3	1 Aug	Telford United		1-1	1-0		Walsh
4	4	BIRMINGHAM CITY		3-1	1-0	1586	Caldwell, Newman, O.G.
5	7	WEST BROMWICH ALB.		2-0	0-0	1495	Marshall, Owen

FINAL LEAGUE TABLE

Sunderland	46	27	12	7	92	48	93
Brighton & H.A.	46	23	15	8	69	47	84
Walsall	46	23	13	10	68	50	82
Notts County	46	23	12	11	82	49	81
Bristol City	46	21	12	13	77	62	75
Northampton Town	46	18	19	9	70	51	73
Wigan Athletic	46	20	12	14	70	61	72
Bristol Rovers	46	18	12	16	68	56	66
Fulham	46	19	9	18	69	60	66
Blackpool	46	17	14	15	71	62	65
Port Vale	46	18	11	17	58	56	65
Brentford	46	16	14	16	53	59	62
Gillingham	46	14	17	15	77	61	59
Bury	46	15	14	17	58	57	59
Chester City	46	14	16	16	51	62	58
Preston North End	46	15	13	18	48	59	58
Southend United	46	14	13	19	65	83	55
Chesterfield	46	15	10	21	41	70	55
Mansfield Town	46	14	12	20	48	59	54
Aldershot	46	15	8	23	64	74	53
Rotherham United	46	12	16	18	50	66	52
Grimsby Town	46	12	14	20	48	58	50
York City	46	8	9	29	48	91	33
Doncaster Rovers	46	8	9	29	40	84	33

1987-88 Season
Back: Lee Rogers, Pearson, Marshall, Newman, Moyes, Waugh, Fitzpatrick, Jordan, Tanner, Walsh.
Front: Hawkins, Harvey, Riley, Cooper, Llewellyn, Owen, Neville, Caldwell.

BACK ROW: Carl Shutt, Russell Bromage, Steve McClaren, Tony Caldwell.
MIDDLE ROW: Jimmy Lumsden (Assistant Manager), Alan Walsh, Rob Newman, Paul Fitzpatrick, Keith Waugh, John Pender,
Paul Mardon, Glenn Humphries, Alan Crawford (Youth Coach).
FRONT ROW: Nigel Hawkins, Ralph Milne, Steve Galliers (Captain), Joe Jordan (Manager), Chris Honor, Andy Llewellyn, Mark Cooper.
BRISTOL CITY 1988-89

SEASON 1988-89

FOOTBALL (BARCLAYS) LEAGUE DIV. THREE

No.	Date	Opposition	Pos.	Res.	H.T.	Att.	Goalscorers	Waugh K.	Llewellyn A.D.	Bromage R.	Humphries G.	Pender J.P.	McClaren S.	Milne R.	Galliers S.	Newman R.N.	Walsh A.	Caldwell A.	Honor C.R.	Mardon P.	Shutt C.S.	Hawkins N.	Fitzpatrick P.J.	McGarvey S.T.	Carter T.D.	Leaning A.J.	Gavin M.	Jordon J.	Balley J.A.	Stanley G.E.	Shepherd A.	Turner R.	Dolan E.	Taylor R.	Eaton J.
1	27 Aug	Notts County		0-0	0-0	6280		1	2	3	4	5	6	7"	8	9	10	11	14																
2	3 Sep	CHESTERFIELD	3	4-0	1-0	7547	LLewellyn, Newman(pen), Walsh(2)	1	2	3		5	6*		8	7	10			4	9	11	12												
3	10	Chester City	11	0-2	0-0	2823		1	2	3		5	6	12	8	7	10			4	9*			11											
4	17	PRESTON NORTH END	12	1-1	1-1	7913	Bromage		2"	3		5	6	7*	8	9	10		14	4	12			11	1										
5	20	Blackpool	12	2-2	2-1	3412	McGarvey(2)		2	3		5	6	7*	8	4	10				9	12		11	1										
6	24	PORT VALE	16	0-1	0-1	7235			2	3		5	6	7	8	4	10				9*	12		11	1										
7	1 Oct	SWANSEA CITY	12	2-0	1-0	7786	Milne, Walsh		2	3		5	6	7	8	4"	10			14	9*	11		12		1									
8	4	Gillingham	7	1-0	1-0	3102	Gavin		2	3*		5	6		8	4	10			12		11"		9		1	7	14							
9	8	FULHAM	13	1-5	0-2	8160	Newman(pen)		2*		12	5	6		8	4	10			3		11		9"		1	7	14							
10	15	Huddersfield Town	11	1-0	0-0	5952	Walsh		2*		4	5	6		8	7	10			12	9"			14		1		11	3						
11	22	Northampton Town	7	3-1	0-1	3668	McGarvey(2), Milne				4	5	6	7	8	2	10							9		1	11"	14	3						
12	25	ALDERSHOT	8	1-1	0-1	8684	McGarvey	1			4	5	6	7	8	2	10				14			9				11"	3						
13	29	Mansfield Town	11	2-2	2-1	3800	McGarvey, Walsh	1			4	5	6	7	8	2	10				14			9"			11		3						
14	5 Nov	BOLTON WANDERERS	9	1-1	1-0	8807	Newman	1	2		4	5	6	7		8	10				9*			12			11		3						
15	8	WOLVERHAMPTON W.	12	0-1	0-0	11336		1	14		4	5	6"	7	8	2	10				9*			12			11		3						
16	12	Wigan Athletic	10	1-0	0-0	2675	Gavin	1	12		4	5			8	2	10				9	14		7"			11		3	6*					
17	26	Sheffield United	12	0-3	0-1	11248		1			4		6		8	5	10				9	12		7"			11		3	2					
18	3 Dec	READING	10	2-1	0-1	8045	Hawkins, Walsh	1			4	5	6		8	2	10				9	12		7*			11		3						
19	17	CARDIFF CITY	7	2-0	1-0	7493	Hawkins, Newman	1	12		4*	5	6			2	10				9"	14		7			11		3	8					
20	26	Bury	10	1-2	1-1	3368	McGarvey	1				5	6			4	10		2		9"	14		7			11		3	8					
21	31	Southend United	9	2-1	1-0	4012	McGarvey, Walsh	1				5	6		12	4	10		2		9			7			11		3	8*					
22	2 Jan	BRISTOL ROVERS	10	0-1	0-0	23191		1				5	6			4	10		2		9	14		7			11"		3	8*	12				
23	14	Chesterfield	11	0-1	0-0	3488		1				5	6		11	4	10		2					7"			9	14	3		8				
24	21	CHESTER CITY	13	0-1	0-0	9586		1				5	6		8	4	10*		2		9			12			11		3		7				
25	28	Preston North End	13	0-2	0-0	6080		1				5	6		7	4	10		2		9						11		3			8			
26	3 Feb	Swansea City	12	1-1	1-0	6523	Turner	1				5	14		7	4	10		2	6				9*			12		3	11"		8			
27	11	GILLINGHAM	11	1-0	0-0	7319	Jordan	1				5	11		7	4	10		2	6				9"			12	14	3				8*		
28	18	Fulham	13	1-3	1-1	4408	McGarvey	1				5	8			4	10		2	6				11*			9		3	12			7		
29	21	Aldershot	11	1-0	1-0	1969	Walsh	1				5	8			4	9		7	12	6							14	3	2"		10	11*		
30	4 Mar	NORTHAMPTON TOWN	12	3-1	3-0	7197	Shutt, Turner, Walsh	1	7			5	8			4	10		2	6	9								3"	14		11			
31	11	Bolton Wanderers	14	0-2	0-0	4432		1	7			5	8			4	10		2*	6	9						12		3			11			
32	18	NOTTS COUNTY	14	0-4	0-1	6407		1				5	8		12	4	10		2	6	9						7*		3			11			
33	21	MANSFIELD TOWN	11	2-0	1-0	5065	Newman(2,1pen)	1			4	5	8*		7	6	10		2	12		9"						14	3			11			
34	25	Bristol Rovers	11	1-1	1-1	8676	Walsh	1			4"	5	8		7*	6	10		2	12		14							3			11		9	
35	27	BURY	10	3-0	1-0	8496	Turner(2), Taylor	1			4	5	7			6	10		2	8									3			11		9	
36	1 Apr	Cardiff City	11	1-1	0-1	6152	Taylor	1			4	5	7			6	10		2	8									3			11		9	
37	4	Brentford	13	0-3	0-2	4627		1			4	5	7		12	6	10		2	8*									3			11		9	
38	8	SOUTHEND UNITED	14	0-2	0-1	6213		1		8	4	5	7"			6	10*		2	14		9		12					3			11			
39	11	BRENTFORD	14	0-1	0-0	4339		1		8	4	5	7			2	10										6		3			11		9	
40	15	BLACKPOOL	14	1-2	1-0	5090	Taylor	1		8	4	5	7			2	10					12					6		3			11*		9	
41	18	HUDDERSFIELD TOWN	13	6-1	5-0	4542	Taylor(3), Gavin, McClaren, Walsh	1				5	7		8	4	10		2								6		3			11		9	
42	21	Port Vale	13	1-0	0-0	6923	Taylor	1				5	7		8	4	10		2								6		3			11		9	
43	29	WIGAN ATHLETIC	13	0-1	0-0	5156		1			14	5	6		7	4	10		2"								8		3			11*		9	12
44	1 May	Wolverhampton Wndrs.	14	0-2	0-1	17351		1			2	5	6		7	4	10					11*					8		3					9	12
45	5	Reading	11	2-1	1-1	3620	Pender, Turner	1		3		5	6		7	4	10		2								8					11		9	
46	13	SHEFFIELD UNITED	11	2-0	0-0	10769	Taylor, Turner			3		5	6		7	4	10		2							1	8					11		9	
							Apps.	37	13	13	20	45	44	10	30	46	46	1	24	13	21	7		20	3	6	26	2	35	8	2	19	3	12	
							Subs.		3		2		1	1	3				2	7	3	10	1	6			3	7		2	1				2
							Goals		1	1		1	1	2		6	11				1	2		9			3	1				6		8	

F.A. CUP

Rd.	Date	Opposition		Res.	H.T.	Att.	Goalscorers	Waugh K.	Llewellyn A.D.	Bromage R.	Humphries G.	Pender J.P.	McClaren S.	Milne R.	Galliers S.	Newman R.N.	Walsh A.	Caldwell A.	Honor C.R.	Mardon P.	Shutt C.S.	Hawkins N.	Fitzpatrick P.J.	McGarvey S.T.	Carter T.D.	Leaning A.J.	Gavin M.	Jordon J.	Balley J.A.	Stanley G.E.	Shepherd A.	Turner R.	Dolan E.	Taylor R.	Eaton J.
1R	19 Nov	SOUTHEND UNITED		3-1	2-0	7027	McGarvey, Shutt, Walsh	1			4	5			8	6	10		2		9			7			11		3						
2R	10 Dec	Aldershot		1-1	0-0	3793	Shutt	1			4	5	6		8*	2	10				9			7			11		3	12					
2Rr	13	ALDERSHOT		0-0	0-0	7299	(extra-time played)	1			4	5	6		8*	2	10				9			7			11		3	12					
2R2r	20	Aldershot		2-2	0-1	3801	Newman,Shutt (extra-time 1-1 end 90 mins)	1	2*			5			8	4	10		12		14	9"		7			11		3	6					
2R3r	22	ALDERSHOT		1-0	1-0	6246	Shutt	1				5	6		12	4	10		2		9			7			11		3	8*					
3R	7 Jan	Hartlepool United		0-1	0-0	4033		1				5	6			4	10		2		9			7"			11	14	3		8				

F.L. (LITTLEWOODS) CUP

Rd.	Date	Opposition		Res.	H.T.	Att.	Goalscorers	Waugh K.	Llewellyn A.D.	Bromage R.	Humphries G.	Pender J.P.	McClaren S.	Milne R.	Galliers S.	Newman R.N.	Walsh A.	Caldwell A.	Honor C.R.	Mardon P.	Shutt C.S.	Hawkins N.	Fitzpatrick P.J.	McGarvey S.T.	Carter T.D.	Leaning A.J.	Gavin M.	Jordon J.	Balley J.A.	Stanley G.E.	Shepherd A.	Turner R.	Dolan E.	Taylor R.	Eaton J.
1R1	30 Aug	EXETER CITY		1-0	1-0	6005	Newman(pen)	1	2	3	4"	5	6	7	8	9	10	11*	14			12													
1R2	7 Sep	Exeter City		1-0	0-0	2749	Walsh	1	2	3		5	6	12	8	7	10			4	9							11*							
2R1	28	Oxford United		4-2	2-1	3705	Hawkins, Milne, Shutt, Walsh		2	3		5	6	7	8	4	10			12	9*	11				1									
2R2	11 Oct	OXFORD UNITED		2-0	1-0	6255	McClaren, Shutt		2		3	5	6		8	4	10			12	9	14				1	7*	11"							
3R	1 Nov	CRYSTAL PALACE		4-1	3-0	12167	Milne(2), Shutt, Walsh	1			4	5	6	7	8	2	10				9						11		3						
4R	29	TRANMERE ROVERS		1-0	1-0	11110	Shutt	1				5	6		8	4	10				9*	7					11	12	3	2					
5R	18 Jan	Bradford City		1-0	1-0	15330	Walsh	1				5	6		7	4	10		2		12						11	9*	3		8				
SF1	15 Feb	Nottingham Forest		1-1	0-0	30016	Mardon	1				5	8		7	4	10		2	6							9	11	3						
SF2	26	NOTTINGHAM FOREST		0-1	0-0	28084	(£97097) (extra-time played)	1				5	8		7	4	10		2	6	12						9*	11	3						

ASSOCIATE MEMBERS (SHERPA VAN) TROPHY

Rd.	Date	Opposition	Pos.	Res.	H.T.	Att.	Goalscorers	Waugh K.	Llewellyn A.D.	Bromage R.	Humphries G.	Pender J.P.	McClaren S.	Milne R.	Galliers S.	Newman R.N.	Walsh A.	Caldwell A.	Honor C.R.	Mardon P.	Shutt C.S.	Hawkins N.	Fitzpatrick P.J.	McGarvey S.T.	Carter T.D.	Leaning A.J.	Gavin M.	Jordon J.	Balley J.A.	Stanley G.E.	Shepherd A.	Turner R.	Dolan E.	Taylor R.	Eaton J.
GM	23 Nov	Bristol Rovers	3	0-1	0-1	3940		1	2"		4	5*	12		8	6	10				9			7			11		3	14					
GM	6 Dec	EXETER CITY	2	2-0	1-0	3642	McGarvey, Newman(pen)	1			4	5	6		8	2	10*				9			7			11		3	12					
1R	24 Jan	Wolverhampton Wndrs		0-3	0-1	14216		1	3			5	6		7	4	10		2		9*			12			11				8				

GLOUCESTERSHIRE CUP FINAL

	Date	Opposition		Res.	H.T.	Att.
	17 Aug	Bristol Rovers		0-3	0-0	1664

FRIENDLIES

No.	Date	Opposition		Res.	H.T.	Att.	Goalscorers
1	29 Jul	Coleford United		15-0	10-0	400	Fitzpatrick(3), Unknown(12)
2	4 Aug	Forest Green Rovers		1-0	0-0		Jordon
3	8	Kilmarnock		4-1	3-1		Jordan(3), Milne
4	10	Celtic		1-1			Caldwell (at Inverclyde National Training Cntr)
5	11	Clyde		1-1	1-1		Caldwell (at Inverclyde National Training Cntr)
6	15	SWINDON TOWN		0-0	0-0	2302	
7	20	SOUTHAMPTON		1-1	1-0	2229	Walsh
8	8 Sep	Clevedon Town		4-1			Bryant, Fitzpatrick, McGarvey, Smith
9	8 May	Yeovil Town		3-1		919	Gavin, Newman, Taylor (D.Linney Benefit)

FINAL LEAGUE TABLE (TOP POSITIONS)

Wolverhampton W.	46	26	14	6	96	49	92
Sheffield United	46	25	9	12	93	54	84
Port Vale	46	24	12	10	78	48	84
Fulham	46	22	9	15	69	67	75
Bristol Rovers	46	19	17	10	67	51	74
Preston North End	46	19	15	12	79	60	72
Brentford	46	18	14	14	66	61	68
Chester City	46	19	11	16	64	61	68
Notts County	46	18	13	15	64	54	67
Bolton Wanderers	46	16	16	14	58	54	64
Bristol City	46	18	9	19	53	55	63
Swansea City	46	15	16	15	51	53	61
Bury	46	16	13	17	55	67	61

SEASON 1989-90
FOOTBALL (BARCLAYS) LEAGUE DIV. THREE

No.	Date	Opposition	Pos.	Res.	H.T.	Att.	Goalscorers
1	19 Aug	Bury		1-1	0-0	3399	Taylor
2	26	BIRMINGHAM CITY	8	1-0	0-0	8938	Taylor
3	2 Sep	Northampton Town	15	0-2	0-0	4088	
4	9	BLACKPOOL	8	2-0	0-0	7172	Newman, Wimbleton
5	16	Cardiff City	6	3-0	1-0	5970	Shelton, Taylor, Turner
6	23	BRISTOL ROVERS	5	0-0	0-0	17432	
7	26	SHREWSBURY TOWN	4	2-1	1-0	9188	Taylor(2)
8	29	Tranmere Rovers	4	0-6	0-2	8974	
9	7 Oct	Brentford	5	2-0	1-0	7421	Turner, Wimbleton
10	14	SWANSEA CITY	6	1-3	1-1	8794	Taylor
11	17	NOTTS COUNTY	5	2-0	1-0	8331	Eaton, O.G.
12	21	Mansfield Town	8	0-1	0-1	2957	
13	28	WIGAN ATHLETIC	6	3-0	2-0	6365	Rennie, Shelton, Turner
14	31	Crewe Alexandra	4	1-0	1-0	3554	Bailey
15	4 Nov	Walsall	1	2-0	1-0	5286	Taylor, Turner
16	11	BOLTON WANDERERS	3	1-1	1-1	11994	Newman
17	25	Reading	4	1-1	1-0	5353	Rennie
18	2 Dec	ROTHERHAM UNITED	6	0-0	0-0	9509	
19	16	LEYTON ORIENT	3	2-1	2-0	7486	Taylor(2)
20	26	Fulham	3	1-0	1-0	6089	Taylor
21	30	Huddersfield Town	3	1-2	0-1	7681	Jones
22	1 Jan	PRESTON NORTH END	3	2-1	1-0	11803	Newman, O.G.
23	13	Birmingham City	1	4-0	1-0	11277	Taylor(2), Newman, Turner
24	20	BURY	1	1-0	1-0	10992	Smith
25	30	CHESTER CITY	1	1-0	0-0	8769	Newman
26	10 Feb	CARDIFF CITY	1	1-0	1-0	11982	Shelton
27	24	READING	1	0-1	0-0	10616	
28	3 Mar	Chester City	1	3-0	2-0	2496	Taylor(3)
29	6	TRANMERE ROVERS	3	1-3	0-1	14376	Shelton
30	10	Shrewsbury Town	2	1-0	0-0	4785	Smith
31	13	Blackpool	1	3-1	1-0	3227	Taylor(2), Shelton
32	17	BRENTFORD	1	2-0	1-0	10813	Gavin, Rennie
33	20	Swansea City	1	5-0	2-0	6867	Taylor(3), Honor, Newman
34	24	Notts County	1	0-0	0-0	9598	
35	27	NORTHAMPTON TOWN	1	3-1	2-1	11965	Shelton, Taylor, Turner
36	31	MANSFIELD TOWN	1	1-0	1-0	11773	Taylor
37	3 Apr	Rotherham United	1	2-1	0-1	5274	Taylor, O.G.
38	7	Wigan Athletic	1	3-2	1-1	3281	Ferguson, Smith(pen), Taylor
39	10	CREWE ALEXANDRA	1	4-1	2-0	13800	Taylor(3), Gavin(pen)
40	14	Preston North End	1	2-2	1-1	7599	Morgan, Shelton
41	16	FULHAM	1	5-1	2-1	16139	Ferguson, Morgan, Newman, Shelton, Smith
42	21	Leyton Orient	1	1-1	0-1	7273	Newman
43	24	HUDDERSFIELD TOWN	1	1-1	0-1	17791	Morgan
44	28	Bolton Wanderers	1	0-1	0-1	11098	
45	2 May	Bristol Rovers	2	0-3	0-1	9813	
46	5	WALSALL	2	4-0	2-0	19480	Gavin(pen), Morgan, Rennie, Shelton

Player appearance/goal summary (columns: Leaning A.J., Llewellyn A.D., Bailey J.A., Wimbleton P., Pender J.P., Rennie D., Gavin M., Newman R.N., Taylor R., Smith D., Turner R., Eaton J., Mardon P., Shelton G., Honor C.R., Bromage R., Humphries G., Mellon M., Jones A.M., Sinclair R., Miller P.A., Horrix D., Jordan J., Ferguson I., Morgan N., Berr: J., Madge M.)

	Leaning	Llewellyn	Bailey	Wimbleton	Pender	Rennie	Gavin	Newman	Taylor	Smith	Turner	Eaton	Mardon	Shelton	Honor	Bromage	Humphries	Mellon	Jones	Sinclair	Miller	Horrix	Jordan	Ferguson	Morgan	Berr	Madge
Apps.	19	46	38	10	10	45	36	46	37	45	26	6	2	43	4	3	36	7	2	27	3			8	7		
Subs.				6			4					7	5	5			10		1	2	2		3	1	3		1
Goals			1	2		4	3	8	27	4	6	1		9	1				1					2	4		

F.A. CUP

	Date	Opposition		Res.	H.T.	Att.	Goalscorers
1R	18 Nov	BARNET		2-0	2-0	7538	Taylor, Turner
2R	9 Dec	FULHAM		2-1	0-1	7662	Taylor, Wimbleton(pen)
3R	6 Jan	SWINDON TOWN		2-1	2-1	17422	Newman, Taylor (£44500)
4R	27	CHELSEA		3-1	1-0	24535	Turner(2), Gavin (£97780)
5R	17 Feb	CAMBRIDGE UNITED		0-0	0-0	20676	
5Rr	21	Cambridge United		1-1	0-0	9796	Taylor (extra-time played, 0-0 end 90 mins)
5R2r	27	Cambridge United		1-5	0-1	9047	Taylor

F.L. (LITTLEWOODS) CUP

	Date	Opposition		Res.	H.T.	Att.	Goalscorers
1R1	22 Aug	READING		2-3	1-2	6318	Smith, Wimbleton(pen)
1R2	29	Reading		2-2	2-0	4457	Taylor(2)

ASSOCIATE MEMBERS (LEYLAND DAF) CUP

	Date	Opposition		Res.	H.T.	Att.	Goalscorers
GM	5 Dec	SWANSEA CITY	1	2-1	2-1	3488	Jones, Shelton
GM	15 Jan	Reading	1	1-0	1-0	1784	Gavin
1R	23	NOTTS COUNTY		0-1	0-0	4902	

GLOUCESTERSHIRE CUP FINAL

	Date	Opposition		Res.	H.T.	Att.	Goalscorers
	8 Aug	BRISTOL ROVERS		1-2	1-0	6153	Taylor

FRIENDLIES

	Date	Opposition		Res.	H.T.	Att.	Goalscorers
1	26 Jul	Trowbridge Town		2-3	1-0		Eaton, Honor
2	1 Aug	Weymouth Town		2-0			Taylor, Wimbleton
3	3	Nuneaton Borough		3-0			Honor, Taylor, Turner
4	11	MANCHESTER UNITED		2-3	0-2	9799	Pender, Rennie

FINAL LEAGUE TABLE

Team	P	W	D	L	F	A	Pts
Bristol Rovers	46	26	15	5	71	35	93
Bristol City	46	27	10	9	76	40	91
Notts County	46	25	12	9	73	53	87
Tranmere Rovers	46	23	11	12	86	49	80
Bury	46	21	11	14	70	49	74
Bolton Wanderers	46	18	15	13	59	48	69
Birmingham City	46	18	12	16	60	59	66
Huddersfield Town	46	17	14	15	61	62	65
Rotherham United	46	17	14	15	71	62	64
Reading	46	15	19	12	57	53	64
Shrewsbury Town	46	16	15	15	59	54	63
Crewe Alexandra	46	15	17	14	56	53	62
Brentford	46	18	7	21	66	66	61
Leyton Orient	46	16	10	20	52	56	58
Mansfield Town	46	16	7	23	50	65	55
Chester City	46	13	15	18	43	55	54
Swansea City	46	14	12	20	45	63	54
Wigan Athletic	46	13	14	19	48	64	53
Preston North End	46	14	10	22	65	79	52
Fulham	46	12	15	19	55	66	51
Cardiff City	46	12	14	20	51	70	50
Northampton Town	46	11	14	21	51	68	47
Blackpool	46	10	16	20	49	73	46
Walsall	46	9	14	23	40	72	41

Back Row: Left to Right. Dave Smith, Matt Bryant, Paul Mardon, Robbie Turner, Cameron Toshack, Paul France, Ronnie McQuilter.
Middle Row: John Pender, David Rennie, Ronnie Sinclair, Rob Newman, Russel Bromage, Andy Leaning, Bob Taylor, Glenn Humphries.
Front Row: Gary Shelton, Mark Gavin, Jason Eaton, Alan Theobald, Micky Mellon, John Bailey, Andy Llewellyn.

1989-90 Season

BRISTOL CITY LINE UP – SEASON 1990-91

Back Row (L-R): *Cameron Toshack, Matt Bryant, Paul Mardon, Wayne Allison, Mark Aizelwood, Murry Jones, Ronnie McQuilter, David Rennie.*
Middle Row (L-R): *Mick Mellon, Louie Donawa, Darren Keeling, Chris Honor, Andy Leaning, Ronnie Sinclair, Steve Weaver, Nicky Morgan, Bob Taylor, Glen Humphries, Jason Eaton.*
Front Row (L-R): *Gary Shelton, Andy Llewellyn, John Bailey, Rob Newman, David Smith, Gerry Mitchell, Mark Madge, Simon Darleston, Junior Bent, Andy May.*

Player columns (left to right): Sinclair R. · Llewellyn A.D. · Aizlewood M. · May A. · Shelton G. · Rennie D. · Donowa L. · Newman R.N. · Taylor R. · Morgan N. · Smith D. · Bent J. · Allison W. · Humphries G. · Bailey J.A. · Leaning A.J. · Scott M. · Bryant M. · Mardon P. · Honor C.R.

No.	Date	Opposition	Pos.	Res.	H.T.	Att.	Goalscorers
1	25 Aug	BLACKBURN ROVERS		4-2	0-1	13755	Taylor(2), Aizlewood, Morgan
2	2 Sep	Swindon Town	4	1-0	1-0	12249	Bent
3	8	PLYMOUTH ARGYLE	5	1-1	1-0	14283	Morgan
4	15	West Bromwich Albion	8	1-2	0-2	12081	Newman
5	22	BRIGHTON & HOVE ALB.	8	3-1	2-0	11522	Taylor(2), Smith
6	29	NEWCASTLE UNITED	5	1-0	1-0	15858	Smith
7	3 Oct	Leicester City	9	0-3	0-1	9815	
8	6	Wolverhampton Wndrs	12	0-4	0-2	17891	
9	13	WEST HAM UNITED	13	1-1	0-1	16838	Morgan
10	20	OLDHAM ATHLETIC	13	1-2	1-2	14021	Morgan
11	24	Millwall	11	2-1	0-1	10335	Aizlewood, O.G.
12	27	Port Vale	13	2-3	1-2	7451	Allison, Smith(pen)
13	3 Nov	WATFORD	11	3-2	1-1	11576	Allison(2), O.G.
14	10	Oxford United	13	1-3	1-2	6834	Shelton
15	17	HULL CITY	10	4-1	0-1	9346	May, Morgan, Newman, Shelton
16	24	Ipswich Town	11	1-1	0-1	10037	Taylor
17	1 Dec	CHARLTON ATHLETIC	13	0-1	0-1	10984	
18	8	SHEFFIELD WEDNESDAY	12	1-1	1-1	11254	O.G.
19	15	Blackburn Rovers	9	1-0	0-0	7072	Newman
20	22	Notts County	11	2-3	1-1	6586	Bent, Smith
21	26	PORTSMOUTH	8	4-1	1-1	11892	Morgan(2), Rennie, Shelton
22	29	MIDDLESBROUGH	7	3-0	1-0	14023	Allison, May, Morgan
23	1 Jan	Barnsley	9	0-2	0-2	8961	
24	12	SWINDON TOWN	9	0-4	0-1	16169	
25	19	Plymouth Argyle	12	0-3	0-0	8041	
26	26	Bristol Rovers	13	2-3	2-2	7054	Newman, Scott(pen)
27	2 Feb	WEST BROMWICH ALB.	9	2-0	1-0	11492	Morgan, Taylor
28	16	Hull City	8	2-0	1-0	5212	May, Newman
29	23	OXFORD UNITED	8	3-1	2-1	10938	Shelton(2), Taylor
30	2 Mar	Charlton Athletic	9	1-2	1-2	5477	Smith
31	5	BRISTOL ROVERS	8	1-0	0-0	22270	Donowa
32	9	IPSWICH TOWN	5	4-2	2-1	11474	Taylor(2), Morgan, Shelton
33	12	LEICESTER CITY	5	1-0	0-0	13297	Taylor
34	16	Newcastle United	5	0-0	0-0	13578	
35	20	West Ham United	7	0-1	0-0	22951	
36	23	WOLVERHAMPTON W.	7	1-1	0-0	15499	Bryant
37	30	Portsmouth	8	1-4	0-0	10418	Morgan
38	1 Apr	NOTTS COUNTY	7	3-2	1-1	13466	Allison, Donowa, Shelton
39	6	Middlesbrough	8	1-2	1-1	13846	Taylor
40	13	BARNSLEY	7	1-0	0-0	12081	Newman
41	20	Oldham Athletic	9	1-2	0-0	14086	Newman
42	23	Brighton & Hove Albion	8	1-0	0-0	7738	Shelton
43	27	MILLWALL	8	1-4	1-0	16741	Morgan
44	4 May	PORT VALE	9	1-1	1-0	11555	Rennie
45	8	Sheffield Wednesday	9	1-3	0-1	31706	Allison
46	11	Watford	9	3-2	0-0	13029	Donowa, Morgan, Newman

Player appearance grid (shirt numbers):

No.	Sin	Lle	Aiz	May	She	Ren	Don	New	Tay	Mor	Smi	Ben	All	Hum	Bai	Lea	Sco	Bry	Mar	Hon
1	1	2	3	4	5	6			8	9	10	11								
2	1	2	3	4	5	6			8	9	10"	11	7	14						
3	1	2	3	4	5	6			8	9"	10	11	7	14						
4	1	2	3	4	5	6			8	9"	10	11	7	14						
5	1	2	3	4	5	6			8	9	10"	11	7	14						
6	1	2	3	4	5	6			8	9	10	11	7							
7	1	2	3	4	5	6			8	9	11"	7	14							
8	1		3	4	5	6	7	2	9	10	11			8*	12					
9		2	4	7	5	6		8	9	10	11						3	1		
10		2	4	7	5	6*	12	8	9"	10	11		14				3	1		
11	1	2	4	7	5	6		8	12	10	11		9				3			
12	1	2	4	7	5	6	14	8		10	11		9				3"			
13	1	2	4	7	5	6	14	8		10"	11		9				3			
14	1	2	4	7	5	6	14	8	12	10	11		9				3"			
15	1	2	3	4	5	6		8		10	11	7	9							
16	1	2	3	4	5	6		8	14	10	11	7	9"							
17	1	2	3	4	5	6		8	9	10"	11	7"	14	12						
18	1	2		4	5	6		8	9	10	11	7*	12				3			
19	1	2		4	5	6		8	9	10	11	7					3			
20		2		4	5	6		8	9	10"	11	7	14				1	3		
21		2	12	4	5	6		8	9"	10	11	7*	14				1	3		
22		2	6	4	5	7"	14	8		10	11		9				1	3		
23		2	6	4	5	7	14	8	12	10"			9				1	3"		
24		2	6	4	5	7	14	8	12	10"	11		9				1	3*		
25		2	6	4		7*	12	8		9							1	3	5	
26		2	6	4			7	8	9	10	11"	14					1	3	5	
27		2	6	4	7			8	9	10"	11		14				1	3	5	
28		2	6	4	7		12	8	9	10	11*						1	3	5	
29		2	6	4	7			8	9	10	11						1	3	5	
30		2	6"	4	7	14		8	9*	10	11		12				1	3	5	
31		2	6	4"	7	14	11	8	9	10*			12				1	3	5	
32		2	6	4"	7		11	8	9	10	14						1	3	5	
33		2	6	4	7"		11	8	9	10"	14		12				1	3	5	
34		2	6	4	7	12		8	9	10"	11*		14				1	3	5	
35		2	6	4	7		11"	8	9	10							1	3	5	
36	2"	6	4	7			11	8	9	10*			14	12			1	3	5	
37	2"	6	4	7	12		11	8	9	10*			14				1		5	3
38		2	6	4	7		11	8	9	10*			12				1		5	3
39			6*	2	7	4	11"	8	9				14	10			1	3	5	12
40		2		4	7			8	9				11	10			1	3	5	6
41		2	6	4"	7			8	9*	12			14	10			1	3	5	11
42	2*	6	12		7			8	11	10				9			1	3	5	4
43		2	6		7			8	11	10			14	9			1	3	5	4"
44			6	2	7	4	14	8	11"	10			9				1	3	5	
45			6	2	7"	4	14	8		10	11		9				1	3	5	
46		2	6	4	7	14		8		10	11"		9				1	3	5	
Apps	17	42	41	44	43	29	11	46	34	43	32	15	18	1	6	29	27	22	6	
Subs		1	1		3	13	5		1	2	5	19	1	1						1
Goals		2	3	8	2	3	8	11	13	5	2	6					1	1		

F.A. CUP

	Date	Opposition		Res.	H.T.	Att.	Goalscorers	Sin	Lle	Aiz	May	She	Ren	Don	New	Tay	Mor	Smi	Ben	All	Hum	Bai	Lea	Sco	Bry	Mar	Hon
3R	5 Jan	Norwich City		1-2	1-1	12630	Allison		2"	6	4	5	7	12	8	10*				11	14		9		3	1	

F.L. (RUMBELOWS) CUP

	Date	Opposition		Res.	H.T.	Att.	Goalscorers	Sin	Lle	Aiz	May	She	Ren	Don	New	Tay	Mor	Smi	Ben	All	Hum
1R1	29 Aug	West Bromwich Albion		2-2	1-1	8721	Morgan(2)	1	2	3	4	5	6			8	9"	10	11	7	14
1R2	5 Sep	WEST BROMWICH ALB.		1-0	0-0	9851	Smith (extra-time played)	1	2	3	4	5	6			8	9	10"	11	7	14
2R1	25	Sunderland		1-0	1-0	10358	Morgan	1	2	3	4	5	6			8	9	10	11	7	
2R2	9 Oct	SUNDERLAND		1-6	1-2	11776	Morgan (£58,734)		2	3	4	5	6	7	8	9"	10	11		14	

FULL MEMBERS (ZENITH DATA SYSTEMS) CUP

	Date	Opposition		Res.	H.T.	Att.	Goalscorers	Sin	Lle	Aiz	May	She	Ren	Don	New	Tay	Mor	Smi	Ben	All	Hum	...	Hon
	21 Nov	Oxford United		2-2	0-0	1323	May(pen), Newman	1	2	3	4	5	6		8	10			12	7	9		11*

Extra-time played following score of 1-1 at end of normal time, Oxford won penalty shoot-out 3-2 to progress to the next round.

GLOUCESTERSHIRE CUP FINAL

	Date	Opposition		Res.	H.T.	Att.	Goalscorers
	15 Aug	Bristol Rovers		4-1	2-1	4209	Morgan(2), Shelton, Smith

FRIENDLIES

	Date	Opposition	Res.	H.T.	Att.	Goalscorers
1	26 Jul	Westbury United	2-1			Shelton, Smith
2	1 Aug	Aylesbury United	2-4	0-0		Allison, Smith
3	6	Clydebank	3-0	1-0		Bent, Morgan, Newman
4	8	Ayr United	2-1	0-0		Allison, Donowa
5	10	Carlisle United	1-0	1-0		Newman
6	13	Stroud	3-0	0-0		Mellon, Taylor, O.G.
7	17	CRYSTAL PALACE	1-1	0-1	4826	Rennie
8	20	ASTON VILLA	2-0	1-0	11739	Allison, Taylor (Robert Newman Benefit)
9	31 Oct	DYNAMO MINSK	3-0	0-0	2564	Donowa, Morgan, Taylor
10	23 Jan	Calne Town	3-0			Aizlewood, Donowa, Scott(pen)

FINAL LEAGUE TABLE

	P	W	D	L	F	A	Pts
Oldham Athletic	46	25	13	8	83	53	88
West Ham United	46	24	15	7	60	34	87
Sheffield Wednesday	46	22	16	8	80	51	82
Notts County	46	23	11	12	76	55	80
Millwall	46	20	13	13	70	51	73
Brighton & Hove Alb.	46	21	7	18	63	69	70
Middlesbrough	46	20	9	17	66	47	69
Barnsley	46	19	12	15	63	48	69
Bristol City	46	20	7	19	68	71	67
Oxford United	46	14	19	13	69	66	61
Newcastle United	46	14	17	15	49	56	59
Wolves	46	13	19	14	63	63	58
Bristol Rovers	46	15	13	18	56	59	58
Ipswich Town	46	13	18	15	60	68	57
Port Vale	46	15	12	19	56	64	57
Charlton Athletic	46	13	17	16	57	61	56
Portsmouth	46	14	11	21	58	70	53
Plymouth Argyle	46	12	17	17	54	68	53
Blackburn Rovers	46	14	10	22	51	66	52
Watford	46	12	15	19	45	59	51
Swindon Town	46	12	14	20	65	73	50
Leicester City	46	14	8	24	60	83	50
West Brom	46	10	18	18	52	61	48
Hull City	46	10	15	21	57	85	45

SEASON 1991-92
FOOTBALL (BARCLAYS) LEAGUE DIVISION TWO

Player columns (left to right): Welch K., Llewellyn A.D., Scott M., May A., Bryant M., Aizlewood M., Shelton G., Rennie D., Allison W., Taylor R., Smith D., Morgan N., Bent J., Edwards R., Harrison G., Caesar G., Connor T., Leaning A.J., Osman R., Gavin M., Dziekanowski D.P., Mellon M., McIntyre J., Cole A.A., Rosenior L., Atteveld R.

No.	Date	Opposition	Pos.	Res.	H.T.	Att.	Goalscorers
1	17 Aug	Southend United		1-1	0-1	6720	Taylor
2	20	BRIGHTON & HOVE ALB.		2-1	1-0	11299	Bryant, Scott
3	24	BLACKBURN ROVERS	2	1-0	1-0	11317	Allison
4	31	Port Vale	4	1-1	0-1	7057	Morgan
5	4 Sep	BRISTOL ROVERS	2	1-0	1-0	20183	Allison
6	7	Leicester City	5	1-2	1-2	17815	Morgan
7	14	TRANMERE ROVERS	5	2-2	2-1	11235	Allison, Shelton
8	17	MILLWALL	6	2-2	1-2	10862	Bryant, Scott(pen)
9	21	Ipswich Town	10	2-4	1-1	9692	Allison, Smith
10	28	PORTSMOUTH	14	0-2	0-2	9830	
11	5 Oct	Derby County	18	1-4	0-1	11880	Edwards
12	12	WATFORD	11	1-0	1-0	7882	Connor
13	19	Barnsley	8	2-1	1-0	6566	May, Shelton
14	26	NEWCASTLE UNITED	9	1-1	0-1	8613	Taylor
15	2 Nov	Cambridge United	9	0-0	0-0	4810	
16	5	PLYMOUTH ARGYLE	9	2-0	2-0	7735	Allison, Morgan
17	9	SUNDERLAND	9	1-0	1-0	10570	Allison
18	16	Oxford United	10	1-1	0-1	5779	Allison
19	23	Middlesbrough	11	1-3	1-2	12928	Taylor
20	30	CHARLTON ATHLETIC	11	0-2	0-1	9123	
21	7 Dec	Grimsby Town	12	1-3	1-1	4866	Rennie
22	21	Bristol Rovers	14	2-3	1-2	6306	Bent, Rennie
23	26	SWINDON TOWN	16	1-1	1-1	14636	Taylor
24	28	PORT VALE	12	3-0	2-0	9235	Allison, Bent, Osman
25	1 Jan	Brighton & Hove Albion	13	0-0	0-0	7555	
26	11	Blackburn Rovers	14	0-4	0-3	12964	
27	18	SOUTHEND UNITED	14	2-2	0-1	9883	Dziekanowski, O.G.
28	1 Feb	BARNSLEY	16	0-2	0-0	9508	
29	4	Swindon Town	16	0-2	0-0	9627	
30	8	Newcastle United	18	0-3	0-0	29263	
31	22	Charlton Athletic	21	1-2	1-0	5900	Shelton
32	29	GRIMSBY TOWN	20	1-1	1-0	8992	Aizlewood
33	7 Mar	Wolverhampton Wndrs	22	1-1	1-1	12542	Osman
34	10	Plymouth Argyle	23	0-1	0-0	9734	
35	14	CAMBRIDGE UNITED	23	1-2	1-0	9579	Scott
36	17	WOLVERHAMPTON W.	21	2-0	0-0	11623	Dziekanowski(2)
37	21	Sunderland	20	3-1	3-0	18933	Allison(2), Cole
38	28	OXFORD UNITED	20	1-1	0-0	12402	Dziekanowski
39	31	Tranmere Rovers	19	2-2	0-0	5797	Cole, Rosenior
40	4 Apr	LEICESTER CITY	17	2-1	1-1	13020	Cole, Rosenior
41	7	MIDDLESBROUGH	17	1-1	0-1	12814	Cole
42	11	Millwall	16	3-2	0-0	6989	Rosenior(2), Cole
43	18	IPSWICH TOWN	17	2-1	1-0	16941	Cole, Rosenior
44	20	Portsmouth	17	0-1	0-1	17151	
45	25	DERBY COUNTY	17	1-2	1-1	16648	Atteveld
46	2 May	Watford	17	2-5	1-1	10582	Cole(2)

Apps. 26 37 46 44 43 34 18 27 37 13 17 15 7 12 9 9 20 30 12 16 12 1 12 5 4
Subs. 1 1 6 5 1 4 10 8 4 1 2 1 2 1 4 3 3
Goals 3 1 2 1 3 2 10 4 1 3 2 1 1 2 4 8 5 1

F.A. CUP

	Date	Opposition		Res.	H.T.	Att.	Goalscorers
3R	4 Jan	WIMBLEDON		1-1	0-1	12679	O.G.
3Rr	11	Wimbledon		1-0	1-0	3747	May
4R	25	Leicester City		2-1	1-0	19313	Bent, Dziekanowski
5R	15 Feb	Nottingham Forest		1-4	0-1	24615	Dziekanowski

F.L. (RUMBELOWS) CUP

	Date	Opposition		Res.	H.T.	Att.	Goalscorers
2R1	25 Sep	Bristol Rovers		3-1	2-1	5155	Allison, Morgan, Smith
2R2	8 Oct	BRISTOL ROVERS		2-4	1-1	9880	Morgan, Smith (ex-time, 1-3 @ 90 min. £57779)

FULL MEMBERS (ZENITH DATA SYSTEMS) CUP

	Date	Opposition		Res.	H.T.	Att.	Goalscorers
2R	22 Oct	SOUTHAMPTON		1-2	1-0	5672	Taylor

GLOUCESTERSHIRE CUP FINAL

	Date	Opposition		Res.	H.T.	Att.	Goalscorers
	7 Aug	BRISTOL ROVERS		3-2	3-2	6796	Taylor(2), Edwards

FRIENDLIES

	Date	Opposition	Res.	H.T.	Att.	Goalscorers
1	17 Jul	Long Ashton	13-1		1000	Allsn(4), Taylr(4), Melln(2), Bent, Dnowa, Edwrds
2	22	Westbury United	2-0			Unknown(2)
3	24	Merthyr Tydfil	6-0			Unknown(6)
4	26	Yate Town	1-0	0-0		Mellon
5	29	Kilmarnock	3-1	1-1		Bryant, Shelton, Smith
6	31	Clydebank	1-4	0-3		Taylor
7	2 Aug	Carlisle United	2-0	1-0		Morgan, Taylor
8	5	Gloucester City	5-1	4-1		Harrison(2) Taylor(2), Allison
9	10	WIMBLEDON	1-1	0-0	2467	Rennie
10	12	STEAUA BUCHAREST	0-2	0-0	3624	

FINAL LEAGUE TABLE

Ipswich Town	46	24	12	10	70	50	84	
Middlesbrough	46	23	11	12	58	41	80	
Derby County	46	23	9	14	69	51	78	
Leicester City	46	23	8	15	62	55	77	
Cambridge United	46	19	17	10	65	47	74	
Blackburn Rvrs	46	21	11	14	70	53	74	
Charlton Athletic	46	20	11	15	54	48	71	
Swindon Town	46	18	15	13	69	55	69	
Portsmouth	46	19	12	15	65	51	69	
Watford	46	18	11	17	51	48	65	
Wolves	46	18	10	18	61	54	64	
Southend United	46	17	11	18	63	63	62	
Bristol Rovers	46	16	14	16	60	63	62	
Tranmere Rovers	46	14	19	13	56	56	61	
Millwall	46	17	10	19	64	71	61	
Barnsley	46	16	11	19	46	57	59	
Bristol City	46	13	15	18	55	71	54	
Sunderland	46	14	11	21	61	65	53	
Grimsby Town	46	14	11	21	47	62	53	
Newcastle United	46	13	13	20	66	84	52	
Oxford United	46	13	11	22	66	73	50	
Plymouth Argyle	46	13	9	24	42	64	48	
Brighton & Hove Alb.	46	12	11	23	56	77	47	
Port Vale	46	10	15	21	42	59	45	

1991-92 Season
Back: Paterson, Donowa, Giles, Gerry Harrison, Vernon, Rennie, Campbell, Graham Smith, Allison, Scott, May.
Middle: Fawthrop (Chief Scout), Bent, Bryant, Edwards, Welch, Weaver, Leaning, Sinclair, Morgan, Taylor,
Aizlewood, Footman (Physiotherapist), Crawford (Youth Coach).
Front: Mellon, Llewellyn, Bailey, Lumsden (Manager), Shelton, Taylor (Asst Manager), Dave Smith, Watkins, Clifford.

1992-93 Season
Back: Mellon, Morgan, Gerry Harrison, McIntyre, Atteveld, Gavin, Connor.
Middle: Footman (Physiotherapist), Denis Smith (Manager), Allison, Dziekanowski, Edwards, Campbell, Leaning,
Welch, Thompson, Bryant, Mitchell, Rosenior, Benton, Mark Harrison (Youth Coach), Crawford (Reserve Team Manager).
Front: Vernon, Paterson, Rouse, Cole, Osman, Shelton, Aizlewood, Llewellyn, Scott, Bent, Hogg.

SEASON 1992-93
FOOTBALL (BARCLAYS) LEAGUE DIV. ONE *

No.	Date	Opposition	Pos.	Res.	H.T.	Att.	Goalscorers
1	15 Aug	PORTSMOUTH		3-3	2-2	15301	Dziekanowski(2), Cole
2	22	Luton Town	7	3-0	1-0	7926	Cole, Mellon, O.G.
3	29	SUNDERLAND	10	0-0	0-0	14076	
4	6 Sep	Derby County	7	4-3	1-2	12738	Allison, Bent, Scott(pen), O.G.
5	12	SOUTHEND UNITED	8	0-1	0-1	9515	
6	15	WEST HAM UNITED	9	1-5	0-3	14130	Scott
7	19	Newcastle United	13	0-5	0-2	29465	
8	26	BARNSLEY	10	2-1	1-1	8049	Allison, Scott(pen)
9	3 Oct	Tranmere Rovers	13	0-3	0-1	5975	
10	10	CHARLTON ATHLETIC	12	2-1	1-1	9282	Dziekanowski, Harrison
11	17	Cambridge United	11	1-2	0-1	3894	Cole
12	24	LEICESTER CITY	11	2-1	0-1	10408	Cole, O.G.
13	31	Brentford	15	1-5	1-2	8726	Cole
14	4 Nov	Millwall	15	1-4	1-1	5934	Cole
15	7	BIRMINGHAM CITY	14	3-0	1-0	10008	Cole, Rosenior, Shelton
16	14	Grimsby Town	15	1-2	0-0	5651	Cole
17	21	SWINDON TOWN	15	2-2	1-1	14066	Rosenior, Shelton
18	28	NOTTS COUNTY	13	1-0	0-0	9065	Shelton
19	5 Dec	Watford	13	0-0	0-0	6746	
20	13	Bristol Rovers	15	0-4	0-1	7106	
21	19	PETERBOROUGH UNITED	17	0-0	0-0	7309	
22	26	OXFORD UNITED	17	1-1	1-1	10737	Rosenior
23	28	Wolverhampton Wndrs	18	0-0	0-0	16419	
24	9 Jan	NEWCASTLE UNITED	18	1-2	1-2	15446	Allison
25	16	Barnsley	18	1-2	0-0	5423	Cole
26	27	West Ham United	18	0-2	0-0	12118	
27	30	LUTON TOWN	19	0-0	0-0	8877	
28	6 Feb	Portsmouth	17	3-2	1-1	10675	Bryant, Gavin, Shelton
29	10	Southend United	18	1-1	1-1	3836	Cole
30	20	Sunderland	20	0-0	0-0	17122	
31	27	Charlton Athletic	20	1-2	1-0	7351	Cole
32	6 Mar	TRANMERE ROVERS	21	1-3	0-2	8810	Cole
33	9	MILLWALL	21	0-1	0-1	8771	
34	13	Birmingham City	20	1-0	0-0	15611	Morgan
35	20	WATFORD	20	2-1	1-1	8265	Bent, Pennyfather
36	24	Swindon Town	22	1-2	0-0	13157	Rosenior
37	28	GRIMSBY TOWN	19	1-0	0-0	6755	Morgan
38	3 Apr	Notts County	20	0-0	0-0	6633	
39	6	BRISTOL ROVERS	15	2-1	0-0	21854	Morgan, Tinnion(pen)
40	10	Oxford United	17	0-2	0-1	6146	
41	12	WOLVERHAMPTON W.	14	1-0	0-0	11756	Bent
42	17	Peterborough United	15	1-1	0-0	5169	Tinnion
43	20	DERBY COUNTY	15	0-0	0-0	8869	
44	24	CAMBRIDGE UNITED	16	0-0	0-0	8995	
45	1 May	Leicester City	16	0-0	0-0	19294	
46	8	BRENTFORD	15	4-1	2-0	12659	Rosenior(3), Allison

* Formerly Football League Division Two.

	Apps.	Subs.	Goals
	(various per player)		

F.A. CUP

	Date		Res.	H.T.	Att.	Goalscorers
3R	19 Jan	Luton Town	0-2	0-1	6094	

F.L. (COCA-COLA) CUP

	Date		Res.	H.T.	Att.	Goalscorers
1R1	18 Aug	Cardiff City	0-1	0-1	7708	
1R2	25	CARDIFF CITY	5-1	3-0	9801	Cole(3), Allison, Rosenior
2R1	22 Sep	SHEFFIELD UNITED	2-1	2-0	6922	Connor, Scott(pen)
2R2	7 Oct	Sheffield United	1-4	1-2	7588	Cole

ANGLO-ITALIAN CUP

	Date		Res.	H.T.	Att.	Goalscorers
PGM	1 Sep	WATFORD	1	1-0	0-0	3588	Shelton
PGM	29	Luton Town	1	1-0	0-0	2538	Allison
IS1	11 Nov	COSENZA		0-2	0-0	3644	
IS2	24	Pisa	8	3-4	2-4	1730	Edwards, Scott(pen), Shelton
IS3	8 Dec	REGGIANA		1-2	1-1	2281	Allison
IS4	16	Cremonese	8	2-2	0-0	535	Cole, Rosenior

PGM = Prelim. round group match. IS = International stage (group B) match.

GLOUCESTERSHIRE CUP FINAL

	Date		Res.	H.T.	Att.	Goalscorers
	5 Aug	Bristol Rovers	1-2	1-0	3722	Cole

FRIENDLIES

	Date		Res.	H.T.	Att.	Goalscorers
1	22 Jul	Newcastle Town	6-1	2-1		Allison(3), Rosenior(2), Cole
2	25	Crewe Alexandra	0-4	0-0	1156	
3	28	Gloucester City	5-2	2-0	500	Scott(2,1pen), Bryant, McIntyre, Vernon
4	1 Aug	Weymouth Town	4-2	2-2		Cole(2), Bryant, McIntyre
5	3	Forest Green Rovers	3-2	2-1		Allison, Bent, Rosenior
6	8	CHELSEA	2-1	1-1	3786	Cole, Scott(pen)
7	14 May	MANCHESTER UNITED	3-3	0-3	21716	Harrison, Rosenior, Wyatt (C.Garland Benefit)

FINAL LEAGUE TABLE

Newcastle United	46	29	9	8	92	38	96
West Ham United	46	26	10	10	81	41	88
Portsmouth	46	26	10	10	80	46	88
Tranmere Rovers	46	23	10	13	72	56	79
Swindon Town	46	21	13	12	74	59	76
Leicester City	46	22	10	14	71	64	76
Millwall	46	18	16	12	65	53	70
Derby County	46	19	9	18	68	57	66
Grimsby Town	46	19	7	20	58	57	64
Peterborough United	46	16	14	16	55	63	62
Wolves	46	16	13	17	57	56	61
Charlton Athletic	46	16	13	17	49	46	61
Barnsley	46	17	9	20	56	60	60
Oxford United	46	14	14	18	53	56	56
Bristol City	46	14	14	18	49	67	56
Watford	46	14	13	19	57	71	55
Notts County	46	12	16	18	55	70	52
Southend United	46	13	13	20	54	64	52
Birmingham City	46	13	12	21	50	72	51
Luton Town	46	10	21	15	48	62	51
Sunderland	46	13	11	22	50	64	50
Brentford	46	13	10	23	52	71	49
Cambridge United	46	11	16	19	48	69	49
Bristol Rovers	46	10	11	25	55	87	41

SEASON 1993-94
FOOTBALL (ENDSLEIGH INS.) LEAGUE DIV. ONE

No.	Date	Opposition	Pos.	Res.	H.T.	Att.	Goalscorers	Welch K.	Munro S.D.	Scott M.	Aizlewood M.	Shail M.	Hewlett M.	Wyatt M.	Shelton G.	Baird I.	Robinson L.	Tinnion B.	Kamara A.	Allison W.	Edwards R.	Bent J.	Brown I.	Harrison G.	Osman R.	Rosenior L.	Gavin M.	Borrows B.	Bryant M.	Martin D.	Llewellyn A.D.	Pennyfather G.	Fowler J.	Harriott M.	Hoyland J.	Partridge S.	Milsom P.
1	14 Aug	Wolverhampton Wndrs		1-3	0-1	21052	Scott	1	2	3	4	5	6*	7"	8	9	10	11	12	14																		
2	21	CRYSTAL PALACE	13	2-0	0-0	12068	Allison, Baird	1	2	3	4	5	6	7	8	9	10"	11		14																		
3	28	Derby County	21	0-1	0-0	15643		1	2	3	4	5			11	9		10		14	6	7"	8															
4	4 Sep	SOUTHEND UNITED	12	2-1	1-0	7396	Osman, Tinnion(pen)	1	2	3		5				9	8"	10			11	7	14	4	6													
5	11	Oxford United	19	2-4	1-2	5464	Baird(2)	1	2	3	4	5				9		10		8	11	7*		6"	12	14												
6	14	LEICESTER CITY	21	1-3	0-2	7899	Scott	1	2	3	4	5				9	7"	10		8	14			6	11													
7	18	CHARLTON ATHLETIC	20	0-0	0-0	7484		1	3	6*		4				9	12	10"		8	14				11	2	5	7										
8	25	Portsmouth	21	0-0	0-0	10702		1	3			4				9	10			8	6				12		11	2	5	7*									
9	2 Oct	BOLTON WANDERERS	15	2-0	1-0	7704	Allison, Scott	1	3	11		4				9	10*	6		8	14					12	2	5	7"									
10	5	Luton Town	8	2-0	0-0	5956	Baird, Tinnion(pen)	1	3	11		4				9	10	6*			12					8	2	5	7									
11	9	Notts County	10	0-2	0-0	6418		1	3	11		4				9	10	6		14						8"	2	5	7									
12	16	BARNSLEY	15	0-2	0-1	6923		1	3	11		4				9		6		8	14					10"	2	5	7									
13	22	Tranmere Rovers	13	2-2	1-1	7123	Allison, Shail	1	3	11		4				9	12	6		10	14	8*					5	7"	2									
14	30	SUNDERLAND	12	2-1	0-0	8162	Allison, Baird	1	3	11		4				9	14	6		10	12	8"					5	7*	2									
15	2 Nov	BIRMINGHAM CITY	9	3-0	1-0	9192	Allison(3)	1	3	11						10		6		9		8					5	7	2									
16	6	Middlesbrough	9	1-0	1-0	9687	Tinnion(pen)	1		3						10		6		9	11	8*					5	7	2	12								
17	13	MILLWALL	8	2-2	1-0	8416	Allison(2)	1		3		4				9	6			10	11	8*					5	7	2	12								
18	20	Watford	10	1-1	0-1	6045	Martin	1	12	3		4*				9	6			10	11	8					5	7	2									
19	27	Peterborough United	8	2-0	2-0	5084	Robinson(2)	1	4	3						9	6			10	11	8					5	7	2									
20	4 Dec	MIDDLESBROUGH	8	0-0	0-0	8441		1	4	3						9	6"			10	11	8*	12				5	7	2	14								
21	11	Leicester City	10	0-3	0-2	13394		1	4	3						9	6			10	11		8"				5		2	7	14							
22	18	WOLVERHAMPTON W.	9	2-1	1-0	15151	Allison, Brown	1	4	3						9	6			10	11	12	8*				5		2	7								
23	27	West Bromwich Albion	9	1-0	1-0	22888	Tinnion	1	4	3					12	9*	6			10	11		8				5		2	7								
24	28	NOTTINGHAM FOREST	11	1-4	0-0	20725	Edwards	1	4	3					12	9"	6			10	11		8*				5		2	7								
25	1 Jan	Grimsby Town	11	0-1	0-0	5469		1	4*	3		12				9	14			10	11					8"	5		7	2	6							
26	3	STOKE CITY	12	0-0	0-0	11132		1	2	3		4				9"	8	6		10	11		14				5		7									
27	15	Barnsley	11	1-1	0-1	5222	Scott	1	4	3		4				9	6			10	11	8			5				7									
28	22	NOTTS COUNTY	11	0-2	0-1	7538		1	5	3		4				9"	6			10	11	8				14			7	2*	12							
29	5 Feb	TRANMERE ROVERS	11	2-0	0-0	8171	Allison, Tinnion	1	5	3		4				9"	6			10	11		14						7	2	8							
30	12	Sunderland	12	0-0	0-0	16816		1	5	3		4				9"	6			10	11		14						12	7*		8		2				
31	22	Crystal Palace	13	1-4	1-1	11508	Shail	1	8	3		4				9	6			10	11		14						5	7			2"					
32	26	Southend United	10	1-0	1-0	4615	Allison	1	8	3		4*				9	6			10	11								5	7		12	2					
33	5 Mar	DERBY COUNTY	12	0-0	0-0	8723		1	4	3"							6			10	11	9*				14			5	7			2	8	12		
34	15	OXFORD UNITED	15	0-1	0-1	6635		1	7*	3						8"		6		10	11	14							5				2	4	12		
35	19	PORTSMOUTH	11	1-0	0-0	6352	Allison	1	3	11		4	8			14	9"	6		10									5				7	2			
36	26	Bolton Wanderers	14	2-2	1-2	10221	Allison(2)	1	3	11		4	8				9"	6		10									5				7	2		14	
37	30	Stoke City	16	0-3	0-1	13208		1	3"	11		4	8*				12	6		10									5	9			7	2		14	
38	2 Apr	WEST BROMWICH ALB.	16	0-0	0-0	8624		1	5	3		4	8				6*			10	12									7			2	11			
39	4	Nottingham Forest	16	0-0	0-0	24162		1	5	3				8			6			10	11									7			2		9		
40	9	GRIMSBY TOWN	16	1-0	0-0	5480	Scott(pen)	1	5	3		4	12	8						10	11									7*			2		9		
41	16	Birmingham City	15	2-2	2-0	20316	Partridge(2)	1	4	5			6	8*			12			10	11									7			2		9		
42	19	LUTON TOWN	11	1-0	1-0	5350	Edwards	1	4	3			6	8			5				11	12								7			2		9		
43	23	WATFORD	13	1-1	0-0	8324	Partridge	1	6	3		4	8	14			5	12			11*									7			2		9		
44	30	Millwall	13	0-0	0-0	11189		1	5	3			8"	14			12	6			11	10								7			2		9*		
45	3 May	Charlton Athletic	13	1-3	1-1	6727	Partridge	1	5	3			8"				12	6			11*	10								7			2		9		
46	8	PETERBOROUGH UNITED	13	4-1	2-0	7790	Bent(2), Robinson(2)	1		5	3		4				8"			12	6			11	10					7*			2		9		

Additional players - League matches: McKop H. - 40/6, 41/3, 45/14, 46/14;
Barclay D. - 42/10*, 43/10"; Brown W. - 46/1

								Welch	Munro	Scott	Aizlewood	Shail	Hewlett	Wyatt	Shelton	Baird	Robinson	Tinnion	Kamara	Allison	Edwards	Bent	Brown	Harrison	Osman	Rosenior	Gavin	Borrows	Bryant	Martin	Llewellyn	Pennyfather	Fowler	Harriott	Hoyland	Partridge	Milsom
							Apps.	45	43	45	5	35	11	8	3	16	31	40		35	31	17	5	1	4	1	6	6	27	33	15	7		17	6	7	1
							Subs.	1			1	1	2		3	9	1		4	8	3	6		1	3	2		1	1	5	1			2	2		
							Goals			5		2				5	4	5		15	2	2	1		1					1						4		

F.A. CUP

								Welch	Munro	Scott	Aizlewood	Shail	Hewlett	Wyatt	Shelton	Baird	Robinson	Tinnion	Kamara	Allison	Edwards	Bent	Brown	Harrison	Osman	Rosenior	Gavin	Borrows	Bryant	Martin
3R	8 Jan	LIVERPOOL		1-1	1-1	20612	Allison (£155,482)	1	2	3		4				9	6			10	11		8						5	7
3Rr	19	LIVERPOOL		1-1	0-0	21718	Allison (£77,348)	1	5	3						9	6			10	11	8							7	2
3Rr	25	Liverpool		1-0	0-0	36720	Tinnion (£337,909.50)	1	5	3						9	6			10	11	8*							7	2	12
4R	9 Feb	Stockport County		4-0	0-1	7691	Allison(3), Shail (£66,807.50)	1	5	3		4				9	6			10	11				2				7	8
5R	19	CHARLTON ATHLETIC		1-1	1-0	20416	Tinnion (£154,907)	1	2	3		4				9	6			10	11	14						5	7	8"
5Rr	2 Mar	Charlton Athletic		0-2	0-1	8205	(£72,268)	1	2	3		4"				9	6			10	11	8			14			5	7

* Abandoned after 65 mins. due to floodlights failure.

F.L. (COCA-COLA) CUP

								Welch	Munro	Scott	Aizlewood	Shail	Hewlett	Wyatt	Shelton	Baird	Robinson	Tinnion	Kamara	Allison	Edwards	Bent	Brown	Harrison	Osman	Rosenior
1R1	17 Aug	Swansea City		1-0	0-0	3746	Robinson	1	2	3*	4	5	6	7	8	9	10	11								12
1R2	24	SWANSEA CITY		0-2	0-1	4633		1	2	3	4	5	6*	7"	8	9	10	11		14						12

ANGLO-ITALIAN CUP

								Welch	Munro	Scott	Aizlewood	Shail	Hewlett	Wyatt	Shelton	Baird	Robinson	Tinnion	Kamara	Allison	Edwards	Bent	Brown	Harrison	Osman	Rosenior	Gavin	Borrows	Bryant	Martin	Llewellyn	Pennyfather
PGM	31 Aug	Portsmouth	3	1-3	1-2	2318	Munro	1	2	3	4	5			11*	9	7			14	12		8		6					10"		
PGM	7 Sep	OXFORD UNITED	2	2-1	1-0	1515	Allison, Rosenior	1				2					7				8			10	11			4			6	3*

PGM = Prelim. round group match. Additional players Anglo/Ital.Cup: (All in Sep 7 match) Thompson D. 5; Morgan N. 9"; McIntyre J. 12; Durbin G. 14.

GLOUCESTERSHIRE CUP FINAL

	5 Aug	BRISTOL ROVERS		1-1	0-0	6698	Bryant (£40,000)

Rovers awarded the Cup by winning penalty shoot-out 5-3. Extra time played after 0-0 score after 90 minutes.

FRIENDLIES

No.	Date	Opposition		Res.	H.T.	Att.	Goalscorers
1	21 Jul	Trowbridge Town		0-1	0-0	603	
2	22	Wimborne Town		4-1			Dziekanowski, Rosenior, Tinnion, Wyatt
3	26	Cobh Rangers		3-1			Brown, Dziekanowski, Robinson
4	28	Limerick		3-2	2-1		Baird, Morgan, Robinson
5	30	Galway		1-0	0-0		Bent
6	3 Aug	Bath City		1-2	0-0	414	Morgan
7	7	Swindon Town		2-1	0-1	4459	Rosenior, Shelton (Steve White Benefit)
8	9	Keynsham Town		6-1	4-0		Scott(2), Allison, Brown, McIntyre, Milsom
9	11	CAPE TOWN SPURS		1-2	0-0	1093	Allison
10	6 May	SWINDON TOWN		3-3	1-1	5032	Robinson(2), Cole (Andy Llewellyn Benefit)
11	22	Highlanders		3-1	2-1	20000	Bent, Sawu, Scott(pen)
12	27	Zimbabwe Select XI		2-2	2-1	5000	Bent, Martin
13	29	Dynamos		2-2	0-0	8000	Fowler, Scott

FINAL LEAGUE TABLE

Crystal Palace	46	27	9	10	73	46	90
Nottingham Forest	46	23	14	9	74	49	83
Millwall	46	19	17	10	58	49	74
Leicester City	46	19	16	11	72	59	73
Tranmere Rovers	46	21	9	16	69	53	72
Derby County	46	20	11	15	73	68	71
Notts County	46	20	8	18	65	69	68
Wolverhampton W.	46	17	17	12	60	47	68
Middlesbrough	46	18	13	15	66	54	67
Stoke City	46	18	13	15	57	59	67
Charlton Athletic	46	19	8	19	61	58	65
Sunderland	46	19	8	19	54	57	65
Bristol City	46	16	16	14	47	50	64
Bolton Wanderers	46	15	14	17	63	64	59
Southend United	46	17	8	21	63	67	59
Grimsby Town	46	13	20	13	52	47	59
Portsmouth	46	15	13	18	52	58	58
Barnsley	46	16	7	23	55	67	55
Watford	46	15	9	22	66	80	54
Luton Town	46	15	9	22	56	60	54
West Bromwich Albion	46	13	12	21	60	69	51
Birmingham City	46	13	12	21	52	69	51
Oxford United	46	13	10	23	54	75	49
Peterborough United	46	8	13	25	48	76	37

1993-94 Season
Back: Scott, Gerry Harrison, Dziekanowski, Allison, David Thompson, Edwards, Bryant, McIntyre.
Middle: Rosenior (Coach), Osman (Player/Manager), Llewellyn, Morgan, Gavin, Welch, Aizlewood, Leaning, Atteveld, Benton, Bent, Whitehead (Coach), Bell (Youth Team Coach), Footman (Physiotherapist).
Front: Shelton, Pennyfather, Tinnion, Baird, Martin, Munro, Shail, Brown, Robinson.

BACK ROW: Marvin Harriott, Scott Partridge, Stuart Duffin, Colin Loss, Mike Wyatt, Ian Brown, Rodney McAree, Junior Bent.
MIDDLE ROW: Russell Osman (Player Manager), Clive Whitehead (First Team Coach), Martin Scott, Jason Fowler, Scott Paterson, Wayne Allison, Keith Welch, Richard Rowe, Henry McKop, Paul Milsom, Matt Hewlett, Leroy Rosenior (Reserve Team Coach), Buster Footman (Physio).
FRONT ROW: Tony Fawthrop (Assistant Manager), Liam Robinson (now Burnley), Matt Bryant, Brian Tinnion, Stuart Munroe, Mark Shail, Dave Martin, Ian Baird, Rob Edwards, Gerry Sweeney (Coach).

BRISTOL CITY RESERVES
Summary, including Bristol South End 1894 -1897)

	P	W	D	L	F	A	Pts	Pos
South Bristol & District League:								
1895/96 Division 1	16	13	2	1	57	19	28	1
1896/97	22	12	5	5	69	30	29	4
Western League:								
1903/04 Division 2	18	15	2	1	64	17	32	1
1904/05	16	14	1	1	46	8	29	2
1905/06	18	14	2	2	79	13	30	2
1906/07	18	11	5	2	54	19	24	3
1907/08	16	12	1	3	55	13	25	1
1908/09	22	15	4	3	59	16	34	1
1909/10 Division 1	24	18	3	3	86	23	39	2
1910/11	18	15	3	0	58	14	33	1
1919/20	18	12	1	5	41	17	25	3
1920/21	30	18	5	7	58	27	41	1
1925/26	18	10	7	1	58	19	27	1
1926/27	22	16	2	4	59	32	34	1
1927/28	20	10	4	6	71	40	24	4
1928/29	14	7	1	6	34	31	15	5
1929/30	14	5	5	4	28	27	15	3
1930/31	12	4	2	6	34	28	10	4
1931/32	14	4	3	7	26	37	11	6
1932/33	16	6	4	6	54	42	16	5
1936/37	8	4	2	2	18	15	10	3
1937/38	8	6	1	1	21	8	13	1
1938/39	10	4	1	5	24	24	9	3
1939/40 Single Division	20	9	2	9	54	43	20	6
1940/41	10	4	2	4	27	24	10	4
1941/42	10	6	2	2	34	16	14	3
1945/46	26	10	6	10	90	69	26	7
1961/62	38	28	7	3	132	36	63	1
1962/63	42	31	5	6	120	56	67	1
1963/64	42	24	15	3	122	43	63	2
1964/65	42	21	4	17	96	82	46	9
1982/83 Division 1 *	36	9	11	16	57	77	29	13
1983/84	40	26	8	6	96	36	60	1
1984/85 Premier Division	42	21	14	7	69	49	56	3
1985/86	42	18	6	18	74	61	42	9
1986/87	42	23	5	14	94	57	51	3
1987/88	42	16	15	11	76	52	47	7
Western League Cup:								
1961/62	5	4	1	0	21	5	Winners	
1982/83	4	2	1	1	10	4	Semi-final	
1983/84	3	2	0	1	9	4	3rd Round	
1984/85	1	0	0	1	0	1	1st Round	
1985/86	1	0	0	1	0	1	1st Round	
1986/87	3	2	0	1	9	3	3rd Round	
1987/88	2	1	0	1	10	8	2nd Round	
Alan Young Cup								
1962/63	2	0	1	1	4	5	Final	
1963/64	2	1	0	1	4	2	Winners	
1964/65	2	0	0	2	0	6	Final	
Bristol Charity League								
1903/04 Single Division	6	4	1	1	18	8	9	1
1904/05	6	3	2	1	15	4	8	2
1905/06	8	6	0	2	24	10	12 Joint Champs.	
1905/06 Champs.play-off	1	0	1	0	1	1	Joint Champs.	
1906/07 Single Division	10	5	5	0	28	6	15 Joint Champs.	
1906/07 Champs.play-off	1	0	1	0	3	3	Joint Champs.	
1907/08 Single Division	10	4	2	4	20	11	10	3
1908/09	12	11	0	1	40	5	22	1
1909/10	6	4	1	1	17	6	9	2
1919/20	10	5	2	3	26	14	12	3

	P	W	D	L	F	A	Pts	Pos
(Bristol Charity League Contd.)								
1927/28	10	9	0	1	67	11	18 Joint Champs.	
1927/28 Champs.play-off	1	1	0	0	4	0	Champs.	
1928/29 Single Division	10	10	0	0	77	9	20	1
1940/41	2	1	0	1	2	5	2	2
1941/42	1	1	0	0	3	2	2	1
South Eastern League:								
1910/11	36	18	6	12	75	52	42	3
1911/12	38	11	8	19	55	76	30	14
1912/13	36	14	7	15	51	55	35	9
1913/14	40	21	5	14	70	60	47	6
1914/15	40	27	4	9	83	43	58	2
Southern League:								
1921/22 English Section	36	18	8	10	73	50	44	2
1922/23 **	38	24	5	9	84	39	53	1
1923/24 Western Sect.	34	17	9	8	63	39	43	5
1924/25	38	18	5	15	51	43	41	10
1925/26	26	16	4	6	48	28	36	2
1926/27	26	14	10	2	77	37	38	2
1927/28 **	30	20	3	7	95	51	43	1
1928/29	26	14	2	10	70	46	30	4
1929/30	28	11	5	12	59	63	27	10
London Combination:								
1930/31 Division 2	26	9	10	7	51	47	28	5
1931/32	22	7	7	8	39	53	21	9
1932/33 Division 1	46	13	10	23	83	108	36	21
1933/34	46	19	12	15	77	91	50	7
1934/35	46	15	10	21	86	93	40	20
1935/36	46	10	5	31	65	140	25	24
1936/37	46	14	8	24	62	96	36	21
1937/38	46	16	9	21	63	81	41	17
1938/39	46	15	5	26	86	130	35	21
1939/40 ***	3	0	0	3	3	13	0	24
Football Combination:								
1946/47 Section B	30	4	11	15	44	65	19	15
1947/48	30	8	7	15	35	49	23	14
1948/49	30	5	6	19	25	47	16	16
1949/50	30	7	11	12	35	49	25	11
1950/51	30	7	6	17	35	50	20	15
1951/52	30	9	1	20	36	66	19	15
1952/53 Division 2	30	7	7	16	34	53	21	15
1953/54	30	14	7	9	45	38	35	3
1954/55 Division 1	30	15	7	8	50	37	37	2
1955/56 Single Division	42	21	13	8	66	43	55	5
1956/57	42	21	12	9	77	62	54	4
1957/58	42	25	7	10	72	48	57	3
1958/59 Division 1	34	15	2	17	56	70	32	8
1959/60	34	12	4	18	56	71	28	14
1960/61	34	10	9	15	60	71	29	14
1965/66 Division 2	38	18	6	14	70	61	42	8
1966/67	24	16	2	6	69	30	34	3
1967/68	40	22	9	9	89	56	53	1
1968/69 Single Division	25	12	3	10	44	36	27	9
1969/70	25	15	4	6	43	30	34	5
1970/71	42	21	11	10	83	55	53	4
1971/72	40	16	10	14	57	50	42	8
1972/73	40	13	7	20	48	66	33	17
1973/74	42	13	6	23	45	75	32	19
1974/75	40	25	8	7	80	43	58	3
1975/76	42	20	11	11	74	44	51	5
1976/77	42	18	10	14	60	51	46	10
1977/78	42	9	13	20	57	87	31	18
1978/79	42	20	8	14	73	69	48	8
1979/80	42	19	10	13	77	58	48	7
1980/81	42	12	6	24	37	64	30	17
1981/82 ****	18	4	4	10	21	30	12	20

		P	W	D	L	F	A	Pts	Pos
(Football Combination Contd.)									
1992/93	Division 1	38	8	12	18	39	60	36	17
1993/94		38	8	9	21	48	84	33	20

Football Combination Cup:

		P	W	D	L	F	A	Pts	Pos
1946/47	Section ?	14	6	4	4	30	29	16	4
1947/48	Section 3	14	6	2	6	19	18	14	4
1948/49	Section 4	14	4	2	8	15	30	10	7
1949/50		14	4	4	6	19	20	12	5
1950/51		14	6	4	4	22	20	16	4
1951/52		14	4	1	9	22	33	9	7
1952/53		14	2	7	5	12	21	11	6
1953/54		14	4	3	7	18	24	11	8
1954/55		14	7	4	3	27	17	18	3
1966/67	Group ?	10	5	2	3	16	12	11	Q/F
1967/68	Knock-out Comp. 5		3	1	1	11	4		S/F
1968/69	Group ?	10	2	3	5	9	11	7	5
1969/70	Group A	10	6	1	3	22	14	13	3

Bristol & Suburban League:

		P	W	D	L	F	A	Pts	Pos
1942/43	Group A	16	15	1	0	78	17	31	1
1943/44		22	20	0	2	96	20	40	1
1944/45	Division 1	26	23	1	2	108	33	47	1

South-West Counties League:

		P	W	D	L	F	A	Pts	Pos
1985/86	Single Division	16	4	4	8	25	43	16	8
1986/87		18	13	4	1	39	17	43	1
1987/88		18	5	4	9	39	45	19	7
1988/89		21	10	2	9	49	36	32	4
1989/90		27	13	8	6	53	27	47	3
1990/91		22	16	5	1	74	21	53	1
1991/92		20	16	3	1	54	12	51	1

South-West Counties League Cup:

		P	W	D	L	F	A	Pts	Pos
1985/86	Group B	2	1	0	1	3	5	3	3
1986/87	Knock-out Comp.	1	0	0	1	1	2		1st Rd.
1987/88		4	2	1	1	4	3		Final
1988/89		1	0	0	1	0	2		1st Rd.
1989/90		3	3	0	0	8	0		Winners
1990/91	Group ?	5	5	0	0	20	7	6	Winners
1991/92		4	1	1	2	11	6	4	Q/F

Gloucestershire Junior Cup:

	P	W	D	L	F	A	Pts	Pos
1894/95	3	2	0	1	8	7		3rd Rd.
1895/96	1	0	0	1	0	1		Prel.Rd.
1896/97	4	2	1	1	15	10		S/F

Gloucestershire Senior Amateur Cup:

	P	W	D	L	F	A	Pts	Pos
1941/42 *****	2	1	1	0	2	2		2nd Rd.
1942/43 *****	3	2	0	1	0	2		S/F
1943/44	5	4	1	0	22	7		Winners
1944/45 *****	6	4	1	1	21	6		Final
1945/46	2	1	0	1	5	1		1st Rd.

Somerset Professional Cup:

	P	W	D	L	F	A	Pts	Pos
1934/35	2	1	0	1	3	2		Group matches
1948/49	1	0	0	1	0	4		1st Rd.
1949/50	2	1	0	1	6	3		S/F
1955/56	3	2	0	1	16	4		Final
1956/57	4	2	2	0	11	5		Joint/winner
1957/58	1	0	0	1	2	5		Q/F
1958/59	3	1	1	1	7	5		S/F
1959/60	3	2	0	1	13	4		S/F
1960/61	2	1	0	1	2	2		2nd Rd.
1961/62	5	3	0	2	10	5		Final
1962/63	4	2	1	1	9	5		Final
1963/64	5	4	1	0	16	3		Winners
1964/65	3	2	0	1	7	2		S/F
1965/66	2	0	1	1	2	4		2nd Rd.
1966/67	2	1	0	1	6	4		2nd Rd.
1967/68	1	0	0	1	1	2		1st Rd.
1968/69	3	1	1	1	8	3		2nd Rd.
1969/70	3	1	1	1	4	2		Final
1970/71	5	4	0	1	16	8		Winners

	P	W	D	L	F	A	Pts	Pos
(Somerset Professional Cup Contd.)								
1971/72	4	4	0	0	15	3		Winners
1972/73	2	1	0	1	4	3		Q/F
1973/74	4	2	1	1	6	2		Final
1974/75	5	4	1	0	13	2		Winners

Somerset Premier Cup:

	P	W	D	L	F	A	Pts	Pos
1975/76	1	0	0	1	1	2		1st Rd.
1977/78	3	2	0	1	4	3		Final
1978/79	2	0	1	1	0	1		Q/F
1979/80	2	0	1	1	0	1		3rd Rd.
1980/81	2	1	0	1	4	4		S/F
1983/84	3	1	1	1	3	3		2nd Rd.
1984/85	6	3	2	1	11	4		S/F
1985/86	5	3	1	1	13	7		S/F
1986/87	3	2	0	1	8	7		S/F
1987/88	2	1	0	1	1	4		Q/F
1989/90	3	2	0	1	10	3		S/F
1990/91	6	4	2	0	13	9		Winners
1991/92	1	0	0	1	0	1		Q/F
1992/93	1	0	0	1	0	4		1st Rd
1993/94	2	1	0	1	4	3		3rd Rd

Berkeley Hunt Charity Cup:

	P	W	D	L	F	A	Pts	Pos
1937/38	1	1	0	0	6	5		Winners
1938/39	1	1	0	0	7	4		Winners

White Hart Cup:

	P	W	D	L	F	A	Pts	Pos
1949/50	1	0	1	0	1	1		Joint Winners

Warminster Challenge Cup

	P	W	D	L	F	A	Pts	Pos
1951/52	1	1	0	0	4	1		Winners
1952/53	1	0	1	0	2	2		Joint Winners
1953/54	1	1	0	0	3	2		Winners
1954/55	1	1	0	0	3	2		Winners
1955/56	1	0	0	1	2	3		Final

Chippenham Sportsmens & Traders Trophy:

	P	W	D	L	F	A	Pts	Pos
1954/55	1	1	0	0	2	1		Winners

Mangotsfield Six-a-side:

	P	W	D	L	F	A	Pts	Pos
1961/62	2	2	0	0	29	13		Winners

Pontins Six-a-side:

	P	W	D	L	F	A	Pts	Pos
1977/78	3	2	0	1	7	6		Group matches

Trend Furnishers Charity Cup:

	P	W	D	L	F	A	Pts	Pos
1982/83	2	0	1	1	0	1		Final
S/F penalty shoot-out	1	1	0	0	4	3		

Clandown Charity Cup:

	P	W	D	L	F	A	Pts	Pos
1983/84	1	0	0	1	2	3		S/F
1983-84 Play-off	1	1	0	0	1	0		3rd place

Friendlies:

	P	W	D	L	F	A	Pts	Pos
1894/95	17	9	2	6	35	25		
1895/96	14	7	0	7	22	22		
1896/97	1	1	0	0	3	2		
1899/00	20	12	2	6	58	36		
1903/04	6	4	1	1	26	8		
1904/05	7	6	0	1	35	8		
1905/06	11	10	0	1	55	12		
1906/07	7	6	1	0	27	5		
1907/08	8	8	0	0	33	7		
1908/09	2	2	0	0	7	3		
1909/10	8	6	2	0	33	8		
1910/11	2	1	0	1	7	4		
1911/12	4	2	1	1	16	5		
1912/13	3	2	0	1	15	7		
1913/14	6	4	1	1	15	9		
1914/15	2	1	0	1	4	4		
1915/16	9	6	2	1	17	9		

	P	W	D	L	F	A
1919/20	10	7	0	3	35	11
1920/21	16	13	2	1	39	19
1921/22	14	11	2	1	57	15
1922/23	5	3	2	0	10	7
1923/24	7	4	1	2	21	11
1924/25	5	4	0	1	20	7
1925/26	10	6	2	2	29	17
1926/27	6	4	1	1	24	11
1927/28	2	1	1	0	5	4
1928/29	2	2	0	0	8	3
1930/31	3	1	0	2	7	8
1931/32	4	3	0	1	28	5
1933/34	2	1	1	0	7	2
1934/35	2	2	0	0	12	4
1935/36	3	3	0	0	17	4
1937/38	2	1	0	1	7	5
1938/39	4	1	1	2	12	12
1940/41	1	1	0	0	11	1
1945/46	1	1	0	0	2	1
1946/47	3	1	0	2	5	5
1948/49	2	2	0	0	9	3
1949/50	1	1	0	0	6	1
1950/51	3	2	0	1	7	2
1951/52	3	2	0	1	8	5
1952/53	2	0	1	1	2	3
1953/54	4	3	0	1	10	2
1954/55	3	2	1	0	12	5
1955/56	2	2	0	0	15	5
1958/59	1	1	0	0	4	1
1962/63	1	1	0	0	5	1
1963/64	5	3	0	2	17	9
1964/65	9	2	1	6	21	24
1965/66	5	2	1	2	13	16
1966/67	2	1	0	1	5	4
1967/68	2	2	0	0	3	0
1970/71	3	3	0	0	18	2
1971/72	2	2	0	0	8	1
1972/73	3	2	0	1	5	3
1973/74	2	1	1	0	2	1
1974/75	4	2	2	0	13	5
1975/76	7	4	1	2	19	12
1976/77	2	1	0	1	2	1
1978/79	2	2	0	0	3	1
1979/80	1	1	0	0	4	2
1980/81	1	1	0	0	4	2
1981/82	1	1	0	0	1	0
1982/83	2	2	0	0	4	0
1984/85	6	5	1	0	15	4
1985/86	4	2	0	2	15	9
1986/87	6	2	1	3	14	16
1988/89	5	3	2	0	8	2
1989/90	5	4	1	0	17	3
1990/91	6	4	0	2	19	10
1991/92	14	6	1	7	32	22
1992/93	7	5	1	1	32	11
1993/94	4	1	2	1	5	4

*   Format changed with formation of Premier League in 1976/77

**   Championship play-offs were held to decide on the overall Champions. These results are not included in the summaries. City lost out on both occasions:- 2-1 to Ebbw Vale (Welsh Section winners), and 5-0 to Kettering Town (Eastern Section winners).

***   Competition abandoned due to Second World War.

****   City Reserves resigned, record expunged.

*****   The record is correct, except it does not reflect all the goals as the actual match score has not always been available.

Note:

(i)   These summaries are from the Author's own researched records, and do not always tie in with official tables.

(ii)   With regard to 'Friendly' matches, a judgement has often had to be made in respect to the status of the team that played, i.e. 1st, 2nd, 3rd or Youth. After further research the Author has changed a number of matches which were previously published as 1st team fixtures to now read as Reserve games.

(iii)   For some Friendly matches, the score has not been traced, despite the known existence of a programme and therefore confirmation of the match having taken place. Therefore this record cannot be considered final, since it is likely that more such games will eventually come to light.

Matches not included in the summaries:

7 Nov 1896 v. Clifton Res.   (h) 6-0 South Bristol & District League
(Match ordered to be replayed on 27 Feb - result 1-3)

2 Jan 1897 v. Clevedon   (a) 0-2 South Bristol & District League
(Match ordered to be replayed on 23 Jan - result 2-2)

29 Oct 1904 v. Warmley   (a) 2-0 Bristol Charity League
(Warmley disbanded in Jan 1905, and their record was expunged)

10 Nov 1906 v. Paulton Rovers   (a) 5-0 Western League
(Abandoned after 83 mins. - failing light. Replayed 15 Apr - result 0-0)

11 Jan 1913 v. Reading Res.   (a) 6-5 South Eastern League
(Abandoned afer 60 mins. - waterlogged pitch. Replayed 24 Mar - result 0-3)

14 Nov 1914 v. Brentford Res.   (h) 7-0 South Eastern League
(Brentford resigned and their record was expunged)

10 Jan 1920 v. Barry Res.   (h) 2-1 Western League
(City fielded L.Hughes an unregistered player. Match ordered to be replayed on 31 Mar - result 4-1)

19 Feb 1921 v. Ton Pentre   (h) 3-0 Western League
(City fielded R.Keen an unregistered player. Match ordered to be replayed on 3 May - result 1-0)

19 Nov 1927 v. Newport County Res.   (a) 1-1 Southern League
(Abandoned after 65 mins. - adverse weather. Replayed 20 Feb - result 1-3)

14 Dec 1946 v. Chelsea Res.   (a) 1-4 Football Combination
(Abandoned after 56 mins. - fog. Replayed 5 Feb - result 2-4)

29 Jan 1949 v. Swindon Town Res.   (h) 0-1 Football Combination Cup
(Abandoned after 86 mins. - fog. Replayed 28 Mar - result 3-1)

25 Nov 1950 v. Watford Res.   (a) 1-1 Football Combination
(Abandoned after 64 mins. - fog. Replayed 26 Apr - result 0-1)

26 Dec 1963 v. Exeter City Res.   (a) 4-1 Western League
(Abandoned after 70 mins. - fog. Replayed 4 Mar - result 4-0)

29 Oct 1968 v. Bournemouth & B.A.Res. (h) 2-0 Football Combination
(Abandoned after 70 mins. - power failure. Replayed 16 Jan - result 1-1)

13 Jan 1977 v. Ipswich Town Res.   (h) 0-0 Football Combination
(Abandoned after 10 mins. - waterlogged pitch. Replayed 21 Apr - result 3-1)

10 Jan 1989 v. Newport County Res.   (h) 1-1 South West Counties League
(Newport County resigned and their record was expunged)

RESERVE SNIPPETS

Bristol City didn't operate a Reserve team in the 1897-98, 1898-99, 1900-01, 1901-02, 1902-03, 1916-17, 1917-18 and 1918-19 seasons.

Following the outbreak of war in 1939, City Colts took on the mantle of the City 2nd Eleven. From the 1943-44 season they became known as 'City Athletic', and it wasn't until the 1945-46 season that a proper Reserve XI was formed again, when they competed in the Western League.

On 30 April 1904, City Res. lost 2-3 against the Club's 1st XI in the last Bristol City match at St. Johns' Lane. As the spectators left at the end of the game, the band played *Auld Lang Syne.*

At the conclusion of the following three matches there was a balloon ascent and parachute descent by Professor Stephens:-
7 Sep 1907 v. Radstock Town   (h) 3-1 Western League, att. 4,250.
12 Sep 1908 v. Aberdare   (h) 1-0 Western League, att. 4,000.
25 Sep 1909 v. Mardy   (h) 3-1 Friendly, att. 'splendid'.

No interval was taken during the 3-1 home win over Tunbridge Wells Rangers on 25 September 1912 in the South Eastern League, as the opposition had a train to catch at the end of the match.

On 22 April 1914, a Combined City and Rovers Reserve XI beat a Gloucestershire XI, 4-1 at Eastville, in a Benefit for the E.J.Clarke Testimonial Fund.

On 3 March 1920, a 'City Old Professionals XI', beat a Police XI, 2-1 at Ashton Gate, after being 1-0 behind at half-time.

The Bristol Charity League was decided by play-offs when teams tied at the top (with the same number of points). City were involved in the following:
1905-06: 3 Apr 1907 v. Bristol Rovers Reserves. Result 1-1, played at the Chequers. (Trophy shared)
1907-08: 27 Apr 1908 v. Bristol Rovers Reserves. Result 3-3, played at the Chequers. (Trophy shared)
1927-28: 10 Oct 1928 v. Welton Rovers. Result 4-0, played at Welton.

The City record in the Bristol Charity League for 1909-10 is not clear in respect of the goals scored, as it has not been possible to ascertain the score in a drawn match at Bath on 28 March (0-0 has been assumed). Differing scores were recorded for the home match with Kingswood Rovers on 29 March ('Western Daily Press' records 4-1, 'Bristol Times and Mirror' and 'Bristol Evening News' both record 9-1) Since the 'Western Daily Press' was the only one to include the goalscorers, the 4-1 result has been assumed correct.

In the Bristol Charity League, 1928-29 season, Clevedon lost 19-0 at Ashton Gate on October 17, and were then defeated 13-0 on their own ground a week later. The City won all their ten matches that season, finishing their programme with a 13-0 victory over Sharpness, at Ashton Gate, on May 1.

City experimented with numbered shirts for the first time on 25 November 1933, for the home London Combination 2-0 victory over Leicester City Reserves. This experiment was described as a success, the only reservation being the small size of the numbers.

The Somerset Professional Cup for 1934-35 appears to have been played on a mini-league basis, since City Reserves played two matches - losing 2-1 at Bath (28 February) and then beating Glastonbury 2-0 at Ashton Gate (20 March).

Following a dispute with B.A.C. over the choice of venue for a 2nd round replay in the Gloucestershire Senior Cup, City Colts withdrew on 3 December 1941. City had forfeited home advantage in the first match (a 2-2 draw on November 29) in order to assist their opponents, but were unwilling to play the replay 'away' as well. In the 1st round City had beaten Southmead Sports, but no details of this away fixture have been found. In the same competition, in 1942-43, City received a 1st round bye, and in the following two rounds beat the 14th Gloucestershire Home Guard and the R.A.F.(Winterbourne) respectively, although no details of the scorelines have come to light. In the Semi-final they lost 0-2 at B.A.C. The tournament was won in the 1943-44 season, after a 1st round bye, and victories over Eden Grove (4-2 away), National Fire Service (6-0 away), B.A.C (5-2 in the Semi-final), and Hollygrove by 5-1 in the Final at the Aero Engines ground. City reached the Final in the following campaign, when they beat R.A.F.(Filton) at home by 5-1, Kleen-E-Ze (10-0 at home), B.A.C. (4-0 at home), and Hollygrove in the Semi-final by an unknown score at home. Before a crowd of 1,300 in the Final at Eastville, City drew 1-1 with R.E.M.E., and at the same venue four days later before an attendance of 1,458, they lost the replay 4-1.

After drawing 3-3 at Yeovil in the 1956-57 Somerset Professional Cup Final, the required replay was played the following season, on 26 November. At the same venue the match finished 1-1, and the two clubs shared the trophy. That same season the two teams met again in this competition, when City lost 5-2 in the Quarter-final.

The first Mangotsfield Six-A-Side Tournament was won by City on 2 November 1961, when Soundwell were beaten 12-9, and Keynsham Town 17-4 in the Semi-final and Final respectively.

On 17 October 1962, Cardiff University were beaten 5-1 in a Friendly played at the County Ground.

The Boxing Day 1963 abandoned game versus Exeter City Res. created an unusual double, as the first XI fixture (at home to Queens Park Rangers) was also brought to a premature halt; both due to fog.

Only 80 minutes was played in the Football Combination 0-0 home draw with Chelsea Reserves on 13 December 1973. The visitors had arrived 20 minutes after the scheduled kick-off time, but the result was allowed to stand.

On 18 May 1977, Bristol Rovers switched their home Football Combination Reserve fixture to Ashton Gate, a move that helped City record a 4-1 victory.

The 4-2 defeat at home to Queens Park Rangers Reserves in the Football Combination on 11 March 1978 took place at 'Stockwood Lane'.

City Manager Alan Dicks played in the 1-0 Somerset Professional Cup Quarter-final victory at Taunton Town on 19 March 1978.

In the 1978 Pontins Six-A-Side Tournament at Brean Down, City beat Aldershot 4-2 and lost to Leicester City 3-0, before beating West Ham United (3-1), the following day.

On 5 April 1979, City Reserves beat Vasteras 1-0 in a Friendly at Bath University, Doyle scoring two minutes before half-time.

Due to an oversight, the match officials were not informed of the Football Combination game at Hereford on 26 April 1979. The fixture started late, with local referee Pat Ellis in charge, and Hereford apprentices Steve Strong and Andy Feeley running the lines; City won 2-1.

Both 1979-80 Football Combination fixtures with Queens Park Rangers were played at Ashton Gate. The Rangers won their 'home' game 5-1 on 14 January. Similarly the City home match with Cardiff City was played at Ninian Park on 21 April, when the Robins won 1-0.

Confusion reigns over the result of the South West Counties League match at Swansea on 22 January 1987. The local press reported a 4-1 defeat to City Reserves although the official record shows the score as 4-3 to City. Bristol City F.C. records the match having been played on 11 February, and have no information of a match in January. In consequence therefore, the 4-1 defeat has been included as a Friendly match.

The South West Counties League match away to Hereford United Reserves on 16 February 1990 was played on the artificial surface pitch at the National Stadium, Cardiff; City Reserves lost 2-1.

WESTERN LEAGUE RECORDS - BRISTOL CITY 3rd ELEVEN

	P	W	D	L	F	A	Pts	Pos		P	W	D	L	F	A	Pts	Pos
1929-30 (Division 2)	18	9	3	6	54	41	21	4	1952-53	34	14	6	14	75	56	34	8
1930-31	32	19	5	8	111	72	43	5	1953-54	34	22	6	6	87	39	50	2
1931-32	34	19	2	13	124	89	40	5	1954-55 (Division 1)	34	11	4	19	53	62	26	12
1932-33	34	18	6	10	91	64	42	3	1955-56	32	8	7	17	43	63	23	13
1933-34	34	10	8	16	60	79	28	14	1956-57	36	13	4	19	58	74	30	17
1934-35	34	15	4	15	87	69	34	10	1957-58	36	16	7	13	70	59	39	8
1935-36	34	14	3	17	71	76	31	12	1958-59	36	12	7	17	75	88	31	14
1936-37	34	11	2	21	62	90	24	13	1959-60	36	12	4	20	65	82	28	17
1937-38	34	15	1	18	86	100	31	12	1960-61 (Single Division)	40	18	10	12	94	70	46	8
1938-39	34	17	6	11	87	58	40	8									
									1965-66	34	4	5	25	33	94	13	18
1946-47 (Division 1) *	24	7	1	16	50	92	15	15	1966-67	40	13	8	19	63	64	34	13
1947-48 (Division 1)	34	11	7	16	69	104	29	11	1967-68	40	9	10	21	33	59	28	17
1948-49	34	7	4	23	57	105	18	18	1968-69	36	13	6	17	64	68	32	14
1949-50 (Division 2)	34	14	8	12	89	60	36	10	1969-70	38	13	7	18	58	76	33	14
1950-51	38	14	5	19	75	84	33	12	1970-71	34	7	8	19	40	78	22	15
1951-52	36	17	7	12	87	58	41	8	1972-73	30	5	4	21	35	76	14	15

* Fixtures in competition not completed due to weather causing many postponements.

N.B.: The official Western league tables incorrectly show Bristol City Reserves playing in the competition 1946-47 and 1947-48.

BRISTOL SOUTH RESERVES - Friendlies

	P	W	D	L	F	A
1891/92	3	0	0	3	3	19
1892/93	3	0	1	2	4	8
1893/94	4	1	0	3	4	14

Bristol City Youth Team - F.A.Youth Cup 1952-53 to 1993-94

Season	Rd	Date	Opposition	Res	HT	Att	Goalscorers
1952-53	1	17 Sep	Trowbridge Town	6-3	3-2		Smith(3), Burgess, Knight, Rawlings
	2	1 Nov	OAK VILLE ATHLETIC	1-0	0-0		Smith
	3	6 Dec	Longfleet St. Mary's	4-0	2-0		Smith(2), Burgess, Rawlings
	4	31 Jan	BRIGGS SPORTS	2-1	0-1	1000	Burgess, Jeremiah
	5	28 Feb	Huntley & Palmers	1-2*	1-1		Rawlings(pen) (*after extra time)
1953-54	1	3 Oct	Bristol Rovers	2-1*	0-0		Munday, Smart (*aet, at Douglas Ground)
	2	19	Portsmouth	0-3	0-1		
1954-55	2	23	BRISTOL ROVERS	4-0	4-0		Gerrish, McCall, Morrison, Watts
	2	11 Dec	ST. AUSTELL	13-0	5-0		McCall(5), Munday(5), Hammond(2), Watts
	3	19 Jan	PINEHURST YOUTH CLUB	4-0	3-0		Morrison, Rowden, Watts, O.G.
	4	5 Feb	Plymouth argyle	1-4*	1-1		Munday (*aet)
1955-56	1	15 Oct	TROWBRIDGE TOWN	8-0	5-0		Fowler(3), Skirton(2), Davis, Oldfield, Taylor
	2	26 Nov	St. Austell	3-0	2-0		Clements, Oldfield, O.G.
	3	10 Dec	PLYMOUTH ARGYLE	2-1	0-0		Skirton, A. Williams(pen)
	4	11 Feb	PORTSMOUTH	3-0	0-2	357	Fowler(2), Gerrish
	5	14 Mar	ARSENAL	4-3	2-2	4012	R.Williams(2), Fowler, Skirton
	SF 1/L	7 Apr	Chesterfield	1-2	1-1	6385	Fowler
	SF 2/L	24	CHESTERFIELD	1-1	0-0		Mawditt
1956-57	1	22 Sep	Southampton	1-7	0-4		
1957-58	2	21 Nov	Newport County	0-9	0-3		
1958-59	1R	13 Oct	NEWPORT COUNTY	2-1	2-0	2903	Burt, Clark
	2	22	TROWBRIDGE TOWN	12-0	5-0	1426	Johnson(5), A.Williams(5), Bryant, Clark
	3	18 Dec	Bristol Rovers	1-1	1-0		O.G. (Played at 'Douglas Ground')
	3R	16	BRISTOL ROVERS	3-0	1-0	2336	A.Williams(3)
	4	20 Jan	Arsenal	1-2	0-1	902	Derrick
1959-60	1	13 Oct	TROWBRIDGE TOWN	5-1	4-0	2387	Bush(2), A.Williams(2), O.G.
	2	10 Nov	HAMWORTHY	14-0	8-0	1945	Bush(6),Clark(3),Davis(2),A.Wllamst(2),Jhnson
	3	8 Dec	READING	2-0	1-0	2126	Bush, A.Williams
	4	3 Feb	Southampton	4-1	2-1		Bush(2), Clark, Derrick
	5	7 Mar	West Ham United	3-3	1-1	13686	Davis, Derrick, A.Williams
	5R	22 Mar	WEST HAM UNITED	3-2	1-1	18181	Bush(2), A.Williams
	SF 1/L	5 Apr	CHELSEA	0-3	0-1	5578	
	SF 2/L	11	Chelsea	0-3	0-2	2544	
1960-61	1	3 Oct	Swindon Town	1-3	1-2		A.Williams
1961-62	1	17 Oct	BRISTOL ROVERS	5-1	3-0	701	Welsh(2), Bryant, Stacey, O.G.
	2	20 Nov	Poole Town	2-1	0-1		Stacey(2)
	3	6 Jan	Dorchester Town	5-0	3-0	2500	Stacey(2), Elson(2)
	4	13 Feb	BRIGHTON & HOVE ALB.	2-0	1-0	2260	Stacey(2)
	5	3 Mar	Portsmouth	1-3	0-0		Peters
1962-63	2	11 Dec	Exeter City	1-5	1-1	639	Sharpe
1963-64	2	20 Nov	Poole Town	3-1	3-0		Watkins(2), Sharpe
	2R	16 Dec	Cardiff City	2-1	0-1		Sharpe, Watkins
	3	18 Jan	Plymouth Argyle	3-5	1-2	2500	Giles(2), Harvey
1964-65	1	17 Nov	Swansea Town	2-2	2-1		Garland, Giles
	1R	24	CARDIFF CITY	4-1	2-1	750	Down(2), Garland, Giles
	2	8 Dec	BRISTOL ROVERS	5-0	3-0	700	Down(2), Garland(2), Bartley
	3	11 Jan	Swansea Town	4-2	2-1	1034	Garland(2), Down, Giles
	4	15 Feb	PLYMOUTH ARGYLE	6-2	2-1	400	Garland(4,1pen), Down, Giles
	5	1 Mar	Arsenal	2-3	1-2	2669	Bartley, Down
1966-67	2	6 Dec	Bristol Rovers	2-2	2-2	1922	Garland, Mannering
	2R	12	Bristol Rovers	1-2	0-0	1058	R.Williams
1967-68	1	7 Nov	Bristol Rovers	0-1	0-0	1240	
1968-69	1	12 Nov	SWINDON TOWN	2-1	1-0	880	K.Fear(pen), Matthews
	2	3 Dec	SWANSEA TOWN	4-2	3-0		Broomfield, K.Fear, Lillington, Matthews
	3	9 Jan	Swansea Town	2-1	0-1		Broomfield, K.Fear
	4	24 Jan	Swindon Town	1-3	1-0		O.G.
1969-70	1	6 Nov	Swindon Town	1-0	1-0		K.Fear
	2	1 Dec	Cardiff City	1-1	2-0		Fry
	2R	15	CARDIFF CITY	3-1	2-0		K.Fear, Fry, T.Richie
	3	30	Plymouth Argyle	2-0	1-0		Bruton, K.Fear
	4	28 Jan	Bournemouth & Bos. Ath.	5-3	2-0	880	Rodgers(3), K.Fear, Griffin
	5	24 Feb	LEEDS UNITED	2-1	1-0	10178	K.Fear, T.Ritchie
	SF 1/L	24 Mar	Tottenham Hotspur	0-2	0-1	3520	
	SF 2/L	6 Apr	TOTTENHAM HOTSPUR	0-1	0-0	9246	
1970-71	2	7 Dec	Bournemouth & Bos. Ath.	0-3	0-1		
1971-72	2	22 Nov	BOURNEMOUTH & BOS. ATH.	1-0	1-0		Howell
	3	20 Dec	Plymouth Argyle	3-2	0-1		Glover, Milne, S.Ritchie
	4	5 Feb	Stoke City	0-0	0-0		
	4R	14	STOKE CITY	2-0	1-0	1240	Glover, Lee
	5	23	Norwich City	1-2	1-0		Griffin
1972-73	2	21 Nov	Southampton	0-0	0-0		
	2R	28	SOUTHAMPTON	2-0	2-0		Crowley, McNeil
	3	2 Jan	NORTHFIELD JUNIORS	2-0	2-0		Crowley(2)
	4	29	Everton	1-0	1-0		Rogers
	5	20 Feb	ARSENAL	2-0	2-0	6781	Collier, Price
	SF 1/L	12 Mar	Sheffield United	2-2	1-1		Pruel(2)
	SF 2/L	21	SHEFFIELD UNITED	0-0	0-0	7906	(Note: United refused to play extra-time)
	SFR	28	Sheffield United	1-0	0-0		Rogers (played at St. Andrew's, Birmingham)
	F 1/L	9 Apr	Ipswich Town	0-3	0-1	5556	
	F 2/L	16	IPSWICH TOWN	1-1	0-1	6032	Rogers
1973-74	2	27 Nov	CARDIFF CITY	4-0	3-0		Lee(2), Teagle(pen), Whitehead
	3	18 Dec	Arsenal	1-4	0-2		McGhee
1974-75	2	21 Nov	Plymouth Argyle	3-2	1-1		Penny(2), McGhee
	3	17 Dec	Ipswich Town	0-1	0-0		
1975-76	3	10 Dec	PLYMOUTH ARGYLE	2-0	1-0		Goatley, Simmons
	3	1 Jan	SWINDON TOWN	4-2	0-1	1000	Penny(2), Pritchard, Simmons
	4	12 Jan	Sunderland	2-2	0-2	1561	Penny(2)
	4R	19	SUNDERLAND	6-2*	0-2		Mabbutt(2),Frenn,Goatly,Pnny,Simms (*aet)
	5	10 Mar	NEWCASTLE UNITED	1-1	1-0	4021	Penny
	5R	15	Newcastle United	1-6	0-3		Goatley
1976-77	2	20 Dec	Southampton	5-4	3-0		Mabbutt(2), Payne(2), Pritchard
	3	26 Jan	Hereford United	0-3	0-0		
1977-78	3	29 Nov	CARDIFF CITY	3-0	0-0	300	Payne(2)
	3	16 Jan	SOUTHAMPTON	1-2	1-0		Payne
1978-79	2	28 Nov	Bristol Rovers	1-5	0-4	1250	Wiffli
1979-80	2	3 Dec	Torquay United	7-1	4-0		Chandler(3), Musker(2), McFall, Smith
	3	8 Jan	Port Vale	6-0	3-0		Biggs(2), McFall(2), Chandler, Smith
	4	29	MIDDLESBROUGH	1-2	1-0		Chandler
1980-81	2	2 Dec	Portsmouth	1-4	0-2		Smith
1981/82	2	23 Nov	Portsmouth	0-1	0-1		
1982-83	1	25 Oct	PLYMOUTH ARGYLE	3-3	3-1		N.Kelly, O.Kelly, Smith
	1R	1 Nov	Plymouth Argyle	2-1	0-0		N.Kelly, O.Kelly
	2	29	BRISTOL ROVERS	1-1	0-1		O.Kelly
	2R	6 Dec	Bristol Rovers	1-2	1-0		N.Kelly
1983-84	1	15 Nov	PLYMOUTH ARGYLE	1-3	1-1		Harris
1984-85	1	10 Nov	Reading	0-4	0-2	71	
1985-86	1Q	26 Sep	SWANSEA CITY	2-2	1-1	114	Hawkins, Thompson
	1QR	30	Swansea City	1-3	1-2		Moore
1986-87	1Q	18	YATE TOWN	6-1	3-1	89	Hawkins(5), Mardon
	2Q	14 Oct	ROMSEY TOWN	6-1	3-1	86	Hawkins(2), Cousins, King, Mardon, O.G.
	1	7 Nov	OXFORD UNITED	1-2	1-0	100	Hawkins
1987-88	1Q	22 Sep	DORCHESTER TOWN	2-0	0-0	86	Bryant, Cousins
	2Q	22 Oct	TORQUAY UNITED	1-0	1-0	51	Weaver
	1	3 Nov	EXETER CITY	2-0	1-0	65	Mardon(2)
	2	9 Dec	SOUTHEND UNITED	2-4	1-2	45	Gorwell, Weaver
1988-89	1	14 Nov	Bristol Rovers	3-1	1-1	270	Darlaston(3)
	2	19 Dec	PLYMOUTH ARGYLE	2-3	1-2	106	Darlaston, Theobald
1989-90	1	24 Oct	HORNDEAN	10-0	2-0		Mellon(4), Darlaston(3), Watkins(2), Smith
	2	21 Nov	PLYMOUTH ARGYLE	0-4	0-2		
1990-91	1	6 Nov	EXETER CITY	1-2	0-1		Proudfoot
1991-92	1	21 Oct	Swindon Town	4-0	1-0		Lumsden(3), Wyatt
	3	19 Nov	EPSOM & EWELL	3-2	1-2		Fowler(2), Wyatt
	3	4 Jan	Southend United	0-3	0-2	153	
1992-93	2	3 Nov	BRISTOL ROVERS	4-1	2-0	362	Hicks(2), Skidmore, Wyatt
	3	25	SWANSEA CITY	5-2	3-2	145	Hicks(2), Fowler, Lumsden, Wyatt
	4	4 Jan	SWINDON TOWN	2-1	1-1	185	Duffin, Milsom
	5	2 Mar	NORWICH CITY	1-0	1-0	478	Milsom
1993-94	2	6 Dec	Reading	3-4	1-2	1057	Duffin(3,2pens)
	3	26 Jan	ASTON VILLA	1-4	0-2	161	Pettit

ADVANCED SUBSCRIBERS

John Treleven
Graham Spackman
David Keats, Thornton Heath
Raymond Shaw
M. J. Cripps
Richard Wells
L.A. Zammit
Derek Hyde
Mark Tyler, Rayleigh, Essex
J. Ringrose
David Jowett
David Earnshaw, Belper, Derbyshire
Steve Emms, Evesham
W.D. Phillips
Jonathan Hall
Jonny Stokkeland, Norway
G.T. Allman
Alan Davies
Dave McPherson, Colchester
Andrew & Janet Waterman
John Rawnsley
Geoffrey Wright
Richard Stocken
Bob Lilliman
Martin Simons, Belgium
Willy Østby, Norway
Christer Svensson, Sweden
Peter Frankland, Shaw, Oldham
Derek Wheatcroft
Chris-Sheila Hooker, Canada
Peter Baxter
Richard Lane, Newark, Notts.
Norman Nicol
G.T. Allman
A.N. Other
Richard Payne
Chris Marsh, Chesterfield
Graham & Ryan James
Roger Hansson, Sweden
Stephen Kieran Byrne
C. Timbrell
Jonathan Morgan
D.M. Woods
Goran Pedersen, Norway
Keith Coburn
Robert M. Smith
David Pottier
Buster Footman, Portishead, Avon
Nicholas Baker
Adam Bigwood, Penryn, Cornwall
Ryan Tutton, Hengrove, Bristol
Robert John Hall
David Arthur Wilshire, Totterdown
Mike Adams, Tickenham, Avon
Roland Jones
Jason Dale Southway, Bristol
John Lloyd, Winterbourne, Bristol
P.T. Knowles, Bristol

Martin Harrington, Withywood, Bristol
Simon Dubber, Shirehampton, Bristol
Russell Wedmore, Bristol
David Orr, Chipping Sodbury
Jason Spillane, Hanham, Bristol
Jonathan & Michael Clapp
Richard Hartill, Hanham, Bristol
Peter Wood
Stephen Franklin, Henleaze, Bristol
Simon Franklin, London Branch
Jeremy Comerford, Uplands, Bristol
Richard Height, Yate, Bristol
N. Bishop, Dilton Marsh, Westbury
Wendy & Garry Smith
Nick & Lin
Benjamin Biggs, Shirehampton, Bristol
(The) Tuckfield Family, Long Ashton
Rob Whitaker
Philip Offer, St. George
W.A. Davies, Bristol
D. Bidgood, Ham, Surrey
Steve Philpott, Uley, Gloucestershire
John Price, Hanham, Bristol
Gill Kendall, Downend, Bristol
Andrew John White
Christopher John White
John Robson, Kingswood, Bristol
Richard Butler, Downend, Bristol
Keith Michael Knight, Nailsea
Matthew Simon Knight, Nailsea
Peter Taylor, Nailsea
Matthew Croker, Backwell
Leslie Albert Knight, Tickenham
Kevin Brake, Lockleaze, Bristol
Andy Jefferson, Keynsham, Bristol
Richard Workman, Brislington, Bristol
Peter Usher, Henbury, Bristol
Andrew D. Langdown, Dursley
Keith Jones, Patchway, Bristol
Julie Clapp, Old Sodbury
John Clapp, Old Sodbury
Richard J. Gabb, Dursley
Martin Pearce, Abbots Langley
Peter John Lomas, Bristol
Mr.P.J. & Mrs.M. Whyham, Gloucester
Chris Ireland, Madrid
Robin Ireland, Portishead
Nigel Wilby, Twerton, Bath
Phillip Edwards, Mark, Somerset
Happy Birthday, Andrew
Ian Williams, Frome, Somerset
David Fudge, Hanham, Bristol
Stephen Fudge, Warmley, Bristol
Paul Tompkins, Oldland Common
Steve Gray, Redfield, Bristol
Lisa Jeffrey
Mike Wright, Thame, Oxfordshire
Malcolm McGivan, Birmingham

Peter Maksimczyk
Alec John McGivan, Oxfordshire
Roger Hayes, Bristol
Paul Tully, Bedminster
Peter Chmielinski, Carshalton Beeches
John Bradbury, Stonehouse, Glos.
Darrell Wayne Sandrone
Duncan James, Warwick
Christopher Bowles, Shepton Mallet
Dave Wyatt, Chepstow
John Turner
C. H. Weaver
M. Bennett, Bristol
'Forever A Robin'
James Smith
G. McDonald, London
Mr. and Mrs. Phillips, Bucks.
G. Parrott
The Two Biggest Fans
Pat Jones, Bristol
R. Turnbull
K. Wright, Bristol
A.N.Other, Gloucester
B. Ashby, West London
Bob and Jane
A. McKenzie
Simon and Family
'Forty Years A Supporter'
J. Draper
Bridge Family
City Fan, West Midlands
R. Bradshaw
Loyal Supporter Since 1960
A Real Bristol Babe
M. Hall, Bristol
Mr. A. Lynch
Brian - Forever City
Mr. Dixon
S. Smith and Family
June and Alec
F. Cook, Bristol
Graham and Carole
Two London Fans
R. Williams
J. and S. Cox
Anthony J. Woods
Mervyn Baker
Jantzen Derrick
Alan Williams
Tom Hopegood
Andrew Woods
Nicholas Woods
Helen Woods
George Kite
Whitehall School
Mick Hunter
Göran Schönhult, Trelleborg, Sweden.
A. Matthews, Tylers Green

A SELECTION OF TITLES

From
'YORE PUBLICATIONS'
12 The Furrows, Harefield,
Middx. UB9 6AT

(Free lists issued 3 times per year. For your first list please send a S.A.E.)

DONNY - The Official History of Doncaster Rovers *(Tony Bluff and Barry Watson)* Written by two supporters of the Club, with the full statistics (from 1879) incl. line-ups (from 1901). The book is well illustrated, with the full written history of the Club. Hardback with dustjacket and 240 pages. Price £14-95 plus £1-80 postage.

COLCHESTER UNITED - The Official History of the 'U's' *(Hal Mason)* With football involvement from the 1920's, the Author - a former journalist and Colchester programme editor - is well qualified to relate this complete history of the Club since its formation in 1937 (including complete statistics and lineups from this season). Large Hardback with dustjacket, 240 pages, priced £14-95 plus £2-70 postage.

AMBER IN THE BLOOD - History of Newport County: *(Tony Ambrosen).* The full written story of football in Newport from the pre-County days up to and including the recently formed Newport AFC club. The text is well illustrated, and a comprehensive statistical section provides all the results, attendances, goalscorers, etc. from 1912 to 1993 - the various Leagues and principal Cup competitions; additionally seasonal total players' appearances are included. A hardback book, containing 176 large pages is exceptional value at only £13-95 plus £2-60 postage.

KILLIE - The Official History (125 Years of Kilmarnock F.C.) *(David Ross).* A very detailed history of Scotland's oldest professional Club. The statistics section (including line-ups) cover the period 1873 to 1994, and over 200 illustrations, incl.a team group for most seasons. A large hardback of 256 pages, priced £15-95 plus £3-50 postage.

REJECTED F.C. VOLUME 1 (Reprint) *(By Dave Twydell)* The revised edition of this popular book - now in hardback - this volume provides the comprehensive histories of: Aberdare Athletic, Ashington, Bootle, Bradford (Park Avenue), Burton (Swifts, Wanderers and United), Gateshead/South Shields, Glossop, Loughborough, Nelson, Stalybridge Celtic and Workington. The 288 well illustrated pages also contain the basic statistical details of each club. Price £12-95 plus £1-30 postage. (Also *Rejected F.C. of Scotland:* Volume 1 covers Edinburgh and The South (Edinburgh City, Leith Athletic, St.Bernards, Armadale, Broxburn United, Bathgate, Peebles Rovers, Mid-Annandale, Nithsdale Wanderers and Solway Star - 288 pages). Volume 2 covers Glasgow and District (Abercorn, Arthurlie, Beith, Cambuslang, Clydebank, Cowlairs, Johnstone, Linthouse, Northern, Third Lanark, and Thistle - 240 pages). Each priced £12-95 plus £1-30 postage.

FOOTBALL LEAGUE - GROUNDS FOR A CHANGE (By Dave Twydell). A 424 page, A5 sized, Hardback book. A comprehensive study of all the Grounds on which the current English Football League clubs previously played. Every Club that has moved Grounds is included, with a 'Potted' history of each, plus 250 illustrations. Plenty of 'reading' material, as well as an interesting reference book. Price £13-95 Plus £1-70 Postage.

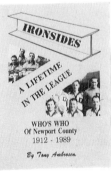

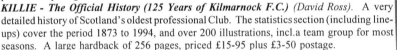

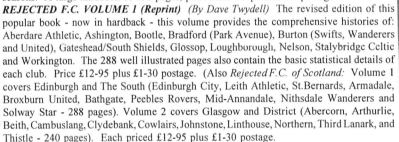

THROUGH THE TURNSTILES *(by Brian Tabner)* This incredible book which provides the average attendance of every English Football League club, for every season from 1888/89 to 1991/92. Well illustrated, and also relates the development of the game (angled towards attendances). Also details of the best supported 'away' teams, season ticket sales over the years, etc. A large format hardback and 208 packed pages. An excellent read at £13-95 plus £1-70 Postage.

COVENTRY CITY FOOTBALLERS (The Complete Who's Who)
By Martin & Paul O'Connor. One of the most detailed books of its type. Every Football (and Southern) League player has been included - around 700. Seasonal appearances of every player, brief personal details, 'pen pictures', together with very detailed information on the movements of the players to other clubs. Plus: around 100 photo's of the Club's most memorable men, and information on the principal players from the very early days. A hardback book with 224 large pages. £13-95 plus £2-60 postage.

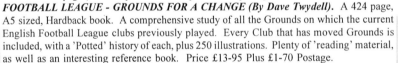

HISTORY OF THE LANCASHIRE FOOTBALL ASSOCIATION 1878-1928. A rare historical and fascinating hardback reprint (first published in 1928). Contains the history of the formative days of Lancashire football. Sections within the 288 pages include the early histories of about 20 Clubs (Manchester Utd., Wigan Borough, Rochdale, etc.), Lancashire Cup competitions, Biographies, etc. For those interested in the development of the game, this is a 'must'. Price £12-95 Plus £1-30 Postage.

THE CODE WAR *(Graham Williams)*
A fascinating look back on football's history - from the earliest days up to the First World War. 'Football' is covered in the broadest sense, for the book delves into the splits over the period to and from Rugby Union and Rugby League, as well as Football (Soccer). Potted histories of many of the Clubs are included, as is a comprehensive index. 192 page hardback, price £10-95 plus £1-20 postage.

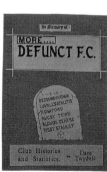